Account Classification and Presentation

Account Title	Classification	Financial Statement	Normal Balance
A			
Accounts Payable	Current Liability	Balance Sheet	Credit
Accounts Receivable	Current Asset	Balance Sheet	Debit
Accumulated Depreciation—Buildings	Plant Asset—Contra	Balance Sheet	Credit
Accumulated Depreciation—Equipment	Plant Asset—Contra	Balance Sheet	Credit
Administrative Expenses	Operating Expense	Income Statement	Debit
Advertising Expense	Operating Expense	Income Statement	Debit
Allowance for Doubtful Accounts	Current Asset—Contra	Balance Sheet	Credit
Amortization Expense	Operating Expense	Income Statement	Debit
B			
Bad Debt Expense	Operating Expense	Income Statement	Debit
Bonds Payable	Long-Term Liability	Balance Sheet	Credit
Buildings	Plant Asset	Balance Sheet	Debit
C			
Cash	Current Asset	Balance Sheet	Debit
Common Stock	Stockholders' Equity	Balance Sheet	Credit
Copyrights	Intangible Asset	Balance Sheet	Debit
Cost of Goods Sold	Cost of Goods Sold	Income Statement	Debit
D			
Debt Investments	Current Asset/Long-Term Investment	Balance Sheet	Debit
Depreciation Expense	Operating Expense	Income Statement	Debit
Discount on Bonds Payable	Long-Term Liability—Contra	Balance Sheet	Debit
Dividend Revenue	Other Income	Income Statement	Credit
Dividends	Temporary account closed to Retained Earnings	Retained Earnings Statement	Debit
Dividends Payable	Current Liability	Balance Sheet	Credit
E			
Equipment	Plant Asset	Balance Sheet	Debit
F			
Freight-Out	Operating Expense	Income Statement	Debit
G			
Gain on Disposal of Plant Assets	Other Income	Income Statement	Credit
Goodwill	Intangible Asset	Balance Sheet	Debit
I			
Income Summary	Temporary account closed to Retained Earnings	Not Applicable	(1)
Income Tax Expense	Income Tax Expense	Income Statement	Debit
Income Taxes Payable	Current Liability	Balance Sheet	Credit
Insurance Expense	Operating Expense	Income Statement	Debit
Interest Expense	Other Expense	Income Statement	Debit
Interest Payable	Current Liability	Balance Sheet	Credit
Interest Receivable	Current Asset	Balance Sheet	Debit
Interest Revenue	Other Income	Income Statement	Credit
Inventory	Current Asset	Balance Sheet (2)	Debit

(continued)

Account Classification and Presentation (continued)

Account Title	Classification	Financial Statement	Normal Balance
L			
Land	Plant Asset	Balance Sheet	Debit
Loss on Disposal of Plant Assets	Other Expense	Income Statement	Debit
M			
Maintenance and Repairs Expense	Operating Expense	Income Statement	Debit
Mortgage Payable	Long-Term Liability	Balance Sheet	Credit
N			
Notes Payable	Current Liability/ Long-Term Liability	Balance Sheet	Credit
P			
Patents	Intangible Asset	Balance Sheet	Debit
Paid-in Capital in Excess of Par—Common Stock	Stockholders' Equity	Balance Sheet	Credit
Paid-in Capital in Excess of Par—Preferred Stock	Stockholders' Equity	Balance Sheet	Credit
Preferred Stock	Stockholders' Equity	Balance Sheet	Credit
Premium on Bonds Payable	Long-Term Liability—Adjunct	Balance Sheet	Credit
Prepaid Insurance	Current Asset	Balance Sheet	Debit
Prepaid Rent	Current Asset	Balance Sheet	Debit
R			
Rent Expense	Operating Expense	Income Statement	Debit
Retained Earnings	Stockholders' Equity	Balance Sheet and Retained Earnings Statement	Credit
S			
Salaries and Wages Expense	Operating Expense	Income Statement	Debit
Salaries and Wages Payable	Current Liability	Balance Sheet	Credit
Sales Discounts	Revenue—Contra	Income Statement	Debit
Sales Returns and Allowances	Revenue—Contra	Income Statement	Debit
Sales Revenue	Revenue	Income Statement	Credit
Selling Expenses	Operating Expense	Income Statement	Debit
Service Revenue	Revenue	Income Statement	Credit
Short-Term Investments	Current Asset	Balance Sheet	Debit
Stock Investments	Current Asset/Long-Term Investment	Balance Sheet	Debit
Supplies	Current Asset	Balance Sheet	Debit
Supplies Expense	Operating Expense	Income Statement	Debit
T			
Treasury Stock	Stockholders' Equity	Balance Sheet	Debit
U			
Unearned Service Revenue	Current Liability	Balance Sheet	Credit
Utilities Expense	Operating Expense	Income Statement	Debit

(1) The normal balance for Income Summary will be credit when there is a net income, debit when there is a net loss. The Income Summary account does not appear on any financial statement.

(2) If a periodic system is used, Inventory also appears on the income statement in the calculation of cost of goods sold.

The following is a sample chart of accounts. It does not represent a comprehensive chart of all the accounts used in this text but rather those accounts that are commonly used. This sample chart of accounts is for a company that generates service revenue as well as sales revenue. It uses the perpetual approach to inventory. If a periodic system was used, the following temporary accounts would be needed to record inventory purchases: Purchases, Freight-In, Purchase Returns and Allowances, and Purchase Discounts.

Chart of Accounts

Assets	Liabilities	Stockholders' Equity	Revenues	Expenses
Cash	Notes Payable	Common Stock	Service Revenue	Administrative Expenses
Accounts Receivable	Accounts Payable	Paid-in Capital in Excess of Par—Common Stock	Sales Revenue	Amortization Expense
Allowance for Doubtful Accounts	Unearned Service Revenue	Preferred Stock	Sales Discounts	Bad Debt Expense
Interest Receivable	Salaries and Wages Payable	Paid-in Capital in Excess of Par—Preferred Stock	Sales Returns and Allowances	Cost of Goods Sold
Inventory	Interest Payable	Treasury Stock	Interest Revenue	Depreciation Expense
Supplies	Dividends Payable	Retained Earnings	Gain on Disposal of Plant Assets	Freight-Out
Prepaid Insurance	Income Taxes Payable	Dividends		Income Tax Expense
Prepaid Rent	Bonds Payable	Income Summary		Insurance Expense
Land	Discount on Bonds Payable			Interest Expense
Equipment	Premium on Bonds Payable			Loss on Disposal of Plant Assets
Accumulated Depreciation—Equipment	Mortgage Payable			Maintenance and Repairs Expense
Buildings				Rent Expense
Accumulated Depreciation—Buildings				Salaries and Wages Expense
Copyrights				Selling Expenses
Goodwill				Supplies Expense
Patents				Utilities Expense

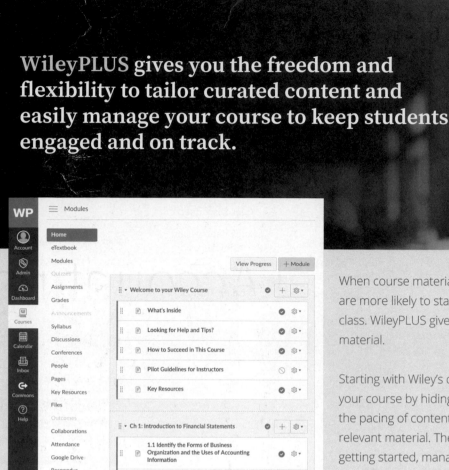

Financial Accounting

Eleventh Edition

JERRY J. WEYGANDT PhD, CPA
University of Wisconsin—Madison
Madison, Wisconsin

PAUL D. KIMMEL PhD, CPA
University of Wisconsin—Madison
Madison, Wisconsin

DONALD E. KIESO PhD, CPA
Northern Illinois University
DeKalb, Illinois

WILEY

DEDICATED TO

Our wives,
Enid, Merlynn, and Donna, for their love,
support, and encouragement.

DIRECTOR AND VICE PRESIDENT	Michael McDonald
EXECUTIVE EDITOR	Zoe Craig
INSTRUCTIONAL DESIGNER	Jenny Welter
DIRECTOR OF MARKETING	Karolina Zarychta Honsa
MARKETING MANAGER	Christina Koop
EDITORIAL SUPERVISOR	Terry Ann Tatro
EDITORIAL ASSISTANT	Megan Joseph
SENIOR CONTENT MANAGER	Dorothy Sinclair
SENIOR PRODUCTION EDITOR	Valerie Vargas
SENIOR DESIGNER	Jon Boylan
COVER IMAGE	Felix Cesare/EyeEm/Getty Images

This text was typeset in 9.5/12 STIX Two Text at Lumina Datamatics, Inc. and printed and bound by Quad Graphics. The cover was printed by Quad Graphics.

Founded in 1807, John Wiley & Sons, Inc. has been a valued source of knowledge and understanding for more than 200 years, helping people around the world meet their needs and fulfill their aspirations. Our company is built on a foundation of principles that include responsibility to the communities we serve and where we live and work. In 2008, we launched a Corporate Citizenship Initiative, a global effort to address the environmental, social, economic, and ethical challenges we face in our business. Among the issues we are addressing are carbon impact, paper specifications and procurement, ethical conduct within our business and among our vendors, and community and charitable support. For more information, please visit our website: www.wiley.com/go/citizenship.

ISBN-13: 9781119594611

The inside back cover will contain printing identification and country of origin if omitted from this page. In addition, if the ISBN on the back cover differs from the ISBN on this page, the one on the back cover is correct.

Library of Congress Cataloging-in-Publication Data

Names: Weygandt, Jerry J., author. | Kimmel, Paul D., author. | Kieso, Donald E., author.
Title: Financial accounting / Jerry J. Weygandt, PhD, CPA, University of Wisconsin-Madison, Madison, Wisconsin, Paul D. Kimmel, PhD, CPA, University of Wisconsin-Madison, Madison, Wisconsin, Donald E. Kieso, PhD, CPA, Northern Illinois University, DeKalb, Illinois.
Description: Eleventh edition. | Hoboken, NJ : Wiley, [2020] | Includes index.
Identifiers: LCCN 2019034991 (print) | LCCN 2019034992 (ebook) | ISBN 9781119594598 (paperback) | ISBN 9781119609292 (Adobe PDF) | ISBN 9781119594611 (epub)
Subjects: LCSH: Accounting.
Classification: LCC HF5636 .W49 2020 (print) | LCC HF5636 (ebook) | DDC 657—dc23
LC record available at https://lccn.loc.gov/2019034991
LC ebook record available at https://lccn.loc.gov/2019034992

Printed in America.

V10015449_110819

Brief Contents

Available in WileyPLUS and Wiley Custom:

From the Authors

Dear Student,

Why This Course? Remember your biology course in high school? Did you have one of those "invisible man" models (or maybe something more high-tech than that) that gave you the opportunity to look "inside" the human body? This accounting course offers something similar. To understand a business, you have to understand the financial insides of a business organization. An accounting course will help you understand the essential financial components of businesses. Whether you are looking at a large multinational company like **Apple** or **Starbucks** or a single-owner software consulting business or coffee shop, knowing the fundamentals of accounting will help you understand what is happening. As an employee, a manager, an investor, a business owner, or a director of your own personal finances—any of which roles you will have at some point in your life—you will make better decisions for having taken this course.

> "Whether you are looking at a large multinational company like **Apple** or **Starbucks** or a single-owner software consulting business or coffee shop, knowing the fundamentals of accounting will help you understand what is happening."

Why This Text? Your instructor has chosen this text for you because of the authors' trusted reputation. The authors have worked hard to write a text that is engaging, timely, and accurate.

How to Succeed? We've asked many students and many instructors whether there is a secret for success in this course. The nearly unanimous answer turns out to be not much of a secret: "Do the homework." This is one course where doing is learning. The more time you spend on the homework assignments—using the various tools that this text provides—the more likely you are to learn the essential concepts, techniques, and methods of accounting. Besides the text itself, WileyPLUS also offers various support resources.

Good luck in this course. We hope you enjoy the experience and that you put to good use throughout a lifetime of success the knowledge you obtain in this course. We are sure you will not be disappointed.

Jerry J. Weygandt
Paul D. Kimmel
Donald E. Kieso

Author Commitment

JERRY J. WEYGANDT, PHD, CPA, is Arthur Andersen Alumni Emeritus Professor of Accounting at the University of Wisconsin—Madison. He holds a Ph.D. in accounting from the University of Illinois. Articles by Professor Weygandt have appeared in *The Accounting Review, Journal of Accounting Research, Accounting Horizons, Journal of Accountancy*, and other academic and professional journals. These articles have examined such financial reporting issues as accounting for price-level adjustments, pensions, convertible securities, stock option contracts, and interim reports. Professor Weygandt is the author of other accounting and financial reporting texts and is a member of the American Accounting Association, the American Institute of Certified Public Accountants, and the Wisconsin Society of Certified Public Accountants. He has served on numerous committees of the American Accounting Association and as a member of the editorial board of *The Accounting Review*; he also has served as President and Secretary-Treasurer of the American Accounting Association. In addition, he has been actively involved with the American Institute of Certified Public Accountants and has been a member of the Accounting Standards Executive Committee (AcSEC) of that organization. He has served on the FASB task force that examined the reporting issues related to accounting for income taxes and served as a trustee of the Financial Accounting Foundation. Professor Weygandt has received the Chancellor's Award for Excellence in Teaching and the Beta Gamma Sigma Dean's Teaching Award. He is on the board of directors of M & I Bank of Southern Wisconsin. He is the recipient of the Wisconsin Institute of CPA's Outstanding Educator's Award and the Lifetime Achievement Award. In 2001 he received the American Accounting Association's Outstanding Educator Award.

PAUL D. KIMMEL, PHD, CPA, received his bachelor's degree from the University of Minnesota and his doctorate in accounting from the University of Wisconsin. He taught at U.W.—Milwaukee for over 25 years and now teaches at U.W.—Madison. He has public accounting experience with Deloitte & Touche (Minneapolis). He was the recipient of the UWM School of Business Advisory Council Teaching Award, the Reggie Taite Excellence in Teaching Award and a three-time winner of the Outstanding Teaching Assistant Award at the University of Wisconsin. He is also a recipient of the Elijah Watts Sells Award for Honorary Distinction for his results on the CPA exam. He is a member of the American Accounting Association and the Institute of Management Accountants and has published articles in *The Accounting Review, Accounting Horizons, Review of Accounting Studies, Advances in Management Accounting, Managerial Finance, Issues in Accounting Education, Journal of Accounting Education*, as well as other journals. His research interests include accounting for financial instruments and innovation in accounting education. He has published papers and given many presentations regarding accounting instruction, and helped prepare a catalog of critical thinking resources for the Federated Schools of Accountancy.

DONALD E. KIESO, PHD, CPA, received his bachelor's degree from Aurora University and his doctorate in accounting from the University of Illinois. He has served as chairman of the Department of Accountancy and is currently the KPMG Emeritus Professor of Accountancy at Northern Illinois University. He has public accounting experience with Price Waterhouse & Co. (San Francisco and Chicago) and Arthur Andersen & Co. (Chicago) and research experience with the Research Division of the American Institute of Certified Public Accountants (New York). He has done postdoctorate work as a Visiting Scholar at the University of California at Berkeley and is a recipient of NIU's Teaching Excellence Award and four Golden Apple Teaching Awards. Professor Kieso is the author of other accounting and business books and is a member of the American Accounting Association, the American Institute of Certified Public Accountants, and the Illinois CPA Society. He has served as a member of the Board of Directors of the Illinois CPA Society, then AACSB's Accounting Accreditation Committees, the State of Illinois Comptroller's Commission, as Secretary-Treasurer of the Federation of Schools of Accountancy, and as Secretary-Treasurer of the American Accounting Association. Professor Kieso is currently serving on the Board of Trustees and Executive Committee of Aurora University, as a member of the Board of Directors of Kishwaukee Community Hospital, and as Treasurer and Director of Valley West Community Hospital. From 1989 to 1993 he served as a charter member of the national Accounting Education Change Commission. He is the recipient of the Outstanding Accounting Educator Award from the Illinois CPA Society, the FSA's Joseph A. Silvoso Award of Merit, the NIU Foundation's Humanitarian Award for Service to Higher Education, a Distinguished Service Award from the Illinois CPA Society, and in 2003 an honorary doctorate from Aurora University.

New to This Edition

Chapter-by-Chapter Changes

Chapter 1: Accounting in Action
- **New** introductory discussion of how financial statement users can use data analytics to improve decision-making.

Chapter 2: The Recording Process
- **New** Helpful Hints, to reinforce student understanding of key concepts.
- **New** Accounting Across the Organization box, on **Hain Celestial Group**'s failure to provide income information to users, which resulted in a significant drop in its stock price.
- Re-ordered example transactions so payment of dividends is last, more reflective of real-world practices.

Chapter 3: Adjusting the Accounts
- **New** discussion and illustration of the five-step revenue recognition process.

Chapter 4: Completing the Accounting Cycle
- Updated definition of worksheet to include its most common form, an electronic spreadsheet.
- Simplified illustration of the closing process for improved understanding.
- **New** End-of-Chapter Problems that review portions of the accounting cycle that are not worksheet-based.

Chapter 5: Accounting for Merchandising Operations
- **New** section on how companies use data analytics to improve business decision-making regarding their policies on credit sales, sales returns and allowances, and sales discounts.
- **New** Comprehensive Accounting Cycle Review for the perpetual inventory method.

Chapter 6: Inventories
- **New** DO IT!s at end of each cost flow method discussion, so students can immediately check their understanding of the FIFO, LIFO, and average-cost methods.
- **New** illustration showing **Walmart**'s recent inventory disclosure, using retail inventory method.

Chapter 7: Fraud, Internal Control, and Cash
- **New** section on how data analytics helps improve internal controls.
- **New** discussion of recent FASB on restricted cash presentation in the statement of cash flows.

Chapter 8: Accounting for Receivables
- **New** Feature Story on how **Nike** has increased its sales through its credit policies.

- **New** section on data analytics and receivables management.
- **New** discussion of FASB expected credit loss model, which requires that companies measure expected uncollectible accounts and record bad debt expense on all receivables, even those with a low risk of loss.

Chapter 9: Plant Assets, Natural Resources, and Intangible Assets
- **New** Feature Story on how equipment can determine financial success in the airline industry.
- **New** discussion and International Note on use of historical cost principle and cash equivalent price in determining the cost of plant assets.
- **New** DO IT!s at end of subsections of depreciation methods, so students can immediately test their understanding of how to calculate straight-line, declining-balance, and units-of-activity depreciation methods.
- **New** discussion and illustration on depreciation disclosure in the notes to the financial statements.
- Expanded discussion of how companies must disclose in the financial statements significant changes in depreciation estimates.
- Moved "Sale of Plant Assets" section before "Retirement of Plant Assets" section for more logical organization of topics.
- Expanded discussion of description of intangible assets and how to account for them.

Chapter 10: Liabilities
- **New** Feature Story on how debt has both helped and hurt **General Motors** and **Ford**.
- **New** discussion of leases and related EOC material.
- **New** discussion of bank line of credit disclosure.

Chapter 11: Corporations: Organization, Stock Transactions, and Stockholders' Equity
- **New** discussion on hybrid forms of business organization.
- **New** discussion on how investors monitor a company's dividend practices.
- **New** discussion on how payment of stock dividend can be viewed as merely a publicity gesture.
- **New** People, Planet, and Profit Insight box on the upward trend of shareholder proposals on corporate responsibility.
- **New** Investor Insight box, on how companies that pay dividends can increase investor wealth.

Chapter 12: Statement of Cash Flows

- Added more T-accounts and journal entries to increase understandability of preparing the statement of cash flows using the indirect method.

- Used 2018 **Apple** financial statements for example in how to analyze the statement of cash flows using free cash flow calculation, for increased student engagement.

Chapter 13: Financial Statement Analysis

- **New** presentation of discontinued operations on the income statement (previously on the statement of comprehensive income) as well as format of the statement of comprehensive income.

- **New** illustration showing the financial ratio classifications, for improved student understanding and engagement.

- Comprehensive example, as well as explanations of ratio calculations, now included in the chapter instead of an appendix.

Appendix H: Investments

- **New** DO IT!s added to appendix discussion as well as end-of-chapter material.

- **New** Review and Practice section includes multiple-choice questions followed by annotated solutions, practice brief exercises with solutions, practice exercises with solutions, and a practice problem with solution.

Proven Pedagogical Features

Financial Accounting, Eleventh Edition, provides a tried and true introduction to financial accounting, while also calling attention to areas of emerging focus such as data analytics. It explains accounting concepts and procedures, starting with recording transactions, reinforces them through practice opportunities, and continues through financial statements and beyond.

In this new edition, all content has been carefully reviewed and revised to ensure maximum student understanding. At the same time, the time-tested features that have proven to be of most help to students have been retained, such as the following.

Financial Statement Transaction Illustrations

Throughout the text, carefully crafted illustrations demonstrate the analysis of business transactions. Each illustration clearly walks the student through the process of (1) basic analysis, (2) equation analysis, and (3) debit-credit analysis, as well as shows the (4) general journal entry and (5) general ledger posting.

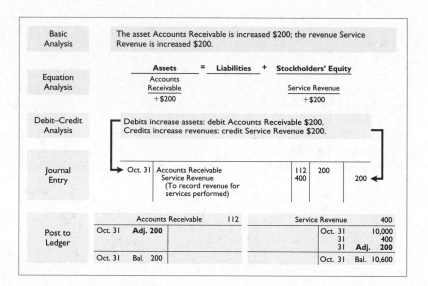

Infographic Learning

Over half of the text is visual, providing students alternative ways of learning about accounting.

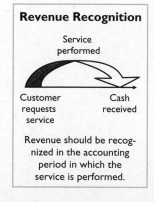

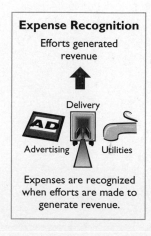

Real-World Decision-Making and Data Analytics

Real-world examples, which illustrate engaging situations in companies, are provided throughout the text. In addition, the text also discusses how managers are increasingly relying on data analytics to make decisions using accounting information.

Investor Insight   Apple Inc.

PhotoAlto/James Hardy/
Getty Images

Reporting Revenue Accurately

Until recently, electronics manufacturer **Apple** was required to spread the revenues from iPhone sales over the two-year period following the sale of the phone. Accounting standards required this because Apple was obligated to provide software updates after the phone was sold. Since Apple had service obligations after the initial date of sale, it was forced to spread the revenue over a two-year period.

As a result, the rapid growth of iPhone sales was not fully reflected in the revenue amounts reported in Apple's income statement. A new accounting standard now enables Apple to report much more of its iPhone revenue at the point of sale. It was estimated that under the new rule revenues would have been about 17% higher and earnings per share almost 50% higher.

In the past, why was it argued that Apple should spread the recognition of iPhone revenue over a two-year period, rather than recording it upfront? (Go to WileyPLUS for this answer and additional questions.)

Data Analytics and Credit Sales

Increased access to ever larger amounts of data about customers, suppliers, products, and virtually every other aspect of a business has resulted in a greater reliance by companies on data analytics to support business decisions. Credit sales, sales returns and allowances, and sales discounts all provide rich opportunities for the use of data analytics.

First, the decision of whom to grant credit is very important. Offering credit to customers can substantially increase sales opportunities. However, some credit customers will ultimately not be able to pay the amounts owed. So offering credit to customers has costs. Effectively analyzing data regarding current as well as potential customers can help a company expand its sales base while minimizing the risk of unpaid receivables.

Similarly, companies must develop policies regarding sales return practices. Merchandisers know that generous return policies can enhance customer loyalty. But if returns become common, the company's profitability will suffer. In recent years, companies such as **Best Buy**, **REI**, and **Costco** have all refined their customer return policies, sometimes with unique rules for specific product types, as a result of data analytics applied to their data on product returns.

Finally, sales discounts are offered to customers to encourage early payment of receivables. Offering these discounts is costly. To achieve the optimal cost-benefit balance on sales discounts, companies statistically analyze past discount practices to determine how large the discount should be, how long the payment period should be, and other factors.

DO IT! Exercises

DO IT! Exercises in the body of the text prompt students to stop and review key concepts. They outline the Action Plan necessary to complete the exercise as well as show a detailed solution.

DO IT! 3 | Adjusting Entries for Accruals

Micro Computer Services Inc. began operations on August 1, 2022. At the end of August 2022, management prepares monthly financial statements. The following information relates to August.

1. At August 31, the company owed its employees $800 in salaries and wages that will be paid on September 1.

2. On August 1, the company borrowed $30,000 from a local bank on a 1-year note payable. The annual interest rate is 10%. Interest will be paid with the note at maturity.

3. Revenue for services performed but unrecorded for August totaled $1,100.

Prepare the adjusting entries needed at August 31, 2022.

ACTION PLAN
- Make adjusting entries at the end of the period to recognize revenues for services performed and for expenses incurred.
- Don't forget to make adjusting entries for accruals. Adjusting entries for accruals will increase both a balance sheet and an income statement account.

Solution

1. Salaries and Wages Expense	800	
Salaries and Wages Payable		800
(To record accrued salaries)		
2. Interest Expense	250	
Interest Payable		250
(To record accrued interest:		
$30,000 \times 10\% \times \frac{1}{12} = \$250$)		
3. Accounts Receivable	1,100	
Service Revenue		1,100
(To record revenue for services performed)		

Related exercise material: **BE3.10, BE3.11, BE3.12, DO IT!** 3.3, E3.5, E3.6, E3.7, E3.8, E3.9, E3.10, E3.11, E3.12, E3.13, E3.14, E3.15, E3.17, E3.18, E3.19, and E3.20.

Review and Practice

Each chapter concludes with a Review and Practice section which includes a review of learning objectives, Decision Tools review, key terms glossary, practice multiple-choice questions with annotated solutions, practice brief exercises with solutions, practice exercises with solutions, and a practice problem with a solution.

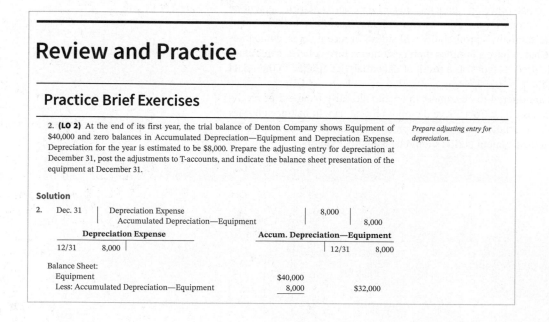

Review and Practice

Practice Brief Exercises

2. (LO 2) At the end of its first year, the trial balance of Denton Company shows Equipment of $40,000 and zero balances in Accumulated Depreciation—Equipment and Depreciation Expense. Depreciation for the year is estimated to be $8,000. Prepare the adjusting entry for depreciation at December 31, post the adjustments to T-accounts, and indicate the balance sheet presentation of the equipment at December 31.

Prepare adjusting entry for depreciation.

Solution

2.	Dec. 31	Depreciation Expense	8,000	
		Accumulated Depreciation—Equipment		8,000

Depreciation Expense		**Accum. Depreciation—Equipment**	
12/31	8,000	12/31	8,000

Balance Sheet:
Equipment	$40,000	
Less: Accumulated Depreciation—Equipment	8,000	$32,000

Digital study tools in the *Financial Accounting* WileyPLUS course include the following.

Real-World Company Videos

Real-world company videos feature both small businesses and larger companies to help students apply content and see how business owners apply concepts from the text in the real world.

Solution Walkthrough Videos

Solution Walkthrough Videos are available as question assistance and help students develop problem-solving techniques. These videos walk students through solutions step-by-step and are based on the most regularly assigned exercises and problems in the text.

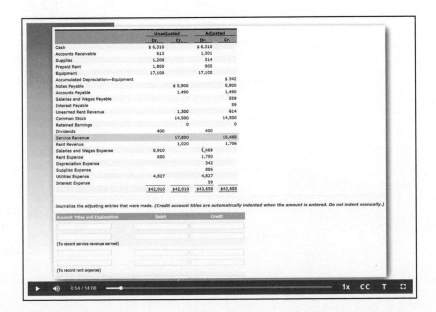

Interactive Tutorials

Interactive tutorials are voice-guided reviews of topics in each learning objective. Check points in the tutorials require students to review and solve simple self-assessment exercises.

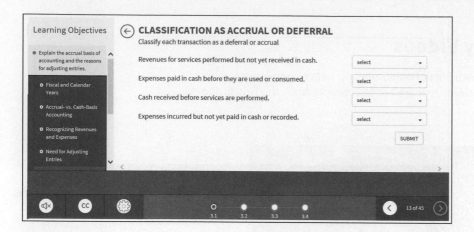

In addition, other WileyPLUS learning opportunities include the following.

- **Cookie Creations** is a continuing case that spans across chapters and shows how a small business grows.
- **Wiley Accounting Updates** (wileyaccountingupdates.com) provide faculty and students with weekly curated news articles and suggested discussion questions.
- **Flashcards and Crossword Puzzles** help students study and master basic vocabulary and concepts.
- **Student Practice** quickly and effectively assesses student understanding of the material.
- **Adaptive Practice** helps students quickly understand what they know and what they do not know, and provides opportunities for practice to effectively prepare for class or quizzes and exams.
- **New Test Bank** questions that analyze transactions using the tabular analysis in the text.

Contents

5   Accounting for Merchandising Operations   5-1

6   Inventories   6-1

7   Fraud, Internal Control, and Cash   7-1

12 Statement of Cash Flows   12-1

13 Financial Analysis: The Big Picture   13-1

Available in WileyPLUS and Wiley Custom:

Acknowledgments

Financial Accounting has benefited greatly from the input of focus group participants, manuscript reviewers, those who have sent comments by letter or e-mail, ancillary authors, and proofers. We greatly appreciate the constructive suggestions and innovative ideas of reviewers and the creativity and accuracy of the ancillary authors and checkers.

Reviewers

Shawn Abbott, *College of the Siskiyous*

Joseph Adamo, *Cazenovia College*

Dawn Addington, *Central New Mexico Community College*

Pushpa Agrawal, *University of Nebraska—Kearney*

Sol Ahiarah, *SUNY—Buffalo State*

Lynn Almond, *Virginia Polytechnic Institute*

Elizabeth Ammann, *Lindenwood University*

Joe Atallah, *Coastline Community College*

Timothy Baker, *California State University—Fresno*

Lisa Banks, *Mott Community College*

Joyce Barden, *DeVry University*

Melody Barta, *Evergreen Valley College*

Jeffrey Beatty, *Fresno City College*

Linda Bell, *Park University*

David Bojarsky, *California State University—Long Beach*

Jack Borke, *University of Wisconsin—Platteville*

Anna Boulware, *St. Charles Community College*

Bruce Bradford, *Fairfield University*

Linda Bressler, *University of Houston—Downtown*

Ann K. Brooks, *University of New Mexico*

Robert Brown, *Evergreen Valley College*

Leroy Bugger, *Edison State College*

Melodi Bunting, *Edgewood College*

Lisa Capozzoli, *College of DuPage*

Renee Castrigano, *Cleveland State University*

Sandy Cereola, *James Madison University*

Gayle Chaky, *Dutchess Community College*

Amy Chang, *San Francisco State University*

Julie Chenier, *Louisiana State University—Baton Rouge*

James Chiafery, *University of Massachusetts—Boston*

Bea Chiang, *The College of New Jersey*

Cheryl Clark, *Point Park University*

Toni Clegg, *Delta College*

Maxine Cohen, *Bergen Community College*

Arthur College, *Evergreen Valley College*

Stephen Collins, *University of Massachusetts—Lowell*

Solveg Cooper, *Cuesta College*

William Cooper, *North Carolina A&T State University*

Cheryl Copeland, *California State University, Fresno*

Alan E. Davis, *Community College of Philadelphia*

Steven Day, *Dixie State University*

Larry DeGaetano, *Montclair State University*

Michael Deschamps, *MiraCosta College*

Bettye Desselle, *Texas Southern University*

Cyril Dibie, *Tarrant County College—Arlington*

Jean Dunn, *Rady School of Management at University of California—San Diego*

Ron Dustin, *Fresno City College*

Barbara Eide, *University of Wisconsin—La Crosse*

Dennis Elam, *Texas A&M University—San Antonio*

James Emig, *Villanova University*

Janet Farler, *Pima Community College*

Charmaine Felder, *Brandman University*

Anthony Fortini, *Camden County College*

Jeanne Franco, *Paradise Valley Community College*

Patrick Geer, *Hawkeye Community College*

Vicki Greshik, *University of Jamestown*

Andrew Griffith, *Iona College*

Jeffrey Haber, *Iona College*

John Hogan, *Fisher College*

Bambi Hora, *University of Central Oklahoma*

M.A. Houston, *Wright State University*

Jeff Hsu, *St. Louis Community College—Meramec*

Kimberly Hurt, *Central Community College*

Hussein Issa, *Rutgers Business School*

Janet Jamieson, *University of Dubuque*

Kevin Jones, *Drexel University*

Don Kovacic, *California State University—San Marcos*

Lynn Krausse, *Bakersfield College*

Craig Krenek, *Elmhurst College*

Jeffrey T. Kunz, *Carroll University*

Steven LaFave, *Augsburg College*

Eric Lee, *University of Northern Iowa*

Jason Lee, *SUNY Plattsburgh*

Harold Little, *Western Kentucky University*

Dennis Lopez, *University of Texas—San Antonio*

Lisa Ludlum, *Western Illinois University*

Michael J. MacDonald, *University of Wisconsin—Whitewater*

Suneel Maheshwari, *Marshall University*

Lois Mahoney, *Eastern Michigan University*

Diane Marker, *University of Toledo*

Christian Mastilak, *Xavier University*

Josephine Mathias, *Mercer County Community College*

Edward McGinnis, *American River College*

Florence McGovern, *Bergen Community College*

Pam Meyer, *University of Louisiana—Lafayette*

Mary Michel, *Manhattan College*

Joan Miller, *William Paterson University*

Earl Mitchell, *Santa Ana College*

Syed Moiz, *University of Wisconsin—Platteville*

Brigitte Muehlmann, *Babson College*

Johnna Murray, *University of Missouri—St. Louis*

Michael Newman, *University of Houston*

Lee Nicholas, *University of Northern Iowa*

Rosemary Nurre, *College of San Mateo*

Cindy Nye, *Bellevue University*

Gary Olsen, *Carroll University*

Sarah O'Rourke, *Rutgers Business School*

Glenn Pate, *Palm Beach State College*

Nori Pearson, *Washington State University*

Joe Pecore, *Rady School of Management at University of California—San Diego*
Obeua Persons, *Rider University*
Judy Peterson, *Monmouth College*
Timothy Peterson, *Gustavus Adolphus College*
Robert Rambo, *Roger Williams University*
Jim Resnik, *Bergen Community College*
Jorge Romero, *Towson University*
Luther Ross, *Central Piedmont Community College*
Maria Roxas, *Central Connecticut State University*
Robert Russ, *Northern Kentucky University*
Susan Sadowski, *Shippensburg University*
Susan Sandblom, *Scottsdale Community College*
Richard Sarkisian, *Camden County College*
Marshall Saunders, *Rutgers Business School*
Karl Schindl, *University of Wisconsin—Manitowoc*
Debbie Seifert, *Illinois State University*
Carl F. Shultz, *Rider University*
Valerie Simmons, *University of Southern Mississippi*
Gregory Sinclair, *San Francisco State University*
Mike Skaff, *College of the Sequoias*
Charles Skender, *University of North Carolina—Chapel Hill*
Karyn Smith, *Georgia Perimeter College*
Kathleen J. Smith, *University of Nebraska—Kearney*
Patrick Stegman, *College of Lake County*
Richard Steingart, *San Jose State University*
Gracelyn Stuart-Tuggle, *Palm Beach State University*
Karen Tabak, *Maryville University*
Diane Tanner, *University of North Florida*
Tom Thompson, *Savannah Technical College*
Mike Tyler, *Barry University*
Jin Ulmer, *Angelina College*
Linda Vaello, *University of Texas—San Antonio*
Manuel Valle, *City College of San Francisco*
Huey L. Van Dine, *Bergen Community College*
Joan Van Hise, *Fairfield University*
Claire Veal, *University of Texas—San Antonio*

Sheila Viel, *University of Wisconsin—Milwaukee*
Suzanne Ward, *University of Louisiana—Lafayette*
Evan Wasserman, *Rutgers Business School*
Dan Way, Central Piedmont Community College
Geri B. Wink, *Colorado State University—Pueblo*
Catherine Wyatt, *Lumina Datamatics*

Ancillary Authors, Contributors, Proofers, and Accuracy Checkers

Ellen Bartley, *St. Joseph's College*
LuAnn Bean, *Florida Institute of Technology*
Jack Borke, *University of Wisconsin—Platteville*
Ann K. Brooks, *University of New Mexico*
Melodi Bunting, *Edgewood College*
Bea Chiang, *The College of New Jersey*
James Emig, *Villanova University*
Larry Falcetto, *Emporia State University*
Heidi Hansel, *Kirkwood Community College*
Coby Harmon, *University of California—Santa Barbara*
Lisa Hewes, *Northern Arizona University*
Derek Jackson, *St. Mary's University of Minnesota*
Craig Krenek, *Elmhurst College*
Kirk Lynch, *Sandhills Community College*
Jill Misuraca, *University of Tampa*
Barbara Muller, *Arizona State University*
Linda Mullins, *Georgia State University—Perimeter College*
Yvonne Phang, *Borough of Manhattan Community College*
Laura Prosser, *Black Hills State University*
Alice Sineath, *University of Maryland University College*
Teresa Speck, *St. Mary's University of Minnesota*
Lynn Stallworth, *Appalachian State University*
Diane Tanner, *University of North Florida*
Sheila Viel, *University of Wisconsin—Milwaukee*
Dick Wasson, *Southwestern College*
Lori Grady Zaher, *Bucks County Community College*

We appreciate the exemplary support and commitment given to us by executive editor Zoe Craig, marketing manager Christina Koop, instructional designer Jenny Welter, editorial supervisor Terry Ann Tatro, designer Jon Boylan, indexer Steve Ingle, senior production editor Valerie Vargas, and Valerie Brandenburg at Lumina. All of these professionals provided innumerable services that helped the text take shape.

We will appreciate suggestions and comments from users—instructors and students alike. You can send your thoughts and ideas about the text to us via email at: *AccountingAuthors@yahoo.com*.

Jerry J. Weygandt
Madison, Wisconsin

Paul D. Kimmel
Madison, Wisconsin

Donald E. Kieso
DeKalb, Illinois

CHAPTER 1

My Good Images/Shutterstock.com

Accounting in Action

The **Chapter Preview** describes the purpose of the chapter and highlights major topics.

Chapter Preview

The following Feature Story about **Columbia Sportswear Company** highlights the importance of having good financial information and knowing how to use it to make effective business decisions. Whatever your pursuits or occupation, the need for financial information is inescapable. You cannot earn a living, spend money, buy on credit, make an investment, or pay taxes without receiving, using, or dispensing financial information. Good decision-making depends on good information. The purpose of this chapter is to show you that accounting is the system used to provide useful financial information.

The **Feature Story** helps you picture how the chapter topic relates to the real world of accounting and business.

Feature Story

Knowing the Numbers

Many students who take this course do not plan to be accountants. If you are in that group, you might be thinking, "If I'm not going to be an accountant, why do I need to know accounting?" Well, consider this quote from Harold Geneen, the former chairman of **IT&T**: "To be good at your business, you have to know the numbers—cold." In business, accounting and financial statements are the means for communicating the numbers. If you don't know how to read financial statements, you can't really know your business.

Knowing the numbers is sometimes even a matter of corporate survival. Consider the story of **Columbia Sportswear Company**, headquartered in Portland, Oregon. Gert Boyle's family fled Nazi Germany when she was 13 years old and then purchased a small hat company in Oregon, Columbia Hat Company. In 1971, Gert's husband, who was then running the company, died suddenly of a heart attack. Gert took over the small, struggling company with help from her son Tim, who was then a senior at the University of Oregon. Somehow, they kept the company afloat. Today, Columbia has more than 4,000 employees and annual sales in excess of $1 billion. Its brands include Columbia, Mountain Hardwear, Sorel, and Montrail.

Columbia doesn't just focus on financial success. Several of its factories have participated in a project to increase health awareness of female factory workers in developing countries. Columbia is also a founding member of the Sustainable Apparel Coalition, which strives to reduce the environmental and social impact of the apparel industry. In addition, the company monitors all of the independent factories that produce its products to ensure that they comply with the company's Standards of Manufacturing Practices. These standards address such issues as forced labor, child labor, harassment, wages and benefits, health and safety, and the environment.

Employers such as Columbia Sportswear generally assume that managers in all areas of the company are "financially literate." To help prepare you for that, this text will help you learn how to read and prepare financial statements, and how to use key tools to evaluate financial results using basic data analytics.

The **Chapter Outline** presents the chapter's topics and subtopics, as well as practice opportunities.

Chapter Outline

LEARNING OBJECTIVES	REVIEW	PRACTICE
LO 1 Identify the activities and users associated with accounting.	• Three activities • Who uses accounting data	**DO IT! 1** Basic Concepts
LO 2 Explain the building blocks of accounting: ethics, principles, and assumptions.	• Ethics • GAAP • Measurement principles • Assumptions	**DO IT! 2** Building Blocks of Accounting
LO 3 State the accounting equation, and define its components.	• Assets • Liabilities • Stockholders' equity	**DO IT! 3** Stockholders' Equity Effects
LO 4 Analyze the effects of business transactions on the accounting equation.	• Accounting transactions • Transaction analysis • Summary of transactions	**DO IT! 4** Tabular Analysis
LO 5 Describe the four financial statements and how they are prepared.	• Income statement • Retained earnings statement • Balance sheet • Statement of cash flows	**DO IT! 5** Financial Statement Items

Go to the Review and Practice section at the end of the chapter for a review of key concepts and practice applications with solutions.

Visit WileyPLUS for additional tutorials and practice opportunities.

Accounting Activities and Users

LEARNING OBJECTIVE 1

Identify the activities and users associated with accounting.

What consistently ranks as one of the top career opportunities in business? What frequently rates among the most popular majors on campus? What was the undergraduate degree chosen by **Nike** founder Phil Knight, **Home Depot** co-founder Arthur Blank, former acting director of the **Federal Bureau of Investigation (FBI)** Thomas Pickard, and numerous members of Congress? Accounting.[1] Why did these people choose accounting? They wanted to understand what was happening financially to their organizations. Accounting is the financial information system that provides these insights. In short, to understand your organization, you have to know the numbers.

    Accounting consists of three basic activities—it **identifies, records, and communicates** the economic events of an organization to interested users. Let's take a closer look at these three activities.

Essential terms are printed in blue when they first appear, and are defined in the end-of-chapter **Glossary Review**.

Three Activities

    As a starting point to the accounting process, a company **identifies the economic events relevant to its business**. Examples of economic events are the sale of snack chips by **PepsiCo**, the provision of telephone services by **AT&T**, and the payment of wages by **Facebook**.

    Once a company like PepsiCo identifies economic events, it **records** those events in order to provide a history of its financial activities. Recording consists of keeping a **systematic, chronological diary of events**, measured in dollars and cents. In recording, PepsiCo also classifies and summarizes economic events.

    Finally, PepsiCo **communicates** the collected information to interested users by means of **accounting reports**. The most common of these reports are called **financial statements**. To make the reported financial information meaningful, PepsiCo reports the recorded data in a standardized way. It accumulates information resulting from similar transactions. For example, PepsiCo accumulates all sales transactions over a certain period of time and reports the data as one amount in the company's financial statements. Such data are said to be reported **in the aggregate**. By presenting the recorded data in the aggregate, the accounting process simplifies a multitude of transactions and makes a series of activities understandable and meaningful.

    A vital element in communicating economic events is the accountant's ability to **analyze and interpret** the reported information. Analysis involves use of ratios, percentages, graphs, and charts to highlight significant financial trends and relationships. Interpretation involves **explaining the uses, meaning, and limitations of reported data**. Appendices A–E show the financial statements of **Apple Inc.**, **PepsiCo, Inc.**, **The Coca-Cola Company**, **Amazon.com, Inc.**, and **Walmart Inc.**, respectively. (In addition, in the *A Look at IFRS* section at the end of each chapter, the French company **LVMH—Louis Vuitton** is analyzed.) We refer to these statements at various places throughout the text. At this point, these financial statements probably strike you as complex and confusing. By the end of this course, you'll be surprised at your ability to understand, analyze, and interpret them.

---

[1] The appendix to this chapter describes job opportunities for accounting majors and explains why accounting is such a popular major.

Illustration 1.1 summarizes the activities of the accounting process.

ILLUSTRATION 1.1 The activities of the accounting process

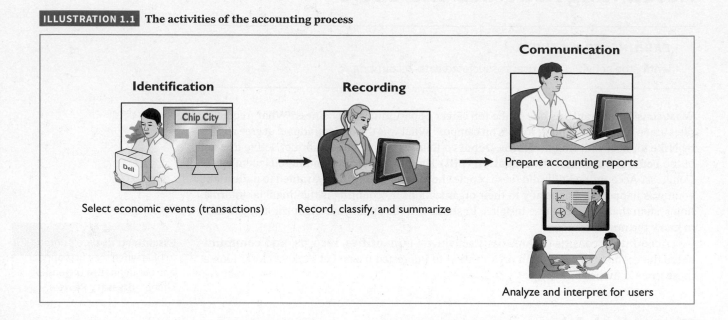

You should understand that the accounting process **includes** the bookkeeping function. **Bookkeeping** usually involves **only** the recording of economic events. It is therefore just one part of the accounting process. In total, accounting involves **the entire process of identifying, recording, and communicating economic events.**[2]

Who Uses Accounting Data

Accounting software systems collect vast amounts of data about the economic events experienced by a company and about the parties with whom the company engages, such as suppliers and customers. Business decision-makers take advantage of this wealth of data by using data analytics to make more informed business decisions. Data analytics involves analyzing data, often employing both software and statistics, to draw inferences. As both data access and analytical software improve, the use of data analytics to support decisions is becoming increasingly common at virtually all types of companies (see **Helpful Hint**).

Users of accounting information can be divided broadly into two groups: internal users and external users.

Internal Users

Internal users of accounting information are the managers who plan, organize, and run a business. These include **marketing managers, production supervisors, finance directors, and company officers.** In running a business, internal users must answer many important questions, as shown in **Illustration 1.2**.

To answer these and other questions, internal users need detailed information on a timely basis. **Managerial accounting** provides internal reports to help users make decisions about their companies. Examples are financial comparisons of operating alternatives, projections of income from new sales campaigns, and forecasts of cash needs for the next year.

---

[2]The origins of accounting are generally attributed to the work of Luca Pacioli, an Italian Renaissance mathematician. Pacioli was a close friend and tutor to Leonardo da Vinci and a contemporary of Christopher Columbus. In his 1494 text *Summa de Arithmetica, Geometria, Proportione et Proportionalite*, Pacioli described a system to ensure that financial information was recorded efficiently and accurately.

ILLUSTRATION 1.2 Questions that internal users ask

Questions Asked by Internal Users

Finance	**Marketing**	**Human Resources**	**Management**
Is cash sufficient to pay dividends to Microsoft stockholders?	What price should Apple charge for an iPhone to maximize the company's net income?	Can General Motors afford to give its employees pay raises this year?	Which PepsiCo product line is the most profitable? Should any product lines be eliminated?

Accounting Across the Organization boxes demonstrate applications of accounting information in various business functions.

Accounting Across the Organization   Clif Bar & Company

iStock.com/Dan Moore

Owning a Piece of the Bar

The original Clif Bar® energy bar was created in 1990 after six months of experimentation by Gary Erickson and his mother in her kitchen. Today, the company has approximately 1,000 employees and was named one of the leading Landor's Breakaway Brands®. One of **Clif Bar & Company**'s proudest moments was the creation of an employee stock ownership plan (ESOP) in 2010. This plan gives its employees 20% ownership of the company. The ESOP also resulted in Clif Bar enacting an open-book management program, including the commitment to educate all employee-owners about its finances. Armed with basic accounting knowledge, employees are more aware of the financial impact of their actions, which leads to better decisions.

What are the benefits to the company and to the employees of making the financial statements available to all employees? (Go to WileyPLUS for this answer and additional questions.)

External Users

External users are individuals and organizations outside a company who want financial information about the company. The two most common types of external users are investors and creditors. **Investors** (owners) use accounting information to decide whether to buy, hold, or sell ownership shares of a company. **Creditors** (such as suppliers and bankers) use accounting information to evaluate the risks of granting credit or lending money. **Illustration 1.3** shows some questions that investors and creditors may ask.

ILLUSTRATION 1.3 Questions that external users ask

Questions Asked by External Users

Investors	**Investors**	**Creditors**
Is General Electric earning satisfactory income?	How does Disney compare in size and profitability with WarnerMedia?	Will United Airlines be able to pay its debts as they come due?

Financial accounting answers these questions. It provides economic and financial information for investors, creditors, and other external users. The information needs of external users vary considerably. **Taxing authorities**, such as the Internal Revenue Service, want to know whether the company complies with tax laws. **Customers** are interested in whether a company like **Tesla, Inc.** will continue to honor product warranties and support its product lines. **Labor unions**, such as the **Major League Baseball Players Association**, want to know whether the owners have the ability to pay increased wages and benefits.

Regulatory agencies, such as the Securities and Exchange Commission or the Federal Trade Commission, want to know whether the company is operating within prescribed rules.

ACTION PLAN

- **Review the basic concepts discussed.**
- **Develop an understanding of the key terms used.**

The **DO IT!** exercises ask you to put newly acquired knowledge to work. They outline the **Action Plan** necessary to complete the exercise, and they show a **Solution**.

DO IT! 1 | Basic Concepts

Indicate whether each of the five statements presented below is true or false. If false, indicate how to correct the statement.

1. The three steps in the accounting process are identification, recording, and communication.
2. Bookkeeping encompasses all steps in the accounting process.
3. Accountants prepare, but do not interpret, financial reports.
4. The two most common types of external users are investors and company officers.
5. Managerial accounting activities focus on reports for internal users.

Solution

1. True.   **2.** False. Bookkeeping involves only the recording step.   **3.** False. Accountants analyze and interpret information in reports as part of the communication step.   **4.** False. The two most common types of external users are investors and creditors.   **5.** True.

Related exercise material: **DO IT! 1.1, E1.1, and E1.2.**

The Building Blocks of Accounting

LEARNING OBJECTIVE 2

Explain the building blocks of accounting: ethics, principles, and assumptions.

A doctor follows certain protocols in treating a patient's illness. An architect follows certain structural guidelines in designing a building. Similarly, an accountant follows certain standards in reporting financial information. These standards are based on specific principles and assumptions. For these standards to work, however, a fundamental business concept must be present—ethical behavior.

Ethics in Financial Reporting

People won't gamble in a casino if they think it is "rigged." Similarly, people won't play the stock market if they think share prices are rigged. At one time, the financial press was full of articles about financial scandals at **Enron**, **WorldCom**, **HealthSouth**, and **AIG**. As more scandals came to light, a mistrust of financial reporting in general seemed to be developing.

One article in the *Wall Street Journal* noted that "repeated disclosures about questionable accounting practices have bruised investors' faith in the reliability of earnings reports, which in turn has sent stock prices tumbling." Imagine trying to carry on a business or invest money if you could not depend on the financial statements to be honestly prepared. Information would have no credibility. There is no doubt that a sound, well-functioning economy depends on accurate and dependable financial reporting.

United States regulators and lawmakers were very concerned that the economy would suffer if investors lost confidence in corporate accounting because of unethical financial reporting. In response, Congress passed the **Sarbanes-Oxley Act (SOX)** to reduce unethical corporate behavior and decrease the likelihood of future corporate scandals. As a result of SOX, top management must now certify the accuracy of financial information. In addition, penalties for fraudulent financial activity are much more severe. Also, SOX increased the independence requirements of the outside auditors who review the accuracy of corporate financial statements and increased the oversight role of boards of directors (see **Ethics Note**).

The standards of conduct by which actions are judged as right or wrong, honest or dishonest, fair or not fair, are **ethics**. Effective financial reporting depends on sound ethical behavior. To sensitize you to ethical situations in business and to give you practice at solving ethical dilemmas, we address ethics in a number of ways in this text:

1. A number of the *Feature Stories* and other parts of the text discuss the central importance of ethical behavior to financial reporting.

2. *Ethics Insight* boxes and marginal *Ethics Notes* highlight ethics situations and issues in actual business settings.

3. Many of the *People, Planet, and Profit Insight* boxes focus on ethical issues that companies face in measuring and reporting social and environmental issues.

4. At the end of the chapter, an *Ethics Case* simulates a business situation and asks you to put yourself in the position of a decision-maker in that case.

When analyzing these various ethics cases and your own ethical experiences, you should apply the three steps outlined in **Illustration 1.4**.

Ethics Notes help sensitize you to some of the ethical issues in accounting.

> **ETHICS NOTE**
>
> Circus-founder P.T. Barnum is alleged to have said, "Trust everyone, but cut the deck." What Sarbanes-Oxley does is to provide measures (like cutting the deck of playing cards) that help ensure that fraud will not occur.

| **ILLUSTRATION 1.4** | Steps in analyzing ethics cases and situations |

1. Recognize an ethical situation and the ethical issues involved.

Use your personal ethics to identify ethical situations and issues. Some businesses and professional organizations provide written codes of ethics for guidance in some business situations.

2. Identify and analyze the principal elements in the situation.

Identify the **stakeholders**—persons or groups who may be harmed or benefited. Ask the question: What are the responsibilities and obligations of the parties involved?

3. Identify the alternatives, and weigh the impact of each alternative on various stakeholders.

Select the most ethical alternative, considering all the consequences. Sometimes there will be one right answer. Other situations involve more than one right solution; these situations require an evaluation of each and a selection of the best alternative.

Insight boxes provide examples of business situations from various perspectives—ethics, investor, international, and corporate social responsibility. Guideline answers to the critical thinking questions as well as additional questions are available in **WileyPLUS**.

Ethics Insight   Dewey & LeBoeuf LLP

Alliance Images/
Shutterstock.com

I Felt the Pressure—Would You?

"I felt the pressure." That's what some of the employees of the now-defunct law firm of **Dewey & LeBoeuf LLP** indicated when they helped to overstate revenue and use accounting tricks to hide losses and cover up cash shortages. These employees worked for the former finance director and former chief financial officer (CFO) of the firm. Here are some of their comments:

- "I was instructed by the CFO to create invoices, knowing they would not be sent to clients. When I created these invoices, I knew that it was inappropriate."

- "I intentionally gave the auditors incorrect information in the course of the audit."

What happened here is that a small group of lower-level employees over a period of years carried out the instructions of their bosses. Their bosses, however, seemed to have no concern about unethical practices as evidenced by various e-mails with one another in which they referred to their financial manipulations as accounting tricks, cooking the books, and fake income.

Sources: Ashby Jones, "Guilty Pleas of Dewey Staff Detail the Alleged Fraud," *Wall Street Journal* (March 28, 2014); and Sara Randazzo, "Dewey CFO Escapes Jail Time in Fraud Case Sentencing," *Wall Street Journal* (October 10, 2017).

Why did these employees lie, and what do you believe should be their penalty for these lies? (Go to WileyPLUS for this answer and additional questions.)

Generally Accepted Accounting Principles

International Note

Over 115 countries use international standards (called IFRS). For example, all companies in the European Union follow IFRS. The differences between U.S. and international standards are not generally significant.

International Notes highlight differences between U.S. and international accounting standards.

The accounting profession has developed standards that are generally accepted and universally practiced. This common set of standards is called **generally accepted accounting principles (GAAP)**. These standards indicate how to report economic events.

The primary accounting standard-setting body in the United States is the **Financial Accounting Standards Board (FASB)**. The **Securities and Exchange Commission (SEC)** is the agency of the U.S. government that oversees U.S. financial markets and accounting standard-setting bodies. The SEC relies on the FASB to develop accounting standards, which public companies must follow. Many countries outside of the United States have adopted the accounting standards issued by the **International Accounting Standards Board (IASB)**. These standards are called **International Financial Reporting Standards (IFRS)** (see **International Note**).

As markets become more global, it is often desirable to compare the results of companies from different countries that report using different accounting standards. In order to increase comparability, in recent years the two standard-setting bodies have made efforts to reduce the differences between U.S. GAAP and IFRS. This process is referred to as **convergence**. As a result of these convergence efforts, it is likely that someday there will be a single set of high-quality accounting standards that are used by companies around the world. Because convergence is such an important issue, we highlight any major differences between GAAP and IFRS in *International Notes* as part of the text discussion as well as provide a more in-depth discussion in the *A Look at IFRS* section at the end of each chapter.

International Insight

Toru Hanai/Pool/Getty Images

The Korean Discount

If you think that accounting standards don't matter, consider recent events in South Korea. For many years, international investors complained that the financial reports of South Korean companies were inadequate and inaccurate. Accounting practices there often resulted in huge differences between stated revenues and actual revenues. Because investors did not have faith in the accuracy of the numbers, they were unwilling to pay as much for the shares of these companies relative to shares of comparable companies in different countries. This difference in share price was often referred to as the "Korean discount."

In response, Korean regulators decided that companies would have to comply with international accounting standards.

This change was motivated by a desire to "make the country's businesses more transparent" in order to build investor confidence and spur economic growth. Many other Asian countries, including China, India, and Japan, have also decided either to adopt international standards or to create standards that are based on the international standards.

Source: Evan Ramstad, "End to 'Korea Discount'?" *Wall Street Journal* (March 16, 2007).

What is meant by the phrase "make the country's businesses more transparent"? Why would increasing transparency spur economic growth? (Go to WileyPLUS for this answer and additional questions.)

HELPFUL HINT

Relevance and *faithful representation* are two primary qualities that make accounting information useful for decision-making.

Measurement Principles

GAAP generally uses one of two measurement principles, the historical cost principle or the fair value principle. Selection of which principle to follow generally relates to trade-offs between relevance and faithful representation (see **Helpful Hint**). **Relevance** means that financial information is capable of making a difference in a decision. **Faithful representation** means that the numbers and descriptions match what really existed or happened—they are factual.

Historical Cost Principle

The **historical cost principle** (or cost principle) dictates that companies record assets at their cost. This is true not only at the time the asset is purchased but also over the time the asset is held. For example, if **Best Buy** purchases land for $360,000, the company initially reports it in its accounting records at $360,000. But what does Best Buy do if, by the end of the next year, the fair value of the land has increased to $400,000? Under the historical cost principle, it continues to report the land at $360,000.

Fair Value Principle

The **fair value principle** states that assets and liabilities should be reported at fair value (the price received to sell an asset or settle a liability). Fair value information may be more useful than historical cost for certain types of assets and liabilities. For example, certain investment securities are reported at fair value because market price information is usually readily available for these types of assets.

In determining which measurement principle to use, companies weigh the factual nature of cost figures versus the relevance of fair value. In general, most companies choose to use cost. Only in situations where assets are actively traded, such as investment securities, do companies apply the fair value principle extensively.

Assumptions

Assumptions provide a foundation for the accounting process. Two main assumptions are the **monetary unit assumption** and the **economic entity assumption**.

Monetary Unit Assumption

The **monetary unit assumption** requires that companies include in the accounting records only transaction data that can be expressed in money terms. This assumption enables accounting to quantify (measure) economic events. The monetary unit assumption is vital to applying the historical cost principle.

This assumption prevents the inclusion of some relevant information in the accounting records. For example, the health of a company's owner, the quality of service, and the morale of employees are not included. The reason: Companies cannot quantify this information in money terms. Though this information is important, companies record only events that can be measured in money.

Economic Entity Assumption

An economic entity can be any organization or unit in society. It may be a company (such as **Crocs, Inc.**), a governmental unit (the state of Ohio), a municipality (Seattle), a school district (St. Louis District 48), or a church (Southern Baptist). The **economic entity assumption** requires that the activities of the entity be kept separate and distinct from the activities of its owner and all other economic entities (see **Ethics Note**). To illustrate, Sally Rider, owner of Sally's Boutique, must keep her personal living costs separate from the expenses of her business. Similarly, **J. Crew** and **Gap Inc.** are segregated into separate economic entities for accounting purposes.

Proprietorship   A business owned by one person is generally a **proprietorship**. The owner is often the manager/operator of the business. Small service-type businesses (plumbing companies, beauty salons, and auto repair shops), farms, and small retail stores (antique shops, clothing stores, and used-book stores) are often proprietorships. **Usually, only a relatively small amount of money (capital) is necessary to start in business as a proprietorship. The owner (proprietor) receives any profits, suffers any losses, and is personally liable for all debts of the business.** There is no legal distinction between the business as an economic unit and the owner, but the accounting records of the business activities are kept separate from the personal records and activities of the owner.

ETHICS NOTE

The importance of the economic entity assumption is illustrated by scandals involving Adelphia. In this case, senior company employees entered into transactions that blurred the line between the employees' financial interests and those of the company. For example, Adelphia guaranteed over $2 billion of loans to the founding family.

Partnership   A business owned by two or more persons associated as partners is a **partnership**. In most respects, a partnership is like a proprietorship except that more than one owner is involved. Typically, a partnership agreement (written or oral) sets forth such terms as initial investment, duties of each partner, division of net income (or net loss), and settlement to be made upon death or withdrawal of a partner. Each partner generally has unlimited personal liability for the debts of the partnership. **Like a proprietorship, for accounting purposes the partnership transactions must be kept separate from the personal activities of the partners.** Partnerships are often used to organize retail and service-type businesses, including professional practices (lawyers, doctors, architects, and certified public accountants).

Corporation   A business organized as a separate legal entity under state corporation law and having ownership divided into transferable shares of stock is a **corporation**. The holders of the shares (stockholders) **enjoy limited liability**; that is, they are not personally liable for the debts of the corporate entity. Stockholders **may transfer all or part of their ownership shares to other investors at any time** (i.e., sell their shares). The ease with which ownership can change adds to the attractiveness of investing in a corporation. Because ownership can be transferred without dissolving the corporation, the corporation **enjoys an unlimited life**.

Although the combined number of proprietorships and partnerships in the United States is more than five times the number of corporations, the revenue produced by corporations is eight times greater. Most of the largest companies in the United States—for example, **ExxonMobil**, **Ford**, **Walmart Inc.**, **Citigroup**, and **Apple**—are corporations.

Accounting Across the Organization

blublaf/E+/Getty Images

Spinning the Career Wheel

How will the study of accounting help you? A working knowledge of accounting is desirable for virtually every field of business. Some examples of how accounting is used in business careers include:

General management: Managers at **Ford Motors, Massachusetts General Hospital, California State University–Fullerton**, a **McDonald's** franchise, and a **Trek** bike shop all need to understand accounting data in order to make wise business decisions.

Marketing: Marketing specialists at **Procter & Gamble** must be sensitive to costs and benefits, which accounting helps them quantify and understand. Making a sale is meaningless unless it is a profitable sale.

Finance: Do you want to be a banker for **Citicorp**, an investment analyst for **Goldman Sachs**, or a stock broker for **Merrill Lynch**? These fields rely heavily on accounting knowledge to analyze financial statements. In fact, it is difficult to get a good job in a finance function without two or three courses in accounting.

Real estate: Are you interested in being a real estate broker for **Prudential Real Estate**? Because a third party—the bank—is almost always involved in financing a real estate transaction, brokers must understand the numbers involved: Can the buyer afford to make the payments to the bank? Does the cash flow from an industrial property justify the purchase price? What are the tax benefits of the purchase?

How might accounting help you? (Go to WileyPLUS for this answer and additional questions.)

ACTION PLAN
- **Review the discussion of ethics and financial reporting standards.**
- **Develop an understanding of the key terms used.**

DO IT! 2 | Building Blocks of Accounting

Indicate whether each of the five statements presented below is true or false. If false, indicate how to correct the statement.

1. Congress passed the Sarbanes-Oxley Act to reduce unethical behavior and decrease the likelihood of future corporate scandals.
2. The primary accounting standard-setting body in the United States is the Financial Accounting Standards Board (FASB).

3. The historical cost principle dictates that companies record assets at their cost. In later periods, however, the fair value of the asset must be used if its fair value is higher than its cost.

4. Relevance means that financial information matches what really happened; the information is factual.

5. A business owner's personal expenses must be separated from expenses of the business to comply with accounting's economic entity assumption.

Solution

1. True.   **2.** True.   **3.** False. The historical cost principle dictates that companies record assets at their cost. Under the historical cost principle, the company must also use cost in later periods. **4.** False. Faithful representation, not relevance, means that financial information matches what really happened; the information is factual.   **5.** True.

Related exercise material: **DO IT! 1.2, E1.3, and E1.4.**

The Accounting Equation

LEARNING OBJECTIVE 3

State the accounting equation, and define its components.

The two basic elements of a business are what it owns and what it owes. **Assets** are the resources a business owns. For example, **Google** has total assets of approximately $93.8 billion. Liabilities and stockholders' equity are the rights or claims against these resources. Thus, Google has $93.8 billion of claims against its $93.8 billion of assets. Claims of those to whom the company owes money (creditors) are called **liabilities**. Claims of owners are called **stockholders' equity**. Google has liabilities of $22.1 billion and stockholders' equity of $71.7 billion.

We can express the relationship of assets, liabilities, and stockholders' equity as an equation, as shown in **Illustration 1.5**.

Assets	=	Liabilities	+	Stockholders' Equity

ILLUSTRATION 1.5

The basic accounting equation

This relationship is the **basic accounting equation**. Assets must equal the sum of liabilities and stockholders' equity. Liabilities appear before stockholders' equity in the basic accounting equation because they are paid first if a business is liquidated.

The accounting equation applies to all **economic entities** regardless of size, nature of business, or form of business organization. It applies to a small proprietorship such as a corner grocery store as well as to a giant corporation such as **PepsiCo**. The equation provides the **underlying framework** for recording and summarizing economic events.

Let's look in more detail at the categories in the basic accounting equation.

Assets

As noted above, **assets** are resources a business owns. The business uses its assets in carrying out such activities as production and sales. The common characteristic possessed by all assets is **the capacity to provide future services or benefits**. In a business, that service potential or future economic benefit eventually results in cash inflows (receipts). For example, consider Campus Pizza, a local restaurant. It owns a delivery include truck that provides economic benefits from delivering pizzas. Other assets of Campus Pizza include tables, chairs, jukebox, cash register, oven, tableware, and, of course, cash.

Liabilities

Liabilities are claims against assets—that is, existing debts and obligations. Businesses of all sizes usually borrow money and purchase merchandise on credit. These economic activities result in payables of various sorts:

- Campus Pizza, for instance, purchases cheese, sausage, flour, and beverages on credit from suppliers. These obligations are called **accounts payable**.
- Campus Pizza also has a **note payable** to First National Bank for the money borrowed to purchase the delivery truck.
- Campus Pizza may also have **salaries and wages payable** to employees and **sales and real estate taxes payable** to the local government.

All of these persons or entities to whom Campus Pizza owes money are its **creditors**.

Creditors may legally force the liquidation of a business that does not pay its debts. In that case, the law requires that creditor claims be paid **before** ownership claims.

Stockholders' Equity

The ownership claim on a corporation's total assets is **stockholders' equity** (see **Helpful Hint**). It is equal to total assets minus total liabilities. Here is why: The assets of a business are claimed by either creditors or stockholders. To find out what belongs to stockholders, we subtract creditors' claims (the liabilities) from the assets. The remainder is the stockholders' claim on the assets—stockholders' equity. It is often referred to as **residual equity**—that is, the equity "left over" after creditors' claims are satisfied.

The stockholders' equity section of a corporation's balance sheet generally consists of (1) common stock and (2) retained earnings.

Common Stock

A corporation may obtain funds by selling shares of stock to investors. **Common stock** is the term used to describe the total amount paid in by stockholders for the shares they purchase.

Retained Earnings

The **retained earnings** section of the balance sheet is determined by three items: revenues, expenses, and dividends.

Revenues **Revenues are the increases in assets or decreases in liabilities resulting from the sale of goods or the performance of services in the normal course of business** (see **Helpful Hint**). Revenues usually result in an increase in an asset. They may arise from different sources and are called various names depending on the nature of the business. Campus Pizza, for instance, has two categories of sales revenues—pizza sales and beverage sales. Other titles for and sources of revenue common to many businesses are sales, fees, services, commissions, interest, dividends, royalties, and rent.

Expenses **Expenses** are the cost of assets consumed or services used in the process of generating revenue. **They are decreases in stockholders' equity that result from operating the business** (see **Helpful Hint**). Like revenues, expenses take many forms and are called various names depending on the type of asset consumed or service used. For example, Campus Pizza recognizes the following types of expenses: cost of ingredients (flour, cheese, tomato paste, meat, mushrooms, etc.); cost of beverages; wages expense; utilities expense (electric, gas, and water expense); telephone expense; delivery expense (gasoline, repairs, licenses, etc.); supplies expense (napkins, detergents, aprons, etc.); rent expense; interest expense; and property tax expense.

Dividends Net income represents an increase in net assets which are then available to distribute to stockholders. The distribution of cash or other assets to stockholders is called a **dividend**. Dividends reduce retained earnings. However, dividends are **not an expense**.

A corporation first determines its revenues and expenses and then computes net income or net loss. If it has net income and decides it has no better use for that income, a corporation may decide to distribute a dividend to its owners (the stockholders).

In summary, the principal sources (increases) of stockholders' equity are investments by stockholders and revenues from business operations. In contrast, reductions (decreases) in stockholders' equity result from expenses and dividends. These relationships are shown in **Illustration 1.6**.

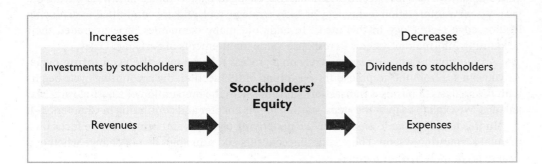

ILLUSTRATION 1.6

Increases and decreases in stockholders' equity

DO IT! 3 | Stockholders' Equity Effects

Classify the following items as issuance of stock (I), dividends (D), revenues (R), or expenses (E). Then indicate whether each item increases or decreases stockholders' equity.

1. Rent Expense.
2. Service Revenue.
3. Dividends.
4. Salaries and Wages Expense.

Solution

1. Rent Expense is an expense (E); it decreases stockholders' equity. **2.** Service Revenue is revenue (R); it increases stockholders' equity. **3.** Dividends is a distribution to stockholders (D); it decreases stockholders' equity. **4.** Salaries and Wages Expense is an expense (E); it decreases stockholders' equity.

Related exercise material: **BE1.1, BE1.2, BE1.3, BE1.4, BE1.5, DO IT! 1.3,** and **E1.5.**

ACTION PLAN

- **Understand the sources of revenue.**
- **Understand what causes expenses.**
- **Review the rules for changes in stockholders' equity.**
- **Recognize that dividends are distributions of cash or other assets to stockholders.**

Analyzing Business Transactions

LEARNING OBJECTIVE 4

Analyze the effects of business transactions on the accounting equation.

Analyze business transactions → JOURNALIZE → POST → TRIAL BALANCE → ADJUSTING ENTRIES → ADJUSTED TRIAL BALANCE → FINANCIAL STATEMENTS → CLOSING ENTRIES → POST-CLOSING TRIAL BALANCE

The system of collecting and processing transaction data and communicating financial information to decision-makers is known as the **accounting information system**. Factors that shape an accounting information system include the nature of the company's business,

This **accounting cycle graphic** illustrates the steps companies follow each period to record transactions and eventually prepare financial statements.

the types of transactions, the size of the company, the volume of data, and the information demands of management and others.

Most businesses use computerized accounting systems—sometimes referred to as electronic data processing (EDP) systems. These systems handle all the steps involved in the recording process, from initial data entry to preparation of the financial statements. In order to remain competitive, companies continually improve their accounting systems to provide accurate and timely data for decision-making. For example, in a recent annual report, **Tootsie Roll** stated, "We also invested in additional processing and data storage hardware during the year. We view information technology as a key strategic tool, and are committed to deploying leading edge technology in this area." In addition, many companies have upgraded their accounting information systems in response to the requirements of Sarbanes-Oxley.

Accounting information systems rely on a process referred to as **the accounting cycle**. As you can see from the graphic at the beginning of this section, the accounting cycle begins with the analysis of business transactions and ends with the preparation of a post-closing trial balance. We explain each of the steps, starting in this chapter and continuing in Chapters 2–4.

In this text, in order to emphasize the underlying concepts and principles, we focus on a manual accounting system. The accounting concepts and principles do not change whether a system is computerized or manual.

Accounting Transactions

Transactions (**business transactions**) are a business's economic events recorded by accountants. Transactions may be external or internal. **External transactions** involve economic events between the company and some outside enterprise. For example, Campus Pizza's purchase of cooking equipment from a supplier, payment of monthly rent to the landlord, and sale of pizzas to customers are external transactions. **Internal transactions** are economic events that occur entirely within one company. The use of cooking and cleaning supplies are internal transactions for Campus Pizza.

Companies carry on many activities that do not represent business transactions. Examples are hiring employees, responding to e-mails, talking with customers, and placing merchandise orders. Some of these activities may lead to business transactions: Employees will earn wages, and suppliers will deliver ordered merchandise. The company must analyze each event to find out if it affects the components of the accounting equation. If it does, the company will record the transaction. **Illustration 1.7** demonstrates the transaction identification process.

ILLUSTRATION 1.7 Transaction identification process

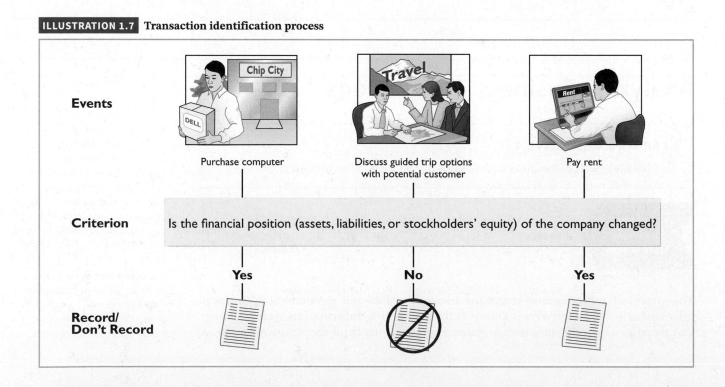

Events

Purchase computer | Discuss guided trip options with potential customer | Pay rent

Criterion: Is the financial position (assets, liabilities, or stockholders' equity) of the company changed?

Yes | No | Yes

Record/ Don't Record

Each transaction must have a dual effect on the accounting equation. For example, if an asset is increased, there must be a corresponding:

- Decrease in another asset, *or*
- Increase in a specific liability, *or*
- Increase in stockholders' equity.

Two or more items could be affected. For example, as one asset is increased $10,000, another asset could decrease $6,000 and a liability could increase $4,000. Any change in a liability or ownership claim is subject to similar analysis.

Transaction Analysis

To demonstrate how to analyze transactions in terms of the accounting equation, we will review the business activities of Softbyte Inc., a smartphone app development business, during its first month of operations. As part of this analysis, we will expand the basic accounting equation. This will allow us to better illustrate the impact of transactions on stockholders' equity. Recall that stockholders' equity is comprised of two parts: common stock and retained earnings. Common stock is affected when the company issues new shares of stock in exchange for cash. Retained earnings is affected when the company earns revenue, incurs expenses, or pays dividends. **Illustration 1.8** shows the **expanded accounting equation**.

ILLUSTRATION 1.8 **Expanded accounting equation**

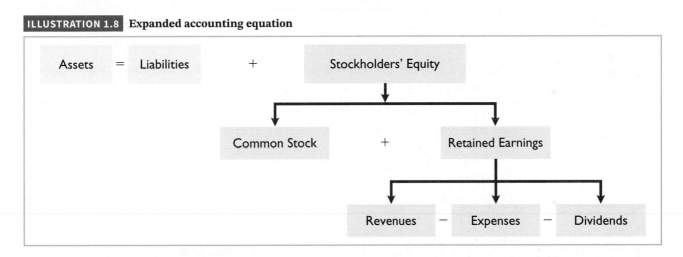

If you are tempted to skip ahead after you've read a few of the following transaction analyses, don't do it (see **Helpful Hint**). Each has something unique to teach, something you'll need later. (We assure you that we've kept them to the minimum needed!)

Transaction 1. Investment of Cash by Stockholders   Ray and Barbara Neal start a smartphone app development company that they incorporate as Softbyte Inc. On September 1, 2020, they invest $15,000 cash in the business in exchange for $15,000 of common stock. The common stock indicates the ownership interest that the Neals have in Softbyte Inc. This transaction results in an equal increase in both assets and stockholders' equity.

HELPFUL HINT

Study these transactions until you are sure you understand them. They are not difficult, but understanding them is important to your success in this course. The ability to analyze transactions in terms of the basic accounting equation is essential in accounting.

Basic Analysis	The asset Cash increases $15,000, and stockholders' equity (specifically, Common Stock) increases $15,000.

		Assets	**=**	**Liabilities**	**+**	**Stockholders' Equity**	
Equation Analysis		Cash	=			Common Stock	
	(1)	+$15,000	=			+$15,000	**Issued Stock**

Observe that the equality of the basic equation has been maintained. Note also that the source of the increase in stockholders' equity (in this case, issued stock) is indicated. Why does this matter? Because investments by stockholders do not represent revenues, and they are excluded in determining net income. Therefore, it is necessary to make clear that the increase is an investment rather than revenue from operations. Additional investments (i.e., investments made by stockholders after the corporation has been initially formed) have the same effect on stockholders' equity as the initial investment.

Transaction 2. Purchase of Equipment for Cash

Softbyte Inc. purchases computer equipment for $7,000 cash. This transaction results in an equal increase and decrease in total assets, though the composition of assets changes.

Basic Analysis	The asset Cash decreases $7,000, and the asset Equipment increases $7,000.

		Assets			=	**Liabilities**	+	**Stockholders' Equity**
		Cash	+	Equipment	=			Common Stock
Equation Analysis		$15,000						$15,000
	(2)	−7,000		+$7,000				
		$ 8,000	+	$7,000	=			$15,000
			$15,000					

Observe that total assets are still $15,000. Common stock also remains at $15,000, the amount of the original investment.

Transaction 3. Purchase of Supplies on Credit

Softbyte Inc. purchases headsets (and other computer accessories expected to last several months) for $1,600 from Mobile Solutions. Mobile Solutions agrees to allow Softbyte to pay this bill in October. This transaction is a purchase on account (a credit purchase). Assets increase because of the expected future benefits of using the headsets and computer accessories, and liabilities increase by the amount due Mobile Solutions.

Basic Analysis	The asset Supplies increases $1,600, and the liability Accounts Payable increases $1,600.

		Assets					=	**Liabilities**	+	**Stockholders' Equity**
		Cash	+	Supplies	+	Equipment	=	Accounts Payable	+	Common Stock
Equation Analysis		$8,000				$7,000				$15,000
	(3)			+$1,600				+$1,600		
		$8,000	+	$1,600	+	$7,000	=	$1,600	+	$15,000
				$16,600				$16,600		

Total assets are now $16,600. This total is matched by a $1,600 creditor's claim and a $15,000 ownership claim.

Transaction 4. Services Performed for Cash

Softbyte Inc. receives $1,200 cash from customers for app development services it has performed. This transaction represents Softbyte's principal revenue-producing activity. Recall that **revenue increases stockholders' equity**.

Basic Analysis	The asset Cash increases $1,200, and stockholders' equity increases $1,200 due to Service Revenue.

			Assets			=	Liabilities	+		Stockholders' Equity				
							Accounts		Common			Retained Earnings		
		Cash	+ Supplies	+ Equipment	=		Payable	+	Stock	+	Rev.	− Exp.	− Div.	
Equation Analysis		$8,000	$1,600	$7,000			$1,600		$15,000					
	(4)	+1,200									+$1,200			Service Revenue
		$9,200 +	$1,600 +	$7,000	=		$1,600	+	$15,000	+	$1,200			
			$17,800						$17,800					

The two sides of the equation balance at $17,800. Service Revenue is included in determining Softbyte's net income.

Note that we do not have room to give details for each individual revenue and expense account in this illustration. Thus, revenues (and expenses when we get to them) are summarized under one column heading for Revenues and one for Expenses. However, it is important to keep track of the category (account) titles affected (e.g., Service Revenue) as they will be needed when we prepare financial statements later in the chapter.

Transaction 5. Purchase of Advertising on Credit   Softbyte Inc. receives a bill for $250 from the *Daily News* for advertising on its online website but postpones payment until a later date. This transaction results in an increase in liabilities and a decrease in stockholders' equity.

Basic Analysis	The liability Accounts Payable increases $250, and stockholders' equity decreases $250 due to Advertising Expense.

			Assets			=	Liabilities	+		Stockholders' Equity				
							Accounts		Common			Retained Earnings		
		Cash	+ Supplies	+ Equipment	=		Payable	+	Stock	+	Rev.	− Exp.	− Div.	
Equation Analysis		$9,200	$1,600	$7,000			$1,600		$15,000		$1,200			
	(5)						+250					−$250		Advertising Expense
		$9,200 +	$1,600 +	$7,000	=		$1,850	+	$15,000	+	$1,200	− $250		
			$17,800						$17,800					

The two sides of the equation still balance at $17,800. Retained Earnings decreases when Softbyte incurs the expense. Expenses do not have to be paid in cash at the time they are incurred. When Softbyte pays at a later date, the liability Accounts Payable will decrease and the asset Cash will decrease (see Transaction 8). The cost of advertising is an expense (rather than an asset) because Softbyte has used the benefits. Advertising Expense is included in determining net income.

Transaction 6. Services Performed for Cash and Credit   Softbyte Inc. performs $3,500 of app development services for customers. The company receives cash of $1,500 from customers, and it bills the balance of $2,000 on account. This transaction results in an equal increase in assets and stockholders' equity.

Basic Analysis	Three specific items are affected: The asset Cash increases $1,500, the asset Accounts Receivable increases $2,000, and stockholders' equity increases $3,500 due to Service Revenue.

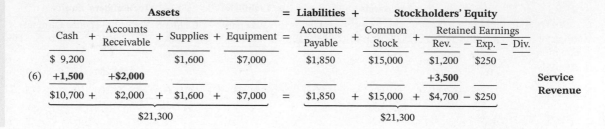

	Assets				=	Liabilities	+	Stockholders' Equity			
	Cash +	Accounts Receivable	+ Supplies +	Equipment =		Accounts Payable	+	Common Stock	+	Retained Earnings	
										Rev. − Exp. − Div.	
	$ 9,200		$1,600	$7,000		$1,850		$15,000		$1,200 $250	
(6)	+1,500	+$2,000								+3,500	Service Revenue
	$10,700 +	$2,000 +	$1,600 +	$7,000 =		$1,850	+	$15,000 +		$4,700 − $250	

$21,300 $21,300

Softbyte recognizes $3,500 in revenues when it performs the service. In exchange for this service, it received $1,500 in Cash and Accounts Receivable of $2,000. This Accounts Receivable represents customers' promises to pay $2,000 to Softbyte in the future. When it later receives collections on account, Softbyte will increase Cash and will decrease Accounts Receivable (see Transaction 9).

Transaction 7. Payment of Expenses Softbyte Inc. pays the following expenses in cash for September: office rent $600, salaries and wages of employees $900, and utilities $200. These payments result in an equal decrease in assets and stockholders' equity.

Basic Analysis	The asset Cash decreases $1,700, and stockholders' equity decreases $1,700 due to the following expenses: Rent Expense, Salaries and Wages Expense, and Utilities Expense.

	Assets				=	Liabilities	−	Stockholders' Equity			
	Cash +	Accounts Receivable	+ Supplies +	Equipment =		Accounts Payable	+	Common Stock	+	Retained Earnings	
										Rev. − Exp. − Div.	
	$10,700	$2,000	$1,600	$7,000		$1,850		$15,000		$4,700 $ 250	
(7)	−1,700									−600	Rent Exp.
										−900	Sal./Wages Exp.
										−200	Utilities Exp.
	$ 9,000 +	$2,000 +	$1,600 +	$7,000 =		$1,850	+	$15,000 +		$4,700 − $1,950	

$19,600 $19,600

The two sides of the equation now balance at $19,600. Three lines are required in the analysis to indicate the different types of expenses that have been incurred.

Transaction 8. Payment of Accounts Payable Softbyte Inc. pays its $250 *Daily News* bill in cash. The company previously (in Transaction 5) recorded the bill as an increase in Accounts Payable and a decrease in stockholders' equity.

Basic Analysis	This cash payment "on account" decreases the asset Cash by $250 and also decreases the liability Accounts Payable by $250.

	Assets				=	Liabilities	+	Stockholders' Equity			
	Cash +	Accounts Receivable	+ Supplies +	Equipment =		Accounts Payable	+	Common Stock	+	Retained Earnings	
										Rev. −Exp. − Div.	
	$9,000	$2,000	$1,600	$7,000		$1,850		$15,000		$4,700 $1,950	
(8)	−250					−250					
	$8,750 +	$2,000 +	$1,600 +	$7,000 =		$1,600	+	$15,000 +		$4,700 − $1,950	

$19,350 $19,350

Observe that the payment of a liability related to an expense that has previously been recorded does not affect stockholders' equity. Softbyte recorded the expense (in Transaction 5) and should not record it again.

Transaction 9. Receipt of Cash on Account   Softbyte Inc. receives $600 in cash from customers who had been billed for services (in Transaction 6). Transaction 9 does not change total assets, but it changes the composition of those assets.

Basic Analysis	The asset Cash increases $600, and the asset Accounts Receivable decreases $600.

Equation Analysis

		Assets				=	Liabilities +		Stockholders' Equity		
	Cash +	Accounts Receivable	+ Supplies +	Equipment =			Accounts Payable	+ Common Stock +	Retained Earnings Rev. − Exp. − Div.		
	$8,750	$2,000	$1,600	$7,000			$1,600	$15,000	$4,700 $1,950		
(9)	+600	−600									
	$9,350 +	$1,400	+ $1,600 +	$7,000	=		$1,600	+ $15,000	+ $4,700 − $1,950		
		$19,350						$19,350			

Note that the collection of an account receivable for services previously billed and recorded does not affect stockholders' equity. Softbyte already recorded this revenue (in Transaction 6) and should not record it again.

Transaction 10. Dividends   The corporation pays a dividend of $1,300 in cash to Ray and Barbara Neal, the stockholders of Softbyte Inc. This transaction results in an equal decrease in assets and stockholders' equity.

Basic Analysis	The asset Cash decreases $1,300, and stockholders' equity decreases $1,300 due to dividends.

Equation Analysis

		Assets				=	Liabilities +		Stockholders' Equity		
	Cash +	Accounts Receivable	+ Supplies +	Equipment =			Accounts Payable	+ Common Stock +	Retained Earnings Rev. − Exp. − Div.		
	$9,350	$1,400	$1,600	$7,000			$1,600	$15,000	$4,700 $1,950		
(10)	−1,300								− $1,300	Dividends	
	$8,050 +	$1,400	+ $1,600 +	$7,000	=		$1,600	+ $15,000	+ $4,700 − $1,950 − $1,300		
		$18,050						$18,050			

Note that the dividend reduces retained earnings, which is part of stockholders' equity. **Dividends are not expenses**. Like stockholders' investments, dividends are excluded in determining net income.

Summary of Transactions

Illustration 1.9 summarizes the September transactions of Softbyte Inc. to show their cumulative effect on the basic accounting equation. It also indicates the transaction number and the specific effects of each transaction. Finally, Illustration 1.9 demonstrates a number of significant facts:

1. Each transaction must be analyzed in terms of its effect on:
    a. The three components of the basic accounting equation (assets, liabilities, and stockholders' equity).
    b. Specific types (kinds) of items within each component (such as the asset Cash).

2. The two sides of the equation must always be equal.

3. The Common Stock and Retained Earnings columns indicate the causes of each change in the stockholders' claim on assets.

ILLUSTRATION 1.9 Tabular summary of Softbyte Inc. transactions

Trans-action	Cash	+	Accounts Receivable	+ Supplies +	Equipment	=	Accounts Payable	+	Common Stock	+	Rev.	− Exp.	− Div.	
				Assets		=	**Liabilities +**				**Stockholders' Equity** Retained Earnings			
(1)	+$15,000							+	$15,000					Issued Stock
(2)	−7,000				+$7,000									
(3)				+$1,600			+$1,600							
(4)	+1,200										+$1,200			Service Revenue
(5)							+250					−$250		Adver. Expense
(6)	+1,500		+$2,000								+3,500			Service Revenue
(7)	−1,700											−600		Rent Expense
												−900		Sal./Wages Exp.
												−200		Utilities Expense
(8)	−250						−250							
(9)	+600		−600											
(10)	−1,300												−$1,300	Dividends
	$ 8,050 +		$1,400 +	$1,600 +	$7,000	=	$1,600	+	$15,000	+	$4,700 −	$1,950 −	$1,300	

$18,050 $18,050

There! You made it through transaction analysis. If you feel a bit shaky on any of the transactions, it might be a good idea at this point to get up, take a short break, and come back again for a brief (10- to 15-minute) review of the transactions, to make sure you understand them before you go on to the next section.

ACTION PLAN

- Analyze the effects of each transaction on the accounting equation.
- Use appropriate category names (not descriptions).
- Keep the accounting equation in balance.

DO IT! 4 | Tabular Analysis

Transactions made by Virmari & Co., a public accounting firm, for the month of August are shown below. Prepare a tabular analysis which shows the effects of these transactions on the expanded accounting equation, similar to that shown in Illustration 1.9.

1. Virmari sold shares of common stock for $25,000 cash.

2. The company purchased $7,000 of office equipment on credit.

3. The company received $8,000 cash in exchange for services performed.

4. The company paid $850 for this month's rent.

5. The company paid a dividend of $1,000 in cash to stockholders.

Solution

Trans-action	Cash	+	Equipment	=	Accounts Payable	+	Common Stock	+	Rev.	− Exp.	− Div.	
		Assets		=	**Liabilities +**				**Stockholders' Equity** Retained Earnings			
(1)	+$25,000						+$25,000					
(2)			+$7,000		+$7,000							
(3)	+8,000								+$8,000			Service Revenue
(4)	−850									−$850		Rent Expense
(5)	−1,000										−$1,000	Dividends
	$31,150 +		$7,000	=	$7,000	+	$25,000	+	$8,000	− $850	− $1,000	

$38,150 $38,150

Related exercise material: **BE1.6, BE1.7, BE1.8, BE1.9, DO IT! 1.4, E1.6, E1.7, and E1.8.**

The Financial Statements

LEARNING OBJECTIVE 5
Describe the four financial statements and how they are prepared.

Companies prepare four financial statements from the summarized accounting data (see **Helpful Hint**):

1. An **income statement** presents the revenues and expenses and resulting net income or net loss for a specific period of time.
2. A **retained earnings statement** summarizes the changes in retained earnings for a specific period of time.
3. A **balance sheet** reports the assets, liabilities, and stockholders' equity of a company at a specific date.
4. A **statement of cash flows** summarizes information about the cash inflows (receipts) and outflows (payments) for a specific period of time.

These statements provide relevant financial data for internal and external users. **Illustration 1.10** shows the financial statements of Softbyte Inc. Note that the statements shown in Illustration 1.10 are interrelated:

1. Net income of $2,750 on the **income statement** is added to the beginning balance of retained earnings in the **retained earnings statement**.
2. Retained earnings of $1,450 at the end of the reporting period shown in the **retained earnings statement** is reported on the **balance sheet**.
3. Cash of $8,050 on the **balance sheet** is reported on the **statement of cash flows**.

Also, explanatory notes and supporting schedules are an integral part of every set of financial statements. We illustrate these notes and schedules in later chapters of this text.

Be sure to carefully examine the format and content of each statement in Illustration 1.10. We describe the essential features of each in the following sections (see **International Note**).

> **HELPFUL HINT**
> The income statement, retained earnings statement, and statement of cash flows are all for a *period* of time, whereas the balance sheet is for a *point* in time.

> **International Note**
> The primary types of financial statements required by GAAP and IFRS are the same. In practice, some format differences do exist in presentations employed by GAAP companies compared to IFRS companies.

Income Statement

The income statement reports the success or profitability of the company's operations over a specific period of time (see **Alternative Terminology**). For example, Softbyte Inc.'s income statement is dated "For the Month Ended September 30, 2022." It is prepared from the data appearing in the revenue and expense columns of Illustration 1.9. The heading of the statement identifies the company, the type of statement, and the time period covered by the statement.

The income statement lists revenues first, followed by expenses. Finally, the statement shows net income (or net loss). When revenues exceed expenses, **net income** results. When expenses exceed revenues, a **net loss** results.

Although practice varies, we have chosen in our illustrations and homework solutions to list expenses in order of magnitude. (We will consider alternative formats for the income statement in later chapters.)

Note that the income statement does not include investment and dividend transactions between the stockholders and the business in measuring net income. For example, as explained earlier, the cash dividend from Softbyte Inc. was not regarded as a business expense. This type of transaction is considered a reduction of retained earnings, which causes a decrease in stockholders' equity.

> **ALTERNATIVE TERMINOLOGY**
> The income statement is sometimes referred to as the *statement of operations, earnings statement, or profit and loss statement.*
>
> **Alternative Terminology** notes present synonymous terms that you may come across in practice.

Financial statements and their interrelationships

The heading of each statement identifies the company, the type of statement, and the specific date or time period covered by the statement.

Note that final sums are double-underlined, and negative amounts (in the statement of cash flows) are presented in parentheses.

The arrows in this illustration show the interrelationships of the four financial statements.

1. Net income is computed first and is needed to determine the ending balance in retained earnings.

2. The ending balance in retained earnings is needed in preparing the balance sheet.

3. The cash shown on the balance sheet is needed in preparing the statement of cash flows.

Softbyte Inc.
Income Statement
For the Month Ended September 30, 2022

Revenues		
Service revenue		$4,700
Expenses		
Salaries and wages expense	$900	
Rent expense	600	
Advertising expense	250	
Utilities expense	200	
Total expenses		1,950
Net income		**$2,750**

Softbyte Inc.
Retained Earnings Statement
For the Month Ended September 30, 2022

Retained earnings, September 1	$ –0–
Add: Net income	2,750
	2,750
Less: Dividends	1,300
Retained earnings, September 30	**$1,450**

Softbyte Inc.
Balance Sheet
September 30, 2022

Assets

Cash	$ 8,050
Accounts receivable	1,400
Supplies	1,600
Equipment	7,000
Total assets	$18,050

Liabilities and Stockholders' Equity

Liabilities		
Accounts payable		$ 1,600
Stockholders' equity		
Common stock	$15,000	
Retained earnings	1,450	16,450
Total liabilities and stockholders' equity		$18,050

Softbyte Inc.
Statement of Cash Flows
For the Month Ended September 30, 2022

Cash flows from operating activities		
Cash receipts from revenues		$ 3,300
Cash payments for expenses		(1,950)
Net cash provided by operating activities		1,350
Cash flows from investing activities		
Purchase of equipment		(7,000)
Cash flows from financing activities		
Sale of common stock	$15,000	
Payment of cash dividends	(1,300)	13,700
Net increase in cash		8,050
Cash at the beginning of the period		0
Cash at the end of the period		$ 8,050

Retained Earnings Statement

Softbyte Inc.'s retained earnings statement reports the changes in retained earnings for a specific period of time. The time period is the same as that covered by the income statement ("For the Month Ended September 30, 2022"). Data for the preparation of the retained earnings statement come from the retained earnings columns of the tabular summary (Illustration 1.9) and from the income statement (Illustration 1.10).

The first line of the statement shows the beginning retained earnings amount. Then come net income and dividends. The retained earnings ending balance is the final amount on the statement. The information provided by this statement indicates the reasons why retained earnings increased or decreased during the period. If there is a net loss, it is deducted with dividends in the retained earnings statement.

Balance Sheet

Softbyte Inc.'s balance sheet reports the assets, liabilities, and stockholders' equity at a specific date (September 30, 2022). The company prepares the balance sheet from the column headings and the month-end data shown in the last line of the tabular summary (Illustration 1.9).

Observe that the balance sheet lists assets at the top, followed by liabilities and stockholders' equity. Total assets must equal total liabilities and stockholders' equity. Softbyte Inc. reports only one liability, Accounts Payable, on its balance sheet. In most cases, there will be more than one liability. When two or more liabilities are involved, a customary way of listing is as shown in **Illustration 1.11**.

Liabilities	
Notes payable	$10,000
Accounts payable	63,000
Salaries and wages payable	18,000
Total liabilities	**$91,000**

ILLUSTRATION 1.11

Presentation of liabilities

The balance sheet is like a snapshot of the company's financial condition at a specific moment in time (usually the month-end or year-end).

Statement of Cash Flows

The primary purpose of a **statement of cash flows** is to provide financial information about the cash receipts and cash payments of a company for a specific period of time (see **Helpful Hint**). To help investors, creditors, and others in their analysis of a company's cash position, the statement of cash flows reports the cash effects of a company's **operating, investing, and financing activities**. In addition, the statement shows the net increase or decrease in cash during the period, and the amount of cash at the end of the period.

Reporting the sources, uses, and change in cash is useful because investors, creditors, and others want to know what is happening to a company's most liquid resource. The statement of cash flows provides answers to the following simple but important questions.

1. Where did cash come from during the period?
2. What was cash used for during the period?
3. What was the change in the cash balance during the period?

As shown in Softbyte Inc.'s statement of cash flows in Illustration 1.10, cash increased $8,050 during the period. Net cash provided by operating activities increased cash $1,350 (cash receipts from revenue less cash payments for expenses). Cash flow from investing activities decreased cash $7,000 (purchase of equipment). Cash flow from financing activities increased cash $13,700 (sale of common stock less payment of cash dividends). At this time, you need not be concerned with how these amounts are determined. Chapter 12 will examine in detail how the statement is prepared.

HELPFUL HINT

The statement of cash flows helps users determine if the company generates enough cash from operations to fund its investing activities.

People, Planet, and Profit Insight

iStock.com/Marek
Uliasz

Beyond Financial Statements

Should we expand our financial statements beyond the income statement, retained earnings statement, balance sheet, and statement of cash flows? Some believe we should take into account ecological and social performance, in addition to financial results, in evaluating a company. The argument is that a company's responsibility lies with anyone who is influenced by its actions. In other words, a company should be interested in benefiting many different parties, instead of only maximizing stockholders' interests.

A socially responsible business does not exploit or endanger any group of individuals. It follows fair trade practices, provides safe environments for workers, and bears responsibility for environmental damage. Granted, measurement of these factors is difficult. How to report this information is also controversial. But, many interesting and useful efforts are underway. Throughout this text, we provide additional insights into how companies are attempting to meet the challenge of measuring and reporting their contributions to society, as well as their financial results, to stockholders.

Why might a company's stockholders be interested in its environmental and social performance? (Go to WileyPLUS for this answer and additional questions.)

ACTION PLAN

- **Remember the basic accounting equation: assets must equal liabilities plus stockholders' equity.**
- **Review previous financial statements to determine how total assets, net income, and stockholders' equity are computed.**

DO IT! 5 | Financial Statement Items

Presented below is selected information related to Flanagan Corporation at December 31, 2022. Flanagan reports financial information monthly.

Equipment	$10,000	Utilities Expense	$ 4,000
Cash	8,000	Accounts Receivable	9,000
Service Revenue	36,000	Salaries and Wages Expense	7,000
Rent Expense	11,000	Notes Payable	16,500
Accounts Payable	2,000	Dividends	5,000

a. Determine the total assets of Flanagan at December 31, 2022.

b. Determine the net income that Flanagan reported for December 2022.

c. Determine the stockholders' equity of Flanagan at December 31, 2022.

Solution

a. The total assets are $27,000, comprised of Cash $8,000, Accounts Receivable $9,000, and Equipment $10,000.

b. Net income is $14,000, computed as follows.

Revenues		
Service revenue		$36,000
Expenses		
Rent expense	$11,000	
Salaries and wages expense	7,000	
Utilities expense	4,000	
Total expenses		22,000
Net income		$14,000

c. The ending stockholders' equity of Flanagan Corporation is $8,500. By rewriting the accounting equation, we can compute stockholders' equity as assets minus liabilities, as follows.

Total assets [as computed in (a)]		$27,000
Less: Liabilities		
Notes payable	$16,500	
Accounts payable	2,000	18,500
Stockholders' equity		$ 8,500

Note that it is not possible to determine the corporation's stockholders' equity in any other way, because the beginning total for stockholders' equity is not provided.

Related exercise material: **BE1.10, BE1.11, DO IT! 1.5, E1.9, E1.10, E1.11, E1.12, E1.13, E1.14, E1.15, E1.16, and E1.17.**

| Appendix 1A | # Career Opportunities in Accounting |

LEARNING OBJECTIVE *6
Explain the career opportunities in accounting.

Why is accounting such a popular major and career choice? First, there are a lot of jobs. In many cities in recent years, the demand for accountants exceeded the supply. Not only are there a lot of jobs, but there are a wide array of opportunities. As one accounting organization observed, "accounting is one degree with 360 degrees of opportunity."

Accounting is also hot because it is obvious that accounting matters. Interest in accounting has increased, ironically, because of the attention caused by the accounting failures of companies such as **Enron** and **WorldCom**. These widely publicized scandals revealed the important role that accounting plays in society. Most people want to make a difference, and an accounting career provides many opportunities to contribute to society. Finally, the Sarbanes-Oxley Act (SOX) significantly increased the accounting and internal control requirements for corporations. This dramatically increased demand for professionals with accounting training.

Accountants are in such demand that it is not uncommon for accounting students to have accepted a job offer a year before graduation. As the following discussion reveals, the job options of people with accounting degrees are virtually unlimited.

Public Accounting

Individuals in **public accounting** offer expert service to the general public, in much the same way that doctors serve patients and lawyers serve clients. A major portion of public accounting involves **auditing**. In auditing, a certified public accountant (CPA) examines company financial statements and provides an opinion as to how accurately the financial statements present the company's results and financial position. Analysts, investors, and creditors rely heavily on these "audit opinions," which CPAs have the exclusive authority to issue.

Taxation is another major area of public accounting. The work that tax specialists perform includes tax advice and planning, preparing tax returns, and representing clients before governmental agencies such as the Internal Revenue Service.

A third area in public accounting is **management consulting**. It ranges from installing basic accounting software or highly complex enterprise resource planning systems, to performing support services for major marketing projects and merger and acquisition activities.

Many CPAs are entrepreneurs. They form small- or medium-sized practices that frequently specialize in tax or consulting services.

Private Accounting

Instead of working in public accounting, you might choose to be an employee of a for-profit company such as **Starbucks**, **Google**, or **PepsiCo**. In **private** (or **managerial**) **accounting**, you would be involved in activities such as cost accounting (finding the cost of producing specific products), budgeting, accounting information system design and support, and tax planning and preparation. You might also be a member of your company's internal audit team. In response to SOX, the internal auditors' job of reviewing the company's operations to ensure compliance with company policies and to increase efficiency has taken on increased importance.

Alternatively, many accountants work for not-for-profit organizations such as the **Red Cross** or the **Bill and Melinda Gates Foundation**, or for museums, libraries, or performing arts organizations.

Governmental Accounting

Another option is to pursue one of the many accounting opportunities in governmental agencies. For example, the Internal Revenue Service (IRS), Federal Bureau of Investigation (FBI), and Securities and Exchange Commission (SEC) all employ accountants. The FBI has a stated goal that at least 15% of its new agents should be CPAs. There is also a very high demand for accounting educators at public colleges and universities and in state and local governments.

Forensic Accounting

Forensic accounting uses accounting, auditing, and investigative skills to conduct investigations into theft and fraud. It is listed among the top 20 career paths of the future. The job of forensic accountants is to catch the perpetrators of the estimated $600 billion per year of theft and fraud occurring at U.S. companies. This includes tracing money-laundering and identity-theft activities as well as tax evasion. Insurance companies hire forensic accountants to detect frauds such as arson, and law offices employ forensic accountants to identify marital assets in divorces. Forensic accountants often have FBI, IRS, or similar government experience.

"Show Me the Money"

How much can a new accountant make? Take a look at the average salaries for college graduates in public and private accounting shown in **Illustration 1A.1**. Keep in mind if you also have a CPA license, you'll make 10–15% more when you start out.

ILLUSTRATION 1A.1

Salary estimates for jobs in public and corporate accounting

Employer	Jr. Level (0–3 yrs.)	Sr. Level (4–6 yrs.)
Public accounting (large firm)	$63,250–$83,250	$78,500–$106,500
Public accounting (medium firm)	$56,500–$67,750	$70,500–$96,000
Public accounting (small company)	$51,500–$60,500	$63,750–$81,500
Corporate accounting (large company)	$53,750–$69,500	$68,750–$87,750

Illustration 1A.2 lists some examples of upper-level salaries for managers in corporate accounting. Note that geographic region, experience, education, CPA certification, and company size each play a role in determining salary.

ILLUSTRATION 1A.2

Upper-level management salaries in corporate accounting

Position	Large Company	Small to Medium Company
Chief financial officer	$207,000–$465,750	$105,250–$208,750
Corporate controller	$140,000–$224,750	$92,000–$161,250
Tax manager	$112,000–$158,250	$88,000–$124,750

The **Review and Practice** section provides opportunities for students to review key concepts and terms as well as complete multiple-choice questions, exercises, and a comprehensive problem. Detailed solutions are also included.

Review and Practice

Learning Objectives Review

1 Identify the activities and users associated with accounting.

Accounting is an information system that identifies, records, and communicates the economic events of an organization to interested users. The major users and uses of accounting are as follows. (a) Management uses accounting information to plan, organize, and run the business. (b) Investors (owners) decide whether to buy, hold, or sell their financial interests on the basis of accounting data. (c) Creditors (suppliers and bankers) evaluate the risks of granting credit or lending money on the basis of accounting information. Other groups that use accounting information are taxing authorities, regulatory agencies, customers, and labor unions.

2 Explain the building blocks of accounting: ethics, principles, and assumptions.

Ethics are the standards of conduct by which actions are judged as right or wrong. Effective financial reporting depends on sound ethical behavior. Generally accepted accounting principles are a common set of standards used by accountants. The primary accounting standard-setting body in the United States is the Financial Accounting Standards Board. The monetary unit assumption requires that companies include in the accounting records only transaction data that can be expressed in terms of money. The economic entity assumption requires that the activities of each economic entity be kept separate from the activities of its owner(s) and other economic entities.

3 State the accounting equation, and define its components.

The basic accounting equation is:

$$\text{Assets} = \text{Liabilities} + \text{Stockholders' Equity}$$

Assets are resources a business owns. Liabilities are creditorship claims on total assets. Stockholders' equity is the ownership claim on total assets.

4 Analyze the effects of business transactions on the accounting equation.

Each business transaction must have a dual effect on the accounting equation. For example, if an individual asset increases, there must be a corresponding (1) decrease in another asset, or (2) increase in a specific liability, or (3) increase in stockholders' equity.

The expanded accounting equation is:

$$\text{Assets} = \text{Liabilities} + \text{Common Stock}$$
$$+ \text{Revenues} - \text{Expenses} - \text{Dividends}$$

Common stock is affected when the company issues new shares of stock in exchange for cash. Revenues are increases in assets resulting from income-earning activities. Expenses are the costs of assets consumed or services used in the process of earning revenue. Dividends are payments the company makes to its stockholders.

5 Describe the four financial statements and how they are prepared.

An income statement presents the revenues and expenses and resulting net income or net loss for a specific period of time. A retained earnings statement summarizes the changes in retained earnings for a specific period of time. A balance sheet reports the assets, liabilities, and stockholders' equity at a specific date. A statement of cash flows summarizes information about the cash inflows (receipts) and outflows (payments) for a specific period of time.

*6 Explain the career opportunities in accounting.

Accounting offers many different jobs in fields such as public and private accounting, governmental accounting, and forensic accounting. Accounting is a popular major because there are many different types of jobs, with unlimited potential for career advancement.

Glossary Review

Accounting   The information system that identifies, records, and communicates the economic events of an organization to interested users. (p. 1-3).

Accounting information system   The system of collecting and processing transaction data and communicating financial information to decision-makers. (p. 1-13).

Assets   Resources a business owns. (p. 1-11).

*Auditing   The examination of financial statements by a certified public accountant in order to express an opinion as to how accurately the financial statements present the company's results and financial position. (p. 1-25).

Balance sheet   A financial statement that reports the assets, liabilities, and stockholders' equity at a specific date. (p. 1-21).

Basic accounting equation   Assets = Liabilities + Stockholders' equity. (p. 1-11).

Bookkeeping   A part of accounting that involves only the recording of economic events. (p. 1-4).

Common stock   Term used to describe the total amount paid in by stockholders for the shares they purchase. (p. 1-12).

Convergence   The process of reducing the differences between U.S. GAAP and IFRS. (p. 1-8).

Corporation   A business organized as a separate legal entity under state corporation law, having ownership divided into transferable shares of stock. (p. 1-10).

Dividend   A distribution by a corporation to its stockholders. (p. 1-12).

Economic entity assumption   An assumption that requires that the activities of the entity be kept separate and distinct from the activities of its owner and all other economic entities. (p. 1-9).

Ethics   The standards of conduct by which one's actions are judged as right or wrong, honest or dishonest, fair or not fair. (p. 1-7).

Expanded accounting equation   Assets = Liabilities + Common stock + Revenues − Expenses − Dividends. (p. 1-15).

Expenses   The cost of assets consumed or services used in the process of generating revenue. (p. 1-12).

Fair value principle   An accounting principle stating that assets and liabilities should be reported at fair value (the price received to sell an asset or settle a liability). (p. 1-9).

Faithful representation   Numbers and descriptions match what really existed or happened—they are factual. (p. 1-8).

Financial accounting The field of accounting that provides economic and financial information for investors, creditors, and other external users. (p. 1-5).

Financial Accounting Standards Board (FASB) A private organization that establishes generally accepted accounting principles (GAAP) in the United States. (p. 1-8).

*__Forensic accounting__ An area of accounting that uses accounting, auditing, and investigative skills to conduct investigations into theft and fraud. (p. 1-26).

Generally accepted accounting principles (GAAP) Common standards that indicate how to report economic events. (p. 1-8).

Historical cost principle An accounting principle that states that companies should record assets at their cost. (p. 1-9).

Income statement A financial statement that presents the revenues and expenses and resulting net income or net loss of a company for a specific period of time. (p. 1-21).

International Accounting Standards Board (IASB) An accounting standard-setting body that issues standards adopted by many countries outside of the United States. (p. 1-8).

International Financial Reporting Standards (IFRS) International accounting standards set by the International Accounting Standards Board (IASB). (p. 1-8).

Liabilities Creditor claims against total assets. (p. 1-12).

*__Management consulting__ An area of public accounting ranging from development of accounting and computer systems to support services for marketing projects and merger and acquisition activities. (p. 1-25).

Managerial accounting The field of accounting that provides internal reports to help users make decisions about their companies. (p. 1-4).

Monetary unit assumption An assumption stating that companies include in the accounting records only transaction data that can be expressed in terms of money. (p. 1-9).

Net income The amount by which revenues exceed expenses. (p. 1-21).

Net loss The amount by which expenses exceed revenues. (p. 1-21).

Partnership A business owned by two or more persons associated as partners. (p. 1-10).

*__Private (or managerial) accounting__ An area of accounting within a company that involves such activities as cost accounting, budgeting, design and support of accounting information systems, and tax planning and preparation. (p. 1-25).

Proprietorship A business owned by one person. (p. 1-9).

*__Public accounting__ An area of accounting in which the accountant offers expert service to the general public. (p. 1-25).

Relevance Financial information that is capable of making a difference in a decision. (p. 1-8).

Retained earnings statement A financial statement that summarizes the changes in retained earnings for a specific period of time. (p. 1-21).

Revenues The increases in assets or decreases in liabilities resulting from the sale of goods or the performance of services in the normal course of business. (p. 1-12).

Sarbanes-Oxley Act (SOX) Law passed by Congress intended to reduce unethical corporate behavior. (p. 1-6).

Securities and Exchange Commission (SEC) A governmental agency that oversees U.S. financial markets and accounting standard-setting bodies. (p. 1-8).

Statement of cash flows A financial statement that summarizes information about the cash inflows (receipts) and cash outflows (payments) for a specific period of time. (p. 1-21).

Stockholders' equity The ownership claim on a corporation's total assets. (p. 1-12).

*__Taxation__ An area of public accounting involving tax advice, tax planning, preparing tax returns, and representing clients before governmental agencies. (p. 1-25).

Transactions The economic events of a business that are recorded by accountants. (p. 1-14).

Practice Multiple-Choice Questions

1. (LO 1) Which of the following is **not** a step in the accounting process?

  a. Identification.   **c.** Recording.

  b. Economic entity.   **d.** Communication.

2. (LO 1) Which of the following statements about users of accounting information is **incorrect**?

  a. Management is an internal user.

  b. Taxing authorities are external users.

  c. Present creditors are external users.

  d. Regulatory authorities are internal users.

3. (LO 2) The historical cost principle states that:

  a. assets should be initially recorded at cost and adjusted when the fair value changes.

  b. activities of an entity are to be kept separate and distinct from its owner.

  c. assets should be recorded at their cost.

  d. only transaction data capable of being expressed in terms of money be included in the accounting records.

4. (LO 2) Which of the following statements about basic assumptions is **correct**?

  a. Basic assumptions are the same as accounting principles.

  b. The economic entity assumption states that there should be a particular unit of accountability.

  c. The monetary unit assumption enables accounting to measure employee morale.

  d. Partnerships are not economic entities.

5. (LO 2) The three types of business entities are:

  a. proprietorships, small businesses, and partnerships.

  b. proprietorships, partnerships, and corporations.

  c. proprietorships, partnerships, and large businesses.

  d. financial, manufacturing, and service companies.

6. (LO 3) Net income will result during a time period when:

  a. assets exceed liabilities.

  b. assets exceed revenues.

  c. expenses exceed revenues.

  d. revenues exceed expenses.

7. (LO 3) As of December 31, 2022, Reed Company has assets of $3,500 and stockholders' equity of $1,500. What are the liabilities for Reed Company as of December 31, 2022?

   a. $1,500.

   b. $1,000.

   c. $2,500.

   d. $2,000.

8. (LO 4) Performing services on account will have the following effects on the components of the basic accounting equation:

   a. increase assets and decrease stockholders' equity.

   b. increase assets and increase stockholders' equity.

   c. increase assets and increase liabilities.

   d. increase liabilities and increase stockholders' equity.

9. (LO 4) Which of the following events is **not** recorded in the accounting records?

   a. Equipment is purchased on account.

   b. An employee is terminated.

   c. A cash investment is made into the business.

   d. The company pays a cash dividend.

10. (LO 4) During 2022, Seisor Company's assets decreased $50,000 and its liabilities decreased $90,000. Its stockholders' equity therefore:

   a. increased $40,000.   **c.** decreased $40,000.

   b. decreased $140,000.   **d.** increased $140,000.

11. (LO 4) Payment of an account payable affects the components of the accounting equation in the following way.

   a. Decreases stockholders' equity and decreases liabilities.

   b. Increases assets and decreases liabilities.

   c. Decreases assets and increases stockholders' equity.

   d. Decreases assets and decreases liabilities.

12. (LO 5) Which of the following statements is **false**?

   a. A statement of cash flows summarizes information about the cash inflows (receipts) and outflows (payments) for a specific period of time.

   b. A balance sheet reports the assets, liabilities, and stockholders' equity at a specific date.

   c. An income statement presents the revenues, expenses, changes in stockholders' equity, and resulting net income or net loss for a specific period of time.

   d. A retained earnings statement summarizes the changes in retained earnings for a specific period of time.

13. (LO 5) On the last day of the period, Alan Cesska Company buys a $900 machine on credit. This transaction will affect the:

   a. income statement only.

   b. balance sheet only.

   c. income statement and retained earnings statement only.

   d. income statement, retained earnings statement, and balance sheet.

14. (LO 5) The financial statement that reports assets, liabilities, and stockholders' equity is the:

   a. income statement.

   b. retained earnings statement.

   c. balance sheet.

   d. statement of cash flows.

*15. (LO 6) Services performed by a public accountant include:

   a. auditing, taxation, and management consulting.

   b. auditing, budgeting, and management consulting.

   c. auditing, budgeting, and cost accounting.

   d. auditing, budgeting, and management consulting.

Solutions

1. b. Economic entity is not one of the steps in the accounting process. The other choices are true because (a) identification is the first step in the accounting process, (c) recording is the second step in the accounting process, and (d) communication is the third and final step in the accounting process.

2. d. Regulatory authorities are external, not internal, users of accounting information. The other choices are true statements.

3. c. The historical cost principle states that assets should be recorded at their cost. The other choices are incorrect because (a) the historical cost principle does not say that assets should be adjusted for changes in fair value, (b) describes the economic entity assumption, and (d) describes the monetary unit assumption.

4. b. The economic entity assumption states that there should be a particular unit of accountability. The other choices are incorrect because (a) basic assumptions are not the same as accounting principles, (c) the monetary unit assumption allows accounting to measure economic events, and (d) partnerships are economic entities.

5. b. Proprietorships, partnerships, and corporations are the three types of business entities. Choices (a) and (c) are incorrect because small and large businesses only denote the sizes of businesses. Choice (d) is incorrect because financial, manufacturing, and service companies are types of businesses, not business entities.

6. d. Net income results when revenues exceed expenses. The other choices are incorrect because (a) assets and liabilities are not used in the computation of net income; (b) revenues, not assets, are included in the computation of net income; and (c) when expenses exceed revenues, a net loss results.

7. d. Using a variation of the basic accounting equation, Assets − Stockholders' equity = Liabilities, $3,500 − $1,500 = $2,000. Therefore, choices (a) $1,500, (b) $1,000, and (c) $2,500 are incorrect.

8. b. When services are performed on account, assets are increased and stockholders' equity is increased. The other choices are incorrect because when services are performed on account (a) stockholders' equity is increased, not decreased; (c) liabilities are not affected; and (d) stockholders' equity is increased and liabilities are not affected.

9. b. If an employee is terminated, this represents an activity of a company, not a business transaction. Assets, liabilities, and stockholders' equity are not affected. Thus, there is no effect on the accounting equation. The other choices are incorrect because they are all recorded: (a) when equipment is purchased on account, both assets and liabilities increase; (c) when a cash investment is made into a business, both assets and stockholders' equity increase; and (d) when a dividend is paid, both assets and stockholders' equity decrease.

10. a. Using the basic accounting equation, Assets = Liabilities + Stockholders' equity, −$50,000 = −$90,000 + Stockholders' equity, so stockholders' equity increased $40,000, not (b) decreased $140,000, (c) decreased $40,000, or (d) increased $140,000.

11. d. Payment of an account payable results in an equal decrease of assets (cash) and liabilities (accounts payable). The other choices are incorrect because payment of an account payable (a) does not affect stockholders' equity, (b) does not increase assets, and (c) does not affect stockholders' equity.

12. c. An income statement represents the revenues, expenses, and resulting net income or net loss for a specific period of time but not the changes in stockholders' equity. The other choices are true statements.

13. b. This transaction will cause assets to increase by $900 and liabilities to increase by $900. The other choices are incorrect because this transaction (a) will have no effect on the income statement, (c) will have no effect on the income statement or the retained earnings statement, and (d) will affect the balance sheet but not the income statement or the retained earnings statement.

14. c. The balance sheet is the statement that reports assets, liabilities and stockholders' equity. The other choices are incorrect because (a) the income statement reports revenues and expenses, (b) the retained earnings statement reports details about stockholders' equity, and (d) the statement of cash flows reports inflows and outflows of cash.

*15. a. Auditing, taxation, and management consulting are all services performed by public accountants. The other choices are incorrect because public accountants do not perform budgeting or cost accounting.

Practice Brief Exercises

Use basic accounting equation.

1. (LO 3) At the beginning of the year, Ortiz Company had total assets of $900,000 and total liabilities of $440,000. Answer the following questions.

a. If total assets decreased $100,000 during the year and total liabilities increased $80,000 during the year, what is the amount of stockholders' equity at the end of the year?

b. During the year, total liabilities decreased $100,000, and stockholders' equity increased $200,000. What is the amount of total assets at the end of the year?

c. If total assets increased $50,000 during the year and stockholders' equity increased $60,000 during the year, what is the amount of total liabilities at the end of the year?

Solution

1. a. ($900,000 − $440,000) − $100,000 − $80,000 = $280,000 stockholders' equity

b. $900,000 − $100,000 + $200,000 = $1,000,000 total assets

c. $440,000 − $60,000 + $50,000 = $430,000 total liabilities

Determine effect of transactions on basic accounting equation.

2. (LO 4) The following are three business transactions. Create a table with rows (a), (b), and (c), and columns for assets, liabilities, and stockholders' equity. For each column, indicate whether the transactions increased (+), decreased (−), or had no effect (NE) on assets, liabilities, and stockholders' equity.

a. Purchased equipment on account.

b. Payment of cash dividends.

c. Paid expenses in cash.

Solution

	Assets	**Liabilities**	**Stockholders' Equity**
2. a.	+	+	NE
b.	−	NE	−
c.	−	NE	−

Determine effect of transactions on basic accounting equation.

3. (LO 4) Follow the same format as in **Practice Brief Exercise 2**. Determine the effect on assets, liabilities, and stockholders' equity of the following three transactions.

a. Performed accounting services for clients for cash.

b. Borrowed cash from a bank on a note payable.

c. Paid cash for rent for the month.

Solution

		Assets	Liabilities	Stockholders' Equity
3.	a.	+	NE	+
	b.	+	+	NE
	c.	−	NE	−

4. **(LO 5)** Indicate whether the following items would appear on the income statement (IS), balance sheet (BS), or retained earnings statement (RES).

Determine where items appear on financial statements.

    a. ____ Common stock.

    b. ____ Cash.

    c. ____ Salaries and wages expense.

    d. ____ Service revenue.

    e. ____ Accounts payable.

Solution

4. a. __BS__ Common stock.

    b. __BS__ Cash.

    c. __IS__ Salaries and wages expense.

    d. __IS__ Service revenue.

    e. __BS__ Accounts payable.

5. **(LO 5)** Presented below in alphabetical order are balance sheet items for Feagler Company at December 31, 2022. Prepare a balance sheet following the format of Illustration 1.10.

Prepare a balance sheet.

Accounts receivable	$12,500
Cash	38,000
Common stock	5,000
Notes payable	40,000
Retained earnings	5,500

Solution

5.

Feagler Company
Balance Sheet
December 31, 2022

Assets

Cash		$38,000
Accounts receivable		12,500
Total assets		$50,500

Liabilities and Stockholders' Equity

Liabilities		
Notes payable	$40,000	
Total liabilities		$40,000
Stockholders' equity		
Common stock	5,000	
Retained earnings	5,500	10,500
Total liabilities and stockholders' equity		$50,500

Practice Exercises

1. **(LO 3, 4)** Selected transactions for Beale Lawn Care Company are as follows.

Analyze the effect of transactions.

1. Sold common stock for cash to start business.

2. Paid monthly utilities.

3. Purchased land on account.

4. Billed customers for services performed.
5. Paid dividends.
6. Received cash from customers billed in (4).
7. Incurred utilities expense on account.
8. Purchased equipment for cash.
9. Received cash from customers when service was performed.

Instructions

List the numbers of the above transactions and describe the effect of each transaction on assets, liabilities, and stockholders' equity. For example, the first answer is (1) Increase in assets and increase in stockholders' equity.

Solution

1. 1. Increase in assets and increase in stockholders' equity.
   2. Decrease in assets and decrease in stockholders' equity.
   3. Increase in assets and increase in liabilities.
   4. Increase in assets and increase in stockholders' equity.
   5. Decrease in assets and decrease in stockholders' equity.
   6. Increase in assets and decrease in assets.
   7. Increase in liabilities and decrease in stockholders' equity.
   8. Increase in assets and decrease in assets.
   9. Increase in assets and increase in stockholders' equity.

Analyze the effect of transactions on assets, liabilities, and stockholders' equity.

2. **(LO 3, 4)** Hayes Computer Timeshare Company entered into the following transactions during May 2022.

1. Purchased office equipment for $10,000 from Office Outfitters on account.
2. Paid $3,000 cash for May rent on storage space.
3. Received $12,000 cash from customers for contracts billed in April.
4. Performed services for Bayliss Construction Company for $4,000 cash.
5. Paid Southern Power Co. $10,000 cash for energy usage in May.
6. Stockholders invested an additional $30,000 in the business.
7. Paid Office Outfitters for the equipment purchased in (1) above.
8. Incurred advertising expense for May of $1,500 on account.

Instructions

Indicate with the appropriate letter whether each of the transactions above results in:

a. An increase in assets and a decrease in assets.
b. An increase in assets and an increase in stockholders' equity.
c. An increase in assets and an increase in liabilities.
d. A decrease in assets and a decrease in stockholders' equity.
e. A decrease in assets and a decrease in liabilities.
f. An increase in liabilities and a decrease in stockholders' equity.
g. An increase in stockholders' equity and a decrease in liabilities.

Solution

2.	1. c	3. a	5. d	7. e
	2. d	4. b	6. b	8. f

Practice Problem

(LO 4, 5) Legal Services Inc. was incorporated on July 1, 2022. During the first month of operations, the following transactions occurred.

Prepare a tabular presentation and financial statements.

1. Legal Services issued common stock in exchange for cash of $10,000.
2. Paid $800 for July rent on office space.
3. Purchased office equipment on account $3,000.
4. Performed legal services for clients for cash $1,500.
5. Borrowed $700 cash from a bank on a note payable.
6. Performed legal services for client on account $2,000.
7. Paid monthly expenses: salaries $500, utilities $300, and advertising $100.

Instructions

a. Prepare a tabular summary of the transactions.

b. Prepare the income statement, retained earnings statement, and balance sheet at July 31, 2022, for Legal Services Inc.

Solution

a.

Trans-action	Cash	+	Accounts Receivable	+	Equipment	=	Notes Payable	+	Accounts Payable	+	Common Stock	+	Rev.	−	Exp.	−	Div.	
(1)	+$10,000					=					+$10,000							Issued Stock
(2)	−800														−$800			Rent Expense
(3)					+$3,000	=			+$3,000									
(4)	+1,500												+$1,500					Service Revenue
(5)	+700						+$700											
(6)			+$2,000										+2,000					Service Revenue
(7)	−500														−500			Sal./Wages Exp.
	−300														−300			Utilities Expense
	−100														−100			Advertising Expense
	$10,500	+	$2,000	+	$3,000	=	$700	+	$3,000	+	$10,000	+	$3,500	−	$1,700			

Assets **$15,500**

Liabilities + Stockholders' Equity **$15,500**

b.

Legal Services Inc.
Income Statement
For the Month Ended July 31, 2022

Revenues		
Service revenue		$3,500
Expenses		
Rent expense	$800	
Salaries and wages expense	500	
Utilities expense	300	
Advertising expense	100	
Total expenses		1,700
Net income		$1,800

Legal Services Inc.
Retained Earnings Statement
For the Month Ended July 31, 2022

Retained earnings, July 1	$ –0–
Add: Net income	1,800
Retained earnings, July 31	$1,800

Legal Services Inc. Balance Sheet July 31, 2022		
Assets		
Cash		$10,500
Accounts receivable		2,000
Equipment		3,000
Total assets		$15,500
Liabilities and Stockholders' Equity		
Liabilities		
Notes payable	$ 700	
Accounts payable	3,000	
Total liabilities		$ 3,700
Stockholders' equity		
Common stock	10,000	
Retained earnings	1,800	11,800
Total liabilities and stockholders' equity		$15,500

WileyPLUS

Brief Exercises, DO IT! Exercises, Exercises, Problems, and many additional resources are available for practice in WileyPLUS.

Questions

1. "Accounting is ingrained in our society and it is vital to our economic system." Explain why this statement is true or false.

2. Identify and describe the activities in the accounting process.

3. **a.** Who are internal users of accounting data?

   b. How does accounting provide relevant data to these users?

4. What uses of financial accounting information are made by (a) investors and (b) creditors?

5. "Bookkeeping and accounting are the same." Explain why this statement is true or false.

6. Harper Travel Agency purchased land for $85,000 cash on December 10, 2022. At December 31, 2022, the land's value has increased to $93,000. What amount should be reported for land on Harper's balance sheet at December 31, 2022? Explain.

7. What is the monetary unit assumption?

8. What is the economic entity assumption?

9. What are the three basic forms of profit-oriented business organizations?

10. Juana Perez is the owner of a successful printing shop. Recently, her business has been increasing, and Juana has been thinking about changing the organization of her business from a proprietorship to a corporation. Discuss some of the advantages Juana would enjoy if she were to incorporate her business.

11. What is the basic accounting equation?

12. **a.** Define the terms assets, liabilities, and stockholders' equity.

    b. What items affect stockholders' equity?

13. Which of the following items are liabilities of jewelry stores?

    a. Cash.

    b. Accounts payable.

    c. Dividends.

    d. Accounts receivable.

    e. Supplies.

    f. Equipment.

    g. Salaries and wages payable.

    h. Service revenue.

    i. Rent expense.

14. Can a business enter into a transaction in which only the left side of the basic accounting equation is affected? If so, give an example.

15. Are the following events recorded in the accounting records? Explain your answer in each case.

    a. The president of the company dies.

    b. Supplies are purchased on account.

    c. An employee is fired.

16. Indicate how the following business transactions affect the basic accounting equation.

    a. Paid cash for janitorial services.

    b. Purchased equipment for cash.

    c. Invested cash in the business for stock.

    d. Paid accounts payable in full.

17. Listed below are some items found in the financial statements of Jonas Co. Indicate in which financial statement(s) the following items would appear.

    a. Service revenue.

    b. Equipment.

    c. Advertising expense.

    d. Accounts receivable.

    e. Retained earnings.

    f. Salaries and wages payable.

18. In February 2022, Rachel Paige invested an additional $10,000 in Drumlin Company. Drumlin's accountant, Liz Cooke, recorded this receipt as an increase in cash and revenues. Is this treatment appropriate? Why or why not?

19. "A company's net income appears directly on the income statement and the retained earnings statement, and it is included indirectly in the company's balance sheet." Do you agree? Explain.

20. Monique Enterprises had a stockholders' equity balance of $158,000 at the beginning of the period. At the end of the accounting period, the stockholders' equity balance was $198,000.

    a. Assuming no additional investment or dividends during the period, what is the net income for the period?

    b. Assuming an additional investment of $16,000 but no dividends during the period, what is the net income for the period?

21. Summarized operations for Lakeview Co. for the month of July are as follows.

    Revenues recognized: for cash $30,000; on account $70,000.
    Expenses incurred: for cash $26,000; on account $38,000.
    Indicate for Lakeview Co. (a) the total revenues, (b) the total expenses, and (c) net income for the month of July.

22. The basic accounting equation is Assets = Liabilities + Stockholders' equity. Replacing the words in that equation with dollar amounts, what is **Apple**'s accounting equation at September 29, 2018?

Brief Exercises

BE1.1 (LO 3), AP The following is the basic accounting equation. Determine the missing amounts.

Use basic accounting equation.

	Assets	=	Liabilities	+	Stockholders' Equity
a.	$78,000		$50,000		?
b.	?		$45,000		$70,000
c.	$94,000		?		$60,000

BE1.2 (LO 3), AP Given the accounting equation, answer each of the following questions.

Use basic accounting equation.

    a. The liabilities of Holland Company are $120,000 and its stockholders' equity is $232,000. What is the amount of Holland Company's total assets?

    b. The total assets of Holland Company are $190,000 and its stockholders' equity is $86,000. What is the amount of its total liabilities?

    c. The total assets of Holland Company are $600,000 and its liabilities are equal to one-half of its total assets. What is the amount of Holland Company's stockholders' equity?

BE1.3 (LO 3), AP At the beginning of the year, Canon Company had total assets of $870,000 and total liabilities of $500,000. Answer the following questions.

Use basic accounting equation.

    a. If total assets increased $150,000 during the year and total liabilities decreased $80,000, what is the amount of stockholders' equity at the end of the year?

    b. During the year, total liabilities increased $100,000 and stockholders' equity decreased $66,000. What is the amount of total assets at the end of the year?

    c. If total assets decreased $80,000 and stockholders' equity increased $120,000 during the year, what is the amount of total liabilities at the end of the year?

BE1.4 (LO 3), AP Use the accounting equation to answer each of the following questions.

Solve accounting equation.

    a. The liabilities of Olga Company are $90,000. Common stock account is $150,000; dividends are $40,000; revenues, $450,000; and expenses, $320,000. What is the amount of Olga Company's total assets?

    b. The total assets of Lafayette Company are $57,000. Common stock account is $23,000; dividends are $7,000; revenues, $50,000; and expenses, $35,000. What is the amount of the company's total liabilities?

    c. The total assets of Dierdorf Co. are $600,000 and its liabilities are equal to two-thirds of its total assets. What is the amount of Dierdorf Co.'s stockholders' equity?

Identify assets, liabilities, and stockholders' equity.

BE1.5 (LO 3), C Indicate whether each of the following items is an asset (A), liability (L), or part of stockholders' equity (SE).

____ **a.** Accounts receivable   ____ **d.** Supplies

____ **b.** Salaries and wages payable   ____ **e.** Dividends

____ **c.** Equipment   ____ **f.** Notes payable

Determine effect of transactions on basic accounting equation.

BE1.6 (LO 4), C The following are three business transactions. Create a table with rows (a), (b), and (c), and columns for assets, liabilities, and stockholders' equity. For each column, indicate whether the transactions increased (+), decreased (−), or had no effect (NE) on assets, liabilities, and stockholders' equity.

a. Purchased supplies on account.

b. Received cash for performing a service.

c. Paid expenses in cash.

Determine effect of transactions on accounting equation.

BE1.7 (LO 4), C The following are three business transactions. Create a table with rows (a), (b), and (c), and columns for assets, liabilities, and stockholders' equity. For each column, indicate whether the transactions increased (+), decreased (−), or had no effect (NE) on assets, liabilities, and stockholders' equity.

a. Stockholders invested cash in the business for common stock.

b. Paid a cash dividend.

c. Received cash from a customer who had previously been billed for services performed.

Classify items affecting stockholders' equity.

BE1.8 (LO 4), C Classify each of the following items as dividends (D), revenue (R), or expense (E).

____ **a.** Advertising expense   ____ **e.** Dividends

____ **b.** Service revenue   ____ **f.** Rent revenue

____ **c.** Insurance expense   ____ **g.** Utilities expense

____ **d.** Salaries and wages expense

Determine effect of transactions on stockholders' equity.

BE1.9 (LO 4), C The following are three transactions. Mark each transaction as affecting common stock (C), dividends (D), revenue (R), expense (E), or not affecting stockholders' equity (NSE).

____ **a.** Received cash for services performed

____ **b.** Paid cash to purchase equipment

____ **c.** Paid employee salaries

Prepare a balance sheet.

BE1.10 (LO 5), AP In alphabetical order below are balance sheet items for Ellerby Company at December 31, 2022. Prepare a balance sheet, following the format of Illustration 1.10.

Accounts payable	$85,000
Accounts receivable	72,500
Cash	44,000
Common stock	21,500
Retained earnings	10,000

Determine where items appear on financial statements.

BE1.11 (LO 5), C Indicate whether the following items would appear on the income statement (IS), balance sheet (BS), or retained earnings statement (RE).

____ **a.** Notes payable   ____ **d.** Cash

____ **b.** Advertising expense   ____ **e.** Service revenue

____ **c.** Common stock   ____ **f.** Dividends

DO IT! Exercises

Review basic concepts.

DO IT! 1.1 (LO 1), K Indicate whether each of the following five statements is true or false. If false, indicate how to correct the statement.

1. The three steps in the accounting process are identification, recording, and examination.

2. The accounting process includes the bookkeeping function.

3. Managerial accounting provides reports to help investors and creditors evaluate a company.

4. The two most common types of external users are investors and creditors.

5. Internal users include human resources managers.

DO IT! 1.2 (LO 2), K Indicate whether each of the following five statements is true or false. If false, indicate how to correct the statement.

Review basic concepts.

1. Congress passed the Sarbanes-Oxley Act to ensure that investors invest only in companies that will be profitable.

2. The standards of conduct by which actions are judged as loyal or disloyal are ethics.

3. The primary accounting standard-setting body in the United States is the Securities and Exchange Commission (SEC).

4. The historical cost principle dictates that companies record assets at their cost and continue to report them at their cost over the time the assets are held.

5. The monetary unit assumption requires that companies record only transactions that can be measured in money terms.

DO IT! 1.3 (LO 3), K Classify the following items as issuance of stock (I), dividends (D), revenues (R), or expenses (E). Then indicate whether each item increases or decreases stockholders' equity.

Evaluate effects of transactions on stockholders' equity.

1. Dividends. **3.** Advertising expense.

2. Rent revenue. **4.** Stockholders invest cash in the business.

DO IT! 1.4 (LO 4), AP Transactions made by Morlan and Co., a law firm, for the month of March are as follows. Prepare a tabular analysis that shows the effects of these transactions on the accounting equation, similar to that shown in Illustration 1.9.

Prepare tabular analysis.

1. The company performed $23,000 of services for customers, on credit.

2. The company received $23,000 in cash from customers who had been billed for services (in transaction 1).

3. The company received a bill for $1,800 of advertising, but will not pay it until a later date.

4. The company paid a dividend of $5,000 in cash to stockholders.

DO IT! 1.5 (LO 5), AP The following is selected information related to Garryowen Company at December 31, 2022. Garryowen reports financial information monthly.

Determine specific amounts on the financial statements.

Accounts Payable	$ 3,000	Salaries and Wages Expense	$16,500
Cash	9,000	Notes Payable	25,000
Advertising Expense	6,000	Rent Expense	9,800
Service Revenue	54,000	Accounts Receivable	13,500
Equipment	29,000	Dividends	7,500

a. Determine the total assets of Garryowen Company at December 31, 2022.

b. Determine the net income that Garryowen Company reported for December 2022.

c. Determine the stockholders' equity of Garryowen Company at December 31, 2022.

Exercises

E1.1 (LO 1), C Callison Company performs the following accounting tasks during the year.

Classify the three activities of accounting.

_____ Analyzing and interpreting information.

_____ Classifying economic events.

_____ Explaining uses, meaning, and limitations of data.

_____ Keeping a systematic chronological diary of events.

_____ Measuring events in dollars and cents.

_____ Preparing accounting reports.

_____ Reporting information in a standard format.

_____ Selecting economic activities relevant to the company.

_____ Summarizing economic events.

Accounting is "an information system that **identifies, records**, and **communicates** the economic events of an organization to interested users."

Instructions

Categorize the accounting tasks performed by Callison as relating to either the identification (I), recording (R), or communication (C) aspects of accounting.

Identify users of accounting information.

E1.2 (LO 1), C a. The following are users of financial statements.

_____ Customers   _____ Securities and Exchange Commission

_____ Internal Revenue Service   _____ Store manager

_____ Labor unions   _____ Suppliers

_____ Marketing manager   _____ Vice president of finance

_____ Production supervisor

Instructions

Identify the users as being either **external users (E)** or **internal users (I)**.

b. The following questions could be asked by an internal user or an external user.

_____ Can we afford to give our employees a pay raise?

_____ Did the company earn a satisfactory income?

_____ Do we need to borrow in the near future?

_____ How does the company's profitability compare to other companies?

_____ What does it cost us to manufacture each unit produced?

_____ Which product should we emphasize?

_____ Will the company be able to pay its short-term debts?

Instructions

Identify each of the questions as being more likely asked by an **internal user (I)** or an **external user (E)**.

Discuss ethics and the historical cost principle.

E1.3 (LO 2), C Sam Cresco, president of Cresco Company, has instructed Sharon Gross, the head of the accounting department for Cresco Company, to report the company's land in the company's accounting reports at its fair value of $170,000 instead of its cost of $100,000. Cresco says, "Showing the land at $170,000 will make our company look like a better investment when we try to attract new investors next month."

Instructions

Explain the ethical situation involved for Sharon Gross, identifying the stakeholders and the alternatives.

Use accounting concepts.

E1.4 (LO 2), C The following situations involve accounting principles and assumptions.

1. Tina Company owns buildings that are worth substantially more than they originally cost. In an effort to provide more relevant information, Tina reports the buildings at fair value in its accounting reports.

2. Fayette Company includes in its accounting records only transaction data that can be expressed in terms of money.

3. Omar Shariff, president of Omar's Oasis, records his personal living costs as expenses of the Oasis.

Instructions

For each of the three situations, state if the accounting method used is correct or incorrect. If correct, identify which principle or assumption supports the method used. If incorrect, identify which principle or assumption has been violated.

Classify accounts as assets, liabilities, and stockholders' equity.

E1.5 (LO 3), C Bailey Cleaners has the following balance sheet items.

Accounts payable	Accounts receivable
Cash	Notes payable
Equipment	Salaries and wages payable
Supplies	Common stock

Instructions

Classify each item as an asset, liability, or stockholders' equity.

Analyze the effect of transactions.

E1.6 (LO 4), C Selected transactions for Verdent Lawn Care Company are as follows.

1. Sold common stock for cash to start business.

2. Paid monthly rent.

3. Purchased equipment on account.

4. Billed customers for services performed.

5. Paid dividends.

6. Received cash from customers billed in (4).

7. Incurred advertising expense on account.

8. Purchased additional equipment for cash.

9. Received cash from customers when service was performed.

Instructions

List the numbers of the above transactions and describe the effect of each transaction on assets, liabilities, and stockholders' equity. For example, the first answer is (1) Increase in assets and increase in stockholders' equity.

E1.7 (LO 4), C Keystone Computer Timeshare Company entered into the following transactions during May 2022.

Analyze the effect of transactions on assets, liabilities, and stockholders' equity.

1. Purchased computers for $20,000 from Data Equipment on account.

2. Paid $3,000 cash for May rent on storage space.

3. Received $15,000 cash from customers for contracts billed in April.

4. Performed computer services for Ryan Construction Company for $2,700 cash.

5. Paid Midland Power Co. $11,000 cash for energy usage in May.

6. Stockholders invested an additional $32,000 in the business.

7. Paid Data Equipment for the computers purchased in (1) above.

8. Incurred advertising expense for May of $840 on account.

Instructions

Indicate with the appropriate letter whether each of the transactions results in:

a. An increase in assets and a decrease in assets.

b. An increase in assets and an increase in stockholders' equity.

c. An increase in assets and an increase in liabilities.

d. A decrease in assets and a decrease in stockholders' equity.

e. A decrease in assets and a decrease in liabilities.

f. An increase in liabilities and a decrease in stockholders' equity.

g. An increase in stockholders' equity and a decrease in liabilities.

E1.8 (LO 4, 5), AP **Writing** An analysis of the transactions made by Foley & Co., a certified public accounting firm, for the month of August is as follows. Each increase and decrease in stockholders' equity is explained.

Analyze transactions and compute net income.

	Assets				= Liabilities +	Stockholders' Equity					
	Cash	+	Accounts Receivable	+ Supplies + Equipment =	Accounts Payable	+	Common Stock	+	Retained Earnings		
									Rev.	− Exp. −	Div.
1.	+$15,000						+$15,000				
2.	−2,000			+$5,000	+$3,000						
3.	−750			+$750							
4.	+4,900		+$4,500						+$9,400			Service Revenue
5.	−1,500				−1,500						
6.	−2,000										−$2,000
7.	−850									−$ 850		Rent Expense
8.	+450		−450								
9.	−3,900									−3,900		Sal./Wages Expense
10.					+500					−500		Utilities Expense

Instructions

a. Describe each transaction that occurred for the month.

b. Determine how much stockholders' equity increased for the month.

c. Compute the amount of net income for the month.

Prepare financial statements.

E1.9 (LO 5), AP An analysis of transactions for Foley & Co., a certified public accounting firm, for the month of August is as follows. Assume that August is the company's first month of business.

	Cash	+	Accounts Receivable	+	Supplies	+	Equipment	=	Accounts Payable	+	Common Stock	+	Rev.	−	Exp.	−	Div.	
					Assets			**= Liabilities +**			**Stockholders' Equity**				**Retained Earnings**			
1.	+$15,000										+$15,000							
2.	−2,000						+$5,000		+$3,000									
3.	−750				+$750													
4.	+4,900		+$4,500										+$9,400					Service Revenue
5.	−1,500								−1,500									
6.	−2,000																−$2,000	
7.	−850														−$ 850			Rent Expense
8.	+450		−450															
9.	−3,900														−3,900			Sal./Wages Expense
10.									+500						−500			Utilities Expense

Instructions

Prepare an income statement and a retained earnings statement for August and a balance sheet at August 31, 2022.

Determine net income (or loss).

E1.10 (LO 5), AP Toth Company had the following assets and liabilities on the dates indicated.

December 31	Total Assets	Total Liabilities
2021	$400,000	$260,000
2022	$480,000	$300,000
2023	$590,000	$400,000

Toth began business on January 1, 2021, with an investment of $100,000 from stockholders.

Instructions

From an analysis of the change in stockholders' equity during the year, compute the net income (or loss) for:

a. 2021, assuming Toth paid $15,000 in dividends for the year.

b. 2022, assuming stockholders made an additional investment of $50,000 and Toth paid no dividends in 2022.

c. 2023, assuming stockholders made an additional investment of $15,000 and Toth paid dividends of $30,000 in 2023.

Analyze financial statements items.

E1.11 (LO 5), AN Two items are omitted from each of the following summaries of balance sheet and income statement data for two corporations for the year 2022, Plunkett Co. and Herring Enterprises.

	Plunkett Co.	Herring Enterprises
Beginning of year:		
Total assets	$ 97,000	$122,000
Total liabilities	85,000	(c)
Total stockholders' equity	(a)	75,000
End of year:		
Total assets	160,000	180,000
Total liabilities	120,000	50,000
Total stockholders' equity	40,000	130,000
Changes during year in stockholders' equity:		
Additional investment	(b)	25,000
Dividends	15,000	(d)
Total revenues	215,000	100,000
Total expenses	175,000	55,000

Instructions

Determine the missing amounts.

E1.12 (LO 5), AP The following information relates to La Greca Co. for the year 2022.

Prepare income statement and retained earnings statement.

Retained earnings, January 1, 2022	$48,000	Advertising expense	$ 1,800
Dividends during 2022	5,000	Rent expense	10,400
Service revenue	62,500	Utilities expense	3,100
Salaries and wages expense	28,000		

Instructions

After analyzing the data, prepare an income statement and a retained earnings statement for the year ending December 31, 2022.

E1.13 (LO 5), AN Robyn Howser is the bookkeeper for Madison Company. Robyn has been trying to determine the correct balance sheet for Madison Company, shown as follows.

Correct an incorrectly prepared balance sheet.

Madison Company
Balance Sheet
December 31, 2022

Assets		Liabilities	
Cash	$14,000	Accounts payable	$15,000
Supplies	3,000	Accounts receivable	(8,500)
Equipment	48,000	Common stock	50,000
Total assets	$65,000	Retained earnings	8,500
		Total liabilities and stockholders' equity	$65,000

Instructions

Prepare a correct balance sheet.

E1.14 (LO 5), AP Wyco Park, a public camping ground near the Four Corners National Recreation Area, has compiled the following financial information as of December 31, 2022.

Compute net income and prepare a balance sheet.

Revenues during 2022—camping fees	$140,000	Notes payable	$ 60,000
Revenues during 2022—general store	47,000	Expenses during 2022	150,000
Accounts payable	11,000	Supplies on hand	2,500
Cash on hand	20,000	Common stock	20,000
Original cost of equipment	105,500	Retained earnings	?
Fair value of equipment	140,000		

Instructions

a. Determine Wyco Park's net income for 2022.

b. Prepare a balance sheet for Wyco Park as of December 31, 2022.

E1.15 (LO 5), AP The following financial information is related to the 2022 operations of Louisa Cruise Company.

Prepare an income statement.

Maintenance and repairs expense	$ 92,000
Utilities expense	10,000
Salaries and wages expense	142,000
Advertising expense	3,500
Ticket revenue	328,000

Instructions

Prepare the 2022 income statement for Louisa Cruise Company.

E1.16 (LO 5), AP The following information is related to Alexis and Ryans, Attorneys at Law.

Prepare a retained earnings statement.

Retained earnings, January 1, 2022	$ 23,000
Legal service revenue—2022	340,000
Total expenses—2022	211,000
Assets, January 1, 2022	85,000
Liabilities, January 1, 2022	62,000
Assets, December 31, 2022	168,000
Liabilities, December 31, 2022	80,000
Dividends—2022	64,000

Instructions

Prepare the 2022 retained earnings statement for Alexis and Ryans, Attorneys at Law.

Prepare a cash flow statement.

E1.17 (LO 5), AP This information is for Paulo Company for the year ended December 31, 2022.

Cash received from revenues from customers	$600,000
Cash received for issuance of common stock	280,000
Cash paid for new equipment	115,000
Cash dividends paid	18,000
Cash paid for expenses	430,000
Cash balance 1/1/22	30,000

Instructions

Prepare the 2022 statement of cash flows for Paulo Company (see Illustration 1.10).

Identify cash flow activities.

E1.18 (LO 5), C The statement of cash flows classifies each transaction as an operating activity, an investing activity, or a financing activity. Operating activities are the types of activities the company performs to generate profits. Investing activities include the purchase of long-lived assets such as equipment or the purchase of investment securities. Financing activities are borrowing money, issuing shares of stock, and paying dividends.

Presented below are the following transactions.

1. Issued stock for $20,000 cash.

2. Issued note payable for $12,000 cash.

3. Purchased office equipment for $11,000 cash.

4. Received $15,000 cash for services performed.

5. Paid $1,000 cash for rent.

6. Paid $600 cash dividend to stockholders.

7. Paid $5,700 cash for salaries.

Instructions

Classify each of these transactions as operating, investing, or financing activities.

Problems

Analyze transactions and compute net income.

P1.1A (LO 4), AP Fredonia Repair Inc. was started on May 1. A summary of May transactions is presented as follows.

1. Stockholders invested $10,000 cash in the business in exchange for common stock.

2. Purchased equipment for $5,000 cash.

3. Paid $400 cash for May office rent.

4. Paid $300 cash for supplies.

5. Incurred $250 of advertising costs in the *Beacon News* on account.

6. Received $4,700 in cash from customers for repair service.

7. Declared and paid a $700 cash dividend.

8. Paid part-time employee salaries $1,000.

9. Paid utility bills $140.

10. Performed repair services worth $1,100 on account.

11. Collected cash of $120 for services billed in transaction (10).

Check figures provide a key number to let you know you are on the right track.

a. Total assets $13,560

b. Net income $4,010

Instructions

a. Prepare a tabular analysis of the transactions using the following column headings: Cash, Accounts Receivable, Supplies, Equipment, Accounts Payable, Common Stock, and Retained Earnings (with separate columns for Revenues, Expenses, and Dividends). Include margin explanations for any changes in stockholders' equity. Revenue is called Service Revenue.

b. From an analysis of the Retained Earnings columns, compute the net income or net loss for May.

Analyze transactions and prepare income statement, retained earnings statement, and balance sheet.

P1.2A (LO 4, 5), AP On August 31, the balance sheet of La Brava Veterinary Clinic showed Cash $9,000, Accounts Receivable $1,700, Supplies $600, Equipment $6,000, Accounts Payable $3,600, Common Stock $13,000, and Retained Earnings $700. During September, the following transactions occurred.

1. Paid $2,900 cash for accounts payable due.

2. Collected $1,300 of accounts receivable.

3. Purchased additional equipment for $2,100, paying $800 in cash and the balance on account.

4. Recognized revenue of $7,300, of which $2,500 is collected in cash and the balance is due in October.

5. Declared and paid a $400 cash dividend.

6. Paid salaries $1,700, rent for September $900, and advertising expense $200.

7. Incurred utilities expense for month on account $170.

8. Received $10,000 from Capital Bank on a 6-month note payable.

Instructions

a. Prepare a tabular analysis of the September transactions beginning with August 31 balances. The column headings should be as follows: Cash + Accounts Receivable + Supplies + Equipment = Notes Payable + Accounts Payable + Common Stock + Retained Earnings + Revenues − Expenses − Dividends.

a. Ending cash $15,900

b. Prepare an income statement for September, a retained earnings statement for September, and a balance sheet at September 30, 2022.

b. Net income $4,330
Total assets $29,800

P1.3A (LO 5), AP On May 1, Nimbus Flying School, a company that provides flying lessons, was started by using common stock in exchange for cash of $45,000. Following are the assets and liabilities of the company on May 31, 2022, and the revenues and expenses for the month of May.

Prepare income statement, retained earnings statement, and balance sheet.

Cash	$ 4,650	Notes Payable	$28,000
Accounts Receivable	7,400	Rent Expense	900
Equipment	64,000	Maintenance and	
Service Revenue	6,800	Repairs Expense	350
Advertising Expense	500	Gasoline Expense	2,500
Accounts Payable	1,400	Utilities Expense	400

No additional investments were made in May, but the company paid dividends of $500 during the month.

Instructions

a. Prepare an income statement and a retained earnings statement for the month of May and a balance sheet at May 31.

a. Net income $2,150
Total assets $76,050

b. Prepare an income statement and a retained earnings statement for May assuming the following data are not included above: (1) $900 worth of services were performed and billed but not collected at May 31, and (2) $1,500 of gasoline expense was incurred but not paid.

b. Net income $1,550

P1.4A (LO 4, 5), AP Nancy Tercek started a delivery service, Tercek Deliveries, on June 1, 2022. The following transactions occurred during the month of June.

Analyze transactions and prepare financial statements.

June	1	Stockholders invested $10,000 cash in the business in exchange for common stock.
	2	Purchased a used van for deliveries for $14,000. Nancy paid $2,000 cash and signed a note payable for the remaining balance.
	3	Paid $500 for office rent for the month.
	5	Performed $4,800 of services on account.
	9	Declared and paid $300 in cash dividends.
	12	Purchased supplies for $150 on account.
	15	Received a cash payment of $1,250 for services performed on June 5.
	17	Purchased gasoline for $100 on account.
	20	Received $1,500 cash for services performed.
	23	Made a cash payment of $500 on the note payable.
	26	Paid $250 for utilities.
	29	Paid for the gasoline purchased on account on June 17.
	30	Paid $1,000 for employee salaries.

Instructions

a. Show the effects of the previous transactions on the accounting equation using the following format.

a. Total assets $25,800

	Assets				=	Liabilities		+	Stockholders' Equity					
											Retained Earnings			
Date	Cash +	Accounts Receivable	+ Supplies +	Equipment =		Notes Payable	+ Accounts Payable	+	Common Stock	+	Rev.	−	Exp.	−	Div.

Include margin explanations for any changes in stockholders' equity in your analysis.

b. Prepare an income statement for the month of June.

b. Net income $4,450

c. Prepare a balance sheet at June 30, 2022.

c. Cash $8,100

Determine financial statement amounts and prepare retained earnings statement.

P1.5A (LO 4, 5), AP **Writing** Financial statement information about four different companies is as follows.

	Donatello Company	Leonardo Company	Michelangelo Company	Raphael Company
January 1, 2022				
Assets	$ 75,000	$110,000	(g)	$150,000
Liabilities	48,000	(d)	$ 75,000	(j)
Stockholders' equity	(a)	60,000	45,000	100,000
December 31, 2022				
Assets	(b)	137,000	200,000	(k)
Liabilities	55,000	75,000	(h)	80,000
Stockholders' equity	40,000	(e)	130,000	140,000
Stockholders' equity changes in year				
Additional investment	(c)	15,000	10,000	15,000
Dividends	6,000	(f)	14,000	10,000
Total revenues	350,000	420,000	(i)	500,000
Total expenses	335,000	382,000	342,000	(l)

Instructions

a. Determine the missing amounts. (*Hint:* For example, to solve for (a), Assets – Liabilities = Stockholders' equity = $27,000.)

b. Retained earnings (ending)
$7,000

b. Prepare the retained earnings statement for Leonardo Company. Assume beginning retained earnings was $20,000.

c. Write a memorandum explaining the sequence for preparing financial statements and the interrelationship of the retained earnings statement with the income statement and balance sheet.

Continuing Case

leungchopan/
Shutterstock.com

The **Cookie Creations** case starts in this chapter and continues through Chapter 13. You also can find this problem in WileyPLUS.

Cookie Creations

CC1 Natalie Koebel spent much of her childhood learning the art of cookie-making from her grandmother. They passed many happy hours mastering every type of cookie imaginable and later creating new recipes that were both healthy and delicious. Now at the start of her second year in college, Natalie is investigating various possibilities for starting her own business as part of the requirements of the entrepreneurship program in which she is enrolled.

A long-time friend insists that Natalie has to include cookies in her business plan. After a series of brainstorming sessions, Natalie settles on the idea of operating a cookie-making school. She will start on a part-time basis and offer her services in people's homes. Now that she has started thinking about it, the possibilities seem endless. During the fall, she will concentrate on holiday cookies. She will offer individual lessons and group sessions (which will probably be more entertainment than education for the participants). Natalie also decides to include children in her target market.

The first difficult decision is coming up with the perfect name for her business. Natalie settles on "Cookie Creations" and then moves on to more important issues.

Instructions

a. What form of business organization—proprietorship, partnership, or corporation—do you recommend that Natalie use for her business? Discuss the benefits and weaknesses of each form and give the reasons for your choice.

b. Will Natalie need accounting information? If yes, what information will she need and why? How often will she need this information?

c. Identify specific asset, liability, and stockholders' equity accounts that Cookie Creations will likely use to record its business transactions.

d. Should Natalie open a separate bank account for the business? Why or why not?

Expand Your Critical Thinking

Financial Reporting Problem: Apple Inc.

CT1.1 The financial statements of **Apple Inc.** for 2018 are presented in Appendix A. The complete annual report, including the notes to the financial statements, is available at the company's website.

Instructions

Refer to Apple's financial statements and answer the following questions.

   a. What were Apple's total assets at September 29, 2018? At September 30, 2017?

   b. How much cash (and cash equivalents) did Apple have on September 29, 2018?

   c. What amount of accounts payable did Apple report on September 29, 2018? On September 30, 2017?

   d. What were Apple's net sales in 2016? In 2017? In 2018?

   e. What is the amount of the change in Apple's net income from 2017 to 2018?

Comparative Analysis Problem: PepsiCo, Inc. vs. The Coca-Cola Company

CT1.2 **PepsiCo**'s financial statements are presented in Appendix B. Financial statements of **The Coca-Cola Company** are presented in Appendix C. The complete annual reports of PepsiCo and Coca-Cola, including the notes to the financial statements, are available at each company's respective website.

Instructions

   a. Based on the information contained in these financial statements, determine the following for each company.

      1. Total assets at December 29, 2018, for PepsiCo and for Coca-Cola at December 31, 2018.

      2. Accounts (notes) receivable, net at December 29, 2018, for PepsiCo and at December 31, 2018, for Coca-Cola.

      3. Net revenues for the year ended in 2018.

      4. Net income for the year ended in 2018.

   b. What conclusions concerning the two companies can be drawn from these data?

Comparative Analysis Problem: Amazon.com, Inc. vs. Walmart Inc.

CT1.3 **Amazon.com, Inc.**'s financial statements are presented in Appendix D. Financial statements of **Walmart Inc.** are presented in Appendix E. The complete annual reports of Amazon and Walmart, including the notes to the financial statements, are available at each company's respective website.

Instructions

   a. Based on the information contained in these financial statements, determine the following for each company.

      1. Total assets at December 31, 2018, for Amazon and for Walmart at January 31, 2019.

      2. Receivables (net) at December 31, 2018, for Amazon and for Walmart at January 31, 2019.

      3. Net sales (product only) for year ended in 2018 (2019 for Walmart).

      4. Net income for the year ended in 2018 (2019 for Walmart).

   b. What conclusions concerning these two companies can be drawn from these data?

Decision-Making Across the Organization

CT1.4 Kathy and James Mohr, local golf stars, opened the Chip-Shot Driving Range Company on March 1, 2022. They invested $25,000 cash and received common stock in exchange for their investment. A caddy shack was constructed for cash at a cost of $8,000, and $800 was spent on golf balls and golf clubs. The Mohrs leased five acres of land at a cost of $1,000 per month and paid the first month's rent. During the first month, advertising costs totaled $750, of which $150 was unpaid at March 31, and $400 was paid to members of the high-school golf team for retrieving golf balls. All revenues from customers were deposited in the company's bank account. On March 15, Kathy and James received a dividend of $1,000. A $100 utility bill was received on March 31 but was not paid. On March 31, the balance in the company's bank account was $18,900.

Kathy and James thought they had a pretty good first month of operations. But, their estimates of profitability ranged from a loss of $6,100 to net income of $2,450.

Instructions

With the class divided into groups, answer the following.

a. How could the Mohrs have concluded that the business operated at a loss of $6,100? Was this a valid basis on which to determine net income?

b. How could the Mohrs have concluded that the business operated at a net income of $2,450? (*Hint:* Prepare a balance sheet at March 31.) Was this a valid basis on which to determine net income?

c. Without preparing an income statement, determine the actual net income for March.

d. What was the revenue recognized in March?

Communication Activity

CT1.5 Ashley Hirano, the bookkeeper for New York Company, has been trying to develop the correct balance sheet for the company. The company's balance sheet is shown as follows.

New York Company			
Balance Sheet			
For the Month Ended December 31, 2022			
Assets		**Liabilities**	
Equipment	$25,500	Common stock	$22,000
Cash	9,000	Accounts receivable	(6,000)
Supplies	2,000	Retained earnings	2,000
Accounts payable	(8,000)	Notes payable	10,500
	$28,500		$28,500

Instructions

Explain to Ashley Hirano in a memo why the original balance sheet is incorrect and what should be done to correct it.

Ethics Case

CT1.6 After numerous campus interviews, Greg Thorpe, a senior at Great Northern College, received two office interview invitations from the Baltimore offices of two large firms. Both firms offered to cover his out-of-pocket expenses (travel, hotel, and meals). He scheduled the interviews for both firms on the same day, one in the morning and one in the afternoon. At the conclusion of each interview, he submitted to both firms his total out-of-pocket expenses for the trip to Baltimore: mileage $112 (280 miles at $0.40), hotel $130, meals $36, and parking and tolls $18, for a total of $296. He believes this approach is appropriate. If he had made two trips, his cost would have been two times $296. He is also certain that neither firm knew he had visited the other on that same trip. Within 10 days, Greg received two checks in the mail, each in the amount of $296.

Instructions

a. Who are the stakeholders (affected parties) in this situation?

b. What are the ethical issues in this case?

c. What would you do in this situation?

All About You

CT1.7 Some people are tempted to make their finances look worse to get college financial aid. Companies sometimes also manage their financial numbers in order to accomplish certain goals. Earnings management is the planned timing of revenues, expenses, gains, and losses to smooth out bumps in net income. In managing earnings, companies' actions vary from being within the range of ethical activity to being both unethical and illegal attempts to mislead investors and creditors.

Instructions

Provide responses for each of the following questions.

  a. Discuss whether you think each of the following actions, taken to increase the chances of receiving financial aid, is ethical.

    1. Spend the student's assets and income first, before spending parents' assets and income.

    2. Accelerate necessary expenses to reduce available cash. For example, if you need a new car, buy it before applying for financial aid.

    3. State that a truly financially dependent child is independent.

    4. Have a parent take an unpaid leave of absence for long enough to get below the "threshold" level of income.

  b. What are some reasons why a **company** might want to overstate its earnings?

  c. What are some reasons why a **company** might want to understate its earnings?

  d. Under what circumstances might an otherwise ethical person decide to illegally overstate or understate earnings?

CT1.8 When companies need money, they go to investors or creditors. Before investors or creditors will give a company cash, they want to know the company's financial position and performance. They want to see the company's financial statements—the balance sheet and the income statement. When students need money for school, they often apply for financial aid. When you apply for financial aid, you must submit your own version of a financial statement—the Free Application for Federal Student Aid (FAFSA) form.

Suppose you have $4,000 in cash and $4,000 in credit card bills. The more cash and other assets that you have, the less likely you are to get financial aid. Also, if you have a lot of consumer debt (credit card bills), schools are less likely to loan you money. To increase your chances of receiving aid, should you use the cash to pay off your credit card bills and therefore make yourself look "worse off" to the financial aid decision-makers?

  YES: You are playing within the rules. You are not hiding assets. You are simply restructuring your assets and liabilities to best conform with the preferences that are built into the federal aid formulas.

  NO: You are engaging in a transaction solely to take advantage of a loophole in the federal aid rules. In doing so, you are potentially depriving someone who is actually worse off than you from receiving aid.

Instructions

Write a response indicating your position regarding this situation. Provide support for your view.

FASB Codification Activity

CT1.9 The FASB has developed the Financial Accounting Standards Board Accounting Standards Codification (or more simply "the Codification"). The FASB's primary goal in developing the Codification is to provide in one place all the authoritative literature related to a particular topic. To provide easy access to the Codification, the FASB also developed the Financial Accounting Standards Board Codification Research System (CRS). CRS is an online, real-time database that provides easy access to the Codification. The Codification and the related CRS provide a topically organized structure, subdivided into topic, subtopics, sections, and paragraphs, using a numerical index system.

You may find this system useful in your present and future studies, and so we have provided an opportunity to use this online system as part of the *Expand Your Critical Thinking* section.

Instructions

Academic access to the FASB Codification is available through university subscriptions, obtained from the American Accounting Association, for an annual fee of $150. This subscription covers an unlimited number of students within a single institution. Once this access has been obtained by your school, you should log in and familiarize yourself with the resources that are accessible at the FASB Codification site.

Considering People, Planet, and Profit

CT1.10 Although **Clif Bar & Company** is not a public company, it does share its financial information with its employees as part of its open-book management approach. Further, although it does not publicly share its financial information, it does provide a different form of an annual report to external users. In this report, the company provides information regarding its sustainability efforts.

Instructions

Go to the Who We Are page of the Clif Bar website and identify the five aspirations.

A Look at IFRS

> ### LEARNING OBJECTIVE 7
> Describe the impact of international accounting standards on U.S. financial reporting.

Most agree that there is a need for one set of international accounting standards. Here is why:

Multinational corporations. Today's companies view the entire world as their market. For example, **Coca-Cola**, **Intel**, and **McDonald's** generate more than 50% of their sales outside the United States. Many foreign companies, such as **Toyota**, **Nestlé**, and **Sony**, find their largest market to be the United States.

Mergers and acquisitions. The mergers between **Fiat/Chrysler** and **Vodafone/Mannesmann** suggest that we will see even more such business combinations of companies from different countries in the future.

Information technology. As communication barriers continue to topple through advances in technology, companies and individuals in different countries and markets are becoming more comfortable buying and selling goods and services from one another.

Financial markets. Financial markets are of international significance today. Whether it is currency, equity securities (stocks), bonds, or derivatives, there are active markets throughout the world trading these types of instruments.

Key Points

Following are the key similarities and differences between GAAP and IFRS as related to accounting fundamentals.

Similarities

- The basic techniques for recording business transactions are the same for U.S. and international companies.
- Both international and U.S. accounting standards emphasize transparency in financial reporting. Both sets of standards are primarily driven by meeting the needs of investors and creditors.
- The three most common forms of business organizations, proprietorships, partnerships, and corporations, are also found in countries that use international accounting standards.

Differences

- International standards are referred to as International Financial Reporting Standards (IFRS), developed by the International Accounting Standards Board. Accounting standards in the United States are referred to as generally accepted accounting principles (GAAP) and are developed by the Financial Accounting Standards Board.
- IFRS tends to be simpler in its accounting and disclosure requirements; some people say it is more "principles-based." GAAP is more detailed; some people say it is more "rules-based."
- The internal control standards applicable to Sarbanes-Oxley (SOX) apply only to large public companies listed on U.S. exchanges. There is continuing debate as to whether non-U.S. companies should have to comply with this extra layer of regulation.

IFRS Practice

IFRS Self-Test Questions

1. Which of the following is **not** a reason why a single set of high-quality international accounting standards would be beneficial?
   a. Mergers and acquisition activity.
   b. Financial markets.
   c. Multinational corporations.
   d. GAAP is widely considered to be a superior reporting system.

2. The Sarbanes-Oxley Act determines:
   a. international tax regulations.
   b. internal control standards as enforced by the IASB.
   c. internal control standards of U.S. publicly traded companies.
   d. U.S. tax regulations.

3. IFRS is considered to be more:
   a. principles-based and less rules-based than GAAP.
   b. rules-based and less principles-based than GAAP.
   c. detailed than GAAP.
   d. None of the answer choices is correct.

IFRS Exercises

IFRS1.1 Who are the two key international players in the development of international accounting standards? Explain their role.

IFRS1.2 What is the benefit of a single set of high-quality accounting standards?

International Financial Reporting Problem: Louis Vuitton

IFRS1.3 The financial statements of **Louis Vuitton** are presented in Appendix F. The complete consolidated financial statements, including the notes to its financial statements, are available at the company's website.

Instructions

Visit Louis Vuitton's corporate website and answer the following questions from the company's 2018 consolidated financial statements.

  a. What accounting firm performed the audit of Louis Vuitton's financial statements?

  b. What is the address of the company's corporate headquarters?

  c. What is the company's reporting currency?

Answers to IFRS Self-Test Questions

1. d   **2.** c   **3.** a

CHAPTER 2

Eva-Katalin/E+/Getty Images

The Recording Process

Chapter Preview

In Chapter 1, we analyzed business transactions in terms of the accounting equation, and we presented the cumulative effects of these transactions in tabular form. Imagine a company like **MF Global** (as in the following Feature Story) using the same tabular format as Softbyte Inc. to keep track of its transactions. In a single day, MF Global engaged in thousands of business transactions. To record each transaction this way would be impractical, expensive, and unnecessary. Instead, companies use a set of procedures and records to keep track of transaction data more easily. This chapter introduces and illustrates these basic procedures and records.

Feature Story

Accidents Happen

How organized are you financially? Take a short quiz. Answer yes or no to each question:

- Does your wallet contain so many cash machine receipts that you've been declared a walking fire hazard?

- Do you wait until your debit card is denied before checking the status of your funds?

- Do you verify the accuracy of your checking account about as often as you clean the space behind your refrigerator?

If you think it is hard to keep track of the many transactions that make up **your** life, imagine how difficult it is for a big corporation to do so. Not only that, but now consider how important it is for a large company to have good accounting records, especially if it has control of **your** life savings. **MF Global Holdings Ltd** was such a company. As a large investment broker, it held billions of dollars of investments for clients. If you had *your* life savings invested at MF Global, you might be slightly displeased if you heard this from one of its representatives: "You know, I kind of remember an account for someone with a name like yours—now what did we do with that?"

Unfortunately, that is almost exactly what happened to MF Global's clients shortly before it filed for bankruptcy. During the days immediately following the bankruptcy filing, regulators and auditors struggled to piece things together. In the words of one regulator, "Their books are a disaster . . . we're trying to figure out what numbers are real numbers." One company that considered buying an interest in MF Global walked away from the deal because it "couldn't get a sense of what was on the balance sheet." That company said the information that should have been instantly available instead took days to produce.

It now appears that MF Global did not properly segregate customer accounts from company accounts. And, because of its sloppy recordkeeping, customers were not protected when the company had financial troubles. Total customer losses were approximately $1 billion. As you can see, accounting matters!

Source: S. Patterson and A. Lucchetti, "Inside the Hunt for MF Global Cash," *Wall Street Journal Online* (November 11, 2011).

Chapter Outline

LEARNING OBJECTIVES	REVIEW	PRACTICE
LO 1 Describe how accounts, debits, and credits are used to record business transactions.	• Debits and credits • Stockholders' equity relationships • Summary of debit/credit rules	**DO IT! 1** Normal Account Balances
LO 2 Indicate how a journal is used in the recording process.	• The recording process • The journal	**DO IT! 2** Recording Business Activities
LO 3 Explain how a ledger and posting help in the recording process.	• The ledger • Posting • Chart of accounts • The recording process illustrated • Summary illustration of journalizing and posting	**DO IT! 3** Posting
LO 4 Prepare a trial balance.	• Limitations of a trial balance • Locating errors • Dollar signs and underlining	**DO IT! 4** Trial Balance

Go to the Review and Practice section at the end of the chapter for a review of key concepts and practice applications with solutions.

Visit WileyPLUS for additional tutorials and practice opportunities.

Accounts, Debits, and Credits

LEARNING OBJECTIVE 1

Describe how accounts, debits, and credits are used to record business transactions.

An **account** is an individual accounting record of increases and decreases in a specific asset, liability, or stockholders' equity item. For example, Softbyte Inc. (the company discussed in Chapter 1) would have separate accounts for Cash, Accounts Receivable, Accounts Payable, Service Revenue, Salaries and Wages Expense, and so on. (Note that whenever we are referring to a specific account, we capitalize the name.)

In its simplest form, an account consists of three parts: (1) a title, (2) a left or debit side, and (3) a right or credit side. Because the format of an account resembles the letter T, we refer to it as a **T-account. Illustration 2.1** shows the basic form of an account.

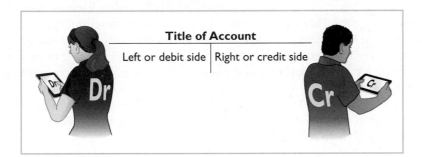

ILLUSTRATION 2.1

Basic form of account

We use this form often throughout this text to explain basic accounting relationships.

Debits and Credits

The term **debit** indicates the left side of an account, and **credit** indicates the right side. They are commonly abbreviated as **Dr.** for debit and **Cr.** for credit. They **do not** mean increase or decrease, as is commonly thought. We use the terms **debit** and **credit** repeatedly in the recording process to describe **where** entries are made in accounts. For example, the act of entering an amount on the left side of an account is called **debiting** the account. Making an entry on the right side is **crediting** the account.

When comparing the totals of the two sides, an account shows a **debit balance** if the total of the debit amounts exceeds the credits. An account shows a **credit balance** if the credit amounts exceed the debits. Note the position of the debit side and credit side in Illustration 2.1.

The procedure of recording debits and credits in an account is shown in **Illustration 2.2** for the transactions affecting the Cash account of Softbyte Inc. The data are taken from the Cash column of the tabular summary in Illustration 1.9.

ILLUSTRATION 2.2

Tabular summary and account form for Softbyte's Cash account

Tabular Summary		Account Form			
Cash			**Cash**		
$15,000		(Debits)	15,000	(Credits)	7,000
−7,000			1,200		1,700
1,200			1,500		250
1,500			600		1,300
−1,700		Balance	8,050		
−250		(Debit)			
600					
−1,300					
$ 8,050					

Every positive item in the tabular summary represents a receipt of cash. Every negative amount represents a payment of cash. **Notice that in the account form, we record the increases in cash as debits and the decreases in cash as credits.** For example, the $15,000 receipt of cash (in blue) is debited to Cash, and the –$7,000 payment of cash (in red) is credited to Cash.

Having increases on one side and decreases on the other reduces recording errors and helps in determining the totals of each side of the account as well as the account balance. The balance is determined by netting the two sides (subtracting one amount from the other). The account balance, a debit of $8,050, indicates that Softbyte had $8,050 more increases than decreases in cash. In other words, Softbyte started with a balance of zero and now has $8,050 in its Cash account.

Debit and Credit Procedure

In Chapter 1, you learned the effect of a transaction on the basic accounting equation. Remember that each transaction must affect two or more accounts to keep the basic accounting equation in balance. In other words, **for each transaction, debits must equal credits**. The equality of debits and credits provides the basis for the **double-entry system** of recording transactions (see **International Note**).

Under the double-entry system, the dual (two-sided) effect of each transaction is recorded in appropriate accounts. This system provides a logical method for recording transactions. As discussed in the Feature Story about **MF Global**, the double-entry system also helps ensure the accuracy of the recorded amounts as well as the detection of errors. If every transaction is recorded with equal debits and credits, the sum of all the debits to the accounts must equal the sum of all the credits.

The double-entry system for determining the equality of the accounting equation is much more efficient than the plus/minus procedure used in Chapter 1. The following discussion illustrates debit and credit procedures in the double-entry system.

International Note

Rules for accounting for specific events sometimes differ across countries. For example, European companies rely less on historical cost and more on fair value than U.S. companies. Despite the differences, the double-entry accounting system is the basis of accounting systems worldwide.

Dr./Cr. Procedures for Assets and Liabilities

In Illustration 2.2 for Softbyte Inc., increases in Cash—an asset—are entered on the left side, and decreases in Cash are entered on the right side. We know that both sides of the basic equation (Assets = Liabilities + Stockholders' Equity) must be equal. It therefore follows that increases and decreases in liabilities have to be recorded **opposite from** increases and decreases in assets. Thus, increases in liabilities are entered on the right or credit side, and decreases in liabilities are entered on the left or debit side. The effects that debits and credits have on assets and liabilities are summarized in **Illustration 2.3**.

ILLUSTRATION 2.3

Debit and credit effects—assets and liabilities

Debits	Credits
Increase assets	Decrease assets
Decrease liabilities	Increase liabilities

Asset accounts normally show debit balances. That is, debits to a specific asset account should exceed credits to that account. Likewise, **liability accounts normally show credit balances.** That is, credits to a liability account should exceed debits to that account. The **normal balance** of an account is on the side where an increase in the account is recorded. **Illustration 2.4** shows the normal balances for assets and liabilities.

ILLUSTRATION 2.4

Normal balances—assets and liabilities

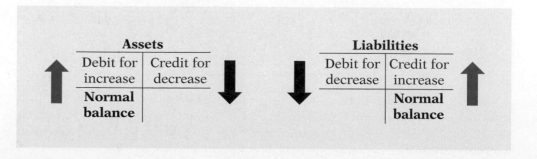

Knowing the normal balance in an account may help when you are trying to identify errors (see **Helpful Hint**). For example, a credit balance in an asset account such as Land or a debit balance in a liability account such as Salaries and Wages Payable usually indicates an error. Occasionally, though, an abnormal balance may be correct. The Cash account, for example, will have a credit balance when a company has overdrawn its bank balance by spending more than it has in its account.

HELPFUL HINT

The normal balance is the side where increases in the account are recorded.

Stockholders' Equity

As Chapter 1 indicated, there are five subdivisions of stockholders' equity: common stock, retained earnings, dividends, revenues, and expenses. In a double-entry system, companies keep accounts for each of these subdivisions, as explained below.

Common Stock   Companies issue **common stock** in exchange for the owners' investment paid in to the corporation. Credits increase the Common Stock account, and debits decrease it. For example, when an owner invests cash in the business in exchange for shares of the corporation's stock, the company debits (increases) Cash and credits (increases) Common Stock.

Illustration 2.5 shows the rules of debit and credit for the Common Stock account.

Debits	Credits
Decrease Common Stock	Increase Common Stock

ILLUSTRATION 2.5

Debit and credit effects— common stock

Illustration 2.6 shows the normal balance for Common Stock.

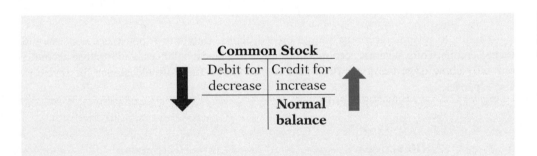

ILLUSTRATION 2.6

Normal balance—common stock

Retained Earnings   **Retained earnings** is net income that is kept (retained) in the business. It represents the portion of stockholders' equity that the company has accumulated through the profitable operation of the business. Credits (net income) increase the Retained Earnings account, and debits (dividends or net losses) decrease it, as **Illustration 2.7** shows (see **Helpful Hint**).

HELPFUL HINT

The rules for debit and credit and the normal balances of common stock and retained earnings are the same as for liabilities.

ILLUSTRATION 2.7

Debit and credit effects and normal balance—retained earnings

Retained Earnings

Debit for decrease	Credit for increase
	Normal balance

Dividends   A **dividend** is a company's distribution to its stockholders on a pro rata (equal) basis. The most common form of a distribution is a **cash dividend**. Dividends reduce the stockholders' claims on retained earnings. Debits increase the Dividends account, and credits decrease it. **Illustration 2.8** shows the normal balance for Dividends.

Debit and credit effect and
normal balance—dividends

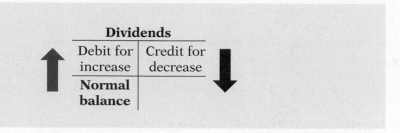

HELPFUL HINT

Because revenues increase
stockholders' equity, a
revenue account has the
same debit/credit rules
as the Common Stock
account. Expenses have the
opposite effect.

Revenues and Expenses The purpose of earning revenues is to benefit the stockholders of the business. When a company recognizes revenues, stockholders' equity increases. Revenues are a subdivision of stockholders' equity and provide information as to **why** stockholders' equity increased. Credits increase revenue accounts and debits decrease them. Therefore, **the effect of debits and credits on revenue accounts is the same as their effect on stockholders' equity** (see **Helpful Hint**).

Expenses have the opposite effect. Expenses decrease stockholders' equity. Since expenses decrease net income and revenues increase it, it is logical that the increase and decrease sides of expense accounts should be the opposite of revenue accounts. Thus, expense accounts are increased by debits and decreased by credits. **Illustration 2.9** shows the rules of debits and credits for revenues and expenses.

Debit and credit effects—
revenues and expenses

Debits	Credits
Decrease revenues	Increase revenues
Increase expenses	Decrease expenses

Credits to revenue accounts should exceed debits. Debits to expense accounts should exceed credits. Thus, revenue accounts normally show credit balances, and expense accounts normally show debit balances. **Illustration 2.10** shows the normal balance for revenues and expenses.

Normal balances—revenues
and expenses

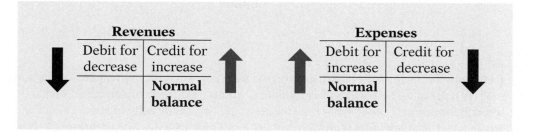

Investor Insight Chicago Cubs

Jonathan Daniel/Getty
Images Sport/Getty
Images

Keeping Score

The **Chicago Cubs** baseball team probably has these major revenue and expense accounts:

Revenues	Expenses
Admissions (ticket sales)	Players' salaries
Concessions	Administrative salaries
Television and radio	Travel
Advertising	Ballpark maintenance

Do you think that the Chicago Bears football team would be likely to have the same major revenue and expense accounts as the Cubs? (Go to WileyPLUS for this answer and additional questions.)

Stockholders' Equity Relationships

As Chapter 1 indicated, companies report the subdivisions of stockholders' equity in various places in the financial statements:

- Common stock and retained earnings in the stockholders' equity section of the balance sheet.
- Dividends on the retained earnings statement.
- Revenues and expenses on the income statement.

Dividends, revenues, and expenses are eventually transferred to retained earnings at the end of the period. As a result, a change in any one of these three items affects stockholders' equity. **Illustration 2.11** shows the relationships related to stockholders' equity.

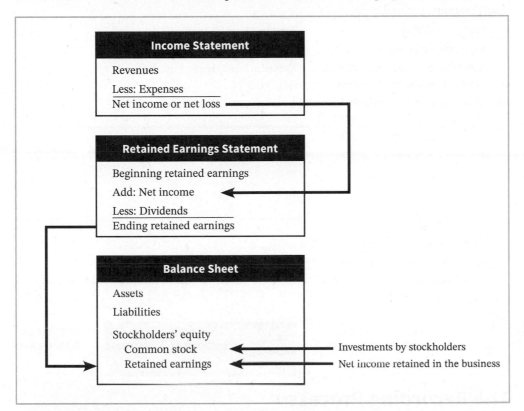

ILLUSTRATION 2.11

Stockholders' equity relationships

Summary of Debit/Credit Rules

HELPFUL HINT

You may want to bookmark Illustration 2.12. You probably will refer to it often.

Illustration 2.12 summarizes the debit/credit rules and effects on each type of account. **Study this diagram carefully.** It will help you understand the fundamentals of the double-entry system (see **Helpful Hint**). No matter what the transaction, total debits must equal total credits in order to keep the accounting equation in balance.

ILLUSTRATION 2.12 Summary of debit/credit rules

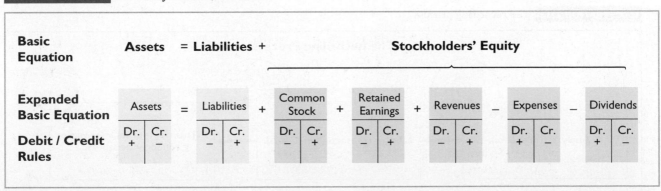

DO IT! 1 | Normal Account Balances

Kate Browne, president of Hair It Is, Inc., has just rented space in a shopping mall in which she will open and operate a beauty salon. A friend has advised Kate to set up a double-entry set of accounting records in which to record all of her business transactions.

Identify the balance sheet accounts that Hair It Is, Inc. will likely use to record the transactions needed to establish and open the business. Also, indicate whether the normal balance of each account is a debit or a credit.

Solution

Hair It Is, Inc. would likely use the following accounts to record the transactions needed to ready the beauty salon for opening day:

Cash (debit balance)   Equipment (debit balance)

Supplies (debit balance)   Accounts Payable (credit balance)

Notes Payable (credit balance),   Common Stock (credit balance)
    if the business borrows money

Related exercise material: **BE2.1, BE2.2, BE2.5, DO IT! 2.1, E2.1, E2.2, E2.4, and E2.7.**

The Journal

ANALYZE | **Journalize the transactions** | POST | TRIAL BALANCE | ADJUSTING ENTRIES | ADJUSTED TRIAL BALANCE | FINANCIAL STATEMENTS | CLOSING ENTRIES | POST-CLOSING TRIAL BALANCE

The Recording Process

Although it is possible to enter transaction information directly into the accounts, few businesses do so. Practically every business uses the basic steps shown in **Illustration 2.13** in the recording process (an integral part of the accounting cycle):

1. Analyze each transaction in terms of its effect on the accounts.
2. Enter the transaction information in a journal.
3. Transfer the journal information to the appropriate accounts in the ledger.

ILLUSTRATION 2.13 The recording process

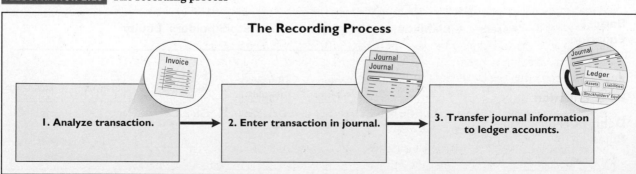

The Recording Process

I. Analyze transaction. → 2. Enter transaction in journal. → 3. Transfer journal information to ledger accounts.

The steps in the recording process occur repeatedly. In Chapter 1, we illustrated the first step, the analysis of transactions, and will give further examples in this and later chapters. The other two steps in the recording process are explained in the next sections.

The Journal

Companies initially record transactions in chronological order (the order in which they occur). Thus, the **journal** is referred to as the book of original entry. For each transaction, the journal shows the debit and credit effects on specific accounts (see **Helpful Hint**).

Companies may use various kinds of journals, but every company has the most basic form of journal, a **general journal**. Typically, a general journal has spaces for dates, account titles and explanations, references, and two amount columns. See the format of the journal in Illustration 2.14. *Whenever we use the term "journal" in this text, we mean the general journal unless we specify otherwise.*

The journal makes several significant contributions to the recording process:

1. It discloses in one place the **complete effects of a transaction**.
2. It provides a **chronological record** of transactions.
3. It helps to **prevent or locate errors** because the debit and credit amounts for each entry can be easily compared.

HELPFUL HINT

In a computerized system, journals are kept as files, and accounts are recorded in electronic databases.

Journalizing

Entering transaction data in the journal is known as **journalizing**. Companies make separate journal entries for each transaction. A complete entry consists of (1) the date of the transaction, (2) the accounts and amounts to be debited and credited, and (3) a brief explanation of the transaction.

Illustration 2.14 shows the technique of journalizing, using the first two transactions of Softbyte Inc. On September 1, stockholders invested $15,000 cash in the corporation in exchange for common stock, and Softbyte purchased computer equipment for $7,000 cash. The number J1 indicates that these two entries are recorded on the first page of the journal. Illustration 2.14 shows the standard form of journal entries for these two transactions. (The boxed numbers correspond to explanations in the list below the illustration.)

GENERAL JOURNAL				J1
Date	**Account Titles and Explanation**	**Ref.**	**Debit**	**Credit**
2022		[5]		
Sept. 1	[2] Cash		15,000	
[1]	[3] Common Stock			15,000
	[4] (Issued common stock for cash)			
1	Equipment		7,000	
	Cash			7,000
	(Purchase of equipment for cash)			

ILLUSTRATION 2.14

Technique of journalizing

[1] The date of the transaction is entered in the Date column.

[2] The debit account title (that is, the account to be debited) is entered first at the extreme left margin of the column headed "Account Titles and Explanation," and the amount of the debit is recorded in the Debit column.

[3] The credit account title (that is, the account to be credited) is indented and entered on the next line in the column headed "Account Titles and Explanation," and the amount of the credit is recorded in the Credit column.

[4] A brief explanation of the transaction appears on the line below the credit account title. A space is left between journal entries. The blank space separates individual journal entries and makes the entire journal easier to read.

[5] The column titled Ref. (which stands for Reference) is left blank when the journal entry is made. This column is used later when the journal entries are transferred to the ledger accounts.

It is important to use correct and specific account titles in journalizing. Erroneous account titles lead to incorrect financial statements. However, some flexibility exists initially in selecting account titles. The main criterion is that each title must appropriately describe the content of the account. Once a company chooses the specific title to use, it should record under that account title all later transactions involving the account. *In homework problems, you should use specific account titles when they are given.* When account titles are not given, you may select account titles that identify the nature and content of each account. The account titles used in journalizing should not contain explanations such as Cash Paid or Cash Received.

Simple and Compound Entries

Some entries involve only two accounts, one debit and one credit. (See, for example, the entries in Illustration 2.14.) This type of entry is called a **simple entry**. Some transactions, however, require more than two accounts in journalizing. An entry that requires three or more accounts is a **compound entry**. To illustrate, assume that on July 1, Butler Company purchases a delivery truck costing $14,000. It pays $8,000 cash now and agrees to pay the remaining $6,000 on account (to be paid later). **Illustration 2.15** shows this compound entry.

ILLUSTRATION 2.15

Compound journal entry

	GENERAL JOURNAL				J1
Date	Account Titles and Explanation	Ref.	Debit		Credit
2022					
July 1	Equipment		14,000		
	Cash				8,000
	Accounts Payable				6,000
	(Purchased truck for cash with balance on account)				

In a compound entry, the standard format requires that all debits be listed before the credits.

ACTION PLAN

- **Understand which activities need to be recorded and which do not. Any activities that affect assets, liabilities, or stockholders' equity should be recorded in a journal.**
- **Analyze the effects of transactions on asset, liability, and stockholders' equity accounts.**

DO IT! 2 | Recording Business Activities

As president and sole stockholder, Kate Browne engaged in the following activities in establishing her salon, Hair It Is, Inc.:

1. Opened a bank account in the name of Hair It Is, Inc. and deposited $20,000 of her own money in this account in exchange for shares of common stock.

2. Purchased equipment on account (to be paid in 30 days) for a total cost of $4,800.

3. Interviewed three people for the position of hair stylist.

Prepare the journal entries to record the transactions.

Solution

The three activities would be recorded as follows.

1.	Cash	20,000	
	Common Stock		20,000
	(Issued common stock for cash)		
2.	Equipment	4,800	
	Accounts Payable		4,800
	(Purchase of equipment on account)		

3. No entry because no transaction has occurred.

Related exercise material: **BE2.3, BE2.4, BE2.5, BE2.6, DO IT! 2.2, E2.3, E2.5, E2.6, E2.7, E2.8, E2.9, E2.12, E2.13, E2.14, and E2.17.**

The Ledger and Posting

ANALYZE → JOURNALIZE → **Post to ledger accounts** → TRIAL BALANCE → ADJUSTING ENTRIES → ADJUSTED TRIAL BALANCE → FINANCIAL STATEMENTS → CLOSING ENTRIES → POST-CLOSING TRIAL BALANCE

The Ledger

The entire group of accounts maintained by a company is the **ledger**. The ledger provides the balance in each of the accounts as well as keeps track of changes in these balances.

Companies may use various kinds of ledgers, but every company has a general ledger. A **general ledger** contains all the asset, liability, and stockholders' equity accounts, as shown in **Illustration 2.16**. *Whenever we use the term "ledger" in this text, we are referring to the general ledger unless we specify otherwise.*

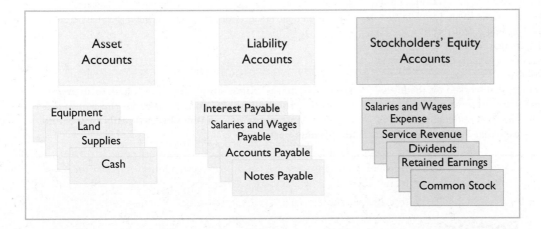

ILLUSTRATION 2.16

The general ledger, which contains all of a company's accounts

Companies arrange the ledger in the sequence in which they present the accounts in the financial statements, beginning with the balance sheet accounts. First in order are the asset accounts, followed by liability accounts, stockholders' equity accounts, revenues, and expenses. Each account is numbered for easier identification.

The ledger provides the balance in each of the accounts. For example, the Cash account shows the amount of cash available to meet current obligations. The Accounts Receivable account shows amounts due from customers. The Accounts Payable account shows amounts owed to creditors.

Standard Form of Account

The simple T-account form used in accounting texts is often very useful for illustration purposes. However, in practice, the account forms used in ledgers are much more structured. **Illustration 2.17** shows a typical form, using assumed data from a cash account.

Three-column form of account

CASH					NO. 101
Date	Explanation	Ref.	Debit	Credit	Balance
2022					
June 1			25,000		25,000
2				8,000	17,000
3			4,200		21,200
9			7,500		28,700
17				11,700	17,000
20				250	16,750
30				7,300	9,450

This format is called the **three-column form of account**. It has three money columns—debit, credit, and balance. The balance in the account is determined after each transaction. Companies use the explanation space and reference columns to provide special information about the transaction.

iordani/Shutterstock.com

A Convenient Overstatement

Sometimes a company's investment securities suffer a permanent decline in value below their original cost. When this occurs, the company is supposed to reduce the recorded value of the securities on its balance sheet ("write them down" in common financial lingo) and record a loss. It appears, however, that during the financial crisis of 2008, employees at some financial institutions chose to look the other way as the value of their investments skidded.

A number of Wall Street traders that worked for the investment bank **Credit Suisse Group** were charged with intentionally overstating the value of securities that had suffered declines of approximately $2.85 billion. One reason that they may have been reluctant to record the losses is out of fear that the company's shareholders and clients would panic if they saw the magnitude of the losses. However, personal self-interest might have been equally to blame—the bonuses of the traders were tied to the value of the investment securities.

Source: S. Pulliam, J. Eaglesham, and M. Siconolfi, "U.S. Plans Changes on Bond Fraud," *Wall Street Journal Online* (February 1, 2012).

What incentives might employees have had to overstate the value of these investment securities on the company's financial statements? (Go to WileyPLUS for this answer and additional questions.)

Posting

The procedure of transferring journal entries to the ledger accounts is called **posting**. **This phase of the recording process accumulates the effects of journalized transactions into the individual accounts.** Posting involves the following steps.

1. In the **ledger**, in the appropriate columns of the account(s) debited, enter the date, journal page, and debit amount shown in the journal.

2. In the reference column of the **journal**, write the account number to which the debit amount was posted.

3. In the **ledger**, in the appropriate columns of the account(s) credited, enter the date, journal page, and credit amount shown in the journal.

4. In the reference column of the **journal**, write the account number to which the credit amount was posted.

Illustration 2.18 shows these four steps using Softbyte Inc.'s first journal entry. The boxed numbers indicate the sequence of the steps.

ILLUSTRATION 2.18

Posting a journal entry

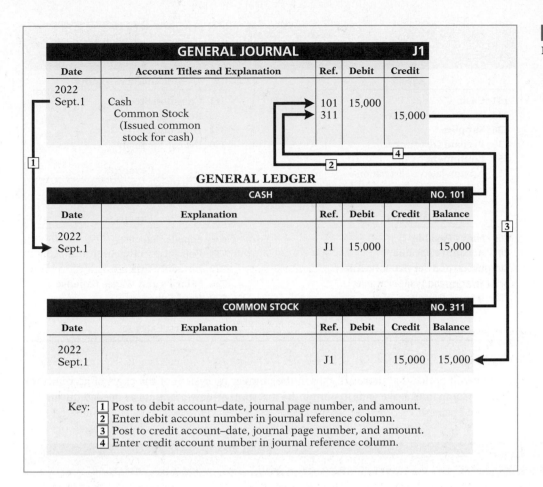

Posting should be performed in chronological order. That is, the company should post all the debits and credits of one journal entry before proceeding to the next journal entry. Postings should be made on a timely basis to ensure that the ledger is up-to-date. *In homework problems, you can journalize all transactions before posting any of the journal entries.*

The reference column of a ledger account indicates the journal page from which the transaction was posted. (After the last entry has been posted, the accountant should scan the reference column **in the journal**, to confirm that all postings have been made.) The explanation space of the ledger account is used infrequently because an explanation already appears in the journal.

Chart of Accounts

The number and type of accounts differ for each company. The number of accounts depends on the amount of detail management desires. For example, the management of one company may want a single account for all types of utility expense. Another may keep separate expense accounts for each type of utility, such as gas, electricity, and water. Similarly, a small company like Softbyte Inc. will have fewer accounts than a corporate giant like **Dell**. Softbyte may be able to manage and report its activities in 20 to 30 accounts, while Dell may require thousands of accounts to keep track of its worldwide activities.

Most companies have a **chart of accounts**. This chart lists the accounts and the account numbers that identify their location in the ledger. The numbering system that identifies the accounts usually starts with the balance sheet accounts and follows with the income statement accounts.

In this and the next two chapters, we will be explaining the accounting for Pioneer Advertising Inc. (a service company). Accounts 101–199 indicate asset accounts; 200–299 indicate liabilities; 301–350 indicate stockholders' equity accounts; 400–499, revenues; 601–799, expenses; 800–899, other revenues; and 900–999, other expenses. **Illustration 2.19** shows Pioneer's chart of accounts. Accounts listed in red are used in this chapter; accounts shown in black are explained in later chapters.

Chart of accounts for Pioneer
Advertising Inc.

Pioneer Advertising Inc.
Chart of Accounts

Assets	Stockholders' Equity
101 Cash	**311 Common Stock**
112 Accounts Receivable	320 Retained Earnings
126 Supplies	**332 Dividends**
130 Prepaid Insurance	350 Income Summary
157 Equipment	
158 Accumulated Depreciation—	**Revenues**
Equipment	**400 Service Revenue**
Liabilities	**Expenses**
200 Notes Payable	631 Supplies Expense
201 Accounts Payable	711 Depreciation Expense
209 Unearned Service Revenue	722 Insurance Expense
212 Salaries and Wages Payable	**726 Salaries and Wages Expense**
230 Interest Payable	**729 Rent Expense**
	732 Utilities Expense
	905 Interest Expense

You will notice that there are gaps in the numbering system of the chart of accounts for Pioneer. Companies leave gaps to permit the insertion of new accounts as needed during the life of the business.

Accounting Across the Organization   Hain Celestial Group

It Starts with the Transaction

Recording financial transactions in a company's records should be straightforward. If a company determines that a transaction involves revenue, it records revenue. If it has an expense, then it records an expense. However, sometimes this is difficult to do. For example, for more than a year, **Hain Celestial Group** (an organic food company) did not provide income information to investors and regulators. The reason was that the company discovered revenue irregularities and said it could not release financial results until it determined when and how to record revenue for certain transactions. When Hain missed four deadlines for reporting earnings information, the food company suffered a 34% drop in its stock price. As one analyst noted, it was hard to fathom why a seemingly simple revenue recognition issue took one year to resolve.

Keith Homan/
Shutterstock.com

In other situations, outright fraud may occur. For example, regulators charged **Obsidian Energy** for fraudulently moving millions of dollars in expenses from operating expenses to capital expenditure accounts. By understating reported operating expenses, Obsidian made it appear that it was efficiently managing its costs as well as increasing its income.

These examples demonstrate that "getting the basic transaction right" is the foundation for relevant and representationally faithful financial statements. Starting with an incorrect or inappropriate transaction leads to distortions in the financial statements.

Sources: Shawn Tully, "The Mystery of Hain Celestial's Accounting," *Fortune.com* (August 20, 2016); and Kelly Cryderman, "U.S. Charges Obsidian, Formerly Penn West, with Accounting Fraud," *Globe and Mail* (June 28, 2017).

Why is it important for companies to record financial transactions completely and accurately? (Go to WileyPLUS for this answer and additional questions.)

The Recording Process Illustrated

Illustrations **2.20** through **2.29** show the basic steps in the recording process, using the October transactions of Pioneer Advertising Inc. A basic analysis, an equation analysis, and a debit-credit analysis precede the journal entry and posting of each transaction. For simplicity, we use the T-account form to show the posting instead of the standard account form.

Study these transaction analyses carefully. **The purpose of transaction analysis is first to identify the type of account involved, and then to determine whether to make a debit or a credit to the account.** You should always perform this type of analysis before preparing a journal entry. Doing so will help you understand the journal entries discussed in this chapter as well as more complex journal entries in later chapters (see **Helpful Hint**).

In addition, an Accounting Cycle Tutorial is available in WileyPLUS. It provides an interactive presentation of the steps in the accounting cycle, using the Pioneer example shown in Illustrations 2.20 through 2.29.

ILLUSTRATION 2.20

Investment of cash by stockholders

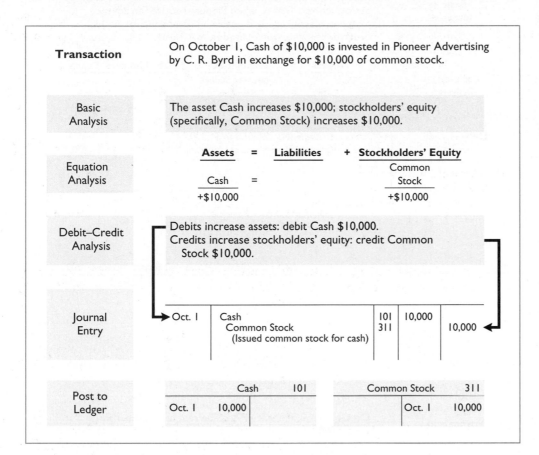

Cash flow analyses show the impact of each transaction on cash.

Cash Flows
+10,000

HELPFUL HINT

Follow these steps:

1. Determine what type of account is involved.
2. Determine what items increased or decreased and by how much.
3. Translate the increases and decreases into debits and credits.

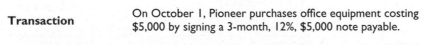

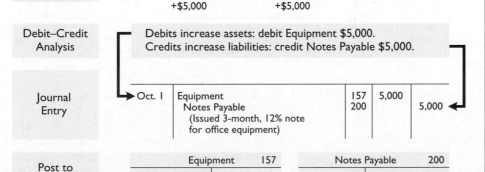

ILLUSTRATION 2.21

Purchase of office equipment

Cash Flows
no effect

ILLUSTRATION 2.22

Receipt of cash for future service

Many liabilities have the word "payable" in their title. But, note that Unearned Service Revenue is considered a liability even though the word *payable* is not used.

Cash Flows
+1,200

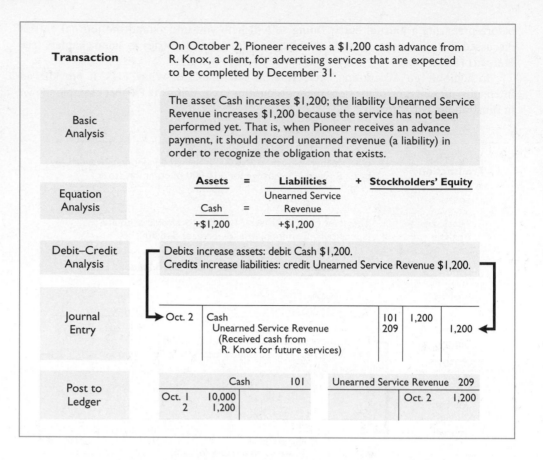

Transaction	On October 2, Pioneer receives a $1,200 cash advance from R. Knox, a client, for advertising services that are expected to be completed by December 31.
Basic Analysis	The asset Cash increases $1,200; the liability Unearned Service Revenue increases $1,200 because the service has not been performed yet. That is, when Pioneer receives an advance payment, it should record unearned revenue (a liability) in order to recognize the obligation that exists.

Equation Analysis

Assets	=	Liabilities	+	Stockholders' Equity
Cash	=	Unearned Service Revenue		
+$1,200		+$1,200		

Debit–Credit Analysis

Debits increase assets: debit Cash $1,200.
Credits increase liabilities: credit Unearned Service Revenue $1,200.

Journal Entry

Oct. 2	Cash	101	1,200	
	Unearned Service Revenue	209		1,200
	(Received cash from R. Knox for future services)			

Post to Ledger

Cash			101		Unearned Service Revenue		209
Oct. 1	10,000					Oct. 2	1,200
2	1,200						

ILLUSTRATION 2.23

Payment of monthly rent

Cash Flows
−900

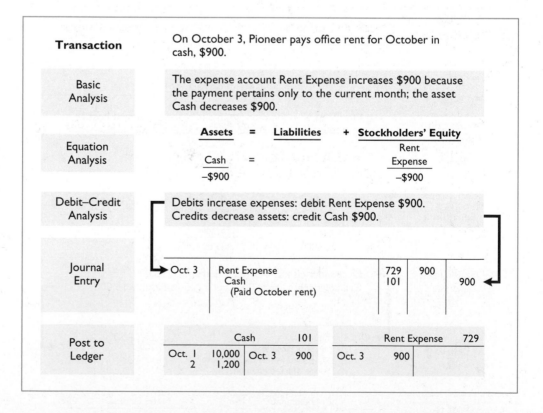

Transaction	On October 3, Pioneer pays office rent for October in cash, $900.
Basic Analysis	The expense account Rent Expense increases $900 because the payment pertains only to the current month; the asset Cash decreases $900.

Equation Analysis

Assets	=	Liabilities	+	Stockholders' Equity
Cash	=			Rent Expense
−$900				−$900

Debit–Credit Analysis

Debits increase expenses: debit Rent Expense $900.
Credits decrease assets: credit Cash $900.

Journal Entry

Oct. 3	Rent Expense	729	900	
	Cash	101		900
	(Paid October rent)			

Post to Ledger

Cash			101		Rent Expense		729
Oct. 1	10,000	Oct. 3	900		Oct. 3	900	
2	1,200						

ILLUSTRATION 2.24
Payment of insurance

Transaction	On October 4, Pioneer pays $600 for a one-year insurance policy that will expire next year on September 30.
Basic Analysis	The asset Cash decreases $600. Payments of expenses that will benefit more than one accounting period are prepaid expenses or prepayments. When a company makes a payment, it debits an asset account in order to show the service or benefit that will be received in the future. Therefore, the asset Prepaid Insurance is increased $600.

Equation Analysis

Assets	=	**Liabilities**	+	**Stockholders' Equity**
Cash + Prepaid Insurance				
−$600 +$600				

Debit–Credit Analysis

Debits increase assets: debit Prepaid Insurance $600.
Credits decrease assets: credit Cash $600.

Journal Entry

Oct. 4	Prepaid Insurance	130	600	
	Cash	101		600
	(Paid one-year policy; effective date October 1)			

Post to Ledger

	Cash		101		Prepaid Insurance	130
Oct. 1	10,000	Oct. 3	900	Oct. 4	600	
2	1,200	4	600			

Cash Flows
−600

ILLUSTRATION 2.25
Purchase of supplies on credit

Transaction	On October 5, Pioneer purchases an estimated 3-month supply of advertising materials on account from Aero Supply for $2,500.
Basic Analysis	The asset Supplies increases $2,500; the liability Accounts Payable increases $2,500.

Equation Analysis

Assets	=	**Liabilities**	+	**Stockholders' Equity**
Supplies	=	Accounts Payable		
+$2,500		+$2,500		

Debit–Credit Analysis

Debits increase assets: debit Supplies $2,500.
Credits increase liabilities: credit Accounts Payable $2,500.

Journal Entry

Oct. 5	Supplies	126	2,500	
	Accounts Payable	201		2,500
	(Purchased supplies on account from Aero Supply)			

Post to Ledger

	Supplies	126		Accounts Payable	201
Oct. 5	2,500			Oct. 5	2,500

Cash Flows
no effect

ILLUSTRATION 2.26

Hiring of employees

Cash Flows
no effect

Event	On October 9, Pioneer hires four employees to begin work on October 15. Each employee is to receive a weekly salary of $500 for a 5-day work week, payable every 2 weeks—first payment made on October 26.
Basic Analysis	This is a business **event**; a business transaction has not occurred. There is only an agreement between the employer and the employees to enter into a business transaction beginning on October 15. Thus, a debit−credit analysis is not needed because there is no accounting entry (see October 26 transaction for first entry).

ILLUSTRATION 2.27

Receipt of cash for services performed

Cash Flows
+10,000

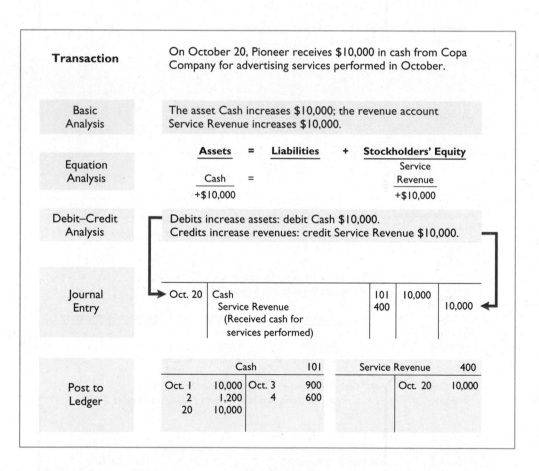

Transaction	On October 20, Pioneer receives $10,000 in cash from Copa Company for advertising services performed in October.
Basic Analysis	The asset Cash increases $10,000; the revenue account Service Revenue increases $10,000.

Assets	=	**Liabilities**	+	**Stockholders' Equity**
				Service
Cash	=			Revenue
+$10,000				+$10,000

Equation Analysis

Debit−Credit Analysis

Debits increase assets: debit Cash $10,000.
Credits increase revenues: credit Service Revenue $10,000.

Journal Entry

Oct. 20	Cash	101	10,000	
	Service Revenue	400		10,000
	(Received cash for services performed)			

Post to Ledger

	Cash		101			Service Revenue		400
Oct. 1	10,000	Oct. 3	900				Oct. 20	10,000
2	1,200	4	600					
20	10,000							

ILLUSTRATION 2.28
Payment of salaries

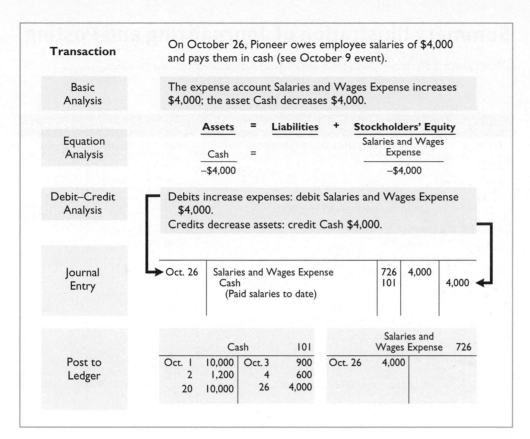

Transaction	On October 26, Pioneer owes employee salaries of $4,000 and pays them in cash (see October 9 event).
Basic Analysis	The expense account Salaries and Wages Expense increases $4,000; the asset Cash decreases $4,000.

Equation Analysis

Assets	=	Liabilities	+	Stockholders' Equity
Cash	=			Salaries and Wages Expense
−$4,000				−$4,000

Debit–Credit Analysis: Debits increase expenses: debit Salaries and Wages Expense $4,000. Credits decrease assets: credit Cash $4,000.

Journal Entry

Oct. 26	Salaries and Wages Expense	726	4,000	
	Cash	101		4,000
	(Paid salaries to date)			

Post to Ledger

Cash 101

Oct. 1	10,000	Oct. 3	900
2	1,200	4	600
20	10,000	26	4,000

Salaries and Wages Expense 726

Oct. 26	4,000	

Cash Flows
−4,000

ILLUSTRATION 2.29
Declaration and payment of dividend

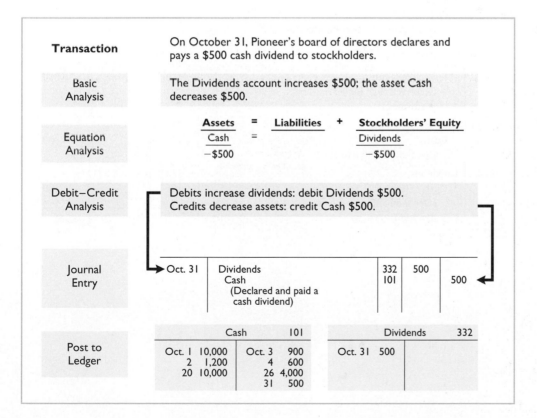

Transaction	On October 31, Pioneer's board of directors declares and pays a $500 cash dividend to stockholders.
Basic Analysis	The Dividends account increases $500; the asset Cash decreases $500.

Equation Analysis

Assets	=	Liabilities	+	Stockholders' Equity
Cash	=			Dividends
−$500				−$500

Debit–Credit Analysis: Debits increase dividends: debit Dividends $500. Credits decrease assets: credit Cash $500.

Journal Entry

Oct. 31	Dividends	332	500	
	Cash	101		500
	(Declared and paid a cash dividend)			

Post to Ledger

Cash 101

Oct. 1	10,000	Oct. 3	900
2	1,200	4	600
20	10,000	26	4,000
		31	500

Dividends 332

Oct. 31	500	

Cash Flows
−500

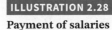 

Summary Illustration of Journalizing and Posting

Illustration 2.30 shows the journal for Pioneer Advertising Inc. for October.

ILLUSTRATION 2.30

General journal entries

	GENERAL JOURNAL			PAGE J1
Date	**Account Titles and Explanation**	**Ref.**	**Debit**	**Credit**
2022				
Oct. 1	Cash	101	10,000	
	Common Stock	311		10,000
	(Issued common stock for cash)			
1	Equipment	157	5,000	
	Notes Payable	200		5,000
	(Issued 3-month, 12% note for office equipment)			
2	Cash	101	1,200	
	Unearned Service Revenue	209		1,200
	(Received advance from R. Knox for future services)			
3	Rent Expense	729	900	
	Cash	101		900
	(Paid cash for October office rent)			
4	Prepaid Insurance	130	600	
	Cash	101		600
	(Paid one-year policy; effective date October 1)			
5	Supplies	126	2,500	
	Accounts Payable	201		2,500
	(Purchased supplies on account from Aero Supply)			
20	Cash	101	10,000	
	Service Revenue	400		10,000
	(Received cash for services performed)			
26	Salaries and Wages Expense	726	4,000	
	Cash	101		4,000
	(Paid salaries to date)			
31	Dividends	332	500	
	Cash	101		500
	(Declared and paid a cash dividend)			

Illustration 2.31 shows the ledger, with all balances in red.

ILLUSTRATION 2.31   **General ledger**

GENERAL LEDGER

Cash   No. 101

Date	Explanation	Ref.	Debit	Credit	Balance
2022					
Oct. 1		J1	10,000		10,000
2		J1	1,200		11,200
3		J1		900	10,300
4		J1		600	9,700
20		J1	10,000		19,700
26		J1		4,000	15,700
31		J1		500	**15,200**

Supplies   No. 126

Date	Explanation	Ref.	Debit	Credit	Balance
2022					
Oct. 5		J1	2,500		**2,500**

Prepaid Insurance   No. 130

Date	Explanation	Ref.	Debit	Credit	Balance
2022					
Oct. 4		J1	600		**600**

Equipment   No. 157

Date	Explanation	Ref.	Debit	Credit	Balance
2022					
Oct. 1		J1	5,000		**5,000**

Notes Payable   No. 200

Date	Explanation	Ref.	Debit	Credit	Balance
2022					
Oct. 1		J1		5,000	**5,000**

Accounts Payable   No. 201

Date	Explanation	Ref.	Debit	Credit	Balance
2022					
Oct. 5		J1		2,500	**2,500**

Unearned Service Revenue   No. 209

Date	Explanation	Ref.	Debit	Credit	Balance
2022					
Oct. 2		J1		1,200	**1,200**

Common Stock   No. 311

Date	Explanation	Ref.	Debit	Credit	Balance
2022					
Oct. 1		J1		10,000	**10,000**

Dividends   No. 332

Date	Explanation	Ref.	Debit	Credit	Balance
2022					
Oct. 31		J1	500		**500**

Service Revenue   No. 400

Date	Explanation	Ref.	Debit	Credit	Balance
2022					
Oct. 20		J1		10,000	**10,000**

Salaries and Wages Expense   No. 726

Date	Explanation	Ref.	Debit	Credit	Balance
2022					
Oct. 26		J1	4,000		**4,000**

Rent Expense   No. 729

Date	Explanation	Ref.	Debit	Credit	Balance
2022					
Oct. 3		J1	900		**900**

DO IT! 3   Posting

Kate Browne recorded the following transactions in a general journal during the month of March.

Mar. 4	Cash	2,280	
	Service Revenue		2,280
15	Salaries and Wages Expenses	400	
	Cash		400
19	Utilities Expense	92	
	Cash		92

Post these entries to the Cash account of the general ledger to determine its ending balance. The beginning balance of Cash on March 1 was $600.

ACTION PLAN

- **Recall that posting involves transferring the journalized debits and credits to specific accounts in the ledger.**
- **Determine the ending balance by netting the total debits and credits.**

Solution

	Cash		
3/1 Bal.	600	3/15	400
3/4	2,280	3/19	92
3/31 Bal.	2,388		

Related exercise material: **BE2.7, BE2.8, DO IT! 2.3, E2.10, E2.11, E2.14, and E2.17.**

The Trial Balance

LEARNING OBJECTIVE 4

Prepare a trial balance.

ANALYZE ▸ JOURNALIZE ▸ POST ▸ **Prepare a trial balance** ▸ ADJUSTING ENTRIES ▸ ADJUSTED TRIAL BALANCE ▸ FINANCIAL STATEMENTS ▸ CLOSING ENTRIES ▸ POST-CLOSING TRIAL BALANCE

A **trial balance** is a list of accounts and their balances at a given time. Companies usually prepare a trial balance at the end of an accounting period. They list accounts in the order in which they appear in the ledger. Debit balances appear in the left column and credit balances in the right column. The totals of the two columns must be equal.

The trial balance proves the mathematical equality of debits and credits after posting. Under the double-entry system, this equality occurs when the sum of the debit account balances equals the sum of the credit account balances. **A trial balance may also uncover errors in journalizing and posting.** For example, a trial balance may well have detected the error at **MF Global** discussed in the Feature Story. **In addition, a trial balance is useful in the preparation of financial statements**, as we will explain in the next two chapters.

The steps for preparing a trial balance are:

1. List the account titles and their balances in the appropriate debit or credit column.
2. Total the debit and credit columns.
3. Verify the equality of the two columns.

Illustration 2.32 shows the trial balance prepared from Pioneer Advertising's ledger (see **Helpful Hint**). Note that the total debits equal the total credits.

ILLUSTRATION 2.32

A trial balance

HELPFUL HINT

Note that the order of presentation in the trial balance is:

Assets
Liabilities
Stockholders' equity
Revenues
Expenses

Pioneer Advertising Inc.
Trial Balance
October 31, 2022

	Debit	Credit
Cash	$15,200	
Supplies	2,500	
Prepaid Insurance	600	
Equipment	5,000	
Notes Payable		$ 5,000
Accounts Payable		2,500
Unearned Service Revenue		1,200
Common Stock		10,000
Dividends	500	
Service Revenue		10,000
Salaries and Wages Expense	4,000	
Rent Expense	900	
	$28,700	$28,700

A trial balance is a necessary checkpoint for uncovering certain types of errors. For example, if only the debit portion of a journal entry has been posted, the trial balance would bring this error to light.

Limitations of a Trial Balance

A trial balance does not guarantee freedom from recording errors, however. Numerous errors may exist even though the totals of the trial balance columns agree (see **Ethics Note**). For example, the trial balance may balance even when:

1. A transaction is not journalized.
2. A correct journal entry is not posted.
3. A journal entry is posted twice.
4. Incorrect accounts are used in journalizing or posting.
5. Offsetting errors are made in recording the amount of a transaction.

As long as equal debits and credits are posted, even to the wrong account or in the wrong amount, the total debits will equal the total credits. **The trial balance does not prove that the company has recorded all transactions or that the ledger is correct.**

ETHICS NOTE

An error is the result of an unintentional mistake; it is neither ethical nor unethical. An irregularity is an intentional misstatement, which is viewed as unethical.

Locating Errors

Errors in a trial balance generally result from mathematical mistakes, incorrect postings, or simply transcribing data incorrectly. What do you do if you are faced with a trial balance that does not balance? First, determine the amount of the difference between the two columns of the trial balance. After this amount is known, the following steps are often helpful:

1. If the error is $1, $10, $100, or $1,000, re-add the trial balance columns and recompute the account balances.
2. If the error is divisible by 2, scan the trial balance to see whether a balance equal to half the error has been entered in the wrong column.
3. If the error is divisible by 9, retrace the account balances on the trial balance to see whether they are incorrectly copied from the ledger. For example, if a balance was $12 and it was listed as $21, a $9 error has been made. Reversing the order of numbers is called a **transposition error**.
4. If the error is not divisible by 2 or 9, scan the ledger to see whether an account balance in the amount of the error has been omitted from the trial balance, and scan the journal to see whether a posting of that amount has been omitted.

Dollar Signs and Underlining

Note that dollar signs do not appear in journals or ledgers. Dollar signs are typically used only in the trial balance and the financial statements. Generally, a dollar sign is shown only for the first item in the column and for the total of that column. A single line (a totaling rule) is placed under the column of figures to be added or subtracted. Total amounts are double-underlined to indicate they are final sums.

Investor Insight Fannie Mae

iStock.com/Enviromatic

Why Accuracy Matters

While most companies record transactions very carefully, the reality is that mistakes still happen. For example, bank regulators fined **Bank One Corporation** (now **JPMorgan Chase**) $1.8 million because they felt that the unreliability of the bank's accounting system caused it to violate regulatory requirements.

Also, in recent years **Fannie Mae**, the government-chartered mortgage association, announced a series of large accounting errors. These announcements caused alarm among investors, regulators, and politicians because they fear that the errors may suggest larger, undetected problems. This is important because the home-mortgage market depends on Fannie Mae to buy hundreds of billions of dollars of mortgages each year from banks, thus enabling the banks to issue new mortgages.

Finally, before a major overhaul of its accounting system, the financial records of **Waste Management, Inc.** were in such disarray that of the company's 57,000 employees, 10,000 were receiving pay slips that were in error.

The Sarbanes-Oxley Act was created to minimize the occurrence of errors like these by increasing every employee's responsibility for accurate financial reporting.

In order for these companies to prepare and issue financial statements, their accounting equations (debits and credits) must have been in balance at year-end. How could these errors or misstatements have occurred? (Go to WileyPLUS for this answer and additional questions.)

ACTION PLAN

- **Determine normal balances and list accounts in the order they appear in the ledger.**
- **Accounts with debit balances appear in the left column, and those with credit balances in the right column.**
- **Total the debit and credit columns to prove equality.**

DO IT! 4 | Trial Balance

The following accounts come from the ledger of SnowGo Corporation at December 31, 2022.

157	Equipment	$88,000		311	Common Stock	$20,000
332	Dividends	8,000		212	Salaries and Wages Payable	2,000
201	Accounts Payable	22,000		200	Notes Payable (due in 3 months)	19,000
726	Salaries and Wages Expense	42,000		732	Utilities Expense	3,000
112	Accounts Receivable	4,000		130	Prepaid Insurance	6,000
400	Service Revenue	95,000		101	Cash	7,000

Prepare a trial balance in good form.

Solution

SnowGo Corporation
Trial Balance
December 31, 2022

	Debit	Credit
Cash	$ 7,000	
Accounts Receivable	4,000	
Prepaid Insurance	6,000	
Equipment	88,000	
Notes Payable		$ 19,000
Accounts Payable		22,000
Salaries and Wages Payable		2,000
Common Stock		20,000
Dividends	8,000	
Service Revenue		95,000
Utilities Expense	3,000	
Salaries and Wages Expense	42,000	
	$158,000	**$158,000**

Related exercise material: **BE2.9, BE2.10, DO IT! 2.4, E2.11, E2.12, E2.13, E2.14, E2.15, E2.16, and E2.17.**

Review and Practice

Learning Objectives Review

1 Describe how accounts, debits, and credits are used to record business transactions.

An account is a record of increases and decreases in specific asset, liability, and stockholders' equity items. The terms debit and credit are synonymous with left and right. Assets, dividends, and expenses are increased by debits and decreased by credits. Liabilities, common stock, retained earnings, and revenues are increased by credits and decreased by debits.

2 Indicate how a journal is used in the recording process.

The basic steps in the recording process are (a) analyze each transaction for its effects on the accounts, (b) enter the transaction information in a journal, and (c) transfer the journal information to the appropriate accounts in the ledger.

The initial accounting record of a transaction is entered in a journal before the data are entered in the accounts. A journal (a) discloses in one place the complete effects of a transaction, (b) provides a chronological record of transactions, and (c) prevents or locates errors because the debit and credit amounts for each entry can be easily compared.

3 Explain how a ledger and posting help in the recording process.

The ledger is the entire group of accounts maintained by a company. The ledger provides the balance in each of the accounts as well as keeps track of changes in these balances. Posting is the transfer of journal entries to the ledger accounts. This phase of the recording process accumulates the effects of journalized transactions in the individual accounts.

4 Prepare a trial balance.

A trial balance is a list of accounts and their balances at a given time. Its primary purpose is to prove the equality of debits and credits after posting. A trial balance also uncovers errors in journalizing and posting and is useful in preparing financial statements.

Glossary Review

Account A record of increases and decreases in specific asset, liability, or stockholders' equity items. (p. 2-3).

Chart of accounts A list of accounts and the account numbers that identify their location in the ledger. (p. 2-13).

Common stock Issued in exchange for the owners' investment paid in to corporation. (p. 2-5)

Compound entry A journal entry that involves three or more accounts. (p. 2-10).

Credit The right side of an account. (p. 2-3).

Debit The left side of an account. (p. 2-3).

Dividend A distribution by a corporation to its stockholders on a pro rata (equal) basis. (p. 2-5).

Double-entry system A system that records in appropriate accounts the dual effect of each transaction. (p. 2-4).

General journal The most basic form of journal. (p. 2-9).

General ledger A ledger that contains all asset, liability, and stockholders' equity accounts. (p. 2-11).

Journal An accounting record in which transactions are initially recorded in chronological order. (p. 2-9).

Journalizing The entering of transaction data in the journal. (p. 2-9).

Ledger The entire group of accounts maintained by a company. (p. 2-11).

Normal balance An account balance on the side where an increase in the account is recorded. (p. 2-4).

Posting The procedure of transferring journal entries to the ledger accounts. (p. 2-12).

Retained earnings Net income that is kept (retained) in the business. (p. 2-5).

Simple entry A journal entry that involves only two accounts. (p. 2-10).

T-account The basic form of an account, consisting of (1) a title, (2) a left or debit side, and (3) a right or credit side. (p. 2-3).

Three-column form of account A form with columns for debit, credit, and balance amounts in an account. (p. 2-12).

Trial balance A list of accounts and their balances at a given time. (p. 2-22).

Practice Multiple-Choice Questions

1. **(LO 1)** Which of the following statements about an account is **true**?

   a. The right side of an account is the debit, or increase, side.

   b. An account is an individual accounting record of increases and decreases in specific asset, liability, and stockholders' equity items.

   c. There are separate accounts for specific assets and liabilities but only one account for stockholders' equity items.

   d. The left side of an account is the credit, or decrease, side.

2. **(LO 1)** Debits:

   a. increase both assets and liabilities.

   b. decrease both assets and liabilities.

   c. increase assets and decrease liabilities.

   d. decrease assets and increase liabilities.

3. **(LO 1)** A revenue account:

   a. is increased by debits.

   b. is decreased by credits.

   c. has a normal balance of a debit.

   d. is increased by credits.

4. **(LO 1)** Accounts that normally have debit balances are:

   a. assets, expenses, and revenues.

   b. assets, expenses, and common stock.

   c. assets, liabilities, and dividends.

   d. assets, dividends, and expenses.

5. **(LO 1)** The expanded accounting equation is:

   a. Assets + Liabilities = Common Stock + Retained Earnings + Revenues + Expenses + Dividends.

   b. Assets = Liabilities + Common Stock + Retained Earnings + Revenues − Expenses + Dividends.

   c. Assets = Liabilities − Common Stock − Retained Earnings − Revenues − Expenses − Dividends.

   d. Assets = Liabilities + Common Stock + Retained Earnings + Revenues − Expenses − Dividends.

6. **(LO 1)** Which of the following is **not** part of the recording process?

   a. Analyzing transactions.

   b. Preparing an income statement.

   c. Entering transactions in a journal.

   d. Posting journal entries.

7. **(LO 2)** Which of the following statements about a journal is **false**?

   a. It is not a book of original entry.

   b. It provides a chronological record of transactions.

   c. It helps to locate errors because the debit and credit amounts for each entry can be readily compared.

   d. It discloses in one place the complete effect of a transaction.

8. **(LO 2)** The purchase of supplies on account should result in:

   a. a debit to Supplies Expense and a credit to Cash.

   b. a debit to Supplies Expense and a credit to Accounts Payable.

   c. a debit to Supplies and a credit to Accounts Payable.

   d. a debit to Supplies and a credit to Accounts Receivable.

9. **(LO 3)** The order of the accounts in the ledger is:

   a. assets, revenues, expenses, liabilities, common stock, dividends.

   b. assets, liabilities, common stock, dividends, revenues, expenses.

   c. common stock, assets, revenues, expenses, liabilities, dividends.

   d. revenues, assets, expenses, liabilities, common stock, dividends.

10. **(LO 3)** A ledger:

    a. contains only asset and liability accounts.

    b. should show accounts in alphabetical order.

    c. is a collection of the entire group of accounts maintained by a company.

    d. is a book of original entry.

11. **(LO 3)** Posting:

    a. normally occurs before journalizing.

    b. transfers ledger transaction data to the journal.

    c. is an optional step in the recording process.

    d. transfers journal entries to ledger accounts.

12. **(LO 3)** Before posting a payment of $5,000, the Accounts Payable of Chola Corporation had a normal balance of $18,000. The balance after posting this transaction was:

    a. $13,000.   c. $23,000.

    b. $5,000.   d. Cannot be determined.

13. **(LO 4)** A trial balance:

    a. is a list of accounts with their balances at a given time.

    b. proves the mathematical accuracy of journalized transactions.

    c. will not balance if a correct journal entry is posted twice.

    d. proves that all transactions have been recorded.

14. **(LO 4)** A trial balance will not balance if:

    a. a correct journal entry is posted twice.

    b. the purchase of supplies on account is debited to Supplies and credited to Cash.

    c. a $100 cash dividend is debited to Dividends for $1,000 and credited to Cash for $100.

    d. a $450 payment on account is debited to Accounts Payable for $45 and credited to Cash for $45.

15. **(LO 4)** The trial balance of Stevens Corporation had accounts with the following normal balances: Cash $5,000, Service Revenue $85,000, Salaries and Wages Payable $4,000, Salaries and Wages Expense $40,000, Rent Expense $10,000, Common Stock $42,000, Dividends $13,000, and Equipment $61,000. In preparing a trial balance, based on these amounts only, the total in the debit column is:

    a. $116,000.   c. $129,000.

    b. $118,000.   d. $131,000.

Solutions

1. b. An account is an individual accounting record of increases and decreases in specific asset, liability, and stockholders' equity items. The other choices are incorrect because (a) the right side of the account is the credit side, not the debit side, and can be the increase or the decrease side, depending on the classification of the account; (c) there are also separate accounts for different stockholders' equity items; and (d) the left side of the account is the debit side, not the credit side, and can be either the decrease or the increase side, depending on the specific classification of the account.

2. c. Debits increase assets but they decrease liabilities. The other choices are incorrect because debits (a) decrease, not increase, liabilities; (b) increase, not decrease, assets; and (d) increase, not decrease, assets and decrease, not increase, liabilities.

3. d. A revenue account is increased by credits. The other choices are incorrect because a revenue account (a) is increased by credits, not debits; (b) is decreased by debits, not credits; and (c) has a normal balance of a credit, not a debit.

4. d. Assets, dividends, and expenses all have normal debit balances. The other choices are incorrect because (a) revenues have normal credit balances, (b) common stock has a normal credit balance, and (c) liabilities have normal credit balances.

5. d. The expanded accounting equation is Assets = Liabilities + Common Stock + Retained Earnings + Revenues − Expenses − Dividends. The other choices are therefore incorrect.

6. b. Preparing an income statement is not part of the recording process. Choices (a) analyzing transactions, (c) entering transactions in a journal, and (d) posting journal entries are all part of the recording process.

7. a. The journal is a book of original entry. The other choices are true statements.

8. c. The purchase of supplies on account results in a debit to Supplies and a credit to Accounts Payable. The other choices are incorrect because the purchase of supplies on account results in (a) a debit to Supplies, not Supplies Expense, and a credit to Accounts Payable, not Cash; (b) a debit to Supplies, not Supplies Expense; and (d) a credit to Accounts Payable, not Accounts Receivable.

9. b. The correct order of the accounts in the ledger is assets, liabilities, common stock, dividends, revenues, expenses. The other choices are incorrect because they do not reflect this order. The order of the accounts in the ledger is (1) balance sheet accounts: assets, liabilities, and stockholders' equity accounts (common stock and dividends), and then (2) income statement accounts: revenues and expenses.

10. c. A ledger is a collection of all the accounts maintained by a company. The other choices are incorrect because a ledger (a) contains all account types—assets, liabilities, stockholders' equity, revenue, and expense accounts—not just asset and liability accounts; (b) usually shows accounts in account number order, not alphabetical order; and (d) is not a book of original entry because entries made in the ledger come from the journals (the books of original entry).

11. d. Posting transfers journal entries to ledger accounts. The other choices are incorrect because posting (a) occurs after journalizing, (b) transfers journal transaction data to the ledger, and (c) is not an optional step in the recording process.

12. a. The balance is $13,000 ($18,000 normal balance − $5,000 payment), not (b) $5,000 or (c) $23,000. Choice (d) is incorrect because the balance can be determined.

13. a. A trial balance is a list of accounts with their balances at a given time. The other choices are incorrect because (b) the trial balance does not prove that journalized transactions are mathematically correct; (c) if a journal entry is posted twice, the trial balance will still balance; and (d) the trial balance does not prove that all transactions have been recorded.

14. c. The trial balance will not balance in this case because the debit of $1,000 to Dividends is not equal to the credit of $100 to Cash. The other choices are incorrect because (a) if a correct journal entry is posted twice, the trial balance will still balance; (b) if the purchase of supplies on account is debited to Supplies and credited to Cash, Cash and Accounts Payable will be understated but the trial balance will still balance; and (d) since the debit and credit amounts are the same, the trial balance will still balance but both Accounts Payable and Cash will be overstated.

15. c. The total debit column = $5,000 (Cash) + $40,000 (Salaries and Wages Expense) + $10,000 (Rent Expense) + $13,000 (Dividends) + $61,000 (Equipment) = $129,000, not (a) $116,000, (b) $118,000, or (d) $131,000.

Practice Brief Exercises

1. (LO 1) Transactions for the Potter Company for the month of May are presented below. Identify the accounts to be debited and credited for each transaction.

Identify accounts to be debited and credited.

May 1   Stockholders invested $22,000 cash in the business in exchange for common stock.
     6   Paid office rent of $900.
    12   Performed consulting services and billed client $4,400.
    18   Purchased equipment on account for $1,200.

Solution

1.

	Account Debited	**Account Credited**
May 1	Cash	Common Stock
6	Rent Expense	Cash
12	Accounts Receivable	Service Revenue
18	Equipment	Accounts Payable

2. (LO 2) Using the data from **Practice Brief Exercise 1**, journalize the transactions (omit explanations).

Journalize transactions.

Solution

2. May	1	Cash		22,000	
		Common Stock			22,000
	6	Rent Expense		900	
		Cash			900
	12	Accounts Receivable		4,400	
		Service Revenue			4,400
	18	Equipment		1,200	
		Accounts Payable			1,200

Post journal entries to T-accounts.

3. (LO 3) Selected transactions for Carlos Santana Company are presented in journal form as follows. Post the transactions to T-accounts. Make one T-account for each and determine each account's ending balance.

					J1
Date	**Account Titles and Explanation**		**Ref.**	**Debit**	**Credit**
June 6	Cash			22,000	
	Common Stock				22,000
	(Investment of cash in business)				
13	Accounts Receivable			8,200	
	Service Revenue				8,200
	(Billed for services performed)				
14	Cash			3,700	
	Accounts Receivable				3,700
	(Received cash in payment of account)				

Solution

3.

Cash				Accounts Receivable			
6/6	22,000			6/13	8,200	6/14	3,700
6/14	3,700			Bal. 4,500			
Bal. 25,700							

Service Revenue				Common Stock			
		6/13	8,200			6/6	22,000
		Bal. 8,200				Bal. 22,000	

Post journal entries to standard form of account.

4. (LO 3) Selected journal entries for Carlos Santana Company are presented in **Practice Brief Exercise 3.** Post the transactions using the standard form of account.

Solution

4. Cash

Date	Explanation	Ref.	Debit	Credit	Balance
June 6		J1	22,000		22,000
14		J1	3,700		25,700

Accounts Receivable

Date	Explanation	Ref.	Debit	Credit	Balance
June 13		J1	8,200		8,200
14		J1		3,700	4,500

Service Revenue

Date	Explanation	Ref.	Debit	Credit	Balance
June 13		J1		8,200	8,200

Common Stock

Date	Explanation	Ref.	Debit	Credit	Balance
June 6		J1		22,000	22,000

5. **(LO 4)** From the following ledger accounts, prepare a trial balance for Bundy Company at December 31, 2022. List the accounts in the order shown in the text. All account balances are normal.

Prepare a trial balance.

Accounts Receivable	$10,000	Salaries and Wages Expense	$ 2,300
Supplies	4,100	Rent Expense	1,200
Accounts Payable	3,500	Common Stock	10,200
Dividends	1,100	Cash	6,000
Service Revenue	11,000		

Solution

5.

Bundy Company
Trial Balance
December 31, 2020

	Debit	Credit
Cash	$ 6,000	
Accounts Receivable	10,000	
Supplies	4,100	
Accounts Payable		$ 3,500
Common Stock		10,200
Dividends	1,100	
Service Revenue		11,000
Salaries and Wages Expense	2,300	
Rent Expense	1,200	
	$24,700	$24,700

Practice Exercises

1. **(LO 1)** The following is information related to Conan Real Estate Agency.

Analyze transactions and determine their effect on accounts.

Oct. 1 Arnold Conan begins business as a real estate agent with a cash investment of $18,000 in exchange for common stock.
   2 Hires an administrative assistant.
   3 Purchases office equipment for $1,700, on account.
   6 Sells a house and lot for B. Clinton; bills B. Clinton $4,200 for realty services performed.
   27 Pays $900 on the balance related to the transaction of October 3.
   30 Pays the administrative assistant $2,800 in salary for October.

Instructions

Journalize the transactions. (You may omit explanations.)

Solution

1.

	GENERAL JOURNAL			J1
Date	**Account Titles and Explanation**	**Ref.**	**Debit**	**Credit**
Oct. 1	Cash		18,000	
	Common Stock			18,000
2	No entry required			
3	Equipment		1,700	
	Accounts Payable			1,700
6	Accounts Receivable		4,200	
	Service Revenue			4,200
27	Accounts Payable		900	
	Cash			900
30	Salaries and Wages Expense		2,800	
	Cash			2,800

Journalize transactions from account data and prepare a trial balance.

2. (LO 2, 4) The following T-accounts summarize the ledger of Garfunkle Landscaping Company at the end of the first month of operations.

Cash			No. 101
4/1	18,000	4/15	700
4/12	800	4/25	1,400
4/29	700		
4/30	1,200		

Unearned Service Revenue		No. 209
	4/30	1,200

Accounts Receivable			No. 112
4/7	3,800	4/29	700

Common Stock		No. 311
	4/1	18,000

Supplies		No. 126
4/4	1,900	

Service Revenue		No. 400
	4/7	3,800
	4/12	800

Accounts Payable			No. 201
4/25	1,400	4/4	1,900

Salaries and Wages Expense		No. 726
4/15	700	

Instructions

a. Prepare the complete general journal (including explanations) from which the postings to Cash were made.

b. Prepare a trial balance at April 30, 2022.

Solution

2. a.

GENERAL JOURNAL

Date	Account Titles and Explanation	Ref.	Debit	Credit
Apr. 1	Cash		18,000	
	Common Stock			18,000
	(Issued common stock for cash)			
12	Cash		800	
	Service Revenue			800
	(Received cash for services performed)			
15	Salaries and Wages Expense		700	
	Cash			700
	(Paid salaries to date)			
25	Accounts Payable		1,400	
	Cash			1,400
	(Paid creditors on account)			
29	Cash		700	
	Accounts Receivable			700
	(Received cash in payment of account)			
30	Cash		1,200	
	Unearned Service Revenue			1,200
	(Received cash for future services)			

b.

Garfunkle Landscaping Company
Trial Balance
April 30, 2022

	Debit	Credit
Cash	$18,600	
Accounts Receivable	3,100	
Supplies	1,900	
Accounts Payable		$ 500
Unearned Service Revenue		1,200
Common Stock		18,000
Service Revenue		4,600
Salaries and Wages Expense	700	
	$24,300	$24,300

Practice Problem

Journalize transactions, post, and prepare a trial balance.

(LO 1, 2, 3, 4) Bob Sample and other student investors opened Campus Laundromat Inc. on September 1, 2022. During the first month of operations, the following transactions occurred.

Sept.	1	Stockholders invested $20,000 cash in the business in exchange for common stock.
	2	The company paid $1,000 cash for store rent for September.
	3	Purchased washers and dryers for $25,000, paying $10,000 in cash and signing a $15,000, 6-month, 12% note payable.
	4	Paid $1,200 for a one-year accident insurance policy.
	10	Received a $200 bill from the *Daily News* for advertising the opening of the laundromat.
	20	Declared and paid a $700 cash dividend to stockholders.
	30	The company determined that cash receipts for laundry services for the month were $6,200.

The chart of accounts for the company is the same as that for Pioneer Advertising Inc. (Illustration 2.19), plus No. 610 Advertising Expense.

Instructions

a. Journalize the September transactions. (Use J1 for the journal page number.)

b. Open ledger accounts and post the September transactions.

c. Prepare a trial balance at September 30, 2022.

Solution

a.

		GENERAL JOURNAL			J1
Date		**Account Titles and Explanation**	**Ref.**	**Debit**	**Credit**
2022					
Sept.	1	Cash	101	20,000	
		Common Stock	311		20,000
		(Issued common stock for cash)			
	2	Rent Expense	729	1,000	
		Cash	101		1,000
		(Paid September rent)			
	3	Equipment	157	25,000	
		Cash	101		10,000
		Notes Payable	200		15,000
		(Purchased laundry equipment for cash and 6-month, 12% note payable)			
	4	Prepaid Insurance	130	1,200	
		Cash	101		1,200
		(Paid one-year insurance policy)			
	10	Advertising Expense	610	200	
		Accounts Payable	201		200
		(Received bill from *Daily News* for advertising)			
	20	Dividends	332	700	
		Cash	101		700
		(Declared and paid a cash dividend)			
	30	Cash	101	6,200	
		Service Revenue	400		6,200
		(Received cash for services performed)			

b.

GENERAL LEDGER

Cash   No. 101

Date	Explanation	Ref.	Debit	Credit	Balance
2022					
Sept. 1		J1	20,000		20,000
2		J1		1,000	19,000
3		J1		10,000	9,000
4		J1		1,200	7,800
20		J1		700	7,100
30		J1	6,200		13,300

Prepaid Insurance   No. 130

Date	Explanation	Ref.	Debit	Credit	Balance
2022					
Sept. 4		J1	1,200		1,200

Equipment   No. 157

Date	Explanation	Ref.	Debit	Credit	Balance
2022					
Sept. 3		J1	25,000		25,000

Notes Payable   No. 200

Date	Explanation	Ref.	Debit	Credit	Balance
2022					
Sept. 3		J1		15,000	15,000

Accounts Payable   No. 201

Date	Explanation	Ref.	Debit	Credit	Balance
2022					
Sept. 10		J1		200	200

Common Stock   No. 311

Date	Explanation	Ref.	Debit	Credit	Balance
2022					
Sept. 1		J1		20,000	20,000

Dividends   No. 332

Date	Explanation	Ref.	Debit	Credit	Balance
2022					
Sept. 20		J1	700		700

Service Revenue   No. 400

Date	Explanation	Ref.	Debit	Credit	Balance
2022					
Sept. 30		J1		6,200	6,200

Advertising Expense   No. 610

Date	Explanation	Ref.	Debit	Credit	Balance
2022					
Sept. 10		J1	200		200

Rent Expense   No. 729

Date	Explanation	Ref.	Debit	Credit	Balance
2022					
Sept. 2		J1	1,000		1,000

c.

Campus Laundromat Inc.
Trial Balance
September 30, 2022

	Debit	Credit
Cash	$13,300	
Prepaid Insurance	1,200	
Equipment	25,000	
Notes Payable		$15,000
Accounts Payable		200
Common Stock		20,000
Dividends	700	
Service Revenue		6,200
Advertising Expense	200	
Rent Expense	1,000	
	$41,400	$41,400

WileyPLUS

Brief Exercises, DO IT! Exercises, Exercises, Problems, and many additional resources are available for practice in WileyPLUS.

Questions

1. Describe the parts of a T-account.

2. "The terms debit and credit mean increase and decrease, respectively." Explain why this statement is true or false.

3. Tom Dingel, a fellow student, contends that the double-entry system means each transaction must be recorded twice. Is Tom correct? Explain.

4. Olga Conrad, a beginning accounting student, believes debit balances are favorable and credit balances are unfavorable. Is Olga correct? Discuss.

5. State the rules of debit and credit as applied to (a) asset accounts, (b) liability accounts, and (c) the stockholders' equity accounts (revenue, expenses, dividends, common stock, and retained earnings).

6. What is the normal balance for each of the following accounts? (a) Accounts Receivable. (b) Cash. (c) Dividends. (d) Accounts Payable. (e) Service Revenue. (f) Salaries and Wages Expense. (g) Common Stock.

7. Indicate whether each of the following accounts is an asset, a liability, or a stockholders' equity account and whether it has a normal debit or credit balance: (a) Accounts Receivable, (b) Accounts Payable, (c) Equipment, (d) Dividends, and (e) Supplies.

8. For the following transactions, indicate the account debited and the account credited.

   a. Supplies are purchased on account.

   b. Cash is received on signing a note payable.

   c. Employees are paid salaries in cash.

9. Indicate whether the following accounts generally will have (a) debit entries only, (b) credit entries only, or (c) both debit and credit entries.

   (1) Cash.

   (2) Accounts Receivable.

   (3) Dividends.

   (4) Accounts Payable.

   (5) Salaries and Wages Expense.

   (6) Service Revenue.

10. What are the basic steps in the recording process?

11. What are the advantages of using a journal in the recording process?

12. **a.** When entering a transaction in the journal, should the debit or credit be written first?

    b. Which should be indented, the debit or credit?

13. Describe a compound entry, and provide an example.

14. **a.** Should business transaction debits and credits be recorded directly in the ledger accounts?

    b. What are the advantages of first recording transactions in the journal and then posting to the ledger?

15. The account number is entered as the last step in posting the amounts from the journal to the ledger. What is the advantage of this step?

16. Journalize the following business transactions.

    a. Mark Stein invests $9,000 cash in the business in exchange for shares of common stock.

    b. Insurance of $800 is paid for the year.

    c. Supplies of $2,000 are purchased on account.

    d. Cash of $7,800 is received for services performed.

17. **a.** What is a ledger?

    b. What is a chart of accounts and why is it important?

18. What is a trial balance and what are its purposes?

19. Juan Kirby is confused about how accounting information flows through the accounting system. He believes the flow of information is as follows.

    a. Debits and credits are posted to the ledger.

    b. A business transaction occurs.

    c. Information is entered in the journal.

    d. Financial statements are prepared.

    e. The trial balance is prepared.

    Is Juan correct? If not, indicate to Juan the proper flow of the information.

20. Two students are discussing the use of a trial balance. They wonder whether the following errors, each considered separately, would prevent the trial balance from balancing. What would you tell them?

    a. The bookkeeper debited Cash for $600 and credited Salaries and Wages Expense for $600 for payment of wages.

    b. Cash collected on account was debited to Cash for $900 and Service Revenue was credited for $90.

21. What are the normal balances for **Apple**'s Cash, Accounts Payable, and Interest Expense accounts?

Brief Exercises

BE2.1 (LO 1), C For each of the following accounts indicate the effects of (a) a debit and (b) a credit on the accounts and (c) the normal balance of the account.

Indicate debit and credit effects and normal balance.

1. Accounts Payable.
2. Advertising Expense.
3. Service Revenue.

4. Accounts Receivable.
5. Common Stock.
6. Dividends.

BE2.2 (LO 1), C Transactions for the Sheldon Cooper Company, which provides welding services, for the month of June are presented as follows. Identify the accounts to be debited and credited for each transaction.

Identify accounts to be debited and credited.

June	1	Sheldon Cooper invests $4,000 cash in exchange for shares of common stock in a small welding business.
	2	Purchases equipment on account for $1,200.
	3	Pays $800 cash to landlord for June rent.
	12	Bills P. Leonard $300 after completing welding work done on account.

Journalize transactions.

BE2.3 (LO 2), AP Transactions for the Sheldon Cooper Company, which provides welding services, for the month of June are presented as follows. Journalize the transactions. (You may omit explanations.)

June	1	Sheldon Cooper invests $4,000 cash in exchange for shares of common stock in a small welding business.
	2	Purchases equipment on account for $1,200.
	3	Pays $800 cash to landlord for June rent.
	12	Bills P. Leonard $300 after completing welding work done on account.

Identify and explain steps in recording process.

BE2.4 (LO 2), C Writing Evan Saunders, a fellow student, is unclear about the basic steps in the recording process. Identify and briefly explain the steps in the order in which they occur.

Indicate basic and debit-credit analysis.

BE2.5 (LO 2), C Bombeck Inc. has the following transactions during August of the current year. Indicate (a) the effect on the accounting equation and (b) the debit-credit analysis (as illustrated in the chapter).

Aug.	1	Opens an office as a financial advisor, investing $5,000 in cash in exchange for common stock.
	4	Pays insurance in advance for 6 months, $1,800 cash.
	16	Receives $1,900 from clients for services performed.
	27	Pays secretary $1,000 salary.

Journalize transactions.

BE2.6 (LO 2), AP Bombeck Inc. has the following transactions during August of the current year. Journalize the transactions. (You may omit explanations.)

Aug.	1	Opens an office as a financial advisor, investing $5,000 in cash in exchange for common stock.
	4	Pays insurance in advance for 6 months, $1,800 cash.
	16	Receives $1,900 from clients for services performed.
	27	Pays secretary $1,000 salary.

Post journal entries to T-accounts.

BE2.7 (LO 3), AP The following selected transactions for Nikolai Company are presented in journal form. Post the transactions to T-accounts. Make one T-account for each item and determine each account's ending balance.

J1

Date		Account Titles and Explanation	Ref.	Debit	Credit
May	5	Accounts Receivable		5,000	
		Service Revenue			5,000
		(Billed for services performed)			
	12	Cash		2,100	
		Accounts Receivable			2,100
		(Received cash in payment of account)			
	15	Cash		3,200	
		Service Revenue			3,200
		(Received cash for services performed)			

Post journal entries to standard form of account.

BE2.8 (LO 3), AP Selected journal entries for Nikolai Company are presented as follows. Post the transactions using the standard form of account.

J1

Date		Account Titles and Explanation	Ref.	Debit	Credit
May	5	Accounts Receivable		5,000	
		Service Revenue			5,000
		(Billed for services performed)			
	12	Cash		2,100	
		Accounts Receivable			2,100
		(Received cash in payment of account)			
	15	Cash		3,200	
		Service Revenue			3,200
		(Received cash for services performed)			

BE2.9 (LO 4), AP From the following ledger balances, prepare a trial balance for the Favre Company at June 30, 2022. List the accounts in the order as indicated in the chapter. All account balances are normal.

Prepare a trial balance.

Accounts Payable $7,000, Cash $5,200, Common Stock $20,000, Dividends $800, Equipment $17,000, Service Revenue $6,000, Accounts Receivable $3,000, Salaries and Wages Expense $6,000, and Rent Expense $1,000.

BE2.10 (LO 4), AN An inexperienced bookkeeper prepared the following trial balance. Prepare a correct trial balance, assuming all account balances are normal.

Prepare a correct trial balance.

Erika Company
Trial Balance
December 31, 2022

	Debit	Credit
Cash	$16,800	
Prepaid Insurance		$ 3,500
Accounts Payable		3,000
Unearned Service Revenue	4,200	
Common Stock		13,000
Dividends		4,500
Service Revenue		25,600
Salaries and Wages Expense	18,600	
Rent Expense		2,400
	$39,600	$52,000

DO IT! Exercises

DO IT! 2.1 (LO 1), C James Mayaguez has just rented space in a strip mall. In this space, he will open a photography studio to be called Picture This! A friend has advised James to set up a double-entry set of accounting records in which to record all of his business transactions.

Identify normal balances.

Identify the balance sheet accounts that James will likely need to record the transactions needed to open his business (a corporation). Indicate whether the normal balance of each account is a debit or credit.

DO IT! 2.2 (LO 2), AP James Mayaguez engaged in the following activities in establishing his photography studio, Picture This!:

Record business activities.

1. Opened a bank account in the name of Picture This! and deposited $8,000 of his own money into this account in exchange for common stock.

2. Purchased photography supplies at a total cost of $1,600. The business paid $300 in cash and the balance is on account.

3. Obtained estimates on the cost of photography equipment from three different manufacturers.

Prepare the journal entries to record the transactions. You may omit explanations.

DO IT! 2.3 (LO 3), AP James Mayaguez recorded the following transactions during the month of April.

Post transaction.

April 3	Cash	3,900	
	Service Revenue		3,900
16	Rent Expense	600	
	Cash		600
20	Salaries and Wages Expense	500	
	Cash		500

Post these entries to the Cash T-account of the general ledger to determine the ending balance in cash. The beginning balance in cash on April 1 was $1,600.

DO IT! 2.4 (LO 4), AP The following accounts are taken from the ledger of Chillin' Company at December 31, 2022.

Prepare a trial balance.

200	Notes Payable	$20,000	101	Cash	$6,000
311	Common Stock	25,000	120	Supplies	5,000
157	Equipment	76,000	522	Rent Expense	2,000
332	Dividends	8,000	220	Salaries and Wages Payable	3,000
726	Salaries and Wages Expense	38,000	201	Accounts Payable	9,000
400	Service Revenue	86,000	112	Accounts Receivable	8,000

Prepare a trial balance in good form.

Exercises

Analyze statements about accounting and the recording process.

E2.1 (LO 1), K Faith Dillon has prepared the following list of statements about accounts.

1. An account is an accounting record of either a specific asset or a specific liability.

2. An account shows only increases, not decreases, in the item it relates to.

3. Some items, such as cash and accounts receivable, are combined into one account.

4. An account has a left, or credit side, and a right, or debit side.

5. A simple form of an account consisting of just the account title, the left side, and the right side is called a T-account.

Instructions

Identify each statement as true or false. If false, indicate how to correct the statement.

Identify debits, credits, and normal balances.

E2.2 (LO 1), C Selected transactions for L. Takemoto, an interior decorating firm, in its first month of business, are as follows.

Jan.	2	Stockholders invested $15,000 cash in the business in exchange for common stock.
	3	Purchased used car for $8,200 cash for use in the business.
	9	Purchased supplies on account for $500.
	11	Billed customers $1,800 for services performed.
	16	Paid $200 cash for advertising.
	20	Received $780 cash from customers billed on January 11.
	23	Paid creditor $300 cash on balance owed.
	28	Declared and paid a $500 cash dividend.

Instructions

For each transaction indicate the following.

a. The basic type of account debited and credited (asset, liability, stockholders' equity).

b. The specific account debited and credited (Cash, Rent Expense, Service Revenue, etc.).

c. Whether the specific account is increased or decreased.

d. The normal balance of the specific account.

Use the following format, in which the January 2 transaction is given as an example.

	Account Debited				Account Credited			
Date	(a) Basic Type	(b) Specific Account	(c) Effect	(d) Normal Balance	(a) Basic Type	(b) Specific Account	(c) Effect	(d) Normal Balance
Jan. 2	Asset	Cash	Increase	Debit	Stockholders' Equity	Common Stock	Increase	Credit

Journalize transactions.

E2.3 (LO 2), AP Data for L. Takemoto, interior decorating, are presented as follows.

Jan.	2	Stockholders invested $15,000 cash in the business in exchange for common stock.
	3	Purchased used car for $8,200 cash for use in the business.
	9	Purchased supplies on account for $500.
	11	Billed customers $1,800 for services performed.
	16	Paid $200 cash for advertising.
	20	Received $780 cash from customers billed on January 11.
	23	Paid creditor $300 cash on balance owed.
	28	Declared and paid a $500 cash dividend.

Instructions

Journalize the transactions using journal page J1. (You may omit explanations.)

E2.4 (LO 1), C The following information is related to Lexington Real Estate Agency.

Analyze transactions and determine their effect on accounts.

Oct. 1 Diane Lexington begins business as a real estate agent with a cash investment of $20,000 in exchange for common stock.

2 Hires an administrative assistant.

3 Purchases office furniture for $2,300, on account.

6 Sells a house and lot for N. Fennig; bills N. Fennig $3,600 for realty services performed.

27 Pays $850 on the balance related to the transaction of October 3.

30 Pays the administrative assistant $2,500 in salary for October.

Instructions

Prepare the debit-credit analysis for each transaction as illustrated in the chapter.

E2.5 (LO 2), AP Transaction data for Lexington Real Estate Agency are presented as follows.

Journalize transactions.

Oct. 1 Diane Lexington begins business as a real estate agent with a cash investment of $20,000 in exchange for common stock.

2 Hires an administrative assistant.

3 Purchases office furniture for $2,300, on account.

6 Sells a house and lot for N. Fennig; bills N. Fennig $3,600 for realty services performed.

27 Pays $850 on the balance related to the transaction of October 3.

30 Pays the administrative assistant $2,500 in salary for October.

Instructions

Journalize the transactions. (You may omit explanations.)

E2.6 (LO 1, 2), AP Fredo Industries had the following transactions.

Analyze transactions and journalize.

1. Borrowed $5,000 from the bank by signing a note.

2. Paid $2,500 cash for a computer.

3. Purchased $450 of supplies on account.

Instructions

a. Indicate what accounts are increased and decreased by each transaction.

b. Journalize each transaction. (Omit explanations.)

E2.7 (LO 1, 2), AP Leppard Enterprises had the following selected transactions.

Analyze transactions and journalize.

1. Kim Leppard invested $5,000 cash in the business in exchange for common stock.

2. Paid office rent of $950.

3. Performed consulting services and billed a client $4,700.

4. Declared and paid a $600 cash dividend.

Instructions

a. Indicate the effect each transaction has on the accounting equation (Assets = Liabilities + Stockholders' Equity), using plus and minus signs.

b. Journalize each transaction. (Omit explanations.)

E2.8 (LO 2), AP Selected transactions for Sophie's Dog Care are as follows during the month of March.

Journalize a series of transactions.

March 1 Paid monthly rent of $1,200.

3 Performed services for $140 on account.

5 Performed services for $75 cash.

8 Purchased equipment for $600. The company paid $80 cash and the balance was on account.

12 Received cash from customers billed on March 3.

14 Paid salaries and wages to employees of $525.

22 Paid utilities of $72.

24 Borrowed $1,500 from Grafton State Bank by signing a note.

27 Paid $220 to repair service for plumbing repairs.

28 Paid balance amount owed from equipment purchase on March 8.

30 Paid $1,800 for 6 months of insurance.

Instructions

Journalize the transactions. Do not provide explanations.

Record journal entries.

E2.9 (LO 2), AP On April 1, Adventures Travel Agency, Inc. began operations. The following transactions were completed during the month.

1. Stockholders invested $24,000 in the business in exchange for common stock.
2. Obtained a bank loan for $7,000 by issuing a note payable.
3. Paid $11,000 cash to buy equipment.
4. Paid $1,200 cash for April office rent.
5. Paid $1,450 for supplies.
6. Purchased $600 of advertising in the *Daily Herald,* on account.
7. Performed services for $18,000: cash of $2,000 was received from customers, and the balance of $16,000 was billed to customers on account.
8. Paid $400 cash dividend to stockholders.
9. Paid the utility bill for the month, $2,000.
10. Paid *Daily Herald* the amount due in transaction (6).
11. Paid $40 of interest on the bank loan obtained in transaction (2).
12. Paid employees' salaries and wages, $6,400.
13. Received $12,000 cash from customers billed in transaction (7).

Instructions

Journalize the transactions. Do not provide explanations.

Analyze statements about the ledger.

E2.10 (LO 3), C Meghan Selzer has prepared the following list of statements about the general ledger.

1. The general ledger contains all the asset and liability accounts, but no stockholders' equity accounts.
2. The general ledger is sometimes referred to as simply the ledger.
3. The accounts in the general ledger are arranged in alphabetical order.
4. Each account in the general ledger is numbered for easier identification.
5. The general ledger is a book of original entry.

Instructions

Identify each statement as true or false. If false, indicate how to correct the statement.

Post journal entries and prepare a trial balance.

E2.11 (LO 3, 4), AP Selected transactions from the journal of Kati Tillman, investment broker, are presented as follows.

Date		Account Titles and Explanation	Ref.	Debit	Credit
Aug.	1	Cash		6,000	
		Common Stock			6,000
		(Issued common stock for cash)			
	10	Cash		2,700	
		Service Revenue			2,700
		(Received cash for services performed)			
	12	Equipment		5,000	
		Cash			800
		Notes Payable			4,200
		(Purchased office equipment for cash and notes payable)			
	25	Account Receivable		1,600	
		Service Revenue			1,600
		(Billed clients for services performed)			
	31	Cash		880	
		Accounts Receivable			880
		(Receipt of cash on account)			

Instructions

a. Post the transactions to T-accounts.
b. Prepare a trial balance at August 31, 2022.

E2.12 (LO 2, 4), AP The following T-accounts summarize the ledger of Santana Landscaping Company at the end of its first month of operations.

Journalize transactions from account data and prepare a trial balance.

Cash			No. 101
4/1	10,000	4/15	720
4/12	900	4/25	1,500
4/29	400		
4/30	1,000		

Accounts Receivable			No. 112
4/7	3,200	4/29	400

Supplies			No. 126
4/4	1,800		

Accounts Payable			No. 201
4/25	1,500	4/4	1,800

Unearned Service Revenue			No. 209
		4/30	1,000

Common Stock			No. 311
		4/1	10,000

Service Revenue			No. 400
		4/7	3,200
		4/12	900

Salaries and Wages Expense			No. 726
4/15	720		

Instructions

a. Prepare the complete general journal (including explanations) from which the postings to Cash were made.

b. Prepare a trial balance at April 30, 2022.

E2.13 (LO 2, 4), AP The ledger for Higgs Co. is as follows.

Journalize transactions from account data and prepare a trial balance.

Cash			No. 101
10/1	5,000	10/4	400
10/10	730	10/12	1,500
10/10	3,000	10/15	280
10/20	500	10/30	300
10/25	2,000	10/31	500

Accounts Receivable			No. 112
10/6	800	10/20	500
10/20	910		

Supplies			No. 126
10/4	400		

Equipment			No. 157
10/3	2,000		

Notes Payable			No. 200
		10/10	3,000

Accounts Payable			No. 201
10/12	1,500	10/3	2,000

Common Stock			No. 311
		10/1	5,000
		10/25	2,000

Dividends			No. 332
10/30	300		

Service Revenue			No. 400
		10/6	800
		10/10	730
		10/20	910

Salaries and Wages Expense			No. 726
10/31	500		

Rent Expense			No. 729
10/15	280		

Instructions

a. Reproduce the journal entries for the transactions that occurred on October 1, 10, and 20, and provide explanations for each.

b. Determine the October 31 balance for each of the accounts above, and prepare a trial balance at October 31, 2022.

E2.14 (LO 2, 3), AP Selected transactions for Alvarado Company during its first month in business are as follows.

Prepare journal entries and post using standard account form.

Sept.	1	Stockholders invested $10,000 cash in the business in exchange for common stock.
	5	Purchased equipment for $12,000 paying $4,000 in cash and the balance on account.
	25	Paid $2,400 cash on balance owed for equipment.
	30	Declared and paid a $500 cash dividend.

Alvarado's chart of accounts shows No. 101 Cash, No. 157 Equipment, No. 201 Accounts Payable, No. 311 Common Stock, and No. 332 Dividends.

Instructions

a. Journalize the transactions on page J1 of the journal. (Omit explanations.)

b. Post the transactions using the standard account form.

Analyze errors and their effects on trial balance.

E2.15 (LO 4), AN The bookkeeper for Brooks Equipment Repair made a number of errors in journalizing and posting, as the following describes.

1. A credit posting of $450 to Accounts Receivable was omitted.

2. A debit posting of $750 for Prepaid Insurance was debited to Insurance Expense.

3. A collection from a customer of $100 in payment of its account owed was journalized and posted as a debit to Cash $100 and a credit to Service Revenue $100.

4. A credit posting of $300 to Property Taxes Payable was made twice.

5. A cash purchase of supplies for $250 was journalized and posted as a debit to Supplies $25 and a credit to Cash $25.

6. A debit of $525 to Advertising Expense was posted as $552.

Instructions

For each error:

a. Indicate whether the trial balance will balance.

b. If the trial balance will not balance, indicate the amount of the difference.

c. Indicate the trial balance column that will have the larger total.

Consider each error separately. Use the following form, in which error (1) is given as an example.

	(a)	**(b)**	**(c)**
Error	**In Balance**	**Difference**	**Larger Column**
(1)	No	$450	debit

Prepare a trial balance.

E2.16 (LO 4), AP The accounts in the ledger of Time Is Money Delivery Service contain the following balances on July 31, 2022.

Accounts Receivable	$10,642	Prepaid Insurance	$ 1,968
Accounts Payable	8,396	Maintenance and Repairs Expense	961
Cash	?	Service Revenue	10,610
Equipment	49,360	Dividends	700
Gasoline Expense	758	Common Stock	40,000
Utilities Expense	523	Salaries and Wages Expense	4,428
Notes Payable	26,450	Salaries and Wages Payable	815
		Retained Earnings	4,636

Instructions

Prepare a trial balance with the accounts arranged as illustrated in the chapter and fill in the missing amount for Cash.

Journalize transactions, post transactions to T-accounts, and prepare trial balance.

E2.17 (LO 2, 3, 4), AP Beyers Corporation provides security services. Selected transactions for Beyers are as follows.

Oct.	1	Issued common stock in exchange for $66,000 cash from investors.
	2	Hired part-time security consultant. Salary will be $2,000 per month. First day of work will be October 15.
	4	Paid one month of rent for building for $2,000.
	7	Purchased equipment for $18,000, paying $4,000 cash and the balance on account.
	8	Paid $500 for advertising.
	10	Received bill for equipment repair cost of $390.
	12	Provided security services for event for $3,200 on account.
	16	Purchased supplies for $410 on account.
	21	Paid balance due from October 7 purchase of equipment.
	24	Received and paid utility bill for $148.
	27	Received payment from customer for October 12 services performed.
	31	Paid employee salaries and wages of $5,100.

Instructions

a. Journalize the transactions. Do not provide explanations.

b. Post the transactions to T-accounts.

c. Prepare a trial balance at October 31, 2022. (*Hint:* Compute ending balances of T-accounts first.)

Problems

P2.1A (LO 2), AP Grandview Park was started on April 1 by R. S. Francis and associates. The following selected events and transactions occurred during April.

Journalize a series of transactions.

Apr.	1	Stockholders invested $50,000 cash in the business in exchange for common stock.
	4	Purchased land costing $34,000 for cash.
	8	Incurred advertising expense of $1,800 on account.
	11	Paid salaries to employees $1,500.
	12	Hired park manager at a salary of $3,500 per month, effective May 1.
	13	Paid $2,400 cash for a one-year insurance policy.
	17	Declared and paid a $1,400 cash dividend.
	20	Received $5,700 in cash for admission fees.
	25	Sold 100 coupon books for $30 each. Each book contains 10 coupons that entitle the holder to one admission to the park.
	30	Received $8,900 in cash admission fees.
	30	Paid $840 on balance owed for advertising incurred on April 8.

Grandview uses the following accounts: Cash, Prepaid Insurance, Land, Accounts Payable, Unearned Service Revenue, Common Stock, Dividends, Service Revenue, Advertising Expense, and Salaries and Wages Expense.

Instructions

Journalize the April transactions.

P2.2A (LO 2, 3, 4), AP Julia Dumars is a licensed CPA. During the first month of operations of her business, Julia Dumars, Inc., the following events and transactions occurred.

Journalize transactions, post, and prepare a trial balance.

May	1	Stockholders invested $20,000 cash in exchange for common stock.
	2	Hired a secretary-receptionist at a salary of $2,000 per month.
	3	Purchased $1,500 of supplies on account from Vincent Supply Company.
	7	Paid office rent of $900 cash for the month.
	11	Completed a tax assignment and billed client $2,800 for services performed.
	12	Received $3,500 advance on a management consulting engagement.
	17	Received cash of $1,200 for services performed for Orville Co.
	31	Paid secretary-receptionist $2,000 salary for the month.
	31	Paid 40% of balance due Vincent Supply Company.

Julia uses the following chart of accounts: No. 101 Cash, No. 112 Accounts Receivable, No. 126 Supplies, No. 201 Accounts Payable, No. 209 Unearned Service Revenue, No. 311 Common Stock, No. 400 Service Revenue, No. 726 Salaries and Wages Expense, and No. 729 Rent Expense.

Instructions

a. Journalize the transactions.

b. Post to the ledger accounts.

c. Prepare a trial balance on May 31, 2022.

c. Trial balance totals $28,400

Journalize and post transactions and prepare a trial balance.

P2.3A (LO 2, 3, 4), AP Tom Zopf owns and manages a computer repair service, which had the following trial balance on December 31, 2021 (the end of its fiscal year).

Tablette Repair Service, Inc.
Trial Balance
December 31, 2021

	Debit	Credit
Cash	$ 8,000	
Accounts Receivable	15,000	
Supplies	11,000	
Prepaid Rent	3,000	
Equipment	21,000	
Accounts Payable		$17,000
Common Stock		30,000
Retained Earnings		11,000
	$58,000	$58,000

Summarized transactions for January 2022 were as follows.

1. Advertising costs, paid in cash, $1,000.
2. Additional supplies acquired on account $3,600.
3. Miscellaneous expenses, paid in cash, $1,700.
4. Cash collected from customers in payment of accounts receivable $13,000.
5. Cash paid to creditors for accounts payable due $14,400.
6. Repair services performed during January: for cash $5,000; on account $9,000.
7. Wages for January, paid in cash, $3,000.
8. Dividends during January were $1,600.

Instructions

a. Open T-accounts for each of the accounts listed in the trial balance, and enter the opening balances for 2022.

b. Prepare journal entries to record each of the January transactions. (Omit explanations.)

c. Post the journal entries to the accounts in the ledger. (Add accounts as needed.)

d. Trial balance totals $61,200

d. Prepare a trial balance as of January 31, 2022.

Prepare a correct trial balance.

P2.4A (LO 4), AN The following trial balance of Dominic Company does not balance.

Dominic Company
Trial Balance
May 31, 2022

	Debit	Credit
Cash	$ 3,850	
Accounts Receivable		$ 2,750
Prepaid Insurance	700	
Equipment	12,000	
Accounts Payable		4,500
Unearned Service Revenue	560	
Common Stock		11,700
Service Revenue	8,690	
Salaries and Wages Expense	4,200	
Advertising Expense		1,100
Utilities Expense	800	
	$30,800	$20,050

Your review of the ledger reveals that each account has a normal balance. You also discover the following errors.

1. The totals of the debit sides of Prepaid Insurance, Accounts Payable, and Utilities Expense were each understated $100.

2. Transposition errors were made in Accounts Receivable and Service Revenue. Based on postings made, the correct balances were $2,570 and $8,960, respectively.

3. A debit posting to Salaries and Wages Expense of $200 was omitted.

4. A $1,000 cash dividend was debited to Common Stock for $1,000 and credited to Cash for $1,000.

5. A $520 purchase of supplies on account was debited to Equipment for $520 and credited to Cash for $520.

6. A cash payment of $450 for advertising was debited to Advertising Expense for $45 and credited to Cash for $45.

7. A collection from a customer for $420 was debited to Cash for $420 and credited to Accounts Payable for $420.

Instructions

Prepare a correct trial balance. Note that the chart of accounts includes the following: Dividends and Supplies. (*Hint:* It helps to prepare the correct journal entry for the transaction described and compare it to the mistake made.)

Trial balance totals $26,720

P2.5A **(LO 2, 3, 4), AP** The Palace Theater opened on April 1. All facilities were completed on March 31. At this time, the ledger showed No. 101 Cash $6,000, No. 140 Land $12,000, No. 145 Buildings (concession stand, projection room, ticket booth, and screen) $8,000, No. 157 Equipment $6,000, No. 201 Accounts Payable $2,000, No. 275 Mortgage Payable $10,000, and No. 311 Common Stock $20,000. During April, the following events and transactions occurred.

Journalize transactions, post, and prepare a trial balance.

Apr. 2 Paid film rental of $800 on first movie.
  3 Ordered two additional films at $950 each.
  9 Received $1,800 cash from admissions.
  10 Made $2,000 payment on mortgage and $1,000 for accounts payable due.
  11 Palace Theater contracted with Dever Company to operate the concession stand. Dever is to pay 18% of gross concession receipts (payable monthly) for the rental of the concession stand.
  12 Paid advertising expenses $320.
  20 Received one of the films ordered on April 3 and was billed $950. The film will be shown in April.
  25 Received $5,200 cash from admissions.
  29 Paid salaries $1,600.
  30 Received statement from Dever showing gross concession receipts of $1,000 and the balance due to the Palace Theater of $180 ($1,000 × 18%) for April. Dever paid one-half of the balance due and will remit the remainder on May 5.
  30 Prepaid $1,000 rental on special film to be run in May.

In addition to the accounts identified above, the chart of accounts shows No. 112 Accounts Receivable, No. 136 Prepaid Rent, No. 400 Service Revenue, No. 429 Rent Revenue, No. 610 Advertising Expense, No. 726 Salaries and Wages Expense, and No. 729 Rent Expense.

Instructions

a. Enter the beginning balances in the ledger as of April 1. Insert a check mark (✓) in the reference column of the ledger for the beginning balance.

b. Journalize the April transactions.

c. Post the April journal entries to the ledger. Assume that all entries are posted from page 1 of the journal.

d. Prepare a trial balance on April 30, 2022.

d. Trial balance totals $37,130

Continuing Case

Cookie Creations

(*Note:* This is a continuation of the Cookie Creations case from Chapter 1.)

CC2 After researching the different forms of business organization, Natalie Koebel decides to operate "Cookie Creations" as a corporation. She then starts the process of getting the business running.

*Go to **WileyPLUS** for complete case details and instructions.*

leungchopan/
Shutterstock.com

Expand Your Critical Thinking

Financial Reporting Problem: Apple Inc.

CT2.1 The financial statements of **Apple Inc.** are presented in Appendix A. The complete annual report, including the notes to the financial statements, is available at the company's website.

Apple's financial statements contain the following selected accounts, stated in millions of dollars.

Accounts Payable   Cash and Cash Equivalents
Accounts Receivable   Research and Development Expense
Property, Plant, and Equipment   Inventories

Instructions

a. Answer the following questions.

1. What is the increase and decrease side for each account?

2. What is the normal balance for each account?

b. Identify the probable other account in the transaction and the effect on that account when:

1. Accounts Receivable is decreased.

2. Accounts Payable is decreased.

3. Inventories are increased.

c. Identify the other account(s) that ordinarily would be involved when:

1. Research and Development Expense is increased.

2. Property, Plant, and Equipment is increased.

Comparative Analysis Problem: PepsiCo, Inc. vs. The Coca-Cola Company

CT2.2 **PepsiCo**'s financial statements are presented in Appendix B. Financial statements of **The Coca-Cola Company** are presented in Appendix C. The complete annual reports of PepsiCo and Coca-Cola, including the notes to the financial statements, are available at each company's respective website.

Instructions

a. Based on the information contained in the financial statements, determine the normal balance of the listed accounts for each company.

PepsiCo	Coca-Cola
1. Inventory	1. Accounts Receivable
2. Property, Plant, and Equipment	2. Cash and Cash Equivalents
3. Accounts Payable	3. Cost of Goods Sold (expense)
4. Interest Expense	4. Sales (revenue)

b. Identify the other account ordinarily involved when:

1. Accounts Receivable is increased.

2. Salaries and Wages Payable is decreased.

3. Property, Plant, and Equipment is increased.

4. Interest Expense is increased.

Comparative Analysis Problem: Amazon.com, Inc. vs. Walmart Inc.

CT2.3 **Amazon.com, Inc.**'s financial statements are presented in Appendix D. Financial statements of **Walmart Inc.** are presented in Appendix E. The complete annual reports of Amazon and Walmart, including the notes to the financial statements, are available at each company's respective website.

Instructions

a. Based on the information contained in the financial statements, determine the normal balance of the listed accounts for each company.

Amazon	Walmart
1. Interest Expense	1. Product Revenues
2. Cash and Cash Equivalents	2. Inventories
3. Accounts Payable	3. Cost of Sales

b. Identify the other account ordinarily involved when:

1. Accounts Receivable is increased.

2. Interest Expense is increased.

3. Salaries and Wages Payable is decreased.

4. Service Revenue is increased.

Real-World Focus

CT2.4 Much information about specific companies is available on the Internet. Such information includes basic descriptions of the company's location, activities, industry, financial health, and financial performance.

Instructions

Go to the **Yahoo! Finance** website, type in a company name (or use the index to find a company name), and then answer the following questions.

a. What is the company's industry?

b. What are the company's total sales?

c. What is the company's net income?

d. What are the names of four of the company's competitors?

e. Choose one of these competitors.

f. What is this competitor's name? What are its sales? What is its net income?

g. Which of these two companies is larger by size of sales? Which one reported higher net income?

CT2.5 The January 27, 2011, edition of the *New York Times* contains an article by Richard Sandomir entitled "N.F.L. Finances, as Seen Through Packers' Records." The author of the article discusses the fact that the **Green Bay Packers** are the only NFL team that publicly publishes its annual report.

Instructions

Read the article and answer the following questions.

a. Why are the Green Bay Packers the only professional football team to publish and distribute an annual report?

b. Why is the football players' labor union particularly interested in the Packers' annual report?

c. In addition to the players' labor union, what other outside party might be interested in the annual report?

d. Even though the Packers' revenue increased, the company's operating profit fell significantly. How does the article explain this decline?

Decision-Making Across the Organization

CT2.6 Dyanna Craig operates Craig Riding Academy. The academy's primary sources of revenue are riding fees and lesson fees, which are paid on a cash basis. Dyanna also boards horses for owners, who are billed monthly for boarding fees. In a few cases, boarders pay in advance of expected use. For its revenue transactions, the academy maintains the following accounts: Cash, Accounts Receivable, and Service Revenue.

The academy owns 10 horses, a stable, a riding corral, riding equipment, and office equipment. These assets are accounted for in these accounts: Horses, Buildings, and Equipment.

The academy also maintains the following accounts: Supplies, Prepaid Insurance, Accounts Payable, Salaries and Wages Expense, Advertising Expense, Utilities Expense, and Maintenance and Repairs Expense.

Dyanna pays periodic cash dividends to stockholders. To record stockholders' equity in the business and dividends, three accounts are maintained: Common Stock, Retained Earnings, and Dividends.

During the first month of operations, an inexperienced bookkeeper was employed. Dyanna Craig asks you to review the following 8 entries of the 50 entries made during the month. In each case, the explanation for the entry is correct.

May	1	Cash	18,000	
		Common Stock		18,000
		(Issued common stock for $18,000 cash)		
	5	Cash	250	
		Service Revenue		250
		(Received $250 cash for lessons provided)		
	7	Cash	300	
		Service Revenue		300
		(Received $300 for boarding of horses		
		beginning June 1)		
	14	Equipment	80	
		Cash		800
		(Purchased desk and other office equipment		
		for $800 cash)		
	15	Salaries and Wages Expense	400	
		Cash		400
		(Issued dividend checks to stockholders)		
	20	Cash	148	
		Service Revenue		184
		(Received $184 cash for riding fees)		
	30	Maintenance and Repairs Expense	75	
		Accounts Payable		75
		(Received bill of $75 from carpenter for repair		
		services performed)		
	31	Supplies	1,700	
		Cash		1,700
		(Purchased an estimated 2-month supply		
		of feed and hay for $1,700 on account)		

Instructions

With the class divided into groups, answer the following.

a. Identify each journal entry that is correct. For each journal entry that is incorrect, prepare the entry that should have been made by the bookkeeper.

b. Which of the incorrect entries would prevent the trial balance from balancing?

c. What was the correct net income for May, assuming the bookkeeper reported net income of $4,500 after posting all 50 entries? (Errors only occur on the 8 entries above.)

d. What was the correct cash balance at May 31, assuming the bookkeeper reported a balance of $12,475 after posting all 50 entries (and the only errors occurred in the items listed above)?

Communication Activity

CT2.7 Keller's Maid Company offers home-cleaning service. Two recurring transactions for the company are billing customers for services performed and paying employee salaries. For example, on March 15, bills totaling $6,000 were sent to customers and $2,000 was paid in salaries to employees.

Instructions

Write a memo to your instructor that explains and illustrates the steps in the recording process for each of the March 15 transactions. Use the format illustrated in the chapter under the heading, "The Recording Process Illustrated."

Ethics Cases

CT2.8 Meredith Ward is the assistant chief accountant at Frazier Company, a manufacturer of computer chips and cellular phones. The company presently has total sales of $20 million. It is the end of the first quarter. Meredith is hurriedly trying to prepare a trial balance so that quarterly financial statements can be prepared and released to management and the regulatory agencies. The total credits on the trial balance exceed the debits by $1,000. In order to meet the 4 P.M. deadline, Meredith decides to force the debits and credits into balance by adding the amount of the difference to the Equipment account. She chooses Equipment because it is one of the larger account balances; percentage-wise, it will be the least misstated. Meredith "plugs" the difference! She believes that the difference will not affect anyone's decisions. She wishes that she had another few days to find the error but realizes that the financial statements are already late.

Instructions

    a. Who are the stakeholders in this situation?

    b. What are the ethical issues involved in this case?

    c. What are Meredith's alternatives?

CT2.9 If you haven't already done so, in the not-too-distant future you will prepare a résumé. In some ways, your résumé is like a company's annual report. Its purpose is to enable others to evaluate your past, in an effort to predict your future.

A résumé is your opportunity to create a positive first impression. It is important that it be impressive—but it should also be accurate. In order to increase their job prospects, some people are tempted to "inflate" their résumés by overstating the importance of some past accomplishments or positions. In fact, you might even think that "everybody does it" and that if you don't do it, you will be at a disadvantage.

David Edmondson, the president and CEO of well-known electronics retailer **Radio Shack**, overstated his accomplishments by claiming that he had earned a bachelor of science degree, when in fact he had not. Apparently, his employer had not done a background check to ensure the accuracy of his résumé. Should Radio Shack have fired him?

    YES: Radio Shack is a publicly traded company. Investors, creditors, employees, and others doing business with the company will not trust it if its leader is known to have poor integrity. The "tone at the top" is vital to creating an ethical organization.

    NO: Mr. Edmondson had been a Radio Shack employee for 11 years. He had served the company in a wide variety of positions, and had earned the position of CEO through exceptional performance. While the fact that he lied 11 years earlier on his résumé was unfortunate, his service since then made this past transgression irrelevant. In addition, the company was in the midst of a massive restructuring, which included closing 700 of its 7,000 stores. It could not afford additional upheaval at this time.

Instructions

Write a response indicating your position regarding this situation. Provide support for your view.

All About You

CT2.10 Every company needs to plan in order to move forward. Its top management must consider where it wants the company to be in 3 to 5 years. Like a company, you need to think about where you want to be 3 to 5 years from now, and you need to start taking steps now in order to get there.

Instructions

Provide responses to each of the following items.

    a. Where would you like to be working in 3 to 5 years? Describe your plan for getting there by identifying between 5 and 10 specific steps that you need to take.

    b. In order to get the job you want, you will need a résumé. Your résumé is the equivalent of a company's annual report. It needs to provide relevant and representationally faithful information about your past accomplishments so that employers can decide whether to "invest" in you. Do a search on the Internet to find a good résumé format. What are the basic elements of a résumé?

    c. A company's annual report provides information about a company's accomplishments. In order for investors to use the annual report, the information must provide a faithful representation; that is, users must have faith that the information is accurate and believable. How can you provide assurance that the information on your résumé is a faithful representation of your accomplishments?

    d. Prepare a résumé assuming that you have accomplished the 5 to 10 specific steps you identified in part (a). Also, provide evidence that would give assurance that the information is a faithful representation of your accomplishments.

Considering People, Planet, and Profit

CT2.11 Auditors provide a type of certification of corporate financial statements. Certification is used in many other aspects of business as well. For example, it plays a critical role in the sustainability movement. The February 7, 2012, issue of the *New York Times* contained an article by S. Amanda Caudill entitled "Better Lives in Better Coffee," which discusses the role of certification in the coffee business.

Instructions

Read the article (available online) and then answer the following questions.

a. The article mentions three different certification types that coffee growers can obtain from three different certification bodies. Using financial reporting as an example, what potential problems might the existence of multiple certification types present to coffee purchasers?

b. According to the author, which certification is most common among coffee growers? What are the possible reasons for this?

c. What social and environmental benefits are coffee certifications trying to achieve? Are there also potential financial benefits to the parties involved?

A Look at IFRS

LEARNING OBJECTIVE 5

Compare the procedures for the recording process under GAAP and IFRS.

International companies use the same set of procedures and records to keep track of transaction data. Thus, the material in Chapter 2 dealing with the account, general rules of debit and credit, and steps in the recording process—the journal, ledger, and chart of accounts—is the same under both GAAP and IFRS.

Key Points

Following are the key similarities and differences between GAAP and IFRS as related to the recording process.

Similarities

- Transaction analysis is the same under IFRS and GAAP.

- Both the IASB and the FASB go beyond the basic definitions provided in the text for the key elements of financial statements, that is, assets, liabilities, equity, revenues, and expenses. The implications of the expanded definitions are discussed in more advanced accounting courses.

- As shown in the text, dollar signs are typically used only in the trial balance and the financial statements. The same practice is followed under IFRS, using the currency of the country where the reporting company is headquartered.

- A trial balance under IFRS follows the same format as shown in the text.

Differences

- IFRS relies less on historical cost and more on fair value than do FASB standards.

- Internal controls are a system of checks and balances designed to prevent and detect fraud and errors. While most public U.S. companies have these systems in place, many non-U.S. companies have never completely documented the controls nor had an independent auditor attest to their effectiveness.

IFRS Practice

IFRS Self-Test Questions

1. Which statement is **correct** regarding IFRS?

    a. IFRS reverses the rules of debits and credits, that is, debits are on the right and credits are on the left.

    b. IFRS uses the same process for recording transactions as GAAP.

    c. The chart of accounts under IFRS is different because revenues follow assets.

    d. None of the above statements are correct.

2. The expanded accounting equation under IFRS is as follows:

    a. Assets = Liabilities + Common Stock + Retained Earnings + Revenues − Expenses + Dividends.

    b. Assets + Liabilities = Common Stock + Retained Earnings + Revenues − Expenses − Dividends.

    c. Assets = Liabilities + Common Stock + Retained Earnings + Revenues − Expenses − Dividends.

    d. Assets = Liabilities + Common Stock + Retained Earnings − Revenues − Expenses − Dividends.

3. A trial balance:

    a. is the same under IFRS and GAAP.

    b. proves that transactions are recorded correctly.

    c. proves that all transactions have been recorded.

    d. will not balance if a correct journal entry is posted twice.

4. One difference between IFRS and GAAP is that:

    a. GAAP uses accrual-accounting concepts and IFRS uses primarily the cash basis of accounting.

    b. IFRS uses a different posting process than GAAP.

    c. IFRS uses more fair value measurements than GAAP.

    d. the limitations of a trial balance are different between IFRS and GAAP.

5. The general policy for using proper currency signs (dollar, yen, pound, etc.) is the same for both IFRS and this text. This policy is as follows:

    a. Currency signs only appear in ledgers and journal entries.

    b. Currency signs are only shown in the trial balance.

    c. Currency signs are shown for all compound journal entries.

    d. Currency signs are shown in trial balances and financial statements.

International Financial Reporting Problem: Louis Vuitton

IFRS2.1 The financial statements of **Louis Vuitton** are presented in Appendix F. The complete consolidated financial statements, including the notes to its financial statements, are available at the company's website.

Instructions

Describe in which statement each of the following items is reported, and the position in the statement (e.g., current asset).

    a. Other operating income and expenses.

    b. Cash and cash equivalents.

    c. Trade accounts payable.

    d. Cost of net financial debt.

Answers to IFRS Self-Test Questions

1. b   **2.** c   **3.** a   **4.** c   **5.** d

Adjusting the Accounts

Chapter Preview

In Chapter 1, you learned a neat little formula: Net income = Revenues − Expenses. In Chapter 2, you learned some rules for recording revenue and expense transactions. Guess what? Things are not really that nice and neat. In fact, it is often difficult for companies to determine in what time period they should report some revenues and expenses. In other words, in measuring net income, timing is everything.

Feature Story

Keeping Track of Groupons

Who doesn't like buying things at a discount? That's why it's not surprising that three years after it started as a company, **Groupon, Inc.** was estimated to be worth $16 billion. This translates into an average increase in value of almost $15 million per day.

Now consider that Groupon had previously been estimated to be worth even more than that. What happened?

Well, accounting regulators and investors began to question the way that Groupon had accounted for some of its transactions. Groupon sells coupons ("groupons"), so how hard can it be to account for that? It turns out that accounting for coupons is not as easy as you might think.

First, consider what happens when Groupon makes a sale. Suppose it sells a groupon for $30 for Highrise Hamburgers. When it receives the $30 from the customer, it must turn over half of that amount ($15) to Highrise Hamburgers. So should Groupon record revenue for the full $30 or just $15? Until recently,

Groupon recorded the full $30. But, in response to an SEC ruling on the issue, Groupon now records revenue of $15 instead. This caused Groupon to restate its previous financial statements. This restatement reduced annual revenue by $312.9 million.

A second issue is a matter of timing. When should Groupon record this $15 revenue? Should it record the revenue when it sells the groupon, or must it wait until the customer uses the groupon at Highrise Hamburgers? The accounting becomes even more complicated when you consider the company's loyalty programs. Groupon offers free or discounted groupons to its subscribers for doing things such as referring new customers or participating in promotions. These grou-pons are to be used for future purchases, yet the company must record the expense at the time the customer receives the groupon.

Finally, Groupon, like all other companies, relies on many estimates in its financial reporting. For example, Groupon reports that "estimates are utilized for, but not limited to, stock-based compensation, income taxes, valuation of acquired goodwill and intangible assets, customer refunds, contingent liabilities and the depreciable lives of fixed assets." It notes that "actual results could differ materially from those estimates." So, next time you use a coupon, think about what that means for the company's accountants!

Chapter Outline

LEARNING OBJECTIVES	REVIEW	PRACTICE
LO 1 Explain the accrual basis of accounting and the reasons for adjusting entries.	• Fiscal and calendar years • Accrual- vs. cash-basis accounting • Recognizing revenues and expenses • Need for adjusting entries • Types of adjusting entries	**DO IT! 1** Timing Concepts
LO 2 Prepare adjusting entries for deferrals.	• Prepaid expenses • Unearned revenues	**DO IT! 2** Adjusting Entries for Deferrals
LO 3 Prepare adjusting entries for accruals.	• Accrued revenues • Accrued expenses • Summary of basic relationships	**DO IT! 3** Adjusting Entries for Accruals
LO 4 Describe the nature and purpose of an adjusted trial balance.	• Preparing the adjusted trial balance • Preparing financial statements	**DO IT! 4** Trial Balance

Go to the Review and Practice section at the end of the chapter for a review of key concepts and practice applications with solutions.

Visit WileyPLUS for additional tutorials and practice opportunities.

Accrual-Basis Accounting and Adjusting Entries

LEARNING OBJECTIVE 1

Explain the accrual basis of accounting and the reasons for adjusting entries.

If we could wait to prepare financial statements until a company ended its operations, no adjustments would be needed. At that point, we could easily determine its final balance sheet and the amount of lifetime income it earned.

However, most companies need feedback about how well they are performing during a period of time. For example, management usually wants monthly financial statements. The Internal Revenue Service requires all businesses to file annual tax returns. Therefore, **accountants divide the economic life of a business into artificial time periods**. This convenient assumption is referred to as the **time period assumption** (see **Alternative Terminology**).

Many business transactions affect more than one of these arbitrary time periods. For example, a new building purchased by **Citigroup** or a new airplane purchased by **Delta Air Lines** will be used for many years. It would not make sense to expense the full cost of these items at the time of purchase because they will be used for many subsequent periods. Instead, companies must allocate the costs to the periods of use (how much of the cost of a building or an airplane contributed to operations this year?).

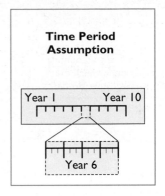

Time Period Assumption

Fiscal and Calendar Years

Both small and large companies prepare financial statements periodically in order to assess their financial condition and results of operations. **Accounting time periods are generally a month, a quarter, or a year.** Monthly and quarterly time periods are called **interim periods**. Most large companies must prepare both quarterly and annual financial statements.

An accounting time period that is one year in length is a **fiscal year**. A fiscal year usually begins with the first day of a month and ends 12 months later on the last day of a month. Many businesses use the **calendar year** (January 1 to December 31) as their fiscal period. Some do not. Companies whose fiscal year differs from the calendar year include **Delta Air Lines**, June 30, and **The Walt Disney Company**, September 30. Sometimes a company's year-end will vary from year to year. For example, **PepsiCo**'s fiscal year ends on the Friday closest to December 31, which was December 30 in 2017 and December 29 in 2018.

Accrual- versus Cash-Basis Accounting

What you will learn in this chapter is **accrual-basis accounting**. Under the accrual basis, companies record transactions that change a company's financial statements **in the periods in which the events occur**. For example, using the accrual basis to determine net income means companies recognize revenues when they perform services (rather than when they receive cash). It also means recognizing expenses when incurred (rather than when paid).

An alternative to the accrual basis is the cash basis. Under **cash-basis accounting**, companies record revenue at the time they receive cash. They record an expense at the time they pay out cash. The cash basis seems appealing due to its simplicity, but it often produces misleading financial statements. For example, it fails to record revenue for a company that has performed services but has not yet received payment. As a result, the cash basis may not recognize revenue in the period that a performance obligation is satisfied.

Accrual-basis accounting is required by generally accepted accounting principles (GAAP). Individuals and some small companies, however, do use cash-basis accounting. The cash basis is justified for small businesses because they often have few receivables and payables. Medium and large companies use accrual-basis accounting.

Recognizing Revenues and Expenses

It can be difficult to determine when to report revenues and expenses. The revenue recognition principle and the expense recognition principle help in this task.

Revenue Recognition

Service
performed

Customer   Cash
requests   received
service

Revenue should be recognized in the accounting period in which the service is performed.

Revenue Recognition Principle

When a company agrees to perform a service or sell a product to a customer, it has a **performance obligation**. When the company meets this performance obligation, it recognizes revenue. The **revenue recognition principle** therefore requires that companies recognize revenue in the accounting period in which the performance obligation is satisfied. A company satisfies its performance obligation by performing a service or providing a good to a customer.

To illustrate, assume Conrad Dry Cleaners performs cleaning services for $100 on June 30, but customers do not claim and pay for their clothes until July 5. Under the revenue recognition principle, Conrad records revenue on June 30 when it satisfies its performance obligation, which is when it performs the service, not in July when it receives the cash. At June 30, Conrad would report a receivable on its balance sheet and revenue in its income statement for the service performed. The journal entries would be as follows.

June 30	Accounts Receivable	100	
	Service Revenue		100
July 5	Cash	100	
	Accounts Receivable		100

Five-Step Revenue Recognition Process—Sierra Corporation Example

Revenue recognition results from a five-step process. This process can best be illustrated with an example. Assume that Sierra Corporation signs a contract with the Lewis family to provide guide services for a one-week backpacking trip for $1,500. **Illustration 3.1** shows the five steps that Sierra follows to recognize revenue.

ILLUSTRATION 3.1 Five steps of revenue recognition

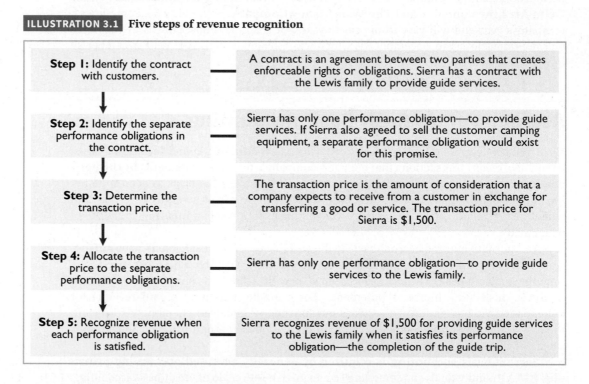

As indicated, Step 5 is when Sierra recognizes revenue related to providing the guide services to the Lewis family. At this point, Sierra completes the trip and satisfies its performance obligation.

Expense Recognition Principle

Accountants follow a simple rule in recognizing expenses: "Let the expenses follow the revenues." Thus, expense recognition is tied to revenue recognition. In the dry cleaning example, this means that Conrad should report the salary expense incurred in performing the June 30 cleaning service in the same period in which it recognizes the service revenue. The critical issue in expense recognition is when the expense makes its contribution to revenue. This may or may not be the same period in which the expense is paid. If Conrad does not pay the salary incurred on June 30 until July, it would report salaries payable on its June 30 balance sheet.

This practice of expense recognition is referred to as the **expense recognition principle**. It requires that companies recognize expenses in the period in which they make efforts (consume assets or incur liabilities) to generate revenue. The term matching is sometimes used in expense recognition to indicate the relationship between the effort expended and the revenue generated. **Illustration 3.2** summarizes the revenue and expense recognition principles.

Expense Recognition

Efforts generated revenue

Delivery

Advertising   Utilities

Expenses are recognized when efforts are made to generate revenue.

ILLUSTRATION 3.2 **GAAP relationships in revenue and expense recognition**

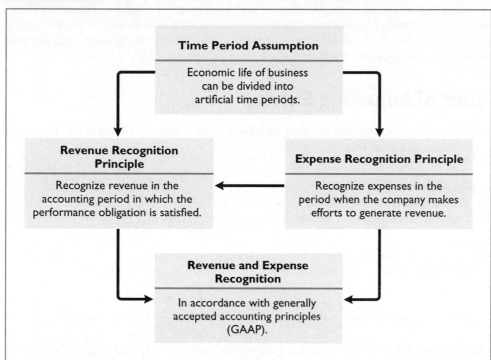

Time Period Assumption

Economic life of business can be divided into artificial time periods.

Revenue Recognition Principle

Recognize revenue in the accounting period in which the performance obligation is satisfied.

Expense Recognition Principle

Recognize expenses in the period when the company makes efforts to generate revenue.

Revenue and Expense Recognition

In accordance with generally accepted accounting principles (GAAP).

Investor Insight   Apple Inc.

Reporting Revenue Accurately

Until recently, electronics manufacturer **Apple** was required to spread the revenues from iPhone sales over the two-year period following the sale of the phone. Accounting standards required this because Apple was obligated to provide software updates after the phone was sold. Since Apple had service obligations after the initial date of sale, it was forced to spread the revenue over a two-year period.

PhotoAlto/James Hardy/ Getty Images

As a result, the rapid growth of iPhone sales was not fully reflected in the revenue amounts reported in Apple's income statement. A new accounting standard now enables Apple to report much more of its iPhone revenue at the point of sale. It was estimated that under the new rule revenues would have been about 17% higher and earnings per share almost 50% higher.

In the past, why was it argued that Apple should spread the recognition of iPhone revenue over a two-year period, rather than recording it upfront? (Go to WileyPLUS for this answer and additional questions.)

The Need for Adjusting Entries

In order for revenues to be recorded in the period in which the performance obligations are satisfied and for expenses to be recognized in the period in which they are incurred, companies make adjusting entries. **Adjusting entries ensure that the revenue recognition and expense recognition principles are followed.**

Adjusting entries are necessary because the **trial balance**—the first pulling together of the transaction data—may not contain up-to-date and complete data. This is true for several reasons:

1. Some events are not recorded daily because it is not efficient to do so. Examples are the use of supplies and the earning of wages by employees.

2. Some costs are not recorded during the accounting period because these costs expire with the passage of time rather than as a result of recurring daily transactions. Examples are charges related to the use of buildings and equipment, rent, and insurance.

3. Some items may be unrecorded. An example is a utility service bill that will not be received until the next accounting period.

Adjusting entries are required every time a company prepares financial statements. The company analyzes each account in the trial balance to determine whether it is complete and up-to-date for financial statement purposes. **Every adjusting entry will include one income statement account and one balance sheet account.**

Types of Adjusting Entries

Adjusting entries are classified as either **deferrals** or **accruals**. As **Illustration 3.3** shows, each of these classes has two subcategories.

ILLUSTRATION 3.3

Categories of adjusting entries

Deferrals:
   1. **Prepaid expenses:** Expenses paid in cash before they are used or consumed.
   2. **Unearned revenues:** Cash received before services are performed.

Accruals:
   1. **Accrued revenues:** Revenues for services performed but not yet received in cash or recorded.
   2. **Accrued expenses:** Expenses incurred but not yet paid in cash or recorded.

Subsequent sections give examples of each type of adjustment. Each example is based on the October 31 trial balance of Pioneer Advertising Inc. from Illustration 2.32. It is reproduced in **Illustration 3.4**. Note that Retained Earning has been added to this trial balance with a zero balance. We will explain its use later.

ILLUSTRATION 3.4

Trial balance

Pioneer Advertising Inc.
Trial Balance
October 31, 2022

	Debit	Credit
Cash	$15,200	
Supplies	2,500	
Prepaid Insurance	600	
Equipment	5,000	
Notes Payable		$ 5,000
Accounts Payable		2,500
Unearned Service Revenue		1,200
Common Stock		10,000
Retained Earnings		–0–
Dividends	500	
Service Revenue		10,000
Salaries and Wages Expense	4,000	
Rent Expense	900	
	$28,700	$28,700

We assume that Pioneer uses an accounting period of one month. Thus, monthly adjusting entries are made. The entries are dated October 31.

DO IT! 1 | Timing Concepts

Below is a list of concepts in the left column, with a description of the concept in the right column. There are more descriptions provided than concepts. Match the description to the concept.

1. ____ Accrual-basis accounting.

2. ____ Calendar year.

3. ____ Time period assumption.

4. ____ Expense recognition principle.

a. Monthly and quarterly time periods.

b. Recognize efforts (expenses) in the period in which a company uses assets or incurs liabilities to generate results (revenues).

c. Accountants divide the economic life of a business into artificial time periods.

d. Companies record revenues when they receive cash and record expenses when they pay out cash.

e. An accounting time period that starts on January 1 and ends on December 31.

f. Companies record transactions in the period in which the events occur.

ACTION PLAN

- Review the key terms identified in the text discussion.

- Study carefully the revenue recognition principle, the expense recognition principle, and the time period assumption.

Solution

1. f   2. e   3. c   4. b

Related exercise material: **BE3.1, BE3.2, BE3.3, BE3.4, DO IT! 3.1, E3.1, E3.2, E3.3, E3.4, and E3.5.**

Adjusting Entries for Deferrals

LEARNING OBJECTIVE 2

Prepare adjusting entries for deferrals.

ANALYZE ▸ JOURNALIZE ▸ POST ▸ **TRIAL BALANCE** ▸ **Journalize and post adjusting entries: deferrals/accruals** ▸ **ADJUSTED TRIAL BALANCE** ▸ **FINANCIAL STATEMENTS** ▸ **CLOSING ENTRIES** ▸ **POST-CLOSING TRIAL BALANCE**

To defer means to postpone or delay. **Deferrals** are expenses or revenues that are recognized at a date later than the point when cash was originally exchanged. Companies make adjusting entries for deferred expenses to record the portion that was incurred during the period. Companies also make adjusting entries for deferred revenues to record services performed during the period. The two types of deferrals are prepaid expenses and unearned revenues.

Prepaid Expenses

When companies pay a future expense that will benefit more than one accounting period, they record an asset called **prepaid expenses** or **prepayments**. When expenses are prepaid, an asset account is increased (debited) to show the service or benefit that the company will receive in the future. Examples of common prepayments are insurance, supplies, advertising, and rent. In addition, companies make prepayments when they purchase buildings and equipment.

Prepaid expenses are costs that expire either with the passage of time (e.g., rent and insurance) **or through use** (e.g., supplies). The expiration of these costs does not require daily entries, which would be impractical and unnecessary. Accordingly, companies postpone the recognition of such cost expirations until they prepare financial statements. At each statement date, they make adjusting entries to record the expenses applicable to the current accounting period and to show the remaining amounts in the asset accounts.

Prior to adjustment, assets are overstated and expenses are understated. Therefore, as shown in **Illustration 3.5**, **an adjusting entry for prepaid expenses results in an increase (a debit) to an expense account and a decrease (a credit) to an asset account**.

ILLUSTRATION 3.5

Adjusting entries for prepaid expenses

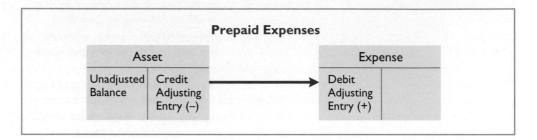

Let's look in more detail at some specific types of prepaid expenses, beginning with supplies.

Supplies

The purchase of supplies, such as paper and envelopes, results in an increase (a debit) to an asset account. During the accounting period, the company uses supplies. Rather than record supplies expense as the supplies are used, companies recognize supplies expense at the **end** of the accounting period. At the end of the accounting period, the company counts the remaining supplies. The difference between the unadjusted balance in the Supplies (asset) account and the actual cost of supplies on hand represents the supplies used (an expense) for that period.

Recall from Chapter 2 that Pioneer Advertising Inc. purchased supplies costing $2,500 on October 5. Pioneer recorded the purchase by increasing (debiting) the asset Supplies. This account shows a balance of $2,500 in the October 31 trial balance. An inventory count at the close of business on October 31 reveals that $1,000 of supplies are still on hand. Thus, the cost of supplies used is $1,500 ($2,500 − $1,000). This use of supplies decreases an asset, Supplies. It also decreases stockholders' equity by increasing an expense account, Supplies Expense (see **Helpful Hint**). This is shown in **Illustration 3.6**.

Supplies

Oct. 5

Supplies purchased; record asset

Oct. 31
Supplies used; record supplies expense

ILLUSTRATION 3.6

Adjustment for supplies

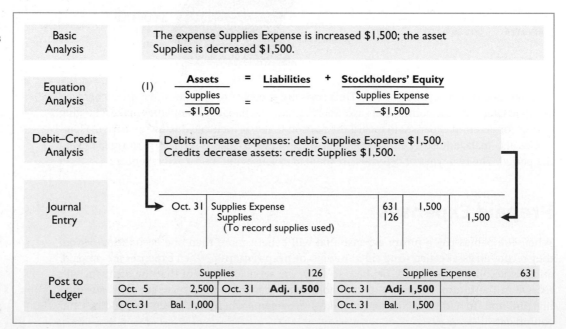

HELPFUL HINT

Due to their nature, adjusting entries have no effect on cash flows. As a result, we do not show the cash flow effects in these illustrations.

After adjustment, the asset account Supplies shows a balance of $1,000, which is equal to the cost of supplies on hand at the statement date. In addition, Supplies Expense shows a balance of $1,500, which equals the cost of supplies used in October. **If Pioneer does not make the adjusting entry, October expenses are understated and net income is overstated by $1,500. Moreover, both assets and stockholders' equity will be overstated by $1,500 on the October 31 balance sheet.**

Insurance

Companies purchase insurance to protect themselves from losses due to fire, theft, and unforeseen events. Insurance must be paid in advance, often for multiple months. The cost of insurance (premiums) paid in advance is recorded as an increase (debit) in the asset account Prepaid Insurance. At the financial statement date, companies increase (debit) Insurance Expense and decrease (credit) Prepaid Insurance for the cost of insurance that has expired during the period.

On October 4, Pioneer Advertising paid $600 for a one-year fire insurance policy. Coverage began on October 1. Pioneer recorded the payment by increasing (debiting) Prepaid Insurance. This account shows a balance of $600 in the October 31 trial balance. Insurance of $50 ($600 ÷ 12) expires each month. The expiration of prepaid insurance decreases an asset, Prepaid Insurance. It also decreases stockholders' equity by increasing an expense account, Insurance Expense.

As shown in **Illustration 3.7**, the asset Prepaid Insurance shows a balance of $550, which represents the unexpired cost for the remaining 11 months of coverage. At the same time, the balance in Insurance Expense equals the insurance cost that expired in October. **If Pioneer does not make this adjustment, October expenses are understated by $50 and net income is overstated by $50. Moreover, both assets and stockholders' equity will be overstated by $50 on the October 31 balance sheet.**

Insurance

Oct. 4

Insurance purchased; record asset

Insurance Policy			
Oct	Nov	Dec	Jan
$50	$50	$50	$50
Feb	March	April	May
$50	$50	$50	$50
June	July	Aug	Sept
$50	$50	$50	$50
Insurance = $600/year			

Oct. 31
      Insurance expired; record insurance expense

ILLUSTRATION 3.7 **Adjustment for insurance**

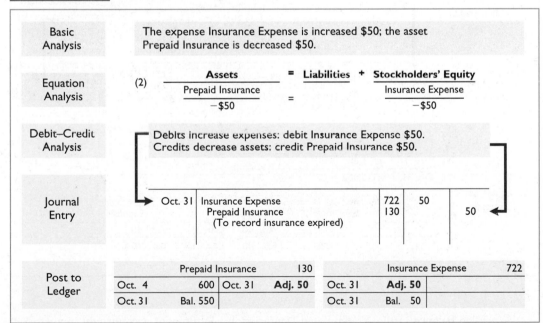

Depreciation

A company typically owns a variety of assets that have long lives, such as buildings, equipment, and motor vehicles. The period of service is referred to as the **useful life** of the asset. Because a building is expected to be of service for many years, it is recorded as an asset, rather than an expense, on the date it is acquired. As explained in Chapter 1, companies record such assets **at cost**, as required by the historical cost principle. To follow the expense recognition principle, companies allocate a portion of this cost to an expense during each period of the asset's useful life. **Depreciation** is the process of allocating the cost of an asset to expense over its useful life.

Depreciation

Oct. 1

Equipment purchased;
record asset

Equipment			
Oct $40	Nov $40	Dec $40	Jan $40
Feb $40	March $40	April $40	May $40
June $40	July $40	Aug $40	Sept $40
Depreciation = $480/year			

Oct. 31

Depreciation recognized;
record depreciation expense

Need for Adjustment The acquisition of a long-lived asset is essentially a long-term pre-payment for the use of that asset. An adjusting entry for depreciation is needed to recognize the cost that has been used (an expense) during the period and to report the unused cost (an asset) at the end of the period. One very important point to understand: **Depreciation is an allocation concept, not a valuation concept.** That is, depreciation **allocates an asset's cost to the periods in which it is used. Depreciation does not attempt to report the actual change in the value of the asset.**

For Pioneer Advertising, assume that depreciation on the equipment is $480 a year, or $40 per month. As shown in **Illustration 3.8**, rather than decrease (credit) the asset account directly, Pioneer instead credits Accumulated Depreciation—Equipment. Accumulated Depreciation is called a **contra asset account**. Such an account is offset against an asset account on the balance sheet. Thus, the Accumulated Depreciation—Equipment account offsets the asset account Equipment. **This account keeps track of the total amount of depreciation expense taken over the life of the asset.** To keep the accounting equation in balance, Pioneer decreases stockholders' equity by increasing an expense account, Depreciation Expense.

ILLUSTRATION 3.8 Adjustment for depreciation

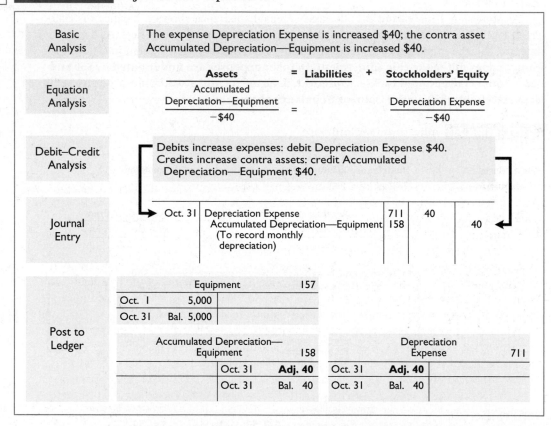

The balance in the Accumulated Depreciation—Equipment account will increase $40 each month, and the balance in Equipment remains $5,000.

Statement Presentation As indicated, Accumulated Depreciation—Equipment is a contra asset account (see **Helpful Hint**). It is offset against Equipment on the balance sheet. The normal balance of a contra asset account is a credit. A theoretical alternative to using a contra asset account would be to decrease (credit) the asset account by the amount of depreciation each period. But using the contra account is preferable for a simple reason: It discloses **both** the original cost of the equipment **and** the total cost that has been expensed to date. Thus, in the balance sheet, Pioneer deducts Accumulated Depreciation—Equipment from the related asset account, as shown in **Illustration 3.9**.

HELPFUL HINT

All contra accounts have increases, decreases, and normal balances opposite to the account to which they relate.

Equipment	$5,000	
Less: Accumulated depreciation—equipment	40	
	$4,960	

ILLUSTRATION 3.9

Balance sheet presentation of accumulated depreciation

Book value is the difference between the cost of any depreciable asset and its related accumulated depreciation (see **Alternative Terminology**). In Illustration 3.9, the book value of the equipment at the balance sheet date is $4,960. The book value and the fair value of the asset are generally two different values. As noted earlier, **the purpose of depreciation is not valuation but a means of cost allocation**.

Depreciation expense identifies the portion of an asset's cost that expired during the period (in this case, in October). The accounting equation shows that **without this adjusting entry, total assets, total stockholders' equity, and net income are overstated by $40 and depreciation expense is understated by $40**.

Illustration 3.10 summarizes the accounting for prepaid expenses.

ALTERNATIVE TERMINOLOGY

Book value is also referred to as *carrying value*.

Accounting for Prepaid Expenses

Examples	Reason for Adjustment	Accounts Before Adjustment	Adjusting Entry
Insurance, supplies, advertising, rent, depreciation	Prepaid expenses originally recorded in asset accounts have been used.	Assets overstated. Expenses understated.	Dr. Expenses Cr. Assets or Contra Assets

ILLUSTRATION 3.10

Accounting for prepaid expenses

Unearned Revenues

When companies receive cash before services are performed, they record a liability by increasing (crediting) a liability account called **unearned revenues**. In other words, a **company now has a performance obligation** (liability) to perform a service for one of its customers. Items like rent, magazine subscriptions, and customer deposits for future service may result in unearned revenues. Airlines such as **United, Southwest**, and **Delta**, for instance, treat receipts from the sale of tickets as unearned revenue until the flight service is provided.

Unearned revenues are the opposite of prepaid expenses. Indeed, unearned revenue on the books of one company is likely to be a prepaid expense on the books of the company that has made the advance payment. For example, if identical accounting periods are assumed, a landlord will have unearned rent revenue when a tenant has prepaid rent.

When a company receives payment for services to be performed in a future accounting period, it increases (credits) an unearned revenue (a liability) account to recognize the liability that exists. The company subsequently recognizes revenues when it performs the service. During the accounting period, it is not practical to make daily entries as the company performs services. Instead, the company delays recognition of revenue until the adjustment process. Then, the company makes an adjusting entry to record the revenue for services performed during the period and to show the liability that remains at the end of the accounting period. Typically, prior to adjustment, liabilities are overstated and revenues are understated. Therefore, as shown in **Illustration 3.11**, **the adjusting entry for unearned revenues results in a decrease (a debit) to a liability account and an increase (a credit) to a revenue account**.

Pioneer Advertising received $1,200 on October 2 from R. Knox for advertising services expected to be completed by December 31. Pioneer credited the payment to Unearned Service Revenue. This liability account shows a balance of $1,200 in the October 31 trial balance. From an evaluation of the services Pioneer performed for Knox during October, the company determines that it should recognize $400 of revenue in October. The liability (Unearned Service Revenue) is therefore decreased, and stockholders' equity (Service Revenue) is increased.

As shown in **Illustration 3.12**, the liability Unearned Service Revenue now shows a balance of $800. That amount represents the remaining advertising services Pioneer is

Unearned Revenues

Oct. 2
Thank you in advance for your work

I will finish by Dec. 31

$1,200

Cash is received in advance; liability is recorded

Oct. 31
Some service has been performed; some revenue is recorded

ILLUSTRATION 3.11

Adjusting entries for unearned revenues

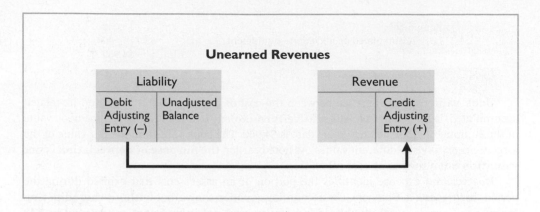

obligated to perform in the future. At the same time, Service Revenue shows total revenue recognized in October of $10,400. **Without this adjustment, revenues and net income are understated by $400 in the income statement. Moreover, liabilities will be overstated and stockholders' equity will be understated by $400 on the October 31 balance sheet.**

ILLUSTRATION 3.12 Service revenue accounts after adjustment

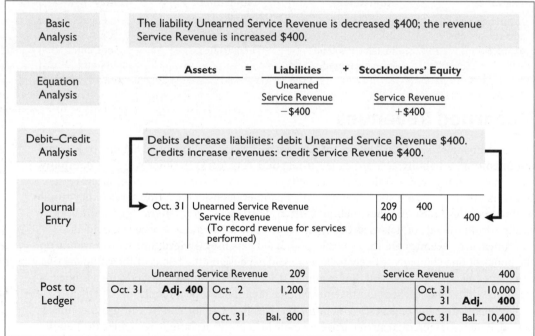

Illustration 3.13 summarizes the accounting for unearned revenues.

ILLUSTRATION 3.13

Accounting for unearned revenues

Accounting for Unearned Revenues

Examples	Reason for Adjustment	Accounts Before Adjustment	Adjusting Entry
Rent, magazine subscriptions, customer deposits for future service	Unearned revenues recorded in liability accounts are now recognized as revenue for services performed.	Liabilities overstated. Revenues understated.	Dr. Liabilities Cr. Revenues

Accounting Across the Organization   Best Buy

Turning Gift Cards into Revenue

Those of you who are marketing majors (and even most of you who are not) know that gift cards are among the hottest marketing tools in merchandising today. Customers purchase gift cards and give them to someone for later use. In a recent year, gift-card sales were expected to exceed $124 billion.

iStock.com/Skip Odonnell

Although these programs are popular with marketing executives, they create accounting questions. Should revenue be recorded at the time the gift card is sold, or when it is exercised? How should expired gift cards be accounted

for? In a recent balance sheet, **Best Buy** reported unearned revenue related to gift cards of $427 million.

Source: "2014 Gift Card Sales to Top $124 Billion, But Growth Slowing," *PR Newswire* (December 10, 2014).

Suppose that Robert Jones purchases a $100 gift card at Best Buy on December 24, 2021, and gives it to his wife, Mary Jones, on December 25, 2021. On January 3, 2022, Mary uses the card to purchase $100 worth of CDs. When do you think Best Buy should recognize revenue and why? (Go to WileyPLUS for this answer and additional questions.)

DO IT! 2 | Adjusting Entries for Deferrals

The ledger of Hammond Inc. on March 31, 2022, includes these selected accounts before adjusting entries are prepared.

	Debit	Credit
Prepaid Insurance	$ 3,600	
Supplies	2,800	
Equipment	25,000	
Accumulated Depreciation—Equipment		$5,000
Unearned Service Revenue		9,200

An analysis of the accounts shows the following.

1. Insurance expires at the rate of $100 per month.
2. Supplies on hand total $800.
3. The equipment depreciates $200 a month.
4. During March, services were performed for $4,000 of the unearned service revenue reported.

Prepare the adjusting entries for the month of March.

ACTION PLAN

- **Make adjusting entries at the end of the period for revenues recognized and expenses incurred in the period.**
- **Don't forget to make adjusting entries for deferrals. Failure to adjust for deferrals leads to overstatement of the asset or liability and understatement of the related expense or revenue.**

Solution

		Debit	Credit
1.	Insurance Expense	100	
	Prepaid Insurance		100
	(To record insurance expired)		
2.	Supplies Expense ($2,800 − $800)	2,000	
	Supplies		2,000
	(To record supplies used)		
3.	Depreciation Expense	200	
	Accumulated Depreciation—Equipment		200
	(To record monthly depreciation)		
4.	Unearned Service Revenue	4,000	
	Service Revenue		4,000
	(To record revenue for services performed)		

Related exercise material: **BE3.5, BE3.6, BE3.7, BE3.8, BE3.9, DO IT! 3.2, E3.5, E3.6, E3.7, E3.8, E3.9, E3.10, E3.11, E3.12, E3.13, E3.14, E3.15, and E3.16.**

Adjusting Entries for Accruals

LEARNING OBJECTIVE 3

Prepare adjusting entries for accruals.

ANALYZE → JOURNALIZE → POST → TRIAL BALANCE → **Journalize and post adjusting entries: deferrals/accruals** → ADJUSTED TRIAL BALANCE → FINANCIAL STATEMENTS → CLOSING ENTRIES → POST-CLOSING TRIAL BALANCE

Accrued Revenues

My fee is $200

Revenue and receivable are recorded for unbilled services

Nov. 10

$200

Cash is received; receivable is reduced

The second category of adjusting entries is **accruals**. Prior to an accrual adjustment, the revenue account (and the related asset account) or the expense account (and the related liability account) are understated. Thus, the adjusting entry for accruals will **increase both a balance sheet and an income statement account**.

Accrued Revenues

Revenues for services performed but not yet recorded at the statement date are **accrued revenues**. Accrued revenues may accumulate (accrue) with the passing of time, as in the case of interest revenue. These are unrecorded because the earning of interest does not involve daily transactions. Companies do not record interest revenue on a daily basis because it is often impractical to do so. Accrued revenues also may result from services that have been performed but not yet billed or collected, as in the case of commissions and fees. These may be unrecorded because only a portion of the total service has been performed and the clients will not be billed until the service has been completed.

An adjusting entry records the receivable that exists at the balance sheet date and the revenue for the services performed during the period. Prior to adjustment, both assets and revenues are understated. As shown in **Illustration 3.14**, an adjusting entry for accrued **revenues results in an increase (a debit) to an asset account and an increase (a credit) to a revenue account** (see **Helpful Hint**).

ILLUSTRATION 3.14

Adjusting entries for accrued revenues

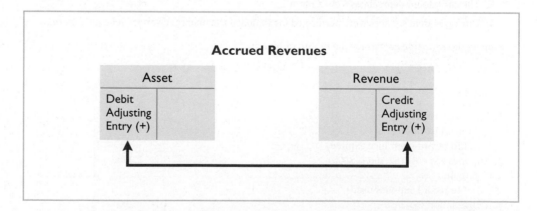

Accrued Revenues

Asset		Revenue	
Debit Adjusting Entry (+)			Credit Adjusting Entry (+)

In October, Pioneer Advertising Inc. performed services worth $200 that were not billed to clients on or before October 31. Because these services were not billed, they were not recorded. The accrual of unrecorded service revenue increases an asset account, Accounts Receivable. It also increases stockholders' equity by increasing a revenue account, Service Revenue, as shown in **Illustration 3.15**.

The asset Accounts Receivable shows that clients owe Pioneer $200 at the balance sheet date. The balance of $10,600 in Service Revenue represents the total revenue for services performed by Pioneer during the month ($10,000 + $400 + $200). **Without the adjusting**

HELPFUL HINT

For accruals, there may have been no prior entry, and the accounts requiring adjustment may both have zero balances prior to adjustment.

ILLUSTRATION 3.15   **Adjustment for accrued revenue**

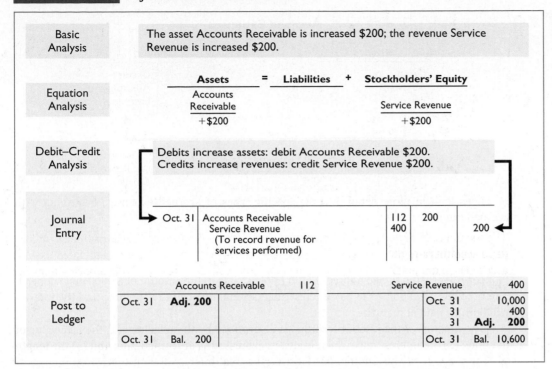

| Basic Analysis | The asset Accounts Receivable is increased $200; the revenue Service Revenue is increased $200. |

Equation Analysis

	Assets	=	Liabilities	+	Stockholders' Equity
	Accounts Receivable				Service Revenue
	+$200				+$200

Debit–Credit Analysis

Debits increase assets: debit Accounts Receivable $200.
Credits increase revenues: credit Service Revenue $200.

Journal Entry

Oct. 31	Accounts Receivable	112	200	
	Service Revenue	400		200
	(To record revenue for services performed)			

Post to Ledger

Accounts Receivable		112
Oct. 31	**Adj. 200**	
Oct. 31	Bal. 200	

Service Revenue		400
	Oct. 31	10,000
	31	400
	31	**Adj. 200**
	Oct. 31	Bal. 10,600

entry, assets and stockholders' equity on the balance sheet and revenues and net income on the income statement are understated.

On November 10, Pioneer receives cash of $200 for the services performed in October and makes the following entry.

Nov. 10	Cash	200	
	Accounts Receivable		200
	(To record cash collected on account)		

The company records the collection of the receivables by a debit (increase) to Cash and a credit (decrease) to Accounts Receivable.

Illustration 3.16 summarizes the accounting for accrued revenues.

Equation analyses summarize the effects of transactions on the three elements of the accounting equation, as well as the effect on cash flows.

A	=	L	+	SE
+200				
−200				

Cash Flows
+ 200

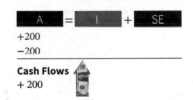

Accounting for Accrued Revenues

Examples	Reason for Adjustment	Accounts Before Adjustment	Adjusting Entry
Interest, rent, services	Services performed but not yet received in cash or recorded.	Assets understated. Revenues understated.	Dr. Assets Cr. Revenues

ILLUSTRATION 3.16

Accounting for accrued revenues

ETHICS NOTE

A report released by **Fannie Mae's** board of directors stated that improper adjusting entries at the mortgage-finance company resulted in delayed recognition of expenses caused by interest rate changes. The motivation for such accounting apparently was the desire to hit earnings estimates.

Accrued Expenses

Expenses incurred but not yet paid or recorded at the statement date are called **accrued expenses**. Interest, taxes, and salaries are common examples of accrued expenses.

Companies make adjustments for accrued expenses to record the obligations that exist at the balance sheet date and to recognize the expenses that apply to the current accounting period (see **Ethics Note**). Prior to adjustment, both liabilities and expenses are understated. Therefore, as **Illustration 3.17** shows, **an adjusting entry for accrued expenses results in an increase (a debit) to an expense account and an increase (a credit) to a liability account**.

ILLUSTRATION 3.17

Adjusting entries for accrued expenses

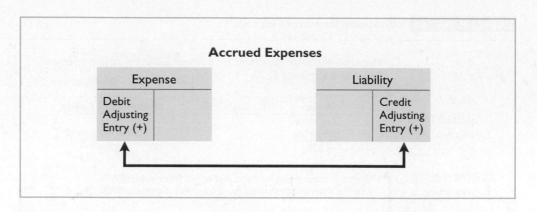

Let's look in more detail at some specific types of accrued expenses, beginning with accrued interest.

Accrued Interest

Pioneer Advertising signed a three-month note payable in the amount of $5,000 on October 1. The note requires Pioneer to pay interest at an annual rate of 12%. The note and the interest will both be paid at maturity.

The amount of the interest recorded is determined by three factors: (1) the face value of the note; (2) the interest rate, which is always expressed as an annual rate; and (3) the length of time the note is outstanding. For Pioneer, the total interest due on the $5,000 note at its maturity date three months in the future is $150 ($5,000 × 12% × $\frac{3}{12}$), or $50 for one month (see **Helpful Hint**). **Illustration 3.18** shows the formula for computing monthly interest expense and its application to Pioneer for the month of October.

HELPFUL HINT

In computing interest, we express the time period as a fraction of a year.

ILLUSTRATION 3.18

Formula for computing interest

Face Value of Note	×	Annual Interest Rate	×	Time in Terms of One Year	=	Interest
$5,000	×	12%	×	$\frac{1}{12}$	=	$50

As **Illustration 3.19** shows, the accrual of interest at October 31 increases a liability account, Interest Payable. It also decreases stockholders' equity by increasing an expense account, Interest Expense.

ILLUSTRATION 3.19

Adjustment for accrued interest

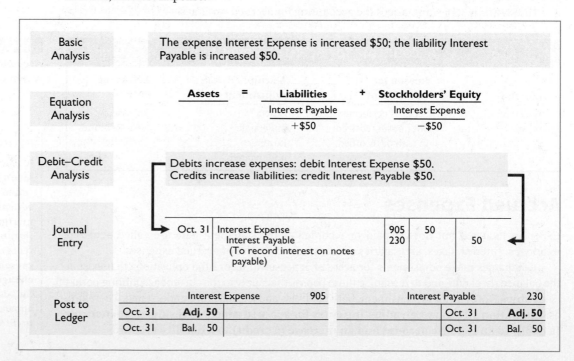

Interest Expense shows the interest charges for the month of October. Interest Payable shows the amount of interest the company owes at the statement date. Pioneer will not pay the interest until the note comes due at the end of three months. Companies use the Interest Payable account, instead of crediting Notes Payable, to disclose the two different types of obligations—interest and principal—in the accounts and statements. **Without this adjusting entry, liabilities and interest expense are understated, and net income and stockholders' equity are overstated.**

Accrued Salaries and Wages

Companies pay for some types of expenses, such as employee salaries and wages, after the services have been performed. Pioneer Advertising paid salaries and wages on October 26 for its employees' first two weeks of work (October 15–October 26). The next payment of salaries will not occur until November 9. As **Illustration 3.20** shows, three working days of unpaid salaries and wages remain in October (October 29–31).

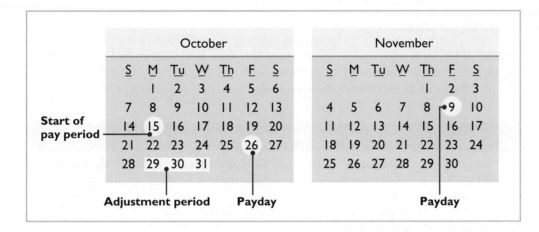

ILLUSTRATION 3.20

Calendar showing Pioneer's pay periods

At October 31, the salaries and wages for these three days represent an accrued expense and a related liability to Pioneer. The employees receive total salaries and wages of $2,000 for a five-day work week, or $400 per day. Thus, accrued salaries and wages at October 31 are $1,200 ($400 × 3). This accrual increases a liability, Salaries and Wages Payable. It also decreases stockholders' equity by increasing an expense account, Salaries and Wages Expense, as shown in **Illustration 3.21**.

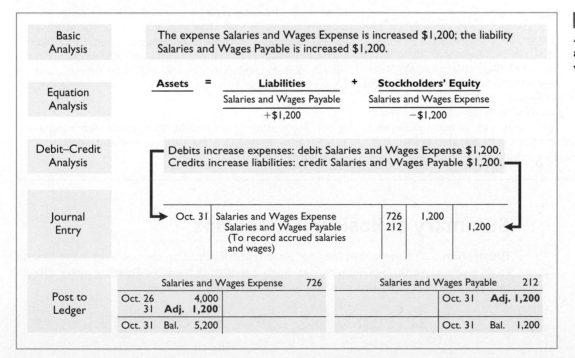

ILLUSTRATION 3.21

Adjustment for accrued salaries and wages

After this adjustment, the balance in Salaries and Wages Expense of $5,200 (13 days × $400) is the actual salary and wages expense for October. The balance in Salaries and Wages Payable of $1,200 is the amount of the liability for salaries and wages Pioneer owes as of October 31. **Without the $1,200 adjustment for salaries and wages, Pioneer's expenses are understated $1,200 and its liabilities are understated $1,200.**

Pioneer pays salaries and wages every two weeks. Consequently, the next payday is November 9, when the company will again pay total salaries and wages of $4,000. The payment consists of $1,200 of salaries and wages payable at October 31 plus $2,800 of salaries and wages expense for November (7 working days, as shown in the November calendar × $400). Therefore, Pioneer makes the following entry on November 9.

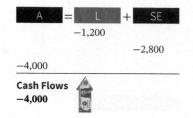

A = L + SE
　　−1,200
　　　　−2,800
−4,000
Cash Flows
−4,000

Nov. 9	Salaries and Wages Payable	1,200	
	Salaries and Wages Expense	2,800	
	Cash		4,000
	(To record November 9 payroll)		

This entry eliminates the liability for Salaries and Wages Payable that Pioneer recorded in the October 31 adjusting entry, and it records the proper amount of Salaries and Wages Expense for the period between November 1 and November 9.

Illustration 3.22 summarizes the accounting for accrued expenses.

ILLUSTRATION 3.22

Accounting for accrued expenses

Accounting for Accrued Expenses			
Examples	**Reason for Adjustment**	**Accounts Before Adjustment**	**Adjusting Entry**
Interest, rent, salaries	Expenses have been incurred but not yet paid in cash or recorded.	Expenses understated. Liabilities understated.	Dr. Expenses Cr. Liabilities

People, Planet, and Profit Insight

iStock.com/Nathan Gleave

Got Junk?

Do you have an old computer or two that you no longer use? How about an old TV that needs replacing? Many people do. Approximately 163,000 computers and televisions become obsolete each day. Yet, in a recent year, only 11% of computers were recycled. It is estimated that 75% of all computers ever sold are sitting in storage somewhere, waiting to be disposed of. Each

of these old TVs and computers is loaded with lead, cadmium, mercury, and other toxic chemicals. If you have one of these electronic gadgets, you have a responsibility, and a probable cost, for disposing of it. Companies have the same problem, but their discarded materials may include lead paint, asbestos, and other toxic chemicals.

What accounting issue might this cause for companies? (Go to WileyPLUS for this answer and additional questions.)

Summary of Basic Relationships

Illustration 3.23 summarizes the four basic types of adjusting entries. Take some time to study and analyze the adjusting entries. Be sure to note that **each adjusting entry affects one balance sheet account and one income statement account.**

Type of Adjustment	Accounts Before Adjustment	Adjusting Entry
Prepaid expenses	Assets overstated.	Dr. Expenses
	Expenses understated.	Cr. Assets or
		Contra Assets
Unearned revenues	Liabilities overstated.	Dr. Liabilities
	Revenues understated.	Cr. Revenues
Accrued revenues	Assets understated.	Dr. Assets
	Revenues understated.	Cr. Revenues
Accrued expenses	Expenses understated.	Dr. Expenses
	Liabilities understated.	Cr. Liabilities

ILLUSTRATION 3.23
Summary of adjusting entries

Illustrations 3.24 and **3.25** show the journalizing and posting of adjusting entries for Pioneer Advertising Inc. on October 31 (see **Helpful Hint**). The ledger identifies all adjustments by the reference J2 because they have been recorded on page 2 of the general journal. The company may insert a center caption "Adjusting Entries" between the last transaction entry and the first adjusting entry in the journal. When you review the general ledger in Illustration 3.25, note that the entries highlighted in red are the adjustments.

ILLUSTRATION 3.24 **General journal showing adjusting entries**

	GENERAL JOURNAL				J2
Date	**Account Titles and Explanation**	**Ref.**	**Debit**	**Credit**	
2022	Adjusting Entries				
Oct. 31	Supplies Expense	631	1,500		
	Supplies	126		1,500	
	(To record supplies used)				
31	Insurance Expense	722	50		
	Prepaid Insurance	130		50	
	(To record insurance expired)				
31	Depreciation Expense	711	40		
	Accumulated Depreciation—Equipment	158		40	
	(To record monthly depreciation)				
31	Unearned Service Revenue	209	400		
	Service Revenue	400		400	
	(To record revenue for services performed)				
31	Accounts Receivable	112	200		
	Service Revenue	400		200	
	(To record revenue for services performed)				
31	Interest Expense	905	50		
	Interest Payable	230		50	
	(To record interest on notes payable)				
31	Salaries and Wages Expense	726	1,200		
	Salaries and Wages Payable	212		1,200	
	(To record accrued salaries and wages)				

HELPFUL HINT

(1) Adjusting entries should not involve debits or credits to Cash.
(2) Evaluate whether the adjustment makes sense. For example, an adjustment to recognize supplies used should increase Supplies Expense.
(3) Double-check all computations.
(4) Each adjusting entry affects one balance sheet account and one income statement account.

ILLUSTRATION 3.25 General ledger after adjustment

GENERAL LEDGER

Cash — No. 101

Date	Explanation	Ref.	Debit	Credit	Balance
2022					
Oct. 1		J1	10,000		10,000
2		J1	1,200		11,200
3		J1		900	10,300
4		J1		600	9,700
20		J1	10,000		19,700
26		J1		4,000	15,700
31		J1		500	15,200

Accounts Receivable — No. 112

Date	Explanation	Ref.	Debit	Credit	Balance
2022					
Oct. 31	Adj. entry	J2	200		200

Supplies — No. 126

Date	Explanation	Ref.	Debit	Credit	Balance
2022					
Oct. 5		J1	2,500		2,500
31	Adj. entry	J2		1,500	1,000

Prepaid Insurance — No. 130

Date	Explanation	Ref.	Debit	Credit	Balance
2022					
Oct. 4		J1	600		600
31	Adj. entry	J2		50	550

Equipment — No. 157

Date	Explanation	Ref.	Debit	Credit	Balance
2022					
Oct. 1		J1	5,000		5,000

Accumulated Depreciation—Equipment — No. 158

Date	Explanation	Ref.	Debit	Credit	Balance
2022					
Oct. 31	Adj. entry	J2		40	40

Notes Payable — No. 200

Date	Explanation	Ref.	Debit	Credit	Balance
2022					
Oct. 1		J1		5,000	5,000

Accounts Payable — No. 201

Date	Explanation	Ref.	Debit	Credit	Balance
2022					
Oct. 5		J1		2,500	2,500

Unearned Service Revenue — No. 209

Date	Explanation	Ref.	Debit	Credit	Balance
2022					
Oct. 2		J1		1,200	1,200
31	Adj. entry	J2	400		800

Salaries and Wages Payable — No. 212

Date	Explanation	Ref.	Debit	Credit	Balance
2022					
Oct. 31	Adj. entry	J2		1,200	1,200

Interest Payable — No. 230

Date	Explanation	Ref.	Debit	Credit	Balance
2022					
Oct. 31	Adj. entry	J2		50	50

Common Stock — No. 311

Date	Explanation	Ref.	Debit	Credit	Balance
2022					
Oct. 1		J1		10,000	10,000

Retained Earnings — No. 320

Date	Explanation	Ref.	Debit	Credit	Balance
2022					

Dividends — No. 332

Date	Explanation	Ref.	Debit	Credit	Balance
2022					
Oct. 31		J1	500		500

Service Revenue — No. 400

Date	Explanation	Ref.	Debit	Credit	Balance
2022					
Oct. 20		J1		10,000	10,000
31	Adj. entry	J2		400	10,400
31	Adj. entry	J2		200	10,600

Supplies Expense — No. 631

Date	Explanation	Ref.	Debit	Credit	Balance
2022					
Oct. 31	Adj. entry	J2	1,500		1,500

Depreciation Expense — No. 711

Date	Explanation	Ref.	Debit	Credit	Balance
2022					
Oct. 31	Adj. entry	J2	40		40

Insurance Expense — No. 722

Date	Explanation	Ref.	Debit	Credit	Balance
2022					
Oct. 31	Adj. entry	J2	50		50

Salaries and Wages Expense — No. 726

Date	Explanation	Ref.	Debit	Credit	Balance
2022					
Oct. 26		J1	4,000		4,000
31	Adj. entry	J2	1,200		5,200

Rent Expense — No. 729

Date	Explanation	Ref.	Debit	Credit	Balance
2022					
Oct. 3		J1	900		900

Interest Expense — No. 905

Date	Explanation	Ref.	Debit	Credit	Balance
2022					
Oct. 31	Adj. entry	J2	50		50

DO IT! 3 | Adjusting Entries for Accruals

Micro Computer Services Inc. began operations on August 1, 2022. At the end of August 2022, management prepares monthly financial statements. The following information relates to August.

1. At August 31, the company owed its employees $800 in salaries and wages that will be paid on September 1.

2. On August 1, the company borrowed $30,000 from a local bank on a 1-year note payable. The annual interest rate is 10%. Interest will be paid with the note at maturity.

3. Revenue for services performed but unrecorded for August totaled $1,100.

Prepare the adjusting entries needed at August 31, 2022.

ACTION PLAN

- Make adjusting entries at the end of the period to recognize revenues for services performed and for expenses incurred.

- Don't forget to make adjusting entries for accruals. Adjusting entries for accruals will increase both a balance sheet and an income statement account.

Solution

1. Salaries and Wages Expense	800	
Salaries and Wages Payable		800
(To record accrued salaries)		
2. Interest Expense	250	
Interest Payable		250
(To record accrued interest:		
$30,000 \times 10\% \times \frac{1}{12} = \$250$)		
3. Accounts Receivable	1,100	
Service Revenue		1,100
(To record revenue for services performed)		

Related exercise material: **BE3.10, BE3.11, BE3.12, DO IT! 3.3, E3.5, E3.6, E3.7, E3.8, E3.9, E3.10, E3.11, E3.12, E3.13, E3.14, E3.15, E3.17, E3.18, E3.19, and E3.20.**

Adjusted Trial Balance and Financial Statements

LEARNING OBJECTIVE 4

Describe the nature and purpose of an adjusted trial balance.

ANALYZE › JOURNALIZE › POST › TRIAL BALANCE › ADJUSTING ENTRIES › **Adjusted trial balance** › **Prepare financial statements** › JOURNALIZE AND POST CLOSING ENTRIES › PREPARE A POST-CLOSING TRIAL BALANCE

After a company has journalized and posted all adjusting entries, it prepares another trial balance from the ledger accounts. This trial balance is called an **adjusted trial balance**. It shows the balances of all accounts, including those adjusted, at the end of the accounting period. The purpose of an adjusted trial balance is to **prove the equality** of the total debit balances and the total credit balances in the ledger after all adjustments. Because the accounts now contain all data needed for financial statements, the adjusted trial balance is the **primary basis for the preparation of financial statements**.

Preparing the Adjusted Trial Balance

Illustration 3.26 presents the adjusted trial balance for Pioneer Advertising Inc. prepared from the ledger accounts in Illustration 3.25. The amounts affected by the adjusting entries are highlighted in red. Compare these amounts to those in the unadjusted trial balance in Illustration 3.4. In this comparison, you will see that there are more accounts in the adjusted trial balance as a result of the adjusting entries made at the end of the month.

ILLUSTRATION 3.26

Adjusted trial balance

Pioneer Advertising Inc.
Adjusted Trial Balance
October 31, 2022

	Debit	Credit
Cash	$15,200	
Accounts Receivable	200	
Supplies	1,000	
Prepaid Insurance	550	
Equipment	5,000	
Accumulated Depreciation—Equipment		$ 40
Notes Payable		5,000
Accounts Payable		2,500
Interest Payable		50
Unearned Service Revenue		800
Salaries and Wages Payable		1,200
Common Stock		10,000
Retained Earnings		–0–
Dividends	500	
Service Revenue		10,600
Salaries and Wages Expense	5,200	
Supplies Expense	1,500	
Rent Expense	900	
Insurance Expense	50	
Interest Expense	50	
Depreciation Expense	40	
	$30,190	$30,190

Preparing Financial Statements

Companies can prepare financial statements directly from the adjusted trial balance. **Illustrations 3.27** and **3.28** present the interrelationships of data in the adjusted trial balance and the financial statements.

As Illustration 3.27 shows, companies prepare the income statement from the revenue and expense accounts. Next, they use the Retained Earnings and Dividends accounts and the net income (or net loss) from the income statement to prepare the retained earnings statement.

ILLUSTRATION 3.27 **Preparation of the income statement and retained earnings statement from the adjusted trial balance**

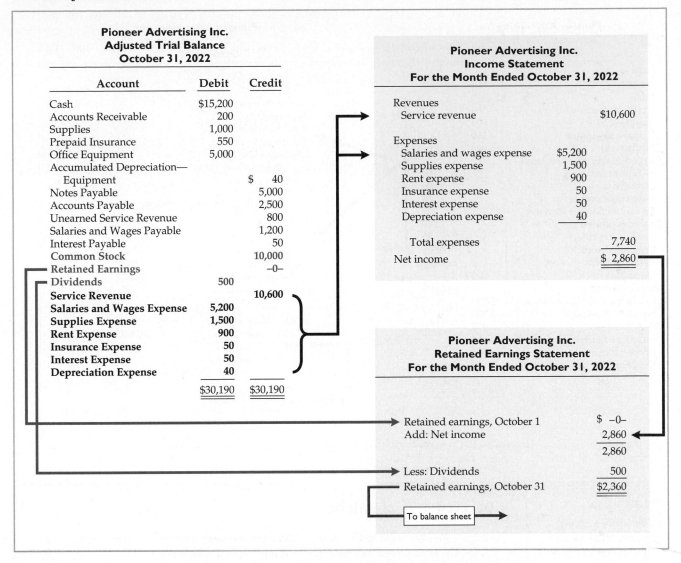

As **Illustration 3.28** shows, companies then prepare the balance sheet from the asset and liability accounts and the ending retained earnings balance as reported in the retained earnings statement.

ILLUSTRATION 3.28 **Preparation of the balance sheet from the adjusted trial balance**

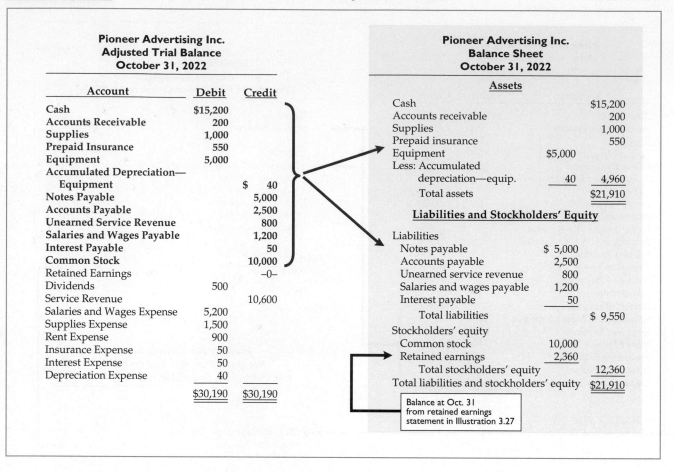

ACTION PLAN	

ACTION PLAN

- In an adjusted trial balance, make sure all asset, liability, revenue, and expense accounts are properly stated.

- To determine the ending balance in Retained Earnings, add net income and subtract dividends.

DO IT! 4 | Trial Balance

Skolnick Co. was organized on April 1, 2022. The company prepares quarterly financial statements. The adjusted trial balance amounts at June 30 are shown below.

	Debit		Credit
Cash	$ 6,700	Accumulated Depreciation—	
Accounts Receivable	600	Equipment	$ 850
Prepaid Rent	900	Notes Payable	5,000
Supplies	1,000	Accounts Payable	1,510
Equipment	15,000	Salaries and Wages Payable	400
Dividends	600	Interest Payable	50
Salaries and Wages Expense	9,400	Unearned Rent Revenue	500
Rent Expense	1,500	Common Stock	14,000
Depreciation Expense	850	Service Revenue	14,200
Supplies Expense	200	Rent Revenue	800
Utilities Expense	510		
Interest Expense	50		
	$37,310		$37,310

a. Determine the net income for the quarter April 1 to June 30.

b. Determine the total assets and total liabilities at June 30, 2022, for Skolnick Co.

c. Determine the amount that appears for retained earnings at June 30, 2022.

Solution

a. The net income is determined by adding revenues and subtracting expenses. The net income is computed as follows.

Revenues		
Service revenue	$14,200	
Rent revenue	800	
Total revenues		$15,000
Expenses		
Salaries and wages expense	9,400	
Rent expense	1,500	
Depreciation expense	850	
Utilities expense	510	
Supplies expense	200	
Interest expense	50	
Total expenses		12,510
Net income		$ 2,490

b. Total assets and liabilities are computed as follows.

Assets			Liabilities	
Cash		$ 6,700	Notes payable	$5,000
Accounts receivable		600	Accounts payable	1,510
Supplies		1,000	Unearned rent	
Prepaid rent		900	revenue	500
Equipment	$15,000		Salaries and wages	
Less: Accumulated			payable	400
depreciation—			Interest payable	50
equipment	850	14,150		
Total assets		$23,350	Total liabilities	$7,460

c. Retained earnings, April 1	$ 0
Add: Net income	2,490
Less: Dividends	600
Retained earnings, June 30	$ 1,890

Related exercise material: **BE3.13, BE3.14, DO IT! 3.4, E3.18, and E3.19.**

Appendix 3A	# Adjusting Entries for the Alternative Treatment of Deferrals

LEARNING OBJECTIVE *5

Prepare adjusting entries for the alternative treatment of deferrals.

In discussing adjusting entries for prepaid expenses and unearned revenues, we illustrated transactions for which companies made the initial entries to balance sheet accounts. In the case of prepaid expenses, the company debited the prepayment to an asset account. In the case of unearned revenue, the company credited a liability account to record the cash received.

Some companies use an alternative treatment. (1) When a company prepays an expense, it debits that amount to an expense account. (2) When it receives payment for future services, it credits the amount to a revenue account. In this appendix, we describe the circumstances that justify such entries and the different adjusting entries that may be required. This alternative treatment of prepaid expenses and unearned revenues has the same effect on the financial statements as the procedures described in the chapter.

Prepaid Expenses

Prepaid expenses become expired costs either through the passage of time (e.g., insurance) or through consumption (e.g., advertising supplies). If at the time of purchase the company expects to consume the supplies before the next financial statement date, **it may choose to debit (increase) an expense account rather than an asset account. This alternative treatment is simply more convenient.**

Assume that Pioneer Advertising Inc. expects that it will use before the end of the month all of the supplies purchased on October 5. A debit of $2,500 to Supplies Expense (rather than to the asset account Supplies) on October 5 will eliminate the need for an adjusting entry on October 31. At October 31, the Supplies Expense account will show a balance of $2,500, which is the cost of supplies used between October 5 and October 31.

But what if the company does not use all the supplies? For example, what if an inventory of $1,000 of advertising supplies remains on October 31? Obviously, the company would need to make an adjusting entry. Prior to adjustment, the expense account Supplies Expense is overstated $1,000, and the asset account Supplies is understated $1,000. Thus, Pioneer makes the following adjusting entry.

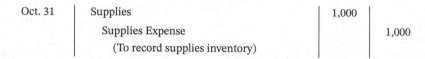

+1,000

+1,000 Exp

Cash Flows
no effect

Oct. 31	Supplies	1,000	
	Supplies Expense		1,000
	(To record supplies inventory)		

Illustration 3A.1 shows the accounts after the company posts the adjusting entry.

ILLUSTRATION 3A.1

Accounts after adjustment

	Supplies				Supplies Expense			
10/31 **Adj.**	**1,000**			10/5	2,500	10/31 **Adj.**	**1,000**
				10/31 **Bal.**	**1,500**		

After adjustment, the asset account Supplies shows a balance of $1,000, which is equal to the cost of supplies on hand at October 31. In addition, Supplies Expense shows a balance of $1,500. This is equal to the cost of supplies used between October 5 and October 31. Without the adjusting entry, expenses are overstated and net income is understated by $1,000 in the October income statement. Also, both assets and stockholders' equity are understated by $1,000 on the October 31 balance sheet.

Illustration 3A.2 compares the entries and accounts for advertising supplies in the two adjustment approaches.

ILLUSTRATION 3A.2

Adjustment approaches—a comparison

	Prepayment Initially Debited to Asset Account (per chapter)				Prepayment Initially Debited to Expense Account (per appendix)		
Oct. 5	Supplies	2,500		Oct. 5	Supplies Expense	2,500	
	Accounts Payable		2,500		Accounts Payable		2,500
Oct. 31	Supplies Expense	1,500		Oct. 31	Supplies	1,000	
	Supplies		1,500		Supplies Expense		1,000

After Pioneer posts the entries, the accounts appear as shown in **Illustration 3A.3**.

ILLUSTRATION 3A.3

Comparison of accounts

	(per chapter) Supplies				(per appendix) Supplies		
10/5	2,500	10/31 **Adj.**	**1,500**	10/31 **Adj.**	**1,000**		
10/31 **Bal.**	**1,000**						

	Supplies Expense				Supplies Expense		
10/31 **Adj.**	**1,500**			10/5	2,500	10/31 **Adj.**	**1,000**
				10/31 **Bal.**	**1,500**		

Note that the account balances under each alternative are the same at October 31: Supplies $1,000 and Supplies Expense $1,500.

Unearned Revenues

Unearned revenues are recognized as revenue at the time services are performed. Similar to the case for prepaid expenses, companies may credit (increase) a revenue account when they receive cash for future services.

To illustrate, assume that Pioneer Advertising Inc. received $1,200 for future services on October 2. Pioneer expects to perform the services before October 31.[1] In such a case, the company credits Service Revenue. If Pioneer in fact performs the service before October 31, no adjustment is needed.

However, if at the statement date Pioneer has not performed $800 of the services, it would make an adjusting entry (see **Helpful Hint**). Without the entry, the revenue account Service Revenue is overstated $800, and the liability account Unearned Service Revenue is understated $800. Thus, Pioneer makes the following adjusting entry.

> **HELPFUL HINT**
> The required adjusted balances here are Service Revenue $400 and Unearned Service Revenue $800.

Oct. 31	Service Revenue	800	
	Unearned Service Revenue		800
	(To record unearned service revenue		

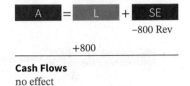

−800 Rev

+800

Cash Flows
no effect

Illustration 3A.4 shows the accounts after Pioneer posts the adjusting entry.

Unearned Service Revenue			**Service Revenue**		
	10/31 **Adj.** 800		10/31 **Adj.** 800	10/2	1,200
				10/31 **Bal.**	**400**

> **ILLUSTRATION 3A.4**
> Accounts after adjustment

The liability account Unearned Service Revenue shows a balance of $800. This equals the services that will be performed in the future. In addition, the balance in Service Revenue equals the services performed in October. Without the adjusting entry, both revenues and net income are overstated by $800 in the October income statement. Also, liabilities are understated by $800 and stockholders' equity is overstated by $800 on the October 31 balance sheet.

Illustration 3A.5 compares the entries and accounts for initially recording unearned service revenue in (1) a liability account or (2) a revenue account.

> **ILLUSTRATION 3A.5**
> Adjustment approaches—a comparison

	Unearned Service Revenue Initially Credited to Liability Account (per chapter)			Unearned Service Revenue Initially Credited to Revenue Account (per appendix)		
Oct. 2	Cash	1,200		Oct. 2 Cash	1,200	
	Unearned Service Revenue		1,200	Service Revenue		1,200
Oct. 31	Unearned Service Revenue	400		Oct. 31 Service Revenue	800	
	Service Revenue		400	Unearned Service Revenue		800

---

[1]This example focuses only on the alternative treatment of unearned revenues. For simplicity, we have ignored the entries to Service Revenue pertaining to the immediate recognition of revenue ($10,000) and the adjusting entry for accrued revenue ($200).

After Pioneer posts the entries, the accounts appear as shown in **Illustration 3A.6**.

ILLUSTRATION 3A.6
Comparison of accounts

(per chapter)				(per appendix)			
Unearned Service Revenue				**Unearned Service Revenue**			
10/31	**Adj.**	400	10/2	1,200		10/31	**Adj.**	800
			10/31	**Bal.**	800			
Service Revenue				**Service Revenue**			
			10/31	**Adj.**	400	10/31	**Adj.**	800	10/2	1,200
									10/31	**Bal.**	400

Note that the balances in the accounts are the same under the two alternatives: Unearned Service Revenue $800 and Service Revenue $400.

Summary of Additional Adjustment Relationships

Illustration 3A.7 provides a summary of basic relationships for deferrals.

ILLUSTRATION 3A.7 Summary of basic relationships for deferrals

Type of Adjustment	Reason for Adjustment	Account Balances before Adjustment	Adjusting Entry
1. Prepaid expenses	(a) Prepaid expenses initially recorded in asset accounts have been used.	Assets overstated. Expenses understated.	Dr. Expenses Cr. Assets
	(b) **Prepaid expenses initially recorded in expense accounts have not been used.**	**Assets understated. Expenses overstated.**	**Dr. Assets Cr. Expenses**
2. Unearned revenues	(a) Unearned revenues initially recorded in liability accounts are now recognized as revenue.	Liabilities overstated. Revenues understated.	Dr. Liabilities Cr. Revenues
	(b) **Unearned revenues initially recorded in revenue accounts are still unearned.**	**Liabilities understated. Revenues overstated.**	**Dr. Revenues Cr. Liabilities**

Alternative adjusting entries **do not apply** to accrued revenues and accrued expenses because **no entries occur before companies make these types of adjusting entries**.

| Appendix 3B | # Financial Reporting Concepts |

LEARNING OBJECTIVE *6
Discuss financial reporting concepts.

This appendix provides a summary of the concepts in action used in this text. In addition, it provides other useful concepts which accountants use as a basis for recording and reporting financial information.

Qualities of Useful Information

The FASB completed the first phase of a project in which it developed a conceptual framework to serve as the basis for future accounting standards. The framework begins by stating that the primary objective of financial reporting is to provide financial information that is **useful** to investors and creditors for making decisions about providing capital. Useful information should possess two fundamental qualities, relevance and faithful representation, as shown in **Illustration 3B.1**.

Relevance Accounting information has **relevance** if it would make a difference in a business decision. Information is considered relevant if it provides information that has **predictive value**, that is, helps provide accurate expectations about the future, and has **confirmatory value**, that is, confirms or corrects prior expectations. **Materiality** is a company-specific aspect of relevance. An item is material when its **size** makes it likely to influence the decision of an investor or creditor.

Faithful Representation **Faithful representation** means that information accurately depicts what really happened. To provide a faithful representation, information must be **complete** (nothing important has been omitted), **neutral** (is not biased toward one position or another), and **free from error**.

ILLUSTRATION 3B.1

Fundamental qualities of useful information

Enhancing Qualities

In addition to the two fundamental qualities, the FASB also describes a number of enhancing qualities of useful information. These include **comparability**, **verifiability**, **timeliness**, and **understandability**. In accounting, **comparability** results when different companies use the same accounting principles. Another type of comparability is consistency. **Consistency** means that a company uses the same accounting principles and methods from year to year. Information is **verifiable** if independent observers, using the same methods, obtain similar results. For accounting information to have relevance, it must be **timely**. That is, it must be available to decision-makers before it loses its capacity to influence decisions. For example, public companies like **Google** or **Best Buy** provide their annual reports to investors within 60 days of their year-end. Information has the quality of **understandability** if it is presented in a clear and concise fashion, so that reasonably informed users of that information can interpret it and comprehend its meaning.

Assumptions in Financial Reporting

To develop accounting standards, the FASB relies on some key assumptions, as shown in **Illustration 3B.2**. These include assumptions about the monetary unit, economic entity, time period, and going concern.

Principles in Financial Reporting

Measurement Principles

GAAP generally uses one of two measurement principles, the historical cost principle or the fair value principle. Selection of which principle to follow generally relates to trade-offs between relevance and faithful representation.

Historical Cost Principle The **historical cost principle** (or cost principle, discussed in Chapter 1) dictates that companies record assets at their cost. This is true not only at the time the asset is purchased but also over the time the asset is held. For example, if land that was purchased for $30,000 increases in value to $40,000, it continues to be reported at $30,000.

Fair Value Principle The **fair value principle** (discussed in Chapter 1) indicates that assets and liabilities should be reported at fair value (the price received to sell an asset or settle a liability). Fair value information may be more useful than historical cost for certain types of assets and liabilities. For example, certain investment securities are reported at fair value

ILLUSTRATION 3B.2

Key assumptions in financial reporting

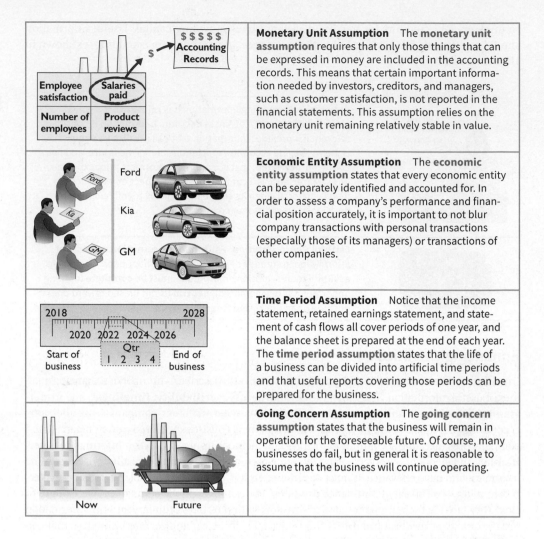

Monetary Unit Assumption The **monetary unit assumption** requires that only those things that can be expressed in money are included in the accounting records. This means that certain important information needed by investors, creditors, and managers, such as customer satisfaction, is not reported in the financial statements. This assumption relies on the monetary unit remaining relatively stable in value.

Economic Entity Assumption The **economic entity assumption** states that every economic entity can be separately identified and accounted for. In order to assess a company's performance and financial position accurately, it is important to not blur company transactions with personal transactions (especially those of its managers) or transactions of other companies.

Time Period Assumption Notice that the income statement, retained earnings statement, and statement of cash flows all cover periods of one year, and the balance sheet is prepared at the end of each year. The **time period assumption** states that the life of a business can be divided into artificial time periods and that useful reports covering those periods can be prepared for the business.

Going Concern Assumption The **going concern assumption** states that the business will remain in operation for the foreseeable future. Of course, many businesses do fail, but in general it is reasonable to assume that the business will continue operating.

because market price information is often readily available for these types of assets. In choosing between cost and fair value, two qualities that make accounting information useful for decision-making are used—relevance and faithful representation. In determining which measurement principle to use, the factual nature of cost figures are weighed versus the relevance of fair value. In general, most assets follow the historical cost principle because fair values may not be representationally faithful. Only in situations where assets are actively traded, such as investment securities, is the fair value principle applied.

Revenue Recognition Principle

The **revenue recognition principle** requires that companies recognize revenue in the accounting period in which the performance obligation is satisfied. As discussed earlier in the chapter, in a service company, revenue is recognized at the time the service is performed. In a merchandising company, the performance obligation is generally satisfied when the goods transfer from the seller to the buyer (discussed in Chapter 5). At this point, the sales transaction is complete and the sales price is established.

Expense Recognition Principle

The **expense recognition principle** (discussed earlier in the chapter) dictates that companies recognize expense in the period in which they make efforts to generate revenue. Thus, expenses follow revenues.

Full Disclosure Principle

The **full disclosure principle** (discussed in Chapter 11) requires that companies disclose all circumstances and events that would make a difference to financial statement users. If an important item cannot reasonably be reported directly in one of the four types of financial statements, then it should be discussed in notes that accompany the statements.

Cost Constraint

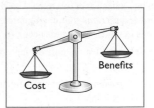

Providing information is costly. In deciding whether companies should be required to provide a certain type of information, accounting standard-setters consider the **cost constraint**. It weighs the cost that companies will incur to provide the information against the benefit that financial statement users will gain from having the information available.

Review and Practice

Learning Objectives Review

1   Explain the accrual basis of accounting and the reasons for adjusting entries.

The time period assumption indicates that the economic life of a business is divided into artificial time periods. Accrual-basis accounting means that companies record events that change a company's financial statements in the periods in which those events occur, rather than in the periods in which the company receives or pays cash.

Companies make adjusting entries at the end of an accounting period. Such entries ensure that companies recognize revenues in the period in which the performance obligation is satisfied and recognize expenses in the period in which they are incurred. The major types of adjusting entries are deferrals (prepaid expenses and unearned revenues) and accruals (accrued revenues and accrued expenses).

2   Prepare adjusting entries for deferrals.

Deferrals are either prepaid expenses or unearned revenues. Companies make adjusting entries for deferrals to record the portion of the prepayment that represents the expense incurred or the revenue for services performed in the current accounting period.

3   Prepare adjusting entries for accruals.

Accruals are either accrued revenues or accrued expenses. Companies make adjusting entries for accruals to record revenues for services performed and expenses incurred in the current accounting period that have not been recognized through daily entries.

4   Describe the nature and purpose of an adjusted trial balance.

An adjusted trial balance shows the balances of all accounts, including those that have been adjusted, at the end of an accounting period. Its purpose is to prove the equality of the total debit balances and total credit balances in the ledger after all adjustments.

*5   Prepare adjusting entries for the alternative treatment of deferrals.

Companies may initially debit prepayments to an expense account. Likewise, they may credit unearned revenues to a revenue account. At the end of the period, these accounts may be overstated. An adjusting entry for prepaid expenses is a debit to an asset account and a credit to an expense account. An adjusting entry for unearned revenues is a debit to a revenue account and a credit to a liability account.

*6   Discuss financial reporting concepts.

To be judged useful, information should have the primary characteristics of relevance and faithful representation. In addition, it should be comparable, consistent, verifiable, timely, and understandable.

The **monetary unit assumption** requires that companies include in the accounting records only transaction data that can be expressed in terms of money. The **economic entity assumption** states that economic events can be identified with a particular unit of accountability. The **time period assumption** states that the economic life of a business can be divided into artificial time periods and that meaningful accounting reports can be prepared for each period. The **going concern assumption** states that the company will continue in operation long enough to carry out its existing objectives and commitments.

The **historical cost principle** states that companies should record assets at their cost. The **fair value principle** indicates that assets and liabilities should be reported at fair value. The **revenue recognition principle** requires that companies recognize revenue in the accounting period in which the performance obligation is satisfied. The **expense recognition principle** dictates that efforts (expenses) be matched with results (revenues). The **full disclosure principle** requires that companies disclose circumstances and events that matter to financial statement users.

The **cost constraint** weighs the cost that companies incur to provide a type of information against its benefits to financial statement users.

Glossary Review

Accrual-basis accounting Accounting basis in which companies record transactions that change a company's financial statements in the periods in which the events occur. (p. 3-3).

Accruals Adjusting entries for either accrued revenues or accrued expenses. (p. 3-6).

Accrued expenses Expenses incurred but not yet paid in cash or recorded. (p. 3-15).

Accrued revenues Revenues for services performed but not yet received in cash or recorded. (p. 3-14).

Adjusted trial balance A list of accounts and their balances after the company has made all adjustments. (p. 3-21).

Adjusting entries Entries made at the end of an accounting period to ensure that companies follow the revenue recognition and expense recognition principles. (p. 3-5).

Book value The difference between the cost of a depreciable asset and its related accumulated depreciation. (p. 3-11).

Calendar year An accounting period that extends from January 1 to December 31. (p. 3-3).

Cash-basis accounting Accounting basis in which companies record revenue when they receive cash and an expense when they pay out cash. (p. 3-3).

*Comparability Ability to compare the accounting information of different companies because they use the same accounting principles. (p. 3-29).

*Consistency Use of the same accounting principles and methods from year to year within a company. (p. 3-29).

Contra asset account An account offset against an asset account on the balance sheet. (p. 3-10).

*Cost constraint Constraint that weighs the cost that companies will incur to provide the information against the benefit that financial statement users will gain from having the information available. (p. 3-31).

Deferrals Adjusting entries for either prepaid expenses or unearned revenues. (p. 3-6).

Depreciation The process of allocating the cost of an asset to expense over its useful life. (p. 3-9).

*Economic entity assumption An assumption that every economic entity can be separately identified and accounted for. (p. 3-30).

Expense recognition principle The principle that companies recognize expense in the period in which they make efforts (consume assets or incur liabilities) to generate revenue. (pp. 3-5, 3-30).

*Fair value principle An accounting principle that assets and liabilities should be reported at fair value (the price received to sell an asset or settle a liability). (p. 3-29).

*Faithful representation Information that accurately depicts what really happened. (p. 3-29).

Fiscal year An accounting period that is one year in length. (p. 3-3).

*Full disclosure principle An accounting principle that dictates that companies disclose circumstances and events that make a difference to financial statement users. (p. 3-30).

*Going concern assumption The assumption that the company will continue in operation for the foreseeable future. (p. 3-30).

*Historical cost principle An accounting principle that states that companies should record assets at their cost. (p. 3-29).

Interim periods Monthly or quarterly accounting time periods. (p. 3-3).

*Materiality A company-specific aspect of relevance. An item is material when its size makes it likely to influence the decision of an investor or creditor. (p. 3-29).

*Monetary unit assumption An assumption that requires that only those things that can be expressed in money are included in the accounting records. (p. 3-30).

Prepaid expenses (prepayments) Future expenses paid in cash before they are used or consumed. (p. 3-7).

*Relevance The quality of information that indicates the information makes a difference in a decision. (p. 3-29).

Revenue recognition principle The principle that companies recognize revenue in the accounting period in which the performance obligation is satisfied. (pp. 3-4, 3-30).

*Timely Describes information that is available to decision-makers before it loses its capacity to influence decisions. (p. 3-29).

Time period assumption An assumption that accountants can divide the economic life of a business into artificial time periods. (pp. 3-3, 3-30).

*Understandability Describes information that is presented in a clear and concise fashion so that users can interpret it and comprehend its meaning. (p. 3-29).

Unearned revenues A liability recorded for cash received before services are performed. (p. 3-11).

Useful life The length of service of a long-lived asset. (p. 3-9).

*Verifiable Describes information that occurs when independent observers, using the same methods, obtain similar results. (p. 3-29).

Practice Multiple-Choice Questions

1. **(LO 1)** The revenue recognition principle states that:
   a. revenue should be recognized in the accounting period in which a performance obligation is satisfied.
   b. expenses should be matched with revenues.
   c. the economic life of a business can be divided into artificial time periods.
   d. the fiscal year should correspond with the calendar year.

2. **(LO 1)** The time period assumption states that:
   a. companies must wait until the calendar year is completed to prepare financial statements.

   b. companies use the fiscal year to report financial information.
   c. the economic life of a business can be divided into artificial time periods.
   d. companies record information in the time period in which the events occur.

3. **(LO 1)** Which of the following statements about the accrual basis of accounting is **false**?
   a. Events that change a company's financial statements are recorded in the periods in which the events occur.
   b. Revenue is recognized in the period in which services are performed.

   c. This basis is in accordance with generally accepted accounting principles.

   d. Revenue is recorded only when cash is received, and expense is recorded only when cash is paid.

4. (LO 1) The principle or assumption dictating that efforts (expenses) should be recognized in the period in which a company consumes assets or incurs liabilities to generate revenue is the:

   a. expense recognition principle.

   b. cost assumption.

   c. time period assumption.

   d. revenue recognition principle.

5. (LO 1) Adjusting entries are made to ensure that:

   a. expenses are recognized in the period in which they are incurred.

   b. revenues are recorded in the period in which services are performed.

   c. balance sheet and income statement accounts have correct balances at the end of an accounting period.

   d. All the responses above are correct.

6. (LO 1) Each of the following is a major type (or category) of adjusting entries **except**:

   a. prepaid expenses.   **c.** accrued expenses.

   b. accrued revenues.   **d.** recognized revenues.

7. (LO 2) The trial balance shows Supplies $1,350 and Supplies Expense $0. If $600 of supplies are on hand at the end of the period, the adjusting entry is:

   a. Supplies   600
        Supplies Expense   600

   b. Supplies   750
        Supplies Expense   750

   c. Supplies Expense   750
        Supplies   750

   d. Supplies Expense   600
        Supplies   600

8. (LO 2) Adjustments for prepaid expenses:

   a. decrease assets and increase revenues.

   b. decrease expenses and increase assets.

   c. decrease assets and increase expenses.

   d. decrease revenues and increase assets.

9. (LO 2) Accumulated Depreciation is:

   a. a contra asset account.

   b. an expense account.

   c. a stockholders' equity account.

   d. a liability account.

10. (LO 2) Rivera Company computes depreciation on delivery equipment at $1,000 for the month of June. The adjusting entry to record this depreciation is as follows.

   a. Depreciation Expense   1,000
        Accumulated Depreciation—
          Rivera Company   1,000

   b. Depreciation Expense   1,000
        Equipment   1,000

   c. Depreciation Expense   1,000
        Accumulated Depreciation—
          Equipment   1,000

   d. Equipment Expense   1,000
        Accumulated Depreciation—
          Equipment   1,000

11. (LO 2) Adjustments for unearned revenues:

   a. decrease liabilities and increase revenues.

   b. have an assets-and-revenues-account relationship.

   c. increase assets and increase revenues.

   d. decrease revenues and decrease assets.

12. (LO 3) Adjustments for accrued revenues:

   a. have a liabilities-and-revenues-account relationship.

   b. have an assets-and-revenues-account relationship.

   c. decrease assets and revenues.

   d. decrease liabilities and increase revenues.

13. (LO 3) Anika Wilson earned a salary of $400 for the last week of September. She will be paid on October 1. The adjusting entry for Anika's employer at September 30 is:

   a. No entry is required.

   b. Salaries and Wages Expense   400
        Salaries and Wages Payable   400

   c. Salaries and Wages Expense   400
        Cash   400

   d. Salaries and Wages Payable   400
        Cash   400

14. (LO 4) Which of the following statements is **incorrect** concerning the adjusted trial balance?

   a. An adjusted trial balance proves the equality of the total debit balances and the total credit balances in the ledger after all adjustments are made.

   b. The adjusted trial balance provides the primary basis for the preparation of financial statements.

   c. The adjusted trial balance lists the account balances segregated by assets and liabilities.

   d. The adjusted trial balance is prepared after the adjusting entries have been journalized and posted.

*15. (LO 5) The trial balance shows Supplies $0 and Supplies Expense $1,500. If $800 of supplies are on hand at the end of the period, the adjusting entry is:

   a. debit Supplies $800 and credit Supplies Expense $800.

   b. debit Supplies Expense $800 and credit Supplies $800.

   c. debit Supplies $700 and credit Supplies Expense $700.

   d. debit Supplies Expense $700 and credit Supplies $700.

*16. (LO 6) Neutrality is a component of:

	Faithful Representation	Relevance
a.	Yes	Yes
b.	No	No
c.	Yes	No
d.	No	Yes

*17. (LO 6) Which item is a constraint in financial accounting?

   a. Comparability.   **c.** Cost.

   b. Materiality.   **d.** Consistency.

Solutions

1. a. Revenue should be recognized in the accounting period in which a performance obligation is satisfied. The other choices are incorrect because (b) defines the expense recognition principle, (c) describes the time period assumption, and (d) a company's fiscal year does not need to correspond with the calendar year.

2. c. The economic life of a business can be divided into artificial time periods. The other choices are incorrect because (a) companies report their activities on a more frequent basis and not necessarily based on a calendar year; (b) companies report financial information more frequently than annually, such as monthly or quarterly, in order to evaluate results of operations; and (d) this statement describes accrual-basis accounting.

3. d. Under the accrual basis of accounting, revenue is recognized when the performance obligation is satisfied, not when cash is received, and expense is recognized when incurred, not when cash is paid. The other choices are true statements.

4. a. The expense recognition principle dictates that companies recognize expenses in the period in which they make efforts to generate revenue. The other choices are incorrect because (b) there is no cost assumption, but the historical cost principle states that assets should be recorded at their cost; (c) the time period assumption states that the economic life of a business can be divided into artificial time periods; and (d) the revenue recognition principle indicates that revenue should be recognized in the accounting period in which a performance obligation is satisfied.

5. d. Adjusting entries are made for all the reasons noted in choices (a), (b), and (c). These choices are all true statements, but (d) is the best answer.

6. d. Unearned revenues, not recognized revenues, is one of the major categories of adjusting entries. The other choices all list one of the major categories of adjusting entries.

7. c. Debiting Supplies Expense for $750 and crediting Supplies for $750 ($1,350 − $600) will decrease Supplies and increase Supplies Expense. The other choices are incorrect because (a) will increase Supplies and decrease Supplies Expense and also for the wrong amounts, (b) will increase Supplies and decrease Supplies Expense, and (d) will cause Supplies to have an incorrect balance of $750 ($1,350 − $600) and Supplies Expense to have an incorrect balance of $600 ($0 + $600).

8. c. Adjustments for prepaid expenses decrease assets and increase expenses. The other choices are incorrect because an adjusting entry for prepaid expenses (a) increases expenses, not revenues; (b) increases, not decreases, expenses and decreases, not increases, assets; and (d) increases, not decreases, revenues and decreases, not increases, assets.

9. a. Accumulated Depreciation is a contra asset account; it is offset against an asset account on the balance sheet. The other choices are incorrect because Accumulated Depreciation is not (b) an expense account or reported on the income statement, (c) a stockholders' equity account, or (d) a liability account.

10. c. The adjusting entry is to debit Depreciation Expense and credit Accumulated Depreciation—Equipment. The other choices are incorrect because (a) the contra asset account title includes the asset being depreciated, not the company name; (b) the credit should be to the contra asset account, not directly to the asset; and (d) the debit for this entry should be Depreciation Expense, not Equipment Expense.

11. a. Adjustments for unearned revenues will consist of a debit (decrease) to unearned revenues (a liability) and a credit (increase) to a revenue account. Choices (b), (c), and (d) are incorrect because adjustments for unearned revenues will increase revenues but will have no effect on assets.

12. b. Adjustments for accrued revenues will have an assets-and-revenues-account relationship. Choices (a) and (d) are incorrect because adjustments for accrued revenues have no effect on liabilities. Choice (c) is incorrect because these adjustments will increase, not decrease, both assets and revenues.

13. b. The adjusting entry should be to debit Salaries and Wages Expense for $400 and credit Salaries and Wages Payable for $400. The other choices are incorrect because (a) if an adjusting entry is not made, the amount of money owed (liability) that is shown on the balance sheet will be understated and the amount of salaries and wages expense will also be understated; (c) the credit account is incorrect as adjusting entries never affect cash; and (d) the debit account should be Salaries and Wages Expense and the credit account should be Salaries and Wages Payable. Adjusting entries never affect cash.

14. c. The accounts on the trial balance can be segregated by the balance in the account—either debit or credit—not whether they are assets or liabilities. All accounts in the ledger are included in the adjusted trial balance, not just assets and liabilities. The other choices are true statements.

*15. a. This adjusting entry correctly states the Supplies account at $800 ($0 + $800) and the Supplies Expense account at $700 ($1,500 − $800). The other choices are incorrect because (b) will cause the Supplies account to have a credit balance (assets have a normal debit balance) and the Supplies Expense account to be stated at $2,300, which is too high; (c) will result in a $700 balance in the Supplies account ($100 too low) and an $800 balance in the Supplies Expense account ($100 too high); and (d) will cause the Supplies account to have a credit balance (assets have a normal debit balance) and the Supplies Expense account to be stated at $2,200, which is too high.

*16. c. Neutrality is one of the enhancing qualities that makes information more representationally faithful, not more relevant. Therefore, choices (a), (b), and (d) are incorrect.

*17. c. Cost is a constraint in financial accounting. The other choices are all enhancing qualities of useful information.

Practice Brief Exercises

Indicate why adjusting entries are needed.

1. (LO 1) The ledger of Dey Company includes the following accounts. Explain why each account may need adjustment.

a. Supplies.

b. Unearned Service Revenue.

c. Salaries and Wages Payable.

d. Interest Payable.

Solution

1. **a.** Supplies: to recognize supplies used during the period.

   b. Unearned Service Revenue: to record revenue for services performed.

   c. Salaries and Wages Payable: to recognize salaries and wages accrual to employees at the end of a reporting period.

   d. Interest Payable: to recognize interest accrued but unpaid on notes payable.

2. **(LO 2)** At the end of its first year, the trial balance of Denton Company shows Equipment of $40,000 and zero balances in Accumulated Depreciation—Equipment and Depreciation Expense. Depreciation for the year is estimated to be $8,000. Prepare the adjusting entry for depreciation at December 31, post the adjustments to T-accounts, and indicate the balance sheet presentation of the equipment at December 31.

Prepare adjusting entry for depreciation.

Solution

2. Dec. 31 | Depreciation Expense   8,000
                   | Accumulated Depreciation—Equipment   8,000

Depreciation Expense	**Accum. Depreciation—Equipment**
12/31 8,000	12/31 8,000

Balance Sheet:

Equipment	$40,000	
Less: Accumulated Depreciation—Equipment	8,000	$32,000

3. **(LO 3)** You are asked to prepare the following accrual adjusting entries at December 31.

   1. Services performed but not recorded are $4,200.

   2. Utility expenses incurred but not paid or recorded are $660.

   3. Salaries and wages earned by employees of $3,000 are unpaid.

Use the following account titles: Accounts Payable, Accounts Receivable, Service Revenue, Salaries and Wages Expense, Salaries and Wages Payable, and Utility Expense.

Prepare adjusting entries for accruals.

Solution

3.	Dec. 31	Accounts Receivable	4,200	
		Service Revenue		4,200
	31	Utility Expense	660	
		Accounts Payable		660
	31	Salaries and Wages Expense	3,000	
		Salaries and Wages Payable		3,000

4. **(LO 1, 2, 3)** The trial balance for Blair Company includes the following balance sheet accounts. Identify the accounts that may require adjustment. For each account that requires adjustment, indicate (a) the type of adjusting entry (prepaid expense, unearned revenue, accrued revenue, or accrued expense) and (b) the related account in the adjusting entry.

Analyze accounts in an unadjusted trial balance.

Accounts Receivable	Interest Payable
Supplies	Unearned Service Revenue
Prepaid Insurance	

Solution

4.	Account	Type of Adjustment	Related Account
	Accounts Receivable	Accrued Revenue	Service Revenue
	Supplies	Prepaid Expense	Supplies Expense
	Prepaid Insurance	Prepaid Expense	Insurance Expense
	Interest Payable	Accrued Expense	Interest Expense
	Unearned Service Revenue	Unearned Revenue	Service Revenue

Prepare an income statement from an adjusted trial balance.

5. (LO 4) The adjusted trial balance of Harmony Company includes the following accounts at December 31, 2022: Cash $12,000, Retained Earnings $22,000, Dividends $3,000, Service Revenue $41,000, Rent Expense $900, Salaries and Wages Expense $6,000, Supplies Expense $700, and Depreciation Expense $1,800. Prepare an income statement for the year.

Solution

5.

Harmony Company
Income Statement
For the Year Ended December 31, 2022

Revenues		
Service revenue		$41,000
Expenses		
Salaries and wages expense	$6,000	
Rent expense	900	
Depreciation expense	1,800	
Supplies expense	700	
Total expenses		9,400
Net income		$31,600

Practice Exercises

Prepare adjusting entries.

1. (LO 2, 3) Wendy Penn, D.D.S., opened a dental practice on January 1, 2022. During the first month of operations, the following transactions occurred.

1. Performed services for patients totaling $785, which had not yet been recorded.

2. Utility expenses incurred but not paid or recorded prior to January 31 totaled $250.

3. Purchased dental equipment on January 1 for $90,000, paying $25,000 in cash and signing a $65,000, 3-year note payable. The equipment depreciates $500 per month. Interest is $550 per month and will be paid when the note is repaid.

4. Purchased a 1-year malpractice insurance policy on January 1 for $15,000.

5. Purchased $1,700 of dental supplies. On January 31, determined that $300 of supplies were on hand.

Instructions

Prepare the adjusting entries on January 31. Account titles are Accumulated Depreciation—Equipment, Depreciation Expense, Service Revenue, Accounts Receivable, Insurance Expense, Interest Expense, Interest Payable, Prepaid Insurance, Supplies, Supplies Expense, Utilities Expense, and Utilities Payable.

Solution

1.	Jan. 31	Accounts Receivable	785	
		Service Revenue		785
	31	Utilities Expense	250	
		Utilities Payable		250
	31	Depreciation Expense	500	
		Accumulated Depreciation—Equipment		500
	31	Interest Expense	550	
		Interest Payable		550
	31	Insurance Expense ($15,000 ÷ 12)	1,250	
		Prepaid Insurance		1,250
	31	Supplies Expense ($1,700 – $300)	1,400	
		Supplies		1,400

2. (LO 2, 3, 4) The income statement of Bragg Co. for the month of July shows net income of $1,400 based on Service Revenue $5,500, Salaries and Wages Expense $2,300, Supplies Expense $1,200, and Utilities Expense $600. In reviewing the statement, you discover the following.

Prepare correct income statement.

1. Insurance expired during July of $450 was omitted.

2. Supplies expense includes $300 of supplies that are still on hand at July 31.

3. Depreciation on equipment of $180 was omitted.

4. Unpaid salaries and wages at July 31 of $400 were not included.

5. Services performed but unrecorded totaled $600.

Instructions

Prepare a correct income statement for July 2022.

Solution

2.

Bragg Co.
Income Statement
For the Month Ended July 31, 2022

Revenues		
Service revenue ($5,500 + $600)		$6,100
Expenses		
Salaries and wages expense ($2,300 + $400)	$2,700	
Supplies expense ($1,200 − $300)	900	
Utilities expense	600	
Insurance expense	450	
Depreciation expense	180	
Total expenses		4,830
Net income		$1,270

Practice Problem

(LO 2, 3) The Green Thumb Lawn Care Inc. began operations on April 1. At April 30, the trial balance shows the following balances for selected accounts.

Prepare adjusting entries from selected data.

Prepaid Insurance	$ 3,600
Equipment	28,000
Notes Payable	20,000
Unearned Service Revenue	4,200
Service Revenue	1,800

Analysis reveals the following additional data.

1. Prepaid insurance is the cost of a 2-year insurance policy, effective April 1.

2. Depreciation on the equipment is $500 per month.

3. The note payable is dated April 1. It is a 6-month, 12% note. Interest will be paid upon note repayment.

4. Seven customers paid for the company's 6-month lawn service package of $600 beginning in April. The company performed services for these customers in April.

5. Lawn services performed for other customers but not recorded at April 30 totaled $1,500.

Instructions

Prepare the adjusting entries for the month of April. Show computations.

Solution

GENERAL JOURNAL					J1
Date	Account Titles and Explanation	Ref.	Debit	Credit	
	Adjusting Entries				
Apr. 30	Insurance Expense		150		
	Prepaid Insurance			150	
	(To record insurance expired:				
	$3,600 ÷ 24 = $150 per month)				
30	Depreciation Expense		500		
	Accumulated Depreciation—Equipment			500	
	(To record monthly depreciation)				
30	Interest Expense		200		
	Interest Payable			200	
	(To record interest on notes payable:				
	$20,000 \times 12\% \times \frac{1}{12} = $200)				
30	Unearned Service Revenue		700		
	Service Revenue			700	
	(To record revenue for services				
	performed: $600 ÷ 6 = $100;				
	$100 per month × 7 = $700)				
30	Accounts Receivable		1,500		
	Service Revenue			1,500	
	(To record revenue for services				
	performed)				

WileyPLUS

Brief Exercises, DO IT! Exercises, Exercises, Problems, and many additional resources are available for practice in WileyPLUS.

Note: All asterisked Questions, Exercises, and Problems relate to material in the appendices to this chapter.

Questions

1. a. How does the time period assumption affect an accountant's analysis of business transactions?

b. Explain the terms fiscal year, calendar year, and interim periods.

2. Identify and state two generally accepted accounting principles that relate to adjusting the accounts.

3. What are the five steps of the revenue recognition principle?

4. Susan Zupan, a lawyer, accepts a legal engagement in March, performs the work in April, and is paid in May. If Zupan's law firm prepares monthly financial statements, when should it recognize revenue from this engagement? Why?

5. Why do accrual-basis financial statements provide more useful information than cash-basis statements?

6. In completing the engagement in Question 4, Zupan incurs and pays no costs in March, incurs and pays $2,000 of costs in April, and pays $2,500 of costs in May (incurred in April). How much expense should the firm deduct from revenues in the month when it recognizes the revenue? Why?

7. "Adjusting entries are required by the historical cost principle of accounting." Explain why this statement is true or false.

8. Why may a trial balance not contain up-to-date and complete financial information?

9. Distinguish between the two categories of adjusting entries, and identify the types of adjustments applicable to each category.

10. What is the debit/credit effect of a prepaid expense adjusting entry?

11. "Depreciation is a valuation process that results in the reporting of the fair value of the asset." Explain why this statement is true or false.

12. Explain the differences between depreciation expense and accumulated depreciation.

13. J. Brownlee Company purchased equipment for $18,000. By the current balance sheet date, $6,000 had been depreciated. Indicate the balance sheet presentation of the data.

14. What is the debit/credit effect of an unearned revenue adjusting entry?

15. Whistler Corp. performed services for a customer but has not yet recorded payment or recorded any entry related to the work. Which of the following accounts are involved in the adjusting entry: (a) asset, (b) liability, (c) revenue, or (d) expense? For the accounts selected, indicate whether they would be debited or credited in the entry.

16. A company fails to recognize an expense incurred but not paid. Indicate which of the following accounts is debited and which is credited in the adjusting entry: (a) asset, (b) liability, (c) revenue, or (d) expense.

17. A company makes an accrued revenue adjusting entry for $900 and an accrued expense adjusting entry for $700. How much was net income understated prior to these entries? Explain.

18. On January 9, a company pays $5,000 for salaries and wages of which $2,000 was reported as Salaries and Wages Payable on December 31. Give the entry to record the payment.

19. For each of the following items before adjustment, indicate the type of adjusting entry (prepaid expense, unearned revenue, accrued revenue, or accrued expense) that is needed to correct the misstatement. If an item could result in more than one type of adjusting entry, indicate each of the types.

a. Assets are understated.

b. Liabilities are overstated.

c. Liabilities are understated.

d. Expenses are understated.

e. Assets are overstated.

f. Revenue is understated.

20. One-half of the adjusting entry is given below. Indicate the account title for the other half of the entry.

a. Salaries and Wages Expense is debited.

b. Depreciation Expense is debited.

c. Interest Payable is credited.

d. Supplies is credited.

e. Accounts Receivable is debited.

f. Unearned Service Revenue is debited.

21. "An adjusting entry may affect more than one balance sheet or income statement account." Explain why this statement is true or false.

22. Why is it possible to prepare financial statements directly from an adjusted trial balance?

*23. Dashan Company debits Supplies Expense for all purchases of supplies and credits Rent Revenue for all advanced rentals. For each type of adjustment, give the adjusting entry.

*24. a. What is the primary objective of financial reporting?

b. Identify the characteristics of useful accounting information.

*25. Dan Fineman, the president of King Company, is pleased. King substantially increased its net income in 2022 while keeping its unit inventory relatively the same. Howard Gross, chief accountant, cautions Dan, however. Gross says that since King changed its method of inventory valuation, there is a consistency problem and it is difficult to determine whether King is better off. Is Gross correct? Why or why not?

*26. What is the distinction between comparability and consistency?

*27. Describe the constraint inherent in the presentation of accounting information.

*28. Laurie Belk is president of Better Books. She has no accounting background. Belk cannot understand why fair value is not used as the basis for all accounting measurement and reporting. Discuss.

*29. What is the economic entity assumption? Give an example of its violation.

Brief Exercises

BE3.1 (LO 1), K Number the following steps of the revenue recognition process (from 1–5) to place in the correct order.

Identify the order of the five steps in the revenue recognition process.

a. _____ Allocate the transaction price to the separate performance obligations.

b. _____ Identify the contract with customers.

c. _____ Identify the separate performance obligations in the contract.

d. _____ Recognize revenue when each performance obligation is satisfied.

e. _____ Determine the transaction price.

BE3.2 (LO 1), C Transactions that affect net income do not necessarily affect cash. Identify the effect, if any, that each of the following transactions would have upon cash and net income. The first transaction has been completed as an example.

Identify impact of transactions on cash and net income.

	Cash	Net Income
a. Purchased $100 of supplies for cash.	−$100	$0

b. Recorded an adjusting entry to record use of $20 of the above supplies.

c. Made sales of $1,300, all on account.

d. Received $800 from customers in payment of their accounts.

e. Purchased equipment for cash, $2,500.

f. Recorded depreciation of building for period used, $600.

Indicate why adjusting entries are needed.

BE3.3 (LO 1), C The ledger of Melmann Company includes the following accounts. Explain why each account may require adjustment.

   a. Prepaid Insurance.

   b. Depreciation Expense.

   c. Unearned Service Revenue.

   d. Interest Payable.

Identify the major types of adjusting entries.

BE3.4 (LO 1), AN Cortina Company accumulates the following adjustment data at December 31. Indicate (1) the type of adjustment (prepaid expense, accrued revenue, and so on) and (2) the status of the accounts before adjustment (for example, "assets understated and revenues understated").

   a. Supplies of $400 are on hand. Supplies account shows $1,600 balance.

   b. Services performed but unbilled total $700.

   c. Interest of $300 has accumulated (and not been paid) on a note payable.

   d. Rent collected in advance totaling $1,100 has been earned.

Prepare adjusting entry for supplies.

BE3.5 (LO 2), AP Lahey Advertising Company's trial balance at December 31 shows Supplies $8,800 and Supplies Expense $0. On December 31, there are $1,100 of supplies on hand. Prepare the adjusting entry at December 31 and, using T-accounts, enter the balances in the accounts, post the adjusting entry, and indicate the adjusted balance in each account.

Prepare adjusting entry for depreciation.

BE3.6 (LO 2), AP At the end of its first year, the trial balance of Rayburn Company shows Equipment $22,000 and zero balances in Accumulated Depreciation—Equipment and Depreciation Expense. Depreciation for the year is estimated to be $2,750. Prepare the annual adjusting entry for depreciation at December 31, post the adjustments to T-accounts, and indicate the balance sheet presentation of the equipment at December 31.

Prepare adjusting entry for prepaid expense.

BE3.7 (LO 2), AP On July 1, 2022, Ling Co. pays $12,400 to Marsh Insurance Co. for a 2-year insurance contract. Both companies have fiscal years ending December 31. For Ling Co., journalize and post the entry on July 1 and the annual adjusting entry on December 31.

Prepare adjusting entry for unearned revenue.

BE3.8 (LO 2), AP On July 1, 2022, Ling Co. pays $12,400 to Marsh Insurance Co. for a 2-year insurance contract. Both companies have fiscal years ending December 31. Journalize and post the entry on July 1 and the annual adjusting entry on December 31 for Marsh Insurance Co. Marsh uses the accounts Unearned Service Revenue and Service Revenue.

Prepare adjusting entries for deferrals.

BE3.9 (LO 2), AP The unadjusted trial balance of Northern Exposure Inc. had these balances for the following selected accounts: Supplies $3,100, Unearned Service Revenue $8,200, and Prepaid Rent $1,200. At the end of the period, a count showed $500 of supplies on hand. Services of $2,900 had been performed related to the unearned revenue account, and one month's rent, worth $400, had been consumed by Northern Exposure. Record the required adjusting entries related to these events.

Prepare adjusting entries for accruals.

BE3.10 (LO 3), AP The bookkeeper for Tran Company asks you to prepare the following accrual adjusting entries at December 31. Use these account titles: Service Revenue, Accounts Receivable, Interest Expense, Interest Payable, Salaries and Wages Expense, and Salaries and Wages Payable.

   a. Interest on notes payable of $300 should be accrued.

   b. Services performed but unbilled totals $1,700.

   c. Salaries of $780 earned by employees have not been recorded or paid.

Prepare adjusting entries for accruals.

BE3.11 (LO 3), AP At December 31 of the current year, Cullen Corporation had a number of items that were not reflected in its accounting records. Maintenance and repair costs of $770 were incurred but not paid. Utilities costing $240 were used but not paid, and use of a warehouse space worth $1,900 was provided to a tenant who had not been billed as of the end of the month. Record the required adjusting entries related to these events.

Analyze accounts in a trial balance.

BE3.12 (LO 2, 3), AN The trial balance of Woods Company includes the following balance sheet accounts. Identify the accounts that might require adjustment. For each account that requires adjustment, indicate (1) the type of adjusting entry (prepaid expense, unearned revenue, accrued revenue, and accrued expense) and (2) the related account in the adjusting entry.

   a. Accounts Receivable.

   b. Prepaid Insurance.

   c. Cash.

   d. Accumulated Depreciation—Equipment.

   e. Dividends.

   f. Interest Payable.

   g. Unearned Service Revenue.

BE3.13 (LO 4), AP The adjusted trial balance of Levin Corporation at December 31, 2022, includes the following selected accounts: Retained Earnings $17,200, Dividends $6,000, Service Revenue $32,600, Salaries and Wages Expense $14,000, Insurance Expense $1,800, Rent Expense $3,900, Supplies Expense $1,500, and Depreciation Expense $1,000. Prepare an income statement for the year.

Prepare an income statement from an adjusted trial balance.

BE3.14 (LO 4), AP The adjusted trial balance of Sharp Corporation at December 31, 2022, includes the following accounts: Retained Earnings $18,000 and Dividends $7,000. The balance in Retained Earnings is the balance as of January 1. Prepare a retained earnings statement for the year assuming net income is $9,000.

Prepare a retained earnings statement from an adjusted trial balance.

*****BE3.15 (LO 5), AP** Mayes Company records all prepayments in income statement accounts. At April 30, the trial balance shows Supplies Expense $2,800, Service Revenue $9,200, and zero balances in related balance sheet accounts. Prepare the adjusting entries at April 30 assuming (a) $700 of supplies on hand and (b) $3,000 of service revenue should be reported as unearned.

Prepare adjusting entries under alternative treatment of deferrals.

*****BE3.16 (LO 6), C** The accompanying chart shows the qualitative characteristics of useful accounting information. Fill in the blanks.

Identify characteristics of useful information.

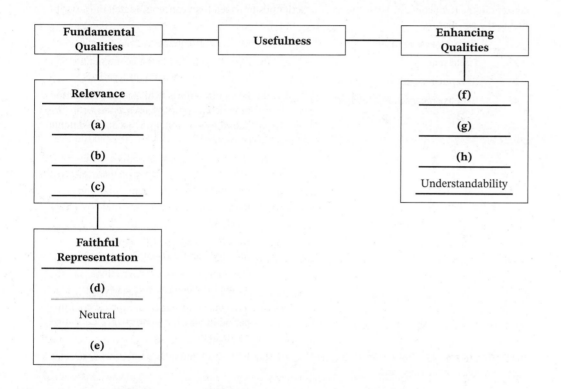

*****BE3.17 (LO 6), C** Given the characteristics of useful accounting information, complete each of the following statements.

Identify characteristics of useful information.

a. For information to be ____, it should have predictive value, confirmatory value, and be material.

b. _____ means that information accurately depicts what really happened.

c. _____ means using the same accounting principles and methods from year to year within a company.

*****BE3.18 (LO 6), C** Here are some qualitative characteristics of useful accounting information:

Identify characteristics of useful information.

1. Predictive value
2. Neutral
3. Verifiable
4. Timely

Match each qualitative characteristic to one of the following statements.

_____ a. Accounting information should help provide accurate expectations about future events.

_____ b. Accounting information cannot be selected, prepared, or presented to favor one set of interested users over another.

_____ c. Independent observers, using the same methods, are able to obtain similar results.

_____ d. Accounting information must be available to decision-makers before it loses its capacity to influence their decisions.

Define full disclosure principle.

* **BE3.19 (LO 6), K** Select the response that completes the following statement correctly. The full disclosure principle dictates that:

a. financial statements should disclose all assets at their cost.

b. financial statements should disclose only those events that can be measured in currency.

c. financial statements should disclose all events and circumstances that would matter to users of financial statements.

d. financial statements should not be relied on unless an auditor has expressed an unqualified opinion on them.

DO IT! Exercises

Identify timing concepts.

DO IT! 3.1 (LO 1), C The following is a list of concepts in the left column, with a description of the concept in the right column. There are more descriptions provided than concepts. Match the description to the concept.

1. _____ Cash-basis accounting.

2. _____ Fiscal year.

3. _____ Revenue recognition principle.

4. _____ Expense recognition principle.

a. Monthly and quarterly time periods.

b. Accountants divide the economic life of a business into artificial time periods.

c. Recognize efforts (expenses) in the period in which a company uses assets or incurs liabilities to generate accomplishments (revenues).

d. Companies record revenues when they receive cash and record expenses when they pay out cash.

e. An accounting time period that is one year in length.

f. An accounting time period that starts on January 1 and ends on December 31.

g. Companies record transactions in the period in which the events occur.

h. Recognize revenue in the accounting period in which a performance obligation is satisfied.

Prepare adjusting entries for deferrals.

DO IT! 3.2 (LO 2), AP The ledger of Herrera, Inc. on March 31, 2022, includes the following selected accounts before adjusting entries.

	Debit	Credit
Prepaid Insurance	$ 2,400	
Supplies	2,500	
Equipment	30,000	
Unearned Service Revenue		$9,000

An analysis of the accounts shows the following.

1. Insurance expires at the rate of $300 per month.

2. Supplies on hand total $1,100.

3. The equipment depreciates at $500 per month.

4. During March, services were performed for two-fifths of the unearned service revenue.

Prepare the adjusting entries for the month of March.

Prepare adjusting entries for accruals.

DO IT! 3.3 (LO 3), AP Javier Computer Services began operations in July 2022. At the end of the month, the company prepares monthly financial statements. It has the following information for the month.

1. At July 31, the company owed employees $1,300 in salaries that the company will pay in August.

2. On July 1, the company borrowed $20,000 from a local bank on a 10-year note. The annual interest rate is 12%. Interest is paid annually.

3. Service revenue unrecorded in July totaled $2,400.

Prepare the adjusting entries needed at July 31, 2022.

DO IT! 3.4 (LO 4), AP Lumina Company was organized on April 1, 2022. The company prepares quarterly financial statements. The adjusted trial balance at June 30 is shown here.

	Debit		Credit
Cash	$ 5,360	Accumulated Depreciation—	
Accounts Receivable	480	Equipment	$ 700
Prepaid Rent	720	Notes Payable	4,000
Supplies	920	Accounts Payable	790
Equipment	12,000	Salaries and Wages Payable	300
Dividends	500	Interest Payable	40
Salaries and Wages Expense	7,400	Unearned Rent Revenue	400
Rent Expense	1,200	Common Stock	11,200
Depreciation Expense	700	Service Revenue	11,360
Supplies Expense	160	Rent Revenue	1,100
Utilities Expense	410		$29,890
Interest Expense	40		
	$29,890		

a. Determine the net income for the quarter April 1 to June 30.

b. Determine the total assets and total liabilities at June 30, 2022, for Lumina Company.

c. Determine the amount that appears for Retained Earnings at June 30, 2022.

Exercises

E3.1 (LO 1), C Ian Muse has prepared the following list of statements about the time period assumption.

1. Adjusting entries would not be necessary if a company's life were not divided into artificial time periods.

2. The IRS requires companies to file annual tax returns.

3. Accountants divide the economic life of a business into artificial time periods, but all transactions affect only one of these periods.

4. Accounting time periods are generally a month, a quarter, or a year.

5. A time period lasting one year is called an interim period.

6. All fiscal years are calendar years, but not all calendar years are fiscal years.

Instructions

Identify each statement as true or false. If false, indicate how to correct the statement.

E3.2 (LO 1), E Writing On numerous occasions, proposals have surfaced to put the federal government on the accrual basis of accounting. This is no small issue. If this basis were used, it would mean that billions in unrecorded liabilities would have to be booked, and the federal deficit would increase substantially.

Instructions

a. What is the difference between accrual-basis accounting and cash-basis accounting?

b. Why would politicians prefer the cash basis over the accrual basis?

c. Write a letter to your senator explaining why the federal government should adopt the accrual basis of accounting.

E3.3 (LO 1), AP Primo Industries collected $105,000 from customers in 2022. Of the amount collected, $25,000 was for services performed in 2021. In addition, Primo performed services worth $40,000 in 2022, which will not be collected until 2023.

Primo Industries also paid $72,000 for expenses in 2022. Of the amount paid, $30,000 was for expenses incurred on account in 2021. In addition, Primo incurred $42,000 of expenses in 2022, which will not be paid until 2023.

Instructions

a. Compute 2022 cash-basis net income.

b. Compute 2022 accrual-basis net income.

Identify point of revenue recognition.

E3.4 (LO 1), C The following independent situations require professional judgment for determining when to recognize revenue from the transactions.

a. **Southwest Airlines** sells you an advance-purchase airline ticket in September for your flight home in December.

b. **Ultimate Electronics** sells you a home theater on a "no money down and full payment in three months" promotional deal.

c. The **Toronto Blue Jays** sell season tickets online to games in the Skydome. Fans can purchase the tickets at any time, although the season doesn't officially begin until April. The major league baseball season runs from April through October.

d. **RBC Financial Group** loans money on August 1. The loan and the interest are repayable in full in November.

e. In August, a customer orders a sweater from the **Target** website, paying with a Target credit card. The sweater arrives in September. Target sends a bill in October and receives payment in October.

Instructions

Determine when revenue should be recognized in each of the above situations.

Determine the type of adjusting entry needed.

E3.5 (LO 2, 3), AP Hart Corporation encounters the following situations:

1. Hart collects $1,300 from a customer in 2022 for services to be performed in 2023.

2. Hart incurs utility expense which is not yet paid in cash or recorded.

3. Hart's employees worked 3 days in 2022 but will not be paid until 2023.

4. Hart performs services for customers but has not yet received cash or recorded the transaction.

5. Hart paid $2,400 rent on December 1 for the 4 months starting December 1.

6. Hart received cash for future services and recorded a liability until the service was performed.

7. Hart performed consulting services for a client in December 2022. On December 31, it had not billed the client for services performed of $1,200.

8. Hart paid cash for an expense and recorded an asset until the item was used up.

9. Hart purchased $900 of supplies in 2022; at year-end, $400 of supplies remain unused.

10. Hart purchased equipment on January 1, 2022; the equipment will be used for 5 years.

11. Hart borrowed $10,000 on October 1, 2022, signing an 8% 1-year note payable. Both the interest and the note will be paid in 1 year.

Instructions

Identify what type of adjusting entry (prepaid expense, unearned revenue, accrued expense, or accrued revenue) is needed in each situation at December 31, 2022.

Prepare adjusting entries from selected data.

E3.6 (LO 2, 3), AN Verne Cova Company has the following balances in selected accounts on December 31, 2022.

Accounts Receivable	$ –0–
Accumulated Depreciation—Equipment	–0–
Equipment	7,000
Interest Payable	–0–
Notes Payable	10,000
Prepaid Insurance	2,100
Salaries and Wages Payable	–0–
Supplies	2,450
Unearned Service Revenue	30,000

All the accounts have normal balances. The following information has been gathered at December 31, 2022.

1. Verne Cova Company borrowed $10,000 by signing a 12%, 1-year note on September 1, 2022. Interest will be paid when the note is repaid.

2. A count of supplies on December 31, 2022, indicates that supplies of $900 are on hand.

3. Depreciation on the equipment for 2022 is $1,000.

4. Verne Cova paid $2,100 for 12 months of insurance coverage on June 1, 2022.

5. On December 1, 2022, Verne Cova collected $30,000 for consulting services to be performed evenly from December 1, 2022, through March 31, 2023.

6. Verne Cova performed consulting services for a client in December 2022. The client will be billed $4,200.

7. Verne Cova pays its employees total salaries of $9,000 every Monday for the preceding 5-day week (Monday through Friday). On Monday, December 29, employees were paid for the week ending December 26. All employees worked the last 3 days of 2022.

Instructions

Prepare adjusting entries for the seven items described above. Verne Cova prepares adjustments annually.

E3.7 (LO 2, 3), AN Wang Company accumulates the following adjustment data at December 31.

Identify types of adjustments and accounts before adjustment.

a. Services performed but unbilled total $600.

b. Store supplies of $160 are on hand. The supplies account shows a $1,900 balance.

c. Utility expenses of $275 are unpaid and unrecorded.

d. Services performed of $490 have been collected in advance.

e. Salaries of $620 are unpaid and unrecorded.

f. Prepaid insurance totaling $400 has expired.

Instructions

For each item, indicate (1) the type of adjustment (prepaid expense, unearned revenue, accrued revenue, or accrued expense) and (2) the status of the accounts before adjustment (overstated or understated).

E3.8 (LO 2, 3), AP The ledger of Howard Rental Agency on March 31 of the current year includes the following selected accounts before adjusting entries have been prepared.

Prepare adjusting entries from selected account data.

	Debit	Credit
Supplies	$ 3,000	
Prepaid Insurance	3,600	
Equipment	25,000	
Accumulated		
Depreciation—Equipment		$ 8,400
Notes Payable		20,000
Unearned Rent Revenue		12,400
Rent Revenue		60,000
Interest Expense	0	
Salaries and Wages Expense	14,000	

An analysis of the accounts shows the following.

1. The equipment depreciates $280 per month.

2. Half of the unearned rent revenue was earned during the quarter.

3. Interest of $400 should be accrued on the notes payable.

4. Supplies on hand total $850.

5. Insurance expires at the rate of $400 per month.

Instructions

Prepare the adjusting entries at March 31, assuming that adjusting entries are made quarterly. Additional accounts are Depreciation Expense, Insurance Expense, Interest Payable, and Supplies Expense.

E3.9 (LO 2, 3), AP Al Medina, D.D.S., opened an incorporated dental practice on January 1, 2022. During the first month of operations, the following transactions occurred.

Prepare adjusting entries.

1. Performed services for patients who had dental plan insurance. At January 31, $760 of such services was completed but not yet billed to the insurance companies.

2. Utility expenses incurred but not paid or recorded prior to January 31 totaled $450.

3. Purchased dental equipment on January 1 for $80,000, paying $20,000 in cash and signing a $60,000, 3-year note payable (interest is paid each December 31). The equipment depreciates $400 per month. Interest is $500 per month.

4. Purchased a 1-year malpractice insurance policy on January 1 for $24,000.

5. Purchased $1,750 of dental supplies (recorded as increase to Supplies). On January 31, determined that $550 of supplies were on hand.

Instructions

Prepare the adjusting entries on January 31. Account titles are Accumulated Depreciation—Equipment, Depreciation Expense, Service Revenue, Accounts Receivable, Insurance Expense, Interest Expense, Interest Payable, Prepaid Insurance, Supplies, Supplies Expense, Utilities Expense, and Accounts Payable.

Prepare adjusting entries.

E3.10 (LO 2, 3), AN The trial balance for Pioneer Advertising Inc. is shown in Illustration 3.4. Instead of the adjusting entries shown in the text at October 31, assume the following adjustment data.

1. Supplies on hand at October 31 total $500.
2. Expired insurance for the month is $100.
3. Depreciation for the month is $50.
4. Services related to unearned service revenue in October worth $600 were performed.
5. Services performed but not recorded at October 31 are $300.
6. Interest to be accrued at October 31 is $95.
7. Salaries to be accrued at October 31 are $1,625.

Instructions

Prepare the adjusting entries for the items above.

Prepare adjusting entries from selected account data.

E3.11 (LO 2, 3), AP The ledger of Armour Lake Lumber Supply on July 31, 2022, includes the following selected accounts before adjusting entries have been prepared.

	Debit	Credit
Supplies	$ 24,000	
Prepaid Rent	3,600	
Buildings	250,000	
Accumulated Depreciation—Buildings		$140,000
Unearned Service Revenue		11,500

An analysis of the company's accounts shows the following.

1. Supplies on hand at the end of the month totaled $18,600.
2. The balance in Prepaid Rent represents 4 months of rent costs.
3. Employees were owed $3,100 related to unpaid and unrecorded salaries and wages.
4. Depreciation on buildings is $6,000 per year.
5. During the month, the company satisfied obligations worth $4,700 related to the Unearned Service Revenue account.
6. Unpaid and unrecorded maintenance and repairs costs were $2,300.

Instructions

Prepare the adjusting entries at July 31 assuming that adjusting entries are made monthly. Use additional accounts as needed.

Prepare a correct income statement.

E3.12 (LO 2, 3), AN The income statement of Norski Co. for the month of July shows net income of $2,000 based on Service Revenue $5,500, Salaries and Wages Expense $2,100, Supplies Expense $900, and Utilities Expense $500. In reviewing the statement, you discover the following:

1. Insurance expired during July of $350 was omitted.
2. Supplies expense includes $200 of supplies that are still on hand at July 31.
3. Depreciation on equipment of $150 was omitted.
4. Unpaid wages at July 31 of $360 were not included.
5. Services performed but unrecorded totaled $700.

Instructions

Prepare a correct income statement for July 2022.

E3.13 (LO 2, 3), AN Selected accounts of Villa Company are shown here.

Journalize basic transactions and adjusting entries.

Supplies Expense	
July 31	750

Salaries and Wages Payable	
July 31	1,000

Salaries and Wages Expense	
July 15	1,000
31	1,000

Accounts Receivable	
July 31	500

Service Revenue	
July 14	3,800
31	900
31	500

Unearned Service Revenue		
July 31	900	July 1	Bal. 1,500
		20	600

Supplies	
July 1	Bal. 1,100	July 31	750
10	200		

Instructions

After analyzing the accounts, journalize (a) the July transactions and (b) the adjusting entries that were made on July 31. (*Hint:* July transactions were for cash.)

E3.14 (LO 2, 3), AN This is a partial adjusted trial balance of Ramon Company.

Analyze adjusted data.

Ramon Company		
Adjusted Trial Balance (partial)		
January 31, 2022		
	Debit	Credit
Supplies	$ 700	
Prepaid Insurance	1,560	
Salaries and Wages Payable		$1,060
Unearned Service Revenue		750
Supplies Expense	950	
Insurance Expense	520	
Salaries and Wages Expense	1,800	
Service Revenue		4,000

Instructions

Answer these questions, assuming the year begins January 1.

a. If the amount in Supplies Expense is the January 31 adjusting entry and $300 of supplies was purchased in January, what was the balance in Supplies on January 1?

b. If the amount in Insurance Expense is the January 31 adjusting entry and the original insurance premium was for 1 year, what was the total premium and when was the policy purchased?

c. If $2,500 of salaries owed were paid in January, what was the balance in Salaries and Wages Payable at December 31, 2021?

d. If $1,800 was received in January for services performed in January (no services are performed on credit), what was the balance in Unearned Service Revenue at December 31, 2021?

E3.15 (LO 2, 3), AN On December 31, 2022, Waters Company prepared an income statement and balance sheet, but failed to take into account three adjusting entries. The balance sheet showed total assets $150,000, total liabilities $70,000, and stockholders' equity $80,000. The incorrect income statement showed net income of $70,000.

Determine effect of adjusting entries.

The data for the three adjusting entries were:

1. Salaries and wages amounting to $10,000 for the last 2 days in December were not paid and not recorded. The next payroll will be in January.

2. Rent payments of $8,000 were received for two months in advance on December 1. The entire amount was credited to Unearned Rent Revenue when received.

3. Depreciation expense for 2022 is $9,000.

Instructions

Complete the following table to correct the financial statement amounts shown (indicate deductions with parentheses).

Item	Net Income	Total Assets	Total Liabilities	Stockholders' Equity
Incorrect amounts	$70,000	$150,000	$70,000	$80,000
Effects of:				
Salaries and wages	‒‒‒‒‒	‒‒‒‒‒	‒‒‒‒‒	‒‒‒‒‒
Rent revenue	‒‒‒‒‒	‒‒‒‒‒	‒‒‒‒‒	‒‒‒‒‒
Depreciation	‒‒‒‒‒	‒‒‒‒‒	‒‒‒‒‒	‒‒‒‒‒
Correct balances	═════	═════	═════	═════

Prepare and post transaction and adjusting entries for prepayments.

E3.16 (LO 2), AP Action Quest Games Inc. adjusts its accounts annually. The following information is available for the year ended December 31, 2022.

1. Purchased a 1-year insurance policy on June 1 for $1,800 cash.

2. Paid $6,500 on August 31 for 5 months' rent in advance.

3. On September 4, received $3,600 cash in advance from a corporation to sponsor a game each month for a total of 9 months for the most improved students at a local school.

4. Signed a contract for cleaning services starting December 1 for $1,000 per month. Paid for the first 2 months on November 30. (*Hint:* Use the account Prepaid Cleaning to record prepayments.)

5. On December 5, received $1,500 in advance from a gaming club. Determined that on December 31, $475 of these games had not yet been played.

Instructions

a. For each of the above transactions, prepare the journal entry to record the initial transaction.

b. For each of the above transactions, prepare the adjusting journal entry that is required on December 31. (*Hint:* Use the account Service Revenue for item 3 and Repairs and Maintenance Expense for item 4.)

c. Post the journal entries in parts (a) and (b) to T-accounts and determine the final balance in each account. (*Note:* Posting to the Cash account is not required.)

Prepare adjusting and subsequent entries for accruals.

E3.17 (LO 3), AP Greenock Limited has the following information available for accruals for the year ended December 31, 2022. The company adjusts its accounts annually.

1. The December utility bill for $425 was unrecorded on December 31. Greenock paid the bill on January 11.

2. Greenock is open 7 days a week and employees are paid a total of $3,500 every Monday for a 7-day (Monday–Sunday) workweek. December 31 is a Thursday, so employees will have worked 4 days (Monday, December 28–Thursday, December 31) that they have not been paid for by year-end. Employees will be paid next on January 4.

3. Greenock signed a $45,000, 5% bank loan on November 1, 2021, due in 2 years. Interest is payable on the first day of each following month. (For example, interest incurred during November would be paid on December 1.)

4. Greenock receives a fee from Pizza Shop next door for all pizzas sold to customers using Greenock's facility. The amount owed for December is $300, which Pizza Shop will pay on January 4. (*Hint:* Use the Service Revenue account.)

5. Greenock rented some of its unused warehouse space to a client for $6,000 a month, payable the first day of the following month. It received the rent payment for the month of December on January 2.

Instructions

a. For each situation, prepare the adjusting entry required at December 31. (Round all calculations to the nearest dollar.)

b. For each situation, prepare the journal entry to record the subsequent cash transaction in 2023.

E3.18 (LO 2, 3, 4), AP The trial balances before and after adjustment for Ryan Company at the end of the fiscal year are as follows.

Prepare adjusting entries.

Ryan Company
Trial Balance
August 31, 2022

	Before Adjustment		After Adjustment	
	Dr.	**Cr.**	**Dr.**	**Cr.**
Cash	$10,900		$10,900	
Accounts Receivable	8,800		9,400	
Supplies	2,500		500	
Prepaid Insurance	4,000		2,500	
Equipment	16,000		16,000	
Accumulated Depreciation—Equipment		$ 3,600		$ 4,800
Accounts Payable		5,800		5,800
Salaries and Wages Payable		0		1,100
Unearned Rent Revenue		1,800		800
Common Stock		10,000		10,000
Retained Earnings		5,500		5,500
Dividends	2,800		2,800	
Service Revenue		34,000		34,600
Rent Revenue		12,100		13,100
Salaries and Wages Expense	17,000		18,100	
Supplies Expense	0		2,000	
Rent Expense	10,800		10,800	
Insurance Expense	0		1,500	
Depreciation Expense	0		1,200	
	$72,800	$72,800	$75,700	$75,700

Instructions

Prepare the adjusting entries that were made.

E3.19 (LO 4), AP The unadjusted and adjusted trial balance for Ryan Company are as follows.

Prepare financial statements from adjusted trial balance.

Ryan Company
Trial Balance
August 31, 2022

	Before Adjustment		After Adjustment	
	Dr.	**Cr.**	**Dr.**	**Cr.**
Cash	$10,900		$10,900	
Accounts Receivable	8,800		9,400	
Supplies	2,500		500	
Prepaid Insurance	4,000		2,500	
Equipment	16,000		16,000	
Accumulated Depreciation—Equipment		$ 3,600		$ 4,800
Accounts Payable		5,800		5,800
Salaries and Wages Payable		0		1,100
Unearned Rent Revenue		1,800		800
Common Stock		10,000		10,000
Retained Earnings		5,500		5,500
Dividends	2,800		2,800	
Service Revenue		34,000		34,600
Rent Revenue		12,100		13,100
Salaries and Wages Expense	17,000		18,100	
Supplies Expense	0		2,000	
Rent Expense	10,800		10,800	
Insurance Expense	0		1,500	
Depreciation Expense	0		1,200	
	$72,800	$72,800	$75,700	$75,700

Instructions

Prepare the income and retained earnings statements for the year and the balance sheet at August 31.

Record transactions on accrual basis; convert revenue to cash receipts.

E3.20 (LO 2, 3), AP The following data are taken from the comparative balance sheets of Cascade Billiards Club, which prepares its financial statements using the accrual basis of accounting.

Account Name	12/31/22 Balance	12/31/21 Balance
Accounts Receivable (from members)	$14,000	$ 9,000
Unearned Service Revenue	17,000	25,000

Members are billed based upon their use of the club's facilities. Unearned service revenues arise from the sale of gift certificates, which members can apply to their future use of club facilities. The 2022 income statement for the club showed that service revenue of $161,000 was recorded during the year.

Instructions

(*Hint:* You will probably find it helpful to use T-accounts to analyze these data.)

   a. Prepare journal entries for each of the following events that took place during 2022.

   1. Accounts receivable from 2021 were all collected.

   2. Gift certificates outstanding at the end of 2021 were all redeemed.

   3. An additional $38,000 worth of gift certificates were sold during 2022. A portion of these was used by the recipients during the year; the remainder was still outstanding at the end of 2022.

   4. Services performed for members for 2022 were billed to members.

   5. Accounts receivable for 2022 (i.e., those billed in item [4] above) were partially collected.

   b. Determine the amount of cash received by the club, with respect to member services, during 2022.

Journalize adjusting entries.

* E3.21 (LO 5), AP Prior to adjustments, Aaron Lynch Company has the following balances in selected accounts on December 31, 2022.

Service Revenue	$40,000
Insurance Expense	2,700
Supplies Expense	2,450

All the accounts have normal balances. Aaron Lynch Company debits prepayments to expense accounts when paid, and credits unearned revenues to revenue accounts when received. The following information has been gathered at December 31, 2022.

   1. Aaron Lynch Company paid $2,700 for 12 months of insurance coverage on June 1, 2022.

   2. On December 1, 2022, Aaron Lynch Company collected $40,000 for consulting services to be performed from December 1, 2022, through March 31, 2023.

   3. A count of supplies on December 31, 2022, indicates that supplies of $900 are on hand.

Instructions

Prepare the adjusting entries needed at December 31, 2022. Adjustments are prepared annually.

Journalize transactions and adjusting entries.

* E3.22 (LO 5), AP At Cambridge Company, prepayments are debited to expense when paid, and unearned revenues are credited to revenue when cash is received. During January of the current year, the following transactions occurred.

Jan.	2	Paid $1,920 for fire insurance protection for the year.
	10	Paid $1,700 for supplies.
	15	Received $6,100 for services to be performed in the future.

On January 31, it is determined that $2,500 of the services were performed and that there are $650 of supplies on hand.

Instructions

   a. Journalize and post the January transactions. (Use T-accounts.)

   b. Journalize and post the adjusting entries at January 31.

   c. Determine the ending balance in each of the accounts.

Identify accounting assumptions and principles.

* E3.23 (LO 6), K The following are the assumptions and principles discussed in Appendix 3B.

   1. Full disclosure principle.   4. Time period assumption.

   2. Going concern assumption.   5. Historical cost principle.

   3. Monetary unit assumption.   6. Economic entity assumption.

Instructions

Identify by number the accounting assumption or principle that is described below. Do not use a number more than once.

_____ **a.** Indicates that a business is expected to operate indefinitely into the future.

_____ **b.** Indicates that personal and business record keeping should be separately maintained.

_____ **c.** Assumes that the monetary unit is the "measuring stick" used to report on financial performance.

_____ **d.** Separates financial information into time periods for reporting purposes.

_____ **e.** Measurement basis used when a reliable estimate of fair value is not available.

_____ **f.** Dictates that companies should disclose all circumstances and events that make a difference to financial statement users.

*E3.24 **(LO 6), C** Rosman Co. had three major business transactions during 2022.

> *Identify the assumption or principle that has been violated.*

a. Reported, at its fair value of $260,000, land with a cost of $208,000.

b. The president of Rosman Co., Jay Rosman, purchased a truck for personal use and charged it to the company's Salaries and Wages Expense account.

c. Rosman Co. wanted to make its 2022 income look better, so it added 2 more weeks to the year (a 54-week year). Previous years were 52 weeks.

Instructions

In each situation, identify the assumption or principle that has been violated, if any, and discuss what the company should have done.

*E3.25 **(LO 6), K** The following characteristics, assumptions, principles, or constraint guide the FASB when it creates accounting standards.

> *Identify financial accounting concepts and principles.*

Relevance	Expense recognition principle
Faithful representation	Time period assumption
Comparability	Going concern assumption
Consistency	Historical cost principle
Monetary unit assumption	Full disclosure principle
Economic entity assumption	Materiality

Match each item above with a description below.

1. _____ Ability to easily evaluate one company's results relative to another's.

2. _____ Requirement that a company will continue to operate for the foreseeable future.

3. _____ The judgment concerning whether an item's size is large enough to matter to decision-makers.

4. _____ The reporting of all information that would make a difference to financial statement users.

5. _____ The practice of preparing financial statements at regular intervals.

6. _____ The quality of information that indicates the information makes a difference in a decision.

7. _____ A belief that items should be reported on the balance sheet at the price that was paid to acquire them.

8. _____ A company's use of the same accounting principles and methods from year to year.

9. _____ Tracing accounting events to particular companies.

10. _____ The desire to minimize bias in financial statements.

11. _____ Reporting only those things that can be measured in monetary units.

12. _____ Dictates that efforts (expenses) be recognized in the period in which a company uses assets or incurs liabilities to generate results (revenues).

*E3.26 **(LO 6), E** Writing Net Nanny Software International Inc., headquartered in Vancouver, Canada, specializes in Internet safety and computer security products for both the home and commercial markets. In a recent balance sheet, it reported a retained earnings deficit of $5,678,288 (in U.S. dollars). It has reported only net losses since its inception. In spite of these losses, Net Nanny's shares of stock have traded anywhere from a high of $3.70 to a low of $0.32 on the Canadian Venture Exchange.

> *Comment on the objective and qualitative characteristics of accounting information.*

Net Nanny's financial statements have historically been prepared in Canadian dollars. Recently, the company adopted the U.S. dollar as its reporting currency.

Instructions

a. What is the objective of financial reporting? How does this objective meet or not meet Net Nanny's investors' needs?

b. Why would investors want to buy Net Nanny's shares if the company has consistently reported losses over the last few years? Include in your answer an assessment of the relevance of the information reported on Net Nanny's financial statements.

c. Comment on how the change in reporting information from Canadian dollars to U.S. dollars likely affected the readers of Net Nanny's financial statements. Include in your answer an assessment of the comparability of the information.

Comment on the objective and qualitative characteristics of financial reporting.

* E3.27 **(LO 6), E** Writing   A friend of yours, Ana Gehrig, recently completed an undergraduate degree in science and has just started working with an international biotechnology company. Ana tells you that the owners of the business are trying to secure new sources of financing which are needed in order for the company to proceed with development of a new healthcare product. Ana said that her boss told her that the company must put together a report to present to potential investors.

Ana thought that the company should include in this package the detailed scientific findings related to the Phase I clinical trials for this product. She said, "I know that the biotech industry sometimes has only a 10% success rate with new products, but if we report all the scientific findings, everyone will see what a sure success this is going to be! The president was talking about the importance of following some set of accounting principles. Why do we need to look at some accounting rules? What they need to realize is that we have scientific results that are quite encouraging, some of the most talented employees around, and the start of some really great customer relationships. We haven't made any sales yet, but we will. We just need the funds to get through all the clinical testing and get government approval for our product. Then these investors will be quite happy that they bought in to our company early!"

Instructions

a. What is accounting information?

b. Comment on how Ana's suggestions for what should be reported to prospective investors conforms to the qualitative characteristics of accounting information. Do you think that the things that Ana wants to include in the information for investors will conform to financial reporting guidelines?

Problems

Prepare adjusting entries, post to ledger accounts, and prepare an adjusted trial balance.

P3.1A (LO 2, 3, 4), AP Deanna Nardelli started her own consulting firm, Nardelli Consulting, on May 1, 2022. The unadjusted trial balance at May 31 is as follows.

Nardelli Consulting
Trial Balance
May 31, 2022

Account Number		Debit	Credit
101	Cash	$ 4,500	
112	Accounts Receivable	6,000	
126	Supplies	1,900	
130	Prepaid Insurance	3,600	
149	Equipment	11,400	
201	Accounts Payable		$ 2,200
209	Unearned Service Revenue		2,000
311	Common Stock		20,000
400	Service Revenue		7,500
726	Salaries and Wages Expense	3,400	
729	Rent Expense	900	
		$31,700	$31,700

In addition to those accounts listed on the trial balance, the chart of accounts for Nardelli Consulting also contains the following accounts and account numbers: No. 150 Accumulated Depreciation—Equipment, No. 212 Salaries and Wages Payable, No. 631 Supplies Expense, No. 717 Depreciation Expense, No. 722 Insurance Expense, and No. 732 Utilities Expense.

Other data:

1. $900 of supplies have been used during the month.

2. Utilities expense incurred but not paid or recorded on May 31, 2022, $250.

3. An insurance policy for 2 years was purchased on May 1.

4. $400 of the balance in the unearned service revenue account remains unearned at the end of the month.

5. May 31 is a Wednesday, and employees are paid on Fridays. Nardelli Consulting has two employees, who are paid $900 each for a 5-day work week.

6. The equipment has a 5-year life with no salvage value. It is being depreciated at $190 per month for 60 months.

7. Invoices representing $1,700 of services performed during the month have not been recorded as of May 31.

Instructions

a. Prepare the adjusting entries for the month of May. Use J4 as the page number for your journal.

b. Enter the totals from the trial balance as beginning account balances and place a check mark in the posting reference column. Post the adjusting entries to the ledger accounts.

c. Prepare an adjusted trial balance at May 31, 2022.

c. Adj. trial balance $34,920

P3.2A (LO 2, 3, 4), AP The Skyline Motel opened for business on May 1, 2022. Its trial balance before adjustment on May 31 is as follows.

Prepare adjusting entries, post, and prepare adjusted trial balance and financial statements.

Skyline Motel
Trial Balance
May 31, 2022

Account Number		Debit	Credit
101	Cash	$ 3,500	
126	Supplies	2,080	
130	Prepaid Insurance	2,400	
140	Land	12,000	
141	Buildings	60,000	
149	Equipment	15,000	
200	Notes Payable		$40,000
201	Accounts Payable		11,180
208	Unearned Rent Revenue		3,300
311	Common Stock		35,000
429	Rent Revenue		10,300
610	Advertising Expense	600	
726	Salaries and Wages Expense	3,300	
732	Utilities Expense	900	
		$99,780	$99,780

In addition to those accounts listed on the trial balance, the chart of accounts for Skyline Motel also contains the following accounts and account numbers: No. 142 Accumulated Depreciation—Buildings, No. 150 Accumulated Depreciation—Equipment, No. 212 Salaries and Wages Payable, No. 230 Interest Payable, No. 619 Depreciation Expense, No. 631 Supplies Expense, No. 718 Interest Expense, and No. 722 Insurance Expense.

Other data:

1. Prepaid insurance is a 1-year policy starting May 1, 2022.

2. A count of supplies shows $750 of unused supplies on May 31.

3. Annual depreciation is $3,000 on the buildings and $1,500 on equipment.

4. The note payable interest rate is 12%. (The note was taken out on May 1 and will be repaid along with interest in 2 years.)

5. Two-thirds of the unearned rent revenue has been earned.

6. Salaries and wages of $750 are unpaid and unrecorded at May 31.

Instructions

a. Journalize the adjusting entries on May 31.

b. Prepare a ledger using the three-column form of account. Enter the trial balance amounts and post the adjusting entries. (Use J1 as the posting reference.)

c. Prepare an adjusted trial balance on May 31.

d. Prepare an income statement and a retained earnings statement for the month of May and a balance sheet at May 31.

c. Adj. trial balance $101,305
d. Net income $4,645
   Ending retained
      earnings $4,645
   Total assets $93,075

Prepare adjusting entries and financial statements.

P3.3A (LO 2, 3, 4), AP Everett Co. was organized on July 1, 2022. Quarterly financial statements are prepared. The unadjusted and adjusted trial balances as of September 30 are shown as follows.

Everett Co.
Trial Balance
September 30, 2022

	Unadjusted		Adjusted	
	Dr.	**Cr.**	**Dr.**	**Cr.**
Cash	$ 8,700		$ 8,700	
Accounts Receivable	10,400		11,500	
Supplies	1,500		650	
Prepaid Rent	2,200		1,200	
Equipment	18,000		18,000	
Accumulated Depreciation—Equipment		$ –0–		$ 700
Notes Payable		10,000		10,000
Accounts Payable		2,500		2,500
Salaries and Wages Payable		–0–		725
Interest Payable		–0–		100
Unearned Rent Revenue		1,900		1,050
Common Stock		22,000		22,000
Dividends	1,600		1,600	
Service Revenue		16,000		17,100
Rent Revenue		1,410		2,260
Salaries and Wages Expense	8,000		8,725	
Rent Expense	1,900		2,900	
Depreciation Expense			700	
Supplies Expense			850	
Utilities Expense	1,510		1,510	
Interest Expense			100	
	$53,810	$53,810	$56,435	$56,435

Instructions

a. Journalize the adjusting entries that were made.

b. Prepare an income statement and a retained earnings statement for the 3 months ending September 30 and a balance sheet at September 30.

c. If the note bears interest at 12%, how many months has it been outstanding? (The note and interest will be paid in 2 years.)

b. Net income $4,575
   Ending retained
      earnings $2,975
   Total assets $39,350

Prepare adjusting entries.

P3.4A (LO 2, 3), AP A review of the ledger of Lewis Company at December 31, 2022, produces the following data pertaining to the preparation of annual adjusting entries.

1. Insurance expense $6,800

1. Prepaid Insurance $15,200. The company has separate insurance policies on its buildings and its motor vehicles. Policy B4564 on the building was purchased on July 1, 2021, for $9,600. The policy has a term of 3 years. Policy A2958 on the vehicles was purchased on January 1, 2022, for $7,200. This policy has a term of 2 years.

2. Rent revenue $84,000

2. Unearned Rent Revenue $429,000. The company began subleasing office space in its new building on November 1, 2022. At December 31, the company had the following rental contracts that are paid in full for the entire term of the lease.

Date	Term (in months)	Monthly Rent Payment	Number of Leases
Nov. 1	9	$5,000	5
Dec. 1	6	$8,500	4

3. Notes Payable $40,000. This balance consists of a note for 6 months at an annual interest rate of 7%, dated November 1. Interest will be paid at note maturity. (Round to nearest dollar.)

4. Salaries and Wages Payable $0. There are eight salaried employees. Salaries are paid every Monday for the prior week. Five employees receive a salary of $600 each per week, and three employees earn $700 each per week. Assume December 31 is a Tuesday. Employees do not work weekends. All employees worked the last 2 days of December.

3. Interest expense $467

4. Salaries and wages expense $2,040

Instructions

Prepare the adjusting entries at December 31, 2022.

P3.5A (LO 2, 3, 4), AP On November 1, 2022, the account balances of Schilling Equipment Repair were as follows.

Journalize transactions and follow through accounting cycle to preparation of financial statements.

No.		Debit	No.		Credit
101	Cash	$ 2,400	154	Accumulated Depreciation—Equipment	$ 2,000
112	Accounts Receivable	4,250	201	Accounts Payable	2,600
126	Supplies	1,800	209	Unearned Service Revenue	1,200
153	Equipment	12,000	212	Salaries and Wages Payable	700
			311	Common Stock	10,000
			320	Retained Earnings	3,950
		$20,450			$20,450

During November, the following summary transactions were completed.

Nov.	8	Paid $1,700 for salaries due employees, of which $700 is for October salaries.
	10	Received $3,420 cash from customers on account.
	12	Received $3,100 cash for services performed in November.
	15	Purchased equipment on account $2,000.
	17	Purchased supplies on account $700.
	20	Paid creditors on account $2,700.
	22	Paid November rent $400.
	25	Paid salaries $1,700.
	27	Performed services on account and billed customers $1,900 for these services.
	29	Received $600 from customers for future service.

Adjustment data consist of:

1. Supplies on hand $1,400.

2. Accrued salaries payable $350.

3. Depreciation for the month is $200.

4. Services related to unearned service revenue of $1,250 were performed.

Instructions

a. Enter the November 1 balances in the ledger accounts.

b. Journalize the November transactions.

c. Post to the ledger accounts. Use J1 for the posting reference. Use the following additional accounts: No. 407 Service Revenue, No. 615 Depreciation Expense, No. 631 Supplies Expense, No. 726 Salaries and Wages Expense, and No. 729 Rent Expense.

d. Prepare a trial balance at November 30.

e. Journalize and post adjusting entries.

f. Prepare an adjusted trial balance.

g. Prepare an income statement and a retained earnings statement for November and a balance sheet at November 30.

d. Trial balance $25,350

f. Adj. trial balance $25,900

g. Net income $1,500
Ending retained earnings $5,450
Total assets $18,950

Prepare adjusting entries, adjusted trial balance, and financial statements using Appendix 3A.

* P3.6A (LO 2, 3, 4, 5), AP Sommer Graphics Company was organized on January 1, 2022, by Krystal Sommer. At the end of the first 6 months of operations, the unadjusted trial balance contained the accounts shown below.

	Debit		Credit
Cash	$ 8,600	Notes Payable	$ 20,000
Accounts Receivable	14,000	Accounts Payable	9,000
Equipment	45,000	Common Stock	22,000
Insurance Expense	2,700	Rent Revenue	52,100
Salaries and Wages Expense	30,000	Service Revenue	6,000
Supplies Expense	3,700		
Advertising Expense	1,900		
Rent Expense	1,500		
Utilities Expense	1,700		
	$109,100		$109,100

Analysis reveals the following additional data.

1. The $3,700 balance in Supplies Expense represents supplies purchased in January. At June 30, $1,500 of supplies are on hand.

2. The note payable was issued on February 1. It is a 9%, 6-month note. Interest is paid when the note matures.

3. The balance in Insurance Expense is the premium on a 1-year policy, dated March 1, 2022.

4. Service Revenue is credited when cash is received from customers. At June 30, service revenue of $1,300 remains unearned.

5. Revenue for services performed but unrecorded at June 30 totals $2,000.

6. Depreciation is $2,250 per year.

b. Adj. trial balance $112,975

c. Net income $18,725
  Ending retained
    earnings $18,725
  Total assets $71,775

Instructions

a. Journalize the adjusting entries at June 30. (Assume adjustments are recorded every 6 months.)

b. Prepare an adjusted trial balance.

c. Prepare an income statement and a retained earnings statement for the 6 months ended June 30 and a balance sheet at June 30.

Continuing Case

leungchopan/
Shutterstock.com

Cookie Creations

(*Note:* This is a continuation of the Cookie Creations case from Chapters 1 and 2.)

CC3 It is the end of November and Natalie has been in touch with her grandmother. Her grandmother asked Natalie how well things went in her first month of business. Natalie, too, would like to know if her business has been profitable or not during November. Natalie realizes that in order to determine Cookie Creations' income, she must first make adjustments.

Go to **WileyPLUS** *for complete case details and instructions.*

Expand Your Critical Thinking

Financial Reporting Problem: Apple Inc.

CT3.1 The financial statements of **Apple Inc.** are presented in Appendix A. The complete annual report, including the notes to the financial statements, is available at the company's website.

Instructions

a. Using the consolidated financial statements and related information, identify items that may result in adjusting entries for prepayments.

b. Using the consolidated financial statements and related information, identify items that may result in adjusting entries for accruals.

c. What has been the trend since 2016 for net income?

Comparative Analysis Problem:

PepsiCo, Inc. vs. The Coca-Cola Company

CT3.2 **PepsiCo**'s financial statements are presented in Appendix B. Financial statements of **The Coca-Cola Company** are presented in Appendix C. The complete annual reports of PepsiCo and Coca-Cola, including the notes to the financial statements, are available at each company's respective website.

Instructions

Based on information contained in these financial statements, determine the following for each company.

a. Net increase (decrease) in property, plant, and equipment (net) from 2017 to 2018.

b. Increase (decrease) in selling, general, and administrative expenses from 2017 to 2018.

c. Increase (decrease) in long-term debt (obligations) from 2017 to 2018.

d. Increase (decrease) in net income from 2017 to 2018.

e. Increase (decrease) in cash and cash equivalents from 2017 to 2018.

Comparative Analysis Problem:

Amazon.com, Inc. vs. Walmart Inc.

CT3.3 **Amazon.com, Inc.**'s financial statements are presented in Appendix D. Financial statements of **Walmart Inc.** are presented in Appendix E. The complete annual reports of Amazon and Walmart, including the notes to the financial statements, are available at each company's respective website.

Instructions

Based on information contained in these financial statements, determine the following for each company.

1. a. Increase (decrease) in interest expense from 2017 to 2018.

b. Increase (decrease) in net income from 2017 to 2018.

c. Increase (decrease) in cash flow from operating activities from 2017 to 2018.

2. Cash flow from operating activities and net income for each company is different. What are some possible reasons for these differences?

Real-World Focus

CT3.4 No financial decision-maker should ever rely solely on the financial information reported in the annual report to make decisions. It is important to keep abreast of financial news. This activity demonstrates how to search for financial news on the Internet.

Instructions

Go to the **Yahoo! Finance** website and then type in either Walmart, Target Corp., or Kmart. Choose **News**, select an article that sounds interesting to you and that would be relevant to an investor in these companies, and then answer the following questions.

a. What was the source of the article (e.g., Reuters, Businesswire, Prnewswire)?

b. Assume that you are a personal financial planner and that one of your clients owns stock in the company. Write a brief memo to your client summarizing the article and explaining the implications of the article for your client's investment.

CT3.5 The July 6, 2011, edition of the *Wall Street Journal Online* includes an article by Michael Rapaport entitled "U.S. Firms Clash Over Accounting Rules." The article discusses why some U.S. companies favored adoption of International Financial Reporting Standards (IFRS) while other companies opposed it.

Instructions

Read the article and answer the following questions.

a. The article says that the switch to IFRS tends to be favored by "larger companies, big accounting firms, and rule makers." What reasons are given for favoring the switch?

b. What two reasons are given by many smaller companies that oppose the switch?

c. What criticism of IFRS is raised with regard to regulated companies?

d. Explain what is meant by "condorsement."

Decision-Making Across the Organization

CT3.6 Abby Park was organized on April 1, 2021, by Trudy Crawford. Trudy is a good manager but a poor accountant. From the trial balance prepared by a junior accountant, Trudy prepared the following income statement for the quarter that ended March 31, 2022.

Abby Park Income Statement For the Quarter Ended March 31, 2022		
Revenues		
Rent revenue		$83,000
Operating expenses		
Advertising expense	$ 4,200	
Salaries and wages expense	27,600	
Utilities expense	1,500	
Depreciation expense	800	
Maintenance and repairs expense	2,800	
Total operating expenses		36,900
Net income		$46,100

Trudy knows that something is wrong with the statement because net income has never exceeded $20,000 in any one quarter. Knowing that you are an experienced accountant, she asks you to review the income statement and other data.

You first look at the trial balance. In addition to the account balances reported above in the income statement, the ledger contains the following additional selected balances at March 31, 2022.

Supplies	$ 4,500
Prepaid Insurance	7,200
Notes Payable	20,000

You then make inquiries and discover the following.

1. Rent revenue includes advanced rentals for summer occupancy of $21,000.

2. There were $600 of supplies on hand at March 31.

3. Prepaid Insurance represents a 1-year policy dated January 1, 2022.

4. The mail on April 1, 2022, included the following bills: advertising for week of March 24, $110; repairs made March 10, $1,040; and March utilities, $240.

5. Salaries and wages expense total $290 per day. At March 31, 2 days' salaries and wages have been incurred but not paid or recorded.

6. The note payable is a 3-month, 17% note dated January 1, 2022. (Interest is paid at note maturity.)

Instructions

With the class divided into groups, answer the following.

a. Prepare a correct income statement for the quarter ended March 31, 2022.

b. Explain to Trudy the generally accepted accounting principles that she did not recognize in preparing her income statement and their effect on her results.

Communication Activity

CT3.7 In reviewing the accounts of Gloria Jean Co. at the end of the year, you discover that adjusting entries have not been made.

Instructions

Write a memo to Gloria Jean Hall, the owner of Gloria Jean Co., that explains the following: the nature and purpose of adjusting entries, why adjusting entries are needed, and the types of adjusting entries that may be made.

Ethics Case

CT3.8 Kellner Company is a pesticide manufacturer. Its sales declined greatly this year due to the passage of legislation outlawing the sale of several of Kellner's chemical pesticides. In the coming year, Kellner will have environmentally safe and competitive chemicals to replace these discontinued products. Sales in the next year are expected to greatly exceed any prior year's. The decline in sales and profits appears to be a one-year aberration. But even so, the company president fears a large dip in the current year's profits. He believes that such a dip could cause a significant drop in the market price of Kellner's stock and make the company a takeover target.

To avoid this possibility, the company president calls in Melissa Ray, controller, to discuss this period's year-end adjusting entries. He urges her to accrue every possible revenue and to defer as many expenses as possible. He says to Melissa, "We need the revenues this year, and next year can easily absorb expenses deferred from this year. We can't let our stock price be hammered down!" Melissa didn't get around to recording the adjusting entries until January 17, but she dated the entries December 31 as if they were recorded then. Melissa also made every effort to comply with the president's request.

Instructions

a. Who are the stakeholders in this situation?

b. What are the ethical considerations of (1) the president's request and (2) Melissa dating the adjusting entries December 31?

c. Can Melissa accrue revenues and defer expenses and still be ethical?

All About You

CT3.9 Companies must report or disclose in their financial statements information about all liabilities, including potential liabilities related to environmental cleanup. There are many situations in which you will be asked to provide personal financial information about your assets, liabilities, revenue, and expenses. Sometimes you will face difficult decisions regarding what to disclose and how to disclose it.

Instructions

Suppose that you are putting together a loan application to purchase a home. Based on your income and assets, you qualify for the mortgage loan, but just barely. How would you address each of the following situations in reporting your financial position for the loan application? Provide responses for each of the following situations.

a. You signed a guarantee for a bank loan that a friend took out for $20,000. If your friend doesn't pay, you will have to pay. Your friend has made all of the payments so far, and it appears he will be able to pay in the future.

b. You were involved in an auto accident in which you were at fault. There is the possibility that you may have to pay as much as $50,000 as part of a settlement. The issue will not be resolved before the bank processes your mortgage request.

c. The company for which you work isn't doing very well, and it has recently laid off employees. You are still employed, but it is quite possible that you will lose your job in the next few months.

Considering People, Planet, and Profit

CT3.10 Many companies have potential pollution or environmental-disposal problems—not only for electronic gadgets, but also for the lead paint or asbestos they sold. How do we fit these issues into the accounting equation? Are these costs and related liabilities that companies should report?

YES: As more states impose laws holding companies responsible, and as more courts levy pollution-related fines, it becomes increasingly likely that companies will have to pay large amounts in the future.

NO: The amounts still are too difficult to estimate. Putting inaccurate estimates on the financial statements reduces their usefulness. Instead, why not charge the costs later, when the actual environmental cleanup or disposal occurs, at which time the company knows the actual cost?

Instructions

Write a response indicating your position regarding this situation. Provide support for your view.

FASB Codification Activity

CT3.11 If your school has a subscription to the FASB Codification, log in and prepare responses to the following.

Instructions

Access the glossary ("Master Glossary") to answer the following.

    a. What is the definition of revenue?

    b. What is the definition of compensation?

A Look at IFRS

LEARNING OBJECTIVE 7
Compare the procedures for adjusting entries under GAAP and IFRS.

The procedure used to adjust the accounting records is essentially the same among countries.

Key Points

Following are the key similarities and differences between GAAP and International Financial Reporting Standards (IFRS) as related to accrual accounting.

Similarities

- In this chapter, you learned accrual-basis accounting applied under GAAP. Companies applying IFRS also use accrual-basis accounting to ensure that they record transactions that affect a company's financial statements in the period in which events occur.

- Similar to GAAP, cash-basis accounting is not allowed under IFRS.

- IFRS also divides the economic life of companies into artificial time periods. Under both GAAP and IFRS, this is referred to as the **time period assumption**.

- The **general** revenue recognition principle required by GAAP that is used in this text is similar to that used under IFRS.

- Revenue recognition fraud is a major issue in U.S. financial reporting. The same situation occurs in other countries, as evidenced by revenue recognition breakdowns at Dutch software company **Baan NV**, Japanese electronics giant **NEC**, and Dutch grocer **Ahold NV**.

Differences

- Under IFRS, revaluation (using fair value) of items such as land and buildings is permitted. IFRS allows depreciation based on revaluation of assets, which is not permitted under GAAP.

- The terminology used for revenues and gains, and expenses and losses, differs somewhat between IFRS and GAAP. For example, income under IFRS includes both revenues, which arise during the normal course of operating activities, and gains, which arise from activities outside of the normal sales of goods and services. The term "income" is not used this way under GAAP. Instead, under GAAP income refers to the net difference between revenues and expenses.

- Under IFRS, expenses include both those costs incurred in the normal course of operations as well as losses that are not part of normal operations. This is in contrast to GAAP, which defines each separately.

IFRS Practice

IFRS Self-Test Questions

1. IFRS:
   a. uses accrual accounting.
   b. uses cash-basis accounting.
   c. allows revenue to be recognized when a customer makes an order.
   d. requires that revenue not be recognized until cash is received.

2. Which of the following statements is **false**?
   a. IFRS employs the time period assumption.
   b. IFRS employs accrual accounting.
   c. IFRS requires that revenues and costs must be capable of being measured reliably.
   d. IFRS uses the cash basis of accounting.

3. GAAP and IFRS require that revenue be recognized:
   a. when the performance obligation is satisfied.
   b. upon receipt of cash from customers.
   c. under cash-basis accounting.
   d. when it is earned and realized.

4. Which of the following is **false**?
   a. Under IFRS, the term income describes both revenues and gains.
   b. Under IFRS, the term expenses includes losses.
   c. Under IFRS, companies do not engage in the adjusting process.
   d. Under IFRS, revenue recognition fraud is a major issue.

5. Accrual-basis accounting:
   a. is optional under IFRS.
   b. results in companies recording transactions that affect a company's financial statements in the period in which events occur.
   c. has been eliminated as a result of the IASB/FASB joint projects.
   d. is no different than cash-basis accounting.

International Financial Reporting Problem: Louis Vuitton

IFRS3.1 The financial statements of **Louis Vuitton** are presented in Appendix F. The complete consolidated financial statements, including the notes to its financial statements, are available at the company's website.

Instructions

Visit Louis Vuitton's corporate website and answer the following questions from Louis Vuitton's 2018 consolidated financial statements.

a. From the notes to the financial statements, how does the company determine the amount of revenue to record at the time of a sale?

b. From the notes to the financial statements, how does the company determine the provision for product returns?

c. Using the consolidated income statement and consolidated statement of financial position, identify items that may result in adjusting entries for deferrals.

d. Using the consolidated income statement, identify two items that may result in adjusting entries for accruals.

Answers to IFRS Self-Test Questions

1. a 2. d 3. a 4. c 5. b

CHAPTER 4

Comstock/Getty Images

Completing the Accounting Cycle

Chapter Preview

As the following Feature Story highlights, at **Rhino Foods, Inc.**, financial statements help employees understand what is happening in the business. In Chapter 3, we prepared financial statements directly from the adjusted trial balance. However, with so many details involved in the end-of-period accounting procedures, it is easy to make errors. One way to minimize errors in the records and to simplify the end-of-period procedures is to use a worksheet.

In this chapter, we will explain the role of the worksheet in accounting. We also will study the remaining steps in the accounting cycle, especially the closing process, again using Pioneer Advertising Inc. as an example. Then we will consider correcting entries and classified balance sheets.

Feature Story

Everyone Likes to Win

When Ted Castle was a hockey coach at the University of Vermont, his players were self-motivated by their desire to win.

But at **Rhino Foods, Inc.**, a bakery-foods company he founded in Burlington, Vermont, he discovered that manufacturing-line workers were not so self-motivated. Ted thought, what if he turned the food-making business into more like a hockey game, with rules, strategies, and trophies?

In a game, knowing the score is all-important. Ted felt that only if the employees know the score—know exactly how the business is doing daily, weekly, monthly—could he turn food-making into a game. But Rhino is a closely held, family-owned business, and its financial statements and profits were confidential. Ted wondered, should he open Rhino's books to the employees?

A consultant put Ted's concerns in perspective when he said, "Imagine you're playing touch football. You play for an hour or two, and the whole time I'm sitting there with a book, keeping score. All of a sudden I blow the whistle, and I say, 'OK, that's it. Everybody go home.' I close my book and walk away. How would you feel?" Ted opened his books and revealed the financial statements to his employees.

The next step was to teach employees the rules and strategies of how to "win" at making food. The first lesson: "Your opponent at Rhino is expenses. You must cut and control expenses." Ted and his staff distilled those lessons into daily scorecards—production reports and income statements—that keep Rhino's employees up-to-date on the game. At noon each day, Ted posts the previous day's results at the entrance to the production room. Everyone checks whether they made or lost money on what they produced the day before. And it's not just an academic exercise: There's a bonus check for each employee at the end of every four-week "game" that meets profitability guidelines.

Rhino has flourished since the first game. Employment has increased from 20 to 130 people, while both revenues and profits have grown dramatically.

Chapter Outline

LEARNING OBJECTIVES	REVIEW	PRACTICE
LO 1 Prepare a worksheet.	• Steps in preparing a worksheet • Preparing financial statements from a worksheet • Preparing adjusting entries from a worksheet	**DO IT! 1** Worksheet
LO 2 Prepare closing entries and a post-closing trial balance.	• Preparing closing entries • Posting closing entries • Preparing a post-closing trial balance	**DO IT! 2** Closing Entries
LO 3 Explain the steps in the accounting cycle and how to prepare correcting entries.	• Summary of the accounting cycle • Reversing entries • Correcting entries	**DO IT! 3** Correcting Entries
LO 4 Identify the sections of a classified balance sheet.	• Current assets • Long-term investments • Property, plant, and equipment • Intangible assets • Current liabilities • Long-term liabilities • Stockholders' (owners') equity	**DO IT! 4** Balance Sheet Classifications

Go to the Review and Practice section at the end of the chapter for a review of key concepts and practice applications with solutions.

Visit WileyPLUS for additional tutorials and practice opportunities.

The Worksheet

LEARNING OBJECTIVE 1

Prepare a worksheet.

We have used T-accounts and trial balances to arrive at the amounts used to prepare financial statements. Accountants, however, frequently use a spreadsheet, called a worksheet, to determine these amounts. A **worksheet** is a multiple-column spreadsheet that may be used in the adjustment process and in preparing financial statements (see **Helpful Hint**).

As its name suggests, the worksheet is a working tool for the accountant. **A worksheet is not a permanent accounting record**; it is neither a journal nor a part of the general ledger. The worksheet is merely a supplemental spreadsheet that is used to make it easier to prepare adjusting entries and the financial statements.

Illustration 4.1 shows the basic form of a worksheet and the five steps for preparing it. The steps are performed in sequence. **The use of a worksheet is optional.** When a company chooses to use one, it prepares financial statements directly from the worksheet. It enters the adjustments in the worksheet columns and then journalizes and posts the adjustments after it has prepared the financial statements. Thus, worksheets make it possible to provide the financial statements to management and other interested parties at an earlier date.

> **HELPFUL HINT**
>
> Companies generally computerize worksheets using a spreadsheet program such as Microsoft Excel.

ILLUSTRATION 4.1 Form and procedure for a worksheet

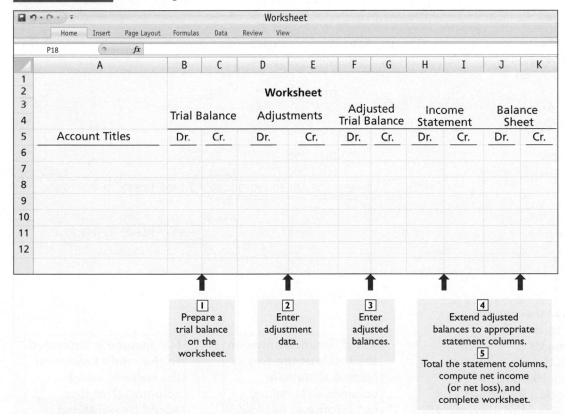

Steps in Preparing a Worksheet

We will use the October 31 trial balance and adjustment data of Pioneer Advertising Inc. from Chapter 3 to illustrate how to prepare a worksheet. We describe each step of the process and demonstrate these steps in **Illustration 4.2**.

ILLUSTRATION 4.2 Preparing a worksheet

	Pioneer Advertising									

Home Insert Page Layout Formulas Data Review View

P18 *fx*

	A	B	C	D	E	F	G	H	I	J	K
1											
2					**Pioneer Advertising Inc.**						
3					Worksheet						
4					For the Month Ended October 31, 2022						
5								Adjusted		Income	Balance
6		Trial Balance		Adjustments		Trial Balance		Statement		Sheet	
7	Account Titles	Dr.	Cr.	Dr.	Cr.	Dr.	Cr.	Dr.	Cr.	Dr.	Cr.
8	Cash	15,200				15,200				15,200	
9	Supplies	2,500			(a) 1,500	1,000				1,000	
10	Prepaid Insurance	600			(b) 50	550				550	
11	Equipment	5,000				5,000				5,000	
12	Notes Payable		5,000				5,000				5,000
13	Accounts Payable		2,500				2,500				2,500
14	Unearned Service Revenue		1,200	(d) 400			800				800
15	Common Stock		10,000				10,000				10,000
16	Dividends	500				500				500	
17	Service Revenue		10,000		(d) 400		10,600		10,600		
18					(e) 200						
19	Salaries and Wages Expense	4,000		(g) 1,200		5,200		5,200			
20	Rent Expense	900				900		900			
21	Totals	28,700	28,700								
22											
23											
24	Supplies Expense			(a) 1,500		1,500		1,500			
25	Insurance Expense			(b) 50		50		50			
26	Accum. Depreciation—										
27	Equipment				(c) 40		40				40
28	Depreciation Expense			(c) 40		40		40			
29	Accounts Receivable			(e) 200		200				200	
30	Interest Expense			(f) 50		50		50			
31	Interest Payable				(f) 50		50				50
32	Salaries and Wages Payable				(g) 1,200		1,200				1,200
33	Totals			3,440	3,440	30,190	30,190	7,740	10,600	22,450	19,590
34											
35	Net Income							2,860			2,860
36	Totals							10,600	10,600	22,450	22,450

Add additional accounts as needed to complete the adjustments:
(a) Supplies Used.
(b) Insurance Expired.
(c) Depreciation Expensed.
(d) Service Revenue Recognized.
(e) Service Revenue Accrued.
(f) Interest Accrued.
(g) Salaries Accrued.

The difference between the totals of the two income statement columns determines net income or net loss.

Net income is extended to the credit column of the balance sheet columns. (Net loss would be extended to the debit column.)

| **Step 1** | # Prepare a Trial Balance on the Worksheet |

Enter all ledger accounts with balances in the account titles column. Enter debit and credit amounts from the ledger in the trial balance columns. Illustration 4.2 shows the worksheet trial balance for Pioneer Advertising Inc. This trial balance is the same one that appears in Illustration 2.32 and Illustration 3.4.

| **Step 2** | # Enter the Adjustments in the Adjustments Columns |

When using a worksheet, enter all adjustments in the adjustments columns. In entering the adjustments, use applicable trial balance accounts. If additional accounts are needed, insert them on the lines immediately below the trial balance totals. A different letter identifies the debit and credit for each adjusting entry. The term used to describe this process is **keying**. **Companies do not journalize the adjustments until after they complete the worksheet and prepare the financial statements.**

The adjustments for Pioneer are the same as the adjustments in Illustration 3.24. They are keyed in the adjustments columns of the worksheet as follows.

a. Pioneer debits an additional account, Supplies Expense, $1,500 for the cost of supplies used, and credits Supplies $1,500.

b. Pioneer debits an additional account, Insurance Expense, $50 for the insurance that has expired, and credits Prepaid Insurance $50.

c. The company needs two additional depreciation accounts. It debits Depreciation Expense $40 for the month's depreciation, and credits Accumulated Depreciation—Equipment $40.

d. Pioneer debits Unearned Service Revenue $400 for services performed, and credits Service Revenue $400.

e. Pioneer debits an additional account, Accounts Receivable, $200 for services performed but not billed, and credits Service Revenue $200.

f. The company needs two additional accounts relating to interest. It debits Interest Expense $50 for accrued interest, and credits Interest Payable $50.

g. Pioneer debits Salaries and Wages Expense $1,200 for accrued salaries, and credits an additional account, Salaries and Wages Payable, $1,200.

After Pioneer has entered all the adjustments, the adjustments columns are totaled to prove their equality.

| **Step 3** | # Enter Adjusted Balances in the Adjusted Trial Balance Columns |

Pioneer determines the adjusted balance of an account by combining the amounts entered in the first four columns of the worksheet for each account. For example, the Prepaid Insurance account in the trial balance columns has a $600 debit balance and a $50 credit in the adjustments columns. The result is a $550 debit balance recorded in the adjusted trial balance columns. **For each account, the amount in the adjusted trial balance columns is the**

balance that will appear in the ledger after journalizing and posting the adjusting entries. The balances in these columns are the same as those in the adjusted trial balance in Illustration 3.26.

After Pioneer has entered all account balances in the adjusted trial balance columns, the columns are totaled to prove their equality. If the column totals do not agree, the financial statement columns will not balance and the financial statements will be incorrect.

Step 4   Extend Adjusted Trial Balance Amounts to Appropriate Financial Statement Columns

HELPFUL HINT

Every adjusted trial balance amount must be extended to one of the four statement columns.

The fourth step is to extend adjusted trial balance amounts to the income statement and balance sheet columns of the worksheet (see **Helpful Hint**). Pioneer enters balance sheet accounts in the appropriate balance sheet debit and credit columns. For instance, it enters Cash in the balance sheet debit column, and Notes Payable in the balance sheet credit column. Pioneer extends Accumulated Depreciation—Equipment to the balance sheet credit column. The reason is that accumulated depreciation is a contra asset account with a credit balance.

Pioneer extends the balances in Common Stock and Retained Earnings, if any, to the balance sheet credit column. In addition, it extends the balance in Dividends to the balance sheet debit column because it is a stockholders' equity account with a debit balance.

The company enters the expense and revenue accounts such as Salaries and Wages Expense and Service Revenue in the appropriate income statement columns.

Step 5   Total the Statement Columns, Compute the Net Income (or Net Loss), and Complete the Worksheet

The company now must total each of the financial statement columns. The net income or net loss for the period is the difference between the totals of the two income statement columns. If total credits exceed total debits, the result is net income. In such a case, as shown in Illustration 4.2, the company inserts the words "Net Income" in the account titles space. It then enters the amount in the income statement debit column and the balance sheet credit column. **The debit amount balances the income statement columns; the credit amount balances the balance sheet columns.** In addition, the credit in the balance sheet column indicates the increase in stockholders' equity resulting from net income.

What if total debits exceed total credits in the income statement columns? In that case, the company has a net loss. It enters the amount of the net loss in the income statement credit column and the balance sheet debit column.

After entering the net income or net loss, the company determines new column totals. The totals shown in the debit and credit income statement columns will match. So will the totals shown in the debit and credit balance sheet columns. If either the income statement columns or the balance sheet columns are not equal after the net income or net loss has been entered, there is an error in the worksheet.

Preparing Financial Statements from a Worksheet

After a company has completed a worksheet, it has at hand all the data required for preparation of financial statements. The income statement is prepared from the income statement columns. The retained earnings statement and balance sheet are prepared from the balance sheet columns. **Illustration 4.3** shows the financial statements prepared from Pioneer Advertising's

ILLUSTRATION 4.3

Financial statements from a worksheet

Pioneer Advertising Inc.
Income Statement
For the Month Ended October 31, 2022

Revenues		
Service revenue		$10,600
Expenses		
Salaries and wages expense	$5,200	
Supplies expense	1,500	
Rent expense	900	
Insurance expense	50	
Interest expense	50	
Depreciation expense	40	
Total expenses		7,740
Net income		$ 2,860

Pioneer Advertising Inc.
Retained Earnings Statement
For the Month Ended October 31, 2022

Retained earnings, October 1	$ –0–
Add: Net income	2,860
	2,860
Less: Dividends	500
Retained earnings, October 31	$2,360

Pioneer Advertising Inc.
Balance Sheet
October 31, 2022

Assets		
Cash		$15,200
Accounts receivable		200
Supplies		1,000
Prepaid insurance		550
Equipment	$ 5,000	
Less: Accumulated depreciation—equipment	40	4,960
Total assets		$21,910
Liabilities and Stockholders' Equity		
Liabilities		
Notes payable	$ 5,000	
Accounts payable	2,500	
Interest payable	50	
Unearned service revenue	800	
Salaries and wages payable	1,200	
Total liabilities		$ 9,550
Stockholders' equity		
Common stock	10,000	
Retained earnings	2,360	
Total stockholders' equity		12,360
Total liabilities and stockholders' equity		$21,910

worksheet. At this point, the company has not journalized or posted adjusting entries. Therefore, ledger balances for some accounts are not the same as the financial statement amounts.

The amount shown for common stock on the worksheet does not change from the beginning to the end of the period unless the company issues additional stock during the period. Because there was no balance in Pioneer's retained earnings, the account is not listed on the worksheet. Only after dividends and net income (or loss) are posted to retained earnings does this account have a balance at the end of the first year of the business.

Using a worksheet, companies can prepare financial statements before they journalize and post adjusting entries. **However, the completed worksheet is not a substitute for formal financial statements.** The format of the data in the financial statement columns of the worksheet is not the same as the format of the financial statements. **A worksheet is essentially a working tool of the accountant**; companies do not distribute it to management and other parties.

Preparing Adjusting Entries from a Worksheet

HELPFUL HINT

Note that writing the explanation of the adjustment at the bottom of the worksheet is not required.

A worksheet is not a journal, and it cannot be used as a basis for posting to ledger accounts. To adjust the accounts, the company must journalize the adjustments and post them to the ledger. **The adjusting entries are prepared from the adjustments columns of the worksheet.** The reference letters in the adjustments columns and the explanations of the adjustments at the bottom of the worksheet help identify the adjusting entries (see **Helpful Hint**). The journalizing and posting of adjusting entries **follow** the preparation of financial statements when a worksheet is used. The adjusting entries on October 31 for Pioneer Advertising Inc. are the same as those shown in Illustration 3.24.

ACTION PLAN

- **Balance sheet: Extend assets to debit column. Extend liabilities to credit column. Extend contra assets to credit column. Extend Dividends account to debit column.**
- **Income statement: Extend expenses to debit column. Extend revenues to credit column.**

DO IT! 1 | Worksheet

Susan Elbe is preparing a worksheet. Explain to Susan how she should extend the following adjusted trial balance accounts to the financial statement columns of the worksheet.

Cash	Dividends
Accumulated Depreciation—Equipment	Service Revenue
Accounts Payable	Salaries and Wages Expense

Solution

Income statement debit column—Salaries and Wages Expense
Income statement credit column—Service Revenue
Balance sheet debit column—Cash; Dividends
Balance sheet credit column—Accumulated Depreciation—Equipment; Accounts Payable

Related exercise material: **BE4.1, BE4.2, BE4.3, DO IT! 4.1, E4.1, E4.2, E4.3, E4.5, and E4.6.**

Closing the Books

LEARNING OBJECTIVE 2

Prepare closing entries and a post-closing trial balance.

ANALYZE ▸ JOURNALIZE ▸ POST ▸ TRIAL BALANCE ▸ ADJUSTING ENTRIES ▸ ADJUSTED TRIAL BALANCE ▸ PREPARE FINANCIAL STATEMENTS ▸ **Journalize and post closing entries** ▸ **Prepare a post-closing trial balance**

At the end of the accounting period, the company makes the accounts ready for the next period. This is called **closing the books.** In closing the books, the company distinguishes between temporary and permanent accounts.

Temporary accounts relate only to a given accounting period. They include all income statement accounts and the Dividends account. **The company closes all temporary accounts at the end of the period.**

In contrast, **permanent accounts** relate to one or more future accounting periods. They consist of all balance sheet accounts, including stockholders' equity accounts. **Permanent accounts are not closed from period to period.** Instead, the company carries forward the balances of permanent accounts into the next accounting period. **Illustration 4.4** identifies the accounts in each category (see **Alternative Terminology**).

ALTERNATIVE TERMINOLOGY

Temporary accounts are sometimes called *nominal accounts*, and permanent accounts are sometimes called *real accounts*.

ILLUSTRATION 4.4
Temporary versus permanent accounts

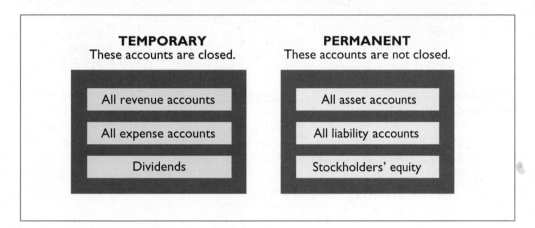

Preparing Closing Entries

At the end of the accounting period, the company transfers temporary account balances to the permanent stockholders' equity account, Retained Earnings, by means of closing entries.

Closing entries formally recognize in the ledger the transfer of net income (or net loss) and Dividends to Retained Earnings. The retained earnings statement shows the results of these entries. **Closing entries also produce a zero balance in each temporary account.** The temporary accounts are then ready to accumulate data in the next accounting period separate from the data of prior periods. Permanent accounts are not closed.

Journalizing and posting closing entries is a required step in the accounting cycle (see Illustration 4.11). The company performs this step after it has prepared financial statements. In contrast to the steps in the cycle that you have already studied, companies generally journalize and post closing entries **only at the end of the annual accounting period**. Thus, all temporary accounts will contain data for the entire accounting period.

In preparing closing entries, companies could close each income statement account directly to Retained Earnings. However, to do so would result in excessive detail in the permanent Retained Earnings account. Instead, companies close the revenue and expense accounts to another temporary account, **Income Summary**, and then transfer the resulting net income or net loss from this account to Retained Earnings (see **Helpful Hint**).

Companies **record closing entries in the general journal**. A center caption, Closing Entries, inserted in the journal between the last adjusting entry and the first closing entry, identifies these entries. Then the company posts the closing entries to the ledger accounts.

Companies generally prepare closing entries directly from the adjusted balances in the ledger. They could prepare separate closing entries for each nominal account, but the following four entries accomplish the desired result more efficiently:

1. Debit each revenue account for its balance, and credit Income Summary for total revenues.
2. Debit Income Summary for total expenses, and credit each expense account for its balance.
3. Debit Income Summary and credit Retained Earnings for the amount of net income.
4. Debit Retained Earnings for the balance in the Dividends account, and credit Dividends for the same amount (see **Helpful Hint**).

HELPFUL HINT

The Income Summary account is used only in the closing process. This temporary account has a zero balance at the end of the process.

HELPFUL HINT

The Dividends account is closed directly to Retained Earnings and *not* to Income Summary because dividends are not an expense.

If there were a net loss (because expenses exceeded revenues), entry 3 would be reversed: there would be a credit to Income Summary and a debit to Retained Earnings. **Illustration 4.5** presents a diagram of the closing process. In it, the boxed numbers refer to the four entries required in the closing process.

ILLUSTRATION 4.5

Diagram of closing process— corporation

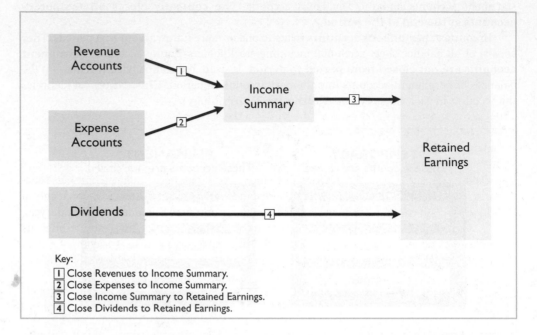

Key:
1 Close Revenues to Income Summary.
2 Close Expenses to Income Summary.
3 Close Income Summary to Retained Earnings.
4 Close Dividends to Retained Earnings.

Closing Entries Illustrated

In practice, companies generally prepare closing entries only at the end of the annual accounting period. However, to illustrate the journalizing and posting of closing entries, we will assume that Pioneer Advertising Inc. closes its books monthly. **Illustration 4.6** shows the closing entries at October 31. (The numbers in parentheses before each entry correspond to the four entries diagrammed in Illustration 4.5.)

ILLUSTRATION 4.6

Closing entries journalized

		GENERAL JOURNAL			J3
Date		**Account Titles and Explanation**	**Ref.**	**Debit**	**Credit**
		Closing Entries			
2022		(1)			
Oct.	31	Service Revenue	400	10,600	
		Income Summary	350		10,600
		(To close revenue account)			
		(2)			
	31	Income Summary	350	7,740	
		Supplies Expense	631		1,500
		Depreciation Expense	711		40
		Insurance Expense	722		50
		Salaries and Wages Expense	726		5,200
		Rent Expense	729		900
		Interest Expense	905		50
		(To close expense accounts)			
		(3)			
	31	Income Summary	350	2,860	
		Retained Earnings	320		2,860
		(To close net income to retained earnings)			
		(4)			
	31	Retained Earnings	320	500	
		Dividends	332		500
		(To close dividends to retained earnings)			

Note that the amounts for Income Summary in entries (1) and (2) are the totals of the income statement credit and debit columns, respectively, in the worksheet.

A couple of cautions in preparing closing entries: (1) Avoid unintentionally doubling the revenue and expense balances rather than zeroing them by ensuring that each revenue account is debited and each expense account is credited. (2) Do not close Dividends through the Income Summary account. **Dividends are not an expense, and they are not a factor in determining net income.**

Posting Closing Entries

Illustration 4.7 shows the posting of the closing entries and the underlining (ruling) of the accounts. Note that all temporary accounts have zero balances after posting the closing entries. In addition, you should realize that the balance in Retained Earnings represents the accumulated undistributed net income of the corporation at the end of the accounting period. This balance is shown on the balance sheet and is the ending amount reported on the retained earnings statement, as shown in Illustration 4.3. Pioneer Advertising uses the Income Summary account only in closing (see **Helpful Hint**). It does not journalize and post entries to this account during the year.

As part of the closing process, Pioneer totals, balances, and double-underlines its temporary accounts—revenues, expenses, and Dividends, as shown in T-account form in Illustration 4.7. It does not close its permanent accounts—assets, liabilities, and stockholders'

> **HELPFUL HINT**
>
> **The balance in Income Summary before it is closed must equal the net income or net loss for the period.**

ILLUSTRATION 4.7   **Posting of closing entries**

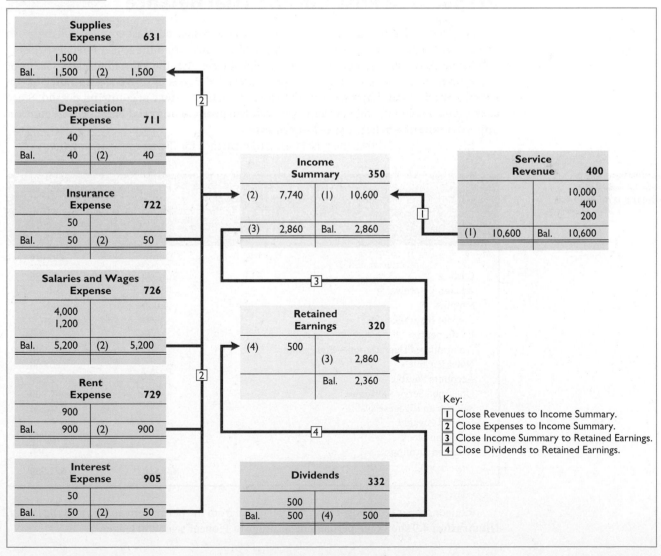

equity (Common Stock and Retained Earnings). Instead, Pioneer draws a single underline beneath the current-period entries for the permanent accounts. The account balance is then entered below the single underline and is carried forward to the next period (for example, see Retained Earnings).

Accounting Across the Organization   Cisco Systems

Performing the Virtual Close

Technology has dramatically shortened the closing process. Recent surveys have reported that the average company now takes only 6 to 7 days to close, rather than the previous 20 days. But a few companies do much better. **Cisco Systems** can perform a "virtual close"—closing within 24 hours on any day in the quarter. The same is true at **Lockheed Martin**, which improved its closing time by 85% in just the last few years. Managers at these companies emphasize that this

iStock.com/Steve Cole

increased speed has not reduced the accuracy and completeness of the data.

This is not just showing off. Knowing exactly where you are financially at any time allows a company to respond faster than its competitors. It also means that the hundreds of people who used to spend 10 to 20 days each quarter tracking transactions can now be more usefully employed on other projects, such as mining data for business intelligence to find new business opportunities.

Who else benefits from a shorter closing process? (Go to WileyPLUS for this answer and additional questions.)

Preparing a Post-Closing Trial Balance

After Pioneer Advertising Inc. has journalized and posted all closing entries, it prepares another trial balance, called a **post-closing trial balance**, from the ledger. The post-closing trial balance lists permanent accounts and their balances after the journalizing and posting of closing entries. The purpose of the post-closing trial balance is **to prove the equality of the permanent account balances carried forward into the next accounting period**. Since all temporary accounts will have zero balances, **the post-closing trial balance will contain only permanent—balance sheet—accounts**.

Illustration 4.8 shows the post-closing trial balance for Pioneer Advertising Inc.

ILLUSTRATION 4.8

Post-closing trial balance

Pioneer Advertising Inc.
Post-Closing Trial Balance
October 31, 2022

	Debit	Credit
Cash	$15,200	
Accounts Receivable	200	
Supplies	1,000	
Prepaid Insurance	550	
Equipment	5,000	
Accumulated Depreciation—Equipment		$ 40
Notes Payable		5,000
Accounts Payable		2,500
Unearned Service Revenue		800
Salaries and Wages Payable		1,200
Interest Payable		50
Common Stock		10,000
Retained Earnings		2,360
	$21,950	**$21,950**

Pioneer prepares the post-closing trial balance from the permanent accounts in the ledger. **Illustration 4.9** shows the permanent accounts in Pioneer's general ledger.

ILLUSTRATION 4.9   **General ledger, permanent accounts**

(Permanent Accounts Only)

GENERAL LEDGER

Cash					No. 101
Date	Explanation	Ref.	Debit	Credit	Balance
2022					
Oct. 1		J1	10,000		10,000
2		J1	1,200		11,200
3		J1		900	10,300
4		J1		600	9,700
20		J1		500	9,200
26		J1		4,000	5,200
31		J1	10,000		**15,200**

Accounts Receivable					No. 112
Date	Explanation	Ref.	Debit	Credit	Balance
2022					
Oct. 31	Adj. entry	J2	**200**		**200**

Supplies					No. 126
Date	Explanation	Ref.	Debit	Credit	Balance
2022					
Oct. 5		J1	2,500		2,500
31	Adj. entry	J2		**1,500**	**1,000**

Prepaid Insurance					No. 130
Date	Explanation	Ref.	Debit	Credit	Balance
2022					
Oct. 4		J1	600		600
31	Adj. entry	J2		**50**	**550**

Equipment					No. 157
Date	Explanation	Ref.	Debit	Credit	Balance
2022					
Oct. 1		J1	5,000		**5,000**

Accumulated Depreciation—Equipment					No. 158
Date	Explanation	Ref.	Debit	Credit	Balance
2022					
Oct. 31	Adj. entry	J2		**40**	**40**

Notes Payable					No. 200
Date	Explanation	Ref.	Debit	Credit	Balance
2022					
Oct. 1		J1		5,000	**5,000**

Accounts Payable					No. 201
Date	Explanation	Ref.	Debit	Credit	Balance
2022					
Oct. 5		J1		2,500	**2,500**

Unearned Service Revenue					No. 209
Date	Explanation	Ref.	Debit	Credit	Balance
2022					
Oct. 2		J1		1,200	1,200
31	Adj. entry	J2	400		800

Salaries and Wages Payable					No. 212
Date	Explanation	Ref.	Debit	Credit	Balance
2022					
Oct. 31	Adj. entry	J2		**1,200**	**1,200**

Interest Payable					No. 230
Date	Explanation	Ref.	Debit	Credit	Balance
2022					
Oct. 31	Adj. entry	J2		**50**	**50**

Common Stock					No. 311
Date	Explanation	Ref.	Debit	Credit	Balance
2022					
Oct. 1		J1		10,000	**10,000**

Retained Earnings					No. 320
Date	Explanation	Ref.	Debit	Credit	Balance
2022					
Oct. 1					–0–
31	**Closing entry**	J3		2,860	**2,860**
31	**Closing entry**	J3	500		**2,360**

Note: The permanent accounts for Pioneer Advertising Inc. are shown here; the temporary accounts are shown in Illustration 4.10. Both permanent and temporary accounts are part of the general ledger; we separate them here to aid in learning.

A post-closing trial balance provides evidence that the company has properly journalized and posted the closing entries. It also shows that the accounting equation is in balance at the end of the accounting period. However, like the trial balance, it does not prove that Pioneer has recorded all transactions or that the ledger is correct. For example, the post-closing trial balance still will balance even if a transaction is not journalized and posted or if a transaction is journalized and posted twice.

The remaining accounts in the general ledger are temporary accounts, shown in **Illustration 4.10**. After Pioneer correctly posts the closing entries, each temporary account has a zero balance. These accounts are double-underlined to finalize the closing process.

ILLUSTRATION 4.10 General ledger, temporary accounts

(Temporary Accounts Only)

GENERAL LEDGER

Dividends — No. 332

Date	Explanation	Ref.	Debit	Credit	Balance
2022					
Oct. 20		J1	500		500
31	Closing entry	J3		500	–0–

Income Summary — No. 350

Date	Explanation	Ref.	Debit	Credit	Balance
2022					
Oct. 31	Closing entry	J3		10,600	10,600
31	Closing entry	J3	7,740		2,860
31	Closing entry	J3	2,860		–0–

Service Revenue — No. 400

Date	Explanation	Ref.	Debit	Credit	Balance
2022					
Oct. 31		J1		10,000	10,000
31	Adj. entry	J2		400	10,400
31	Adj. entry	J2		200	10,600
31	Closing entry	J3	10,600		–0–

Supplies Expense — No. 631

Date	Explanation	Ref.	Debit	Credit	Balance
2022					
Oct. 31	Adj. entry	J2	1,500		1,500
31	Closing entry	J3		1,500	–0–

Depreciation Expense — No. 711

Date	Explanation	Ref.	Debit	Credit	Balance
2022					
Oct. 31	Adj. entry	J2	40		40
31	Closing entry	J3		40	–0–

Insurance Expense — No. 722

Date	Explanation	Ref.	Debit	Credit	Balance
2022					
Oct. 31	Adj. entry	J2	50		50
31	Closing entry	J3		50	–0–

Salaries and Wages Expense — No. 726

Date	Explanation	Ref.	Debit	Credit	Balance
2022					
Oct. 26		J1	4,000		4,000
31	Adj. entry	J2	1,200		5,200
31	Closing entry	J3		5,200	–0–

Rent Expense — No. 729

Date	Explanation	Ref.	Debit	Credit	Balance
2022					
Oct. 3		J1	900		900
31	Closing entry	J3		900	–0–

Interest Expense — No. 905

Date	Explanation	Ref.	Debit	Credit	Balance
2022					
Oct. 31	Adj. entry	J2	50		50
31	Closing entry	J3		50	–0–

Note: The temporary accounts for Pioneer Advertising Inc. are shown here. Illustration 4.9 shows the permanent accounts. Both permanent and temporary accounts are part of the general ledger; we separate them here to aid in learning.

ACTION PLAN

- **Close revenue and expense accounts to Income Summary.**
- **Close Income Summary to Retained Earnings.**
- **Close Dividends to Retained Earnings.**

DO IT! 2 | Closing Entries

Hancock Company has the following balances in selected accounts of its adjusted trial balance.

Accounts Payable	$27,000	Dividends	$15,000
Service Revenue	98,000	Retained Earnings	42,000
Rent Expense	22,000	Accounts Receivable	38,000
Salaries and Wages Expense	51,000	Supplies Expense	7,000

Prepare the closing entries at December 31.

Solution

Date		Debit	Credit
Dec. 31	Service Revenue	98,000	
	Income Summary		98,000
	(To close revenue account to Income Summary)		
31	Income Summary	80,000	
	Salaries and Wages Expense		51,000
	Rent Expense		22,000
	Supplies Expense		7,000
	(To close expense accounts to Income Summary)		

31	Income Summary ($98,000 − $80,000)	18,000	
	Retained Earnings		18,000
	(To close net income to retained earnings)		
31	Retained Earnings	15,000	
	Dividends		15,000
	(To close dividends to retained earnings)		

Related exercise material: **BE4.4, BE4.5, BE4.6, BE4.7, DO IT! 4.2, E4.4, E4.7, E4.8, and E4.11.**

The Accounting Cycle and Correcting Entries

LEARNING OBJECTIVE 3

Explain the steps in the accounting cycle and how to prepare correcting entries.

Summary of the Accounting Cycle

Illustration 4.11 summarizes the steps in the accounting cycle. You can see that the cycle begins with the analysis of business transactions and ends with the preparation of a post-closing trial balance. Companies perform the steps in the cycle in sequence and repeat them in each accounting period.

Steps 1–3 may occur daily during the accounting period. Companies perform Steps 4–7 on a periodic basis, such as monthly, quarterly, or annually. Steps 8 and 9—closing entries and a post-closing trial balance—usually take place only at the end of a company's **annual** accounting period.

There are also two **optional steps** in the accounting cycle. As you have seen, companies may use a worksheet in preparing adjusting entries and financial statements. In addition, they may use reversing entries, as explained below.

Reversing Entries—An Optional Step

Some accountants prefer to reverse certain adjusting entries by making a **reversing entry** at the beginning of the next accounting period. A reversing entry is the exact opposite of the adjusting entry made in the previous period. **Use of reversing entries is an optional bookkeeping procedure; it is not a required step in the accounting cycle.** Accordingly, we have chosen to cover this topic in Appendix 4A at the end of this chapter.

Correcting Entries—An Avoidable Step

Unfortunately, errors may occur in the recording process. Companies should correct errors, **as soon as they discover them**, by journalizing and posting **correcting entries** (see **Ethics Note**). If the accounting records are free of errors, no correcting entries are needed.

You should recognize several differences between correcting entries and adjusting entries. First, adjusting entries are an integral part of the accounting cycle. Correcting entries, on the other hand, are unnecessary if the records are error-free. Second, companies journalize and post adjustments **only at the end of an accounting period**. In contrast, companies make correcting entries **whenever they discover an error**. Finally, adjusting entries always affect at least one balance sheet account and one income statement account. In contrast, correcting entries may involve any combination of accounts in need of correction. **Correcting entries must be posted before closing entries.**

ETHICS NOTE

When companies find errors in previously released income statements, they restate those numbers. Perhaps because of the increased scrutiny caused by Sarbanes-Oxley, in a recent year companies filed a record 1,195 restatements.

ILLUSTRATION 4.11

Required steps in the accounting cycle

The Accounting Cycle

ILLUSTRATION 4.11

Required steps in the accounting cycle

To determine the correcting entry, it is useful to compare the incorrect entry with the correct entry. Doing so helps identify the accounts and amounts that should—and should not—be corrected. After comparison, the accountant makes an entry to correct the accounts. The following two cases for Mercato Co. illustrate this approach.

Case 1

On May 10, Mercato Co. journalized and posted a $50 cash collection on account from a customer as a debit to Cash $50 and a credit to Service Revenue $50 (see **Illustration 4.12**). The company discovered the error on May 20, when the customer paid the remaining balance in full.

ILLUSTRATION 4.12

Comparison of entries

Incorrect Entry (May 10)			Correct Entry (May 10)		
Cash	50		Cash	50	
Service Revenue		50	Accounts Receivable		50

Comparison of the incorrect entry with the correct entry reveals that the debit to Cash $50 is correct. However, the $50 credit to Service Revenue should have been credited to Accounts Receivable. As a result, both Service Revenue and Accounts Receivable are overstated in the ledger. Mercato makes the correcting entry shown in **Illustration 4.13**.

ILLUSTRATION 4.13

Correcting entry

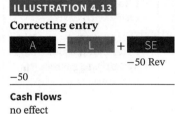

A = L + SE
                  −50 Rev
−50

Cash Flows
no effect

	Correcting entry		
May 20	Service Revenue	50	
	Accounts Receivable		50
	(To correct entry of May 10)		

Case 2

On May 18, Mercato purchased on account equipment costing $450. The transaction was journalized and posted as a debit to Equipment $45 and a credit to Accounts Payable $45 (see **Illustration 4.14**). The error was discovered on June 3, when Mercato received the monthly statement for May from the creditor.

ILLUSTRATION 4.14

Comparison of entries

Incorrect Entry (May 18)			Correct Entry (May 18)		
Equipment	45		Equipment	450	
Accounts Payable		45	Accounts Payable		450

Comparison of the two entries shows that two accounts are incorrect. Equipment is understated $405, and Accounts Payable is understated $405. Mercato makes the correcting entry shown in **Illustration 4.15**.

ILLUSTRATION 4.15

Correcting entry

A = L + SE
+405
      +405

Cash Flows
no effect

	Correcting entry		
June 3	Equipment	405	
	Accounts Payable		405
	(To correct entry of May 18)		

Instead of preparing one correcting entry, **it is possible to reverse the incorrect entry and then prepare the correct entry**. This approach will result in more entries and postings than a correcting entry, but it will accomplish the desired result.

Accounting Across the Organization   Yale Express

iStock.com/christian Lagereek

Lost in Transportation

Yale Express, a short-haul trucking firm, turned over much of its cargo to local truckers to complete deliveries. Yale collected the entire delivery charge. When billed by the local trucker, Yale sent payment for the final phase to the local trucker. Yale used a cutoff period of 20 days into the next accounting period in making its adjusting entries for accrued liabilities. That is, it waited 20 days to receive the local truckers' bills to determine the amount of the unpaid but incurred delivery charges as of the balance sheet date.

On the other hand, **Republic Carloading**, a nationwide, long-distance freight forwarder, frequently did not receive transportation bills from truckers to whom it passed on cargo until months after the year-end. In making its year-end adjusting entries, Republic waited for months in order to include all of these outstanding transportation bills.

When Yale Express merged with Republic Carloading, Yale's vice president employed the 20-day cutoff procedure for both firms. As a result, millions of dollars of Republic's accrued transportation bills went unrecorded. When the company detected the error and made correcting entries, these and other errors changed a reported profit of $1.14 million into a loss of $1.88 million!

What might Yale Express's vice president have done to produce more accurate financial statements without waiting months for Republic's outstanding transportation bills? (Go to WileyPLUS for this answer and additional questions.)

ACTION PLAN

- **Compare the incorrect entry with correct entry.**
- **After comparison, make an entry to correct the accounts.**

DO IT! 3 | Correcting Entries

Sanchez Company discovered the following errors made in January 2022.

1. A payment of Salaries and Wages Expense of $600 was debited to Supplies and credited to Cash, both for $600.

2. A collection of $3,000 from a client on account was debited to Cash $200 and credited to Service Revenue $200.

3. The purchase of supplies on account for $860 was debited to Supplies $680 and credited to Accounts Payable $680.

Correct the errors without reversing the incorrect entry.

Solution

1. Salaries and Wages Expense	600	
Supplies		600
2. Service Revenue	200	
Cash	2,800	
Accounts Receivable		3,000
3. Supplies ($860 − $680)	180	
Accounts Payable		180

Related exercise material: **BE4.8, BE4.9, DO IT! 4.3, E4.10, E4.12, and E4.13.**

Classified Balance Sheet

LEARNING OBJECTIVE 4

Identify the sections of a classified balance sheet.

The balance sheet presents a snapshot of a company's financial position at a point in time. To improve users' understanding of a company's financial position, companies often use a classified balance sheet. A **classified balance sheet** groups together similar assets and similar liabilities, using a number of standard classifications and sections. This is useful because items within a group have similar economic characteristics. A classified balance sheet generally contains the standard classifications listed in **Illustration 4.16**.

Assets	Liabilities and Stockholders' Equity
Current assets	Current liabilities
Long-term investments	Long-term liabilities
Property, plant, and equipment	Stockholders' equity
Intangible assets	

ILLUSTRATION 4.16

Standard balance sheet classifications

These groupings help financial statement readers determine such things as (1) whether the company has enough assets to pay its debts as they come due, and (2) the claims of short- and long-term creditors on the company's total assets. Many of these groupings can be seen in the balance sheet of Franklin Corporation shown in **Illustration 4.17**. In the sections that follow, we explain each of these groupings.

ILLUSTRATION 4.17

Classified balance sheet

Franklin Corporation
Balance Sheet
October 31, 2022

Assets

Current assets

Cash		$ 6,600	
Debt investments		2,000	
Accounts receivable		7,000	
Notes receivable		1,000	
Inventory		3,000	
Supplies		2,100	
Prepaid insurance		400	
Total current assets			$22,100

Long-term investments

Stock investments		5,200	
Investment in real estate		2,000	7,200

Property, plant, and equipment

Land		10,000	
Equipment	$24,000		
Less: Accumulated depreciation—			
equipment	5,000	19,000	29,000

Intangible assets

Patents			3,100
Total assets			$61,400

Liabilities and Stockholders' Equity

Current liabilities

Notes payable		$11,000	
Accounts payable		2,100	
Unearned service revenue		900	
Salaries and wages payable		1,600	
Interest payable		450	
Total current liabilities			$16,050

Long-term liabilities

Mortgage payable		10,000	
Notes payable		1,300	
Total long-term liabilities			11,300
Total liabilities			27,350

Stockholders' equity

Common stock		20,000	
Retained earnings		14,050	
Total stockholders' equity			34,050
Total liabilities and stockholders' equity			$61,400

Current Assets

Current assets are assets that a company expects to convert to cash or use up within one year or its operating cycle, whichever is longer. In Illustration 4.17, Franklin Corporation had current assets of $22,100. For most businesses, the cutoff for classification as current assets is one year from the balance sheet date. For example, accounts receivable are current assets because the company will collect them and convert them to cash within one year. Supplies is a current asset because the company expects to use them up in operations within one year.

Some companies use a period longer than one year to classify assets and liabilities as current because they have an operating cycle longer than one year. The **operating cycle** of a company is the average time that it takes to purchase inventory, sell it on account, and then collect cash from customers. For most businesses, this cycle takes less than a year so they use a one-year cutoff. But for some businesses, such as vineyards or airplane manufacturers, this period may be longer than a year. **Except where noted, we will assume that companies use one year to determine whether an asset or liability is current or long-term.**

Common types of current assets are (1) cash, (2) investments (such as short-term U.S. government securities), (3) receivables (notes receivable, accounts receivable, and interest receivable), (4) inventories, and (5) prepaid expenses (supplies and insurance). **On the balance sheet, companies usually list these items in the order in which they expect to convert them into cash** (*follow this rule when doing your homework*). **Illustration 4.18** presents the current assets of **Southwest Airlines Co.**

ILLUSTRATION 4.18

Current assets section

Real World

Southwest Airlines Co.	
Balance Sheet (partial)	
(in millions)	
Current assets	
Cash and cash equivalents	$1,355
Short-term investments	1,797
Accounts receivable	419
Inventories	467
Prepaid expenses and other current assets	418
Total current assets	$4,456

Long-Term Investments

ALTERNATIVE TERMINOLOGY

Long-term investments are often referred to simply as *investments*.

Long-term investments are generally (1) investments in stocks and bonds of other companies that are held for more than one year, (2) long-term assets such as land or buildings that a company is not currently using in its operating activities, and (3) long-term notes receivable (see **Alternative Terminology**). In Illustration 4.17, Franklin Corporation reported total long-term investments of $7,200 on its balance sheet.

Alphabet Inc. reported long-term investments in its balance sheet, as shown in **Illustration 4.19**.

ILLUSTRATION 4.19

Long-term investments section

Real World

Alphabet Inc.	
Balance Sheet (partial)	
(in millions)	
Long-term investments	
Non-marketable investments	$5,183

ALTERNATIVE TERMINOLOGY

Property, plant, and equipment is sometimes called *fixed assets* or *plant assets*.

Property, Plant, and Equipment

Property, plant, and equipment are assets with relatively long useful lives that a company is currently using in operating the business (see **Alternative Terminology**). This category includes land, buildings, machinery and equipment, delivery equipment, and furniture. In Illustration 4.17, Franklin Corporation reported property, plant, and equipment of $29,000.

Depreciation is the practice of allocating the cost of assets to a number of years. Companies do this by systematically assigning a portion of an asset's cost as an expense each year (rather than expensing the full purchase price in the year of purchase). The assets that the company depreciates are reported on the balance sheet at cost less accumulated depreciation. The **accumulated depreciation** account shows the total amount of depreciation that the company has expensed thus far in the asset's life. In Illustration 4.17, Franklin Corporation reported accumulated depreciation of $5,000 related to its equipment.

Illustration 4.20 presents the property, plant, and equipment of **Tesla Motors, Inc.** *In your homework, present each accumulated depreciation account immediately below the related plant asset, as shown in Illustration 4.17.*

Tesla Motors, Inc.
Balance Sheet (partial)
(in thousands)

Property, plant, and equipment

Machinery, equipment and office furniture	$322,394
Tooling	230,385
Leasehold improvements	94,763
Building and building improvements	67,707
Land	45,020
Computer equipment and software	42,073
Construction in progress	76,294
	878,636
Less: Accumulated depreciation	140,142
Total	$738,494

ILLUSTRATION 4.20
Property, plant, and equipment section
Real World

Intangible Assets

Many companies have long-lived assets that do not have physical substance yet often are very valuable. We call these assets **intangible assets** (see **Helpful Hint**). One significant intangible asset is goodwill. Others include patents, copyrights, and trademarks or trade names that give the company **exclusive right** of use for a specified period of time. In Illustration 4.17, Franklin Corporation reported intangible assets of $3,100.

Illustration 4.21 shows the intangible assets of media and theme park giant **The Walt Disney Company** in a recent year.

HELPFUL HINT

Sometimes intangible assets are reported under a broader heading called "Other assets."

The Walt Disney Company
Balance Sheet (partial)
(in millions)

Intangible assets and goodwill

Character/franchise intangibles and copyrights	$ 5,830
Other amortizable intangible assets	903
Less: Accumulated amortization	1,204
Net amortizable intangible assets	5,529
FCC licenses	667
Trademarks	1,218
Other indefinite lived intangible assets	20
	7,434
Goodwill	27,881
	$35,315

ILLUSTRATION 4.21
Intangible assets section
Real World

People, Planet, and Profit Insight

Regaining Goodwill

iStock.com/Gehringj

After falling to unforeseen lows amidst scandals, recalls, and economic crises, the reputation of corporate America is recovering in the eyes of the American public. Overall corporate reputation is experiencing rehabilitation as the American public gives high marks overall to corporate America, specific industries, and the largest number of individual companies in a dozen years. This is according to the findings of the *2011 Harris Interactive RQ Study*, which measures the reputations of the 60 most visible companies in the United States.

The survey focuses on six reputational dimensions that influence reputation and consumer behavior. Four of these dimensions, along with the five corporations that ranked highest within each, are as follows.

- **Social Responsibility:** (1) Whole Foods Market, (2) Johnson & Johnson, (3) Google, (4) The Walt Disney Company, (5) Procter & Gamble Co.
- **Emotional Appeal:** (1) Johnson & Johnson, (2) Amazon.com, (3) UPS, (4) General Mills, (5) Kraft Foods
- **Financial Performance:** (1) Google, (2) Berkshire Hathaway, (3) Apple, (4) Intel, (5) The Walt Disney Company
- **Products and Services:** (1) Intel Corporation, (2) 3M Company, (3) Johnson & Johnson, (4) Google, (5) Procter & Gamble Co.

Source: www.harrisinteractive.com.

Name two industries today that are probably rated low on the reputational characteristics of "being trusted" and "having high ethical standards." (Go to WileyPLUS for this answer and additional questions.)

Current Liabilities

ETHICS NOTE

A company that has more current assets than current liabilities can increase the ratio of current assets to current liabilities by using cash to pay off some current liabilities. This gives the appearance of being more liquid. Do you think this move is ethical?

In the liabilities and stockholders' equity section of the balance sheet, the first grouping is current liabilities. **Current liabilities** are obligations that the company is to pay within the coming year or its operating cycle, whichever is longer (see **Ethics Note**). Common examples are accounts payable, salaries and wages payable, notes payable, interest payable, and income taxes payable. Also included as current liabilities are current maturities of long-term obligations—payments to be made within the next year on long-term obligations. In Illustration 4.17, Franklin Corporation reported five different types of current liabilities, for a total of $16,050.

Illustration 4.22 shows the current liabilities section adapted from the balance sheet of **The Marcus Corporation**.

ILLUSTRATION 4.22

Current liabilities section

Real World

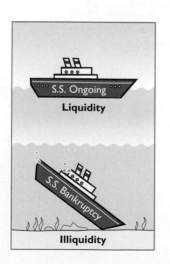

Liquidity

Illiquidity

The Marcus Corporation
Balance Sheet (partial)
(in thousands)

Current liabilities	
Notes payable	$ 239
Accounts payable	24,242
Current maturities of long-term debt	57,250
Other current liabilities	27,477
Income taxes payable	11,215
Salaries and wages payable	6,720
Total current liabilities	$127,143

Users of financial statements look closely at the relationship between current assets and current liabilities. This relationship is important in evaluating a company's **liquidity**—its ability to pay obligations expected to be due within the next year. When current assets exceed current liabilities, the likelihood of paying the liabilities is favorable. When the reverse is true, short-term creditors may not be paid, and the company may ultimately be forced into bankruptcy.

Can a Company Be Too Liquid?

There actually is a point where a company can be too liquid—that is, it can have too much working capital (current assets less current liabilities). While it is important to be liquid enough to be able to pay short-term bills as they come due, a company does not want to tie up its cash in extra inventory or receivables that are not earning the company money.

iStock.com/Jorge Salcedo

By one estimate from the **REL Consultancy Group**, the thousand largest U.S. companies have on their books cumulative excess working capital of $764 billion. Based on this figure, companies could have reduced debt by 36% or increased net income by 9%. Given that managers throughout a company are interested in improving profitability, it is clear that they should have an eye toward managing working capital. They need to aim for a "Goldilocks solution"—not too much, not too little, but just right.

Source: K. Richardson, "Companies Fall Behind in Cash Management," *Wall Street Journal* (June 19, 2007).

What can various company managers do to ensure that working capital is managed efficiently to maximize net income? (Go to WileyPLUS for this answer and additional questions.)

Long-Term Liabilities

Long-term liabilities (long-term debt) are obligations that a company expects to pay **after** one year. Liabilities in this category include bonds payable, mortgages payable, long-term notes payable, lease liabilities, and pension liabilities. Many companies report long-term debt maturing after one year as a single amount in the balance sheet and show the details of the debt in notes that accompany the financial statements. Others list the various types of long-term liabilities. In Illustration 4.17, Franklin Corporation reported long-term liabilities of $11,300.

Illustration **4.23** shows the long-term liabilities that **Nike, Inc.** reported in its balance sheet in a recent year.

Nike, Inc.	
Balance Sheet (partial)	
(in millions)	
Long-term liabilities	
Bonds payable	$1,106
Notes payable	51
Deferred income taxes and other	1,544
Total long-term liabilities	$2,701

ILLUSTRATION 4.23

Long-term liabilities section

Real World

Stockholders' (Owners') Equity

The content of the owners' equity section varies with the form of business organization. In a proprietorship, there is one capital account. In a partnership, there is a capital account for each partner. Corporations divide owners' equity into two accounts—Common Stock (sometimes referred to as Capital Stock) and Retained Earnings. Corporations record stockholders' investments in the company by debiting an asset account (typically Cash) and crediting the Common Stock account. They record in the Retained Earnings account income retained for use in the business. Corporations combine the Common Stock and Retained Earnings accounts and report them on the balance sheet as **stockholders' equity**. (We discuss these corporation accounts in later chapters.) **Nordstrom, Inc.** recently reported its stockholders' equity section as shown in **Illustration 4.24**.

Stockholders' equity section

Real World

Nordstrom, Inc.
Balance Sheet (partial)
($ in thousands)

Stockholders' equity

Common stock, 271,331 shares	$ 685,934
Retained earnings	1,406,747
Total stockholders' equity	$2,092,681

ACTION PLAN

- **Analyze whether each financial statement item is an asset, liability, or stockholders' equity.**
- **Determine whether asset and liability items are short-term or long-term.**

DO IT! 4 | Balance Sheet Classifications

The following accounts were taken from the financial statements of Callahan Company.

_____ Salaries and wages payable
_____ Service revenue
_____ Interest payable
_____ Goodwill
_____ Debt investments (short-term)
_____ Mortgage payable (due in 3 years)

_____ Stock investments (long-term)
_____ Equipment
_____ Accumulated depreciation—equipment
_____ Depreciation expense
_____ Common stock
_____ Unearned service revenue

Match each of the accounts to its proper balance sheet classification, shown below. If the item would not appear on a balance sheet, use "NA."

Current assets (CA)
Long-term investments (LTI)
Property, plant, and equipment (PPE)
Intangible assets (IA)

Current liabilities (CL)
Long-term liabilities (LTL)
Stockholders' equity (SE)

Solution

__CL__ Salaries and wages payable
__NA__ Service revenue
__CL__ Interest payable
__IA__ Goodwill
__CA__ Debt investments (short-term)
__LTL__ Mortgage payable (due in 3 years)

__LTI__ Stock investments (long-term)
__PPE__ Equipment
__PPE__ Accumulated depreciation—equipment
__NA__ Depreciation expense
__SE__ Common stock
__CL__ Unearned service revenue

Related exercise material: **BE4.10, BE4.11, DO IT! 4.4, E4.9, E4.14, E4.15, E4.16, and E4.17.**

Appendix 4A

Reversing Entries

LEARNING OBJECTIVE *5

Prepare reversing entries.

After preparing the financial statements and closing the books, it is often helpful to reverse some of the adjusting entries before recording the regular transactions of the next period. Such entries are **reversing entries**. Companies make **a reversing entry at the beginning of the next accounting period**. Each reversing entry **is the exact opposite of the adjusting entry made in the previous period**. The recording of reversing entries is an **optional step** in the accounting cycle.

The purpose of reversing entries is to simplify the recording of a subsequent transaction related to an adjusting entry. For example, in Chapter 3, the payment of salaries after an adjusting entry resulted in two debits: one to Salaries and Wages Payable and the other to Salaries and Wages Expense. With reversing entries, the company can debit the entire subsequent payment to Salaries and Wages Expense. **The use of reversing entries does not change the amounts reported in the financial statements.** What it does is simplify the recording of subsequent transactions.

Reversing Entries Example

Companies most often use reversing entries to reverse two types of adjusting entries: accrued revenues and accrued expenses. To illustrate the optional use of reversing entries for accrued expenses, we will use the salaries expense transactions for Pioneer Advertising Inc. as illustrated in Chapters 2, 3, and 4. The transaction and adjustment data are as follows.

1. October 26 (initial salary entry): Pioneer pays $4,000 of salaries and wages earned between October 15 and October 26.

2. October 31 (adjusting entry): Salaries and wages earned between October 29 and October 31 are $1,200. The company will pay these in the November 9 payroll.

3. November 9 (subsequent salary entry): Salaries and wages paid are $4,000. Of this amount, $1,200 applied to accrued salaries and wages payable, and $2,800 was earned between November 1 and November 9.

Illustration 4A.1 shows the entries with and without reversing entries.

ILLUSTRATION 4A.1   Comparative entries—without and with reversing

Without Reversing Entries (per chapter)				With Reversing Entries (per appendix)		
Initial Salary Entry				Initial Salary Entry		
Oct. 26	Salaries and Wages Expense	4,000		Oct. 26	(Same entry)	
	Cash		4,000			
Adjusting Entry				Adjusting Entry		
Oct. 31	Salaries and Wages Expense	1,200		Oct. 31	(Same entry)	
	Salaries and Wages Payable		1,200			
Closing Entry				Closing Entry		
Oct. 31	Income Summary	5,200		Oct. 31	(Same entry)	
	Salaries and Wages Expense		5,200			
Reversing Entry				Reversing Entry		
Nov. 1	No reversing entry is made.			Nov. 1	**Salaries and Wages Payable**	1,200
Subsequent Salary Entry					**Salaries and Wages Expense**	1,200
Nov. 9	Salaries and Wages Payable	1,200		Subsequent Salary Entry		
	Salaries and Wages Expense	2,800		Nov. 9	**Salaries and Wages Expense**	4,000
	Cash		4,000		**Cash**	4,000

The first three entries are the same whether or not Pioneer uses reversing entries. The last two entries are different. The November 1 **reversing entry** eliminates the $1,200 balance in Salaries and Wages Payable created by the October 31 adjusting entry. The reversing entry also creates a $1,200 credit balance in the Salaries and Wages Expense account. As you know, it is unusual for an expense account to have a credit balance. The balance is correct in this instance, though, because it anticipates that the entire amount of the first salaries and wages payment in the new accounting period will be debited to Salaries and Wages Expense. This debit will eliminate the credit balance. The resulting debit balance in the expense account will equal the salaries and wages expense incurred in the new accounting period ($2,800 in this example).

If Pioneer makes reversing entries, it can debit all cash payments of expenses to the expense account. This means that on November 9 (and every payday) Pioneer can debit Salaries and Wages Expense for the amount paid, without regard to any accrued salaries and wages payable. Being able to make the **same entry each time** simplifies the recording process. The company can record subsequent transactions as if the related adjusting entry had never been made.

Illustration 4A.2 shows the posting of the entries with reversing entries.

ILLUSTRATION 4A.2   **Postings with reversing entries**

Salaries and Wages Expense					
10/26	Paid	4,000			
31	Adjusting	1,200			
Bal.		5,200	10/31	Closing	5,200
11/9	Paid	4,000	**11/1**	**Reversing**	**1,200**

Salaries and Wages Payable					
11/1	**Reversing**	**1,200**	10/31	Adjusting	1,200

A company can also use reversing entries for accrued revenue adjusting entries. For Pioneer, the adjusting entry was Accounts Receivable (Dr.) $200 and Service Revenue (Cr.) $200. Thus, the reversing entry on November 1 is:

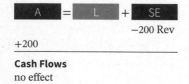

A = L + SE

−200 Rev
+200

Cash Flows
no effect

Nov. 1	Service Revenue	200	
	Accounts Receivable		200
	(To reverse October 31 adjusting entry)		

When Pioneer collects the accrued service revenue, it debits Cash and credits Service Revenue.

Review and Practice

Learning Objectives Review

1 Prepare a worksheet.

The steps in preparing a worksheet are as follows. (a) Prepare a trial balance on the worksheet. (b) Enter the adjustments in the adjustments columns. (c) Enter adjusted balances in the adjusted trial balance columns. (d) Extend adjusted trial balance amounts to appropriate financial statement columns. (e) Total the statement columns, compute net income (or net loss), and complete the worksheet.

2 Prepare closing entries and a post-closing trial balance.

Closing the books occurs at the end of an accounting period. The process is to journalize and post closing entries and then underline and balance all accounts. In closing the books, companies make separate entries to close revenues and expenses to Income Summary, Income Summary to Retained Earnings, and Dividends to Retained Earnings. Only temporary accounts are closed. A post-closing trial balance contains the balances in permanent accounts that are carried forward to the next accounting period. The purpose of this trial balance is to prove the equality of these balances.

3 Explain the steps in the accounting cycle and how to prepare correcting entries.

The required steps in the accounting cycle are (1) analyze business transactions, (2) journalize the transactions, (3) post to ledger accounts, (4) prepare a trial balance, (5) journalize and post adjusting entries, (6) prepare an adjusted trial balance, (7) prepare financial statements, (8) journalize and post closing entries, and (9) prepare a post-closing trial balance.

One way to determine the correcting entry is to compare the incorrect entry with the correct entry. After comparison, the company makes a correcting entry to correct the accounts. An alternative to one correcting entry is to reverse the incorrect entry and then prepare the correct entry.

4   Identify the sections of a classified balance sheet.

A classified balance sheet categorizes assets as current assets; long-term investments; property, plant, and equipment; and intangible assets. Liabilities are classified as either current or long-term. There is also a stockholders' (owners') equity section, which varies with the form of business organization.

*5   Prepare reversing entries.

Reversing entries are the opposite of the adjusting entries made in the preceding period. Some companies choose to make reversing entries at the beginning of a new accounting period to simplify the recording of later transactions related to the adjusting entries. In most cases, only accrued adjusting entries are reversed.

Glossary Review

Classified balance sheet A balance sheet that contains standard classifications or sections. (p. 4-18).

Closing entries Entries made at the end of an accounting period to transfer the balances of temporary accounts to a permanent stockholders' equity account, Retained Earnings. (p. 4-9).

Correcting entries Entries to correct errors made in recording transactions. (p. 4-15).

Current assets Assets that a company expects to convert to cash or use up within one year or its operating cycle, whichever is longer. (p. 4-20).

Current liabilities Obligations that a company expects to pay within the coming year or its operating cycle, whichever is longer. (p. 4-22).

Income Summary A temporary account used in closing revenue and expense accounts. (p. 4-9).

Intangible assets Long-lived assets that do not have physical substance. (p. 4-21).

Liquidity The ability of a company to pay obligations expected to be due within the next year. (p. 4-22).

Long-term investments Generally, (1) investments in stocks and bonds of other companies that are normally held for many years; (2) long-term assets, such as land and buildings, not currently being used in operating activities; and (3) long-term notes receivable. (p. 4-20).

Long-term liabilities Obligations that a company expects to pay after one year. (p. 4-23).

Operating cycle The average time that it takes to purchase inventory, sell it on account, and then collect cash from customers. (p. 4-20).

Permanent (real) accounts Accounts that relate to one or more future accounting periods. Consist of all balance sheet accounts. Balances are carried forward to the next accounting period. (p. 4-9).

Post-closing trial balance A list of permanent accounts and their balances after a company has journalized and posted closing entries. (p. 4-12).

Property, plant, and equipment Assets with relatively long useful lives that are currently being used in operations. (p. 4-20).

Reversing entry An entry, made at the beginning of the next accounting period that is the exact opposite of the adjusting entry made in the previous period. (p. 4-15).

Stockholders' equity The ownership claim of shareholders on total assets. It is to a corporation what owner's equity is to a proprietorship. (p. 4-23).

Temporary (nominal) accounts Accounts that relate only to a given accounting period. Consist of all income statement accounts, the Dividends account, and the Income Summary account. All temporary accounts are closed at the end of the accounting period. (p. 4-9).

Worksheet A multiple-column form that may be used in making adjustments and in preparing financial statements. (p. 4-3).

Practice Multiple-Choice Questions

1. **(LO 1)** Which of the following statements is **incorrect** concerning the worksheet?
   a. The worksheet is essentially a working tool of the accountant.
   b. The worksheet is distributed to management and other interested parties.
   c. The worksheet cannot be used as a basis for posting to ledger accounts.
   d. Financial statements can be prepared directly from the worksheet before journalizing and posting the adjusting entries.

2. **(LO 1)** In a worksheet, net income is entered in the following columns:
   a. income statement (Dr.) and balance sheet (Dr.).
   b. income statement (Cr.) and balance sheet (Dr.).
   c. income statement (Dr.) and balance sheet (Cr.).
   d. income statement (Cr.) and balance sheet (Cr.).

3. **(LO 1)** In the unadjusted trial balance of its worksheet for the year ended December 31, 2022, Knox Company reported Equipment of $120,000. The year-end adjusting entries require an adjustment of $15,000 for depreciation expense for the equipment. After the adjusted

trial balance is completed, what amount should be shown in the financial statement columns?

    a. A debit of $105,000 for Equipment in the balance sheet column.

    b. A credit of $15,000 for Depreciation Expense in the income statement column.

    c. A debit of $120,000 for Equipment in the balance sheet column.

    d. A debit of $15,000 for Accumulated Depreciation—Equipment in the balance sheet column.

4. (LO 2) An account that will have a zero balance after closing entries have been journalized and posted is:

    a. Service Revenue.

    b. Supplies.

    c. Prepaid Insurance.

    d. Accumulated Depreciation—Equipment.

5. (LO 2) When a net loss has occurred, Income Summary is:

    a. debited and Retained Earnings is credited.

    b. credited and Retained Earnings is debited.

    c. debited and Dividends is credited.

    d. credited and Dividends is debited.

6. (LO 2) The closing process involves separate entries to close (1) expenses, (2) dividends, (3) revenues, and (4) income summary. The correct sequencing of the entries is:

    a. (4), (3), (2), (1).

    b. (1), (2), (3), (4).

    c. (3), (1), (4), (2).

    d. (3), (2), (1), (4).

7. (LO 2) Which types of accounts will appear in the post-closing trial balance?

    a. Permanent (real) accounts.

    b. Temporary (nominal) accounts.

    c. Accounts shown in the income statement columns of a worksheet.

    d. None of these answer choices is correct.

8. (LO 3) All of the following are required steps in the accounting cycle **except**:

    a. journalizing and posting closing entries.

    b. preparing financial statements.

    c. journalizing the transactions.

    d. preparing a worksheet.

9. (LO 3) The proper order of the following steps in the accounting cycle is:

    a. prepare unadjusted trial balance, journalize transactions, post to ledger accounts, journalize and post adjusting entries.

    b. journalize transactions, prepare unadjusted trial balance, post to ledger accounts, journalize and post adjusting entries.

    c. journalize transactions, post to ledger accounts, prepare unadjusted trial balance, journalize and post adjusting entries.

    d. prepare unadjusted trial balance, journalize and post adjusting entries, journalize transactions, post to ledger accounts.

10. (LO 3) When Ramirez Company purchased supplies worth $5,000, it incorrectly recorded a credit to Supplies for $5,000 and a debit to Cash for $5,000. Before correcting this error:

    a. Cash is overstated and Supplies is overstated.

    b. Cash is understated and Supplies is understated.

    c. Cash is understated and Supplies is overstated.

    d. Cash is overstated and Supplies is understated.

11. (LO 3) Cash of $100 received at the time the service was performed was journalized and posted as a debit to Cash $100 and a credit to Accounts Receivable $100. Assuming the incorrect entry is not reversed, the correcting entry is:

    a. debit Service Revenue $100 and credit Accounts Receivable $100.

    b. debit Accounts Receivable $100 and credit Service Revenue $100.

    c. debit Cash $100 and credit Service Revenue $100.

    d. debit Accounts Receivable $100 and credit Cash $100.

12. (LO 4) The correct order of presentation in a classified balance sheet for the following current assets is:

    a. accounts receivable, cash, prepaid insurance, inventory.

    b. cash, inventory, accounts receivable, prepaid insurance.

    c. cash, accounts receivable, inventory, prepaid insurance.

    d. inventory, cash, accounts receivable, prepaid insurance.

13. (LO 4) A company has purchased a tract of land. It expects to build a production plant on the land in approximately 5 years. During the 5 years before construction, the land will be idle. The land should be reported as:

    a. property, plant, and equipment.

    b. land expense.

    c. a long-term investment.

    d. an intangible asset.

14. (LO 4) In a classified balance sheet, assets are usually classified using the following categories:

    a. current assets; long-term assets; property, plant, and equipment; and intangible assets.

    b. current assets; long-term investments; property, plant, and equipment; and tangible assets.

    c. current assets; long-term investments; tangible assets; and intangible assets.

    d. current assets; long-term investments; property, plant, and equipment; and intangible assets.

15. (LO 4) Current assets are listed:

    a. by expected conversion to cash.   **c.** by longevity.

    b. by importance.   **d.** alphabetically.

*16. (LO 5) On December 31, Kevin Hartman Company correctly made an adjusting entry to recognize $2,000 of accrued salaries payable. On January 8 of the next year, total salaries of $3,400 were paid. Assuming the correct reversing entry was made on January 1, the entry on January 8 will result in a credit to Cash $3,400 and the following debit(s):

a. Salaries and Wages Payable $1,400 and Salaries and Wages Expense $2,000.

b. Salaries and Wages Payable $2,000 and Salaries and Wages Expense $1,400.

c. Salaries and Wages Expense $3,400.

d. Salaries and Wages Payable $3,400.

Solutions

1. **b.** The worksheet is a working tool of the accountant; it is not distributed to management and other interested parties. The other choices are all true statements.

2. **c.** Net income is entered in the Dr. column of the income statement and the Cr. column of the balance sheet. The other choices are incorrect because net income is entered in the (a) Cr. (not Dr.) column of the balance sheet, (b) Dr. (not Cr.) column of the income statement and in the Cr. (not Dr.) column of the balance sheet, and (d) Dr. (not Cr.) column of the income statement.

3. **c.** A debit of $120,000 for Equipment would appear in the balance sheet column. The other choices are incorrect because (a) Equipment, less accumulated depreciation of $15,000, would total $105,000 under assets on the balance sheet, not on the worksheet; (b) a debit, not credit, for Depreciation Expense would appear in the income statement column; and (d) a credit, not debit, of $15,000 for Accumulated Depreciation—Equipment would appear in the balance sheet column.

4. **a.** The Service Revenue account will have a zero balance after closing entries have been journalized and posted because it is a temporary account. The other choices are incorrect because (b) Supplies, (c) Prepaid Insurance, and (d) Accumulated Depreciation—Equipment are all permanent accounts and therefore not closed in the closing process.

5. **b.** The effect of a net loss is a credit to Income Summary and a debit to Retained Earnings. The other choices are incorrect because (a) Income Summary is credited, not debited, and Retained Earnings is debited, not credited; (c) Income Summary is credited, not debited, and Dividends is not affected; and (d) Retained Earnings, not Dividends, is debited.

6. **c.** The correct order is (3) revenues, (1) expenses, (4) income summary, and (2) dividends. Therefore, choices (a), (b), and (d) are incorrect.

7. **a.** Permanent accounts appear in the post-closing trial balance. The other choices are incorrect because (b) temporary accounts and (c) income statement accounts are closed to a zero balance and are therefore not included in the post-closing trial balance. Choice (d) is wrong as there is a correct answer for this question.

8. **d.** Preparing a worksheet is not a required step in the accounting cycle. The other choices are all required steps in the accounting cycle.

9. **c.** The proper order of the steps in the accounting cycle is (1) journalize transactions, (2) post to ledger accounts, (3) prepare unadjusted trial balance, and (4) journalize and post adjusting entries. Therefore, choices (a), (b), and (d) are incorrect.

10. **d.** This entry causes Cash to be overstated and Supplies to be understated. Supplies should have been debited (increasing supplies) and Cash should have been credited (decreasing cash). The other choices are incorrect because (a) Supplies is understated, not overstated; (b) Cash is overstated, not understated; and (c) Cash is overstated, not understated, and Supplies is understated, not overstated.

11. **b.** The correcting entry is to debit Accounts Receivable $100 and credit Service Revenue $100. The other choices are incorrect because (a) Service Revenue should be credited, not debited, and Accounts Receivable should be debited, not credited; (c) Service Revenue should be credited for $100, and Cash should not be included in the correcting entry as it was recorded properly; and (d) Accounts Receivable should be debited for $100 and Cash should not be included in the correcting entry as it was recorded properly.

12. **c.** Companies list current assets on the balance sheet in the order of liquidity: cash, accounts receivable, inventory, and prepaid insurance. Therefore, choices (a), (b), and (d) are incorrect.

13. **c.** Long term investments include long-term assets such as land that a company is not currently using in its operating activities. The other choices are incorrect because (a) land is reported as property, plant, and equipment only if it is being currently used in the business; (b) land is an asset, not an expense; and (d) land has physical substance and thus is a tangible property.

14. **d.** These are the categories usually used in a classified balance sheet. The other choices are incorrect because the categories (a) "long-term assets" and (b) and (c) "tangible assets" are generally not used.

15. **a.** Current assets are listed in order of their liquidity, not (b) by importance, (c) by longevity, or (d) alphabetically.

*16. c. The use of reversing entries simplifies the recording of the first payroll following the end of the year by eliminating the need to make an entry to the Salaries and Wages Payable account. The other choices are incorrect because (a) Salaries and Wages Payable is not part of the payroll entry on January 8, and the debit to Salaries and Wages Expense should be for $3,400, not $2,000; and (b) and (d) the Salaries and Wages Expense account, not the Salaries and Wages Payable account, should be debited.

Practice Exercises

1. **(LO 2)** Arapaho Company ended its fiscal year on July 31, 2022. The company's adjusted trial balance as of the end of its fiscal year is as shown below.

Journalize and post closing entries and prepare a post-closing trial balance.

Arapaho Company
Adjusted Trial Balance
July 31, 2022

No.	Account Titles	Debit	Credit
101	Cash	$ 15,940	
112	Accounts Receivable	8,580	
157	Equipment	16,900	
158	Accumulated Depreciation—Equipment		$ 7,500
201	Accounts Payable		4,420
208	Unearned Rent Revenue		1,600
311	Common Stock		20,500
320	Retained Earnings		25,000
332	Dividends	14,000	
400	Service Revenue		64,000
429	Rent Revenue		5,500
711	Depreciation Expense	4,500	
726	Salaries and Wages Expense	54,700	
732	Utilities Expense	13,900	
		$128,520	$128,520

Instructions

a. Prepare the closing entries using page J15 in a general journal.

b. Post to Retained Earnings and No. 350 Income Summary accounts. (Use the three-column form.)

c. Prepare a post-closing trial balance at July 31, 2022.

Solution

1. a.

GENERAL JOURNAL   **J15**

Date	Account Titles	Ref.	Debit	Credit
July 31	Service Revenue	400	64,000	
	Rent Revenue	429	5,500	
	Income Summary	350		69,500
	(To close revenue accounts)			
31	Income Summary	350	73,100	
	Depreciation Expense	711		4,500
	Salaries and Wages Expense	726		54,700
	Utilities Expense	732		13,900
	(To close expense accounts)			
31	Retained Earnings ($73,100 − $69,500)	320	3,600	
	Income Summary	350		3,600
	(To close net loss to retained earnings)			
31	Retained Earnings	320	14,000	
	Dividends	332		14,000
	(To close dividends to retained earnings)			

b.   **Retained Earnings**   **No. 320**

Date	Explanation	Ref.	Debit	Credit	Balance
July 31	Balance				25,000
31	Close net loss	J15	3,600		21,400
31	Close dividends	J15	14,000		7,400

Income Summary   **No. 350**

Date	Explanation	Ref.	Debit	Credit	Balance
July 31	Close revenue	J15		69,500	69,500
31	Close expenses	J15	73,100		(3,600)
31	Close net loss	J15		3,600	0

c.

Arapaho Company
Post-Closing Trial Balance
July 31, 2022

	Debit	Credit
Cash	$15,940	
Accounts Receivable	8,580	
Equipment	16,900	
Accumulated Depreciation—Equipment		$ 7,500
Accounts Payable		4,420
Unearned Rent Revenue		1,600
Common Stock		20,500
Retained Earnings		7,400
	$41,420	$41,420

2. **(LO 4)** The adjusted trial balance for Arapaho Company is presented in **Practice Exercise 1**.

Prepare financial statements.

Instructions

a. Prepare an income statement and a retained earnings statement for the year ended July 31, 2022.

b. Prepare a classified balance sheet at July 31, 2022.

Solution

2. a.

Arapaho Company
Income Statement
For the Year Ended July 31, 2022

Revenues		
Service revenue	$64,000	
Rent revenue	5,500	
Total revenues		$69,500
Expenses		
Salaries and wages expense	54,700	
Utilities expense	13,900	
Depreciation expense	4,500	
Total expenses		73,100
Net loss		($ 3,600)

Arapaho Company
Retained Earnings Statement
For the Year Ended July 31, 2022

Retained earnings, August 1, 2021		$25,000
Less: Net loss	$ 3,600	
Dividends	14,000	17,600
Retained earnings, July 31, 2022		$ 7,400

b.

Arapaho Company
Balance Sheet
July 31, 2022

Assets

Current assets			
Cash		$15,940	
Accounts receivable		8,580	
Total current assets			$24,520
Property, plant, and equipment			
Equipment		16,900	
Less: Accumulated depreciation—equipment		7,500	9,400
Total assets			$33,920

Liabilities and Stockholders' Equity

Current liabilities			
Accounts payable		$ 4,420	
Unearned rent revenue		1,600	
Total current liabilities			$ 6,020
Stockholders' equity			
Common stock		20,500	
Retained earnings		7,400	
Total stockholders' equity			27,900
Total liabilities and stockholders' equity			$33,920

Practice Problem

Prepare worksheet and classified balance sheet, and journalize closing entries.

(LO 1, 2, 4) At the end of its first month of operations, Pampered Pet Service Inc. has the following unadjusted trial balance.

Pampered Pet Service Inc.
August 31, 2022
Trial Balance

	Debit	Credit
Cash	$ 5,400	
Accounts Receivable	2,800	
Supplies	1,300	
Prepaid Insurance	2,400	
Equipment	60,000	
Notes Payable		$40,000
Accounts Payable		2,400
Common Stock		30,000
Dividends	1,000	
Service Revenue		4,900
Salaries and Wages Expense	3,200	
Utilities Expense	800	
Advertising Expense	400	
	$77,300	$77,300

Other data:

1. Insurance expires at the rate of $200 per month.
2. $1,000 of supplies are on hand at August 31.
3. Monthly depreciation on the equipment is $900.
4. Interest of $500 on the notes payable has accrued during August.

Instructions

    a. Prepare a worksheet.

    b. Prepare a classified balance sheet assuming $35,000 of the notes payable are long-term.

    c. Journalize the closing entries.

Solution

a.

Pampered Pet Service Inc.
Worksheet
For the Month Ended August 31, 2022

Account Titles	Trial Balance Dr.	Trial Balance Cr.	Adjustments Dr.	Adjustments Cr.	Adjusted Trial Balance Dr.	Adjusted Trial Balance Cr.	Income Statement Dr.	Income Statement Cr.	Balance Sheet Dr.	Balance Sheet Cr.
Cash	5,400				5,400				5,400	
Accounts Receivable	2,800				2,800				2,800	
Supplies	1,300			(b) 300	1,000				1,000	
Prepaid Insurance	2,400			(a) 200	2,200				2,200	
Equipment	60,000				60,000				60,000	
Notes Payable		40,000				40,000				40,000
Accounts Payable		2,400				2,400				2,400
Common Stock		30,000				30,000				30,000
Dividends	1,000				1,000				1,000	
Service Revenue		4,900				4,900		4,900		
Salaries and Wages Expense	3,200				3,200		3,200			
Utilities Expense	800				800		800			
Advertising Expense	400				400		400			
Totals	77,300	77,300								
Insurance Expense			(a) 200		200		200			
Supplies Expense			(b) 300		300		300			
Depreciation Expense			(c) 900		900		900			
Accumulated Depreciation— Equipment				(c) 900		900				900
Interest Expense			(d) 500		500		500			
Interest Payable				(d) 500		500				500
Totals			1,900	1,900	78,700	78,700	6,300	4,900	72,400	73,800
Net Loss								1,400	1,400	
Totals							6,300	6,300	73,800	73,800

Explanation: (a) insurance expired, (b) supplies used, (c) depreciation expensed, and (d) interest accrued.

b.

Pampered Pet Service Inc.
Balance Sheet
August 31, 2022

Assets

Current assets		
Cash	$ 5,400	
Accounts receivable	2,800	
Supplies	1,000	
Prepaid insurance	2,200	
Total current assets		$11,400
Property, plant, and equipment		
Equipment	60,000	
Less: Accumulated depreciation—equipment	900	59,100
Total assets		$70,500

Liabilities and Stockholders' Equity

Current liabilities		
Notes payable	$ 5,000	
Accounts payable	2,400	
Interest payable	500	
Total current liabilities		$ 7,900
Long-term liabilities		
Notes payable		35,000
Total liabilities		42,900
Stockholders' equity		
Common stock	30,000	
Retained earnings	(2,400)*	
Total stockholders' equity		27,600
Total liabilities and stockholders' equity		$70,500

*Net loss of $1,400 plus dividends of $1,000 equals negative retained earnings (deficit).

c.

Aug. 31	Service Revenue	4,900	
	Income Summary		4,900
	(To close revenue account)		
31	Income Summary	6,300	
	Salaries and Wages Expense		3,200
	Depreciation Expense		900
	Utilities Expense		800
	Interest Expense		500
	Advertising Expense		400
	Supplies Expense		300
	Insurance Expense		200
	(To close expense accounts)		
31	Retained Earnings	1,400	
	Income Summary		1,400
	(To close net loss to retained earnings)		
31	Retained Earnings	1,000	
	Dividends		1,000
	(To close dividends to retained earnings)		

WileyPLUS

Brief Exercises, DO IT! Exercises, Exercises, Problems, and many additional resources are available for practice in WileyPLUS.

Note: All asterisked Questions, Exercises, and Problems relate to material in the appendix to the chapter.

Questions

1. "A worksheet is a permanent accounting record and its use is required in the accounting cycle." Do you agree? Explain.

2. Explain the purpose of the worksheet.

3. What is the relationship, if any, between the amount shown in the adjusted trial balance column for an account and that account's ledger balance?

4. If a company's revenues are $125,000 and its expenses are $113,000, in which financial statement columns of the worksheet will the net

income of $12,000 appear? When expenses exceed revenues, in which columns will the difference appear?

5. Why is it necessary to prepare formal financial statements if all of the data are in the statement columns of the worksheet?

6. Identify the account(s) debited and credited in each of the four closing entries, assuming the company has net income for the year.

7. Describe the nature of the Income Summary account and identify the types of summary data that may be posted to this account.

8. What are the content and purpose of a post-closing trial balance?

9. Which of the following accounts would not appear in the post-closing trial balance? Interest Payable, Equipment, Depreciation Expense, Dividends, Unearned Service Revenue, Accumulated Depreciation—Equipment, and Service Revenue.

10. Distinguish between a reversing entry and an adjusting entry. Are reversing entries required?

11. Indicate, in the sequence in which they are made, the three required steps in the accounting cycle that involve journalizing.

12. Identify, in the sequence in which they are prepared, the three trial balances that are used in the accounting cycle.

13. How do correcting entries differ from adjusting entries?

14. What standard classifications are used in preparing a classified balance sheet?

15. What is meant by the term "operating cycle"?

16. Define current assets. What basis is used for arranging individual items within the current assets section?

17. Distinguish between long-term investments and property, plant, and equipment.

18. (a) What is the term used to describe the owners' equity section of a corporation? (b) Identify the two owners' equity accounts in a corporation and indicate the purpose of each.

19. Using **Apple**'s annual report, determine its current liabilities at September 30, 2017, and September 29, 2018. Were current liabilities higher or lower than current assets in these two years?

*20. Cigale Company prepares reversing entries. If the adjusting entry for interest payable is reversed, what type of an account balance, if any, will there be in Interest Payable and Interest Expense after the reversing entry is posted?

*21. At December 31, accrued salaries payable totaled $3,500. On January 10, total salaries of $8,000 are paid. (a) Assume that reversing entries are made at January 1. Give the January 10 entry, and indicate the Salaries and Wages Expense account balance after the entry is posted. (b) Repeat part (a) assuming reversing entries are not made.

Brief Exercises

BE4.1 (LO 1), K The steps in using a worksheet are presented in random order below. List the steps in the proper order by placing numbers 1–5 in the blank spaces.

List the steps in preparing a worksheet.

a. _____ Prepare a trial balance on the worksheet.

b. _____ Enter adjusted balances.

c. _____ Extend adjusted balances to appropriate statement columns.

d. _____ Total the statement columns, compute net income (loss), and complete the worksheet.

e. _____ Enter adjustment data.

BE4.2 (LO 1), AP The ledger of Clayton Company includes the following unadjusted balances: Prepaid Insurance $3,000, Service Revenue $58,000, and Salaries and Wages Expense $25,000. Adjusting entries are required for (a) expired insurance $1,800; (b) services performed $1,100, but unbilled and uncollected; and (c) accrued salaries payable $800. Enter the unadjusted balances and adjustments into a worksheet and complete the worksheet for all accounts. (Note: You will need to add the following accounts: Accounts Receivable, Salaries and Wages Payable, and Insurance Expense.)

Prepare partial worksheet.

BE4.3 (LO 1), C The following selected accounts appear in the adjusted trial balance columns of the worksheet for Goulet Company: Accumulated Depreciation—Equipment, Depreciation Expense, Common Stock, Dividends, Service Revenue, Supplies, and Accounts Payable. Indicate the financial statement column (income statement Dr., balance sheet Cr., etc.) to which each balance should be extended.

Identify worksheet columns for selected accounts.

BE4.4 (LO 2), AP The ledger of Rios Company contains the following balances: Retained Earnings $30,000, Dividends $2,000, Service Revenue $50,000, Salaries and Wages Expense $27,000, and Supplies Expense $7,000. Prepare the closing entries at December 31.

Prepare closing entries from ledger balances.

BE4.5 (LO 2), AP The ledger of Rios Company contains the following balances: Retained Earnings $30,000, Dividends $2,000, Service Revenue $50,000, Salaries and Wages Expense $27,000, and Supplies Expense $7,000. Enter the balances in T-accounts, post the closing entries, and underline and balance the accounts.

Post closing entries; underline and balance T-accounts.

BE4.6 (LO 2), AP The income statement for Weeping Willow Golf Club for the month ending July 31 shows Service Revenue $16,400, Salaries and Wages Expense $8,200, Maintenance and Repairs Expense $2,500, and Net Income $5,700. Prepare the entries to close the revenue and expense accounts. Post the entries to the revenue and expense accounts, and complete the closing process for these accounts using the three-column form of account.

Journalize and post closing entries using the three-column form of account.

BE4.7 (LO 2), C The following selected accounts appear in the adjusted trial balance columns of the worksheet for Goulet Company: Accumulated Depreciation—Equipment, Depreciation Expense, Common Stock, Dividends, Service Revenue, Supplies, and Accounts Payable. Identify the accounts that would be included in a post-closing trial balance.

Identify post-closing trial balance accounts.

List the required steps in the accounting cycle in sequence.

BE4.8 (LO 3), K The steps in the accounting cycle are listed in random order below. List the steps in proper sequence, assuming no worksheet is prepared, by placing numbers 1–9 in the blank spaces.

a. _____ Prepare a trial balance.

b. _____ Journalize the transactions.

c. _____ Journalize and post closing entries.

d. _____ Prepare financial statements.

e. _____ Journalize and post adjusting entries.

f. _____ Post to ledger accounts.

g. _____ Prepare a post-closing trial balance.

h. _____ Prepare an adjusted trial balance.

i. _____ Analyze business transactions.

Prepare correcting entries.

BE4.9 (LO 3), AP At Creighton Company, the following errors were discovered after the transactions had been journalized and posted. Prepare the correcting entries.

1. A collection on account from a customer for $870 was recorded as a debit to Cash $870 and a credit to Service Revenue $870.

2. The purchase of store supplies on account for $1,570 was recorded as a debit to Supplies $1,750 and a credit to Accounts Payable $1,750.

Prepare the current assets section of a balance sheet.

BE4.10 (LO 4), AP The balance sheet debit column of the worksheet for Hamidi Company includes the following accounts: Accounts Receivable $12,500, Prepaid Insurance $3,600, Cash $4,100, Supplies $5,200, and Debt Investments (short-term) $6,700. Prepare the current assets section of the balance sheet, listing the accounts in proper sequence.

Classify accounts on balance sheet.

BE4.11 (LO 4), C The following are the major balance sheet classifications:

Current assets (CA)   Current liabilities (CL)
Long-term investments (LTI)   Long-term liabilities (LTL)
Property, plant, and equipment (PPE)   Stockholders' equity (SE)
Intangible assets (IA)

Match each of the following accounts to its proper balance sheet classification.

_____ Accounts payable   _____ Income taxes payable
_____ Accounts receivable   _____ Debt investments (long-term)
_____ Accumulated depreciation—buildings _____ Land
_____ Buildings   _____ Inventory
_____ Cash   _____ Patents
_____ Copyrights   _____ Supplies

Prepare reversing entries.

* **BE4.12 (LO 5), AP** At October 31, Burgess Company made an accrued expense adjusting entry of $2,100 for salaries. Prepare the reversing entry on November 1, and indicate the balances in Salaries and Wages Payable and Salaries and Wages Expense after posting the reversing entry.

DO IT! Exercises

Prepare a worksheet.

DO IT! 4.1 (LO 1), C Bradley Decker is preparing a worksheet. Explain to Bradley how he should extend the following adjusted trial balance accounts to the financial statement columns of the worksheet.

Service Revenue   Accounts Receivable
Notes Payable   Accumulated Depreciation—Buildings
Common Stock   Utilities Expense

Prepare closing entries.

DO IT! 4.2 (LO 2), AP Paloma Company shows the following balances in selected accounts of its adjusted trial balance.

Supplies	$32,000	Service Revenue	$108,000
Supplies Expense	6,000	Salaries and Wages Expense	40,000
Accounts Receivable	12,000	Utilities Expense	8,000
Dividends	22,000	Rent Expense	18,000
Retained Earnings	70,000		

Prepare the closing entries at December 31.

DO IT! 4.3 (LO 3), AN Hanson Company has an inexperienced accountant. During the first months on the job, the accountant made the following errors in journalizing transactions. All entries were posted as made.

Prepare correcting entries.

1. The purchase of supplies for $650 cash was debited to Equipment $210 and credited to Cash $210.

2. A $500 dividend was debited to Salaries and Wages Expense $900 and credited to Cash $900.

3. A payment on account of $820 to a creditor was debited to Accounts Payable $280 and credited to Cash $280.

Prepare the correcting entries.

DO IT! 4.4 (LO 4), C The following accounts were taken from the financial statements of Lee Company.

Match accounts to balance sheet classifications.

_____ Interest revenue	_____ Common stock
_____ Utilities payable	_____ Accumulated depreciation—equipment
_____ Accounts payable	_____ Equipment
_____ Supplies	_____ Salaries and wages expense
_____ Bonds payable	_____ Debt investments (long-term)
_____ Goodwill	_____ Unearned rent revenue

Match each of the accounts to its proper balance sheet classification, as shown below. If the item would not appear on a balance sheet, use "NA."

Current assets (CA)	Current liabilities (CL)
Long-term investments (LTI)	Long-term liabilities (LTL)
Property, plant, and equipment (PPE)	Stockholders' equity (SE)
Intangible assets (IA)	

Exercises

E4.1 (LO 1), AP The trial balance columns of the worksheet for Nanduri Company at June 30, 2022, are as follows.

Complete the worksheet.

Nanduri Company
Worksheet
For the Month Ended June 30, 2022

	Trial Balance	
Account Titles	**Dr.**	**Cr.**
Cash	2,320	
Accounts Receivable	2,440	
Supplies	1,880	
Accounts Payable		1,120
Unearned Service Revenue		240
Common Stock		3,600
Service Revenue		2,400
Salaries and Wages Expense	560	
Miscellaneous Expense	160	
	7,360	7,360

Other data:

1. A physical count reveals $500 of supplies on hand.

2. $100 of the unearned revenue is still unearned at month-end.

3. Accrued salaries are $210.

Instructions

Enter the trial balance on a worksheet and complete the worksheet.

Complete the worksheet.

E4.2 (LO 1), AP The adjusted trial balance columns of the worksheet for DeSousa Company are as follows.

DeSousa Company
Worksheet (partial)
For the Month Ended April 30, 2022

Account Titles	Adjusted Trial Balance		Income Statement		Balance Sheet	
	Dr.	Cr.	Dr.	Cr.	Dr.	Cr.
Cash	10,000					
Accounts Receivable	7,840					
Prepaid Rent	2,280					
Equipment	23,050					
Accumulated Depreciation—Equip.		4,921				
Notes Payable (due in October 2022)		5,700				
Accounts Payable		4,920				
Common Stock		20,000				
Retained Earnings		7,960				
Dividends	3,650					
Service Revenue		15,590				
Salaries and Wages Expense	10,840					
Rent Expense	760					
Depreciation Expense	671					
Interest Expense	57					
Interest Payable		57				
Totals	59,148	59,148				

Instructions

Complete the worksheet.

Prepare financial statements from worksheet.

E4.3 (LO 1, 4), AP Worksheet data for DeSousa Company are presented in E4.2.

Instructions

Prepare an income statement, a retained earnings statement, and a classified balance sheet.

Journalize and post closing entries and prepare a post-closing trial balance.

E4.4 (LO 2), AP Worksheet data for DeSousa Company are presented in E4.2.

Instructions

a. Journalize the closing entries at April 30.

b. Post the closing entries to Income Summary and Retained Earnings. (Use T-accounts.)

c. Prepare a post-closing trial balance at April 30.

Prepare adjusting entries from financial statement columns, and extend balances to worksheet columns.

E4.5 (LO 1), AP The adjustments columns of the worksheet for Misra Company are shown here.

Account Titles	Adjustments	
	Debit	Credit
Accounts Receivable	1,100	
Prepaid Insurance		300
Accumulated Depreciation—Equipment		900
Salaries and Wages Payable		500
Service Revenue		1,100
Salaries and Wages Expense	500	
Insurance Expense	300	
Depreciation Expense	900	
	2,800	2,800

Instructions

a. Prepare the adjusting entries.

b. Assuming the adjusted trial balance amount for each account is normal, indicate the financial statement column to which each balance should be extended.

E4.6 (LO 1), AN Selected spreadsheet data for Elsayed Company are presented here.

Derive adjusting entries from spreadsheet data.

Account Titles	Trial Balance Dr.	Trial Balance Cr.	Adjusted Trial Balance Dr.	Adjusted Trial Balance Cr.
Accounts Receivable	?		34,000	
Prepaid Insurance	26,000		20,000	
Supplies	7,000		?	
Accumulated Depreciation—Equipment		12,000		?
Salaries and Wages Payable		?		5,600
Service Revenue		88,000		97,000
Insurance Expense			?	
Depreciation Expense			10,000	
Supplies Expense			4,500	
Salaries and Wages Expense	?		49,000	

Instructions

a. Fill in the missing amounts.

b. Prepare the adjusting entries that were made.

E4.7 (LO 2), AP Kay Magill Company had the following adjusted trial balance.

Prepare closing entries and a post-closing trial balance.

Kay Magill Company
Adjusted Trial Balance
For the Year Ended June 30, 2022

Account Titles	Adjusted Trial Balance Debit	Adjusted Trial Balance Credit
Cash	$ 3,712	
Accounts Receivable	3,904	
Supplies	480	
Accounts Payable		$ 1,556
Unearned Service Revenue		160
Common Stock		4,000
Retained Earnings		1,760
Dividends	628	
Service Revenue		4,300
Salaries and Wages Expense	1,344	
Miscellaneous Expense	256	
Supplies Expense	1,900	
Salaries and Wages Payable		448
	$12,224	$12,224

Instructions

a. Prepare closing entries at June 30, 2022.

b. Prepare a post-closing trial balance.

E4.8 (LO 2), AP Plevin Company ended its fiscal year on July 31, 2022. The company's adjusted trial balance as of the end of its fiscal year is shown as follows.

Journalize and post closing entries and prepare a post-closing trial balance.

Plevin Company
Adjusted Trial Balance
July 31, 2022

No.	Account Titles	Debit	Credit
101	Cash	$ 9,840	
112	Accounts Receivable	8,780	
157	Equipment	15,900	
158	Accumulated Depreciation—Equip.		$ 7,400
201	Accounts Payable		4,220
208	Unearned Rent Revenue		1,800
311	Common Stock		20,000
320	Retained Earnings		25,200
332	Dividends	16,000	
400	Service Revenue		64,000
429	Rent Revenue		6,500
711	Depreciation Expense	8,000	
726	Salaries and Wages Expense	55,700	
732	Utilities Expense	14,900	
		$129,120	$129,120

Instructions

a. Prepare the closing entries using page J15.

b. Post to the Retained Earnings and No. 350 Income Summary accounts. (Use the three-column form.)

c. Prepare a post-closing trial balance at July 31.

Prepare financial statements.

E4.9 (LO 4), AP The adjusted trial balance for Plevin Company is presented in E4.8.

Instructions

a. Prepare an income statement and a retained earnings statement for the year.

b. Prepare a classified balance sheet at July 31.

Answer questions related to the accounting cycle.

E4.10 (LO 3), C Janis Engle has prepared the following list of statements about the accounting cycle.

1. "Journalize the transactions" is the first step in the accounting cycle.

2. Reversing entries are a required step in the accounting cycle.

3. Correcting entries do not have to be part of the accounting cycle.

4. If a worksheet is prepared, some steps of the accounting cycle are incorporated into the worksheet.

5. The accounting cycle begins with the analysis of business transactions and ends with the preparation of a post-closing trial balance.

6. All steps of the accounting cycle occur daily during the accounting period.

7. The step of "post to the ledger accounts" occurs before the step of "journalize the transactions."

8. Closing entries must be prepared before financial statements can be prepared.

Instructions

Identify each statement as true or false. If false, indicate how to correct the statement.

Prepare closing entries.

E4.11 (LO 2), AP Selected accounts for Heather's Salon are presented here. All June 30 postings are from closing entries.

Salaries and Wages Expense

6/10	3,200			
6/28	5,600			
Bal.	8,800	6/30	8,800	

Service Revenue

		6/15	9,700	
		6/24	8,400	
6/30	18,100	Bal.	18,100	

Retained Earnings

6/30	2,500	6/1	12,000	
		6/30	5,000	
		Bal.	14,500	

Supplies Expense

6/12	600			
6/24	700			
Bal.	1,300	6/30	1,300	

Rent Expense

6/1	3,000			
Bal.	3,000	6/30	3,000	

Dividends

6/13	1,000			
6/25	1,500			
Bal.	2,500	6/30	2,500	

Instructions

a. Prepare the closing entries that were made.

b. Post the closing entries to Income Summary.

E4.12 (LO 3), AN Andrew Clark Company discovered the following errors made in January 2022.

Prepare correcting entries.

1. A payment of Salaries and Wages Expense of $700 was debited to Equipment and credited to Cash, both for $700.

2. A collection of $1,000 from a client on account was debited to Cash $100 and credited to Service Revenue $100.

3. The purchase of equipment on account for $760 was debited to Equipment $670 and credited to Accounts Payable $670.

Instructions

a. Correct the errors by reversing the incorrect entry and preparing the correct entry.

b. Correct the errors without reversing the incorrect entry.

E4.13 (LO 3), AN Keenan Company has an inexperienced accountant. During the first 2 weeks on the job, the accountant made the following errors in journalizing transactions. All entries were posted as made.

Prepare correcting entries.

1. A payment on account of $840 to a creditor was debited to Accounts Payable $480 and credited to Cash $480.

2. The purchase of supplies on account for $560 was debited to Equipment $56 and credited to Accounts Payable $56.

3. A $500 cash dividend was debited to Salaries and Wages Expense $500 and credited to Cash $500.

Instructions

Prepare the correcting entries.

E4.14 (LO 4), AP Writing The adjusted trial balance for Martell Bowling Alley at December 31, 2022, contains the following accounts.

Prepare a classified balance sheet.

	Debit			Credit
Buildings	$128,800	Common Stock		$ 90,000
Accounts Receivable	14,520	Retained Earnings		25,000
Prepaid Insurance	4,680	Accumulated Depreciation—Buildings		42,600
Cash	18,040	Accounts Payable		12,300
Equipment	62,400	Notes Payable		97,780
Land	67,000	Accumulated Depreciation—Equipment		18,720
Insurance Expense	780	Interest Payable		2,600
Depreciation Expense	7,360	Service Revenue		17,180
Interest Expense	2,600			$306,180
	$306,180			

Instructions

a. Prepare a classified balance sheet; assume that $22,000 of the note payable will be paid in 2023.

b. Comment on the liquidity of the company.

E4.15 (LO 4), C The following are the major balance sheet classifications.

Classify accounts on balance sheet.

Current assets (CA)   Current liabilities (CL)
Long-term investments (LTI) Long-term liabilities (LTL)
Property, plant, and equipment (PPE) Stockholders' equity (SE)
Intangible assets (IA)

Instructions

Classify each of the following accounts taken from Raman Company's balance sheet.

_____ Accounts payable	_____ Accumulated depreciation—equipment
_____ Accounts receivable	_____ Buildings
_____ Cash	_____ Land (in use)
_____ Common stock	_____ Notes payable (due in 2 years)
_____ Patents	_____ Supplies
_____ Salaries and wages payable	_____ Equipment
_____ Inventory	_____ Prepaid expenses
_____ Stock investments (to be sold in 7 months)	

Prepare a classified balance sheet.

E4.16 (LO 4), AP The following items were taken from the financial statements of D. Gygi Company. (All amounts are in thousands.)

Long-term debt	$ 1,000	Accumulated depreciation—equipment	$ 5,655
Prepaid insurance	880	Accounts payable	1,444
Equipment	11,500	Notes payable (due after 2023)	400
Stock investments (long-term)	264	Common stock	10,000
Debt investments (short-term)	3,690	Retained earnings	2,955
Notes payable (due in 2023)	500	Accounts receivable	1,696
Cash	2,668	Inventory	1,256

Instructions

Prepare a classified balance sheet in good form as of December 31, 2022.

Prepare financial statements.

E4.17 (LO 4), AP These financial statement items are for Norsted Company at year-end, July 31, 2022.

Salaries and wages payable	$ 2,080	Notes payable (long-term)	$ 1,800
Salaries and wages expense	51,700	Cash	14,200
Utilities expense	22,600	Accounts receivable	9,780
Equipment	30,400	Accumulated depreciation—equipment	6,000
Accounts payable	4,100	Dividends	3,000
Service revenue	62,000	Depreciation expense	4,000
Rent revenue	8,500	Retained earnings (beginning of the year)	21,200
Common stock	30,000		

Instructions

a. Prepare an income statement and a retained earnings statement for the year.

b. Prepare a classified balance sheet at July 31.

Use reversing entries.

* **E4.18 (LO 5), AP** Reblin Company pays salaries of $12,000 every Monday for the preceding 5-day week (Monday through Friday). Assume December 31 falls on a Tuesday, so Reblin's employees have worked 2 days without being paid at the end of the fiscal year.

Instructions

a. Assume the company does not use reversing entries. Prepare the December 31 adjusting entry and the entry on Monday, January 6, when Reblin pays the payroll.

b. Assume the company does use reversing entries. Prepare the December 31 adjusting entry, the January 1 reversing entry, and the entry on Monday, January 6, when Reblin pays the payroll.

Prepare closing and reversing entries.

* **E4.19 (LO 2, 5), AP** On December 31, the adjusted trial balance of Cisneros Employment Agency shows the following selected data.

Accounts Receivable	$24,500	Service Revenue	$92,500
Interest Expense	8,300	Interest Payable	2,000

Analysis shows that adjusting entries were made to (1) accrue $5,000 of service revenue and (2) accrue $2,000 interest expense.

Instructions

a. Prepare the closing entries for the temporary accounts shown above at December 31.

b. Prepare the reversing entries on January 1.

c. Post the entries in (a) and (b), excluding the Income Summary account. Underline and balance the accounts. (Use T-accounts.)

d. Prepare the entries to record (1) the collection of the accrued revenue on January 10 and (2) the payment of all interest due ($2,000) on January 15.

e. Post the entries in (d) to the temporary accounts.

Problems

P4.1A (LO 1, 2, 4), AP The trial balance columns of the worksheet for Lampert Roofing at March 31, 2022, are as follows.

Prepare a worksheet, financial statements, and adjusting and closing entries.

Lampert Roofing Worksheet For the Month Ended March 31, 2022		
	Trial Balance	
Account Titles	**Dr.**	**Cr.**
Cash	4,500	
Accounts Receivable	3,200	
Supplies	2,000	
Equipment	11,000	
Accumulated Depreciation—Equipment		1,250
Accounts Payable		2,500
Unearned Service Revenue		550
Common Stock		10,000
Retained Earnings		2,900
Dividends	1,100	
Service Revenue		6,300
Salaries and Wages Expense	1,300	
Miscellaneous Expense	400	
	23,500	23,500

Other data:

1. A physical count reveals only $550 of roofing supplies on hand.
2. Depreciation for March is $250.
3. Unearned service revenue amounted to $210 at March 31.
4. Accrued salaries are $700.

Instructions

a. Enter the trial balance on a worksheet and complete the worksheet.

b. Prepare an income statement and a retained earnings statement for the month of March and a classified balance sheet at March 31.

c. Journalize the adjusting entries from the adjustments columns of the worksheet.

d. Journalize the closing entries from the financial statement columns of the worksheet.

a. Adjusted trial balance $24,450

b. Net income $2,540
   Total assets $17,750

P4.2A (LO 1, 2, 4), AP The adjusted trial balance columns of the worksheet for Alshwer Company are as follows.

Complete worksheet; prepare financial statements, closing entries, and post-closing trial balance.

Alshwer Company
Worksheet
For the Year Ended December 31, 2022

Account No.	Account Titles	Adjusted Trial Balance Dr.	Adjusted Trial Balance Cr.
101	Cash	5,300	
112	Accounts Receivable	10,800	
126	Supplies	1,500	
130	Prepaid Insurance	2,000	
157	Equipment	27,000	
158	Accumulated Depreciation—Equipment		5,600
200	Notes Payable		15,000
201	Accounts Payable		6,100
212	Salaries and Wages Payable		2,400
230	Interest Payable		600
311	Common Stock		10,000
320	Retained Earnings		3,000
332	Dividends	7,000	
400	Service Revenue		61,000
610	Advertising Expense	8,400	
631	Supplies Expense	4,000	
711	Depreciation Expense	5,600	
722	Insurance Expense	3,500	
726	Salaries and Wages Expense	28,000	
905	Interest Expense	600	
	Totals	103,700	103,700

Instructions

a. Net income $10,900

b. Current assets $19,600
   Current liabilities $14,100

e. Post-closing trial balance
   $46,600

Complete all steps in accounting cycle.

a. Complete the worksheet by extending the balances to the financial statement columns.

b. Prepare an income statement, a retained earnings statement, and a classified balance sheet. (*Note:* $5,000 of the notes payable become due in 2023.)

c. Prepare the closing entries. Use J14 for the journal page.

d. Post the closing entries. (Use the three-column form of account.) Income Summary is account No. 350.

e. Prepare a post-closing trial balance.

P4.3A (LO 1, 2, 3, 4), AP Heidi Jara opened Jara's Cleaning Service on July 1, 2022. During July, the following transactions were completed.

July 1 Stockholders invested $20,000 cash in the business in exchange for common stock.
   1 Purchased used truck for $9,000, paying $4,000 cash and the balance on account.
   3 Purchased cleaning supplies for $2,100 on account.
   5 Paid $1,800 cash on a 1-year insurance policy effective July 1.
   12 Billed customers $4,500 for cleaning services.
   18 Paid $1,500 cash on amount owed on truck and $1,400 on amount owed on cleaning supplies.
   20 Paid $2,500 cash for employee salaries.
   21 Collected $3,400 cash from customers billed on July 12.
   25 Billed customers $6,000 for cleaning services.
   31 Paid $350 for the monthly gasoline bill for the truck.
   31 Paid a $5,600 cash dividend.

The chart of accounts for Jara's Cleaning Service contains the following accounts: No. 101 Cash, No. 112 Accounts Receivable, No. 126 Supplies, No. 130 Prepaid Insurance, No. 157 Equipment, No. 158 Accumulated Depreciation—Equipment, No. 201 Accounts Payable, No. 212 Salaries and Wages Payable, No. 311 Common Stock, No. 320 Retained Earnings, No. 332 Dividends, No. 350 Income Summary, No. 400 Service Revenue, No. 631 Supplies Expense, No. 633 Gasoline Expense, No. 711 Depreciation Expense, No. 722 Insurance Expense, and No. 726 Salaries and Wages Expense.

Instructions

a. Journalize and post the July transactions. Use page J1 for the journal and the three-column form of account.

b. Trial balance $34,700

b. Prepare a trial balance at July 31 on a worksheet.

c. Enter the following adjustments on the worksheet and complete the worksheet.

   1. Unbilled and uncollected revenue for services performed at July 31 were $2,700.

   2. Depreciation on equipment for the month was $500.

   3. One-twelfth of the insurance expired.

   4. An inventory count shows $600 of cleaning supplies on hand at July 31.

   5. Unpaid employee salaries of $1,000 should be accrued.

d. Prepare an income statement and a retained earnings statement for July and a classified balance sheet at July 31.

e. Journalize and post adjusting entries. Use page J2 for the journal.

f. Journalize and post closing entries and complete the closing process. Use page J3 for the journal.

g. Prepare a post-closing trial balance at July 31.

c. Adjusted trial balance $38,900

d. Net income $7,200 Total assets $26,800

g. Post-closing trial balance $27,300

P4.4A (LO 1, 2, 4), AP Jarmuz Management Services began business on January 1, 2021, with a capital investment of $90,000. The company manages condominiums for owners (service revenue) and rents space in its own office building (rent revenue). The trial balance and adjusted trial balance columns of the worksheet at the end of 2022 are as follows.

Complete worksheet; prepare classified balance sheet, entries, and post-closing trial balance.

Jarmuz Management Services
Worksheet
For the Year Ended December 31, 2022

Account Titles	Trial Balance Dr.	Trial Balance Cr.	Adjusted Trial Balance Dr.	Adjusted Trial Balance Cr.
Cash	13,800		13,800	
Accounts Receivable	28,300		28,300	
Prepaid Insurance	3,600		2,400	
Land	67,000		67,000	
Buildings	127,000		127,000	
Equipment	59,000		59,000	
Accounts Payable		12,500		12,500
Unearned Rent Revenue		6,000		1,500
Notes Payable		120,000		120,000
Common Stock		90,000		90,000
Retained Earnings		54,000		54,000
Dividends	22,000		22,000	
Service Revenue		90,700		90,700
Rent Revenue		29,000		33,500
Salaries and Wages Expense	42,000		42,000	
Advertising Expense	20,500		20,500	
Utilities Expense	19,000		19,000	
Totals	402,200	402,200		
Insurance Expense			1,200	
Depreciation Expense			6,600	
Accumulated Depreciation—Buildings				3,000
Accumulated Depreciation—Equipment				3,600
Interest Expense			10,000	
Interest Payable				10,000
Totals			418,800	418,800

Instructions

a. Prepare a classified balance sheet. (*Note:* $30,000 of the notes payable is due for payment next year.)

b. Journalize the adjusting entries.

c. Journalize the closing entries.

d. Prepare a post-closing trial balance.

a. Total current assets $44,500

d. Post-closing trial balance $297,500

Prepare financial statements, closing entries, and post-closing trial balance.

P4.5A (LO 2, 4), AP The completed financial statement columns of the spreadsheet for Fleming Company are as follows.

Fleming Company
For the Year Ended December 31, 2022

Account No.	Account Titles	Income Statement Dr.	Income Statement Cr.	Balance Sheet Dr.	Balance Sheet Cr.
101	Cash			8,900	
112	Accounts Receivable			10,800	
130	Prepaid Insurance			2,800	
157	Equipment			24,000	
158	Accumulated Depreciation—Equip.				4,500
201	Accounts Payable				9,000
212	Salaries and Wages Payable				2,400
311	Common Stock				12,000
320	Retained Earnings				7,500
332	Dividends			11,000	
400	Service Revenue		60,000		
622	Maintenance and Repairs Expense	1,600			
711	Depreciation Expense	3,100			
722	Insurance Expense	1,800			
726	Salaries and Wages Expense	30,000			
732	Utilities Expense	1,400			
	Totals	37,900	60,000	57,500	35,400
	Net Income	22,100			22,100
		60,000	60,000	57,500	57,500

Instructions

a. Ending retained earnings $18,600
Total current assets $22,500

d. Post-closing trial balance $46,500

a. Prepare an income statement, a retained earnings statement, and a classified balance sheet.

b. Prepare the closing entries.

c. Post the closing entries and underline and balance the accounts. (Use T-accounts.) Income Summary is account No. 350.

d. Prepare a post-closing trial balance.

Prepare adjusting entries, post to ledger accounts, and prepare adjusted trial balance.

P4.6A (LO 3), AP Len Kumar started his own consulting firm, Kumar Consulting, on June 1, 2022. The trial balance at June 30 is as follows.

Kumar Consulting
Trial Balance
June 30, 2022

	Debit	Credit
Cash	$ 6,850	
Accounts Receivable	7,000	
Supplies	2,000	
Prepaid Insurance	2,880	
Equipment	15,000	
Accounts Payable		$ 4,230
Unearned Service Revenue		5,200
Common Stock		22,000
Service Revenue		8,300
Salaries and Wages Expense	4,000	
Rent Expense	2,000	
	$39,730	$39,730

In addition to those accounts listed on the trial balance, the chart of accounts for Kumar also contains the following accounts: Accumulated Depreciation—Equipment, Salaries and Wages Payable, Depreciation Expense, Insurance Expense, Utilities Expense, and Supplies Expense.

Other data:

1. Supplies on hand at June 30 total $720.

2. A utility bill for $180 has not been recorded and will not be paid until next month.

3. The insurance policy is for a year.

4. Services were performed for $4,100 of unearned service revenue by the end of the month.

5. Salaries of $1,250 are accrued at June 30.

6. The equipment has a 5-year life with no salvage value and is being depreciated at $250 per month for 60 months.

7. Invoices representing $3,900 of services performed by Kumar during the month have not been recorded as of June 30.

Instructions

a. Prepare the adjusting entries for the month of June.

b. Post the adjusting entries to the ledger accounts. Enter the totals from the trial balance as beginning account balances. (Use T-accounts.)

c. Prepare an adjusted trial balance at June 30, 2022.

b. Service rev.　$16,300

c. Tot. trial balance　$45,310

P4.7A (LO 2, 4), AP The Moto Hotel opened for business on May 1, 2022. Here is its trial balance before adjustment on May 31.

Prepare adjusting entries, adjusted trial balance, and financial statements.

Moto Hotel
Trial Balance
May 31, 2022

	Debit	Credit
Cash	$ 2,500	
Supplies	2,600	
Prepaid Insurance	1,800	
Land	15,000	
Buildings	70,000	
Equipment	16,800	
Accounts Payable		$ 4,700
Unearned Rent Revenue		3,300
Notes Payable		36,000
Common Stock		60,000
Rent Revenue		9,000
Salaries and Wages Expense	3,000	
Utilities Expense	800	
Advertising Expense	500	
	$113,000	$113,000

Other data:

1. Insurance expires at the rate of $450 per month.

2. A count of supplies shows $1,050 of unused supplies on May 31.

3. Annual depreciation is $3,600 on the building and $3,000 on equipment.

4. The interest rate of the notes payable is 6%. (The note was taken out on May 1 and will be repaid in 2025.)

5. Unearned rent of $2,500 has been earned.

6. Salaries of $900 are accrued and unpaid at May 31.

Instructions

a. Journalize the adjusting entries on May 31.

b. Prepare a ledger using T-accounts. Enter the trial balance amounts and post the adjusting entries.

c. Prepare an adjusted trial balance on May 31.

d. Prepare (1) an income statement and (2) a retained earnings statement for the month of May and (3) a classified balance sheet at May 31.

e. If Moto closed its accounts monthly, which accounts should be closed in May?

c. Rent revenue　$11,500
Tot. adj. trial
　balance　$114,630

d. Net income　$3,570

Prepare adjusting entries and financial statements; identify accounts to be closed.

P4.8A (LO 2, 4), AP Salt Creek Golf Inc. was organized on July 1, 2022. Quarterly financial statements are prepared. The trial balance and adjusted trial balance on September 30 are shown as follows.

Salt Creek Golf Inc.
Trial Balance
September 30, 2022

	Unadjusted Dr.	Unadjusted Cr.	Adjusted Dr.	Adjusted Cr.
Cash	$ 6,700		$ 6,700	
Accounts Receivable	400		1,000	
Supplies	1,200		180	
Prepaid Rent	1,800		900	
Equipment	15,000		15,000	
Accumulated Depreciation—Equipment				$ 350
Notes Payable		$ 5,000		5,000
Accounts Payable		1,070		1,070
Salaries and Wages Payable				600
Interest Payable				50
Unearned Rent Revenue		1,000		800
Common Stock		14,000		14,000
Retained Earnings		0		0
Dividends	600		600	
Service Revenue		14,100		14,700
Rent Revenue		700		900
Salaries and Wages Expense	8,800		9,400	
Rent Expense	900		1,800	
Depreciation Expense			350	
Supplies Expense			1,020	
Utilities Expense	470		470	
Interest Expense			50	
	$35,870	$35,870	$37,470	$37,470

Instructions

a. Journalize the adjusting entries that were made.

b. Prepare an income statement and a retained earnings statement for the 3 months ending September 30 and a classified balance sheet at September 30.

c. Identify which accounts should be closed on September 30, assuming Salt Creek Golf closes its books quarterly.

d. If the note bears interest at 12%, how many months has it been outstanding?

b. Net income $2,510
   Tot. assets $23,430

Journalize transactions and follow through accounting cycle to preparation of financial statements.

P4.9A (LO 2, 4), AP On November 1, 2022, the following were the account balances of Soho Equipment Repair.

	Debit		Credit
Cash	$ 2,790	Accumulated Depreciation—Equipment	$ 500
Accounts Receivable	2,910	Accounts Payable	2,300
Supplies	1,120	Unearned Service Revenue	400
Equipment	10,000	Salaries and Wages Payable	620
		Common Stock	10,000
		Retained Earnings	3,000
	$16,820		$16,820

During November, the following summary transactions were completed.

Nov. 8	Paid $1,220 for salaries due employees, of which $600 is for November and $620 is for October salaries payable.
10	Received $1,800 cash from customers in payment of account.
12	Received $3,700 cash for services performed in November.
15	Purchased store equipment on account $3,600.
17	Purchased supplies on account $1,300.
20	Paid creditors $2,500 of accounts payable due.
22	Paid November rent $480.
25	Paid salaries $1,000.
27	Performed services on account worth $900 and billed customers.
29	Received $750 from customers for services to be performed in the future.

Adjustment data:

1. Supplies on hand are valued at $1,100.

2. Accrued salaries payable are $480.

3. Depreciation for the month is $250.

4. Services were performed to satisfy $500 of unearned service revenue.

Instructions

a. Enter the November 1 balances in the ledger accounts. (Use T-accounts.)

b. Journalize the November transactions.

c. Post to the ledger accounts. Use the following additional accounts: Service Revenue, Depreciation Expense, Supplies Expense, Salaries and Wages Expense, and Rent Expense.

d. Prepare a trial balance at November 30.

e. Journalize and post adjusting entries.

f. Prepare an adjusted trial balance.

g. Prepare an income statement and a retained earnings statement for November and a classified balance sheet at November 30.

f. Cash	$3,840
Tot. adj. trial balance	$24,680
g. Net income	$970

P4.10A (LO 3), AN Dao Vang, CPA, was retained by Universal Cable to prepare financial statements for April 2022. Vang accumulated all the ledger balances per Universal's records and found the following.

Analyze errors and prepare correcting entries and trial balance.

Universal Cable
Trial Balance
April 30, 2022

	Debit	Credit
Cash	$ 4,100	
Accounts Receivable	3,200	
Supplies	800	
Equipment	10,600	
Accumulated Depreciation—Equip.		$ 1,350
Accounts Payable		2,100
Salaries and Wages Payable		700
Unearned Service Revenue		890
Common Stock		10,000
Retained Earnings		2,900
Service Revenue		5,450
Salaries and Wages Expense	3,300	
Advertising Expense	600	
Miscellaneous Expense	290	
Depreciation Expense	500	
	$23,390	$23,390

Dao Vang reviewed the records and found the following errors.

1. Cash received from a customer on account was recorded as $950 instead of $590.

2. A payment of $75 for advertising expense was entered as a debit to Miscellaneous Expense $75 and a credit to Cash $75.

3. The first salary payment in April was for $1,900, which included $700 of salaries payable on March 31. The payment was recorded as a debit to Salaries and Wages Expense $1,900 and a credit to Cash $1,900. (No reversing entries were made on April 1.)

4. The purchase on account of a printer costing $310 was recorded as a debit to Supplies and a credit to Accounts Payable for $310.

5. A cash payment of repair expense on equipment for $96 was recorded as a debit to Equipment $69 and a credit to Cash $69.

Instructions

a. Prepare an analysis of each error showing (1) the incorrect entry, (2) the correct entry, and (3) the correcting entry. Items 4 and 5 occurred on April 30, 2022.

b. Trial balance $22,690   b. Prepare a correct trial balance.

Continuing Case

leungchopan/
Shutterstock.com

Cookie Creations

(*Note:* This is a continuation of the Cookie Creations case from Chapters 1 through 3.)

CC4 Natalie had a very busy December. At the end of the month, after journalizing and posting the December transactions and adjusting entries, Natalie then prepared an adjusted trial balance.

Go to **WileyPLUS** *for complete case details and instructions.*

Comprehensive Accounting Cycle Review

Complete all steps in accounting cycle.

ACR4.1 Mike Greenberg opened Kleene Window Washing Inc. on July 1, 2022. During July, the following transactions occurred.

July 1   Issued 12,000 shares of common stock for $12,000 cash.
      1   Purchased used truck for $8,000, paying $2,000 cash and the balance on account.
      3   Purchased cleaning supplies for $900 on account.
      5   Paid $1,800 cash on a 1-year insurance policy effective July 1.
     12   Billed customers $3,700 for cleaning services performed.
     18   Paid $1,000 cash on amount owed on truck and $500 on amount owed on cleaning supplies.
     20   Paid $2,000 cash for employee salaries.
     21   Collected $1,600 cash from customers billed on July 12.
     25   Billed customers $2,500 for cleaning services performed.
     31   Paid $290 for maintenance of the truck during month.
     31   Declared and paid $600 cash dividend.

The chart of accounts for Kleene Window Washing contains the following accounts: Cash, Accounts Receivable, Supplies, Prepaid Insurance, Equipment, Accumulated Depreciation—Equipment, Accounts Payable, Salaries and Wages Payable, Common Stock, Retained Earnings, Dividends, Income Summary, Service Revenue, Maintenance and Repairs Expense, Supplies Expense, Depreciation Expense, Insurance Expense, and Salaries and Wages Expense.

Instructions

a. Journalize the July transactions.

b. Post to the ledger accounts. (Use T-accounts.)

c. Prepare a trial balance at July 31.

d. Journalize the following adjustments.

   1. Services performed but unbilled and uncollected at July 31 were $1,700.

   2. Depreciation on equipment for the month was $180.

   3. One-twelfth of the insurance expired.

4. A count shows $320 of cleaning supplies on hand at July 31.

5. Accrued but unpaid employee salaries were $400.

e. Post adjusting entries to the T-accounts.

f. Prepare an adjusted trial balance.

g. Prepare the income statement and a retained earnings statement for July and a classified balance sheet at July 31.

h. Journalize and post closing entries and complete the closing process.

i. Prepare a post-closing trial balance at July 31.

f. Cash $5,410

g. Tot. assets $21,500

ACR4.2 Lars Linken opened Lars Cleaners on March 1, 2022. During March, the following transactions occurred.

Complete all steps in accounting cycle.

Mar.	1	Issued 10,000 shares of common stock for $15,000 cash.
	1	Borrowed $6,000 cash by signing a 6-month, 6%, $6,000 note payable. Interest will be paid the first day of each subsequent month.
	1	Purchased a used truck for $8,000 cash.
	2	Paid $1,500 cash to cover rent from March 1 through May 31.
	3	Paid $2,400 cash on a 6-month insurance policy effective March 1.
	6	Purchased cleaning supplies for $2,000 on account.
	14	Billed customers $3,700 for cleaning services performed.
	18	Paid $500 on amount owed on cleaning supplies.
	20	Paid $1,750 cash for employee salaries.
	21	Collected $1,600 cash from customers billed on March 14.
	28	Billed customers $4,200 for cleaning services performed.
	31	Paid $350 for gas and oil used in the truck during the month (use Maintenance and Repairs Expense).
	31	Declared and paid a $900 cash dividend.

The chart of accounts for Lars Cleaners contains the following accounts: Cash, Accounts Receivable, Supplies, Prepaid Insurance, Prepaid Rent, Equipment, Accumulated Depreciation—Equipment, Accounts Payable, Salaries and Wages Payable, Notes Payable, Interest Payable, Common Stock, Retained Earnings, Dividends, Income Summary, Service Revenue, Maintenance and Repairs Expense, Supplies Expense, Depreciation Expense, Insurance Expense, Salaries and Wages Expense, Rent Expense, and Interest Expense.

Instructions

a. Journalize the March transactions.

b. Post to the ledger accounts. (Use T-accounts.)

c. Prepare a trial balance at March 31.

d. Journalize the following adjustments.

1. Services performed but unbilled and uncollected at March 31 were $200.

2. Depreciation on equipment for the month was $250.

3. One-sixth of the insurance expired.

4. An inventory count shows $280 of cleaning supplies on hand at March 31.

5. Accrued but unpaid employee salaries were $1,080.

6. One month of the prepaid rent has expired.

7. One month of interest expense related to the note payable has accrued and will be paid April 1. (*Hint:* Use the formula from Illustration 3.18 to compute interest.)

e. Post adjusting entries to the T-accounts.

f. Prepare an adjusted trial balance.

g. Prepare the income statement and a retained earnings statement for March and a classified balance sheet at March 31.

h. Journalize and post closing entries and complete the closing process.

i. Prepare a post-closing trial balance at March 31.

f. Tot. adj. trial balance $31,960

g. Tot. assets $24,730

Journalize transactions and follow through accounting cycle to preparation of financial statements.

ACR4.3 On August 1, 2022, the following were the account balances of B&B Repair Services.

	Debit		Credit
Cash	$ 6,040	Accumulated Depreciation—Equipment	$ 600
Accounts Receivable	2,910	Accounts Payable	2,300
Notes Receivable	4,000	Unearned Service Revenue	1,260
Supplies	1,030	Salaries and Wages Payable	1,420
Equipment	10,000	Common Stock	12,000
		Retained Earnings	6,400
	$23,980		$23,980

During August, the following transactions occurred.

Aug. 1 Paid $400 cash for advertising in local newspapers. Advertising flyers will be included with newspapers delivered during August and September.

3 Paid August rent $380.

5 Received $1,200 cash from customers in payment on account.

10 Paid $3,120 for salaries due employees, of which $1,700 is for August and $1,420 is for July salaries payable.

12 Received $2,800 cash for services performed in August.

15 Purchased store equipment on account $2,000.

20 Paid creditors $2,000 of accounts payable due.

22 Purchased supplies on account $800.

25 Paid $2,900 cash for employees' salaries.

27 Billed customers $3,760 for services performed.

29 Received $780 from customers for services to be performed in the future.

Adjustment data:

1. A count shows supplies on hand of $960.

2. Accrued but unpaid employees' salaries are $1,540.

3. Depreciation on equipment for the month is $320.

4. Services were performed to satisfy $800 of unearned service revenue.

5. One month's worth of advertising services has been received.

6. One month of interest revenue related to the $4,000 note receivable should be accrued. The 4-month note has a 6% annual interest rate. (*Hint:* Use the formula from Illustration 3.18 to compute interest.)

Instructions

a. Enter the August 1 balances in the ledger accounts. (Use T-accounts.)

b. Journalize the August transactions.

c. Post to the ledger accounts. B&B's chart of accounts includes Prepaid Advertising, Interest Receivable, Service Revenue, Interest Revenue, Advertising Expense, Depreciation Expense, Supplies Expense, Salaries and Wages Expense, and Rent Expense.

d. Prepare a trial balance at August 31.

e. Journalize and post adjusting entries.

f. Prepare an adjusted trial balance.

g. Prepare an income statement and a retained earnings statement for August and a classified balance sheet at August 31.

h. Journalize and post closing entries and complete the closing process.

i. Prepare a post-closing trial balance at August 31.

f. Cash $2,020
Tot. adj. trial
    balance $32,580

g. Net loss $530

Record and post transaction, adjusting, and closing journal entries; prepare adjusted trial balance and financial statements.

ACR4.4 At June 30, 2022, the end of its most recent fiscal year, Green River Computer Consultants' post-closing trial balance was as follows:

	Debit	Credit
Cash	$5,230	
Accounts receivable	1,200	
Supplies	690	
Accounts payable		$ 400
Unearned service revenue		1,120
Common stock		3,600
Retained earnings		2,000
	$7,120	$7,120

The company underwent a major expansion in July. New staff was hired and more financing was obtained. Green River conducted the following transactions during July 2022, and adjusts its accounts monthly.

July 1 Purchased equipment, paying $4,000 cash and signing a 2-year note payable for $20,000. The equipment has a 4-year useful life. The note has a 6% interest rate, with interest payable on the first day of each following month.

2 Issued 20,000 shares of common stock for $50,000 cash.

3 Paid $3,600 cash for a 12-month insurance policy effective July 1.

3 Paid the first 2 months' rent (July and August 2022) for an annual lease of office space for $4,000 per month.

6 Paid $3,800 for supplies.

9 Visited client offices and agreed on the terms of a consulting project. Green River will bill the client, Connor Productions, on the 20th of each month for services performed.

10 Collected $1,200 cash on account from Milani Brothers. This client was billed in June when Green River performed the service.

13 Performed services for Fitzgerald Enterprises. This client paid $1,120 in advance last month. All services relating to this payment are now completed.

14 Paid $400 cash for a utility bill. This related to June utilities that were accrued at the end of June.

16 Met with a new client, Thunder Bay Technologies. Received $12,000 cash in advance for future services to be performed.

18 Paid semi-monthly salaries for $11,000.

20 Performed services worth $28,000 on account and billed customers.

20 Received a bill for $2,200 for advertising services received during July. The amount is not due until August 15.

23 Performed the first phase of the project for Thunder Bay Technologies. Recognized $10,000 of revenue from the cash advance received July 16.

27 Received $15,000 cash from customers billed on July 20.

Adjustment data:

1. Adjustment of prepaid insurance.

2. Adjustment of prepaid rent.

3. Supplies used, $1,250.

4. Equipment depreciation, $500 per month.

5. Accrual of interest on note payable. (*Hint:* Use the formula from Illustration 3.18 to compute interest.)

6. Salaries for the second half of July, $11,000, to be paid on August 1.

7. Estimated utilities expense for July, $800 (invoice will be received in August).

8. Income tax for July, $1,200, will be paid in August. (*Hint:* Use the accounts Income Tax Expense and Income Taxes Payable.)

The chart of accounts for Green River Computer Consultants contains the following accounts: Cash, Accounts Receivable, Supplies, Prepaid Insurance, Prepaid Rent, Equipment, Accumulated Depreciation—Equipment, Accounts Payable, Notes Payable, Interest Payable, Income Taxes Payable, Salaries and Wages Payable, Unearned Service Revenue, Common Stock, Retained Earnings, Income Summary, Service Revenue, Supplies Expense, Depreciation Expense, Insurance Expense, Salaries and Wages Expense, Advertising Expense, Income Tax Expense, Interest Expense, Rent Expense, and Utilities Expense.

Instructions

a. Enter the July 1 balances in the ledger accounts. (Use T-accounts.)

b. Journalize the July transactions.

c. Post to the ledger accounts.

d. Prepare a trial balance at July 31.

e. Journalize and post adjusting entries for the month ending July 31.

f. Prepare an adjusted trial balance.

g. Prepare an income statement and a retained earnings statement for July and a classified balance sheet at July 31.

g. Net income $6,770
Tot. assets $99,670

h. Journalize and post closing entries and complete the closing process.

i. Prepare a post-closing trial balance at July 31.

Expand Your Critical Thinking

Financial Reporting Problem: Apple Inc.

CT4.1 The financial statements of **Apple Inc.** are presented in Appendix A. The complete annual report, including the notes to the financial statements, is available at the company's website.

Instructions

Answer the questions below using Apple's Consolidated Balance Sheets.

a. What were Apple's total current assets at September 29, 2018, and September 30, 2017?

b. Are assets that Apple included under current assets listed in proper order? Explain.

c. How are Apple's assets classified?

d. What was Apple's "Cash and cash equivalents" at September 29, 2018?

e. What were Apple's total current liabilities at September 29, 2018, and September 30, 2017?

Comparative Analysis Problem: PepsiCo, Inc. vs. The Coca-Cola Company

CT4.2 **PepsiCo**'s financial statements are presented in Appendix B. Financial statements of **The Coca-Cola Company** are presented in Appendix C. The complete annual reports of PepsiCo and Coca-Cola, including the notes to the financial statements, are available at each company's respective website.

Instructions

a. Based on the information contained in these financial statements, determine each of the following for PepsiCo at December 29, 2018, and for Coca-Cola at December 31, 2018.

1. Total current assets.

2. Net amount of property, plant, and equipment (land, buildings, and equipment).

3. Total current liabilities.

4. Total equity.

b. What conclusions concerning the companies' respective financial positions can be drawn?

Comparative Analysis Problem: Amazon.com, Inc. vs. Walmart Inc.

CT4.3 **Amazon.com, Inc.**'s financial statements are presented in Appendix D. Financial statements of **Walmart Inc.** are presented in Appendix E. The complete annual reports of Amazon and Walmart, including the notes to the financial statements, are available at each company's respective website.

Instructions

a. Based on the information contained in these financial statements, determine the following for Amazon at December 31, 2018, and Walmart at January 31, 2019.

1. Total current assets.

2. Net amount of property and equipment (fixed assets).

3. Total current liabilities.

4. Total equity.

b. What conclusions concerning these two companies can be drawn from these data?

Real-World Focus

CT4.4 Numerous companies have established home pages on the Internet, e.g., the soda companies **Capt'n Eli Soda** and **Cheerwine**.

Instructions

Examine the home pages of any two companies and answer the following questions.

a. What type of information is available?

b. Is any accounting-related information presented?

c. Would you describe the home page as informative, promotional, or both? Why?

Decision-Making Across the Organization

CT4.5 Whitegloves Janitorial Service was started 2 years ago by Lynn Sanders. Because business has been exceptionally good, Lynn decided on July 1, 2022, to expand operations by acquiring an additional truck and hiring two more assistants. To finance the expansion, Lynn obtained on July 1, 2022, a $25,000, 10% bank loan, payable $10,000 on July 1, 2023, and the balance on July 1, 2024. The terms of the loan require the borrower to have $10,000 more current assets than current liabilities at December 31, 2022. If these terms are not met, the bank loan will be refinanced at 15% interest. At December 31, 2022, the accountant for Whitegloves Janitorial Service Inc. prepared the following balance sheet.

Whitegloves Janitorial Service
Balance Sheet
December 31, 2022

Assets			Liabilities and Stockholders' Equity		
Current assets			Current liabilities		
Cash	$ 6,500		Notes payable	$10,000	
Accounts receivable	9,000		Accounts payable	2,500	
Supplies	5,200		Total current liabilities		$12,500
Prepaid insurance	4,800		Long-term liability		
Total current assets		$25,500	Notes payable		15,000
Property, plant, and equipment			Total liabilities		27,500
Equipment (net)	22,000		Stockholders' equity		
Delivery trucks (net)	34,000		Common stock	30,000	
Total property, plant, and equipment		56,000	Retained earnings	24,000	
			Total stockholders' equity		54,000
Total assets		$81,500	Total liabilities and stockholders' equity		$81,500

Lynn presented the balance sheet to the bank's loan officer on January 2, 2023, confident that the company had met the terms of the loan. The loan officer was not impressed. She said, "We need financial statements audited by a CPA." A CPA was hired and immediately realized that the balance sheet had been prepared from a trial balance and not from an adjusted trial balance. The adjustment data at the balance sheet date consisted of the following.

1. Unbilled janitorial services performed were $3,700.
2. Janitorial supplies on hand were $2,500.
3. Prepaid insurance was a 3-year policy dated January 1, 2022.
4. December expenses incurred but unpaid and unrecorded at December 31, $500.
5. Interest on the bank loan was not recorded.
6. The amounts for property, plant, and equipment presented in the balance sheet were reported net of accumulated depreciation (cost less accumulated depreciation). These amounts included accumulated depreciation of $4,000 for cleaning equipment and $5,000 for delivery trucks as of January 1, 2022. Depreciation expense for 2022 was $2,000 for cleaning equipment and $5,000 for delivery trucks.

Instructions

With the class divided into groups, answer the following.

a. Prepare a correct balance sheet.
b. Were the terms of the bank loan met? Explain.

Communication Activity

CT4.6 The accounting cycle is important in understanding the accounting process.

Instructions

Write a memorandum to your instructor that lists the steps of the accounting cycle in the order they should be completed. End with a paragraph that explains the optional steps in the cycle.

Ethics Case

CT4.7 As the controller of Take No Prisoners Perfume Company, you discover a misstatement that overstated net income in the prior year's financial statements. The misleading financial statements appear in the company's annual report, which was issued to banks and other creditors less than a month ago. After much thought about the consequences of telling the president, Jeb Wilde, about this misstatement, you gather your courage to inform him. Jeb says, "Hey! What they don't know won't hurt them. But, just so we set the record straight, we'll adjust this year's financial statements for last year's misstatement. We can absorb that misstatement better in this year than in last year anyway! Just don't make such a mistake again."

Instructions

a. Who are the stakeholders in this situation?

b. What are the ethical issues in this situation?

c. What would you do as a controller in this situation?

All About You

CT4.8 Companies prepare balance sheets in order to know their financial position at a specific point in time. This enables them to make a comparison to their position at previous points in time, and gives them a basis for planning for the future. In order to evaluate your financial position, you need to prepare a personal balance sheet. Assume that you have compiled the following information regarding your finances. (*Note:* Some of the items might not be used in your personal balance sheet.)

Amount owed on student loan (long-term)	$ 5,000
Balance in checking account	1,200
Certificate of deposit (6-month)	3,000
Annual earnings from part-time job	11,300
Automobile	7,000
Balance on automobile loan (current portion)	1,500
Balance on automobile loan (long-term portion)	4,000
Home computer	800
Amount owed to you by younger brother	300
Balance in money market account	1,800
Annual tuition	6,400
Video and stereo equipment	1,250
Balance owed on credit card (current portion)	150
Balance owed on credit card (long-term portion)	1,650

Instructions

Prepare a personal balance sheet using the format you have learned for a classified balance sheet for a company. For the equity account, use Owner's Equity and determine its balance using the accounting equation.

FASB Codification Activity

CT4.9 If your school has a subscription to the FASB Codification, log in and prepare responses to the following.

Instructions

a. Access the glossary ("Master Glossary") at the FASB Codification website to answer the following.

    1. What is the definition of current assets?

    2. What is the definition of current liabilities?

b. A company wants to offset its accounts payable against its cash account and show a cash amount net of accounts payable on its balance sheet. Identify the criteria (found in the FASB Codification) under which a company has the right of set off. Does the company have the right to offset accounts payable against the cash account?

A Look at IFRS

LEARNING OBJECTIVE 6
Compare the procedures for the closing process under GAAP and IFRS.

The classified balance sheet, although generally required internationally, contains certain variations in format when reporting under IFRS.

Key Points

Following are the key similarities and differences between GAAP and IFRS related to the closing process and the financial statements.

Similarities

- The procedures of the closing process are applicable to all companies, whether they are using IFRS or GAAP.
- IFRS generally requires a classified statement of financial position similar to the classified balance sheet under GAAP.
- IFRS follows the same guidelines as this text for distinguishing between current and non-current assets and liabilities.

Differences

- IFRS recommends but does not require the use of the title "statement of financial position" rather than "balance sheet."
- The format of statement of financial position information is often presented differently under IFRS. Although no specific format is required, many companies that follow IFRS present statement of financial position information in this order:
  - Non-current assets
  - Current assets
  - Equity
  - Non-current liabilities
  - Current liabilities
- Under IFRS, current assets are usually listed in the reverse order of liquidity. For example, under GAAP cash is listed first, but under IFRS it is listed last.
- IFRS has many differences in terminology from what is shown in your text. For example, in the following sample statement of financial position, notice in the investment category that stock is called shares.

Franklin AG			
Statement of Financial Position			
October 31, 2022			
Assets			
Intangible assets			
Patents			€ 3,100
Property, plant, and equipment			
Land		€10,000	
Equipment	€24,000		
Less: Accumulated depreciation	5,000	19,000	29,000
Long-term investments			
Share investments		5,200	
Investment in real estate		2,000	7,200

Current assets		
Prepaid insurance	400	
Supplies	2,100	
Inventory	3,000	
Notes receivable	1,000	
Accounts receivable	7,000	
Debt investments	2,000	
Cash	6,600	22,100
Total assets		€61,400

Equity and Liabilities

Equity		
Share capital	€20,000	
Retained earnings	14,050	€34,050
Non-current liabilities		
Mortgage payable	10,000	
Notes payable	1,300	11,300
Current liabilities		
Notes payable	11,000	
Accounts payable	2,100	
Salaries and wages payable	1,600	
Unearned service revenue	900	
Interest payable	450	16,050
Total equity and liabilities		€61,400

- Both GAAP and IFRS are increasing the use of fair value to report assets. However, at this point IFRS has adopted it more broadly. As examples, under IFRS companies can apply fair value to property, plant, and equipment, and in some cases to intangible assets.

IFRS Practice

IFRS Self-Test Questions

1. A company has purchased a tract of land and expects to build a production plant on the land in approximately 5 years. During the 5 years before construction, the land will be idle. Under IFRS, the land should be reported as:

   a. land expense.

   b. property, plant, and equipment.

   c. an intangible asset.

   d. a long-term investment.

2. Current assets under IFRS are listed generally:

   a. by importance.

   b. in the reverse order of their expected conversion to cash.

   c. by longevity.

   d. alphabetically.

3. Companies that follow IFRS:

   a. use the term stock instead of shares for investments.

   b. may offset assets against liabilities and show net assets and net liabilities on their statements of financial position, rather than the underlying detailed line items.

   c. may report non-current assets before current assets on the statement of financial position.

   d. do not have any guidelines as to what should be reported on the statement of financial position.

4. Companies that follow IFRS to prepare a statement of financial position generally use the following order of classification:

   a. current assets, current liabilities, non-current assets, non-current liabilities, equity.

   b. non-current assets, non-current liabilities, current assets, current liabilities, equity.

   c. non-current assets, current assets, equity, non-current liabilities, current liabilities.

   d. equity, non-current assets, current assets, non-current liabilities, current liabilities.

IFRS Exercises

IFRS4.1 In what ways does the format of a statement of financial of position under IFRS often differ from a balance sheet presented under GAAP?

IFRS4.2 What term is commonly used under IFRS in reference to the balance sheet?

IFRS4.3 The statement of financial position for Sundell Company at December 31, 2022, includes the following accounts (in British pounds): Accounts Receivable £12,500, Prepaid Insurance £3,600, Cash £15,400, Supplies £5,200, and Debt Investments (short-term) £6,700. Prepare the current assets section of the statement of financial position, listing the accounts in proper sequence.

IFRS4.4 The following information is available for Lessila Bowling Alley at December 31, 2022.

Buildings	$128,800	Share Capital	$100,000
Accounts Receivable	14,520	Retained Earnings (beginning)	15,000
Prepaid Insurance	4,680	Accumulated Depreciation—Buildings	42,600
Cash	18,040	Accounts Payable	12,300
Equipment	62,400	Notes Payable	97,780
Land	64,000	Accumulated Depreciation—Equipment	18,720
Insurance Expense	780	Interest Payable	2,600
Depreciation Expense	7,360	Bowling Revenues	14,180
Interest Expense	2,600		

Prepare a classified statement of financial position. Assume that $13,900 of the notes payable will be paid in 2023.

International Comparative Analysis Problem: Apple vs. Louis Vuitton

IFRS4.5 The financial statements of **Louis Vuitton** are presented in Appendix F. The complete consolidated financial statements, including the notes to its financial statements, are available at the company's website.

Instructions

Identify five differences in the format of the statement of financial position used by Louis Vuitton compared with that of a company, such as **Apple**, that follows GAAP. (Apple's financial statements are available in Appendix A.)

Answers to IFRS Self-Test Questions

1. d   **2.** b   **3.** c   **4.** c

iStock.com/omgimages

Accounting for Merchandising Operations

Chapter Preview

Merchandising is one of the largest and most influential industries in the United States. It is likely that a number of you will work for a merchandiser. Therefore, understanding the financial statements of merchandising companies is important. In this chapter, you will learn the basics about reporting merchandising transactions. In addition, you will learn how to prepare and analyze a commonly used form of the income statement—the multiple-step income statement.

Feature Story

Buy Now, Vote Later

Have you ever shopped for outdoor gear at an **REI (Recreational Equipment, Inc.)** store? If so, you might have been surprised if a salesclerk asked if you were a member. A

member? What do you mean a member? REI is a consumer cooperative, or "co-op" for short. To figure out what that means, consider this:

As a cooperative, the Company is owned by its members. Each member is entitled to one vote in the election of the Company's Board of Directors. Recent data show that we have more than 18 million members.

Voting rights? Now that's something you don't get from shopping at **Walmart**. REI members get other benefits as well, including sharing in the company's profits through a dividend at the end of the year. The more you spend, the bigger your dividend.

Since REI is a co-op, you might also wonder whether management's incentives might be a little different than at other stores. Management is still concerned about making a profit, as it ensures the long-term viability of the company. REI's members also want the company to be run efficiently, so that prices remain low. In order for its members to evaluate just how well management is doing, REI publishes an audited annual report, just like publicly traded companies do.

How well is this business model working for REI? Well, it has consistently been rated as one of the best places to work in the United States by *Fortune* magazine. It is one of only five companies named each year since the list was created in 1998. Also, REI had sustainable business practices long before social responsibility became popular at other companies. As the CEO's stewardship report states, "we reduced the absolute amount of energy we use despite opening four new stores and growing our business; we grew the amount of FSC-certified paper we use to 58.4 percent of our total paper footprint—including our cash register receipt paper; we facilitated 2.2 million volunteer hours and we provided $3.7 million to more than 330 conservation and recreation nonprofits."

So, while REI, like other retailers, closely monitors its financial results, it also strives to succeed in other areas. And, with over 10 million votes at stake, REI's management knows that it has to deliver.

Chapter Outline

LEARNING OBJECTIVES	REVIEW	PRACTICE
LO 1 Describe merchandising operations and inventory systems.	• Operating cycles • Flow of costs	**DO IT! 1** Merchandising Operations and Inventory Systems
LO 2 Record purchases under a perpetual inventory system.	• Freight costs • Purchase returns and allowances • Purchase discounts • Summary of purchasing transactions	**DO IT! 2** Purchase Transactions
LO 3 Record sales under a perpetual inventory system.	• Sales returns and allowances • Sales discounts • Data analytics and credit sales	**DO IT! 3** Sales Transactions
LO 4 Apply the steps in the accounting cycle to a merchandising company.	• Adjusting entries • Closing entries • Summary of merchandising entries	**DO IT! 4** Closing Entries
LO 5 Prepare a multiple-step income statement.	• Multiple-step income statement • Single-step income statement • Classified balance sheet	**DO IT! 5** Multiple-Step Income Statement

Go to the Review and Practice section at the end of the chapter for a review of key concepts and practice applications with solutions.

Visit WileyPLUS for additional tutorials and practice opportunities.

Merchandising Operations and Inventory Systems

LEARNING OBJECTIVE 1
Describe merchandising operations and inventory systems.

REI, **Walmart Inc.**, and **Amazon.com** are called merchandising companies because they buy and sell merchandise rather than perform services as their primary source of revenue. Merchandising companies that purchase and sell directly to consumers are called **retailers**. Merchandising companies that sell to retailers are known as **wholesalers**. For example, retailer **Walgreens** might buy goods from wholesaler **McKesson**. Retailer **Office Depot** might buy office supplies from wholesaler **United Stationers**. The primary source of revenue for merchandising companies is the sale of merchandise, often referred to simply as **sales revenue** or **sales**. A merchandising company has two categories of expenses: cost of goods sold and operating expenses.

Cost of goods sold is the total cost of merchandise sold during the period. This expense is directly related to the revenue recognized from the sale of goods. **Illustration 5.1** shows the income measurement process for a merchandising company. The items in the two blue boxes are unique to a merchandising company; they are not used by a service company.

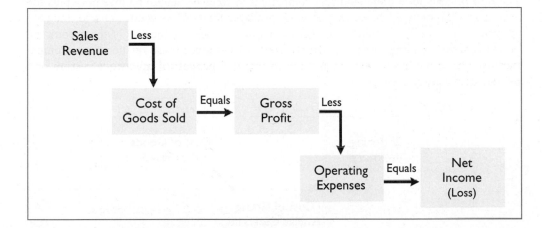

ILLUSTRATION 5.1

Income measurement process for a merchandising company

Operating Cycles

The operating cycle of a merchandising company is ordinarily longer than that of a service company. The purchase of merchandise inventory and its eventual sale lengthen the cycle. **Illustration 5.2** shows the operating cycle of a service company.

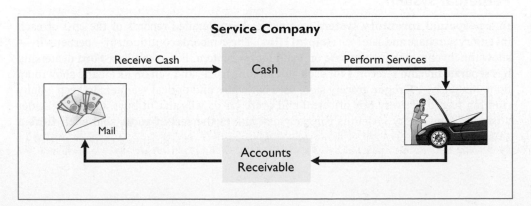

ILLUSTRATION 5.2

Operating cycle for a service company

Illustration 5.3 shows the operating cycle of a merchandising company.

ILLUSTRATION 5.3
Operating cycle for a merchandising company

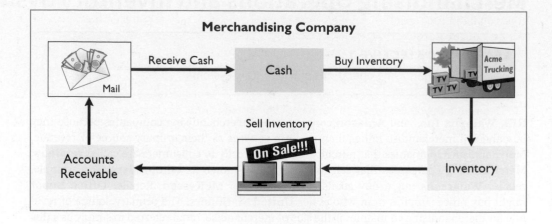

Note that the added asset account for a merchandising company is the Inventory account. Companies report inventory as a current asset on the balance sheet.

Flow of Costs

The flow of costs for a merchandising company is as follows. Beginning inventory plus the cost of goods purchased is the cost of goods available for sale. As goods are sold, they are assigned to cost of goods sold. Those goods that are not sold by the end of the accounting period represent ending inventory. **Illustration 5.4** describes these relationships. Companies use one of two systems to account for inventory: a **perpetual inventory system** or a **periodic inventory system**.

ILLUSTRATION 5.4

Flow of costs

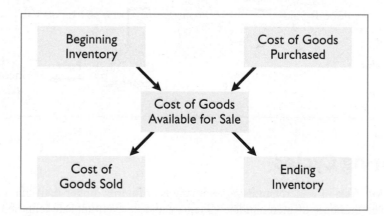

Perpetual System

In a **perpetual inventory system**, companies keep detailed records of the cost of each inventory purchase and sale (see **Helpful Hint**). These records continuously—perpetually—show the inventory that should be on hand for every item. For example, a **Ford** dealership has separate inventory records for each automobile, truck, and van on its lot and showroom floor. Similarly, a **Kroger** grocery store uses bar codes and optical scanners to keep a daily running record of every box of cereal and every jar of jelly that it buys and sells. Under a perpetual inventory system, a company determines the cost of goods sold **each time a sale occurs**.

HELPFUL HINT

Even under perpetual inventory systems, companies take a physical inventory count. This is done as a control procedure to verify inventory levels, in order to detect theft or "shrinkage."

Periodic System

In a **periodic inventory system**, companies do not keep detailed inventory records of the goods on hand throughout the period. Instead, they determine the cost of goods sold **only at the end of the accounting period**—that is, periodically. At that point, the company takes a physical inventory count to determine the cost of goods on hand.

To determine the cost of goods sold under a periodic inventory system, the following steps are necessary:

1. Determine the cost of goods on hand at the beginning of the accounting period.
2. Add to it the cost of goods purchased.
3. Subtract the cost of goods on hand as determined by the physical inventory count at the end of the accounting period.

Illustration 5.5 compares the sequence of activities and the timing of the cost of goods sold computation under the two inventory systems.

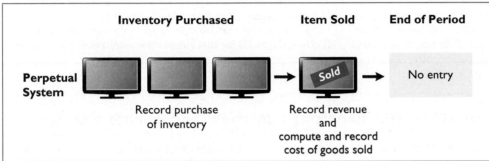

ILLUSTRATION 5.5

Comparing perpetual and periodic inventory systems

Advantages of the Perpetual System

Companies that sell merchandise with high unit values, such as automobiles, furniture, and major home appliances, have traditionally used perpetual systems. The growing use of computers and electronic scanners has enabled many more companies to install perpetual inventory systems. The perpetual inventory system is so named because the accounting records continuously—perpetually—show the quantity and cost of the inventory that should be on hand at any time.

A perpetual inventory system provides better control over inventories than a periodic system. Since the inventory records show the quantities that should be on hand, the company can count the goods at any time to see whether the amount of goods actually on hand agrees with the inventory records. If shortages are uncovered, the company can investigate immediately. Although a perpetual inventory system requires both additional clerical work and expense to maintain the subsidiary records, a computerized system can minimize this cost. Much of **Amazon.com**'s success is attributed to its sophisticated inventory system.

Some businesses find it either unnecessary or uneconomical to invest in a sophisticated, computerized perpetual inventory system such as Amazon's. Many small merchandising businesses now use basic accounting software, which provides some of the essential benefits of a perpetual inventory system. Also, managers of some small businesses still find that they can control their merchandise and manage day-to-day operations using a periodic inventory system.

Because of the widespread use of the perpetual inventory system, we illustrate it in this chapter. We discuss and illustrate the periodic system in Appendix 5B.

Investor Insight   Morrow Snowboards, Inc.

iStock.com/Ben Blankenburg

Improving Stock Appeal

Investors are often eager to invest in a company that has a hot new product. However, when snowboard-maker **Morrow Snowboards, Inc.** (now part of **K2 Sports**) issued shares of stock to the public for the first time, some investors expressed reluctance to invest in Morrow because of a number of accounting control problems. To reduce investor concerns, Morrow implemented a perpetual inventory system to improve its control over inventory. In addition, the company stated that it would perform a physical inventory count every quarter until it felt that its perpetual inventory system was reliable.

If a perpetual system keeps track of inventory on a daily basis, why do companies ever need to do a physical count? (Go to WileyPLUS for this answer and additional questions.)

ACTION PLAN

- **Review merchandising concepts.**
- **Understand the flow of costs in a merchandising company.**

DO IT! 1 | Merchandising Operations and Inventory Systems

Indicate whether the following statements are true or false. If false, indicate how to correct the statement.

1. The primary source of revenue for a merchandising company results from performing services for customers.
2. The operating cycle of a service company is usually shorter than that of a merchandising company.
3. Sales revenue less cost of goods sold equals gross profit.
4. Ending inventory plus the cost of goods purchased equals cost of goods available for sale.

Solution

1. False. The primary source of revenue for a service company (not a merchandising company) results from performing services for customers. Merchandising companies sell products.   **2.** True. **3.** True.   **4.** False. Beginning inventory plus the cost of goods purchased equals cost of goods available for sale.

Related exercise material: **BE5.1, BE5.2, DO IT! 5.1, and E5.1.**

Recording Purchases Under a Perpetual System

LEARNING OBJECTIVE 2
Record purchases under a perpetual inventory system.

Companies purchase inventory using cash or credit (on account). They normally record purchases when they receive the goods from the seller. Every purchase should be supported by business documents that provide written evidence of the transaction. Each cash purchase should be supported by a canceled check or a cash register receipt indicating the items purchased and amounts paid. Companies record cash purchases by an increase in Inventory and a decrease in Cash.

A **purchase invoice** should support each credit purchase. This invoice indicates the total purchase price and other relevant information. However, the purchaser does not prepare a separate purchase invoice. Instead, the purchaser uses as a purchase invoice a copy of the sales invoice sent by the seller. In **Illustration 5.6**, for example, Sauk Stereo (the buyer) uses as a purchase invoice the sales invoice prepared by PW Audio Supply, Inc. (the seller).

ILLUSTRATION 5.6

Sales invoice used as purchase invoice by Sauk Stereo

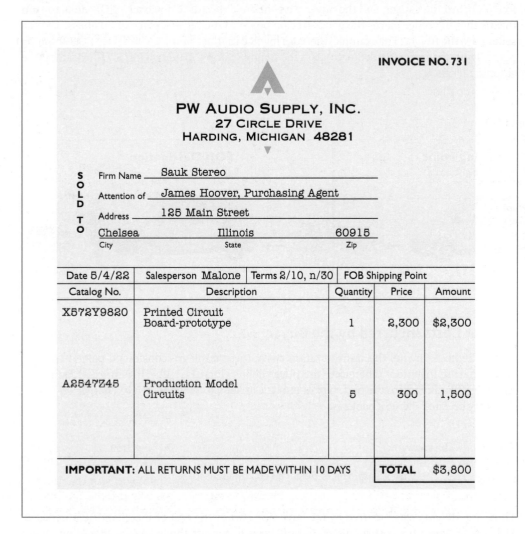

INVOICE NO. 731

PW AUDIO SUPPLY, INC.
27 CIRCLE DRIVE
HARDING, MICHIGAN 48281

SOLD TO		
Firm Name	Sauk Stereo	
Attention of	James Hoover, Purchasing Agent	
Address	125 Main Street	
Chelsea	Illinois	60915
City	State	Zip

Date 5/4/22	Salesperson Malone	Terms 2/10, n/30	FOB Shipping Point		
Catalog No.	Description		Quantity	Price	Amount
X572Y9820	Printed Circuit Board-prototype		1	2,300	$2,300
A2547Z45	Production Model Circuits		5	300	1,500

IMPORTANT: ALL RETURNS MUST BE MADE WITHIN 10 DAYS	**TOTAL**	**$3,800**

To better understand the contents of this invoice, identify these items:
1. Seller
2. Invoice date
3. Purchaser
4. Salesperson
5. Credit terms
6. Freight terms
7. Goods sold: catalog number, description, quantity, price per unit
8. Total invoice amount

Sauk Stereo makes the following journal entry to record its purchase from PW Audio Supply on account. The entry increases (debits) Inventory and increases (credits) Accounts Payable.

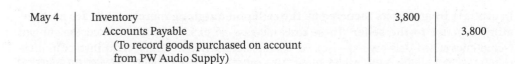

May 4	Inventory	3,800	
	Accounts Payable		3,800
	(To record goods purchased on account from PW Audio Supply)		

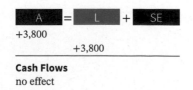

A	=	L	+	SE
+3,800				
		+3,800		

Cash Flows
no effect

Under the perpetual inventory system, companies record purchases of merchandise for resale in the Inventory account. Not all purchases are debited to Inventory, however. Recall that companies record purchases of assets acquired for use and not for resale, such as supplies and equipment, as increases to specific asset accounts rather than to Inventory. For example, to record the purchase of materials used to make shelf signs or for cash register receipt paper, Sauk Stereo would increase (debit) Supplies.

Freight Costs

The sales agreement should indicate who—the seller or the buyer—is to pay for transporting the goods to the buyer's place of business. When a common carrier such as a railroad, trucking company, or airline transports the goods, the carrier prepares a freight bill in accord with the sales agreement.

Freight terms are expressed as either FOB shipping point or FOB destination. The letters FOB mean **free on board**. Thus, **FOB shipping point** means that the seller places the goods free on board the carrier, and the buyer pays the freight costs. Conversely, **FOB destination** means that the seller places the goods free on board to the buyer's place of business, and the seller pays the freight. For example, the sales invoice in Illustration 5.6 indicates FOB shipping point. Thus, the buyer (Sauk Stereo) pays the freight charges. **Illustration 5.7** illustrates these shipping terms.

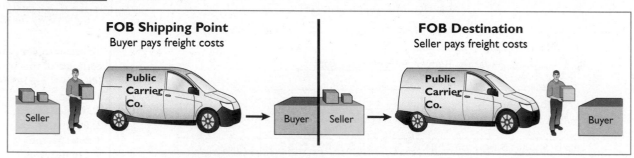

ILLUSTRATION 5.7 Shipping terms

Freight Costs Incurred by the Buyer

When the buyer incurs the transportation costs, these costs are considered part of the cost of purchasing inventory. Therefore, the buyer debits (increases) the Inventory account. For example, if Sauk Stereo (the buyer) pays Public Carrier Co. $150 for freight charges on May 6, the entry on Sauk Stereo's books is:

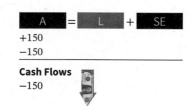

May 6	Inventory	150	
	Cash		150
	(To record payment of freight on goods purchased)		

Thus, any freight costs incurred by the buyer are part of the cost of merchandise purchased. The reason: Inventory cost should include all costs to acquire the inventory, including freight necessary to deliver the goods to the buyer. Companies recognize these costs as cost of goods sold when inventory is sold.

Freight Costs Incurred by the Seller

In contrast, **freight costs incurred by the seller on outgoing merchandise are an operating expense to the seller**. These costs increase an expense account titled Freight-Out (sometimes called Delivery Expense). For example, if the freight terms on the invoice in Illustration 5.6 had required PW Audio Supply (the seller) to pay the freight charges, the entry by PW Audio Supply would be:

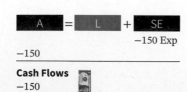

May 4	Freight-Out (or Delivery Expense)	150	
	Cash		150
	(To record payment of freight on goods sold)		

When the seller pays the freight charges, the seller will usually establish a higher invoice price for the goods to cover the shipping expense.

Purchase Returns and Allowances

A purchaser may be dissatisfied with the merchandise received because the goods are damaged or defective, of inferior quality, or do not meet the purchaser's specifications. In such cases, the purchaser may return the goods to the seller for credit if the sale was made on credit, or for a cash refund if the purchase was for cash. This transaction is known as a **purchase return**. Alternatively, the purchaser may choose to keep the merchandise if the seller is willing to grant an allowance (deduction) from the purchase price. This transaction is known as a **purchase allowance**.

Assume that Sauk Stereo returned goods costing $300 to PW Audio Supply on May 8. The following entry by Sauk Stereo for the returned merchandise decreases (debits) Accounts Payable and decreases (credits) Inventory.

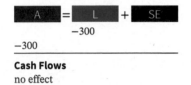

Cash Flows
no effect

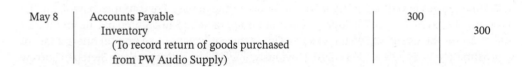

May 8	Accounts Payable	300	
	Inventory		300
	(To record return of goods purchased from PW Audio Supply)		

Because Sauk Stereo increased Inventory when the goods were received, Inventory is now decreased when Sauk Stereo returns the goods.

Suppose instead that Sauk Stereo chose to keep the goods after being granted a $50 allowance (reduction in price). It would reduce (debit) Accounts Payable and reduce (credit) Inventory for $50.

Purchase Discounts

The credit terms of a purchase on account may permit the buyer to claim a cash discount for prompt payment. The buyer calls this cash discount a **purchase discount**. This incentive offers advantages to both parties. The purchaser saves money, and the seller is able to shorten its operating cycle by converting the accounts receivable into cash more quickly.

Credit terms specify the amount of the cash discount and time period in which it is offered. They also indicate the time period in which the purchaser is expected to pay the full invoice price if the discount is not taken. In the sales invoice in Illustration 5.6, credit terms are 2/10, n/30, which is read "two-ten, net thirty" (see **Helpful Hint**). This means that the buyer may take a 2% cash discount on the invoice price, less ("net of") any returns or allowances, if payment is made within 10 days of the invoice date (the **discount period**). Otherwise, the invoice price, less any returns or allowances, is due 30 days from the invoice date.

Alternatively, the discount period may extend to a specified number of days following the month in which the sale occurs. For example, 1/10 EOM (end of month) means that a 1% discount is available if the invoice is paid within the first 10 days of the next month.

When the seller elects not to offer a cash discount for prompt payment, credit terms will specify only the maximum time period for paying the balance due. For example, the invoice may state the time period as n/30, n/60, or n/10 EOM. This means, respectively, that the buyer must pay the net amount in 30 days, 60 days, or within the first 10 days of the next month.

When the buyer pays an invoice within the discount period, the amount of the discount decreases Inventory. Why? Because companies record inventory at cost, and by paying within the discount period, the buyer has reduced its cost. To illustrate, assume Sauk Stereo pays the balance due of $3,500 (gross invoice price of $3,800 less purchase returns and allowances of $300) on May 14, the last day of the discount period. Since the terms are 2/10, n/30, the cash discount is $70 ($3,500 × 2%) and Sauk Stereo pays $3,430 ($3,500 − $70). The entry Sauk Stereo makes to record its May 14 payment decreases (debits) Accounts Payable by the

HELPFUL HINT

The term *net* in "net 30" means the remaining amount due after subtracting any sales returns and allowances and partial payments.

net amount owed, reduces (credits) Inventory by the $70 discount, and reduces (credits) Cash by the net amount paid.

A = L + SE
−3,500
−3,430
−70

Cash Flows
−3,430

May 14	Accounts Payable	3,500	
	Cash		3,430
	Inventory		70
	(To record payment within discount period)		

If Sauk Stereo failed to take the discount and instead made full payment of $3,500 on June 3 (after the expiration of the discount period), it would debit Accounts Payable and credit Cash for $3,500 each.

A = L + SE
−3,500
−3,500

Cash Flows
−3,500

June 3	Accounts Payable	3,500	
	Cash		3,500
	(To record payment with no discount taken)		

A merchandising company should usually take all available discounts. Passing up the discount may be viewed as **paying interest** for use of the money. For example, passing up the discount offered by PW Audio Supply would be comparable to Sauk Stereo paying an interest rate of 2% for the use of $3,500 for 20 days. This is the equivalent of an annual interest rate of approximately 36.5% [2% × (365 ÷ 20)]. Obviously, it would be better for Sauk Stereo to borrow at prevailing bank interest rates of 6% to 10% than to lose the discount.

Summary of Purchasing Transactions

The following T-account (with transaction descriptions in red) provides a summary of the effect of the previous transactions on Inventory. Sauk Stereo originally purchased $3,800 of inventory on account. It then returned $300 of goods. It paid $150 in freight charges, and finally, it received a $70 discount off the balance owed because it paid within the discount period. This results in a balance in Inventory of $3,580.

		Inventory			
Purchase	May 4	3,800	May 8	300	Purchase return
Freight-in	6	150	14	70	Purchase discount
Balance		3,580			

ACTION PLAN

- **Purchaser records goods at cost.**
- **When goods are returned, purchaser reduces Inventory.**

DO IT! 2 | Purchase Transactions

On September 5, De La Hoya Company buys merchandise on account from Junot Diaz Company. The purchase price of the goods paid by De La Hoya is $1,500, and the cost to Diaz Company was $800. On September 8, De La Hoya returns defective goods with a selling price of $200. Record the transactions on the books of De La Hoya Company.

Solution

Sept. 5	Inventory	1,500	
	Accounts Payable		1,500
	(To record goods purchased on account)		
8	Accounts Payable	200	
	Inventory		200
	(To record return of defective goods)		

Related exercise material: **BE5.3, BE5.5, DO IT! 5.2, E5.2, E5.3, E5.4, and E5.11.**

Recording Sales Under a Perpetual System

LEARNING OBJECTIVE 3

Record sales under a perpetual inventory system.

In accordance with the revenue recognition principle, companies record sales revenue when the performance obligation is satisfied. Typically, the performance obligation is satisfied when the goods transfer from the seller to the buyer. At this point, the sales transaction is complete and the sales price established.

Sales may be made on credit or for cash. A **business document** should support every sales transaction, to provide written evidence of the sale. **Cash register documents** provide evidence of cash sales. A **sales invoice**, like the one shown in Illustration 5.6, provides support for a credit sale. The original copy of the invoice goes to the customer, and the seller keeps a copy for use in recording the sale. The invoice shows the date of sale, customer name, total sales price, and other relevant information.

The seller makes two entries for each sale. **The first entry records the sale**: The seller increases (debits) Cash (or Accounts Receivable if a credit sale) and also increases (credits) Sales Revenue. **The second entry records the cost of the merchandise sold**: The seller increases (debits) Cost of Goods Sold and also decreases (credits) Inventory for the cost of those goods. As a result, the Inventory account will show at all times the amount of inventory that should be on hand.

To illustrate a credit sales transaction, PW Audio Supply, Inc. records its May 4 sale of $3,800 to Sauk Stereo (see Illustration 5.6) as follows (assume the merchandise cost PW Audio Supply $2,400).

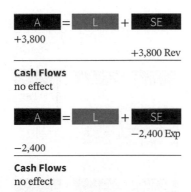

May 4	Accounts Receivable	3,800	
	Sales Revenue		3,800
	(To record credit sale to Sauk Stereo per invoice #731)		

4	Cost of Goods Sold	2,400	
	Inventory		2,400
	(To record cost of merchandise sold on invoice #731 to Sauk Stereo)		

For internal decision-making purposes, merchandising companies may use more than one sales revenue account. For example, PW Audio Supply may decide to keep separate sales revenue accounts for its sales of TVs, Blu-ray players, and headsets. **REI** might use separate accounts for camping gear, children's clothing, and ski equipment—or it might have even more narrowly defined accounts. By using separate sales revenue accounts for major product lines, rather than a single combined sales revenue account, company management can more closely monitor sales trends and respond to changes in sales patterns more strategically. For example, if TV sales are increasing while Blu-ray player sales are decreasing, PW Audio Supply might reevaluate both its advertising and pricing policies on these items to ensure they are optimal.

On its income statement presented to outside investors, a merchandising company normally would report only a single sales figure—the sum of all of its individual sales revenue accounts. This is done for two reasons. First, providing detail on all of its individual sales revenue accounts would add considerable length to its income statement. Second, companies do not want their competitors to know the details of their operating results. However, **Microsoft** recently expanded its disclosure of revenue from three to five types. The reason: The additional categories enabled financial statement users to better evaluate the growth of the company's consumer and Internet businesses (see **Ethics Note**).

ETHICS NOTE

Many companies are trying to improve the quality of their financial reporting. For example, **General Electric** now provides more detail on its revenues and operating profits.

At the end of "Anatomy of a Fraud" stories, which describe some recent real-world frauds, we discuss the missing control activities that would likely have prevented or uncovered the fraud.

Anatomy of a Fraud[1]

Holly Harmon was a cashier at a national superstore for only a short time when she began stealing merchandise using three methods. Under the first method, her husband or friends took UPC labels from cheaper items and put them on more expensive items. Holly then scanned the goods at the register. Using the second method, Holly scanned an item at the register but then voided the sale and left the merchandise in the shopping cart. A third approach was to put goods into large plastic containers. She scanned the plastic containers but not the goods within them. After Holly quit, a review of past surveillance tapes enabled the store to observe the thefts and to identify the participants.

Total take: $12,000

The Missing Controls

Human resource controls. A background check would have revealed Holly's previous criminal record. She would not have been hired as a cashier.

Physical controls. Software can flag high numbers of voided transactions or a high number of sales of low-priced goods. Random comparisons of video records with cash register records can ensure that the goods reported as sold on the register are the same goods that are shown being purchased on the video recording. Finally, employees should be aware that they are being monitored.

Source: Adapted from Wells, *Fraud Casebook* (2007), pp. 251–259.

Sales Returns and Allowances

We now look at the "flip side" of purchase returns and allowances, which the seller records as **sales returns and allowances**. These are transactions where the seller either accepts goods back from the buyer (a return) or grants a reduction in the purchase price (an allowance) so the buyer will keep the goods. PW Audio Supply's entries to record returned goods involve two journal entries: (1) an increase (debit) in Sales Returns and Allowances (a contra account to Sales Revenue) and a decrease (credit) in Accounts Receivable at the $300 selling price, and (2) an increase (debit) in Inventory (assume a $140 cost) and a decrease (credit) in Cost of Goods Sold, as shown below (assuming that the goods were not defective).

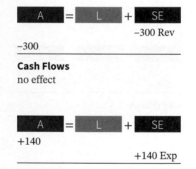

May 8	Sales Returns and Allowances	300	
	Accounts Receivable		300
	(To record credit granted to Sauk Stereo		
	for returned goods)		
8	Inventory	140	
	Cost of Goods Sold		140
	(To record cost of goods returned)		

If Sauk Stereo returns goods because they are damaged or defective, then PW Audio Supply's entry to Inventory and Cost of Goods Sold should be for the fair value of the returned goods, rather than their cost. For example, if the returned goods were defective and had a fair value of $50, PW Audio Supply would debit Inventory for $50 and credit Cost of Goods Sold for $50.

What happens if the goods are not returned but the seller grants the buyer an allowance by reducing the purchase price? In this case, the seller debits Sales Returns and Allowances and credits Accounts Receivable for the amount of the allowance. An allowance has no impact on Inventory or Cost of Goods Sold since no items are returned.

---

[1] The "Anatomy of a Fraud" stories in this text are adapted from *Fraud Casebook: Lessons from the Bad Side of Business,* edited by Joseph T. Wells (Hoboken, NJ: John Wiley & Sons, Inc., 2007). Used by permission. The names of some of the people and organizations in the stories are fictitious, but the facts in the stories are true.

Sales Returns and Allowances is a **contra revenue account** to Sales Revenue. This means that it is offset against a revenue account on the income statement. The normal balance of Sales Returns and Allowances is a debit. Companies use a contra account, instead of debiting Sales Revenue, to track separately in the accounts and to report separately in the income statement the amount of sales returns and allowances. Disclosure of this information is important to management. Excessive returns and allowances may suggest problems—inferior merchandise, inaccuracies in filling orders, errors in billing customers, or delivery or shipment mistakes. Moreover, a decrease (debit) recorded directly to Sales Revenue would obscure the relative importance of sales returns and allowances as a percentage of sales. It also could distort comparisons between total sales in different accounting periods.

At the end of the accounting period, if the company anticipates that future sales returns and allowances will be material, the company should make an adjusting entry to estimate the amount of these returns. In some industries, such as those relating to the sale of books and periodicals, returns are often material. The accounting for situations where returns must be estimated is addressed in advanced accounting courses.

Accounting Across the Organization   Costco Wholesale

iStock.com/Yuri

The Point of No Return?

In most industries, sales returns are relatively minor. But returns of consumer electronics can really take a bite out of profits. At one time, the marketing executives at **Costco Wholesale** faced a difficult decision. Costco always prided itself on its generous return policy. Most goods had an unlimited grace period for returns. However, a new policy requires that certain electronics must be returned within 90 days of their purchase. The reason? The cost of returned products such as high-definition TVs, computers, and iPods cut an estimated 8¢ per share off Costco's earnings per share, which was $2.30.

Online sales have accentuated the return problem. Many retailers have found that to compete, they must offer free shipping for returned goods.

Sources: Kris Hudson, "Costco Tightens Policy on Returning Electronics," *Wall Street Journal* (February 27, 2007), p. B4; and Loretta Chao, "More Retailers Offering Free Shipping on Returns," *Wall Street Journal* (October 11, 2015).

If a company expects significant returns, what are the implications for revenue recognition? (Go to WileyPLUS for this answer and additional questions.)

Sales Discounts

As mentioned in our discussion of purchase transactions, the seller may offer the customer a cash discount—called by the seller a **sales discount**—for the prompt payment of the balance due. Like a purchase discount, a sales discount is based on the invoice price less returns and allowances, if any. The seller increases (debits) the Sales Discounts account for discounts that are taken. For example, PW Audio Supply makes the following entry to record the cash receipt on May 14 from Sauk Stereo within the discount period.

May 14	Cash	3,430		
	Sales Discounts	70		
	Accounts Receivable		3,500	
	(To record collection within the			
	discount period from Sauk Stereo)			

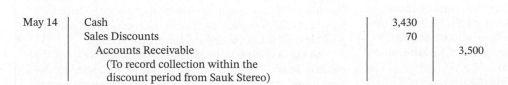

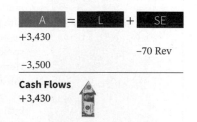

A = L + SE
+3,430
−70 Rev
−3,500

Cash Flows
+3,430

Like Sales Returns and Allowances, Sales Discounts is a **contra revenue account** to Sales Revenue. Its normal balance is a debit. PW Audio Supply uses this account, instead of debiting Sales Revenue, to track the amount of cash discounts taken by customers. If Sauk Stereo does not take the discount, PW Audio Supply increases (debits) Cash for $3,500 and decreases (credits) Accounts Receivable for the same amount at the date of collection.

At the end of the accounting period, if the amount of potential discounts is material, the company should make an adjusting entry to estimate the discounts. This would not usually be the case for sales discounts but might be necessary for other types of discounts, such as volume discounts, which are addressed in more advanced accounting courses.

The following T-accounts summarize the three sales-related transactions and show their combined effect on net sales for PW Audio Supply.

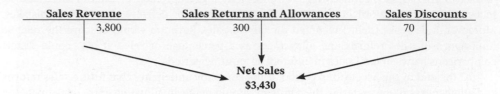

Sales Revenue	Sales Returns and Allowances	Sales Discounts
3,800	300	70

Net Sales
$3,430

Data Analytics and Credit Sales

Increased access to ever larger amounts of data about customers, suppliers, products, and virtually every other aspect of a business has resulted in a greater reliance by companies on data analytics to support business decisions. Credit sales, sales returns and allowances, and sales discounts all provide rich opportunities for the use of data analytics.

First, the decision of whom to grant credit is very important. Offering credit to customers can substantially increase sales opportunities. However, some credit customers will ultimately not be able to pay the amounts owed. So offering credit to customers has costs. Effectively analyzing data regarding current as well as potential customers can help a company expand its sales base while minimizing the risk of unpaid receivables.

Similarly, companies must develop policies regarding sales return practices. Merchandisers know that generous return policies can enhance customer loyalty. But if returns become common, the company's profitability will suffer. In recent years, companies such as **Best Buy**, **REI**, and **Costco** have all refined their customer return policies, sometimes with unique rules for specific product types, as a result of data analytics applied to their data on product returns.

Finally, sales discounts are offered to customers to encourage early payment of receivables. Offering these discounts is costly. To achieve the optimal cost-benefit balance on sales discounts, companies statistically analyze past discount practices to determine how large the discount should be, how long the payment period should be, and other factors.

People, Planet, and Profit Insight   PepsiCo

Helen Sessions/Alamy Stock Photo

Selling Green

Here is a question an executive of PepsiCo was asked: Should **PepsiCo** market green? The executive indicated that the company should, as he believes it's the No. 1 thing consumers all over the world care about. Here are some of his thoughts on this issue:

"Sun Chips are part of the food business I run. It's a 'healthy snack.' We decided that Sun Chips, if it's a healthy snack, should be made in facilities that have a net-zero footprint. In other words, I want off the electric grid everywhere we make Sun Chips. We did that. Sun Chips should be made in a facility that puts back more water than it uses. It does that. And we

partnered with our suppliers and came out with the world's first compostable chip package.

Now, there was an issue with this package: It was louder than the New York subway, louder than jet engines taking off. What would a company that's committed to green do: walk away or stay committed? If your people are passionate, they're going to fix it for you as long as you stay committed. Six months later, the compostable bag has half the noise of our current package.

So the view today is: we should market green, we should be proud to do it . . . it has to be a 360-degree process, both internal and external. And if you do that, you can monetize environmental sustainability for the shareholders."

Source: "Four Problems—and Solutions," *Wall Street Journal* (March 7, 2011), p. R2.

What is meant by "monetize environmental sustainability" for shareholders? (Go to WileyPLUS for this answer and additional questions.)

DO IT! 3 | Sales Transactions

On September 5, De La Hoya Company buys merchandise on account from Junot Diaz Company. The selling price of the goods is $1,500, and the cost to Diaz Company was $800. On September 8, De La Hoya returns defective goods with an initial selling price of $200 and a fair value of $30. Record the transactions on the books of Junot Diaz Company.

ACTION PLAN

- Seller records both the sale and the cost of goods sold at the time of the sale.
- When goods are returned, the seller records the return in a contra account, Sales Returns and Allowances, and reduces Accounts Receivable.
- Any goods returned increase Inventory and reduce Cost of Goods Sold. Defective or damaged inventory is recorded at fair value (scrap value).

Solution

Sept. 5	Accounts Receivable	1,500	
	Sales Revenue		1,500
	(To record credit sale)		
5	Cost of Goods Sold	800	
	Inventory		800
	(To record cost of goods sold)		
8	Sales Returns and Allowances	200	
	Accounts Receivable		200
	(To record credit granted for receipt of returned goods)		
8	Inventory	30	
	Cost of Goods Sold		30
	(To record fair value of goods returned)		

Related exercise material: **BE5.3, BE5.4, DO IT! 5.3, E5.3, E5.4, E5.5, and E5.11.**

The Accounting Cycle for a Merchandising Company

LEARNING OBJECTIVE 4

Apply the steps in the accounting cycle to a merchandising company.

Up to this point, we have illustrated the basic entries for transactions relating to purchases and sales in a perpetual inventory system. Now we consider the remaining steps in the accounting cycle for a merchandising company. Each of the required steps described in Chapter 4 for service companies applies to merchandising companies. Appendix 5A to this chapter shows the use of a worksheet by a merchandiser (an optional step).

Adjusting Entries

A merchandising company generally has the same types of adjusting entries as a service company. However, a merchandiser using a perpetual system will require one additional adjustment to make the records agree with the actual inventory on hand. Here's why: At the end of each period, for control purposes, a merchandising company that uses a perpetual system will take a physical count of its goods on hand. The company's unadjusted balance in Inventory usually does not agree with the actual amount of inventory on hand. The perpetual inventory records may be incorrect due to recording errors, theft, or waste. Thus, the company needs to adjust the perpetual records to make the recorded inventory amount agree with the inventory on hand. **This involves adjusting Inventory and Cost of Goods Sold.**

For example, suppose that PW Audio Supply, Inc. has an unadjusted balance of $40,500 in Inventory. Through a physical count, PW Audio Supply determines that its actual merchandise inventory at December 31 is $40,000. The company would make an adjusting entry as follows.

Dec. 31	Cost of Goods Sold	500	
	Inventory ($40,500 − $40,000)		500
	(To adjust inventory to physical count)		

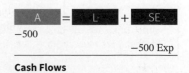

A = L + SE

−500

−500 Exp

Cash Flows
no effect

Closing Entries

A merchandising company, like a service company, closes to Income Summary all accounts that affect net income. In journalizing, the company credits all temporary accounts with debit balances, and debits all temporary accounts with credit balances. It also closes both Income Summary and Dividends to Retained Earnings. The following are the closing entries for PW Audio Supply using assumed amounts from its year-end adjusted trial balance. Recall that Cost of Goods Sold is an expense account with a normal debit balance, and Sales Returns and Allowances and Sales Discounts are contra revenue accounts with normal debit balances (see **Helpful Hint**).

			Dr.	Cr.
Dec. 31	Sales Revenue		480,000	
	Income Summary			480,000
	(To close income statement accounts			
	with credit balances)			
31	Income Summary		450,000	
	Sales Returns and Allowances			12,000
	Sales Discounts			8,000
	Cost of Goods Sold			316,000
	Salaries and Wages Expense			64,000
	Freight-Out			7,000
	Advertising Expense			16,000
	Utilities Expense			17,000
	Depreciation Expense			8,000
	Insurance Expense			2,000
	(To close income statement accounts			
	with debit balances)			
31	Income Summary		30,000	
	Retained Earnings			30,000
	(To close net income to retained earnings)			
31	Retained Earnings		15,000	
	Dividends			15,000
	(To close dividends to retained earnings)			

After PW Audio Supply has posted the closing entries, all temporary accounts have zero balances. Also, Retained Earnings has a balance that is carried over to the next period.

Summary of Merchandising Entries

Illustration 5.8 summarizes the entries for the merchandising accounts using a perpetual inventory system.

ILLUSTRATION 5.8 Daily recurring and adjusting and closing entries

	Transactions	Daily Recurring Entries	Dr.	Cr.
Sales Transactions	Selling merchandise to customers.	Cash or Accounts Receivable	XX	
		Sales Revenue		XX
		Cost of Goods Sold	XX	
		Inventory		XX
	Granting sales returns or allowances to customers.	Sales Returns and Allowances	XX	
		Cash or Accounts Receivable		XX
		Inventory	XX	
		Cost of Goods Sold		XX
	Paying freight costs on sales; FOB destination.	Freight-Out	XX	
		Cash		XX
	Receiving payment from customers within discount period.	Cash	XX	
		Sales Discounts	XX	
		Accounts Receivable		XX

(continues)

ILLUSTRATION 5.8 *(continued)*

Transactions	Daily Recurring Entries	Dr.	Cr.
Purchase Transactions — Purchasing merchandise for resale.	Inventory Cash or Accounts Payable	XX	XX
Paying freight costs on merchandise purchased; FOB shipping point.	Inventory Cash	XX	XX
Receiving purchase returns or allowances from suppliers.	Cash or Accounts Payable Inventory	XX	XX

Paying suppliers within discount period.	Accounts Payable
	  Inventory
	  Cash
		XX	XX
			XX

Events	Adjusting and Closing Entries	Dr.	Cr.
Adjust because book amount is higher than the inventory amount determined to be on hand.	Cost of Goods Sold Inventory	XX	XX
Closing temporary accounts with credit balances.	Sales Revenue Income Summary	XX	XX

Closing temporary accounts with debit balances.	Income Summary
	  Sales Returns and Allowances
	  Sales Discounts
	  Cost of Goods Sold
	  Freight-Out
	  Expenses
		XX	XX
			XX
			XX
			XX
			XX

DO IT! 4 | Closing Entries

The adjusted trial balance of Celine's Sports Wear Shop at December 31 shows Inventory $25,000, Sales Revenue $162,400, Sales Returns and Allowances $4,800, Sales Discounts $3,600, Cost of Goods Sold $110,000, Rent Revenue $6,000, Freight-Out $1,800, Rent Expense $8,800, and Salaries and Wages Expense $22,000. Prepare the closing entries for the income statement accounts.

ACTION PLAN
- Close all temporary accounts with credit balances to Income Summary by debiting these accounts.
- Close all temporary accounts with debit balances, except dividends, to Income Summary by crediting these accounts.

Solution

The two closing entries are:

Dec. 31	Sales Revenue	162,400	
	Rent Revenue	6,000	
	Income Summary		168,400
	(To close accounts with credit balances)		
31	Income Summary	151,000	
	Cost of Goods Sold		110,000
	Sales Returns and Allowances		4,800
	Sales Discounts		3,600
	Freight-Out		1,800
	Rent Expense		8,800
	Salaries and Wages Expense		22,000
	(To close accounts with debit balances)		

Related exercise material: **BE5.6, BE5.7, DO IT! 5.4, E5.6, E5.7, and E5.8.**

Multiple-Step Income Statement

LEARNING OBJECTIVE 5

Prepare a multiple-step income statement.

Merchandising companies widely use the classified balance sheet introduced in Chapter 4 and one of two forms for the income statement. This section explains the preparation of these financial statements by merchandisers.

Multiple-Step Income Statement

The **multiple-step income statement** is so named because it shows several steps in determining net income. Two of these steps relate to the company's principal operating activities. A multiple-step statement also distinguishes between **operating** and **nonoperating activities**. Finally, the statement highlights intermediate components of net income and shows subgroupings of expenses.

Income Statement Presentation of Sales

The multiple-step income statement begins by presenting **sales revenue**. It then deducts contra revenue accounts—sales returns and allowances and sales discounts—from sales revenue to arrive at **net sales**. **Illustration 5.9** presents the sales section for PW Audio Supply, Inc., using assumed data from its adjusted trial balance at year-end.

ILLUSTRATION 5.9

Computation of net sales

Sales		
Sales revenue		$480,000
Less: Sales returns and allowances	$12,000	
Sales discounts	8,000	20,000
Net sales		**$460,000**

Gross Profit

ALTERNATIVE TERMINOLOGY

Gross profit is sometimes referred to as *gross margin*.

From Illustration 5.1, you learned that companies deduct cost of goods sold from sales revenue to determine **gross profit** (see **Alternative Terminology**). For this computation, companies use **net sales** (which takes into consideration Sales Returns and Allowances and Sales Discounts) as the amount of sales revenue. On the basis of the sales data in Illustration 5.9 (net sales of $460,000) and cost of goods sold under the perpetual inventory system (assume $316,000), PW Audio Supply's gross profit is $144,000, computed as shown in **Illustration 5.10**.

ILLUSTRATION 5.10

Computation of gross profit

Net sales	$460,000
Cost of goods sold	316,000
Gross profit	**$144,000**

We also can express a company's gross profit as a percentage, called the **gross profit rate**. To do so, we divide the amount of gross profit by net sales. For PW Audio Supply, the **gross profit rate** is 31.3%, computed as shown in **Illustration 5.11**.

ILLUSTRATION 5.11

Gross profit rate formula and computation

Gross Profit	÷	**Net Sales**	=	**Gross Profit Rate**
$144,000	÷	$460,000	=	31.3%

Analysts generally consider the gross profit **rate** to be more useful than the gross profit **amount**. The rate expresses a more meaningful (qualitative) relationship between net sales and gross profit. For example, a gross profit of $1,000,000 may sound impressive. But if it is the result of a gross profit rate of only 7%, it is not so impressive. The gross profit rate tells how many cents of each net sales dollar contribute to gross profit.

Gross profit represents the **merchandising profit** of a company. It is not a measure of the overall profitability because operating expenses are not yet deducted. But managers and other interested parties closely watch the amount and trend of gross profit. They compare current gross profit with amounts reported in past periods. They also compare the company's gross profit rate with rates of competitors and with industry averages. Such comparisons provide information about the effectiveness of a company's purchasing function and the soundness of its pricing policies.

Operating Expenses and Income from Operations

Operating expenses are the next component in measuring net income for a merchandising company. They are the expenses incurred in the process of earning sales revenue. These expenses are similar in merchandising and service companies. Companies sometimes segregate operating expenses into selling expenses and administrative expenses to provide additional information. Selling expenses include such items as expenses for sales salaries and advertising. Administrative expenses include such items as insurance expense, utility expense, and freight-out.

At PW Audio Supply, operating expenses were $114,000. The company determines its income from operations by subtracting operating expenses from gross profit. Thus, as **Illustration 5.12** shows, income from operations is $30,000.

Gross profit		$144,000
Operating expenses		
Salaries and wages expense	64,000	
Utilities expense	17,000	
Advertising expense	16,000	
Depreciation expense	8,000	
Freight-out	7,000	
Insurance expense	2,000	
Total operating expenses		114,000
Income from operations		$ 30,000

ILLUSTRATION 5.12

Operating expenses in computing income from operations

Nonoperating Activities

Nonoperating activities consist of various revenues and expenses and gains and losses that are unrelated to the company's main line of operations. When nonoperating items are included, the label "**Income from operations**" (or "Operating income") precedes them. This label clearly identifies the results of the company's normal operations, an amount determined by subtracting cost of goods sold and operating expenses from net sales. The results of nonoperating activities are shown in the categories "**Other revenues and gains**" and "**Other expenses and losses**." **Illustration 5.13** lists examples of each.

Other Revenues and Gains
Interest revenue from notes receivable and marketable securities.
Dividend revenue from investments in common stock.
Rent revenue from subleasing a portion of the store.
Gain from the sale of property, plant, and equipment.

Other Expenses and Losses
Interest expense on notes and loans payable.
Casualty losses from recurring causes, such as vandalism and accidents.
Loss from the sale or abandonment of property, plant, and equipment.
Loss from strikes by employees and suppliers.

ILLUSTRATION 5.13

Other items of nonoperating activities

Merchandising companies report the nonoperating activities in the income statement immediately after the company's operating activities. **Illustration 5.14** shows these sections for PW Audio Supply, Inc., using assumed data. The net amount resulting from Other revenues and gains and Other expenses and losses is added to or subtracted from Income from operations to arrive at net income. The net income amount is the so-called "bottom line" of a company's income statement.

ILLUSTRATION 5.14

Multiple-step income statement

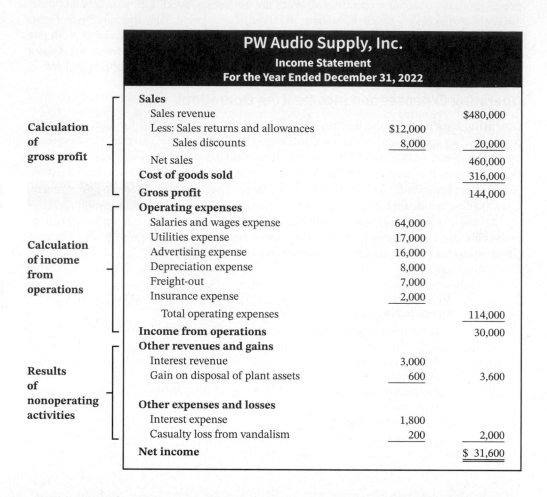

PW Audio Supply, Inc. **Income Statement** **For the Year Ended December 31, 2022**		
Sales		
Sales revenue		$480,000
Less: Sales returns and allowances	$12,000	
Sales discounts	8,000	20,000
Net sales		460,000
Cost of goods sold		316,000
Gross profit		144,000
Operating expenses		
Salaries and wages expense	64,000	
Utilities expense	17,000	
Advertising expense	16,000	
Depreciation expense	8,000	
Freight-out	7,000	
Insurance expense	2,000	
Total operating expenses		114,000
Income from operations		30,000
Other revenues and gains		
Interest revenue	3,000	
Gain on disposal of plant assets	600	3,600
Other expenses and losses		
Interest expense	1,800	
Casualty loss from vandalism	200	2,000
Net income		$ 31,600

Calculation of gross profit

Calculation of income from operations

Results of nonoperating activities

Ethics Insight   IBM

ImageRite RF/Getty Images

Disclosing More Details

After **Enron**, increased investor criticism and regulator scrutiny forced many companies to improve the clarity of their financial disclosures. For example, **IBM** began providing more detail regarding its "Other gains and losses." It had previously included these items in its selling, general, and administrative expenses, with little disclosure. For example, previously if IBM sold off one of its buildings at a gain, it included this gain in the selling, general, and administrative expense line item, thus reducing that expense. This made it appear that the company had done a better job of controlling operating expenses than it actually had.

As another example, when **eBay** sold the remainder of its investment in **Skype** to **Microsoft**, it reported a gain in "Other revenues and gains" of $1.7 billion. Since eBay's total income from operations was $2.4 billion, it was very important that the gain from the Skype sale not be buried in operating income.

Why have investors and analysts demanded more accuracy in isolating "Other gains and losses" from operating items? (Go to WileyPLUS for this answer and additional questions.)

The distinction between operating and nonoperating activities is crucial to many external users of financial data. These users view operating income as sustainable and many nonoperating activities as non-recurring (see **Ethics Note**). Therefore, when forecasting next year's income, analysts put the most weight on this year's income from operations and less weight on this year's nonoperating activities.

Single-Step Income Statement

Another income statement format is the **single-step income statement**. The statement is so named because only one step—subtracting total expenses from total revenues—is required in determining net income.

In a single-step statement, all data are classified into two categories: (1) **revenues**, which include both operating revenues and other revenues and gains; and (2) **expenses**, which include cost of goods sold, operating expenses, and other expenses and losses. **Illustration 5.15** shows a single-step statement for PW Audio Supply, Inc.

PW Audio Supply, Inc. Income Statement For the Year Ended December 31, 2022		
Revenues		
Net sales		$460,000
Interest revenue		3,000
Gain on disposal of plant assets		600
Total revenues		463,600
Expenses		
Cost of goods sold	$316,000	
Operating expenses	114,000	
Interest expense	1,800	
Casualty loss from vandalism	200	
Total expenses		432,000
Net income		$ 31,600

ILLUSTRATION 5.15

Single-step income statement

There are two primary reasons for using the single-step format. (1) A company does not realize any type of profit or income until total revenues exceed total expenses, so it makes sense to divide the statement into these two categories. (2) The format is simpler and easier to read. *For homework problems, however, you should use the single-step format only when specifically instructed to do so.*

Classified Balance Sheet

In the balance sheet, merchandising companies report inventory as a current asset immediately below accounts receivable. Recall from Chapter 4 that companies generally list current asset items in the order of their closeness to cash (liquidity). Inventory is less close to cash than accounts receivable because the goods must first be sold and then collection made from the customer. **Illustration 5.16** presents the assets section of a classified balance sheet for PW Audio Supply, Inc.

ETHICS NOTE

Companies manage earnings in various ways. **Conagra Brands** recorded a non-recurring gain for $186 million from the sale of **Pilgrim's Pride** stock to help meet an earnings projection for the quarter.

ILLUSTRATION 5.16 Assets section of a classified balance sheet

PW Audio Supply, Inc
Balance Sheet (Partial)
December 31, 2022

Assets

Current assets		
Cash		$ 9,500
Accounts receivable		16,100
Inventory		40,000
Prepaid insurance		1,800
Total current assets		67,400
Property, plant, and equipment		
Equipment	$80,000	
Less: Accumulated depreciation—equipment	24,000	56,000
Total assets		$123,400

The $40,000 is the cost of the inventory on hand, not its expected selling price.

ACTION PLAN

- Subtract cost of goods sold from net sales to determine gross profit.
- Subtract operating expenses from gross profit to determine income from operations.
- Add/subtract nonoperating items to determine net income.

DO IT! 5 | Multiple-Step Income Statement

The following information is available for Art Center Corp. for the year ended December 31, 2022.

Other revenues and gains	$ 8,000		Sales revenue	$462,000
Other expenses and losses	3,000		Operating expenses	187,000
Cost of goods sold	147,000		Sales discounts	20,000

Prepare a multiple-step income statement for Art Center Corp.

Solution

Art Center Corp.
Income Statement
For the Year Ended December 31, 2022

Sales		
Sales revenue		$462,000
Sales discounts		20,000
Net sales		442,000
Cost of goods sold		147,000
Gross profit		295,000
Operating expenses		187,000
Income from operations		108,000
Other revenues and gains	$8,000	
Other expenses and losses	3,000	5,000
Net income		$113,000

Related exercise material: **BE5.8, BE5.9, BE5.10, DO IT! 5.5, E5.9, E5.10, E5.12, E5.13, and E5.14.**

Appendix 5A | Merchandising Company Worksheet

LEARNING OBJECTIVE *6
Prepare a worksheet for a merchandising company.

Using a Worksheet

As indicated in Chapter 4, a worksheet enables companies to prepare financial statements before they journalize and post adjusting entries. The steps in preparing a worksheet for a merchandising company are the same as for a service company. **Illustration 5A.1** shows the

ILLUSTRATION 5A.1 Worksheet for merchandising company—perpetual inventory system

PW Audio Supply

PW Audio Supply, Inc.
Worksheet
For the Year Ended December 31, 2022

Accounts	Trial Balance Dr.	Trial Balance Cr.	Adjustments Dr.	Adjustments Cr.	Adjusted Trial Balance Dr.	Adjusted Trial Balance Cr.	Income Statement Dr.	Income Statement Cr.	Balance Sheet Dr.	Balance Sheet Cr.
Cash	9,500				9,500				9,500	
Accounts Receivable	16,100				16,100				16,100	
Inventory	40,500			(a) 500	40,000				40,000	
Prepaid Insurance	3,800			(b) 2,000	1,800				1,800	
Equipment	80,000				80,000				80,000	
Accumulated Depreciation—Equipment		16,000		(c) 8,000		24,000				24,000
Accounts Payable		20,400				20,400				20,400
Common Stock		50,000				50,000				50,000
Retained Earnings		33,000				33,000				33,000
Dividends	15,000				15,000				15,000	
Sales Revenue		480,000				480,000		480,000		
Sales Returns and Allowances	12,000				12,000		12,000			
Sales Discounts	8,000				8,000		8,000			
Cost of Goods Sold	315,500		(a) 500		316,000		316,000			
Freight-Out	7,000				7,000		7,000			
Advertising Expense	16,000				16,000		16,000			
Salaries and Wages Expense	59,000		(d) 5,000		64,000		64,000			
Utilities Expense	17,000				17,000		17,000			
Totals	599,400	599,400								
Insurance Expense			(b) 2,000		2,000		2,000			
Depreciation Expense			(c) 8,000		8,000		8,000			
Salaries and Wages Payable				(d) 5,000		5,000				5,000
Totals			15,500	15,500	612,400	612,400	450,000	480,000	162,400	132,400
Net Income							30,000			30,000
Totals							480,000	480,000	162,400	162,400

Key: (a) Adjustment to inventory on hand. (b) Insurance expired. (c) Depreciation expense. (d) Salaries and wages accrued.

worksheet for PW Audio Supply, Inc. (excluding nonoperating items). The unique accounts for a merchandiser using a **perpetual inventory system** are in red.

Trial Balance Columns

Data for the trial balance come from the ledger balances of PW Audio Supply at December 31. The amount shown for Inventory, $40,500, is the year-end inventory amount from the perpetual inventory system.

Adjustments Columns

A merchandising company generally has the same types of adjustments as a service company. As you see in the worksheet, adjustments (b), (c), and (d) are for insurance, depreciation, and salaries and wages. Pioneer Advertising Inc., as illustrated in Chapters 3 and 4, also had these adjustments. Adjustment (a) was required to adjust the perpetual inventory carrying amount to the actual count.

After PW Audio Supply enters all adjustments data on the worksheet, it establishes the equality of the adjustments column totals. It then extends the balances in all accounts to the adjusted trial balance columns.

Adjusted Trial Balance

The adjusted trial balance shows the balance of all accounts after adjustment at the end of the accounting period.

Income Statement Columns

Next, the merchandising company transfers the accounts and balances that affect the income statement from the adjusted trial balance columns to the income statement columns. PW Audio Supply shows Sales Revenue of $480,000 in the credit column. It shows the contra revenue accounts Sales Returns and Allowances $12,000 and Sales Discounts $8,000 in the debit column. The difference of $460,000 is the net sales shown on the income statement (Illustration 5.14).

Finally, the company totals all the credits in the income statement column and compares those totals to the total of the debits in the income statement column. If the credits exceed the debits, the company has net income. PW Audio Supply has net income of $30,000. If the debits exceed the credits, the company would report a net loss.

Balance Sheet Columns

The major difference between the balance sheets of a service company and a merchandiser is inventory. PW Audio Supply shows the ending inventory amount of $40,000 in the balance sheet debit column. The information to prepare the retained earnings statement is also found in these columns. That is, the retained earnings beginning balance is $33,000. Dividends are $15,000. Net income results when the total of the debit column exceeds the total of the credit column in the balance sheet columns. A net loss results when the total of the credits exceeds the total of the debit balances.

Appendix 5B	# Periodic Inventory System

LEARNING OBJECTIVE *7

Record purchases and sales under a periodic inventory system.

As described in this chapter, companies may use one of two basic systems of accounting for inventories: (1) the perpetual inventory system or (2) the periodic inventory system. In the chapter, we focused on the characteristics of the perpetual inventory system. In this appendix, we discuss and illustrate the **periodic inventory system**. One key difference between the two systems is the point at which the company computes cost of goods sold. For a visual reminder of this difference, refer back to Illustration 5.5.

Determining Cost of Goods Sold Under a Periodic System

Determining cost of goods sold is different when a periodic inventory system is used rather than a perpetual system. As you have seen, a company using a **perpetual system** makes an entry to record cost of goods sold and to reduce inventory each time a sale is made. A company using a **periodic system** does not record cost of goods sold with each sale. Instead, at the end of the period, the company performs a count to determine the ending balance of inventory. It then **calculates cost of goods sold by subtracting ending inventory from the cost of goods available for sale**. Cost of goods available for sale is the sum of beginning inventory plus purchases, as shown in **Illustration 5B.1**.

	Beginning inventory
+	Cost of goods purchased
	Cost of goods available for sale
−	Ending inventory
	Cost of goods sold

ILLUSTRATION 5B.1

Basic formula for cost of goods sold using the periodic system

Another difference between the two approaches is that the perpetual system directly adjusts the Inventory account for any transaction that affects inventory (such as purchases, freight costs, returns, and discounts). The periodic system does not do this. Instead, it uses separate accounts for purchases, freight costs, returns, and discounts. These various accounts are shown in Illustration 5B.2, which presents the calculation of cost of goods sold for PW Audio Supply, Inc., using the periodic approach and assumed data.

Note that the basic elements from Illustration 5B.1 are highlighted in **Illustration 5B.2**. You will learn more in Chapter 6 about how to determine cost of goods sold using the periodic system.

PW Audio Supply, Inc.
Cost of Goods Sold
For the Year Ended December 31, 2022

Cost of goods sold			
Inventory, January 1			$ 36,000
Purchases		$325,000	
Less: Purchase returns and allowances	$10,400		
Purchase discounts	6,800	17,200	
Net purchases		307,800	
Add: Freight-in		12,200	
Cost of goods purchased			320,000
Cost of goods available for sale			356,000
Less: Inventory, December 31			40,000
Cost of goods sold			$316,000

ILLUSTRATION 5B.2

Cost of goods sold for a merchandiser using a periodic inventory system

The far-right column identifies the primary items that are used to determine cost of goods sold of $316,000. The middle column explains cost of goods purchased of $320,000. The left column reports contra purchase items of $17,200.

The use of the periodic inventory system does not affect the form of presentation in the balance sheet. As under the perpetual system, a company reports inventory in the current assets section. PW Audio Supply would report inventory of $40,000 at December 31, 2022.

Recording Merchandise Transactions

In a **periodic inventory system**, companies record revenues from the sale of merchandise when sales are made, just as in a perpetual system. Unlike the perpetual system, however, companies **do not record the cost of the merchandise sold**. Instead, they take a physical inventory count at the **end of the period** to determine (1) the cost of the merchandise then on hand and (2) the cost of the goods sold during the period. And, **under a periodic system, companies record purchases of merchandise in the Purchases account rather than in the Inventory account**. Purchase returns and allowances, purchase discounts, and freight costs on purchases are recorded in separate accounts as well.

To illustrate the recording of merchandise transactions under a periodic inventory system, we will use purchase/sales transactions between PW Audio Supply, Inc. and Sauk Stereo, as illustrated for the perpetual inventory system in this chapter.

Recording Purchases of Merchandise

On the basis of the sales invoice (Illustration 5.6) and receipt of the merchandise ordered from PW Audio Supply, Sauk Stereo records the $3,800 purchase as follows (see **Helpful Hint**).

May 4	Purchases	3,800	
	Accounts Payable		3,800
	(To record goods purchased on account		
	from PW Audio Supply)		

Purchases is a temporary account whose normal balance is a debit. Recall that all temporary accounts are closed during the closing process.

Freight Costs

When the purchaser directly incurs the freight costs, it debits the account Freight-In (or Transportation-In). For example, if Sauk Stereo pays Public Carrier Co. $150 for freight charges on its purchase from PW Audio Supply on May 6, the entry on Sauk Stereo's books is as follows.

May 6	Freight-In (Transportation-In)	150	
	Cash		150
	(To record payment of freight on goods		
	purchased)		

Like Purchases, Freight-In is a temporary account whose normal balance is a debit. **Freight-In is part of cost of goods purchased.** The reason is that cost of goods purchased should include any freight charges necessary to bring the goods to the purchaser. Freight costs are not subject to a purchase discount. Purchase discounts apply only to the invoice cost of the merchandise.

Purchase Returns and Allowances

Sauk Stereo returns goods costing $300 to PW Audio Supply and prepares the following entry to recognize the return.

May 8	Accounts Payable	300	
	Purchase Returns and Allowances		300
	(To record return of goods purchased		
	from PW Audio Supply)		

Purchase Returns and Allowances is a temporary account whose normal balance is a credit.

Purchase Discounts

On May 14, Sauk Stereo pays the balance due on account to PW Audio Supply, taking the 2% cash discount allowed by PW Audio Supply for payment within 10 days. Sauk Stereo records the payment and discount as follows.

May 14	Accounts Payable ($3,800 − $300)	3,500	
	Purchase Discounts ($3,500 × .02)		70
	Cash		3,430
	(To record payment within the discount period)		

Purchase Discounts is a temporary account whose normal balance is a credit.

Recording Sales of Merchandise

The seller, PW Audio Supply, records the sale of $3,800 of merchandise to Sauk Stereo on May 4 (sales invoice No. 731, Illustration 5.6) as follows.

May 4	Accounts Receivable	3,800	
	Sales Revenue		3,800
	(To record credit sales per invoice #731 to Sauk Stereo)		

Sales Returns and Allowances

To record the returned goods received from Sauk Stereo on May 8, PW Audio Supply records the $300 sales return as follows. Note that there is no second entry for Cost of Goods Sold and Inventory.

May 8	Sales Returns and Allowances	300	
	Accounts Receivable		300
	(To record credit granted to Sauk Stereo for returned goods)		

Sales Discounts

On May 14, PW Audio Supply receives payment of $3,430 on account from Sauk Stereo. PW Audio Supply honors the 2% cash discount and records the payment of Sauk Stereo's account receivable in full as follows.

May 14	Cash	3,430	
	Sales Discounts ($3,500 × .02)	70	
	Accounts Receivable ($3,800 − $300)		3,500
	(To record collection within 2/10, n/30 discount period from Sauk Stereo)		

Comparison of Entries—Perpetual vs. Periodic

Illustration 5B.3 summarizes the periodic inventory entries shown in this appendix and compares them to the perpetual system entries from the chapter. Entries that differ in the two systems are shown in color.

ILLUSTRATION 5B.3 Comparison of entries for perpetual and periodic inventory systems

	Entries on Sauk Stereo's Books				
Transaction	**Perpetual Inventory System**		**Periodic Inventory System**		

May 4 Purchase of merchandise on credit.	Inventory
	    Accounts Payable
		3,800	3,800	Purchases
				    Accounts Payable
					3,800	3,800

6 Freight costs on purchases.	Inventory
	    Cash
		150	150	Freight-In
				    Cash
					150	150

8 Purchase returns and allowances.	Accounts Payable
	    Inventory
		300	300	Accounts Payable
				    Purchase Returns and Allowances
					300	300

14 Payment on account with a discount.	Accounts Payable
	    Cash
	    Inventory
		3,500	3,430
			70
				Accounts Payable
				    Cash
				    Purchase Discounts
					3,500	3,430
						70

	Entries on PW Audio Supply's Books				
Transaction	**Perpetual Inventory System**		**Periodic Inventory System**		

May 4 Sale of merchandise on credit.	Accounts Receivable
	    Sales Revenue
		3,800	3,800	Accounts Receivable
				    Sales Revenue
					3,800	3,800

	Cost of Goods Sold Inventory	2,400	2,400	**No entry for Cost of Goods Sold and Inventory**		

8 Return of merchandise sold.	Sales Returns and
	    Allowances
	    Accounts Receivable
		300	300	Sales Returns and
				    Allowances
				    Accounts Receivable
					300	300

	Inventory Cost of Goods Sold	140	140	**No entry for Cost of Goods Sold and Inventory**		

14 Cash received on account with a discount.	Cash
	Sales Discounts
	    Accounts Receivable
		3,430
		70
			3,500	Cash
				Sales Discounts
				    Accounts Receivable
					3,430
					70
						3,500

Journalizing and Posting Closing Entries

For a merchandising company, like a service company, all accounts that affect the determination of net income are closed to Income Summary. Data for the preparation of closing entries may be obtained from the income statement columns of the worksheet. In journalizing, all debit column amounts are credited, and all credit columns amounts are debited. To close the merchandise inventory in a periodic inventory system:

1. The beginning inventory balance is debited to Income Summary and credited to Inventory.

2. The ending inventory balance, as determined by the physical count, is debited to Inventory and credited to Income Summary.

The two entries for PW Audio Supply are as follows.

(1)

Dec. 31	Income Summary	36,000	
	Inventory		36,000
	(To close beginning inventory)		

(2)

31	Inventory	40,000	
	Income Summary		40,000
	(To record ending inventory)		

Illustration 5B.4 shows the Inventory and Income Summary accounts after posting.

Inventory				Income Summary				
1/1	Bal.	36,000	12/31 Close **36,000**	12/31	Close	**36,000**	12/31 Close	**40,000**
12/31	Close	**40,000**						
12/31	Bal.	40,000						

Posting closing entries for merchandise inventory

Often, the closing of Inventory is included with other closing entries, as shown below for PW Audio Supply (see **Helpful Hint**). (*Close Inventory with other accounts in homework problems unless stated otherwise.*)

HELPFUL HINT

Except for merchandise inventory, the easiest way to prepare the first two closing entries is to identify the temporary accounts by their balances and then prepare one entry for the credits and one for the debits.

Dec. 31	**Inventory (Dec. 31)**	40,000	
	Sales Revenue	480,000	
	Purchase Returns and Allowances	10,400	
	Purchase Discounts	6,800	
	Income Summary		537,200
	(To record ending inventory and close accounts with credit balances)		
31	Income Summary	507,200	
	Inventory (Jan. 1)		**36,000**
	Sales Returns and Allowances		12,000
	Sales Discounts		8,000
	Purchases		325,000
	Freight-In		12,200
	Salaries and Wages Expense		64,000
	Freight-Out		7,000
	Advertising Expense		16,000
	Utilities Expense		17,000
	Depreciation Expense		8,000
	Insurance Expense		2,000
	(To close beginning inventory and other income statement accounts with debit balances)		
31	Income Summary	30,000	
	Retained Earnings		30,000
	(To transfer net income to retained earnings)		
31	Retained Earnings	15,000	
	Dividends		15,000
	(To close dividends to retained earnings)		

After the closing entries are posted, all temporary accounts have zero balances. In addition, Retained Earnings has a credit balance of $48,000: beginning balance + net income − dividends ($33,000 + $30,000 − $15,000). The Inventory account has a $40,000 balance, which corresponds to the physical count.

Using a Worksheet

As indicated in Chapter 4, a worksheet enables companies to prepare financial statements before journalizing and posting adjusting entries. The steps in preparing a worksheet for a merchandising company are the same as they are for a service company.

Trial Balance Columns

Data for the trial balance come from the ledger balances of PW Audio Supply at December 31. The amount shown for Inventory, $36,000, is the beginning inventory amount from the periodic inventory system.

Adjustments Columns

A merchandising company generally has the same types of adjustments as a service company. As you see in the worksheet in **Illustration 5B.5**, adjustments (a), (b), and (c) are for insurance, depreciation, and salaries and wages. These adjustments were also required for Pioneer Advertising Inc., as illustrated in Chapters 3 and 4. The unique accounts for a merchandiser using a **periodic inventory system** are shown in capital red letters. Note, however, that this example excludes nonoperating items.

After all adjustment data are entered on the worksheet, the equality of the adjustment column totals is established. The balances in all accounts are then extended to the adjusted trial balance columns.

ILLUSTRATION 5B.5 Worksheet for merchandising company—periodic inventory system

PW Audio Supply

Home Insert Page Layout Formulas Data Review View

P18   fx

PW Audio Supply, Inc.
Worksheet
For the Year Ended December 31, 2022

	Trial Balance		Adjustments		Adjusted Trial Balance		Income Statement		Balance Sheet	
Accounts	Dr.	Cr.	Dr.	Cr.	Dr.	Cr.	Dr.	Cr.	Dr.	Cr.
Cash	9,500				9,500				9,500	
Accounts Receivable	16,100				16,100				16,100	
INVENTORY	36,000				36,000		36,000	40,000	40,000	
Prepaid Insurance	3,800			(a) 2,000	1,800				1,800	
Equipment	80,000				80,000				80,000	
Accumulated Depreciation—Equipment		16,000		(b) 8,000		24,000				24,000
Accounts Payable		20,400				20,400				20,400
Common Stock		50,000				50,000				50,000
Retained Earnings		33,000				33,000				33,000
Dividends	15,000				15,000				15,000	
SALES REVENUE		480,000				480,000		480,000		
SALES RETURNS AND ALLOWANCES	12,000				12,000		12,000			
SALES DISCOUNTS	8,000				8,000		8,000			
PURCHASES	325,000				325,000		325,000			
PURCHASE RETURNS AND ALLOWANCES		10,400				10,400		10,400		
PURCHASE DISCOUNTS		6,800				6,800		6,800		
FREIGHT-IN	12,200				12,200		12,200			
Freight-Out	7,000				7,000		7,000			
Advertising Expense	16,000				16,000		16,000			
Salaries and Wages Expense	59,000		(c) 5,000		64,000		64,000			
Utilities Expense	17,000				17,000		17,000			
Totals	616,600	616,600								
Insurance Expense			(a) 2,000		2,000		2,000			
Depreciation Expense			(b) 8,000		8,000		8,000			
Salaries and Wages Payable				(c) 5,000		5,000				5,000
Totals			15,000	15,000	629,600	629,600	507,200	537,200	162,400	132,400
Net Income							30,000			30,000
Totals							537,200	537,200	162,400	162,400

Key: (a) Insurance expired. (b) Depreciation expense. (c) Salaries and wages accrued.

Income Statement Columns

Next, PW Audio Supply transfers the accounts and balances that affect the income statement from the adjusted trial balance columns to the income statement columns. The company shows Sales Revenue of $480,000 in the credit column. It shows the contra revenue accounts, Sales Returns and Allowances of $12,000 and Sales Discounts of $8,000, in the debit column. The difference of $460,000 is the net sales shown on the income statement (Illustration 5.9). Similarly, Purchases of $325,000 and Freight-In of $12,200 are extended to the debit column. The contra purchase accounts, Purchase Returns and Allowances of $10,400 and Purchase Discounts of $6,800, are extended to the credit columns.

The worksheet procedures for the Inventory account merit specific comment as follows.

1. The beginning balance, $36,000, is extended from the adjusted trial balance column to the **income statement debit column**. From there, it can be added in reporting cost of goods available for sale in the income statement.

2. The ending inventory, $40,000, is added to the worksheet by an **income statement credit and a balance sheet debit**. The credit makes it possible to deduct ending inventory from the cost of goods available for sale in the income statement to determine cost of goods sold. The debit means the ending inventory can be reported as an asset on the balance sheet.

These two procedures are specifically shown in **Illustration 5B.6**.

	Income Statement		Balance Sheet	
	Dr.	Cr.	Dr.	Cr.
Inventory	(1) 36,000	40,000 ⟵ (2) ⟶	40,000	

ILLUSTRATION 5B.6

Worksheet procedures for inventories

The computation for cost of goods sold, taken from the items in the income statement column in Illustration 5B.5, is shown in **Illustration 5B.7** (see **Helpful Hint**).

Debit Column		Credit Column	
Beginning inventory	$ 36,000	Ending inventory	$40,000
Purchases	325,000	Purchase returns and allowances	10,400
Freight-in	12,200	Purchase discounts	6,800
Total debits	373,200	Total credits	$57,200
Less: Total credits	57,200		
Cost of goods sold	**$316,000**		

ILLUSTRATION 5B.7

Computation of cost of goods sold from worksheet columns

> **HELPFUL HINT**
>
> In a periodic system, cost of goods sold is a computation—it is not a separate account with a balance.

Finally, PW Audio Supply totals all the credits in the income statement column and compares these totals to the total of the debits in the income statement column. If the credits exceed the debits, the company has net income. PW Audio Supply has net income of $30,000. If the debits exceed the credits, the company would report a net loss.

Balance Sheet Columns

The major difference between the balance sheets of a service company and a merchandising company is inventory. PW Audio Supply shows ending inventory of $40,000 in the balance sheet debit column. The information to prepare the retained earnings statement is also found in these columns. That is, the retained earnings beginning balance is $33,000. Dividends are $15,000. Net income results when the total of the debit column exceeds the total of the credit column in the balance sheet columns. A net loss results when the total of the credits exceeds the total of the debit balances.

Review and Practice

Learning Objectives Review

1 Describe merchandising operations and inventory systems.

Because of inventory, a merchandising company has sales revenue, cost of goods sold, and gross profit. To account for inventory, a merchandising company must choose between a perpetual and a periodic inventory system.

2 Record purchases under a perpetual inventory system.

The company debits the Inventory account for all purchases of merchandise and freight-in, and credits it for purchase discounts and purchase returns and allowances.

3 Record sales under a perpetual inventory system.

When a merchandising company sells inventory, it debits Accounts Receivable (or Cash) and credits Sales Revenue for the **selling price** of the merchandise. At the same time, it debits Cost of Goods Sold and credits Inventory for the **cost** of the inventory items sold. Sales Returns and Allowances and Sales Discounts are debited and are contra revenue accounts.

4 Apply the steps in the accounting cycle to a merchandising company.

Each of the required steps in the accounting cycle for a service company applies to a merchandising company. A worksheet is again an optional step. Under a perpetual inventory system, the company must adjust the Inventory account to agree with the physical count.

5 Prepare a multiple-step income statement.

A multiple-step income statement shows numerous steps in determining net income, including nonoperating activities sections. A single-step income statement classifies all data under two categories, revenues or expenses, and determines net income in one step.

*6 Prepare a worksheet for a merchandising company.

The steps in preparing a worksheet for a merchandising company are the same as for a service company. The unique accounts for a merchandiser are Inventory, Sales Revenue, Sales Returns and Allowances, Sales Discounts, and Cost of Goods Sold.

*7 Record purchases and sales under a periodic inventory system.

In recording purchases under a periodic system, companies must make entries for (a) cash and credit purchases, (b) purchase returns and allowances, (c) purchase discounts, and (d) freight costs using separate accounts and *not* the Inventory account. In recording sales, companies must make entries for (a) cash and credit sales, (b) sales returns and allowances, and (c) sales discounts only. The Inventory and Cost of Goods Sold accounts are not used.

Glossary Review

Contra revenue account An account that is offset against a revenue account on the income statement. (p. 5-13).

Cost of goods sold The total cost of merchandise sold during the period. (p. 5-3).

FOB destination Freight terms indicating that the seller places the goods free on board to the buyer's place of business, and the seller pays the freight. (p. 5-8).

FOB shipping point Freight terms indicating that the seller places goods free on board the carrier, and the buyer pays the freight costs. (p. 5-8).

Gross profit The excess of net sales over the cost of goods sold. (p. 5-18).

Gross profit rate Gross profit expressed as a percentage, calculated by dividing the amount of gross profit by net sales. (p. 5-18).

Income from operations Income from a company's principal operating activity, determined by subtracting cost of goods sold and operating expenses from gross profit. (p. 5-19).

Multiple-step income statement An income statement that shows several steps in determining net income. (p. 5-18).

Net sales Sales revenue less sales returns and allowances and sales discounts. (p. 5-18).

Nonoperating activities Various revenues, expenses, gains, and losses that are unrelated to a company's main line of operations. (p. 5-19).

Operating expenses   Expenses incurred in the process of earning sales revenue. (p. 5-19).

Other expenses and losses   A nonoperating-activities section of the income statement that shows expenses and losses unrelated to the company's main line of operations. (p. 5-19).

Other revenues and gains   A nonoperating-activities section of the income statement that shows revenues and gains unrelated to the company's main line of operations. (p. 5-19).

Periodic inventory system   An inventory system under which the company does not keep detailed inventory records in the Inventory account throughout the accounting period but determines the cost of goods sold only at the end of an accounting period. (p. 5-5).

Perpetual inventory system   An inventory system under which the company keeps detailed records of the cost of each inventory purchase and sale in the Inventory account, and the records continuously show the inventory that should be on hand. (p. 5-4).

Purchase allowance   A deduction made to the selling price of merchandise, granted by the seller so that the buyer will keep the merchandise. (p. 5-9).

Purchase discount   A cash discount claimed by a buyer for prompt payment of a balance due. (p. 5-9).

Purchase invoice   A document that supports each credit purchase. (p. 5-7).

Purchase return   A return of goods from the buyer to the seller for a cash or credit refund. (p. 5-9).

Sales discount   A reduction given by a seller for prompt payment of a credit sale. (p. 5-13).

Sales invoice   A document that supports each credit sale. (p. 5-11).

Sales returns and allowances   Purchase returns and allowances from the seller's perspective. See *Purchase return* and *Purchase allowance*. (p. 5-12).

Sales revenue (Sales)   The primary source of revenue in a merchandising company. (p. 5-3).

Single-step income statement   An income statement that shows only one step in determining net income. (p. 5-21).

Practice Multiple-Choice Questions

1. **(LO 1)** Gross profit will result if:
   a. operating expenses are less than net income.
   b. net sales are greater than operating expenses.
   c. net sales are greater than cost of goods sold.
   d. operating expenses are greater than cost of goods sold.

2. **(LO 2)** Under a perpetual inventory system, when goods are purchased for resale by a company:
   a. purchases on account are debited to Inventory.
   b. purchases on account are debited to Purchases.
   c. purchase returns are debited to Purchase Returns and Allowances.
   d. freight costs are debited to Freight-Out.

3. **(LO 3)** The sales revenue accounts that normally have a debit balance are:
   a. Sales Discounts.
   b. Sales Returns and Allowances.
   c. both Sales Discounts and Sales Returns and Allowances.
   d. neither Sales Discounts nor Sales Returns and Allowances.

4. **(LO 3)** A credit sale of $750 is made on June 13, terms 2/10, net/30. A return of $50 is granted on June 16. The amount received as payment in full on June 23 is:
   a. $700.   c. $685.
   b. $686.   d. $650.

5. **(LO 2)** Which of the following accounts will normally appear in the ledger of a merchandising company that uses a perpetual inventory system?
   a. Purchases.   c. Cost of Goods Sold.
   b. Freight-In.   d. Purchase Discounts.

6. **(LO 3)** To record the sale of goods for cash in a perpetual inventory system:
   a. only one journal entry is necessary to record cost of goods sold and reduction of inventory.
   b. only one journal entry is necessary to record the receipt of cash and the sales revenue.
   c. two journal entries are necessary: one to record the receipt of cash and sales revenue, and one to record the cost of goods sold and reduction of inventory.
   d. two journal entries are necessary: one to record the receipt of cash and reduction of inventory, and one to record the cost of goods sold and sales revenue.

7. **(LO 4)** The steps in the accounting cycle for a merchandising company are the same as those in a service company **except**:
   a. an additional adjusting journal entry for inventory may be needed in a merchandising company.
   b. closing journal entries are not required for a merchandising company.
   c. a post-closing trial balance is not required for a merchandising company.
   d. a multiple-step income statement is required for a merchandising company.

8. **(LO 5)** The multiple-step income statement for a merchandising company shows each of the following items **except**:
   a. gross profit.
   b. cost of goods sold.
   c. a sales section.
   d. an investing activities section.

9. (LO 5) If net sales are $400,000, cost of goods sold is $310,000, and operating expenses are $60,000, the gross profit is:

 a. $30,000. c. $340,000.

 b. $90,000. d. $400,000.

10. (LO 5) A single-step income statement:

 a. reports gross profit.

 b. does not report cost of goods sold.

 c. reports sales revenue and all other revenues and gains in the revenues section of the income statement.

 d. reports income from operations separately.

11. (LO 5) Which of the following appears on both a single-step and a multiple-step income statement?

 a. Inventory. c. Income from operations.

 b. Gross profit. d. Cost of goods sold.

*12. (LO 6) In a worksheet using a perpetual inventory system, Inventory is shown in the following columns:

 a. adjusted trial balance debit and balance sheet debit.

 b. income statement debit and balance sheet debit.

 c. income statement credit and balance sheet debit.

 d. income statement credit and adjusted trial balance debit.

*13. (LO 7) In determining cost of goods sold in a periodic system:

 a. purchase discounts are deducted from net purchases.

 b. freight-out is added to net purchases.

 c. purchase returns and allowances are deducted from net purchases.

 d. freight-in is added to net purchases.

*14. (LO 7) If beginning inventory is $60,000, cost of goods purchased is $380,000, and ending inventory is $50,000, cost of goods sold is:

 a. $390,000. c. $330,000.

 b. $370,000. d. $420,000.

*15 (LO 7) When goods are purchased for resale by a company using a periodic inventory system:

 a. purchases on account are debited to Inventory.

 b. purchases on account are debited to Purchases.

 c. purchase returns are debited to Purchase Returns and Allowances.

 d. freight costs are debited to Purchases.

Solutions

1. c. Gross profit will result if net sales are greater than cost of goods sold. The other choices are incorrect because (a) operating expenses and net income are not used in the computation of gross profit; (b) gross profit results when net sales are greater than cost of goods sold, not operating expenses; and (d) gross profit results when net sales, not operating expenses, are greater than cost of goods sold.

2. a. Under a perpetual inventory system, when a company purchases goods for resale, purchases on account are debited to the Inventory account, not (b) Purchases or (c) Purchase Returns and Allowances. Choice (d) is incorrect because freight costs related to purchases are also debited to the Inventory account, not the Freight-Out account.

3. c. Both Sales Discounts and Sales Returns and Allowances normally have a debit balance. Choices (a) and (b) are both correct, but (c) is the better answer. Choice (d) is incorrect as both Sales Discounts and Sales Returns and Allowances, not neither, are correct.

4. b. The amount of $686 is paid within 10 days of the purchase ($750 − $50) − [($750 − $50) × 2%]. The other choices are incorrect because (a) does not consider the discount of $14; (c) the amount of the discount is based upon the amount after the return is granted ($700 × 2%), not the amount before the return of merchandise ($750 × 2%); and (d) does not constitute payment in full on June 23.

5. c. The Cost of Goods Sold account normally appears in the ledger of a merchandising company using a perpetual inventory system. The other choices are incorrect because (a) the Purchases account, (b) the Freight-In account, and (d) the Purchase Discounts account all appear in the ledger of a merchandising company that uses a periodic inventory system.

6. c. Two journal entries are necessary: one to record the receipt of cash and sales revenue, and one to record the cost of goods sold and reduction of inventory. The other choices are incorrect because (a) only considers the recognition of the expense and ignores the revenue,

(b) only considers the recognition of revenue and leaves out the expense or cost of merchandise sold, and (d) the receipt of cash and sales revenue, not reduction of inventory, are paired together, and the cost of goods sold and reduction of inventory, not sales revenue, are paired together.

7. a. An additional adjusting journal entry for inventory may be needed in a merchandising company to adjust for a physical inventory count, but it is not needed for a service company. The other choices are incorrect because (b) closing journal entries and (c) a post-closing trial balance are required for both types of companies. Choice (d) is incorrect because while a multiple-step income statement is not required for a merchandising company, it is useful to distinguish income generated from operating the business versus income or loss from non-recurring, nonoperating items.

8. d. An investing activities section appears on the statement of cash flows, not on a multiple-step income statement. Choices (a) gross profit, (b) cost of goods sold, and (c) a sales section are all items reported on a multiple-step income statement.

9. b. Gross profit = Net sales of $400,000 − Cost of goods sold $310,000 = $90,000, not (a) $30,000, (c) $340,000, or (d) $400,000.

10. c. Both sales revenue and "Other revenues and gains" are reported in the revenues section of a single-step income statement. The other choices are incorrect because (a) gross profit is not reported on a single-step income statement, (b) cost of goods sold is included in the expenses section of a single-step income statement, and (d) income from operations is not shown separately on a single-step income statement.

11. d. Cost of goods sold appears on both a single-step and a multiple-step income statement. The other choices are incorrect because (a) inventory does not appear on either a single-step or a multiple-step income statement and (b) gross profit and (c) income from operations appear on a multiple-step income statement but not on a single-step income statement.

12. a. In a worksheet using a perpetual inventory system, inventory is shown in the adjusted trial balance debit column and in the balance sheet debit column. The other choices are incorrect because the Inventory account is not shown in the income statement columns.

*13. d. In determining cost of goods sold in a periodic system, freight-in is added to net purchases. The other choices are incorrect because (a) purchase discounts are deducted from purchases, not net purchases; (b) freight-out is a cost of sales, not a cost of purchases; and (c) purchase returns and allowances are deducted from purchases, not net purchases.

*14. a. Beginning inventory of $60,000 + Cost of goods purchased $380,000 − Ending inventory $50,000 = Cost of goods sold $390,000, not (b) $370,000, (c) $330,000, or (d) $420,000.

*15. b. Purchases for resale are debited to the Purchases account. The other choices are incorrect because (a) purchases on account are debited to Purchases, not Inventory; (c) Purchase Returns and Allowances are always credited; and (d) freight costs are debited to Freight-In, not Purchases.

Practice Brief Exercises

1. (LO 1, 4) The following are the components in determining cost of goods sold for (a) Frazier Company, (b) Todd Company, and (c) Abreu Enterprises. Determine the missing amounts.

Compute the missing amounts in determining cost of goods sold.

	Beginning Inventory	Purchases	Cost of Goods Available for Sale	Ending Inventory	Cost of Goods Sold
a.	$120,000	$150,000	?	?	$160,000
b.	$ 50,000	?	$125,000	$45,000	?
c.	?	$220,000	$330,000	$61,000	?

Solution

1. a. Cost of goods available for sale = $120,000 + $150,000 = $270,000
   Ending inventory = $270,000 − $160,000 = $110,000

b. Purchases = $125,000 − $50,000 = $75,000
   Cost of goods sold = $125,000 − $45,000 = $80,000

c. Beginning inventory = $330,000 − $220,000 = $110,000
   Cost of goods sold = $330,000 − $61,000 = $269,000

2. (LO 2) Prepare the journal entries to record the following transactions on Robertson Company's books using a perpetual inventory system.

Journalize purchase transactions.

a. On March 2, Melky Company sold $800,000 of merchandise to Robertson Company, terms 2/10, n/30.

b. On March 6, Robertson Company returned $100,000 of the merchandise purchased on March 2.

c. On March 12, Robertson Company paid the balance due to Melky Company.

Solution

2. a. Inventory	800,000	
Accounts Payable		800,000
b. Accounts Payable	100,000	
Inventory		100,000
c. Accounts Payable ($800,000 − $100,000)	700,000	
Inventory ($700,000 × 2%)		14,000
Cash ($700,000 − $14,000)		686,000

3. (LO 3) Prepare the journal entries to record the following transactions on Wendel Company's books using a perpetual inventory system.

Journalize sales transactions.

a. On March 2, Wendel Company sold $700,000 of merchandise to Krista Company, terms 2/10, n/30. The cost of the merchandise sold was $460,000.

b. On March 6, Krista Company returned $80,000 of the merchandise purchased on March 2. The cost of the merchandise returned was $54,000.

c. On March 12, Wendel Company received the balance due from Krista Company.

Solution

3. a. March	2	Accounts Receivable	700,000	
		Sales Revenue		700,000
	2	Cost of Goods Sold	460,000	
		Inventory		460,000
b.	6	Sales Returns and Allowances	80,000	
		Accounts Receivable		80,000
	6	Inventory	54,000	
		Cost of Goods Sold		54,000
c.	12	Cash ($620,000 − $12,400)	607,600	
		Sales Discounts ($620,000 × 2%)	12,400	
		Accounts Receivable ($700,000 − $80,000)		620,000

Prepare closing entries.

4. (LO 4) Cabrera Company uses the perpetual inventory system and has the following account balances: Sales Revenue $300,000, Sales Returns and Allowances $10,000, Cost of Goods Sold $174,000, and Inventory $50,000. Prepare the entries to record the closing of these items to Income Summary.

Solution

4.	Sales Revenue	300,000	
	Income Summary		300,000
	Income Summary	184,000	
	Cost of Goods Sold		174,000
	Sales Returns and Allowances		10,000

Compute net sales, gross profit, income from operations, and gross profit rate.

5. (LO 5) Assume Yoan Company has the following reported amounts: Sales revenue $400,000, Sales discounts $10,000, Cost of goods sold $234,000, and Operating expenses $60,000. Compute the following: (a) net sales, (b) gross profit, (c) income from operations, and (d) gross profit rate. (Round to one decimal place.)

Solution

5. **a.** Net sales = $400,000 − $10,000 = $390,000

   b. Gross profit = $390,000 − $234,000 = $156,000

   c. Income from operations = $156,000 − $60,000 = $96,000

   d. Gross profit rate = $156,000 ÷ $390,000 = 40%

Practice Exercises

Prepare purchase and sales entries.

1. (LO 2, 3) On June 10, Vareen Company purchased $8,000 of merchandise on account from Harrah Company, FOB shipping point, terms 3/10, n/30. Vareen pays the freight costs of $400 on June 11. Damaged goods totaling $300 are returned to Harrah for credit on June 12. The fair value of these goods is $70. On June 19, Vareen pays Harrah Company in full, less the purchase discount. Both companies use a perpetual inventory system.

Instructions

a. Prepare separate entries for each transaction on the books of Vareen Company.

b. Prepare separate entries for each transaction for Harrah Company. The merchandise purchased by Vareen on June 10 had cost Harrah $4,800.

Solution

1. a.

June 10	Inventory	8,000	
	Accounts Payable		8,000
11	Inventory	400	
	Cash		400

	12	Accounts Payable	300	
		Inventory		300
	19	Accounts Payable ($8,000 − $300)	7,700	
		Inventory ($7,700 × 3%)		231
		Cash ($7,700 − $231)		7,469

b.

June 10		Accounts Receivable	8,000	
		Sales Revenue		8,000
		Cost of Goods Sold	4,800	
		Inventory		4,800
	12	Sales Returns and Allowances	300	
		Accounts Receivable		300
		Inventory	70	
		Cost of Goods Sold		70
	19	Cash ($7,700 − $231)	7,469	
		Sales Discounts ($7,700 × 3%)	231	
		Accounts Receivable ($8,000 − $300)		7,700

2. (LO 5) In its income statement for the year ended December 31, 2022, Marten Company reported the following condensed data.

Prepare multiple-step and single-step income statements.

Interest expense	$ 70,000	Net sales	$2,200,000
Operating expenses	725,000	Interest revenue	25,000
Cost of goods sold	1,300,000	Loss on disposal of plant assets	17,000

Instructions

a. Prepare a multiple-step income statement.

b. Prepare a single-step income statement.

Solution

2. a.

Marten Company
Income Statement
For the Year Ended December 31, 2022

Net sales		$2,200,000
Cost of goods sold		1,300,000
Gross profit		900,000
Operating expenses		725,000
Income from operations		175,000
Other revenues and gains		
Interest revenue		25,000
Other expenses and losses		
Interest expense	$70,000	
Loss on disposal of plant assets	17,000	87,000
Net income		$ 113,000

b.

Marten Company
Income Statement
For the Year Ended December 31, 2022

Revenues		
Net sales		$2,200,000
Interest revenue		25,000
Total revenues		2,225,000
Expenses		
Cost of goods sold	$1,300,000	
Operating expenses	725,000	
Interest expense	70,000	
Loss on disposal of plant assets	17,000	
Total expenses		2,112,000
Net income		$ 113,000

Practice Problem

Prepare a multiple-step income statement.

(LO 5) The adjusted trial balance columns of Falcetto Company for the year ended December 31, 2022, are as follows.

	Debit		Credit
Cash	14,500	Accumulated Depreciation—	
Accounts Receivable	11,100	Equipment	18,000
Inventory	29,000	Notes Payable	25,000
Prepaid Insurance	2,500	Accounts Payable	10,600
Equipment	95,000	Common Stock	50,000
Dividends	12,000	Retained Earnings	31,000
Sales Returns and Allowances	6,700	Sales Revenue	536,800
Sales Discounts	5,000	Interest Revenue	2,500
Cost of Goods Sold	363,400		673,900
Freight-Out	7,600		
Advertising Expense	12,000		
Salaries and Wages Expense	56,000		
Utilities Expense	18,000		
Rent Expense	24,000		
Depreciation Expense	9,000		
Insurance Expense	4,500		
Interest Expense	3,600		
	673,900		

Instructions

Prepare a multiple-step income statement for Falcetto Company.

Solution

Falcetto Company
Income Statement
For the Year Ended December 31, 2022

Sales		
Sales revenue		$536,800
Less: Sales returns and allowances	$ 6,700	
Sales discounts	5,000	11,700
Net sales		525,100
Cost of goods sold		363,400
Gross profit		161,700
Operating expenses		
Salaries and wages expense	56,000	
Rent expense	24,000	
Utilities expense	18,000	
Advertising expense	12,000	
Depreciation expense	9,000	
Freight-out	7,600	
Insurance expense	4,500	
Total operating expenses		131,100
Income from operations		30,600
Other revenues and gains		
Interest revenue		2,500
Other expenses and losses		
Interest expense		3,600
Net income		$ 29,500

WileyPLUS

Brief Exercises, DO IT! Exercises, Exercises, Problems, and many additional resources are available for practice in WileyPLUS.

Note: All asterisked Questions, Exercises, and Problems relate to material in the appendices to the chapter.

Questions

1. (a) "The steps in the accounting cycle for a merchandising company are different from the accounting cycle for a service company." (b) "The measurement of net income for a merchandising company is conceptually the same as for a service company." Explain why each statement is true or false.

2. Why is the normal operating cycle for a merchandising company likely to be longer than for a service company?

3. What components of revenues and expenses are different between merchandising and service companies?

4. How does income measurement differ between a merchandising and a service company?

5. When is cost of goods sold determined in a perpetual inventory system?

6. Distinguish between FOB shipping point and FOB destination. Identify the freight terms that will result in a debit to Inventory by the buyer and a debit to Freight-Out by the seller.

7. Explain the meaning of the credit terms 2/10, n/30.

8. Goods costing $2,000 are purchased on account on July 15 with credit terms of 2/10, n/30. On July 18, a $200 credit memo is received from the supplier for damaged goods. Give the journal entry on July 24 to record payment of the balance due within the discount period using a perpetual inventory system.

9. Masie Ascot believes revenues from credit sales may be recorded before they are collected in cash. Explain why Masie is correct or incorrect.

10. (a) What is the primary source document for recording (1) cash sales and (2) credit sales? (b) Using XXs for amounts, give the journal entry for each of the transactions in part (a).

11. A credit sale is made on July 10 for $900, terms 1/15, n/30. On July 12 the purchaser returns $100 of goods for credit. Give the journal entry on July 19 to record the receipt of the balance due within the discount period.

12. Explain why the Inventory account will usually require adjustment at year-end for a merchandiser that uses the perpetual inventory system.

13. Prepare the closing entries for the Sales Revenue account, assuming a balance of $200,000 and the Cost of Goods Sold account with a $145,000 balance.

14. What merchandising account(s) will appear in the post-closing trial balance?

15. Minnick Co. has net sales of $105,000, cost of goods sold of $70,000, and operating expenses of $20,000. What is its gross profit and its gross profit rate?

16. Scribe Company reports net sales of $800,000, gross profit of $560,000, and net income of $230,000. What are its operating expenses, assuming that there are no nonoperating activities?

17. Identify the distinguishing features of a multiple-step income statement for a merchandising company.

18. Identify the sections of a multiple-step income statement that relate to (a) operating activities, and (b) nonoperating activities.

19. How does the single-step form of income statement differ from the multiple-step form?

20. What title does **Apple** use for gross profit? By how much did its 2018 gross profit change, and in what direction, when compared to 2017?

*21. Indicate the columns of the worksheet in a perpetual system in which (a) inventory and (b) cost of goods sold will be shown.

*22. Identify the accounts that are added to or deducted from Purchases in a periodic system to determine the cost of goods purchased. For each account, indicate whether it is added or deducted.

*23. On July 15, a company purchases on account goods costing $1,900, with credit terms of 2/10, n/30. On July 18, the company receives a $400 credit memo from the supplier for damaged goods. Give the journal entry on July 24 to record payment of the balance due within the discount period assuming a periodic inventory system.

Brief Exercises

BE5.1 (LO 1), AP The following are the components in determining cost of goods sold. Determine the missing amounts.

Compute missing amounts in determining cost of goods sold.

	Beginning Inventory	Purchases	Cost of Goods Available for Sale	Ending Inventory	Cost of Goods Sold
a.	$80,000	$100,000	?	?	$120,000
b.	$50,000	?	$115,000	$35,000	?
c.	?	$110,000	$160,000	$29,000	?

Compute missing amounts in determining net income.

BE5.2 (LO 1), AP The following are the components in Gates Company's income statement. Determine the missing amounts, assuming that there are no nonoperating activities.

	Sales Revenue	Cost of Goods Sold	Gross Profit	Operating Expenses	Net Income
a.	$ 75,000	?	$ 30,000	?	$12,100
b.	$108,000	$70,000	?	?	$29,500
c.	?	$71,900	$109,600	$46,200	?

Journalize perpetual inventory entries.

BE5.3 (LO 2, 3), AP Rita Company buys merchandise on account from Linus Company. The selling price of the goods is $900, and the cost of the goods is $590. Both companies use perpetual inventory systems. Journalize the transaction on the books of both companies.

Journalize sales transactions.

BE5.4 (LO 3), AP Prepare the journal entries to record the following transactions on Borst Company's books using a perpetual inventory system.

a. On March 2, Borst Company sold $800,000 of merchandise on account to McLeena Company, terms 2/10, n/30. The cost of the merchandise sold was $540,000.

b. On March 6, McLeena Company returned $140,000 of the merchandise purchased on March 2. The cost of the returned merchandise was $94,000.

c. On March 12, Borst Company received the balance due from McLeena Company.

Journalize purchase transactions.

BE5.5 (LO 2), AP Prepare the journal entries to record the following transactions on McLeena Company's books under a perpetual inventory system.

a. On March 2, Borst Company sold $800,000 of merchandise on account to McLeena Company, terms 2/10, n/30. The cost of the merchandise sold was $540,000.

b. On March 6, McLeena Company returned $140,000 of the merchandise purchased on March 2. The cost of the returned merchandise was $94,000.

c. On March 12, Borst Company received the balance due from McLeena Company.

Prepare adjusting entry for inventory.

BE5.6 (LO 4), AP At year-end, the perpetual inventory records of Litwin Company showed merchandise inventory of $98,000. The company determined, however, that its actual inventory on hand was $95,700. Record the necessary adjusting entry.

Prepare closing entries for accounts.

BE5.7 (LO 4), AP Hudson Company has the following account balances: Sales Revenue $195,000, Sales Discounts $2,000, Cost of Goods Sold $117,000, and Inventory $40,000. Prepare the entries to record the closing of these accounts to Income Summary under a perpetual inventory system.

Prepare sales section of income statement.

BE5.8 (LO 5), AP Barto Company provides the following information for the month ended October 31, 2022; sales on credit $300,000, cash sales $150,000, sales discounts $5,000, and sales returns and allowances $19,000. Prepare the sales section of a multiple-step income statement based on this information.

Explain the presentation of a multiple-step income statement.

BE5.9 (LO 5), C [Writing] Explain where each of the following items would appear on a multiple-step income statement: gain on disposal of plant assets, cost of goods sold, depreciation expense, and sales returns and allowances.

Compute net sales, gross profit, income from operations, and gross profit rate.

BE5.10 (LO 5), AP Assume Kader Company has the following reported amounts: Sales revenue $510,000, Sales returns and allowances $15,000, Cost of goods sold $330,000, and Operating expenses $110,000. Compute the following: (a) net sales, (b) gross profit, (c) income from operations, and (d) gross profit rate. (Round to one decimal place.)

Identify worksheet columns for selected accounts.

*BE5.11 (LO 6), C Presented below is the format of a partial worksheet using the perpetual inventory system presented in Appendix 5A.

	Trial Balance		Adjusted Trial Balance		Income Statement		Balance Sheet	
	Dr.	Cr.	Dr.	Cr.	Dr.	Cr.	Dr.	Cr.

Indicate where the following items will appear on the worksheet: (a) Cash, (b) Inventory, (c) Sales revenue, and (d) Cost of goods sold.

Example:

Cash: Trial balance debit column; Adjusted trial balance debit column; and Balance sheet debit column.

Compute net purchases and cost of goods purchased.

*BE5.12 (LO 7), AP Assume that Space Company uses a periodic inventory system and has these account balances: Purchases $404,000, Purchase Returns and Allowances $13,000, Purchase Discounts $9,000, and Freight-In $16,000. Determine net purchases and cost of goods purchased.

*BE5.13 (LO 7), AP Assume that Space Company uses a periodic inventory system and has these account balances: Purchases $404,000, Purchase Returns and Allowances $13,000, Purchase Discounts $9,000, and Freight-In $16,000. Assume also that Space Company has beginning inventory of $60,000, ending inventory of $90,000, and net sales of $612,000. Determine the amounts to be reported for cost of goods sold and gross profit.

Compute cost of goods sold and gross profit.

*BE5.14 (LO 7), AP Prepare the journal entries to record these transactions on Kimble Company's books using a periodic inventory system.

Journalize purchase transactions.

a. On March 2, Kimble Company purchased $800,000 of merchandise on account from Poe Company, terms 2/10, n/30.

b. On March 6, Kimble Company returned $130,000 of the merchandise purchased on March 2.

c. On March 12, Kimble Company paid the balance due to Poe Company.

*BE5.15 (LO 7), AP A. Hall Company has the following merchandise account balances: Sales Revenue $180,000, Sales Discounts $2,000, Purchases $120,000, and Purchases Returns and Allowances $30,000. In addition, it has a beginning inventory of $40,000 and an ending inventory of $30,000. Prepare the entries to record the closing of these items to Income Summary using the periodic inventory system.

Prepare closing entries for merchandise accounts.

*BE5.16 (LO 7), C The following is the format of a partial worksheet using the periodic inventory system presented in Appendix 5B.

Identify worksheet columns for selected accounts.

Trial Balance		Adjusted Trial Balance		Income Statement		Balance Sheet	
Dr.	Cr.	Dr.	Cr.	Dr.	Cr.	Dr.	Cr.

Indicate where the following items will appear on the worksheet: (a) Cash, (b) Beginning inventory, (c) Accounts payable, and (d) Ending inventory.

Example
Cash: Trial balance debit column; Adjustment trial balance debit column; and Balance sheet debit column.

DO IT! Exercises

DO IT! 5.1 (LO 1), C Indicate whether the following statements are true or false. If false, indicate how to correct the statement.

Answer general questions about merchandisers.

1. A merchandising company reports gross profit but a service company does not.

2. Under a periodic inventory system, a company determines the cost of goods sold each time a sale occurs.

3. A service company is likely to use accounts receivable but a merchandising company is not likely to do so.

4. Under a periodic inventory system, the cost of goods on hand at the beginning of the accounting period plus the cost of goods purchased less the cost of goods on hand at the end of the accounting period equals cost of goods sold.

DO IT! 5.2 (LO 2), AP On October 5, Iverson Company buys merchandise on account from Lasse Company. The selling price of the goods is $5,000, and the cost to Lasse Company is $3,000. On October 8, Iverson returns defective goods with a selling price of $640 and a fair value of $240. Record the transactions on the books of Iverson Company.

Record transactions of purchasing company.

DO IT! 5.3 (LO 3), AP On October 5, Iverson Company buys merchandise on account from Lasse Company. The selling price of the goods is $5,000, and the cost to Lasse Company is $3,000. On October 8, Iverson returns defective goods with a selling price of $640 and a fair value of $240. Record the transactions on the books of Lasse Company.

Record transactions of selling company.

DO IT! 5.4 (LO 4), AP The adjusted trial balance of Optique Boutique at December 31 shows Inventory $21,000, Sales Revenue $156,000, Sales Returns and Allowances $4,000, Sales Discounts $3,000, Cost of Goods Sold $92,400, Interest Revenue $5,000, Freight-Out $1,500, Utilities Expense $7,400, and Salaries and Wages Expense $19,500. Prepare the closing entries for Optique for these accounts.

Prepare closing entries for a merchandising company.

Prepare a multiple-step income statement.

DO IT! 5.5 (LO 5), AP The following information is available for Berlin Corp. for the year ended December 31, 2022:

Other revenues and gains	$ 12,700	Sales revenue	$592,000
Other expenses and losses	13,300	Operating expenses	186,000
Cost of goods sold	156,000	Sales returns and allowances	40,000

Prepare a multiple-step income statement for Berlin Corp.

Exercises

Answer general questions about merchandisers.

E5.1 (LO 1), C Mr. Etemadi has prepared the following list of statements about service companies and merchandisers.

1. Measuring net income for a merchandiser is conceptually the same as for a service company.
2. For a merchandiser, sales less operating expenses is called gross profit.
3. For a merchandiser, the primary source of revenue is the sale of inventory.
4. Sales salaries and wages is an example of an operating expense.
5. The operating cycle of a merchandiser is the same as that of a service company.
6. In a perpetual inventory system, no detailed inventory records of goods on hand are maintained in the Inventory account.
7. In a periodic inventory system, the cost of goods sold is determined only at the end of the reporting period.
8. A periodic inventory system provides better control over inventories than a perpetual system.

Instructions

Identify each statement as true or false. If false, indicate how to correct the statement.

Journalize purchase transactions.

E5.2 (LO 2), AP Information related to Rice Co. is presented below.

1. On April 5, purchased merchandise on account from Jax Company for $28,000, terms 2/10, net/30, FOB shipping point.
2. On April 6, paid freight costs of $700 on merchandise purchased from Jax.
3. On April 7, purchased equipment on account for $30,000.
4. On April 8, returned $3,600 of merchandise to Jax Company.
5. On April 15, paid the amount due to Jax Company in full.

Instructions

a. Prepare the journal entries to record these transactions on the books of Rice Co. under a perpetual inventory system.
b. Assume that Rice Co. paid the balance due to Jax Company on May 4 instead of April 15. Prepare the journal entry to record this payment.

Journalize perpetual inventory entries.

E5.3 (LO 2, 3), AP Assume that on September 1, **Office Depot** had an inventory that included a variety of calculators. The company uses a perpetual inventory system. During September, these transactions occurred.

Sept. 6	Purchased calculators from Dragoo Co. at a total cost of $1,600, on account, terms n/30, FOB shipping point.
9	Paid freight of $50 on calculators purchased from Dragoo Co.
10	Returned calculators to Dragoo Co. for $66 credit because they did not meet specifications.
12	Sold calculators costing $520 for $690 to Fryer Book Store, on account, terms n/30.
14	Granted credit of $45 to Fryer Book Store for the return of one calculator that was not ordered. The calculator cost $34.
20	Sold calculators costing $570 for $760 to Heasley Card Shop, on account, terms n/30.

Instructions

Journalize the September transactions for Office Depot.

E5.4 (LO 2, 3), AP On June 10, Pais Company purchased $9,000 of merchandise on account from McGiver Company, FOB shipping point, terms 3/10, n/30. Pais pays the freight costs of $400 on June 11. Goods totaling $600 are returned to McGiver for credit on June 12. On June 19, Pais pays McGiver Company in full, less the discount. Both companies use a perpetual inventory system.

Journalize perpetual inventory entries.

Instructions

a. Prepare separate entries for each transaction on the books of Pais Company.

b. Prepare separate entries for each transaction for McGiver Company. The merchandise purchased by Pais on June 10 cost McGiver $5,000, and the goods returned cost McGiver $310.

E5.5 (LO 3), AP The following transactions are for Alonzo Company.

Journalize sales transactions.

1. On December 3, Alonzo Company sold $500,000 of merchandise to Arte Co., on account, terms 1/10, n/30. The cost of the merchandise sold was $330,000.

2. On December 8, Arte Co. was granted an allowance of $25,000 for merchandise purchased on December 3.

3. On December 13, Alonzo Company received the balance due from Arte Co.

Instructions

a. Prepare the journal entries to record these transactions on the books of Alonzo Company using a perpetual inventory system.

b. Assume that Alonzo Company received the balance due from Arte Co. on January 2 of the following year instead of December 13. Prepare the journal entry to record the receipt of payment on January 2.

E5.6 (LO 4, 5), AP The adjusted trial balance of Doge Company shows the following data pertaining to sales at the end of its fiscal year October 31, 2022: Sales Revenue $900,000, Freight-Out $14,000, Sales Returns and Allowances $22,000, and Sales Discounts $13,500.

Prepare sales section and closing entries.

Instructions

a. Prepare the sales section of the multiple-step income statement.

b. Prepare separate closing entries for (1) sales revenue, and (2) the contra accounts to sales revenue.

E5.7 (LO 4), AP Juan Morales Company had the following account balances at year-end: Cost of Goods Sold $60,000, Inventory $15,000, Utilities Expense $29,000, Sales Revenue $115,000, Sales Discounts $1,200, and Sales Returns and Allowances $1,700. A physical count of inventory determines that merchandise inventory on hand is $13,900.

Prepare adjusting and closing entries.

Instructions

a. Prepare the adjusting entry necessary as a result of the physical count.

b. Prepare closing entries.

E5.8 (LO 4), AP Presented below is selected information related to Garland Co. for the year ended January 31, 2022.

Prepare adjusting and closing entries.

Ending inventory per		Insurance expense	$ 12,000
perpetual records	$ 21,600	Rent expense	20,000
Ending inventory actually		Salaries and wages expense	55,000
on hand	21,000	Sales discounts	10,000
Cost of goods sold	218,000	Sales returns and allowances	13,000
Freight-out	7,000	Sales revenue	380,000

Instructions

a. Prepare the necessary adjusting entry for inventory.

b. Prepare the necessary closing entries.

E5.9 (LO 5), AP Presented below is selected information for Lien Co. for the month of January 2022.

Prepare an income statement and calculate the gross profit rate.

Cost of goods sold	$212,000	Rent expense	$ 32,000
Freight-out	7,000	Sales discounts	8,000
Insurance expense	12,000	Sales returns and allowances	20,000
Salaries and wages expense	60,000	Sales revenue	370,000

Instructions

a. Prepare an income statement using the format presented in Illustration 5.14.

b. Compute the gross profit rate.

Prepare income statements.

Excel

E5.10 (LO 5), AP In its income statement for the year ended December 31, 2022, Laine Inc. reported the following condensed data.

Operating expenses	$ 725,000	Interest revenue	$ 33,000
Cost of goods sold	1,256,000	Loss on disposal of plant assets	17,000
Interest expense	70,000	Net sales	2,200,000

Instructions

a. Prepare a multiple-step income statement.

b. Prepare a single-step income statement.

Prepare correcting entries for sales and purchases.

E5.11 (LO 2, 3), AN An inexperienced accountant for Huang Company made the following errors in recording merchandising transactions.

1. A $195 refund to a customer for faulty merchandise was debited to Sales Revenue $195 and credited to Cash $195.

2. A $180 credit purchase of supplies was debited to Inventory $180 and credited to Cash $180.

3. A $215 sales discount was debited to Sales Revenue.

4. A cash payment of $20 for freight on merchandise purchases was debited to Freight-Out $200 and credited to Cash $200. Huang uses the perpetual inventory system.

Instructions

Prepare separate correcting entries for each error, assuming that the incorrect entry is not reversed. (Omit explanations.)

Compute various income measures.

E5.12 (LO 5), AP In 2022, Matt Cruz Company had net sales of $900,000 and cost of goods sold of $522,000. Operating expenses were $225,000, and interest expense was $11,000. Cruz prepares a multiple-step income statement.

Instructions

a. Compute Cruz's gross profit.

b. Compute the gross profit rate. Why is this rate computed by financial statement users?

c. What is Cruz's income from operations and net income?

d. If Cruz prepared a single-step income statement, what amount would it report for net income?

e. In what section of its classified balance sheet should Cruz report inventory?

Compute missing amounts and compute gross profit rate.

E5.13 (LO 5), AN Financial information is presented here for two different companies.

	Yoste Company	Noone Company
Sales revenue	$90,000	$ (d)
Sales returns and allowances	(a)	5,000
Net sales	84,000	100,000
Cost of goods sold	58,000	(e)
Gross profit	(b)	40,000
Operating expenses	14,380	(f)
Net income	(c)	17,000

Instructions

a. Fill in the missing amounts. Assume that there are no nonoperating activities.

b. Calculate the gross profit rate for each company. (Round to one decimal place.)

Compute missing amounts.

E5.14 (LO 5), AN The following financial information is presented for three different companies.

	Allen Cosmetics	Bast Grocery	Corr Wholesalers
Sales revenue	$90,000	$ (e)	$122,000
Sales returns and allowances	(a)	5,000	12,000
Net sales	86,000	95,000	(i)
Cost of goods sold	56,000	(f)	(j)
Gross profit	(b)	38,000	24,000
Operating expenses	15,000	(g)	18,000
Income from operations	(c)	(h)	(k)
Other expenses and losses	4,000	7,000	(l)
Net income	(d)	11,000	5,000

Instructions

Determine the missing amounts.

*E5.15 (LO 6), AP Presented below are selected accounts for Salazar Company as reported in the work-sheet using a perpetual inventory system at the end of May 2022.

Complete worksheet using a perpetual inventory system.

Accounts	Adjusted Trial Balance		Income Statement		Balance Sheet	
	Dr.	Cr.	Dr.	Cr.	Dr.	Cr.
Cash	11,000					
Inventory	76,000					
Sales Revenue		480,000				
Sales Returns and Allowances	10,000					
Sales Discounts	9,000					
Cost of Goods Sold	300,000					

Instructions

Complete the worksheet by extending amounts reported in the adjusted trial balance to the appropriate columns in the worksheet. Do not total individual columns.

*E5.16 (LO 6), AP The trial balance columns of the worksheet using a perpetual inventory system for Marquez Company at June 30, 2022, are as follows.

Prepare a worksheet using a perpetual inventory system.

Marquez Company
Worksheet
For the Month Ended June 30, 2022

Account Titles	Trial Balance	
	Debit	Credit
Cash	1,920	
Accounts Receivable	2,440	
Inventory	11,640	
Accounts Payable		1,120
Common Stock		3,500
Sales Revenue		42,500
Cost of Goods Sold	20,560	
Utilities Expense	10,560	
	47,120	47,120

Adjustment data:

Utility costs incurred on account, but not yet recorded, total $1,500.

Instructions

Enter the trial balance on a worksheet and complete the worksheet.

*E5.17 (LO 7), AP The adjusted trial balance of Mendez Company at the end of its fiscal year, August 31, 2022, includes these accounts: Inventory $18,700, Purchases $154,000, Sales Revenue $190,000, Freight-In $8,000, Sales Returns and Allowances $3,000, Freight-Out $1,000, and Purchase Returns and Allowances $5,000. The ending inventory is $21,000.

Prepare cost of goods sold section.

Instructions

Prepare a cost of goods sold section on the income statement for the year ending August 31, 2022 (periodic inventory system).

*E5.18 (LO 7), AP On January 1, 2022, Christel Madan Corporation had inventory of $50,000. At December 31, 2022, Christel Madan had the following account balances.

Compute various income statement items.

Freight-in	$ 4,000
Purchases	509,000
Purchase discounts	6,000
Purchase returns and allowances	2,000
Sales revenue	840,000
Sales discounts	5,000
Sales returns and allowances	10,000

At December 31, 2022, Christel Madan determines that its ending inventory is $60,000. Christel Madan uses the periodic inventory system.

Instructions

a. Compute Christel Madan's 2022 gross profit.

b. Compute Christel Madan's 2022 operating expenses if net income is $130,000 and there are no non-operating activities.

Prepare cost of goods sold section.

*E5.19 (LO 7), AN Below is a series of cost of goods sold sections for companies B, M, O, and S.

	B	M	O	S
Beginning inventory	$ 250	$ 120	$ 700	$ (j)
Purchases	1,500	1,080	(g)	43,590
Purchase returns and allowances	80	(d)	290	(k)
Net purchases	(a)	1,040	7,410	42,290
Freight-in	130	(e)	(h)	2,240
Cost of goods purchased	(b)	1,230	8,050	(l)
Cost of goods available for sale	1,800	1,350	(i)	49,530
Ending inventory	310	(f)	1,150	6,230
Cost of goods sold	(c)	1,230	7,600	43,300

Instruction

Fill in the lettered blanks to complete the cost of goods sold sections.

Journalize purchase transactions.

*E5.20 (LO 7), AP This information relates to Alfie Co.

1. On April 5, purchased merchandise from Bach Company for $27,000, on account, terms 2/10, net/30, FOB shipping point.
2. On April 6, paid freight costs of $1,200 on merchandise purchased from Bach Company.
3. On April 7, purchased equipment on account for $30,000.
4. On April 8, returned $3,600 of the April 5 merchandise to Bach Company.
5. On April 15, paid the amount due to Bach Company in full.

Instructions

a. Prepare the journal entries to record these transactions on the books of Alfie Co. using a periodic inventory system.

b. Assume that Alfie Co. paid the balance due to Bach Company on May 4 instead of April 15. Prepare the journal entry to record this payment.

Journalize purchase transactions.

*E5.21 (LO 7), AP The following information is related to Lor Co.

1. On April 5, purchased merchandise on account from Garcia Company for $19,000, terms 2/10, net/30, FOB shipping point.
2. On April 6, paid freight costs of $800 on merchandise purchased from Garcia.
3. On April 7, purchased equipment on account from Holifield Mfg. Co. for $23,000.
4. On April 8, returned merchandise that cost $4,000 to Garcia Company.
5. On April 15, paid the amount due to Garcia Company in full.

Instructions

a. Prepare the journal entries to record the preceding transactions on the books of Lor Co. using a periodic inventory system.

b. Assume that Lor Co. paid the balance due to Garcia Company on May 4 instead of April 15. Prepare the journal entry to record this payment.

Complete worksheet.

*E5.22 (LO 6, 7), AP The following are selected accounts for B. Midler Company as reported in the worksheet at the end of May 2022. Ending inventory is $75,000.

Accounts	Adjusted Trial Balance		Income Statement		Balance Sheet	
	Dr.	Cr.	Dr.	Cr.	Dr.	Cr.
Cash	9,000					
Inventory	80,000					
Purchases	240,000					
Purchase Returns and Allowances		30,000				
Sales Revenue		450,000				
Sales Returns and Allowances	10,000					
Sales Discounts	5,000					
Rent Expense	42,000					

Instructions

Complete the worksheet by extending amounts reported in the adjusted trial balance columns to the appropriate columns in the worksheet. The company uses the periodic inventory system.

Problems

P5.1A (LO 2, 3), AP Powell's Warehouse distributes hardback books to retail stores and extends credit terms of 2/10, n/30 to all of its customers. During the month of June, the following merchandising transactions occurred.

Journalize purchase and sales transactions under a perpetual inventory system.

Excel

June	1	Purchased books on account for $1,040 from Catlin Publishers, terms 2/10, n/30.
	3	Sold books on account to Garfunkle Bookstore for $1,200. The cost of the books sold was $720.
	6	Received $40 credit for books returned to Catlin Publishers.
	9	Paid Catlin Publishers in full.
	15	Received payment in full from Garfunkle Bookstore.
	17	Sold books on account to Bell Tower for $1,200. The cost of the merchandise sold was $730.
	20	Purchased books on account for $800 from Priceless Book Publishers, terms 1/15, n/30.
	24	Received payment in full from Bell Tower.
	26	Paid Priceless Book Publishers in full.
	28	Sold books on account to General Bookstore for $1,300. The cost of the merchandise sold was $780.
	30	Granted General Bookstore $130 credit for books returned costing $80.

Instructions

Journalize the transactions for the month of June for Powell's Warehouse using a perpetual inventory system.

P5.2A (LO 2, 3, 5), AP Winters Hardware Store completed the following merchandising transactions in the month of May. At the beginning of May, the ledger of Winters showed Cash of $8,000 and Common Stock of $8,000.

Journalize, post, and prepare a partial income statement.

May	1	Purchased merchandise on account from Black Wholesale Supply for $8,000, terms 1/10, n/30.
	2	Sold merchandise on account $4,400, terms 2/10, n/30. The cost of the merchandise sold was $3,300.
	5	Received credit from Black Wholesale Supply for merchandise returned $200.
	9	Received collections in full, less discounts, from customers billed on May 2.
	10	Paid Black Wholesale Supply in full, less discount.
	11	Purchased supplies for cash $900.
	12	Purchased merchandise for cash $3,100.
	15	Received $230 refund for return of poor-quality merchandise from supplier on cash purchase.
	17	Purchased merchandise on account from Wilhelm Distributors for $2,500, terms 2/10, n/30, FOB shipping point.
	19	Paid freight on May 17 purchase $250.
	24	Sold merchandise for cash $5,500. The merchandise sold had a cost of $4,100.
	25	Purchased merchandise on account from Clasps, Inc. for $800, terms 3/10, n/30.
	27	Paid Wilhelm Distributors in full, less discount.
	29	Made refunds to cash customers for returned merchandise $124. The returned merchandise cost $90.
	31	Sold merchandise on account for $1,280 terms n/30. The cost of the merchandise sold was $830.

Winters Hardware's chart of accounts includes the following: No. 101 Cash, No. 112 Accounts Receivable, No. 120 Inventory, No. 126 Supplies, No. 201 Accounts Payable, No. 311 Common Stock, No. 401 Sales Revenue, No. 412 Sales Returns and Allowances, No. 414 Sales Discounts, and No. 505 Cost of Goods Sold.

Instructions

a. Journalize the transactions using a perpetual inventory system.

b. Enter the beginning cash and common stock balances and post the transactions. (Use J1 for the journal reference.)

c. Prepare an income statement through gross profit for the month of May 2022.

c. Gross profit $2,828

Prepare financial statements and adjusting and closing entries.

P5.3A (LO 4, 5), AP The Deluxe Store is located in midtown Madison. At the end of the company's fiscal year on November 30, 2022, the following accounts with normal balances appeared in two of its trial balances.

	Unadjusted	Adjusted
Accounts Payable	$ 25,200	$ 25,200
Accounts Receivable	30,500	30,500
Accumulated Depr.—Equip.	34,000	45,000
Cash	26,000	26,000
Common Stock	40,000	40,000
Cost of Goods Sold	507,000	507,000
Dividends	10,000	10,000
Freight-Out	6,500	6,500
Equipment	146,000	146,000
Depreciation Expense		11,000
Insurance Expense		7,000
Interest Expense	6,400	6,400
Interest Revenue	8,000	8,000
Inventory	29,000	29,000
Notes Payable	37,000	37,000
Prepaid Insurance	10,500	3,500
Property Tax Expense		2,500
Property Taxes Payable		2,500
Rent Expense	15,000	15,000
Retained Earnings	61,700	61,700
Salaries and Wages Expense	96,000	96,000
Sales Commissions Expense	6,500	11,000
Sales Commissions Payable		4,500
Sales Returns and Allowances	8,000	8,000
Sales Revenue	700,000	700,000
Utilities Expense	8,500	8,500

Instructions

a. Net income $29,100
   Retained earnings $80,800
   Total assets $190,000

a. Prepare a multiple-step income statement, a retained earnings statement, and a classified balance sheet. Notes payable are due in 2025. The Deluxe Store uses the perpetual inventory system.

b. Journalize the adjusting entries that were made.

c. Journalize the closing entries that are necessary.

Journalize, post, and prepare a trial balance.

P5.4A (LO 2, 3, 4), AP At the beginning of the current season on April 1, the ledger of Granite Hills Pro Shop showed Cash $2,500, Inventory $3,500, and Common Stock $6,000. The following transactions were completed during April 2022.

Apr.	5	Purchased golf discs, bags, and other inventory on account from Arnie Co. $1,500, FOB shipping point, terms 3/10, n/60.
	7	Paid freight on the Arnie purchase $80.
	9	Received credit from Arnie Co. for merchandise returned $200.
	10	Sold merchandise on account for $1,340, terms n/30. The merchandise sold had a cost of $820.
	12	Purchased disc golf shirts and other accessories on account from Woods Sportswear $830, terms 1/10, n/30.
	14	Paid Arnie Co. in full, less discount.
	17	Received credit from Woods Sportswear for merchandise returned $30.
	20	Made sales on account to members for $810, terms n/30. The cost of the merchandise sold was $550.
	21	Paid Woods Sportswear in full, less discount.
	27	Granted an allowance to members for clothing that did not fit $80.
	30	Received payments on account from members $1,220.

The chart of accounts for the store includes the following: No. 101 Cash, No. 112 Accounts Receivable, No. 120 Inventory, No. 201 Accounts Payable, No. 311 Common Stock, No. 401 Sales Revenue, No. 412 Sales Returns and Allowances, and No. 505 Cost of Goods Sold.

Instructions

a. Journalize the April transactions using a perpetual inventory system.

b. Enter the beginning balances in the ledger accounts and post the April transactions. (Use J1 for the journal reference.)

c. Prepare a trial balance on April 30, 2022.

c. Total debits $8,150

*P5.5A (LO 4, 5, 6), AP The trial balance of Valdez Fashion Center contained the following accounts at November 30, the end of the company's fiscal year. Valdez adjusts its accounts annually and uses the perpetual inventory system.

Complete accounting cycle beginning with a worksheet.

Valdez Fashion Center
Trial Balance
November 30, 2022

	Debit	Credit
Cash	$ 8,700	
Accounts Receivable	30,700	
Inventory	44,700	
Supplies	6,200	
Equipment	133,000	
Accumulated Depreciation—Equipment		$ 28,000
Notes Payable		51,000
Accounts Payable		48,500
Common Stock		50,000
Retained Earnings		40,000
Dividends	12,000	
Sales Revenue		755,200
Sales Returns and Allowances	8,800	
Cost of Goods Sold	497,400	
Salaries and Wages Expense	140,000	
Advertising Expense	24,400	
Utilities Expense	14,000	
Maintenance and Repairs Expense	12,100	
Freight-Out	16,700	
Rent Expense	24,000	
Totals	$972,700	$972,700

Adjustment data:

1. Supplies on hand totaled $2,000.

2. Annual depreciation is $11,500 on the equipment.

3. Interest of $4,000 is accrued on notes payable at November 30.

4. Inventory actually on hand is $44,400.

Instructions

a. Enter the trial balance on a worksheet, and complete the worksheet.

b. Prepare a multiple-step income statement and a retained earnings statement for the year, and a classified balance sheet as of November 30, 2022. Notes payable of $20,000 are due in January 2023.

c. Journalize the adjusting entries.

d. Journalize the closing entries.

e. Prepare a post-closing trial balance.

a. Adj. trial balance $988,200
   Net loss $2,200

b. Gross profit $248,700
   Total assets $179,300

*P5.6A (LO 5, 7), AP At the end of Oates Department Store's fiscal year on November 30, 2022, these accounts appeared in its adjusted trial balance.

Determine cost of goods sold and gross profit under periodic approach.

Freight-In	$ 5,060
Inventory	41,300
Purchases	613,000
Purchase Discounts	7,000
Purchase Returns and Allowances	6,760
Sales Revenue	902,000
Sales Returns and Allowances	20,000

Additional facts:

1. Per a physical count, merchandise inventory on November 30, 2022, is $36,200.

2. Note that Oates Department Store uses a periodic system.

Instructions

Gross profit $272,600

Prepare an income statement through gross profit for the year ended November 30, 2022.

Calculate missing amounts and assess profitability.

*P5.7A (LO 5, 7), AN Zhou Inc. operates a retail operation that purchases and sells snowmobiles, among other outdoor products. The company purchases all inventory on credit and uses a periodic inventory system. The Accounts Payable account is used for recording inventory purchases only; all other current liabilities are accrued in separate accounts. You are provided with the following selected information for the fiscal years 2020 through 2023, inclusive.

	2020	2021	2022	2023
Income Statement Data				
Net sales revenue		$96,890	$ (e)	$82,220
Cost of goods sold		(a)	28,060	26,490
Gross profit		67,800	59,620	(i)
Operating expenses		63,640	(f)	52,870
Net income		$ (b)	$ 3,510	$ (j)
Balance Sheet Data				
Inventory	$13,000	$ (c)	$14,700	$ (k)
Accounts payable	5,800	6,500	4,600	(l)
Additional Information				
Purchases of merchandise inventory on account		$25,890	$ (g)	$24,050
Cash payments to suppliers		(d)	(h)	24,650

c. $9,800
g. $32,960
i. $55,730

Instructions

a. Calculate the missing amounts. Assume that there are no nonoperating activities.

b. Sales declined over the 3-year fiscal period, 2021–2023. Does that mean that profitability necessarily also declined? Explain, computing the gross profit rate and the profit margin (Net income ÷ Net sales revenue) for each fiscal year to help support your answer. (Round to one decimal place.)

Journalize, post, and prepare trial balance and partial income statement using periodic approach.

*P5.8A (LO 7), AP At the beginning of the current season on April 1, the ledger of Granite Hills Pro Shop showed Cash $2,500, Inventory $3,500, and Common Stock $6,000. These transactions occurred during April 2022.

Apr.	5	Purchased golf bags, clubs, and balls on account from Arnie Co. $1,500, terms 3/10, n/60, FOB shipping point.
	7	Paid freight on Arnie Co. purchases $80.
	9	Received credit from Arnie Co. for merchandise returned $200.
	10	Sold merchandise on account to members $1,340, terms n/30.
	12	Purchased golf shoes, sweaters, and other accessories on account from Woods Sportswear $830, terms 1/10, n/30.
	14	Paid Arnie Co. in full.
	17	Received credit from Woods Sportswear for merchandise returned $30.
	20	Made sales on account to members $810, terms n/30.
	21	Paid Woods Sportswear in full.
	27	Granted credit to customers for clothing that did not fit properly $80.
	30	Received payments on account from members $1,220.

The chart of accounts for the pro shop includes Cash, Accounts Receivable, Inventory, Accounts Payable, Common Stock, Sales Revenue, Sales Returns and Allowances, Purchases, Purchase Returns and Allowances, Purchase Discounts, and Freight-In.

Instructions

a. Journalize the April transactions using a periodic inventory system.

b. Using T-accounts, enter the beginning balances in the ledger accounts and post the April transactions.

c. Tot. trial balance $8,427
d. Gross profit $700

c. Prepare a trial balance on April 30, 2022.

d. Prepare an income statement through gross profit, assuming merchandise inventory on hand at April 30 is $4,263.

Continuing Case

Cookie Creations

(*Note:* This is a continuation of the Cookie Creations case from Chapters 1 through 4.)

CC5 Because Natalie has had such a successful first few months, she is considering other opportunities to develop her business. One opportunity is to become the exclusive distributor of a line of fine European mixers. The current cost of a mixer is approximately $525 (U.S.), and Natalie would sell each one for $1,050. Natalie comes to you for advice on how to account for these mixers.

Go to **WileyPLUS** *for complete case details and instructions.*

leungchopan/
Shutterstock.com

Comprehensive Accounting Cycle Review

ACR5.1 On December 1, 2022, Divine Distributing Company had the following account balances.

	Debit		Credit
Cash	$ 7,200	Accumulated Depreciation—	
Accounts Receivable	4,600	Equipment	$ 2,200
Inventory	12,000	Accounts Payable	4,500
Supplies	1,200	Salaries and Wages Payable	1,000
Equipment	22,000	Common Stock	15,000
	$47,000	Retained Earnings	24,300
			$47,000

During December, the company completed the following transactions.

Dec.	6	Paid $1,600 for salaries and wages due employees, of which $600 is for December and $1,000 is for November salaries and wages payable.
	8	Received $1,900 cash from customers in payment of account (no discount allowed).
	10	Sold merchandise for cash $6,300. The cost of the merchandise sold was $4,100.
	13	Purchased merchandise on account from Hecht Co. $9,000, terms 2/10, n/30.
	15	Purchased supplies for cash $2,000.
	18	Sold merchandise on account $12,000, terms 3/10, n/30. The cost of the merchandise sold was $8,000.
	20	Paid salaries and wages $1,800.
	23	Paid Hecht Co. in full, less discount.
	27	Received collections in full, less discounts, from customers billed on December 18.

Adjustment data:

1. Accrued salaries and wages payable were $800.
2. Depreciation was $200 per month.
3. Supplies on hand were $1,500.

Instructions

a. Journalize the December transactions using a perpetual inventory system.

b. Enter the December 1 balances in the ledger T-accounts and post the December transactions. Use these additional accounts: Cost of Goods Sold, Depreciation Expense, Salaries and Wages Expense, Sales Revenue, Sales Discounts, and Supplies Expense.

c. Journalize and post adjusting entries.

d. Prepare an adjusted trial balance.

e. Prepare an income statement and a retained earnings statement for December and a classified balance sheet at December 31.

d. Totals $65,300

e. Net income $740

ACR5.2 On November 1, 2022, IKonk, Inc. had the following account balances. The company uses the perpetual inventory method.

	Debit		Credit
Cash	$ 9,000	Accumulated Depreciation—	
Accounts Receivable	2,240	Equipment	$ 1,000
Supplies	860	Accounts Payable	3,400
Equipment	25,000	Unearned Service Revenue	4,000
	$37,100	Salaries and Wages Payable	1,700
		Common Stock	20,000
		Retained Earnings	7,000
			$37,100

During November, the following transactions were completed.

Nov.	8	Paid $3,550 for salaries and wages, of which $1,850 is for November and $1,700 is for October.
	10	Received $1,900 cash from customers in payment of account. No discount was allowed.
	11	Purchased merchandise on account from Dimas Discount Supply for $8,000, terms 2/10, n/30.
	12	Sold merchandise on account for $5,500, terms 2/10, n/30. The cost of the merchandise sold was $4,000.
	15	Received credit from Dimas Discount Supply for merchandise returned $300.
	19	Received collections in full, less discounts, from customers billed on sales of $5,500 on November 12.
	20	Paid Dimas Discount Supply in full, less discount.
	22	Received $2,300 cash for services performed in November.
	25	Purchased equipment on account $5,000.
	27	Purchased supplies on account $1,700.
	28	Paid creditors $3,000 of accounts payable due. No discount was taken.
	29	Paid November rent $375.
	29	Paid salaries and wages $1,300.
	29	Performed services on account and billed customers $700 for those services.
	29	Received $675 from customers for services to be performed in the future.

Adjustment data:

1. Supplies on hand total $1,600.

2. Accrued salaries and wages payable are $500.

3. Depreciation for the month is $250.

4. $650 of services related to unearned service revenue was performed by month-end.

Instructions

a. Enter the November 1 balances in ledger T-accounts.

b. Journalize the November transactions.

c. Post to the ledger accounts. You will need to add some accounts.

d. Journalize and post adjusting entries.

e. Tot. adj. trial bal. $49,025

e. Prepare an adjusted trial balance at November 30.

f. Tot. assets $38,430

f. Prepare a multiple-step income statement and a retained earnings statement for November and a classified balance sheet at November 30.

g. Journalize and post closing entries.

Expand Your Critical Thinking

Financial Reporting Problem: Apple Inc.

CT5.1 The financial statements of **Apple Inc.** are presented in Appendix A. The complete annual report, including the notes to the financial statements, is available at the company's website.

Instructions

Answer the following questions using Apple's Consolidated Statements of Operations.

a. What was the percentage change in (1) net sales and in (2) net income from 2016 to 2017 and from 2017 to 2018?

b. What was the company's gross profit rate in 2016, 2017, and 2018?

c. What was the company's percentage of net income to net sales in 2016, 2017, and 2018? Comment on any trend in this percentage.

Comparative Analysis Problem: PepsiCo, Inc. vs. The Coca-Cola Company

CT5.2 **PepsiCo**'s financial statements are presented in Appendix B. Financial statements of **The Coca-Cola Company** are presented in Appendix C. The complete annual reports of PepsiCo and Coca-Cola, including the notes to the financial statements, are available at each company's respective website.

Instructions

a. Based on the information contained in these financial statements, determine each of the following for each company.

    1. Gross profit for 2018.

    2. Gross profit rate for 2018.

    3. Income from operations (or operating profit) for 2018.

    4. Percentage change in operating profit from 2017 to 2018.

b. What conclusions concerning the relative profitability of the two companies can you draw from these data?

Comparative Analysis Problem: Amazon.com, Inc. vs. Walmart Inc.

CT5.3 **Amazon.com, Inc.**'s financial statements are presented in Appendix D. Financial statements of **Walmart Inc.** are presented in Appendix E. (Use Walmart's January 31, 2019, financial statements for comparative purposes.) The complete annual reports of Amazon and Walmart, including the notes to the financial statements, are available at each company's respective website.

Instructions

a. Based on the information contained in these financial statements, determine each of the following for each company. Use Amazon's net product sales and Walmart's net sales to compute gross profit information.

    1. Gross profit for 2018.

    2. Gross profit rate for 2018.

    3. Operating income for 2018.

    4. Percentage change in operating income from 2017 to 2018.

b. What conclusions concerning the relative profitability of the two companies can you draw from these data?

Real-World Focus

CT5.4 No financial decision-maker should ever rely solely on the financial information reported in a company's annual report to make decisions. It is important to keep abreast of financial news. This activity demonstrates how to search for financial news on the Internet.

Instructions

Search the Internet for an article on either **PepsiCo** or **Coca-Cola** that sounds interesting to you and that would be relevant to an investor in these companies. Then, answer the following questions.

a. What was the source of the article (e.g., Reuters, Businesswire, PR Newswire)?

b. Assume that you are a personal financial planner and that one of your clients owns stock in the company. Write a brief memo to your client, summarizing the article and explaining the implications of the article for his or her investment.

Decision-Making Across the Organization

CT5.5 Three years ago, Karen Suez and her brother-in-law Reece Jones opened Gigasales Department Store. For the first two years, business was good, but the following condensed income results for 2022 were disappointing.

Gigasales Department Store
Income Statement
For the Year Ended December 31, 2022

Net sales		$700,000
Cost of goods sold		560,000
Gross profit		140,000
Operating expenses		
Selling expenses	$100,000	
Administrative expenses	20,000	120,000
Net income		$ 20,000

Karen believes the problem lies in the relatively low gross profit rate (gross profit divided by net sales) of 20%. Reece believes the problem is that operating expenses are too high.

Karen thinks the gross profit rate can be improved by making two changes for 2023. She does not anticipate that these changes will have any effect on operating expenses.

1. Increase average selling prices by 15%. This increase is expected to lower sales volume so that net sales will increase only 4%.

2. Buy merchandise in larger quantities and take all purchase discounts. These changes to selling prices and purchasing practices are expected to increase the gross profit rate from 20% to a new rate of 25%.

Reece thinks expenses can be cut by making the following two changes for 2023. He feels that these changes will not have any effect on net sales or cost of goods sold.

1. Cut the 2022 sales salaries of $60,000 in half and give sales personnel a commission of 2% of net sales.

2. Reduce store deliveries to one day per week rather than twice a week. This change will reduce 2022 delivery expenses of $40,000 by 40%. (Recall that delivery costs to customers are selling expenses.)

Karen and Reece come to you for help in deciding the best way to improve net income.

Instructions

With the class divided into groups, answer the following.

a. Prepare a condensed income statement for 2023, assuming (1) Karen's changes are implemented and (2) Reece's ideas are adopted.

b. What is your recommendation to Karen and Reece?

c. Prepare a condensed income statement for 2023, assuming both sets of proposed changes are made.

d. Discuss the impact that other factors might have. For example, would increasing the quantity of inventory increase costs? Would a salary cut affect employee morale? Would decreased morale affect sales? Would decreased store deliveries decrease customer satisfaction? What other suggestions might be considered?

Communication Activity

CT5.6 The following events are in chronological order.

1. Aikan decides to buy a surfboard.

2. He calls Surfing Hawaii Co. to inquire about its surfboards.

3. Two days later, he requests Surfing Hawaii Co. to make a surfboard.

4. Three days later, Surfing Hawaii Co. sends him a purchase order to fill out.

5. He sends back the purchase order.

6. Surfing Hawaii Co. receives the completed purchase order.

7. Surfing Hawaii Co. completes the surfboard.

8. Aikan picks up the surfboard.

9. Surfing Hawaii Co. bills Aikan.

10. Surfing Hawaii Co. receives payment from Aikan.

Instructions

In a memorandum to the president of Surfing Hawaii Co., answer the following.

   a. When should Surfing Hawaii Co. record the sale?

   b. Suppose that with his purchase order, Aikan is required to make a down payment. Would that change your answer?

Ethics Case

CT5.7 Tabitha Andes was just hired as the assistant treasurer of Southside Stores, a specialty chain store that has nine retail stores concentrated in one metropolitan area. Among other things, the payment of all invoices is centralized in one of the departments Tabitha will manage. Her primary responsibility is to maintain the company's high credit rating by paying all bills when due and to take advantage of all cash discounts.

Pete Wilson, the former assistant treasurer who has been promoted to treasurer, is training Tabitha in her new duties. He instructs Tabitha that she is to continue the practice of preparing all checks "net of discount" and dating the checks the last day of the discount period. "But," Pete continues, "we always hold the checks at least 4 days beyond the discount period before mailing them. That way, we get another 4 days of interest on our money. Most of our creditors need our business and don't complain. And, if they scream about our missing the discount period, we blame it on the mailroom or the post office. We've only lost one discount out of every hundred we take that way. I think everybody does it. By the way, welcome to our team!"

Instructions

   a. What are the ethical considerations in this case?

   b. What stakeholders are harmed or benefitted?

   c. Should Tabitha continue the practice started by Pete? Does she have any choice?

All About You

CT5.8 There are many situations in business where it is difficult to determine the proper period in which to record revenue. Suppose that after graduation with a degree in finance, you take a job as a manager at a consumer electronics store called FarWest Electronics. The company has expanded rapidly in order to compete with **Best Buy**.

FarWest has also begun selling gift cards. The cards are available in any dollar amount and allow the holder of the card to purchase an item for up to 2 years from the time the card is purchased. If the card is not used during that 2 years, it expires.

Instructions

At what point should the revenue from the gift cards be recognized? Include the reasoning to support your answers.

FASB Codification Activity

CT5.9 If your school has a subscription to the FASB Codification, log in and prepare responses to the following.

Instructions

   a. Access the glossary ("Master Glossary") to answer the following:

      1. What is the definition provided for inventory?

      2. What is a customer?

   b. What guidance does the Codification provide concerning reporting inventories above cost?

A Look at IFRS

LEARNING OBJECTIVE 8
Compare the accounting for merchandising under GAAP and IFRS.

The basic accounting entries for merchandising are the same under both GAAP and IFRS. The income statement is a required statement under both sets of standards. The basic format is similar although some differences do exist.

Key Points

Following are the key similarities and differences between GAAP and IFRS related to inventories.

Similarities

- Under both GAAP and IFRS, a company can choose to use either a perpetual or a periodic inventory system.
- The definition of inventories is basically the same under GAAP and IFRS.
- As indicated above, the basic accounting entries for merchandising are the same under both GAAP and IFRS.
- Both GAAP and IFRS require that income statement information be presented for multiple years. For example, IFRS requires that 2 years of income statement information be presented, whereas GAAP requires 3 years.

Differences

- Under GAAP, companies generally classify income statement items by function. Classification by function leads to descriptions like administration, distribution, and manufacturing. Under IFRS, companies must classify expenses either by nature or by function. Classification by nature leads to descriptions such as the following: salaries, depreciation expense, and utilities expense. If a company uses the functional-expense method on the income statement, disclosure by nature is required in the notes to the financial statements.
- Presentation of the income statement under GAAP follows either a single-step or multiple-step format. IFRS does not mention a single-step or multiple-step approach.
- Under IFRS, revaluation of land, buildings, and intangible assets is permitted.

IFRS Practice

IFRS Self-Test Questions

1. Which of the following would **not** be included in the definition of inventory under IFRS?
   a. Photocopy paper held for sale by an office-supply store.
   b. Stereo equipment held for sale by an electronics store.
   c. Used office equipment held for sale by the human resources department of a plastics company.
   d. All of the answer choices would meet the definition.

2. Which of the following would **not** be a line item of a company reporting costs by nature?
   a. Depreciation expense.
   c. Interest expense.
   b. Salaries expense.
   d. Manufacturing expense.

3. Which of the following would **not** be a line item of a company reporting costs by function?
   a. Administration.
   c. Utilities expense.
   b. Manufacturing.
   d. Distribution.

4. Which of the following statements is **false**?
   a. IFRS specifically requires use of a multiple-step income statement.
   b. Under IFRS, companies can use either a perpetual or periodic system.
   c. IFRS does not require the use of a single-step income statement.
   d. IFRS does not prohibit the revaluation of land.

IFRS Exercises

IFRS5.1 Explain the difference between the "nature-of-expense" and "function-of-expense" classifications.

IFRS5.2 For each of the following income statement line items, state whether the item is a "by nature" expense item or a "by function" expense item.

_____ Cost of goods sold.
_____ Depreciation expense.
_____ Salaries and wages expense.
_____ Selling expenses.

_____ Utilities expense.
_____ Delivery expense.
_____ General and administrative expenses.

International Financial Reporting Problem: Louis Vuitton

IFRS5.3 The financial statements of **Louis Vuitton** are presented in Appendix F. The complete consolidated financial statements, including the notes to its financial statements, are available at the company's website.

Instructions

Use Louis Vuitton's 2018 consolidated financial statements to answer the following questions.

a. Does Louis Vuitton use a multiple-step or a single-step income statement format? Explain how you made your determination.

b. Instead of "interest expense," what label does Louis Vuitton use for interest costs that it incurs?

c. Using the notes to the company's financial statements, determine the following:

1. Composition of the inventory.

2. Amount of inventory (net).

Answers to IFRS Self-Test Questions

1. c **2.** d **3.** c **4.** a

CHAPTER 6

James Porter/Stone/Getty Images

Inventories

Chapter Preview

In the previous chapter, we discussed the accounting for merchandise inventory using a perpetual inventory system. In this chapter, we explain the methods used to calculate the cost of inventory on hand at the balance sheet date and the cost of goods sold.

Feature Story

"Where Is That Spare Bulldozer Blade?"

Let's talk inventory—big, bulldozer-size inventory. **Caterpillar Inc.** is the world's largest manufacturer of construction and mining equipment, diesel and natural gas engines, and industrial gas turbines. It sells its products in over 200 countries, making it one of the most successful U.S. exporters. More

than 70% of its productive assets are located domestically, and nearly 50% of its sales are foreign.

In the past, Caterpillar's profitability suffered, but today it is very successful. A big part of this turnaround can be attributed to effective management of its inventory. Imagine what it costs Caterpillar to have too many bulldozers sitting around in inventory—a situation the company definitely wants to avoid. Yet Caterpillar must also make sure it has enough inventory to meet demand.

At one time during a 7-year period, Caterpillar's sales increased by 100% while its inventory increased by only 50%. To achieve this dramatic reduction in the amount of resources tied up in inventory while continuing to meet customers' needs, Caterpillar used a two-pronged approach. First, it completed a factory modernization program, which greatly increased its production efficiency. The program reduced by 60% the amount of inventory the company processes at any one time. It also reduced by an incredible 75% the time it takes to manufacture a part.

Second, Caterpillar dramatically improved its parts distribution system. It ships more than 100,000 items daily from its 23 distribution centers strategically located around the world (10 million square feet of warehouse space—remember, we're talking bulldozers). The company can virtually guarantee that it can get any part to anywhere in the world within 24 hours.

These changes led to record exports, profits, and revenues for Caterpillar. It would seem that things couldn't be better. But industry analysts, as well as the company's managers, thought otherwise. In order to maintain Caterpillar's position as the industry leader, management began another major overhaul of inventory production and inventory management processes. The goal: to cut the number of repairs in half, increase productivity by 20%, and increase inventory turnover by 40%.

In short, Caterpillar's ability to manage its inventory has been a key reason for its past success and will very likely play a huge part in its future profitability as well.

Chapter Outline

LEARNING OBJECTIVES	REVIEW	PRACTICE
LO 1 Discuss how to classify and determine inventory.	• Classifying inventory • Determining inventory quantities	**DO IT! 1** Rules of Ownership
LO 2 Apply inventory cost flow methods and discuss their financial effects.	• Specific identification • Cost flow assumptions • Financial statement and tax effects • Using inventory cost flow methods consistently	**DO IT! 2** Cost Flow Methods
LO 3 Indicate the effects of inventory errors on the financial statements.	• Income statement effects • Balance sheet effects	**DO IT! 3** Inventory Errors
LO 4 Explain the statement presentation and analysis of inventory.	• Presentation • Lower-of-cost-or-net realizable value • Analysis	**DO IT! 4a** LCNRV **DO IT! 4b** Inventory Turnover

Go to the Review and Practice section at the end of the chapter for a review of key concepts and practice applications with solutions.

Visit WileyPLUS for additional tutorials and practice opportunities.

Classifying and Determining Inventory

LEARNING OBJECTIVE 1
Discuss how to classify and determine inventory.

Two important steps in the reporting of inventory at the end of the accounting period are the classification of inventory based on its degree of completeness and the determination of inventory amounts.

Classifying Inventory

How a company classifies its inventory depends on whether the firm is a merchandiser or a manufacturer. In a **merchandising** company, such as those described in Chapter 5, inventory consists of many different items. For example, in a grocery store, canned goods, dairy products, meats, and produce are just a few of the inventory items on hand. These items have two common characteristics: (1) they are owned by the company, and (2) they are in a form ready for sale to customers in the ordinary course of business. Thus, merchandisers need only one inventory classification, **merchandise inventory**, to describe the many different items that make up the total inventory.

In a **manufacturing** company, some inventory may not yet be ready for sale. As a result, manufacturers usually classify inventory into three categories: finished goods, work in process, and raw materials. **Finished goods inventory** is manufactured items that are completed and ready for sale. **Work in process** is that portion of manufactured inventory that has been placed into the production process but is not yet complete. **Raw materials** are the basic goods that will be used in production but have not yet been placed into production.

For example, **Caterpillar** classifies earth-moving tractors completed and ready for sale as **finished goods**. It classifies the tractors on the assembly line in various stages of production as **work in process**. The steel, glass, tires, and other components that are on hand waiting to be used in the production of tractors are identified as **raw materials** (see **Helpful Hint**). **Illustration 6.1** shows an adapted excerpt from Note 7 of Caterpillar's annual report.

HELPFUL HINT

Regardless of the classification, companies report all inventories under Current Assets on the balance sheet.

ILLUSTRATION 6.1

Composition of Caterpillar's inventory

	December 31		
(millions of dollars)	**2018**	**2017**	**2016**
Raw materials	$ 3,382	$ 2,802	$2,102
Work in process	2,674	2,254	1,719
Finished goods	5,241	4,761	4,576
Other	232	201	217
Total inventories	**$11,529**	**$10,018**	**$8,614**

By observing the levels and changes in the levels of these three inventory types, financial statement users can gain insight into management's production plans. For example, low levels of raw materials and high levels of finished goods suggest that management believes it has enough inventory on hand and production will be slowing down—perhaps in anticipation of a recession. Conversely, high levels of raw materials and low levels of finished goods probably signal that management is planning to step up production.

Many companies have significantly lowered inventory levels and costs using **just-in-time (JIT) inventory** methods. Under a just-in-time method, companies manufacture or purchase goods only when needed. **Dell** is famous for having developed a system for making computers in response to individual customer requests. Even though it makes each computer to meet each customer's particular specifications, Dell is able to assemble the computer and put it on a truck in less than 48 hours. The success of the JIT system depends on reliable suppliers. By integrating its information systems with those of its suppliers, Dell reduced its inventories to nearly zero. This is a huge advantage in an industry where products become obsolete nearly overnight.

The accounting concepts discussed in this chapter apply to the inventory classifications of both merchandising and manufacturing companies. Our focus here is on merchandise inventory. Additional issues specific to manufacturing companies are discussed in managerial accounting courses.

iStock.com/PeskyMonkey

A Big Hiccup

JIT can save a company a lot of money, but it isn't without risk. An unexpected disruption in the supply chain can cost a company a lot of money. Japanese automakers experienced just such a disruption when a 6.8-magnitude earthquake caused major damage to the company that produces 50% of their piston rings. The rings themselves cost only $1.50, but you can't make a car without them. As a result, the automakers were forced to shut down production for a few days—a loss of tens of thousands of cars.

Similarly, a major snowstorm halted production at the Canadian plants of **Ford**. A Ford spokesperson said, "Because the plants run with just-in-time inventory, we don't have large stockpiles of parts sitting around. When you have a somewhat significant disruption, you can pretty quickly run out of parts."

Sources: Amy Chozick, "A Key Strategy of Japan's Car Makers Backfires," *Wall Street Journal* (July 20, 2007); and Kate Linebaugh, "Canada Military Evacuates Motorists Stranded by Snow," *Wall Street Journal* (December 15, 2010).

What steps might the companies take to avoid such a serious disruption in the future? (Go to WileyPLUS for this answer and additional questions.)

Determining Inventory Quantities

Companies take a physical inventory at the end of the accounting period. Taking a physical inventory involves actually counting, weighing, or measuring each kind of inventory on hand (see **Ethics Note**). If using a perpetual system, companies might take a physical inventory at other times during the accounting period for the following reasons:

1. To check the accuracy of their perpetual inventory records.
2. To determine the amount of inventory lost due to wasted raw materials, shoplifting, or employee theft.

Companies using a periodic inventory system take a physical inventory for **two different purposes**: to determine the inventory on hand at the balance sheet date, and to determine the cost of goods sold for the period.

Determining inventory quantities involves two steps: (1) taking a physical inventory of goods on hand and (2) determining the ownership of goods.

Taking a Physical Inventory

In many companies, taking an inventory is a formidable task. Retailers such as **Target**, **True Value Hardware**, or **Home Depot** have thousands of different inventory items. An inventory count is generally more accurate when goods are not being sold or received during the counting. Consequently, companies often "take inventory" when the business is closed or when business is slow. Many retailers close early on a chosen day in January—after the holiday sales and returns, when inventories are at their lowest level—to count inventory. **Walmart Inc.**, for example, has a year-end of January 31.

Determining Ownership of Goods

One challenge in computing inventory quantities is determining what inventory a company owns. To determine ownership of goods, two questions must be answered: Do all of the goods included in the count belong to the company? Does the company own any goods that were not included in the count?

Goods in Transit   A complication in determining ownership is **goods in transit** (on board a truck, train, ship, or plane) at the end of the period. The company may have purchased goods that have not yet been received, or it may have sold goods that have not yet been delivered

Ethics Insight   Leslie Fay

iStock.com/Greg Brookes

Falsifying Inventory to Boost Income

Managers at women's apparel maker **Leslie Fay** were convicted of falsifying inventory records to boost net income in an attempt to increase management bonuses. In another case, executives at **Craig Electronics** were accused of defrauding lenders by manipulating inventory records. The indictment said the company classified "defective goods as new or refurbished" and claimed that

it owned certain shipments "from overseas suppliers" when, in fact, Craig either did not own the shipments or the shipments did not exist.

What effect does an overstatement of inventory have on a company's financial statements? (Go to WileyPLUS for this answer and additional questions.)

to its customer. To arrive at an accurate count, the company must determine ownership of these goods.

Goods in transit should be included in the inventory of the company that has legal title to the goods. Legal title is determined by the terms of the sale, as shown in **Illustration 6.2** and described below.

ILLUSTRATION 6.2 **Terms of sale**

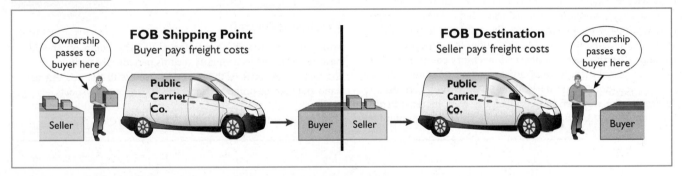

1. When the terms are **FOB (free on board) shipping point**, ownership of the goods passes to the buyer when the public carrier accepts the goods from the seller.

2. When the terms are **FOB destination**, ownership of the goods remains with the seller until the goods reach the buyer.

If goods in transit at the statement date are ignored, inventory quantities may be seriously miscounted. Assume, for example, that Hargrove Company has 20,000 units of inventory on hand on December 31. It also has the following goods in transit:

1. Sales of 1,500 units shipped December 31 FOB destination.

2. Purchases of 2,500 units shipped FOB shipping point by the seller on December 31.

Hargrove has legal title to both the 1,500 units sold and the 2,500 units purchased. If the company ignores the units in transit, it would understate inventory quantities by 4,000 units (1,500 + 2,500).

As we will see later in the chapter, inaccurate inventory counts affect not only the inventory amount shown on the balance sheet but also the cost of goods sold calculation on the income statement.

Consigned Goods   In some lines of business, it is common to hold the goods of other parties and try to sell the goods for them for a fee, but without taking ownership of the goods. These are called **consigned goods**.

For example, you might have a used car that you would like to sell. If you take the item to a dealer, the dealer might be willing to put the car on its lot and charge you a commission if it is sold. Under this agreement, the dealer **would not take ownership** of the car, which would still belong to you. Therefore, if an inventory count were taken, the car would not be included in the dealer's inventory because the dealer does not own it.

Many car, boat, and antique dealers sell goods on consignment to keep their inventory costs down and to avoid the risk of purchasing an item that they will not be able to sell. Today, even some manufacturers are making consignment agreements with their suppliers in order to keep their inventory levels low. For example, prior to filing bankruptcy, **Sports Authority Inc.** became embroiled in lawsuits with suppliers over goods that it was holding on consignment. A judge ruled that Sports Authority had to comply with the suppliers' wishes since the consigned goods belonged to the suppliers.

Anatomy of a Fraud

Ted Nickerson, CEO of clock manufacturer Dally Industries, had expensive tastes. To support this habit, Ted took out large loans, which he collateralized with his shares of Dally Industries stock. If the price of Dally's stock fell, he was required to provide the bank with more shares of stock. To achieve target net income figures and thus maintain the stock price, Ted coerced employees in the company to alter inventory figures. Inventory quantities were manipulated by changing the amounts on inventory control tags after the year-end physical inventory count. For example, if a tag said there were 20 units of a particular item, the tag was changed to 220. Similarly, the unit costs that were used to determine the value of ending inventory were increased from, for example, $125 per unit to $1,250. Both of these fraudulent changes had the effect of increasing the amount of reported ending inventory. This reduced cost of goods sold and increased net income.

Total take: $245,000

The Missing Control

Independent internal verification. The company should have spot-checked its inventory records periodically, verifying that the number of units in the records agreed with the amount on hand and that the unit costs agreed with vendor price sheets.

Source: Adapted from Wells, *Fraud Casebook* (2007), pp. 502–509.

ACTION PLAN

- **Apply the rules of ownership to goods held on consignment.**
- **Apply the rules of ownership to goods in transit.**

DO IT! 1 | Rules of Ownership

Hasbeen Company completed its inventory count. It arrived at a total inventory value of $200,000. As a new member of Hasbeen's accounting department, you have been given the information listed below. Discuss how this information affects the reported cost of inventory.

1. Hasbeen included in the inventory goods held on consignment for Falls Co., costing $15,000.
2. The company did not include in the count purchased goods of $10,000 which were in transit (terms: FOB shipping point).
3. The company did not include in the count sold inventory with a cost of $12,000 which was in transit (terms: FOB shipping point).

Solution

The goods of $15,000 held on consignment should be deducted from the inventory count. The goods of $10,000 purchased FOB shipping point should be added to the inventory count. Sold goods of $12,000 which were in transit FOB shipping point should not be included in the ending inventory. Thus, inventory should be reported at $195,000 ($200,000 − $15,000 + $10,000).

Related exercise material: **BE6.1, BE6.2, DO IT! 6.1, E6.1, E6.2, and E6.3.**

Inventory Methods and Financial Effects

LEARNING OBJECTIVE 2

Apply inventory cost flow methods and discuss their financial effects.

Inventory is accounted for at cost. Cost includes all expenditures necessary to acquire goods and place them in a condition ready for sale. For example, freight costs incurred to acquire inventory are added to the cost of inventory, but the cost of shipping goods to a customer is a selling expense.

After a company has determined the quantity of units of inventory, it applies unit costs to the quantities to compute the total cost of the inventory and the cost of goods sold. This process can be complicated if a company has purchased inventory items at different times with different costs.

For example, assume that Crivitz TV Company purchased three identical 50-inch TVs on different dates at costs of $700, $750, and $800. During the year, Crivitz sold two TVs at $1,200 each. These facts are summarized in **Illustration 6.3**.

ILLUSTRATION 6.3

Data for inventory costing example

Purchases			
February 3	1 TV	at	$700
March 5	1 TV	at	$750
May 22	1 TV	at	$800
Sales			
June 1	2 TVs	for	$2,400 ($1,200 × 2)

Cost of goods sold will differ depending on which two TVs the company sold. For example, it might be $1,450 ($700 + $750), or $1,500 ($700 + $800), or $1,550 ($750 + $800). In this section, we discuss alternative costing methods available to Crivitz.

Specific Identification

If Crivitz can positively identify which particular units it sold and which are still in ending inventory, it can use the **specific identification method** of inventory costing. For example, if Crivitz sold the TVs it purchased on February 3 and May 22, then its cost of goods sold is $1,500 ($700 + $800), and its ending inventory is $750 (see **Illustration 6.4**). Using this method, companies can accurately determine ending inventory and cost of goods sold.

ILLUSTRATION 6.4

Specific identification method

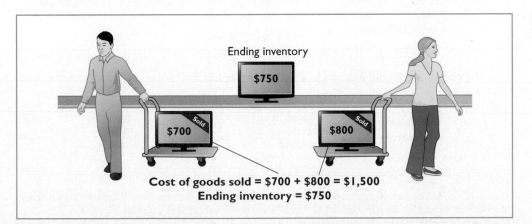

Ending inventory

$750

$700   Sold

$800   Sold

Cost of goods sold = $700 + $800 = $1,500
Ending inventory = $750

Specific identification requires that companies keep records of the original cost of each individual inventory item. Historically, specific identification was possible only when a company sold a limited variety of high-unit-cost items that could be identified clearly from the time of purchase through the time of sale. Examples of such products are cars, pianos, or expensive antiques (see **Ethics Note**).

Today, bar coding, electronic product codes, and radio frequency identification make it theoretically possible to apply specific identification with nearly any type of product. The reality is, however, that this practice is still relatively rare. Instead, rather than keep track of the cost of each particular item sold, most companies make assumptions, called **cost flow assumptions**, about which units were sold.

Cost Flow Assumptions

Because specific identification is often impractical, other cost flow methods are permitted. These differ from specific identification in that they **assume** flows of costs that may be unrelated to the physical flow of goods. There are three assumed cost flow methods:

1. First-in, first-out (FIFO).
2. Last-in, first-out (LIFO).
3. Average-cost.

There is no accounting requirement that the cost flow assumption be consistent with the physical movement of the goods. Company management selects the appropriate cost flow method to be used for accounting purposes.

To demonstrate the three cost flow methods, we will use a **periodic** inventory system. We assume a periodic system because **very few companies use perpetual LIFO, FIFO, or average-cost** to cost their inventory and related cost of goods sold. Instead, companies that use perpetual systems often use an assumed cost (called a standard cost) to record cost of goods sold at the time of sale. Then, at the end of the period when they count their inventory, they **recalculate cost of goods sold using periodic FIFO, LIFO, or average-cost** as shown in this chapter and adjust cost of goods sold to this recalculated number.[1]

To illustrate the three inventory cost flow methods, we will use the data for Houston Electronics' Astro condensers, shown in **Illustration 6.5**.

ILLUSTRATION 6.5

Data for Houston Electronics

Houston Electronics
Astro Condensers

Date	Explanation	Units	Unit Cost	Total Cost
Jan. 1	Beginning inventory	100	$10	$ 1,000
Apr. 15	Purchase	200	11	2,200
Aug. 24	Purchase	300	12	3,600
Nov. 27	Purchase	400	13	5,200
	Total units available for sale	1,000		$12,000
	Units in ending inventory	(450)		
	Units sold	550		

The cost of goods sold formula in a periodic system is:

Beginning Inventory	+	Cost of Goods Purchased	−	Ending Inventory	=	Cost of Goods Sold

---

[1]Also, some companies use a perpetual system to keep track of units, but they do not make an entry for perpetual cost of goods sold. In addition, firms that employ LIFO tend to use **dollar-value LIFO**, a method discussed in upper-level courses. FIFO periodic and FIFO perpetual give the same result. Therefore, companies should not incur the additional cost to use FIFO perpetual. Few companies use perpetual average-cost because of the added cost of recordkeeping. Finally, for instructional purposes, we believe it is easier to demonstrate the cost flow assumptions under the periodic system, which makes it more pedagogically appropriate.

Houston Electronics had a total of 1,000 units available to sell during the period (beginning inventory plus purchases). The total cost of these 1,000 units is $12,000, referred to as **cost of goods available for sale**. A physical inventory taken at December 31 determined that there were 450 units in ending inventory. Therefore, Houston sold 550 units (1,000 – 450) during the period. To determine the cost of the 550 units that were sold (the cost of goods sold), we assign a cost to the ending inventory and subtract that value from the cost of goods available for sale. The value assigned to the ending inventory **depends on which cost flow method we use**. No matter which cost flow assumption we use, though, the sum of cost of goods sold plus the cost of the ending inventory must equal the cost of goods available for sale—in this case, $12,000.

First-In, First-Out (FIFO)

The **first-in, first-out (FIFO) method** assumes that the **earliest goods** purchased are the first to be sold. FIFO often parallels the actual physical flow of merchandise. That is, it generally is good business practice to sell the oldest units first. Under the FIFO method, therefore, the **costs** of the earliest goods purchased are the first to be recognized in determining cost of goods sold. (This does not necessarily mean that the oldest units **are** sold first, but that the costs of the oldest units are **recognized** first. In a bin of picture hangers at the hardware store, for example, no one really knows, nor would it matter, which hangers are sold first.) **Illustration 6.6** shows the allocation of the cost of goods available for sale at Houston Electronics under FIFO (see **Helpful Hint**).

ILLUSTRATION 6.6
Allocation of costs—FIFO method

Cost of Goods Available for Sale				
Date	Explanation	Units	Unit Cost	Total Cost
Jan. 1	Beginning inventory	100	$10	$ 1,000
Apr. 15	Purchase	200	11	2,200
Aug. 24	Purchase	300	12	3,600
Nov. 27	Purchase	400	13	5,200
	Total	1,000		$12,000

Step 1: Ending Inventory				Step 2: Cost of Goods Sold	
Date	Units	Unit Cost	Total Cost		
Nov. 27	400	$13	$5,200	Cost of goods available for sale	$12,000
Aug. 24	50	12	600	Less: Ending inventory	5,800
Total	450		$5,800	Cost of goods sold	$ 6,200

$1,000
$2,200
$3,000
$600
$5,200

Cost of goods sold

$6,200

$5,800 Warehouse

Ending inventory

HELPFUL HINT

Note the sequencing of the allocation: (1) compute ending inventory, and (2) determine cost of goods sold.

Under FIFO, since it is assumed that the first goods purchased were the first goods sold, ending inventory is based on the costs of the most recent units purchased (see **Helpful Hint**). That is, **under FIFO, companies determine the cost of the ending inventory by taking the unit cost of the most recent purchase and working backward until all units of inventory have been costed**. In this example, Houston Electronics accounts for the 450 units of ending inventory using the **most recent** costs. The last purchase was 400 units at

HELPFUL HINT

Another way of thinking about the calculation of FIFO ending inventory is the LISH assumption—last in still here.

$13 on November 27. The remaining 50 units use the unit cost of the second most recent purchase, $12, on August 24. Next, Houston Electronics calculates cost of goods sold by subtracting the cost of the units **not sold** (ending inventory) from the cost of all goods available for sale.

Illustration 6.7 demonstrates that Houston can also calculate the cost of the 550 units sold by using the costs of the first 550 units acquired. Note that of the 300 units purchased on August 24, only 250 units are assumed sold. This agrees with our calculation of the cost of ending inventory, where 50 of these units were assumed unsold and thus included in ending inventory.

ILLUSTRATION 6.7

Proof of cost of goods sold— FIFO method

Date	Units	Unit Cost	Total Cost
Jan. 1	100	$10	$1,000
Apr. 15	200	11	2,200
Aug. 24	250	12	3,000
Total	550		**$6,200**

ACTION PLAN

- **Understand the periodic inventory system.**
- **Allocate costs between goods sold and goods on hand (ending inventory) for the FIFO method.**
- **Compute cost of goods sold for the FIFO method.**

DO IT! 2 | Cost Flow Methods—FIFO Method

Part 1: The accounting records of Shumway Ag Implements show the following data.

Beginning inventory	4,000 units at $3
Purchases	6,000 units at $4
Sales	7,000 units at $12

Determine the cost of goods sold during the period under a periodic inventory system using the FIFO method.

Solution

Cost of goods available for sale = (4,000 × $3) + (6,000 × $4) = $36,000

Ending inventory = 10,000 − 7,000 = 3,000 units

Cost of goods sold FIFO: $36,000 − (3,000 × $4) = $24,000

Related exercise material: **BE6.3, BE6.4, BE6.5, BE6.6, DO IT! 6.2, E6.4, E6.5, E.6.6, E6.7, and E6.8.**

Last-In, First-Out (LIFO)

The **last-in, first-out (LIFO) method** assumes that the **latest goods** purchased are the first to be sold. LIFO seldom coincides with the actual physical flow of inventory. (Exceptions include goods stored in piles, such as coal or hay, where goods are removed from the top of the pile as they are sold.) Under the LIFO method, the **costs** of the latest goods purchased are the first to be recognized in determining cost of goods sold. **Illustration 6.8** shows the allocation of the cost of goods available for sale at Houston Electronics under LIFO.

ILLUSTRATION 6.8

Allocation of costs— LIFO method

	Cost of Goods Available for Sale			
Date	Explanation	Units	Unit Cost	Total Cost
Jan. 1	Beginning inventory	100	$10	$ 1,000
Apr. 15	Purchase	200	11	2,200
Aug. 24	Purchase	300	12	3,600
Nov. 27	Purchase	400	13	5,200
	Total	1,000		**$12,000**

(continues)

ILLUSTRATION 6.8

(continued)

Step 1: Ending Inventory				Step 2: Cost of Goods Sold	
Date	Units	Unit Cost	Total Cost		
Jan. 1	100	$10	$1,000	Cost of goods available for sale	$12,000
Apr. 15	200	11	2,200	Less: Ending inventory	5,000
Aug. 24	150	12	1,800	Cost of goods sold	$ 7,000
Total	450		$5,000		

Under LIFO, since it is assumed that the first goods sold were those that were most recently purchased, ending inventory is based on the costs of the oldest units purchased (see **Helpful Hint**). That is, **under LIFO, companies determine the cost of the ending inventory by taking the unit cost of the earliest goods available for sale and working forward until all units of inventory have been costed**. In this example, Houston Electronics accounts for the 450 units of ending inventory using the **earliest** costs. The first purchase was 100 units at $10 in the January 1 beginning inventory. Then, 200 units were purchased at $11. The remaining 150 units needed have a $12 per unit cost (August 24 purchase). Next, Houston Electronics calculates cost of goods sold by subtracting the cost of the units **not sold** (ending inventory) from the cost of all goods available for sale.

Illustration 6.9 demonstrates that Houston can also calculate the cost of the 550 units sold by using the costs of the last 550 units acquired. Note that of the 300 units purchased on August 24, only 150 units are assumed sold. This agrees with our calculation of the cost of ending inventory, where 150 of these units were assumed unsold and thus included in ending inventory.

HELPFUL HINT

Another way of thinking about the calculation of LIFO ending inventory is the FISH assumption—first in still here.

Date	Units	Unit Cost	Total Cost
Nov. 27	400	$13	$5,200
Aug. 24	150	12	1,800
Total	550		$7,000

ILLUSTRATION 6.9

Proof of cost of goods sold—LIFO method

Under a periodic inventory system, which we are using here, **all goods purchased during the period are assumed to be available for the first sale, regardless of the date of purchase**.

ACTION PLAN

- Understand the periodic inventory system.
- Allocate costs between goods sold and goods on hand (ending inventory) for the LIFO method.
- Compute cost of goods sold for the LIFO method.

DO IT! 2 | Cost Flow Methods—LIFO Method

Part 2: The accounting records of Shumway Ag Implements show the following data.

Beginning inventory	4,000 units at $3
Purchases	6,000 units at $4
Sales	7,000 units at $12

Determine the cost of goods sold during the period under a periodic inventory system using the LIFO method.

Solution

Cost of goods available for sale = (4,000 × $3) + (6,000 × $4) = $36,000

Ending inventory = 10,000 − 7,000 = 3,000 units

Cost of goods sold LIFO: $36,000 − (3,000 × $3) = $27,000

Related exercise material: **BE6.3, BE6.4, BE6.5, BE6.6, DO IT! 6.2, E6.5, E6.6, E6.7, and E6.8.**

Average-Cost

The **average-cost method** allocates the cost of goods available for sale on the basis of the **weighted-average unit cost** incurred. The average-cost method assumes that goods are similar in nature. **Illustration 6.10** presents the formula and a sample computation of the weighted-average unit cost.

ILLUSTRATION 6.10

Formula for weighted-average unit cost

Cost of Goods Available for Sale	÷	Total Units Available for Sale	=	Weighted-Average Unit Cost
$12,000	÷	1,000	=	$12

The company then applies the weighted-average unit cost to the units on hand to determine the cost of the ending inventory. **Illustration 6.11** shows the allocation of the cost of goods available for sale at Houston Electronics using average-cost.

ILLUSTRATION 6.11

Allocation of costs—average-cost method

Cost of Goods Available for Sale				
Date	Explanation	Units	Unit Cost	Total Cost
Jan. 1	Beginning inventory	100	$10	$ 1,000
Apr. 15	Purchase	200	11	2,200
Aug. 24	Purchase	300	12	3,600
Nov. 27	Purchase	400	13	5,200
	Total	1,000		$12,000

Step 1: Ending Inventory				Step 2: Cost of Goods Sold	
$12,000	÷ 1,000 =	$12		Cost of goods available for sale	$12,000
				Less: Ending inventory	5,400
		Total		Cost of goods sold	$ 6,600
Units	**Unit Cost**	**Cost**			
450	$12	**$5,400**			

(continues)

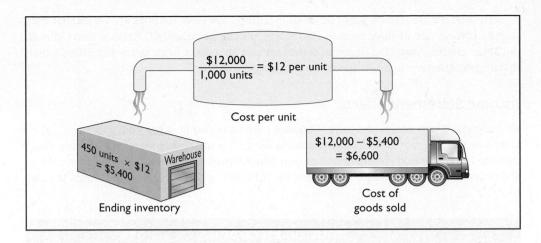

ILLUSTRATION 6.11

(continued)

We can verify the cost of goods sold under this method by multiplying the units sold by the weighted-average unit cost ($550 \times \$12 = \$6,600$). Note that this method does **not** use the average of the unit costs. That average is $11.50 ($10 + $11 + $12 + $13 = $46; $46 ÷ 4). The average-cost method instead uses the average **weighted by** the quantities purchased at each unit cost.

DO IT! 2 | Cost Flow Methods—Average-Cost Method

Part 3: The accounting records of Shumway Ag Implements show the following data.

Beginning inventory	4,000 units at $3
Purchases	6,000 units at $4
Sales	7,000 units at $12

Determine the cost of goods sold during the period under a periodic inventory system using the average-cost method.

Solution

Cost of goods available for sale = (4,000 × $3) + (6,000 × $4) = $36,000
Ending inventory = 10,000 – 7,000 = 3,000 units

Weighted-average unit cost: [(4,000 @ $3) + (6,000 @ $4)] ÷ 10,000 = $3.60
Cost of goods sold average-cost: $36,000 – (3,000 × $3.60) = $25,200

Related exercise material: **BE6.3, BE6.4, BE6.5, BE6.6, DO IT! 6.2, E6.5, E6.6, E6.7, and E6.8.**

ACTION PLAN

- **Understand the periodic inventory system.**
- **Allocate costs between goods sold and goods on hand (ending inventory) for the average-cost method.**
- **Compute cost of goods sold for the average-cost method.**

Financial Statement and Tax Effects of Cost Flow Methods

Each of the three assumed cost flow methods is acceptable under GAAP. For example, **Reebok International Ltd.** and **Wendy's International** currently use the FIFO method of inventory costing. **Campbell Soup Company**, **Kroger**, and **Walgreens** use LIFO for part or all of their inventory. **Bristol-Myers Squibb**, **Starbucks**, and **Motorola** use the average-cost method. In fact, a company may also use more than one cost flow method at the same time for different types of inventory. **Stanley Black & Decker Manufacturing Company**, for example, uses LIFO for domestic inventories and FIFO for foreign inventories. **Illustration 6.12** shows the use of the three cost flow methods in 500 large U.S. companies.

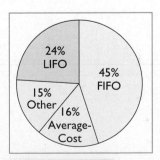

ILLUSTRATION 6.12

Use of cost flow methods in major U.S. companies

The reasons companies adopt different inventory cost flow methods are varied, but they usually involve one of three factors: (1) income statement effects, (2) balance sheet effects, or (3) tax effects. Analyzing financial statement and tax effects helps users determine which inventory costing method best meets the company's objectives.

Income Statement Effects

To understand why companies might choose a particular cost flow method, let's examine the effects of the different cost flow assumptions on the financial statements of Houston Electronics. The condensed income statements in **Illustration 6.13** assume that Houston sold its 550 units for $18,500, had operating expenses of $9,000, and is subject to an income tax rate of 20%.

ILLUSTRATION 6.13

Comparative effects of cost flow methods

Houston Electronics			
Condensed Income Statements			
	FIFO	**LIFO**	**Average-Cost**
Sales revenue	$18,500	$18,500	$18,500
Beginning inventory	1,000	1,000	1,000
Purchases	11,000	11,000	11,000
Cost of goods available for sale	12,000	12,000	12,000
Ending inventory	**5,800**	**5,000**	**5,400**
Cost of goods sold	6,200	7,000	6,600
Gross profit	12,300	11,500	11,900
Operating expenses	9,000	9,000	9,000
Income before income taxes*	3,300	2,500	2,900
Income tax expense (20%)	660	500	580
Net income	**$ 2,640**	**$ 2,000**	**$ 2,320**

*We are assuming that Houston Electronics is a corporation, and corporations are required to pay income taxes.

In this example, which assumes equal beginning inventories, the cost of goods available for sale ($12,000) is the same under each of the three inventory cost flow methods. However, the ending inventories and the costs of goods sold are different. This difference is due to the unit costs that the company allocated to cost of goods sold and to ending inventory. Each dollar of difference in ending inventory results in a corresponding dollar difference in income before income taxes. For Houston, an $800 difference exists between FIFO and LIFO cost of goods sold.

In periods when costs change, the cost flow assumption can have significant impacts both on income and on evaluations of income, such as the following.

1. In a period of inflation, FIFO produces a higher net income because lower unit costs of the first units purchased are matched against revenue.

2. In a period of inflation, LIFO produces a lower net income because higher unit costs of the last goods purchased are matched against revenue.

3. If costs are falling, the results from the use of FIFO and LIFO are reversed. FIFO will report the lowest net income and LIFO the highest.

4. Regardless of whether costs are rising or falling, average-cost produces net income between FIFO and LIFO.

As shown in the Houston example (Illustration 6.13), in a period of rising costs, FIFO reports the highest net income ($2,640) and LIFO the lowest ($2,000); average-cost falls between these two amounts ($2,320).

To management, higher net income is an advantage. It causes external users to view the company more favorably. In addition, management bonuses, if based on net income, will be higher. Therefore, when costs are rising (which is usually the case), companies tend to prefer FIFO because it results in higher net income.

Others believe that LIFO presents a more realistic net income number. That is, LIFO matches the more recent costs against current revenues to provide a better measure of net income. During periods of inflation, many challenge the quality of non-LIFO earnings, noting that failing to match current costs against current revenues leads to an understatement of cost of goods sold and an overstatement of net income. As some indicate, additional net income computed using FIFO creates **"paper or phantom profits"**—that is, earnings that do not really exist.

Balance Sheet Effects

A major advantage of the FIFO method is that in a period of inflation, the costs allocated to ending inventory will approximate their current cost. For example, for Houston Electronics, 400 of the 450 units in the ending inventory are costed under FIFO at the higher November 27 unit cost of $13.

Conversely, a major shortcoming of the LIFO method is that in a period of inflation, the costs allocated to ending inventory may be significantly understated in terms of current cost. The understatement becomes greater over prolonged periods of inflation if the inventory includes goods purchased in one or more prior accounting periods. For example, **Caterpillar** has used LIFO for more than 50 years. Its balance sheet shows ending inventory of $9,700 million. But the inventory's actual current cost if FIFO had been used is $12,189 million.

Tax Effects

We have seen that both inventory on the balance sheet and net income on the income statement are higher when companies use FIFO in a period of inflation. Yet, many companies have selected LIFO. Why? The reason is that LIFO results in the lowest income taxes (because of lower net income) during times of rising costs (see **Helpful Hint**). For example, at Houston Electronics, income taxes are $500 under LIFO, compared to $660 under FIFO. The tax savings of $160 makes more cash available for use in the business.

HELPFUL HINT

A tax rule, often referred to as the LIFO conformity rule, requires that if companies use LIFO for tax purposes they must also use it for financial reporting purposes. This means that if a company chooses the LIFO method to reduce its tax bills, it will also have to report lower net income in its financial statements.

Using Inventory Cost Flow Methods Consistently

Whatever cost flow method a company chooses, it should use that method consistently from one accounting period to another. This approach is often referred to as the **consistency concept**, which means that a company uses the same accounting principles and methods from year to year. Consistent application enhances the comparability of financial statements over successive time periods. In contrast, using the FIFO method one year and the LIFO method the next year would make it difficult to compare the net incomes of the two years.

Although consistent application is preferred, it does not mean that a company may never change its inventory costing method. When a company adopts a different method, it should disclose in the financial statements the change and its effects on net income. **Illustration 6.14** shows a typical disclosure, using information from recent financial statements of **Quaker Oats** (a unit of **PepsiCo**).

ILLUSTRATION 6.14

Disclosure of change in cost flow method

`Real World`

Quaker Oats
Notes to the Financial Statements

Note 1: Effective July 1, the Company adopted the LIFO cost flow assumption for valuing the majority of U.S. Grocery Products inventories. The Company believes that the use of the LIFO method better matches current costs with current revenues. The effect of this change on the current year was to decrease net income by $16.0 million.

International Insight ExxonMobil Corporation

Mike Fuentes/Bloomberg/
Getty Images

Is LIFO Fair?

ExxonMobil Corporation, like many U.S. companies, uses LIFO to value its inventory for financial reporting and tax purposes. In one recent year, this resulted in a cost of goods sold figure that was $5.6 billion higher than under FIFO. By increasing cost of goods sold, ExxonMobil reduces net income, which reduces taxes. Critics say that LIFO provides an unfair "tax dodge." As Congress looks for more sources of tax revenue, some lawmakers favor the elimination of LIFO. Supporters of LIFO argue that the method is conceptually sound because it matches current costs with current revenues. In addition, they point out that this matching provides protection against inflation.

International accounting standards do not allow the use of LIFO. Because of this, the net income of foreign oil companies such as **BP** and **Royal Dutch Shell** are not directly comparable to U.S. companies, which can make analysis difficult.

Source: David Reilly, "Big Oil's Accounting Methods Fuel Criticism," *Wall Street Journal* (August 8, 2006), p. C1.

What are the arguments for and against the use of LIFO? (Go to WileyPLUS for this answer and additional questions.)

ACTION PLAN

- **Understand the periodic inventory system.**
- **Allocate costs between goods sold and goods on hand (ending inventory) for each cost flow method.**
- **Compute cost of goods sold for each method.**

DO IT! 2 | Cost Flow Methods

Part 4: London Company sold 600 units of inventory in April. In addition, the following information is available.

April 1 inventory	250	$10	$ 2,500
April 15 purchases	400	12	4,800
April 23 purchases	350	13	4,550
	1,000		$11,850

Determine the cost of goods sold during the period under a periodic inventory system using (a) the FIFO method, (b) the LIFO method, and (c) the average-cost method.

Solution

Cost of goods available for sale = $11,850
Ending inventory = 1,000 – 600 = 400 units

a. FIFO: $11,850 – $4,550 (350 × $13) – $600 (50 × $12) = $6,700

b. LIFO: $11,850 – $2,500 (250 × $10) – $1,800 (150 × $12) = $7,550

c. Weighted-average unit cost: $11,850 ($2,500 + $4,800 + $4,550) ÷ 1,000 = $11.85

   Average-cost: $11,850 – (400 × $11.85) = $7,110

Related exercise material: **BE6.3, BE6.4, BE6.5, BE6.6, DO IT! 6.2, E6.4, E6.5, E6.6, E6.7, E6.8, and E6.9.**

Effects of Inventory Errors

LEARNING OBJECTIVE 3

Indicate the effects of inventory errors on the financial statements.

Unfortunately, errors occasionally occur in accounting for inventory. In some cases, errors are caused by failure to count or cost the inventory correctly. In other cases, errors occur because companies do not properly recognize the transfer of legal title to goods that are in transit. When errors occur, they affect both the income statement and the balance sheet.

Income Statement Effects

The ending inventory of one period automatically becomes the beginning inventory of the next period. Thus, inventory errors affect the computation of cost of goods sold and net income in two periods.

The effects on cost of goods sold can be computed by first entering incorrect data in the formula in **Illustration 6.15** and then substituting the correct data.

ILLUSTRATION 6.15 **Formula for cost of goods sold**

Beginning Inventory	+	Cost of Goods Purchased	–	Ending Inventory	=	Cost of Goods Sold

> **ETHICS NOTE**
> Inventory fraud increases during recessions. Such fraud includes costing inventory at amounts in excess of its actual value, or claiming to have inventory when no inventory exists. Inventory fraud usually overstates ending inventory, thereby understating cost of goods sold and creating higher net income.

If **beginning** inventory is understated, cost of goods sold will be understated. If **ending** inventory is understated, cost of goods sold will be overstated. **Illustration 6.16** shows the effects of inventory errors on the current year's income statement (see **Ethics Note**).

ILLUSTRATION 6.16

Effects of inventory errors on current year's income statement

When Inventory Error:	Cost of Goods Sold Is:	Net Income Is:
Understates beginning inventory	Understated	Overstated
Overstates beginning inventory	Overstated	Understated
Understates ending inventory	Overstated	Understated
Overstates ending inventory	Understated	Overstated

An error in the ending inventory of the current period will have a **reverse effect on net income of the next accounting period**. **Illustration 6.17** shows this effect. Note that the understatement of ending inventory in 2021 results in an understatement of beginning inventory in 2022 and an overstatement of net income in 2022.

ILLUSTRATION 6.17 **Effects of inventory errors on two years' income statements**

Veronique Unique, Inc.
Condensed Income Statements

	2021 Incorrect		2021 Correct		2022 Incorrect		2022 Correct	
Sales revenue		$80,000		$80,000		$90,000		$90,000
Beginning inventory	$20,000		$20,000		**$12,000**		**$15,000**	
Cost of goods purchased	40,000		40,000		68,000		68,000	
Cost of goods available for sale	60,000		60,000		80,000		83,000	
Ending inventory	**12,000**		**15,000**		23,000		23,000	
Cost of goods sold		48,000		45,000		57,000		60,000
Gross profit		32,000		35,000		33,000		30,000
Operating expenses		10,000		10,000		20,000		20,000
Net income		$22,000		$25,000		$13,000		$10,000

$(3,000)
Net income
understated

$3,000
Net income
overstated

The errors cancel. Thus, the combined total income for the 2-year period is correct.

Over the two years, though, total net income is correct because the errors **offset each other**. Notice that total net income using incorrect data is $35,000 ($22,000 + $13,000), which is the same as the total net income of $35,000 ($25,000 + $10,000) using correct data. Also note in this example that an error in the beginning inventory does not result in a corresponding error in the ending inventory for that period. The correctness of the ending inventory depends entirely on the accuracy of counting and costing the inventory at the balance sheet date under the periodic inventory system.

Balance Sheet Effects

Companies can determine the effect of ending inventory errors on the balance sheet by using the basic accounting equation: Assets = Liabilities + Stockholders' Equity. Errors in the ending inventory have the effects shown in **Illustration 6.18**.

ILLUSTRATION 6.18

Effects of ending inventory errors on balance sheet

Ending Inventory Error	Assets	Liabilities	Stockholders' Equity
Overstated	Overstated	No effect	Overstated
Understated	Understated	No effect	Understated

The effect of an error in ending inventory on the subsequent period was shown in Illustration 6.17. Note that if the error is not corrected, the combined total net income for the two periods would be correct. Thus, total stockholders' equity reported on the balance sheet at the end of 2022 will also be correct.

ACTION PLAN

- **An ending inventory error in one period will have an equal and opposite effect on cost of goods sold and net income in the next period.**
- **After two years, the errors have offset each other.**

DO IT! 3 | Inventory Errors

Visual Company overstated its 2021 ending inventory by $22,000. Determine the impact this error has on ending inventory, cost of goods sold, and stockholders' equity in 2021 and 2022.

Solution

	2021	2022
Ending inventory	$22,000 overstated	No effect
Cost of goods sold	$22,000 understated	$22,000 overstated
Stockholders' equity	$22,000 overstated	No effect

Related exercise material: **BE6.7, DO IT! 6.3, E6.9, and E6.10.**

Inventory Presentation and Analysis

LEARNING OBJECTIVE 4

Explain the statement presentation and analysis of inventory.

Presentation

Recall that inventory is classified in the balance sheet as a current asset immediately below accounts receivable. In a multiple-step income statement, cost of goods sold is subtracted from net sales. There also should be disclosure of (1) the major inventory classifications, (2) the basis of accounting (cost, or lower-of-cost-or-net realizable value), and (3) the cost method (FIFO, LIFO, or average-cost).

Walmart Inc., for example, in its January 31, 2017, balance sheet reported inventories of $43,046 million under current assets. The accompanying notes to the financial statements, as shown in **Illustration 6.19**, disclosed the following information.

ILLUSTRATION 6.19
Inventory disclosures by Walmart
Real World

Walmart Inc.
Notes to the Financial Statements

Note 1. Summary of Significant Accounting Policies

Inventories

The Company values inventories at the lower of cost or market as determined primarily by the retail method of accounting, using the last-in, first-out ("LIFO") method for substantially all of the Walmart U.S. segment's inventories. The inventory at the Walmart International segment is valued primarily by the retail inventory method of accounting, using the first-in, first-out ("FIFO") method. The retail method of accounting results in inventory being valued at the lower of cost or market since permanent markdowns are immediately recorded as a reduction of the retail value of inventory. The inventory at the Sam's Club segment is valued using the LIFO method. At January 31, 2017 and 2016, the Company's inventories valued at LIFO approximate those inventories as if they were valued at FIFO.

Lower-of-Cost-or-Net Realizable Value

The value of inventory for companies selling high-technology or fashion goods can drop very quickly due to continual changes in technology or fashion. These circumstances sometimes call for inventory valuation methods other than those presented so far. For example, at one time, purchasing managers at **Ford** decided to make a large purchase of palladium, a precious metal used in vehicle emission devices. They made this purchase because they feared a future shortage. The shortage did not materialize, and by the end of the year the cost of palladium had plummeted. Ford's inventory was then worth $1 billion less than its original cost. Do you think Ford's inventory should have been stated at cost, in accordance with the historical cost principle, or at its lower net realizable value?

As you probably reasoned, this situation requires a departure from the cost basis of accounting. When the value of inventory is lower than its cost, companies must "write down" the inventory to its net realizable value. This is done by valuing the inventory at the **lower-of-cost-or-net realizable value (LCNRV)** in the period in which the cost decline occurs. LCNRV is an example of accounting **conservatism**. Conservatism means that accountants select a method of reporting that is least likely to overstate assets and net income. Critics of accounting conservatism argue that it introduces bias into accounting numbers. This can reduce the representational faithfulness as well as the relevance of financial reports.

Under the LCNRV basis, **net realizable value** refers to the net amount that a company expects to realize (receive) from the sale of inventory. Specifically, net realizable value is the estimated selling price in the normal course of business, less estimated costs to complete and sell.

Companies apply LCNRV to the items in inventory after they have used one of the inventory costing methods (specific identification, FIFO, or average-cost) to determine cost. To illustrate the application of LCNRV, assume that Ken Tuckie TV has the following lines of merchandise with costs and net realizable values as indicated. LCNRV produces the results shown in **Illustration 6.20**. Note that the amounts shown in the final column are the lower-of-cost-or-net realizable value amounts for each item.

ILLUSTRATION 6.20
Computation of lower-of-cost-or-net realizable value

	Units	Cost per Unit	Net Realizable Value per Unit	Lower-of-Cost-or-Net Realizable Value	
Flat-screen TVs	100	$600	$550	$ 55,000	($550 × 100)
Satellite radios	500	90	104	45,000	($90 × 500)
DVD recorders	850	50	48	40,800	($48 × 850)
DVDs	3,000	5	6	15,000	($5 × 3,000)
Total inventory				$155,800	

Companies that use the LIFO method or the retail inventory method (discussed in Appendix 6B and shown in Illustration 6.19) are not required to use lower-of-cost-or-net realizable value for inventory valuation. Instead, they use a lower-of-cost-or-market approach which is a more complex calculation. The computation for the lower-of-cost-or-market method is discussed in more advanced accounting courses.

ACTION PLAN

- **Determine whether cost or net realizable value is lower for each inventory type.**
- **Sum the lowest value of each inventory type to determine the total value of inventory.**

DO IT! 4a │ LCNRV

Tracy Company sells three different types of home heating stoves (gas, wood, and pellet). The cost and net realizable value of its inventory of stoves are as follows.

	Cost	Net Realizable Value
Gas	$ 84,000	$ 79,000
Wood	250,000	280,000
Pellet	112,000	101,000

Determine the value of the company's inventory under the lower-of-cost-or-net realizable value approach.

Solution

The lowest value for each inventory type is gas $79,000, wood $250,000, and pellet $101,000. The total inventory value is the sum of these amounts, $430,000.

Related exercise material: **BE6.8, DO IT! 6.4a, E6.11, and E6.12.**

Analysis

The amount of inventory carried by a company has significant economic consequences. And inventory management is a double-edged sword that requires constant attention. On the one hand, management wants to have a great variety and quantity available so that customers have a wide selection and items are always in stock. But, such a policy may incur high carrying costs (e.g., investment, storage, insurance, obsolescence, and damage). On the other hand, low inventory levels lead to stock-outs and lost sales. Common ratios used to manage and evaluate inventory levels are the inventory turnover ratio and a related measure, days in inventory.

Inventory turnover measures the number of times on average the inventory is sold during the period. Its purpose is to measure the liquidity of the inventory. The inventory turnover is computed by dividing cost of goods sold by the average inventory during the period. Unless seasonal factors are significant, average inventory can be computed from the beginning and ending inventory balances. For example, **Walmart** reported in its January 31, 2016, annual report a beginning inventory of $45,141 million, an ending inventory of $44,469 million, and cost of goods sold for the year ended January 31, 2016, of $360,984 million. The inventory turnover formula and computation for Walmart are shown in **Illustration 6.21**.

ILLUSTRATION 6.21

Inventory turnover formula and computation for Walmart

Cost of Goods Sale	÷	Average Inventory	=	Inventory Turnover
$360,984	÷	$\dfrac{\$45,141 + \$44,469}{2}$	=	8.1 times

A variant of the inventory turnover is **days in inventory**. This measures the average number of days inventory is held. It is calculated as 365 divided by the inventory turnover.

For example, Walmart's inventory turnover of 8.1 times divided into 365 is 45.1 days. This is the approximate time that it takes a company to sell the inventory once it arrives at the store.

There are typical levels of inventory in every industry. Companies that are able to keep their inventory at lower levels and higher turnovers and still satisfy customer needs are the most successful.

Accounting Across the Organization   Sony

iStock.com/Dmitry Kutlayev

Too Many TVs or Too Few?

Financial analysts closely monitor the inventory management practices of companies. For example, some analysts following **Sony** expressed concern because the company built up its inventory of televisions in an attempt to sell 25 million liquid crystal display (LCD) TVs—a 60% increase over the prior year. In that prior year, Sony had cut its inventory levels so that its quarterly days in inventory was down to 38 days, compared to 61 days for the same quarter a year before that. Now, as a result of its inventory build-up, days in inventory rose to 59 days. Management said that it didn't think that Sony's inventory levels were too high. However, analysts were concerned that the company would have to engage in very heavy discounting in order to sell off its inventory. Analysts noted that the losses from discounting can be "punishing."

Source: Daisuke Wakabayashi, "Sony Pledges to Corral Inventory," *Wall Street Journal Online* (November 2, 2010).

For Sony, what are the advantages and disadvantages of having a low days in inventory measure? (Go to WileyPLUS for this answer and additional questions.)

DO IT! 4b | Inventory Turnover

Early in 2022, Westmoreland Company switched to a just-in-time inventory system. Its sales revenue, cost of goods sold, and inventory amounts for 2021 and 2022 are shown below.

	2021	2022
Sales revenue	$2,000,000	$1,800,000
Cost of goods sold	1,000,000	910,000
Beginning inventory	290,000	210,000
Ending inventory	210,000	50,000

Determine the inventory turnover and days in inventory for 2021 and 2022. Discuss the changes in the amount of inventory, the inventory turnover and days in inventory, and the amount of sales across the two years.

Solution

	2021	2022
Inventory turnover	$\dfrac{\$1,000,000}{(\$290,000 + \$210,000) \div 2} = 4$	$\dfrac{\$910,000}{(\$210,000 + \$50,000) \div 2} = 7$
Days in inventory	$365 \div 4 = 91.3$ days	$365 \div 7 = 52.1$ days

The company experienced a very significant decline in its ending inventory as a result of the just-in-time inventory. This decline improved its inventory turnover and its days in inventory. However, its sales declined by 10%. It is possible that this decline was caused by the dramatic reduction in the amount of inventory that was on hand, which increased the likelihood of stock-outs (failure to have inventory on hand). To determine the optimal inventory level, management must weigh the benefits of reduced inventory against the potential lost sales caused by stock-outs.

Related exercise material: **BE6.9, DO IT! 6.4b, E6.12, E6.13, and E6.14.**

ACTION PLAN

- **To find the inventory turnover, divide cost of goods sold by average inventory.**
- **To determine days in inventory, divide 365 days by the inventory turnover.**
- **Just-in-time inventory reduces the amount of inventory on hand, which reduces carrying costs. Reducing inventory levels by too much has potential negative implications for sales.**

Appendix 6A	# Inventory Cost Flow Methods in Perpetual Inventory Systems

> ### LEARNING OBJECTIVE *5
> Apply the inventory cost flow methods to perpetual inventory records.

What inventory cost flow methods can companies employ if they use a perpetual inventory system? Simple—they can use any of the inventory cost flow methods described in the chapter. To illustrate the application of the three assumed cost flow methods (FIFO, LIFO, and average-cost), we will use the data shown in **Illustration 6A.1** and in this chapter for Houston Electronics' Astro condensers.

ILLUSTRATION 6A.1
Inventoriable units and costs

Houston Electronics
Astro Condensers

Date	Explanation	Units	Unit Cost	Total Cost	Balance in Units
1/1	Beginning inventory	100	$10	$ 1,000	100
4/15	Purchases	200	11	2,200	300
8/24	Purchases	300	12	3,600	600
9/10	Sale	550			50
11/27	Purchases	400	13	5,200	450
				$12,000	

First-In, First-Out (FIFO)

Under perpetual FIFO, the company charges to cost of goods sold the cost of the earliest goods on hand **prior to each sale**. Therefore, the cost of goods sold on September 10 consists of the units on hand January 1 and the units purchased April 15 and August 24. **Illustration 6A.2** shows the inventory under a FIFO method perpetual system.

ILLUSTRATION 6A.2
Perpetual system—FIFO

Date	Purchases		Cost of Goods Sold	Inventory Balance (in units and cost)	
January 1				(100 @ $10)	$1,000
April 15	(200 @ $11)	$2,200		(100 @ $10) (200 @ $11)	$3,200
August 24	(300 @ $12)	$3,600		(100 @ $10) (200 @ $11) (300 @ $12)	$6,800
September 10			(100 @ $10) (200 @ $11) (250 @ $12)	(50 @ $12)	$ 600
			$6,200		
November 27	(400 @ $13)	$5,200		(50 @ $12) (400 @ $13)	**$5,800**

Cost of goods sold → **$6,200**

Ending inventory → **$5,800**

The ending inventory in this situation is $5,800, and the cost of goods sold is $6,200 [(100 @ $10) + (200 @ $11) + (250 @ $12)].

Compare Illustrations 6.6 and 6A.2. You can see that the results under FIFO in a perpetual system are the **same as in a periodic system**. In both cases, the ending inventory is $5,800 and cost of goods sold is $6,200. The observation is always true: the FIFO method yields the same results for both the periodic and perpetual systems. Regardless of the system, the first costs in are the costs assigned to cost of goods sold.

Last-In, First-Out (LIFO)

Under the LIFO method using a perpetual system, the company charges to cost of goods sold the cost of the most recent purchase **prior** to the sale. Therefore, the cost of the goods sold on September 10 consists of all the units from the August 24 and April 15 purchases plus 50 of the units in beginning inventory. **Illustration 6A.3** shows the computation of the ending inventory under the LIFO method.

ILLUSTRATION 6A.3

Perpetual system—LIFO

Date	Purchases		Cost of Goods Sold	Inventory Balance (in units and cost)	
January 1				(100 @ $10)	$1,000
April 15	(200 @ $11)	$2,200		(100 @ $10) (200 @ $11)	$3,200
August 24	(300 @ $12)	$3,600		(100 @ $10) (200 @ $11) (300 @ $12)	$6,800
September 10			(300 @ $12) (200 @ $11) (50 @ $10)	(50 @ $10)	$ 500
			$6,300		⟶ Cost of goods sold
November 27	(400 @ $13)	$5,200		(50 @ $10) (400 @ $13)	$5,700 ⟶ Ending inventory

The use of LIFO in a perpetual system will usually produce cost allocations that differ from those using LIFO in a periodic system. In a perpetual system, the latest units purchased **prior to each sale** are allocated to cost of goods sold. In contrast, in a periodic system, the latest units purchased **during the period** are allocated to cost of goods sold. Thus, when a purchase is made after the last sale, the LIFO method under the periodic system will apply this purchase to the period's sales. See Illustration 6.9, which shows the proof that the 400 units at $13 purchased on November 27 applied to the sale of 550 units on September 10.

Under the LIFO perpetual system in Illustration 6A.3, the 400 units at $13 purchased on November 27 are all allocated to the ending inventory. The ending inventory in this LIFO perpetual illustration is $5,700, and cost of goods sold is $6,300, as compared to the LIFO periodic Illustration 6.8, where the ending inventory is $5,000 and cost of goods sold is $7,000.

Average-Cost

The average-cost method in a perpetual inventory system is called the **moving-average method**. Under this method, the company computes a new weighted-average unit cost **after each purchase**, by dividing the cost of goods available for sale by the units on hand. The weighted-average unit cost is then applied to (1) the units sold, to determine the cost of goods sold, and (2) the remaining units on hand, to determine the ending inventory cost. **Illustration 6A.4** shows the application of the moving-average cost method by Houston Electronics (computations of the moving-average unit cost are shown after Illustration 6A.4).

ILLUSTRATION 6A.4

Perpetual system—moving-average method

Date	Purchases		Cost of Goods Sold	Inventory Balance (in units and cost)	
January 1				(100 @ $10)	$1,000
April 15	(200 @ $11)	$2,200		(300 @ $10.667)	$3,200
August 24	(300 @ $12)	$3,600		(600 @ $11.333)	$6,800
September 10			(550 @ $11.333)	(50 @ $11.333)	$ 567
			$6,233		
November 27	(400 @ $13)	$5,200		(450 @ $12.816)	**$5,767**

Cost of goods sold

Ending inventory

As indicated, Houston Electronics computes **a new weighted-average unit cost each time it makes a purchase**.

1. On April 15, after Houston buys 200 units for $2,200, a total of 300 units costing $3,200 ($1,000 + $2,200) are on hand. The weighted-average unit cost is $10.667 ($3,200 ÷ 300).

2. On August 24, after Houston buys 300 units for $3,600, a total of 600 units costing $6,800 ($1,000 + $2,200 + $3,600) are on hand. The weighted-average unit cost is $11.333 ($6,800 ÷ 600).

3. On September 10, to compute cost of goods sold, Houston uses this unit cost of $11.333 in costing the units sold until it makes another purchase, at which time the company computes a new unit cost. Accordingly, the unit cost of the 550 units sold on September 10 is $11.333, and the total cost of goods sold is $6,233.

4. On November 27, following the purchase of 400 units for $5,200, there are 450 units on hand costing $5,767 ($567 + $5,200) with a new weighted-average unit cost of $12.816 ($5,767 ÷ 450).

Compare this moving-average cost under the perpetual inventory system to Illustration 6.11, which shows the average-cost method under a periodic inventory system.

Appendix 6B

Estimating Inventories

LEARNING OBJECTIVE *6

Describe the two methods of estimating inventories.

In the chapter, we assumed that a company would be able to physically count its inventory. What if it cannot? What if the inventory were destroyed by fire or flood, for example? In that case, the company would use an estimate to determine the cost of the lost inventory.

Two circumstances explain why companies sometimes estimate inventories. First, a casualty such as fire, flood, or earthquake may make it impossible to take a physical inventory. Second, managers may want monthly or quarterly financial statements, but a physical inventory is taken only annually. The need for estimating inventories occurs primarily with a periodic inventory system because of the absence of perpetual inventory records.

There are two widely used methods of estimating inventories: (1) the gross profit method, and (2) the retail inventory method.

Gross Profit Method

The **gross profit method** estimates the cost of ending inventory by applying a gross profit rate to net sales. This method is relatively simple but effective. Accountants, auditors, and managers frequently use the gross profit method to test the reasonableness of the ending inventory amount. It will detect large errors.

To use this method, a company needs to know its net sales, cost of goods available for sale, and gross profit rate. The company then can estimate its gross profit for the period. **Illustration 6B.1** shows the formulas for using the gross profit method.

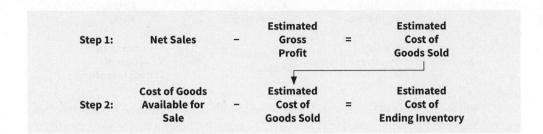

To illustrate, assume that Kishwaukee Company wishes to prepare an income statement for the month of January. Its records show net sales of $200,000, beginning inventory $40,000, and cost of goods purchased $120,000. In the preceding year, the company realized a 30% gross profit rate. It expects to earn the same rate this year. Given these facts and assumptions, Kishwaukee can compute the estimated cost of the ending inventory at January 31 under the gross profit method as shown in **Illustration 6B.2**.

Step 1:

Net sales	$200,000
Less: Estimated gross profit (30% × $200,000)	60,000
Estimated cost of goods sold	**$140,000**

Step 2:

Beginning inventory	$ 40,000
Cost of goods purchased	120,000
Cost of goods available for sale	160,000
Less: Estimated cost of goods sold	140,000
Estimated cost of ending inventory	**$ 20,000**

The gross profit method is based on the assumption that the gross profit rate will remain constant. But, it may not remain constant, due to a change in merchandising policies or in market conditions. In such cases, the company should adjust the rate to reflect current operating conditions. In some cases, companies can obtain a more accurate estimate by applying this method on a department or product-line basis.

Note that companies should not use the gross profit method to prepare financial statements at the end of the year. These statements should be based on a physical inventory count.

Retail Inventory Method

A retail store such as **Home Depot**, **Ace Hardware**, or **Walmart** has thousands of different types of merchandise at low unit costs. In such cases, it is difficult and time-consuming to apply unit costs to inventory quantities. An alternative is to use the **retail inventory method** to estimate the cost of inventory. Most retail companies can establish a relationship between cost and sales price. The company then applies the cost-to-retail percentage to the ending inventory at retail prices to determine inventory at cost.

Under the retail inventory method, a company's records must show both the cost and retail value of the goods available for sale. **Illustration 6B.3** presents the formulas for using the retail inventory method.

ILLUSTRATION 6B.3
Retail inventory method
formulas

Step 1:	Goods Available for Sale at Retail	−	Net Sales	=	Ending Inventory at Retail	
Step 2:	Goods Available for Sale at Cost	÷	Goods Available for Sale at Retail	=	Cost-to-Retail Ratio	
Step 3:	Ending Inventory at Retail	×	Cost-to-Retail Ratio	=	Estimated Cost of Ending Inventory	

We can demonstrate the logic of the retail method by using unit-cost data. Assume that Ortiz Inc. has marked 10 units purchased at $7 to sell for $10 per unit. Thus, the cost-to-retail ratio is 70% ($70 ÷ $100). If four units remain unsold, their retail value is $40 (4 × $10), and their cost is $28 ($40 × 70%). This amount agrees with the total cost of goods on hand on a per unit basis (4 × $7).

Illustration 6B.4 shows application of the retail method for Valley West. Note that it is not necessary to take a physical inventory to determine the estimated cost of goods on hand at any given time.

ILLUSTRATION 6B.4
Application of retail inventory
method

	At Cost	At Retail
Beginning inventory	$14,000	$ 21,500
Goods purchased	61,000	78,500
Goods available for sale	$75,000	100,000
Less: Net sales		70,000
Step (1) Ending inventory at retail =		**$ 30,000**

Step (2) Cost-to-retail ratio = $75,000 ÷ $100,000 = 75%
Step (3) Estimated cost of ending inventory = $30,000 × 75% = $22,500

HELPFUL HINT
In determining inventory at retail, companies use selling prices of the units.

The retail inventory method also facilitates taking the inventory at the end of an accounting period. Valley West can value the goods on hand at the prices marked on the merchandise, and then apply the cost-to-retail ratio to the goods on hand at retail to determine the ending inventory at cost (see **Helpful Hint**).

The major disadvantage of the retail method is that it is an averaging technique. Thus, it may produce an incorrect inventory valuation if the mix of the ending inventory is not representative of the mix in the goods available for sale. Assume, for example, that the cost-to-retail ratio of 75% for Valley West consists of equal proportions of inventory items that have cost-to-retail ratios of 70%, 75%, and 80%. If the ending inventory contains only items with a 70% ratio, an incorrect inventory cost will result. Companies can minimize this problem by applying the retail method on a department or product-line basis.

Review and Practice

Learning Objectives Review

1 Discuss how to classify and determine inventory.

Merchandisers need only one inventory classification, merchandise inventory, to describe the different items that make up total inventory. Manufacturers, on the other hand, usually classify inventory into three categories: finished goods, work in process, and raw materials. To determine inventory quantities, companies (1) take a physical inventory of goods on hand and (2) determine the ownership of goods in transit or on consignment.

2 Apply inventory cost flow methods and discuss their financial effects.

The primary basis of accounting for inventories is cost. Cost of goods available for sale includes (a) cost of beginning inventory and (b) cost of goods purchased. The inventory cost flow methods are specific identification and three assumed cost flow methods—FIFO, LIFO, and average-cost.

When costs are rising, the first-in, first-out (FIFO) method results in lower cost of goods sold and higher net income than the other methods. The last-in, first-out (LIFO) method results in the lowest income taxes. The reverse is true when costs are falling. In the balance sheet, FIFO results in an ending inventory that is closest to current value. Inventory under LIFO is the farthest from current value.

3   Indicate the effects of inventory errors on the financial statements.

In the income statement of the current year: (a) If beginning inventory is understated, net income is overstated. The reverse occurs if beginning inventory is overstated. (b) If ending inventory is overstated, net income is overstated. If ending inventory is understated, net income is understated. In the following period, its effect on net income for that period is reversed, and total net income for the two years will be correct.

In the balance sheet: Ending inventory errors will have the same effect on total assets and total stockholders' equity and no effect on liabilities.

4   Explain the statement presentation and analysis of inventory.

Inventory is classified in the balance sheet as a current asset immediately below accounts receivable. There also should be disclosure in the notes for (1) the major inventory classifications, (2) the basis of accounting, and (3) the cost method.

Companies use the lower-of-cost-or-net realizable value (LCNRV) basis when the net realizable value is less than cost. Under LCNRV, companies recognize the loss in the period in which the cost decline occurs.

The inventory turnover is cost of goods sold divided by average inventory. To convert it to average days in inventory, divide 365 days by the inventory turnover.

*5   Apply the inventory cost flow methods to perpetual inventory records.

Under FIFO and a perpetual inventory system, companies charge to cost of goods sold the cost of the earliest goods on hand prior to each sale. Under LIFO and a perpetual system, companies charge to cost of goods sold the cost of the most recent purchase prior to sale. Under the moving-average (average-cost) method and a perpetual system, companies compute a new weighted-average unit cost after each purchase.

*6   Describe the two methods of estimating inventories.

The two methods of estimating inventories are the gross profit method and the retail inventory method. Under the gross profit method, companies apply a gross profit rate to net sales to determine estimated cost of goods sold. They then subtract estimated cost of goods sold from cost of goods available for sale to determine the estimated cost of the ending inventory.

Under the retail inventory method, companies compute a cost-to-retail ratio by dividing the cost of goods available for sale by the retail value of the goods available for sale. They then apply this ratio to the ending inventory at retail to determine the estimated cost of the ending inventory.

Glossary Review

Average-cost method   Inventory costing method that uses the weighted-average unit cost to allocate to ending inventory and cost of goods sold the cost of goods available for sale. (p. 6-12).

Consigned goods   Goods held for sale by one party although ownership of the goods is retained by another party. (p. 6-6).

Consistency concept   Dictates that a company use the same accounting principles and methods from year to year. (p. 6-15).

Days in inventory   Measure of the average number of days inventory is held; calculated as 365 divided by inventory turnover. (p. 6-20).

Finished goods inventory   Manufactured items that are completed and ready for sale. (p. 6-3).

First-in, first-out (FIFO) method   Inventory costing method that assumes that the costs of the earliest goods purchased are the first to be recognized as cost of goods sold. (p. 6-9).

FOB (free on board) destination   Freight terms indicating that ownership of the goods remains with the seller until the goods reach the buyer. (p. 6-5).

FOB (free on board) shipping point   Freight terms indicating that ownership of the goods passes to the buyer when the public carrier accepts the goods from the seller. (p. 6-5).

*****Gross profit method**   A method for estimating the cost of the ending inventory by applying a gross profit rate to net sales and subtracting estimated cost of goods sold from cost of goods available for sale. (p. 6-24).

Inventory turnover   A ratio that measures the number of times on average the inventory sold during the period; computed by dividing cost of goods sold by the average inventory during the period. (p. 6-20).

Just-in-time (JIT) inventory   Inventory system in which companies manufacture or purchase goods only when needed for use. (p. 6-3).

Last-in, first-out (LIFO) method   Inventory costing method that assumes the costs of the latest units purchased are the first to be allocated to cost of goods sold. (p. 6-10).

Lower-of-cost-or-net realizable value (LCNRV)   A basis whereby inventory is stated at the lower of either its cost or its net realizable value. (p. 6-19).

*****Moving-average method**   Inventory costing method in which a new weighted-average unit cost is computed after each purchase, by dividing the cost of goods available for sale by the units on hand. (p. 6-23).

Net realizable value   Net amount that a company expects to realize (receive) from the sale of inventory. Specifically, it is the estimated selling price in the normal course of business, less estimated costs to complete and sell. (p. 6-19)

Raw materials   Basic goods that will be used in production but have not yet been placed into production. (p. 6-3).

*****Retail inventory method**   A method for estimating the cost of the ending inventory by applying a cost-to-retail ratio to the ending inventory at retail. (p. 6-25).

Specific identification method   An actual physical flow costing method in which items still in inventory are specifically tracked and costed to arrive at the total cost of the ending inventory. (p. 6-7).

Weighted-average unit cost   Average cost that is weighted by the number of units purchased at each unit cost. (p. 6-12).

Work in process   That portion of manufactured inventory that has been placed into the production process but is not yet complete. (p. 6-3).

Practice Multiple-Choice Questions

1. **(LO 1)** When is a physical inventory usually taken?

   a. When the company has its greatest amount of inventory.

   b. When a limited number of goods are being sold or received.

   c. At the end of the company's fiscal year.

   d. Both when a limited number of goods are being sold or received, and at the end of the company's fiscal year.

2. **(LO 1)** Which of the following should **not** be included in the physical inventory of a company?

   a. Goods held on consignment from another company.

   b. Goods shipped on consignment to another company.

   c. Goods in transit from another company shipped FOB shipping point.

   d. None of the answer choices is correct.

3. **(LO 1)** As a result of a thorough physical inventory, Railway Company determined that it had inventory of $180,000 at December 31, 2022. This count did not take into consideration the following facts: Rogers Consignment Store currently has goods worth $35,000 on its sales floor that belong to Railway but are being sold on consignment by Rogers. The selling price of these goods is $50,000. Railway purchased $13,000 of goods that were shipped on December 27, FOB destination, that will be received by Railway on January 3. Determine the correct amount of inventory that Railway should report.

   a. $230,000.

   b. $215,000.

   c. $228,000.

   d. $193,000.

4. **(LO 2)** Cost of goods available for sale consists of two elements: beginning inventory and:

   a. ending inventory.

   b. cost of goods purchased.

   c. cost of goods sold.

   d. All of the answer choices are correct.

5. **(LO 2)** Kam Company has the following:

	Units	Unit Cost
Inventory, Jan. 1	8,000	$11
Purchase, June 19	13,000	12
Purchase, Nov. 8	5,000	13

   If 9,000 units are on hand at December 31, the cost of the ending inventory under FIFO is:

   a. $99,000.

   b. $108,000.

   c. $113,000.

   d. $117,000.

6. **(LO 2)** Kam Company has the following:

	Units	Unit Cost
Inventory, Jan. 1	8,000	$11
Purchase, June 19	13,000	12
Purchase, Nov. 8	5,000	13

   If 9,000 units are on hand, the cost of the ending inventory under LIFO is:

   a. $113,000.

   b. $108,000.

   c. $99,000.

   d. $100,000.

7. **(LO 2)** Davidson Electronics has the following:

	Units	Unit Cost
Inventory, Jan. 1	5,000	$ 8
Purchase, April 2	15,000	$10
Purchase, Aug. 28	20,000	$12

   If Davidson has 7,000 units on hand at December 31, the cost of ending inventory under the average-cost method is:

   a. $84,000.

   b. $70,000.

   c. $56,000.

   d. $75,250.

8. **(LO 2)** In periods of rising costs, LIFO will produce:

   a. higher net income than FIFO.

   b. the same net income as FIFO.

   c. lower net income than FIFO.

   d. higher net income than average-cost.

9. **(LO 2)** Considerations that affect the selection of an inventory costing method do **not** include:

   a. tax effects.

   b. balance sheet effects.

   c. income statement effects.

   d. perpetual vs. periodic inventory system.

10. **(LO 3)** Fran Company's ending inventory is understated $4,000. The effects of this error on the current year's cost of goods sold and net income, respectively, are:

    a. understated, overstated.

    b. overstated, understated.

    c. overstated, overstated.

    d. understated, understated.

11. **(LO 3)** Harold Company overstated its ending inventory by $15,000 at December 31, 2021. It did not correct the error in 2021 or 2022. As a result, Harold's stockholders' equity was:

    a. overstated at December 31, 2021, and understated at December 31, 2022.

    b. overstated at December 31, 2021, and properly stated at December 31, 2022.

    c. understated at December 31, 2021, and understated at December 31, 2022.

    d. overstated at December 31, 2021, and overstated at December 31, 2022.

12. **(LO 4)** The lower-of-cost-or-net realizable value rule for inventory is an example of the application of:

    a. the conservatism convention.

    b. the historical cost principle.

    c. the materiality concept.

    d. the economics entity assumption.

13. **(LO 4)** Norton Company purchased 1,000 widgets and has 200 widgets in its ending inventory at a cost of $91 each and a net realizable value of $80 each. The ending inventory under lower-of-cost-or-net realizable value is:

    a. $91,000.

    b. $80,000.

    c. $18,200.

    d. $16,000.

14. (LO 4) Carlos Company had beginning inventory of $80,000, ending inventory of $110,000, cost of goods sold of $285,000, and sales of $475,000. Carlos's days in inventory is:

a. 73 days.

c. 102.5 days.

b. 121.7 days.

d. 84.5 days.

15. (LO 4) Which of these would cause the inventory turnover to increase the most?

a. Increasing the amount of inventory on hand.

b. Keeping the amount of inventory on hand constant but increasing sales.

c. Keeping the amount of inventory on hand constant but decreasing sales.

d. Decreasing the amount of inventory on hand and increasing sales.

*16. (LO 5) In a perpetual inventory system:

a. LIFO cost of goods sold will be the same as in a periodic inventory system.

b. average costs are a simple average of unit costs incurred.

c. a new average is computed under the average-cost method after each sale.

d. FIFO cost of goods sold will be the same as in a periodic inventory system.

*17. (LO 6) King Company has sales of $150,000 and cost of goods available for sale of $135,000. If the gross profit rate is 30%, the estimated cost of the ending inventory under the gross profit method is:

a. $15,000.

c. $45,000.

b. $30,000.

d. $75,000.

Solutions

1. d. A physical inventory is usually taken when a limited number of goods are being sold or received, and at the end of the company's fiscal year. Choice (a) is incorrect because a physical inventory count is usually taken when the company has the least, not greatest, amount of inventory. Choices (b) and (c) are correct, but (d) is the better answer.

2. a. Goods held on consignment should not be included because another company has title (ownership) to the goods. The other choices are incorrect because (b) goods shipped on consignment to another company and (c) goods in transit from another company shipped FOB shipping point should be included in a company's ending inventory. Choice (d) is incorrect because (a) is not included in the physical inventory.

3. b. The inventory held on consignment by Rogers should be included in Railway's inventory balance at cost ($35,000). The purchased goods of $13,000 should not be included in inventory until January 3 because the goods are shipped FOB destination. Therefore, the correct amount of inventory is $215,000 ($180,000 + $35,000), not (a) $230,000, (c) $228,000, or (d) $193,000.

4. b. Cost of goods available for sale consists of beginning inventory and cost of goods purchased, not (a) ending inventory or (c) cost of goods sold. Therefore, choice (d) is also incorrect.

5. c. Under FIFO, ending inventory will consist of 5,000 units from the Nov. 8 purchase and 4,000 units from the June 19 purchase. Therefore, ending inventory is (5,000 × $13) + (4,000 × $12) = $113,000, not (a) $99,000, (b) $108,000, or (d) $117,000.

6. d. Under LIFO, ending inventory will consist of 8,000 units from the inventory at Jan. 1 and 1,000 units from the June 19 purchase. Therefore, ending inventory is (8,000 × $11) + (1,000 × $12) = $100,000, not (a) $113,000, (b) $108,000, or (c) $99,000.

7. d. Under the average-cost method, total cost of goods available for sale needs to be calculated in order to determine the weighted-average unit cost. The total cost of goods available is $430,000 = (5,000 × $8) + (15,000 × $10) + (20,000 × $12). The weighted-average unit cost = ($430,000 ÷ 40,000 total units available for sale) = $10.75. Therefore, ending inventory is ($10.75 × 7,000) = $75,250, not (a) $84,000, (b) $70,000, or (c) $56,000.

8. c. In periods of rising costs, LIFO will produce lower net income than FIFO, not (a) higher than FIFO or (b) the same as FIFO. Choice

(d) is incorrect because in periods of rising costs, LIFO will produce lower net income than average-cost. LIFO therefore charges the highest inventory cost against revenues in a period of rising costs.

9. d. Perpetual vs. periodic inventory system is not one of the factors that affect the selection of an inventory costing method. The other choices are incorrect because (a) tax effects, (b) balance sheet effects, and (c) income statement effects all affect the selection of an inventory costing method.

10. b. Because ending inventory is too low, cost of goods sold will be too high (overstated) and since cost of goods sold (an expense) is too high, net income will be too low (understated). Therefore, the other choices are incorrect.

11. b. Stockholders' equity is overstated by $15,000 at December 31, 2021, and is properly stated at December 31, 2022. An ending inventory error in one period will have an equal and opposite effect on cost of goods sold and net income in the next period; after two years, the errors have offset each other. The other choices are incorrect because stockholders' equity (a) is properly stated, not understated, at December 31, 2022; (c) is overstated, not understated, by $15,000 at December 31, 2021, and is properly stated, not understated, at December 31, 2022; and (d) is properly stated at December 31, 2022, not overstated.

12. a. Conservatism means to use the lowest value for assets and revenues when in doubt. The other choices are incorrect because (b) historical cost means that companies value assets at the original cost, (c) materiality means that an amount is large enough to affect a decision-maker, and (d) economic entity means to keep the company's transactions separate from the transactions of other entities.

13. d. Under the LCNRV basis, inventory is reported at lower-of-cost-or-net realizable value. Therefore, ending inventory would be valued at 200 widgets × $80 each = $16,000 not (a) $91,000, (b) $80,000, or (c) $18,200.

14. b. Carlos's days in inventory = 365 ÷ Inventory turnover = 365 ÷ {$285,000 ÷ [($80,000 + $110,000) ÷ 2]} = 121.7 days, not (a) 73 days, (c) 102.5 days, or (d) 84.5 days.

15. d. Decreasing the amount of inventory on hand will cause the denominator to decrease, causing inventory turnover to increase. Increasing sales will cause the numerator of the ratio to increase (higher sales means higher COGS), thus causing inventory turnover to increase even more. The other choices are incorrect because (a) increasing the amount of inventory on hand causes the denominator of the ratio to increase while the numerator stays the same, causing inventory turnover to decrease; (b) keeping the amount of inventory on hand constant but increasing sales will cause inventory turnover to increase because the numerator of the ratio will increase (higher sales means higher COGS) while the denominator stays the same, which will result in a lesser inventory increase than decreasing amount of inventory on hand and increasing sales; and (c) keeping the amount of inventory on hand constant but decreasing sales will cause inventory turnover to decrease because the numerator of the ratio will decrease (lower sales means lower COGS) while the denominator stays the same.

*16. **d.** FIFO cost of goods sold is the same under both a periodic and a perpetual inventory system. The other choices are incorrect because (a) LIFO cost of goods sold is not the same under a periodic and a perpetual inventory system; (b) average costs are based on a moving average of unit costs, not an average of unit costs; and (c) a new average is computed under the average-cost method after each purchase, not sale.

*17. **b.** COGS = Sales ($150,000) – Gross profit ($150,000 × 30%) = $105,000. Ending inventory = Cost of goods available for sale ($135,000) – COGS ($105,000) = $30,000, not (a) $15,000, (c) $45,000, or (d) $75,000.

Practice Brief Exercises

Determine ending inventory amount.

1. (LO 1) Fylus Company took a physical inventory on December 31 and determined that goods costing $180,000 were on hand. Not included in the physical count were $18,000 of goods purchased from Rake Corporation, FOB destination, and $27,000 of goods sold to Shovel Company for $40,000, FOB destination. Both the Rake purchase and the Shovel sale were in transit at year-end. What amount should Fylus report as its December 31 inventory?

Solution

1.
Physical inventory	$180,000
Add: Goods sold to Shovel	27,000
Fylus ending inventory	$207,000

The $18,000 of goods purchased from Rake are excluded from ending inventory because the terms are FOB destination, which means Fylus takes title at the time the goods are received. Goods sold to Shovel FOB destination means that the goods are still Fylus's until delivered.

Compute ending inventory using FIFO and LIFO.

2. (LO 2) In its first month of operations, Moncada Company made three purchases of merchandise in the following sequence: (1) 200 units at $7, (2) 300 units at $8, and (3) 150 units at $9. Assuming there are 220 units on hand, compute the cost of the ending inventory under the (a) FIFO method and (b) LIFO method. Moncada use a periodic inventory system.

Solution

2. **a.** The ending inventory under FIFO consists of (150 units at $9) + (70 units at $8) for a total allocation of $1,910 ($1,350 + $560).

   b. The ending inventory under LIFO consists of (200 units at $7) + (20 units at $8) for a total allocation of $1,560 ($1,400 + $160).

Compute inventory turnover and days in inventory.

3. (LO 4) At December 31, 2022, the following information was available for Garcia Company: ending inventory $30,000, beginning inventory $42,000, cost of goods sold $240,000, and sales revenue $400,000. Calculate inventory turnover and days in inventory for Garcia Company.

Solution

3. Inventory turnover: $\dfrac{\$240,000}{(\$30,000 + \$42,000) \div 2} = \dfrac{\$240,000}{\$36,000} = 6.67$

Days in inventory: $\dfrac{365}{6.67} = 54.7$ days

Practice Exercises

1. **(LO 1)** Mika Sorbino, an auditor with Martinez CPAs, is performing a review of Sergei Company's inventory account. Sergei's did not have a good year and top management is under pressure to boost reported income. According to its records, the inventory balance at year-end was $650,000. However, the following information was not considered when determining that amount.

Determine the correct inventory amount.

1. Included in the company's count were goods with a cost of $200,000 that the company is holding on consignment. The goods belong to Bosnia Corporation.

2. The physical count did not include goods purchased by Sergei with a cost of $40,000 that were shipped FOB shipping point on December 28 and did not arrive at Sergei's warehouse until January 3.

3. Included in the inventory account was $15,000 of office supplies that were stored in the warehouse and were to be used by the company's supervisors and managers during the coming year.

4. The company received an order on December 28 that was boxed and was sitting on the loading dock awaiting pick-up on December 31. The shipper picked up the goods on January 1 and delivered them on January 6. The shipping terms were FOB shipping point. The goods had a selling price of $40,000 and a cost of $30,000. The goods were not included in the count because they were sitting on the dock.

5. On December 29, Sergei shipped goods with a selling price of $80,000 and a cost of $60,000 to Oman Sales Corporation FOB shipping point. The goods arrived on January 3. Oman Sales had only ordered goods with a selling price of $10,000 and a cost of $8,000. However, a Sergei's sales manager had authorized the shipment and said that if Oman wanted to ship the goods back next week, it could.

6. Included in the count was $30,000 of goods that were parts for a machine that the company no longer made. Given the high-tech nature of Sergei's products, it was unlikely that these obsolete parts had any other use. However, management would prefer to keep them on the books at cost, "since that is what we paid for them, after all."

Instructions

Prepare a schedule to determine the correct inventory amount. Provide explanations for each item above, saying why you did or did not make an adjustment for each item.

Solution

1. Ending inventory—as reported	$650,000
1. Subtract from inventory: The goods belong to Bosnia Corporation. Sergei is merely holding them for Bosnia.	(200,000)
2. Add to inventory: The goods belonged to Sergei when they were shipped.	40,000
3. Subtract from inventory: Office supplies should be carried in a separate account. They are not considered inventory held for resale.	(15,000)
4. Add to inventory: The goods belong to Sergei until they are shipped (Jan. 1).	30,000
5. Add to inventory: Oman Sales ordered goods with a cost of $8,000. Sergei should record the corresponding sales revenue of $10,000. Sergei's decision to ship extra "unordered" goods does not constitute a sale. The manager's statement that Oman could ship the goods back indicates that Sergei knows this overshipment is not a legitimate sale. The manager acted unethically in an attempt to improve Sergei's reported income by overshipping.	52,000
6. Subtract from inventory: GAAP requires that inventory be valued at the lower-of-cost-or-net realizable value. Obsolete parts should be adjusted from cost to zero if they have no other use.	(30,000)
Correct inventory	$527,000

Determine effects of inventory errors.

2. (LO 3) Abel's Hardware reported cost of goods sold as follows.

	2021	2022
Beginning inventory	$ 20,000	$ 30,000
Cost of goods purchased	150,000	175,000
Cost of goods available for sale	170,000	205,000
Less: Ending inventory	30,000	35,000
Cost of goods sold	$140,000	$170,000

Abel's made two errors: (1) 2021 ending inventory was overstated $2,500, and (2) 2022 ending inventory was understated $5,500.

Instructions

Compute the correct cost of goods sold for each year.

Solution

2.

	2021	2022
Beginning inventory	$ 20,000	$ 27,500
Cost of goods purchased	150,000	175,000
Cost of goods available for sale	170,000	202,500
Less: Corrected ending inventory	27,500[a]	40,500[b]
Cost of goods sold	$142,500	$162,000

[a]$30,000 − $2,500 = $27,500; [b]$35,000 + $5,500 = $40,500

Determine LCNRV valuation.

3. (LO 4) Creve Couer Camera Inc. uses the lower-of-cost-or-net realizable value basis for its inventory. The following data are available at December 31.

	Units	Cost per Unit	Net Realizable Value per Unit
Cameras:			
Minolta	5	$160	$156
Canon	7	145	153
Light Meters:			
Vivitar	12	120	114
Kodak	10	130	142

Instructions

What amount should be reported for inventory on Creve Couer Camera's financial statements, assuming the lower-of-cost-or-net realizable value rule is applied?

Solution

3.

	Cost per Unit	Net Realizable Value per Unit	Lower-of-Cost or-Net Realizable Value	Units	Inventory at Lower-of-Cost-or-Net Realizable Value
Cameras:					
Minolta	$160	$156	$156	5	$ 780
Canon	145	153	145	7	1,015
Light Meters:					
Vivitar	120	114	114	12	1,368
Kodak	130	142	130	10	1,300
Total					$4,463

Practice Problems

1. (LO 2) Englehart Company has the following inventory, purchases, and sales data for the month of March.

Compute inventory and cost of goods sold using three cost flow methods in a periodic inventory system.

Inventory:	March 1	200 units @ $4.00	$ 800
Purchases:	March 10	500 units @ $4.50	2,250
	March 20	400 units @ $4.75	1,900
	March 30	300 units @ $5.00	1,500
Sales:	March 15	500 units	
	March 25	400 units	

The physical inventory count on March 31 shows 500 units on hand.

Instructions

Under a **periodic inventory system**, determine the cost of inventory on hand at March 31 and the cost of goods sold for March under (a) FIFO, (b) LIFO, and (c) average-cost. (For average-cost, carry weighted-average unit cost to three decimal places.)

Solution

1. The cost of goods available for sale is $6,450, as follows.

Inventory:		200 units @ $4.00	$ 800
Purchases:	March 10	500 units @ $4.50	2,250
	March 20	400 units @ $4.75	1,900
	March 30	300 units @ $5.00	1,500
	Total goods available for sale		$6,450

a.   **FIFO Method**

Ending inventory:

Date	Units	Unit Cost	Total Cost	
March 30	300	$5.00	$1,500	
March 20	200	4.75	950	$2,450
	Cost of goods sold: $6,450 – $2,450 =			$4,000

b.   **LIFO Method**

Ending inventory:

Date	Units	Unit Cost	Total Cost	
March 1	200	$4.00	$ 800	
March 10	300	4.50	1,350	$2,150
	Cost of goods sold: $6,450 – $2,150 =			$4,300

c.   **Average-Cost Method**

Weighted-average unit cost: $6,450 ÷ 1,400 = $4.607

Ending inventory: 500 × $4.607 =	$2,303.50
Cost of goods sold: $6,450 – $2,303.50 =	$4,146.50

*2. (LO 5) Practice Problem 1 showed cost of goods sold computations under a periodic inventory system. Now let's assume that Englehart Company uses a perpetual inventory system. The company has the same inventory, purchases, and sales data for the month of March as shown earlier:

Compute inventory and cost of goods sold using three cost flow methods in a perpetual inventory system.

Inventory:	March 1	200 units @ $4.00	$ 800
Purchases:	March 10	500 units @ $4.50	2,250
	March 20	400 units @ $4.75	1,900
	March 30	300 units @ $5.00	1,500
Sales:	March 15	500 units	
	March 25	400 units	

The physical inventory count on March 31 shows 500 units on hand.

Instructions

Under a **perpetual inventory system**, determine the cost of inventory on hand at March 31 and the cost of goods sold for March under (a) FIFO, (b) LIFO, and (c) moving-average cost.

Solution

2. The cost of goods available for sale at March 31 is $6,450, as follows.

Inventory:		200 units @ $4.00	$ 800
Purchases:	March 10	500 units @ $4.50	2,250
	March 20	400 units @ $4.75	1,900
	March 30	300 units @ $5.00	1,500
	Total:	1,400	$6,450

Under a **perpetual inventory system**, the cost of goods sold under each cost flow method is as follows.

a.

FIFO Method

Date	Purchases	Cost of Goods Sold	Inventory Balance
March 1			(200 @ $4.00) $ 800
March 10	(500 @ $4.50) $2,250		(200 @ $4.00) (500 @ $4.50) }$3,050
March 15		(200 @ $4.00) (300 @ $4.50) —————— $2,150	(200 @ $4.50) $ 900
March 20	(400 @ $4.75) $1,900		(200 @ $4.50) (400 @ $4.75) }$2,800
March 25		(200 @ $4.50) (200 @ $4.75) —————— $1,850	(200 @ $4.75) $ 950
March 30	(300 @ $5.00) $1,500		(200 @ $4.75) (300 @ $5.00) }$2,450
Ending inventory $2,450		Cost of goods sold: $2,150 + $1,850 = $4,000	

b.

LIFO Method

Date	Purchases	Cost of Goods Sold	Inventory Balance
March 1			(200 @ $4.00) $ 800
March 10	(500 @ $4.50) $2,250		(200 @ $4.00) (500 @ $4.50) }$3,050
March 15		(500 @ $4.50) $2,250	(200 @ $4.00) $ 800
March 20	(400 @ $4.75) $1,900		(200 @ $4.00) (400 @ $4.75) }$2,700
March 25		(400 @ $4.75) $1,900	(200 @ $4.00) $ 800
March 30	(300 @ $5.00) $1,500		(200 @ $4.00) (300 @ $5.00) }$2,300
Ending inventory $2,300		Cost of goods sold: $2,250 + $1,900 = $4,150	

c.

Moving-Average Cost Method

Date	Purchases	Cost of Goods Sold	Inventory Balance
March 1			(200 @ $ 4.00) $ 800
March 10	(500 @ $4.50) $2,250		(700 @ $4.357) $3,050
March 15		(500 @ $4.357) $2,179	(200 @ $4.357) $ 871
March 20	(400 @ $4.75) $1,900		(600 @ $4.618) $2,771
March 25		(400 @ $4.618) $1,847	(200 @ $4.618) $ 924
March 30	(300 @ $5.00) $1,500		(500 @ $4.848) $2,424
Ending inventory $2,424		Cost of goods sold: $2,179 + $1,847 = $4,026	

WileyPLUS

Brief Exercises, DO IT! Exercises, Exercises, Problems, and many additional resources are available for practice in WileyPLUS.

Note: All asterisked Questions, Exercises, and Problems relate to material in the appendices to the chapter.

Questions

1. "The key to successful business operations is effective inventory management." Do you agree? Explain.

2. An item must possess two characteristics to be classified as inventory by a merchandiser. What are these two characteristics?

3. Your friend Wil Juritz has been hired to help take the physical inventory in Byrd's Hardware Store. Explain to Wil what this job will entail.

4. **a.** Bonita Company ships merchandise to Myan Company on December 30. The merchandise reaches the buyer on January 6. Indicate the terms of sale that will result in the goods being included in (1) Bonita's December 31 inventory, and (2) Myan's December 31 inventory.

   b. Under what circumstances should Bonita Company include consigned goods in its inventory?

5. Nona Hat Shop received a shipment of hats for which it paid the wholesaler $2,970. The price of the hats was $3,000, but Nona was given a $30 cash discount and required to pay freight charges of $50. What amount should Nona record for inventory? Why?

6. Explain the difference between the terms FOB shipping point and FOB destination.

7. Ken McCall believes that the allocation of cost of goods available for sale should be based on the actual physical flow of the goods. Explain to Ken why this may be both impractical and inappropriate.

8. What is the major advantage and major disadvantage of the specific identification method of inventory costing?

9. "The selection of an inventory cost flow method is a decision made by accountants." Explain why this statement is true or false. Once a method has been selected, what accounting requirement applies?

10. Which assumed inventory cost flow method:

   a. usually coincides with the actual physical flow of merchandise?

   b. divides cost of goods available for sale by total units available for sale to determine a unit cost?

   c. assumes that the latest units purchased are the first to be sold?

11. In a period of rising costs, the inventory reported in Short Company's balance sheet is close to the current cost of the inventory, whereas King Company's inventory is considerably below its current cost. Identify the inventory cost flow method being used by each company. Which company probably has been reporting the higher gross profit?

12. Mamosa Corporation has been using the FIFO cost flow method during a prolonged period of inflation. During the same time period, Mamosa has been paying out all of its net income as dividends. What adverse effects may result from this policy?

13. Hank Artisan is studying for the next accounting mid-term examination. What should Hank know about (a) departing from the cost basis of accounting for inventories and (b) the meaning of "net realizable value" in the lower-of-cost-or-net realizable value method?

14. Jackson Music Center has 5 TVs on hand at the balance sheet date that cost $400 each. The net realizable value is $350 per unit. Under the lower-of-cost-or-net realizable value basis of accounting for inventories, what value should Jackson report for the TVs on the balance sheet? Why?

15. Bonnie Stores has 20 toasters on hand at the balance sheet date. Each costs $27. The net realizable value is $30 per unit. Under the lower-of-cost-or-net realizable value basis of accounting for inventories, what value should Bonnie report for the toasters on the balance sheet? Why?

16. Kuzu Company discovers in 2022 that its ending inventory at December 31, 2021, was $7,000 understated. What effect will this error have on (a) 2021 net income, (b) 2022 net income, and (c) the combined net income for the 2 years?

17. Tilton Company's balance sheet shows Inventory $162,800. What additional disclosures should be made?

18. Under what circumstances might inventory turnover be too high? That is, what possible negative consequences might occur?

19. What inventory cost flow method does **Apple** use for its inventories? (*Hint:* You will need to examine the notes for Apple's financial statements.)

*20. "When perpetual inventory records are kept, the results under the FIFO and LIFO methods are the same as they would be in a periodic inventory system." Explain why this statement is true or false.

*21. How does the average-cost method of inventory costing differ between a perpetual inventory system and a periodic inventory system?

*22. When is it necessary to estimate inventories?

*23. Both the gross profit method and the retail inventory method are based on averages. For each method, indicate the average used, how it is determined, and how it is applied.

*24. Wiggins Company has net sales of $400,000 and cost of goods available for sale of $300,000. If the gross profit rate is 35%, what is the estimated cost of the ending inventory? Show computations.

*25. Emporia Shoe Shop had goods available for sale in 2020 with a retail price of $120,000. The cost of these goods was $84,000. If sales during the period were $80,000, what is the estimated cost of ending inventory using the retail inventory method?

Brief Exercises

Identify items to be included in taking a physical inventory.

BE6.1 (LO 1), C Peete Company identifies the following items for possible inclusion in the taking of a physical inventory. Indicate whether each item should be included or excluded from the inventory taking.

  a. Goods shipped on consignment by Peete to another company.

  b. Goods in transit from a supplier shipped FOB destination.

  c. Goods sold but being held for customer pickup.

  d. Goods held on consignment from another company.

Determine ending inventory amount.

BE6.2 (LO 1), AP Stallman Company took a physical inventory on December 31 and determined that goods costing $200,000 were on hand. Not included in the physical count were $25,000 of goods purchased from Pelzer Corporation, FOB shipping point, and $22,000 of goods sold to Alvarez Company for $30,000, FOB destination. Both the Pelzer purchase and the Alvarez sale were in transit at year-end. What amount should Stallman report as its December 31 inventory?

Compute ending inventory using FIFO and LIFO.

BE6.3 (LO 2), AP In its first month of operations, McLanie Company made three purchases of merchandise in the following sequence: (1) 300 units at $6, (2) 400 units at $8, and (3) 500 units at $9. Assuming there are 200 units on hand, compute the cost of the ending inventory under the (a) FIFO method and (b) LIFO method. McLanie uses a periodic inventory system.

Compute the ending inventory using average-cost.

BE6.4 (LO 2), AP In its first month of operations, McLanie Company made three purchases of merchandise in the following sequence: (1) 300 units at $6, (2) 400 units at $8, and (3) 500 units at $9. Assuming there are 200 units on hand, compute the cost of the ending inventory under the average-cost method. (Round weighted-average unit cost to three decimal places.)

Explain the financial statement effect of inventory cost flow assumptions.

BE6.5 (LO 2), C The management of Milque Corp. is considering the effects of inventory-costing methods on its financial statements and its income tax expense. Assuming that the cost the company pays for inventory is increasing, which method will:

  a. Provide the highest net income?

  b. Provide the highest ending inventory?

  c. Result in the lowest income tax expense?

Explain the financial statement effect of inventory cost flow assumptions.

BE6.6 (LO 2), AP In its first month of operation, Hoffman Company purchased 100 units of inventory for $6, then 200 units for $7, and finally 140 units for $8. At the end of the month, 180 units remained. Compute the amount of phantom profit that would result if the company used FIFO rather than LIFO. Explain why this amount is referred to as phantom profit. The company uses the periodic system.

Determine correct income statement amounts.

BE6.7 (LO 3), AN Fennick Company reports net income of $92,000 in 2022. However, ending inventory was understated $7,000. What is the correct net income for 2022? What effect, if any, will this error have on total assets as reported in the balance sheet at December 31, 2022?

Determine the LCNRV valuation using inventory categories.

BE6.8 (LO 4), AP Wahlowitz Video Center accumulates the following cost and net realizable value data at December 31.

Inventory Categories	Cost Data	Net Realizable Value Data
Cameras	$12,500	$13,400
Camcorders	9,000	9,500
Blu-ray players	13,000	12,200

Compute the lower-of-cost-or-net realizable value for the company's total inventory.

Compute inventory turnover and days in inventory.

BE6.9 (LO 4), AP Suppose at December 31 of a recent year, the following information (in thousands) was available for sunglasses manufacturer **Oakley, Inc.**: ending inventory $155,377, beginning inventory $119,035, cost of goods sold $349,114, and sales revenue $761,865. Calculate the inventory turnover and days in inventory for Oakley, Inc. (Round inventory turnover to two decimal places.)

Apply cost flow methods to a perpetual inventory system.

***BE6.10 (LO 5), AP** Loggins Department Store uses a perpetual inventory system and had no beginning inventory. Data for product E2-D2 include the following purchases.

Date	Number of Units	Unit Cost
May 7	50	$10
July 28	30	15

On June 1, Loggins sold 25 units, and on August 27, 30 more units. Compute the cost of goods sold using (a) FIFO, (b) LIFO, and (c) average-cost. (Round the cost per unit to three decimal places.)

*BE6.11 **(LO 6), AP** At May 31, Suarez Company has net sales of $330,000 and cost of goods available for sale of $230,000. Compute the estimated cost of the ending inventory, assuming the gross profit rate is 35%.

Apply the gross profit method.

*BE6.12 **(LO 6), AP** On June 30, Calico Fabrics has the following data pertaining to the retail inventory method. Goods available for sale: at cost $38,000; at retail $50,000; net sales $40,000; and ending inventory at retail $10,000. Compute the estimated cost of the ending inventory using the retail inventory method.

Apply the retail inventory method.

DO IT! Exercises

DO IT! 6.1 (LO 1), AN Sheldon Company just took its physical inventory on December 31. The count of inventory items on hand at the company's business locations resulted in a total inventory cost of $300,000. In reviewing the details of the count and related inventory transactions, you have discovered the following items had not been considered.

Apply rules of ownership to determine inventory cost.

1. Sheldon has sent inventory costing $28,000 on consignment to Richfield Company. All of this inventory was at Richfield's showrooms on December 31.

2. The company did not include in the count inventory (cost, $20,000) that was sold on December 28, terms FOB shipping point. The goods were in transit on December 31.

3. The company did not include in the count inventory (cost, $13,000) that was purchased with terms of FOB shipping point. The goods were in transit on December 31.

Compute the correct December 31 inventory.

DO IT! 6.2 (LO 2), AP The accounting records of Ohm Electronics show the following data.

Compute cost of goods sold under different cost flow methods.

Beginning inventory	3,000 units at $5
Purchases	8,000 units at $7
Sales	9,400 units at $10

Determine cost of goods sold during the period under a periodic inventory system using (a) the FIFO method, (b) the LIFO method, and (c) the average-cost method. (Round unit cost to three decimal places.)

DO IT! 6.3 (LO 3), AN Janus Company understated its 2021 ending inventory by $31,000. Determine the impact this error has on ending inventory, cost of goods sold, and stockholders' equity in 2021 and 2022.

Determine effect of inventory error.

DO IT! 6.4a (LO 4), AP Jeri Company sells three different categories of tools (small, medium, and large). The cost and net realizable value of its inventory of tools are as follows.

Compute inventory value under LCNRV.

	Cost	Net Realizable Value
Small	$ 64,000	$ 61,000
Medium	290,000	260,000
Large	152,000	167,000

Determine the value of the company's inventory under the lower-of-cost-or-net realizable value approach.

DO IT! 6.4b (LO 4), AP Early in 2022, Fedor Company switched to a just-in-time inventory system. Its sales revenue, cost of goods sold, and inventory amounts for 2021 and 2022 are shown below.

Compute inventory turnover and days in inventory, and assess inventory level.

	2021	2022
Sales revenue	$3,120,000	$3,713,000
Cost of goods sold	1,200,000	1,425,000
Beginning inventory	170,000	210,000
Ending inventory	210,000	90,000

Determine the inventory turnover and days in inventory for 2021 and 2022. Discuss the changes in the amount of inventory, the inventory turnover and days in inventory, and the amount of sales revenue across the two years.

Exercises

Determine the correct inventory amount.

E6.1 (LO 1), AN Umatilla Bank and Trust is considering giving Pohl Company a loan. Before doing so, it decides that further discussions with Pohl's accountant may be desirable. One area of particular concern is the Inventory account, which has a year-end balance of $275,000. Discussions with the accountant reveal the following.

1. Pohl shipped goods costing $55,000 to Hemlock Company FOB shipping point on December 28. The goods are not expected to reach Hemlock until January 12. The goods were not included in the physical inventory because they were not in the warehouse.

2. The physical count of the inventory did not include goods costing $95,000 that were shipped to Pohl FOB destination on December 27 and were still in transit at year-end.

3. Pohl received goods costing $25,000 on January 2. The goods were shipped FOB shipping point on December 26 by Yanice Co. The goods were not included in the physical count.

4. Pohl shipped goods costing $51,000 to Ehler of Canada FOB destination on December 30. The goods were received in Canada on January 8. They were not included in Pohl's physical inventory.

5. Pohl received goods costing $42,000 on January 2 that were shipped FOB destination on December 29. The shipment was a rush order that was supposed to arrive December 31. This purchase was included in the ending inventory of $275,000.

Instructions

Determine the correct inventory amount on December 31.

Determine the correct inventory amount.

E6.2 (LO 1), AN Farley Bains, an auditor with Nolls CPAs, is performing a review of Ryder Company's Inventory account. Ryder did not have a good year, and top management is under pressure to boost reported income. According to its records, the inventory balance at year-end was $740,000. However, the following information was not considered when determining that amount.

1. Included in the company's count were goods with a cost of $228,000 that the company is holding on consignment. The goods belong to Nader Corporation.

2. The physical count did not include goods purchased by Ryder with a cost of $40,000 that were shipped FOB shipping point on December 28 and did not arrive at Ryder's warehouse until January 3.

3. Included in the Inventory account was $17,000 of office supplies that were stored in the warehouse and were to be used by the company's supervisors and managers during the coming year.

4. The company received an order on December 29 that was boxed and was sitting on the loading dock awaiting pick-up on December 31. The shipper picked up the goods on January 1 and delivered them on January 6. The shipping terms were FOB shipping point. The goods had a selling price of $40,000 and a cost of $29,000. The goods were not included in the count because they were sitting on the dock.

5. Included in the count was $50,000 of goods that were parts for a machine that the company no longer made. Given the high-tech nature of Ryder's products, it was unlikely that these obsolete parts had any other use. However, management would prefer to keep them on the books at cost, "since that is what we paid for them, after all."

Instructions

Prepare a schedule to determine the correct inventory amount. Provide explanations for each item above, stating why you did or did not make an adjustment for each item.

Identify items in inventory.

E6.3 (LO 1), AN Gato Inc. had the following inventory situations to consider at January 31, its year-end.

a. Goods held on consignment for Steele Corp. since December 12.

b. Goods shipped on consignment to Logan Holdings Inc. on January 5.

c. Goods shipped to a customer, FOB destination, on January 29 that are still in transit.

d. Goods shipped to a customer, FOB shipping point, on January 29 that are still in transit.

e. Goods purchased FOB destination from a supplier on January 25 that are still in transit.

f. Goods purchased FOB shipping point from a supplier on January 25 that are still in transit.

g. Office supplies on hand at January 31.

Instructions

Identify which of the preceding items should be included in inventory. If the item should not be included in inventory, state in what account, if any, it should have been recorded.

E6.4 (LO 2), AN On December 1, Premium Electronics has three DVD players left in stock. All are identical, all are priced to sell at $85. One of the three DVD players left in stock, with serial #1012, was purchased on June 1 at a cost of $52. Another, with serial #1045, was purchased on November 1 for $48. The last player, serial #1056, was purchased on November 30 for $40.

Calculate cost of goods sold using specific identification and FIFO periodic.

Instructions

a. Calculate the cost of goods sold using the FIFO periodic inventory method, assuming that two of the three players were sold by the end of December, Premium Electronics' year-end.

b. If Premium Electronics used the specific identification method instead of the FIFO method, how might it alter its earnings by "selectively choosing" which particular players to sell to the two customers? What would Premium's cost of goods sold be if the company wished to minimize earnings? Maximize earnings?

c. Which inventory method, FIFO or specific identification, do you recommend that Premium use? Explain why.

E6.5 (LO 2), AP Mather sells a snowboard, EZslide, that is popular with snowboard enthusiasts. The following is information relating to Mather's beginning inventory and purchases of EZslide snowboards during September. During the same month, 102 EZslide snowboards were sold. Mather uses a periodic inventory system.

Compute inventory and cost of goods sold using periodic FIFO, LIFO, and average-cost.

Date	Explanation	Units	Unit Cost	Total Cost
Sept. 1	Inventory	12	$100	$ 1,200
Sept. 12	Purchases	45	103	4,635
Sept. 19	Purchases	50	104	5,200
Sept. 26	Purchases	20	105	2,100
	Totals	127		$13,135

Instructions

Compute the ending inventory at September 30 and the cost of goods sold using the FIFO, LIFO, and average-cost methods. (For average-cost, round the weighted-average unit cost to three decimal places.) Prove the amount allocated to cost of goods sold under each method.

E6.6 (LO 2), AP Rusthe Inc. uses a periodic inventory system. Its records show the following for the month of May, in which 74 units were sold.

Calculate inventory and cost of goods sold using FIFO, average-cost, and LIFO in a periodic inventory system.

Date	Explanation	Units	Unit Cost	Total Cost
May 1	Inventory	30	$ 9	$270
15	Purchase	25	10	250
24	Purchase	38	11	418
	Total	93		$938

Instructions

Calculate the ending inventory at May 31 using the (a) FIFO, (b) LIFO, and (c) average-cost methods. (For average-cost, round the weighted-average unit cost to three decimal places.) Prove the amount allocated to cost of goods sold under each method.

E6.7 (LO 2), AP Jeters Company uses a periodic inventory system and reports the following for the month of June.

Compute inventory and cost of goods sold using periodic FIFO, LIFO, and average-cost.

Date	Explanation	Units	Unit Cost	Total Cost
June 1	Inventory	120	$5	$ 600
12	Purchase	370	6	2,220
23	Purchase	200	7	1,400
30	Inventory	230		

Instructions

a. Compute the cost of the ending inventory and the cost of goods sold under (1) FIFO, (2) LIFO, and (3) average-cost. (Round weighted-average unit cost to three decimal places.)

b. Which costing method gives the highest ending inventory? The highest cost of goods sold? Why?

c. How do the average-cost values for ending inventory and cost of goods sold relate to ending inventory and cost of goods sold for FIFO and LIFO?

d. Explain why the unit cost is not $6 per the average-cost method.

E6.8 (LO 2), AP Lisa Company had 100 units in beginning inventory at a total cost of $10,000. The company purchased 200 units at a total cost of $26,000. At the end of the year, Lisa had 80 units in ending inventory.

Compute inventory under FIFO, LIFO, and average-cost.

Instructions

a. Compute the cost of the ending inventory and the cost of goods sold under (1) FIFO, (2) LIFO, and (3) average-cost.

b. Which cost flow method would result in the highest net income?

c. Which cost flow method would result in inventories approximating current cost in the balance sheet?

d. Which cost flow method would result in Lisa paying the least taxes?

Determine effects of inventory errors.

E6.9 (LO 3), AN Dowell Hardware reported cost of goods sold as follows.

	2022	2021
Beginning inventory	$ 30,000	$ 20,000
Cost of goods purchased	175,000	164,000
Cost of goods available for sale	205,000	184,000
Less: Ending inventory	37,000	30,000
Cost of goods sold	$168,000	$154,000

Dowell made two errors:

1. 2021 ending inventory was overstated by $2,000.

2. 2022 ending inventory was understated by $5,000.

Instructions

Compute the correct cost of goods sold for each year.

Prepare correct income statements.

E6.10 (LO 3), AN **Writing** Sheen Company reported these income statement data for a 2-year period.

	2022	2021
Sales revenue	$250,000	$210,000
Beginning inventory	40,000	32,000
Cost of goods purchased	202,000	173,000
Cost of goods available for sale	242,000	205,000
Less: Ending inventory	55,000	40,000
Cost of goods sold	187,000	165,000
Gross profit	$ 63,000	$ 45,000

Sheen Company uses a periodic inventory system. The inventories at January 1, 2021, and December 31, 2022, are correct. However, the ending inventory at December 31, 2021, is overstated by $8,000.

Instructions

a. Prepare correct income statement data for the 2 years.

b. What is the cumulative effect of the inventory error on total gross profit for the 2 years?

c. Explain in a letter to the president of Sheen Company what has happened—that is, the nature of the error and its effect on the financial statements.

Determine LCNRV valuation.

E6.11 (LO 4), AP Digital Camera Shop Inc. uses the lower-of-cost-or-net realizable value basis for its inventory. The following data are available at December 31.

	Units	Cost per Unit	Net Realizable Value per Unit
Cameras			
Minolta	5	$170	$158
Canon	7	145	152
Light Meters			
Vivitar	12	125	114
Kodak	10	120	135

Instructions

What amount should be reported for inventory on Digital Camera Shop's balance sheet, assuming the lower-of-cost-or-net realizable value rule is applied?

Compute lower-of-cost-or-net realizable value.

E6.12 (LO 4), AP Serebin Company applied FIFO to its inventory and got the following results for its ending inventory.

Cameras	100 units at a cost per unit of $65
Blu-ray players	150 units at a cost per unit of $75
iPods	125 units at a cost per unit of $80

The net realizable value of each of these products at year-end was cameras $71, Blu-ray players $67, and iPods $78.

Instructions

Determine the amount of ending inventory at lower-of-cost-or-net realizable value.

E6.13 (LO 4), AP Suppose this information is available for **PepsiCo, Inc.** for 2020, 2021, and 2022.

(in millions)	**2020**	**2021**	**2022**
Beginning inventory	$ 1,926	$ 2,290	$ 2,522
Ending inventory	2,290	2,522	2,618
Cost of goods sold	18,038	20,351	20,099
Net sales revenue	39,474	43,251	43,232

Compute inventory turnover, days in inventory, and gross profit rate.

Instructions

a. Calculate the inventory turnover for 2020, 2021, and 2022. (Round to one decimal place.)

b. Calculate the days in inventory for 2020, 2021, and 2022. (Round to one decimal place.)

c. Calculate the gross profit rate for 2020, 2021, and 2022. (Round to one decimal place.)

d. Comment on any trends observed in your answers to parts (a), (b), and (c).

E6.14 (LO 4), AP The cost of goods sold computations for Alpha Company and Omega Company are as follows.

Compute inventory turnover and days in inventory.

	Alpha Company	**Omega Company**
Beginning inventory	$ 45,000	$ 71,000
Cost of goods purchased	200,000	290,000
Cost of goods available for sale	245,000	361,000
Ending inventory	55,000	69,000
Cost of goods sold	$190,000	$292,000

Instructions

a. Compute inventory turnover (round to two decimal places) and days in inventory (round to nearest day) for each company.

b. Which company moves its inventory more quickly?

*E6.15 (LO 5), AP Bufford Appliance uses a perpetual inventory system. For its flat-screen television sets, the January 1 inventory was 3 sets at $600 each. On January 10, Bufford purchased 6 units at $660 each. The company sold 2 units on January 8 and 4 units on January 15.

Apply cost flow methods to a perpetual inventory system.

Instructions

Compute the ending inventory under (a) FIFO, (b) LIFO, and (c) moving-average cost. (For moving-average, round the weighted-average unit cost to three decimal places.)

*E6.16 (LO 5), AP Inventory data for Jeters Company are presented as follows.

Calculate inventory and cost of goods sold using three cost flow methods in a perpetual inventory system.

Date	Explanation	Units	Unit Cost	Total Cost
June 1	Inventory	120	$5	$ 600
12	Purchase	370	6	2,220
23	Purchase	200	7	1,400
30	Inventory	230		

Instructions

a. Calculate the cost of the ending inventory and the cost of goods sold for each cost flow assumption, using a perpetual inventory system. Assume a sale of 410 units occurred on June 15 for a selling price of $8 and a sale of 50 units on June 27 for $9. (For the moving-average method, round the weighted-average unit cost to three decimal places.)

b. How do the results differ from E6.7?

c. Why is the average unit cost not $6 [($5 + $6 + $7) ÷ 3 = $6]?

*E6.17 (LO 5), AP Mather sells a snowboard, EZslide, that is popular with snowboard enthusiasts. The following is information relating to Mather's purchases of EZslide snowboards during September. During the same month, 102 EZslide snowboards were sold.

Apply cost flow methods to a perpetual inventory system.

Date	Explanation	Units	Unit Cost	Total Cost
Sept. 1	Inventory	12	$100	$ 1,200
Sept. 12	Purchases	45	103	4,635
Sept. 19	Purchases	50	104	5,200
Sept. 26	Purchases	20	105	2,100
	Totals	127		$13,135

Additional data regarding the company's sales of EZslide snowboards are provided below. Assume that Mather uses a perpetual inventory system.

Date		Units
Sept. 5	Sale	8
Sept. 16	Sale	48
Sept. 29	Sale	46
	Totals	102

Instructions

Compute ending inventory at September 30 using FIFO, LIFO, and moving-average. (For moving-average, round the weighted-average unit cost to three decimal places.)

Use the gross profit method to estimate inventory.

*E6.18 (LO 6), AP Brenda Company reported the following information for November and December 2022.

	November	December
Cost of goods purchased	$536,000	$ 610,000
Inventory, beginning-of-month	130,000	120,000
Inventory, end-of-month	120,000	?
Net sales revenue	840,000	1,000,000

Brenda's ending inventory at December 31 was destroyed in a fire.

Instructions

a. Compute the gross profit rate for November.

b. Using the gross profit rate for November, determine the estimated cost of inventory lost in the fire.

Determine merchandise lost using the gross profit method of estimating inventory.

*E6.19 (LO 6), AP The inventory of Hauser Company was destroyed by fire on March 1. From an examination of the accounting records, the following data for the first 2 months of the year are obtained: Sales Revenue $51,000, Sales Returns and Allowances $1,000, Purchases $31,200, Freight-In $1,200, and Purchase Returns and Allowances $1,400.

Instructions

Determine the merchandise lost by fire, assuming:

a. A beginning inventory of $20,000 and a gross profit rate of 40% on net sales.

b. A beginning inventory of $30,000 and a gross profit rate of 30% on net sales.

Determine ending inventory at cost using retail method.

*E6.20 (LO 6), AP Gepetto Shoe Store uses the retail inventory method for its two departments, Women's Shoes and Men's Shoes. The following information for each department is obtained.

	Women's Shoes	Men's Shoes
Beginning inventory at cost	$ 25,000	$ 45,000
Cost of goods purchased at cost	110,000	136,300
Net sales	178,000	185,000
Beginning inventory at retail	46,000	60,000
Cost of goods purchased at retail	179,000	185,000

Instructions

Compute the estimated cost of the ending inventory for each department under the retail inventory method.

Problems

Determine items and amounts to be recorded in inventory.

P6.1A (LO 1), AN Pitt Limited is trying to determine its ending inventory as of February 28, 2022, the company's year-end. The accountant counted everything that was in the warehouse as of February 28, which resulted in an ending inventory of $48,000. However, she needed help in determining how to handle the following items.

a. On February 26, Pitt shipped to a customer goods costing $800. The goods were shipped FOB shipping point, and the customer received the goods on March 2.

b. On February 26, Martine Inc. shipped goods to Pitt FOB destination. The invoice price was $350 plus $25 for freight. The receiving report indicates that the goods were received by Pitt on March 2.

c. Pitt had $500 of inventory at a customer's warehouse "on approval." The customer was going to let Pitt know whether it wanted the merchandise by the end of the week, March 4.

d. Pitt also had $400 of inventory at a Belle craft shop, on consignment from Pitt.

e. On February 26, Pitt ordered goods costing $750. The goods were shipped FOB shipping point on February 27. Pitt received the goods on March 1.

f. On February 28, Pitt packaged goods and had them ready for shipping to a customer FOB destination. The invoice price was $350 plus $25 for freight; the cost of the items was $280. The goods were received by the customer on March 2.

g. Pitt had damaged goods set aside in the warehouse because they are no longer saleable. These goods originally cost $400 and, originally, Pitt expected to sell these items for $600.

Instructions

For each of the above transactions, specify whether the item in question should be included in ending inventory, and if so, at what amount. For each item that is not included in ending inventory, indicate who owns it and what account, if any, it should have been recorded in.

P6.2A (LO 2), AP Mullins Distribution markets CDs of numerous performing artists. At the beginning of March, Mullins had in beginning inventory 2,500 CDs with a unit cost of $7. During March, Mullins made the following purchases of CDs.

Determine cost of goods sold and ending inventory using FIFO, LIFO, and average-cost with analysis.

March 5	2,000 @ $8	March 21	5,000 @ $10
March 13	3,500 @ $9	March 26	2,000 @ $11

During March 12,000 units were sold. Mullins uses a periodic inventory system.

Instructions

a. Determine the cost of goods available for sale.

b. Determine (1) the ending inventory and (2) the cost of goods sold under each of the assumed cost flow methods (FIFO, LIFO, and average-cost). Prove the accuracy of the cost of goods sold under the FIFO and LIFO methods. (For average-cost, round the weighted-average unit cost to three decimal places.)

b. Cost of goods sold:
FIFO $105,000
LIFO $115,500
Average $109,601

c. Which cost flow method results in (1) the highest inventory amount for the balance sheet and (2) the highest cost of goods sold for the income statement?

P6.3A (LO 2), AP Vista Company Inc. had a beginning inventory of 100 units of Product RST at a cost of $8 per unit. During the year, purchases were:

Determine cost of goods sold and ending inventory using FIFO, LIFO, and average-cost in a periodic inventory system and assess financial statement effects.

Feb. 20	600 units at $9	Aug. 12	400 units at $11
May 5	500 units at $10	Dec. 8	100 units at $12

Vista Company uses a periodic inventory system. Sales totaled 1,500 units.

Instructions

a. Determine the cost of goods available for sale.

b. Determine the ending inventory and the cost of goods sold under each of the assumed cost flow methods (FIFO, LIFO, and average-cost). Prove the accuracy of the cost of goods sold under the FIFO and LIFO methods. (Round the weighted-average unit cost to three decimal places.)

b. Cost of goods sold:
FIFO $14,500
LIFO $15,100
Average $14,824

c. Which cost flow method results in the lowest inventory amount for the balance sheet? The lowest cost of goods sold for the income statement?

P6.4A (LO 2), AP Writing The management of Felipe Inc. is reevaluating the appropriateness of using its present inventory cost flow method, which is average-cost. The company requests your help in determining the results of operations for 2022 if either the FIFO or the LIFO method had been used. For 2022, the accounting records show these data:

Compute ending inventory, prepare income statements, and answer questions using FIFO and LIFO.

Inventories		Purchases and Sales	
Beginning (7,000 units)	$14,000	Total net sales (180,000 units)	$747,000
Ending (17,000 units)		Total cost of goods purchased	
		(190,000 units)	466,000

Purchases were made quarterly as follows.

Quarter	Units	Unit Cost	Total Cost
1	50,000	$2.20	$110,000
2	40,000	2.35	94,000
3	40,000	2.50	100,000
4	60,000	2.70	162,000
	190,000		$466,000

Operating expenses were $130,000, and the company's income tax rate is 20%.

a. Net income:
FIFO $146,320
LIFO $138,400

Instructions

a. Prepare comparative condensed income statements for 2022 under FIFO and LIFO. (Show computations of ending inventory.)

b. Answer the following questions for management.
1. Which cost flow method (FIFO or LIFO) produces the more meaningful inventory amount for the balance sheet? Why?
2. Which cost flow method (FIFO or LIFO) produces the more meaningful net income? Why?
3. Which cost flow method (FIFO or LIFO) is more likely to approximate the actual physical flow of goods? Why?
4. How much more cash will be available for management under LIFO than under FIFO? Why?
5. Will gross profit under the average-cost method be higher or lower than FIFO? Than LIFO? (*Note:* It is not necessary to quantify your answer.)

Calculate ending inventory, cost of goods sold, gross profit, and gross profit rate under a periodic inventory system; compare results.

P6.5A (LO 2), AP You have the following information for Van Gogh Inc. for the month ended October 31, 2022. Van Gogh uses a periodic inventory system for inventory.

Date	Description	Units	Unit Cost or Selling Price
Oct. 1	Beginning inventory	60	$24
Oct. 9	Purchase	120	26
Oct. 11	Sale	100	35
Oct. 17	Purchase	100	27
Oct. 22	Sale	60	40
Oct. 25	Purchase	70	29
Oct. 29	Sale	110	40

Instructions

a. Gross profit:
LIFO $2,970
FIFO $3,310
Average $3,133

a. Calculate (i) ending inventory, (ii) cost of goods sold, (iii) gross profit, and (iv) gross profit rate under each of the following methods.
1. LIFO.
2. FIFO.
3. Average-cost. (Round weighted-average unit cost to three decimal places.)

b. Compare results for the three cost flow assumptions.

Compare specific identification, FIFO, and LIFO under a periodic inventory system; use cost flow assumption to influence gross profit.

P6.6A (LO 2), AP You have the following information for Jewels Gems. Jewels uses the periodic method of accounting for its inventory transactions. Jewels only carries one brand and size of diamonds—all are identical. Each batch of diamonds purchased is carefully coded and marked with its purchase cost.

March 1	Beginning inventory 150 diamonds at a cost of $310 per diamond.
March 3	Purchased 200 diamonds at a cost of $350 each.
March 5	Sold 180 diamonds for $600 each.
March 10	Purchased 330 diamonds at a cost of $375 each.
March 25	Sold 390 diamonds for $650 each.

Instructions

a. Gross profit:
Maximum $162,500
Minimum $155,350

a. Assume that Jewels Gems uses the specific identification cost flow method.
1. Demonstrate how Jewels could maximize its gross profit for the month by specifically selecting which diamonds to sell on March 5 and March 25.
2. Demonstrate how Jewels could minimize its gross profit for the month by selecting which diamonds to sell on March 5 and March 25.

b. Assume that Jewels uses the FIFO cost flow assumption. Calculate cost of goods sold. How much gross profit would Jewels report under this cost flow assumption?

c. Assume that Jewels uses the LIFO cost flow assumption. Calculate cost of goods sold. How much gross profit would the company report under this cost flow assumption?

d. Which cost flow method should Jewels Gems select? Explain.

Compute ending inventory, prepare income statements, and answer questions using FIFO and LIFO.

P6.7A (LO 2), AN **Writing** The management of National Inc. asks your help in determining the comparative effects of the FIFO and LIFO inventory cost flow methods. For 2022, the accounting records show these data.

Inventory, January 1 (10,000 units)	$ 35,000
Cost of 120,000 units purchased	468,500
Sales revenue on 98,000 units	750,000
Operating expenses	124,000

Units purchased consisted of 35,000 units at $3.70 on May 10, 60,000 units at $3.90 on August 15, and 25,000 units at $4.20 on November 20. Income taxes are 20%.

Instructions

a. Prepare comparative condensed income statements for 2022 under FIFO and LIFO. (Show computations of ending inventory.)

b. Answer the following questions for management in the form of a business letter.

   1. Which inventory cost flow method produces the inventory amount that most closely approximates the amount that would have to be paid to replace the inventory? Why?

   2. Which inventory cost flow method produces the net income amount that is a more likely indicator of next period's net income? Why?

   3. Which inventory cost flow method is most likely to approximate the actual physical flow of the goods? Why?

   4. How much more cash will be available under LIFO than under FIFO? Why?

   5. How much of the gross profit under FIFO is illusory in comparison with the gross profit under LIFO?

a. Net income:
FIFO $203,840
LIFO $191,120

*P6.8A (LO 5), AP Bieber Inc. is a retailer operating in Calgary, Alberta. Bieber uses the perpetual inventory system. Assume that there are no credit transactions; all amounts are settled in cash. You are provided with the following information for Bieber for the month of January 2022.

Calculate cost of goods sold, ending inventory, and gross profit for LIFO, FIFO, and moving-average under the perpetual system; compare results.

Date	Description	Quantity	Unit Cost or Selling Price
Dec. 31	Ending inventory	160	$20
Jan. 2	Purchase	100	22
Jan. 6	Sale	180	40
Jan. 9	Purchase	75	24
Jan. 10	Sale	50	45
Jan. 23	Purchase	100	25
Jan. 30	Sale	130	48

Instructions

a. For each of the following cost flow assumptions, calculate (i) cost of goods sold, (ii) ending inventory, and (iii) gross profit.

   1. LIFO.

   2. FIFO.

   3. Moving-average. (Round weighted-average unit cost to three decimal places.)

b. Compare results for the three cost flow assumptions.

a. Gross profit:
LIFO $7,490
FIFO $7,865
Average $7,763

*P6.9A (LO 5), AP Lyon Center began operations on July 1. It uses a perpetual inventory system. During July, the company had the following purchases and sales.

Determine ending inventory under a perpetual inventory system.

Date	Purchases		Sales Units
	Units	Unit Cost	
July 1	7	$62	
July 6			5
July 11	3	$66	
July 14			3
July 21	4	$71	
July 27			3

Instructions

a. Determine the ending inventory under a perpetual inventory system using (1) FIFO, (2) moving-average (round weighted-average unit cost to three decimal places), and (3) LIFO.

b. Which costing method produces the highest ending inventory?

a. FIFO $213
Average $207
LIFO $195

*P6.10A (LO 6), AP Suzuki Company lost all of its inventory in a fire on December 26, 2022. The accounting records showed the following inventory-related data for November and December.

Compute gross profit rate and inventory loss using gross profit method.

Excel

	November	December (to 12/26)
Net sales	$600,000	$700,000
Beginning inventory	32,000	36,000
Purchases	389,000	420,000
Purchase returns and allowances	13,300	14,900
Purchase discounts	8,500	9,500
Freight-in	8,800	9,900
Ending inventory	36,000	?

Suzuki is fully insured for fire losses but must prepare a report for the insurance company.

Instructions

a. Gross profit rate 38%

a. Compute the gross profit rate for November.

b. Using the gross profit rate for November, determine the estimated cost of the inventory lost in the fire.

Compute ending inventory using retail method.

*P6.11A (LO 6), AP Dixon Books uses the retail inventory method to estimate its monthly ending inventories. The following information is available for two of its departments at **October 31, 2022**.

	Hardcovers		Paperbacks	
	Cost	Retail	Cost	Retail
Beginning inventory	$ 420,000	$ 700,000	$ 280,000	$ 360,000
Purchases	2,135,000	3,200,000	1,155,000	1,540,000
Freight-in	24,000		12,000	
Purchase discounts	44,000		22,000	
Net sales		3,100,000		1,570,000

At **December 31**, Dixon Books takes a physical inventory at retail. The actual retail values of the inventories in each department are Hardcovers $790,000 and Paperbacks $335,000.

Instructions

a. Hardcovers: end. inv. $520,000

a. Determine the estimated cost of the ending inventory for each department at **October 31**, 2022, using the retail inventory method.

b. Compute the ending inventory at cost for each department at **December 31**, assuming the cost-to-retail ratios for the year are 65% for Hardcovers and 75% for Paperbacks.

Continuing Case

Cookie Creations

(*Note:* This is a continuation of the Cookie Creations case from Chapters 1 through 5.)

CC6 Natalie is busy establishing both divisions of her business (cookie classes and mixer sales) and completing her business degree. Her goals for the next 11 months are to sell one mixer per month and to give two to three classes per week.

The cost of the fine European mixers is expected to increase. Natalie has just negotiated new terms with Kzinski that include shipping costs in the negotiated purchase price (mixers will be shipped FOB destination). Natalie must choose a cost flow assumption for her mixer inventory.

Go to **WileyPLUS** *for complete case details and instructions.*

leungchopan/
Shutterstock.com

Comprehensive Accounting Cycle Review

ACR6 On December 1, 2022, Matthias Company had the following account balances.

	Debit		Credit
Cash	$ 4,800	Accumulated Depreciation—Equipment	$ 1,500
Accounts Receivable	3,900	Accounts Payable	3,000
Inventory	1,800*	Common Stock	20,000
Equipment	21,000	Retained Earnings	7,000
	$31,500		$31,500

*3,000 × $0.60

The following transactions occurred during December.

Dec. 3 Purchased 4,000 units of inventory on account at a cost of $0.72 per unit.
  5 Sold 4,400 units of inventory on account for $0.90 per unit. (Matthias sold 3,000 of the $0.60 units and 1,400 of the $0.72.)
  7 Granted the December 5 customer $180 credit for 200 units of inventory returned costing $144. These units were returned to inventory.
  17 Purchased 2,200 units of inventory for cash at $0.80 each.
  22 Sold 2,000 units of inventory on account for $0.95 per unit. (Matthias sold 2,000 of the $0.72 units.)

Adjustment data:

1. Recognized accrued salaries payable of $400.

2. Recognized depreciation of $200 per month.

Instructions

a. Journalize the December transactions and adjusting entries, assuming Matthias uses the perpetual inventory system.

b. Enter the December 1 balances in the ledger T-accounts and post the December transactions. In addition to the accounts mentioned above, use the following additional accounts: Cost of Goods Sold, Depreciation Expense, Salaries and Wages Expense, Salaries and Wages Payable, Sales Revenue, and Sales Returns and Allowances.

c. Prepare an adjusted trial balance as of December 31, 2022.

d. Prepare a multiple-step income statement for December 2022 and a classified balance sheet at December 31, 2022.

e. Compute ending inventory and cost of goods sold under FIFO, assuming Matthias Company uses the periodic inventory system.

f. Compute ending inventory and cost of goods sold under LIFO, assuming Matthias Company uses the periodic inventory system.

Expand Your Critical Thinking

Financial Reporting Problem: Apple Inc.

CT6.1 The notes that accompany a company's financial statements provide informative details that would clutter the amounts and descriptions presented in the statements. Refer to the financial statements of **Apple Inc.** in Appendix A as well as its annual report. The complete annual report, including the notes to the financial statements, is available at the company's website.

Instructions

Answer the following questions. Complete the requirements in millions of dollars, as shown in Apple's annual report.

a. What did Apple report for the amount of inventories in its consolidated balance sheet at September 30, 2017? At September 29, 2018?

b. Compute the dollar amount of change and the percentage change in inventories between 2017 and 2018. Compute inventory as a percentage of current assets at September 29, 2018.

c. Which inventory cost flow method does Apple use? (See Notes to the Financial Statements.)

d. What is the cost of sales (cost of goods sold) reported by Apple for 2018, 2017, and 2016? Compute the percentage of cost of sales to net sales in 2018.

Comparative Analysis Problem: PepsiCo, Inc. vs. The Coca-Cola Company

CT6.2 **PepsiCo**'s financial statements are presented in Appendix B. Financial statements of **The Coca-Cola Company** are presented in Appendix C. The complete annual reports of PepsiCo and Coca-Cola, including the notes to the financial statements, are available at each company's respective website.

Instructions

a. Based on the information contained in these financial statements, compute the following 2018 ratios for each company.

   1. Inventory turnover.

   2. Days in inventory.

b. What conclusions concerning the management of the inventory can you draw from these data?

Comparative Analysis Problem: Amazon.com, Inc. vs. Walmart Inc.

CT6.3 Amazon.com, Inc.'s financial statements are presented in Appendix D. Financial statements of **Walmart Inc.** are presented in Appendix E. The complete annual reports of Amazon and Walmart, including the notes to the financial statements, are available at each company's respective website.

Instructions

a. Based on the information contained in these financial statements, compute the following ratios for each company.

   1. Inventory turnover.

   2. Days in inventory.

b. What conclusions concerning the management of the inventory can you draw from these data?

Real-World Focus

CT6.4 A company's annual report usually will identify the inventory method used. Knowing that, you can analyze the effects of the inventory method on the income statement and balance sheet.

Instructions

Answer the following questions based on the current year's annual report available at **Cisco**'s website.

a. At Cisco's fiscal year-end, what was the inventory on the balance sheet?

b. How has this changed from the previous fiscal year-end?

c. How much of the inventory was finished goods?

Decision-Making Across the Organization

CT6.5 On April 10, 2022, fire damaged the office and warehouse of Corvet Company. Most of the accounting records were destroyed, but the following balances were determined as of March 31, 2022: inventory (January 1, 2022), $80,000; net sales revenue (January 1–March 31, 2022), $180,000; purchases (January 1–March 31, 2022), $94,000.

The company's fiscal year ends on December 31. It uses a periodic inventory system.

From an analysis of the April bank statement, you discover cancelled checks of $4,200 for cash purchases during the period April 1–10. Deposits during the same period totaled $18,500. Of that amount, 60% were collections on accounts receivable, and the balance was cash sales.

Correspondence with the company's principal suppliers revealed $12,400 of purchases on account from April 1 to April 10. Of that amount, $1,600 was for merchandise in transit on April 10 that was shipped FOB destination.

Correspondence with the company's principal customers produced acknowledgments of credit sales totaling $37,000 from April 1 to April 10. It was estimated that $5,600 of credit sales would never be acknowledged or recovered from customers.

Corvet Company reached an agreement with the insurance company that its fire-loss claim should be based on the average of the gross profit rates for the preceding 2 years. The financial statements for 2020 and 2021 showed the following data.

	2021	2020
Net sales	$600,000	$480,000
Cost of goods purchased	404,000	356,000
Beginning inventory	60,000	40,000
Ending inventory	80,000	60,000

Inventory with a cost of $17,000 was salvaged from the fire.

Instructions

With the class divided into groups, answer the following.

a. Determine the balances of (1) net sales revenue and (2) purchases at April 10, 2022.

*b. Determine the average gross profit rate for the years 2020 and 2021. (*Hint:* Find the gross profit rate for each year and divide the sum by 2.)

*c. Determine the inventory loss as a result of the fire, using the gross profit method.

Communication Activity

CT6.6 You are the controller of Small Toys Inc. Marta Johns, the president, recently mentioned to you that she found an error in the 2021 financial statements which she believes has corrected itself. She determined, in discussions with the Purchasing Department, that 2021 ending inventory was overstated by $1 million. Marta says that the 2022 ending inventory is correct. Thus, she assumes that 2022 income is correct. Marta says to you, "What happened has happened—there's no point in worrying about it anymore."

Instructions

You conclude that Marta is incorrect. Write a brief, tactful memo to Marta, clarifying the situation. The company uses the periodic inventory system.

Ethics Case

CT6.7 Nixon Wholesale Corp. uses the LIFO periodic inventory system for inventory costing purposes. In the current year, profit at Nixon is running unusually high. The corporate tax rate is also high this year, but it is scheduled to decline significantly next year. In an effort to lower the current year's net income and to take advantage of the changing income tax rate, the president of Nixon Wholesale instructs the plant accountant to recommend to the purchasing department a large purchase of inventory for delivery 3 days before the end of the year. The cost of the inventory to be purchased has doubled during the year, and the purchase will represent a major portion of the cost of goods available for sale during the period.

Instructions

a. What is the effect of this transaction on this year's and next year's income statement and income tax expense? Why?

b. If Nixon Wholesale had been using the FIFO method of inventory costing, would the president give the same directive?

c. Should the plant accountant order the inventory purchase to lower income? What are the ethical implications of this order?

All About You

CT6.8 Some of the largest business frauds ever perpetrated have involved the misstatement of inventory. Two classics were at **Leslie Fay** and **McKesson Corporation**.

Instructions

There is considerable information regarding inventory frauds available on the Internet. Search for information about one of the two cases mentioned above, or inventory fraud at any other company, and prepare a short explanation of the nature of the inventory fraud.

FASB Codification Activity

CT6.9 If your school has a subscription to the FASB Codification, log in and prepare responses to the following.

Instructions

a. The primary basis for accounting for inventories is cost. How is cost defined in the Codification?

b. What does the Codification state regarding the use of consistency in the selection or employment of a basis for inventory?

A Look at IFRS

LEARNING OBJECTIVE 7

Compare the accounting for inventories under GAAP and IFRS.

The major IFRS requirements related to accounting and reporting for inventories are the same as GAAP. The major difference is that IFRS prohibits the use of the LIFO cost flow assumption.

Key Points

Following are the key similarities and differences between GAAP and IFRS related to inventories.

Similarities

- IFRS and GAAP account for inventory acquisitions at historical cost and report inventory at the lower-of-cost-or-net realizable value subsequent to acquisition.
- Who owns the goods—goods in transit or consigned goods—as well as the costs to include in inventory are essentially accounted for the same under IFRS and GAAP.

Differences

- The requirements for accounting for and reporting inventories are more principles-based under IFRS. That is, GAAP provides more detailed guidelines in inventory accounting.
- A major difference between IFRS and GAAP relates to the LIFO cost flow assumption. GAAP permits the use of LIFO for inventory costing. IFRS prohibits its use. FIFO and average-cost are the only two acceptable cost flow assumptions permitted under IFRS. Both sets of standards permit specific identification where appropriate.

IFRS Practice

IFRS Self-Test Questions

1. Which of the following should **not** be included in the inventory of a company using IFRS?

   a. Goods held on consignment from another company.

   b. Goods shipped on consignment to another company.

   c. Goods in transit from another company shipped FOB shipping point.

   d. None of the above.

2. Which method of inventory costing is prohibited under IFRS?

   a. Specific identification.

   b. LIFO.

   c. FIFO.

   d. Average-cost.

IFRS Exercises

IFRS6.1 Briefly describe some of the similarities and differences between GAAP and IFRS with respect to the accounting for inventories.

IFRS6.2 LaTour Inc. is based in France and prepares its financial statements (in euros) in accordance with IFRS. In 2022, it reported cost of goods sold of €578 million and average inventory of €154 million. Briefly discuss how analysis of LaTour's inventory turnover (and comparisons to a company using GAAP) might be affected by differences in inventory accounting between IFRS and GAAP.

International Financial Reporting Problem: Louis Vuitton

IFRS6.3 The financial statements of **Louis Vuitton** are presented in Appendix F. The complete consolidated financial statements, including the notes to its financial statements, are available at the company's website.

Instructions

Using the notes to the company's 2018 consolidated financial statements, answer the following questions.

   a. What cost flow assumption does the company use to value inventory other than wine?

   b. What net amount of goods purchased for resale and finished products did the company report at December 31, 2018?

Answers to IFRS Self-Test Questions

1. a   **2.** b

CHAPTER 7

Tom Werner/DigitalVision/Getty Images

Fraud, Internal Control, and Cash

Chapter Preview

As the following Feature Story about recording cash sales at **Barriques** indicates, control of cash is important to ensure that fraud does not occur. Companies also need controls to safeguard other types of assets. For example, Barriques undoubtedly has controls to prevent the theft of food and supplies, and controls to prevent the theft of tableware and dishes from its kitchen.

In this chapter, we explain the essential features of an internal control system and how it prevents fraud. We also describe how those controls apply to a specific asset—cash. These applications include some controls with which you may be already familiar, such as the use of a bank.

Feature Story

Minding the Money in Madison

For many years, **Barriques** in Madison, Wisconsin, has been named the city's favorite coffeehouse. Barriques not only does a booming business in coffee but also has wonderful baked goods, delicious sandwiches, and a fine selection of wines.

"Our customer base ranges from college students to neighborhood residents as well as visitors to our capital city," says bookkeeper Kerry Stoppleworth, who joined the company shortly after it was founded in 1998. "We are unique because we have customers who come in early on their way to work for a cup of coffee and then will stop back after work to pick up a bottle of wine for dinner. We stay very busy throughout all three parts of the day."

Like most businesses where purchases are low-cost and high-volume, cash control has to be simple. "We use a computerized point-of-sale (POS) system to keep track of our inventory and allow us to efficiently ring through an order for a customer," explains Stoppleworth. "You can either scan a barcode for an item or enter in a code for items that don't

have a barcode such as cups of coffee or bakery items." The POS system also automatically tracks sales by department and maintains an electronic journal of all the sales transactions that occur during the day.

"There are two POS stations at each store, and throughout the day any of the staff may operate them," says Stoppleworth. At the end of the day, each POS station is reconciled separately. The staff counts the cash in the drawer and enters this amount into the closing totals in the POS system. The POS system then compares the cash and credit amounts, less the cash being carried forward to the next day (the float), to the shift total in the electronic journal. If there are discrepancies, a recount is done and the journal is reviewed transaction by transaction to identify the problem. The staff then creates a deposit ticket for the cash less the float and puts this in a drop safe with the electronic journal summary report for the manager to review and take to the bank the next day. Ultimately, the bookkeeper reviews all of these documents as well as the deposit receipt that the bank produces to make sure they are all in agreement.

As Stoppleworth concludes, "We keep the closing process and accounting simple so that our staff can concentrate on taking care of our customers and making great coffee and food."

Chapter Outline

LEARNING OBJECTIVES	REVIEW	PRACTICE
LO 1 Define fraud and the principles of internal control.	• Fraud • The Sarbanes-Oxley Act • Internal control • Principles of internal control activities • Data analytics and internal controls • Limitations of internal control	**DO IT! 1** Principles of Control Activities
LO 2 Apply internal control principles to cash.	• Cash receipts controls • Cash disbursements controls • Petty cash fund	**DO IT! 2a** Control over Cash Receipts **DO IT! 2b** Petty Cash Fund
LO 3 Identify the control features of a bank account.	• Making bank deposits • Writing checks • EFT system • Bank statements • Reconciling the bank account	**DO IT! 3** Bank Reconciliation
LO 4 Explain the reporting of cash.	• Cash equivalents • Restricted cash	**DO IT! 4** Reporting Cash

Go to the Review and Practice section at the end of the chapter for a review of key concepts and practice applications with solutions.

Visit WileyPLUS for additional tutorials and practice opportunities.

Fraud and Internal Control

LEARNING OBJECTIVE 1

Define fraud and the principles of internal control.

The Feature Story describes many of the internal control procedures used by **Barriques**. These procedures are necessary to discourage employees from fraudulent activities.

Fraud

A **fraud** is a dishonest act by an employee that results in personal benefit to the employee at a cost to the employer. Examples of fraud reported in the financial press include the following.

- A bookkeeper in a small company diverted $750,000 of bill payments to a personal bank account over a three-year period.
- A shipping clerk with 28 years of service shipped $125,000 of merchandise to himself.
- A computer operator embezzled $21 million from **Wells Fargo Bank** over a two-year period.
- A church treasurer "borrowed" $150,000 of church funds to finance a friend's business dealings.

Why does fraud occur? The three main factors that contribute to fraudulent activity are depicted by the **fraud triangle** in **Illustration 7.1**.

The most important element of the fraud triangle is **opportunity**. For an employee to commit fraud, the workplace environment must provide opportunities that an employee can take advantage of. Opportunities occur when the workplace lacks sufficient controls to deter and detect fraud. For example, inadequate monitoring of employee actions can create opportunities for theft and can embolden employees because they believe they will not be caught.

A second factor that contributes to fraud is **financial pressure**. Employees sometimes commit fraud because of personal financial problems caused by too much debt. Or, they might commit fraud because they want to lead a lifestyle that they cannot afford on their current salary.

The third factor that contributes to fraud is **rationalization**. In order to justify their fraud, employees rationalize their dishonest actions. For example, employees sometimes justify fraud because they believe they are underpaid while the employer is making lots of money. Employees feel justified in stealing because they believe they deserve to be paid more.

ILLUSTRATION 7.1

Fraud triangle

The Sarbanes-Oxley Act

What can be done to prevent or to detect fraud? After numerous corporate scandals came to light in the early 2000s, Congress addressed this issue by passing the **Sarbanes-Oxley Act (SOX)**. Under SOX, all publicly traded U.S. corporations are required to maintain an adequate system of internal control. Corporate executives and boards of directors must ensure that these controls are reliable and effective. In addition, independent outside auditors must attest to the adequacy of the internal control system. Companies that fail to comply are subject to fines, and company officers can be imprisoned. SOX also created the Public Company Accounting Oversight Board (PCAOB) to establish auditing standards and regulate auditor activity.

One poll found that 60% of investors believe that SOX helps safeguard their stock investments. Many say they would be unlikely to invest in a company that fails to follow SOX requirements. Although some corporate executives have criticized the time and expense involved in following SOX requirements, SOX appears to be working well. For example, the chief accounting officer of **Eli Lilly** noted that SOX triggered a comprehensive review of how the company documents its controls. This review uncovered redundancies and pointed out controls that needed to be added. In short, it added up to time and money well spent.

Internal Control

Internal control is a process designed to provide reasonable assurance regarding the achievement of company objectives related to operations, reporting, and compliance. In more detail, the purposes of internal control are to safeguard assets, enhance the reliability of accounting records, increase efficiency of operations, and ensure compliance with laws and regulations. Internal control systems have five primary components, as listed below.[1]

- **A control environment.** It is the responsibility of top management to make it clear that the organization values integrity and that unethical activity will not be tolerated. This component is often referred to as the "tone at the top."
- **Risk assessment.** Companies must identify and analyze the various factors that create risk for the business and must determine how to manage these risks.
- **Control activities.** To reduce the occurrence of fraud, management must design policies and procedures to address the specific risks faced by the company.
- **Information and communication.** The internal control system must capture and communicate all pertinent information both down and up the organization, as well as communicate information to appropriate external parties.
- **Monitoring.** Internal control systems must be monitored periodically for their adequacy. Significant deficiencies need to be reported to top management and/or the board of directors.

People, Planet, and Profit Insight

iStock.com/Karl Dolenc

And the Controls Are . . .

Internal controls are important for an effective financial reporting system. The same is true for sustainability reporting. An effective system of internal controls for sustainability reporting will help in the following ways: (1) prevent the unauthorized use of data; (2) provide reasonable assurance that the information is accurate, valid, and complete; and (3) report information that is consistent with overall sustainability accounting policies. With these types of controls, users will have the confidence that they can use the sustainability information effectively.

Some regulators are calling for even more assurance through audits of this information. Companies that potentially can cause environmental damage through greenhouse gases, as well as companies in the mining and extractive industries, are subject to reporting requirements. And, as demand for more information in the sustainability area expands, the need for audits of this information will grow.

Why is sustainability information important to investors? (Go to WileyPLUS for this answer and additional questions.)

Principles of Internal Control Activities

Each of the five components of an internal control system is important. Here, we will focus on one component, the control activities. The reason? These activities are the backbone of the company's efforts to address the risks it faces, such as fraud. The specific control activities

---

[1]The Committee of Sponsoring Organizations of the Treadway Commission, "Internal Control—Integrated Framework," *www.coso.org/documents/990025P_Executive_Summary_final_may20_e.pdf*; and Stephen J. McNally, "The 2013 COSO Framework and SOX Compliance," *Strategic Finance* (June 2013).

used by a company will vary, depending on management's assessment of the risks faced. This assessment is heavily influenced by the size and nature of the company.

The six principles of control activities are as follows.

- Establishment of responsibility
- Segregation of duties
- Documentation procedures
- Physical controls
- Independent internal verification
- Human resource controls

We explain these principles in the following sections. You should recognize that they apply to most companies and are relevant to both manual and computerized accounting systems.

Establishment of Responsibility

An essential principle of internal control is to assign responsibility to specific employees. **Control is most effective when only one person is responsible for a given task.**

To illustrate, assume that the cash on hand at the end of the day in a **Safeway** supermarket is $10 short of the cash entered in the cash register. If only one person has operated the register, the shift manager can quickly determine responsibility for the shortage. If two or more individuals have worked the register, it may be impossible to determine who is responsible for the error.

Many retailers solve this problem by having registers with multiple drawers. This makes it possible for more than one person to operate a register but still allows identification of a particular employee with a specific drawer. Only the signed-in cashier has access to his or her drawer.

Establishing responsibility often requires limiting access only to authorized personnel, and then identifying those personnel. For example, the automated systems used by many companies have mechanisms such as identifying passcodes that keep track of who made a journal entry, who entered a sale, or who went into an inventory storeroom at a particular time. Use of identifying passcodes enables the company to establish responsibility by identifying the particular employee who carried out the activity.

It's your shift now. I'm turning in my cash drawer and heading home.

Transfer of cash drawers

Anatomy of a Fraud

Maureen Frugali was a training supervisor for claims processing at Colossal Healthcare. As a standard part of the claims-processing training program, Maureen created fictitious claims for use by trainees. These fictitious claims were then sent to the accounts payable department. After the training claims had been processed, she was to notify Accounts Payable of all fictitious claims, so that they would not be paid. However, she did not inform Accounts Payable about every fictitious claim. She created some fictitious claims for entities that she controlled (that is, she would receive the payment), and she let Accounts Payable pay her.

Total take: $11 million

The Missing Control

Establishment of responsibility. The healthcare company did not adequately restrict the responsibility for authorizing and approving claims transactions. The training supervisor should not have been authorized to create claims in the company's "live" system.

Source: Adapted from Wells, *Fraud Casebook* (2007), pp. 61–70.

Segregation of Duties

Segregation of duties is indispensable in an internal control system. There are two common applications of this principle:

1. Different individuals should be responsible for related activities.
2. The responsibility for recordkeeping for an asset should be separate from the physical custody of that asset.

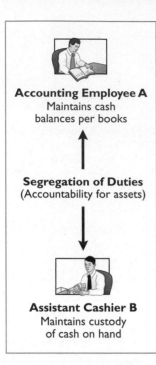

Accounting Employee A
Maintains cash
balances per books

↑
Segregation of Duties
(Accountability for assets)
↓

Assistant Cashier B
Maintains custody
of cash on hand

The rationale for segregation of duties is this: **The work of one employee should, without a duplication of effort, provide a reliable basis for evaluating the work of another employee.** For example, the personnel who design and program computerized systems should not be assigned duties related to day-to-day use of the systems. Otherwise, they could design the systems to benefit them personally and conceal the fraud through day-to-day use.

Segregation of Related Activities   Making one individual responsible for related activities increases the potential for errors and irregularities.

Purchasing Activities   Companies should, for example, assign related **purchasing activities** to different individuals. Related purchasing activities include ordering merchandise, approving orders, receiving goods, authorizing payment, and paying for goods or services. Various frauds are possible when one person handles related purchasing activities:

- If a purchasing agent is allowed to order goods without obtaining supervisory approval, the likelihood of the purchasing agent receiving kickbacks from suppliers increases.
- If an employee who orders goods also handles the invoice and receipt of the goods, as well as payment authorization, he or she might authorize payment for a fictitious invoice.

These abuses are less likely to occur when companies divide the purchasing tasks.

Sales Activities   Similarly, companies should assign related **sales activities** to different individuals. Related selling activities include making a sale, shipping (or delivering) the goods to the customer, billing the customer, and receiving payment. Various frauds are possible when one person handles related sales activities:

- If a salesperson can make a sale without obtaining supervisory approval, he or she might make sales at unauthorized prices to increase sales commissions.
- A shipping clerk who also has access to accounting records could ship goods to himself.
- A billing clerk who handles billing and receipt could understate the amount billed for sales made to friends and relatives.

These abuses are less likely to occur when companies divide the sales tasks. The salespeople make the sale, the shipping department ships the goods on the basis of the sales order, and the billing department prepares the sales invoice after comparing the sales order with the report of goods shipped.

Anatomy of a Fraud

Lawrence Fairbanks, the assistant vice-chancellor of communications at Aesop University, was allowed to make purchases of under $2,500 for his department without external approval. Unfortunately, he also sometimes bought items for himself, such as expensive antiques and other collectibles. How did he do it? He replaced the vendor invoices he received with fake vendor invoices that he created. The fake invoices had descriptions that were more consistent with the communications department's purchases. He submitted these fake invoices to the accounting department as the basis for their journal entries and to the accounts payable department as the basis for payment.

Total take: $475,000

The Missing Control

Segregation of duties. The university had not properly segregated related purchasing activities. Lawrence was ordering items, receiving the items, and receiving the invoice. By receiving the invoice, he had control over the documents that were used to account for the purchase and thus was able to substitute a fake invoice.

Source: Adapted from Wells, *Fraud Casebook* (2007), pp. 3–15.

Segregation of Recordkeeping from Physical Custody   The accountant should have neither physical custody of the asset nor access to it. Likewise, the custodian of the asset should not maintain or have access to the accounting records. **The custodian of the asset is not likely to convert the asset to personal use when one employee maintains the record of the asset, and a different employee has physical custody of the asset.** The separation of accounting responsibility from the custody of assets is especially important for cash and inventories because these assets are very vulnerable to fraud.

Anatomy of a Fraud

Angela Bauer was an accounts payable clerk for Aggasiz Construction Company. Angela prepared and issued checks to vendors and reconciled bank statements. She perpetrated a fraud in this way: She wrote checks for costs that the company had not actually incurred (e.g., fake taxes). A supervisor then approved and signed the checks. Before issuing the check, though, Angela would "white-out" the payee line on the check and change it to personal accounts that she controlled. She was able to conceal the theft because she also reconciled the bank account. That is, nobody else ever saw that the checks had been altered.

Total take: $570,000

The Missing Control

Segregation of duties. Aggasiz Construction Company did not properly segregate recordkeeping from physical custody. Angela had physical custody of the checks, which essentially was control of the cash. She also had recordkeeping responsibility because she prepared the bank reconciliation.

Source: Adapted from Wells, *Fraud Casebook* (2007), pp. 100–107.

Documentation Procedures

Documents provide evidence that transactions and events have occurred. For example, point-of-sale terminals are networked with a company's computing and accounting records, which results in direct documentation.

Similarly, a shipping document indicates that the goods have been shipped, and a sales invoice indicates that the company has billed the customer for the goods. By requiring signatures (or initials) on the documents, the company can identify the individual(s) responsible for the transaction or event. Companies should document transactions when they occur.

Companies should establish procedures for documents. First, whenever possible, companies should use **prenumbered documents, and all documents should be accounted for**. Prenumbering helps to prevent a transaction from being recorded more than once, or conversely, from not being recorded at all. Second, the control system should require that employees **promptly forward source documents for accounting entries to the accounting department. This control measure helps to ensure timely recording of the transaction** and contributes directly to the accuracy and reliability of the accounting records.

Prenumbered invoices

Anatomy of a Fraud

To support their reimbursement requests for travel costs incurred, employees at Mod Fashions Corporation's design center were required to submit receipts. The receipts could include the detailed bill provided for a meal, the credit card receipt provided when the credit card payment was made, or a copy of the employee's monthly credit card bill that listed the item. A number of the designers who frequently traveled together came up with a fraud scheme: They submitted claims for the same expenses. For example, if they had a meal together that cost $200, one person submitted the detailed meal bill, another submitted the credit card receipt, and a third submitted a monthly credit card bill showing the meal as a line item. Thus, all three received a $200 reimbursement.

Total take: $75,000

The Missing Control

Documentation procedures. Mod Fashions should require the original, detailed receipt. It should not accept photocopies, and it should not accept credit card statements. In addition, documentation procedures could be further improved by requiring the use of a corporate credit card (rather than a personal credit card) for all business expenses.

Source: Adapted from Wells, *Fraud Casebook* (2007), pp. 79–90.

Physical Controls

Use of physical controls is essential. **Physical controls** relate to the safeguarding of assets and enhance the accuracy and reliability of the accounting records. **Illustration 7.2** shows examples of these controls.

ILLUSTRATION 7.2 **Physical controls**

Physical Controls

 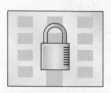  

| Safes, vaults, and safety deposit boxes for cash and business papers | Locked warehouses and storage cabinets for inventories and records | Computer facilities with passkey access or fingerprint or eyeball scans | Alarms to prevent break-ins | Television monitors and garment sensors to deter theft | Time clocks for recording time worked |

Anatomy of a Fraud

At Centerstone Health, a large insurance company, the mailroom each day received insurance applications from prospective customers. Mailroom employees scanned the applications into electronic documents before the applications were processed. Once the applications were scanned, they could be accessed online by authorized employees.

Insurance agents at Centerstone Health earn commissions based upon successful applications. The sales agent's name is listed on the application. However, roughly 15% of the applications are from customers who did not work with a sales agent. Two friends—Alex, an employee in recordkeeping, and Parviz, a sales agent—thought up a way to perpetrate a fraud. Alex identified scanned applications that did not list a sales agent. After business hours, he entered the mailroom and found the hard-copy applications that did not show a sales agent. He wrote in Parviz's name as the sales agent and then rescanned the application for processing. Parviz received the commission, which the friends then split.

Total take: $240,000

The Missing Control

Physical controls. Centerstone Health lacked two basic physical controls that could have prevented this fraud. First, the mailroom should have been locked during nonbusiness hours, and access during business hours should have been tightly controlled. Second, the scanned applications supposedly could be accessed only by authorized employees using their passwords. However, the password for each employee was the same as the employee's user ID. Since employee user-ID numbers were available to all other employees, all employees knew each other's passwords. Thus, Alex could enter the system using another employee's password and access the scanned applications.

Source: Adapted from Wells, *Fraud Casebook* (2007), pp. 316–326.

Independent Internal Verification

Most internal control systems provide for **independent internal verification**. This principle involves the review of data prepared by employees. To obtain maximum benefit from independent internal verification:

1. Companies should verify records periodically or on a surprise basis.
2. An employee who is independent of the personnel responsible for the information should make the verification.
3. Discrepancies and exceptions should be reported to a management level that can take appropriate corrective action.

Independent internal verification is especially useful in comparing recorded accountability with existing assets. The reconciliation of the electronic journal with the cash in the point-of-sale terminal at **Barriques** is an example of this internal control principle. Other common examples are the reconciliation of a company's cash balance per books with the cash balance per bank, and the verification of the perpetual inventory records through a count of physical inventory. **Illustration 7.3** shows the relationship between this principle and the segregation of duties principle.

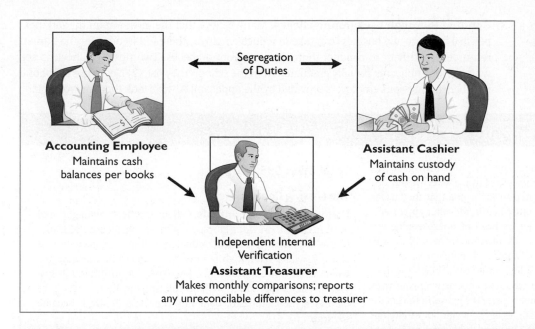

Anatomy of a Fraud

Bobbi Jean Donnelly, the office manager for Mod Fashions Corporation's design center, was responsible for preparing the design center budget and reviewing expense reports submitted by design center employees. Her desire to upgrade her wardrobe got the better of her, and she perpetrated a fraud that involved filing expense-reimbursement requests for her own personal clothing purchases. Bobbi Jean was able to conceal the fraud because she was responsible for reviewing all expense reports, including her own. In addition, she sometimes was given ultimate responsibility for signing off on the expense reports when her boss was "too busy." Also, because she controlled the budget, when she submitted her expenses, she coded them to budget items that she knew were running under budget, so that they would not catch anyone's attention.

Total take: $275,000

The Missing Control

Independent internal verification. Bobbi Jean's boss should have verified her expense reports. When asked what he thought her expenses for a year were, the boss said about $10,000. At $115,000 per year, her actual expenses were more than 10 times what would have been expected. However, because he was "too busy" to verify her expense reports or to review the budget, he never noticed.

Source: Adapted from Wells, *Fraud Casebook* (2007), pp. 79–90.

Large companies often assign independent internal verification to internal auditors. **Internal auditors** are company employees who continuously evaluate the effectiveness of the company's internal control systems. They review the activities of departments and individuals to determine whether prescribed internal controls are being followed. They also recommend improvements when needed. For example, **WorldCom** was at one time the second largest U.S. telecommunications company. The fraud that caused its bankruptcy (the largest ever when it occurred) involved billions of dollars. It was uncovered by an internal auditor.

Human Resource Controls

Human resource control activities include the following.

1. **Bond employees who handle cash. Bonding** involves obtaining insurance protection against theft by employees. It contributes to the safeguarding of cash in two ways. First, the insurance company carefully screens all individuals before adding them to the policy and may reject risky applicants. Second, bonded employees know that the insurance company will vigorously prosecute all offenders.

2. **Rotate employees' duties and require employees to take vacations.** These measures deter employees from attempting thefts since they will not be able to permanently conceal their improper actions. Many banks, for example, have discovered employee thefts when the employee was on vacation or assigned to a new position.

3. **Conduct thorough background checks.** Many believe that the most important and inexpensive measure any business can take to reduce employee theft and fraud is for the human resource department to conduct thorough background checks. Two tips: (1) Check to see whether job applicants actually graduated from the schools they list. (2) Never use telephone numbers for previous employers provided by the applicant. Always look them up yourself.

Anatomy of a Fraud

Ellen Lowry was the desk manager and Josephine Rodriguez was the head of housekeeping at the Excelsior Inn, a luxury hotel. The two best friends were so dedicated to their jobs that they never took vacations, and they frequently filled in for other employees. In fact, Ms. Rodriguez, whose job as head of housekeeping did not include cleaning rooms, often cleaned rooms herself, "just to help the staff keep up." These two "dedicated" employees, working as a team, found a way to earn a little more cash. Ellen, the desk manager, provided significant discounts to guests who paid with cash. She kept the cash and did not register the guests in the hotel's computerized system. Instead, she took the room out of circulation "due to routine maintenance." Because the room did not show up as being used, it did not receive a normal housekeeping assignment. Instead, Josephine, the head of housekeeping, cleaned the rooms during the guests' stay.

Total take: $95,000

The Missing Control

Human resource controls. Ellen, the desk manager, had been fired by a previous employer after being accused of fraud. If the Excelsior Inn had conducted a thorough background check, it would not have hired her. The hotel fraud was detected when Ellen missed work for a few days due to illness. A system of mandatory vacations and rotating days off would have increased the chances of detecting the fraud before it became so large.

Source: Adapted from Wells, *Fraud Casebook* (2007), pp. 145–155.

Accounting Across the Organization

SOX Boosts the Role of Human Resources

Stockbyte/Getty Images

Under SOX, a company needs to keep track of employees' degrees and certifications to ensure that employees continue to meet the specified requirements of a job. Also, to ensure proper employee supervision and proper separation of duties, companies must develop and monitor an organizational chart. When one corporation went through this exercise, it found that out of 17,000 employees, there were 400 people who did not report to anyone. The corporation also had 35 people who reported to each other. In addition, if an employee complains of an unfair firing and mentions financial issues at the company, the human resource department must refer the case to the company audit committee and possibly to its legal counsel.

Why would unsupervised employees or employees who report to each other represent potential internal control threats? (Go to WileyPLUS for this answer and additional questions.)

Data Analytics and Internal Controls

Data analytics has dramatically changed many aspects of internal control practices. In the past, internal and external auditors tended to rely heavily on investigations of period-end samples of transactions to identify potential violations. Now, rather than wait for a period-end sample, many companies employ continuous monitoring of virtually every transaction. As a result, spikes in certain types of activity or developing trends are more quickly identified and investigated.

Many different aspects of journal entries can be monitored continuously. For example, systems can automatically identify who recorded a particular journal entry. This is important to ensure that the segregation of duties control principle is not violated, that is, that the entry is only made by a current (as opposed to recently terminated) employee and that the employee is authorized to make that type of entry.

Large dollar amounts in risky areas can also be flagged and investigated quickly. Recipients of payments can be easily screened to ensure, for example, that bonus amounts are correctly determined based on results and bonus formulas, and that bonuses are only paid to employees who are designated for bonus payments. Similarly, vendor payments can be easily screened to ensure that payments only go to authorized vendors and that amounts are within an anticipated range. Sophisticated models can be used to continually estimate critical measures, and those estimates are then compared to actual results to identify outliers.

Limitations of Internal Control

Companies generally design their systems of internal control to provide **reasonable assurance** of proper safeguarding of assets and reliability of the accounting records. The concept of reasonable assurance rests on the premise that the costs of establishing control procedures should not exceed their expected benefit (see **Helpful Hint**).

To illustrate, consider shoplifting losses in retail stores. Stores could eliminate such losses by having a security guard stop and search customers as they leave the store. But store managers have concluded that the negative effects of such a procedure cannot be justified. Instead, they have attempted to control shoplifting losses by less costly procedures. They post signs saying, "We reserve the right to inspect all packages" and "All shoplifters will be prosecuted." They use hidden cameras and store detectives to monitor customer activity, and they install sensor equipment at exits.

The **human element** is an important factor in every system of internal control. A good system can become ineffective as a result of employee fatigue, carelessness, or indifference. For example, a receiving clerk may not bother to count goods received and may just "fudge" the counts. Occasionally, two or more individuals may work together to get around prescribed controls. Such **collusion** can significantly reduce the effectiveness of a system, eliminating the protection offered by segregation of duties. No system of internal control is perfect.

The **size of the business** also may impose limitations on internal control. Small companies often find it difficult to segregate duties or to provide for independent internal verification. A study by the Association of Certified Fraud Examiners indicates that businesses with fewer than 100 employees are most at risk for employee theft. In fact, 29% of frauds occurred at companies with fewer than 100 employees. The median loss at small companies was $154,000, which was nearly as high as the median fraud at companies with more than 10,000 employees ($160,000). A $154,000 loss can threaten the very existence of a small company.

HELPFUL HINT

Controls may vary with the risk level of the activity. For example, management may consider cash to be high risk and maintaining inventories in the stockroom as low risk. Thus, management would have stricter controls for cash.

DO IT! 1 | Principles of Control Activities

Identify which principles of control activities are violated in each of the following situations, and explain how each situation creates an opportunity for a fraud.

1. The person with primary responsibility for reconciling the bank account and making all bank deposits is also the company's accountant.

2. Wellstone Company's treasurer received an award for distinguished service because he had not taken a vacation in 30 years.

3. In order to save money spent on order slips and to reduce time spent keeping track of order slips, a local bar/restaurant does not buy prenumbered order slips.

ACTION PLAN

- Familiarize yourself with each of the principles of control activities discussed.
- Understand the nature of the frauds that each principles of control activity is intended to address.

Solution

1. Violates the segregation of duties control principle. Recordkeeping should be separate from physical custody. As a consequence, the employee could embezzle cash and make journal entries to hide the theft.

2. Violates the human resource control principle. Key employees must take vacations. Otherwise, the treasurer, who manages the company's cash, might embezzle cash and use his position to conceal the theft.

3. Violates the documentation procedures control principle. If prenumbered documents are not used, then it is virtually impossible to account for the documents. As a consequence, an employee could write up a dinner sale, receive the cash from the customer, and then throw away the order slip and keep the cash.

Related exercise material: **BE7.1, BE7.2, BE7.3, BE7.4, DO IT! 7.1, E7.1, E7.2, E7.3, E7.5, and E7.6.**

Cash Controls

LEARNING OBJECTIVE 2
Apply internal control principles to cash.

Cash is the one asset that is readily convertible into any other type of asset. It also is easily concealed and transported, and is highly desired. Because of these characteristics, **cash is the asset most susceptible to fraudulent activities**. In addition, because of the large volume of cash transactions, numerous errors may occur in executing and recording them. To safeguard cash and to ensure the accuracy of the accounting records for cash, effective internal control over cash is critical.

Cash Receipts Controls

Illustration 7.4 shows how the internal control principles explained earlier apply to cash receipts transactions. As you might expect, companies vary considerably in how they apply these principles. To illustrate internal control over cash receipts, we will examine control activities for a retail store with both over-the-counter and mail receipts.

ILLUSTRATION 7.4 **Application of internal control principles to cash receipts**

Cash Receipts Controls

 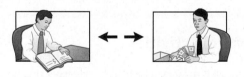 

Establishment of Responsibility
Only designated personnel are authorized to handle cash receipts (cashiers)

Segregation of Duties
Different individuals receive cash, record cash receipts, and hold the cash

Documentation Procedures
Use remittance advice (mail receipts), cash register tapes or computer records, and deposit slips

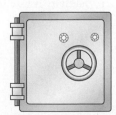  

Physical Controls
Store cash in safes and bank vaults; limit access to storage areas; use cash registers or point-of-sale terminals

Independent Internal Verification
Supervisors count cash receipts daily; assistant treasurer compares total receipts to bank deposits daily

Human Resource Controls
Bond personnel who handle cash; require employees to take vacations; conduct background checks

Over-the-Counter Receipts

In retail businesses, control of over-the-counter receipts centers on cash registers that are visible to customers. A cash sale is entered in a cash register (or point-of-sale terminal), with the amount clearly visible to the customer. This activity prevents the sales clerk from entering a lower amount and pocketing the difference. The customer receives an itemized cash register receipt and is expected to count the change received. (One weakness at **Barriques** in the Feature Story is that customers are only given a receipt if requested.) The cash register's tape is locked in the register until a supervisor removes it. This tape accumulates the daily transactions and totals.

At the end of the clerk's shift, the clerk counts the cash and sends the cash and the count to the cashier. The cashier counts the cash, prepares a deposit slip, and deposits the cash at the bank. The cashier also sends a duplicate of the deposit slip to the accounting department to indicate cash received. The supervisor removes the cash register tape and sends it to the accounting department as the basis for a journal entry to record the cash received. (For point-of-sale systems, the accounting department receives information on daily transactions and totals through the computer network.) **Illustration 7.5** summarizes this process (see **Helpful Hint**).

HELPFUL HINT

Flowcharts such as this one enhance the understanding of the flow of documents, the processing steps, and the internal control procedures.

ILLUSTRATION 7.5
Control of over-the-counter receipts

This system for handling cash receipts uses an important internal control principle—segregation of recordkeeping from physical custody. The supervisor has access to the cash register tape but **not** to the cash. The clerk and the cashier have access to the cash but **not** to the register tape. In addition, the cash register tape provides documentation and enables independent internal verification. Use of these three principles of internal control (segregation of recordkeeping from physical custody, documentation, and independent internal verification) provides an effective system of internal control. Any attempt at fraudulent activity should be detected unless there is collusion among the employees.

In some instances, the amount deposited at the bank will not agree with the cash recorded in the accounting records based on the cash register tape. These differences often result because the clerk hands incorrect change back to the retail customer. In this case, the difference between the actual cash and the amount reported on the cash register tape is reported in a Cash Over and Short account. For example, suppose that the cash register tape indicated sales of $6,956.20 but the amount of cash was only $6,946.10. A cash shortfall of $10.10 exists. To account for this cash shortfall and related cash sales, the company makes the following entry.

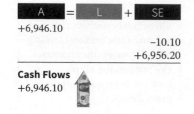

	A	=	L	+	SE
+6,946.10					
					−10.10
					+6,956.20

Cash Flows
+6,946.10

Cash	6,946.10	
Cash Over and Short	10.10	
Sales Revenue		6,956.20
(To record cash shortfall and cash sales)		

Cash Over and Short is an income statement item. It is reported as miscellaneous expense when there is a cash shortfall, and as miscellaneous revenue when there is an overage. Clearly, the amount should be small. Any material amounts in this account should be investigated.

Mail Receipts

All mail receipts should be opened in the presence of at least two mail clerks. These receipts are generally in the form of checks. A mail clerk should endorse each check "For Deposit Only." This restrictive endorsement reduces the likelihood that someone could divert the check to personal use. Banks will not give an individual cash when presented with a check that has this type of endorsement.

The mail clerks prepare, in triplicate, a list of the checks received each day. This list shows the name of the check issuer, the purpose of the payment, and the amount of the check. Each mail clerk signs the list to establish responsibility for the data. The original copy of the list, along with the checks, is then sent to the cashier's department. A copy of the list is sent to the accounting department for recording in the accounting records. The mail clerks also keep a copy.

This process provides excellent internal control for the company. By employing at least two clerks, the chance of fraud is reduced. Each clerk knows he or she is being observed by the other clerk(s). To engage in fraud, they would have to collude. The customers who submit payments also provide control because they will contact the company with a complaint if they are not properly credited for payment. Because the cashier has access to the cash but not the records, and the accounting department has access to the records but not the cash, neither can engage in undetected fraud.

ACTION PLAN

- **Differentiate among the internal control principles of (1) establishing responsibility, (2) using physical controls, and (3) independent internal verification.**

- **Design an effective system of internal control over cash receipts.**

DO IT! 2a | Control over Cash Receipts

L. R. Cortez is concerned about the control over cash receipts in his fast-food restaurant, Big Cheese. The restaurant has two cash registers. At no time do more than two employees take customer orders and enter sales. Work shifts for employees range from 4 to 8 hours. Cortez asks your help in installing a good system of internal control over cash receipts.

Solution

Cortez should assign a separate cash register drawer to each employee at the start of each work shift, with register totals set at zero. Each employee should have access to only the assigned register drawer to enter all sales. Each customer should be given a receipt. At the end of the shift, the employee should do a cash count. A separate employee should compare the cash count with the register tape (or point-of-sale records) to be sure they agree. In addition, Cortez should install an automated point-of-sale system that would enable the company to compare orders entered in the register to orders processed by the kitchen.

Related exercise material: **BE7.5, BE7.6, BE7.7, BE7.8, DO IT! 7.2a, E7.2, E7.3, E7.4, E7.5, and E7.6.**

Cash Disbursements Controls

Companies disburse cash for a variety of reasons, such as to pay expenses and liabilities or to purchase assets. **Generally, internal control over cash disbursements is more effective when companies pay by check or electronic funds transfer (EFT) rather than by cash.** One exception is **payments for incidental amounts that are paid out of petty cash.**[2]

Companies generally issue checks only after following specified control procedures. **Illustration 7.6** shows how principles of internal control apply to cash disbursements.

ILLUSTRATION 7.6 Application of internal control principles to cash disbursements

Cash Disbursements Controls

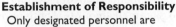
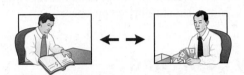

Establishment of Responsibility
Only designated personnel are authorized to sign checks (treasurer) and approve vendors

Segregation of Duties
Different individuals approve and make payments; check-signers do not record disbursements

Documentation Procedures
Use prenumbered checks and account for them in sequence; each check must have an approved invoice; require employees to use corporate credit cards for reimbursable expenses; stamp invoices "paid"

Physical Controls
Store blank checks in safes, with limited access; print check amounts by machine in indelible ink

Independent Internal Verification
Compare checks to invoices; reconcile bank statement monthly

Human Resource Controls
Bond personnel who handle cash; require employees to take vacations; conduct background checks

---

Voucher System Controls

Most medium and large companies use vouchers as part of their internal control over cash disbursements. A **voucher system** is a network of approvals by authorized individuals, acting independently, to ensure that all disbursements by check are proper.

The system begins with the authorization to incur a cost or expense. It ends with the issuance of a check for the liability incurred. A **voucher** is an authorization form prepared for each expenditure. Companies require vouchers for all types of cash disbursements except those from petty cash.

The starting point in preparing a voucher is to fill in the appropriate information about the liability on the face of the voucher. The vendor's invoice provides most of the needed

---

[2] We explain the operation of a petty cash fund later in the chapter.

information. Then, an employee in the accounts payable department records the liability related to the voucher (in a journal called a **voucher register**) and files it according to the date on which it is to be paid. The company issues and sends a check on that date, and stamps the voucher "paid." The paid voucher is sent to the accounting department for recording (in a journal called the **check register**). A voucher system involves two journal entries, one to record the liability in the voucher register when the voucher is issued, and a second in the check register to pay the liability that relates to the voucher.

The use of a voucher system, whether done manually or electronically, improves internal control over cash disbursements. First, the authorization process inherent in a voucher system establishes responsibility. Each individual has responsibility to review the underlying documentation to ensure that it is correct. In addition, the voucher system keeps track of the documents that back up each transaction. By keeping these documents in one place, a supervisor can independently verify the authenticity of each transaction. Consider, for example, the case of Aesop University presented earlier in the Anatomy of a Fraud box. Aesop did not use a voucher system for transactions under $2,500. As a consequence, there was no independent verification of the documents, which enabled the employee to submit fake invoices to hide his unauthorized purchases.

Petty Cash Fund

As you just learned, better internal control over cash disbursements is possible when companies make payments by check. However, using checks to pay small amounts is both impractical and a nuisance. For instance, a company would not want to write checks to pay for postage due, working lunches, or taxi fares. A common way of handling such payments, while maintaining satisfactory control, is to use a **petty cash fund** to pay relatively small amounts (see **Ethics Note**). The operation of a petty cash fund, often called an **imprest system**, involves (1) establishing the fund, (2) making payments from the fund, and (3) replenishing the fund.[3]

Establishing the Petty Cash Fund

Two essential steps in establishing a petty cash fund are (1) appointing a petty cash custodian who will be responsible for the fund, and (2) determining the size of the fund. Ordinarily, a company expects the amount in the fund to cover anticipated disbursements for a three- to four-week period.

To establish the fund, a company issues a check payable to the petty cash custodian for the stipulated amount. For example, if Laird Company decides to establish a $100 fund on March 1, the general journal entry is as follows.

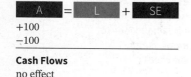

+100
−100

Cash Flows
no effect

Mar. 1	Petty Cash	100	
	Cash		100
	(To establish a petty cash fund)		

The fund custodian cashes the check and places the proceeds in a locked petty cash box or drawer. Most petty cash funds are established on a fixed-amount basis. The company will make no additional entries to the Petty Cash account unless management changes the stipulated amount of the fund. For example, if Laird decides on July 1 to increase the size of the fund to $250, it would debit Petty Cash $150 and credit Cash $150.

Making Payments from the Petty Cash Fund

The petty cash custodian has the authority to make payments from the fund that conform to prescribed management policies. Usually, management limits the size of expenditures that come from petty cash. Likewise, it may not permit use of the fund for certain types of transactions (such as making short-term loans to employees).

[3] The term "imprest" means an advance of money for a designated purpose.

Each payment from the fund must be documented on a prenumbered petty cash receipt (or petty cash voucher), as shown in **Illustration 7.7**. The signatures of both the fund custodian and the person receiving payment are required on the receipt. If other supporting documents such as a freight bill or invoice are available, they should be attached to the petty cash receipt (see **Helpful Hint**).

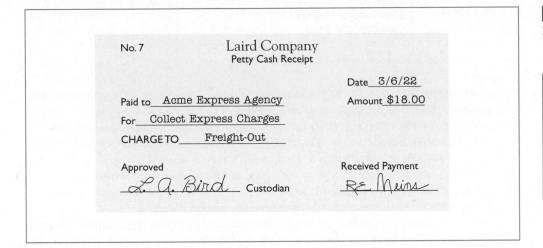

ILLUSTRATION 7.7
Petty cash receipt

HELPFUL HINT

The petty cash receipt satisfies two internal control principles: (1) establishment of responsibility (signature of custodian), and (2) documentation procedures.

The petty cash custodian keeps the receipts in the petty cash box until the fund is replenished. The sum of the petty cash receipts and the money in the fund should equal the established total at all times. Management can (and should) make surprise counts at any time by an independent person, such as an internal auditor, to determine the correctness of the fund.

The company does not make an accounting entry to record a payment when it is made from petty cash. It is considered both inexpedient and unnecessary to do so. Instead, the company recognizes the accounting effects of each payment when it replenishes the fund.

Replenishing the Petty Cash Fund

When the money in the petty cash fund reaches a minimum level, the company replenishes the fund (see **Helpful Hint**). The petty cash custodian initiates a request for reimbursement. The custodian prepares a schedule (or summary) of the payments that have been made and sends the schedule, supported by petty cash receipts and other documentation, to the treasurer's office. The treasurer's office examines the receipts and supporting documents to verify that proper payments from the fund were made. The treasurer then approves the request and issues a check to restore the fund to its established amount. At the same time, all supporting documentation is stamped "paid" so that it cannot be submitted again for payment.

To illustrate, assume that on March 15 Laird's petty cash custodian requests a check for $87 because the fund contains $13 cash. Petty cash receipts also total $87: postage $44, freight-out $38, and miscellaneous expenses $5. This replenishment will reestablish the desired total of $100 in the fund. The journal entry to record the replenishment is as follows.

HELPFUL HINT

Replenishing the petty cash fund involves three internal control principles: (1) segregation of duties, (2) documentation procedures, and (3) independent internal verification.

A	=	L	+	SE

Mar. 15	Postage Expense	44	
	Freight-Out	38	
	Miscellaneous Expense	5	
	Cash		87
	(To replenish petty cash fund)		

−44 Exp
−38 Exp
−5 Exp
−87

Cash Flows
−87

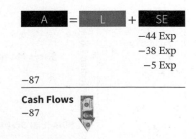

Note that the replenishment entry does not affect the Petty Cash account. Replenishment changes the composition of the fund by replacing the petty cash receipts with cash. It does not change the balance in the fund.

Occasionally, in replenishing a petty cash fund, the company may need to recognize a cash shortage or overage. This results when the total of the cash plus receipts in the petty cash box does not equal the established amount of the petty cash fund. To illustrate, assume that Laird's petty cash custodian has only $12 in cash in the fund plus the receipts as listed. The request for reimbursement would therefore be for $88 to reestablish the $100 cash total. Laird would make the following entry.

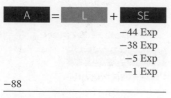

−44 Exp
−38 Exp
−5 Exp
−1 Exp

−88

Cash Flows
−88

Mar. 15	Postage Expense	44	
	Freight-Out	38	
	Miscellaneous Expense	5	
	Cash Over and Short	1	
	Cash		88
	(To replenish petty cash fund)		

Conversely, if the custodian has $14 in cash, the reimbursement request would be for $86. The company would credit Cash Over and Short for $1 (overage). A company reports a debit balance in Cash Over and Short in the income statement as miscellaneous expense (see **Helpful Hint**). It reports a credit balance in the account as miscellaneous revenue. The company closes Cash Over and Short to Income Summary at the end of the year.

Companies should replenish a petty cash fund **at the end of the accounting period, regardless of the cash in the fund**. Replenishment at this time is necessary in order to recognize the effects of the petty cash payments on the financial statements.

Internal control over a petty cash fund is strengthened by (1) having a supervisor make surprise counts of the fund to ascertain whether the paid petty cash receipts and fund cash equal the designated amount, and (2) cancelling or defacing the paid petty cash receipts so they cannot be resubmitted for reimbursement.

HELPFUL HINT

Cash over and short situations result from mathematical errors or from failure to keep accurate records.

Ethics Insight

How Employees Steal

Occupational fraud is using your own occupation for personal gain through the misuse or misapplication of the company's resources or assets. This type of fraud is one of three types:

1. **Asset misappropriation**, such as theft of cash on hand, fraudulent disbursements, false refunds, ghost employees, personal purchases, and fictitious employees. This fraud is the most common but the least costly.

iStock.com/Chris Fertnig

2. **Corruption**, such as bribery, illegal gratuities, and economic extortion. This fraud generally falls in the middle between asset misappropriation and financial statement fraud as regards frequency and cost.

3. **Financial statement fraud**, such as fictitious revenues, concealed liabilities and expenses, improper disclosures, and improper asset values. This fraud occurs less frequently than other types of fraud, but it is the most costly.

The following graph shows the frequency and the median loss for each type of occupational fraud. (Note that the sum of percentages exceeds 100% because some cases of fraud involved more than one type.)

Source: *2016 Report to the Nations on Occupational Fraud and Abuse*, Association of Certified Fraud Examiners, p. 12.

How can companies reduce the likelihood of occupational fraud? (Go to WileyPLUS for this answer and additional questions.)

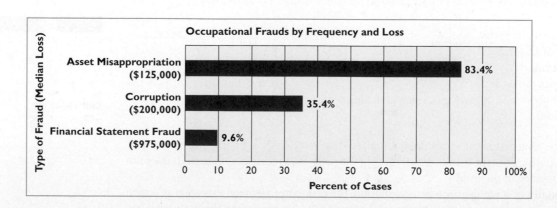

DO IT! 2b | Petty Cash Fund

Bateer Company established a $50 petty cash fund on July 1. On July 30, the fund had $12 cash remaining and petty cash receipts for postage $14, office supplies $10, and delivery expense to customers $15. Prepare journal entries to establish the fund on July 1 and to replenish the fund on July 30.

Solution

July	1	Petty Cash	50	
		Cash		50
		(To establish petty cash fund)		
	30	Postage Expense	14	
		Supplies	10	
		Freight-Out	15	
		Cash Over and Short		1
		Cash ($50 – $12)		38
		(To replenish petty cash)		

Related exercise material: **BE7.9, DO IT! 7.2b, E7.7, and E7.8.**

ACTION PLAN

- To establish the fund, set up a separate general ledger account.
- Determine how much cash is needed to replenish the fund: subtract the cash remaining from the established petty cash fund balance.
- Total the petty cash receipts. Determine any cash over or short—the difference between the cash needed to replenish the fund and the total of the petty cash receipts.
- Record the expenditures incurred according to the petty cash receipts when replenishing the fund.

Control Features of a Bank Account

LEARNING OBJECTIVE 3

Identify the control features of a bank account.

The use of a bank contributes significantly to good internal control over cash. A company safeguards its cash by using a bank as a depository and clearinghouse for checks received and checks written. The use of a bank checking account minimizes the amount of cash that must be kept on hand. It also facilitates control of cash because a double record is maintained of all bank transactions—one by the business and the other by the bank. The asset account Cash maintained by the company is the "flipside" of the bank's liability account for that company. A **bank reconciliation** is the process of comparing the bank's balance with the company's balance, and explaining the differences to make them agree.

Many companies have more than one bank account. For efficiency of operations and better control, national retailers like **Walmart** and **Target** often have regional bank accounts. Similarly, a company such as **ExxonMobil** with more than 100,000 employees may have a payroll bank account as well as one or more general bank accounts. In addition, a company may maintain several bank accounts in order to have more than one source for short-term loans.

Making Bank Deposits

An authorized employee, such as the head cashier, should make a company's bank deposits. Each deposit must be documented by a deposit slip (ticket), as shown in **Illustration 7.8**.

ILLUSTRATION 7.8
Deposit slip

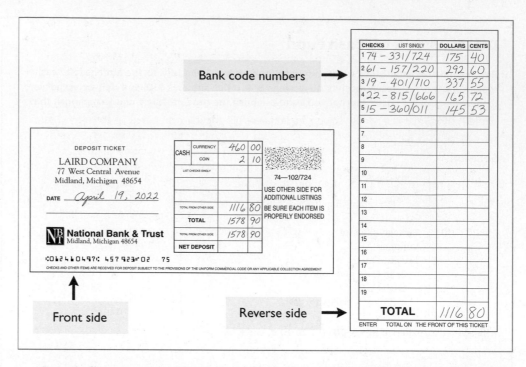

Deposit slips are prepared in duplicate. The bank retains the original; the depositor keeps the duplicate, machine-stamped by the bank to establish its authenticity.

Writing Checks

A **check** is a written order signed by the depositor directing the bank to pay a specified sum of money to a designated recipient. There are three parties to a check: (1) the **maker** (or drawer) who issues the check, (2) the **bank** (or payer) on which the check is drawn, and (3) the **payee** to whom the check is payable. A check is a **negotiable instrument** that one party can transfer to another party by endorsement. Each check should be accompanied by an explanation of its purpose. In many companies, a remittance advice attached to the check, as shown in **Illustration 7.9**, explains the check's purpose.

ILLUSTRATION 7.9
Check with remittance advice

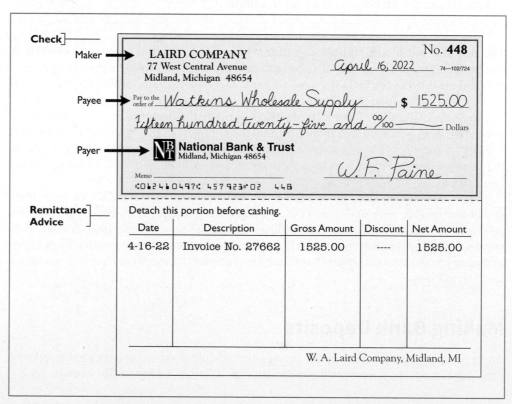

Electronic Funds Transfer (EFT) System

It is not surprising that companies and banks have developed approaches to transfer funds among parties without the use of paper (deposit tickets, checks, etc.). Such procedures, called **electronic funds transfers (EFTs)**, are disbursement systems that use wire, telephone, or computers to transfer cash from one location to another. Use of EFT is quite common. For example, many employees receive no formal payroll checks from their employers. Instead, employers send electronic payroll data to the appropriate employee banks. Also, companies now frequently make regular payments such as those for utilities, rent, and insurance by EFT.

EFT transactions normally result in better internal control since no cash or checks are handled by company employees. This does not mean that opportunities for fraud are eliminated. In fact, the same basic principles related to internal control apply to EFT transactions. For example, without proper segregation of duties and authorizations, an employee might be able to redirect electronic payments into a personal bank account and conceal the theft with fraudulent accounting entries.

Bank Statements

Each month, the company receives from the bank a **bank statement** showing its bank transactions and balances.[4] For example, the statement for Laird Company in **Illustration 7.10**

ILLUSTRATION 7.10

Bank statement

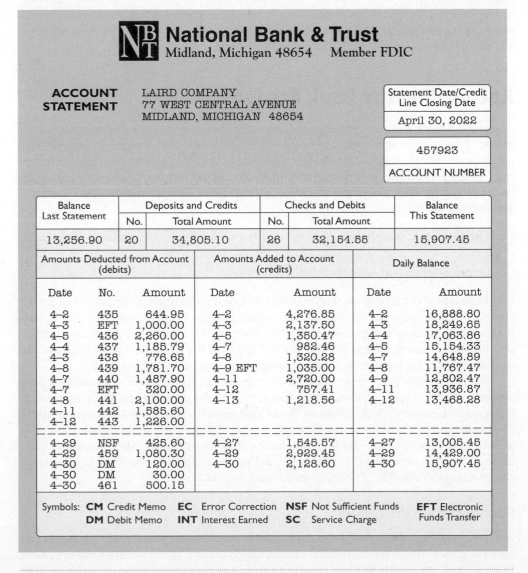

---

[4]Our presentation assumes that a company makes all adjustments at the end of the month. In practice, a company may also make journal entries during the month as it reviews online information from the bank regarding its account.

shows the following: (1) checks paid and other debits (such as debit card transactions or electronic funds transfers for bill payments) that reduce the balance in the depositor's account, (2) deposits (by direct deposit, automated teller machine, or electronic funds transfer) and other credits that increase the balance in the depositor's account, and (3) the account balance after each day's transactions.

Remember that **bank statements are prepared from the** *bank's* **perspective**. For example, **every deposit the bank receives is an increase in the bank's liabilities (an account payable to the depositor)**. Therefore, in Illustration 7.10, National Bank and Trust **credits** to Laird Company every deposit it received from Laird. The reverse occurs when the bank "pays" a check issued by Laird Company on its checking account balance: Payment reduces the bank's liability and is therefore **debited** to Laird's account with the bank.

The bank statement lists in numerical sequence all paid checks along with the date the check was paid and its amount. Upon paying a check, the bank stamps the check "paid"; a paid check is sometimes referred to as a **canceled** check. In addition, the bank includes with the bank statement memoranda explaining other debits and credits it made to the depositor's account (see **Helpful Hint**).

HELPFUL HINT

Essentially, the bank statement is a copy of the bank's records sent to the customer or made available online for review.

A check that is not paid by a bank because of insufficient funds in a bank account is called an **NSF check** (not sufficient funds). The bank uses a debit memorandum when a previously deposited customer's check "bounces" because of insufficient funds. In such a case, the customer's bank marks the check NSF (not sufficient funds) and returns it to the depositor's bank. The bank then debits (decreases) the depositor's account, as shown by the symbol NSF in Illustration 7.10, and sends the NSF check and debit memorandum to the depositor as notification of the charge. The NSF check reestablishes an account receivable for the depositor and reduces its cash in the bank account.

Reconciling the Bank Account

Because the bank and the company maintain independent records of the company's cash account, you might assume that the respective balances will always agree. In fact, the two balances are seldom the same at any given time, and both balances differ from the "correct or true" balance. Therefore, it is necessary to make the balance per books and the balance per bank agree with the correct or true amount—a process called **reconciling the bank account**. The need for reconciliation has two causes:

1. **Time lags** that prevent one of the parties from recording the transaction in the same period.
2. **Errors** by either party in recording transactions.

Time lags occur frequently. For example, several days may elapse between the time a company pays by check and the date the bank pays the check. Similarly, when a company uses the bank's night depository to make its deposits, there will be a difference of one day between the time the company records the receipts and the time the bank does so. A time lag also occurs whenever the bank mails a debit or credit memorandum to the company.

You might think that if a company never writes checks (for example, if a small company uses only a debit card or electronic funds transfers), it does not need to reconcile its account. However, **the possibility of errors or fraud still necessitates periodic reconciliation**. The incidence of errors or fraud depends on the effectiveness of the internal controls maintained by the company and the bank. Bank errors are infrequent. However, either party could accidentally record a $450 check as $45 or $540. In addition, the bank might mistakenly charge a check drawn by C. D. Berg to the account of C. D. Burg.

Reconciliation Procedure

In reconciling the bank account, it is customary to reconcile the balance per books and balance per bank to their adjusted (correct or true) cash balances. **To obtain maximum benefit from a bank reconciliation, an employee who has no other responsibilities related to cash should prepare the reconciliation**. When companies do not follow the internal control principle of independent internal verification in preparing the reconciliation, cash embezzlements may escape unnoticed. For example, in the Anatomy of a Fraud box about Aggasiz Construction Company presented earlier, a bank reconciliation by someone other than Angela Bauer might have exposed her embezzlement.

Illustration 7.11 shows the reconciliation process (see **Helpful Hint**). The starting point in preparing the reconciliation is to enter the balance per bank statement and balance per books on a schedule. The following steps should reveal all the reconciling items that cause the difference between the two balances.

HELPFUL HINT

Deposits in transit and outstanding checks are reconciling items because of time lags.

ILLUSTRATION 7.11
Bank reconciliation process

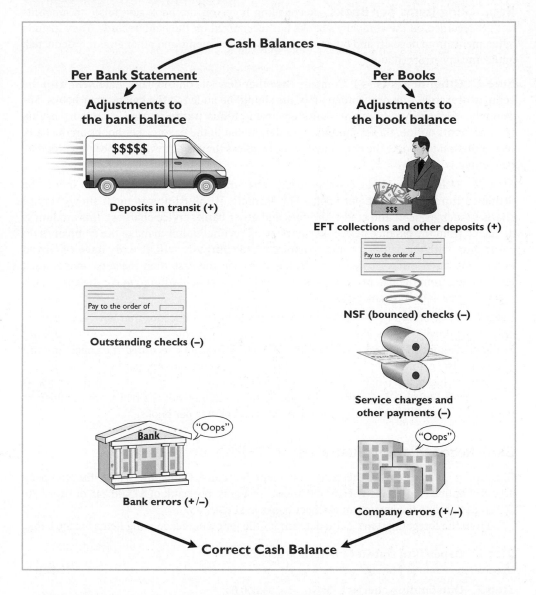

Reconciling Items per Bank   On the bank side of the reconciliation, the items to reconcile are deposits in transit (amounts added), outstanding checks (amounts deducted), and bank errors (if any). By adjusting the bank balance for these items, a company brings that balance up to date.

Step 1   Deposits in transit (+). Compare the individual deposits on the bank statement with the deposits in transit from the preceding bank reconciliation and with the deposits per company records or copies of duplicate deposit slips for the current period. Deposits recorded by the depositor that have not been recorded by the bank represent **deposits in transit**. Add these deposits to the balance per bank.

Step 2   Outstanding checks (−). Compare the paid checks shown on the bank statement or the paid checks returned with the bank statement with (a) checks outstanding from the preceding bank reconciliation, and (b) checks issued by the company recorded as cash payments in the current period. Issued checks recorded by the company that have not been paid by the bank represent **outstanding checks**. Deduct outstanding checks from the balance per bank.

Step 3 Bank errors (+/−). Note any errors made by the bank that were discovered in the previous steps. For example, if the bank processed a deposit of $1,693 as $1,639 in error, the difference of $54 ($1,693 − $1,639) is added to the balance per bank on the bank reconciliation. All errors made by the bank are reconciling items in determining the adjusted cash balance per the bank.

Reconciling Items per Books Reconciling items on the book side relate to amounts not yet recorded on the company's books but recognized on the bank records. They include adjustments from deposits and other amounts added, payments and other amounts deducted, and company errors (if any).

Step 1 Other deposits (+). Compare the other deposits on the bank statement with the company records. Any unrecorded amounts should be added to the balance per books. For example, if the bank statement shows electronic funds transfers from customers paying their accounts online, these amounts should be added to the balance per books on the bank reconciliation to update the company's records unless they had previously been recorded by the company.

Step 2 Other payments (−). Similarly, any unrecorded other payments should be deducted from the balance per books. For example, if the bank statement shows service charges (such as debit and credit card fees and other bank service charges), this amount is deducted from the balance per books on the bank reconciliation to make the company's records agree with the bank's records. **Normally, the company will already have recorded electronic payments.** However, if this has not been the case then these payments must be deducted from the balance per books on the bank reconciliation to make the company's records agree with the bank's records.

Step 3 Book errors (+/−). Note any errors made by the depositor that have been discovered in the previous steps. For example, say the company wrote check No. 443 to a supplier in the amount of $1,226 on April 12, but the accounting clerk recorded the check amount as $1,262. The error of $36 ($1,262 − $1,226) is added to the balance per books because the company reduced the balance per books by $36 too much when it recorded the check as $1,262 instead of $1,226. Only errors made by the company, not the bank, are included as reconciling items in determining the adjusted cash balance per books.

Bank Reconciliation Illustrated

Illustration 7.10 presented the bank statement for Laird Company, which the company accessed online (see **Helpful Hint**). It shows a balance per bank of $15,907.45 on April 30, 2022. On this date the balance of cash per books is $11,709.45.

From the foregoing steps, Laird determines the following reconciling items for the bank.

Step 1 Deposits in transit (+): April 30 deposit (received by bank on May 1).	$2,201.40
Step 2 Outstanding checks (−): No. 453, $3,000.00; No. 457, $1,401.30; No. 460, $1,502.70.	5,904.00

Step 3 Bank errors (+/−): None.

Reconciling items per books are as follows:

Step 1 Other deposits (+): Unrecorded electronic receipt from customer on account on April 9 determined from the bank statement.	$1,035.00

Step 2 Other payments (−): The electronic payments on April 3 and 7 were previously recorded by the company when they were initiated. Unrecorded charges determined from the bank statement are as follows:

Returned NSF check on April 29	425.60
Debit and credit card fees on April 30	120.00
Bank service charges on April 30	30.00

HELPFUL HINT

Note in the bank statement in Illustration 7.10 that the bank has paid checks No. 459 and 461, but check No. 460 is not listed. Thus, this check is outstanding. If a complete bank statement were provided, checks No. 453 and 457 also would not be listed. Laird obtains the amounts for these three checks from its cash payments records.

Step 3 **Company errors (+):** Check No. 443 was correctly written
by Laird for $1,226 and was correctly paid by the bank on April 12.
However, it was recorded as $1,262 on Laird's books.   36.00

Illustration 7.12 shows Laird's bank reconciliation (see **Alternative Terminology**).

Laird Company
Bank Reconciliation
April 30, 2022

Cash balance per bank statement		$15,907.45
Add: Deposits in transit		2,201.40
		18,108.85
Less: Outstanding checks		
No. 453	$3,000.00	
No. 457	1,401.30	
No. 460	1,502.70	5,904.00
Adjusted cash balance per bank		**$12,204.85**
Cash balance per books		$ 11,709.45
Add: Electronic funds transfer received	$1,035.00	
Error in recording check No. 443	36.00	1,071.00
		12,780.45
Less: NSF check	425.60	
Debit and credit card fees	120.00	
Bank service charge	30.00	575.60
Adjusted cash balance per books		**$12,204.85**

ILLUSTRATION 7.12
Bank reconciliation

ALTERNATIVE TERMINOLOGY
The terms *adjusted* cash *balance, true cash balance,* and *correct cash balance* are used interchangeably.

Entries from Bank Reconciliation

The depositor (that is, the company) next must record each reconciling item used to determine the **adjusted cash balance per books**. If the company does not journalize and post these items, the Cash account will not show the correct balance. The adjusting entries for the Laird Company bank reconciliation on April 30 are as follows. Note that every entry involves cash.

Collection of Electronic Funds Transfer   A payment of an account by a customer is recorded in the same way, whether the cash is received through the mail or electronically. The entry is as follows.

Apr. 30	Cash	1,035	
	Accounts Receivable		1,035
	(To record receipt of electronic funds transfer)		

A = L + SE
+1,035
−1,035

Cash Flows
+1,035

Book Error   An examination of the cash disbursements journal shows that check No. 443 was a payment on account to Andrea Company, a supplier. The correcting entry is as follows.

Apr. 30	Cash	36	
	Accounts Payable		36
	(To correct error in recording check No. 443)		

A = L + SE
+36
+36

Cash Flows
+36

NSF Check As indicated earlier, an NSF check becomes an accounts receivable to the depositor. The entry is as follows.

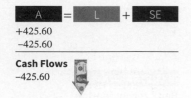

A = L + SE
+425.60
−425.60
_____
Cash Flows
−425.60

Apr. 30	Accounts Receivable	425.60	
	Cash		425.60
	(To record NSF check)		

Bank Charge Expense Fees for processing debit and credit card transactions are normally debited to the Bank Charge Expense account, as are bank service charges. We have chosen to combine and record these in one journal entry, as shown below, although they also could be journalized separately.

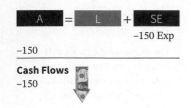

A = L + SE
−150 Exp
−150
_____
Cash Flows
−150

Apr. 30	Bank Charge Expense	150	
	Cash		150
	(To record charges for debit and credit card fees of $120 and bank service charges of $30)		

After Laird posts the entries, the Cash account will appear as in **Illustration 7.13**. The adjusted cash balance in the ledger should agree with the adjusted cash balance per books in the bank reconciliation in Illustration 7.12.

ILLUSTRATION 7.13

Adjusted balance in Cash account

	Cash			
Apr. 30 Bal.	11,709.45	Apr. 30		425.60
30	1,035.00	30		150.00
30	36.00			
Apr. 30 Bal.	**12,204.85**			

What entries does the bank make? If the company discovers any bank errors in preparing the reconciliation, it should notify the bank so the bank can make the necessary corrections on its records. The bank does not make any entries for deposits in transit or outstanding checks. Only when these items reach the bank will the bank record these items.

Investor Insight

AP Images/Mary Altaffer

Madoff's Ponzi Scheme

No recent fraud has generated more notoriety and rage than the one perpetrated by Bernard Madoff. Madoff was an elite New York investment fund manager who was highly regarded by securities regulators. Investors flocked to him because he delivered steady returns of between 10% and 15%, no matter whether the market was going up or going down. However, for many years, Madoff did not actually invest the cash that people gave to him. Instead, he was running a Ponzi scheme: He paid returns to existing investors using cash received from new investors. As long as the size of his investment fund continued to grow from new investments at a rate that exceeded the amounts that he needed to pay out in returns, Madoff was able to operate his fraud smoothly.

To conceal his misdeeds, Madoff fabricated false investment statements that were provided to investors. In addition, Madoff hired an auditor that never verified the accuracy of the investment records but automatically issued unqualified opinions each year. A competing fund manager warned the SEC a number of times over a nearly 10-year period that he thought Madoff was engaged in fraud. The SEC never aggressively investigated the allegations. Investors, many of which were charitable organizations, lost more than $18 billion. Madoff was sentenced to a jail term of 150 years.

How was Madoff able to conceal such a giant fraud? (Go to WileyPLUS for this answer and additional questions.)

DO IT! 3 | Bank Reconciliation

ACTION PLAN
- **Understand the items on a bank reconciliation.**
- **Identify time lags and explain how they cause reconciling items.**

Sally Kist owns Linen Kist Fabrics. Sally asks you to explain how she should treat the following reconciling items when reconciling the company's bank account: (1) a debit memorandum for an NSF check, (2) a credit memorandum for an electronic funds transfer from one of the company's customers received by the bank, (3) outstanding checks, and (4) a deposit in transit.

Solution

Sally should treat the reconciling items as follows.

1. NSF check: Deduct from balance per books.
2. Electronic funds transfer received by bank: Add to balance per books.
3. Outstanding checks: Deduct from balance per bank.
4. Deposit in transit: Add to balance per bank.

Related exercise material: **BE7.10, BE7.11, BE7.12, BE7.13, BE7.14, BE7.15, DO IT! 7.3, E7.9, E7.10, E7.11, E7.12, and E7.13.**

Reporting Cash

LEARNING OBJECTIVE 4

Explain the reporting of cash.

Cash consists of coins, currency (paper money), checks, money orders, and money on hand or on deposit in a bank or similar depository. Companies report cash in two different statements: the balance sheet and the statement of cash flows. The balance sheet reports the amount of cash available at a given point in time. The statement of cash flows shows the sources and uses of cash during a period of time. The statement of cash flows was introduced in Chapter 1 and will be discussed in much detail in Chapter 12. In this section, we discuss some important points regarding the presentation of cash in the balance sheet.

When presented in a balance sheet, cash on hand, cash in banks, and petty cash are often combined and reported simply as **Cash**. Because it is the most liquid asset owned by the company, cash is listed first in the current assets section of the balance sheet.

Cash Equivalents

Many companies use the designation "Cash and cash equivalents" in reporting cash. (See **Illustration 7.14** for an example.) **Cash equivalents** are short-term, highly liquid investments that are both:

1. Readily convertible to known amounts of cash, and
2. So near their maturity that their market value is relatively insensitive to changes in interest rates. (Generally, only investments with maturities of three months or less qualify under this definition.)

Examples of cash equivalents are Treasury bills, commercial paper (short-term corporate notes), and money market funds. All typically are purchased with cash that is in excess of immediate needs (see **Ethics Note**).

ETHICS NOTE

Recently, some companies were forced to restate their financial statements because they had too broadly interpreted which types of investments could be treated as cash equivalents. By reporting these items as cash equivalents, the companies made themselves look more liquid.

ILLUSTRATION 7.14
Balance sheet presentation
of cash

Real World

Delta Air Lines, Inc.	
Balance Sheet	
(partial, in millions)	
Assets	
Current assets	
Cash and cash equivalents	**$2,844**
Short-term investments	959
Restricted cash	**122**

Occasionally, a company will have a net negative balance in its bank account. In this case, the company should report the negative balance among current liabilities. For example, farm equipment manufacturer **Ag-Chem** at one time reported "Checks outstanding in excess of cash balances" of $2,145,000 among its current liabilities.

Restricted Cash

A company may have **restricted cash**, cash that is not available for general use but rather is restricted for a special purpose. For example, landfill companies are often required to maintain a fund of restricted cash to ensure they will have adequate resources to cover closing and clean-up costs at the end of a landfill site's useful life. **McKesson Corp.** recently reported restricted cash of $962 million to be paid out as the result of investor lawsuits.

Cash restricted in use should be reported separately on the balance sheet as restricted cash. If the company expects to use the restricted cash within the next year, it reports the amount as a current asset. When this is not the case, it reports the restricted funds as a noncurrent asset. The FASB now requires that restricted cash be included with cash and cash equivalents when reconciling the beginning and ending amounts on a statement of cash flows.

Illustration 7.14 shows restricted cash reported in the financial statements of **Delta Air Lines**. The company is required to maintain restricted cash as collateral to support insurance obligations related to workers' compensation claims. Delta does not have access to these funds for general use, and so it must report them separately, rather than as part of cash and cash equivalents.

ACTION PLAN
- **Understand how companies present cash and restricted cash on the balance sheet.**
- **Review the designations of cash equivalents and restricted cash, and how companies typically handle them.**

DO IT! 4 | Reporting Cash

Indicate whether each of the following statements is true or false. If false, indicate how to correct the statement.

1. Cash and cash equivalents are comprised of coins, currency (paper money), money orders, and NSF checks.

2. Restricted cash is classified as either a current asset or noncurrent asset, depending on the circumstances.

3. A company may have a negative balance in its bank account. In this case, it should offset this negative balance against cash and cash equivalents on the balance sheet.

4. Because cash equivalents often include short-term investments, accounts receivable should be reported as the first item on the balance sheet.

Solution

1. False. NSF checks should be reported as receivables, not cash and cash equivalents.   2. True.
3. False. Companies that have a negative balance in their bank accounts should report the negative balance as a current liability.   4. False. Cash equivalents are readily convertible to known amounts of cash, and so near maturity (less than 3 months) that they are considered more liquid than accounts receivable and therefore are reported before accounts receivable on the balance sheet.

Related exercise material: **BE7.16, DO IT! 7.4, E7.14, and E7.15.**

Review and Practice

Learning Objectives Review

1 Define fraud and the principles of internal control.

A fraud is a dishonest act by an employee that results in personal benefit to the employee at a cost to the employer. The fraud triangle refers to the three factors that contribute to fraudulent activity by employees: opportunity, financial pressure, and rationalization. Internal control consists of all the related methods and measures adopted within an organization to safeguard its assets, enhance the reliability of its accounting records, increase efficiency of operations, and ensure compliance with laws and regulations.

The principles of internal control are establishment of responsibility, segregation of duties, documentation procedures, physical controls, independent internal verification, and human resource controls such as bonding and requiring employees to take vacations.

2 Apply internal control principles to cash.

Internal controls over cash receipts include (a) designating specific personnel to handle cash; (b) assigning different individuals to receive cash, record cash, and maintain custody of cash; (c) using remittance advices for mail receipts, cash register tapes for over-the-counter receipts, and deposit slips for bank deposits; (d) using company safes and bank vaults to store cash with access limited to authorized personnel, and using cash registers or point-of-sale terminals in executing over-the-counter receipts; (e) making independent daily counts of register receipts and daily comparison of total receipts with total deposits; and (f) bonding personnel that handle cash and requiring them to take vacations.

Internal controls over cash disbursements include (a) having specific individuals such as the treasurer authorized to sign checks and approve vendors; (b) assigning different individuals to approve items for payment, make the payment, and record the payment; (c) using prenumbered checks and accounting for all checks, with each check supported by an approved invoice; (d) storing blank checks in a safe or vault with access restricted to authorized personnel, and using a check-writing machine to imprint amounts on checks; (e) comparing each check with the approved invoice before issuing the check, and making monthly reconciliations of bank and book balances; and (f) bonding personnel who handle cash, requiring employees to take vacations, and conducting background checks.

Companies operate a petty cash fund to pay relatively small amounts of cash. They must establish the fund, make payments from the fund, and replenish the fund when the cash in the fund reaches a minimum level.

3 Identify the control features of a bank account.

A bank account contributes to good internal control by providing physical controls for the storage of cash. It minimizes the amount of currency that a company must keep on hand, and it creates a double record of a depositor's bank transactions. It is customary to reconcile the balance per books and balance per bank to their adjusted balances. The steps in the reconciling process are to determine deposits in transit, electronic funds transfers received by bank, outstanding checks, errors by the depositor or the bank, and unrecorded bank memoranda.

4 Explain the reporting of cash.

Companies list cash first in the current assets section of the balance sheet. In some cases, they report cash together with cash equivalents. Cash restricted for a special purpose is reported separately as a current asset or as a noncurrent asset, depending on when the cash is expected to be used.

Glossary Review

Bank reconciliation The process of comparing the bank's balance with the company's balance and explaining any differences to make them agree. (p. 7-19).

Bank statement A monthly statement from the bank that shows the depositor's bank transactions and balances. (p. 7-21).

Bonding Obtaining insurance protection against theft by employees. (p. 7-9).

Cash Resources that consist of coins, currency, checks, money orders, and money on hand or on deposit in a bank or similar depository. (p. 7-27).

Cash equivalents Short-term, highly liquid investments that can be converted to a specific amount of cash. (p. 7-27).

Check A written order signed by a bank depositor, directing the bank to pay a specified sum of money to a designated recipient. (p. 7-20).

Deposits in transit Deposits recorded by the depositor but not yet recorded by the bank. (p. 7-23).

Electronic funds transfer (EFT) A disbursement system that uses wire, telephone, or computers to transfer funds from one location to another. (p. 7-21).

Fraud A dishonest act by an employee that results in personal benefit to the employee at a cost to the employer. (p. 7-3).

Fraud triangle The three factors that contribute to fraudulent activity by employees: opportunity, financial pressure, and rationalization. (p. 7-3).

Internal auditors Company employees who continuously evaluate the effectiveness of the company's internal control system. (p. 7-9).

Internal control A process designed to provide reasonable assurance regarding the achievement of company objectives related to operations, reporting, and compliance. (p. 7-4).

NSF check A check that is not paid by a bank because of insufficient funds in a customer's bank account. (p. 7-22).

Outstanding checks Checks issued and recorded by a company but not yet paid by the bank. (p. 7-24).

Petty cash fund A cash fund used to pay relatively small amounts. (p. 7-16).

Restricted cash Cash that must be used for a special purpose. (p. 7-28).

Sarbanes-Oxley Act (SOX) Regulations passed by Congress to try to reduce unethical corporate behavior. (p. 7-3).

Voucher An authorization form prepared for each payment in a voucher system. (p. 7-15).

Voucher system A network of approvals by authorized individuals acting independently to ensure that all disbursements by check are proper. (p. 7-15).

Practice Multiple-Choice Questions

1. **(LO 1)** Which of the following is **not** an element of the fraud triangle?
   a. Rationalization.
   b. Financial pressure.
   c. Segregation of duties.
   d. Opportunity.

2. **(LO 1)** An organization uses internal control to enhance the accuracy and reliability of accounting records and to:
   a. safeguard assets.
   b. prevent fraud.
   c. produce correct financial statements.
   d. deter employee dishonesty.

3. **(LO 1)** Which of the following was **not** a result of the Sarbanes-Oxley Act?
   a. Companies must file financial statements with the Internal Revenue Service.
   b. All publicly traded companies must maintain adequate internal controls.
   c. The Public Company Accounting Oversight Board was created to establish auditing standards and regulate auditor activity.
   d. Corporate executives and board of directors must ensure that controls are reliable and effective, and they can be fined or imprisoned for failure to do so.

4. **(LO 1)** The principles of internal control do **not** include:
   a. establishment of responsibility.
   b. documentation procedures.
   c. management responsibility.
   d. independent internal verification.

5. **(LO 1)** Physical controls do **not** include:
   a. safes and vaults to store cash.
   b. independent bank reconciliations.
   c. locked warehouses for inventories.
   d. bank safety deposit boxes for important papers.

6. **(LO 1)** Which of the following control activities is **not** relevant when a company uses a computerized (rather than manual) accounting system?
   a. Establishment of responsibility.
   b. Segregation of duties.
   c. Independent internal verification.
   d. All of these control activities are relevant to a computerized system.

7. **(LO 2)** Permitting only designated personnel to handle cash receipts is an application of the principle of:
   a. segregation of duties.
   b. establishment of responsibility.
   c. independent internal verification.
   d. human resource controls.

8. **(LO 2)** The use of prenumbered checks in disbursing cash is an application of the principle of:
   a. establishment of responsibility.
   b. segregation of duties.
   c. physical controls.
   d. documentation procedures.

9. **(LO 2)** A company writes a check to replenish a $100 petty cash fund when the fund contains receipts of $94 and $4 in cash. In recording the replenishment, the company should:
   a. debit Cash Over and Short for $2.
   b. debit Petty Cash for $94.
   c. credit Cash for $94.
   d. credit Petty Cash for $2.

10. **(LO 3)** The control features of a bank account do **not** include:
    a. having bank auditors verify the correctness of the bank balance per books.
    b. minimizing the amount of cash that must be kept on hand.
    c. providing a double record of all bank transactions.
    d. safeguarding cash by using a bank as a depository.

11. **(LO 3)** In a bank reconciliation, deposits in transit are:
    a. deducted from the book balance.
    b. added to the book balance.
    c. added to the bank balance.
    d. deducted from the bank balance.

12. **(LO 3)** The reconciling item in a bank reconciliation that will result in an adjusting entry by the depositor is:
    a. outstanding checks.   c. a bank error.
    b. deposit in transit.   d. bank service charges.

13. (LO 4) Which of the following items in a cash drawer at November 30 is **not** cash?

    a. Money orders.

    b. Coins and currency.

    c. An NSF check.

    d. A customer check dated November 28.

14. (LO 4) Which of the following statements correctly describes the reporting of cash?

    a. Cash cannot be combined with cash equivalents.

    b. Restricted cash funds may be combined with cash.

    c. Cash is listed first in the current assets section.

    d. Restricted cash funds cannot be reported as a current asset.

Solutions

1. c. Segregation of duties is not an element of the fraud triangle. The other choices are fraud triangle elements.

2. a. Safeguarding assets is one of the purposes of using internal control. The other choices are incorrect because while internal control can help to (b) prevent fraud, (c) produce correct financial statements, and (d) deter employee dishonesty, these are not the main purposes of using it.

3. a. Filing financial statements with the IRS is not a result of the Sarbanes-Oxley Act (SOX); SOX focuses on the prevention or detection of fraud. The other choices are results of SOX.

4. c. Management responsibility is not one of the principles of internal control. The other choices are true statements.

5. b. Independent bank reconciliations are not a physical control. The other choices are true statements.

6. d. Establishment of responsibility, segregation of duties, and independent internal verification are all relevant to a computerized system.

7. b. Permitting only designated personnel to handle cash receipts is an application of the principle of establishment of responsibility, not (a) segregation of duties, (c) independent internal verification, or (d) human resource controls.

8. d. The use of prenumbered checks in disbursing cash is an application of the principle of documentation procedures, not (a) establishment of responsibility, (b) segregation of duties, or (c) physical controls.

9. a. When the replenishment check is recorded, the company should debit Cash Over and Short for the shortage of $2 (total of the receipts plus cash in the drawer ($98) versus $100), not (b) debit Petty Cash for $94, (c) credit Cash for $94, or (d) credit Petty Cash for $2.

10. a. Having bank auditors verify the correctness of the bank balance per books is not one of the control features of a bank account. The other choices are true statements.

11. c. Deposits in transit are added to the bank balance on a bank reconciliation, not (a) deducted from the book balance, (b) added to the book balance, or (d) deducted from the bank balance.

12. d. Because the depositor does not know the amount of the bank service charges until the bank statement is received, an adjusting entry must be made when the statement is received. The other choices are incorrect because (a) outstanding checks do not require an adjusting entry by the depositor because the checks have already been recorded in the depositor's books, (b) deposits in transit do not require an adjusting entry by the depositor because the deposits have already been recorded in the depositor's books, and (c) bank errors do not require an adjusting entry by the depositor, but the depositor does need to inform the bank of the error so it can be corrected.

13. c. An NSF check should not be considered cash. The other choices are true statements.

14. c. Cash is listed first in the current assets section. The other choices are incorrect because (a) cash and cash equivalents can be appropriately combined when reporting cash on the balance sheet, (b) restricted cash is not to be combined with cash when reporting cash on the balance sheet, and (d) restricted funds can be reported as current assets if they will be used within one year.

Practice Brief Exercises

1. (LO 2) On May 31, Tyler's petty cash fund of $200 is replenished when the fund contains $7 in cash and receipts for postage $105, freight-out $49, and miscellaneous expense $40. Prepare the journal entry to record the replenishment of the petty cash fund.

Prepare entry to replenish a petty cash fund.

Solution

1.	May 31	Postage Expense	105	
		Freight-Out	49	
		Miscellaneous Expense	40	
		Cash		193
		Cash Over and Short		1

2. (LO 3) At August 31, Saladino Company has the following bank information: cash balance per bank $5,200, outstanding checks $1,462, deposits in transit $1,211, and a bank debit memo $110. Determine the adjusted cash balance per bank at July 31.

Prepare partial bank reconciliation.

Solution

2.

Cash balance per bank	$5,200
Add: Deposits in transit	1,211
	6,411
Less: Outstanding checks	1,462
Adjusted cash balance per bank	$4,949

Explain the statement presentation of cash balances.

3. (LO 4) Zian Company has the following cash balances: Cash in Bank $18,762, Payroll Bank Account $8,000, Petty Cash $150, and Plant Expansion Fund Cash $30,000 to be used 2 years from now. Explain how each balance should be reported on the balance sheet.

Solution

3. Zian Company should report Cash in Bank, Payroll Bank Account, and Petty Cash as current assets (usually combined as one Cash amount). Plant Expansion Fund Cash should be reported as a noncurrent asset, assuming the fund is not expected to be used until 2 years from now.

Practice Exercises

Indicate whether procedure is good or weak internal control.

1. (LO 1, 2) Listed below are five procedures followed by Shepherd Company.

1. Total cash receipts are compared to bank deposits daily by someone who has no other cash responsibilities.
2. Time clocks are used for recording time worked by employees.
3. Employees are required to take vacations.
4. Any member of the sales department can approve credit sales.
5. Sam Hill ships goods to customers, bills customers, and receives payment from customers.

Instructions

Indicate whether each procedure is an example of good internal control or of weak internal control. If it is an example of good internal control, indicate which internal control principle is being followed. If it is an example of weak internal control, indicate which internal control principle is violated. Use the table below.

Procedure	IC Good or Weak?	Related Internal Control Principle
1.		
2.		
3.		
4.		
5.		

Solution

1.	Procedure	IC Good or Weak?	Related Internal Control Principle
	1.	Good	Independent internal verification
	2.	Good	Physical controls
	3.	Good	Human resource controls
	4.	Weak	Establishment of responsibility
	5.	Weak	Segregation of duties

Prepare bank reconciliation and adjusting entries.

2. (LO 3) The information below relates to the Cash account in the ledger of Ansel Company for June 2022.

Balance June 1—$17,450; Cash deposited—$64,000.
Balance June 30—$17,704; Checks written—$63,746.

The June bank statement shows a balance of $16,422 on June 30 and the following memoranda.

Credits		Debits	
Collection of electronic funds transfer	$1,530	NSF check: Anne Adams	$425
Interest earned on checking account	35	Safety deposit box rent	55

At June 30, deposits in transit were $4,750, and outstanding checks totaled $2,383.

Instructions

a. Prepare the bank reconciliation at June 30.

b. Prepare the adjusting entries at June 30, assuming (1) the NSF check was from a customer on account, and (2) no interest had been accrued on the note.

Solution

2. a.

Ansel Company
Bank Reconciliation
June 30, 2022

Cash balance per bank statement		$16,422
Add: Deposits in transit		4,750
		21,172
Less: Outstanding checks		2,383
Adjusted cash balance per bank		$18,789
Cash balance per books		$17,704
Add: Electronic funds transfer received	$1,530	
Interest earned	35	1,565
		19,269
Less: NSF check	425	
Safety deposit box rent	55	480
Adjusted cash balance per books		$18,789

b.

June 30	Cash		1,530	
		Accounts Receivable		1,530
	30	Cash	35	
		Interest Revenue		35
	30	Accounts Receivable (Anne Adams)	425	
		Cash		425
	30	Bank Charge Expense	55	
		Cash		55

Practice Problem

(LO 3) Trillo Company's bank statement for May 2022 shows the following selected data.

Prepare bank reconciliation and journalize entries.

Balance 5/1	$12,650	Balance 5/31	$14,280
Debit memorandum:		Credit memorandum:	
NSF check	175	Collection of electronic funds	
		transfer	505

The cash balance per books at May 31 is $13,319. Your review of the data reveals the following.

1. The NSF check was from Hup Co., a customer.
2. Outstanding checks at May 31 total $2,410.
3. Deposits in transit at May 31 total $1,752.
4. A Trillo Company check written for $352, dated May 10, cleared the bank on May 25. The company recorded this check, which was a payment on account, for $325.

Instructions

a. Prepare a bank reconciliation at May 31.

b. Journalize the entries required by the reconciliation.

Solution

a.

Trillo Company
Bank Reconciliation
May 31, 2022

Cash balance per bank statement		$14,280
Add: Deposits in transit		1,752
		16,032
Less: Outstanding checks		2,410
Adjusted cash balance per bank		$13,622
Cash balance per books		$13,319
Add: Electronic funds transfer received		505
		13,824
Less: NSF check	$175	
Error in recording check ($352 − $325)	27	202
Adjusted cash balance per books		$13,622

b.

May	31	Cash	505	
		Accounts Receivable		505
		(To record receipt of electronic funds transfer)		
	31	Accounts Receivable	175	
		Cash		175
		(To record NSF check)		
	31	Accounts Payable	27	
		Cash		27
		(To correct error in recording check)		

WileyPLUS

Brief Exercises, DO IT! Exercises, Exercises, Problems, and many additional resources are available for practice in WileyPLUS.

Questions

1. A local bank reported that it lost $150,000 as the result of an employee fraud. Ray Fairburn is not clear on what is meant by an "employee fraud." Explain the meaning of fraud to Ray and give an example of a fraud that might occur at a bank.

2. Fraud experts often say that there are three primary factors that contribute to employee fraud. Identify the three factors and explain what is meant by each.

3. Identify the five components of a good internal control system.

4. "Internal control is concerned only with enhancing the accuracy of the accounting records." Explain why this statement is true or false.

5. Discuss how the Sarbanes-Oxley Act has increased the importance of internal control to top managers of a company.

6. What principles of internal control apply to most businesses?

7. In the corner grocery store, all sales clerks make change out of one cash register drawer. Is this a violation of internal control? Why?

8. Branden Doyle is reviewing the principle of segregation of duties. What are the two common applications of this principle?

9. How do documentation procedures contribute to good internal control?

10. What internal control objectives are met by physical controls?

11. (a) Explain the control principle of independent internal verification. (b) What practices are important in applying this principle?

12. The management of Ortiz Company asks you, the company accountant, to explain (a) the concept of reasonable assurance in internal control and (b) the importance of the human factor in internal control.

13. What principle(s) of internal control is (are) involved in making daily cash counts of over-the-counter receipts?

14. Assume that **Kohl's** installed new electronic cash registers in its department stores. How do cash registers improve internal control over cash receipts?

15. At Lazlo Wholesale Company, two mail clerks open all mail receipts. How does this strengthen internal control?

16. "To have maximum effective internal control over cash disbursements, all payments should be made by check." Explain why this statement is true or false.

17. Pauli Company's internal controls over cash disbursements provide for the treasurer to sign checks imprinted by a checkwriter after comparing the check with the approved invoice. Identify the internal control principles that are present in these controls.

18. Explain how these principles apply to cash disbursements: (a) physical controls, and (b) human resource controls.

19. (a) What is a voucher system? (b) What principles of internal control apply to a voucher system?

20. What is the essential feature of an electronic funds transfer (EFT) procedure?

21. (a) Identify the three activities that pertain to a petty cash fund, and indicate an internal control principle that is applicable to each activity. (b) When are journal entries required in the operation of a petty cash fund?

22. "The use of a bank contributes significantly to good internal control over cash." Explain why this statement is true or false.

23. Hank Cook is confused about the lack of agreement between the cash balance per books and the balance per bank. Explain the causes for the lack of agreement to Hank, and give an example of each cause.

24. Trisha Massey asks for your help concerning an NSF check. Explain to Trisha (a) what an NSF check is, (b) how it is treated in a bank reconciliation, and (c) whether it will require an adjusting entry.

25. a. Describe cash equivalents and explain how they are reported.

   b. How should restricted cash funds be reported on the balance sheet?

26. Robbins Inc. owns the following assets at the balance sheet date.

Cash in bank—savings account	$ 8,000
Cash on hand	1,100
Cash refund due from the IRS	1,000
Checking account balance	12,000

What amount should be reported as Cash in the balance sheet?

27. What was **Apple**'s balance in cash and cash equivalents at September 29, 2018? Did it report any restricted cash? How did Apple define cash equivalents?

Brief Exercises

BE7.1 (LO 1), C Match each situation with the fraud triangle factor—opportunity, financial pressure, or rationalization—that best describes it.

Identify fraud triangle concepts.

   a. An employee's monthly credit card payments are nearly 75% of his or her monthly earnings.

   b. An employee earns minimum wage at a firm that has reported record earnings for each of the last five years.

   c. An employee has an expensive gambling habit.

   d. An employee has check-writing and check-signing responsibilities for a small company, as well as reconciling the bank account.

BE7.2 (LO 1), C Shelly Eckert has prepared the following list of statements about internal control.

Identify internal control objectives.

   a. One of the objectives of internal control is to safeguard assets from employee theft, robbery, and unauthorized use.

   b. One of the objectives of internal control is to enhance the accuracy and reliability of the accounting records.

   c. No laws require U.S. corporations to maintain an adequate system of internal control.

Identify each statement as true or false. If false, indicate how to correct the statement.

BE7.3 (LO 1), C Pat Buhn is the new owner of Young Co. She has heard about internal control but is not clear about its importance for her business. Explain to Pat the four purposes of internal control and give her one application of each purpose for Young Co.

Explain the importance of internal control.

BE7.4 (LO 1), C The internal control procedures in Dayton Company result in the following situations. Identify the principles of internal control that are being followed in each case.

Identify internal control principles.

   a. Employees who have physical custody of assets do not have access to the accounting records.

   b. Each month, the assets on hand are compared to the accounting records by an internal auditor.

   c. A prenumbered shipping document is prepared for each shipment of goods to customers.

BE7.5 (LO 2), C Jolson Company has the following internal control procedures over cash receipts. Identify the internal control principle that is applicable to each procedure.

Identify the internal control principles applicable to cash receipts.

   a. All over-the-counter receipts are entered in cash registers.

   b. All cashiers are bonded.

    c. Daily cash counts are made by cashier department supervisors.

    d. The duties of receiving cash, recording cash, and custody of cash are assigned to different individuals.

    e. Only cashiers may operate cash registers.

Make journal entries for cash overage and shortfall.

BE7.6 (LO 2), AP The cash register tape for Bluestem Industries reported sales of $6,871.50. Record the journal entry that would be necessary for each of the following situations. (a) Sales per cash register tape exceeds cash on hand by $50.75. (b) Cash on hand exceeds cash reported by cash register tape by $28.32.

Make journal entry using cash count sheet.

BE7.7 (LO 2), AP While examining cash receipts information, the accounting department determined the following information: cash on hand $1,125.74 and cash sales per register tape $988.62. Prepare the required journal entry.

Identify the internal control principles applicable to cash disbursements.

BE7.8 (LO 2), C Tott Company has the following internal control procedures over cash disbursements. Identify the internal control principle that is applicable to each procedure.

    a. Company checks are prenumbered.

    b. The bank statement is reconciled monthly by an internal auditor.

    c. Blank checks are stored in a safe in the treasurer's office.

    d. Only the treasurer or assistant treasurer may sign checks.

    e. Check-signers are not allowed to record cash disbursement transactions.

Prepare entry to replenish a petty cash fund.

BE7.9 (LO 2), AP On March 20, Harbor's petty cash fund of $100 is replenished when the fund contains $19 in cash and receipts for postage $40, supplies $26, and travel expense $15. Prepare the journal entry to record the replenishment of the petty cash fund.

Identify the control features of a bank account.

BE7.10 (LO 3), C Luke Roye is uncertain about the control features of a bank account. Explain the control benefits of (a) a check and (b) a bank statement.

Indicate location of reconciling items in a bank reconciliation.

BE7.11 (LO 3), C The following reconciling items are applicable to the bank reconciliation for Forde Co. Indicate how each item should be shown on a bank reconciliation.

    a. Outstanding checks.

    b. Bank debit memorandum for service charge.

    c. Bank credit memorandum for collecting an electronic funds transfer.

    d. Deposits in transit.

Identify reconciling items that require adjusting entries.

BE7.12 (LO 3), C The following reconciling items are applicable to the bank reconciliation for Forde Co. Indicate (1) the items that will result in an adjustment to the depositor's records and (2) why the other items do not require adjustment.

    a. Outstanding checks.

    b. Bank debit memorandum for service charge.

    c. Bank credit memorandum for collecting an electronic funds transfer.

    d. Deposits in transit.

Prepare partial bank reconciliation.

BE7.13 (LO 3), AP At July 31, Planter Company has this bank information: cash balance per bank $7,291, outstanding checks $762, deposits in transit $1,350, and a bank service charge $40. Determine the adjusted cash balance per bank at July 31.

Prepare partial bank reconciliation.

BE7.14 (LO 3), AP At August 31, Pratt Company has a cash balance per books of $9,500 and the following additional data from the bank statement: charge for printing Pratt Company checks $35 and interest earned on checking account balance $40. In addition, Pratt Company has outstanding checks of $800. Determine the adjusted cash balance per books at August 31.

Compute outstanding checks.

BE7.15 (LO 3), AN In the month of November, Fiesta Company Inc. wrote checks in the amount of $9,750. In December, checks in the amount of $11,762 were written. In November, $8,800 of these checks were presented to the bank for payment, and $10,889 in December. There were no outstanding checks at the beginning of November. What is the amount of outstanding checks at the end of November? At the end of December?

Explain the statement presentation of cash balances.

BE7.16 (LO 4), C Spahn Company has the following cash balances: Cash in Bank $12,742, Payroll Bank Account $6,000, and Plant Expansion Fund Cash $25,000 to be used two years from now. Explain how each balance should be reported on the balance sheet.

DO IT! Exercises

DO IT! 7.1 (LO 1), C Identify which control activity is violated in each of the following situations, and explain how the situation creates an opportunity for fraud or inappropriate accounting practices.

Identify violations of control activities.

1. Once a month, the sales department sends sales invoices to the accounting department to be recorded.

2. Steve Nicoles orders merchandise for Binn Company; he also receives merchandise and authorizes payment for merchandise.

3. Several clerks at Draper's Groceries use the same cash register drawer.

DO IT! 7.2a (LO 2), C Wes Unsel is concerned with control over mail receipts at Wooden Sporting Goods. All mail receipts are opened by Mel Blount. Mel sends the checks to the accounting department, where they are stamped "For Deposit Only." The accounting department records and deposits the mail receipts weekly. Wes asks for your help in establishing a good system of internal control over mail receipts.

Design system of internal control over cash receipts.

DO IT! 7.2b (LO 2), AP Wilkinson Company established a $100 petty cash fund on August 1. On August 31, the fund had $7 cash remaining and petty cash receipts for postage $31, office supplies $42, and miscellaneous expense $16. Prepare journal entries to establish the fund on August 1 and replenish the fund on August 31.

Make journal entries for petty cash fund.

DO IT! 7.3 (LO 3), C Ned Douglas owns Ned's Blankets. He asks you to explain how he should treat the following reconciling items when reconciling the company's bank account.

Explain treatment of items in bank reconciliation.

1. Outstanding checks.

2. A deposit in transit.

3. The bank charged to the company account a check written by another company.

4. A debit memorandum for a bank service charge.

DO IT! 7.4 (LO 4), C Indicate whether each of the following statements is true or false. If false, indicate how to correct the statement.

Analyze statements about the reporting of cash.

1. A company has the following assets at the end of the year: cash on hand $40,000, cash refund due from supplier $30,000, and checking account balance $22,000. Cash and cash equivalents is therefore $62,000.

2. A company that has received NSF checks should report these checks as a current liability on the balance sheet.

3. Restricted cash that is a current asset is reported as part of cash and cash equivalents.

4. A company has cash in the bank of $50,000, petty cash of $400, and stock investments of $100,000. Total cash and cash equivalents is therefore $50,400.

Exercises

E7.1 (LO 1), C Ricci's Pizza operates strictly on a carryout basis. Customers pick up their orders at a counter where a clerk exchanges the pizza for cash. While at the counter, the customer can see other employees making the pizzas and the large ovens in which the pizzas are baked.

Identify the principles of internal control.

Instructions

Identify the six principles of internal control and give an example of each principle that you might observe when picking up your pizza. (*Note:* It may not be possible to observe all the principles.)

E7.2 (LO 1, 2), E The following control procedures are used at Torres Company for over-the-counter cash receipts.

Identify internal control weaknesses over cash receipts and suggest improvements.

1. To minimize the risk of robbery, cash in excess of $100 is stored in an unlocked briefcase in the stockroom until it is deposited in the bank.

2. All over-the-counter receipts are processed by three clerks who use a cash register with a single cash drawer.

3. The company accountant makes the bank deposit and then records the day's receipts.

4. At the end of each day, the total receipts are counted by the cashier on duty and reconciled to the cash register total.

5. Cashiers are experienced; they are not bonded.

Instructions

a. For each procedure, explain the weakness in internal control, and identify the control principle that is violated.

b. For each weakness, suggest a change in procedure that will result in good internal control.

Identify internal control weaknesses over cash disbursements and suggest improvements.

E7.3 (LO 1, 2), E The following control procedures are used in Bunny's Boutique Shoppe for cash disbursements.

1. Company checks are stored in an unmarked envelope on a shelf behind the cash register.

2. The store manager personally approves all payments before she signs and issues checks.

3. The store purchases used goods for resale from people that bring items to the store. Since that can occur anytime that the store is open, all employees are authorized to purchase goods for resale by disbursing cash from the register. The purchase is documented by having the store employee write on a piece of paper a description of the item that was purchased and the amount that was paid. The employee then signs the paper and puts it in the register.

4. After payment, bills are "filed" in a paid invoice folder.

5. The company accountant prepares the bank reconciliation and reports any discrepancies to the owner.

Instructions

a. For each procedure, explain the weakness in internal control and identify the internal control principle that is violated.

b. For each weakness, suggest a change in the procedure that will result in good internal control.

Identify internal control weaknesses for cash disbursements and suggest improvements.

E7.4 (LO 2), E At Martinez Company, checks are not prenumbered because both the purchasing agent and the treasurer are authorized to issue checks. Each signer has access to unissued checks kept in an unlocked file cabinet. The purchasing agent pays all bills pertaining to goods purchased for resale. Prior to payment, the purchasing agent determines that the goods have been received and verifies the mathematical accuracy of the vendor's invoice. After payment, the invoice is filed by vendor name and the purchasing agent records the payment in the cash disbursements journal. The treasurer pays all other bills following approval by authorized employees. After payment, the treasurer stamps all bills "paid," files them by payment date, and records the checks in the cash disbursements journal. Martinez Company maintains one checking account that is reconciled by the treasurer.

Instructions

a. List the weaknesses in internal control over cash disbursements.

b. Identify improvements for correcting these weaknesses.

Indicate whether procedure is good or weak internal control.

E7.5 (LO 1, 2), C Consider the following five procedures followed by Eikenberry Company.

1. Several individuals operate the cash register using the same register drawer.

2. A monthly bank reconciliation is prepared by someone who has no other cash responsibilities.

3. Joe Cockrell writes checks and also records cash payment entries.

4. One individual orders inventory, while a different individual authorizes payments.

5. Unnumbered sales invoices from credit sales are forwarded to the accounting department every four weeks for recording.

Instructions

Indicate whether each procedure is an example of good internal control or of weak internal control. If it is an example of good internal control, indicate which internal control principle is being followed. If it is an example of weak internal control, indicate which internal control principle is violated. Use the table below.

Procedure	IC Good or Weak?	Related Internal Control Principle
1.		
2.		
3.		
4.		
5.		

E7.6 (LO 1, 2), C The following are five procedures followed by Gilmore Company. *Indicate whether procedure is good or weak internal control.*

1. Employees are required to take vacations.
2. Any member of the sales department can approve credit sales.
3. Paul Jaggard ships goods to customers, bills customers, and receives payment from customers.
4. Total cash receipts are compared to bank deposits daily by someone who has no other cash responsibilities.
5. Time clocks are used for recording time worked by employees.

Instructions

Indicate whether each procedure is an example of good internal control or of weak internal control. If it is an example of good internal control, indicate which internal control principle is being followed. If it is an example of weak internal control, indicate which internal control principle is violated. Use the table below.

Procedure	IC Good or Weak?	Related Internal Control Principle
1.		
2.		
3.		
4.		
5.		

E7.7 (LO 2), AP Setterstrom Company established a petty cash fund on May 1 for $100. The company reimbursed the fund on June 1 and July 1 with the following results. *Prepare journal entries for a petty cash fund.*

June 1: Cash in fund $1.75. Receipts: delivery expense $31.25, postage expense $39.00, and miscellaneous expense $25.00.

July 1: Cash in fund $3.25. Receipts: delivery expense $21.00, entertainment expense $51.00, and miscellaneous expense $24.75.

On July 10, Setterstrom increased the fund from $100 to $130.

Instructions

Prepare journal entries for Setterstrom Company for May 1, June 1, July 1, and July 10.

E7.8 (LO 2), AP Horvath Company uses an imprest petty cash system. The fund was established on March 1 with a balance of $100. During March, the following petty cash receipts were found in the petty cash box. *Prepare journal entries for a petty cash fund.*

Date	Receipt No.	For	Amount
3/5	1	Stamps	$39
7	2	Freight-Out	21
9	3	Miscellaneous Expense	6
11	4	Travel Expense	24
14	5	Miscellaneous Expense	5

The fund was replenished on March 15 when the fund contained $2 in cash. On March 20, the fund was increased to $175.

Instructions

Journalize the entries in March that pertain to the operation of the petty cash fund.

E7.9 (LO 3), AN Rachel Sells is unable to reconcile the bank balance at January 31. Rachel's reconciliation is shown here. *Prepare bank reconciliation and adjusting entries.*

Cash balance per bank	$3,677.20
Add: NSF check	450.00
Less: Bank service charge	28.00
Adjusted balance per bank	$4,099.20
Cash balance per books	$3,975.20
Less: Deposits in transit	590.00
Add: Outstanding checks	770.00
Adjusted balance per books	$4,155.20

Instructions

a. What is the proper adjusted cash balance per bank?
b. What is the proper adjusted cash balance per books?
c. Prepare the adjusting journal entries necessary to determine the adjusted cash balance per books.

Determine outstanding checks.

E7.10 (LO 3), AP At April 30, the bank reconciliation of Back 40 Company shows three outstanding checks: No. 254 $650, No. 255 $700, and No. 257 $410. The May bank statement and the May cash disbursements journal are given here.

Bank Statement Checks Paid			Cash Disbursements Journal Checks Issued		
Date	Check No.	Amount	Date	Check No.	Amount
5-4	254	$650	5-2	258	$159
5-2	257	410	5-5	259	275
5-17	258	159	5-10	260	925
5-12	259	275	5-15	261	500
5-20	260	925	5-22	262	750
5-29	263	480	5-24	263	480
5-30	262	750	5-29	264	360

Instructions

Determine the outstanding checks at May 31.

Prepare bank reconciliation and adjusting entries.

E7.11 (LO 3), AP The following information pertains to Lance Company.

1. Cash balance per bank, July 31, $8,732.

2. July bank service charge not recorded by the depositor $45.

3. Cash balance per books, July 31, $8,768.

4. Deposits in transit, July 31, $3,500.

5. $2,023 collected from a customer for Lance Company in July by the bank through electronic funds transfer. The collection has not been recorded by Lance Company.

6. Outstanding checks, July 31, $1,486.

Instructions

a. Prepare a bank reconciliation at July 31, 2022.

b. Journalize the adjusting entries at July 31 on the books of Lance Company.

Prepare bank reconciliation and adjusting entries.

E7.12 (LO 3), AP This information relates to the Cash account in the ledger of Howard Company.

Balance September 1—$16,400; Cash deposited—$64,000
Balance September 30—$17,600; Checks written—$62,800

The September bank statement shows a balance of $16,500 at September 30 and the following memoranda.

Credits		Debits	
Collection from customer of electronic funds transfer	$1,830	NSF check: H. Kane	$560
Interest earned on checking account	45	Safety deposit box rent	60

At September 30, deposits in transit were $4,738 and outstanding checks totaled $2,383.

Instructions

a. Prepare the bank reconciliation at September 30, 2022.

b. Prepare the adjusting entries at September 30, assuming the NSF check was from a customer on account.

Compute deposits in transit and outstanding checks for two bank reconciliations.

E7.13 (LO 3), AN The cash records of Upton Company show the following.

For July:

1. The June 30 bank reconciliation indicated that deposits in transit total $580. During July, the general ledger account Cash shows deposits of $16,900, but the bank statement indicates that only $15,600 in deposits were received during the month.

2. The June 30 bank reconciliation also reported outstanding checks of $940. During the month of July, Upton Company's books show that $17,500 of checks were issued, yet the bank statement shows that $16,400 of checks cleared the bank in July.

For September:

3. In September, deposits per the bank statement totaled $25,900, deposits per the books were $26,400, and deposits in transit at September 30 were $2,200.

4. In September, cash disbursements per the books were $23,500, checks clearing the bank were $24,000, and outstanding checks at September 30 were $2,100.

There were no bank debit or credit memoranda, and no errors were made by either the bank or Upton Company.

Instructions

Answer the following questions.

a. In situation 1, what were the deposits in transit at July 31?

b. In situation 2, what were the outstanding checks at July 31?

c. In situation 3, what were the deposits in transit at August 31?

d. In situation 4, what were the outstanding checks at August 31?

E7.14 (LO 4), AP Wynn Company has recorded the following items in its financial records.

Show presentation of cash in financial statements.

Cash in bank	$ 42,000
Cash in plant expansion fund	100,000
Cash on hand	12,000
Highly liquid investments	34,000
Petty cash	500
Receivables from customers	89,000
Stock investments	61,000

The highly liquid investments had maturities of 3 months or less when they were purchased. The stock investments will be sold in the next 6 to 12 months. The plant expansion project will begin in 3 years.

Instructions

a. What amount should Wynn report as "Cash and cash equivalents" on its balance sheet?

b. Where should the items not included in part (a) be reported on the balance sheet?

E7.15 (LO 4), AP A new accountant at Wyne Inc. is trying to identify which of the amounts shown below should be reported as the current asset "Cash and cash equivalents" in the year-end balance sheet, as of April 30, 2022.

Identify reporting of cash.

1. $60 of currency and coin in a locked box used for incidental cash transactions.

2. A $10,000 U.S. Treasury bill, due May 31, 2022.

3. $260 of checks that Wyne has received from customers but not yet deposited.

4. $2,500 in the company's checking account.

5. $4,800 in its savings account.

6. $75 of prepaid postage in its postage meter.

7. A $25 IOU from the company receptionist.

Instructions

a. What amount should Wyne report for "Cash and cash equivalents" at April 30, 2022?

b. In what account(s) and in what financial statement(s) should the items not included in "Cash and cash equivalents" be reported?

Problems

P7.1A (LO 1, 2), C Bolz Office Supply Company recently changed its system of internal control over cash disbursements. The system includes the following features.

Identify internal control principles applicable to cash disbursements.

Instead of being unnumbered and manually prepared, all checks must now be prenumbered and prepared by using the new accounts payable software purchased by the company. Before a check can be issued, each invoice must have the approval of Kathy Moon, the purchasing agent, and Robin Self, the receiving department supervisor. Checks must be signed by either Jennifer Edwards, the treasurer, or Rich Woodruff, the assistant treasurer. Before signing a check, the signer is expected to compare the amount of the check with the amount on the invoice.

After signing a check, the signer stamps the invoice PAID and inserts (within the stamp) the date, check number, and amount of the check. The "paid" invoice is then sent to the accounting department for recording.

Blank checks are stored in a safe in the treasurer's office. The combination to the safe is known only by the treasurer and assistant treasurer. Each month, the bank statement is reconciled with the general ledger cash balance by the assistant chief accountant. All employees who handle or account for cash are bonded.

Instructions

Identify the internal control principles and their application to cash disbursements of Bolz Office Supply Company.

Identify internal control weaknesses in cash receipts and cash disbursements.

P7.2A (LO 1, 2), E Blue Bayou Middle School wants to raise money for a new sound system for its auditorium. The primary fundraising event is a dance at which the famous disc jockey Kray Zee will play classic and not-so-classic dance tunes. Grant Hill, the music and theater instructor, has been given the responsibility for coordinating the fundraising efforts. This is Grant's first experience with fundraising. He decides to put the eighth-grade choir in charge of the event; he will be a relatively passive observer.

Grant had 500 unnumbered tickets printed for the dance. He left the tickets in a box on his desk and told the choir students to take as many tickets as they thought they could sell for $5 each. In order to ensure that no extra tickets would be floating around, he told them to dispose of any unsold tickets. When the students received payment for the tickets, they were to bring the cash back to Grant and he would put it in a locked box in his desk drawer.

Some of the students were responsible for decorating the gymnasium for the dance. Grant gave each of them a key to the money box and told them that if they took money out to purchase materials, they should put a note in the box saying how much they took and what it was used for. After 2 weeks, the money box appeared to be getting full, so Grant asked Lynn Dandi to count the money, prepare a deposit slip, and deposit the money in a bank account Grant had opened.

The day of the dance, Grant wrote a check from the account to pay Kray Zee. The D.J. said, however, that he accepted only cash and did not give receipts. So Grant took $200 out of the cash box and gave it to the D.J. At the dance, Grant had Dana Uhler working at the entrance to the gymnasium, collecting tickets from students, and selling tickets to those who had not prepurchased them. Grant estimated that 400 students attended the dance.

The following day, Grant closed out the bank account, which had $250 in it, and gave that amount plus the $180 in the cash box to Principal Sanchez. Principal Sanchez seemed surprised that, after generating roughly $2,000 in sales, the dance netted only $430 in cash. Grant did not know how to respond.

Instructions

Identify as many internal control weaknesses as you can in this scenario, and suggest how each could be addressed.

Journalize and post petty cash fund transactions.

P7.3A (LO 2), AP Kael Company maintains a petty cash fund for small expenditures. These transactions occurred during the month of August.

Aug. 1 Established the petty cash fund by writing a check payable to the petty cash custodian for $200.
    15 Replenished the petty cash fund by writing a check for $175. On this date, the fund consisted of $25 in cash and these petty cash receipts: freight-out $74.40, entertainment expense $36, postage expense $33.70, and miscellaneous expense $27.50.
    16 Increased the amount of the petty cash fund to $400 by writing a check for $200.
    31 Replenished the petty cash fund by writing a check for $283. On this date, the fund consisted of $117 in cash and these petty cash receipts: postage expense $145, entertainment expense $90.60, and freight-out $46.40.

Instructions

a. Journalize the petty cash transactions.

b. Post to the Petty Cash account.

c. What internal control features exist in a petty cash fund?

P7.4A (LO 3), AP On July 31, 2022, Keeds Company had a cash balance per books of $6,140. The statement from Dakota State Bank on that date showed a balance of $7,690.80. A comparison of the bank statement with the Cash account revealed the following facts.

Prepare a bank reconciliation and adjusting entries.

1. The bank service charge for July was $25.

2. The bank collected $1,520 for Keeds Company through electronic funds transfer.

3. The July 31 cash receipts of $1,193.30 were not included in the bank statement for July. These receipts were deposited by the company in a night deposit vault on July 31.

4. Company check No. 2480 issued to L. Taylor, a creditor, for $384 that cleared the bank in July was incorrectly recorded as a cash payment on July 10 for $348.

5. Checks outstanding on July 31 totaled $1,860.10.

6. On July 31, the bank statement showed an NSF charge of $575 for a check received by the company from W. Krueger, a customer, on account.

Instructions

a. Prepare the bank reconciliation as of July 31.

b. Prepare the necessary adjusting entries at July 31.

a. Adjusted cash bal. $7,024.00

P7.5A (LO 3), AP The bank portion of the bank reconciliation for Bogalusa Company at October 31, 2022, is as follows.

Prepare a bank reconciliation and adjusting entries from detailed data.

Bogalusa Company
Bank Reconciliation
October 31, 2022

Cash balance per bank		$12,367.90
Add: Deposits in transit		1,530.20
		13,898.10
Less: Outstanding checks		

Check Number	Check Amount	
2451	$1,260.40	
2470	684.20	
2471	844.50	
2472	426.80	
2474	1,050.00	4,265.90
Adjusted cash balance per bank		$ 9,632.20

The adjusted cash balance per bank agreed with the adjusted cash balance per books at October 31. All necessary journal entries were made at the end of October. The November bank statement showed the following checks and deposits.

Bank Statement

	Checks and Debits			Deposits and Credits	
Date	**Number**	**Amount**		**Date**	**Amount**
11-1	2470	$ 684.20		11-1	$ 1,530.20
11-2	2471	844.50		11-4	1,211.60
11-5	2474	1,050.00		11-8	990.10
11-4	2475	1,640.70		11-13	2,575.00
11-8	2476	2,830.00		11-18	1,472.70
11-10	2477	600.00		11-19 EFT	2,242.00
11-15	2479	1,750.00		11-21	2,945.00
11-18	2480	1,330.00		11-25	2,567.30
11-27	2481	695.40		11-28	1,650.00
11-28	SC	85.00		11-30	1,186.00
11-30	2483	575.50		Total	$18,369.90
11-29	2486	940.00			
	Total	$13,025.30			

The cash records per books for November showed the following.

Cash Payments							Cash Receipts	
Date	Number	Amount	Date	Number	Amount		Date	Amount
11-1	2475	$1,640.70	11-20	2483	$ 575.50		11-3	$ 1,211.60
11-2	2476	2,830.00	11-22	2484	829.50		11-7	990.10
11-2	2477	600.00	11-23	2485	974.80		11-12	2,575.00
11-4	2478	538.20	11-24	2486	940.00		11-17	1,472.70
11-8	2479	1,705.00	11-29	2487	398.00		11-20	2,954.00
11-10	2480	1,330.00	11-30	2488	800.00		11-24	2,567.30
11-15	2481	695.40	Total		$14,469.10		11-27	1,650.00
11-18	2482	612.00					11-29	1,186.00
							11-30	1,304.00
							Total	$15,910.70

The November bank statement contained two bank memoranda:

1. A credit of $2,242 for the collection for Bogalusa Company of an electronic funds transfer.

2. A debit for the printing of additional company checks $85.

At November 30, the cash balance per books was $11,073.80 and the cash balance per the bank statement was $17,712.50. The bank did not make any errors, but **Bogalusa Company made two errors.**

Instructions

a. Adjusted cash bal. $13,176.80

a. Prepare a bank reconciliation at November 30, 2022.

b. Prepare the adjusting entries based on the reconciliation. (*Note:* The correction of any errors pertaining to recording checks should be made to Accounts Payable. The correction of any errors relating to recording cash receipts should be made to Accounts Receivable.)

Prepare a bank reconciliation and adjusting entries.

P7.6A (LO 3), AP Timmins Company of Emporia, Kansas, spreads herbicides and applies liquid fertilizer for local farmers. On May 31, 2022, the company's Cash account per its general ledger showed a balance of $6,738.90.

The bank statement from Emporia State Bank on that date showed the following balance.

Emporia State Bank		
Checks and Debits	Deposits and Credits	Daily Balance
XXX	XXX	5-31 6,968.00

A comparison of the details on the bank statement with the details in the Cash account revealed the following facts.

1. The statement included a debit memo of $40 for the printing of additional company checks.

2. Cash sales of $883.15 on May 12 were deposited in the bank. The cash receipts entry and the deposit slip were incorrectly made for $933.15. The bank credited Timmins Company for the correct amount.

3. Outstanding checks at May 31 totaled $276.25, and deposits in transit were $1,880.15.

4. On May 18, the company issued check No. 1181 for $685 to H. Moses, on account. The check, which cleared the bank in May, was incorrectly journalized and posted by Timmins Company for $658.

5. $2,690 was collected from a customer's note receivable by the bank for Timmins Company on May 31 through electronic funds transfer.

6. Included with the canceled checks was a check issued by Tomins Company to C. Pernod for $360 that was incorrectly charged to Timmins Company by the bank.

7. On May 31, the bank statement showed an NSF charge of $380 for a check issued by Sara Ballard, a customer, to Timmins Company on account.

Instructions

a. Adjusted cash bal. $8,931.90

a. Prepare the bank reconciliation at May 31, 2022.

b. Prepare the necessary adjusting entries for Timmins Company at May 31, 2022.

Prepare a comprehensive bank reconciliation with theft and internal control deficiencies.

P7.7A (LO 1, 2, 3), AN Daisey Company is a very profitable small business. It has not, however, given much consideration to internal control. For example, in an attempt to keep clerical and office expenses to a minimum, the company has combined the jobs of cashier and bookkeeper. As a result, Bret Turrin handles all cash receipts, keeps the accounting records, and prepares the monthly bank reconciliations.

The balance per the bank statement on October 31, 2022, was $18,380. Outstanding checks were No. 62 for $140.75, No. 183 for $180, No. 284 for $253.25, No. 862 for $190.71, No. 863 for $226.80, and No. 864 for $165.28. Included with the statement was a credit memorandum of $185 indicating the collection of a note receivable for Daisey Company by the bank on October 25. This memorandum has not been recorded by Daisey.

The company's ledger showed one Cash account with a balance of $21,877.72. The balance included undeposited cash on hand. Because of the lack of internal controls, Bret took for personal use all of the undeposited receipts in excess of $3,795.51. He then prepared the following bank reconciliation in an effort to conceal his theft of cash.

Cash balance per books, October 31		$21,877.72
Add: Outstanding checks		
No. 862	$190.71	
No. 863	226.80	
No. 864	165.28	482.79
		22,360.51
Less: Undeposited receipts		3,795.51
Unadjusted balance per bank, October 31		18,565.00
Less: Bank credit memorandum		185.00
Cash balance per bank statement, October 31		$18,380.00

Instructions

a. Prepare a correct bank reconciliation. (*Hint:* Deduct the amount of the theft from the adjusted balance per books.)

b. Indicate the three ways that Bret attempted to conceal the theft and the dollar amount involved in each method.

c. What principles of internal control were violated in this case?

a. Adjusted cash bal. $21,018.72

Continuing Case

Cookie Creations

(*Note:* This is a continuation of the Cookie Creations case from Chapters 1 through 6.)

CC7 Part 1   Natalie is struggling to keep up with the recording of her accounting transactions. She is spending a lot of time marketing and selling mixers and giving her cookie classes. Her friend John is an accounting student who runs his own accounting service. He has asked Natalie if she would like to have him do her accounting. John and Natalie meet and discuss her business.

Part 2   Natalie decides that she cannot afford to hire John to do her accounting. One way that she can ensure that her cash account does not have any errors and is accurate and up-to-date is to prepare a bank reconciliation at the ledger of each month. Natalie would like you to help her.

Go to **WileyPLUS** *for complete case details and instructions.*

leungchopan/
Shutterstock.com

Comprehensive Accounting Cycle Review

ACR7 On December 1, 2022, Fullerton Company had the following account balances.

	Debit		Credit
Cash	$18,200	Accumulated Depreciation—	
Notes Receivable	2,200	Equipment	$ 3,000
Accounts Receivable	7,500	Accounts Payable	6,100
Inventory	16,000	Common Stock	50,000
Prepaid Insurance	1,600	Retained Earnings	14,400
Equipment	28,000		$73,500
	$73,500		

During December, the company completed the following transactions.

Dec.
7   Received $3,600 cash from customers in payment of account (no discount allowed).
12   Purchased merchandise on account from Vance Co. $12,000, terms 1/10, n/30.
17   Sold merchandise on account $16,000, terms 2/10, n/30. The cost of the merchandise sold was $10,000.
19   Paid salaries $2,200.
22   Paid Vance Co. in full, less discount.
26   Received collections in full, less discounts, from customers billed on December 17.
31   Received $2,700 cash from customers in payment of account (no discount allowed).

Adjustment data:

1. Depreciation was $200 per month.

2. Insurance of $400 expired in December.

Instructions

a. Journalize the December transactions. (Assume a perpetual inventory system.)

b. Enter the December 1 balances in the ledger T-accounts and post the December transactions. Use these additional accounts: Cost of Goods Sold, Depreciation Expense, Insurance Expense, Salaries and Wages Expense, Sales Revenue, and Sales Discounts.

c. The statement from Jackson County Bank on December 31 showed a balance of $26,130. A comparison of the bank statement with the Cash account revealed the following facts.

    1. The bank collected a note receivable of $2,200 for Fullerton Company on December 15 through electronic funds transfer.

    2. The December 31 receipts were deposited in a night deposit vault on December 31. These deposits were recorded by the bank in January.

    3. Checks outstanding on December 31 totaled $1,210.

    4. On December 31, the bank statement showed an NSF charge of $680 for a check received by the company from L. Bryan, a customer, on account.

Prepare a bank reconciliation as of December 31 based on the available information. (*Hint:* The cash balance per books is $26,100. This can be proven by finding the balance in the Cash account from parts (a) and (b).)

d. Journalize the adjusting entries resulting from the bank reconciliation and adjustment data.

e. Post the adjusting entries to the ledger T-accounts.

f. Prepare an adjusted trial balance.

g. Prepare a multiple-step income statement for December and a classified balance sheet at December 31.

Expand Your Critical Thinking

Financial Reporting Problem: Apple Inc.

CT7.1 The financial statements of **Apple Inc.** are presented in Appendix A. The complete annual report, including the notes to the financial statements, is available at the company's website.

Instructions

a. What comments, if any, are made about cash in the "Report of the Independent Registered Public Accounting Firm"?

b. What data about cash and cash equivalents are shown in the 2017 and 2018 consolidated balance sheets?

c. In its Notes to Consolidated Financial Statements, how does Apple define cash equivalents?

d. In "Management's Annual Report on Internal Control over Financial Reporting," what does Apple's management say about internal control for 2018?

Comparative Analysis Problem:

PepsiCo, Inc. vs. The Coca-Cola Company

CT7.2 **PepsiCo**'s financial statements are presented in Appendix B. Financial statements of **The Coca-Cola Company** are presented in Appendix C. The complete annual reports of PepsiCo and Coca-Cola, including the notes to the financial statements, are available at each company's respective website.

Instructions

a. Based on the information contained in these financial statements, determine each of the following for each company:

1. Cash and cash equivalents balance for 2018.

2. Increase (decrease) in cash and cash equivalents from 2017 to 2018 per the balance sheet.

3. Net cash provided by operating activities during the year ended December 2018 (from statement of cash flows).

b. What conclusions concerning the management of cash can be drawn from these data?

Comparative Analysis Problem:

Amazon.com, Inc. vs. Walmart Inc.

CT7.3 **Amazon.com, Inc.**'s financial statements are presented in Appendix D. Financial statements of **Walmart Inc.** are presented in Appendix E. The complete annual reports of Amazon and Walmart, including the notes to the financial statements, are available at each company's respective website.

Instructions

a. Based on the information contained in these financial statements, determine each of the following for each company:

1. Cash and cash equivalents balance at December 31, 2018, for Amazon and at January 31, 2019, for Walmart.

2. Increase (decrease) in cash and cash equivalents from 2017 to 2018 per the balance sheet.

3. Net cash provided by operating activities during the year ended December 31, 2018, for Amazon and January 31, 2019, for Walmart from statement of cash flows.

b. What conclusions concerning the management of cash can be drawn from these data?

Real-World Focus

CT7.4 The **Public Company Accounting Oversight Board (PCAOB)** was created as a result of the Sarbanes-Oxley Act. It has oversight and enforcement responsibilities over accounting firms in the United States.

Instructions

Go to the PCAOB website and then answer the following questions.

a. What is the mission of the PCAOB?

b. Briefly summarize the PCAOB's responsibilities related to inspections.

c. Briefly summarize the PCAOB's responsibilities related to enforcement.

Decision-Making Across the Organization

CT7.5 The board of trustees of a local church is concerned about the internal accounting controls for the offering collections made at weekly services. The trustees ask you to serve on a three-person audit team with the internal auditor of a local college and a CPA who has just joined the church.

At a meeting of the audit team and the board of trustees, you learn the following.

1. The church's board of trustees has delegated responsibility for the financial management and audit of the financial records to the finance committee. This group prepares the annual budget and approves major disbursements. It is not involved in collections or recordkeeping. No audit has been made in recent years because the same trusted employee has kept church records and served as financial secretary for 15 years. The church does not carry any fidelity insurance.

2. The collection at the weekly service is taken by a team of ushers who volunteer to serve one month. The ushers take the collection plates to a basement office at the rear of the church. They hand their plates to the head usher and return to the church service. After all plates have been turned in, the head usher counts the cash received. The head usher then places the cash in the church safe along with a notation of the amount counted. The head usher volunteers to serve for 3 months.

3. The next morning, the financial secretary opens the safe and recounts the collection. The secretary withholds $150–$200 in cash, depending on the cash expenditures expected for the week, and deposits the remainder of the collections in the bank. To facilitate the deposit, church members who contribute by check are asked to make their checks payable to "Cash."

4. Each month, the financial secretary reconciles the bank statement and submits a copy of the reconciliation to the board of trustees. The reconciliations have rarely contained any bank errors and have never shown any errors per books.

Instructions

With the class divided into groups, answer the following.

a. Indicate the weaknesses in internal accounting control over the handling of collections.

b. List the improvements in internal control procedures that you plan to make at the next meeting of the audit team for (1) the ushers, (2) the head usher, (3) the financial secretary, and (4) the finance committee.

c. What church policies should be changed to improve internal control?

Communication Activity

CT7.6 As a new auditor for the CPA firm of Blacke and Whyte, you have been assigned to review the internal controls over mail cash receipts of Simon Company. Your review reveals the following. Checks are promptly endorsed "For Deposit Only," but no list of the checks is prepared by the person opening the mail. The mail is opened either by the cashier or by the employee who maintains the accounts receivable records. Mail receipts are deposited in the bank weekly by the cashier.

Instructions

Write a letter to Frank Simon, owner of Simon Company, explaining the weaknesses in internal control and your recommendations for improving the system.

Ethics Case

CT7.7 You are the assistant controller in charge of general ledger accounting at Linbarger Bottling Company. Your company has a large loan from an insurance company. The loan agreement requires that the company's cash account balance be maintained at $200,000 or more, as reported monthly.

At June 30, the cash balance is $80,000, which you report to Lisa Infante, the financial vice president. Lisa excitedly instructs you to keep the cash receipts book open for one additional day for purposes of the June 30 report to the insurance company. Lisa says, "If we don't get that cash balance over $200,000, we'll default on our loan agreement. They could close us down, put us all out of our jobs!" Lisa continues, "I talked to Oconto Distributors (one of Linbarger's largest customers) this morning. They said they sent us a check for $150,000 yesterday. We should receive it tomorrow. If we include just that one check in our cash balance, we'll be in the clear. It's in the mail!"

Instructions

a. Who will suffer negative effects if you do not comply with Lisa Infante's instructions? Who will suffer if you do comply?

b. What are the ethical considerations in this case?

c. What alternatives do you have?

All About You

CT7.8 The print and electronic media are full of stories about potential security risks that may arise from your computer or smartphone. It is important to keep in mind, however, that there are also many other ways that your identity can be stolen. The federal government provides many resources to help protect you from identity thieves.

Instructions

Search the Internet for "ID Theft Faceoff Game" and then complete the quiz provided.

FASB Codification Activity

CT7.9 If your school has a subscription to the FASB Codification, log in and prepare responses to the following.

  a. How is cash defined in the Codification?

  b. How are cash equivalents defined in the Codification?

  c. What are the disclosure requirements related to cash and cash equivalents?

A Look at IFRS

LEARNING OBJECTIVE 5
Compare the accounting for fraud, internal control, and cash under GAAP and IFRS.

Fraud can occur anywhere. Because the three main factors that contribute to fraud are universal in nature, the principles of internal control activities are used globally by companies. While Sarbanes-Oxley (SOX) does not apply to non-U.S. companies, most large international companies have internal controls similar to those presented in this chapter. IFRS and GAAP are also very similar in accounting for cash. *IAS No. 1 (revised),* "Presentation of Financial Statements," is the only standard that discusses issues specifically related to cash.

Key Points

The following are the key similarities and differences between GAAP and IFRS related to fraud, internal control, and cash.

Similarities

- The fraud triangle discussed in this chapter is applicable to all international companies. Some of the major frauds on an international basis are **Parmalat** (Italy), **Royal Ahold** (the Netherlands), and **Satyam Computer Services** (India).

- Rising economic crime poses a growing threat to companies, with 34% of all organizations worldwide being victims of fraud in a recent 12-month period.

- Accounting scandals both in the United States and internationally have reignited the debate over the relative merits of GAAP, which takes a "rules-based" approach to accounting, versus IFRS, which takes a "principles-based" approach. The FASB announced that it intends to introduce more principles-based standards.

- On a lighter note, at one time the Ig Nobel Prize in Economics went to the CEOs of those companies involved in the corporate accounting scandals of that year for "adapting the mathematical concept of imaginary numbers for use in the business world." A parody of the Nobel Prizes, the Ig Nobel Prizes (read Ignoble, as in not noble) are given each year in early October for 10 achievements that "first make people laugh, and then make them think." Organized by the scientific humor magazine *Annals of Improbable Research (AIR)*, they are presented by a group that includes genuine Nobel laureates at a ceremony at Harvard University's Sanders Theater.

- Internal controls are a system of checks and balances designed to prevent and detect fraud and errors. While most companies have these systems in place, many have never completely documented them, nor had an independent auditor attest to their effectiveness. Both of these actions are required under SOX.

- Companies find that internal control review is a costly process but badly needed. One study estimates the cost of SOX compliance for U.S. companies at over $35 billion, with audit fees doubling in the first year of compliance. At the same time, examination of internal controls indicates lingering problems in the way companies operate. One study of first compliance with the internal-control testing provisions documented material weaknesses for about 13% of companies reporting in a two-year period (*PricewaterhouseCoopers' Global Economic Crime Survey*, 2005).

- The accounting and internal control procedures related to cash are essentially the same under both IFRS and this text. In addition, the definition used for cash equivalents is the same.
- Most companies report cash and cash equivalents together under IFRS, as shown in this text. In addition, IFRS follows the same accounting policies related to the reporting of restricted cash.

Differences

- The SOX internal control standards apply only to companies listed on U.S. exchanges. There is continuing debate over whether foreign issuers should have to comply with this extra layer of regulation.

IFRS Practice

IFRS Self-Test Questions

1. Non-U.S companies that follow IFRS:
    a. do not normally use the principles of internal control activities described in this text.
    b. often offset cash with accounts payable on the balance sheet.
    c. are not required to follow SOX.
    d. None of the answer choices is correct.

2. The Sarbanes-Oxley Act applies to:
    a. all U.S. companies listed on U.S. exchanges.
    b. all companies that list stock on any stock exchange in any country.
    c. all European companies listed on European exchanges.
    d. all U.S. companies listed on U.S. exchanges and all European companies listed on European exchanges.

IFRS Exercise

IFRS7.1 Some people argue that the internal control requirements of the Sarbanes-Oxley Act (SOX) put U.S. companies at a competitive disadvantage to companies outside the United States. Discuss the competitive implications (both pros and cons) of SOX.

International Financial Reporting Problem: Louis Vuitton

IFRS7.2 The financial statements of **Louis Vuitton** are presented in Appendix F. The complete consolidated financial statements, including the notes to its financial statements, are available at the company's website.

Instructions

Using the notes to the company's 2018 consolidated financial statements, what are Louis Vuitton's accounting policies related to cash and cash equivalents?

Answers to IFRS Self-Test Questions

1. c   **2.** a

arsenik/E+/Getty Images

Accounting for Receivables

Chapter Preview

As indicated in the following Feature Story, receivables are a significant asset for **Nike** as well as many other retail companies. Because a large portion of sales in the United States are credit sales, receivables are important to companies in other industries as well. As a consequence, companies must pay close attention to their receivables and manage them carefully. In this chapter, you will learn what journal entries companies make when they sell products, when they collect cash from those sales, and when they write off accounts they cannot collect.

Feature Story

What's Cooking?

What major U.S corporation got its start 38 years ago with a waffle iron? *Hint:* It doesn't sell food. *Another hint:* Swoosh. *Another hint:* "Just do it." That's right, **Nike**. In 1971, Nike co-founder Bill Bowerman put a piece of rubber into a kitchen waffle iron,

and the trademark waffle sole was born. It seems fair to say that at Nike, "They don't make 'em like they used to."

Nike was co-founded by Bowerman and Phil Knight, a member of Bowerman's University of Oregon track team. Each began in the shoe business independently during the early 1960s. Bowerman got his start by making hand-crafted running shoes for his University of Oregon track team. Knight, after completing graduate school, started a small business importing low-cost, high-quality shoes from Japan. In 1964, the two joined forces, each contributing $500, and formed Blue Ribbon Sports, a partnership that marketed Japanese shoes.

It wasn't until 1971 that the company began manufacturing its own line of shoes. With the new shoes came a new corporate name—Nike—the Greek goddess of victory. It is hard to imagine that the company that now boasts a stable full of world-class athletes as promoters at one time had part-time employees selling shoes out of car trunks at track meets on a cash-and-carry basis.

As the business grew, Nike sold its shoes to sporting good shops and department stores on a credit basis. This necessitated receivables management. Today, with sales of $20.8 billion and accounts receivable of $3.1 billion, managing accounts receivable is vitally important to Nike's success. If it makes a major mistake with its receivables, it will definitely affect the bottom line.

In recent years, Nike has expanded its product line to a diverse range of products, including performance equipment such as soccer balls and golf clubs. While this has increased sales revenue, it has also complicated Nike's receivables management efforts. Now, instead of selling shoes at a limited number of retail outlets, it sells its vast number of products to a diverse array of stores, large and small. For example, Nike golf clubs are sold at local country clubs and golf shops across the country, while soccer equipment can be sold directly to customers through Internet sales. This diversification of its customer list complicates matters because Nike has to approve each new store or customer for credit sales, monitor cash collections, and pursue slow-paying accounts. That's a lot of work. Maybe cash-and-carry wasn't so bad after all.

Chapter Outline

LEARNING OBJECTIVES	REVIEW	PRACTICE
LO 1 Explain how companies recognize accounts receivable.	• Types of receivables • Recognizing accounts receivable	**DO IT! 1** Recognizing Accounts Receivable
LO 2 Describe how companies value accounts receivable and record their disposition.	• Valuing accounts receivable • Disposing of accounts receivable	**DO IT! 2a** Bad Debt Expense **2b** Factoring
LO 3 Explain how companies recognize, value, and dispose of notes receivable.	• Determining the maturity date • Computing interest • Recognizing notes receivable • Valuing notes receivable • Disposing of notes receivable	**DO IT! 3** Recognizing Notes Receivable
LO 4 Describe the statement presentation and analysis of receivables.	• Presentation • Analysis • Data analytics and receivables management	**DO IT! 4** Analysis of Receivables

Go to the Review and Practice section at the end of the chapter for a review of key concepts and practice applications with solutions.

Visit WileyPLUS for additional tutorials and practice opportunities.

Recognition of Accounts Receivable

The term **receivables** refers to amounts due from individuals and companies. Receivables are claims that are expected to be collected in cash. The management of receivables is a very important activity for any company that sells goods or services on credit.

Receivables are important because they represent one of a company's most liquid assets. For many companies, receivables are also one of the largest assets. For example, receivables represent 13.7% of the current assets of pharmaceutical giant **Rite Aid**. **Illustration 8.1** lists receivables as a percentage of total assets for five other well-known companies in a recent year.

Company	Receivables as a Percentage of Total Assets
Ford Motor Company	43.2%
General Electric	41.5
Minnesota Mining and Manufacturing Company (3M)	12.7
DuPont Co.	11.7
Intel Corporation	3.9

ILLUSTRATION 8.1

Receivables as a percentage of assets

Types of Receivables

The relative significance of a company's receivables as a percentage of its assets depends on various factors: its industry, the time of year, whether it extends long-term financing, and its credit policies. To reflect important differences among receivables, they are frequently classified as (1) accounts receivable, (2) notes receivable, and (3) other receivables.

Accounts receivable are amounts customers owe on account. They result from the sale of goods and services. Companies generally expect to collect accounts receivable within 30 to 60 days. They are usually the most significant type of claim held by a company.

Notes receivable are a written promise (as evidenced by a formal instrument) for amounts to be received. The note normally requires the collection of interest and extends for time periods of 60–90 days or longer. Notes and accounts receivable that result from sales transactions are often called **trade receivables**.

Other receivables include nontrade receivables such as interest receivable, loans to company officers, advances to employees, and income taxes refundable. These do not generally result from the operations of the business. Therefore, they are generally classified and reported as separate items in the balance sheet (see **Ethics Note**).

ETHICS NOTE

Companies report receivables from employees separately in the financial statements. The reason: Sometimes these receivables are not the result of an "arm's-length" transaction.

Recognizing Accounts Receivable

Recognizing accounts receivable is relatively straightforward. A service organization records a receivable when it performs a service on account. A merchandiser records accounts receivable at the point of sale of merchandise on account. When a merchandiser sells goods, it increases (debits) Accounts Receivable and increases (credits) Sales Revenue.

Recall that sellers sometimes offer sales discounts to encourage early payment by the buyer. If the buyer pays during the discount period, the receivable balance will be satisfied with a smaller cash payment. Also, the buyer might find some of the goods unacceptable and choose to return the unwanted goods. When a buyer returns goods that it previously purchased on credit, the receivable balance is reduced.

To review, assume that Jordache Co. on July 1, 2022, sells merchandise on account to Polo Company for $1,000, terms 2/10, n/30. On July 5, Polo returns merchandise with a sales price of $100 to Jordache Co. On July 11, Jordache receives payment from Polo Company for the balance due. The journal entries to record these transactions on the books of Jordache Co. are as follows (see **Helpful Hint**). **(Cost of goods sold entries are omitted.)**

HELPFUL HINT

These entries are the same as those described in Chapter 5. For simplicity, we have omitted inventory and cost of goods sold from this set of journal entries and from end-of-chapter material.

July 1	Accounts Receivable	1,000	
	Sales Revenue		1,000
	(To record sales on account)		
July 5	Sales Returns and Allowances	100	
	Accounts Receivable		100
	(To record merchandise returned)		
July 11	Cash ($900 − $18)	882	
	Sales Discounts ($900 × .02)	18	
	Accounts Receivable		900
	(To record collection of accounts receivable)		

Some retailers issue their own credit cards. When you use a retailer's credit card (**JCPenney**, for example), the retailer charges interest on the balance due if not paid within a specified period (usually 25–30 days).

To illustrate, assume that you use your JCPenney credit card to purchase clothing with a sales price of $300 on June 1, 2022. JCPenney will increase (debit) Accounts Receivable for $300 and increase (credit) Sales Revenue for $300 (cost of goods sold entry omitted) as follows.

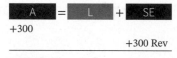

+300

+300 Rev

Cash Flows
no effect

June 1	Accounts Receivable	300	
	Sales Revenue		300
	(To record sale of merchandise)		

Assuming that you owe $300 at the end of the month and JCPenney charges 1.5% per month on the balance due, the adjusting entry that JCPenney makes to record interest revenue of $4.50 ($300 × 1.5%) on June 30 is as follows.

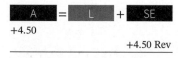

+4.50

+4.50 Rev

Cash Flows
no effect

June 30	Accounts Receivable	4.50	
	Interest Revenue		4.50
	(To record interest on amount due)		

Interest revenue is often substantial for many retailers.

Anatomy of a Fraud

Tasanee was the accounts receivable clerk for a large nonprofit foundation that provided performance and exhibition space for the performing and visual arts. Her responsibilities included activities normally assigned to an accounts receivable clerk, such as recording revenues from various sources (donations, facility rental fees, ticket revenue, and bar receipts). However, she was also responsible for handling all cash and checks from the time they were received until the time she deposited them, as well as preparing the bank reconciliation. Tasanee took advantage of her situation by falsifying bank deposits and bank reconciliations so that she could steal cash from the bar receipts. Since nobody else logged the donations or matched the donation receipts to pledges prior to Tasanee receiving them, she was able to offset the cash that was stolen against donations that she received but didn't record. Her crime was made easier by the fact that her boss, the company's controller, only did a very superficial review of the bank reconciliation

and thus didn't notice that some numbers had been cut out from other documents and taped onto the bank reconciliation.

Total take: $1.5 million

The Missing Controls

Segregation of duties. The foundation should not have allowed an accounts receivable clerk, whose job was to record receivables, to also handle cash, record cash, make deposits, and especially prepare the bank reconciliation.

Independent internal verification. The controller was supposed to perform a thorough review of the bank reconciliation. Because he did not, he was terminated from his position.

Source: Adapted from Wells, *Fraud Casebook* (2007), pp. 183–194.

DO IT! 1 | Recognizing Accounts Receivable

On May 1, Wilton sold merchandise on account to Bates for $50,000 terms 3/15, n/45. On May 4, Bates returns merchandise with a sales price of $2,000. On May 14, Wilton receives payment from Bates for the balance due. Prepare journal entries to record the May transactions on Wilton's books. (You may ignore cost of goods sold entries and explanations.)

Solution

Date		Account	Debit	Credit
May 1		Accounts Receivable	50,000	
		Sales Revenue		50,000
4		Sales Returns and Allowances	2,000	
		Accounts Receivable		2,000
14		Cash ($48,000 − $1,440)	46,560	
		Sales Discounts ($48,000 × .03)	1,440	
		Accounts Receivable		48,000

Related exercise material: **BE8.1, BE8.2, DO IT! 8.1, E8.1, E8.2, and E8.3.**

Valuation and Disposition of Accounts Receivable

LEARNING OBJECTIVE 2
Describe how companies value accounts receivable and record their disposition.

Valuing Accounts Receivable

Once companies record receivables in the accounts, the next question is: How should they report receivables in the financial statements? Companies report accounts receivable on the balance sheet as an asset. But determining the **amount** to report is sometimes difficult because some receivables will become uncollectible.

Each customer must satisfy the credit requirements of the seller before the credit sale is approved. Inevitably, though, some accounts receivable become uncollectible. For example, a customer may not be able to pay because of a decline in its sales revenue due to a downturn in the economy. Similarly, individuals may be laid off from their jobs or faced with unexpected hospital bills. Companies record credit losses as **Bad Debt Expense** (or Uncollectible Accounts Expense). Such losses are a normal and necessary risk of doing business on a credit basis.

When U.S. home prices fell, home foreclosures rose, and the economy in general slowed as a result of the financial crisis of 2008, lenders experienced huge increases in their bad debt expense. For example, during one quarter **Wachovia** (a large U.S. bank now owned by **Wells Fargo**) increased bad debt expense from $108 million to $408 million. Similarly, **American Express** increased its bad debt expense by 70%.

Two methods are used in accounting for uncollectible accounts: (1) the direct write-off method (not GAAP) and (2) the allowance method (GAAP). The following sections explain these methods.

Direct Write-Off Method for Uncollectible Accounts

Under the **direct write-off method**, when a company determines a particular account to be uncollectible, it charges the loss to Bad Debt Expense. Assume, for example, that Warden Co. writes off as uncollectible M. E. Doran's $200 balance on December 12. Warden's entry is as follows.

A = L + SE
−200 Exp

−200

Cash Flows
no effect

Dec. 12	Bad Debt Expense	200	
	Accounts Receivable		200
	(To record write-off of M. E. Doran account)		

Under this method, Bad Debt Expense will show only **actual losses** from specific customer uncollectibles. The company will report accounts receivable at its gross amount, shown in the Accounts Receivable account.

Use of the direct write-off method can reduce the relevance of both the income statement and the balance sheet. Consider the following example. In 2022, Quick Buck Computer Company decided it could increase its revenues by offering computers to college students without requiring any money down and with no credit-approval process. On campuses across the country, it sold one million computers with a selling price of $800 each. This increased Quick Buck's revenues and receivables by $800 million. The promotion was a huge success! The 2022 balance sheet and income statement looked great. Unfortunately, during 2023, nearly 40% of the customers defaulted on their loans. This made the 2023 income statement and balance sheet look terrible. **Illustration 8.2** shows the effect of these events on the financial statements if the direct write-off method is used.

ILLUSTRATION 8.2

Effects of direct write-off method

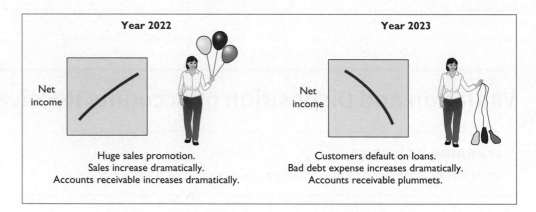

Year 2022

Net income

Huge sales promotion.
Sales increase dramatically.
Accounts receivable increases dramatically.

Year 2023

Net income

Customers default on loans.
Bad debt expense increases dramatically.
Accounts receivable plummets.

Under the direct write-off method, companies often record bad debt expense in a period different from the period in which they record the related revenue. The method does not attempt to match bad debt expense to sales revenue in the income statement. Nor does the direct write-off method show accounts receivable in the balance sheet at the amount the company actually expects to receive in cash. **Consequently, unless uncollectibles are insignificant, the direct write-off method is not acceptable for financial reporting purposes.**

Allowance Method for Uncollectible Accounts

The **allowance method** of accounting for uncollectibles involves estimating uncollectible accounts at the end of each period. This provides better matching of expenses with revenues on the income statement. It also ensures that companies state receivables on the balance sheet at their cash (net) realizable value. **Cash (net) realizable value** is the net amount the company expects to receive in cash. It excludes amounts that the company estimates it will not collect. Thus, this method reduces receivables in the balance sheet by the amount of estimated uncollectible receivables.

Companies must use the allowance method for financial reporting purposes when uncollectibles are material in amount (see **Helpful Hint**). This method has three essential features:

1. Companies **estimate** uncollectible accounts receivable. They match estimated expense **against revenues** in the same accounting period in which they record the revenues.

2. Companies debit Bad Debt Expense and credit Allowance for Doubtful Accounts through an adjusting entry at the end of each period. Allowance for Doubtful Accounts is a contra account to Accounts Receivable.

3. When companies write off a specific customer account, they debit actual uncollectibles to Allowance for Doubtful Accounts and credit that amount to Accounts Receivable.

Recording Estimated Uncollectibles   To illustrate the allowance method, assume that Hampson Furniture has credit sales of $1,200,000 in 2022, its first year of operations. Of this amount, $200,000 of receivables remains uncollected at December 31. The credit manager estimates that $12,000 of these receivables will be uncollectible. The adjusting entry to record the estimated uncollectibles increases (debits) Bad Debt Expense and increases (credits) Allowance for Doubtful Accounts, as follows.

Dec. 31	Bad Debt Expense	12,000	
	Allowance for Doubtful Accounts		12,000
	(To record estimate of uncollectible accounts)		

A = L + SE
−12,000 Exp
−12,000

Cash Flows
no effect

Hampson reports Bad Debt Expense in the income statement as an operating expense. Thus, the estimated uncollectibles are matched with the sales revenue in 2022. Hampson records the expense in the same year it made the sales.

Allowance for Doubtful Accounts shows the estimated amount of claims on customers that the company expects will become uncollectible in the future. Companies use a contra account instead of a direct credit to Accounts Receivable because they do not know which specific customers will not pay. The credit balance in the allowance account will absorb the specific write-offs when they occur. As **Illustration 8.3** shows, the company deducts the allowance account from accounts receivable in the current assets section of the balance sheet.

| Hampson Furniture | | |
Balance Sheet (partial)		
Current assets		
Cash		$ 14,800
Accounts receivable	$200,000	
Less: Allowance for doubtful accounts	12,000	188,000
Inventory		310,000
Supplies		25,000
Total current assets		$537,800

ILLUSTRATION 8.3
Presentation of allowance for doubtful accounts

The amount of $188,000 in Illustration 8.3 represents the expected **cash realizable value** of the accounts receivable at the statement date (see **Helpful Hint**). **Companies do not close Allowance for Doubtful Accounts at the end of the fiscal year as it is a permanent account.**

HELPFUL HINT
Cash realizable value is sometimes referred to as *accounts receivable (net)*.

Recording the Write-Off of an Uncollectible Account   Companies use various methods of collecting past-due accounts, such as letters, calls, and legal action. When they have exhausted all means of collecting a past-due account and collection appears impossible, the company writes off the account. In the credit card industry, for example, it is standard practice to write off accounts that are 210 days past due. To prevent premature or unauthorized write-offs, authorized management personnel should formally approve each write-off. **To maintain segregation of duties, the employee authorized to write off accounts should not have daily responsibilities related to cash or receivables.**

To illustrate a receivables write-off, assume that the financial vice president of Hampson Furniture authorizes a write-off of the $500 balance owed by R. A. Ware on March 1, 2023. The entry to record the write-off is as follows.

Mar. 1	Allowance for Doubtful Accounts	500	
	Accounts Receivable		500
	(Write-off of R. A. Ware account)		

A = L + SE
+500
−500

Cash Flows
no effect

The company does not increase Bad Debt Expense when the write-off occurs. **Under the allowance method, companies debit every specific customer write-off to Allowance for Doubtful Accounts rather than to Bad Debt Expense.** A debit to Bad Debt

Expense would be incorrect because the company has already recognized the expense when it made the adjusting entry for estimated uncollectibles. Instead, the entry to record the write-off of an uncollectible account reduces both Accounts Receivable and Allowance for Doubtful Accounts. After posting, the general ledger accounts for 2023 appear as shown in **Illustration 8.4**.

ILLUSTRATION 8.4

General ledger balances after write-off

Accounts Receivable				Allowance for Doubtful Accounts			
Jan. 1 Bal.	200,000	Mar. 1	500	Mar. 1	500	Jan. 1 Bal.	12,000
Mar. 1 Bal.	199,500					Mar. 1 Bal.	11,500

A write-off affects **only balance sheet accounts**—not income statement accounts. The write-off of the account reduces both Accounts Receivable and Allowance for Doubtful Accounts. Cash realizable value in the balance sheet, therefore, remains the same, as **Illustration 8.5** shows.

ILLUSTRATION 8.5

Cash realizable value comparison

	Before Write-Off	After Write-Off
Accounts receivable	$200,000	$199,500
Allowance for doubtful accounts	12,000	11,500
Cash realizable value	**$188,000**	**$188,000**

Recovery of an Uncollectible Account Occasionally, a company collects from a customer after it has written off the account as uncollectible. The company makes two entries to record the recovery of a previously written off customer account. (1) It reverses the entry made in writing off the account. This reinstates the customer's account. (2) It journalizes the cash collection in the usual manner.

To illustrate, assume that on July 1, 2023, R. A. Ware pays the $500 amount that Hampson had written off on March 1. Hampson makes the following entries.

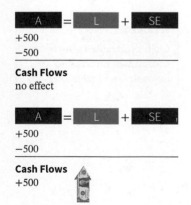

A = L + SE
+500
−500

Cash Flows
no effect

		(1)		
July 1	Accounts Receivable		500	
	Allowance for Doubtful Accounts			500
	(To reverse write-off of R. A. Ware account)			

A = L + SE
+500
−500

Cash Flows
+500

		(2)		
July 1	Cash		500	
	Accounts Receivable			500
	(To record collection from R. A. Ware)			

Note that the recovery of a customer account, like the write-off of a customer account, affects **only balance sheet accounts**. The net effect of the two entries above is a debit to Cash and a credit to Allowance for Doubtful Accounts for $500.

Estimating the Allowance For Hampson Furniture in Illustration 8.3, the amount of the expected uncollectibles was given. However, in "real life," companies must estimate the amount of expected uncollectible accounts if they use the allowance method. **Illustration 8.6** shows an excerpt from the notes to **Nike**'s financial statements discussing its use of the allowance method.

ILLUSTRATION 8.6
Nike's allowance method disclosure
Real World

Nike, Inc.

Notes to the Financial Statements

Allowance for Uncollectible Accounts Receivable

We make ongoing estimates relating to the ability to collect our accounts receivable and maintain an allowance for estimated losses resulting from the inability of our customers to make required payments. In determining the amount of the allowance, we consider our historical level of credit losses and make judgments about the creditworthiness of significant customers based on ongoing credit evaluations. Since we cannot predict future changes in the financial stability of our customers, actual future losses from uncollectible accounts may differ from our estimates.

Frequently, companies estimate the allowance as a percentage of the outstanding receivables. Under the **percentage-of-receivables basis**, management establishes a percentage relationship between the amount of receivables and expected losses from uncollectible accounts (see **Helpful Hint**). For example, suppose Steffen Company has an ending balance in Accounts Receivable of $200,000 and an unadjusted credit balance in Allowance for Doubtful Accounts of $1,500. It estimates that 5% of its accounts receivable will eventually be uncollectible. It should report a **balance** in Allowance for Doubtful Accounts of $10,000 (.05 × $200,000). To increase the balance in Allowance for Doubtful Accounts from its unadjusted amount of $1,500 to $10,000, the company debits (increases) Bad Debt Expense and credits (increases) Allowance for Doubtful Accounts by $8,500 ($10,000 − $1,500).

To more accurately estimate the ending balance in the allowance account, a company often prepares a schedule called **aging the accounts receivable**. This schedule classifies customer balances by the length of time they have been unpaid.

After the company arranges the accounts by age, it determines the expected uncollectible accounts by applying percentages, based on past experience, to the totals of each category. The longer a receivable is past due, the less likely it is to be collected. As a result, the estimated percentage of uncollectible accounts increases as the number of days past due increases (see **Helpful Hint**). **Illustration 8.7** shows an aging schedule for Dart Company at December 31, 2022. Note the increasing uncollectible percentages from 2% to 40%.

> **HELPFUL HINT**
> Where appropriate, the percentage-of-receivables basis may use only a single percentage rate.

> **Allowance for Doubtful Accounts**
>
> | | |
> |---|---|
> | Dec. 31 Unadj. Bal. | 1,500 |
> | Dec. 31 Adj. | **8,500** |
> | Dec. 31 Bal. | 10,000 |

> **HELPFUL HINT**
> The older categories have higher percentages because the longer an account is past due, the less likely it is to be collected.

ILLUSTRATION 8.7
Aging schedule

	A	B	C	D	E	F	G
1			**Dart Company**				
2			Aging Schedule				
3			December 31, 2022				
4				Number of Days Past Due			
5			Not				
6	Customer	Total	Yet Due	1–30	31–60	61–90	Over 90
7	T. E. Adert	$ 600		$ 300		$ 200	$ 100
8	R. C. Bortz	300	$ 300				
9	B. A. Carl	450		200	$ 250		
10	O. L. Diker	700	500			200	
11	T. O. Ebbet	600			300		300
12	Others	36,950	26,200	5,200	2,450	1,600	1,500
13		$39,600	$27,000	$5,700	$3,000	$2,000	$1,900
14	Estimated percentage uncollectible		2%	4%	10%	20%	40%
15	Total estimated uncollectible accounts	$ 2,228	$ 540	$ 228	$ 300	$ 400	$ 760
16							

Total estimated uncollectible accounts for Dart Company ($2,228) represent the existing customer claims expected to become uncollectible in the future. Thus, this amount represents the **required balance** in Allowance for Doubtful Accounts at the balance sheet date. Accordingly, **the amount of bad debt expense that should be recorded in the adjusting entry is the difference between the required balance and the existing balance in the allowance account**. The existing, unadjusted balance in Allowance for Doubtful Accounts is the net result of the beginning balance (a normal credit balance) less the write-offs of specific accounts during the year (debits to the allowance account).

For example, if the unadjusted trial balance shows Allowance for Doubtful Accounts with a credit balance of $528, then an adjusting entry for $1,700 ($2,228 − $528) is necessary:

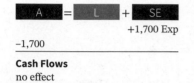

A = L + SE

+1,700 Exp

−1,700

Cash Flows
no effect

Dec. 31	Bad Debt Expense	1,700	
	Allowance for Doubtful Accounts		1,700
	(To adjust allowance account to total estimated uncollectibles)		

After Dart posts the adjusting entry, its accounts appear as shown in **Illustration 8.8**.

ILLUSTRATION 8.8

Bad debt expense accounts after posting

Bad Debt Expense		**Allowance for Doubtful Accounts**	
Dec. 31 Adj. **1,700**			Dec. 31 Unadj. Bal. 528
			Dec. 31 Adj. **1,700**
			Dec. 31 Bal. 2,228

An important aspect of accounts receivable management is simply maintaining a close watch on the accounts. Studies have shown that customer accounts more than 60 days past due lose approximately 50% of their value if no payment activity occurs within the next 30 days. For each additional 30 days that pass, the collectible value halves once again.

Occasionally, the allowance account will have a **debit balance** prior to adjustment. This occurs because the debits to the allowance account from write-offs during the year **exceeded** the beginning balance in the account, which was based on previous estimates for uncollectibles. In such a case, the company **adds the debit balance to the required balance** when it makes the adjusting entry. Thus, if there was a $500 **debit** balance in the allowance account before adjustment, the adjusting entry would be for $2,728 ($2,228 + $500) to arrive at an adjusted credit balance of $2,228 as shown below.

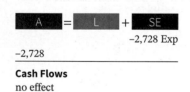

A = L + SE

−2,728 Exp

−2,728

Cash Flows
no effect

Dec. 31	Bad Debt Expense	2,728	
	Allowance for Doubtful Accounts		2,728
	(To adjust allowance account to total estimated uncollectibles)		

After Dart posts the adjusting entry, its accounts appear as shown in **Illustration 8.9**.

ILLUSTRATION 8.9

Bad debt expense accounts after posting

Bad Debt Expense		**Allowance for Doubtful Accounts**	
Dec. 31 Adj. **2,728**		Dec. 31 Unadj. Bal. 500	Dec. 31 Adj. **2,728**
			Dec. 31 Bal. 2,228

The percentage-of-receivables basis provides an estimate of the cash realizable value of the receivables. The FASB now employs an expected credit loss model which requires that companies must measure expected uncollectible accounts and record bad debt expense on all receivables, even those with a low risk of loss. Companies use sophisticated models employing data analytics to arrive at accurate estimates on a timely basis.

The note in **Illustration 8.10** regarding accounts receivable comes from the annual report of the shoe company **Skechers USA**.

Skechers USA's note disclosure of accounts receivable

Real World

Skechers USA
Notes to the Financial Statements

The likelihood of a material loss on an uncollectible account would be mainly dependent on deterioration in the overall economic conditions in a particular country or region. Reserves are fully provided for all probable losses of this nature. For receivables that are not specifically identified as high risk, we provide a reserve based upon our historical loss rate as a percentage of sales. Gross trade accounts receivable were $293.1 million and $241.9 million, and the allowance for bad debts, returns, sales allowances and customer chargebacks were $21.0 million and $15.9 million, at December 31, 2014 and 2013, respectively. Our credit losses charged to expense for the years ended December 31, 2014, 2013 and 2012 were $11.8 million, $2.6 million and $1.5 million, respectively. In addition, we recorded sales return and allowance expense (recoveries) for the years ended December 31, 2014, 2013 and 2012 of $2.3 million, $0.2 million and $(0.4) million, respectively.

Ethics Insight

Christy Thompson/
Shutterstock.com

Cookie Jar Allowances

There are many pressures on companies to achieve earnings targets. For managers, poor earnings can lead to dismissal or lack of promotion. It is thus not surprising that management may be tempted to look for ways to boost their earnings number.

One way a company can achieve greater earnings is to lower its estimate of what is needed in its Allowance for Doubtful Accounts (sometimes referred to as "tapping the cookie jar"). For example, suppose a company has an Allowance for Doubtful Accounts of $10 million and decides to reduce this balance to $9 million. As a result of this change,

Bad Debt Expense decreases by $1 million and earnings increase by $1 million.

Large banks such as **JPMorgan Chase**, **Wells Fargo**, and **Bank of America** recently decreased their Allowance for Doubtful Accounts by over $4 billion. These reductions came at a time when these big banks were still suffering from lower mortgage lending and trading activity, both of which led to lower earnings. They justified these reductions in the allowance balances by noting that credit quality and economic conditions had improved. This may be so, but it sure is great to have a cookie jar that might be tapped when a boost in earnings is needed.

How might investors determine that a company is managing its earnings? (Go to WileyPLUS for this answer and additional questions.)

DO IT! 2a | Bad Debt Expense

Brule Corporation has been in business for 5 years. The unadjusted trial balance at the end of the current year shows Accounts Receivable $30,000, Sales Revenue $180,000, and Allowance for Doubtful Accounts with a debit balance of $2,000. Brule estimates uncollectibles to be 10% of accounts receivable. Prepare the entry necessary to adjust Allowance for Doubtful Accounts.

Solution

Brule should make the following entry to bring the debit balance in Allowance for Doubtful Accounts up to a normal, credit balance of $3,000 (10% × $30,000):

Bad Debt Expense [(10% × $30,000) + $2,000]	5,000	
Allowance for Doubtful Accounts		5,000
(To adjust allowance account to total estimated		
uncollectibles)		

Related exercise material: **BE8.3, BE8.4, BE8.5, BE8.6, DO IT! 8.2a, E8.4, E8.5, E8.6, E8.7, and E8.8.**

ACTION PLAN

- **Estimate the amount the company does not expect to collect.**
- **Consider the existing balance in the allowance account when using the percentage-of-receivables basis.**
- **Report receivables at their cash (net) realizable value—that is, the amount the company expects to collect in cash.**

Disposing of Accounts Receivable

In the normal course of events, companies collect accounts receivable in cash and remove the receivables from the books. However, as credit sales and receivables have grown in significance, the "normal course of events" has changed. Companies now frequently sell their receivables to another company for cash, thereby shortening the cash-to-cash operating cycle.

Companies sell receivables for two major reasons. First, **they may be the only reasonable source of cash**. When money is tight, companies may not be able to borrow money in the usual credit markets. Or, if money is available, the cost of borrowing may be prohibitive.

A second reason for selling receivables is that **billing and collection are often time-consuming and costly**. It is often easier for a retailer to sell the receivables to another party with expertise in billing and collection matters. Credit card companies such as **MasterCard**, **Visa**, and **Discover** specialize in billing and collecting accounts receivable.

Sale of Receivables to a Factor

A common sale of receivables is a sale to a factor. A **factor** is a finance company or bank that buys receivables from businesses and then collects the payments directly from the customers. Factoring is a multibillion dollar business.

Factoring arrangements vary widely. Typically, the factor charges a fee to the company that is selling the receivables. This fee often ranges from 1–3% of the amount of receivables purchased. To illustrate, assume that Hendredon Furniture factors $600,000 of receivables to Federal Factors. Federal Factors assesses a service charge of 2% of the amount of receivables sold. The journal entry to record the sale by Hendredon Furniture on April 2, 2022, is as follows.

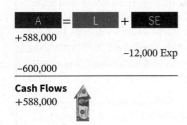

A = L + SE
+588,000
                  −12,000 Exp
−600,000

Cash Flows
+588,000

Apr. 2	Cash	588,000	
	Service Charge Expense (2% × $600,000)	12,000	
	Accounts Receivable		600,000
	(To record the sale of accounts receivable)		

If Hendredon often sells its receivables, it reports the service charge expense as an operating expense. If the company infrequently sells receivables, it may report this amount in the "Other expenses and losses" section of the income statement.

National Credit Card Sales

Over one billion credit cards are in use in the United States—more than three credit cards for every man, woman, and child in this country. **Visa, MasterCard**, and **American Express** are the national credit cards that most individuals use. Three parties are involved when national credit cards are used in retail sales: (1) the credit card issuer, who is independent of the retailer; (2) the retailer; and (3) the customer. **A retailer's acceptance of a national credit card is another form of selling (factoring) the receivable**.

Illustration 8.11 shows the major advantages of national credit cards to the retailer. In exchange for these advantages, the retailer pays the credit card issuer a fee of 2–4% of the invoice price for its services (see **Ethics Note**).

Accounting for Credit Card Sales
The retailer generally considers sales from the use of national credit cards as **cash sales**. The retailer must pay to the bank that issues the card a fee for processing the transactions. The retailer records the credit card slips in a similar manner as checks deposited from a cash sale.

ILLUSTRATION 8.11

Advantages of credit cards to the retailer

To illustrate, Anita Ferreri purchases $1,000 of compact discs for her restaurant from Karen Kerr Music Co., using her Visa First Bank Card. First Bank charges a service fee of 3%. The entry to record this transaction by Karen Kerr Music on March 22, 2022, is as follows.

Mar. 22	Cash	970	
	Service Charge Expense	30	
	Sales Revenue		1,000
	(To record Visa credit card sales)		

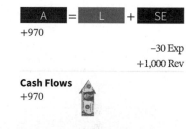

A = L + SE
+970
                    −30 Exp
                    +1,000 Rev

Cash Flows
+970

Accounting Across the Organization   Nordstrom

Zibedik/iStock/
Getty Images

How Does a Credit Card Work?

Most of you know how to use a credit card, but do you know what happens in the transaction and how the transaction is processed? Suppose that you use a **Visa** card to purchase some new ties at **Nordstrom**. The customer swipes or taps the credit card (or inserts it if it is a chip card), which allows the information to be read. The salesperson enters the amount of the purchase. The machine contacts the Visa computer, which routes the call back to the bank that issued your Visa card. The issuing bank verifies that the account exists, that the card is not stolen, and that you have not exceeded your credit limit. At this point, you then complete the sale by signing the receipt.

Visa acts as the clearing agent for the transaction. It transfers funds from the issuing bank to Nordstrom's bank account. Generally this transfer of funds, from sale to the receipt of funds in the merchant's account, takes two to three days.

In the meantime, Visa puts a pending charge on your account for the amount of the tie purchase; that amount counts immediately against your available credit limit. At the end of the billing period, Visa sends you an invoice (your credit card bill), which shows the various charges you made, and the amounts that Visa expended on your behalf, for the month. You then must "pay the piper" for your stylish new ties.

Assume that Nordstrom prepares a bank reconciliation at the end of each month. If some credit card sales have not been processed by the bank, how should Nordstrom treat these transactions on its bank reconciliation? (Go to WileyPLUS for this answer and additional questions.)

ACTION PLAN

- **Consider sale of receivables to a factor.**
- **Weigh cost of factoring against benefit of having cash in hand.**

DO IT! 2b | Factoring

Peter M. Kell Wholesalers Co. needs to raise $120,000 in cash to safely cover next Friday's employee payroll. Kell has reached its debt ceiling with its lenders. Kell's present balance of outstanding receivables totals $750,000. Kell decides to factor $125,000 of its receivables on September 7, 2022, to alleviate this cash crunch. Record the entry that Kell would make when it raises the needed cash. (Assume a 1% service charge.)

Solution

Assuming that Kell Co. factors $125,000 of its accounts receivable at a 1% service charge, it would make this entry:

Sept. 7	Cash	123,750	
	Service Charge Expense (1% × $125,000)	1,250	
	Accounts Receivable		125,000
	(To record sale of receivables to factor)		

Related exercise material: **BE8.7, DO IT! 8.2b, E8.9, E8.10, and E8.11.**

Notes Receivable

LEARNING OBJECTIVE 3

Explain how companies recognize, value, and dispose of notes receivable.

Companies may also grant credit in exchange for a formal credit instrument known as a promissory note. A **promissory note** is a written promise to pay a specified amount of money on demand or at a definite time. Promissory notes may be used (1) when individuals and companies lend or borrow money, (2) when the amount of the transaction and the credit period exceed normal limits, or (3) in settlement of accounts receivable.

In a promissory note, the party making the promise to pay is called the **maker**. The party to whom payment is to be made is called the **payee**. The note may specifically identify the payee by name or may designate the payee simply as the bearer of the note.

In the note shown in **Illustration 8.12**, Calhoun Company is the maker and Wilma Company is the payee. To Wilma Company, the promissory note is a note receivable. To Calhoun Company, it is a note payable (see **Helpful Hint**).

ILLUSTRATION 8.12

Promissory note

HELPFUL HINT

For this note, the maker, Calhoun Company, debits Cash and credits Notes Payable. The payee, Wilma Company, debits Notes Receivable and credits Cash.

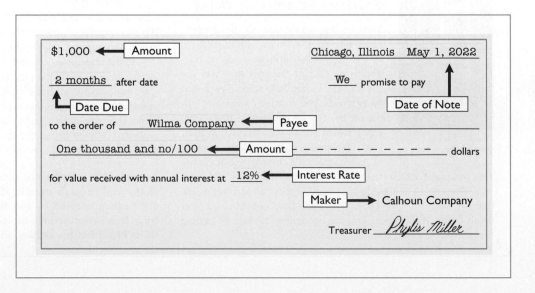

Notes receivable give the holder a stronger legal claim to assets than do accounts receivable. Like accounts receivable, notes receivable can be readily sold to another party. Promissory notes are negotiable instruments (as are checks), which means that they can be transferred to another party by endorsement.

Companies frequently accept notes receivable from customers who need to extend the payment of an outstanding account receivable. They often require such notes from high-risk customers. In some industries (such as the pleasure and sport boat industry), all credit sales are supported by notes. The majority of notes, however, originate from lending transactions.

The basic issues in accounting for notes receivable are the same as those for accounts receivable. On the following pages, we look at these issues. Before we do, however, we need to consider two issues that do not apply to accounts receivable: determining the maturity date and computing interest.

Determining the Maturity Date

Illustration 8.13 shows three ways of stating the maturity date of a promissory note.

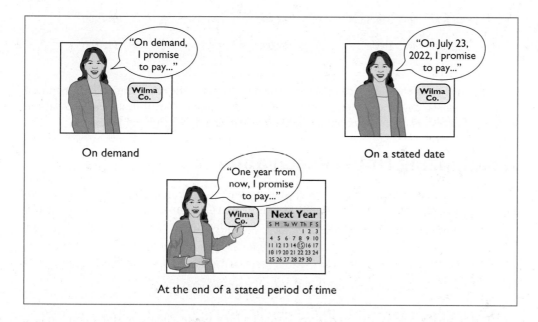

ILLUSTRATION 8.13

Maturity date of different notes

When the life of a note is expressed in terms of months, you find the date when it matures by counting the months from the date of issue. For example, the maturity date of a three-month note dated May 1 is August 1. A note drawn on the last day of a month matures on the last day of its repayment month. That is, a July 31 note due in two months matures on September 30.

When the due date is stated in terms of days, you need to count the exact number of days to determine the maturity date. In counting, **omit the date the note is issued but include the due date**. For example, the maturity date of a 60-day note dated July 17 is September 15, computed as shown in **Illustration 8.14**.

Term of note		60 days
July (31–17)	14	
August	31	45
Maturity date: September		**15**

ILLUSTRATION 8.14

Computation of maturity date

Computing Interest

Illustration 8.15 gives the basic formula for computing interest on an interest-bearing note.

ILLUSTRATION 8.15
Formula for computing interest

Face Value of Note	×	Annual Interest Rate	×	Time in Terms of One Year	=	Interest

HELPFUL HINT
The interest rate specified is the *annual* rate.

The interest rate specified in a note is an **annual** rate of interest (see **Helpful Hint**). The time factor in the formula in Illustration 8.15 expresses the fraction of a year that the note is outstanding. When the maturity date is stated in days, the time factor is often the number of days divided by 360. Remember that when counting days, omit the date that the note is issued but include the due date. When the due date is stated in months, the time factor is the number of months divided by 12. **Illustration 8.16** shows computation of interest for various time periods.

ILLUSTRATION 8.16
Computation of interest

Terms of Note		Interest Computation				
	Face	×	Rate	×	Time	= Interest
$730, 12%, 120 days	$730	×	12%	×	$\frac{120}{360}$	= $ 29.20
$1,000, 9%, 6 months	$1,000	×	9%	×	$\frac{6}{12}$	= $ 45.00
$2,000, 6%, 1 year	$2,000	×	6%	×	$\frac{1}{1}$	= $120.00

There are different ways to calculate interest. For example, the computation in Illustration 8.15 assumes 360 days for the length of the year. Most financial institutions use 365 days to compute interest. *For homework problems, assume 360 days to simplify computations.*

Recognizing Notes Receivable

To illustrate the basic entry for notes receivable, we will use Calhoun Company's $1,000, two-month, 12% promissory note dated May 1. Assuming that Calhoun Company wrote the note to settle an open account, Wilma Company makes the following entry for the receipt of the note.

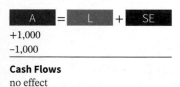

A = L + SE
+1,000
−1,000

Cash Flows
no effect

May 1	Notes Receivable	1,000	
	Accounts Receivable		1,000
	(To record acceptance of Calhoun Company note)		

The company records the note receivable at its **face value**, the value shown on the face of the note. No interest revenue is reported when the note is accepted because the revenue recognition principle requires that revenue be recognized only when the performance obligation is satisfied. Interest is therefore recognized (accrued) as time passes.

If a company lends cash in exchange for a note, the entry is a debit to Notes Receivable and a credit to Cash in the amount of the loan.

Valuing Notes Receivable

Valuing short-term notes receivable is the same as valuing accounts receivable. Like accounts receivable, companies report short-term notes receivable at their **cash (net) realizable value**. The notes receivable allowance account is Allowance for Doubtful Accounts. The estimations involved in determining cash realizable value and in recording bad debt expense and the related allowance are done similarly to accounts receivable.

Disposing of Notes Receivable

Notes may be held to their maturity date, at which time the face value plus accrued interest is due. In some situations, the maker of the note defaults, and the payee must make an appropriate adjustment. In other situations, similar to accounts receivable, the holder of the note speeds up the conversion to cash by selling the receivables (as described earlier in this chapter).

Honor of Notes Receivable

A note is **honored** when its maker pays in full at its maturity date. For each interest-bearing note, the **amount due at maturity** is the face value of the note plus interest for the length of time specified on the note.

To illustrate, assume that Wolder Co. lends Higley Co. $10,000 on June 1, accepting a five-month, 9% interest note. In this situation, interest is $375 ($10,000 × 9% × $\frac{5}{12}$). The amount due, **the maturity value**, is $10,375 ($10,000 + $375). To obtain payment, Wolder (the payee) must present the note either to Higley Co. (the maker) or to the maker's agent, such as a bank. If Wolder presents the note to Higley Co. on November 1, the maturity date, Wolder's entry to record the collection is as follows.

Nov. 1	Cash	10,375	
	Notes Receivable		10,000
	Interest Revenue ($10,000 × 9% × $\frac{5}{12}$)		375
	(To record collection of Higley note and interest)		

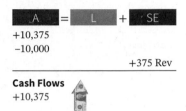

A = L + SE
+10,375
−10,000
+375 Rev

Cash Flows
+10,375

Accrual of Interest Receivable

Suppose instead that Wolder Co. prepares financial statements as of September 30, necessitating an interest-adjusting entry. The timeline in **Illustration 8.17** presents the revenue analysis for this situation.

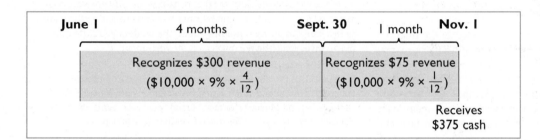

ILLUSTRATION 8.17

Timeline of interest earned

To reflect interest earned but not yet received, Wolder must accrue interest on September 30. In this case, the adjusting entry by Wolder is for four months of interest, or $300, as shown below.

Sept. 30	Interest Receivable ($10,000 × 9% × $\frac{4}{12}$)	300	
	Interest Revenue		300
	(To accrue 4 months' interest on Higley note)		

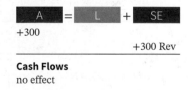

A = L + SE
+300
+300 Rev

Cash Flows
no effect

At the note's maturity on November 1, Wolder receives $10,375. This amount represents repayment of the $10,000 note as well as all five months of interest, or $375, as shown below. The $375 is comprised of the $300 Interest Receivable accrued on September 30 plus $75 earned during October. Wolder's entry to record the honoring of the Higley note on November 1 is as follows.

Nov. 1	Cash [$10,000 + ($10,000 × 9% × $\frac{5}{12}$)]	10,375	
	Notes Receivable		10,000
	Interest Receivable		300
	Interest Revenue ($10,000 × 9% × $\frac{1}{12}$)		75
	(To record collection of Higley note and interest)		

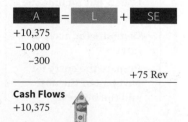

A = L + SE
+10,375
−10,000
−300
+75 Rev

Cash Flows
+10,375

In this case, Wolder credits Interest Receivable for the $300 that was established in the adjusting entry on September 30.

Dishonor of Notes Receivable

A **dishonored (defaulted) note** is a note that is not paid in full at maturity. A dishonored note receivable is no longer negotiable. However, the payee still has a claim against the maker of the note for both the note and the interest. Therefore, the note holder usually transfers the customer's debt from the Notes Receivable account to an Accounts Receivable account.

To illustrate, assume that Higley Co. on November 1 indicates that it cannot pay at the present time. The entry to record the dishonor of the note depends on whether Wolder Co. expects eventual collection. If it does expect eventual collection, Wolder Co. recognizes interest revenue and debits the amount due (face value and interest) on the note to Accounts Receivable. It would make the following entry at the time the note is dishonored (assuming no previous accrual of interest).

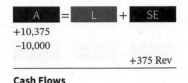

+10,375
−10,000

+375 Rev

Cash Flows
no effect

Nov. 1	Accounts Receivable	10,375	
	Notes Receivable		10,000
	Interest Revenue		375
	(To record the dishonor of Higley note)		

If instead on November 1 there is no hope of collection, the note holder would write off the face value of the note by debiting Allowance for Doubtful Accounts. No interest revenue would be recorded because collection is not expected to occur.

Accounting Across the Organization   Countrywide Financial Corporation

Steve Debenport/E+/
Getty Images

Bad Information Can Lead to Bad Loans

Many factors contributed to the financial crisis of 2008. One significant factor that resulted in many bad loans was a failure by lenders to investigate loan customers sufficiently. For example, **Countrywide Financial Corporation** wrote many loans under its "Fast and Easy" loan program. That program allowed borrowers to provide little or no documentation for their income or their assets. Other lenders had similar programs, which earned the nickname "liars' loans." One study found that in these situations, 60% of applicants overstated their incomes by more than 50% in order to qualify for a loan. Critics of the banking industry say that because loan officers were compensated for loan volume and because banks were selling the loans to investors rather than holding them, the lenders had little incentive to investigate the borrowers' creditworthiness.

Sources: Glenn R. Simpson and James R. Hagerty, "Countrywide Loss Focuses Attention on Underwriting," *Wall Street Journal* (April 30, 2008), p. B1; and Michael Corkery, "Fraud Seen as Driver in Wave of Foreclosures," *Wall Street Journal* (December 21, 2007), p. A1.

What steps should the banks have taken to ensure the accuracy of financial information provided on loan applications? (Go to WileyPLUS for this answer and additional questions.)

ACTION PLAN

- **Count the exact number of days to determine the maturity date. Omit the date the note is issued, but include the due date.**
- **Compute the accrued interest.**
- **Prepare the entry for payment of the note and the interest.**

DO IT! 3 | Recognizing Notes Receivable

Gambit Stores accepts from Leonard Co. a $3,400, 90-day, 6% note dated May 10 in settlement of Leonard's overdue receivable. (a) What is the maturity date of the note? (b) What is the interest to be received at the maturity date? (c) What entry does Gambit make at the maturity date, assuming Leonard pays the note and interest in full at that time?

Solution

a. The maturity date is August 8, computed as follows.

		90 days
Term of note:		
May (31−10)	21	
June	30	
July	31	82
Maturity date: August		8

b. The interest to be received at the maturity date is $51, computed as follows.

$$\text{Face} \times \text{Rate} \times \text{Time} = \text{Interest}$$
$$\$3,400 \times 6\% \times \tfrac{90}{360} = \$51$$

c. Gambit Stores records this entry at the maturity date:

Cash	3,451	
Notes Receivable		3,400
Interest Revenue		51
(To record collection of Leonard note and interest)		

Related exercise material: **BE8.8, BE8.9, BE8.10, DO IT! 8.3, E8.12, E8.13, E8.14, and E8.15.**

Presentation and Analysis of Receivables

LEARNING OBJECTIVE 4
Describe the statement presentation and analysis of receivables.

If a company has significant receivables, analysts carefully review the company's financial statement disclosures to evaluate how well the company is managing its receivables.

Presentation

Companies should identify in the balance sheet or in the notes to the financial statements each of the major types of receivables. Short-term receivables appear in the current assets section of the balance sheet. Short-term investments appear before short-term receivables because these investments are more liquid (nearer to cash). Companies report both the gross amount of receivables and the allowance for doubtful accounts.

In the income statement, companies report bad debt expense and service charge expense as operating expenses. Interest revenue appears under "Other revenues and gains" in the nonoperating activities section of the income statement.

Presented below are examples of different types of information provided to help users understand the issues related to receivables. **Illustration 8.18**, for example, shows the composition of **Deere & Company**'s net receivables. Given that receivables represent 60% of the total assets of this heavy equipment manufacturer, investors are interested in the types of receivables and their significance.

ILLUSTRATION 8.18
Balance sheet presentation of receivables
Real World

Deere & Company	
Balance Sheet (partial)	
(in millions)	
Receivables	
Receivables from unconsolidated subsidiaries	$ 30
Trade accounts and notes receivable	3,278
Financing receivables	27,583
Restricted financing receivables	4,616
Other receivables	1,500
Total receivables	37,007
Less: Allowance for doubtful trade receivables	175
Net receivables	$36,832

Illustration 8.19 contains an excerpt from the notes to the financial statements of **Skechers**, discussing how it monitors receivables.

Skechers USA
Notes to the Financial Statements

To minimize the likelihood of uncollectibility, customers' credit-worthiness is reviewed periodically based on external credit reporting services, financial statements issued by the customer and our experience with the account, and it is adjusted accordingly. When a customer's account becomes significantly past due, we generally place a hold on the account and discontinue further shipments to that customer, minimizing further risk of loss.

If a company has significant concentrations of credit risk, it must discuss this risk in the notes to its financial statements. A **concentration of credit risk** is a threat of nonpayment from a single large customer or class of customers that could adversely affect the financial health of the company. **Illustration 8.20** shows an excerpt from the credit risk note from Skechers' 2015 annual report. The company reports that its five largest customers account for 14.6% of its net sales.

Skechers USA
Notes to the Financial Statements

During 2015, 2014 and 2013, no customer accounted for 10.0% or more of net sales. As of December 31, 2015, one customer accounted for 10.6% of gross trade receivables. No other customer accounted for more than 10% of net trade receivables at December 31, 2015 or 2014. During 2015, 2014 and 2013, net sales to the five largest customers were approximately 14.6%, 15.7% and 18.1%, respectively.

This note to Skechers' financial statements indicates it has a relatively high concentration of credit risk. A default by any of these large customers could have a significant negative impact on its financial performance.

Analysis

Investors and corporate managers compute financial ratios to evaluate the liquidity of a company's accounts receivable. They use the **accounts receivable turnover** to assess the liquidity of the receivables. This ratio measures the number of times, on average, the company collects accounts receivable during the period. It is computed by dividing net credit sales (net sales less cash sales) by the average net accounts receivable during the year. Unless seasonal factors are significant, average net accounts receivable outstanding can be computed from the beginning and ending balances of net accounts receivable.

For example, **Cisco Systems** recently had net sales of $37,750 million for the year. It had a beginning accounts receivable (net) balance of $5,157 million and an ending accounts receivable (net) balance of $5,344 million. Assuming that Cisco's sales were all on credit, its accounts receivable turnover is computed as shown in **Illustration 8.21**.

Net Credit Sales	÷	Average Net Accounts Receivable	=	Accounts Receivable Turnover
$37,750	÷	$\dfrac{\$5,157 + \$5,344}{2}$	=	7.2 times

The result indicates an accounts receivable turnover of 7.2 times per year. The higher the turnover, the more liquid the company's receivables.

A variant of the accounts receivable turnover that makes the liquidity even more evident is its conversion into an **average collection period** in terms of days. This is done by dividing the accounts receivable turnover into 365 days. For example, Cisco's turnover of 7.2 times is divided into 365 days, as shown in **Illustration 8.22**, to obtain approximately 51 days. This means that it takes Cisco 51 days to collect its accounts receivable.

Days in Year	÷	Accounts Receivable Turnover	=	Average Collection Period in Days
365 days	÷	7.2 times	=	51 days

ILLUSTRATION 8.22

Average collection period for receivables formula and computation

Companies frequently use the average collection period to assess the effectiveness of a company's credit and collection policies. The general rule is that the collection period should not greatly exceed the credit term period (that is, the time allowed for payment).

Data Analytics and Receivables Management

Opportunities abound to improve receivables management through data analytics. Software packages promise increases in working capital, improved revenues, and enhanced customer relations. So-called visualization software, which presents data in sophisticated graph format, enables managers to more quickly identify issues and obtain a deeper understanding of the factors that influence successful receivables management. Use of such software helps identify which currencies, sales representatives, customers, product lines, or geographic regions need closer attention. This sometimes enables management to do a more granular investigation of the cash-to-cash cycle time to evaluate which product lines are meeting company goals.

Data analytics of receivables is particularly valuable for predictive analysis, which allows improved evaluation of customers' risk profiles. In many instances, the company can identify risky customers and take corrective action before problems arise. Software provided by companies such as **Workday** use artificial intelligence to forecast which customers are likely to pay late.

DO IT! 4 | Analysis of Receivables

In 2022, Lebron James Company has net credit sales of $923,795 for the year. It had a beginning accounts receivable (net) balance of $38,275 and an ending accounts receivable (net) balance of $35,988. Compute Lebron James Company's (a) accounts receivable turnover and (b) average collection period in days.

Solution

a.

Net credit sales	÷	Average net accounts receivable	=	Accounts receivable turnover
$923,795	÷	$\dfrac{\$38,275 + \$35,988}{2}$	=	24.9 times

b.

Days in year	÷	Accounts receivable turnover	=	Average collection period in days
365	÷	24.9 times	=	14.7 days

Related exercise material: **BE8.11, BE8.12, DO IT! 8.4, E8.16, and E8.17.**

ACTION PLAN

- **Review the formula to compute the accounts receivable turnover.**
- **Make sure that both the beginning and ending accounts receivable balances are considered in the computation.**
- **Review the formula to compute the average collection period in days.**

Review and Practice

Learning Objectives Review

1 Explain how companies recognize accounts receivable.

Receivables are frequently classified as (1) accounts, (2) notes, and (3) other. Accounts receivable are amounts customers owe on account. Notes receivable are claims for which lenders issue formal instruments of credit as proof of the debt. Other receivables include nontrade receivables such as interest receivable, loans to company officers, advances to employees, and income taxes refundable.

Companies record accounts receivable when they perform a service on account or at the point of sale of merchandise on account. Accounts receivable are reduced by sales returns and allowances. Cash discounts reduce the amount received on accounts receivable. When interest is charged on a past due receivable, the company adds this interest to the accounts receivable balance and recognizes it as interest revenue.

2 Describe how companies value accounts receivable and record their disposition.

There are two methods of accounting for uncollectible accounts: the allowance method (GAAP) and the direct write-off method (not GAAP). Companies use the percentage-of-receivables basis to apply the allowance method. The percentage-of-receivables basis emphasizes the cash realizable value of the accounts receivable. An aging schedule is often used with this basis.

When a company collects an account receivable, it credits Accounts Receivable. When a company sells (factors) an account receivable, a service charge expense reduces the amount received.

3 Explain how companies recognize, value, and dispose of notes receivable.

For a note stated in months, the maturity date is found by counting the months from the date of issue. For a note stated in days, the number of days is counted, omitting the issue date and counting the due date. The formula for computing interest is Face value × Interest rate × Time. Interest rates are always stated in annual terms.

Companies record notes receivable at face value. In some cases, it is necessary to accrue interest prior to maturity. In this case, companies debit Interest Receivable and credit Interest Revenue.

Notes can be held to maturity. At that time the face value plus accrued interest is due, and the note is removed from the accounts. In many cases, the holder of the note speeds up the conversion by selling the receivable to another party (a factor). In some situations, the maker of the note dishonors the note (defaults), in which case the company transfers the note and accrued interest to an account receivable or writes off the note, depending on anticipated collectibility.

4 Describe the statement presentation and analysis of receivables.

As with accounts receivable, companies report notes receivable at their cash (net) realizable value. The notes receivable allowance account is Allowance for Doubtful Accounts. The computation and estimations involved in valuing notes receivable at cash realizable value, and in recording the proper amount of bad debt expense and the related allowance, are similar to those for accounts receivable.

Companies should identify in the balance sheet or in the notes to the financial statements each major type of receivable. Short-term receivables are considered current assets. Companies report the gross amount of receivables and the allowance for doubtful accounts. They report bad debt expense and service charge expenses in the multiple-step income statement as operating (selling) expenses. Interest revenue appears under other revenues and gains in the nonoperating activities section of the statement. Managers and investors evaluate accounts receivable for liquidity by computing a turnover ratio and an average collection period.

Glossary Review

Accounts receivable Amounts owed by customers on account. (p. 8-3).

Accounts receivable turnover A measure of the liquidity of accounts receivable; computed by dividing net credit sales by average net accounts receivable. (p. 8-20).

Aging the accounts receivable The analysis of receivable balances by the length of time they have been unpaid. (p. 8-9).

Allowance method A GAAP method of accounting for uncollectibles that involves estimating uncollectible accounts at the end of each period. (p. 8-6).

Average collection period The average amount of time that a receivable is outstanding; calculated by dividing 365 days by the accounts receivable turnover. (p. 8-21).

Bad Debt Expense An expense account to record uncollectible receivables. (p. 8-5).

Cash (net) realizable value The net amount a company expects to receive in cash. (p. 8-6).

Direct write-off method A non-GAAP method of accounting for uncollectibles that involves expensing accounts at the time they are determined to be uncollectible. (p. 8-5).

Dishonored (defaulted) note A note that is not paid in full at maturity. (p. 8-18).

Factor A finance company or bank that buys receivables from businesses and then collects the payments directly from the customers. (p. 8-12).

Maker   The party in a promissory note who is making the promise to pay. (p. 8-14).

Notes receivable   Written promise (as evidenced by a formal instrument) for amounts to be received. (p. 8-3).

Other receivables   Various forms of nontrade receivables, such as interest receivable and income taxes refundable. (p. 8-3).

Payee   The party to whom payment of a promissory note is to be made. (p. 8-14).

Percentage-of-receivables basis   A method by which management estimates what percentage of receivables will result in losses from uncollectible accounts. (p. 8-9).

Promissory note   A written promise to pay a specified amount of money on demand or at a definite time. (p. 8-14).

Receivables   Amounts due from individuals and other companies. (p. 8-3).

Trade receivables   Notes and accounts receivable that result from sales transactions. (p. 8-3).

Practice Multiple-Choice Questions

1. (LO 1) A receivable that is evidenced by a formal instrument and that normally requires the payment of interest is a(n):

    a. account receivable.

    b. trade receivable.

    c. note receivable.

    d. classified receivable.

2. (LO 1) Receivables are frequently classified as:

    a. accounts receivable, company receivables, and other receivables.

    b. accounts receivable, notes receivable, and employee receivables.

    c. accounts receivable and general receivables.

    d. accounts receivable, notes receivable, and other receivables.

3. (LO 1) Kersee Company on June 15 sells merchandise on account to Eng Co. for $1,000, terms 2/10, n/30. On June 20, Eng Co. returns merchandise with a sales price of $300 to Kersee Company. On June 24, payment is received from Eng Co. for the balance due. What is the amount of cash received?

    a. $700.   **c.** $686.

    b. $680.   **d.** None of the above.

4. (LO 2) Accounts and notes receivable are reported in the current assets section of the balance sheet at:

    a. cash (net) realizable value.

    b. net book value.

    c. lower-of-cost-or-market value.

    d. invoice cost.

5. (LO 2) Hughes Company has a credit balance of $5,000 in its Allowance for Doubtful Accounts before any adjustments are made at the end of the year. Based on review and aging of its accounts receivable at the end of the year, Hughes estimates that $60,000 of its receivables are uncollectible. The amount of bad debt expense which should be reported for the year is:

    a. $5,000.   **c.** $60,000.

    b. $55,000.   **d.** $65,000.

6. (LO 2) Hughes Company has a debit balance of $5,000 in its Allowance for Doubtful Accounts before any adjustments are made at the end of the year. Based on review and aging of its accounts receivable at the end of the year, Hughes estimates that $60,000 of its receivables are uncollectible. In this situation, the amount of bad debt expense that should be reported for the year is:

    a. $5,000.   **c.** $60,000.

    b. $55,000.   **d.** $65,000.

7. (LO 2) Net credit sales for the month are $800,000. The accounts receivable balance is $160,000. The allowance is calculated as 7.5% of the receivables balance using the percentage-of-receivables basis.

If Allowance for Doubtful Accounts has a credit balance of $5,000 before adjustment, what is the balance after adjustment?

    a. $12,000.   **c.** $17,000.

    b. $7,000.   **d.** $31,000.

8. (LO 2) In 2022, Patterson Wholesale Company had net credit sales of $750,000. On January 1, 2022, Allowance for Doubtful Accounts had a credit balance of $18,000. During 2022, $30,000 of uncollectible accounts receivable were written off. Past experience indicates that the allowance should be 10% of the balance in receivables (percentage-of-receivables basis). If the accounts receivable balance was $200,000, what is the required adjustment to Allowance for Doubtful Accounts at December 31, 2022?

    a. $20,000.   **c.** $32,000.

    b. $75,000.   **d.** $30,000.

9. (LO 2) An analysis and aging of the accounts receivable of Prince Company at December 31 reveals the following data.

Accounts receivable	$800,000
Allowance for doubtful accounts per books before adjustment	50,000
Amounts expected to become uncollectible	65,000

The cash realizable value of the accounts receivable at December 31, after adjustment, is:

    a. $685,000.   **c.** $800,000.

    b. $750,000.   **d.** $735,000.

10. (LO 2) Which of the following statements about Visa credit card sales is **incorrect**?

    a. The credit card issuer makes the credit investigation of the customer.

    b. The retailer is not involved in the collection process.

    c. Two parties are involved.

    d. The retailer receives cash more quickly than it would from individual customers on account.

11. (LO 2) Good Stuff Retailers accepted $50,000 of **Citibank Visa** credit card charges for merchandise sold on July 1. Citibank charges 4% for its credit card use. The entry to record this transaction by Good Stuff Retailers will include a credit to Sales Revenue of $50,000 and a debit(s) to:

a. Cash	$48,000
and Service Charge Expense	$2,000
b. Accounts Receivable	$48,000
and Service Charge Expense	$2,000
c. Cash	$50,000
d. Accounts Receivable	$50,000

12. (LO 3) One of the following statements about promissory notes is incorrect. The **incorrect** statement is:

   a. The party making the promise to pay is called the maker.

   b. The party to whom payment is to be made is called the payee.

   c. A promissory note is not a negotiable instrument.

   d. A promissory note is often required from high-risk customers.

13. (LO 3) Michael Co. accepts a $1,000, 3-month, 6% promissory note in settlement of an account with Tani Co. The entry to record this transaction is as follows.

a. Notes Receivable	1,015	
Accounts Receivable		1,015
b. Notes Receivable	1,000	
Accounts Receivable		1,000
c. Notes Receivable	1,000	
Sales Revenue		1,000
d. Notes Receivable	1,030	
Accounts Receivable		1,030

14. (LO 3) Schleis Co. holds Murphy Inc.'s $10,000, 120-day, 9% note. The entry made by Schleis Co. when the note is collected, assuming no interest has been previously accrued, is:

a. Cash	10,300	
Notes Receivable		10,300
b. Cash	10,000	
Notes Receivable		10,000
c. Accounts Receivable	10,300	
Notes Receivable		10,000
Interest Revenue		300
d. Cash	10,300	
Notes Receivable		10,000
Interest Revenue		300

15. (LO 4) Prall Corporation sells its goods on terms of 2/10, n/30. It has an accounts receivable turnover of 7. What is its average collection period (days)?

   a. 2,555.   **c.** 52.

   b. 30.   **d.** 210.

16. (LO 4) Eddy Corporation had net credit sales during the year of $800,000 and cost of goods sold of $500,000. The net balance of accounts receivable at the beginning of the year was $100,000, and at the end of the year it was $150,000. What were the accounts receivable turnover and the average collection period in days?

   a. 4.0 and 91.3 days.   **c.** 6.4 and 57 days.

   b. 5.3 and 68.9 days.   **d.** 8.0 and 45.6 days.

Solutions

1. c. A note receivable represents claims for which formal instruments of credit are issued as evidence of the debt. The note normally requires the payment of the principal and interest on a specific date. Choices (a) account receivable, (b) trade receivable, and (d) classified receivable rarely require the payment of interest if paid within a 30-day period.

2. d. Receivables are frequently classified as accounts receivable, notes receivable, and other receivables. The other choices are incorrect because receivables are not frequently classified as (a) company receivables, (b) employee receivables, or (c) general receivables.

3. c. Because payment is made within the discount period of 10 days, the amount received is $700 ($1,000 – $300 return) minus the discount of $14 ($700 × 2%), for a cash amount of $686, not (a) $700 or (b) $680. Choice (d) is wrong as there is a correct answer.

4. a. Accounts and notes receivable are reported in the current assets section of the balance sheet at cash (net) realizable value, not (b) net book value, (c) lower-of-cost-or-market value, or (d) invoice cost.

5. b. By crediting Allowance for Doubtful Accounts for $55,000, the new balance will be the required balance of $60,000. This adjusting entry debits Bad Debt Expense for $55,000 and credits Allowance for Doubtful Accounts for $55,000, not (a) $5,000, (c) $60,000, or (d) $65,000.

6. d. By crediting Allowance for Doubtful Accounts for $65,000, the new balance will be the required balance of $60,000. This adjusting entry debits Bad Debt Expense for $65,000 and credits Allowance for Doubtful Accounts for $65,000, not (a) $5,000, (b) $55,000, or (c) $60,000.

7. a. The ending balance required in the allowance account is 7.5% × $160,000, or $12,000. Since there is already a balance of $5,000 in Allowance for Doubtful Accounts, the difference of $7,000 should be added, resulting in a balance of $12,000, not (b) $7,000, (c) $17,000, or (d) $31,000.

8. c. After the write-offs are recorded, Allowance for Doubtful Accounts will have a debit balance of $12,000 ($18,000 credit beginning balance combined with a $30,000 debit for the write-offs). The desired balance, using the percentage-of-receivables basis, is a credit balance of $20,000 ($200,000 × 10%). In order to have an ending balance of $20,000, the required adjustment to Allowance for Doubtful Accounts is $32,000, not (a) $20,000, (b) $75,000, or (d) $30,000.

9. d. Accounts Receivable less the expected uncollectible amount equals the cash realizable value of $735,000 ($800,000 – $65,000), not (a) $685,000, (b) $750,000, or (c) $800,000.

10. c. There are three parties, not two, involved in Visa credit card sales: the credit card company, the retailer, and the customer. The other choices are true statements.

11. a. Credit card sales are considered cash sales. Cash is debited $48,000 for the net amount received ($50,000 – $2,000 for credit card use fee), and Service Charge Expense is debited $2,000 for the 4% credit card use fee ($50,000 × 4%). The other choices are therefore incorrect.

12. c. A promissory note is a negotiable instrument. The other choices are true statements.

13. b. Notes Receivable is recorded at face value ($1,000). No interest on the note is recorded until it is earned. Accounts Receivable is credited because no new sales have been made. The other choices are therefore incorrect.

14. d. Cash is debited for its maturity value [$10,000 + interest earned ($10,000 × $\frac{120}{360}$ × 9%)], Notes Receivable is credited for its face value, and Interest Revenue is credited for the amount of interest earned. The other choices are therefore incorrect.

15. c. Average collection period = Number of days in the year (365) ÷ Accounts receivable turnover (7) = 52 days, not (a) 2,555, (b) 30, or (d) 210.

16. c. The accounts receivable turnover is 6.4 {$800,000 ÷ [($100,000 + $150,000) ÷ 2]}. The average collection period in days is 57 days (365 ÷ 6.4). The other choices are therefore incorrect.

Practice Brief Exercises

1. (LO 1) Record the following transactions on the books of Gonzalez Co. (Ignore cost of goods sold entries.)

Record basic accounts receivable transactions.

    a. On August 1, Gonzalez Co. sold merchandise on account to Miguel Inc. for $15,500, terms 1/10, n/30.

    b. On August 8, Miguel Inc. returned merchandise with a sales price of $3,100 to Gonzalez Co.

    c. On August 11, Miguel Inc. paid the balance due.

Solution

1.			
a.	Accounts Receivable	15,500	
	Sales Revenue		15,500
b.	Sales Returns and Allowances	3,100	
	Accounts Receivable		3,100
c.	Cash ($12,400 − $124)	12,276	
	Sales Discounts ($12,400 × 1%)	124	
	Accounts Receivable ($15,500 − $3,100)		12,400

2. (LO 2) Sanchez Co. uses the percentage-of-receivables basis in 2022 to record bad debt expense. It estimates that 3% of accounts receivable will become uncollectible. Sales revenues are $900,000 for 2022, and sales returns and allowances are $50,000 for 2022. Accounts receivable has a balance of $139,000, and the allowance for doubtful accounts has a credit balance of $3,000. Prepare the adjusting entry to record bad debt expense in 2022.

Prepare entry using percentage-of-receivables method.

Solution

2.	Bad Debt Expense	1,170	
	Allowance for Doubtful Accounts		
	[($139,000 × 3%) − $3,000]		1,170

3. (LO 3) On January 20, 2022, Carlos Co. sold merchandise on account to Carson Co. for $20,000, n/30. On February 19, Carson Co. gave Carlos Co. an 8% promissory note in settlement of this account. Prepare the journal entries to record the sale and the settlement of the account receivable. (Ignore cost of goods sold entries).

Prepare entries for notes receivable exchanged for accounts receivable.

Solution

Jan. 20	Accounts Receivable	20,000	
	Sales Revenue		20,000
Feb. 19	Notes Receivable	20,000	
	Accounts Receivable		20,000

Practice Exercises

1. (LO 2) The ledger of J.C. Cobb Company at the end of the current year shows Accounts Receivable $150,000, Sales Revenue $850,000, and Sales Returns and Allowances $30,000.

Journalize entries to record allowance for doubtful accounts using two different bases.

Instructions

    a. If J.C. Cobb uses the direct write-off method to account for uncollectible accounts, journalize the entry at December 31 if J.C. Cobb determines that M. Jack's $1,500 balance is uncollectible.

b. If Allowance for Doubtful Accounts has a credit balance of $2,400 in the trial balance, journalize the adjusting entry at December 31, assuming uncollectibles are expected to be 10% of accounts receivable.

c. If Allowance for Doubtful Accounts has a debit balance of $200 in the trial balance, journalize the adjusting entry at December 31, assuming uncollectibles are expected to be 6% of accounts receivable.

Solution

1. **a.**	Dec. 31	Bad Debt Expense		1,500	
		Accounts Receivable			1,500
b.	Dec. 31	Bad Debt Expense		12,600	
		Allowance for Doubtful Accounts			12,600
		[($150,000 × 10%) – $2,400]			
c.	Dec. 31	Bad Debt Expense		9,200	
		Allowance for Doubtful Accounts			9,200
		[($150,000 × 6%) + $200]			

Journalize entries for notes receivable transactions.

2. (LO 3) Troope Supply Co. has the following transactions related to notes receivable during the last 3 months of 2022.

Oct.   1   Loaned $16,000 cash to Juan Vasquez on a 1-year, 10% note.
Dec. 11   Sold goods to A. Palmer, Inc., receiving a $6,750, 90-day, 8% note.
    31   Accrued interest revenue on all notes receivable.

Instructions

a. Journalize the transactions for Troope Supply Co. (Ignore cost of goods sold entries.)

b. Record the collection of the Vasquez note at its maturity in 2023.

Solution

2. a.

		2022		
Oct. 1	Notes Receivable		16,000	
	Cash			16,000
Dec. 11	Notes Receivable		6,750	
	Sales Revenue			6,750
31	Interest Receivable		430	
	Interest Revenue*			430

*Calculation of interest revenue:

Vasquez's note: $16,000 × 10% × $\frac{3}{12}$ = $400

Palmer's note: 6,750 × 8% × $\frac{20}{360}$ =   30

Total accrued interest $430

b.

		2023		
Oct. 1	Cash		17,600	
	Interest Receivable			400
	Interest Revenue**			1,200
	Notes Receivable			16,000

**$16,000 × 10% × $\frac{9}{12}$

Practice Problem

Prepare entries for various receivables transactions.

(LO 1, 2, 3) The following selected transactions relate to B. Dylan Corporation.

Mar.	1	Sold $20,000 of merchandise to Potter Company, terms 2/10, n/30.
	11	Received payment in full from Potter Company for the balance related to the March 1 sale.
	12	Accepted Juno Company's $20,000, 6-month, 12% note for balance due on outstanding accounts receivable.
	13	Made B. Dylan Corporation credit card sales for $13,200.
	15	Made Visa credit card sales totaling $6,700. A 5% service fee is charged by Visa.
Apr.	11	Sold accounts receivable of $8,000 to Harcot Factor. Harcot Factor assesses a service charge of 2% of the amount of receivables sold.
	13	Received collections of $8,200 on B. Dylan Corporation credit card sales and added finance charges of 1.5% to the remaining balances.
May	10	Wrote off as uncollectible $16,000 of accounts receivable. (B. Dylan Corporation uses the percentage-of-receivables basis to estimate uncollectibles.)
June	30	An aging schedule indicates total uncollectibles of $23,500. At June 30, the balance in the allowance account is $3,500 before adjustment.
July	16	One of the accounts receivable written off in May was from J. Simon, who pays the amount due, $4,000, in full.

Instructions

Prepare the journal entries for the transactions. (Ignore entries for cost of goods sold.)

Solution

Mar.	1	Accounts Receivable	20,000	
		Sales Revenue		20,000
		(To record sales on account)		
	11	Cash	19,600	
		Sales Discounts (2% × $20,000)	400	
		Accounts Receivable		20,000
		(To record collection of accounts receivable)		
	12	Notes Receivable	20,000	
		Accounts Receivable		20,000
		(To record acceptance of Juno Company note)		
	13	Accounts Receivable	13,200	
		Sales Revenue		13,200
		(To record company credit card sales)		
	15	Cash	6,365	
		Service Charge Expense (5% × $6,700)	335	
		Sales Revenue		6,700
		(To record credit card sales)		
Apr.	11	Cash	7,840	
		Service Charge Expense (2% × $8,000)	160	
		Accounts Receivable		8,000
		(To record sale of receivables to factor)		
	13	Cash	8,200	
		Accounts Receivable		8,200
		(To record collection of accounts receivable)		
		Accounts Receivable [($13,200 − $8,200) × 1.5%]	75	
		Interest Revenue		75
		(To record interest on amount due)		
May	10	Allowance for Doubtful Accounts	16,000	
		Accounts Receivable		16,000
		(To record write-off of accounts receivable)		

June 30	Bad Debt Expense ($23,500 – $3,500)		20,000	
	Allowance for Doubtful Accounts			20,000
	(To record estimate of uncollectible accounts)			
July 16	Accounts Receivable		4,000	
	Allowance for Doubtful Accounts			4,000
	(To reverse write-off of accounts receivable)			
	Cash		4,000	
	Accounts Receivable			4,000
	(To record collection of accounts receivable)			

WileyPLUS

Brief Exercises, DO IT! Exercises, Exercises, Problems, and many additional resources are available for practice in WileyPLUS.

Questions

1. What is the difference between an account receivable and a note receivable?

2. What are some common types of receivables other than accounts receivable and notes receivable?

3. **Texaco** issues its own credit cards. Assume that Texaco charges you $40 interest on an unpaid balance. Prepare the journal entry that Texaco makes to record this revenue.

4. What are the essential features of the allowance method of accounting for uncollectibles?

5. Lance Morrow cannot understand why cash realizable value does not decrease when an uncollectible account is written off under the allowance method. Clarify this point for Lance.

6. What types of receivables does **Apple** report on its balance sheet? Does it use the allowance method or the direct write-off method to account for uncollectibles?

7. Sarasota Company has a credit balance of $2,200 in Allowance for Doubtful Accounts before adjustment. The total estimated uncollectibles under the percentage-of-receivables basis is $5,100. Prepare the adjusting entry to record bad debt expense.

8. How are uncollectibles accounted for under the direct write-off method? What are the disadvantages of this method?

9. Tawyna Dobbs, the vice president of sales for Tropical Pools and Spas, wants the company's credit department to be less restrictive in granting credit. "How can we sell anything when you guys won't approve anybody?" she asks. Discuss the pros and cons of easy credit. What are the accounting implications?

10. **JCPenney** accepts both its own credit cards and national credit cards. What are the advantages of accepting both types of cards?

11. An article that was published in the *Wall Street Journal* indicated that companies are selling their receivables at a record rate. Why are companies selling their receivables?

12. **Calico Corners** decides to sell $400,000 of its accounts receivable to Fast Cash Factors Inc. Fast Cash Factors assesses a service charge of 3% of the amount of receivables sold. Prepare the journal entry that Calico Corners makes to record this sale.

13. Your roommate is uncertain about the advantages of a promissory note. Compare the advantages of a note receivable with those of an account receivable.

14. How may the maturity date of a promissory note be stated?

15. Indicate the maturity date of each of the following promissory notes:

Date of Note	Terms
a. March 13	one year after date of note
b. May 4	3 months after date
c. June 20	30 days after date
d. July 1	60 days after date

16. Compute the missing amounts for each of the following notes.

Principal	Annual Interest Rate	Time	Total Interest
(a)	6%	60 days	$ 270
$60,000	(b)	5 months	$2,500
$50,000	11%	(c)	$2,750
$30,000	8%	3 years	(d)

17. Mendosa Company dishonors a note at maturity. What are the options available to the lender?

18. **General Motors** has accounts receivable and notes receivable. How should the receivables be reported on the balance sheet?

19. The accounts receivable turnover is 8.14, and average net accounts receivable during the period is $400,000. What is the amount of net credit sales for the period?

Brief Exercises

BE8.1 (LO 1), C The following are three receivables transactions. Indicate whether these receivables are reported as accounts receivable, notes receivable, or other receivables on a balance sheet.

  a. Sold merchandise on account for $64,000 to a customer.

  b. Received a promissory note of $57,000 for services performed.

  c. Advanced $10,000 to an employee.

Identify different types of receivables.

BE8.2 (LO 1), AP Record the following transactions on the books of Jarvis Co. (Omit cost of goods sold entries.)

  a. On July 1, Jarvis Co. sold merchandise on account to Stacey Inc. for $23,000, terms 2/10, n/30.

  b. On July 8, Stacey Inc. returned merchandise with a sales price of $2,400 to Jarvis Co.

  c. On July 11, Stacey Inc. paid the balance due.

Record basic accounts receivable transactions.

BE8.3 (LO 2), AP Bayfiew Corp uses the percentage-of-receivables basis to record bad debt expense.

Accounts receivable (ending balance)	$550,000 (debit)
Allowance for doubtful accounts (unadjusted)	4,200 (debit)

The company estimates that 3% of accounts receivable will become uncollectible.

  a. Prepare the adjusting journal entry to record bad debt expense for the year.

  b. What is the ending (adjusted) balance in Allowance for Doubtful Accounts?

  c. What is the cash (net) realizable value?

Prepare entry using the percentage-of-receivables method.

BE8.4 (LO 2), AP At the end of 2021, Safer Co. has accounts receivable of $700,000 and an allowance for doubtful accounts of $25,000. On January 24, 2022, it is learned that the company's receivable from Madonna Inc. is not collectible and therefore management authorizes a write-off of $4,300.

  a. Prepare the journal entry to record the write-off.

  b. What is the cash realizable value of the accounts receivable (1) before the write-off and (2) after the write-off?

Prepare entry for write-off, and determine cash realizable value.

BE8.5 (LO 2), AP At the end of 2021, Safer Co. has accounts receivable of $700,000 and an allowance for doubtful accounts of $25,000. On January 24, 2022, it is learned that the company's receivable from Madonna Inc. is not collectible and therefore management authorizes a write-off of $4,300. On March 4, 2022, Safer Co. receives payment of $4,300 in full from Madonna Inc. Prepare the journal entries to record this transaction.

Prepare entries for collection of customer account write-off.

BE8.6 (LO 2), AP Byrd Co. uses the percentage-of-receivables basis to record bad debt expense and concludes that 2% of accounts receivable will become uncollectible. Accounts receivable are $400,000 at the end of the year, and the allowance for doubtful accounts has a credit balance of $2,800.

  a. Prepare the adjusting journal entry to record bad debt expense for the year.

  b. If the allowance for doubtful accounts had a debit balance of $900 instead of a credit balance of $2,800, prepare the adjusting journal entry for bad debt expense.

Prepare entry using percentage-of-receivables method.

BE8.7 (LO 2), AP Consider these transactions:

  a. Tastee Restaurant accepted a Visa card in payment of a $200 lunch bill. The bank charges a 3% fee. What entry should Tastee make?

  b. Martin Company sold its accounts receivable of $65,000. What entry should Martin make, given a service charge of 3% on the amount of receivables sold?

Prepare entries for credit card sale and sale of accounts receivable.

BE8.8 (LO 3), AP Compute interest and find the maturity date for the following notes.

Compute interest and determine maturity dates on notes.

Date of Note	Face Value	Interest Rate (%)	Terms
a. June 10	$80,000	6%	60 days
b. July 14	$50,000	7%	90 days
c. April 27	$12,000	8%	75 days

Determine maturity dates and compute interest and rates on notes.

BE8.9 (LO 3), AN The following are data on three promissory notes. Determine the missing amounts.

	Date of Note	Terms	Maturity Date	Face Value	Annual Interest Rate	Total Interest
a.	April 1	60 days	?	$600,000	9%	?
b.	July 2	30 days	?	90,000	?	$600
c.	March 7	6 months	?	120,000	10%	?

Prepare entry for note receivable exchanged for accounts receivable.

BE8.10 (LO 3), AP On January 10, 2022, Masterson Co. sold merchandise on account to Tompkins for $8,000, terms n/30. On February 9, Tompkins gave Masterson Co. a 7% promissory note in settlement of this account. Prepare the journal entry to record the sale and the settlement of the accounts receivable. (Omit cost of goods sold entries.)

Prepare entry for estimated uncollectibles and classifications, and compute ratios.

BE8.11 (LO 2, 4), AP During its first year of operations, Fertig Company had net credit sales of $3,000,000, of which $400,000 remained uncollected at year-end. The credit manager estimates that $18,000 of these receivables will become uncollectible.

a. Prepare the journal entry to record the estimated uncollectibles. (Assume an unadjusted balance of zero in Allowance for Doubtful Accounts.)

b. Prepare the current assets section of the balance sheet for Fertig Company, assuming that in addition to the receivables it has cash of $90,000, merchandise inventory of $180,000, and supplies of $13,000.

c. Calculate the accounts receivable turnover and average collection period. Assume that average net accounts receivable were $300,000. Explain what these measures tell us.

Analyze accounts receivable.

BE8.12 (LO 4), AP Suppose the 2022 financial statements of **3M Company** report net credit sales of $23.1 billion. Accounts receivable (net) are $3.2 billion at the beginning of the year and $3.25 billion at the end of the year. Compute 3M's accounts receivable turnover. Compute 3M's average collection period for accounts receivable in days.

DO IT! Exercises

Prepare entries to recognize accounts receivable.

DO IT! 8.1 (LO 1), AP On March 1, Lincoln sold merchandise on account to Amelia Company for $28,000, terms 1/10, n/45. On March 6, Amelia returns merchandise with a sales price of $1,000. On March 11, Lincoln receives payment from Amelia for the balance due. Prepare journal entries to record the March transactions on Lincoln's books. (You may ignore cost of goods sold entries and explanations.)

Prepare entry for uncollectible accounts.

DO IT! 8.2a (LO 2), AP Mantle Company has been in business several years. At the end of the current year, the unadjusted trial balance shows:

Accounts Receivable	$ 310,000 Dr.
Sales Revenue	2,200,000 Cr.
Allowance for Doubtful Accounts	5,700 Cr.

Uncollectibles are estimated to be 7% of receivables. Prepare the entry to adjust Allowance for Doubtful Accounts.

Prepare entry for factored accounts.

DO IT! 8.2b (LO 2), AP Neumann Distributors is a growing company whose ability to raise capital has not been growing as quickly as its expanding assets and sales. Neumann's local banker has indicated that the company cannot increase its borrowing for the foreseeable future. Neumann's suppliers are demanding payment for goods acquired within 30 days of the invoice date, but Neumann's customers are slow in paying for their purchases (60–90 days). As a result, Neumann has a cash flow problem.

Neumann needs $160,000 to cover next Friday's payroll. Its balance of outstanding accounts receivable totals $800,000. To alleviate this cash crunch, the company sells $170,000 of its receivables. Record the entry that Neumann would make. (Assume a 2% service charge.)

Prepare entries for notes receivable.

DO IT! 8.3 (LO 3), AP Buffet Wholesalers accepts from Gates Stores a $6,200, 4-month, 9% note dated May 31 in settlement of Gates' overdue account. The maturity date of the note is September 30. What entry does Buffet make at the maturity date, assuming Gates pays the note and interest in full at that time?

Compute ratios for receivables.

DO IT! 8.4 (LO 4), AP In 2022, Bismark Company has net credit sales of $1,600,000 for the year. It had a beginning accounts receivable (net) balance of $108,000 and an ending accounts receivable (net) balance of $120,000. Compute Bismark Company's (a) accounts receivable turnover and (b) average collection period in days.

Exercises

E8.1 (LO 1), AP On January 6, Jacob Co. sells merchandise on account to Harley Inc. for $9,200, terms 1/10, n/30. On January 16, Harley pays the amount due.

Prepare entries for recognizing accounts receivable.

Instructions

Prepare the entries on Jacob Co.'s books to record the sale and related collection. (Omit cost of goods sold entries.)

E8.2 (LO 1), AP The following are selected transactions of Molina Company. Molina sells in large quantities to other companies and also sells its product in a small retail outlet.

Journalize entries related to accounts receivable.

March	1	Sold merchandise on account to Dodson Company for $5,000, terms 2/10, n/30.
	3	Dodson Company returned merchandise with a sales price of $500 to Molina.
	9	Molina collected the amount due from Dodson Company from the March 1 sale.
	15	Molina sold merchandise for $400 in its retail outlet. The customer used his Molina credit card.
	31	Molina added 1.5% monthly interest to the customer's credit card balance.

Instructions

Prepare journal entries for the transactions above. (Ignore cost of goods sold entries and explanations.)

E8.3 (LO 1), AP The following are two independent situations.

Journalize entries for recognizing accounts receivable.

Instructions

a. On January 6, Brumbaugh Co. sells merchandise on account to Pryor Inc. for $7,000, terms 2/10, n/30. On January 16, Pryor Inc. pays the amount due. Prepare the entries on Brumbaugh's books to record the sale and related collection. (Omit cost of goods sold entries.)

b. On January 10, Andrew Farley uses his Paltrow Co. credit card to purchase merchandise from Paltrow Co. for $9,000. On February 10, Farley is billed for the amount due of $9,000. On February 12, Farley pays $5,000 on the balance due. On March 10, Farley is billed for the amount due, including interest at 1% per month on the unpaid balance as of February 12. Prepare the entries on Paltrow Co.'s books related to the transactions that occurred on January 10, February 12, and March 10. (Omit cost of goods sold entries.)

E8.4 (LO 1, 2), AP At the beginning of the current period, Rose Corp. had balances in Accounts Receivable of $200,000 and in Allowance for Doubtful Accounts of $9,000 (credit). During the period, it had credit sales of $800,000 and collections of $763,000. It wrote off as uncollectible accounts receivable of $7,300. However, a $3,100 account previously written off as uncollectible was recovered before the end of the current period. Uncollectible accounts are estimated to total $25,000 at the end of the period. (Omit cost of goods sold entries.)

Journalize receivables transactions.

Instructions

a. Prepare the entries to record sales and collections during the period.

b. Prepare the entry to record the write-off of uncollectible accounts during the period.

c. Prepare the entries to record the recovery of the uncollectible account during the period.

d. Prepare the entry to record bad debt expense for the period.

e. Determine the ending balances in Accounts Receivable and Allowance for Doubtful Accounts.

f. What is the net realizable value of the receivables at the end of the period?

E8.5 (LO 2), AP The ledger of Macarty Company at the end of the current year shows Accounts Receivable $78,000, Credit Sales $810,000, and Sales Returns and Allowances $40,000.

Journalize entries to record allowance for doubtful accounts using two different bases.

Instructions

a. If Macarty uses the direct write-off method to account for uncollectible accounts, journalize the entry at December 15 if Macarty determines that Matisse's $900 balance is uncollectible.

b. If Allowance for Doubtful Accounts has a credit balance of $1,100 in the trial balance, journalize the adjusting entry at December 31, assuming uncollectibles are expected to be 10% of accounts receivable.

c. If Allowance for Doubtful Accounts has a debit balance of $500 in the trial balance, journalize the adjusting entry at December 31, assuming uncollectibles are expected to be 8% of accounts receivable.

Determine bad debt expense, and prepare the adjusting entry.

E8.6 (LO 2), AP Godfreid Company has accounts receivable of $95,400 at March 31, 2022. Credit terms are 2/10, n/30. At March 31, 2022, there is a $2,100 credit balance in Allowance for Doubtful Accounts prior to adjustment. The company uses the percentage-of-receivables basis for estimating uncollectible accounts. The company's estimates of uncollectibles are as shown below.

| | Balance, March 31 | | Estimated Percentage |
Age of Accounts	2022	2021	Uncollectible
Current	$65,000	$75,000	2%
1–30 days past due	12,900	8,000	5
31–90 days past due	10,100	2,400	30
Over 90 days past due	7,400	1,100	50
	$95,400	$86,500	

Instructions

a. Determine the total estimated uncollectibles at March 31, 2022.

b. Prepare the adjusting entry at March 31, 2022, to record bad debt expense.

c. Discuss the implications of the changes in the aging schedule from 2021 to 2022.

Journalize write-off and recovery.

E8.7 (LO 2), AP At December 31, 2021, Blanda Company had a credit balance of $15,000 in Allowance for Doubtful Accounts. During 2022, Blanda wrote off accounts totaling $11,000. One of those accounts of $1,800 was later collected. At December 31, 2022, an aging schedule indicated that the balance in Allowance for Doubtful Accounts should be $19,000.

Instructions

Prepare journal entries to record the 2022 transactions of Blanda Company.

Prepare entries for estimated uncollectibles, write-off, and recovery.

E8.8 (LO 2), AP On December 31, 2021, when its Allowance for Doubtful Accounts had a debit balance of $1,400, Dallas Co. estimates that 9% of its accounts receivable balance of $90,000 will become uncollectible and records the necessary adjustment to Allowance for Doubtful Accounts. On May 11, 2022, Dallas Co. determined that B. Jared's account was uncollectible and wrote off $1,200. On June 12, 2022, Jared paid the amount previously written off.

Instructions

Prepare the journal entries on December 31, 2021, May 11, 2022, and June 12, 2022.

Journalize entries for the sale of accounts receivable.

E8.9 (LO 2), AP The following are two independent situations. (Ignore cost of goods sold entries.)

Instructions

a. On March 3, Kitselman Appliances sells $650,000 of its receivables to Ervay Factors Inc. Ervay Factors assesses a finance charge of 3% of the amount of receivables sold. Prepare the entry on Kitselman Appliances' books to record the sale of the receivables.

b. On May 10, Fillmore Company sold merchandise for $3,000 and accepted the customer's America Bank MasterCard. America Bank charges a 4% service charge for credit card sales. Prepare the entry on Fillmore Company's books to record the sale of merchandise.

Journalize entries for credit card sales.

E8.10 (LO 2), AP The following are two independent situations.

Instructions

a. On April 2, Jennifer Elston uses her **JCPenney** credit card to purchase merchandise from a JCPenney store for $1,500. On May 1, Elston is billed for the $1,500 amount due. Elston pays $500 on the balance due on May 3. Elston receives a bill dated June 1 for the amount due, including interest at 1.0% per month on the unpaid balance as of May 3. Prepare the entries on JCPenney Co.'s books related to the transactions that occurred on April 2, May 3, and June 1.

b. On July 4, Spangler's Restaurant accepts a Visa card for a $200 dinner bill. Visa charges a 2% service fee. Prepare the entry on Spangler's books related to this transaction.

Journalize credit card sales.

E8.11 (LO 2), AP Colaw Stores accepts both its own and national credit cards. During the year, the following selected summary transactions occurred.

Jan. 15 Made Colaw credit card sales totaling $18,000. (There were no balances prior to January 15.)

  20 Made Visa credit card sales (service charge fee 2%) totaling $4,500.

Feb. 10 Collected $10,000 on Colaw credit card sales.

  15 Added finance charges of 1.5% to Colaw credit card account balances.

Instructions

Journalize the transactions for Colaw Stores.

E8.12 (LO 3), AP Moses Supply Co. has the following transactions related to notes receivable during the last 2 months of the year. The company does not make entries to accrue interest except at December 31.

Prepare entries for notes receivable transactions.

Nov. 1   Loaned $60,000 cash to C. Bohr on a 12-month, 7% note.
Dec. 11   Sold goods to K. R. Pine, Inc., receiving a $3,600, 90-day, 8% note.
    16   Received a $12,000, 180-day, 9% note to settle an open account from A. Murdock.
    31   Accrued interest revenue on all notes receivable.

Instructions

Journalize the transactions for Moses Supply Co. (Omit cost of goods sold entries.)

E8.13 (LO 3), AP These transactions took place for Bramson Co.

Journalize notes receivable transactions.

2021

May 1   Received a $5,000, 12-month, 6% note in exchange for an outstanding account receivable from R. Stoney.
Dec. 31   Accrued interest revenue on the R. Stoney note.

2022

May 1   Received principal plus interest on the R. Stoney note. (No interest has been accrued since December 31, 2021.)

Instructions

Record the transactions in the general journal. The company does not make entries to accrue interest except at December 31.

E8.14 (LO 3), AP Vandiver Company had the following selected transactions.

Prepare entries for notes receivable transactions.

Apr. 1, 2022   Accepted Goodwin Company's 12-month, 6% note in settlement of a $30,000 account receivable.
July 1, 2022   Loaned $25,000 cash to Thomas Slocombe on a 9-month, 10% note.
Dec. 31, 2022   Accrued interest on all notes receivable.
Apr. 1, 2023   Received principal plus interest on the Goodwin note.
Apr. 1, 2023   Thomas Slocombe dishonored its note; Vandiver expects it will eventually collect.

Instructions

Prepare journal entries to record the transactions. Vandiver prepares adjusting entries once a year on December 31.

E8.15 (LO 3), AP On May 2, McLain Company lends $9,000 to Chang, Inc., issuing a 6-month, 7% note. At the November 2 maturity date, Chang indicates that it cannot pay.

Journalize entries for dishonor of notes receivable.

Instructions

a. Prepare the entry to record the issuance of the note.

b. Prepare the entry to record the dishonor of the note, assuming that McLain Company expects collection will occur.

c. Prepare the entry to record the dishonor of the note, assuming that McLain Company does not expect collection in the future.

E8.16 (LO 4), AP Eileen Corp. had the following balances in receivable accounts at October 31, 2022 (in thousands): Allowance for Doubtful Accounts $52, Accounts Receivable $2,910, Other Receivables $189, and Notes Receivable $1,353.

Prepare a balance sheet presentation of receivables.

Instructions

Prepare the balance sheet presentation of Eileen Corp.'s receivables in good form.

E8.17 (LO 4), AN Kerwick Company had net accounts receivable of $100,000 on January 1, 2022. The only transactions that affected accounts receivable during 2022 were net credit sales of $1,000,000. At December 31, 2022, the company had net receivables of $150,000.

Compute accounts receivable turnover and average collection period.

Instructions

a. Compute the accounts receivable turnover for 2022.

b. Compute the average collection period in days.

Problems

Prepare journal entries related to bad debt expense, and compute ratios.

P8.1A (LO 1, 2, 4), AP At December 31, 2021, Suisse Imports reported this information on its balance sheet.

Accounts receivable	$600,000
Less: Allowance for doubtful accounts	37,000

During 2022, the company had the following transactions related to receivables.

1. Sales on account	$2,500,000
2. Sales returns and allowances	50,000
3. Collections of accounts receivable	2,200,000
4. Write-offs of accounts receivable deemed uncollectible	41,000
5. Recovery of accounts previously written off as uncollectible	15,000

Instructions

a. Prepare the journal entries to record each of these five transactions. Assume that no cash discounts were taken on the collections of accounts receivable. (Omit cost of goods sold entries.)

b. A/R bal. $809,000

b. Enter the January 1, 2022, balances in Accounts Receivable and Allowance for Doubtful Accounts, post the entries to the two accounts (use T-accounts), and determine the balances.

c. Prepare the journal entry to record bad debt expense for 2022, assuming that aging the accounts receivable indicates that estimated uncollectibles are $46,000.

d. Compute the accounts receivable turnover and average collection period.

Compute bad debt expense amounts.

P8.2A (LO 2), AP Writing Here is information related to Morgane Company for 2022.

Total credit sales	$1,500,000
Accounts receivable at December 31	840,000
Uncollectibles written off	37,000

Instructions

a. What amount of bad debt expense will Morgane Company report if it uses the direct write-off method of accounting for uncollectibles?

b. Bad Debt Exp. $30,600

b. Assume that Morgane Company uses the percentage-of-receivables basis to record bad debt expense and concludes that 4% of accounts receivable will become uncollectible. What amount of bad debt expense will the company record if Allowance for Doubtful Accounts has a credit balance of $3,000?

c. Assume the same facts as in part (b), except that there is a $1,000 debit balance in Allowance for Doubtful Accounts. What amount of bad debt expense will Morgane record?

d. What is a weakness of the direct write-off method of recording bad debt expense?

Journalize transactions related to uncollectibles.

P8.3A (LO 2), AP Presented below is an aging schedule for Bryan Company at December 31, 2021.

Customer	Total	Not Yet Due	Number of Days Past Due			
			1–30	**31–60**	**61–90**	**Over 90**
Aneesh	$ 24,000		$ 9,000	$15,000		
Bird	30,000	$ 30,000				
Cope	50,000	5,000	5,000		$40,000	
DeSpears	38,000					$38,000
Others	120,000	72,000	35,000	13,000		
	$262,000	$107,000	$49,000	$28,000	$40,000	$38,000
Estimated percentage uncollectible		3%	7%	12%	24%	60%
Total estimated uncollectibles	$ 42,400	$ 3,210	$ 3,430	$ 3,360	$ 9,600	$22,800

At December 31, 2021, the unadjusted balance in Allowance for Doubtful Accounts is a credit of $8,000.

Instructions

a. Journalize and post the adjusting entry for uncollectibles at December 31, 2021. (Use T-accounts.)

b. Journalize and post to the allowance account these 2022 selected events and transactions:

 1. March 1, a $600 customer balance originating in 2021 is judged uncollectible.

 2. May 1, a check for $600 is received from the customer whose account was written off as uncollectible on March 1.

c. Journalize the adjusting entry for uncollectibles at December 31, 2022, assuming that the unadjusted balance in Allowance for Doubtful Accounts is a debit of $1,400 and the aging schedule indicates that total estimated uncollectibles will be $36,700.

a. Bad Debt Exp. $34,400

P8.4A (LO 2), AP Rianna.com uses the allowance method of accounting for uncollectibles. The company produced the following aging of the accounts receivable at year-end.

Journalize transactions related to uncollectibles.

	Total	Number of Days Outstanding				
		0–30	**31–60**	**61–90**	**91–120**	**Over 120**
Accounts receivable	$377,000	$222,000	$90,000	$38,000	$15,000	$12,000
% uncollectible		1%	4%	5%	8%	10%

Instructions

a. Calculate the total estimated uncollectibles based on the above information.

b. Prepare the year-end adjusting journal entry to record Bad Debt Expense using the aged uncollectible accounts receivable determined in (a). Assume the unadjusted balance in Allowance for Doubtful Accounts is a $4,000 debit.

c. Of the above accounts, $5,000 is determined to be specifically uncollectible. Prepare the journal entry to write off the uncollectible account.

d. The company collects $5,000 subsequently on a specific account that had previously been determined to be uncollectible in (c). Prepare the journal entry or entries necessary to restore the account and record the cash collection.

e. Comment on how your answers to (a)–(d) would change if Rianna.com used 3% of total accounts receivable, rather than aging the accounts receivable. What are the advantages to the company of aging the accounts receivable rather than applying a percentage to total accounts receivable?

*a. Tot. est.
uncollectibles $10,120*

P8.5A (LO 2), AP Writing At December 31, 2022, the trial balance of Malone Company contained the following amounts before adjustment.

Journalize entries to record transactions related to uncollectibles.

	Debit	Credit
Accounts Receivable	$180,000	
Allowance for Doubtful Accounts		$ 1,500
Sales Revenue		875,000

Instructions

a. Prepare the adjusting entry at December 31, 2022, to record bad debt expense, assuming that the aging schedule indicates that $10,200 of accounts receivable will be uncollectible.

b. Repeat part (a), assuming that instead of a credit balance there is a $1,500 debit balance in Allowance for Doubtful Accounts.

c. During the next month, January 2023, a $2,100 account receivable is written off as uncollectible. Prepare the journal entry to record the write-off.

d. Repeat part (c), assuming that Malone Company uses the direct write-off method instead of the allowance method in accounting for uncollectible accounts receivable.

e. What are the advantages of using the allowance method in accounting for uncollectible accounts as compared to the direct write-off method?

b. Bad Debt Exp. $11,700

P8.6A (LO 1, 2, 3, 4), AP Milton Company closes its books on its July 31 year-end. The company does not make entries to accrue for interest except at its year-end. On June 30, the Notes Receivable account balance is $23,800. Notes Receivable includes the following.

Prepare entries for various credit card and notes receivable transactions.

Date	Maker	Face Value	Term	Maturity Date	Interest Rate
April 21	Coote Inc.	$ 6,000	90 days	July 20	8%
May 25	Brady Co.	7,800	60 days	July 24	10%
June 30	BMG Corp.	10,000	6 months	December 31	6%

During July, the following transactions were completed.

July   5   Made sales of $4,500 on Milton credit cards.
     14   Made sales of $600 on Visa credit cards. The credit card service charge is 3%.
     20   Received payment in full from Coote Inc. on the amount due.
     24   Received payment in full from Brady Co. on the amount due.

Instructions

a. Journalize the July transactions and the July 31 adjusting entry to accrue interest receivable. (Interest is computed using 360 days for terms expressed in days; omit cost of goods sold entries.)

b. A/R bal. $4,500

b. Enter the balances at July 1 in the receivable accounts and post the entries to all of the receivable accounts. (Use T-accounts.)

c. Tot. receivables $14,550

c. Show the balance sheet presentation of the receivable accounts at July 31, 2022.

Journalize various receivables transactions.

P8.7A (LO 1, 2, 3), AP On January 1, 2022, Harvee Company had Accounts Receivable of $54,200 and Allowance for Doubtful Accounts of $3,700. Harvee Company prepares financial statements annually. During the year, the following selected transactions occurred.

Jan.   5   Sold $4,000 of merchandise to Rian Company, terms n/30.
Feb.   2   Accepted a $4,000, 4-month, 9% promissory note from Rian Company for balance due.
     12   Sold $12,000 of merchandise to Cato Company and accepted Cato's $12,000, 2-month, 10% note.
     26   Sold $5,200 of merchandise to Malcolm Co., terms n/10.
Apr.   5   Accepted a $5,200, 3-month, 8% note from Malcolm Co.
     12   Collected Cato Company note in full.
June   2   Collected Rian Company note in full.
     15   Sold $2,000 of merchandise to Gerri Inc. and accepted a $2,000, 6-month, 12% note.

Instructions

Journalize the transactions. (Omit cost of goods sold entries.)

Calculate and interpret various ratios.

P8.8A (LO 4), AN Suppose the amounts presented here are basic financial information (in millions) from the 2022 annual reports of **Nike** and **adidas**.

	Nike	adidas
Sales revenue (net)	$19,176.1	$10,381
Allowance for doubtful accounts, beginning	78.4	119
Allowance for doubtful accounts, ending	110.8	124
Accounts receivable balance (gross), beginning	2,873.7	1,743
Accounts receivable balance (gross), ending	2,994.7	1,553

Instructions

Calculate the accounts receivable turnover and average collection period for both companies. Comment on the difference in their collection experiences.

Prepare financial statements.

P8.9A (LO 4), AP The adjusted trial balance of Gibson Company for the year ended December 31, 2022, is as follows:

	Debit	Credit
Cash	$ 6,400	
Accounts Receivable	2,700	
Notes Receivable	6,300	
Inventory	10,000	
Equipment	7,500	
Allowance for Doubtful Accounts		$ 300
Accumulated Depreciation—Equipment		1,000
Notes Payable		1,100
Accounts Payable		600
Common Stock		17,000

	Debit	Credit
Retained Earnings		11,000
Dividends	1,000	
Sales Revenue		13,000
Interest Revenue		100
Cost of Goods Sold	8,000	
Salaries and Wages Expense	1,400	
Rent Expense	700	
Bad Debt Expense	60	
Service Charge Expense	40	
	$44,100	$44,100

Instructions

Prepare a multiple-step income statement, retained earnings statement, and classified balance sheet. The notes payable is due on January 10, 2023. The notes receivable is due on June 30, 2023. Allowance for Doubtful Accounts applies to Accounts Receivable only.

Retained earnings $12,900

Continuing Case

Cookie Creations

(*Note:* This is a continuation of the Cookie Creations case from Chapters 1 through 7.)

CC8 One of Natalie's friends, Curtis Lesperance, runs a coffee shop where he sells specialty coffees and prepares and sells muffins and cookies. He is eager to buy one of Natalie's fine European mixers, which would enable him to make larger batches of muffins and cookies. However, Curtis cannot afford to pay for the mixer for at least 30 days. He asks Natalie if she would be willing to sell him the mixer on credit. Natalie comes to you for advice.

Go to **WileyPLUS** *for complete case details and instructions.*

leungchopan/
Shutterstock.com

Comprehensive Accounting Cycle Review

ACR8 Winter Company's balance sheet at December 31, 2021, is presented as follows.

Winter Company
Balance Sheet
December 31, 2021

Cash	$13,100	Accounts payable	$ 8,750
Accounts receivable	19,780	Common stock	20,000
Allowance for doubtful accounts	(800)	Retained earnings	12,730
Inventory	9,400		$41,480
	$41,480		

During January 2022, the following transactions occurred. Winter uses the perpetual inventory system.

Jan. 1 Winter accepted a 4-month, 8% note from Merando Company in payment of Merando's $1,200 account.

3 Winter wrote off as uncollectible the accounts of Inwood Corporation ($450) and Goza Company ($280).

8 Winter purchased $17,200 of inventory on account.

11 Winter sold for $28,000 on account inventory that cost $19,600.

15 Winter sold inventory that cost $700 to Mark Lauber for $1,000. Lauber charged this amount on his Visa First Bank card. The service fee charged Winter by First Bank is 3%.

17 Winter collected $22,900 from customers on account. No sales discounts were allowed.

21 Winter paid $14,300 on accounts payable. No purchase discounts were taken.

24 Winter received payment in full ($280) from Goza Company on the account written off on January 3.

27 Winter purchased supplies for $1,400 cash.

31 Winter paid other operating expenses, $3,718.

Adjustment data:

1. Interest is recorded for the month on the note from January 1.
2. Uncollectibles are expected to be 6% of the January 31, 2022, accounts receivable.
3. A count of supplies on January 31, 2022, reveals that $560 remains unused.

Instructions

(You may want to set up T-accounts to determine ending balances.)

a. Prepare journal entries for the transactions listed above and adjusting entries. (Include entries for cost of goods sold using the perpetual system.)

b. Totals $74,765

b. Prepare an adjusted trial balance at January 31, 2022.

c. Total assets $47,473

c. Prepare a multiple-step income statement and a retained earnings statement for the month ended January 31, 2022, and a balance sheet as of January 31, 2022.

Expand Your Critical Thinking

Financial Reporting Problem: Apple Inc.

CT8.1 Refer to the financial statements of **Apple Inc.** in Appendix A. The complete annual report, including the notes to the financial statements, is available at the company's website.

Instructions

a. Calculate the accounts receivable turnover and average collection period for the year ended September 29, 2018. (Assume all sales were credit sales.)

b. Did Apple have any potentially significant credit risks during the same period as specified in (a)? (*Hint*: Refer to the notes to the financial statements.)

c. What conclusions can you draw from the information in parts (a) and (b)?

Comparative Analysis Problem: PepsiCo, Inc. vs. The Coca-Cola Company

CT8.2 **PepsiCo, Inc.**'s financial statements are presented in Appendix B. Financial statements of **The Coca-Cola Company** are presented in Appendix C. The complete annual reports of PepsiCo and Coca-Cola, including the notes to the financial statements, are available at each company's respective website.

Instructions

a. Based on the information in these financial statements, compute the following 2018 ratios for each company. (Assume that all sales are credit sales and that PepsiCo's receivables on its balance sheet are all trade receivables.)

1. Accounts receivable turnover.   2. Average collection period for receivables.

b. What conclusions about managing accounts receivable can you draw from these data?

Comparative Analysis Problem: Amazon.com, Inc. vs. Walmart Inc.

CT8.3 **Amazon.com, Inc.**'s financial statements are presented in Appendix D. Financial statements of **Walmart Inc.** are presented in Appendix E. The complete annual reports of Amazon and Walmart, including the notes to the financial statements, are available at each company's respective website.

Instructions

a. Based on the information in these financial statements, compute the following ratios for each company (for the most recent year shown). (Assume all sales are credit sales.)

1. Accounts receivable turnover.   2. Average collection period for receivables.

b. What conclusions about managing accounts receivable can you draw from these data?

Interpreting Financial Statements

CT8.4 RLF Company sells office equipment and supplies to many organizations in the city and surrounding area on contract terms of 2/10, n/30. In the past, over 75% of the credit customers have taken advantage of the discount by paying within 10 days of the invoice date.

The number of customers taking the full 30 days to pay has increased within the last year. Current indications are that less than 60% of the customers are now taking the discount. Uncollectibles as a percentage of gross credit sales have risen from the 2.5% average in past years to about 4.5% in the current year.

The company's Finance Committee has requested more information on the collections of accounts receivable. The controller responded to this request with the following report.

RLF Company
Accounts Receivable Collections
May 31, 2020

The fact that some credit accounts will prove uncollectible is normal. Annual customer account write-offs have been 2.5% of gross credit sales over the past 5 years. During the last fiscal year, this percentage increased to slightly less than 4.5%. The current Accounts Receivable balance is $1,400,000. The distribution of this balance in terms of age and probability of collection is as follows.

Proportion of Total	Age Categories	Estimated Percentage of Collection
60%	not yet due	98%
22%	less than 30 days past due	96%
9%	30 to 60 days past due	94%
5%	61 to 120 days past due	91%
2½%	121 to 180 days past due	75%
1½%	over 180 days past due	30%

Allowance for Doubtful Accounts had a credit balance of $29,500 on June 1, 2019. RLF has provided for a monthly bad debt expense accrual during the current fiscal year based on the assumption that 4.5% of gross credit sales will be uncollectible. Total gross credit sales for the 2019–2020 fiscal year amounted to $2,900,000. Write-offs of uncollectible accounts during the year totaled $102,000.

Instructions

a. Prepare an accounts receivable aging schedule for RLF Company using the age categories identified in the controller's report to the Finance Committee showing the following.

1. The amount of accounts receivable outstanding for each age category and in total.

2. The estimated amount that is uncollectible for each category and in total.

b. Compute the amount of the year-end adjustment necessary to bring Allowance for Doubtful Accounts to the balance indicated by the age analysis. Then prepare the necessary journal entry to adjust the accounting records.

c. In a recessionary environment with tight credit and high interest rates:

1. Identify steps RLF Company might consider to improve the accounts receivable situation.

2. Then evaluate each step identified in terms of the risks and costs involved.

Real-World Focus

CT8.5 Purpose: To learn more about factoring.

Instructions

Go to the **Commercial Capital LLC** website, click on **Invoice Factoring**, and then answer the following questions.

a. What are some of the benefits of factoring?

b. What is the range of the percentages of the typical discount rate?

c. If a company factors its receivables, what percentage of the value of the receivables can it expect to receive from the factor in the form of cash, and how quickly will it receive the cash?

Decision-Making Across the Organization

CT8.6 Emilio and René Santos own Club Fandango. From its inception, Club Fandango has sold merchandise on either a cash or credit basis, but no credit cards have been accepted. During the past several months, the Santos have begun to question their credit-sales policies. First, they have lost some sales because of their refusal to accept credit cards. Second, representatives of two metropolitan banks have convinced them to accept their national credit cards. One bank, Business National Bank, has stated that (1) its credit card fee is 4% and (2) it pays the retailer 96 cents on each $1 of sales within 3 days of receiving the credit card billings.

The Santos decide to determine how much it costs to extend credit to customers. From the accounting records of the past 3 years, they accumulate these data:

	2022	2021	2020
Net credit sales	$500,000	$600,000	$400,000
Collection agency fees for slow-paying customers	2,900	2,600	1,600
Salary of part-time accounts receivable clerk	4,400	4,400	4,400

Credit and collection expenses as a percentage of net credit sales are as follows: uncollectible accounts 1.6%, billing and mailing costs .5%, and credit investigation fee on new customers .2%.

Emilio and René also determine that the average accounts receivable balance outstanding during the year is 5% of net credit sales. The Santos estimate that they could earn an average of 10% annually on cash invested in other business opportunities.

Instructions

With the class divided into groups, answer the following.

a. Prepare a tabulation for each year showing total credit and collection expenses in dollars and as a percentage of net credit sales.

b. Determine the net credit and collection expenses in dollars and as a percentage of net credit sales after considering the revenue not earned from other investment opportunities. (*Note:* The income lost on the cash held by the bank for 3 days is considered to be immaterial.)

c. Discuss both the financial and nonfinancial factors that are relevant to the decision.

Communication Activity

CT8.7 Jill Epp, a friend of yours, overheard a discussion at work about changes her employer wants to make in accounting for uncollectible accounts. Jill knows little about accounting, and she asks you to help make sense of what she heard. Specifically, she asks you to explain the differences between the percentage-of-receivables and the direct write-off methods for uncollectible accounts.

Instructions

In a letter of one page (or less), explain to Jill the two methods of accounting for uncollectibles. Be sure to discuss differences between these methods.

Ethics Case

CT8.8 The controller of Diaz Co. believes that the yearly allowance for doubtful accounts for Diaz Co. should be 2% of accounts receivable. The president of Diaz Co., nervous that the stockholders might expect the company to sustain its 10% growth rate, suggests that the controller increase the allowance for doubtful accounts to 4%. The president thinks that the lower net income, which reflects a 6% growth rate, will be a more sustainable rate for Diaz Co.

Instructions

a. Who are the stakeholders in this case?

b. Does the president's request pose an ethical dilemma for the controller?

c. Should the controller be concerned with Diaz Co.'s growth rate? Explain your answer.

All About You

CT8.9 Credit card usage in the United States is substantial. Many startup companies use credit cards as a way to help meet short-term financial needs. The most common forms of debt for startups are use of credit cards and loans from relatives.

Suppose that you start up Brothers Sandwich Shop. You invest your savings of $20,000 and borrow $70,000 from your relatives. Although sales in the first few months are good, you see that you may not have sufficient cash to pay expenses and maintain your inventory at acceptable levels, at least in the short term. You decide you may need to use one or more credit cards to fund the possible cash shortfall.

Instructions

a. Go to the Internet and find two sources that provide insight into how to compare credit card terms.

b. Develop a list, in descending order of importance, as to what features are most important to you in selecting a credit card for your business.

c. Examine the features of your present credit card. (If you do not have a credit card, select a likely one online for this exercise.) Given your analysis above, what are the three major disadvantages of your present credit card?

FASB Codification Activity

CT8.10 If your school has a subscription to the FASB Codification, log in and prepare responses to the following.

    a. How are receivables defined in the Codification?

    b. What are the conditions under which losses from uncollectible receivables (Bad Debt Expense) should be reported?

A Look at IFRS

LEARNING OBJECTIVE 5
Compare the accounting for receivables under GAAP and IFRS.

The basic accounting and reporting issues related to the recognition, measurement, and disposition of receivables are essentially the same between IFRS and GAAP.

Key Points

Following are the key similarities and differences between GAAP and IFRS related to the accounting for receivables.

Similarities

- The recording of receivables, the recognition of sales returns and allowances and sales discounts, and the allowance method to record uncollectibles are the same between GAAP and IFRS.

- Both IFRS and GAAP often use the term impairment to indicate that a receivable or a percentage of receivables may not be collectible.

- The FASB and IASB have worked to implement fair value measurement for financial instruments (the amount they currently could be sold for), such as receivables. Both Boards have faced bitter opposition from various factions.

Differences

- Although IFRS implies that receivables with different characteristics should be reported separately, there is no standard that mandates this segregation.

- IFRS and GAAP differ in the criteria used to determine how to record a factoring transaction. IFRS uses a combination approach focused on risks and rewards and loss of control. GAAP uses loss of control as the primary criterion. In addition, IFRS permits partial derecognition of receivables; GAAP does not.

IFRS Practice

IFRS Self-Test Questions

1. Which of the following statements is **false** under IFRS?

    a. Receivables include equity securities purchased by the company.

    b. Receivables include credit card receivables.

    c. Receivables include amounts owed by employees as a result of company loans to employees.

    d. Receivables include amounts resulting from transactions with customers.

2. In recording a factoring transaction:

    a. IFRS focuses on loss of control.

    b. GAAP focuses on loss of control and risks and rewards.

    c. IFRS and GAAP allow partial derecognition.

    d. IFRS allows partial derecognition.

3. Under IFRS:

    a. the entry to record estimated uncollectible accounts is the same as GAAP.

    b. it is always acceptable to use the direct write-off method.

    c. all financial instruments are recorded at fair value.

    d. None of the answer choices is correct.

International Financial Reporting Problem: Louis Vuitton

IFRS8.1 The financial statements of **Louis Vuitton** are presented in Appendix F. The complete consolidated financial statements, including the notes to its financial statements, are available at the company's website.

Instructions

Use the company's 2018 consolidated financial statements to answer the following questions.

- **a.** What is the accounting policy related to accounting for trade accounts receivable?

- **b.** According to the notes to the financial statements, what accounted for the difference between gross trade accounts receivable and net accounts receivable?

- **c.** According to the notes to the financial statements, what was the major reason why the balance in receivables increased relative to the previous year?

- **d.** Using information in the notes to the financial statements, determine what percentage the provision for impairment of receivables was as a percentage of gross trade receivables for 2018 and 2017. How did the ratio change from 2017 to 2018, and what does this suggest about the company's receivables?

Answers to IFRS Self-Test Questions

1. a **2.** d **3.** a

iStock.com/travellinglight

Plant Assets, Natural Resources, and Intangible Assets

Chapter Preview

The accounting for long-term assets has important implications for a company's reported results. In this chapter, we explain the application of the historical cost principle of accounting to property, plant, and equipment, such as **Southwest Airlines** airplanes, as well as to natural resources and intangible assets, such as the "Southwest Airlines heart" trademark. We also describe the methods that companies may use to allocate an asset's cost over its useful life. In addition, we discuss the accounting for expenditures incurred during the useful lives of assets, such as the cost of replacing tires on airplanes.

Feature Story

A Tale of Two Airlines

So, you're interested in starting a new business. Have you thought about the airline industry? Today, the most profitable airlines in the industry are not well-known major players like **American Airlines** and **United**. In fact, most giant, older airlines seem to be either bankrupt or on the verge of bankruptcy. In a recent year, five major airlines representing 24% of total U.S. capacity were operating under bankruptcy protection.

Not all airlines are hurting. The growth and profitability in the airline industry today is found at relative newcomers like **Southwest Airlines** and **JetBlue Airways**. These and other newer airlines compete primarily on ticket prices. During a recent five-year period, the low-fare airline market share increased by 47%, reaching 22% of U.S. airline capacity.

Southwest was the first upstart to make it big. It did so by taking a different approach. It bought small, new, fuel-efficient planes. Also, instead of the "hub-and-spoke" approach used by the major airlines, it opted for direct, short hop, no frills flights. It was all about controlling costs—getting the most out of its efficient new planes.

JetBlue, founded by former employees of Southwest, was recently ranked as the number 1 airline in the United States by the airline rating company **SkyTrax**. Management initially attempted to differentiate JetBlue by offering amenities not found on other airlines, such as seatback entertainment systems, while adopting Southwest's low-fare model. This approach was successful during JetBlue's early years, as it enjoyed both profitability and rapid growth. However, more recently the company has had to take aggressive steps to rein in costs in order to return to profitability.

In the past, upstarts such as **ValuJet** chose a different approach. The company bought planes that were 20 to 30 years old (known in the industry as *zombies*), which allowed it to quickly add planes to its fleet. ValuJet started with a $3.4 million investment and grew to be worth $630 million in its first three years.

But with high fuel costs, airlines are no longer in the market for old planes, which generally cannot be operated efficiently. Today, success in the airline business comes from owning the newest and most efficient equipment, and knowing how to get the most out of it.

Chapter Outline

LEARNING OBJECTIVES	REVIEW	PRACTICE
LO 1 Explain the accounting for plant asset expenditures.	• Determining the cost of plant assets • Expenditures during useful life	**DO IT! 1** Cost of Plant Assets
LO 2 Apply depreciation methods to plant assets.	• Factors in computing depreciation • Depreciation methods • Depreciation and income taxes • Revising periodic depreciation • Impairments	**DO IT! 2a** Depreciation Methods **2b** Revised Depreciation
LO 3 Explain how to account for the disposal of plant assets.	• Sale of plant assets • Retirement of plant assets	**DO IT! 3** Plant Asset Disposal
LO 4 Describe how to account for natural resources and intangible assets.	• Natural resources • Depletion • Intangible assets • Accounting for intangible assets • Types of intangible assets • Research and development costs	**DO IT! 4** Classification Concepts
LO 5 Discuss how plant assets, natural resources, and intangible assets are reported and analyzed.	• Presentation • Analysis	**DO IT! 5** Asset Turnover

Go to the Review and Practice section at the end of the chapter for a review of key concepts and practice applications with solutions.

Visit WileyPLUS for additional tutorials and practice opportunities.

Plant Asset Expenditures

LEARNING OBJECTIVE 1

Explain the accounting for plant asset expenditures.

Plant assets are resources that have three characteristics. They have physical substance (a definite size and shape), are used in the operations of a business, and are not intended for sale to customers. They are also called **property, plant, and equipment**; **plant and equipment**; and **fixed assets**. These assets are expected to be of use to the company for a number of years. Except for land, plant assets decline in service potential over their useful lives.

Because plant assets play a key role in ongoing operations, companies keep plant assets in good operating condition. They also replace worn-out or outdated plant assets, and expand productive resources as needed. Many companies have substantial investments in plant assets. **Illustration 9.1** shows the percentages of plant assets in relation to total assets of companies in a number of industries.

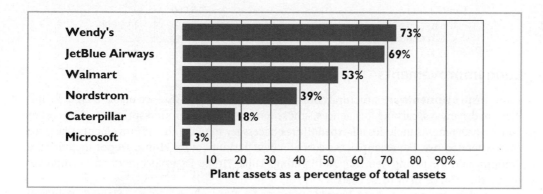

ILLUSTRATION 9.1

Percentages of plant assets in relation to total assets

Determining the Cost of Plant Assets

The **historical cost principle** requires that companies record plant assets at cost. Thus, JetBlue Airways and Southwest Airlines record their planes at cost. **Cost consists of all expenditures necessary to acquire an asset and make it ready for its intended use.** For example, when **Boeing** buys equipment, the purchase price, freight costs paid by Boeing, and installation costs are all part of the cost of the equipment.

Cost is measured by the cash paid in a cash transaction or by the **cash equivalent price** paid when companies use noncash assets in payment. **The cash equivalent price is equal to the fair value of the asset given up or the fair value of the asset received, whichever is more clearly determinable.** Once cost is established, it becomes the basis of accounting for the plant asset over its useful life. Current fair value is not used to increase the recorded cost after acquisition. We explain the application of the historical cost principle to each of the major classes of plant assets in the following sections (see **International Note**).

> **International Note**
>
> IFRS is more flexible regarding asset valuation. Companies revalue to fair value when they believe this information is more relevant.

Land

Companies often use **land** as a building site for a manufacturing plant or office building. The cost of land includes (1) the cash purchase price, (2) closing costs such as title and attorney fees, (3) real estate broker commissions, and (4) accrued property taxes and other liens assumed by the purchaser. For example, if the cash price is $50,000 and the purchaser agrees to pay accrued taxes of $5,000, the cost of the land is $55,000.

Companies record as debits (increases) to the Land account all necessary costs incurred to make land **ready for its intended use** (see **Helpful Hint**). When a company acquires vacant land, these costs include expenditures for clearing, draining, filling, and grading.

> **HELPFUL HINT**
>
> Management's intended use is important in applying the historical cost principle.

Sometimes the land has a building on it that must be removed before construction of a new building. In this case, the company debits to the Land account all demolition and removal costs, less any proceeds from salvaged materials.

To illustrate, assume that Hayes Company acquires real estate at a cash cost of $100,000. The property contains an old warehouse that is razed at a net cost of $6,000 ($7,500 in demolition costs less $1,500 proceeds from salvaged materials). Additional expenditures are the attorney's fee, $1,000, and the real estate broker's commission, $8,000. The cost of the land is $115,000, computed as shown in **Illustration 9.2**.

ILLUSTRATION 9.2

Computation of cost of land

Land	
Cash price of property	$100,000
Net removal cost of warehouse ($7,500 − $1,500)	6,000
Attorney's fee	1,000
Real estate broker's commission	8,000
Cost of land	**$115,000**

Hayes makes the following entry to record the acquisition of the land.

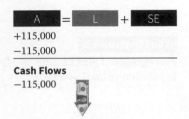

+115,000
−115,000

Cash Flows

−115,000

Land	115,000	
Cash		115,000
(To record purchase of land)		

Land Improvements

Land improvements are structural additions with limited lives that are made to land. Examples are driveways, parking lots, fences, landscaping, and underground sprinklers. The cost of land improvements includes all expenditures necessary to make the improvements ready for their intended use. For example, the cost of a new parking lot for **Home Depot** includes the amount paid for paving, fencing, and lighting. Thus, Home Depot debits to Land Improvements the total of all of these costs.

Land improvements have limited useful lives. Even when well-maintained, they will eventually need to be replaced. As a result, companies expense (depreciate) the cost of land improvements over their useful lives.

Buildings

Buildings are facilities used in operations, such as stores, offices, factories, warehouses, and airplane hangars. Companies debit to the Buildings account all necessary expenditures related to the purchase or construction of a building. When a building is **purchased**, such costs include the purchase price, closing costs (attorney's fee, title insurance, etc.), and the real estate broker's commission. Costs to make the building ready for its intended use include expenditures for remodeling and replacing or repairing the roof, floors, electrical wiring, and plumbing. When a new building is **constructed**, its cost consists of the contract price plus payments for architects' fees, building permits, and excavation costs.

In addition, companies charge certain interest costs to the Buildings account. Interest costs incurred to finance the project are included in the cost of the building when a significant period of time is required to get the building ready for use. In these circumstances, interest costs are considered as necessary as materials and labor. However, the inclusion of interest costs in the cost of a constructed building is **limited to interest costs incurred during the construction period**. When construction has been completed, the company records subsequent interest payments on funds borrowed to finance the construction as debits (increases) to Interest Expense.

Equipment

Equipment includes assets used in operations, such as store check-out counters, office furniture, factory machinery, and delivery trucks. **JetBlue Airways'** equipment includes aircraft, in-flight entertainment systems, and trucks for ground operations. The cost of equipment consists of the cash purchase price, sales taxes, freight charges, and insurance during transit paid by the purchaser. It also includes expenditures required in assembling, installing, and testing the equipment. However, companies treat as expenses the costs of motor vehicle licenses and accident insurance on company trucks and cars. Such items are **annual recurring expenditures and do not benefit future periods**. Two criteria apply in determining the cost of equipment: (1) the frequency of the cost—one time or recurring, and (2) the benefit period—the life of the asset or one year.

To illustrate, assume that Lenard Company purchases a delivery truck on January 1 at a cash price of $22,000. Related expenditures are sales taxes $1,320, painting and lettering $500, motor vehicle license $80, and a three-year accident insurance policy $1,600. The cost of the delivery truck is $23,820, computed as shown in **Illustration 9.3**.

ILLUSTRATION 9.3

Computation of cost of delivery truck

Delivery Truck	
Cash price	$22,000
Sales taxes	1,320
Painting and lettering	500
Cost of delivery truck	**$23,820**

Lenard treats the cost of a motor vehicle license as an expense and the cost of an insurance policy as a prepaid asset. Thus, the company records the purchase of the truck and related expenditures as follows.

Equipment	23,820	
License Expense	80	
Prepaid Insurance	1,600	
Cash		25,500
(To record purchase of delivery truck and related expenditures)		

A = L + SE
+23,820
          −80 Exp
+1,600
−25,500

Cash Flows
−25,500

For another example, assume Merten Company purchases factory machinery at a cash price of $50,000. Related expenditures are sales taxes $3,000, insurance during shipping $500, and installation and testing $1,000. The cost of the factory machinery is $54,500, computed as shown in **Illustration 9.4**.

ILLUSTRATION 9.4

Computation of cost of factory machinery

Factory Machinery	
Cash price	$50,000
Sales taxes	3,000
Insurance during shipping	500
Installation and testing	1,000
Cost of factory machinery	**$54,500**

Thus, Merten records the purchase and related expenditures as follows.

Equipment	54,500	
Cash		54,500
(To record purchase of factory machinery and related expenditures)		

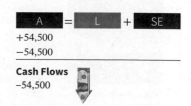

A = L + SE
+54,500
−54,500

Cash Flows
−54,500

Expenditures During Useful Life

During the useful life of a plant asset, a company may incur costs for ordinary repairs, additions, or improvements. **Ordinary repairs** are expenditures to **maintain** the operating efficiency and productive life of the asset. They usually are small amounts that occur frequently. Examples are motor tune-ups and oil changes, the painting of buildings, and the replacing of worn-out gears on machinery. Companies record such repairs as debits to Maintenance and Repairs Expense as they are incurred. Because they are immediately charged as an expense against revenues, these costs are often referred to as **revenue expenditures**.

In contrast, **additions and improvements** are costs incurred to **increase** the operating efficiency, productive capacity, or useful life of a plant asset. They are usually material in amount and occur infrequently. Additions and improvements increase the company's investment in productive facilities. Companies generally debit these amounts to the plant asset affected. They are often referred to as **capital expenditures**.

Companies must use good judgment in deciding between a revenue expenditure and capital expenditure. For example, assume that Rodriguez Co. purchases a number of wastepaper baskets. The proper accounting would appear to be to capitalize and then depreciate these wastepaper baskets over their useful lives. However, Rodriguez will generally expense these wastepaper baskets immediately. This practice is justified on the basis of **materiality**. Materiality refers to the impact of an item's size on a company's financial operations. The **materiality concept** states that if an item would not make a difference in decision-making, the company does not have to follow GAAP in reporting that item.

Anatomy of a Fraud

Bernie Ebbers was the founder and CEO of the phone company **WorldCom**. The company engaged in a series of increasingly large, debt-financed acquisitions of other companies. These acquisitions made the company grow quickly, which made the stock price increase dramatically. However, because the acquired companies all had different accounting systems, WorldCom's financial records were a mess. When WorldCom's performance started to flatten out, Bernie coerced WorldCom's accountants to engage in a number of fraudulent activities to make net income look better than it really was and thus prop up the stock price. One of these frauds involved treating $7 billion of line costs as capital expenditures. The line costs, which were rental fees paid to other phone companies to use their phone lines, had always been properly expensed in previous years. Capitalization delayed expense recognition to future periods and thus boosted current-period profits.

Total take: $7 billion

The Missing Controls

Documentation procedures. The company's accounting system was a disorganized collection of non-integrated systems, which resulted from a series of corporate acquisitions. Top management took advantage of this disorganization to conceal its fraudulent activities.

Independent internal verification. A fraud of this size should have been detected by a routine comparison of the actual physical assets with the list of physical assets shown in the accounting records.

Accounting Across the Organization

iStock.com/Brian Raisbeck

Many U.S. Firms Use Leases

Leases, which are formal rental agreements, allow companies to use plant assets without actually purchasing them. Leasing is big business for U.S. companies. For example, business investment in equipment in a recent year totaled $800 billion. Leasing accounted for about 33% of all business investment ($264 billion).

Who does the most leasing? Interestingly, major banks such as **Continental National Bank**, **JPMorgan Chase**, and **US Bancorp** are the major lessors. Also, many companies have established separate leasing companies, such as **Boeing Capital Corporation**, **Dell Financial Services**, and **John Deere Capital Corp**. And, as an excellent example of the magnitude of leasing, leased planes account for nearly 40% of the U.S. fleet of commercial airlines. **International Lease Finance Corporation** in Los Angeles owns more planes than any airline in the world. Leasing is also becoming increasingly common in the hotel industry. **Marriott**, **Hilton**, and **Inter-Continental** are choosing to lease hotels that are owned by someone else.

Why might airline managers choose to lease rather than purchase their planes? (Go to WileyPLUS for this answer and additional questions.)

DO IT! 1 | Cost of Plant Assets

Assume that Drummond Heating and Cooling Co. purchases a delivery truck for $15,000 cash, plus sales taxes of $900 and delivery costs of $500. The buyer also pays $200 for painting and lettering, $600 for an annual insurance policy, and $80 for a motor vehicle license. Explain how each of these costs would be accounted for.

Solution

The first four payments ($15,000 purchase price, $900 sales taxes, $500 delivery costs, and $200 painting and lettering) are expenditures necessary to make the truck ready for its intended use. Thus, the cost of the truck is $16,600. The payment for insurance is reported as a separate asset, prepaid insurance, and allocated to expense as appropriate. The payment for the license should be treated as an expense.

Related exercise material: **BE9.1, BE9.2, BE9.3, DO IT! 9.1, E9.1, E9.2, and E9.3.**

Depreciation Methods

LEARNING OBJECTIVE 2

Apply depreciation methods to plant assets.

As explained in Chapter 3, **depreciation is the process of allocating to expense the cost of a plant asset over its useful (service) life in a rational and systematic manner.** Such cost allocation enables companies to properly record expenses (efforts) with associated revenues (results) in accordance with the expense recognition principle, as shown in **Illustration 9.5**.

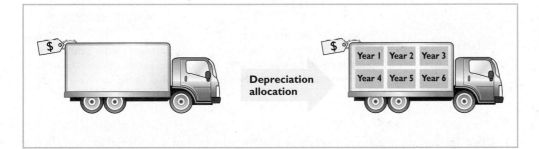

Depreciation allocation

Year 1 Year 2 Year 3
Year 4 Year 5 Year 6

ILLUSTRATION 9.5

Depreciation as a cost allocation concept

Depreciation affects the balance sheet through accumulated depreciation, which companies report as a deduction from plant assets. It affects the income statement through depreciation expense.

It is important to understand that **depreciation is a process of cost allocation. It is not a process of asset valuation.** No attempt is made to measure the change in an asset's fair value during ownership. So, the **book value** (cost less accumulated depreciation) of a plant asset may be quite different from its **fair value**. In fact, if an asset is fully depreciated, it can have a zero book value but still have a fair value.

Depreciation applies to three classes of plant assets: land improvements, buildings, and equipment. Each asset in these classes is considered to be a **depreciable asset**. Why? Because the usefulness to the company and revenue-producing ability of each asset will decline over the asset's useful life. Depreciation **does not apply to land** because its usefulness and revenue-producing ability generally remain intact over time. In fact, in many cases, the usefulness of land increases over time because of the scarcity of good land sites. Thus, **land is not a depreciable asset**.

During a depreciable asset's useful life, its revenue-producing ability declines because of **wear and tear**. A delivery truck that has been driven 100,000 miles will be less useful to a company than one driven only 800 miles.

Revenue-producing ability may also decline because of obsolescence. **Obsolescence** occurs when an asset becomes out of date before it physically wears out. The rerouting of airlines from Chicago's Midway Airport to Chicago-O'Hare International Airport because Midway's runways were too short for giant jets is an example. Similarly, many companies replace their computers long before they originally planned to do so because technological improvements make the old hardware obsolete.

Recognizing depreciation on an asset does not result in an accumulation of cash for replacement of the asset. The balance in Accumulated Depreciation represents the total amount of the asset's cost that the company has charged to expense. **It is not a cash fund.**

Note that the concept of depreciation is consistent with the going concern assumption. The **going concern assumption** states that the company will continue in operation for the foreseeable future. If a company does not use a going concern assumption, then plant assets should be reported at their fair value. In that case, depreciation of these assets is not needed.

Factors in Computing Depreciation

Three factors affect the computation of depreciation, as shown in **Illustration 9.6** (see **Helpful Hint**).

ILLUSTRATION 9.6

Three factors in computing depreciation

HELPFUL HINT

Depreciation expense is reported on the income statement. Accumulated depreciation is reported on the balance sheet as a deduction from plant assets.

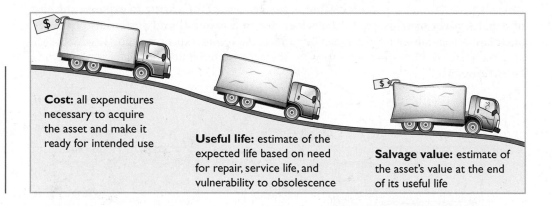

Cost: all expenditures necessary to acquire the asset and make it ready for intended use

Useful life: estimate of the expected life based on need for repair, service life, and vulnerability to obsolescence

Salvage value: estimate of the asset's value at the end of its useful life

1. **Cost.** Earlier, we explained the issues affecting the cost of a depreciable asset. Recall that companies record plant assets at cost, in accordance with the historical cost principle.

2. **Useful life. Useful life** is an estimate of the expected productive life, also called service life, of the asset for its owner. Useful life may be expressed in terms of time, units of activity (such as machine hours), or units of output. Useful life is an estimate. In making the estimate, management considers such factors as the intended use of the asset, repair and maintenance policies, and vulnerability of the asset to obsolescence. The company's past experience with similar assets is often helpful in deciding on expected useful life.

ALTERNATIVE TERMINOLOGY

Another term sometimes used for salvage value is *residual value*.

3. **Salvage value. Salvage value** is an estimate of the asset's value at the end of its useful life (see **Alternative Terminology**). Companies may base the value on the asset's worth as scrap or on its expected trade-in value. Like useful life, salvage value is an estimate. In making the estimate, management considers how it plans to dispose of the asset and its experience with similar assets.

Depreciation Methods

Depreciation is generally computed using one of the following methods:

1. Straight-line.
2. Units-of-activity.
3. Declining-balance.

Each method is acceptable under generally accepted accounting principles. Management selects the method that it believes best measures an asset's contribution to revenue over its useful life. Once a company chooses a method, it should apply that method consistently over the useful life of the asset. Consistency enhances the ability to analyze financial statements over multiple years.

We will compare the three depreciation methods using the data presented in **Illustration 9.7** for a small delivery truck purchased by Barb's Florists on January 1, 2022.

ILLUSTRATION 9.7

Delivery truck data

Cost	$13,000
Expected salvage value	$1,000
Estimated useful life in years	5
Estimated useful life in miles	100,000

Illustration 9.8 shows the use of the primary depreciation methods in a sample of the largest companies in the United States. No matter what method is used, the total amount depreciated over the useful life of the asset is its depreciable cost. **Depreciable cost** is equal to the cost of the asset less its salvage value.

ILLUSTRATION 9.8

Use of depreciation methods in large U.S. companies

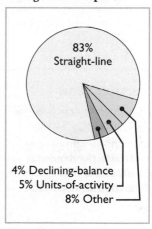

83%
Straight-line

4% Declining-balance
5% Units-of-activity
8% Other

Straight-Line Method

Under the **straight-line method**, companies expense the same amount of depreciation for each year of the asset's useful life. It is measured solely by the passage of time.

To compute depreciation expense under the straight-line method, companies need to determine depreciable cost. As indicated above, **depreciable cost** is the cost of the asset less its salvage value. It represents the total amount subject to depreciation. Under the straight-line method, to determine depreciation expense, we divide depreciable cost by the asset's useful life as measured in years. **Illustration 9.9** shows the computation of the first year's depreciation expense for Barb's Florists.

ILLUSTRATION 9.9   **Formula for straight-line method**

Cost	−	Salvage Value	=	Depreciable Cost
$13,000	−	$1,000	=	$12,000

Depreciable Cost	÷	Useful Life (in years)	=	Depreciation Expense
$12,000	÷	5	=	$2,400

Alternatively, we also can compute an annual **rate** of depreciation. In this case, the rate is 20% (100% ÷ 5 years). When a company uses an annual straight-line rate, it applies the percentage rate to the depreciable cost of the asset. **Illustration 9.10** shows a **depreciation schedule** using an annual rate.

ILLUSTRATION 9.10
Straight-line depreciation schedule

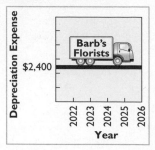

	Computation			Annual	End of Year	
Year	Depreciable Cost	×	Depreciation Rate =	Depreciation Expense	Accumulated Depreciation	Book Value
2022	$12,000		20%	**$2,400**	$ 2,400	$10,600*
2023	12,000		20	**2,400**	4,800	8,200
2024	12,000		20	**2,400**	7,200	5,800
2025	12,000		20	**2,400**	9,600	3,400
2026	12,000		20	**2,400**	12,000	**1,000**

Barb's Florists

*Book value = Cost − Accumulated depreciation = ($13,000 − $2,400).

Note that the depreciation expense of $2,400 is the same each year. The book value (computed as cost minus accumulated depreciation) at the end of the useful life is equal to the expected $1,000 salvage value.

What happens to these computations for an asset purchased **during** the year, rather than on January 1? In that case, it is necessary to **prorate the annual depreciation** on a time basis. If Barb's Florists had purchased the delivery truck on April 1, 2022, the company would own the truck for nine months of the first year (April–December). Thus, depreciation for 2022 would be $1,800 ($12,000 × 20% × $\frac{9}{12}$ of a year).

The straight-line method predominates in practice. Large companies like **Campbell Soup**, **Marriott**, and **General Mills** use the straight-line method. It is simple to apply, and it records expenses with associated revenues appropriately when the use of the asset is reasonably uniform throughout the service life. Generally, the types of assets that provide equal benefits over their useful lives are those for which daily use does not affect productivity. Examples are office furniture and fixtures, buildings, warehouses, and garages for motor vehicles.

ACTION PLAN

• Calculate depreciable cost (Cost − Salvage value).

• Divide the depreciable cost by the asset's estimated useful life.

DO IT! 2a | Depreciation Methods—Straight-Line Depreciation

Part 1: On January 1, 2022, Iron Mountain Ski Corporation purchased a new snow-grooming machine for $50,000. The machine is estimated to have a 10-year life with a $2,000 salvage value. What adjusting entry would Iron Mountain Ski Corporation make at December 31, 2022, if it uses the straight-line method of depreciation and adjusts its accounts annually?

Solution

$$\text{Depreciation expense} = \frac{\text{Cost} - \text{Salvage value}}{\text{Useful life}} = \frac{\$50,000 - \$2,000}{10} = \$4,800$$

The entry to record the first year's depreciation would be:

Dec. 31	Depreciation Expense	4,800	
	Accumulated Depreciation—Equipment		4,800
	(To record depreciation on snow-grooming machine)		

Related exercise material: **BE9.4, BE9.5, and DO IT! 9.2a.**

ALTERNATIVE TERMINOLOGY

Another term often used is the *units-of-production method.*

Units-of-Activity Method

Under the **units-of-activity method**, useful life is expressed in terms of the total units of production or use expected from the asset, rather than as a time period (see **Alternative Terminology**). The units-of-activity method is ideally suited to factory machinery. Manufacturing companies can measure production in units of output or in machine hours used in operating machinery. This method can also be used for such assets as delivery equipment (miles driven) and airplanes (hours in use). The units-of-activity method is generally not suitable for buildings or furniture because depreciation for these assets is more a function of time than of use (see **Helpful Hint**).

To use this method, companies estimate the total units of activity for the entire useful life, and then divide these units into depreciable cost. The resulting number represents the depreciable cost per unit. The depreciable cost per unit is then applied to the actual units of activity during the year to determine the annual depreciation expense.

To illustrate, assume that Barb's Florists drives its delivery truck 15,000 miles in the first year. **Illustration 9.11** shows the units-of-activity formula and the computation of the first year's depreciation expense.

Depreciable Cost	÷	Total Units of Activity	=	Depreciable Cost per Unit
$12,000	÷	100,000 miles	=	$0.12

Depreciable Cost per Unit	×	Units of Activity During the Year	=	Depreciation Expense
$0.12	×	15,000 miles	=	$1,800

LLUSTRATION 9.11
Formula for units-of-activity method

Illustration 9.12 shows the units-of-activity depreciation schedule, using assumed mileage. The depreciable cost per unit remains constant for all years.

Barb's Florists

	Computation				Annual	End of Year	
Year	Units of Activity	×	Depreciable Cost/Unit	=	Depreciation Expense	Accumulated Depreciation	Book Value
2022	15,000		$0.12		**$1,800**	$ 1,800	$11,200*
2023	30,000		0.12		**3,600**	5,400	7,600
2024	20,000		0.12		**2,400**	7,800	5,200
2025	25,000		0.12		**3,000**	10,800	2,200
2026	10,000		0.12		**1,200**	12,000	**1,000**

*$13,000 − $1,800.

LLUSTRATION 9.12
Units-of-activity depreciation schedule

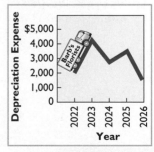

This method is easy to apply for assets purchased mid-year. In such a case, the company computes the depreciation using the productivity of the asset for the partial year.

The units-of-activity method is not nearly as popular as the straight-line method (see Illustration 9.8) primarily because it is often difficult for companies to reasonably estimate total activity. However, some very large companies, such as **Chevron** and **Boise Cascade** (a forestry company), do use this method. When the productivity of an asset varies significantly from one period to another, the units-of-activity method results in the best matching of expenses with revenues.

ACTION PLAN

- Calculate depreciable cost (Cost − Salvage value).
- Divide the depreciable cost by the asset's estimated useful hours.
- Multiply depreciable cost per hour by actual hours used.

DO IT! 2a | Depreciation Methods—Units-of-Activity

Part 2: On January 1, 2022, Iron Mountain Ski Corporation purchased a new snow-grooming machine for $50,000. The machine is estimated to have a 100,000-hour life with a $2,000 salvage value. The machine is used for 12,000 hours during 2022. What journal entry would Iron Mountain Ski Corporation make at December 31, 2022, if it uses the units-of-activity method of depreciation and adjusts its accounts annually?

Solution

$$\text{Depreciable cost per hour} = \frac{\text{Cost} - \text{Salvage value}}{\text{Useful life}} = \frac{\$50,000 - \$2,000}{100,000 \text{ hours}} = \$0.48/\text{hour}$$

$$\text{Depreciation expense} = \text{Depreciable cost per unit} \times \text{Hours of activity during the year}$$
$$= \$0.48 \times 12,000 \text{ hours} = \$5,760$$

Iron Mountains would record the first year's depreciation as follows.

Dec. 31	Depreciation Expense	5,760	
	Accumulated Depreciation—Equipment		5,760
	(To record depreciation on snow-grooming machine)		

Related exercise material: **BE9.7, E9.5, and E9.7.**

Declining-Balance Method

The **declining-balance method** produces a decreasing annual depreciation expense over the asset's useful life. The method is so named because the periodic depreciation is based on a **declining book value** (cost less accumulated depreciation) of the asset. With this method, companies compute annual depreciation expense by multiplying the book value at the beginning of the year by the declining-balance depreciation rate. **The depreciation rate remains constant from year to year, but the book value to which the rate is applied declines each year.**

At the beginning of the first year, book value is the cost of the asset. This is because the balance in accumulated depreciation at the beginning of the asset's useful life is zero. In subsequent years, book value is the difference between cost and accumulated depreciation to date. Unlike the other depreciation methods, the declining-balance method **ignores salvage value in determining the amount to which the declining-balance rate is applied**. Salvage value, however, does limit the total depreciation that can be taken. Depreciation stops when the asset's book value equals expected salvage value.

A common declining-balance rate is double the straight-line rate. The method is often called the **double-declining-balance method**. If Barb's Florists uses the double-declining-balance method, it uses a depreciation rate of 40% (2 × the straight-line rate of 20%). **Illustration 9.13** shows the declining-balance formula and the computation of the first year's depreciation on the delivery truck.

ILLUSTRATION 9.13

Formula for declining-balance method

Book Value at Beginning of Year	×	Declining-Balance Rate	=	Depreciation Expense
$13,000	×	40%	=	$5,200

Illustration 9.14 shows the depreciation schedule under this method and indicates that the delivery equipment is 69% depreciated ($8,320 ÷ $12,000) at the end of the second year. Under the straight-line method, the truck would be depreciated 40% ($4,800 ÷ $12,000) at that time. Because the declining-balance method produces higher depreciation expense in the early years than in the later years, it is considered an **accelerated-depreciation method**.

Barb's Florists					
	Computation		**Annual**	**End of Year**	
Year	Book Value Beginning of Year	× Depreciation Rate	= Depreciation Expense	Accumulated Depreciation	Book Value
2022	$13,000	40%	**$5,200**	$ 5,200	$7,800
2023	7,800	40	**3,120**	8,320	4,680
2024	4,680	40	**1,872**	10,192	2,808
2025	2,808	40	**1,123**	11,315	1,685
2026	1,685	40	**685***	12,000	**1,000**

*Computation of $674 ($1,685 × 40%) is adjusted to $685 in order for book value to equal salvage value.

ILLUSTRATION 9.14

Double-declining-balance depreciation schedule

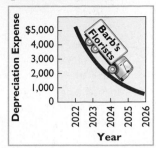

The declining-balance method is compatible with the expense recognition principle. It matches the higher depreciation expense in early years with the higher benefits received in these years. It also recognizes lower depreciation expense in later years, when the asset's contribution to revenue is less. Some assets lose usefulness rapidly because of obsolescence. In these cases, the declining-balance method provides the most appropriate depreciation amount (see **Helpful Hint**).

HELPFUL HINT

The method recommended for an asset that is expected to be significantly more productive in the first half of its useful life is the declining-balance method.

When a company purchases an asset during the year, it must prorate the first year's declining-balance depreciation on a time basis. For example, if Barb's Florists had purchased the truck on April 1, 2022, depreciation for 2022 would become $3,900 ($13,000 × 40% × $\frac{9}{12}$). The book value at the beginning of 2023 is then $9,100 ($13,000 − $3,900), and the 2023 depreciation is $3,640 ($9,100 × 40%). Subsequent computations would follow from those amounts.

DO IT! 2a | Depreciation Methods—Declining-Balance

Part 3: On January 1, 2022, Iron Mountain Ski Corporation purchased a new snow-grooming machine for $50,000. The machine is estimated to have a 10-year life with a $2,000 salvage value. What journal entry would Iron Mountain Ski Corporation make at December 31, 2022, if it uses the double-declining-balance method of depreciation and adjusts its accounts annually?

ACTION PLAN

- Calculate the declining-balance depreciation rate.
- Determine the book value at the beginning of each year.
- Multiply the depreciation rate by the book value.

Solution

Depreciation rate = 2 × straight-line rate = 2 × 10% = 20%
Book value at beginning of 2022 = Cost − Accumulated depreciation = $50,000 − $0 = $50,000
Depreciation expense = Depreciation rate × Book value = 20% × $50,000 = $10,000

Iron Mountains would record the first year's depreciation as follows.

Dec. 31	Depreciation Expense	10,000	
	Accumulated Depreciation—Equipment		10,000
	(To record depreciation on		
	snow-grooming machine)		

Related exercise material: **BE9.6 and E9.7.**

Comparison of Methods

Illustration 9.15 compares annual and total depreciation expense under each of the three methods for Barb's Florists.

Annual depreciation varies considerably among the methods, but **total depreciation expense is the same ($12,000) for the five-year period** under all three methods. Each method is acceptable in accounting because each recognizes in a rational and systematic

ILLUSTRATION 9.15

Comparison of depreciation methods

Year	Straight-Line	Units-of-Activity	Declining-Balance
2022	$ 2,400	$ 1,800	$ 5,200
2023	2,400	3,600	3,120
2024	2,400	2,400	1,872
2025	2,400	3,000	1,123
2026	2,400	1,200	685
	$12,000	**$12,000**	**$12,000**

manner the decline in service potential of the asset. **Illustration 9.16** graphs the depreciation expense pattern under each method.

ILLUSTRATION 9.16

Patterns of depreciation expense

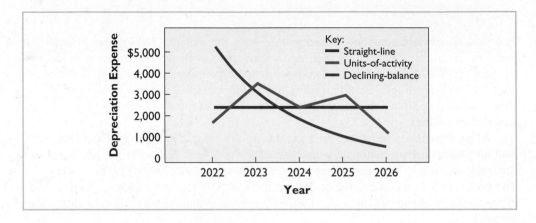

ACTION PLAN

- **For straight-line, calculate depreciable cost and then divide that by the asset's useful life.**

- **For units-of-activity, calculate depreciable cost, divide that by the asset's estimated useful hours, and then multiply depreciable cost per hour by actual hours used.**

- **For declining-balance, calculate the declining-balance depreciation rate, determine the book value at the beginning of each year, and then multiply the depreciation rate by the book value.**

DO IT! 2a | Depreciation Methods

Part 4: Mendez Corporation purchased a truck at the beginning of 2022 for $100,000. The truck is estimated to have a salvage value of $12,000 and a useful life of 160,000 miles or 8 years. It was driven 23,000 miles in 2022 and 31,000 miles in 2023. Compute depreciation expense for 2023 using the:

a. Straight-line method.

b. Units-of-activity method.

c. Double-declining-balance (DDB) method.

Solution

a. $\dfrac{\text{Cost} - \text{Salvage value}}{\text{Useful life}} = \dfrac{\$100,000 - \$12,000}{8 \text{ years}} = \$11,000$

b. $\dfrac{\text{Cost} - \text{Salvage value}}{\text{Useful life}} = \dfrac{\$100,000 - \$12,000}{160,000 \text{ miles}} = \$0.55/\text{mile}$

Depreciable cost per mile × Actual miles = $0.55 × 31,000 miles = $17,050

c. Depreciation rate = 2 × Straight-line rate = 2 × 12.5% (100% ÷ 8 years) = 25%

DDB depreciation rate × Book value at beginning of 2023
25% × $75,000* = $18,750

*Depreciation in 2022: 25% × $100,000 = $25,000; Book value at end of 2022: $100,000 − $25,000 = $75,000

Related exercise material: **BE9.4, BE9.6, BE9.7, DO IT! 9.2a, E9.5, and E9.7.**

HELPFUL HINT

Depreciation per financial statements is usually different from depreciation per tax returns.

Depreciation and Income Taxes

The Internal Revenue Service (IRS) allows corporate taxpayers to deduct depreciation expense when they compute taxable income. However, the IRS does not require taxpayers to use the same depreciation method on the tax return that is used in preparing financial statements (see **Helpful Hint**).

Many corporations use the straight-line method in their financial statements to maximize net income reported to investors. At the same time, they use a special accelerated-depreciation method on their tax returns to minimize their income taxes paid to the IRS. Taxpayers must use on their tax returns either the straight-line method or a special accelerated-depreciation method called the **Modified Accelerated Cost Recovery System** (MACRS).

Depreciation Disclosure in the Notes

Companies must disclose the choice of depreciation method in their financial statements or in related notes that accompany the statements. **Illustration 9.17** shows excerpts from the "Property and equipment" notes from the financial statements of **Southwest Airlines**.

ILLUSTRATION 9.17

Disclosure of depreciation policies

`Real World`

Southwest Airlines
Notes to the Financial Statements
Property and equipment Depreciation is provided by the straight-line method to estimated residual values over periods generally ranging from 23 to 25 years for flight equipment.

From this note, we learn that Southwest Airlines uses the straight-line method to depreciate its planes over periods of 23 to 25 years.

Revising Periodic Depreciation

Depreciation is one example of the use of estimation in the accounting process. Management should periodically review annual depreciation expense, as well as the underlying useful life and salvage value estimates used in its computation. If wear and tear or obsolescence indicates that annual depreciation estimates are inadequate or excessive, the company should change the amount of depreciation expense.

When a change in an estimate is required, the company makes the change in **current and future years. It does not change depreciation in prior periods.** The rationale is that continual restatement of prior periods would adversely affect confidence in financial statements.

To determine the new annual depreciation expense, the company first computes the asset's depreciable cost at the time of the revision. It then allocates the revised depreciable cost to the remaining useful life (see **Helpful Hint**).

To illustrate, assume that Barb's Florists decides at the end of 2025 (prior to the year-end adjusting entries) to extend the useful life of the truck by one year (a total life of six years) and increase its salvage value to $2,200. The company has used the straight-line method to depreciate the asset to date. Depreciation per year was $2,400 [($13,000 − $1,000) ÷ 5]. Accumulated depreciation after three years (2022–2024) is $7,200 ($2,400 × 3), and book value is $5,800 ($13,000 − $7,200). The new annual depreciation is $1,200, computed as shown in **Illustration 9.18**.

> **HELPFUL HINT**
>
> Use a step-by-step approach: (1) determine new depreciable cost; (2) divide by remaining useful life.

ILLUSTRATION 9.18

Revised depreciation computation

Book value, 1/1/25	$ 5,800	
Less: New salvage value	2,200	
Depreciable cost	$ 3,600	
New remaining useful life	3 years	(2025–2027)
Revised annual depreciation ($3,600 ÷ 3)	**$ 1,200**	

Barb's Florists makes no journal entry for the change in useful life and salvage value estimates. On December 31, 2025, during the preparation of adjusting entries, it records depreciation expense of $1,200.

Companies must disclose in the financial statements significant changes in estimates. Although a company may have a legitimate reason for changing an estimated life, financial statement users should be aware that some companies might change an estimate simply to achieve financial statement goals. For example, extending an asset's estimated life reduces depreciation expense and increases current period income.

At one time, **AirTran Airways** (now owned by **Southwest Airlines**) increased the estimated useful lives of some of its planes from 25 to 30 years and increased the estimated lives of related aircraft parts from 5 years to 30 years. It disclosed that the change in estimate decreased its net loss for the year by approximately $0.6 million, or about $0.01 per share. Whether these changes were appropriate depends on how reasonable it is to assume that planes will continue to be used for a long time. Our Feature Story suggests that although in the past many planes lasted a long time, it is also clear that because of high fuel costs, airlines are now scrapping many of their old, inefficient planes.

Impairments

As noted earlier, the book value of plant assets is rarely the same as the fair value. In instances where the value of a plant asset declines substantially, its fair value might fall materially below book value. This may happen because a machine has become obsolete, or the market for the product made by the machine has dried up or has become very competitive. A **permanent decline** in the fair value of an asset is referred to as an **impairment**. So as not to overstate the asset on the books, the company records a write-down, whereby the asset's book value is reduced to its new fair value during the year in which the decline in value occurs. **Disney** recorded a $200 million write-down on its action movie *John Carter*. Disney spent more than $300 million producing the film.

ACTION PLAN

- **Calculate new depreciable cost.**
- **Divide new depreciable cost by new remaining life.**

DO IT! 2b │ Revised Depreciation

Chambers Corporation purchased a piece of equipment for $36,000. It estimated a 6-year life and $6,000 salvage value. Thus, straight-line depreciation was $5,000 per year [($36,000 − $6,000) ÷ 6]. At the end of year three (before the depreciation adjustment), it estimated the new total life to be 10 years and the new salvage value to be $2,000. Compute the revised depreciation.

Solution

Original depreciation expense = [($36,000 − $6,000) ÷ 6] = $5,000
Accumulated depreciation after 2 years = 2 × $5,000 = $10,000
Book value = $36,000 − $10,000 = $26,000

Book value after 2 years of depreciation	$26,000
Less: New salvage value	2,000
Depreciable cost	$24,000
New remaining useful life (10 − 2)	8 years
Revised annual depreciation ($24,000 ÷ 8)	$ 3,000

Related exercise material: **BE9.8, DO IT! 9.2b, and E9.8.**

Plant Asset Disposals

LEARNING OBJECTIVE 3

Explain how to account for the disposal of plant assets.

Companies dispose of plant assets that are no longer useful to them. **Illustration 9.19** shows the three types of asset disposals.

ILLUSTRATION 9.19 **Methods of plant asset disposal**

Retirement	**Sale**	**Exchange**
Equipment is scrapped or discarded.	Equipment is sold to another party.	Existing equipment is traded for new equipment.

Whatever the disposal method, the company must determine the book value of the plant asset at the disposal date to determine the gain or loss on disposal. Recall that the book value is the difference between the cost of the plant asset and the accumulated depreciation to date. If the disposal does not occur on the first day of the year, the company must record depreciation for the fraction of the year to the date of disposal. The company then eliminates the book value by reducing (debiting) Accumulated Depreciation for the total depreciation associated with that asset to the date of disposal and reducing (crediting) the asset account for the cost of the asset.

In this chapter, we examine the accounting for the retirement and sale of plant assets. In the appendix to the chapter, we discuss and illustrate the accounting for exchanges of plant assets.

Sale of Plant Assets

In a disposal by sale, the company compares the book value of the asset with the proceeds received from the sale. If the proceeds of the sale **exceed** the book value of the plant asset, **a gain on disposal occurs**. If the proceeds of the sale **are less than** the book value of the plant asset sold, **a loss on disposal occurs** (see **Helpful Hint**).

Only by coincidence will the book value and the fair value of the asset be the same when the asset is sold. Gains and losses on sales of plant assets are therefore quite common. For example, **Delta Airlines** reported a $94 million gain on the sale of five **Boeing** B727-200 aircraft and five **Lockheed Martin** L-1011-1 aircraft.

Gain on Sale

To illustrate a gain on sale of plant assets, assume that on July 1, 2022, Wright Company sells office furniture for $16,000 cash. The office furniture originally cost $60,000. As of January 1, 2022, it had accumulated depreciation of $41,000. Depreciation for the first six months of 2022 is $8,000. Wright records depreciation expense and updates accumulated depreciation to July 1 with the following entry.

July 1	Depreciation Expense	8,000	
	Accumulated Depreciation—Equipment		8,000
	(To record depreciation expense for the first 6 months of 2022)		

After the accumulated depreciation balance is updated, the company computes the gain or loss. The gain or loss is the difference between the proceeds from the sale and the book value at the date of disposal. **Illustration 9.20** shows this computation for Wright Company, which has a gain on disposal of $5,000.

Cost of office furniture	$60,000
Less: Accumulated depreciation ($41,000 + $8,000)	49,000
Book value at date of disposal	11,000
Proceeds from sale	16,000
Gain on disposal of plant asset	**$ 5,000**

> **HELPFUL HINT**
>
> When disposing of a plant asset, the company removes in the accounting records all amounts related to the asset. This includes the original cost and the total depreciation to date in the Accumulated Depreciation account.

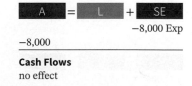

−8,000 Exp
−8,000

Cash Flows
no effect

ILLUSTRATION 9.20

Computation of gain on disposal

Wright records the sale and the gain on disposal of the plant asset as follows.

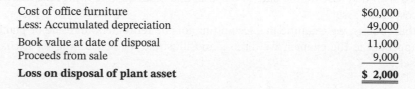

July 1	Cash	16,000	
	Accumulated Depreciation—Equipment	49,000	
	Equipment		60,000
	Gain on Disposal of Plant Assets		5,000
	(To record sale of office furniture at a gain)		

A = L + SE
+16,000
+49,000
−60,000
             +5,000 Rev

Cash Flows
+16,000

Companies report a gain on disposal of plant assets in the "Other revenues and gains" section of the income statement.

Loss on Sale

Assume that instead of selling the office furniture for $16,000, Wright sells it for $9,000. In this case, Wright computes a loss of $2,000 as shown in **Illustration 9.21**.

ILLUSTRATION 9.21

Computation of loss on disposal

Cost of office furniture	$60,000
Less: Accumulated depreciation	49,000
Book value at date of disposal	11,000
Proceeds from sale	9,000
Loss on disposal of plant asset	**$ 2,000**

Wright records the sale and the loss on disposal of the plant asset as follows.

A = L + SE
 +9,000
+49,000
             −2,000 Exp
−60,000

Cash Flows
+9,000

July 1	Cash	9,000	
	Accumulated Depreciation—Equipment	49,000	
	Loss on Disposal of Plant Assets	2,000	
	Equipment		60,000
	(To record sale of office furniture at a loss)		

Companies report a loss on disposal of plant assets in the "Other expenses and losses" section of the income statement.

Retirement of Plant Assets

To illustrate the retirement of plant assets, assume that Hobart Company retires its computer printers, which cost $32,000. The accumulated depreciation on these printers is $32,000. The equipment, therefore, is fully depreciated (zero book value). The entry to record this retirement is as follows.

A = L + SE
+32,000
−32,000

Cash Flows
no effect

	Accumulated Depreciation—Equipment	32,000	
	Equipment		32,000
	(To record retirement of fully depreciated equipment)		

     What happens if a fully depreciated plant asset is still useful to the company? In this case, the asset and its accumulated depreciation continue to be reported on the balance sheet, without further depreciation adjustment, until the company retires the asset. Reporting the asset and related accumulated depreciation on the balance sheet informs the financial statement reader that the asset is still in use. Once fully depreciated, no additional depreciation should be taken, even if an asset is still being used. In no situation can the accumulated depreciation on a plant asset exceed its cost.

If a company retires a plant asset before it is fully depreciated and no cash is received for scrap or salvage value, a loss on disposal occurs. For example, assume that Sunset Company discards delivery equipment that cost $18,000 and has accumulated depreciation of $14,000. The entry is as follows.

Accumulated Depreciation—Equipment	14,000	
Loss on Disposal of Plant Assets	4,000	
Equipment		18,000
(To record retirement of delivery equipment at a loss)		

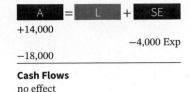

+14,000

−4,000 Exp

−18,000

Cash Flows
no effect

Companies report a loss on disposal of plant assets in the "Other expenses and losses" section of the income statement.

DO IT! 3 | Plant Asset Disposals

Overland Trucking has an old truck that cost $30,000 and has accumulated depreciation of $16,000 at the disposal date. Assume two different situations:

1. The company sells the old truck for $17,000 cash.

2. The truck is worthless, so the company simply retires it.

What entry should Overland use to record each scenario?

Solution

1. Sale of truck for cash:

Cash	17,000	
Accumulated Depreciation—Equipment	16,000	
Equipment		30,000
Gain on Disposal of Plant Assets		3,000
[$17,000 − ($30,000 − $16,000)]		
(To record sale of truck at a gain)		

2. Retirement of truck:

Accumulated Depreciation—Equipment	16,000	
Loss on Disposal of Plant Assets	14,000	
Equipment		30,000
(To record retirement of truck at a loss)		

Related exercise material: **BE9.9, BE9.10, DO IT! 9.3, E9.9, and E9.10.**

ACTION PLAN

- **Compare the asset's book value and its fair value to determine whether a gain or loss has occurred.**

- **Make sure that both the Equipment account and Accumulated Depreciation—Equipment are reduced upon disposal.**

Natural Resources and Intangible Assets

LEARNING OBJECTIVE 4
Describe how to account for natural resources and intangible assets.

Natural Resources

Natural resources consist of standing timber and underground deposits of oil, gas, and minerals (see **Helpful Hint**). These long-lived productive assets have two distinguishing characteristics: (1) they are physically extracted in operations (such as mining, cutting, or pumping), and (2) they are replaceable only by an act of nature.

HELPFUL HINT

On a balance sheet, natural resources may be described more specifically as *timberlands, mineral deposits, oil reserves,* and so on.

The acquisition cost of a natural resource is the price needed to acquire the resource **and** prepare it for its intended use. For an already-discovered resource, such as an existing coal mine, cost is the price paid for the property.

Depletion

The allocation of the cost of natural resources in a rational and systematic manner over the resource's useful life is called **depletion**. (That is, depletion is to natural resources as depreciation is to plant assets.) **Companies generally use the units-of-activity method** (learned earlier in the chapter) **to compute depletion.** The reason is that **depletion generally is a function of the units extracted during the year**.

Under the units-of-activity method, companies divide the total cost of the natural resource minus salvage value by the number of units estimated to be in the resource. The result is a **depletion cost per unit**. To compute depletion, the cost per unit is then multiplied by the number of units extracted.

To illustrate, assume that Lane Coal Company invests $5 million in a mine estimated to have 1 million tons of coal and no salvage value. **Illustration 9.22** shows the computation of the depletion cost per unit.

ILLUSTRATION 9.22

Computation of depletion cost per unit

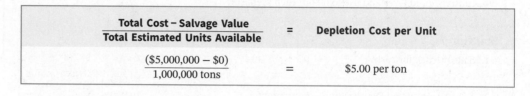

$\dfrac{\text{Total Cost} - \text{Salvage Value}}{\text{Total Estimated Units Available}}$	=	**Depletion Cost per Unit**
$\dfrac{(\$5,000,000 - \$0)}{1,000,000 \text{ tons}}$	=	$5.00 per ton

If Lane extracts 250,000 tons in the first year, then the depletion for the year is $1,250,000 (250,000 tons × $5). It records the depletion as follows.

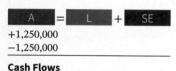

+1,250,000
−1,250,000

Cash Flows
no effect

Inventory (coal)	1,250,000	
Accumulated Depletion		1,250,000
(To record depletion of coal mine)		

Lane debits Inventory for the total depletion for the year and credits Accumulated Depletion to reduce the carrying value of the natural resource. Accumulated Depletion is a contra asset similar to Accumulated Depreciation. Lane credits Inventory when it sells the inventory and debits Cost of Goods Sold. The amount not sold remains in inventory and is reported in the current assets section of the balance sheet.

Some companies do not use an Accumulated Depletion account. In such cases, the company credits the amount of depletion directly to the natural resources account.

Intangible Assets

Intangible assets are rights, privileges, and competitive advantages that result from ownership of long-lived assets that do not possess physical substance. Many companies' most valuable assets are intangible. Some widely known intangible assets are **Microsoft**'s patents, **McDonald's** franchises, the trade name iPod, and **Nike**'s trademark "swoosh."

Financial statements report numerous intangible assets. Yet, many other financially significant intangibles are not reported. To give an example, according to its financial statements in a recent year, **Google** had total stockholders' equity of $22.7 billion. But its market value—the total market value of all its shares on that same date—was roughly $178.5 billion. Thus, its actual market value was about $155.8 billion greater than the amount reported for stockholders' equity on the balance sheet. It is not uncommon for a company's reported book value to differ from its market value because balance sheets are reported at historical cost. But such an extreme difference seriously diminishes the usefulness of the balance sheet to decision-makers. In the case of Google, the difference is due to unrecorded intangibles. For many high-tech or so-called intellectual-property companies, most of their value is from intangibles, many of which are not reported under current accounting rules.

Intangibles may be evidenced by contracts, licenses, and other documents. They may arise from the following sources:

1. Government grants, such as patents, copyrights, licenses, trademarks, and trade names.

2. Acquisition of another business in which the purchase price includes a payment for goodwill.

3. Private monopolistic arrangements arising from contractual agreements, such as franchises and leases.

Accounting for Intangible Assets

Companies record intangible assets at cost. This cost consists of all expenditures necessary for the company to acquire the right, privilege, or competitive advantage. Intangibles are categorized as having either a limited life or an indefinite life. If an intangible has a **limited life**, the company allocates its cost over the asset's useful life using a process similar to depreciation. The process of allocating the cost of intangibles is referred to as **amortization** (see **Helpful Hint**). The cost of intangible assets with **indefinite lives should not be amortized**.

> **HELPFUL HINT**
> *Amortization* is to intangibles what *depreciation* is to plant assets and *depletion* is to natural resources.

To record amortization of an intangible asset, a company increases (debits) Amortization Expense and decreases (credits) the specific intangible asset. (Alternatively, some companies choose to credit a contra account, such as Accumulated Amortization. *For homework purposes, you should directly credit the specific intangible asset.*)

Intangible assets are typically amortized on a straight-line basis. For example, the legal life of a patent is 20 years. Companies **amortize the cost of a patent over its 20-year life or its useful life, whichever is shorter**. To illustrate the computation of patent amortization, assume that National Labs purchases a patent at a cost of $60,000 on June 30. If National estimates the useful life of the patent to be eight years, the annual amortization expense is $7,500 ($60,000 ÷ 8) per year. National records $3,750 ($7,500 × $\frac{6}{12}$) of amortization for the six-month period ended December 31 as follows.

Dec. 31	Amortization Expense	3,750	
	Patents		3,750
	(To record patent amortization)		

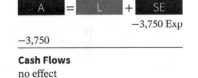

−3,750 Exp
−3,750

Cash Flows
no effect

Companies classify Amortization Expense as an operating expense in the income statement.

There is a difference between intangible assets and plant assets in determining cost. For plant assets, cost includes both the purchase price of the asset and the costs incurred in designing and constructing the asset. In contrast, the initial cost for an intangible asset includes **only the purchase price**. Companies expense any costs incurred in developing an intangible asset.

When a company has significant intangibles, analysts evaluate the reasonableness of the useful life estimates that the company discloses in the notes to its financial statements. In determining useful life, the company should consider obsolescence, inadequacy, and other factors. These may cause a patent or other intangible to become economically ineffective before the end of its legal life.

For example, suppose **Intel** purchased a patent on a new computer chip. The legal life of the patent is 20 years. From experience, however, we know that the useful life of a computer chip patent is rarely more than five years. Because new superior chips are developed so rapidly, existing chips become obsolete. Consequently, we would question the amortization expense of Intel if it amortized its patent on a computer chip for a life significantly longer than a five-year period. Amortizing an intangible over a period that is too long will understate amortization expense, overstate Intel's net income, and overstate its assets.

Types of Intangible Assets

Patents

A **patent** is an exclusive right issued by the U.S. Patent Office that enables the recipient to manufacture, sell, or otherwise control an invention for a period of 20 years from the date of the grant. A patent is nonrenewable. **The initial cost of a patent is the cash or cash equivalent price paid to acquire the patent.**

The saying, "A patent is only as good as the money you're prepared to spend defending it," is very true. Many patents are subject to litigation by competitors. Any legal costs an owner incurs in successfully defending a patent in an infringement suit are considered necessary to establish the patent's validity. **The owner adds those costs to the Patents account and amortizes them over the remaining life of the patent.**

The patent holder amortizes the cost of a patent over its 20-year legal life or its useful life, whichever is shorter. Companies consider obsolescence and inadequacy in determining useful life. These factors may cause a patent to become economically ineffective before the end of its legal life.

Copyrights

The federal government grants **copyrights**, which give the owner the exclusive right to reproduce and sell an artistic or published work. Copyrights last for the life of the creator plus 70 years. The cost of a copyright is the **cost of acquiring and successfully defending it**. The cost may be only the small fee paid to the U.S. Copyright Office, or it may amount to a great deal more if a copyright is acquired from another party. The useful life of a copyright generally is significantly shorter than its legal life. Therefore, copyrights usually are amortized over a relatively short period of time.

Trademarks and Trade Names

A **trademark** or **trade name** is a word, phrase, jingle, or symbol that identifies a particular enterprise or product. Trade names like Wheaties, Monopoly, Big Mac, Kleenex, Coca-Cola, and Jeep create immediate product identification and generally enhance the sale of the product. The creator or original user may obtain exclusive legal right to the trademark or trade name by registering it with the U.S. Patent Office. Such registration provides 20 years of protection. The registration may be renewed indefinitely as long as the trademark or trade name is in use.

If a company purchases the trademark or trade name, its cost is the purchase price. If a company develops and maintains the trademark or trade name, any costs related to these activities are expensed as incurred. Because trademarks and trade names have indefinite lives, they are not amortized.

Accounting Across the Organization   Google

Hattanas/
Shutterstock.com

We Want to Own Glass

Google, which trademarked the term "Google Glass," then wanted to trademark the term "Glass." Why? Because the simple word Glass has marketing advantages over the term Google Glass. It is easy to remember and is more universal. Regulators, however, balked at Google's request. They said that the possible trademark is too similar to other existing or pending software trademarks that contain the word "glass." Also, regulators suggested that the term Glass is merely descriptive and therefore lacks trademark protection. For example, regulators noted that a company that makes salsa could not trademark the term "Spicy Salsa."

BorderStylo LLC, which developed a Web-browser extension called Write on Glass, filed a notice of opposition to Google's request. In the end, the case will probably not be resolved because Google Glass as a company product appears to have failed.

Source: Jacob Gershman, "Google Wants to Own 'Glass'," *Wall Street Journal* (April 4, 2014), p. B5.

If Google had been initially successful in registering the term Glass, where would this trademark be reported on its financial statements? (Go to WileyPLUS for this answer and additional questions.)

Franchises

When you fill up your tank at the corner **Shell** station, eat lunch at **Subway**, or make a reservation at a **Marriott**, you are dealing with franchises. A franchise is a contractual arrangement between a franchisor and a franchisee. The franchisor grants the franchisee the right to sell certain products, to perform specific services, or to use certain trademarks or trade names, usually within a designated geographic area.

Another type of franchise is a **license**. A license granted by a governmental body permits a company to use public property in performing its services. Examples are the use of city streets for a bus line or taxi service; the use of public land for telephone, electric, and cable television lines; and the use of airwaves for radio or TV broadcasting. In a recent license agreement, **FOX**, **CBS**, and **NBC** agreed to pay $27.9 billion for the right to broadcast **NFL** football games over an eight-year period. Franchises and licenses may be granted for a definite period of time, an indefinite period, or perpetually.

When a company incurs costs in connection with the acquisition of the franchise or license, it should recognize an intangible asset. Companies record as **operating expenses** annual payments made under a franchise agreement in the period in which they are incurred. In the case of a limited life, a company amortizes the cost of a franchise (or license) as operating expense over the useful life. If the life is indefinite or perpetual, the cost is not amortized.

Goodwill

Usually, the largest intangible asset that appears on a company's balance sheet is goodwill. Goodwill represents the value of all favorable attributes that relate to a company that are not attributable to any other specific asset. These include exceptional management, desirable location, good customer relations, skilled employees, high-quality products, and harmonious relations with labor unions. Goodwill is unique. Unlike assets such as investments and plant assets, which can be sold **individually** in the marketplace, goodwill can be identified only with the business **as a whole**.

If goodwill can be identified only with the business as a whole, how can its amount be determined? One could try to put a dollar value on the factors listed above (exceptional management, desirable location, and so on). But, the results would be very subjective, and such subjective valuations would not contribute to the reliability of financial statements. **Therefore, companies record goodwill only when an entire business is purchased. When the entire business is purchased, goodwill is the excess of cost over the fair value of the net assets (assets less liabilities) acquired.**

In recording the purchase of a business, the company debits (increases) the identifiable acquired assets at their fair values, credits liabilities at their fair values, credits cash for the purchase price, and records the difference as the cost of goodwill. **Goodwill is not amortized** because it is considered to have an indefinite life. However, goodwill must be written down if a company determines that its value has been permanently impaired.

Research and Development Costs

Research and development costs are expenditures that may lead to patents, copyrights, new processes, and new products (see Helpful Hint). Many companies spend considerable sums of money on research and development (R&D). For example, in a recent year, **Google** spent over $9.8 billion on R&D.

HELPFUL HINT

Research and development (R&D) costs are not intangible assets. But because they may lead to patents and copyrights, we discuss them in this section.

Research and development costs present accounting challenges. For one thing, it is sometimes difficult to assign the costs to specific projects. Also, there are uncertainties in identifying the extent and timing of future benefits. As a result, companies usually record R&D costs **as an expense when incurred** (instead of as an asset), whether the research and development is successful or not.

To illustrate, assume that Laser Scanner Company spent $3 million on R&D that resulted in two highly successful patents. It spent $20,000 on legal fees for the patents. The company would add the lawyers' fees to the Patents account. The R&D costs, however, cannot be

International Note

IFRS allows capitalization of some development costs. This may contribute to differences in R&D expenditures across nations.

included in the cost of the patents. Instead, the company would record the R&D costs as an expense when incurred.

Many disagree with this accounting approach (see **International Note**). They argue that expensing R&D costs leads to understated assets and net income. Others believe that capitalizing these costs will lead to highly speculative assets on the balance sheet. Who is right is difficult to determine.

ACTION PLAN

- **Know that the accounting for an intangible asset often depends on whether the item has a finite or indefinite life.**
- **Recognize the many similarities and differences between the accounting for natural resources, plant assets, and intangible assets.**

DO IT! 4 | Classification Concepts

Match the statement with the term most directly associated with it. Use each term only once.

Copyrights	Depletion
Intangible assets	Franchises
Research and development costs	

1. _____ The allocation of the cost of a natural resource in a rational and systematic manner.

2. _____ Rights, privileges, and competitive advantages that result from the ownership of long-lived assets that do not possess physical substance.

3. _____ An exclusive right granted by the federal government to reproduce and sell an artistic or published work.

4. _____ A right to sell certain products or services or to use certain trademarks or trade names within a designated geographic area.

5. _____ Costs incurred by a company that often lead to patents or new products. These costs must be expensed as incurred.

Solution

1. Depletion
2. Intangible assets
3. Copyrights

4. Franchises
5. Research and development costs

Related exercise material: **BE9.11, BE9.12, DO IT! 9.4, E9.11, E9.12, and E9.13.**

Statement Presentation and Analysis

LEARNING OBJECTIVE 5

Discuss how plant assets, natural resources, and intangible assets are reported and analyzed.

Presentation

Usually, companies combine plant assets and natural resources under "Property, plant, and equipment" in the balance sheet. They show intangible assets separately. **Illustration 9.23** shows the assets section from the balance sheet of Artex Company, with emphasis on the reporting of plant assets.

When a plant asset is fully depreciated, the plant asset and related accumulated depreciation should continue to be reported on the balance sheet without further depreciation or adjustment until the asset is retired. Intangibles do not usually use a contra asset account, such as the contra asset account Accumulated Depreciation used for plant

ILLUSTRATION 9.23
Presentation of property, plant, and equipment, and intangible assets

Artex Company
Balance Sheet (partial)
(in thousands)

Current assets			
Cash		$ 430	
Accounts receivable		100	
Inventory		910	
Total current assets			$ 1,440
Property, plant, and equipment			
Gold mine	$ 530		
Less: Accumulated depletion	210	320	
Land		600	
Buildings	7,600		
Less: Accumulated depreciation—buildings	500	7,100	
Equipment	3,870		
Less: Accumulated depreciation—equipment	620	3,250	
Total property, plant, and equipment			11,270
Intangible assets			
Patents		440	
Trademarks		180	
Goodwill		900	1,520
Total assets			$14,230

assets. Instead, companies record amortization of intangibles as a direct decrease (credit) to the asset account.

Companies may disclose in the balance sheet or the notes to the financial statements the major classes of assets such as land, land improvements, buildings and equipment, and accumulated depreciation (by major classes or in total). In addition, they should describe the depreciation and amortization methods that were used, as well as disclose the amount of depreciation and amortization expense for the period. *For homework purposes, use the format in Illustration 9.23 for preparing balance sheet information.*

Analysis

Using ratios, we can analyze how efficiently a company uses its assets to generate sales. The **asset turnover** analyzes the productivity of a company's assets. It tells us how many dollars of net sales a company generates for each dollar invested in assets. This ratio is computed by dividing net sales by average total assets for the period. **Illustration 9.24** shows the computation of the asset turnover for **Procter & Gamble**. P&G's net sales for a recent year were $76,279 million. Its total ending assets were $129,495 million, and beginning assets were $144,266 million.

ILLUSTRATION 9.24
Asset turnover formula and computation

Net Sales	÷	Average Total Assets	=	Asset Turnover
$76,279	÷	$\dfrac{\$144,266 + \$129,495}{2}$	=	.56 times

Thus, each dollar invested in assets produced $0.56 in net sales for P&G. If a company is using its assets efficiently, each dollar of assets will create a high amount of net sales. This ratio varies greatly among different industries—from those that are asset-intensive (utilities) to those that are not (services).

People, Planet, and Profit Insight BHP

iStock.com/Christian Uhrig

Sustainability Report Please

Sustainability reports identify how the company is meeting its corporate social responsibilities. Many companies, both large and small, are now issuing these reports. For example, companies such as **Disney**, **Best Buy**, **Microsoft**, **Ford**, and **ConocoPhillips** issue these reports. Presented below is an adapted section of a recent **BHP** (a global mining, oil, and gas company) sustainability report on its environmental policies. These policies are to (1) take action to address the challenges of climate change, (2) set and achieve targets that reduce pollution, and (3) enhance biodiversity by assessing and considering ecological values and land-use aspects. Here is how BHP measures the success or failure of some of these policies:

Social Responsibility	Target	Target Date
Safety	• Zero work-related fatalities. • Year-on-year improvement of our total recordable injury frequency (TRIF).	Annual Annual
Health	For our most material exposures of respirable silica, diesel particulate and coal mine dust, we will achieve a 50 percent reduction in the number of workers potentially exposed as compared with the FY2017 baseline.	30 June 2022
Community	Zero significant community events.	Annual
	Our social investment will contribute to improved quality of life in host communities and support achievement of the UN Sustainable Development Goals. We will invest not less than one percent of pre-tax profit (three-year rolling average) in meeting these objectives.	30 June 2022
	Regional Indigenous Peoples Plans will be developed, which support implementation of BHP's Indigenous Peoples Strategy. Plans will include all geographically relevant assets.	30 June 2022
Climate change	Maintain FY2022 greenhouse gas (GHG) emissions at or below FY2017 levels while we continue to grow our business.	30 June 2022
	Longer-term goal: In line with international commitments, BHP aims to achieve net-zero operational GHG emissions in the second half of this century.	The second half of this century.

In addition to the environment, BHP has sections in its sustainability report that discuss people, safety, health, and community.

Why do you believe companies issue sustainability reports? (Go to WileyPLUS for this answer and additional questions.)

ACTION PLAN	DO IT! 5 ⏐ Asset Turnover
• Recognize that the asset turnover analyzes the productivity of a company's assets. • Know the formula Net sales ÷ Average total assets = Asset turnover.	Paramour Company reported net income of $180,000, net sales of $420,000, and total assets of $460,000 on January 1, 2022, and total assets of $540,000 on December 31, 2022. Determine Paramour's asset turnover for 2022.

Solution

The asset turnover for Paramour Company is computed as follows.

Net Sales	÷	Average Total Assets	=	Asset Turnover
$420,000	÷	$\dfrac{\$460,000 + \$540,000}{2}$	=	.84 times

Related exercise material: **BE9.14, DO IT! 9.5, and E9.14.**

| Appendix 9A | Exchange of Plant Assets |

LEARNING OBJECTIVE *6

Explain how to account for the exchange of plant assets.

Ordinarily, companies record a gain or loss on the exchange of plant assets. The rationale for recognizing a gain or loss is that most exchanges have **commercial substance**. An exchange has commercial substance if the future cash flows change as a result of the exchange.

To illustrate, Ramos Co. exchanges some of its equipment for land held by Brodhead Inc. It is likely that the timing and amount of the cash flows arising from the land will differ significantly from the cash flows arising from the equipment. As a result, both Ramos and Brodhead are in different economic positions after the exchange. Therefore, **the exchange has commercial substance**, and the companies recognize a gain or loss in the exchange. Because most exchanges have commercial substance (even when similar assets are exchanged), we illustrate only this type of situation for both a loss and a gain.

Loss Treatment

To illustrate an exchange that results in a loss, assume that Roland Company exchanged a set of used trucks plus cash for a new semi-truck. The used trucks have a combined book value of $42,000 (cost $64,000 less $22,000 accumulated depreciation). Roland's purchasing agent, experienced in the secondhand market, indicates that the used trucks have a fair value of $26,000. In addition to the trucks, Roland must pay $17,000 for the new semi-truck. Roland computes the cost of the new semi-truck as shown in **Illustration 9A.1**.

Fair value of used trucks	$26,000
Cash paid	17,000
Cost of new semi-truck	$43,000

ILLUSTRATION 9A.1

Cost of new semi-truck

Roland incurs a loss on disposal of plant assets of $16,000 on this exchange. The reason is that the book value of the used trucks is greater than the fair value of these trucks. **Illustration 9A.2** shows the computation.

Book value of used trucks ($64,000 − $22,000)	$42,000
Fair value of used trucks	26,000
Loss on disposal of plant assets	**$16,000**

ILLUSTRATION 9A.2

Computation of loss on disposal

In recording an exchange with a loss, four steps are required: (1) eliminate the book value of the asset given up, (2) record the cost of the asset acquired, (3) recognize the loss on disposal of plant assets, and (4) record cash paid or received. Roland Company thus records the exchange as follows.

Equipment (new)	43,000		+43,000	
Accumulated Depreciation—Equipment	22,000		+22,000	
Loss on Disposal of Plant Assets	16,000			−16,000 Exp
Equipment (old)		64,000	−64,000	
Cash		17,000	−17,000	
(To record exchange of used trucks for semi-truck)				

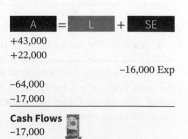

A = L + SE

Cash Flows

−17,000

Gain Treatment

To illustrate a gain situation, assume that Mark Express Delivery decides to exchange its old delivery equipment plus cash of $3,000 for new delivery equipment. The book value of the old delivery equipment is $12,000 (cost $40,000 less accumulated depreciation $28,000). The fair value of the old delivery equipment is $19,000.

The cost of the new asset is the fair value of the old asset exchanged plus any cash paid (or other consideration given up). The cost of the new delivery equipment is $22,000, computed as shown in **Illustration 9A.3**.

ILLUSTRATION 9A.3

Cost of new delivery equipment

Fair value of old delivery equipment	$19,000
Cash paid	3,000
Cost of new delivery equipment	**$22,000**

A gain results when the fair value of the old delivery equipment is greater than its book value. For Mark Express, there is a gain of $7,000 on disposal of plant assets, computed as shown in **Illustration 9A.4**.

ILLUSTRATION 9A.4

Computation of gain on disposal

Fair value of old delivery equipment	$19,000
Book value of old delivery equipment ($40,000 − $28,000)	12,000
Gain on disposal of plant assets	**$ 7,000**

Mark Express records the exchange as follows.

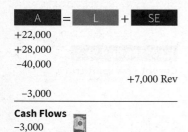

A	=	L	+	SE
+22,000				
+28,000				
−40,000				
				+7,000 Rev
−3,000				

Cash Flows
−3,000

Equipment (new)	22,000	
Accumulated Depreciation—Equipment (old)	28,000	
Equipment (old)		40,000
Gain on Disposal of Plant Assets		7,000
Cash		3,000
(To record exchange of old delivery equipment for new delivery equipment)		

In recording an exchange with a gain, the following four steps are involved: (1) eliminate the book value of the asset given up, (2) record the cost of the asset acquired, (3) recognize the gain on disposal of plant assets, and (4) record cash paid or received.

Review and Practice

Learning Objectives Review

1 Explain the accounting for plant asset expenditures.

The cost of plant assets includes all expenditures necessary to acquire the asset and make it ready for its intended use. Once cost is established, the company uses that amount as the basis of accounting for the plant assets over its useful life.

Companies incur revenue expenditures to maintain the operating efficiency and productive life of an asset. They debit these expenditures to Maintenance and Repairs Expense as incurred. Capital expenditures increase the operating efficiency, productive capacity, or expected useful life of the asset. Companies generally debit these expenditures to the plant asset affected.

2 Apply depreciation methods to plant assets.

Depreciation is the allocation of the cost of a plant asset to expense over its useful (service) life in a rational and systematic manner. Depreciation is not a process of valuation, nor is it a process that results in an accumulation of cash.

Three depreciation methods are:

Method	Effect on Annual Depreciation	Formula
Straight-line	Constant amount	Depreciable cost ÷ Useful life (in years)
Units-of-activity	Varying amount	Depreciable cost per unit × Units of activity during the year
Declining-balance	Decreasing amount	Book value at beginning of year × Declining-balance rate

Companies make revisions of periodic depreciation in present and future periods, not retroactively. They determine the new annual depreciation by dividing the depreciable cost at the time of the revision by the remaining useful life.

3 Explain how to account for the disposal of plant assets.

The accounting for disposal of a plant asset through retirement or sale is as follows. (a) Eliminate the book value of the plant asset at the date of disposal. (b) Record cash proceeds, if any. (c) Account for the difference between the book value and the cash proceeds as a gain or loss on disposal.

4 Describe how to account for natural resources and intangible assets.

Companies compute depletion cost per unit by dividing the total cost of the natural resource minus salvage value by the number of units estimated to be in the resource. They then multiply the depletion cost per unit by the number of units extracted and sold.

The process of allocating the cost of an intangible asset is referred to as amortization. The cost of intangible assets with indefinite lives is not amortized. Companies normally use the straight-line method for amortizing intangible assets.

5 Discuss how plant assets, natural resources, and intangible assets are reported and analyzed.

Companies usually combine plant assets and natural resources under property, plant, and equipment. They show intangible assets separately. Either within the balance sheet or in the notes, companies should disclose the balances of the major classes of assets, such as land, buildings, and equipment, and accumulated depreciation by major classes or in total. They also should describe the depreciation and amortization methods used, and should disclose the amount of depreciation and amortization expense for the period. The asset turnover measures the productivity of a company's assets in generating sales.

*6 Explain how to account for the exchange of plant assets.

Ordinarily, companies record a gain or loss on the exchange of plant assets. The rationale for recognizing a gain or loss is that most exchanges have commercial substance. An exchange has commercial substance if the future cash flows change as a result of the exchange.

Glossary Review

Accelerated-depreciation method Depreciation method that produces higher depreciation expense in the early years than in the later years. (p. 9-12).

Additions and improvements Costs incurred to increase the operating efficiency, productive capacity, or useful life of a plant asset. (p. 9-6).

Amortization The allocation of the cost of an intangible asset to expense over its useful life in a systematic and rational manner. (p. 9-21).

Asset turnover A measure of how efficiently a company uses its assets to generate sales; calculated as net sales divided by average total assets. (p. 9-25).

Capital expenditures Expenditures that increase the company's investment in productive facilities. (p. 9-6).

Cash equivalent price The fair value of the asset given up or the fair value of the asset received, whichever is more clearly determinable. (p. 9-3).

Copyrights Exclusive grant from the federal government that allows the owner to reproduce and sell an artistic or published work. (p. 9-22).

Declining-balance method Depreciation method that applies a constant rate to the declining book value of the asset and produces a decreasing annual depreciation expense over the useful life of the asset. (p. 9-12).

Depletion The allocation of the cost of a natural resource in a rational and systematic manner over the resource's useful life. (p. 9-20).

Depreciable cost The cost of a plant asset less its salvage value. (p. 9-9).

Depreciation The process of allocating to expense the cost of a plant asset over its useful (service) life in a rational and systematic manner. (p. 9-7).

Franchise (license) A contractual arrangement under which the franchisor grants the franchisee the right to sell certain products, perform specific services, or use certain trademarks or trade names, usually within a designated geographic area. (p. 9-23).

Going concern assumption The company will continue in operation for the foreseeable future. (p. 9-8).

Goodwill The value of all favorable attributes that relate to a company that is not attributable to any other specific asset. (p. 9-23).

Impairment A permanent decline in the fair value of an asset. (p. 9-16).

Intangible assets Rights, privileges, and competitive advantages that result from the ownership of long-lived assets that do not possess physical substance. (p. 9-20).

Materiality concept If an item would not make a difference in decision-making, a company does not have to follow GAAP in reporting it. (p. 9-6).

Natural resources Assets that consist of standing timber and underground deposits of oil, gas, and minerals. (p. 9-19).

Ordinary repairs Expenditures to maintain the operating efficiency and productive life of the long-lived asset. (p. 9-5).

Patent An exclusive right issued by the U.S. Patent Office that enables the recipient to manufacture, sell, or otherwise control an invention for a period of 20 years from the date of the grant. (p. 9-22).

Plant assets Tangible resources that are used in the operations of the business and are not intended for sale to customers. (p. 9-3).

Research and development (R&D) costs Expenditures that may lead to patents, copyrights, new processes, or new products. These costs are expensed as incurred. (p. 9-23).

Revenue expenditures Expenditures that are immediately charged against revenues as an expense. (p. 9-6).

Salvage value An estimate of an asset's value at the end of its useful life. (p. 9-8).

Straight-line method Depreciation method in which periodic depreciation is the same for each year of the asset's useful life. (p. 9-9).

Trademark (trade name) A word, phrase, jingle, or symbol that identifies a particular enterprise or product. (p. 9-22).

Units-of-activity method Depreciation method in which useful life is expressed in terms of the total units of production or use expected from an asset. (p. 9-10).

Useful life An estimate of the expected productive life, also called service life, of an asset. (p. 9-8).

Practice Multiple-Choice Questions

1. (LO 1) Corrieten Company purchased equipment and incurred the following costs.

Cash price	$24,000
Sales taxes	1,200
Insurance during transit	200
Installation and testing	400
Total costs	$25,800

What amount should be recorded as the cost of the equipment?

a. $24,000.

b. $25,200.

c. $25,400.

d. $25,800.

2. (LO 1) Additions to plant assets are:

a. revenue expenditures.

b. debited to the Maintenance and Repairs Expense account.

c. debited to the Purchases account.

d. capital expenditures.

3. (LO 2) Depreciation is a process of:

a. valuation.

b. cost allocation.

c. cash accumulation.

d. appraisal.

4. (LO 2) Cuso Company purchased equipment on January 1, 2021, at a total cost of $400,000. The equipment has an estimated salvage value of $10,000 and an estimated useful life of 5 years. The amount of accumulated depreciation at December 31, 2022, if the straight-line method of depreciation is used, is:

a. $80,000.

b. $160,000.

c. $78,000.

d. $156,000.

5. (LO 2) Kant Enterprises purchased a truck for $11,000 on January 1, 2021. The truck has an estimated salvage value of $1,000 at the end of 5 years. Using the units-of-activity method, the balance in accumulated depreciation at December 31, 2022, can be computed by the following formula:

a. ($11,000 ÷ Total estimated activity) × Units of activity for 2022.

b. ($10,000 ÷ Total estimated activity) × Units of activity for 2022.

c. ($11,000 ÷ Total estimated activity) × Units of activity for 2021 and 2022.

d. ($10,000 ÷ Total estimated activity) × Units of activity for 2021 and 2022.

6. (LO 2) Jefferson Company purchased a piece of equipment on January 1, 2022. The equipment cost $60,000 and has an estimated life of 8 years and a salvage value of $8,000. What was the depreciation expense for the asset for 2023 under the double-declining-balance method?

a. $6,500.

b. $11,250.

c. $15,000.

d. $6,562.

7. (LO 2) When there is a change in estimated depreciation:

a. previous depreciation should be corrected.

b. current and future years' depreciation should be revised.

c. only future years' depreciation should be revised.

d. None of the answer choices is correct.

8. (LO 2) Able Towing Company purchased a tow truck for $60,000 on January 1, 2022. It was originally depreciated on a straight-line basis over 10 years with an assumed salvage value of $12,000. On December 31, 2024, before adjusting entries had been made, the company decided to change the remaining estimated life to 4 years (including 2024) and the salvage value to $2,000. What was the depreciation expense for 2024?

a. $6,000.

b. $4,800.

c. $15,000.

d. $12,100.

9. (LO 3) Bennie Razor Company has decided to sell one of its old manufacturing machines on June 30, 2022. The machine was purchased for $80,000 on January 1, 2018, and was depreciated on a straight-line basis for 10 years assuming no salvage value. If the machine was sold for $26,000, what was the amount of the gain or loss recorded at the time of the sale?

a. $18,000.

b. $54,000.

c. $22,000.

d. $46,000.

10. (LO 4) Maggie Sharrer Company expects to extract 20 million tons of coal from a mine that cost $12 million. If no salvage value is expected and 2 million tons are mined in the first year, the entry to record depletion will include a:

a. debit to Accumulated Depletion of $2,000,000.

b. credit to Depletion Expense of $1,200,000.

c. debit to Inventory of $1,200,000.

d. credit to Accumulated Depletion of $2,000,000.

11. (LO 4) Which of the following statements is **false**?

a. If an intangible asset has a finite life, it should be amortized.

b. The amortization period of an intangible asset can exceed 20 years.

c. Goodwill is recorded only when a business is purchased.

d. Research and development costs are expensed when incurred, except when the research and development expenditures result in a successful patent.

12. (LO 4) Martha Beyerlein Company incurred $150,000 of research and development costs in its laboratory to develop a patent granted on January 2, 2022. On July 31, 2022, Beyerlein paid $35,000 for legal fees in a successful defense of the patent. The total amount debited to Patents through July 31, 2022, should be:

 a. $150,000.

 b. $35,000.

 c. $185,000.

 d. $170,000.

13. (LO 5) Indicate which of the following statements is **true**.

 a. Since intangible assets lack physical substance, they need be disclosed only in the notes to the financial statements.

 b. Goodwill should be reported as a contra account in the stockholders' equity section.

 c. Totals of major classes of assets can be shown in the balance sheet, with asset details disclosed in the notes to the financial statements.

 d. Intangible assets are typically combined with plant assets and natural resources, and shown in the property, plant, and equipment section.

14. (LO 5) Lake Coffee Company reported net sales of $180,000, net income of $54,000, beginning total assets of $200,000, and ending total assets of $300,000. What was the company's asset turnover?

 a. 0.90.

 b. 0.20.

 c. 0.72.

 d. 1.39.

*15. (LO 6) Schopenhauer Company exchanged an old machine, with a book value of $39,000 and a fair value of $35,000, and paid $10,000 cash for a similar new machine. The transaction has commercial substance. At what amount should the machine acquired in the exchange be recorded on Schopenhauer's books?

 a. $45,000.

 b. $46,000.

 c. $49,000.

 d. $50,000.

*16. (LO 6) In exchanges of assets in which the exchange has commercial substance:

 a. neither gains nor losses are recognized immediately.

 b. gains, but not losses, are recognized immediately.

 c. losses, but not gains, are recognized immediately.

 d. both gains and losses are recognized immediately.

Solutions

1. d. All of the costs ($1,200 + $200 + $400) in addition to the cash price ($24,000) should be included in the cost of the equipment because they were necessary expenditures to acquire the asset and make it ready for its intended use. The other choices are therefore incorrect.

2. d. When an addition is made to plant assets, it is intended to increase productive capacity, increase the assets' useful life, or increase the efficiency of the assets. This is called a capital expenditure. The other choices are incorrect because (a) additions to plant assets are not revenue expenditures because the additions will have a long-term useful life whereas revenue expenditures are minor repairs and maintenance that do not prolong the life of the assets; (b) additions to plant assets are debited to Plant Assets, not Maintenance and Repairs Expense, because the Maintenance and Repairs Expense account is used to record expenditures not intended to increase the life of the assets; and (c) additions to plant assets are debited to Plant Assets, not Purchases, because the Purchases account is used to record assets intended for resale (inventory).

3. b. Depreciation is a process of allocating the cost of an asset over its useful life, not a process of (a) valuation, (c) cash accumulation, or (d) appraisal.

4. d. Accumulated depreciation will be the sum of 2 years of depreciation expense. Annual depreciation for this asset is ($400,000 – $10,000) ÷ 5 = $78,000. The sum of 2 years' depreciation is therefore $156,000 ($78,000 + $78,000), not (a) $80,000, (b) $160,000, or (c) $78,000.

5. d. The units-of-activity method takes salvage value into consideration; therefore, the depreciable cost is $10,000. This amount is divided by total estimated activity. The resulting number is multiplied by the units of activity used in 2021 and 2022 to compute the accumulated depreciation at the end of 2022, the second year of the asset's use. The other choices are therefore incorrect.

6. b. For the double-declining-balance method, the depreciation rate would be 25% or $\left(\frac{1}{8} \times 2\right)$. For 2022, annual depreciation expense is $15,000 ($60,000 book value × 25%); for 2023, annual depreciation expense is $11,250 [($60,000 – $15,000) × 25%], not (a) $6,500, (c) $15,000, or (d) $6,562.

7. b. When there is a change in estimated depreciation, the current and future years' depreciation computation should reflect the new estimates. The other choices are incorrect because (a) previous years' depreciation should not be adjusted when new estimates are made for

depreciation, and (c) when there is a change in estimated depreciation, the current and future years' depreciation computation should reflect the new estimates. Choice (d) is wrong because there is a correct answer.

8. d. First, calculate accumulated depreciation from January 1, 2022, through December 31, 2023, which is $9,600 {[($60,000 – $12,000) ÷ 10 years] × 2 years}. Next, calculate the revised depreciable cost, which is $48,400 ($60,000 – $9,600 – $2,000). Thus, the depreciation expense for 2024 is $12,100 ($48,400 ÷ 4), not (a) $6,000, (b) $4,800, or (c) $15,000.

9. a. First, the book value needs to be determined. The accumulated depreciation as of June 30, 2022, is $36,000 [($80,000 ÷ 10) × 4.5 years]. Thus, the cost of the machine less accumulated depreciation equals $44,000 ($80,000 – $36,000). The loss recorded at the time of sale is $18,000 ($26,000 – $44,000), not (b) $54,000, (c) $22,000, or (d) $46,000.

10. c. The amount of depletion is determined by computing the depletion per unit ($12 million ÷ 20 million tons = $0.60 per ton) and then multiplying that amount by the number of units extracted during the year (2 million tons × $0.60 = $1,200,000). This amount is debited to Inventory and credited to Accumulated Depletion. The other choices are therefore incorrect.

11. d. Research and development (R&D) costs are expensed when incurred, regardless of whether the research and development expenditures result in a successful patent or not. The other choices are true statements.

12. b. Because the $150,000 was spent developing the patent rather than buying it from another firm, it is debited to Research and Development Expense. Only the $35,000 spent on the successful defense can be debited to Patents, not (a) $150,000, (c) $185,000, or (d) $170,000.

13. c. Reporting only totals of major classes of assets in the balance sheet is appropriate. Additional details can be shown in the notes to the financial statements. The other choices are false statements.

14. c. Asset turnover = Net sales ($180,000) ÷ Average total assets [($200,000 + $300,000) ÷ 2] = 0.72 times, not (a) 0.90, (b) 0.20, or (d) 1.39 times.

*15. a. When an exchange has commercial substance, the debit to the new asset is equal to the fair value of the old asset plus the cash paid ($35,000 + $10,000 = $45,000), not (b) $46,000, (c) $49,000, or (d) $50,000.

*16. d. Both gains and losses are recognized immediately when an exchange of assets has commercial substance. The other choices are therefore incorrect.

Practice Brief Exercises

Compute straight-line and double-declining-balance depreciation.

1. (LO 2) Fulmer Company acquires a delivery truck at a cost of $50,000 on January 1, 2022. The truck is expected to have a salvage value of $5,000 at the end of its 5-year useful life.

   a. Compute annual depreciation expense for the first and second years using the straight-line method.

   b. Compute annual depreciation expense for the first and second years using double-declining-balance.

Solution

1. a. Depreciable cost of $45,000 ($50,000 − $5,000). With a 5-year useful life, annual depreciation is $9,000 ($45,000 ÷ 5). Under the straight-line method, depreciation is the same each year. Thus, depreciation is $9,000 for both the first and second years.

   b. The double-declining-balance rate is 40% (20% × 2), which is applied to book value at the beginning of the year. The computations are:

	Book Value	×	Rate	=	Depreciation Expense
Year 1	$50,000		40%		$20,000
Year 2	($50,000 − $20,000)		40%		$12,000

Prepare entries for disposal by sale.

2. (LO 3) Giolito Company sells equipment on August 31, 2022, for $20,000 cash. The equipment originally cost $60,000 and as of January 1, 2022, had accumulated depreciation of $38,000. Depreciation for the first 8 months of 2022 is $6,000. Prepare the journal entries to (a) update depreciation to August 31, 2022, and (b) record the sale of the equipment.

Solution

2. a. Depreciation Expense   6,000

        Accumulated Depreciation—Equipment   6,000

   b. Cash   20,000

        Accumulated Depreciation—Equipment   44,000

        Equipment   60,000

        Gain on Disposal of Plant Assets   4,000

Cost of equipment	$60,000	
Less: Accumulated depreciation	44,000*	
Book value at date of disposal	16,000	
Proceeds from sale	20,000	
Gain on disposal	$ 4,000	

*$38,000 + $6,000

Prepare amortization expense entry and balance sheet presentation for intangible assets.

3. (LO 4) Lucas Company acquires a limited-life franchise for $200,000 on January 2, 2022. Its estimated useful life is 10 years. (a) Prepare the journal entry to record amortization expense for the first year. (b) Show how this franchise is reported on the balance sheet at the end of the first year.

Solution

3. a. Amortization Expense ($200,000 ÷ 10)   20,000

        Franchises   20,000

   b. Intangible assets

        Franchises $180,000

Practice Exercises

1. (LO 2) Winston Company purchased a new machine on October 1, 2022, at a cost of $120,000. The company estimated that the machine will have a salvage value of $12,000. The machine is expected to be used for 12,000 working hours during its 4-year life.

Determine depreciation for partial periods.

Instructions

Compute the depreciation expense under the following methods for the year indicated, assuming that Winston prepares adjusting entries annually.

   a. Straight-line for 2022.

   b. Units-of-activity for 2022, assuming machine usage was 1,700 hours.

   c. Declining-balance using double the straight-line rate for 2022 and 2023.

Solution

1. a. Straight-line method:

$$\left(\frac{\$120{,}000 - \$12{,}000}{4}\right) = \$27{,}000 \text{ per year}$$

2022 depreciation $= \$27{,}000 \times \frac{3}{12} = \underline{\$6{,}750}$

   b. Units-of-activity method:

$$\left(\frac{\$120{,}000 - \$12{,}000}{12{,}000}\right) = \$9 \text{ per hour}$$

2022 depreciation $= 1{,}700 \text{ hours} \times \$9 = \underline{\$15{,}300}$

   c. Declining-balance method:

2022 depreciation $= \$120{,}000 \times 50\% \times \frac{3}{12} = \underline{\$15{,}000}$

Book value January 1, 2023 $= \$120{,}000 - \$15{,}000 = \underline{\$105{,}000}$

2023 depreciation $= \$105{,}000 \times 50\% = \underline{\$52{,}500}$

2. (LO 4) Lake Company, organized in 2022, has the following transactions related to intangible assets.

Prepare entries to set up appropriate accounts for different intangibles; amortize intangible assets.

1/2/22	Purchased patent (8-year life)	$560,000
4/1/22	Goodwill purchased (indefinite life)	360,000
7/1/22	Acquired 10-year franchise; expiration date 7/1/2032	440,000
9/1/22	Incurred research and development costs	85,000

Instructions

Prepare the necessary entries to record these transactions. All costs incurred were for cash. Make the annual adjusting entries as of December 31, 2022, recording any necessary amortization and reflecting all balances accurately as of that date.

Solution

2.	1/2/22	Patents	560,000	
		Cash		560,000
	4/1/22	Goodwill	360,000	
		Cash		360,000
		(Part of the entry to record purchase of another company)		
	7/1/22	Franchises	440,000	
		Cash		440,000
	9/1/22	Research and Development Expense	85,000	
		Cash		85,000
	12/31/22	Amortization Expense	92,000	
		($560,000 ÷ 8) + [($440,000 ÷ 10) × $\frac{1}{2}$]		
		Patents		70,000
		Franchises		22,000

Ending balances. 12/31/22:
 Patents = $490,000 ($560,000 – $70,000)
 Goodwill = $360,000
 Franchises = $418,000 ($440,000 – $22,000)
 R&D expense = $85,000

Practice Problems

Compute depreciation under different methods.

1. (LO 2) DuPage Company purchases a factory machine at a cost of $18,000 on January 1, 2022. DuPage expects the machine to have a salvage value of $2,000 at the end of its 4-year useful life.

During its useful life, the machine is expected to be used 160,000 hours. Actual annual hourly usage was 2022, 40,000; 2023, 60,000; 2024, 35,000; and 2025, 25,000.

Instructions

Prepare depreciation schedules for the following methods: (a) straight-line, (b) units-of-activity, and (c) declining-balance using double the straight-line rate.

Solution

1. a.

Straight-Line Method

| | Computation | | | Annual | End of Year | |
| | Depreciable | | Depreciation | Depreciation | Accumulated | Book |
Year	Cost*	×	Rate	= Expense	Depreciation	Value
2022	$16,000		25%	$4,000	$ 4,000	$14,000**
2023	16,000		25	4,000	8,000	10,000
2024	16,000		25	4,000	12,000	6,000
2025	16,000		25	4,000	16,000	2,000

  *$18,000 – $2,000
 **$18,000 – $4,000

b.

Units-of-Activity Method

| | Computation | | | Annual | End of Year | |
| | Units of | | Depreciable | Depreciation | Accumulated | Book |
Year	Activity	×	Cost/Unit	= Expense	Depreciation	Value
2022	40,000		$0.10*	$4,000	$ 4,000	$14,000
2023	60,000		0.10	6,000	10,000	8,000
2024	35,000		0.10	3,500	13,500	4,500
2025	25,000		0.10	2,500	16,000	2,000

 *($18,000 – $2,000) ÷ 160,000

c.

Declining-Balance Method

	Computation			Annual	End of Year	
	Book Value			Depreciation	Accumulated	Book
	Beginning of		Depreciation	Depreciation	Accumulated	Book
Year	Year	×	Rate*	= Expense	Depreciation	Value
2022	$18,000		50%	$9,000	$ 9,000	$9,000
2023	9,000		50	4,500	13,500	4,500
2024	4,500		50	2,250	15,750	2,250
2025	2,250		50	250**	16,000	2,000

 *$\frac{1}{4} \times 2$
 **Adjusted to $250 because ending book value should not be less than expected salvage value.

2. (LO 3) On January 1, 2019, Skyline Limousine Co. purchased a limo at an acquisition cost of $28,000. The vehicle has been depreciated by the straight-line method using a 4-year service life and a $4,000 salvage value. The company's fiscal year ends on December 31.

Record disposal of plant asset.

Instructions

Prepare the journal entry or entries to record the disposal of the limousine assuming that it was:

a. Retired and scrapped with no salvage value on January 1, 2023.

b. Sold for $5,000 on July 1, 2022.

Solution

2. a. 1/1/23	Accumulated Depreciation—Equipment		24,000	
	Loss on Disposal of Plant Assets		4,000	
	Equipment			28,000
	(To record retirement of limousine)			
b. 7/1/22	Depreciation Expense*		3,000	
	Accumulated Depreciation—Equipment			3,000
	(To record depreciation to date			
	of disposal)			
	Cash		5,000	
	Accumulated Depreciation—Equipment**		21,000	
	Loss on Disposal of Plant Assets		2,000	
	Equipment			28,000
	(To record sale of limousine)			

$*[(\$28,000 - \$4,000) \div 4] \times \frac{1}{2}$
$**[(\$28,000 - \$4,000) \div 4] \times 3 = \$18,000; \$18,000 + \$3,000$

WileyPLUS

Brief Exercises, DO IT! Exercises, Exercises, Problems, and many additional resources are available for practice in WileyPLUS.

Note: All asterisked Questions, Exercises, and Problems relate to material in the appendix to the chapter.

Questions

1. Ms. Harcross is uncertain about the applicability of the historical cost principle to plant assets. Explain the principle to Ms. Harcross.

2. What are some examples of land improvements?

3. Barrister Company acquires the land and building owned by Noble Company. What types of costs may be incurred to make the asset ready for its intended use if Barrister Company wants to use only the land? If it wants to use both the land and the building?

4. In a recent newspaper release, the president of Magnusson Company asserted that something has to be done about depreciation. The president said, "Depreciation does not come close to accumulating the cash needed to replace the asset at the end of its useful life." What is your response to the president?

5. Melanie is studying for the next accounting examination. She asks your help on two questions: (a) What is salvage value? (b) How is salvage value used in determining depreciable cost under the straight-line method? Answer Melanie's questions.

6. Contrast the straight-line method and the units-of-activity method as to (a) useful life, and (b) the pattern of periodic depreciation over useful life.

7. Contrast the effects of the three depreciation methods on annual depreciation expense.

8. In the fourth year of an asset's 5-year useful life, the company decides that the asset will have a 6-year service life. How should the revision of this estimate be recorded? Why?

9. Distinguish between ordinary repairs and capital expenditures during an asset's useful life.

10. How is a gain or loss on the sale of a plant asset computed?

11. Marsh Corporation owns a machine that is fully depreciated but is still being used. How should Marsh account for this asset and report it in the financial statements?

12. What are natural resources, and what are their distinguishing characteristics?

13. Explain the concept of depletion and how it is computed.

14. What are the similarities and differences between the terms depreciation, depletion, and amortization?

15. Warwick Company hires an accounting intern who says that intangible assets should always be amortized over their legal lives. Is the intern correct? Explain.

16. Goodwill has been defined as the value of all favorable attributes that relate to a business that cannot be attributed to specific identifiable assets. What types of attributes could result in goodwill?

17. Kathy Malone, a business major, is working on a case problem for one of her classes. In the case problem, the company needs to raise cash to market a new product it developed. Doug Price, an engineering major, takes one look at the company's balance sheet and says, "This company has an awful lot of goodwill. Why don't you recommend that it sell some of it to raise cash?" How should Kathy respond to Doug?

18. Under what conditions is goodwill recorded? What is the proper accounting treatment for amortizing goodwill?

19. Often, research and development costs provide companies with lasting benefits. (For example, these costs can lead to the development of a patent that will increase the company's income for many years.) However, generally accepted accounting principles require that such costs be recorded as an expense when incurred. Why?

20. **McDonald's Corporation** reports total average assets of $28.9 billion and net sales of $20.5 billion. What is the company's asset turnover?

21. Peyton Corporation and Rogers Corporation operate in the same industry. Peyton uses the straight-line method to account for depreciation; Rogers uses an accelerated method. Explain what complications might arise in trying to compare the results of these two companies.

22. Mesa Corporation uses straight-line depreciation for financial reporting purposes but an accelerated method for tax purposes. Is it acceptable to use different methods for the two purposes? What is Mesa Corporation's motivation for doing this?

23. You are comparing two companies in the same industry. You have determined that Gore Corp. depreciates its plant assets over a 40-year life, whereas Ross Corp. depreciates its plant assets over a 20-year life. Discuss the implications this has for comparing the results of the two companies.

24. Sosa Company is doing significant work to revitalize its warehouses. It is not sure whether it should capitalize these costs or expense them. What are the implications for current-year net income and future net income of expensing versus capitalizing these costs?

25. What does **Apple** use as the estimated useful life on its buildings? On its machinery and equipment? (*Hint:* You will need to use the notes to Apple's financial statements, available at the company's website.)

* 26. When assets are exchanged in a transaction involving commercial substance, how is the gain or loss on disposal of plant assets computed?

* 27. Unruh Refrigeration Company trades in an old machine for a new model when the fair value of the old machine is greater than its book value. The transaction has commercial substance. Should Unruh recognize a gain on disposal of plant assets? If the fair value of the old machine is less than its book value, should Unruh recognize a loss on disposal of plant assets?

Brief Exercises

Determine the cost of land.

BE9.1 (LO 1), AP These expenditures were incurred by Dobbin Company in purchasing land: cash price $60,000, assumed accrued taxes $5,000, attorney's fees $2,100, real estate broker's commission $3,300, and clearing and grading $3,500. What is the cost of the land?

Determine the cost of a truck.

BE9.2 (LO 1), AP Thoms Company incurs these expenditures in purchasing a truck: cash price $24,000, accident insurance (during use) $2,000, sales taxes $1,080, motor vehicle license $300, and painting and lettering $1,700. What is the cost of the truck?

Prepare entries for delivery truck costs.

BE9.3 (LO 1), AP Krieg Company had the following two transactions related to its delivery truck.

1. Paid $38 for an oil change.

2. Paid $400 to install special shelving units, which increase the operating efficiency of the truck.

Prepare Krieg's journal entries to record these two transactions.

Compute straight-line depreciation.

BE9.4 (LO 2), AP Gordon Chemicals Company acquires a delivery truck at a cost of $31,000 on January 1, 2022. The truck is expected to have a salvage value of $4,000 at the end of its 4-year useful life. Compute annual depreciation for the first and second years using the straight-line method.

Compute depreciation and evaluate treatment.

BE9.5 (LO 2), AN Ivy Company purchased land and a building on January 1, 2022. Management's best estimate of the value of the land was $100,000 and of the building $250,000. However, management told the accounting department to record the land at $230,000 and the building at $120,000. The building is being depreciated on a straight-line basis over 20 years with no salvage value. Why do you suppose management requested this accounting treatment? Is it ethical?

Compute declining-balance depreciation.

BE9.6 (LO 2), AP Gordon Chemicals Company acquires a delivery truck at a cost of $31,000 on January 1, 2022. The truck is expected to have a salvage value of $4,000 at the end of its 4-year useful life. Assuming the declining-balance depreciation rate is double the straight-line rate, compute annual depreciation for the first and second years under the declining-balance method.

Compute depreciation using units-of-activity method.

BE9.7 (LO 2), AP Kwik Taxi Service uses the units-of-activity method in computing depreciation on its taxicabs. Each cab is expected to be driven 150,000 miles. Taxi 10 cost $27,500 and is expected to have a salvage value of $500. Taxi 10 was driven 32,000 miles in 2021 and 33,000 miles in 2022. Compute the depreciation for each year.

BE9.8 (LO 2), AP On January 1, 2022, the Hermann Company general ledger shows Equipment $36,000 and Accumulated Depreciation $13,600. The depreciation resulted from using the straight-line method with a useful life of 10 years and a salvage value of $2,000. On this date, the company concludes that the equipment has a remaining useful life of only 2 years with the same salvage value. Compute the revised annual depreciation.

Compute revised depreciation.

BE9.9 (LO 3), AP Prepare journal entries to record these transactions. (a) Echo Company retires its delivery equipment, which cost $41,000. Accumulated depreciation is also $41,000 on this delivery equipment. No salvage value is received. (b) Assume the same information as in part (a), except that accumulated depreciation for the equipment is $37,200 instead of $41,000.

Journalize entries for disposal of plant assets.

BE9.10 (LO 3), AP Antone Company sells office equipment on July 31, 2022, for $21,000 cash. The office equipment originally cost $72,000 and as of January 1, 2022, had accumulated depreciation of $42,000. Depreciation for the first 7 months of 2022 is $4,600. Prepare the journal entries to (a) update depreciation to July 31, 2022, and (b) record the sale of the equipment.

Journalize entries for sale of plant assets.

BE9.11 (LO 4), AP Franceour Mining Co. purchased for $7 million a mine that is estimated to have 35 million tons of ore and no salvage value. In the first year, 5 million tons of ore are extracted.

a. Prepare the journal entry to record depletion for the first year.

b. Show how this mine is reported on the balance sheet at the end of the first year.

Prepare depletion entry and balance sheet presentation for natural resources.

BE9.12 (LO 4), AP Campanez Company purchases a patent for $140,000 on January 2, 2022. Its estimated useful life is 10 years.

a. Prepare the journal entry to record amortization expense for the first year.

b. Show how this patent is reported on the balance sheet at the end of the first year.

Prepare amortization expense entry and balance sheet presentation for intangible assets.

BE9.13 (LO 5), AP Information related to plant assets, natural resources, and intangible assets at the end of 2022 for Dent Company is as follows: buildings $1,100,000, accumulated depreciation—buildings $600,000, goodwill $410,000, coal mine $500,000, and accumulated depletion—coal mine $108,000. Prepare a partial balance sheet of Dent Company for these items.

Classify long-lived assets on balance sheet.

BE9.14 (LO 5), AP In a recent annual report, **Target** reported beginning total assets of $44.1 billion, ending total assets of $44.5 billion, and net sales of $63.4 billion. Compute Target's asset turnover.

Calculate asset turnover.

*BE9.15 (LO 6), AP** Olathe Company exchanges old delivery equipment for new delivery equipment. The book value of the old delivery equipment is $31,000 (cost $61,000 less accumulated depreciation $30,000). Its fair value is $24,000, and cash of $5,000 is paid. Prepare the entry to record the exchange, assuming the transaction has commercial substance.

Prepare entry for disposal by exchange.

*BE9.16 (LO 6), AP** Olathe Company exchanges old delivery equipment for new delivery equipment. The book value of the old delivery equipment is $31,000 (cost $61,000 less accumulated depreciation $30,000). Its fair value is $33,000, and cash of $5,000 is paid. Prepare the entry to record the exchange.

Prepare entry for disposal by exchange.

DO IT! Exercises

DO IT! 9.1 (LO 1), C Hummer Company purchased a delivery truck. The total cash payment was $30,020, including the following items.

Explain accounting for cost of plant assets.

Negotiated purchase price	$24,000
Installation of special shelving	1,100
Painting and lettering	900
Motor vehicle license	180
Two-year insurance policy	2,400
Sales tax	1,440
Total paid	$30,020

Explain how each of these costs should be accounted for.

DO IT! 9.2a (LO 2), AP On January 1, 2022, Salt Creek Country Club purchased a new riding mower for $15,000. The mower is expected to have a 10-year life with a $1,000 salvage value. What journal entry would Salt Creek make on December 31, 2022, if it uses straight-line depreciation?

Calculate depreciation expense and make journal entry.

DO IT! 9.2b (LO 2), AP Fordon Corporation purchased a piece of equipment for $50,000. It estimated an 8-year life and $2,000 salvage value. At the end of year 4 (before the depreciation adjustment), it estimated the new total life to be 10 years and the new salvage value to be $4,000. Compute the revised depreciation, assuming Fordon uses the straight-line method.

Calculate revised depreciation

Make journal entries to record plant asset disposal.

DO IT! 9.3 (LO 3), AP Bylie Company has an old factory machine that cost $50,000. The machine has accumulated depreciation of $28,000. Bylie has decided to sell the machine.

a. What entry would Bylie make to record the sale of the machine for $25,000 cash?

b. What entry would Bylie make to record the sale of the machine for $15,000 cash?

Match classifications to concepts.

DO IT! 9.4 (LO 4), K Match the statement with the term most directly associated with it. Use each term only once.

Goodwill Amortization
Intangible assets Franchises
Research and development costs

1. _____ Rights, privileges, and competitive advantages that result from the ownership of long-lived assets that do not possess physical substance.

2. _____ The allocation of the cost of an intangible asset to expense in a rational and systematic manner.

3. _____ A right to sell certain products or services, or use certain trademarks or trade names, within a designated geographic area.

4. _____ Costs incurred by a company that often lead to patents or new products. These costs must be expensed as incurred.

5. _____ The excess of the cost of a company over the fair value of the net assets acquired.

Calculate asset turnover.

DO IT! 9.5 (LO 5), AP For 2022, Sale Company reported beginning total assets of $300,000 and ending total assets of $340,000. Its net income for this period was $50,000, and its net sales were $400,000. Compute the company's asset turnover for 2022.

Exercises

Determine cost of plant acquisitions.

E9.1 (LO 1), C Writing The following expenditures relating to plant assets were made by Glenn Company during the first 2 months of 2022.

1. Paid $7,000 of accrued taxes at the time the plant site was acquired.

2. Paid $200 insurance to cover a possible accident loss on new factory machinery while the machinery was in transit.

3. Paid $850 sales taxes on a new delivery truck.

4. Paid $21,000 for parking lots and driveways on the new plant site.

5. Paid $250 to have the company name and slogan painted on the new delivery truck.

6. Paid $8,000 for installation of new factory machinery.

7. Paid $900 for a 2-year accident insurance policy on the new delivery truck.

8. Paid $75 motor vehicle license fee on the new truck.

Instructions

a. Explain the application of the historical cost principle in determining the acquisition cost of plant assets.

b. List the numbers of the transactions, and opposite each indicate the account title to which each expenditure should be debited.

Determine property, plant, and equipment costs.

E9.2 (LO 1), C Adama Company incurred the following costs.

1. Sales tax on factory machinery purchased	$ 5,000
2. Painting of and lettering on truck immediately upon purchase	700
3. Installation and testing of factory machinery	2,000
4. Real estate broker's commission on land purchased	3,500
5. Insurance premium paid for first year's insurance on new truck	880
6. Cost of landscaping on property purchased	7,200
7. Cost of paving parking lot for new building constructed	17,900
8. Cost of clearing, draining, and filling land	13,300
9. Architect's fees on self-constructed building	10,000

Instructions

Indicate to which account Adama would debit each of the costs.

E9.3 (LO 1), AP On March 1, 2022, Boyd Company acquired real estate, on which it planned to construct a small office building, by paying $80,000 in cash. An old warehouse on the property was demolished at a cost of $8,200; the salvaged materials were sold for $1,700. Additional expenditures before construction began included $1,900 attorney's fee for work concerning the land purchase, $5,200 real estate broker's fee, $9,100 architect's fee, and $14,000 to put in driveways and a parking lot.

Determine acquisition costs of land.

Instructions

a. Determine the amount to be recorded as the cost of the land.

b. For each cost not used in part (a), indicate the account to be debited.

E9.4 (LO 2), C Alysha Monet has prepared the following list of statements about depreciation.

Understand depreciation concepts.

1. Depreciation is a process of asset valuation, not cost allocation.

2. Depreciation provides for the proper recording of expenses (efforts) with revenues (results).

3. The book value of a plant asset should approximate its fair value.

4. Depreciation applies to three classes of plant assets: land, buildings, and equipment.

5. Depreciation does not apply to a building because its usefulness and revenue-producing ability generally remain intact over time.

6. The revenue-producing ability of a depreciable asset will decline due to wear and tear and to obsolescence.

7. Recognizing depreciation on an asset results in an accumulation of cash for replacement of the asset.

8. The balance in accumulated depreciation represents the total cost that has been charged to expense since placing the asset in service.

9. Depreciation expense and accumulated depreciation are reported on the income statement.

10. Three factors affect the computation of depreciation: cost, useful life, and salvage value.

Instructions

Identify each statement as true or false. If false, indicate how to correct the statement.

E9.5 (LO 2), AP Yello Bus Lines uses the units-of-activity method in depreciating its buses. One bus was purchased on January 1, 2022, at a cost of $148,000. Over its 4-year useful life, the bus is expected to be driven 100,000 miles. Salvage value is expected to be $8,000.

Compute depreciation under units-of-activity method.

Instructions

a. Compute the depreciable cost per unit.

b Prepare a depreciation schedule assuming actual mileage was: 2022, 26,000; 2023, 32,000; 2024, 25,000; and 2025, 17,000.

E9.6 (LO 2), AP Rottino Company purchased a new machine on October 1, 2022, at a cost of $150,000. The company estimated that the machine will have a salvage value of $12,000. The machine is expected to be used for 10,000 working hours during its 5-year life.

Determine depreciation for partial periods.

Instructions

Compute the depreciation expense under the following methods for the year indicated.

a. Straight-line for 2022.

b. Units-of-activity for 2022, assuming machine usage was 1,700 hours.

c. Declining-balance using double the straight-line rate for 2022 and 2023.

E9.7 (LO 2), AP Linton Company purchased a delivery truck for $34,000 on January 1, 2022. The truck has an expected salvage value of $2,000, and is expected to be driven 100,000 miles over its estimated useful life of 8 years. Actual miles driven were 15,000 in 2022 and 12,000 in 2023.

Compute depreciation using different methods.

Instructions

a. Compute depreciation expense for 2022 and 2023 using (1) the straight-line method, (2) the units-of-activity method, and (3) the double-declining-balance method.

b. Assume that Linton uses the straight-line method.

1. Prepare the journal entry to record 2022 depreciation expense.

2. Show how the truck would be reported in the December 31, 2022, balance sheet.

Compute revised annual depreciation.

E9.8 (LO 2), AP Victor Mineli, the new controller of Santorini Company, has reviewed the expected useful lives and salvage values of selected depreciable assets at the beginning of 2022. Here are his findings:

Type of Asset	Date Acquired	Cost	Accumulated Depreciation, Jan. 1, 2022	Useful Life (in years)		Salvage Value	
				Old	Proposed	Old	Proposed
Building	Jan. 1, 2014	$700,000	$130,000	40	58	$50,000	$35,000
Warehouse	Jan. 1, 2017	120,000	23,000	25	20	5,000	3,600

All assets are depreciated by the straight-line method. Santorini Company uses a calendar year in preparing annual adjusting entries and financial statements. After discussion, management has agreed to accept Victor's proposed changes. (The "Proposed" useful life is total life, not remaining life.)

Instructions

a. Compute the revised annual depreciation on each asset in 2022. (Round to nearest dollar.)

b. Prepare the entry (or entries) to record depreciation on the building in 2022.

Record disposal of equipment.

E9.9 (LO 3), AP Here are selected 2022 transactions of Akron Corporation.

Jan. 1   Retired a piece of machinery that was purchased on January 1, 2012. The machine cost $62,000 and had a useful life of 10 years with no salvage value.

June 30   Sold a computer that was purchased on January 1, 2020. The computer cost $36,000 and had a useful life of 3 years with no salvage value. The computer was sold for $5,000 cash.

Dec. 31   Sold a delivery truck for $9,000 cash. The truck cost $25,000 when it was purchased on January 1, 2019, and was depreciated based on a 5-year useful life with a $4,000 salvage value.

Instructions

Journalize all entries required on the above dates, including entries to update depreciation on assets disposed of, where applicable. Akron Corporation uses straight-line depreciation. (Assume depreciation is up to date as of December 31, 2021).

Journalize entries for disposal of equipment.

E9.10 (LO 3), AP Pryce Company owns equipment that cost $65,000 when purchased on January 1, 2019. It has been depreciated using the straight-line method based on an estimated salvage value of $5,000 and an estimated useful life of 5 years.

Instructions

Prepare Pryce Company's journal entries to record the sale of the equipment in these four independent situations.

a. Sold for $31,000 on January 1, 2022.

b. Sold for $31,000 on May 1, 2022.

c. Sold for $11,000 on January 1, 2022.

d. Sold for $11,000 on October 1, 2022.

Journalize entries for natural resources depletion.

E9.11 (LO 4), AP On July 1, 2022, Friedman Inc. invested $720,000 in a mine estimated to have 900,000 tons of ore of uniform grade. During the last 6 months of 2022, 100,000 tons of ore were mined.

Instructions

a. Prepare the journal entry to record depletion.

b. Assume that the 100,000 tons of ore were mined, but only 80,000 units were sold. How are the costs applicable to the 20,000 unsold units reported?

Prepare adjusting entries for amortization.

E9.12 (LO 4), AP These are selected 2022 transactions for Wyle Corporation:

Jan. 1   Purchased a copyright for $120,000. The copyright has a useful life of 6 years and a remaining legal life of 30 years.

Mar. 1   Purchased a patent with an estimated useful life of 4 years and a legal life of 20 years for $54,000.

Sept. 1   Purchased a small company and recorded goodwill of $150,000. Its useful life is indefinite.

Instructions

Prepare all adjusting entries at December 31 to record amortization required by the events.

E9.13 (LO 4), AP Gill Company, organized in 2022, has the following transactions related to intangible assets.

Prepare entries to set up appropriate accounts for different intangibles; amortize intangible assets.

1/2/22	Purchased patent (7-year life)	$595,000	
4/1/22	Goodwill purchased (indefinite life)	360,000	
7/1/22	Acquired 10-year franchise; expiration date 7/1/2032	480,000	
9/1/22	Incurred research and development costs	185,000	

Instructions

Prepare the necessary entries to record these transactions. All costs incurred were for cash. Make the adjusting entries as of December 31, 2022, recording any necessary amortization and reflecting all balances accurately as of that date.

E9.14 (LO 5), AP During 2022, Paola Corporation reported net sales of $3,500,000 and net income of $1,500,000. Its balance sheet reported average total assets of $1,400,000.

Calculate asset turnover.

Instructions

Calculate the asset turnover.

** E9.15 (LO 6), AP** Presented below are two independent transactions. Both transactions have commercial substance.

Journalize entries for exchanges.

1. Mercy Co. exchanged old trucks (cost $64,000 less $22,000 accumulated depreciation) plus cash of $17,000 for new trucks. The old trucks had a fair value of $38,000.

2. Pence Inc. trades its used machine (cost $12,000 less $4,000 accumulated depreciation) for a new machine. In addition to exchanging the old machine (which had a fair value of $11,000), Pence also paid cash of $3,000.

Instructions

a. Prepare the entry to record the exchange of assets by Mercy Co.

b. Prepare the entry to record the exchange of assets by Pence Inc.

** E9.16 (LO 6), AP** Rizzo's Delivery Company and Overland's Express Delivery exchanged delivery trucks on January 1, 2022. Rizzo's truck cost $22,000. It has accumulated depreciation of $15,000 and a fair value of $3,000. Overland's truck cost $10,000. It has accumulated depreciation of $8,000 and a fair value of $3,000. The transaction has commercial substance.

Journalize entries for the exchange of plant assets.

Instructions

a. Journalize the exchange for Rizzo's Delivery Company.

b. Journalize the exchange for Overland's Express Delivery.

Problems

P9.1A (LO 1), AP Peete Company was organized on January 1. During the first year of operations, the following plant asset expenditures and receipts were recorded in random order.

Determine acquisition costs of land and building.

Debit	
1. Excavation costs for new building	$ 23,000
2. Architect's fees on building plans	33,000
3. Full payment to building contractor	640,000
4. Cost of real estate purchased as a plant site	280,000
5. Cost of parking lots and driveways	29,000
6. Accrued real estate taxes paid at time of purchase of land	3,170
7. Installation cost of fences around property	6,800
8. Cost of demolishing building to make land suitable for construction of new building	31,000
9. Real estate taxes paid for the current year on land	6,400
	$1,052,370

Credit	
10. Proceeds from salvage of demolished building	$ 12,000

Instructions

Analyze the transactions using the following table column headings. Enter the number of each transaction in the Item column, and enter the amounts in the appropriate columns. For amounts in the Other Accounts column, also indicate the account title.

Land $302,170

Item	Land	Buildings	Other Accounts

Compute depreciation under different methods.

P9.2A (LO 2), AP In recent years, Jayme Company has purchased three machines. Because of frequent employee turnover in the accounting department, a different accountant was in charge of selecting the depreciation method for each machine, and various methods have been used. Information concerning the machines is summarized in the table below.

Machine	Acquired	Cost	Salvage Value	Useful Life (in years)	Depreciation Method
1	Jan. 1, 2020	$96,000	$12,000	8	Straight-line
2	July 1, 2021	85,000	10,000	5	Declining-balance
3	Nov. 1, 2021	66,000	6,000	6	Units-of-activity

For the declining-balance method, Jayme Company uses the double-declining rate. For the units-of-activity method, total machine hours are expected to be 30,000. Actual hours of use in the first 3 years were 2021, 800; 2022, 4,500; and 2023, 6,000.

Instructions

a. Machine 2 $60,520

a. Compute the amount of accumulated depreciation on each machine at December 31, 2023.

b. If machine 2 was purchased on April 1 instead of July 1, what would be the depreciation expense for this machine in 2021? In 2022?

Compute depreciation under different methods.

P9.3A (LO 1, 2), AP On January 1, 2022, Evers Company purchased the following two machines for use in its production process.

Machine A: The cash price of this machine was $48,000. Related expenditures also paid in cash included: sales tax $1,700, shipping costs $150, insurance during shipping $80, installation and testing costs $70, and $100 of oil and lubricants to be used with the machinery during its first year of operations. Evers estimates that the useful life of the machine is 5 years with a $5,000 salvage value remaining at the end of that time period. Assume that the straight-line method of depreciation is used.

Machine B: The recorded cost of this machine was $180,000. Evers estimates that the useful life of the machine is 4 years with a $10,000 salvage value remaining at the end of that time period.

Instructions

a. Prepare the following for Machine A.

1. The journal entry to record its purchase on January 1, 2022.

2. The journal entry to record annual depreciation at December 31, 2022.

b. Calculate the amount of depreciation expense that Evers should record for Machine B each year of its useful life under the following assumptions.

1. Evers uses the straight-line method of depreciation.

b. 2. 2022 DDB depreciation $90,000

2. Evers uses the declining-balance method. The rate used is twice the straight-line rate.

3. Evers uses the units-of-activity method and estimates that the useful life of the machine is 125,000 units. Actual usage is as follows: 2022, 45,000 units; 2023, 35,000 units; 2024, 25,000 units; and 2025, 20,000 units.

c. Which method used to calculate depreciation on Machine B reports the highest amount of depreciation expense in year 1 (2022)? The highest amount in year 4 (2025)? The highest total amount over the 4-year period?

Calculate revisions to depreciation expense.

P9.4A (LO 2), AP At the beginning of 2020, Mazzaro Company acquired equipment costing $120,000. It was estimated that this equipment would have a useful life of 6 years and a salvage value of $12,000 at that time. The straight-line method of depreciation was considered the most appropriate to use with this type of equipment. Depreciation is to be recorded at the end of each year.

During 2022 (the third year of the equipment's life), the company's engineers reconsidered their expectations and estimated that the equipment's useful life would probably be 7 years (in total) instead of 6 years. The estimated salvage value was not changed at that time. However, during 2025, the estimated salvage value was reduced to $5,000.

Instructions

Indicate how much depreciation expense should be recorded each year for this equipment, by completing the following table.

Year	Depreciation Expense	Accumulated Depreciation
2020		
2021		
2022		
2023		
2024		
2025		
2026		

2026 depreciation expense
$17,900

P9.5A (LO 2, 3, 5), AP At December 31, 2022, Arnold Corporation reported the following plant assets.

Journalize equipment transactions related to purchase, sale, retirement, and depreciation.

Land		$ 3,000,000
Buildings	$26,500,000	
Less: Accumulated depreciation—buildings	11,925,000	14,575,000
Equipment	40,000,000	
Less: Accumulated depreciation—equipment	5,000,000	35,000,000
Total plant assets		$52,575,000

During 2023, the following selected cash transactions occurred.

Apr.	1	Purchased land for $2,200,000.
May	1	Sold equipment that cost $600,000 when purchased on January 1, 2016. The equipment was sold for $170,000.
June	1	Sold land for $1,600,000. The land cost $1,000,000.
July	1	Purchased equipment for $1,100,000.
Dec. 31		Retired equipment that cost $700,000 when purchased on December 31, 2013. No salvage value was received.

Instructions

a. Journalize the transactions. (*Hint:* You may wish to set up T-accounts, post beginning balances, and then post 2023 transactions.) Arnold uses straight-line depreciation for buildings and equipment. The buildings are estimated to have a 40-year useful life and no salvage value; the equipment is estimated to have a 10-year useful life and no salvage value. Update depreciation on assets disposed of at the time of sale or retirement.

b. Record adjusting entries for depreciation for 2023.

c. Prepare the plant assets section of Arnold's balance sheet at December 31, 2023.

c. Tot. plant assets $50,037,500

P9.6A (LO 3), AP Ceda Co. has equipment that cost $80,000 and that has been depreciated $50,000.

Record disposals.

Instructions

Record the disposal under the following assumptions.

a. It was discarded with no cash received.

b. It was sold for $21,000.

c. It was sold for $31,000.

b. $9,000 loss

P9.7A (LO 4, 5), AP The intangible assets section of Amato Corporation's balance sheet at December 31, 2022, is presented here.

Prepare entries to record transactions related to acquisition and amortization of intangibles; prepare the intangible assets section and note.

Patents ($60,000 cost less $6,000 amortization)	$54,000
Copyrights ($36,000 cost less $25,200 amortization)	10,800
Total	$64,800

The patent was acquired in January 2022 and has a useful life of 10 years. The copyright was acquired in January 2016 and also has a useful life of 10 years. The following cash transactions may have affected intangible assets during 2023.

Jan.	2	Paid $46,800 legal costs to successfully defend the patent against infringement by another company.
Jan.–July		Developed a new product, incurring $230,000 in research and development costs during February. A patent was granted for the product on July 1, and its useful life is equal to its legal life. Legal and other costs for the patent were $20,000.

Sept. 1 Paid $40,000 to a quarterback to appear in commercials advertising the company's products. The commercials aired in September.

Oct. 1 Acquired a copyright for $200,000. The copyright has a useful life and legal life of 50 years.

Instructions

a. Prepare journal entries to record the transactions.

b. Prepare journal entries to record the 2023 amortization expense for intangible assets.

c. Tot. intangibles $315,300

c. Prepare the intangible assets section of the balance sheet at December 31, 2023.

d. Prepare the note to the financial statements on Amato Corporation's intangible assets as of December 31, 2023.

Prepare entries to correct errors in recording and amortizing intangible assets.

P9.8A (LO 4), AP Due to rapid employee turnover in the accounting department, the following transactions involving intangible assets were improperly recorded by Inland Corporation.

1. Inland developed a new manufacturing process, incurring research and development costs of $160,000. The company also purchased a patent for $40,000. In early January, Inland capitalized $200,000 as the cost of the patents. Patent amortization expense of $10,000 was recorded based on a 20-year useful life.

2. On July 1, 2022, Inland purchased a small company and as a result recorded goodwill of $80,000. Inland recorded a half-year's amortization in 2022, based on a 20-year life ($2,000 amortization).

Instructions

Prepare all journal entries necessary to correct any errors made during 2022. Assume the books have not yet been closed for 2022.

Calculate and comment on asset turnover.

P9.9A (LO 5), AP **Writing** LaPorta Company and Lott Corporation, two corporations of roughly the same size, are both involved in the manufacture of in-line skates. Each company depreciates its plant assets using the straight-line approach. An investigation of their financial statements reveals the following information.

	LaPorta Co.	Lott Corp.
Net income	$ 800,000	$1,000,000
Net sales	1,300,000	1,180,000
Average total assets	2,500,000	2,000,000
Average plant assets	1,800,000	1,000,000

Instructions

a. LaPorta .52 times

a. For each company, calculate the asset turnover.

b. Based on your calculations in part (a), comment on the relative effectiveness of the two companies in using their assets to generate net sales.

Prepare financial statements.

P9.10A (LO 5), AP The adjusted trial balance of Feagler Company for the year ended December 31, 2022, is as follows.

	Debit	Credit
Cash	$ 5,500	
Accounts Receivable	3,100	
Note Receivable (due February 20, 2023)	2,000	
Inventory	6,000	
Timberland	21,000	
Land	14,000	
Equipment	35,400	
Patents	11,000	
Accumulated Depletion		$ 3,900
Allowance for Doubtful Accounts		1,000
Accumulated Depreciation—Equipment		8,300
Notes Payable (due January 15, 2023)		4,600
Accounts Payable		2,300
Common Stock		60,000
Retained Earnings		8,500
Sales Revenue		52,000
Interest Revenue		400

	Debit	Credit
Cost of Goods Sold	$ 23,000	
Salaries and Wages Expense	11,400	
Depreciation Expense	2,100	
Amortization Expense	1,600	
Research and Development Expense	1,300	
Bad Debt Expense	500	
License Expense	300	
Interest Expense	800	
Loss on Disposal of Plant Assets	2,000	
Total	$141,000	$141,000

Instructions

Prepare a multiple-step income statement and retained earnings statement for 2022, and a classified balance sheet as of December 31, 2022.

Net income $9,400

Continuing Case

Cookie Creations

(*Note:* This is a continuation of the Cookie Creations case from Chapters 1 through 8.)

CC9 Natalie is also thinking of buying a van that will be used only for business. Natalie is concerned about the impact of the van's cost on her income statement and balance sheet. She has come to you for advice on calculating the van's depreciation.

Go to **WileyPLUS** *for complete case details and instructions.*

leungchopan/
Shutterstock.com

Comprehensive Accounting Cycle Review

ACR9 Milo Corporation's unadjusted trial balance at December 1, 2022, is presented below.

	Debit	Credit
Cash	$ 22,000	
Accounts Receivable	36,800	
Notes Receivable	10,000	
Interest Receivable	–0–	
Inventory	36,200	
Prepaid Insurance	3,600	
Land	20,000	
Buildings	150,000	
Equipment	60,000	
Patent	9,000	
Allowance for Doubtful Accounts		$ 500
Accumulated Depreciation—Buildings		50,000
Accumulated Depreciation—Equipment		24,000
Accounts Payable		27,300
Salaries and Wages Payable		–0–
Notes Payable (due April 30, 2023)		11,000
Interest Payable		–0–
Notes Payable (due in 2028)		35,000
Common Stock		50,000
Retained Earnings		63,600
Dividends	12,000	
Sales Revenue		900,000
Interest Revenue		–0–
Gain on Disposal of Plant Assets		–0–

	Debit	Credit
Bad Debt Expense	–0–	
Cost of Goods Sold	630,000	
Depreciation Expense	–0–	
Insurance Expense	–0–	
Interest Expense	–0–	
Other Operating Expenses	61,800	
Amortization Expense	–0–	
Salaries and Wages Expense	110,000	
	$1,161,400	$1,161,400

The following transactions occurred during December.

Dec. 2   Purchased equipment for $16,000, plus sales taxes of $800 (paid in cash).

    2   Milo sold for $3,500 equipment which originally cost $5,000. Accumulated depreciation on this equipment at January 1, 2022, was $1,800; 2022 depreciation prior to the sale of equipment was $825.

  15   Milo sold for $5,000 on account inventory that cost $3,500.

  23   Salaries and wages of $6,600 were paid for December.

Adjustment data:

1. Milo estimates that uncollectible accounts receivable at year-end are $4,000.

2. The note receivable is a 1-year, 8% note dated April 1, 2022. No interest has been recorded.

3. The balance in prepaid insurance represents payment of a $3,600, 6-month premium on September 1, 2022.

4. The building is being depreciated using the straight-line method over 30 years. The salvage value is $30,000.

5. The equipment owned prior to this year is being depreciated using the straight-line method over 5 years. The salvage value is 10% of cost.

6. The equipment purchased on December 2, 2022, is being depreciated using the straight-line method over 5 years, with a salvage value of $1,800.

7. The patent was acquired on January 1, 2022, and has a useful life of 9 years from that date.

8. Unpaid salaries at December 31, 2022, total $2,200.

9. Both the short-term and long-term notes payable are dated January 1, 2022, and carry a 10% interest rate. All interest is payable in the next 12 months.

10. Income tax expense was $15,000. It was unpaid at December 31.

Instructions

  a. Prepare journal entries for the transactions listed above and adjusting entries.

b. Totals $1,190,775   **b.** Prepare an adjusted trial balance at December 31, 2022.

c. Net income $66,150   **c.** Prepare a 2022 income statement and a 2022 retained earnings statement.

d. Total assets $247,850   **d.** Prepare a December 31, 2022, balance sheet.

Expand Your Critical Thinking

Financial Reporting Problem: Apple Inc.

CT9.1 The financial statements of **Apple Inc.** are presented in Appendix A. The complete annual report, including the notes to the financial statements, is available at the company's website.

Instructions

Answer the following questions.

  a. What were the total cost and book value of property, plant, and equipment at September 29, 2018?

  b. Using the notes to the financial statements, what method of depreciation is used by Apple for financial reporting purposes?

  c. What was the amount of depreciation and amortization expense for each of the 3 years 2016–2018? (*Hint:* Use the statement of cash flows.)

d. Using the statement of cash flows, what are the amounts of property, plant, and equipment purchased in 2018 and 2017?

Comparative Analysis Problem: PepsiCo, Inc. vs. The Coca-Cola Company

CT9.2 PepsiCo, Inc.'s financial statements are presented in Appendix B. Financial statements of **The Coca-Cola Company** are presented in Appendix C. The complete annual reports of PepsiCo and Coca-Cola, including the notes to the financial statements, are available at each company's respective website.

Instructions

a. Compute the asset turnover for each company for 2018.

b. What conclusions concerning the efficiency of assets can be drawn from these data?

Comparative Analysis Problem: Amazon.com, Inc. vs. Walmart Inc.

CT9.3 Amazon.com, Inc.'s financial statements are presented in Appendix D. Financial statements of **Walmart Inc.** are presented in Appendix E. The complete annual reports of Amazon and Walmart, including the notes to the financial statements, are available at each company's respective website.

Instructions

a. Compute the asset turnover for each company using the financial statements at December 31, 2018, for Amazon and at January 31, 2019, for Walmart in Appendices D and E, respectively.

b. What conclusions concerning the efficiency of assets can be drawn from these data?

Real-World Focus

CT9.4 A company's annual report identifies the amount of its plant assets and the depreciation method used.

Instructions

Select a well-known company, search the Internet for the company's website address, and then answer the following questions.

a. What is the name of the company?

b. What is the Internet address of the annual report?

c. At fiscal year-end, what is the net amount of its plant assets?

d. What is the accumulated depreciation?

e. Which method of depreciation does the company use?

Decision-Making Across the Organization

CT9.5 Pinson Company and Estes Company are two companies that are similar in many respects. One difference is that Pinson Company uses the straight-line method and Estes Company uses the declining-balance method at double the straight-line rate. On January 2, 2020, both companies acquired the depreciable assets shown below.

Asset	Cost	Salvage Value	Useful Life
Buildings	$360,000	$20,000	40 years
Equipment	130,000	10,000	10 years

Including the appropriate depreciation charges, annual net income for the companies in the years 2020, 2021, and 2022 and total income for the 3 years were as follows.

	2020	2021	2022	Total
Pinson Company	$84,000	$88,400	$90,000	$262,400
Estes Company	68,000	76,000	85,000	229,000

At December 31, 2022, the balance sheets of the two companies are similar except that Estes Company has more cash than Pinson Company, and the companies' net property, plant, and equipment are different.

Lynda Peace is interested in buying one of the companies. She comes to you for advice.

Instructions

With the class divided into groups, answer the following.

  a. Determine the annual and total depreciation recorded by each company during the 3 years.

  b. Assuming that Estes Company also uses the straight-line method of depreciation instead of the declining-balance method as in (a), prepare comparative income data for the 3 years.

  c. Which company should Lynda Peace buy? Why?

Communication Activity

CT9.6 The chapter presented some concerns regarding the current accounting standards for research and development expenditures.

Instructions

Assume that you are either (a) the president of a company that is very dependent on ongoing research and development, writing a memo to the FASB complaining about the current accounting standards regarding research and development, or (b) the FASB member defending the current standards regarding research and development. Your memo should address the following questions.

  1. By requiring expensing of R&D, do you think companies will spend less on R&D? Why or why not? What are the possible implications for the competitiveness of U.S. companies?

  2. If a company makes a commitment to spend money for R&D, it must believe it has future benefits. Shouldn't these costs therefore be capitalized just like the purchase of any long-lived asset that is believed to have future benefits?

Ethics Case

CT9.7 Clean Aire Anti-Pollution Company is suffering declining sales of its principal product, non-biodegradable plastic cartons. The president, Wade Truman, instructs his controller, Kate Rollins, to lengthen asset lives to reduce depreciation expense. A processing line of automated plastic extruding equipment, purchased for $3.5 million in January 2022, was originally estimated to have a useful life of 8 years and a salvage value of $400,000. Depreciation has been recorded for 2 years on that basis. Wade wants the estimated life changed to 12 years total and the straight-line method continued with no change in the salvage value. Kate is hesitant to make the change, believing it is unethical to increase net income in this manner. Wade says, "Hey, the life is only an estimate, and I've heard that our competition uses a 12-year life on their production equipment."

Instructions

  a. Who are the stakeholders in this situation?

  b. Is the proposed change in asset life unethical, or is it simply a good business practice by an astute president?

  c. What is the effect of Wade's proposed change on net income in the year of change?

All About You

CT9.8 Companies invest substantial sums to ensure that their product is well-known to the consumer. Test your knowledge of who owns some famous brands and their impact on the financial statements.

Instructions

  a. Provide an answer to the four multiple-choice questions below.

  1. Which company owns both Taco Bell and Pizza Hut?

a. McDonald's.	**c.** Yum Brands.
b. CKE.	**d.** Wendy's.

  2. Dairy Queen belongs to:

a. Breyers.	**c.** GE.
b. Berkshire Hathaway.	**d.** The Coca-Cola Company.

  3. Philip Morris, the cigarette maker, is owned by:

a. Altria.	**c.** Boeing.
b. GE.	**d.** ExxonMobil.

4. AOL, a major Internet provider, belongs to:

    a. Microsoft.   **c.** NBC.

    b. Cisco.   **d.** Verizon Communications.

b. How do you think the value of these brands is reported on the appropriate company's balance sheet?

FASB Codification Activity

CT9.9 If your school has a subscription to the FASB Codification, log in and prepare responses to the following.

a. What does it mean to capitalize an item?

b. What is the definition provided for an intangible asset?

c. Your great-uncle, who is a CPA, is impressed that you are taking an accounting class. Based on his experience, he believes that depreciation is something that companies do based on past practice, not on the basis of authoritative guidance. Provide the authoritative literature to support the practice of fixed-asset depreciation.

A Look at IFRS

LEARNING OBJECTIVE 7
Compare the accounting for long-lived assets under GAAP and IFRS.

IFRS follows most of the same principles as GAAP in the accounting for property, plant, and equipment. There are, however, some significant differences in the implementation. IFRS allows the use of revaluation of property, plant, and equipment, and it also requires the use of component depreciation. In addition, there are some significant differences in the accounting for both intangible assets and impairments.

Key Points

The following are the key similarities and differences between GAAP and IFRS as related to the accounting for long-lived assets.

Similarities

- The definition for plant assets for both IFRS and GAAP is essentially the same.
- Both IFRS and GAAP follow the historical cost principle when accounting for property, plant, and equipment at date of acquisition. Cost consists of all expenditures necessary to acquire the asset and make it ready for its intended use.
- Under both IFRS and GAAP, interest costs incurred during construction are capitalized. Recently, IFRS converged to GAAP requirements in this area.
- IFRS also views depreciation as an allocation of cost over an asset's useful life. IFRS permits the same depreciation methods (e.g., straight-line, accelerated, and units-of-activity) as GAAP.
- Under both GAAP and IFRS, changes in the depreciation method used and changes in useful life and salvage value are handled in current and future periods. Prior periods are not affected.
- The accounting for subsequent expenditures (such as ordinary repairs and additions) are essentially the same under IFRS and GAAP.
- The accounting for plant asset disposals is essentially the same under IFRS and GAAP.
- Initial costs to acquire natural resources are recorded in essentially the same manner under IFRS and GAAP.
- The definition of intangible assets is essentially the same under IFRS and GAAP.
- The accounting for exchanges of nonmonetary assets has recently converged between IFRS and GAAP. GAAP now requires that gains on exchanges of nonmonetary assets be recognized if the exchange has commercial substance. This is the same framework used in IFRS.

Differences

- IFRS uses the term **residual value** rather than salvage value to refer to an owner's estimate of an asset's value at the end of its useful life for that owner.

- IFRS allows companies to revalue plant assets to fair value at the reporting date. Companies that choose to use the revaluation framework must follow revaluation procedures. If revaluation is used, it must be applied to all assets in a class of assets. Assets that are experiencing rapid price changes must be revalued on an annual basis; otherwise, less frequent revaluation is acceptable.

- IFRS requires component depreciation. **Component depreciation** specifies that any significant parts of a depreciable asset that have different estimated useful lives should be separately depreciated. Component depreciation is allowed under GAAP but is seldom used.

- As in GAAP, under IFRS the costs associated with research and development are segregated into the two components. Costs in the research phase are always expensed under both IFRS and GAAP. Under IFRS, however, costs in the development phase are capitalized as Development Costs once technological feasibility is achieved.

- IFRS permits revaluation of intangible assets (except for goodwill). GAAP prohibits revaluation of intangible assets.

IFRS Practice

IFRS Self-Test Questions

1. Which of the following statements is **correct**?

   a. Both IFRS and GAAP permit revaluation of property, plant, and equipment and intangible assets (except for goodwill).

   b. IFRS permits revaluation of property, plant, and equipment and intangible assets (except for goodwill).

   c. Both IFRS and GAAP permit revaluation of property, plant, and equipment but not intangible assets.

   d. GAAP permits revaluation of property, plant, and equipment but not intangible assets.

2. Research and development costs are:

   a. expensed under GAAP.

   b. expensed under IFRS.

   c. expensed under both GAAP and IFRS.

   d. None of the answer choices is correct.

IFRS Exercises

IFRS9.1 What is component depreciation, and when must it be used?

IFRS9.2 What is revaluation of plant assets? When should revaluation be applied?

IFRS9.3 Some product development expenditures are recorded as development expenses and others as development costs. Explain the difference between these accounts and how a company decides which classification is appropriate.

International Financial Statement Analysis: Louis Vuitton

IFRS9.4 The financial statements of **Louis Vuitton** are presented in Appendix F. The complete consolidated financial statements, including the notes to its financial statements, are available at the company's website.

Instructions

Use the company's 2018 consolidated financial statements to answer the following questions.

   a. According to the notes to the financial statements, what method or methods does the company use to depreciate "property, plant, and equipment?" What useful lives does it use to depreciate property, plant, and equipment?

   b. Using the notes to the financial statements, explain how the company accounted for its intangible assets with indefinite lives.

   c. Using the notes to the financial statements, determine (1) the balance in Accumulated Amortization and Impairment for intangible assets (other than goodwill), and (2) the balance in Depreciation (and impairment) for property, plant, and equipment.

Answers to IFRS Self-Test Questions

1. b   2. a

monkeybusinessimages/Getty Images

Liabilities

Chapter Preview

The following Feature Story suggests that **General Motors (GM)** and **Ford** accumulated tremendous amounts of debt in their pursuit of auto industry dominance. It is unlikely that they could have grown so large without this debt, but at times the debt threatened their very existence. Given this risk, why do companies borrow money? Why do they sometimes borrow short-term and other times long-term? Besides bank borrowings, what other kinds of debts do companies incur? In this chapter, we address these issues.

Feature Story

And Then There Were Two

Debt can help a company acquire the things it needs to grow. But, it is often the very thing that can also kill a company. A brief history of **Maxwell Car Company** illustrates the role of debt in the U.S. auto industry. In 1920, Maxwell Car Company was on the brink of financial ruin. Because it

was unable to pay its bills, its creditors stepped in and took over. They hired a former **General Motors (GM)** executive named Walter Chrysler to reorganize the company. By 1925, he had taken over the company and renamed it Chrysler. By 1933, **Chrysler** was booming, with sales surpassing even those of **Ford**.

But the next few decades saw Chrysler make a series of blunders. By 1980, with its creditors pounding at the gates, Chrysler was again on the brink of financial ruin.

At that point, Chrysler brought in a former Ford executive named Lee Iacocca to save the company. Iacocca argued that the United States could not afford to let Chrysler fail because of the loss of jobs. He convinced the federal government to grant loan guarantees—promises that if Chrysler failed to pay its creditors, the government would pay them. Iacocca then streamlined operations and brought out some profitable products. Chrysler repaid all of its government-guaranteed loans by 1983, seven years ahead of the scheduled final payment.

To compete in today's global vehicle market, you must be big—really big. So in 1998, Chrysler merged with German automaker **Daimler-Benz** to form **DaimlerChrysler**. For a time, this left just two U.S.-based auto manufacturers—GM and Ford. But in 2007, DaimlerChrysler sold 81% of Chrysler to **Cerberus**, an investment group, to provide much-needed cash infusions to the automaker. In 2009, Daimler turned over its remaining stake to Cerberus. Three days later, Chrysler filed for bankruptcy. But by 2010, it was beginning to show signs of a turnaround.

The car companies are giants. GM and Ford typically rank among the top five U.S. firms in total assets. But GM and Ford accumulated truckloads of debt on their way to getting big. Although debt made it possible to get so big, the Chrysler story, and GM's bankruptcy in 2009, make it clear that debt can also threaten a company's survival.

Chapter Outline

LEARNING OBJECTIVES	REVIEW	PRACTICE
LO 1 Explain how to account for current liabilities.	• What is a current liability? • Notes payable • Sales taxes payable • Unearned revenues • Current maturities of long-term debt • Payroll and payroll taxes payable	**DO IT! 1a** Current Liabilities **1b** Wages and Payroll Taxes
LO 2 Describe the major characteristics of bonds.	• Types of bonds • Issuing procedures • Bond trading • Determining the market price of a bond	**DO IT! 2** Bond Terminology
LO 3 Explain how to account for bond transactions.	• Issuing bonds at face value • Discount or premium on bonds • Issuing bonds at a discount • Issuing bonds at a premium • Redeeming bonds at maturity • Redeeming bonds before maturity	**DO IT! 3a** Bond Issuance **3b** Bond Redemption
LO 4 Explain how to account for long-term notes payable.	• Mortgage notes payable • Lease liabilities	**DO IT! 4** Long-Term Notes
LO 5 Discuss how liabilities are reported and analyzed.	• Presentation • Analysis • Debt and equity financing	**DO IT! 5** Analyzing Liabilities

Go to the Review and Practice section at the end of the chapter for a review of key concepts and practice applications with solutions.

Visit WileyPLUS for additional tutorials and practice opportunities.

Accounting for Current Liabilities

LEARNING OBJECTIVE 1

Explain how to account for current liabilities.

What Is a Current Liability?

You have learned that liabilities are defined as "creditors' claims on total assets" and as "existing debts and obligations." Companies must settle or pay these claims, debts, and obligations at some time in the future by transferring assets or services. The future date on which they are due or payable (the maturity date) is a significant feature of liabilities.

Recall that a **current liability** is a debt that a company expects to pay within one year or the operating cycle, whichever is longer. Debts that do not meet these criteria are **long-term liabilities**.

Financial statement users want to know whether a company's obligations are current or long-term. A company that has more current liabilities than current assets often lacks liquidity, or short-term debt-paying ability. In addition, users want to know the types of liabilities a company has. If a company declares bankruptcy, a specific, predetermined order of payment to creditors exists. Thus, the amount and type of liabilities are of critical importance.

The different types of current liabilities include notes payable, accounts payable, unearned revenues, and accrued liabilities such as taxes, salaries and wages, and interest payable. In the sections that follow, we discuss common types of current liabilities (see **Helpful Hint**).

HELPFUL HINT

In previous chapters, we explained the entries for accounts payable and the adjusting entries for some current liabilities.

Notes Payable

Companies record obligations in the form of written notes as **notes payable**. Notes payable are often used instead of accounts payable because they give the lender formal proof of the obligation in case legal remedies are needed to collect the debt. Companies frequently issue notes payable to meet short-term financing needs. Notes payable usually require the borrower to pay interest.

Notes are issued for varying periods of time. **Those due for payment within one year of the balance sheet date are usually classified as current liabilities.**

To illustrate the accounting for notes payable, assume that First National Bank agrees to lend $100,000 on September 1, 2022, if Cole Williams Co. signs a $100,000, 12%, four-month note maturing on January 1. When a company issues an interest-bearing note, the amount of assets it receives upon issuance of the note generally equals the note's face value. Cole Williams therefore will receive $100,000 cash and will make the following journal entry.

Sept. 1	Cash	100,000	
	Notes Payable		100,000
	(To record issuance of 12%, 4-month note to First National Bank)		

A	=	L	+	SE
+100,000				
		+100,000		

Cash Flows
+ 100,000

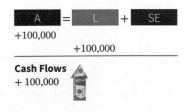

Interest expense accrues over the life of the note, and the company must periodically record that accrual. If Cole Williams prepares financial statements annually, it makes an adjusting entry at December 31 to recognize interest expense and interest payable of $4,000 ($100,000 $\times$ 12% $\times \frac{4}{12}$). **Illustration 10.1** shows the formula for computing interest and its application to Cole Williams' note.

Face Value of Note	$\times$	Annual Interest Rate	$\times$	Time in Terms of One Year	=	Interest
$100,000	$\times$	12%	$\times$	$\frac{4}{12}$	=	$4,000

ILLUSTRATION 10.1

Formula for computing interest expense

Cole Williams makes an adjusting entry as follows.

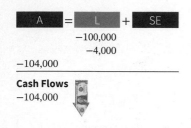

Cash Flows
no effect

Dec. 31	Interest Expense	4,000	
	Interest Payable		4,000
	(To accrue interest for 4 months on First National Bank note)		

In the December 31 financial statements, the current liabilities section of the balance sheet will show notes payable $100,000 and interest payable $4,000. In addition, the company will report interest expense of $4,000 under "Other expenses and losses" in the income statement. If Cole Williams prepared financial statements monthly, the adjusting entry at the end of each month would be $1,000 ($100,000 × 12% × $\frac{1}{12}$).

At maturity (January 1, 2023), Cole Williams must pay the face value of the note ($100,000) plus $4,000 interest ($100,000 × 12% × $\frac{4}{12}$). It records payment of the note and accrued interest as follows.

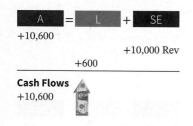

Cash Flows
−104,000

Jan. 1	Notes Payable	100,000	
	Interest Payable	4,000	
	Cash		104,000
	(To record payment of First National Bank interest-bearing note and accrued interest at maturity)		

Sales Taxes Payable

Many of the products we purchase at retail stores are subject to sales taxes. Many states also are now collecting sales taxes on purchases made on the Internet as well. Sales taxes are expressed as a percentage of the sales price. The selling company collects the tax from the customer when the sale occurs. Periodically (usually monthly), the retailer remits the collections to the state's department of revenue. Collecting sales taxes is important. For example, the State of New York recently sued **Sprint Corporation** for $300 million for its alleged failure to collect sales taxes on phone calls.

Under most state sales tax laws, the selling company must enter separately in the cash register the amount of the sale and the amount of the sales tax collected (see **Helpful Hint**). (Gasoline sales are a major exception.) The company then uses the cash register readings to credit Sales Revenue and Sales Taxes Payable. For example, if the March 25 cash register reading for Cooley Grocery shows sales of $10,000 and sales taxes of $600 (sales tax rate of 6%), the journal entry is as follows.

HELPFUL HINT

For point-of-sale systems, the company receives sales information through the computer network.

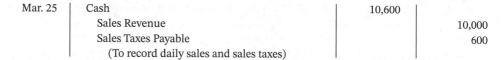

Cash Flows
+10,600

Mar. 25	Cash	10,600	
	Sales Revenue		10,000
	Sales Taxes Payable		600
	(To record daily sales and sales taxes)		

When the company remits the taxes to the taxing agency, it debits Sales Taxes Payable and credits Cash. The company does not report sales taxes as an expense. It simply forwards to the government the amount paid by the customers. Thus, Cooley Grocery serves only as a **collection agent** for the taxing authority.

Sometimes companies do not enter sales taxes separately in the cash register. To determine the amount of sales in such cases, divide total receipts by 100% plus the sales tax percentage. For example, assume that Cooley Grocery enters total receipts of $10,600. The receipts from the sales are equal to the sales price (100%) plus the tax percentage (6% of sales), or 1.06 times the sales total. We can compute the sales amount as follows.

$$\$10,600 \div 1.06 = \$10,000$$

Thus, we can find the sales tax amount of $600 by either (1) subtracting sales from total receipts ($10,600 − $10,000) or (2) multiplying sales by the sales tax rate ($10,000 × .06).

Unearned Revenues

A magazine publisher, such as **Sports Illustrated**, receives customers' checks when they order magazines. An airline company, such as **Southwest Airlines**, often receives cash when it sells tickets for future flights. Season tickets for concerts, sporting events, and theater programs are also paid for in advance. How do companies account for customer cash payments that are received before goods are delivered or services are performed?

1. When a company receives the advance payment, it debits Cash and credits a current liability account identifying the source of the unearned revenue.

2. When the company recognizes revenue by satisfying its performance obligation, it debits an unearned revenue account and credits a revenue account.

To illustrate, assume that Superior University sells 10,000 season football tickets at $50 each for its five-game home schedule. The university makes the following entry for the sale of season tickets.

Aug. 6	Cash (10,000 × $50)	500,000	
	Unearned Ticket Revenue		500,000
	(To record sale of 10,000 season tickets)		

As each game is completed, Superior records the recognition of revenue with the following entry.

Sept. 7	Unearned Ticket Revenue ($500,000 ÷ 5)	100,000	
	Ticket Revenue		100,000
	(To record football ticket revenue)		

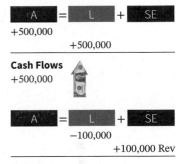

A	=	L	+	SE
+500,000				
		+500,000		

Cash Flows
+500,000

A	=	L	+	SE
		−100,000		
				+100,000 Rev

Cash Flows
no effect

The account Unearned Ticket Revenue represents unearned revenue, and Superior reports it as a current liability. As the school recognizes revenue, it reclassifies the amount from unearned revenue to Ticket Revenue. Unearned revenue is substantial for some companies. In the airline industry, for example, tickets sold for future flights represent almost 50% of total current liabilities. At **United Air Lines**, unearned ticket revenue is its largest current liability, recently amounting to over $1 billion.

Illustration 10.2 shows specific unearned revenue and revenue accounts used in selected types of businesses.

| Type of Business | Account Title | |
	Unearned Revenue	Revenue
Airline	Unearned Ticket Revenue	Ticket Revenue
Magazine publisher	Unearned Subscription Revenue	Subscription Revenue
Hotel	Unearned Rent Revenue	Rent Revenue

ILLUSTRATION 10.2
Unearned revenue and revenue accounts

Current Maturities of Long-Term Debt

Companies often have a portion of long-term debt that comes due in the current year. That amount is considered a current liability. As an example, assume that Wendy Construction issues a five-year, interest-bearing $25,000 note on January 1, 2022. This note specifies that each January 1, starting January 1, 2023, Wendy should pay $5,000 of the note. When the company prepares financial statements on December 31, 2022, it should report $5,000 as a current liability and $20,000 as a long-term liability. (The $5,000 amount is the portion of the note that is due to be paid within the next 12 months.) Companies often identify current maturities of long-term debt on the balance sheet as **long-term debt due within one year**. In a recent year, **General Motors** had $724 million of such debt.

It is not necessary to prepare an adjusting entry to recognize the current maturity of long-term debt. At the balance sheet date, all obligations due within one year are classified as current, and all other obligations as long-term.

ACTION PLAN

- Use the interest formula: Face value of note × Annual interest rate × Time in terms of one year.
- Divide total receipts by 100% plus the tax rate to determine sales revenue; then subtract sales revenue from the total receipts.
- Determine what fraction of the total unearned rent should be recognized this year.

DO IT! 1a | Current Liabilities

You and several classmates are studying for the next accounting examination. They ask you to answer the following questions.

1. If cash is borrowed on a $50,000, 6-month, 12% note on September 1, how much interest expense would be incurred by December 31?
2. How is the sales tax amount determined when the cash register total includes sales taxes?
3. If $15,000 is collected in advance on November 1 for 3 months' rent, what amount of rent revenue should be recognized by December 31?

Solution

1. $\$50,000 \times 12\% \times \frac{4}{12} = \$2,000$
2. First, divide the total cash register receipts by 100% plus the sales tax percentage to find the sales revenue amount. Second, subtract the sales revenue amount from the total cash register receipts to determine the sales taxes.
3. $\$15,000 \times \frac{2}{3} = \$10,000$

Related exercise material: **BE10.1, BE10.2, BE10.3, BE10.4, DO IT! 10.1a, E10.1, E10.2, E10.3, E10.4, and E10.5.**

Payroll and Payroll Taxes Payable

Assume that Susan Alena works 40 hours this week for Pepitone Inc., earning a wage of $10 per hour. Will Susan receive a $400 check at the end of the week? Not likely. The reason: Pepitone is required to withhold amounts from her wages to pay various governmental authorities. For example, Pepitone will withhold amounts for FICA taxes (Social Security and Medicare)[1] and for federal and state income taxes. If these withholdings total $100, Susan will receive a check for only $300. **Illustration 10.3** summarizes the types of payroll deductions that normally occur for most companies.

ILLUSTRATION 10.3

Payroll deductions

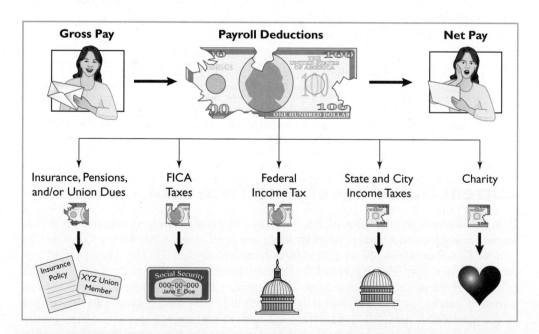

Gross Pay	Payroll Deductions	Net Pay

Insurance, Pensions, and/or Union Dues   FICA Taxes   Federal Income Tax   State and City Income Taxes   Charity

[1]Social Security and Medicare taxes are commonly called FICA taxes. In 1937, Congress enacted the Federal Insurance Contribution Act (FICA) whereby both the employee and employer must make equal contributions to Social Security and Medicare. The recent combined Social Security and Medicare rate was 7.65%. *Our examples and homework use 7.65% for both.*

As a result of these deductions, companies withhold from employee paychecks amounts that must be paid to other parties. Pepitone therefore has incurred a liability to pay these third parties and must report this liability in its balance sheet.

As a second illustration, assume that Cargo Corporation records its payroll for the week of March 7 with the journal entry shown below.

Mar. 7	Salaries and Wages Expense	100,000	
	FICA Taxes Payable		7,650
	Federal Income Taxes Payable		21,864
	State Income Taxes Payable		2,922
	Salaries and Wages Payable		67,564
	(To record payroll and withholding taxes for the week ending March 7)		

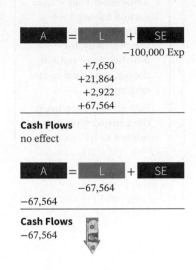

A = L + SE

−100,000 Exp
+7,650
+21,864
+2,922
+67,564

Cash Flows
no effect

Cargo then records payment of this payroll on March 7 as follows.

Mar. 7	Salaries and Wages Payable	67,564	
	Cash		67,564
	(To record payment of the March 7 payroll)		

A = L + SE

−67,564

−67,564

Cash Flows
−67,564

In this case, Cargo records $100,000 in salaries and wages expense. In addition, it records liabilities for the salaries and wages payable as well as liabilities to governmental agencies. Rather than pay the employees $100,000, Cargo instead must withhold the taxes and make the tax payments directly. In summary, Cargo is essentially serving as a tax collector.

In addition to the liabilities incurred as a result of withholdings, employers also incur a second type of payroll-related liability. With every payroll, the **employer** incurs liabilities to pay various **payroll taxes** levied upon the employer. These payroll taxes include the **employer's share** of FICA (Social Security and Medicare) taxes and state and federal unemployment taxes. Based on Cargo Corp.'s $100,000 payroll, the company would record the employer's expense and liability for its payroll taxes as follows.

Mar. 7	Payroll Tax Expense	13,850	
	FICA Taxes Payable		7,650
	Federal Unemployment Taxes Payable		800
	State Unemployment Taxes Payable		5,400
	(To record employer's payroll taxes on March 7 payroll)		

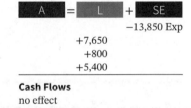

A = L + SE

−13,850 Exp
+7,650
+800
+5,400

Cash Flows
no effect

Companies classify the payroll and payroll tax liability accounts as current liabilities because they must be paid to employees or remitted to taxing authorities periodically and in the near term. Taxing authorities impose substantial fines and penalties on employers if the withholding and payroll taxes are not computed correctly and paid on time.

Anatomy of a Fraud

Art was a custodial supervisor for a large school district. The district was supposed to employ between 35 and 40 regular custodians, as well as 3 or 4 substitute custodians to fill in when regular custodians were absent. Instead, in addition to the regular custodians, Art "hired" 77 substitutes. In fact, almost none of these people worked for the district. Instead, Art submitted time cards for these people, collected their checks at the district office, and personally distributed the checks to the "employees." If a substitute's check was for $1,200, that person would cash the check, keep $200, and pay Art $1,000.

Total take: $150,000

The Missing Controls

Human resource controls. Thorough background checks should be performed. No employees should begin work until they

have been approved by the Board of Education and entered into the payroll system. No employees should be entered into the payroll system until they have been approved by a supervisor. All paychecks should be distributed directly to employees at the official school locations by designated employees or direct-deposited into approved employee bank accounts.

Independent internal verification. Budgets should be reviewed monthly to identify situations where actual costs significantly exceed budgeted amounts.

Source: Adapted from Wells, *Fraud Casebook* (2007), pp. 164–171.

DO IT! 1b | Wages and Payroll Taxes

During the month of September, Lake Corporation's employees earned wages of $60,000. Withholdings related to these wages were $4,590 for FICA, $6,500 for federal income tax, and $2,000 for state income tax. Costs incurred for unemployment taxes were $90 for federal and $150 for state.

Prepare the September 30 journal entries for (a) salaries and wages expense and salaries and wages payable, assuming that all September wages will be paid in October, and (b) the company's payroll tax expense.

Solution

a. To determine wages payable, reduce wages expense by the withholdings for FICA, federal income tax, and state income tax.

Sept. 30	Salaries and Wages Expense	60,000	
	FICA Taxes Payable		4,590
	Federal Income Taxes Payable		6,500
	State Income Taxes Payable		2,000
	Salaries and Wages Payable		46,910

b. Payroll taxes would be for the company's share of FICA, as well as for federal and state unemployment tax.

Sept. 30	Payroll Tax Expense	4,830	
	FICA Taxes Payable		4,590
	Federal Unemployment Taxes Payable		90
	State Unemployment Taxes Payable		150

Related exercise material: **BE10.5, BE10.6, BE10.7, DO IT! 10.1b, E10.6,** and **E10.7.**

Major Characteristics of Bonds

> **LEARNING OBJECTIVE 2**
> Describe the major characteristics of bonds.

Long-term liabilities are obligations that a company expects to pay more than one year in the future. In this section, we explain the accounting for the principal types of obligations reported in the long-term liabilities section of the balance sheet. These obligations often are in the form of bonds or long-term notes.

Bonds are a form of interest-bearing note payable issued by corporations, universities, and governmental agencies. Typically, interest payments are made to the bondholders throughout the term of the bond, and the face value is repaid upon maturity. Bonds, like common stock, are sold in small denominations (usually $1,000 or multiples of $1,000). As a result, bonds attract many investors. When a corporation issues bonds, it is borrowing money. The person who buys the bonds (the bondholder) is lending money.

Types of Bonds

Bonds may have many different features. In the following sections, we describe the types of bonds commonly issued.

Secured and Unsecured Bonds

Secured bonds have specific assets of the issuer pledged as collateral for the bonds. A bond secured by real estate, for example, is called a **mortgage bond**. A bond secured by specific assets set aside to redeem (retire) the bonds is called a **sinking fund bond**.

Unsecured bonds, also called **debenture bonds**, are issued against the general credit of the borrower. Companies with good credit ratings use these bonds extensively. For example, at one time, **DuPont** reported over $2 billion of debenture bonds outstanding.

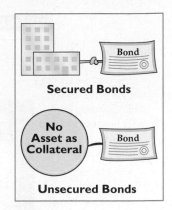

Secured Bonds

Unsecured Bonds

Convertible and Callable Bonds

Bonds that can be converted into common stock at the bondholder's option are **convertible bonds**. Convertible bonds have features that are attractive both to bondholders and to the issuer. The conversion feature often gives bondholders an opportunity to benefit if the market price of the common stock increases substantially. Furthermore, until conversion, the bondholder receives interest on the bond. For the issuer, the bonds sell at a higher price and pay a lower rate of interest than comparable debt securities that do not have a conversion option. Many corporations, such as **USAir**, **United States Steel**, and **General Motors**, have issued convertible bonds.

Bonds that the issuing company can redeem (buy back) at a stated dollar amount prior to maturity are **callable bonds**. Typically, bonds are repaid at the maturity date. The call feature allows companies to repay their debt early.

Convertible Bonds

Callable Bonds

Issuing Procedures

State laws grant corporations the power to issue bonds. Both the board of directors and stockholders usually must approve bond issues. **In authorizing the bond issue, the board of directors must stipulate the number of bonds authorized, total face value, and contractual interest rate**. The total bond authorization often exceeds the number of bonds the company originally issues. This gives the corporation the flexibility to issue more bonds, if needed, to meet future cash requirements.

The **face value** is the amount of principal due at the maturity date. The **maturity date** is the date that the final payment is due to the investor from the issuing company. The **contractual interest rate**, often referred to as the **stated rate**, is the rate used to determine the amount of cash interest the issuing company pays and the investor receives. Usually, the contractual rate is stated as an annual rate.

The terms of the bond issue are set forth in a legal document called a **bond indenture**. The indenture shows the terms and summarizes the rights of the bondholders and their trustees, and the obligations of the issuing company. The **trustee** (usually a financial institution) keeps records of each bondholder, maintains custody of unissued bonds, and holds conditional title to pledged property.

In addition, the issuing company arranges for the printing of **bond certificates**. The indenture and the certificate are separate documents. As shown in **Illustration 10.4**, a bond certificate provides the following information: name of the issuer, face value (par value), contractual interest rate, and maturity date. An investment company that specializes in selling securities generally sells the bonds for the issuing company.

Bond Trading

Bondholders have the opportunity to convert their holdings into cash at any time by selling the bonds at the current market price on national securities exchanges. **Bond prices are quoted as a percentage of the face value of the bond, which is usually $1,000**. A $1,000 face value bond with a quoted price of 97 means that the selling price of the bond is 97% of face value, or $970. Newspapers and the financial press publish bond prices and trading activity daily, as shown in **Illustration 10.5**.

ILLUSTRATION 10.4 **Bond certificate**

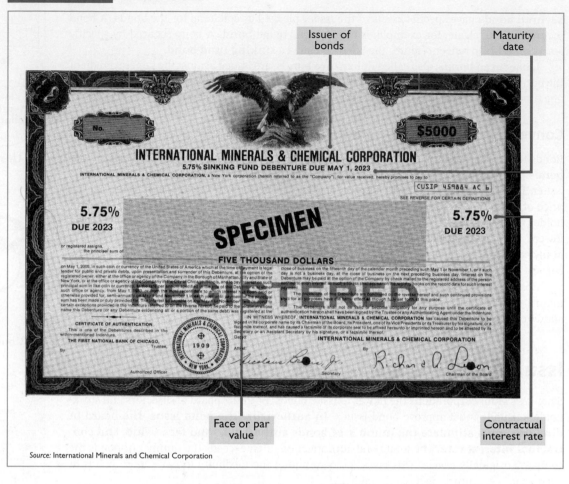

Source: International Minerals and Chemical Corporation

ILLUSTRATION 10.5

Market information for bonds

Issuer	Bonds	Maturity	Close	Yield
Time Warner Cable	6.75	June 15, 2039	116.4	5.49

HELPFUL HINT

The price of a $1,000 bond trading at $95\frac{1}{4}$ is $952.50.

This bond listing indicates that **Time Warner Cable** has outstanding 6.75% (contractual interest rate), $1,000 (face value) bonds that mature in 2039 (see **Helpful Hint**). They currently yield a 5.49% return. At the close of trading, the price was 116.4% of face value, or $1,164.

A corporation makes journal entries **only when it issues or buys back bonds**, when interest is accrued or paid, and when bondholders convert bonds into common stock. For example, **DuPont does not journalize** transactions between its bondholders and other investors. If Tom Smith sells his DuPont bonds to Faith Jones, DuPont does not journalize the transaction.

Determining the Market Price of a Bond

Same dollars at different times are not equal.

If your company needed financing and wanted to attract investors to purchase your bonds, how would the market set the price for these bonds? To be more specific, assume that Coronet, Inc. issues a **zero-interest bond** (pays no interest) with a face value of $1,000,000 due in 20 years. For this bond, the only cash Coronet pays to bond investors is one million dollars at the end of 20 years. Would investors pay one million dollars for this bond? We hope not because one million dollars received 20 years from now is not the same as one million dollars received today.

The term **time value of money** is used to indicate the relationship between time and money—that a dollar received today is worth more than a dollar to be received at some time in the future. If you had $1 million today, you would invest it. From that investment, you would earn interest such that at the end of 20 years, you would have much more than $1 million. Thus, if someone is going to pay you $1 million 20 years from now, you would want to find its equivalent today, or its present value. In other words, you would want to determine the value today of the amount to be received in the future after taking into account current interest rates.

The current market price (present value) of a bond is the value at which it should sell in the marketplace. Market price therefore is a function of the three factors that determine present value: (1) the dollar amounts to be received, (2) the length of time until the amounts are received, and (3) the market rate of interest. The **market interest rate** is the rate investors demand for loaning funds. In most cases, the market interest rate will differ from its contractual interest rate.

To illustrate, assume that Acropolis Company on January 1, 2022, issues $100,000 of 9% bonds, due in five years, with interest payable annually at year-end. The purchaser of the bonds would receive the following two types of cash payments: (1) **principal** of $100,000 to be paid at maturity, and (2) five $9,000 **interest payments** ($100,000 × 9%) over the term of the bonds. **Illustration 10.6** shows a time diagram depicting both cash flows.

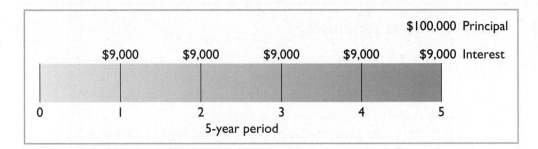

ILLUSTRATION 10.6

Time diagram depicting cash flows

The current market price of a bond is equal to the present value of all the future cash payments promised by the bond. **Illustration 10.7** lists and totals the present values of these amounts, assuming the market rate of interest is 9%.

Present value of $100,000 received in 5 years	$ 64,993
Present value of $9,000 received annually for 5 years	35,007
Market price of bonds	**$100,000**

ILLUSTRATION 10.7

Computing the market price of bonds

Present value calculations involve the use of present value factors. Tables are available to provide the present value numbers to be used, or these values can be determined mathematically or with financial calculators.[2] Appendix G provides further discussion of the concepts and the mechanics of the time value of money computations.

Investor Insight

alphaspirit/Shutterstock.com

Running Hot!

Recently, the market for bonds was running hot. For example, consider these two large deals: **Apple Inc.** sold $17 billion of debt, which at the time was the largest corporate bond ever issued. But shortly thereafter, it was beaten by **Verizon Communications Inc.**, which sold $49 billion of debt. The chart highlights the increased issuance of bonds.

As one expert noted about these increases, "Companies are taking advantage of this lower-rate environment in the limited period of time it is going to be around." An interesting aspect of these bond issuances is that some companies, like

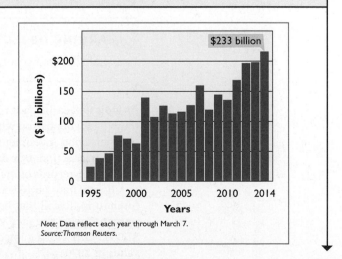

[2]For those knowledgeable in the use of present value tables, the computations in the example shown in Illustration 10.7 are $100,000 × .64993 = $64,993, and $9,000 × 3.88965 = $35,007 (rounded).

Philip Morris International, **Medtronic**, and **Simon Property Group**, are even selling 30-year bonds. These bond issuers are benefitting from "a massive sentiment shift," says one bond expert. The belief that the economy will continue to improve is making investors more comfortable holding longer-term bonds, as they search for investments that offer better returns than U.S. Treasury bonds.

Sources: Vipal Monga, "The Big Number," *Wall Street Journal* (March 20, 2012), p. B5; and Mike Cherney, "Renewed Embrace of Bonds Sparks Boom," *Wall Street Journal* (March 8–9, 2014), p. B5.

What are the advantages for companies of issuing 30-year bonds instead of 5-year bonds? (Go to WileyPLUS for this answer and additional questions.)

ACTION PLAN

- **Review the types of bonds and the basic terms associated with bonds.**

DO IT! 2 | Bond Terminology

State whether each of the following statements is true or false. If false, indicate how to correct the statement.

_____ **1.** Mortgage bonds and sinking fund bonds are both examples of secured bonds.

_____ **2.** Unsecured bonds are also known as debenture bonds.

_____ **3.** The contractual interest rate is the rate investors demand for loaning funds.

_____ **4.** The face value is the amount of principal the issuing company must pay at the maturity date.

_____ **5.** The market price of a bond is equal to its face value.

Solution

1. True.   **2.** True.   **3.** False. The contractual interest rate is used to determine the amount of cash interest the borrower pays.   **4.** True.   **5.** False. The market price of a bond is the value at which it should sell in the marketplace. As a result, the market price of the bond and its face value are often different.

Related exercise material: **DO IT! 10.2 and E10.8.**

Accounting for Bond Transactions

LEARNING OBJECTIVE 3

Explain how to account for bond transactions.

As indicated earlier, a corporation records bond transactions when it issues (sells) or redeems (buys back) bonds and when bondholders convert bonds into common stock. If bondholders sell their bond investments to other investors, the issuing company receives no further cash on this transaction, **nor does the issuing company journalize the transaction** (although it does keep records of the names of bondholders in some cases).

Bonds may be issued at face value, below face value (discount), or above face value (premium). Recall that bond prices for both new issues and existing bonds are quoted as **a percentage of the face value of the bond, and that face value is usually $1,000.** Thus, a $1,000 bond with a quoted price of 97 means that the selling price of the bond is 97% of face value, or $970.

Issuing Bonds at Face Value

To illustrate the accounting for bonds issued at face value, assume that on January 1, 2022, Candlestick Inc. issues $100,000, five-year, 10% bonds at 100 (100% of face value). The entry to record the sale is as follows.

Jan. 1	Cash	100,000	
	Bonds Payable		100,000
	(To record sale of bonds at face value)		

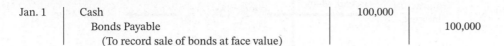

Candlestick reports bonds payable in the long-term liabilities section of the balance sheet because the maturity date is January 1, 2027 (more than one year away).

Over the term (life) of the bonds, companies make entries to record bond interest. Interest on bonds payable is computed in the same manner as interest on notes payable. Assume that interest is payable annually on January 1 on the Candlestick bonds. In that case, Candlestick accrues interest of $10,000 ($100,000 × 10%) on December 31. At December 31, Candlestick recognizes the $10,000 of interest expense incurred with the following entry.

Dec. 31	Interest Expense	10,000	
	Interest Payable		10,000
	(To accrue bond interest)		

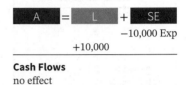

The company classifies interest payable as a current liability because it is scheduled for payment within the next year on January 1. When Candlestick pays the interest on January 1, 2023, it debits (decreases) Interest Payable and credits (decreases) Cash for $10,000.

Candlestick records the payment on January 1 as follows.

Jan. 1	Interest Payable	10,000	
	Cash		10,000
	(To record payment of bond interest)		

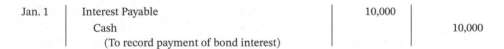

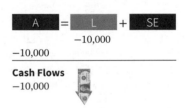

Discount or Premium on Bonds

The previous example assumed that the contractual (stated) interest rate and the market (effective) interest rate paid on the bonds were the same. Recall that the **contractual interest rate** is the rate applied to the face (par) value to arrive at the interest paid in a year. The **market interest rate** is the rate investors demand for loaning funds to the corporation. When the contractual interest rate and the market interest rate are the same, bonds sell **at face value (par value)**.

However, market interest rates change daily. The type of bond issued, the state of the economy, current industry conditions, and the company's performance all affect market interest rates. As a result, contractual and market interest rates often differ. To make bonds salable when the two rates differ, bonds sell below or above face value.

To illustrate, suppose that a company issues 10% bonds at a time when other bonds of similar risk are paying 12%. Investors will not be interested in buying the 10% bonds, so their value will fall below their face value. When a bond is sold for less than its face value, the difference between its face value and selling price is called a **discount**. As a result of the decline in the bonds' selling price, the actual interest rate incurred by the company increases to the level of the current market interest rate.

Conversely, if the market rate of interest is **lower than** the contractual interest rate, investors will have to pay more than face value for the bonds. That is, if the market rate of interest is 8% but the contractual interest rate on the bonds is 10%, the price of the bonds will be bid up. When a bond is sold for more than its face value, the difference between its face value and selling price is called a **premium**. **Illustration 10.8** shows these relationships.

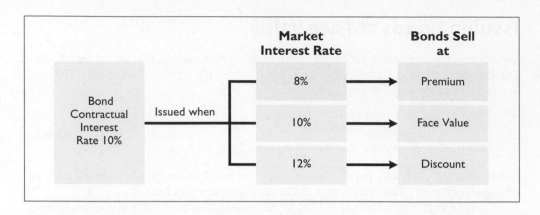

Issuance of bonds at an amount different from face value is quite common. By the time a company prints the bond certificates and markets the bonds, it will be a coincidence if the market rate and the contractual rate are the same. Thus, the issuance of bonds at a discount does not mean that the issuer's financial strength is suspect. Conversely, the sale of bonds at a premium does not indicate that the financial strength of the issuer is exceptional.

Issuing Bonds at a Discount

To illustrate issuance of bonds at a discount, assume that on January 1, 2022, Candlestick Inc. sells $100,000, five-year, 10% bonds for $98,000 (98% of face value). Interest is payable annually on January 1. The entry to record the issuance is as follows (see **Helpful Hint**).

Jan. 1	Cash	98,000	
	Discount on Bonds Payable	2,000	
	Bonds Payable		100,000
	(To record sale of bonds at a discount)		

HELPFUL HINT

Discount on Bonds Payable

Increase Debit	Decrease Credit
↓	
Normal Balance	

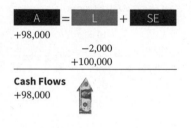

+98,000

−2,000
+100,000

Cash Flows
+98,000

Although Discount on Bonds Payable has a debit balance, **it is not an asset**. Rather, it is a **contra account**. This account is **deducted from bonds payable** on the balance sheet, as shown in **Illustration 10.9**.

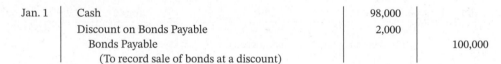

Candlestick Inc.
Balance Sheet (partial)

Long-term liabilities		
Bonds payable	$100,000	
Less: Discount on bonds payable	**2,000**	$98,000

The $98,000 represents the **carrying (or book) value** of the bonds (see **Helpful Hint**). On the date of issue, this amount equals the market price of the bonds.

The issuance of bonds below face value—at a discount—causes the total cost of borrowing to differ from the bond interest paid. That is, the issuing corporation must pay not only the contractual interest rate over the term of the bonds but also the face value (rather than the issuance price) at maturity. Therefore, the difference between the issuance price and face value of the bonds—the discount—is an **additional cost of borrowing**. The company records this additional cost as **interest expense** over the life of the bonds. The total cost of borrowing $98,000 for Candlestick is therefore $52,000, computed as shown in **Illustration 10.10**.

HELPFUL HINT

Carrying value (book value) of bonds issued at a discount is determined by subtracting the balance of the discount account from the balance of the Bonds Payable account.

Bonds Issued at a Discount

Annual interest payments	
($100,000 × 10% = $10,000; $10,000 × 5)	$50,000
Add: Bond discount ($100,000 − $98,000)	2,000
Total cost of borrowing	**$52,000**

Alternatively, we can compute the total cost of borrowing as shown in **Illustration 10.11**.

ILLUSTRATION 10.11

Alternative computation of total cost of borrowing—bonds issued at a discount

Bonds Issued at a Discount	
Principal at maturity	$100,000
Annual interest payments ($10,000 × 5)	50,000
Cash to be paid to bondholders	150,000
Less: Cash received from bondholders	98,000
Total cost of borrowing	**$ 52,000**

To follow the expense recognition principle, companies allocate bond discount to expense in each period in which the bonds are outstanding. This is referred to as **amortizing the discount**. Amortization of the discount **increases** the amount of interest expense reported each period. That is, after the company amortizes the discount, the amount of interest expense it reports in a period will exceed the contractual amount. As shown in Illustration 10.10, for the bonds issued by Candlestick, total interest expense will exceed the contractual interest by $2,000 over the life of the bonds.

As the discount is amortized, its balance declines. As a consequence, the carrying value of the bonds will increase, until at maturity the carrying value of the bonds equals their face amount. This is shown in **Illustration 10.12**. Appendices 10A and 10B at the end of this chapter discuss procedures for amortizing bond discount.

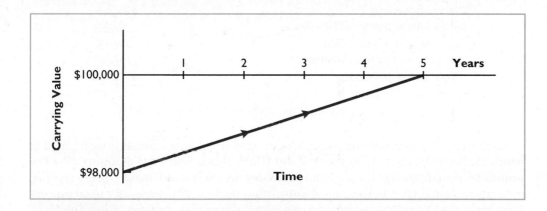

ILLUSTRATION 10.12

Amortization of bond discount

Issuing Bonds at a Premium

To illustrate the issuance of bonds at a premium, we now assume the Candlestick Inc. bonds described above sell for $102,000 (102% of face value) rather than for $98,000. The entry to record the sale is as follows.

Jan. 1	Cash	102,000	
	Bonds Payable		100,000
	Premium on Bonds Payable		2,000
	(To record sale of bonds at a premium)		

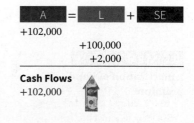

Candlestick adds the premium on bonds payable **to the bonds payable amount** on the balance sheet, as shown in **Illustration 10.13**.

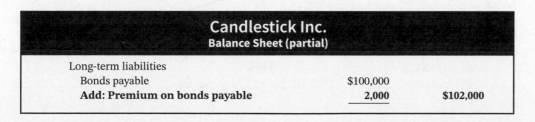

ILLUSTRATION 10.13

Statement presentation of bond premium

Candlestick Inc.		
Balance Sheet (partial)		
Long-term liabilities		
Bonds payable	$100,000	
Add: Premium on bonds payable	**2,000**	**$102,000**

ILLUSTRATION 10.14

Total cost of borrowing— bonds issued at a premium

The sale of bonds above face value causes the total cost of borrowing to be **less than the bond interest paid**. The reason: The borrower is not required to pay the bond premium at the maturity date of the bonds. Thus, the bond premium is considered to be **a reduction in the cost of borrowing** that reduces bond interest over the life of the bonds. The total cost of borrowing $102,000 for Candlestick is shown in **Illustration 10.14** (see **Helpful Hint**).

Bonds Issued at a Premium	
Annual interest payments	
($100,000 × 10% = $10,000; $10,000 × 5)	$50,000
Less: Bond premium ($102,000 − $100,000)	2,000
Total cost of borrowing	**$48,000**

Alternatively, we can compute the cost of borrowing as shown in **Illustration 10.15**.

ILLUSTRATION 10.15

Alternative computation of total cost of borrowing—bonds issued at a premium

Bonds Issued at a Premium	
Principal at maturity	$100,000
Annual interest payments ($10,000 × 5)	50,000
Cash to be paid to bondholders	150,000
Less: Cash received from bondholders	102,000
Total cost of borrowing	**$ 48,000**

Similar to bond discount, companies allocate bond premium to expense in each period in which the bonds are outstanding (see **Helpful Hint**). This is referred to as **amortizing the premium**. Amortization of the premium **decreases** the amount of interest expense reported each period. That is, after the company amortizes the premium, the amount of interest expense it reports in a period will be less than the contractual amount. As shown in Illustration 10.14, for the bonds issued by Candlestick, contractual interest will exceed the interest expense by $2,000 over the life of the bonds.

As the premium is amortized, its balance declines. As a consequence, the carrying value of the bonds will decrease, until at maturity the carrying value of the bonds equals their face amount. This is shown in **Illustration 10.16**. Appendices 10A and 10B at the end of this chapter discuss procedures for amortizing bond premium.

ILLUSTRATION 10.16

Amortization of bond premium

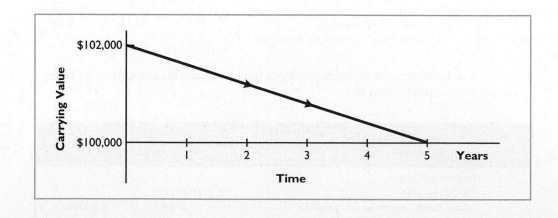

DO IT! 3a | Bond Issuance

Giant Corporation issues $200,000 of bonds for $189,000. (a) Prepare the journal entry to record the issuance of the bonds, and (b) show how the bonds would be reported on the balance sheet at the date of issuance.

Solution

a.

Cash	189,000	
Discount on Bonds Payable	11,000	
Bonds Payable		200,000
(To record sale of bonds at a discount)		

b.

Long-term liabilities		
Bonds payable	$200,000	
Less: Discount on bonds payable	11,000	$189,000

Related exercise material: **BE10.8, BE10.9, BE10.10, BE10.11, BE10.12, DO IT! 10.3a, E10.9, E10.10, and E10.11.**

Redeeming Bonds at Maturity

Regardless of the issue price of bonds, the book value of the bonds at maturity will equal their face value. Assuming that the company pays and records separately the interest for the last interest period, Candlestick Inc. records the redemption of its bonds at maturity as follows.

Jan. 1	Bonds Payable	100,000	
	Cash		100,000
	(To record redemption of bonds at maturity)		

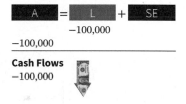

A = L + SE
−100,000
−100,000

Cash Flows
−100,000

Redeeming Bonds Before Maturity

Bonds may be redeemed before maturity. A company may decide to redeem bonds before maturity to reduce interest cost and to remove debt from its balance sheet. A company should redeem debt early only if it has sufficient cash resources.

When a company redeems bonds before maturity, it is necessary to (1) eliminate the carrying value of the bonds at the redemption date, (2) record the cash paid, and (3) recognize the gain or loss on redemption. The **carrying value** of the bonds is the face value of the bonds less any remaining bond discount or plus any remaining bond premium at the redemption date (see **Helpful Hint**).

To illustrate, assume that Candlestick Inc. has sold its bonds at a premium. At the end of the fourth period, Candlestick redeems these bonds at 103 after paying the annual interest. Assume that the carrying value of the bonds at the redemption date is $100,400 (principal $100,000 and premium $400). Candlestick records the redemption at the end of the fourth interest period (January 1, 2026) as follows.

Jan. 1	Bonds Payable	100,000	
	Premium on Bonds Payable	400	
	Loss on Bond Redemption	2,600	
	Cash		103,000
	(To record redemption of bonds at 103)		

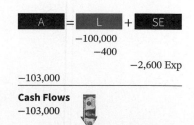

A = L + SE
−100,000
−400
−2,600 Exp
−103,000

Cash Flows
−103,000

Note that the loss of $2,600 is the difference between the cash paid of $103,000 and the carrying value of the bonds of $100,400. Gains and losses from bond redemptions are reported in the income statement as "Other revenues and gains" or "Other expenses and losses."

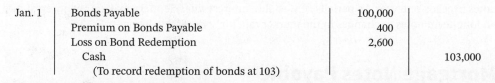

People, Planet, and Profit Insight

CarpathianPrince/
Shutterstock.com

How About Some Green Bonds?

Green bonds are debt used to fund activities such as renewable-energy projects. For example, a company may use the proceeds from the sale of green bonds to clean up its manufacturing operations and cut waste (such as that related to energy consumption).

The use of green bonds has taken off as companies now have guidelines as to how to disclose and report on these green-bond proceeds. These standardized disclosures provide transparency as to how these bonds are used and their effect on overall profitability.

Investors are taking a strong interest in these bonds. Investing companies are installing socially responsible investing teams and have started to integrate sustainability into their investment processes. The disclosures of how companies are using the bond proceeds help investors to make better financial decisions.

Source: Ben Edwards, "Green Bonds Catch On," *Wall Street Journal* (April 3, 2014), p. C5.

Why might standardized disclosure help investors to better understand how proceeds from the sale or issuance of bonds are used? (Go to WileyPLUS for this answer and additional questions.)

ACTION PLAN

- **Determine and eliminate the carrying value of the bonds.**
- **Record the cash paid.**
- **Compute and record the gain or loss (the difference between the first two items).**

DO IT! 3b ⏐ Bond Redemption

R & B Inc. issued $500,000, 10-year bonds at a discount. Prior to maturity, when the carrying value of the bonds is $496,000, the company redeems the bonds at 98. Prepare the entry to record the redemption of the bonds.

Solution

There is a gain on redemption. The cash paid, $490,000 ($500,000 × 98%), is less than the carrying value of $496,000. The entry is:

Bonds Payable	500,000	
Discount on Bonds Payable		4,000
Gain on Bond Redemption		6,000
Cash		490,000
(To record redemption of bonds at 98)		

Related exercise material: **BE10.13, DO IT! 10.3b, E10.12, and E10.13.**

Accounting for Long-Term Notes Payable

LEARNING OBJECTIVE 4

Explain how to account for long-term notes payable.

The use of notes payable in long-term debt financing is quite common. **Long-term notes payable** are similar to short-term interest-bearing notes payable except that the term of the notes exceeds one year. In periods of unstable interest rates, lenders may tie the interest rate on long-term notes to changes in the market rate for comparable loans.

Mortgage Notes Payable

A long-term note may be secured by a **mortgage** that pledges title to specific assets as security for a loan. Individuals widely use **mortgage notes payable** to purchase homes, and many small and some large companies use them to acquire plant assets. At one time, approximately 18% of **McDonald's** long-term debt related to mortgage notes on land, buildings, and improvements.

Like other long-term notes payable, the mortgage loan terms may stipulate either a **fixed** or an **adjustable** interest rate. The interest rate on a fixed-rate mortgage remains the same over the life of the mortgage. The interest rate on an adjustable-rate mortgage is adjusted periodically to reflect changes in the market rate of interest. Typically, the terms require the borrower to make equal installment payments over the term of the loan. Each payment consists of (1) interest on the unpaid balance of the loan and (2) a reduction of loan principal. While the total amount of the payment remains constant, the interest decreases each period, and the portion applied to the loan principal increases.

Companies initially record mortgage notes payable at face value. They subsequently make entries for each installment payment. To illustrate, assume that Porter Technology Inc. issues a $500,000, 8%, 20-year mortgage note on December 31, 2022, to obtain needed financing for a new research laboratory. The terms provide for annual installment payments of $50,926 (not including real estate taxes and insurance). **Illustration 10.17** shows the installment payment schedule for the first four years.

Interest Period	(A) Cash Payment	(B) Interest Expense (D) × 8%	(C) Reduction of Principal (A) − (B)	(D) Principal Balance (D) − (C)
Issue date				$500,000
1	$50,926	$40,000	$10,926	489,074
2	50,926	39,126	11,800	477,274
3	50,926	38,182	12,744	464,530
4	50,926	37,162	13,764	450,766

ILLUSTRATION 10.17

Mortgage installment payment schedule

Porter records the mortgage loan on December 31, 2022, as follows.

Dec. 31	Cash	500,000	
	Mortgage Payable		500,000
	(To record mortgage loan)		

On December 31, 2023, Porter records the first installment payment as follows.

Dec. 31	Interest Expense	40,000	
	Mortgage Payable	10,926	
	Cash		50,926
	(To record annual payment on mortgage)		

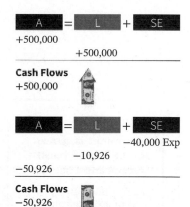

A = L + SE
+500,000
+500,000

Cash Flows
+500,000

A = L + SE
−40,000 Exp
−10,926
−50,926

Cash Flows
−50,926

In the balance sheet, the company reports the reduction in principal for the next year as a current liability, and it classifies the remaining unpaid principal balance as a long-term liability. At December 31, 2023, the total liability is $489,074. Of that amount, $11,800 is current and $477,274 ($489,074 − $11,800) is long-term.

Lease Liabilities

A **lease** is a contractual agreement between a lessor (owner of a property) and a lessee (renter of the property). This arrangement gives the lessee the right to use specific property, which is owned by the **lessor**, for a specified period of time. In return for the use of the property, the **lessee** makes rental payments over the lease term to the lessor.

Leasing has grown tremendously in popularity. Today, it is the fastest growing form of capital investment. Instead of borrowing money to buy an airplane, computer, nuclear core, or satellite, a company makes periodic payments to lease these assets. Even gambling casinos lease their slot machines. The global equipment-leasing market is over a $900 billion business, with the United States accounting for about one-third of the global market.

Accounting for Lease Arrangements

For all leases greater than one year, the lessee records a right-of-use asset and a lease liability. The lease liability is computed as the present value of the lease payments. The right-of-use asset is equal to the lease liability. To illustrate, assume that Gonzalez Company decides to lease new equipment. The lease term is four years; the economic life of the equipment is estimated to be five years. The present value of the lease payments is $190,000.

Gonzalez records the lease arrangement as follows.

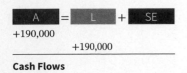

+190,000

      +190,000

Cash Flows
no effect

Right-of-Use Asset	190,000	
Lease Liability		190,000
(To record leased asset and lease liability)		

Balance Sheet Presentation

Gonzalez reports its leased asset on the balance sheet in the long-term assets section. It reports the lease liability on the balance sheet as a liability. The portion of the lease liability expected to be paid in the next year is a current liability. The remainder is classified as a long-term liability.

Income Statement Presentation

The income statement presentation of leases by lessees depends on whether the lease is considered a finance or operating lease. The lease is a finance lease if it meets one of five criteria (discussed in more advanced accounting courses). Leases that do not meet any of these five criteria are considered operating leases.

Under finance lease treatment, the right-of-use asset is amortized (depreciated) in a fashion similar to other fixed assets, and the interest expense is determined in a fashion similar to other long-term liabilities. Under operating lease treatment, a single expense amount is determined. The calculation of this expense amount is complex and is addressed in advanced accounting courses.

ACTION PLAN

- **Record the issuance of the note as a cash receipt and a liability.**
- **Each installment payment consists of interest and payment of principal.**

DO IT! 4 | Long-Term Notes

Cole Research issues a $250,000, 6%, 20-year mortgage note to obtain needed financing for a new lab. The terms call for annual payments of $21,796 each. Prepare the entries to record the mortgage loan and the first payment.

Solution

Cash	250,000	
Mortgage Payable		250,000
(To record mortgage loan)		
Interest Expense	15,000*	
Mortgage Payable	6,796	
Cash		21,796
(To record annual payment on mortgage)		

*Interest expense = $250,000 × 6% = $15,000

Related exercise material: **BE10.14, DO IT! 10.4, and E10.14.**

Reporting and Analyzing Liabilities

Presentation

Current liabilities is the first category under liabilities on the balance sheet. Companies list each of the principal types of current liabilities separately within the category. In addition, companies disclose the terms of notes payable and other key information about the individual items in the notes to the financial statements.

Companies seldom list current liabilities in the order of liquidity. The reason is that varying maturity dates may exist for specific obligations such as notes payable. Or, as a matter of custom, many companies show notes payable first and then accounts payable, regardless of amount. **Illustration 10.18** shows an example.

ILLUSTRATION 10.18

Balance sheet presentation of liabilities

Marais Company		
Balance Sheet (partial)		
Liabilities		
Current liabilities		
Notes payable	$250,000	
Accounts payable	125,000	
Current maturities of long-term debt	300,000	
Salaries and wages payable	75,000	
Total current liabilities		$ 750,000
Long-term liabilities		
Bonds payable	$1,000,000	
Less: Discount on bonds payable	80,000	920,000
Notes payable, secured by plant assets		500,000
Lease liability		440,000
Total long-term liabilities		1,860,000
Total liabilities		$2,610,000

Disclosure of debt is very important. Failures at **Enron**, **WorldCom**, and **Global Crossing** have made investors very concerned about companies' debt obligations (see **Ethics Note**). Summary data regarding debts are reported in the balance sheet with detailed data (such as interest rates, maturity dates, conversion privileges, and assets pledged as collateral) reported in supporting schedules in the notes. Recall that companies should report current maturities of long-term debt as a current liability.

ETHICS NOTE

Some companies try to minimize the amount of debt reported on their balance sheets by not reporting certain types of commitments as liabilities. This subject is of intense interest in the financial community.

Analysis

Careful examination of debt obligations helps you assess a company's ability to pay its current and long-term obligations. It also helps you determine whether a company can obtain debt financing in order to grow. We will use the information from the financial statements of **General Motors** (see **Illustration 10.19**) to illustrate the analysis of a company's liquidity and solvency.

ILLUSTRATION 10.19

Simplified balance sheets for
General Motors

Real World

General Motors Company
Balance Sheets
December 31, 2017 and 2016
(in millions)

Assets	2017	2016
Total current assets	$ 68,744	$ 76,203
Noncurrent assets	143,738	145,487
Total assets	$212,482	$221,690
Liabilities and Stockholders' Equity		
Total current liabilities	$ 76,890	$ 85,181
Noncurrent liabilities	99,392	92,434
Total liabilities	176,282	177,615
Total stockholders' equity	36,200	44,075
Total liabilities and stockholders' equity	$212,482	$221,690

Liquidity

Use of current and noncurrent classifications makes it possible to analyze a company's liquidity. **Liquidity** refers to the ability to pay maturing obligations and meet unexpected needs for cash. The relationship of current assets to current liabilities is critical in analyzing liquidity. We can express this relationship as a dollar amount (working capital) and as a ratio (the current ratio).

The excess of current assets over current liabilities is **working capital**. Illustration 10.20 shows the formula for the computation of **General Motors'** working capital (dollar amounts in millions).

ILLUSTRATION 10.20

Working capital formula and
computation

Current Assets	–	Current Liabilities	=	Working Capital
$68,744	–	$76,890	=	$(8,146)

As an absolute dollar amount, working capital offers limited informational value. For example, $1 million of working capital may be more than needed for a small company but inadequate for a large corporation. Also, $1 million of working capital may be adequate for a company at one time but inadequate at another time.

The **current ratio** permits us to compare the liquidity of different-sized companies and of a single company at different times. The current ratio is calculated as current assets divided by current liabilities. **Illustration 10.21** shows the formula for this ratio, along with its computation using General Motors' current asset and current liability data (dollar amounts in millions).

ILLUSTRATION 10.21

Current ratio formula and
computation

Current Assets	÷	Current Liabilities	=	Current Ratio
$68,744	÷	$76,890	=	.89:1

Historically, companies and analysts considered a current ratio of 2:1 to be the standard for a good credit rating. In recent years, however, many healthy companies have maintained ratios well below 2:1 by improving management of their current assets and liabilities. General Motors' ratio of .89:1 is quite low.

Companies that keep fewer liquid assets on hand must rely on other sources of liquidity. One such source is a **bank line of credit**. A line of credit is a prearranged agreement between a company and a lender that permits the company, should it be necessary, to borrow up to an agreed-upon amount. For example, a recent disclosure regarding debt in General Motors' annual report stated that it had $12 billion of unused lines of credit.

Solvency

Next, we look at two ratios that provide information about a company's long-run solvency. **Solvency** refers to the ability of a company to survive over a long period of time. Long-term creditors and stockholders are interested in a company's long-run solvency. Of particular interest is the company's ability to pay interest as it comes due and to repay the face value of its debt at maturity.

The **debt to assets ratio** measures the percentage of the total assets provided by creditors. It is computed by dividing total liabilities (both current and long-term liabilities) by total assets. To illustrate, we use data from Illustration 10.19. General Motors reported total liabilities of $176,282 million and total assets of $212,482 million. As shown in **Illustration 10.22**, General Motors' debt to assets ratio is 83%. The higher the percentage of debt to assets, the greater the risk that the company may be unable to meet its maturing obligation.

Total Liabilities	÷	Total Assets	=	Debt to Assets Ratio
$176,282	÷	$212,482	=	83%

ILLUSTRATION 10.22

Debt to assets ratio

Times interest earned indicates the company's ability to meet interest payments as they come due. It is computed by dividing the sum of net income, interest expense, and income tax expense by interest expense. General Motors in 2017 reported a net loss of $3,882 million, interest expense of $575 million, and income tax expense of $11,533 million. As shown in **Illustration 10.23**, General Motors' times interest earned is 14.3 times. This interest coverage is considered safe.

Net Income + Interest Expense + Income Tax Expense	÷	Interest Expense	=	Times Interest Earned
$(3,882) + $575 + $11,533	÷	$575	=	14.3 times

ILLUSTRATION 10.23

Times interest earned

Investor Insight

iStock.com/yenwen lu

Debt Masking

In the wake of the financial crisis of 2008, many financial institutions are wary of reporting too much debt on their financial statements, for fear that investors will consider them too risky. The Securities and Exchange Commission (SEC) is concerned that some companies engage in "debt masking" to make it appear that they have less debt than they actually do. These companies enter into transactions at the end of the accounting period that essentially remove debt from their books. Shortly after the end of the period, they reverse the transaction and the debt goes back on their books. The *Wall Street Journal* reported that 18 large banks "had consistently lowered one type of debt at the end of each of the past five quarters, reducing it on average by 42% from quarterly peaks."

Source: Tom McGinty, Kate Kelly, and Kara Scannell, "Debt 'Masking' Under Fire," *Wall Street Journal Online* (April 21, 2010).

What implications does debt masking have for an investor that is using the debt to assets ratio to evaluate a company's solvency? (Go to WileyPLUS for this answer and additional questions.)

Debt and Equity Financing

To obtain large amounts of long-term capital, corporate management has to decide whether to issue additional common stock (equity financing), bonds or notes (debt financing), or a combination of the two. This decision is important to the company, investors, and creditors. The capital structure of a company provides clues as to the potential profit that can be achieved and the risks taken by the company. Debt financing offers these advantages over common stock, as shown in **Illustration 10.24**.

Bond Financing	Advantages
Ballot	1. **Stockholder control is not affected.** Bondholders do not have voting rights, so current owners (stockholders) retain full control of the company.
Tax Bill	2. **Tax savings result.** Bond interest is deductible for tax purposes; dividends on stock are not.
Income Statement / EPS	3. **Earnings per share (EPS) may be higher.** Although bond interest expense reduces net income, earnings per share often is higher under bond financing because no additional shares of common stock are issued.

HELPFUL HINT

Besides corporations, governmental agencies and universities also issue bonds to raise capital.

As Illustration 10.24 shows, one reason to issue bonds is that they do not affect stockholder control. Because bondholders do not have voting rights, owners can raise capital with bonds and still maintain corporate control (see **Helpful Hint**). In addition, bonds are attractive to corporations because the cost of bond interest is tax-deductible. As a result of this tax treatment, which stock dividends do not offer, bonds may result in a lower cost of financing than equity financing.

To illustrate another advantage of bond financing, assume that Microsystems, Inc. is considering two plans for financing the construction of a new $5 million plant. Plan A involves issuance of 200,000 shares of common stock at the current market price of $25 per share. Plan B involves issuance of $5 million, 8% bonds at face value. Income before interest and taxes on the new plant will be $1.5 million. Income taxes are expected to be 30%. Microsystems currently has 100,000 shares of common stock outstanding. **Illustration 10.25** shows the alternative effects on earnings per share.

	Plan A Issue Stock	Plan B Issue Bonds
Income before interest and taxes	$1,500,000	$1,500,000
Interest (8% × $5,000,000)	—	400,000
Income before income taxes	1,500,000	1,100,000
Income tax expense (30%)	450,000	330,000
Net income	$1,050,000	$ 770,000
Outstanding shares	300,000	100,000
Earnings per share	**$3.50**	**$7.70**

Note that net income is $280,000 less ($1,050,000 − $770,000) with long-term debt financing (bonds). However, earnings per share is higher because there are 200,000 fewer shares of common stock outstanding.

One disadvantage in using bonds is that the company must **pay interest** on a periodic basis. In addition, the company must also **repay the principal** at the due date. A company with fluctuating earnings and a relatively weak cash position may have great difficulty making interest payments when earnings are low. Furthermore, when the economy, stock market, or a company's revenues stagnate, debt payments can gobble up cash quickly and limit a company's ability to meet its financial obligations.

ACTION PLAN

- **Use the formula for the current ratio: Current assets ÷ Current liabilities.**
- **Use the formula for working capital: Current assets − Current liabilities.**
- **Use the formula for the debt to assets ratio: Total liabilities ÷ Total assets.**

DO IT! 5 | Analyzing Liabilities

Trout Company provides you with the following balance sheet information as of December 31, 2022.

Current assets	$10,500	Current liabilities	$ 8,000
Long-term assets	24,200	Long-term liabilities	16,000
Total assets	$34,700	Stockholders' equity	10,700
		Total liabilities and stockholders' equity	$34,700

In addition, Trout reported net income for 2022 of $14,000, income tax expense of $2,800, and interest expense of $900.

Instructions

a. Compute the current ratio and working capital for Trout for 2022.

b. Assume that at the end of 2022, Trout used $2,000 cash to pay off $2,000 of accounts payable. How would the current ratio and working capital have changed?

c. Compute the debt to assets ratio and the times interest earned for Trout for 2022.

Solution

a. Current ratio is 1.31:1 ($10,500 ÷ $8,000). Working capital is $2,500 ($10,500 − $8,000).

b. Current ratio is 1.42:1 [($10,500 − $2,000) ÷ ($8,000 − $2,000)]. Working capital is $2,500 ($8,500 − $6,000).

c. Debt to assets ratio is 69.2% ($24,000 ÷ $34,700). Times interest earned is 19.67 times [($14,000 + $2,800 + $900) ÷ $900].

Related exercise material: **BE10.18, DO IT! 10.5, E10.18, and E10.19.**

Appendix 10A | Straight-Line Amortization

LEARNING OBJECTIVE *6
Apply the straight-line method of amortizing bond discount and bond premium.

Amortizing Bond Discount

To follow the expense recognition principle, companies allocate bond discount to expense in each period in which the bonds are outstanding. The **straight-line method of amortization** allocates the same amount to interest expense in each interest period. The calculation is presented in **Illustration 10A.1.**

Bond Discount	÷	Number of Interest Periods	=	Bond Discount Amortization

ILLUSTRATION 10A.1

Formula for straight-line method of bond discount amortization

In the Candlestick Inc. example, the company sold $100,000, five-year, 10% bonds on January 1, 2022, for $98,000. This resulted in a $2,000 bond discount ($100,000 − $98,000). The bond discount amortization is $400 ($2,000 ÷ 5) for each of the five amortization periods. Candlestick records the first accrual of bond interest and the amortization of bond discount on December 31 as follows.

Dec. 31	Interest Expense	10,400	
	Discount on Bonds Payable		400
	Interest Payable ($100,000 × 10%)		10,000
	(To record accrued bond interest and amortization of bond discount)		

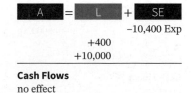

$$A = L + SE$$
−10,400 Exp
+400
+10,000

Cash Flows
no effect

Over the term of the bonds, the balance in Discount on Bonds Payable will decrease annually by the same amount until it has a zero balance at the maturity date of the bonds (see **Alternative Terminology**). Thus, the carrying value of the bonds at maturity will be equal to the face value of the bonds.

Preparing a bond discount amortization schedule, as shown in **Illustration 10A.2**, is useful to determine interest expense, discount amortization, and the carrying value of the bond. As indicated, the interest expense recorded each period is $10,400. Also note that the carrying value of the bond increases $400 each period until it reaches its face value of $100,000 at the end of period 5.

ALTERNATIVE TERMINOLOGY

The balance in the Discount on Bonds Payable account is often referred to as *Unamortized Discount on Bonds Payable.*

Candlestick Inc.

Home   Insert   Page Layout   Formulas   Data   Review   View

P18   fx

Candlestick Inc.
Bond Discount Amortization Schedule
Straight-Line Method—Annual Interest Payments
$100,000 of 10%, 5-Year Bonds

Interest Periods	(A) Interest to Be Paid (10% × $100,000)	(B) Interest Expense to Be Recorded (A) + (C)	(C) Discount Amortization ($2,000 ÷ 5)	(D) Unamortized Discount (D) − (C)	(E) Bond Carrying Value ($100,000 − D)
Issue date				$2,000	$ 98,000
1	$10,000	$10,400	$ 400	1,600	98,400
2	10,000	10,400	400	1,200	98,800
3	10,000	10,400	400	800	99,200
4	10,000	10,400	400	400	99,600
5	10,000	10,400	400	0	100,000
	$50,000	$52,000	$2,000		

Column **(A)** remains constant because the face value of the bonds ($100,000) is multiplied by the annual contractual interest rate (10%) each period.

Column **(B)** is computed as the interest paid (Column A) plus the discount amortization (Column C).

Column **(C)** indicates the discount amortization each period.

Column **(D)** decreases each period by the same amount until it reaches zero at maturity.

Column **(E)** increases each period by the amount of discount amortization until it equals the face value at maturity.

Amortizing Bond Premium

The amortization of bond premium parallels that of bond discount. **Illustration 10A.3** presents the formula for determining bond premium amortization under the straight-line method.

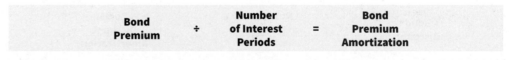

Bond Premium	÷	Number of Interest Periods	=	Bond Premium Amortization

Continuing our example, assume Candlestick Inc., sells the bonds described above for $102,000, rather than $98,000. This results in a bond premium of $2,000 ($102,000 − $100,000). The premium amortization for each interest period is $400 ($2,000 ÷ 5). Candlestick records the first accrual of interest on December 31 as follows.

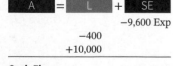

A   =   L   +   SE

−9,600 Exp

−400

+10,000

Cash Flows
no effect

Dec. 31	Interest Expense	9,600	
	Premium on Bonds Payable	400	
	Interest Payable ($100,000 × 10%)		10,000
	(To record accrued bond interest and		
	amortization of bond premium)		

Over the term of the bonds, the balance in Premium on Bonds Payable will decrease annually by the same amount until it has a zero balance at maturity.

A bond premium amortization schedule, as shown in **Illustration 10A.4**, is useful to determine interest expense, premium amortization, and the carrying value of the bond. As indicated, the interest expense Candlestick records each period is $9,600. Note that the carrying value of the bond decreases $400 each period until it reaches its face value of $100,000 at the end of period 5.

ILLUSTRATION 10A.4

Bond premium amortization schedule

Candlestick Inc.

Home | Insert | Page Layout | Formulas | Data | Review | View

P18   fx

	A	B	C	D	E	F
1			**Candlestick Inc.**			
2			**Bond Premium Amortization Schedule**			
3			**Straight-Line Method—Annual Interest Payments**			
4			**$100,000 of 10%, 5-Year Bonds**			
5		(A)	(B)	(C)	(D)	(E)
6		Interest to	Interest Expense	Premium	Unamortized	Bond
7	Interest	Be Paid	to Be Recorded	Amortization	Premium	Carrying Value
8	Periods	(10% × $100,000)	(A) – (C)	($2,000 ÷ 5)	(D) – (C)	($100,000 + D)
9	Issue date				$2,000	$102,000
10	1	$10,000	$ 9,600	$ 400	1,600	101,600
11	2	10,000	9,600	400	1,200	101,200
12	3	10,000	9,600	400	800	100,800
13	4	10,000	9,600	400	400	100,400
14	5	10,000	9,600	400	0	100,000
15		$50,000	$48,000	$2,000		
16						
17	Column **(A)** remains constant because the face value of the bonds ($100,000) is multiplied by the annual contractual interest rate (10%) each period.					
18	Column **(B)** is computed as the interest paid (Column A) less the premium amortization (Column C).					
19	Column **(C)** indicates the premium amortization each period.					
20	Column **(D)** decreases each period by the same amount until it reaches zero at maturity.					
21	Column **(E)** decreases each period by the amount of premium amortization until it equals the face value at maturity.					

Appendix 10B	# Effective-Interest Amortization

LEARNING OBJECTIVE *7

Apply the effective-interest method of amortizing bond discount and bond premium.

To follow the expense recognition principle, companies allocate bond discount and bond premium to expense in each period in which the bonds are outstanding. However, to completely comply with the expense recognition principle, interest expense **as a percentage of carrying value** should not change over the life of the bonds.

This percentage, referred to as the **effective-interest rate**, is established when the bonds are issued and remains constant in each interest period. Unlike the straight-line method, the effective-interest method of amortization accomplishes this result.

Under the **effective-interest method of amortization**, the amortization of bond discount or bond premium results in periodic interest expense equal to a constant percentage of the carrying value of the bonds. The effective-interest method results in **varying amounts** of amortization and interest expense per period but a **constant percentage rate**. In contrast, the straight-line method results in constant amounts of amortization and interest expense per period but a varying percentage rate.

Companies follow three steps under the effective-interest method:

1. Compute the **bond interest expense** by multiplying the carrying value of the bonds at the beginning of the interest period by the effective-interest rate.

2. Compute the **bond interest paid** (or accrued) by multiplying the face value of the bonds by the contractual interest rate.

3. Compute the **amortization amount** by determining the difference between the amounts computed in Steps 1 and 2.

Illustration 10B.1 depicts these steps.

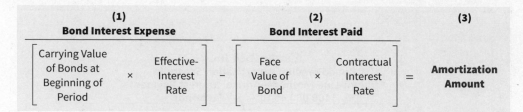

Both the straight-line and effective-interest methods of amortization result in the same total amount of interest expense over the term of the bonds. Furthermore, interest expense each interest period is generally comparable in amount. However, **when the amounts are materially different**, generally accepted accounting principles (GAAP) require use of the effective-interest method.

HELPFUL HINT

Note that the amount of periodic interest expense increases over the life of the bonds when the effective-interest method is used for bonds issued at a discount. The reason is that a constant percentage is applied to an increasing bond carrying value to compute interest expense. The carrying value is increasing because of the amortization of the discount.

Amortizing Bond Discount

In the Candlestick Inc. example, the company sold $100,000, five-year, 10% bonds on January 1, 2022, for $98,000. This resulted in a $2,000 bond discount ($100,000 − $98,000). This discount results in an effective-interest rate of approximately 10.5348%. (The effective-interest rate can be computed using the techniques shown in Appendix G.)

Preparing a bond discount amortization schedule as shown in **Illustration 10B.2** facilitates the recording of interest expense and the discount amortization. Note that interest expense as a percentage of carrying value remains constant at 10.5348% (see **Helpful Hint**).

ILLUSTRATION 10B.2 Bond discount amortization schedule

Candlestick Inc.
Bond Discount Amortization Schedule
Effective-Interest Method—Annual Interest Payments
10% Bonds Issued at 10.5348%

Interest Periods	(A) Interest to Be Paid (10% × $100,000)	(B) Interest Expense to Be Recorded (10.5348% × Preceding Bond Carrying Value)		(C) Discount Amortization (B) − (A)	(D) Unamortized Discount (D) − (C)	(E) Bond Carrying Value ($100,000 − D)
Issue date					$2,000	$ 98,000
1	$10,000	$10,324	(10.5348% × $98,000)	$ 324	1,676	98,324
2	10,000	10,358	(10.5348% × $98,324)	358	1,318	98,682
3	10,000	10,396	(10.5348% × $98,682)	396	922	99,078
4	10,000	10,438	(10.5348% × $99,078)	438	484	99,516
5	10,000	10,484	(10.5348% × $99,516)	484	–0–	100,000
	$50,000	$52,000		$2,000		

Column **(A)** remains constant because the face value of the bonds ($100,000) is multiplied by the annual contractual interest rate (10%) each period.

Column **(B)** is computed as the preceding bond carrying value times the annual effective-interest rate (10.5348%).

Column **(C)** indicates the discount amortization each period.

Column **(D)** decreases each period until it reaches zero at maturity.

Column **(E)** increases each period until it equals face value at maturity.

For the first interest period, **Illustration 10B.3** shows the computations of bond interest expense and the bond discount amortization.

Bond interest expense ($98,000 × 10.5348%)	$10,324	
Less: Bond interest paid ($100,000 × 10%)	10,000	
Bond discount amortization	$ 324	

ILLUSTRATION 10B.3

Computation of bond discount amortization

As a result, Candlestick records the accrual of interest and amortization of bond discount on December 31 as follows.

Dec. 31	Interest Expense	10,324	
	Discount on Bonds Payable		324
	Interest Payable		10,000
	(To record accrued interest and		
	amortization of bond discount)		

−10,324 Exp

+324
+10,000

Cash Flows
no effect

For the second interest period, bond interest expense will be $10,358 ($98,324 × 10.5348%), and the discount amortization will be $358. At December 31, Candlestick makes the following adjusting entry.

Dec. 31	Interest Expense	10,358	
	Discount on Bonds Payable		358
	Interest Payable		10,000
	(To record accrued interest and		
	amortization of bond discount)		

−10,358 Exp

+358
+10,000

Cash Flows
no effect

Amortizing Bond Premium

Continuing our example, assume Candlestick Inc. sells the bonds described above for $102,000 rather than $98,000. This would result in a bond premium of $2,000 ($102,000 − $100,000). This premium results in an effective-interest rate of approximately 9.4794%. (The effective-interest rate can be solved for using the techniques shown in Appendix G.) **Illustration 10B.4** shows the bond premium amortization schedule.

ILLUSTRATION 10B.4 **Bond premium amortization schedule**

Candlestick Inc.
Bond Premium Amortization Schedule
Effective-Interest Method—Annual Interest Payments
10% Bonds Issued at 9.4794%

Interest Periods	(A) Interest to Be Paid (10% × $100,000)	(B) Interest Expense to Be Recorded (9.4794% × Preceding Bond Carrying Value)	(C) Premium Amortization (A) − (B)	(D) Unamortized Premium (D) − (C)	(E) Bond Carrying Value ($100,000 + D)
Issue date				$2,000	$102,000
1	$10,000	$ 9,669 (9.4794% × $102,000)	$ 331	1,669	101,669
2	10,000	9,638 (9.4794% × $101,669)	362	1,307	101,307
3	10,000	9,603 (9.4794% × $101,307)	397	910	100,910
4	10,000	9,566 (9.4794% × $100,910)	434	476	100,476
5	10,000	9,524 * (9.4794% × $100,476)	476*	–0–	100,000
	$50,000	$48,000	$2,000		

Column **(A)** remains constant because the face value of the bonds ($100,000) is multiplied by the contractual interest rate (10%) each period.

Column **(B)** is computed as the carrying value of the bonds times the annual effective-interest rate (9.4794%).

Column **(C)** indicates the premium amortization each period.

Column **(D)** decreases each period until it reaches zero at maturity.

Column **(E)** decreases each period until it equals face value at maturity.

*Rounded to eliminate remaining discount resulting from rounding the effective rate.

For the first interest period, **Illustration 10B.5** shows the computations of bond interest expense and the bond premium amortization.

ILLUSTRATION 10B.5

Computation of bond premium amortization

Bond interest paid ($100,000 × 10%)	$10,000
Less: Bond interest expense ($102,000 × 9.4794%)	9,669
Bond premium amortization	**$ 331**

The entry Candlestick makes on December 31 is:

A	=	L	+	SE
				−9,669 Exp
−331				
+10,000				

Cash Flows
no effect

Dec. 31	Interest Expense	9,669	
	Premium on Bonds Payable	331	
	Interest Payable		10,000
	(To record accrued interest and amortization		
	of bond premium)		

For the second interest period, interest expense will be $9,638, and the premium amortization will be $362. Note that the amount of periodic interest expense decreases over the life of the bond when companies apply the effective-interest method to bonds issued at a premium. The reason is that a constant percentage is applied to a decreasing bond carrying value to compute interest expense. The carrying value is decreasing because of the amortization of the premium.

Review and Practice

Learning Objectives Review

1 Explain how to account for current liabilities.

A current liability is a debt that a company expects to pay within one year or the operating cycle, whichever is longer. The major types of current liabilities are notes payable, accounts payable, sales taxes payable, unearned revenues, and accrued liabilities such as taxes, salaries and wages, and interest payable.

When a promissory note is interest-bearing, the amount of assets received upon the issuance of the note is generally equal to the face value of the note. Interest expense accrues over the life of the note. At maturity, the amount paid equals the face value of the note plus accrued interest.

Companies record sales taxes payable at the time the related sales occur. The company serves as a collection agent for the taxing authority. Sales taxes are not an expense to the company. Companies initially record unearned revenues in an unearned revenue account. As a company recognizes revenue by satisfying its performance obligation, a transfer from unearned revenue to revenue occurs. Companies report the current maturities of long-term debt as a current liability in the balance sheet.

2 Describe the major characteristics of bonds.

Bonds can have many different features and may be secured, unsecured, convertible, or callable. The terms of the bond issue are set forth in a bond indenture, and a bond certificate provides the specific information about the bond itself.

3 Explain how to account for bond transactions.

When companies issue bonds, they debit Cash for the cash proceeds and credit Bonds Payable for the face value of the bonds. The account Premium on Bonds Payable shows a bond premium. Discount on Bonds Payable shows a bond discount.

When bondholders redeem bonds at maturity, the issuing company credits Cash and debits Bonds Payable for the face value of the bonds. When bonds are redeemed before maturity, the issuing company (a) eliminates the carrying value of the bonds at the redemption date, (b) records the cash paid, and (c) recognizes the gain or loss on redemption.

4 Explain how to account for long-term notes payable.

Long-term notes payable are similar to short-term notes payable except the term of the note payable exceeds one year. Each payment consists of (1) interest expense on the unpaid balance of the loan and (2) a reduction of loan principal. The interest expense decreases each period, while the portion applied to the loan principal increases.

5 Describe how liabilities are reported and analyzed.

Companies should report the nature and amount of each long-term debt in the balance sheet or in the notes accompanying the financial statements.

Companies may sell bonds to investors to raise long-term capital. Bonds offer the following advantages over common stock: (a) stockholder control is not affected, (b) tax savings result, and (c) earnings per share of common stock may be higher.

Stockholders and long-term creditors are interested in a company's long-run solvency. Debt to assets and times interest earned are two ratios that provide information about debt-paying ability and long-run solvency.

*6 Apply the straight-line method of amortizing bond discount and bond premium.

The straight-line method of amortization results in a constant amount of amortization and interest expense per period.

*7 Apply the effective-interest method of amortizing bond discount and bond premium.

The effective-interest method results in varying amounts of amortization and interest expense per period but a constant percentage rate of interest. When the difference between the straight-line and effective-interest method is material, GAAP requires use of the effective-interest method.

Glossary Review

Bond certificate A legal document that indicates the name of the issuer, the face value of the bonds, the contractual interest rate, and the maturity date of the bonds. (p. 10-9).

Bond indenture A legal document that sets forth the terms of the bond issue. (p. 10-9).

Bonds A form of interest-bearing notes payable issued by corporations, universities, and governmental entities. (p. 10-8).

Callable bonds Bonds that are subject to redemption (buy back) at a stated dollar amount prior to maturity at the option of the issuer. (p. 10-9).

Contractual interest rate Rate used to determine the amount of cash interest the borrower pays and the investor receives. (p. 10-9).

Convertible bonds Bonds that permit bondholders to convert them into common stock at the bondholders' option. (p. 10-9).

Current ratio A measure of a company's liquidity; computed as current assets divided by current liabilities. (p. 10-22).

Debenture bonds Bonds issued against the general credit of the borrower. Also called unsecured bonds. (p. 10-9).

Debt to assets ratio A solvency measure that indicates the percentage of total assets provided by creditors; computed as total liabilities divided by total assets. (p. 10-23).

Discount (on a bond) The difference between the face value of a bond and its selling price, when the bond is sold for less than its face value. (p. 10-13).

*Effective-interest method of amortization A method of amortizing bond discount or bond premium that results in periodic interest expense equal to a constant percentage of the carrying value of the bonds. (p. 10-27).

*Effective-interest rate Rate established when bonds are issued that maintains a constant value for interest expense as a percentage of bond carrying value in each interest period. (p. 10-27).

Face value Amount of principal due at the maturity date of the bond. (p. 10-9).

Long-term liabilities Obligations expected to be paid more than one year in the future. (p. 10-8).

Market interest rate The rate investors demand for loaning funds to the corporation. (p. 10-11).

Maturity date The date on which the final payment on the bond is due from the bond issuer to the investor. (p. 10-9).

Mortgage bond A bond secured by real estate. (p. 10-9).

Mortgage notes payable A long-term note secured by a mortgage that pledges title to specific assets as security for a loan. (p. 10-18).

Notes payable Obligations in the form of written notes. (p. 10-3).

Premium (on a bond) The difference between the selling price and the face value of a bond, when the bond is sold for more than its face value. (p. 10-13).

Secured bonds Bonds that have specific assets of the issuer pledged as collateral. (p. 10-9).

Sinking fund bonds Bonds secured by specific assets set aside to redeem them. (p. 10-9).

*Straight-line method of amortization A method of amortizing bond discount or bond premium that allocates the same amount to interest expense in each interest period. (p. 10-25).

Times interest earned A solvency measure that indicates a company's ability to meet interest payments; computed by dividing the sum of net income, interest expense, and income tax expense by interest expense. (p. 10-23).

Time value of money The relationship between time and money. A dollar received today is worth more than a dollar promised at some time in the future. (p. 10-10).

Unsecured bonds Bonds issued against the general credit of the borrower. Also called debenture bonds. (p. 10-9).

Working capital A measure of a company's liquidity; computed as current assets minus current liabilities. (p. 10-22).

Practice Multiple-Choice Questions

1. (LO 1) The time period for classifying a liability as current is one year or the operating cycle, whichever is:

   a. longer.   **c.** probable.

   b. shorter.   **d.** possible.

2. (LO 1) To be classified as a current liability, a debt must be expected to be paid within:

   a. one year.

   b. the operating cycle.

   c. 2 years.

   d. one year or the operating cycle, whichever is longer.

3. (LO 1) Ottman Company borrows $88,500 on September 1, 2022, from Sandwich State Bank by signing an $88,500, 12%, one-year note, interest to be paid at maturity. What is the interest at December 31, 2022?

   a. $2,655.   **c.** $4,425.

   b. $3,540.   **d.** $10,620.

4. (LO 1) JD Company borrowed $70,000 on December 1 on a 6-month, 12% note, interest to be paid at maturity. At December 31:

   a. neither the note payable nor the interest payable is a current liability.

   b. the note payable is a current liability but the interest payable is not.

   c. the interest payable is a current liability but the note payable is not.

   d. both the note payable and the interest payable are current liabilities.

5. (LO 1) Alexis Company has total proceeds from sales of $4,515. If the proceeds include sales taxes of 5%, the amount to be credited to Sales Revenue is:

   a. $4,000.   **c.** $4,289.25.

   b. $4,300.   **d.** No correct answer given.

6. (LO 1) No Fault Insurance Company collected a premium of $18,000 for a 1-year insurance policy on April 1, 2022. What amount should No Fault report as a current liability for Unearned Service Revenue at December 31, 2022?

   a. $0.   **c.** $13,500.

   b. $4,500.   **d.** $18,000.

7. (LO 1) Employer payroll taxes do **not** include:

   a. federal unemployment taxes.

   b. state unemployment taxes.

   c. federal income taxes.

   d. FICA taxes.

8. (LO 1) When recording payroll:

   a. gross earnings are recorded as salaries and wages payable.

   b. net pay is recorded as salaries and wages expense.

   c. payroll deductions are recorded as liabilities.

   d. More than one of the answers is correct.

9. (LO 2) The term used for bonds that are unsecured is:

   a. callable bonds.   **c.** debenture bonds.

   b. U.S. Treasury bonds.   **d.** convertible bonds.

10. (LO 3) Karson Inc. issues 10-year bonds with a face value of $200,000. If the bonds are issued at a premium, this indicates that:

   a. the contractual interest rate exceeds the market interest rate.

   b. the market interest rate exceeds the contractual interest rate.

   c. the contractual interest rate and the market interest rate are the same.

   d. no relationship exists between the two rates.

11. (LO 3) On January 1, 2022, Kelly Corp. issues $200,000, 5-year, 7% bonds at face value. The entry to record the issuance of the bonds would include a:

   a. debit to Cash for $14,000.

   b. debit to Bonds Payable for $200,000.

   c. credit to Bonds Payable for $200,000.

   d. credit to Interest Expense of $14,000.

12. (LO 3) Prescher Corporation issued bonds that pay interest every July 1 and January 1. The entry to accrue bond interest at December 31 includes a:

   a. debit to Interest Payable.

   b. credit to Cash.

   c. credit to Interest Expense.

   d. credit to Interest Payable.

13. (LO 3) Goethe Corporation redeems its $100,000 face value bonds at 105 on January 1, following the payment of annual interest. The carrying value of the bonds at the redemption date is $103,745. The entry to record the redemption will include a:

   a. credit of $3,745 to Loss on Bond Redemption.

   b. debit of $3,745 to Premium on Bonds Payable.

   c. credit of $1,255 to Gain on Bond Redemption.

   d. debit of $5,000 to Premium on Bonds Payable.

14. (LO 4) Andrews Inc. issues a $497,000, 10%, 3-year mortgage note on January 1. The note will be paid in three annual installments of $200,000, each payable at the end of the year. What is the amount of interest expense that should be recognized by Andrews Inc. in the second year?

   a. $16,567.   **c.** $34,670.

   b. $49,700.   **d.** $346,700.

15. (LO 4) Howard Corporation issued a 20-year mortgage note payable on January 1, 2022. At December 31, 2022, the unpaid principal balance will be reported as:

   a. a current liability.

   b. a long-term liability.

   c. part current and part long-term liability.

   d. interest payable.

16. (LO 5) For 2022, Corn Flake Corporation reported net income of $300,000. Interest expense was $40,000 and income taxes were $100,000. The times interest earned was:

    a. 3 times.   **c.** 7.5 times.

    b. 4.4 times.   **d.** 11 times.

*17. (LO 6) On December 31, 2022, Hurley Corporation issues $500,000, 5-year, 12% bonds at 96 with interest payable each December 31. The entry on December 31, 2023, to record payment of bond interest and the amortization of bond discount using the straight-line method will include a:

    a. debit to Interest Expense $30,000.

    b. debit to Interest Expense $60,000.

    c. credit to Discount on Bonds Payable $4,000.

    d. credit to Discount on Bonds Payable $2,000.

*18. (LO 6) On December 31, 2022, Hurley Corporation issues $500,000, 5-year, 12% bonds at 96 with interest payable each December 31. What is the carrying value of the bonds at the end of the third interest period using straight-line amortization?

    a. $492,000.   **c.** $486,000.

    b. $488,000.   **d.** $464,000.

*19. (LO 7) On January 1, Holly Ester Inc. issued $1,000,000, 9% bonds for $938,554. The market rate of interest for these bonds is 10%. Interest is payable annually on December 31. Holly Ester uses the effective-interest method of amortizing bond discount. At the end of the first year, Holly Ester should report unamortized bond discount of:

    a. $54,900.

    b. $57,591.

    c. $51,610.

    d. $51,000.

*20. (LO 7) Dias Corporation issued $1,000,000, 14%, 5-year bonds with interest payable annually on December 31. The bonds sold for $1,072,096. The market rate of interest for these bonds was 12%. On the first interest date, using the effective-interest method, the debit entry to Interest Expense is for:

    a. $120,000.

    b. $125,581.

    c. $128,652.

    d. $140,000.

Solutions

1. a. The time period for classifying a liability as current is one year or the operating cycle, whichever is longer, not (b) shorter, (c) probable, or (d) possible.

2. d. To be classified as a current liability, a debt must be expected to be paid within one year or the operating cycle. Choices (a) and (b) are both correct, but (d) is the better answer. Choice (c) is incorrect.

3. b. Accrued interest at 12/31/22 is computed as the face value ($88,500) times the interest rate (12%) times the portion of the year the debt was outstanding (4 months out of 12), or $3,540 ($88,500 × 12% × $\frac{4}{12}$), not (a) $2,655, (c) $4,425, or (d) $10,620.

4. d. A current liability is a debt the company reasonably expects to pay (1) from existing current assets or through the creation of other current liabilities, and (2) within the next year or the operating cycle, whichever is longer. Since both the interest payable and the note payable are expected to be paid within one year, they both will be considered current liabilities. The other choices are therefore incorrect.

5. b. Dividing the total proceeds ($4,515) by one plus the sales tax rate (1.05) will result in the amount of sales to be credited to the Sales Revenue account of $4,300 ($4,515 ÷ 1.05). The other choices are therefore incorrect.

6. b. The monthly premium is $1,500 ($18,000 ÷ 12). Because No Fault has recognized 9 months of insurance revenue (April 1–December 31), 3 months' insurance premium is still unearned. The amount that No Fault should report as Unearned Service Revenue is therefore $4,500 (3 months × $1,500), not (a) $0, (c) $13,500, or (d) $18,000.

7. c. Federal income taxes are an employee payroll deduction, not an employer payroll tax. The employer is merely a collection agent. The other choices are all included in employer payroll taxes.

8. c. Payroll deductions are recorded as liabilities. The other choices are incorrect because (a) gross earnings are recorded as salaries and wages expense, and (b) net pay is recorded as salaries and wages payable. Choice (d) is wrong as there is only one correct answer.

9. c. Debenture bonds are not secured by any collateral. The other choices are incorrect because (a) callable bonds can be paid off or retired by the issuer before they reach their maturity date, (b) U.S. Treasury bonds are secured by the federal government, and (d) convertible bonds permit bondholders to convert them into common stock at the bondholders' option.

10. a. When bonds are issued at a premium, this indicates that the contractual interest rate is higher than the market interest rate. The other choices are incorrect because (b) when the market interest rate exceeds the contractual interest rate, bonds are sold at a discount; (c) when the contractual interest rate and the market interest rate are the same, bonds will be issued at par; and (d) the relationship between the market rate of interest and the contractual rate of interest determines whether bonds are issued at par, a discount, or a premium.

11. c. The issuance entry for the bonds includes a debit to Cash for $200,000 and a credit to Bonds Payable for $200,000. The other choices are therefore incorrect.

12. d. Since the interest has not been paid, it must be accrued as an increase in expenses and liabilities. The entry would be a debit to Interest Expense and a credit to Interest Payable. The other choices are incorrect because (a) an interest accrual will increase, not decrease, Interest Payable; (b) interest accruals do not affect Cash; and (c) an interest accrual will increase, not decrease, Interest Expense.

13. b. The entry to record the retirement of bonds will include a debit to Bonds Payable of $100,000, a debit to Premium on Bonds Payable of $3,745 ($103,745 − $100,000), a credit to Cash of $105,000 ($100,000 × 1.05), and a debit to Loss on Bond Redemption of $1,255 ($105,000 − $103,745). The other choices are therefore incorrect.

14. c. In the first year, Andrews will recognize $49,700 of interest expense ($497,000 × 10%). After the first payment is made, the amount remaining on the note will be $346,700 [$497,000 principal − ($200,000 payment − $49,700 interest)]. The remaining balance ($346,700) is multiplied by the interest rate (10%) to compute the interest expense to be recognized for the second year, $34,670 ($346,700 × 10%), not (a) $16,567, (b) $49,700, or (d) $346,700.

15. c. Howard Corporation reports the reduction in principal for the next year as a current liability, and it classifies the remaining unpaid principal balance as a long-term liability. The other choices are therefore incorrect.

16. d. Times interest earned = Net income + Interest expense + Income tax expense ($300,000 + $40,000 + $100,000 = $440,000) ÷ Interest expense ($40,000), which equals 11 times, not (a) 3, (b) 4.4, or (c) 7.5 times.

***17. c.** [$500,000 − (96% × $500,000)] = $20,000; $20,000 ÷ 5 = $4,000 of discount to amortize annually. As a result, the entry would involve a credit to Discount on Bonds Payable $4,000. The other choices are therefore incorrect.

***18. a.** The carrying value of bonds increases by the amount of the periodic discount amortization. Discount amortization using the straight-line method is $4,000 each period. Total discount amortization for three periods is $12,000 ($4,000 × 3 periods) which is added to the initial carrying value ($480,000) to arrive at $492,000, the carrying value at the end of the third interest period, not (b) $488,000, (c) $486,000, or (d) $464,000.

***19. b.** The beginning balance of unamortized bond discount is $61,446 ($1,000,000 − $938,554). The discount amortization is $3,855, the difference between the cash interest payment of $90,000 ($1,000,000 × 9%) and the interest expense recorded of $93,855 ($938,554 × 10%). This discount amortization ($3,855) is then subtracted from the beginning balance of unamortized discount ($61,446) to arrive at a balance of $57,591 at the end of the first year, not (a) $54,900, (c) $51,610, or (d) $51,000.

***20. c.** The debit to Interest Expense = $1,072,096 (initial carrying value of bond) × 12% (market rate) = $128,652, not (a) $120,000, (b) $125,581, or (d) $140,000.

Practice Brief Exercises

Compute and record sales taxes payable.

1. (LO 1) Amy Pond Discounts does not segregate sales and sales taxes at the time of sale. The cash receipts for March 17 total $19,928. All sales are subject to a 6% sales tax. Compute sales taxes payable and make the entry to record sales taxes payable and sales revenue.

Solution

1. Sales taxes payable:
Sales = $18,800 ($19,928 ÷ 1.06)
Sales taxes payable = $1,128 ($18,800 × 6%)

Mar. 17	Cash	19,928	
	Sales Revenue		18,800
	Sales Taxes Payable		1,128

Compute gross earnings and net pay.

2. (LO 2) Ben Borke's regular hourly wage rate is $20, and he receives an hourly rate of $30 for work in excess of 40 hours. During a January pay period, Ben works 46 hours. Ben's federal income tax withholding is $123, he has no voluntary deductions, and the FICA tax rate is 7.65%. There are no state income taxes. Compute Ben's gross earnings and net pay for the pay period.

Solution

2. Gross earnings:

Regular pay (40 hours × $20)		$800.00
Overtime pay (6 hours × $30)		180.00
Gross earnings		$980.00
Less: FICA taxes withheld ($980 × 7.65%)	$ 74.97	
Federal income taxes withheld	123.00	197.97
Net pay		$782.03

3. (LO 3) Kahnle Corporation issued 3,000, 7%, 5-year, $1,000 bonds dated January 1, 2022, at 100. Interest is paid each January 1. (a) Prepare the journal entry to record the sale of these bonds on January 1, 2022. (b) Prepare the adjusting journal entry on December 31, 2022, to record interest expense. (c) Prepare the journal entry on January 1, 2023, to record interest paid.

Prepare entries for bonds issued at face value.

Solution

3. a. 2022

Jan. 1	Cash	3,000,000	
	Bonds Payable (3,000 × $1,000)		3,000,000

b. 2022

Dec. 31	Interest Expense	210,000	
	Interest Payable ($3,000,000 × 7%)		210,000

c. 2023

Jan. 1	Interest Payable	210,000	
	Cash ($3,000,000 × 7%)		210,000

4. (LO 4) Tyler-Danish Inc. issues a $600,000, 10%, 10-year mortgage note on December 31, 2022, to obtain financing for a new building. The terms provide for annual installment payments of $97,647, Prepare the entry to record the mortgage loan on December 31, 2022, and the first installment payment on December 31, 2023.

Prepare entries for long-term notes payable.

Solution

4.

Annual Interest Period	(A) Cash Payment	(B) Interest Expense (D) × 10%	(C) Reduction of Principal (A) − (B)	(D) Principal Balance (D) − (C)
Issue Date				$600,000
1	$97,647	$60,000	$37,647	562,353

2022

Dec. 31	Cash	600,000	
	Mortgage Payable		600,000

2023

Dec. 31	Interest Expense	60,000	
	Mortgage Payable	37,647	
	Cash		97,647

5. (LO 5) The following are liabilities for Rymer Company at December 31, 2022. Prepare the long-term liabilities section of the balance sheet for Rymer Company.

Prepare statement presentation of long-term liabilities.

Bonds payable, due 2024	$700,000
Accounts payable	100,000
Lease liability, due after 2023	120,000
Notes payable, due 2027	110,000
Premium on bonds payable	40,000

Solution

5. Long-term liabilities*

Bonds payable, due 2024	$700,000	
Plus: Premium on bonds payable	40,000	$740,000
Notes payable, due 2027		110,000
Lease liability		120,000
Total long-term liabilities		$970,000

*Accounts Payable is a current liability.

Practice Exercises

1. (LO 1) On June 1, JetSet Company borrows $150,000 from First Bank on a 6-month, $150,000, 8% note. Interest is paid at maturity.

Instructions

a. Prepare the entry on June 1.

b. Prepare the adjusting entry on June 30.

c. Prepare the entry at maturity (December 1), assuming monthly adjusting entries have been made through November 30.

d. What was the total financing cost (interest expense)?

Solution

1. a.	June 1	Cash	150,000	
		Notes Payable		150,000
b.	June 30	Interest Expense	1,000	
		Interest Payable		
		($150,000 × 8% × $\frac{1}{12}$)		1,000
c.	Dec. 1	Notes Payable	150,000	
		Interest Payable		
		($150,000 × 8% × $\frac{6}{12}$)	6,000	
		Cash		156,000

d. $6,000

2. (LO 3) Global Airlines Company issued $900,000 of 8%, 10-year bonds on January 1, 2022, at face value. Interest is payable annually each January 1.

Instructions

Prepare the journal entries to record the following events.

a. The issuance of the bonds.

b. The accrual of interest on December 31.

c. The payment of interest on January 1, 2023.

d. The redemption of bonds at maturity, assuming interest for the last interest period has been paid and recorded.

Solution

2. a.	2022			
	Jan. 1	Cash	900,000	
		Bonds Payable		900,000
b.	2022			
	Dec. 31	Interest Expense	72,000	
		Interest Payable ($900,000 × 8%)		72,000
c.	2023			
	Jan. 1	Interest Payable	72,000	
		Cash		72,000
d.	2032			
	Jan. 1	Bonds Payable	900,000	
		Cash		900,000

3. (LO 4) Trawler Company borrowed $500,000 on December 31, 2022, by issuing a $500,000, 7% mortgage note payable. The terms call for annual installment payments of $80,000 each December 31.

Instructions

a. Prepare the journal entries to record the mortgage loan and the first two installment payments.

b. Indicate the amount of mortgage note payable to be reported as a current liability and as a long-term liability at December 31, 2023.

Solution

3. a. 2022

Dec. 31	Cash	500,000	
	Mortgage Payable		500,000

2023

Dec. 31	Interest Expense ($500,000 × 7%)	35,000	
	Mortgage Payable	45,000	
	Cash		80,000

2024

Dec. 31	Interest Expense [($500,000 − $45,000) × 7%]	31,850	
	Mortgage Payable	48,150	
	Cash		80,000

b. Current: $48,150

Long-term: $406,850 ($500,000 − $45,000 − $48,150)

Practice Problem

(LO 3, 4) Snyder Software Inc. has successfully developed a new spreadsheet software application. To produce and market the application, the company needed $1.9 million of additional financing. On January 1, 2022, Snyder borrowed money as follows.

Prepare entries to record issuance of bonds and long-term notes, interest accrued, and bond redemption.

1. Snyder issued $1 million, 10%, 10-year bonds at face value. Interest is payable each January 1.

2. Snyder also issued a $400,000, 6%, 15-year mortgage payable. The terms provide for annual installment payments of $41,185 on December 31.

Instructions

1. For the 10-year, 10% bonds:

   a. Journalize the issuance of the bonds on January 1, 2022.

   b. Prepare the journal entry for interest expense in 2022.

   c. Prepare the entry for the redemption of the bonds at 101 on January 1, 2025, after paying the interest due on this date.

2. For the mortgage payable:

   a. Prepare the entry for the issuance of the note on January 1, 2022.

   b. Prepare a payment schedule for the first four installment payments.

   c. Indicate the current and noncurrent amounts for the mortgage payable at December 31, 2022.

Solution

1. a. 2022

Jan. 1	Cash	1,000,000	
	Bonds Payable		1,000,000
	(To record issuance of bonds)		

b. 2022

Dec. 31	Interest Expense	100,000	
	Interest Payable ($1,000,000 × 10%)		100,000
	(To record accrual of annual interest)		

c. 2025

Jan. 1	Bonds Payable	1,000,000	
	Loss on Bond Redemption	10,000*	
	Cash		1,010,000
	(To record redemption of bonds at 101)		

*$1,010,000 − $1,000,000

2. **a.** 2022

Jan. 1	Cash		400,000	
	Mortgage Payable			400,000
	(To record issuance of mortgage payable)			

b.

Interest Period	Cash Payment	Interest Expense	Reduction of Principal	Principal Balance
Issue date				$400,000
1	$41,185	$24,000	$17,185	382,815
2	41,185	22,969	18,216	364,599
3	41,185	21,876	19,309	345,290
4	41,185	20,717	20,468	324,822

c. Current liability: $18,216
Long-term liability: $364,599

WileyPLUS

Brief Exercises, DO IT! Exercises, Exercises, Problems, and many additional resources are available for practice in WileyPLUS.

Note: All asterisked Questions, Exercises, and Problems relate to material in the appendices to the chapter.

Questions

1. Jenny Perez believes a current liability is a debt that can be expected to be paid in one year. Is Jenny correct? Explain.

2. Rayborn Company obtains $20,000 in cash by signing a 9%, 6-month, $20,000 note payable to First Bank on July 1. Rayborn's fiscal year ends on September 30. What information should be reported for the note payable in the annual financial statements?

3. **a.** Your roommate says, "Sales taxes are reported as an expense in the income statement." Do you agree? Explain.

   b. Leiana's Cafe has cash proceeds from sales of $8,550. This amount includes $550 of sales taxes. Give the entry to record the proceeds.

4. Carolina University sold 9,000 season football tickets at $100 each for its five-game home schedule. What entries should be made (a) when the tickets are sold and (b) after each game?

5. Identify three taxes commonly withheld by the employer from an employee's gross pay.

6. (a) What are long-term liabilities? Give three examples. (b) What is a bond?

7. Contrast the following types of bonds: (a) secured and unsecured, and (b) convertible and callable.

8. The following terms are important in issuing bonds: (a) face value, (b) contractual interest rate, (c) bond indenture, and (d) bond certificate. Explain each of these terms.

9. Describe the two major obligations related to bonds.

10. Assume that Acorn Inc. sold bonds with a face value of $100,000 for $104,000. Was the market interest rate equal to, less than, or greater than the bonds' contractual interest rate? Explain.

11. If a 6%, 10-year, $800,000 bond is issued at face value and interest is paid annually, what is the amount of the interest payment at the end of the first period?

12. If the Bonds Payable account has a balance of $700,000 and the Discount on Bonds Payable account has a balance of $36,000, what is the carrying value of the bonds?

13. Which accounts are debited and which are credited if a bond issue originally sold at a premium is redeemed before maturity at 97 immediately following the payment of interest?

14. Rattigan Corporation is considering issuing a convertible bond. What is a convertible bond? Discuss the advantages of a convertible bond from the standpoint of (a) the bondholders and (b) the issuing corporation.

15. Tim Rian, a friend of yours, has recently purchased a home for $125,000, paying $25,000 down and the remainder financed by a 6.5%, 20-year mortgage, payable at $745.57 per month. At the end of the first month, Tim receives a statement from the bank indicating that only $203.90 of principal was paid during the month. At this rate, he calculates that it will take over 40 years to pay off the mortgage. Is he right? Discuss.

16. (a) What is a lease agreement? (b) What are the two common types of leases?

17. Benedict Company entered into an agreement to lease 12 computers from Haley Electronics, Inc. The present value of the lease payments is $186,300. Assuming that this is a finance lease, what entry would Benedict Company make on the date of the lease agreement?

18. **a.** In general, what are the requirements for the financial statement presentation of long-term liabilities?

    b. What ratios may be computed to evaluate a company's liquidity and solvency?

19. Identify the liabilities classified by **Apple** as current in 2018.

20. (a) As a source of long-term financing, what are the major advantages of bonds over common stock? (b) What are the major disadvantages in using bonds for long-term financing?

21. What is liquidity? What are two measures of liquidity?

*22. Explain the straight-line method of amortizing discount and premium on bonds payable.

*23. Robbins Corporation issues $200,000 of 6%, 5-year bonds on January 1, 2022, at 103. Assuming that the straight-line method is used to amortize the premium, what is the total amount of interest expense for 2022?

*24. Honore Draper is discussing the advantages of the effective-interest method of bond amortization with her accounting staff. What points do you think Honore is making to argue her case?

*25. Dotsin Corporation issues $400,000 of 9%, 5-year bonds on January 1, 2022, at 104. If Dotsin uses the effective-interest method in amortizing the premium, will the annual interest expense increase or decrease over the life of the bonds? Explain.

Brief Exercises

BE10.1 (LO 1), C Busch Company has these obligations at December 31: (a) a note payable for $100,000 due in 2 years with an annual interest rate of 6%, (b) interest payable of $6,000 on a long-term note payable due next year, and (c) accounts payable of $60,000. For each obligation, indicate whether it should be classified as a current liability, long-term liability, or both.

Identify whether obligations are current liabilities.

BE10.2 (LO 1), AP Hive Company borrows $90,000 on July 1 from the bank by signing a $90,000, 7%, 1-year note payable. Interest will be repaid at maturity. Prepare the journal entries to record (a) the proceeds of the note and (b) accrued interest at December 31, assuming adjusting entries are made only at the end of the year.

Prepare entries for an interest-bearing note payable.

BE10.3 (LO 1), AP Greenspan Supply does not segregate sales and sales taxes at the time of sale. The register total for March 16 is $10,388. All sales are subject to a 6% sales tax. Compute sales taxes payable and make the entry to record sales taxes payable and sales.

Compute and record sales taxes payable.

BE10.4 (LO 1), AP Bramble University sells 3,500 season basketball tickets at $80 each for its 10-game home schedule. Give the entry to record (a) the sale of the season tickets and (b) the revenue recognized after playing the first home game.

Prepare entries for unearned revenues.

BE10.5 (LO 1), AP Betsy Strand's regular hourly wage rate is $16, and she receives an hourly rate of $24 for work in excess of 40 hours. During a January pay period, Betsy works 47 hours. Betsy's federal income tax withholding is $95, and she has no voluntary deductions. Compute Betsy Strand's gross earnings and net pay for the pay period. Assume that the FICA tax rate is 7.65%.

Compute gross earnings and net pay.

BE10.6 (LO 1), AP Betsy Strand's regular hourly wage rate is $16, and she receives an hourly rate of $24 for work in excess of 40 hours. During a January pay period, Betsy works 47 hours. Betsy's federal income tax withholding is $95, and she has no voluntary deductions. Prepare the employer's journal entries to record (a) Betsy's pay for the period and (b) the payment of Betsy's wages. Use January 15 for the end of the pay period and the payment date. Assume that the FICA tax rate is 7.65%.

Record a payroll and the payment of wages.

BE10.7 (LO 1), AP Betsy Strand's regular hourly wage rate is $16, and she receives an hourly rate of $24 for work in excess of 40 hours. During a January pay period, Betsy works 47 hours. Betsy's federal income tax withholding is $95, and she has no voluntary deductions. Prepare the employer's journal entry to record payroll taxes for the period. Assume the FICA tax rate is 7.65%. Ignore unemployment taxes.

Prepare entries for payroll taxes.

BE10.8 (LO 3), AP Bridle Inc. issues $300,000, 10-year, 8% bonds at 98. Prepare the journal entry to record the sale of these bonds on March 1, 2022.

Prepare entry for bonds issued.

BE10.9 (LO 3), AP Ravine Company issues $400,000, 20-year, 7% bonds at 101. Prepare the journal entry to record the sale of these bonds on June 1, 2022.

Prepare entry for bonds issued.

BE10.10 (LO 3), AP Clooney Corporation issued 3,000 7%, 5-year, $1,000 bonds dated January 1, 2022, at face value. Interest is paid each January 1.

Prepare journal entries for bonds issued at face value.

   a. Prepare the journal entry to record the sale of these bonds on January 1, 2022.

   b. Prepare the adjusting journal entry on December 31, 2022, to record interest expense.

   c. Prepare the journal entry on January 1, 2023, to record interest paid.

Prepare entries for bonds sold at a discount and a premium.

BE10.11 (LO 3), AP Nasreen Company issues $2 million, 10-year, 8% bonds at 97, with interest payable each January 1.

    a. Prepare the journal entry to record the sale of these bonds on January 1, 2022.

    b. Assuming instead that the above bonds sold for 104, prepare the journal entry to record the sale of these bonds on January 1, 2022.

Prepare entries for bonds issued.

BE10.12 (LO 3), AP Frankum Company has issued three different bonds during 2022. Interest is payable annually on each of these bonds.

    1. On January 1, 2022, 1,000, 8%, 5-year, $1,000 bonds dated January 1, 2022, were issued at face value.

    2. On July 1, $900,000, 9%, 5-year bonds dated July 1, 2022, were issued at 102.

    3. On September 1, $400,000, 7%, 5-year bonds dated September 1, 2022, were issued at 98.

Prepare the journal entry to record each bond transaction at the date of issuance.

Prepare entry for redemption of bonds.

BE10.13 (LO 3), AP The balance sheet for Miley Consulting reports the following information on July 1, 2022.

Long-term liabilities		
Bonds payable	$1,000,000	
Less: Discount on bonds payable	60,000	$940,000

Miley decides to redeem these bonds at 101 after paying annual interest. Prepare the journal entry to record the redemption on July 1, 2022.

Prepare entries for long-term notes payable.

BE10.14 (LO 4), AP Jenseng Inc. issues an $800,000, 10%, 10-year mortgage note on December 31, 2022, to obtain financing for a new building. The terms provide for annual installment payments of $130,196. Prepare the entry to record the mortgage loan on December 31, 2022, and the first installment payment on December 31, 2023.

Account for finance lease.

BE10.15 (LO 4), AP Imhoff Company leases a new building from Noble Construction, Inc. The present value of the lease payments is $700,000. The lease is a finance lease. Prepare the journal entry that the lessee should make to record this transaction.

Prepare statement presentation of long-term liabilities.

BE10.16 (LO 5), AP Presented here are long-term liability items for Stevens Inc. at December 31, 2022. Prepare the long-term liabilities section of the balance sheet for Stevens Inc.

Bonds payable (due 2026)	$700,000
Lease liability (due after 2023)	70,000
Notes payable (due 2024)	80,000
Discount on bonds payable	28,000

Compare bond versus stock financing.

BE10.17 (LO 5), AN Moby Inc. is considering two alternatives to finance its construction of a new $2 million plant.

    a. Issuance of 200,000 shares of common stock at the market price of $10 per share.

    b. Issuance of $2 million, 8% bonds at face value.

Complete the following table, and indicate which alternative is preferable.

	Issue Stock	**Issue Bond**
Income before interest and taxes	$700,000	$700,000
Interest expense from bonds	_____	_____
Income before income taxes		
Income tax expense (30%)	_____	_____
Net income	$_____	$_____
Outstanding shares	_____	500,000
Earnings per share	_____	_____

Prepare liabilities section of balance sheet.

BE10.18 (LO 5), AP Presented here are liability items for O'Brian Inc. at December 31, 2022. Prepare the liabilities section of O'Brian's balance sheet.

Accounts payable	$157,000	FICA taxes payable	$ 7,800
Notes payable	20,000	Interest payable	40,000
(due May 1, 2023)		Notes payable (due 2024)	80,000
Bonds payable (due 2026)	900,000	Income taxes payable	3,500
Unearned rent revenue	240,000	Sales taxes payable	1,700
Discount on bonds payable	41,000		

BE10.19 (LO 5), AN Suppose the 2022 **adidas** financial statements contain the following selected data (in millions).

Analyze liquidity and solvency.

Current assets	$4,485	Interest expense	$169
Total assets	8,875	Income tax expense	113
Current liabilities	2,836	Net income	245
Total liabilities	5,099		
Cash	775		

Compute the following values and provide a brief interpretation of each.

a. Working capital. **c.** Debt to assets ratio.

b. Current ratio. **d.** Times interest earned.

*BE10.20 (LO 6), AP Alpine Company issues $2 million, 10-year, 7% bonds at 99, with interest payable each December 31. The straight-line method is used to amortize bond discount.

Prepare journal entries for bonds issued at a discount.

a. Prepare the journal entry to record the sale of these bonds on January 1, 2022.

b. Prepare the journal entry to record interest expense and bond discount amortization on December 31, 2022, assuming no previous accrual of interest.

*BE10.21 (LO 6), AP Harvard Inc. issues $4 million, 5-year, 8% bonds at 102, with interest payable each January 1. The straight-line method is used to amortize bond premium.

Prepare journal entries for bonds issued at a premium.

a. Prepare the journal entry to record the sale of these bonds on January 1, 2022.

b. Prepare the journal entry to record interest expense and bond premium amortization on December 31, 2022, assuming no previous accrual of interest.

*BE10.22 (LO 7), AP Writing The following is the partial bond discount amortization schedule for Rohr Corp. Rohr uses the effective-interest method of amortization.

Use effective-interest method of bond amortization.

Interest Periods	Interest to Be Paid	Interest Expense to Be Recorded	Discount Amortization	Unamortized Discount	Bond Carrying Value
Issue date				$38,609	$961,391
1	$45,000	$48,070	$3,070	35,539	964,461
2	45,000	48,223	3,223	32,316	967,684

a. Prepare the journal entry to record the payment of interest and the discount amortization at the end of period 1.

b. Explain why interest expense is greater than interest paid.

c. Explain why interest expense will increase each period.

DO IT! Exercises

DO IT! 10.1a (LO 1), AP You and several classmates are studying for the next accounting exam. They ask you to answer the following questions.

Answer questions about current liabilities.

1. If cash is borrowed on a $60,000, 9-month, 10% note on August 1, how much interest expense would be incurred by December 31?

2. The cash register total including sales taxes is $42,000, and the sales tax rate is 5%. What is the sales taxes payable?

3. If $42,000 is collected in advance on November 1 for 6-month magazine subscriptions, what amount of subscription revenue should be recognized on December 31?

DO IT! 10.1b (LO 1), AP During the month of February, Hennesey Corporation's employees earned wages of $74,000. Withholdings related to these wages were $5,661 for FICA, $7,100 for federal income tax, and $1,900 for state income tax. Costs incurred for unemployment taxes were $110 for federal and $160 for state.

Prepare entries for payroll and payroll taxes.

Prepare the February 28 journal entries for (a) salaries and wages expense and salaries and wages payable assuming that all February wages will be paid in March and (b) the company's payroll tax expense.

Evaluate statements about bonds.

DO IT! 10.2 (LO 2), C State whether each of the following statements is true or false. If false, indicate how to correct the statement.

_____ **1.** Mortgage bonds and sinking fund bonds are both examples of debenture bonds.

_____ **2.** Convertible bonds are also known as callable bonds.

_____ **3.** The market rate is the rate investors demand for loaning funds.

_____ **4.** Annual interest on bonds is equal to the face value times the stated rate.

_____ **5.** The present value of a bond is the value at which it should sell in the market.

Prepare journal entry for bond issuance and show balance sheet presentation.

DO IT! 10.3a (LO 3), AP Smiley Corporation issues $300,000 of bonds for $315,000. (a) Prepare the journal entry to record the issuance of the bonds, and (b) show how the bonds would be reported on the balance sheet at the date of issuance.

Prepare entry for bond redemption.

DO IT! 10.3b (LO 3), AP Farmland Corporation issued $400,000 of 10-year bonds at a discount. Prior to maturity, when the carrying value of the bonds was $388,000, the company redeemed the bonds at 99. Prepare the entry to record the redemption of the bonds.

Prepare entries for mortgage note and installment payment on note.

DO IT! 10.4 (LO 4), AP Detwiler Orchard issues a $700,000, 6%, 15-year mortgage note to obtain needed financing for a new lab. The terms call for annual payments of $72,074 each. Prepare the entries to record the mortgage loan and the first installment payment.

Analyze liabilities.

DO IT! 10.5 (LO 5), AN Grouper Company provides you with the following balance sheet information as of December 31, 2022.

Current assets	$11,500	Current liabilities	$12,000
Long-term assets	26,500	Long-term liabilities	14,000
Total assets	$38,000	Stockholders' equity	12,000
		Total liabilities and stockholders' equity	$38,000

In addition, Grouper reported net income for 2022 of $16,000, income tax expense of $3,200, and interest expense of $1,300.

a. Compute the current ratio and working capital for Grouper for 2022.

b. Assume that at the end of 2022, Grouper used $3,000 cash to pay off $3,000 of accounts payable. How would the current ratio and working capital have changed?

c. Compute the debt to assets ratio and the times interest earned ratio for Grouper for 2022. (Do not use the information from (b) to determine the solution.)

Exercises

Prepare entries for interest-bearing notes.

E10.1 (LO 1), AP C.S. Lewis Company had the following transactions involving notes payable.

July 1, 2022	Borrows $50,000 from First National Bank by signing a 9-month, 8% note.
Nov. 1, 2022	Borrows $60,000 from Lyon County State Bank by signing a 3-month, 6% note.
Dec. 31, 2022	Prepares annual adjusting entries.
Feb. 1, 2023	Pays principal and interest to Lyon County State Bank.
Apr. 1, 2023	Pays principal and interest to First National Bank.

Instructions

Prepare journal entries for each of the transactions.

Prepare entries for interest-bearing notes.

E10.2 (LO 1), AP On June 1, Marchon Company Ltd. borrows $60,000 from Acme Bank on a 6-month, $60,000, 8% note. The note matures on December 1.

Instructions

a. Prepare the entry on June 1.

b. Prepare the adjusting entry on June 30.

c. Prepare the entry at maturity (December 1), assuming monthly adjusting entries have been made through November 30.

d. What was the total financing cost (interest expense)?

E10.3 (LO 1), AP In performing accounting services for small businesses, you encounter the following situations pertaining to cash sales.

Journalize sales and related taxes.

1. Cerviq Company enters sales and sales taxes separately on its cash register. On April 10, the register totals are sales $22,000 and sales taxes $1,100.

2. Quartz Company does not segregate sales and sales taxes. Its register total for April 15 is $13,780, which includes a 6% sales tax.

Instructions

Prepare the entries to record the sales transactions and related taxes for (a) Cerviq Company and (b) Quartz Company.

E10.4 (LO 1), AP Season tickets for the Dingos are priced at $320 and include 16 home games. An equal amount of revenue is recognized after each game is played. When the season began, the amount credited to Unearned Ticket Revenue was $1,728,000. By the end of October, $1,188,000 of the Unearned Ticket Revenue had been recognized as revenue.

Journalize unearned revenue transactions.

Instructions

a. How many season tickets did the Dingos sell?

b. How many home games had the Dingos played by the end of October?

c. Prepare the entry for the initial recording of the Unearned Ticket Revenue.

d. Prepare the entry to recognize the revenue after the first home game had been played.

E10.5 (LO 1), AP Cassini Company Ltd. publishes a monthly sports magazine, *Fishing Preview*. Subscriptions to the magazine cost $28 per year. During November 2022, Cassini sells 6,300 subscriptions for cash, beginning with the December issue. Cassini prepares financial statements quarterly and recognizes subscription revenue at the end of the quarter. The company uses the accounts Unearned Subscription Revenue and Subscription Revenue. The company has a December 31 year-end.

Journalize unearned subscription revenue.

Instructions

a. Prepare the entry in November for the receipt of the subscriptions.

b. Prepare the adjusting entry at December 31, 2022, to record subscription revenue in December 2022.

c. Prepare the adjusting entry at March 31, 2023, to record subscription revenue in the first quarter of 2023.

E10.6 (LO 1), AP Dan Noll's gross earnings for the week were $1,780, his federal income tax withholding was $303, and his FICA total was $136. There were no state income taxes.

Calculate and record net pay.

Instructions

a. What was Noll's net pay for the week?

b. Journalize the entry for the recording of his pay in the general journal. (*Note:* Use Salaries and Wages Payable, not Cash.)

c. Record the issuing of the check for Noll's pay in the general journal.

E10.7 (LO 1), AP According to the accountant of Ulster Inc., its payroll taxes for the week were as follows: $137.68 for FICA taxes, $13.77 for federal unemployment taxes, and $92.93 for state unemployment taxes.

Record accrual of payroll taxes.

Instructions

Journalize the entry to record payroll taxes.

E10.8 (LO 2), C Nick Bosch has prepared the following list of statements about bonds.

Evaluate statements about bonds.

1. Bonds are a form of interest-bearing notes payable.

2. Secured bonds have specific assets of the issuer pledged as collateral for the bonds.

3. Secured bonds are also known as debenture bonds.

4. A conversion feature may be added to bonds to make them more attractive to bond buyers.

5. The rate used to determine the amount of cash interest the borrower pays is called the stated rate.

6. Bond prices are usually quoted as a percentage of the face value of the bond.

7. The present value of a bond is the value at which it should sell in the marketplace.

Instructions

Identify each statement as true or false. If false, indicate how to correct the statement.

Prepare journal entries for issuance of bonds and payment and accrual of interest.

E10.9 (LO 3), AP On August 1, 2022, Gonzaga Corporation issued $600,000, 7%, 10-year bonds at face value. Interest is payable annually on August 1. Gonzaga's year-end is December 31.

Instructions

Prepare journal entries to record the following events.

a. The issuance of the bonds.

b. The annual accrual of interest on December 31, 2022.

c. The payment of interest on August 1, 2023.

Prepare journal entries for issuance of bonds and payment and accrual of interest.

E10.10 (LO 3), AP On January 1, Kirkland Company issued $300,000, 8%, 10-year bonds at face value. Kirkland's year-end is December 31. Interest is payable annually on January 1.

Instructions

Prepare journal entries to record the following events.

a. The issuance of the bonds.

b. The annual accrual of interest on December 31.

c. The payment of interest on January 1.

Prepare entries to record issuance of bonds at discount and premium.

E10.11 (LO 3), AP Whitmore Company issued $500,000 of 5-year, 8% bonds at 97 on January 1, 2022. The bonds pay interest annually.

Instructions

a. 1. Prepare the journal entry to record the issuance of the bonds.

   2. Compute the total cost of borrowing for these bonds.

b. Repeat the requirements from part (a), assuming the bonds were issued at 105.

Prepare entries for bond interest and redemption.

E10.12 (LO 3), AP The following information is taken from Ohlman Corp.'s balance sheet at December 31, 2021.

Current liabilities	
Interest payable	$ 112,000
Long-term liabilities	
Bonds payable, 7%, due January 1, 2024	1,600,000

Bond interest is payable annually on January 1. The bonds are callable on any interest date.

Instructions

a. Journalize the payment of the bond interest on January 1, 2022.

b. Assume that on January 1, 2022, after paying interest, Ohlman calls bonds having a face value of $600,000. The call price is 103. Record the redemption of the bonds.

c. Prepare the entry to record the annual accrual of interest on December 31, 2022.

Prepare journal entries for redemption of bonds.

E10.13 (LO 3), AP The following situations are independent of each other.

Instructions

For each situation, prepare the appropriate journal entry for the redemption of the bonds.

a. Mikhail Corporation redeemed $140,000 face value, 9% bonds on April 30, 2022, at 101. The carrying value of the bonds at the redemption date was $126,500. The bonds pay annual interest, and the interest payment due on April 30, 2022, has been made and recorded.

b. Oldman, Inc., redeemed $170,000 face value, 12.5% bonds on June 30, 2022, at 98. The carrying value of the bonds at the redemption date was $184,000. The bonds pay annual interest, and the interest payment due on June 30, 2022, has been made and recorded.

Prepare entries to record mortgage note and payments.

E10.14 (LO 4), AP Yancey Co. receives $300,000 when it issues a $300,000, 10% mortgage note payable to finance the construction of a building at December 31, 2022. The terms provide for annual installment payments of $50,000 on December 31.

Instructions

Prepare the journal entries to record the mortgage loan and the first two payments.

Prepare long-term liabilities section.

E10.15 (LO 5), AP The adjusted trial balance for Karr Farm Corporation at the end of 2022 contained the following accounts.

Interest Payable	$ 9,000
Lease Liability, due after 2023	89,500
Bonds Payable, due 2026	180,000
Premium on Bonds Payable	32,000

Instructions

Prepare the long-term liabilities section of the balance sheet.

E10.16 (LO 5), AP Sanchez, Inc. reports the following liabilities (in thousands) on its December 31, 2022, balance sheet.

Prepare liabilities section of balance sheet.

Accounts payable	$4,263.9	Mortgage payable (due after 2023)	$6,746.7
Unearned rent revenue	1,058.1	Notes payable (due in 2025)	335.6
Bonds payable	1,961.2	Salaries and wages payable	858.1
Current portion of		Notes payable (due in 2023)	2,563.6
mortgage payable	1,992.2	Warranty liability—current	1,417.3
Income taxes payable	265.2		

Instructions

a. Identify which of the above liabilities are likely current and which are likely long-term. List any items that do not fit in either category. Explain the reasoning for your selection.

b. Prepare the liabilities section of Sanchez's balance sheet as at December 31, 2022.

E10.17 (LO 5), AN Gilliland Airlines is considering two alternatives for the financing of a purchase of a fleet of airplanes. These two alternatives are:

Compare two alternatives of financing—issuance of common stock vs. issuance of bonds.

1. Issue 90,000 shares of common stock at $30 per share. (Cash dividends have not been paid nor is the payment of any contemplated.)

2. Issue 10%, 10-year bonds at face value for $2,700,000.

It is estimated that the company will generate $800,000 of income before interest and taxes as a result of this purchase. The company has an estimated tax rate of 30% and has 120,000 shares of common stock outstanding prior to the new financing.

Instructions

Determine the effect on net income and earnings per share for these two methods of financing.

E10.18 (LO 5), AN Suppose the following financial data were reported by **3M Company** for 2021 and 2022 (dollars in millions).

Calculate current ratio and working capital before and after paying accounts payable.

3M Company
Balance Sheets (partial)

	2022	2021
Current assets		
Cash and cash equivalents	$ 3,040	$1,849
Accounts receivable, net	3,250	3,195
Inventories	2,639	3,013
Other current assets	1,866	1,541
Total current assets	$10,795	$9,598
Current liabilities	$ 4,897	$5,839

Instructions

a. Calculate the current ratio and working capital for 3M for 2021 and 2022.

b. Suppose that at the end of 2022, 3M management used $300 million cash to pay off $300 million of accounts payable. How would its current ratio and working capital have changed?

E10.19 (LO 5), AN Suppose **McDonald's** 2022 financial statements contain the following selected data (in millions).

Calculate liquidity and solvency ratios; discuss impact of unrecorded obligations on liquidity and solvency.

Current assets	$ 3,416.3	Interest expense	$ 473.2
Total assets	30,224.9	Income tax expense	1,936.0
Current liabilities	2,988.7	Net income	4,551.0
Total liabilities	16,191.0		

Instructions

Compute the following values and provide a brief interpretation of each.

a. Working capital.

c. Debt to assets ratio.

b. Current ratio.

d. Times interest earned.

Prepare journal entries to record issuance of bonds, payment of interest, amortization of premium using straight-line, and redemption at maturity.

*E10.20 (LO 6), AP Sehr Company issued $500,000, 6%, 30-year bonds on January 1, 2022, at 103. Interest is payable annually on January 1. Sehr uses straight-line amortization for bond premium or discount.

Instructions

Prepare the journal entries to record the following events.

a. The issuance of the bonds.

b. The accrual of interest and the premium amortization on December 31, 2022.

c. The payment of interest on January 1, 2023.

d. The redemption of the bonds at maturity, assuming interest for the last interest period has been paid and recorded.

Prepare journal entries to record issuance of bonds, payment of interest, amortization of discount using straight-line, and redemption at maturity.

*E10.21 (LO 6), AP Motley Company issued $300,000, 8%, 15-year bonds on December 31, 2021, for $288,000. Interest is payable annually on December 31. Motley uses the straight-line method to amortize bond premium or discount.

Instructions

Prepare the journal entries to record the following events.

a. The issuance of the bonds.

b. The payment of interest and the discount amortization on December 31, 2022.

c. The redemption of the bonds at maturity, assuming interest for the last interest period has been paid and recorded.

Prepare entries for issuance of bonds, payment of interest, and amortization of discount using effective-interest method.

*E10.22 (LO 7), AP Woode Corporation issued $400,000, 7%, 20-year bonds on January 1, 2022, for $360,727. This price resulted in an effective-interest rate of 8% on the bonds. Interest is payable annually on January 1. Woode uses the effective-interest method to amortize bond premium or discount.

Instructions

Prepare the journal entries to record the following. (Round to the nearest dollar.)

a. The issuance of the bonds.

b. The accrual of interest and the discount amortization on December 31, 2022.

c. The payment of interest on January 1, 2023.

Prepare entries for issuance of bonds, payment of interest, and amortization of premium using effective-interest method.

*E10.23 (LO 7), AP Hernandez Company issued $380,000, 7%, 10-year bonds on January 1, 2022, for $407,968. This price resulted in an effective-interest rate of 6% on the bonds. Interest is payable annually on January 1. Hernandez uses the effective-interest method to amortize bond premium or discount.

Instructions

Prepare the journal entries to record the following. (Round to the nearest dollar.)

a. The issuance of the bonds.

b. The accrual of interest and the premium amortization on December 31, 2022.

c. The payment of interest on January 1, 2023.

Problems

Prepare current liability entries, adjusting entries, and current liabilities section.

P10.1A (LO 1, 5), AP On January 1, 2022, the ledger of Romada Company contained these liability accounts.

Accounts Payable	$42,500
Sales Taxes Payable	6,600
Unearned Service Revenue	19,000

During January, the following selected transactions occurred.

Jan. 1	Borrowed $18,000 in cash from Apex Bank on a 4-month, 5%, $18,000 note. Interest will be paid at maturity.
5	Sold merchandise for cash totaling $6,254, which includes 6% sales taxes.
12	Performed services for customers who had made advance payments of $10,000. (Credit Service Revenue.)
14	Paid state treasurer's department for sales taxes collected in December 2021, $6,600.
20	Sold 500 units of a new product on credit at $48 per unit, plus 6% sales tax.

During January, the company's employees earned wages of $70,000. Withholdings related to these wages were $5,355 for FICA, $5,000 for federal income tax, and $1,500 for state income tax. The company owed no money related to these earnings for federal or state unemployment tax. Assume that wages earned during January will be paid during February. No entry had been recorded for wages or payroll tax expense as of January 31.

Instructions

a. Journalize the January transactions.

b. Journalize the adjusting entries at January 31 for the outstanding note payable and for salaries and wages expense and payroll tax expense.

c. Prepare the current liabilities section of the balance sheet at January 31, 2022. Assume no change in Accounts Payable.

c. Tot. current liabilities $146,724

P10.2A (LO 1, 5), AP The following are selected transactions of Blanco Company. Blanco prepares financial statements **quarterly**. Interest on all notes is paid at maturity.

Journalize and post note transactions; show balance sheet presentation.

Jan. 2	Purchased merchandise on account from Nunez Company, $30,000, terms 2/10, n/30. (Blanco uses the perpetual inventory system.)
Feb. 1	Issued a 9%, 2-month, $30,000 note to Nunez in payment of account.
Mar. 31	Accrued interest for 2 months on Nunez note.
Apr. 1	Paid face value and interest on Nunez note.
July 1	Purchased equipment from Marson Equipment, paying $11,000 in cash and signing a 10%, 3-month, $60,000 note.
Sept. 30	Accrued interest for 3 months on Marson note.
Oct. 1	Paid face value and interest on Marson note.
Dec. 1	Borrowed $24,000 from the Paola Bank by issuing a 3-month, 8% note with a face value of $24,000.
Dec. 31	Recognized interest expense for 1 month on Paola Bank note.

Instructions

a. Prepare journal entries for the listed transactions and events.

b. Post to the accounts Notes Payable, Interest Payable, and Interest Expense.

c. Show the balance sheet presentation of notes and interest payable at December 31, 2022.

d. What is total interest expense for the year?

d. $2,110

P10.3A (LO 3, 5), AP On October 1, 2021, Kristal Corp. issued $700,000, 5%, 10-year bonds at face value. The bonds were dated October 1, 2021, and pay interest annually on October 1. Financial statements are prepared annually on December 31.

Prepare journal entries to record issuance of bonds, interest, balance sheet presentation, and bond redemption.

Instructions

a. Prepare the journal entry to record the issuance of the bonds.

b. Prepare the adjusting entry to record the accrual of interest on December 31, 2021.

c. Show the balance sheet presentation of bonds payable and bond interest payable on December 31, 2021.

d. Prepare the journal entry to record the payment of interest on October 1, 2022.

e. Prepare the adjusting entry to record the accrual of interest on December 31, 2022.

f. Assume that on January 1, 2023, Kristal pays the accrued bond interest and calls the bonds. The call price is 104. Record the payment of interest and redemption of the bonds.

f. Loss $28,000

P10.4A (LO 3, 5), AP Malcolm Company sold $6,000,000, 7%, 15-year bonds on January 1, 2022. The bonds were dated January 1, 2022, and pay interest each December 31. The bonds were sold at 98.

Prepare journal entries to record issuance of bonds, show balance sheet presentation, and record bond redemption.

Instructions

a. Prepare the journal entry to record the issuance of the bonds on January 1, 2022.

b. At December 31, 2022, $8,000 of the bond discount had been amortized. Show the long-term liability balance sheet presentation of the bond liability at December 31, 2022.

c. Loss $224,000

c. At January 1, 2024, when the carrying value of the bonds was $5,896,000, the company redeemed the bonds at 102. Record the redemption of the bonds assuming that interest for the year had already been paid.

Journalize and post note transactions; show balance sheet presentation.

P10.5A (LO 1, 5), AP Ehler Corporation sells rock-climbing products and also operates an indoor climbing facility for climbing enthusiasts. During the last part of 2022, Ehler had the following transactions related to notes payable. Interest on all notes is paid at maturity.

Sept. 1	Issued a $12,000 note to Pippen to purchase inventory. The 3-month note payable bears interest of 6% and is due December 1. (Ehler uses a perpetual inventory system.)
Sept. 30	Accrued interest for the Pippen note.
Oct. 1	Issued a $16,500, 8%, 4-month note to Prime Bank to finance the purchase of a new climbing wall for advanced climbers. The note is due February 1.
Oct. 31	Accrued interest for the Pippen note and the Prime Bank note.
Nov. 1	Issued a $26,000 note and paid $8,000 cash to purchase a vehicle to transport clients to nearby climbing sites as part of a new series of climbing classes. This note bears interest of 6% and matures in 12 months.
Nov. 30	Accrued interest for the Pippen note, the Prime Bank note, and the vehicle note.
Dec. 1	Paid principal and interest on the Pippen note.
Dec. 31	Accrued interest for the Prime Bank note and the vehicle note.

Instructions

a. Prepare journal entries for the above transactions.

b. Interest Payable $590

b. Post the above entries to the Notes Payable, Interest Payable, and Interest Expense accounts. (Use T-accounts.)

c. Show the balance sheet presentation of notes payable and interest payable at December 31.

d. How much interest expense relating to notes payable did Ehler incur during the year?

Prepare journal entries to record interest payments and redemption of bonds.

P10.6A (LO 3), AP The following information is taken from Hardesty's balance sheet at December 31, 2021.

Current liabilities	
Interest payable	$ 40,000
Long-term liabilities	
Bonds payable (8%, due January 1, 2025)	500,000

Interest is payable annually on January 1. The bonds are callable on any annual interest payment date.

Instructions

a. Journalize the payment of the bond interest on January 1, 2022.

b. Loss $6,000

b. Assume that on January 1, 2022, after paying interest, Hardesty calls bonds having a face value of $200,000. The call price is 103. Record the redemption of the bonds.

c. Prepare the adjusting entry on December 31, 2022, to accrue the interest on the remaining bonds.

Prepare installment payments schedule, journal entries, and balance sheet presentation for a mortgage payable.

P10.7A (LO 4, 5), AP Laverne Inc. purchased a new piece of equipment to be used in its new facility. The $370,000 piece of equipment was purchased with a $50,000 down payment and with cash received through the issuance of a $320,000, 8%, 5-year mortgage payable issued on January 1, 2022. The terms provide for annual installment payments of $80,146 each December 31.

Instructions

(Round all computations to the nearest dollar.)

a. Prepare an installment payments schedule for the first three payments of the mortgage payable.

b. Prepare the journal entry related to the notes payable for December 31, 2022.

c. Current portion $58,910

c. Show the balance sheet presentation for this obligation for December 31, 2022. (*Hint:* Be sure to distinguish between the current and long-term portions of the mortgage.)

Prepare financial statements from an adjusted trial balance.

P10.8A (LO 5), AP The adjusted trial balance of Ubben Company for the year ended December 31, 2022, is as follows.

	Debit	Credit
Cash	$ 32,000	
Accounts Receivable	30,000	
Inventory	9,000	
Equipment	50,000	
Allowance for Doubtful Accounts		$ 1,000
Accumulated Depreciation—Equipment		4,000
Notes Payable		3,000
Accounts Payable		11,000
Unearned Service Revenue		6,600
Sales Taxes Payable		2,100
Salaries and Wages Payable		1,800
FICA Taxes Payable		500
Interest Payable		400
Bonds Payable		12,000
Mortgage Notes Payable		8,000
Common Stock		15,000
Retained Earnings		12,900
Sales Revenue		220,000
Cost of Goods Sold	120,000	
Salaries and Wages Expense	40,000	
Depreciation Expense	10,000	
Rent Expense	5,000	
Bad Debt Expense	1,200	
Interest Expense	300	
Dividends	200	
Discount on Bonds Payable	600	
	$298,300	$298,300

Instructions

Prepare a multiple-step income statement and retained earnings statement for 2022, and a classified balance sheet as of December 31, 2022. The notes payable is due on January 10, 2023. The mortgage notes payable matures in 2028, with a principal payment of $1,000 due in March 2023.

*P10.9A (LO 5, 6), AP Paris Electric sold $3,000,000, 10%, 10-year bonds on January 1, 2022. The bonds were dated January 1 and pay interest annually on January 1. Paris Electric uses the straight-line method to amortize bond premium or discount. The bonds were sold at 104.

Prepare entries to record issuance of bonds, interest accrual, and straight-line amortization for 2 years.

Instructions

a. Prepare the journal entry to record the issuance of the bonds on January 1, 2022.

b. Prepare a bond premium amortization schedule for the first four interest periods.

b. Amortization $12,000

c. Prepare the journal entries for interest expense and the amortization of the premium in 2022 and 2023. Also, prepare the journal entry for interest payment in 2023.

d. Show the balance sheet presentation of the bond liability at December 31, 2023.

d. Premium on bonds payable $96,000

*P10.10A (LO 5, 6), AP Fong Corporation sold $2,000,000, 7%, 5-year bonds on January 1, 2022. The bonds were dated January 1, 2022, and pay interest each January 1. Fong Corporation uses the straight-line method to amortize bond premium or discount.

Prepare journal entries to record issuance of bonds, interest, and straight-line amortization, and show balance sheet presentation.

Instructions

a. Prepare all the necessary journal entries to record the issuance of the bonds and bond interest expense for 2022, assuming that the bonds sold at 102.

b. Prepare journal entries as in part (a) assuming that the bonds sold at 97.

c. Show the balance sheet presentation for the bond issue at December 31, 2022, using (1) the 102 selling price, and then (2) the 97 selling price.

Prepare journal entries to record interest payments, straight-line discount amortization, and redemption of bonds.

*P10.11A (LO 6), AP The following information is taken from Lassen Corp.'s balance sheet at December 31, 2021.

Current liabilities		
Interest payable		$ 96,000
Long-term liabilities		
Bonds payable (4%, due January 1, 2032)	$2,400,000	
Less: Discount on bonds payable	24,000	2,376,000

Interest is payable annually on January 1. The bonds are callable on any annual interest payment date. Lassen uses straight-line amortization for any bond premium or discount. From December 31, 2021, the bonds will be outstanding for an additional 10 years (120 months).

Instructions

(Round all computations to the nearest dollar.)

a. Journalize the payment of bond interest on January 1, 2022.

b. Prepare the entry to amortize bond discount and to accrue the interest on December 31, 2022.

c. Loss $11,600

c. Assume that on January 1, 2023, after paying interest, Lassen Corp. calls bonds having a face value of $400,000. The call price is 102. Record the redemption of the bonds.

d. Prepare the adjusting entry at December 31, 2023, to amortize bond discount and to accrue interest on the remaining bonds.

Prepare journal entries to record issuance of bonds, payment of interest, and amortization of bond discount using effective-interest method.

→ Excel

*P10.12A (LO 7), AP On January 1, 2022, Lachte Corporation issued $1,800,000 face value, 5%, 10-year bonds at $1,667,518. This price resulted in an effective-interest rate of 6% on the bonds. Lachte uses the effective-interest method to amortize bond premium or discount. The bonds pay interest each January 1.

Instructions

(Round all computations to the nearest dollar.)

a. Prepare the journal entry to record the issuance of the bonds on January 1, 2022.

b. Prepare an amortization table through December 31, 2024 (three interest periods) for this bond issue.

c. Interest Expense $100,051

c. Prepare the journal entry to record the accrual of interest and the amortization of the discount on December 31, 2022.

d. Prepare the journal entry to record the payment of interest on January 1, 2023.

e. Prepare the journal entry to record the accrual of interest and the amortization of the discount on December 31, 2023.

Prepare journal entries to record issuance of bonds, payment of interest, and effective-interest amortization, and show balance sheet presentation.

*P10.13A (LO 5, 7), AP Writing On January 1, 2022, Opal Company issued $2,000,000 face value, 7%, 10-year bonds at $2,147,202. This price resulted in a 6% effective-interest rate on the bonds. Opal uses the effective-interest method to amortize bond premium or discount. The bonds pay annual interest on each January 1.

Instructions

a. Prepare the journal entries to record the following transactions.

1. The issuance of the bonds on January 1, 2022.

2. Accrual of interest and amortization of the premium on December 31, 2022.

3. The payment of interest on January 1, 2023.

a. 4. Interest Expense $128,162

4. Accrual of interest and amortization of the premium on December 31, 2023.

b. Show the proper long-term liabilities balance sheet presentation for the liability for bonds payable at December 31, 2023.

c. Provide the answers to the following questions in narrative form.

1. What amount of interest expense is reported for 2023?

2. Would the bond interest expense reported in 2023 be the same as, greater than, or less than the amount that would be reported if the straight-line method of amortization were used?

Continuing Case

Cookie Creations

leungchopan/
Shutterstock.com

(*Note:* This is a continuation of the Cookie Creations case from Chapters 1 through 9.)

CC10 Recall that Cookie Creations sells fine European mixers that it purchases from Kzinski Supply Co. Kzinski warrants the mixers to be free of defects in material and workmanship for a period of one year from the date of original purchase. If the mixer has such a defect, Kzinski will repair or replace the mixer free of charge for parts and labor.

Go to **WileyPLUS** *for complete case details and instructions.*

Comprehensive Accounting Cycle Review

ACR10.1 Aimes Corporation's balance sheet at December 31, 2021, is presented below.

Aimes Corporation			
Balance Sheet			
December 31, 2021			
Cash	$ 30,000	Accounts payable	$ 13,750
Inventory	30,750	Interest payable	2,500
Prepaid insurance	5,600	Bonds payable	50,000
Equipment	38,000	Common stock	25,000
		Retained earnings	13,100
	$104,350		$104,350

During 2022, the following transactions occurred. Aimes uses a perpetual inventory system.

1. Aimes paid $2,500 interest on the bonds on January 1, 2022.
2. Aimes purchased $241,100 of inventory on account.
3. Aimes sold for $480,000 cash inventory which cost $265,000. Aimes also collected $28,800 sales taxes.
4. Aimes paid $230,000 on accounts payable.
5. The prepaid insurance ($5,600) expired on July 31.
6. On August 1, Aimes paid $10,200 for insurance coverage from August 1, 2022, through July 31, 2023.
7. Aimes paid $17,000 sales taxes to the state.
8. Paid other operating expenses, $91,000.
9. Redeemed the bonds on December 31, 2022, by paying $48,000 plus $2,500 interest.
10. Issued $90,000 of 8% bonds on December 31, 2022, at 103. The bonds pay interest every June 30 and December 31.

Adjustment data:

1. Recorded the insurance expired from item 7.
2. The equipment was acquired on December 31, 2021, and will be depreciated on a straight-line basis over 5 years with a $3,000 salvage value.

Instructions

(You may want to set up T-accounts to determine ending balances.)

a. Prepare journal entries for the transactions listed above and adjusting entries.

b. Prepare an adjusted trial balance at December 31, 2022.

c. Prepare an income statement and a retained earnings statement for the year ending December 31, 2022, and a classified balance sheet as of December 31, 2022.

b. Totals $656,450

c. N.I. $106,650

ACR10.2 Writing Eastland Company and Westside Company are competing businesses. Both began operations 6 years ago and are quite similar in most respects. The current balance sheet data for the two companies are shown as follows.

	Eastland Company	Westside Company
Cash	$ 63,300	$ 48,400
Accounts receivable	304,700	302,500
Allowance for doubtful accounts	(13,600)	–0–
Inventory	463,900	515,200
Plant and equipment	255,300	257,300
Accumulated depreciation—plant and equipment	(112,650)	(189,850)
Total assets	$960,950	$933,550
Current liabilities	$440,200	$431,500
Long-term liabilities	78,000	82,000
Total liabilities	518,200	513,500
Stockholders' equity	442,750	420,050
Total liabilities and stockholders' equity	$960,950	$933,550

You have been engaged as a consultant to conduct a review of the two companies. Your goal is to determine which of them is in the stronger financial position. Both companies use the FIFO inventory method.

Your review of their financial statements quickly reveals that the two companies have not followed the same accounting practices. The differences and your conclusions regarding them are summarized below.

1. Eastland Company has used the allowance method of accounting for uncollectibles. A review shows that the amount of its write-offs each year has been quite close to the allowances that have been provided. It therefore seems reasonable to have confidence in its current estimate of uncollectibles.

   Westside Company has used the direct write-off method for uncollectibles, and it has been somewhat slow to write off its uncollectible accounts. Based upon an aging analysis and review of its accounts receivable, it is estimated that $18,000 of its existing accounts will probably prove to be uncollectible.

2. Eastland Company estimated a useful life of 12 years and a salvage value of $30,000 for its plant and equipment. It has been depreciating them on a straight-line basis.

   Westside Company has the same type of plant and equipment, with the same age. However, it estimated a useful life of 10 years and a salvage value of $10,000. It has been depreciating its plant and equipment using the double-declining-balance method. Westside's percentage of accumulated depreciation to plant and equipment is a better representation of cost allocation.

   Based upon engineering studies of these types of plant and equipment, you conclude that Westside's estimates and method for calculating depreciation are the more appropriate. If Eastland Company used the double-declining-balance method of depreciation, its accumulated depreciation balance would be $188,374.

3. Among its current liabilities, Eastland has included the portions of long-term liabilities that become due within the next year. Westside has not done so.

   You find that $16,000 of Westside's $82,000 of long-term liabilities are due to be repaid in the current year.

Instructions

a. Total assets:
Eastland $885,226
Westside $915,550

a. Revise the balance sheets presented above so that the data are comparable and reflect the current financial position for each of the two companies.

b. Prepare a brief report to your client stating your conclusions.

Expand Your Critical Thinking

Financial Reporting Problem: Apple Inc.

CT10.1 The financial statements of **Apple Inc.** are presented in Appendix A. The complete annual report, including the notes to the financial statements, is available at the company's website.

Instructions

Refer to Apple's financial statements and answer the following questions about current liabilities.

a. What were Apple's total current liabilities at September 29, 2018? What was the increase/decrease in Apple's total current liabilities from the prior year?

b. How much were the accounts payable at September 29, 2018?

c. What were the components of total current liabilities on September 29, 2018 (other than accounts payable already discussed in (b))?

Comparative Analysis Problem: PepsiCo, Inc. vs. The Coca-Cola Company

CT10.2 **PepsiCo, Inc.**'s financial statements are presented in Appendix B. Financial statements of **The Coca-Cola Company** are presented in Appendix C.

Instructions

a. At December 29, 2018, what was PepsiCo's largest current liability? What were its total current liabilities? At December 31, 2018, what was Coca-Cola's largest current liability? What were its total current liabilities?

b. Based on information contained in those financial statements, compute the following 2018 values for each company:

  1. Working capital.

  2. Current ratio.

c. What conclusions concerning the relative liquidity of these companies can be drawn from these data?

d. Based on the information contained in these financial statements, compute the following 2018 ratios for each company.

  1. Debt to assets.

  2. Times interest earned.

e. What conclusions concerning the companies' long-run solvency can be drawn from these ratios?

Comparative Analysis Problem: Amazon.com, Inc. vs. Walmart Inc.

CT10.3 The financial statements of **Amazon.com, Inc.** are presented in Appendix D. Financial statements of **Walmart Inc.** are presented in Appendix E.

Instructions

a. Based on the information contained in these financial statements, compute the current ratio for the most recent fiscal year provided for each company. What conclusions concerning the companies' liquidity can be drawn from these ratios?

b. Based on the information contained in these financial statements, compute the following ratios for each company's most recent fiscal year.

  1. Debt to assets ratio.

  2. Times interest earned.

  What conclusions about the companies' long-run solvency can be drawn from the ratios?

Real-World Focus

CT10.4 Bond or debt securities pay a stated rate of interest. This rate of interest is dependent on the risk associated with the investment. Also, bond prices change when the risks associated with those bonds change. **Standard & Poor's** provides ratings for companies that issue debt securities.

Instructions

Go to the Standard & Poor's website and then answer the following questions.

   a. Explain the meaning of an "A" rating. Explain the meaning of a "C" rating.

   b. What types of things can cause a change in a company's credit rating?

   c. Explain the relationship between a company's credit rating and the merit of an investment in that company's bonds.

Decision-Making Across the Organization

*****CT10.5** On January 1, 2020, Picard Corporation issued $3,000,000, 5-year, 8% bonds at 97. The bonds pay interest annually on January 1. By January 1, 2022, the market rate of interest for bonds of risk similar to those of Picard Corporation had risen. As a result, the market price of these bonds was $2,500,000 on January 1, 2022—below their carrying value of $2,946,000.

   Geoff Marquis, president of the company, suggests repurchasing all of these bonds in the open market at the $2,500,000 price. But to do so the company will have to issue $2,500,000 (face value) of new 10-year, 12% bonds at par. The president asks you, as controller, "What is the feasibility of my proposed repurchase plan?"

Instructions

With the class divided into groups, answer the following.

   a. Prepare the journal entry to redeem the 5-year bonds on January 1, 2022. Prepare the journal entry to issue the new 10-year bonds.

   b. Prepare a short memo to the president in response to his request for advice. List the economic factors that you believe should be considered for his repurchase proposal.

Communication Activity

CT10.6 Jerry Hogan, president of Norwest, Inc., is considering the issuance of bonds to finance an expansion of his business. He has asked you to (1) discuss the advantages of bonds over common stock financing, (2) indicate the types of bonds he might issue, and (3) explain the issuing procedures used in bond transactions.

Instructions

Write a memo to the president, answering his request.

Ethics Case

CT10.7 Ken Iwig is the president, founder, and majority owner of Olathe Medical Corporation, an emerging medical technology products company. Olathe is in dire need of additional capital to keep operating and to bring several promising products to final development, testing, and production. Ken, as owner of 51% of the outstanding stock, manages the company's operations. He places heavy emphasis on research and development and on long-term growth. The other principal stockholder is Barb Lowery who, as a nonemployee investor, owns 40% of the stock. Barb would like to deemphasize the R&D functions and emphasize the marketing function, to maximize short-run sales and profits from existing products. She believes this strategy would raise the market price of Olathe's stock.

   All of Ken's personal capital and borrowing power is tied up in his 51% stock ownership. He knows that any offering of additional shares of stock will dilute his controlling interest because he won't be able to participate in such an issuance. But, Barb has money and would likely buy enough shares to gain control of Olathe. She then would dictate the company's future direction, even if it meant replacing Ken as president and CEO.

   The company already has considerable debt. Raising additional capital with debt will be costly, will adversely affect Olathe's credit rating, and will increase the company's reported losses due to the growth in interest expense. Barb and the other minority stockholders express opposition to the assumption of additional debt, fearing the company will be pushed to the brink of bankruptcy. Wanting to maintain his control and to preserve the direction of "his" company, Ken is doing everything to avoid a stock issuance. He is contemplating a large issuance of bonds, even if it means the bonds are issued with a high effective-interest rate.

Instructions

a. Who are the stakeholders in this situation?

b. What are the ethical issues in this case?

c. What would you do if you were Ken?

All About You

CT10.8 Medical costs are substantial and rising. But will they be the most substantial expense over your lifetime? Not likely. Will it be housing or food? Again, not likely. The answer is taxes. On average, Americans work 107 days per year to afford their taxes. Companies, too, have large tax burdens. They look very hard at tax issues in deciding where to build their plants and where to locate their administrative headquarters.

Instructions

a. Determine what your state income taxes are if your taxable income is $60,000 and you file as a single taxpayer in the state in which you live.

b. Assume that you own a home worth $200,000 in your community and the tax rate is 2.1%. Compute the property taxes you would pay.

c. Assume that the total gasoline bill for your automobile is $1,200 a year (300 gallons at $4 per gallon). What are the amounts of state and federal taxes that you pay on the $1,200?

d. Assume that your purchases for the year total $9,000. Of this amount, $5,000 was for food and prescription drugs. What is the amount of sales tax you would pay on these purchases? (Many states do not levy a sales tax on food or prescription drugs. Does yours?)

e. Determine what your FICA taxes are if your income is $60,000.

f. Determine what your federal income taxes are if your taxable income is $60,000 and you file as a single taxpayer.

g. Determine your total taxes paid based on the above calculations, and determine the percentage of income that you would pay in taxes based on the following formula: Total taxes paid ÷ Total income.

CT10.9 Numerous articles have been written that identify early warning signs that you might be getting into trouble with your personal debt load. You can find many good articles on this topic on the Internet.

Instructions

Find an article that identifies early warning signs of personal debt trouble. Write a summary of the article and bring your summary and the article to class to share.

FASB Codification Activity

CT10.10 If your school has a subscription to the FASB Codification, log in and prepare responses to the following.

a. What is the definition of current liabilities?

b. What is the definition of long-term obligation?

c. What guidance does the Codification provide for the disclosure of long-term liabilities?

A Look at IFRS

LEARNING OBJECTIVE 8

Compare the accounting for liabilities under GAAP and IFRS.

IFRS and GAAP have similar definitions of liabilities but have a different approach for recording certain liabilities.

Key Points

Following are the key similarities and differences between GAAP and IFRS as related to accounting for liabilities.

Similarities

- The basic definition of a liability under GAAP and IFRS is very similar. In a more technical way, liabilities are defined by the IASB as a present obligation of the entity arising from past events, the settlement of which is expected to result in an outflow from the entity of resources embodying economic benefits.

- The accounting for current liabilities such as notes payable, unearned revenue, and payroll taxes payable is similar between GAAP and IFRS.

- IFRS requires that companies classify liabilities as current or noncurrent on the face of the statement of financial position (balance sheet), except in industries where a **presentation** based on liquidity would be considered to provide more useful information (such as financial institutions). When current liabilities (also called short-term liabilities) are presented, they are generally presented in order of liquidity.

- Under IFRS, liabilities are classified as current if they are expected to be paid within 12 months.

- Similar to GAAP, items are normally reported in order of liquidity. Companies sometimes show liabilities before assets. Also, they will sometimes show long-term liabilities before current liabilities.

- The basic calculation for bond valuation is the same under GAAP and IFRS. In addition, the accounting for bond liability transactions is essentially the same between GAAP and IFRS.

- IFRS requires use of the effective-interest method for amortization of bond discounts and premiums. GAAP also requires the effective-interest method, except that it allows use of the straight-line method where the difference is not material. Under IFRS, companies do not use a premium or discount account but instead show the bond at its net amount. For example, if a $100,000 bond was issued at 97, under IFRS a company would record:

Cash	97,000	
Bonds Payable		97,000

Differences

- The accounting for convertible bonds differs between IFRS and GAAP. Unlike GAAP, IFRS splits the proceeds from the convertible bond between an equity component and a debt component. The equity conversion rights are reported in equity.

  To illustrate, assume that Harris Corp. issues convertible 7% bonds with a face value of $1,000,000 and receives $1,000,000. Comparable bonds without a conversion feature would have required a 9% rate of interest. To determine how much of the proceeds would be allocated to debt and how much to equity, the promised payments of the bond obligation would be discounted at the market rate of 9%. Suppose that this results in a present value of $850,000. The entry to record the issuance would be:

Cash	1,000,000	
Bonds Payable		850,000
Share Premium—Conversion Equity		150,000

- Under IFRS, companies sometimes will net current liabilities against current assets to show working capital on the face of the statement of financial position.

- Leases classified as operating leases under GAAP are accounted for differently under IFRS. Also, IFRS allows alternative measurement bases for right-of-use assets (e.g., the revaluation model).

- Both Boards share the same objective of recording leases by lessees and lessors according to their economic substance—that is, according to the definitions of assets and liabilities. However, GAAP for leases is much more "rules-based" with specific criteria to determine if a lease arrangement is a finance or operating lease. IFRS is more conceptual in its provisions.

IFRS Practice

IFRS Self-Test Questions

1. Which of the following is **false**?

    a. Under IFRS, current liabilities must always be presented before noncurrent liabilities.

    b. Under IFRS, an item is a current liability if it will be paid within the next 12 months.

    c. Under IFRS, current liabilities are sometimes netted against current assets on the statement of financial position.

    d. Under IFRS, a liability is only recognized if it is a present obligation.

2. The accounting for bonds payable is:

    a. essentially the same under IFRS and GAAP.

    b. different under IFRS as GAAP requires use of the straight-line method for amortization of bond premium and discount.

    c. the same under IFRS and GAAP, except that market prices may be different because the present value calculations are different between IFRS and GAAP.

    d. not covered by IFRS.

3. Which of the following is **true** regarding accounting for amortization of bond discount and premium?

    a. Both IFRS and GAAP must use the effective-interest method.

    b. GAAP must use the effective-interest method, but IFRS may use either the effective-interest method or the straight-line method.

    c. IFRS is required to use the effective-interest method.

    d. GAAP is required to use the straight-line method.

4. The leasing standards employed by IFRS:

    a. rely more heavily on interpretation of the conceptual meaning of assets and liabilities than GAAP.

    b. are more "rules based" than those of GAAP.

    c. employ the same "bright-line test" as GAAP.

    d. are identical to those of GAAP.

IFRS Exercises

IFRS10.1 Briefly describe some of the similarities and differences between GAAP and IFRS with respect to the accounting for liabilities.

IFRS10.2 Ratzlaff Company issues (in euros) €2 million, 10-year, 8% bonds at 97, with interest payable annually on January 1.

Instructions

a. Prepare the journal entry to record the sale of these bonds on January 1, 2022.

b. Assuming instead that the above bonds sold for 104, prepare the journal entry to record the sale of these bonds on January 1, 2022.

International Financial Reporting Problem: Louis Vuitton

IFRS10.3 The financial statements of **Louis Vuitton** are presented in Appendix F. The complete consolidated financial statements, including the notes to its financial statements, are available at the company's website.

Instructions

Use the company's 2018 consolidated financial statements to answer the following questions.

a. What were the total current liabilities for the company as of December 31, 2018? What portion of these current liabilities related to provisions?

b. According to the notes to the financial statements, what is the composition of long-term gross borrowings?

c. According to the accounting policy note to the financial statements, how are borrowings measured?

d. Determine the amount of fixed-rate and adjustable-rate (floating) borrowings (gross) that the company reports.

Answers to IFRS Self-Test Questions

1. a   **2.** a   **3.** c   **4.** a

Corporations: Organization, Stock Transactions, and Stockholders' Equity

Chapter Preview

Corporations like **Facebook** and **Google** have substantial resources at their disposal. In fact, the corporation is the dominant form of business organization in the United States in terms of sales, earnings, and number of employees. All of the 500 largest U.S. companies are corporations. In this chapter, we look at the essential features of a corporation and explain the accounting for a corporation's capital stock transactions.

Feature Story

Oh Well, I Guess I'll Get Rich

Suppose you started one of the fastest-growing companies in the history of business. Now suppose that by "going public"—issuing stock of your company to outside investors who are foaming at the mouth for the chance to buy its shares—you would instantly become one of the richest people in the world. Would you hesitate?

That is exactly what Mark Zuckerberg, the founder of **Facebook**, did. Many people who start high-tech companies go public as soon as possible to cash in on their riches. But Zuckerberg was reluctant to do so. To understand why, you need to understand the advantages and disadvantages of being a public company.

The main motivation for issuing shares to the public is to raise money so you can grow your business. However, unlike a manufacturer or even an online retailer, Facebook doesn't need major physical resources, it doesn't have inventory, and it doesn't really need much money for marketing. But why not go public anyway, so the company would have some extra cash on hand—and so you personally get rich? As head of a closely held, nonpublic company, Zuckerberg was subject to far fewer regulations than a public company. Prior to going public, Zuckerberg could basically run the company however he wanted to.

For example, early in 2012, Facebook shocked the investment community by purchasing the photo-sharing service Instagram. The purchase was startling both for its speed (over a weekend) and price ($1 billion). Zuckerberg basically didn't seek anyone's approval. He thought it was a good idea, so he just did it. The structured decision-making process of a public company would make it very difficult for a public company to move that fast.

Speed is useful, but it is likely that Facebook will make even bigger acquisitions in the future. The reason: To survive among the likes of **Microsoft**, **Google**, and **Apple**, Facebook needs lots of cash. To raise that amount of money, the company really needed to go public. So in 2012, Mark Zuckerberg reluctantly made Facebook a public company, thus becoming one of the richest people in the world.

Chapter Outline

LEARNING OBJECTIVES	REVIEW	PRACTICE
LO 1 Discuss the major characteristics of a corporation.	• Characteristics of a corporation • Forming a corporation • Stockholder rights • Stock issue considerations • Corporate capital	**DO IT! 1a** Corporate Organization **1b** Corporate Capital
LO 2 Explain how to account for the issuance of common, preferred, and treasury stock.	• Accounting for common stock • Accounting for preferred stock • Accounting for treasury stock	**DO IT! 2a** Issuance of Stock **2b** Treasury Stock
LO 3 Explain how to account for cash dividends, stock dividends, and stock splits.	• Cash dividends • Dividend preferences • Stock dividends • Stock splits	**DO IT! 3a** Dividends on Preferred and Common Stock **3b** Stock Dividends and Stock Splits
LO 4 Discuss how stockholders' equity is reported and analyzed.	• Retained earnings • Retained earnings restrictions • Balance sheet presentation of stockholders' equity • Analysis of stockholders' equity	**DO IT! 4a** Stockholders' Equity Section **4b** Analyzing Stockholders' Equity

Go to the Review and Practice section at the end of the chapter for a review of key concepts and practice applications with solutions.

Visit WileyPLUS for additional tutorials and practice opportunities.

Corporate Form of Organization

LEARNING OBJECTIVE 1

Discuss the major characteristics of a corporation.

In 1819, Chief Justice John Marshall defined a corporation as "an artificial being, invisible, intangible, and existing only in contemplation of law." This definition is the foundation for the prevailing legal interpretation that a **corporation** is an **entity separate and distinct from its owners**.

A corporation is created by law, and its continued existence depends upon the statutes of the state in which it is incorporated. As a legal entity, a corporation has most of the rights and privileges of a person. The major exceptions relate to privileges that only a living person can exercise, such as the right to vote or to hold public office. A corporation is subject to the same duties and responsibilities as a person. For example, it must abide by the laws, and it must pay taxes.

Two common ways to classify corporations are by **purpose** and by **ownership**. A corporation may be organized for the purpose of making a profit, or it may be not-for-profit. For-profit corporations include such well-known companies as **McDonald's**, **Nike**, **PepsiCo**, and **Google**. Not-for-profit corporations are organized for charitable, medical, or educational purposes. Examples are the **Salvation Army** and the **American Cancer Society**.

Classification by ownership differentiates publicly held and privately held corporations. A **publicly held corporation** may have thousands of stockholders. Its stock is regularly traded on a national securities exchange such as the New York Stock Exchange or NASDAQ. Examples are **IBM**, **Caterpillar**, and **Apple**.

In contrast, a **privately held corporation** usually has only a few stockholders, and does not offer its stock for sale to the general public (see **Alternative Terminology**). Privately held companies are generally much smaller than publicly held companies, although some notable exceptions exist. **Cargill Inc.**, a private corporation that trades in grain and other commodities, is one of the largest companies in the United States.

ALTERNATIVE TERMINOLOGY

Privately held corporations are also referred to as *closely held corporations.*

Characteristics of a Corporation

In 1964, when **Nike**'s founders Phil Knight and Bill Bowerman were just getting started in the running shoe business, they formed their original organization as a partnership. In 1968, they reorganized the company as a corporation. A number of characteristics distinguish corporations from proprietorships and partnerships. We explain the most important of these characteristics below.

Separate Legal Existence

As an entity separate and distinct from its owners, the corporation acts under its own name rather than in the name of its stockholders. **Facebook** may buy, own, and sell property. It may borrow money, and it may enter into legally binding contracts in its own name. It may also sue or be sued, and it pays its own taxes.

In a partnership, the acts of the owners (partners) bind the partnership. In contrast, the acts of its owners (stockholders) do not bind the corporation unless such owners are **agents** of the corporation. For example, if you owned shares of Nike stock, you would not have the right to purchase inventory for the company unless you were designated as an agent of the corporation.

Stockholders

Legal existence separate from owners

Limited Liability of Stockholders

Since a corporation is a separate legal entity, creditors have recourse only to corporate assets to satisfy their claims. The liability of stockholders is normally limited to their investment in the

Stockholders

Limited liability of stockholders

corporation. Creditors have no legal claim on the personal assets of the owners unless fraud has occurred. Even in the event of bankruptcy, stockholders' losses are generally limited to their capital investment in the corporation.

Transferable Ownership Rights

Transferable ownership rights

Shares of capital stock represent ownership in a corporation. These shares are transferable units. Stockholders may dispose of part or all of their interest in a corporation simply by selling their stock. The transfer of an ownership interest in a partnership requires the consent of each owner. In contrast, the transfer of stock is entirely at the discretion of the stockholder. It does not require the approval of either the corporation or other stockholders.

The transfer of ownership rights between stockholders normally has no effect on the daily operating activities of the corporation. Nor does it affect the corporation's assets, liabilities, and total ownership equity. The transfer of these ownership rights is a transaction between individual owners. The company does not participate in the transfer of these ownership rights after the original sale of the capital stock.

Ability to Acquire Capital

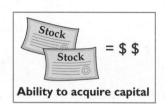

Ability to acquire capital

It is relatively easy for a corporation to obtain capital through the issuance of stock. Buying stock in a corporation is often attractive to an investor because a stockholder has limited liability and shares of stock are readily transferable. Also, numerous individuals can become stockholders by investing relatively small amounts of money.

Continuous Life

Continuous life

The life of a corporation is stated in its charter. The life may be perpetual, or it may be limited to a specific number of years. If it is limited, the company can extend the life through renewal of the charter. Since a corporation is a separate legal entity, its continuance as a going concern is not affected by the withdrawal, death, or incapacity of a stockholder, employee, or officer. As a result, a successful company can have a continuous and perpetual life.

Corporation Management

Stockholders legally own the corporation. However, they manage the corporation indirectly through a board of directors they elect. Mark Zuckerberg is the chairman of **Facebook**'s board of directors. The board, in turn, formulates the operating policies for the company. The board also selects officers, such as a president and one or more vice presidents, to execute policy and to perform daily management functions. As a result of the Sarbanes-Oxley Act, the board is now required to monitor management's actions more closely. Many feel that the failures of **Enron**, **WorldCom**, and **MF Global** could have been avoided by more diligent boards.

Illustration 11.1 presents a typical organization chart showing the delegation of responsibility. The chief executive officer (CEO) has overall responsibility for managing the business. As the organization chart shows, the CEO delegates responsibility to other officers. The chief accounting officer is the **controller**. The controller's responsibilities include (1) maintaining the accounting records, (2) ensuring an adequate system of internal control, and (3) preparing financial statements, tax returns, and internal reports. The **treasurer** has custody of the corporation's funds and is responsible for maintaining the company's cash position.

The organizational structure of a corporation enables a company to hire professional managers to run the business (see **Ethics Note**). On the other hand, the separation of ownership and management often reduces an owner's ability to actively manage the company.

ETHICS NOTE

Managers who are not owners are often compensated based on the performance of the firm. They thus may be tempted to exaggerate firm performance by inflating income figures.

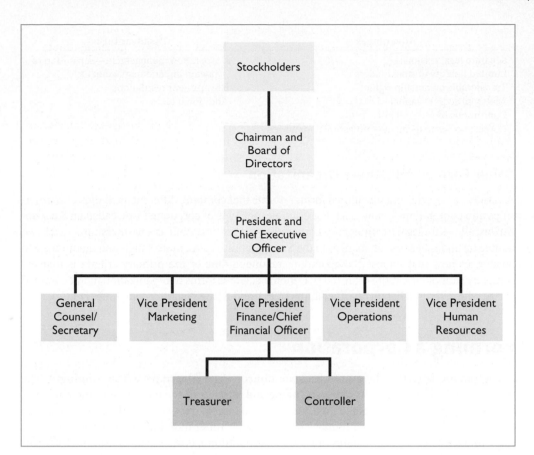

ILLUSTRATION 11.1
Corporation organization chart

Government Regulations

A corporation is subject to numerous state and federal regulations. For example, state laws usually prescribe the requirements for issuing stock, the distributions of earnings permitted to stockholders, and the acceptable methods for buying back and retiring stock. Federal securities laws govern the sale of capital stock to the general public. Also, most publicly held corporations are required to make extensive disclosure of their financial affairs to the Securities and Exchange Commission (SEC) through quarterly and annual reports (Forms 10Q and 10K). In addition, when a corporation lists its stock on organized securities exchanges, it must comply with the reporting requirements of these exchanges. Government regulations are designed to protect the owners of the corporation.

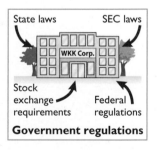

Government regulations

Additional Taxes

Owners of proprietorships and partnerships report their share of earnings on their personal income tax returns. The individual owner then pays taxes on this amount. Corporations, on the other hand, must pay federal and state income taxes **as a separate legal entity**. These taxes can be substantial. They can amount to as much as 40% of taxable income.

In addition, stockholders must pay taxes on cash dividends (pro rata distributions of net income). Thus, many argue that the government taxes corporate income **twice (double taxation)**—once at the corporate level and again at the individual level.

In summary, **Illustration 11.2** shows the advantages and disadvantages of a corporation compared to a proprietorship and a partnership.

Additional taxes

ILLUSTRATION 11.2

Advantages and disadvantages of a corporation

Advantages	Disadvantages
Separate legal existence	Corporation management—separation of ownership and management
Limited liability of stockholders	Government regulations
Transferable ownership rights	Additional taxes
Ability to acquire capital	
Continuous life	
Corporation management—professional managers	

Other Forms of Business Organization

A variety of "hybrid" organizational forms—forms that combine different attributes of partnerships and corporations—now exist. For example, one type of corporate form, called an **S corporation**, allows for legal treatment as a corporation but tax treatment as a partnership—that is, no double taxation. Because of changes to the S corporation's rules, more small- and medium-sized businesses now may choose S corporation treatment. One of the primary criteria is that the company cannot have more than 100 shareholders. Other forms of organization include limited partnerships, limited liability partnerships (LLPs), and limited liability companies (LLCs).

Forming a Corporation

A corporation is formed by grant of a state **charter** (see **Alternative Terminology**). The charter is a document that describes the name and purpose of the corporation, the types and number of shares of stock that are authorized to be issued, the names of the individuals that formed the company, and the number of shares that these individuals agreed to purchase. Regardless of the number of states in which a corporation has operating divisions, it is incorporated in only one state.

> **ALTERNATIVE TERMINOLOGY**
>
> The charter is often referred to as the *articles of incorporation.*

It is to the company's advantage to incorporate in a state whose laws are favorable to the corporate form of business organization. For example, although **Facebook** has its headquarters in California, it is incorporated in Delaware. In fact, more and more corporations have been incorporating in states with rules that favor existing management. For example, **Gulf Oil** changed its state of incorporation to Delaware to thwart possible unfriendly takeovers. There, certain defensive tactics against takeovers can be approved by the board of directors alone, without a vote by shareholders.

Upon receipt of its charter from the state of incorporation, the corporation establishes **by-laws**. The by-laws establish the internal rules and procedures for conducting the affairs of the corporation. Corporations engaged in interstate commerce must also obtain a **license** from each state in which they do business. The license subjects the corporation's operating activities to the general corporation laws of the state.

Costs incurred in the formation of a corporation are called **organization costs**. These costs include legal and state fees, and promotional expenditures involved in the organization of the business. **Corporations expense organization costs as incurred.** Determining the amount and timing of future benefits is so difficult that it is standard procedure to take a conservative approach of expensing these costs immediately.

Stockholder Rights

When chartered, the corporation may begin selling shares of stock. When a corporation has only one class of stock, it is **common stock**. Each share of common stock gives the stockholder the ownership rights pictured in **Illustration 11.3**. The articles of incorporation or the by-laws state the ownership rights of a share of stock.

Proof of stock ownership is evidenced by a form known as a **stock certificate**. As **Illustration 11.4** shows, the face of the certificate shows the name of the corporation, the stockholder's name, the class and special features of the stock, the number of shares owned, and the signatures of authorized corporate officials. Prenumbered certificates facilitate accountability. They may be issued for any quantity of shares.

ILLUSTRATION 11.3 Ownership rights of stockholders

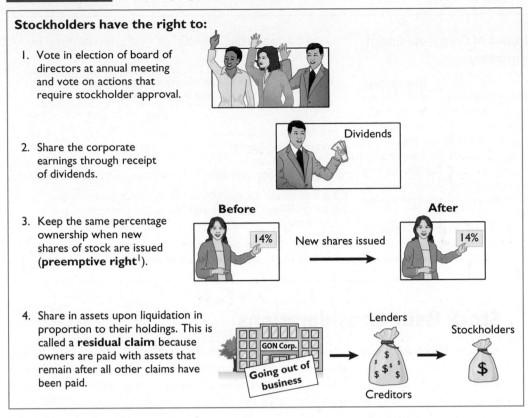

Stockholders have the right to:

1. Vote in election of board of directors at annual meeting and vote on actions that require stockholder approval.

2. Share the corporate earnings through receipt of dividends.

   Dividends

3. Keep the same percentage ownership when new shares of stock are issued (**preemptive right**[1]).

   Before — 14% — New shares issued — After — 14%

4. Share in assets upon liquidation in proportion to their holdings. This is called a **residual claim** because owners are paid with assets that remain after all other claims have been paid.

   GON Corp. Going out of business — Lenders — Stockholders — Creditors

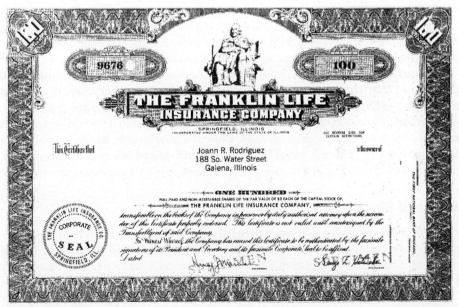

ILLUSTRATION 11.4

A stock certificate

9676 — 100

THE FRANKLIN LIFE INSURANCE COMPANY

SPRINGFIELD, ILLINOIS
INCORPORATED UNDER THE LAWS OF THE STATE OF ILLINOIS

SEE REVERSE SIDE FOR CERTAIN DEFINITIONS

This Certifies that

Joann R. Rodriguez
188 So. Water Street
Galena, Illinois

is the owner of

ONE HUNDRED

FULL-PAID AND NON-ASSESSABLE SHARES OF THE PAR VALUE OF $2 EACH OF THE CAPITAL STOCK OF,
THE FRANKLIN LIFE INSURANCE COMPANY,

Source: The Franklin Life Insurance Company

[1]A number of companies have eliminated the preemptive right because they believe it makes an unnecessary and cumbersome demand on management. For example, by stockholder approval, **IBM** has dropped its preemptive right for stockholders.

People, Planet, and Profit Insight

iStock.com/Robert Churchill

The Impact of Corporate Social Responsibility

A survey conducted by **Institutional Shareholder Services**, a proxy advisory firm, shows that 83% of investors now believe environmental and social factors can significantly impact shareholder value over the long term. This belief is clearly visible in the rising level of support for shareholder proposals requesting action related to social and environmental issues.

The following table shows that the number of corporate social responsibility (CSR) related shareholder proposals rose from 150 in 2000 to 191 in 2010. Moreover, those proposals received average voting support of 18.4% of votes cast versus just 7.5% a decade earlier.

Trends in Shareholder Proposals on Corporate Responsibility			
	2000	**2005**	**2010**
Number of proposals voted	150	155	191
Average voting support	7.5%	9.9%	18.4%
Percent proposals receiving >10% support	16.7%	31.2%	52.1%

Source: Investor Responsibility Research Center, Ernst & Young, *Seven Questions CEOs and Boards Should Ask About: "Triple Bottom Line" Reporting.*

Why are CSR-related shareholder proposals increasing? (Go to WileyPLUS for this answer and additional questions.)

Stock Issue Considerations

Although **Facebook** incorporated in 2004, it did not sell stock to the public until 2012. At that time, Facebook evidently decided it would benefit from the infusion of cash that a public sale would bring. When a corporation decides to issue stock, it must resolve a number of basic questions: How many shares should it authorize for sale? How should it issue the stock? What value should the corporation assign to the stock? We address these questions in the following sections.

Authorized Stock

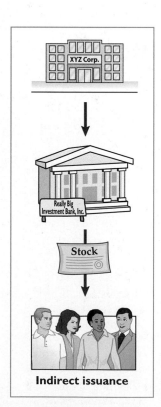

Indirect issuance

The charter indicates the maximum number of shares that a corporation is **authorized** to sell. The total amount of **authorized stock** at the time of incorporation normally anticipates both initial and subsequent capital needs. As a result, the number of shares authorized generally exceeds the number initially sold. If it sells all authorized stock, a corporation must obtain consent of the state to amend its charter before it can issue additional shares.

The authorization of capital stock does not result in a formal accounting entry. The reason is that the event has no immediate effect on either corporate assets or stockholders' equity. However, the number of authorized shares is often reported in the stockholders' equity section of the balance sheet. It is then simple to determine the number of unissued shares that the corporation can issue without amending the charter: subtract the total shares issued from the total authorized. For example, if **Advanced Micro** was authorized to sell 100,000 shares of common stock and issued 80,000 shares, 20,000 shares would remain unissued.

Issuance of Stock

A corporation can issue common stock **directly** to investors. Alternatively, it can issue the stock **indirectly** through an investment banking firm that specializes in bringing securities to the attention of prospective investors. Direct issue is typical in closely held companies. Indirect issue is customary for a publicly held corporation.

In an indirect issue, the investment banking firm may agree to **underwrite** the entire stock issue. In this arrangement, the investment banker buys the stock from the corporation at a stipulated price and resells the shares to investors. The corporation thus avoids any risk of being unable to sell the shares. Also, it obtains immediate use of the cash received from the underwriter. The investment banking firm, in turn, assumes the risk of reselling the shares, in return for an underwriting fee.[2] For example, **Google** (the world's number-one Internet

---

[2]Alternatively, the investment banking firm may agree only to enter into a **best-efforts contract** with the corporation. In such cases, the banker agrees to sell as many shares as possible at a specified price. The corporation bears the risk of unsold stock. Under a best-efforts arrangement, the banking firm is paid a fee or commission for its services.

search engine) used underwriters when it issued a highly successful initial public offering, raising $1.67 billion. The underwriters charged a 3% underwriting fee (approximately $50 million) on Google's stock offering.

How does a corporation set the price for a new issue of stock? Among the factors to be considered are (1) the company's anticipated future earnings, (2) its expected dividend rate per share, (3) its current financial position, (4) the current state of the economy, and (5) the current state of the securities market. The calculation can be complex and is properly the subject of a finance course.

Anatomy of a Fraud

The president, chief operating officer, and chief financial officer of **SafeNet**, a software encryption company, were each awarded employee stock options by the company's board of directors as part of their compensation package. Stock options enable an employee to buy a company's stock sometime in the future at the price that existed when the stock option was awarded. For example, suppose that you received stock options today, when the stock price of your company was $30. Three years later, if the stock price rose to $100, you could "exercise" your options and buy the stock for $30 per share, thereby making $70 per share. After being awarded their stock options, the three employees changed the award dates in the company's records to dates in the past, when the company's stock was trading at historical lows. For instance, using the previous example, they would choose a past date when the stock was selling for $10 per share, rather than the $30 price on the actual award date. This would increase the profit from exercising the options to $90 per share.

Total take: $1.7 million

The Missing Control

Independent internal verification. The company's board of directors should have ensured that the awards were properly administered. For example, the date on the minutes from the board meeting could be compared to the dates that were recorded for the awards. In addition, the dates should again be confirmed upon exercise.

Par and No-Par Value Stocks

Par value stock is capital stock to which the charter has assigned a value per share. Years ago, par value determined the **legal capital** per share that a company must retain in the business for the protection of corporate creditors. That amount was not available for withdrawal by stockholders. Thus, in the past, most states required the corporation to sell its shares at par or above.

However, par value was often immaterial relative to the actual value of the company's stock—even at the time of issuance. Thus, its usefulness as a protective device to creditors was questionable. For example, **Facebook**'s par value is $0.000006 per share, yet its market price recently was $84. Thus, par has no relationship with market price. In the vast majority of cases, it is an immaterial amount. As a consequence, today many states do not require a par value. Instead, they use other means to protect creditors.

No-par value stock is capital stock to which the charter has not assigned a value. No-par value stock is fairly common today. For example, **Nike** and **Procter & Gamble** both have no-par stock. In many states, the board of directors assigns a **stated value** to no-par shares.

DO IT! 1a | Corporate Organization

Indicate whether each of the following statements is true or false. If false, indicate how to correct the statement.

_____ 1. Similar to partners in a partnership, stockholders of a corporation have unlimited liability.

_____ 2. It is relatively easy for a corporation to obtain capital through the issuance of stock.

_____ 3. The separation of ownership and management is an advantage of the corporate form of business.

_____ 4. The journal entry to record the authorization of capital stock includes a credit to the appropriate capital stock account.

_____ 5. All states require a par value per share for capital stock.

ACTION PLAN

• Review the characteristics of a corporation to understand which are advantages and which are disadvantages.

• Understand that corporations raise capital through the issuance of stock, which can be par or no-par.

Solution

1. False. The liability of stockholders is normally limited to their investment in the corporation. **2.** True. **3.** False. The separation of ownership and management is a disadvantage of the corporate form of business. **4.** False. The authorization of capital stock does not result in a formal accounting entry. **5.** False. Many states do not require a par value.

Related exercise material: **BE11.1, DO IT! 11.1a, E11.1, and E11.2.**

Corporate Capital

Owners' equity for a corporation is identified by various names: **stockholders' equity**, **shareholders' equity**, or **corporate capital**. The stockholders' equity section of a corporation's balance sheet consists of two parts: (1) paid-in (contributed) capital and (2) retained earnings (earned capital).

The distinction between **paid-in capital** and **retained earnings** is important from both a legal and a financial point of view. Legally, corporations can make distributions of earnings (declare dividends) out of retained earnings in all states. However, in many states they cannot declare dividends out of paid-in capital. Management, stockholders, and others often look to retained earnings for the continued existence and growth of the corporation.

Paid-In Capital

Paid-in capital is the total amount of cash and other assets paid in to the corporation by stockholders in exchange for capital stock. As noted earlier, when a corporation has only one class of stock, it is **common stock**.

Retained Earnings

Retained earnings is net income that a corporation retains for future use. Net income is recorded in Retained Earnings by a closing entry that debits Income Summary and credits Retained Earnings. For example, assuming that net income for Delta Robotics in its first year of operations is $130,000, the closing entry is:

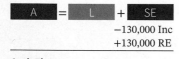

−130,000 Inc
+130,000 RE

Cash Flows
no effect

Income Summary	130,000	
Retained Earnings		130,000
(To close Income Summary and transfer net income		
to Retained Earnings)		

If Delta Robotics has a balance of $800,000 in common stock at the end of its first year, its stockholders' equity section is as shown in **Illustration 11.5.**

ILLUSTRATION 11.5

Stockholders' equity section

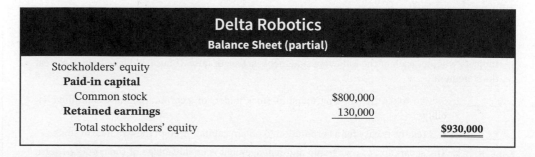

Delta Robotics		
Balance Sheet (partial)		
Stockholders' equity		
Paid-in capital		
Common stock	$800,000	
Retained earnings	130,000	
Total stockholders' equity		**$930,000**

Illustration 11.6 compares the owners' equity (stockholders' equity) accounts reported on a balance sheet for a proprietorship and a corporation.

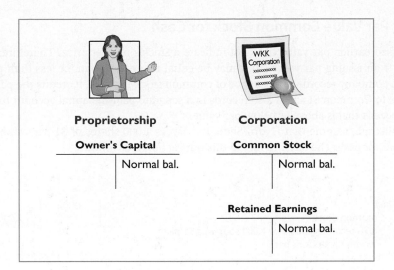

ILLUSTRATION 11.6
Comparison of owners' equity accounts

DO IT! 1b | Corporate Capital

At the end of its first year of operation, Doral Corporation has $750,000 of common stock and net income of $122,000. Prepare (a) the closing entry for net income and (b) the stockholders' equity section at year-end.

Solution

a. Income Summary	122,000	
Retained Earnings		122,000
(To close Income Summary and transfer net income to Retained Earnings)		

b. Stockholders' equity
    Paid-in capital

Common stock	$750,000	
Retained earnings	122,000	
Total stockholders' equity		$872,000

Related exercise material: **DO IT! 11.1b.**

ACTION PLAN

- Record net income in Retained Earnings by a closing entry in which Income Summary is debited and Retained Earnings is credited.
- In the stockholders' equity section, show (1) paid-in capital and (2) retained earnings.

Accounting for Stock Issuances

LEARNING OBJECTIVE 2
Explain how to account for the issuance of common, preferred, and treasury stock.

Accounting for Common Stock

Let's now look at how to account for issues of common stock. The primary objectives in accounting for the issuance of common stock are (1) to identify the specific sources of paid-in capital, and (2) to maintain the distinction between paid-in capital and retained earnings. **The issuance of common stock affects only paid-in capital accounts.**

Issuing Par Value Common Stock for Cash

As discussed earlier, par value does not indicate a stock's market price. Therefore, the cash proceeds from issuing par value stock may be equal to, greater than, or less than par value. When the company records the issuance of common stock for cash, it credits the par value of the shares to Common Stock. It also records in a separate paid-in capital account the portion of the proceeds that is above or below par value.

To illustrate, assume that Hydro-Slide, Inc. issues 1,000 shares of $1 par value common stock at par for cash. The entry to record this transaction is as follows.

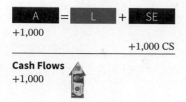

+1,000

           +1,000 CS

Cash Flows
+1,000

Cash	1,000	
Common Stock		1,000
(To record issuance of 1,000 shares of $1 par		
common stock at par)		

Now assume that Hydro-Slide issues an additional 1,000 shares of the $1 par value common stock for cash at $5 per share. The amount received above the par value, in this case $4 ($5 – $1), is credited to Paid-in Capital in Excess of Par—Common Stock. The entry is as follows.

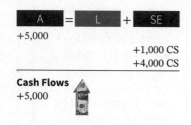

+5,000

           +1,000 CS
           +4,000 CS

Cash Flows
+5,000

Cash	5,000	
Common Stock		1,000
Paid-in Capital in Excess of Par—Common Stock		4,000
(To record issuance of 1,000 shares of $1 par		
common stock)		

ALTERNATIVE TERMINOLOGY

Paid-in Capital in Excess of Par is also called *Premium on Stock*.

ILLUSTRATION 11.7

Stockholders' equity—paid-in capital in excess of par

The total paid-in capital from these two transactions is $6,000, and the legal capital is $2,000 (see **Alternative Terminology**). Assuming Hydro-Slide, Inc. has retained earnings of $27,000, **Illustration 11.7** shows the company's stockholders' equity section.

Hydro-Slide, Inc.	
Balance Sheet (partial)	
Stockholders' equity	
Paid-in capital	
Common stock	$ 2,000
Paid-in capital in excess of par—	
common stock	**4,000**
Total paid-in capital	6,000
Retained earnings	27,000
Total stockholders' equity	$33,000

When a corporation issues stock for less than par value, it debits the account Paid-in Capital in Excess of Par—Common Stock if a credit balance exists in this account. If a credit balance does not exist, then the corporation debits to Retained Earnings the amount less than par. This situation occurs only rarely. Most states do not permit the sale of common stock below par value because stockholders may be held personally liable for the difference between the price paid upon original sale and par value.

Issuing No-Par Common Stock for Cash

When no-par common stock has a stated value, the entries are similar to those illustrated for par value stock. The corporation credits the stated value to Common Stock. Also, when the selling price of no-par stock exceeds stated value, the corporation credits the excess to Paid-in Capital in Excess of Stated Value—Common Stock.

For example, assume that instead of $1 par value stock, Hydro-Slide, Inc. has $5 stated value no-par stock and the company issues 5,000 shares at $8 per share for cash. The entry is as follows.

Cash	40,000	
Common Stock		25,000
Paid-in Capital in Excess of Stated Value—Common Stock		15,000
(To record issuance of 5,000 shares of $5 stated		
value no-par stock)		

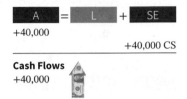

```
A       =   L   +   SE
+40,000
                        +25,000 CS
                        +15,000 CS

Cash Flows
+40,000
```

Hydro-Slide, Inc. reports Paid-in Capital in Excess of Stated Value—Common Stock as part of paid-in capital in the stockholders' equity section.

What happens when no-par stock does not have a stated value? In that case, the corporation credits the entire proceeds to Common Stock. Thus, if Hydro-Slide does not assign a stated value to its no-par stock, it records the issuance of the 5,000 shares at $8 per share for cash as follows.

Cash	40,000	
Common Stock		40,000
(To record issuance of 5,000 shares of no-par stock)		

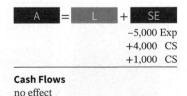

```
A       =   L   +   SE
+40,000
                        +40,000 CS

Cash Flows
+40,000
```

Issuing Common Stock for Services or Noncash Assets

Corporations also may issue stock for services (compensation to attorneys or consultants) or for noncash assets (land, buildings, and equipment). In such cases, what cost should be recognized in the exchange transaction? To comply with the **historical cost principle**, in a non-cash transaction **cost is the cash equivalent price**. Thus, **cost is either the fair value of the consideration given up or the fair value of the consideration received**, whichever is more clearly determinable.

To illustrate, assume that attorneys have helped Jordan Company incorporate. They have billed the company $5,000 for their services. They agree to accept 4,000 shares of $1 par value common stock in payment of their bill. At the time of the exchange, there is no established market price for the stock. In this case, the fair value of the consideration received ($5,000 attorney services) is more clearly evident. Accordingly, Jordan Company makes the following entry.

Organization Expense	5,000	
Common Stock		4,000
Paid-in Capital in Excess of Par—Common Stock		1,000
(To record issuance of 4,000 shares of $1 par value		
stock to attorneys)		

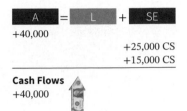

```
A       =   L   +   SE
                        −5,000 Exp
                        +4,000  CS
                        +1,000  CS

Cash Flows
no effect
```

As explained earlier, organization costs are expensed as incurred.

In contrast, assume that Athletic Research Inc. is an existing publicly held corporation. Its $5 par value common stock is actively traded at $8 per share. The company issues 10,000 shares of stock to acquire land recently advertised for sale at $90,000. The most clearly evident value in this noncash transaction is the market price of the consideration given ($80,000 common stock; the advertised price of the land is not necessarily indicative of its value). The company records the transaction as follows.

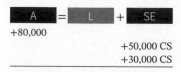

Cash Flows
no effect

Land	80,000	
Common Stock		50,000
Paid-in Capital in Excess of Par—Common Stock		30,000
(To record issuance of 10,000 shares of $5 par value		
stock for land)		

As illustrated in these examples, **the par value of the stock is never a factor in determining the cost of the assets or services received in noncash transactions**. This is also true of the stated value of no-par stock.

Accounting for Preferred Stock

To appeal to a larger segment of potential investors, a corporation may issue an additional class of stock, called preferred stock. **Preferred stock** has contractual provisions that give it some preference or priority over common stock. Typically, preferred stockholders have a priority as to (1) distributions of earnings (dividends) and (2) assets in the event of liquidation. However, they generally do not have voting rights.

Like common stock, corporations may issue preferred stock for cash or for noncash assets. The entries for these transactions are similar to the entries for common stock. When a corporation has more than one class of stock, each paid-in capital account title should identify the stock to which it relates. A company might have the following accounts: Preferred Stock, Common Stock, Paid-in Capital in Excess of Par—Preferred Stock, and Paid-in Capital in Excess of Par—Common Stock.

For example, if Stine Corporation issues 10,000 shares of $10 par value preferred stock for $12 cash per share, the entry to record the issuance is as follows.

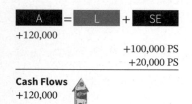

Cash Flows
+120,000

Cash	120,000	
Preferred Stock		100,000
Paid-in Capital in Excess of Par—Preferred Stock		20,000
(To record issuance of 10,000 shares of $10 par value		
preferred stock)		

Preferred stock may have either a par value or no-par value. In the stockholders' equity section of the balance sheet, companies list preferred stock first because of its dividend and liquidation preferences over common stock.

Investor Insight   Facebook

Emmanuel Dunand/
AFP/Getty Images

How to Read Stock Quotes

Organized exchanges trade the stock of publicly held companies at dollar prices per share established by the interaction between buyers and sellers. For each listed security, the financial press reports the high and low prices of the stock during the year, the total volume of stock traded on a given day, the high and low prices for the day, and the closing market price, with the net change for the day. **Facebook** is listed on the NASDAQ exchange. Here is a listing for Facebook:

	52 Weeks						
Stock	High	Low	Volume	High	Low	Close	Net Change
Facebook	86.07	54.66	54,156,600	85.59	83.11	84.63	.629

These numbers indicate the following. The high and low market prices for the last 52 weeks have been $86.07 and $54.66. The trading volume for the day was 54,156,600 shares. The high, low, and closing prices for that date were $85.59, $83.11, and $84.63, respectively. The net change for the day was a decrease of $0.629 per share.

For stocks traded on organized exchanges, how are the dollar prices per share established? What factors might influence the price of shares in the marketplace? (Go to WileyPLUS for this answer and additional questions.)

DO IT! 2a | Issuance of Stock

Cayman Corporation begins operations on March 1 by issuing 100,000 shares of $1 par value common stock for cash at $12 per share. On March 15, it issues 5,000 shares of common stock to attorneys in settlement of their bill of $50,000 for organization costs. On March 28, Cayman Corporation issues 1,500 shares of $10 par value preferred stock for cash at $30 per share. Journalize the issuance of the common and preferred shares, assuming the shares are not publicly traded.

Solution

Mar. 1	Cash	1,200,000	
	Common Stock (100,000 × $1)		100,000
	Paid-in Capital in Excess of Par—Common Stock		1,100,000
	(To record issuance of 100,000 shares at $12 per share)		
Mar. 15	Organization Expense	50,000	
	Common Stock (5,000 × $1)		5,000
	Paid-in Capital in Excess of Par—Common Stock		45,000
	(To record issuance of 5,000 shares for attorneys' fees)		
Mar. 28	Cash	45,000	
	Preferred Stock (1,500 × $10)		15,000
	Paid-in Capital in Excess of Par—Preferred Stock		30,000
	(To record issuance of 1,500 shares at $30 per share)		

Related exercise material: **BE11.2, BE11.3, BE11.4, BE11.5, DO IT! 11.2a, E11.3, E11.4, E11.6, and E11.8.**

ACTION PLAN

- **In issuing shares for cash, credit Common Stock or Preferred Stock for par value per share.**
- **Credit any additional proceeds in excess of par to a separate paid-in capital account.**
- **When stock is issued for services, use the cash equivalent price.**
- **For the cash equivalent price, use either the fair value of what is given up or the fair value of what is received, whichever is more clearly determinable.**

Accounting for Treasury Stock

Treasury stock is a corporation's own stock that it has issued and subsequently reacquired from shareholders but not retired (see **Helpful Hint**). A corporation may acquire treasury stock for various reasons:

1. To reissue the shares to officers and employees under bonus and stock compensation plans.
2. To increase trading of the company's stock in the securities market. Companies expect that buying their own stock will signal that management believes the stock is underpriced, which they hope will enhance its market price.
3. To have additional shares available for use in the acquisition of other companies.
4. To reduce the number of shares outstanding and thereby increase earnings per share.

A less frequent reason for purchasing treasury shares is to eliminate hostile shareholders by buying them out.

Many corporations have treasury stock. For example, approximately 65% of U.S. companies have treasury stock. In a recent year, **Nike** purchased more than 6 million treasury shares.

HELPFUL HINT

Treasury shares do not have dividend rights or voting rights.

Purchase of Treasury Stock

Companies generally account for treasury stock by **the cost method**. This method uses the cost of the shares purchased to value the treasury stock. Under the cost method, the company debits **Treasury Stock** for the **price paid to reacquire the shares**. When the company disposes of the shares, it credits to Treasury Stock **the same amount** it paid to reacquire the shares.

To illustrate, assume that on January 1, 2022, the stockholders' equity section of Mead, Inc. has 400,000 shares authorized and 100,000 shares of $5 par value common stock outstanding (all issued at par value) and Retained Earnings of $200,000. **Illustration 11.8** shows the stockholders' equity section before purchase of treasury stock.

Mead, Inc.
Balance Sheet (partial)

Stockholders' equity	
Paid-in capital	
Common stock, $5 par value, 400,000 shares	
authorized, 100,000 shares issued and outstanding	$500,000
Retained earnings	200,000
Total stockholders' equity	$700,000

On February 1, 2022, Mead acquires 4,000 shares of its common stock at $8 per share. The entry is as follows.

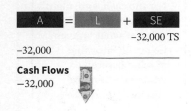

A	=	L	+	SE
				−32,000 TS
−32,000				

Cash Flows
−32,000

Feb. 1	Treasury Stock	32,000	
	Cash		32,000
	(To record purchase of 4,000 shares of treasury stock at $8 per share)		

Mead debits Treasury Stock for the cost of the shares purchased ($32,000). Is the original paid-in capital account, Common Stock, affected? No, because **the number of issued shares does not change**.

In the stockholders' equity section of the balance sheet, Mead deducts treasury stock from total paid-in capital and retained earnings. Treasury Stock is a **contra stockholders' equity account**. Thus, the acquisition of treasury stock reduces stockholders' equity. The stockholders' equity section of Mead, Inc. after purchase of treasury stock is as shown in **Illustration 11.9**.

Mead, Inc.
Balance Sheet (partial)

Stockholders' equity	
Paid-in capital	
Common stock, $5 par value, 400,000 shares authorized,	
100,000 shares issued, and 96,000 shares outstanding	$500,000
Retained earnings	200,000
Total paid-in capital and retained earnings	700,000
Less: Treasury stock (4,000 shares)	**32,000**
Total stockholders' equity	$668,000

Mead discloses in the balance sheet both the number of shares issued (100,000) and the number of shares in the treasury (4,000). The difference is the number of shares of stock outstanding (96,000). The term **outstanding stock** means the number of shares of issued stock that are being held by stockholders.

Some maintain that companies should report treasury stock as an asset because it can be sold for cash. But under this reasoning, companies would also show unissued stock as an asset, which is clearly incorrect. Rather than being an asset, treasury stock reduces stockholder claims on corporate assets. This effect is correctly shown by reporting treasury stock as a deduction from total paid-in capital and retained earnings (see **Ethics Note**).

Disposal of Treasury Stock

Treasury stock is usually sold. The accounting for its sale differs when treasury stock is sold above cost than when it is sold below cost (see **Helpful Hint**).

Sale of Treasury Stock Above Cost   If the selling price of the treasury stock is equal to its cost, the company records the sale of the shares by a debit to Cash and a credit to Treasury

ETHICS NOTE

The purchase of treasury stock reduces the cushion for creditors. To protect creditors, many states require that a portion of retained earnings equal to the cost of the treasury stock purchased be restricted from being paid as dividends.

HELPFUL HINT

Treasury stock transactions are classified as capital stock transactions. As in the case when stock is issued, the income statement is not involved.

Stock. When the selling price of the stock is greater than its cost, the company credits the difference to Paid-in Capital from Treasury Stock.

To illustrate, assume that on July 1, Mead, Inc. sells for $10 per share 1,000 of the 4,000 shares of its treasury stock previously acquired at $8 per share. The entry is as follows.

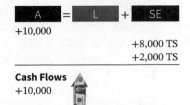

July 1	Cash (1,000 × $10)	10,000	
	Treasury Stock (1,000 × $8)		8,000
	Paid-in Capital from Treasury Stock		2,000
	(To record sale of 1,000 shares of treasury stock above cost)		

A = L + SE
+10,000
　　　　　+8,000 TS
　　　　　+2,000 TS
Cash Flows
+10,000

Mead does not record a $2,000 gain on sale of treasury stock because (1) gains on sales occur when **assets** are sold, and treasury stock is not an asset, and (2) a corporation does not realize a gain or suffer a loss from stock transactions with its own stockholders. Thus, companies should **not** include in net income any paid-in capital arising from the sale of treasury stock. Instead, they report Paid-in Capital from Treasury Stock separately on the balance sheet, as a part of paid-in capital.

Sale of Treasury Stock Below Cost When a company sells treasury stock below its cost, it usually debits to Paid-in Capital from Treasury Stock the excess of cost over selling price. Thus, if Mead, Inc. sells an additional 800 shares of treasury stock on October 1 at $7 per share, it makes the following entry.

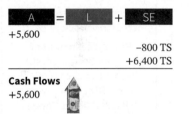

Oct. 1	Cash (800 × $7)	5,600	
	Paid-in Capital from Treasury Stock	800	
	Treasury Stock (800 × $8)		6,400
	(To record sale of 800 shares of treasury stock below cost)		

A = L + SE
+5,600
　　　　　−800 TS
　　　　　+6,400 TS
Cash Flows
+5,600

Observe the following from the two sales entries. (1) Mead credits Treasury Stock at cost in each entry. (2) Mead uses Paid-in Capital from Treasury Stock for the difference between cost and the resale price of the shares. (3) The original paid-in capital account, Common Stock, is not affected. **The sale of treasury stock increases both total assets and total stockholders' equity.**

Illustration 11.10 shows the treasury stock account balances on October 1 after posting the foregoing entries.

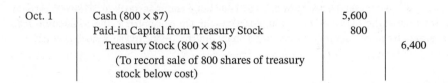

	Treasury Stock				Paid-in Capital from Treasury Stock		
Feb. 1	32,000	July 1	8,000	Oct. 1	800	July 1	2,000
		Oct. 1	6,400			Oct. 1 Bal.	1,200
Oct. 1 Bal.	17,600						

ILLUSTRATION 11.10
Treasury stock accounts

When a company fully depletes the credit balance in Paid-in Capital from Treasury Stock, it debits to Retained Earnings any additional excess of cost over selling price. To illustrate, assume that Mead, Inc. sells its remaining 2,200 shares at $7 per share on December 1. The excess of cost over selling price is $2,200 [2,200 × ($8 – $7)]. In this case, Mead debits $1,200 of the excess to Paid-in Capital from Treasury Stock. It debits the remainder to Retained Earnings. The entry is as follows.

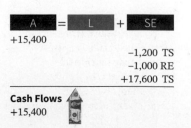

Dec. 1	Cash (2,200 × $7)	15,400	
	Paid-in Capital from Treasury Stock	1,200	
	Retained Earnings	1,000	
	Treasury Stock (2,200 × $8)		17,600
	(To record sale of 2,200 shares of treasury stock at $7 per share)		

A = L + SE
+15,400
　　　　　−1,200 TS
　　　　　−1,000 RE
　　　　　+17,600 TS
Cash Flows
+15,400

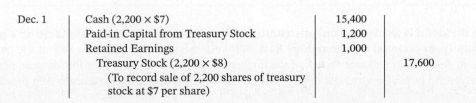

Accounting Across the Organization   Reebok

Han Myung-Gu/
WireImage/Getty Images

A Bold Repurchase Strategy

In a bold (and some would say risky) move, **Reebok** at one time bought back nearly a third of its shares. This repurchase of shares dramatically reduced Reebok's available cash. In fact, the company borrowed significant funds to accomplish the repurchase. In a press release, management stated that it was repurchasing the shares because it believed its stock was severely underpriced. The repurchase of so many shares was meant to signal management's belief in good future earnings.

Skeptics, however, suggested that Reebok's management was repurchasing shares to make it less likely that another company would acquire Reebok (in which case Reebok's top managers would likely lose their jobs). By depleting its cash, Reebok became a less attractive acquisition target. Acquiring companies like to purchase companies with large cash balances so they can pay off debt used in the acquisition.

What signal might a large stock repurchase send to investors regarding management's belief about the company's growth opportunities? (Go to WileyPLUS for this answer and additional questions.)

ACTION PLAN

- **Record the purchase of treasury stock at cost.**
- **When treasury stock is sold above its cost, credit the excess of the selling price over cost to Paid-in Capital from Treasury Stock. If Paid-in Capital from Treasury Stock is depleted, then debit Retained Earnings.**
- **When treasury stock is sold below its cost, debit the excess of cost over selling price to Paid-in Capital from Treasury Stock.**

DO IT! 2b | Treasury Stock

Santa Anita Inc. purchases 3,000 shares of its $50 par value common stock for $180,000 cash on July 1. It will hold the shares in the treasury until resold. On November 1, the corporation sells 1,000 shares of treasury stock for cash at $70 per share. Journalize the treasury stock transactions.

Solution

July 1	Treasury Stock	180,000	
	Cash		180,000
	(To record the purchase of 3,000 shares at $60 per share)		
Nov. 1	Cash	70,000	
	Treasury Stock		60,000
	Paid-in Capital from Treasury Stock		10,000
	(To record the sale of 1,000 shares of treasury stock at $70 per share)		

Related exercise material: **BE11.6, DO IT! 11.2b, E11.7, E11.8 and E11.9.**

Cash Dividends, Stock Dividends, and Stock Splits

LEARNING OBJECTIVE 3

Explain how to account for cash dividends, stock dividends, and stock splits.

A **dividend** **is a corporation's distribution of cash or stock to its stockholders on a pro rata (proportional to ownership) basis.** Pro rata means that if you own 10% of the common shares, you will receive 10% of the dividend. Dividends can take four forms: cash, property, scrip (a promissory note to pay cash), or stock. Cash dividends predominate in practice although companies also declare stock dividends with some frequency. These two forms of dividends are therefore the focus of our discussion.

Investors are very interested in a company's dividend practices. In the financial press, **dividends are generally reported quarterly as a dollar amount per share**. (Sometimes they are reported on an annual basis.) For example, the recent **quarterly** dividend rate was 24 cents per share for **Nike**, 22 cents per share for **GE**, and 25 cents per share for **Conagra Brands**.

Cash Dividends

A **cash dividend** is a pro rata distribution of cash to stockholders. Cash dividends are not paid on treasury shares. For a corporation to pay a cash dividend, it must have the following.

1. **Retained earnings.** The legality of a cash dividend depends on the laws of the state in which the company is incorporated. Payment of cash dividends from retained earnings is legal in all states. In general, cash dividend distributions from only the balance in common stock (legal capital) are illegal.

   A dividend declared out of paid-in capital is termed a **liquidating dividend**. Such a dividend reduces or "liquidates" the amount originally paid in by stockholders. Statutes vary considerably with respect to cash dividends based on paid-in capital in excess of par or stated value. Many states permit such dividends.

2. **Adequate cash.** Recently, Facebook had a balance in retained earnings of $6,099 million but a cash balance of only $4,315 million. If it had wanted to pay a dividend equal to its retained earnings, Facebook would have had to raise $1,784 million more in cash. It would have been unlikely to do this because it would not be able to pay this much in dividends in future years. In addition, such a dividend would completely deplete Facebook's balance in retained earnings, so it would not be able to pay a dividend in the next year unless it had positive net income.

3. **Declared dividends.** A company does not pay dividends unless its board of directors decides to do so, at which point the board "declares" the dividend. The board of directors has full authority to determine the amount of income to distribute in the form of a dividend and the amount to retain in the business. Dividends do not accrue like interest on a note payable, and they are not a liability until declared.

The amount and timing of a dividend are important issues for management to consider. The payment of a large cash dividend could lead to liquidity problems for the company. On the other hand, a small dividend or a missed dividend may cause unhappiness among stockholders. Many stockholders expect to receive a reasonable cash payment from the company on a periodic basis. Many companies declare and pay cash dividends quarterly. On the other hand, a number of high-growth companies pay no dividends, preferring to conserve cash to finance future capital expenditures.

Investors monitor a company's dividend practices. For example, regular dividend boosts in the face of irregular earnings can be a warning signal. Companies with high dividends and rising debt may be borrowing money to pay shareholders. On the other hand, low dividends may not be a negative sign because it may mean the company is reinvesting in itself, which may result in high returns through increases in the stock price. Presumably, investors seeking regular dividends buy stock in companies that pay periodic dividends, and those seeking growth in the stock price (capital gains) buy stock in companies that retain their earnings rather than pay dividends.

Entries for Cash Dividends

Three dates are important in connection with dividends: (1) the declaration date, (2) the record date, and (3) the payment date. Normally, there are two to four weeks between each date. Companies make accounting entries on the declaration date and the payment date. Companies do not make any entries on the record date.

On the **declaration date**, the board of directors formally declares (authorizes) the cash dividend and announces it to stockholders. The declaration of a cash dividend **commits**

the corporation to a legal obligation. The company must make an entry to recognize the increase in Cash Dividends and the increase in the liability Dividends Payable.

To illustrate, assume that on December 1, 2022, the directors of Media General declare a 50 cents per share cash dividend on 100,000 outstanding shares of $10 par value common stock. The dividend is $50,000 (100,000 × $0.50). The entry to record the declaration is as follows.

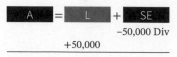

−50,000 Div
+50,000

Cash Flows
no effect

Declaration Date

Dec. 1	Cash Dividends	50,000	
	Dividends Payable		50,000
	(To record declaration of cash dividend)		

Media General debits the account Cash Dividends. Cash dividends decrease retained earnings. We use the specific title Cash Dividends to differentiate it from other types of dividends, such as stock dividends. Dividends Payable is a current liability. It will normally be paid within the next several months. *For homework problems, you should use the Cash Dividends account for recording dividend declarations.*

At the **record date**, the company determines ownership of the outstanding shares for dividend purposes (see **Helpful Hint**). The stockholders' records maintained by the corporation supply this information. In the interval between the declaration date and the record date, the corporation updates its stock ownership records. For Media General, the record date is December 22. No entry is required on this date because the corporation's liability recognized on the declaration date is unchanged.

HELPFUL HINT

The purpose of the record date is to identify the persons or entities that will receive the dividend, not to determine the amount of the dividend liability.

Record Date

| Dec. 22 | | No entry | | |

On the **payment date**, the company makes cash dividend payments to the stockholders of record (as of December 22) and records the payment of the dividend. If January 20 is the payment date for Media General, the entry on that date is as follows.

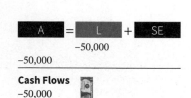

−50,000
−50,000

Cash Flows
−50,000

Payment Date

Jan. 20	Dividends Payable	50,000	
	Cash		50,000
	(To record payment of cash dividend)		

Note that payment of the dividend reduces both current assets and current liabilities. It has no effect on stockholders' equity. The cumulative effect of the declaration and payment of a cash dividend is to **decrease both stockholders' equity and total assets**. **Illustration 11.11** summarizes the three important dates associated with dividends for Media General.

ILLUSTRATION 11.11
Key dividend dates

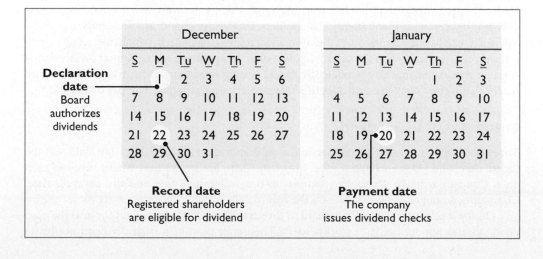

When using a Cash Dividends account, Media General should transfer the balance of that account to Retained Earnings at the end of the year by a closing entry. The entry for Media General at closing on December 31, 2022, is as follows.

Dec. 31	Retained Earnings	50,000	
	Cash Dividends		50,000
	(To close Cash Dividends to Retained Earnings)		

Investor Insight

iStock.com/Palto

What About Dividends?

If you have some excess dollars that you want to invest, you might consider stocks that pay dividends. According to data from the **Standard & Poor's (S&P)** Dow Jones Indices, dividend income made up 33% of the monthly return of the S&P 500 between 1926 and 2015. What that means is that dividends comprise one-third of the return to shareholders.

In addition, data from 1927 to 2014 indicate that dividend payers outperformed non-dividend payers, averaging 10.4% annual growth versus 8.5%. If you do not think that difference is much, the table indicates how an annual investment of $10,000 would grow at each of these rates.

Growth Over	8.5% Annual Growth Rate	10.4% Annual Growth Rate
10 years	$ 161,000	$ 179,400
20 years	524,900	661,800
30 years	1,300,000	2,000,000

Some companies have strong dividend yields, such as **Ford Motor Company** and **AT&T**. Others have been increasing dividend payouts at a strong clip, such as **UPS**, **Microsoft**, and **Boeing**. Good luck in your future investing!

Source: Selena Maranjian, "Dividend Stocks in 2017: 7 Stats Everyone Should Know," *The Motley Fool* (December 14, 2016).

What factors must management consider in deciding how large a dividend to pay? (Go to WileyPLUS for this answer and additional questions.)

Dividend Preferences

Preferred stockholders have the right to receive dividends before common stockholders. For example, if the dividend rate on preferred stock is $5 per share, common shareholders cannot receive any dividends in the current year until preferred stockholders have received $5 per share. The first claim to dividends does not, however, **guarantee** the payment of dividends. Dividends depend on many factors, such as adequate retained earnings and availability of cash. If a company does not pay dividends to preferred stockholders, it cannot pay dividends to common stockholders.

For preferred stock, companies state the per share dividend amount as a percentage of the par value or as a specified dollar amount. For example, **EarthLink** (before it merged with **Windstream Holdings**) specified a 3% dividend on its $100 par value preferred stock. **PepsiCo** pays $4.56 per share on its no-par preferred stock.

Most preferred stocks also have a preference on corporate assets if the corporation fails. This feature provides security for the preferred stockholder. The preference to assets may be for the par value of the shares or for a specified liquidating value. For example, **Commonwealth Edison**'s preferred stock entitles its holders to receive $31.80 per share, plus accrued and unpaid dividends, in the event of liquidation. The liquidation preference establishes the respective claims of creditors and preferred stockholders in litigation involving bankruptcy lawsuits.

Preferred stockholders — Common stockholders

Dividend preferences

Cumulative Dividend

Preferred stock often contains a **cumulative dividend** feature. This feature stipulates that preferred stockholders must be paid both current-year dividends and any unpaid prior-year dividends before common stockholders are paid any dividends. When preferred stock is cumulative, preferred dividends not declared in a given period are called **dividends in arrears**.

To illustrate, assume that Scientific Leasing has 5,000 shares of 7%, $100 par value, cumulative preferred stock outstanding. Each $100 share pays a $7 dividend (.07 × $100 par value). The annual dividend is $35,000 (5,000 × $7 per share). If dividends are two years in arrears, preferred stockholders are entitled to receive the dividends shown in **Illustration 11.12**.

ILLUSTRATION 11.12

Computation of total dividends to preferred stock

Dividends in arrears ($35,000 × 2)	$ 70,000
Current-year dividends	35,000
Total preferred dividends	**$105,000**

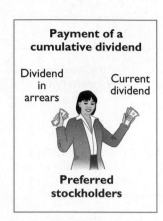

Payment of a cumulative dividend

Dividend in arrears

Current dividend

Preferred stockholders

The company cannot pay dividends to common stockholders until it pays the entire preferred dividend. In other words, companies cannot pay dividends to common stockholders while any preferred dividends are in arrears.

Dividends in arrears are not considered a liability. No payment obligation exists until the board of directors formally declares that the corporation will pay a dividend. However, companies should disclose in the notes to the financial statements the amount of dividends in arrears. Doing so enables investors to assess the potential impact of this commitment on the corporation's financial position.

The investment community does not look favorably on companies that are unable to meet their dividend obligations. As a financial officer noted in discussing one company's failure to pay its cumulative preferred dividend for a period of time, "Not meeting your obligations on something like that is a major black mark on your record."

Allocating Cash Dividends Between Preferred and Common Stock

As indicated, preferred stock has priority over common stock in regard to dividends. Holders of cumulative preferred stock must be paid any unpaid prior-year dividends and their current-year dividend before common stockholders receive dividends.

To illustrate, assume that at December 31, 2022, IBR Inc. has 1,000 shares of 8%, $100 par value cumulative preferred stock outstanding. It also has 50,000 shares of $10 par value common stock outstanding. The dividend per share for preferred stock is $8 ($100 par value × 8%). The required annual dividend for preferred stock is therefore $8,000 (1,000 shares × $8). At December 31, 2022, the directors declare a $6,000 cash dividend. In this case, the entire dividend amount goes to preferred stockholders because of their dividend preference. The entry to record the declaration of the dividend is as follows.

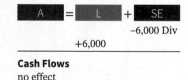

A = L + SE

−6,000 Div

+6,000

Cash Flows
no effect

Dec. 31	Cash Dividends	6,000	
	Dividends Payable		6,000
	(To record $6 per share cash dividend to preferred stockholders)		

Because of the cumulative feature, dividends of $2 ($8 − $6) per share are in arrears on preferred stock for 2022. IBR must pay this $2,000 of dividends to preferred stockholders before it can pay any future dividends to common stockholders. IBR should disclose dividends in arrears in the financial statements.

At December 31, 2023, IBR declares a $50,000 cash dividend. The allocation of the dividend to the two classes of stock is as shown in **Illustration 11.13**.

ILLUSTRATION 11.13

Allocating dividends to preferred and common stock

Total dividend		$50,000
Allocated to preferred stock		
Dividends in arrears, 2022 (1,000 × $2)	**$2,000**	
2023 dividend (1,000 × $8)	**8,000**	**10,000**
Remainder allocated to common stock		$40,000

The entry to record the declaration of the dividend is as follows.

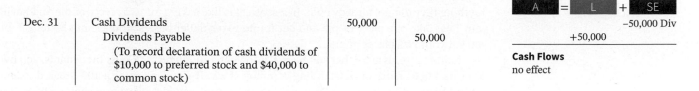

Dec. 31	Cash Dividends	50,000	
	Dividends Payable		50,000
	(To record declaration of cash dividends of $10,000 to preferred stock and $40,000 to common stock)		

A = L + SE

−50,000 Div

+50,000

Cash Flows
no effect

If IBR's preferred stock is not cumulative, preferred stockholders receive only $8,000 in dividends in 2023. Common stockholders receive $42,000.

DO IT! 3a | Dividends on Preferred and Common Stock

MasterMind Corporation has 2,000 shares of 6%, $100 par value preferred stock outstanding at December 31, 2022. At December 31, 2022, the company declared a $60,000 cash dividend. Determine the dividend paid to preferred stockholders and common stockholders under each of the following scenarios.

1. The preferred stock is noncumulative, and the company has not missed any dividends in previous years.

2. The preferred stock is noncumulative, and the company did not pay a dividend in each of the two previous years.

3. The preferred stock is cumulative, and the company did not pay a dividend in each of the two previous years.

Solution

1. The company has not missed past dividends and the preferred stock is noncumulative. Thus, the preferred stockholders are paid only this year's dividend. The dividend paid to preferred stockholders would be $12,000 (2,000 × .06 × $100). The dividend paid to common stockholders would be $48,000 ($60,000 − $12,000).

2. The preferred stock is noncumulative. Thus, past unpaid dividends do not have to be paid. The dividend paid to preferred stockholders would be $12,000 (2,000 × .06 × $100). The dividend paid to common stockholders would be $48,000 ($60,000 − $12,000).

3. The preferred stock is cumulative. Thus, dividends that have been missed (dividends in arrears) must be paid. The dividend paid to preferred stockholders would be $36,000 (3 × 2,000 × .06 × $100). Of the $36,000, $24,000 relates to dividends in arrears and $12,000 relates to the current year's dividend on preferred stock. The dividend paid to common stockholders would be $24,000 ($60,000 − $36,000).

Related exercise material: **BE11.7, DO IT! 11.3a, and E11.13.**

ACTION PLAN

- **Determine dividends on preferred shares by multiplying the dividend rate times the par value of the stock times the number of outstanding preferred shares.**

- **Understand the cumulative feature. If preferred stock is cumulative, then any missed dividends (dividends in arrears) and the current year's dividend must be paid to preferred stockholders before dividends are paid to common stockholders.**

Stock Dividends

A **stock dividend** is a pro rata (proportional to ownership) distribution of the corporation's own stock to stockholders. Whereas a company pays cash in a cash dividend, a company issues shares of stock in a stock dividend. **A stock dividend results in a decrease in retained earnings and an increase in paid-in capital.** Unlike a cash dividend, a stock dividend does not decrease total stockholders' equity or total assets.

Because a stock dividend does not result in a distribution of assets, some view it as nothing more than a publicity gesture. Stock dividends are often issued by companies that do not have adequate cash to issue a cash dividend. Such companies may not want to announce that they are not going to issue a cash dividend at their expected time. By issuing a stock dividend, they "save face" by giving the appearance of distributing a dividend. Note that since a stock dividend neither increases nor decreases the assets in the company, investors are not receiving anything they did not already own. In a sense, it is like asking for two pieces of pie and having your host take one piece of pie and cut it into two smaller pieces. You are not better off, but you got your two pieces of pie.

To illustrate, assume that you have a 2% ownership interest in Cetus Inc. That is, you own 20 of its 1,000 shares of outstanding common stock. If Cetus declares a 10% stock dividend, it would issue 100 shares (1,000 × 10%) of stock. You would receive two shares (2% × 100). Would your ownership interest change? No, it would remain at 2% (22 ÷ 1,100). **You now own more shares of stock, but your ownership interest has not changed.**

Cetus has disbursed no cash and has assumed no liabilities. What, then, are the purposes and benefits of a stock dividend? Corporations issue stock dividends generally for one or more of the following reasons.

1. To satisfy stockholders' dividend expectations without spending cash.

2. To increase the marketability of the corporation's stock. When the number of shares outstanding increases, the market price per share decreases. Decreasing the market price of the stock makes it easier for smaller investors to purchase the shares.

3. To emphasize that a company has permanently reinvested in the business a portion of stockholders' equity, which therefore is unavailable for cash dividends.

When the dividend is declared, the board of directors determines the size of the stock dividend and the value assigned to each dividend. In order to meet legal requirements, the per share amount must be at least equal to the par or stated value.

Generally, if the company issues a **small stock dividend** (less than 20–25% of the corporation's outstanding stock), the value assigned to the dividend is the fair value (market price) per share. This treatment is based on the assumption that a small stock dividend will have little effect on the market price of the shares previously outstanding. Thus, many stockholders consider small stock dividends to be distributions of earnings equal to the market price of the shares distributed. If a company issues a **large stock dividend** (greater than 20–25%), the price assigned to the dividend is the par or stated value. Small stock dividends predominate in practice. Thus, we will illustrate only entries for small stock dividends.

Entries for Stock Dividends

To illustrate the accounting for small stock dividends, assume that Medland Corporation has a balance of $300,000 in retained earnings. It declares a 10% stock dividend on its 50,000 shares of $10 par value common stock. The current market price of its stock is $15 per share. The number of shares to be issued is 5,000 (10% × 50,000). Therefore, the total amount to be debited to Stock Dividends is $75,000 (5,000 × $15). The entry to record the declaration of the stock dividend is as follows.

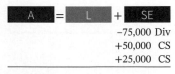

-75,000 Div
+50,000 CS
+25,000 CS

Cash Flows
no effect

Stock Dividends	75,000	
Common Stock Dividends Distributable		50,000
Paid-in Capital in Excess of Par—Common Stock		25,000
(To record declaration of 10% stock dividend)		

Medland debits Stock Dividends for the market price of the stock issued ($15 × 5,000). (Similar to cash dividends, stock dividends decrease retained earnings.) Medland also credits Common Stock Dividends Distributable for the par value of the dividend shares ($10 × 5,000) and credits Paid-in Capital in Excess of Par—Common Stock for the excess of the market price over par ($5 × 5,000).

Common Stock Dividends Distributable is a **stockholders' equity account**. It is not a liability because assets will not be used to pay the dividend. If the company prepares a balance sheet before it issues the dividend shares, it reports the distributable account under paid-in capital as shown in **Illustration 11.14**.

Paid-in capital	
Common stock	$500,000
Common stock dividends distributable	**50,000**
Paid-in capital in excess of par—common stock	25,000
Total paid-in capital	$575,000

When Medland issues the dividend shares, it debits Common Stock Dividends Distributable and credits Common Stock, as follows.

Common Stock Dividends Distributable	50,000	
Common Stock		50,000
(To record issuance of 5,000 shares in a stock dividend)		

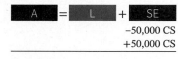

−50,000 CS
+50,000 CS

Cash Flows
no effect

Effects of Stock Dividends

How do stock dividends affect stockholders' equity? They **change the composition of stockholders' equity** because they transfer a portion of retained earnings to paid-in capital. However, **total stockholders' equity remains the same**. Stock dividends also have no effect on the par or stated value per share, but the number of shares outstanding increases. **Illustration 11.15** shows these effects for Medland.

	Before Dividend	Change	After Dividend
Stockholders' equity			
Paid-in capital			
Common stock, $10 par	$500,000	$ 50,000	$550,000
Paid-in capital in excess of par	—	25,000	25,000
Total paid-in capital	500,000	+75,000	575,000
Retained earnings	300,000	−75,000	225,000
Total stockholders' equity	**$800,000**	**$ 0**	**$800,000**
Outstanding shares	**50,000**	**+5,000**	**55,000**
Par value per share	**$10.00**	**$0**	**$10.00**

ILLUSTRATION 11.15

Stock dividend effects

In this example, total paid-in capital increases by $75,000 (50,000 shares × 10% × $15) and retained earnings decreases by the same amount. Note also that total stockholders' equity remains unchanged at $800,000. The number of shares increases by 5,000 (50,000 × 10%).

Stock Splits

A **stock split**, like a stock dividend, involves issuance of additional shares to stockholders according to their percentage ownership. **However, a stock split results in a reduction in the par or stated value per share** (see **Helpful Hint**). The purpose of a stock split is to increase the marketability of the stock by lowering its market price per share. This, in turn, makes it easier for the corporation to issue additional stock.

The effect of a split on market price is generally **inversely proportional** to the size of the split. For example, after a 2-for-1 stock split, the market price of **Nike's** stock fell from $111 to

HELPFUL HINT

A stock split changes the par value per share but does not affect any balances in stockholders' equity accounts.

approximately $55. The lower market price stimulated market activity. Within one year, the stock was trading above $100 again. **Illustration 11.16** shows the effect of a 4-for-1 stock split for stockholders.

ILLUSTRATION 11.16

Effect of stock split for stockholders

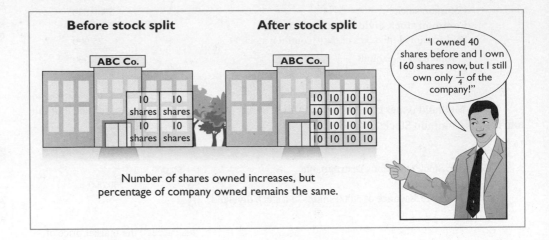

In a stock split, the company increases the number of shares in the same proportion that par or stated value per share decreases. For example, in a 2-for-1 split, the company exchanges one share of $10 par value stock for two shares of $5 par value stock. **A stock split does not have any effect on total paid-in capital, retained earnings, or total stockholders' equity.** However, the number of shares outstanding increases, and par value per share decreases. **Illustration 11.17** shows these effects for Medland Corporation, assuming that it splits its 50,000 shares of common stock on a 2-for-1 basis.

ILLUSTRATION 11.17

Stock split effects

	Before Stock Split	Change	After Stock Split
Stockholders' equity			
Paid-in capital			
Common stock,	$500,000		$500,000
Paid-in capital in excess of par—common stock	–0–		–0–
Total paid-in capital	500,000	$ –0–	500,000
Retained earnings	300,000	–0–	300,000
Total stockholders' equity	$800,000	$ –0–	$800,000
Outstanding shares	50,000	+50,000	100,000
Par value per share	$10.00	−$5.00	$5.00

A stock split does not affect the balances in any stockholders' equity accounts. Therefore, **a company does not need to journalize a stock split**.

Illustration 11.18 summarizes the differences between stock dividends and stock splits.

ILLUSTRATION 11.18

Differences between the effects of stock dividends and stock splits

Item	Stock Dividend	Stock Split
Total paid-in capital	Increase	No change
Total retained earnings	Decrease	No change
Total par value (common stock)	Increase	No change
Par value per share	No change	Decrease
Outstanding shares	Increase	Increase
Total stockholders' equity	No change	No change

Investor Insight   Berkshire Hathaway

iStock.com/Hiob

A No-Split Philosophy

Warren Buffett's company, **Berkshire Hathaway**, has two classes of shares. Until recently, the company had never split either class of stock. As a result, the class A stock had a market price of $97,000 and the class B sold for about $3,200 per share. Because the price per share is so high, the stock does not trade as frequently as the stock of other companies. Buffett has always opposed stock splits because he feels that a lower stock price attracts short-term investors. He appears to be correct. For example, while more than 6 million shares of **IBM** are exchanged on the average day, only about 1,000 class A shares of Berkshire are traded. Despite Buffett's aversion to splits, in order to accomplish a recent acquisition, Berkshire decided to split its class B shares 50 to 1.

Source: Scott Patterson, "Berkshire Nears Smaller Baby B's," *Wall Street Journal Online* (January 19, 2010).

Why does Warren Buffett usually oppose stock splits? (Go to WileyPLUS for this answer and additional questions.)

DO IT! 3b | Stock Dividends and Stock Splits

Sing CD Company has had five years of record earnings. Due to this success, the market price of its 500,000 outstanding shares of $2 par value common stock has tripled from $15 per share to $45. During this period, paid-in capital remained the same at $2,000,000. Retained earnings increased from $1,500,000 to $10,000,000. President Joan Elbert is considering either a 10% stock dividend or a 2-for-1 stock split. She asks you to show the before-and-after effects of each option on retained earnings, total stockholders' equity, shares outstanding, and par value per share.

Solution

The stock dividend amount is $2,250,000 [(500,000 × 10%) × $45]. The new balance in retained earnings is $7,750,000 ($10,000,000 − $2,250,000). The retained earnings balance after the stock split is the same as it was before the split: $10,000,000. Total stockholders' equity does not change. The effects on the stockholders' equity accounts are as follows.

	Original Balances	After Dividend	After Split
Paid-in capital	$ 2,000,000	$ 4,250,000	$ 2,000,000
Retained earnings	10,000,000	7,750,000	10,000,000
Total stockholders' equity	$12,000,000	$12,000,000	$12,000,000
Shares outstanding	500,000	550,000	1,000,000
Par value per share	$2.00	$2.00	$1.00

Related exercise material: **BE11.8, BE11.9, DO IT! 11.3b, E11.14, E11.15, and E11.16.**

ACTION PLAN

- Calculate the stock dividend's effect on retained earnings by multiplying the number of new shares times the market price of the stock (or par value for a large stock dividend).
- Recall that a stock dividend increases the number of shares without affecting total stockholders' equity.
- Recall that a stock split only increases the number of shares outstanding and decreases the par value per share.

Reporting and Analyzing Stockholders' Equity

LEARNING OBJECTIVE 4

Discuss how stockholders' equity is reported and analyzed.

Retained Earnings

Recall that **retained earnings** is net income that a company retains in the business. The balance in retained earnings is part of the stockholders' claim on the total assets of the corporation. It does not, however, represent a claim on any specific asset. Nor can the amount of retained earnings be associated with the balance of any asset account. For example, a $100,000 balance in retained earnings does not mean that there should be $100,000 in cash.

The reason is that the company may have used the cash resulting from the excess of revenues over expenses to purchase buildings, equipment, and other assets.

To demonstrate that retained earnings and cash may be quite different, **Illustration 11.19** shows recent amounts of retained earnings and cash in selected companies.

ILLUSTRATION 11.19

Retained earnings and cash balances

	(in millions)	
Company	Retained Earnings	Cash
Facebook	$ 3,159	$3,323
Google	61,262	8,989
Nike	5,695	3,337
Starbucks	4,130	2,576
Amazon	2,190	8,658

HELPFUL HINT

Remember that Retained Earnings is a stockholders' equity account; its normal balance is a credit.

Remember that when a company has net income, it closes net income to retained earnings. The closing entry is a debit to Income Summary and a credit to Retained Earnings.

When a company has a **net loss** (expenses exceed revenues), it also closes this amount to retained earnings. The closing entry is a debit to Retained Earnings and a credit to Income Summary (see **Helpful Hint**). To illustrate, assume that Rendle Corporation has a net loss of $400,000 in 2022. The closing entry to record this loss is as follows.

Retained Earnings	400,000	
Income Summary		400,000
(To close net loss to Retained Earnings)		

This closing entry is done even if it results in a debit balance in Retained Earnings. **Companies do not debit net losses to paid-in capital accounts.** To do so would destroy the distinction between paid-in and earned capital. If cumulative losses exceed cumulative income over a company's life, a debit balance in Retained Earnings results. A debit balance in Retained Earnings is identified as a **deficit**. A company reports a deficit as a deduction in the stockholders' equity section, as shown in **Illustration 11.20** for Ursula, Inc.

ILLUSTRATION 11.20

Stockholders' equity with deficit

Ursula, Inc.	
Balance Sheet (partial)	
Stockholders' equity	
Paid-in capital	
Common stock	$800,000
Retained earnings (deficit)	**(50,000)**
Total stockholders' equity	$750,000

Retained Earnings Restrictions

The balance in retained earnings is generally available for dividend declarations. Some companies state this fact. In some circumstances, however, there may be **retained earnings restrictions**. These make a portion of the balance currently unavailable for dividends. Restrictions result from one or more of these causes: legal, contractual, or voluntary.

Companies generally disclose retained earnings restrictions in the notes to the financial statements. For example, as shown in **Illustration 11.21**, **Tektronix, Inc.**, a manufacturer of electronic measurement devices, recently had total retained earnings of $774 million, but the unrestricted portion was only $223.8 million.

Tektronix, Inc.
Notes to the Financial Statements
Certain of the Company's debt agreements require compliance with debt covenants. The Company had unrestricted retained earnings of $223.8 million after meeting those requirements.

Balance Sheet Presentation of Stockholders' Equity

In the stockholders' equity section of the balance sheet, companies report paid-in capital, retained earnings, and treasury stock. Within paid-in capital, two classifications are recognized:

1. **Capital stock**, which consists of preferred and common stock. Companies show preferred stock before common stock because of its preferential rights. They report information about the par value, shares authorized, shares issued, and shares outstanding for each class of stock.

2. **Additional paid-in capital**, which includes the excess of amounts paid in over par or stated value.

Illustration 11.22 presents the stockholders' equity section of the balance sheet of Graber Inc. (see **International Note**). The company discloses a retained earnings restriction in the notes. The stockholders' equity section for Graber Inc. includes most of the accounts discussed in this chapter. The disclosures pertaining to Graber's common stock indicate that 400,000 shares are issued, 100,000 shares are unissued (500,000 authorized less 400,000 issued), and 390,000 shares are outstanding (400,000 issued less 10,000 shares in treasury).

> **International Note**
> Like GAAP, companies using IFRS typically disclose separate categories of capital on the balance sheet. However, because of varying accounting treatments of certain transactions (such as treasury stock or asset revaluations), some categories used under IFRS vary from those under GAAP.

ILLUSTRATION 11.22
Stockholders' equity section of balance sheet

Graber Inc.		
Balance Sheet (partial)		
Stockholders' equity		
Paid-in capital		
Capital stock		
9% preferred stock, $100 par value, cumulative, 10,000 shares authorized, 6,000 shares issued and outstanding		$ 600,000
Common stock, no par, $5 stated value, 500,000 shares authorized, 400,000 shares issued, and 390,000 outstanding		2,000,000
Total capital stock		2,600,000
Additional paid-in capital		
Paid-in capital in excess of par—preferred stock	$ 30,000	
Paid-in capital in excess of stated value—common stock	1,050,000	
Total additional paid-in capital		1,080,000
Total paid-in capital		3,680,000
Retained earnings **(see Note R)**		1,050,000
Total paid-in capital and retained earnings		4,730,000
Less: Treasury stock (10,000 common shares)		80,000
Total stockholders' equity		$4,650,000
Note R: Retained earnings is restricted for the cost of treasury stock, $80,000.		

DO IT! 4a | Stockholders' Equity Section

Jennifer Corporation has issued 300,000 shares of $3 par value common stock. It is authorized to issue 600,000 shares. The paid-in capital in excess of par value on the common stock is $380,000. The corporation has reacquired 15,000 shares of common stock at a cost of $50,000 and is currently holding those shares.

  The corporation also has 4,000 shares issued and outstanding of 8%, $100 par value preferred stock. It is authorized to issue 10,000 shares. The paid-in capital in excess of par value on the preferred stock is $97,000. Retained earnings is $610,000.

  Prepare the stockholders' equity section of the balance sheet.

Solution

Jennifer Corporation			
Balance Sheet (partial)			
Stockholders' equity			
Paid-in capital			
Capital stock			
8% preferred stock, $100 par value,			
10,000 shares authorized, 4,000 shares			
issued and outstanding		$400,000	
Common stock, $3 par value, 600,000 shares			
authorized, 300,000 shares issued, and			
285,000 shares outstanding		900,000	
Total capital stock			$1,300,000
Additional paid-in capital			
Paid-in capital in excess of par—preferred stock		97,000	
Paid-in capital in excess of par value—common stock		380,000	
Total additional paid-in capital			477,000
Total paid-in capital			1,777,000
Retained earnings			610,000
Total paid-in capital and retained earnings			2,387,000
Less: Treasury stock (15,000 common shares) (at cost)			50,000
Total stockholders' equity			$2,337,000

Related exercise material: **BE11.11, DO IT! 11.4a, E11.19, E11.20, and E11.21.**

Analysis of Stockholders' Equity

Investors are interested in both a company's dividend record and its earnings performance. Although those two measures are often parallel, that is not always the case. Thus, investors should investigate each one separately.

Payout Ratio

One way that companies reward stockholders for their investment is to pay them dividends. The **payout ratio** measures the percentage of earnings a company distributes in the form of cash dividends to common stockholders. It is computed by **dividing total cash dividends declared to common shareholders by net income**.

  To illustrate, **Nike**'s dividends were recently $1,133 million and net income was $4,240 million. **Illustration 11.23** shows Nike's payout ratio.

Cash Dividends Declared on Common Stock	÷	Net Income	=	Payout Ratio
$1,133	÷	$4,240	=	26.7%

Companies attempt to set their dividend rate at a level that will be sustainable. Companies that have high growth rates are characterized by low payout ratios because they reinvest most of their net income in the business. Thus, a low payout ratio is not necessarily bad news. Companies that believe they have many good opportunities for growth, such as **Facebook**, will reinvest those funds in the company rather than pay dividends. However, low dividend payments, or a cut in dividend payments, might signal that a company has liquidity or solvency problems and is trying to conserve cash by not paying dividends. Thus, investors and analysts should investigate the reason for low dividend payments.

Illustration 11.24 lists recent payout ratios of four well-known companies.

Company	Payout Ratio
Microsoft	24.5%
Kellogg	43.3%
Facebook	0.0%
Walmart	49.0%

ILLUSTRATION 11.24

Payout ratios of companies

Return on Common Stockholders' Equity

Investors and analysts can measure profitability from the viewpoint of the common stockholder by the **return on common stockholders' equity**. This ratio, as shown in Illustration 11.25, indicates how many dollars of net income the company earned for each dollar invested by the common stockholders. It is computed by dividing **net income available to common stockholders** (which is net income minus preferred dividends) by average common stockholders' equity.

To illustrate, **Walt Disney Company**'s beginning-of-the-year and end-of-the-year common stockholders' equity were $31,820 and $30,753 million, respectively. Its net income was $4,687 million, and no preferred stock was outstanding. The return on common stockholders' equity is computed as shown in **Illustration 11.25**.

Net Income minus Preferred Dividends	÷	Average Common Stockholders' Equity	=	Return on Common Stockholders' Equity
($4,687 – $0)	÷	$\dfrac{(\$31,820 + \$30,753)}{2}$	=	15.0%

ILLUSTRATION 11.25

Disney's return on common stockholders' equity

As shown above, if a company has preferred stock, we would deduct the amount of **preferred dividends** from the company's net income to compute income available to common stockholders. Also, the par value of preferred stock is deducted from total stockholders' equity when computing the average common stockholders' equity.

DO IT! 4b | Analyzing Stockholders' Equity

On January 1, 2022, Siena Corporation purchased 2,000 shares of treasury stock. Other information regarding Siena Corporation is provided below.

	2021	2022
Net income	$110,000	$110,000
Dividends on preferred stock	10,000	10,000
Dividends on common stock	2,000	1,600
Common stockholders' equity, beginning of year	500,000	400,000*
Common stockholders' equity, end of year	500,000	400,000

*Adjusted for purchase of treasury stock.

(a) Compute return on common stockholders' equity for each year, and (b) discuss its change from 2021 to 2022.

ACTION PLAN

- Determine return on common stockholders' equity by dividing net income available to common stockholders by average common stockholders' equity.

Solution

a.

	2021	2022
Return on common stock- holders' equity	$\dfrac{(\$110,000 - \$10,000)}{(\$500,000 + \$500,000) \div 2} = 20\%$	$\dfrac{(\$110,000 - \$10,000)}{(\$400,000 + \$400,000) \div 2} = 25\%$

b. Between 2021 and 2022, return on common stockholders' equity improved from 20% to 25%. While this would appear to be good news for the company's common stockholders, this increase should be carefully evaluated. It is important to note that net income did not change during this period. The increase in the ratio was due to the purchase of treasury shares, which reduced the denominator of the ratio. As the company repurchases its own shares, it becomes more reliant on debt and thus increases its risk.

Related exercise material: **DO IT! 11.4b, E11.22, E11.23, and E11.24.**

Appendix 11A	# Stockholders' Equity Statement

LEARNING OBJECTIVE *5

Describe the use and content of the stockholders' equity statement.

When balance sheets and income statements are presented by a corporation, changes in the separate accounts comprising stockholders' equity should also be disclosed. Disclosure of such changes is necessary to make the financial statements sufficiently informative for users. The disclosures may be made in an additional statement or in the notes to the financial statements.

Many corporations make the disclosures in a **stockholders' equity statement**. The statement shows the changes in **each** stockholders' equity account and in **total** stockholders' equity during the year. As shown in **Illustration 11A.1**, the stockholders' equity statement is prepared in columnar form. It contains columns for each account and for total stockholders' equity. The transactions are then identified and their effects are shown in the appropriate columns.

ILLUSTRATION 11A.1 Stockholders' equity statement

Hampton Corporation
Stockholders' Equity Statement
For the Year Ended December 31, 2022

	Common Stock ($5 Par)	Paid-in Capital in Excess of Par—Common Stock	Retained Earnings	Treasury Stock	Total
Balance January 1	$300,000	$200,000	$650,000	$(34,000)	$1,116,000
Issued 5,000 shares of common stock at $15	25,000	50,000			75,000
Declared a $40,000 cash dividend			(40,000)		(40,000)
Purchased 2,000 shares for treasury at $16				(32,000)	(32,000)
Net income for year			240,000		240,000
Balance December 31	$325,000	$250,000	$850,000	$(66,000)	$1,359,000

In practice, additional columns are usually provided to show the number of shares of issued stock and treasury stock. The stockholders' equity statement for **PepsiCo** for a three-year period is shown in Appendix B. **When a stockholders' equity statement is presented, a retained earnings statement is not necessary** because the retained earnings column explains the changes in this account.

| **Appendix 11B** | # Book Value per Share |

LEARNING OBJECTIVE *6
Compute book value per share.

You have learned about a number of per share amounts in this chapter. Another per share amount of some importance is **book value per share**. It represents **the equity a common stockholder has in the net assets of the corporation** from owning one share of stock. Remember that the net assets (total assets minus total liabilities) of a corporation must be equal to total stockholders' equity. **Illustration 11B.1** shows the formula for computing book value per share when a company has only one class of stock outstanding.

| **Total Stockholders' Equity** | ÷ | **Number of Common Shares Outstanding** | = | **Book Value per Share** |

ILLUSTRATION 11B.1
Book value per share formula

Thus, if Marlo Corporation has total stockholders' equity of $1,500,000 (common stock $1,000,000 and retained earnings $500,000) and 50,000 shares of common stock outstanding, book value per share is $30 ($1,500,000 ÷ 50,000).

When a company has both preferred and common stock, the computation of book value is more complex. Since preferred stockholders have a prior claim on net assets over common stockholders, their equity must be deducted from total stockholders' equity. Then, we can determine the stockholders' equity that applies to the common stock. The computation of book value per share involves the following steps.

1. **Compute the preferred stock equity.** This equity is equal to the sum of the call price of all outstanding shares of preferred stock plus any cumulative dividends in arrears. If the preferred stock does not have a call price, the par value of the stock is used.

2. **Determine the common stock equity.** Subtract the preferred stock equity from total stockholders' equity.

3. **Determine book value per share.** Divide common stock equity by shares of common stock outstanding.

Book Value per Share Example

We will use the stockholders' equity section of Graber Inc. shown in Illustration 11.22. Assume that Graber's preferred stock is callable at $120 per share and is cumulative, and that dividends on Graber's preferred stock were in arrears for one year, $54,000 (6,000 × $9). **Illustration 11B.2** shows the computation of preferred stock equity (Step 1 in the preceding list).

Call price (6,000 shares × $120)	$720,000
Dividends in arrears (6,000 shares × $9)	54,000
Preferred stock equity	**$774,000**

ILLUSTRATION 11B.2
Computation of preferred stock equity—Step 1

The computation of book value per share (Steps 2 and 3) is shown in **Illustration 11B.3**.

Total stockholders' equity	$4,760,000
Less: **Preferred stock equity**	774,000
Common stock equity	**$3,986,000**
Shares of common stock outstanding	390,000
Book value per share ($3,986,000 ÷ 390,000)	**$10.22**

ILLUSTRATION 11B.3
Computation of book value per share with preferred stock—Steps 2 and 3

Note that we used a call price of $120 instead of the par value of $100. Note also that the paid-in capital in excess of par value of preferred stock, $30,000, **is not assigned to the preferred stock equity**. Preferred stockholders ordinarily do not have a right to amounts paid-in in excess of par value. Therefore, such amounts are assigned to the common stock equity in computing book value per share.

Book Value versus Market Price

Be sure you understand that **book value per share generally does not equal market price per share**. Book value generally is based on recorded costs. Market price reflects the subjective judgments of thousands of stockholders and prospective investors about a company's potential for future earnings and dividends. Market price per share may exceed book value per share, but that fact does not necessarily mean that the stock is overpriced. The correlation between book value and the annual range of a company's market price per share is often remote, as indicated by the data shown in **Illustration 11B.4**.

ILLUSTRATION 11B.4

Book value per share and market prices compared

Company	Book Value (year-end)	Market Range (for the year)
The Limited	$13.38	$31.03–$22.89
H. J. Heinz	$ 7.48	$40.61–$34.53
Cisco Systems	$ 3.66	$21.24–$17.01
Walmart	$12.79	$50.87–$42.31

Book value per share **is useful** in determining the trend of a stockholder's per share equity in a corporation. It is also significant in many contracts and in court cases where the rights of individual parties are based on cost information.

Review and Practice

Learning Objectives Review

1 Discuss the major characteristics of a corporation.

The major characteristics of a corporation are separate legal existence, limited liability of stockholders, transferable ownership rights, ability to acquire capital, continuous life, corporation management, government regulations, and additional taxes.

2 Explain how to account for the issuance of common, preferred, and treasury stock.

Common Stock. When companies record the issuance of common stock for cash, they credit the par value of the shares to Common Stock. They record in a separate paid-in capital account the portion of the proceeds that is above or below par value. When no-par common stock has a stated value, the entries are similar to those for par value stock. When no-par stock does not have a stated value, companies credit the entire proceeds to Common Stock.

Preferred Stock. Like common stock, companies may issue preferred stock for cash or noncash assets. The entries for these transactions are similar to the entries for common stock. Preferred stock has contractual provisions that give it priority over common stock in certain areas. Typically, preferred stockholders have preferences (1) to dividends and (2) to assets in liquidation. They usually do not have voting rights.

Treasury Stock. The cost method is generally used in accounting for treasury stock. Under this approach, companies debit Treasury Stock at the price paid to reacquire the shares. They credit the same amount to Treasury Stock when they sell the shares. The difference between the sales price and cost is recorded in stockholders' equity accounts, not in income statement accounts.

3 Explain how to account for cash dividends, stock dividends, and stock splits.

Cash Dividends. Companies make entries for cash dividends at the declaration date and at the payment date. At the **declaration date**, the entry is debit Cash Dividends and credit Dividends Payable. At the **payment date**, the entry is debit Dividends Payable and credit Cash.

Stock Dividends. At the declaration date, the entry for a small stock dividend is debit Stock Dividends, credit Paid-in Capital in

Excess of Par (or Stated Value)—Common Stock, and credit Common Stock Dividends Distributable. At the distribution date, the entry for a small stock dividend is debit Common Stock Dividends Distributable and credit Common Stock.

Stock Splits. A stock split reduces the par or stated value per share and increases the number of shares but does not affect balances in stockholders' equity accounts. As a result, no entry is needed.

---

4 Discuss how stockholders' equity is reported and analyzed.

Additions to retained earnings consist of net income. Deductions consist of net loss and cash and stock dividends. In some instances, portions of retained earnings are restricted, making that portion unavailable for the payment of dividends.

In the stockholders' equity section of the balance sheet, companies report paid-in capital and retained earnings and identify specific sources of paid-in capital. Within paid-in capital, companies show two classifications: capital stock and additional paid-in capital. If a corporation has treasury stock, it deducts the cost of treasury stock from total paid-in capital and retained earnings to determine total stockholders' equity.

A company's dividend record can be evaluated by looking at what percentage of net income it chooses to pay out in dividends,

as measured by the payout ratio (dividends divided by net income). Earnings performance is measured with the return on common stockholders' equity (income available to common stockholders divided by average common stockholders' equity).

---

*5 Describe the use and content of the stockholders' equity statement.

Corporations must disclose changes in stockholders' equity accounts and may choose to do so by issuing a separate stockholders' equity statement. This statement, prepared in columnar form, shows changes in each stockholders' equity account and in total stockholders' equity during the accounting period. When this statement is presented, a retained earnings statement is not necessary.

---

*6 Compute book value per share.

Book value per share represents the equity a common stockholder has in the net assets of a corporation from owning one share of stock. When there is only common stock outstanding, the formula for computing book value per share is Total stockholders' equity ÷ Number of common shares outstanding = Book value per share.

Glossary Review

Authorized stock The amount of stock that a corporation is authorized to sell as indicated in its charter. (p. 11-8).

*Book value per share The equity a common stockholder has in the net assets of the corporation from owning one share of stock. (p. 11-33).

Cash dividend A pro rata distribution of cash to stockholders. (p. 11-19).

Charter A document that is issued by the state to set forth important terms and features regarding the creation of a corporation. (p. 11-6).

Corporation A business organized as a legal entity separate and distinct from its owners under state corporation law. (p. 11-3).

Cumulative dividend A feature of preferred stock entitling the stockholder to receive current and unpaid prior-year dividends before common stockholders receive dividends. (p. 11-21).

Declaration date The date the board of directors formally declares (authorizes) a dividend and announces it to stockholders. (p. 11-19).

Deficit A debit balance in Retained Earnings. (p. 11-28).

Dividend A corporation's distribution of cash or stock to its stockholders on a pro rata (proportional) basis. (p. 11-18).

Liquidating dividend A dividend declared out of paid-in capital. (p. 11-19).

No-par value stock Capital stock that has not been assigned a value in the corporate charter. (p. 11-9).

Organization costs Costs incurred in the formation of a corporation. (p. 11-6).

Outstanding stock Capital stock that has been issued and is being held by stockholders. (p. 11-16).

Paid-in capital Total amount of cash and other assets paid in to the corporation by stockholders in exchange for capital stock. (p. 11-10).

Par value stock Capital stock that has been assigned a value per share in the corporate charter. (p. 11-9).

Payment date The date dividends are transferred to stockholders. (p. 11-20).

Payout ratio A measure of the percentage of earnings a company distributes in the form of cash dividends to common stockholders. (p. 11-30).

Preferred stock Capital stock that has some preferences over common stock. (p. 11-14).

Privately held corporation A corporation that has only a few stockholders and whose stock is not available for sale to the general public. (p. 11-3).

Publicly held corporation A corporation that may have thousands of stockholders and whose stock is regularly traded on a national securities exchange. (p. 11-3).

Record date The date when ownership of outstanding shares is determined for dividend purposes. (p. 11-20).

Retained earnings Net income that the corporation retains for future use. (p. 11-10).

Retained earnings restrictions Circumstances that make a portion of retained earnings currently unavailable for dividends. (p. 11-28).

Return on common stockholders' equity A measure of profitability that shows how many dollars of net income were earned for each dollar invested by the owners; computed as net income minus preferred dividends divided by average common stockholders' equity. (p. 11-31).

Stated value The amount per share assigned by the board of directors to no-par value stock. (p. 11-9).

Stock dividend A pro rata distribution to stockholders of the corporation's own stock. (p. 11-23).

*Stockholders' equity statement A statement that shows the changes in each stockholders' equity account and in total stockholders' equity during the year. (p. 11-32).

Stock split The issuance of additional shares of stock to stockholders according to their percentage ownership. It is accompanied by a reduction in the par or stated value per share. (p. 11-25).

Treasury stock A corporation's own stock that has been issued and subsequently reacquired from shareholders by the corporation but not retired. (p. 11-15).

Practice Multiple-Choice Questions

1. (LO 1) Which of the following is **not** a major advantage of a corporate form of organization?

    a. Separate legal existence.

    b. Continuous life.

    c. Government regulations.

    d. Transferable ownership rights.

2. (LO 1) A major **disadvantage** of a corporation is:

    a. limited liability of stockholders.

    b. additional taxes.

    c. transferable ownership rights.

    d. separate legal existence.

3. (LO 1) Which of the following statements is **false**?

    a. Ownership of common stock gives the owner a voting right.

    b. The stockholders' equity section begins with a paid-in capital section.

    c. The authorization of capital stock does not result in a formal accounting entry.

    d. Par value and market price of a company's stock are always the same.

4. (LO 2) ABC Corporation issues 1,000 shares of $10 par value common stock at $12 per share. In recording the transaction, credits are made to:

    a. Common Stock $10,000 and Paid-in Capital in Excess of Stated Value $2,000.

    b. Common Stock $12,000.

    c. Common Stock $10,000 and Paid-in Capital in Excess of Par $2,000.

    d. Common Stock $10,000 and Retained Earnings $2,000.

5. (LO 2) Preferred stock may have priority over common stock **except** in:

    a. dividends.

    b. assets in the event of liquidation.

    c. cumulative dividend features.

    d. voting.

6. (LO 2) XYZ, Inc. sells 100 shares of $5 par value treasury stock at $13 per share. If the cost of acquiring the shares was $10 per share, the entry for the sale should include credits to:

    a. Treasury Stock $1,000 and Paid-in Capital from Treasury Stock $300.

    b. Treasury Stock $500 and Paid-in Capital from Treasury Stock $800.

    c. Treasury Stock $1,000 and Retained Earnings $300.

    d. Treasury Stock $500 and Paid-in Capital in Excess of Par $800.

7. (LO 2) In the stockholders' equity section of the balance sheet, the cost of treasury stock is deducted from:

    a. total paid-in capital and retained earnings.

    b. retained earnings.

    c. total stockholders' equity.

    d. common stock in paid-in capital.

8. (LO 3) U-Bet Corporation has 10,000 shares of 8%, $100 par value, cumulative preferred stock outstanding at December 31, 2022. No dividends were declared in 2020 or 2021. If U-Bet wants to pay $375,000 of dividends in 2022, common stockholders will receive:

    a. $0.   **c.** $215,000.

    b. $295,000.   **d.** $135,000.

9. (LO 3) Entries for cash dividends are required on the:

    a. declaration date and the payment date.

    b. record date and the payment date.

    c. declaration date, record date, and payment date.

    d. declaration date and the record date.

10. (LO 3) Which of the following statements about small stock dividends is **true**?

    a. A debit to Retained Earnings for the par value of the shares issued should be made.

    b. A small stock dividend decreases total stockholders' equity.

    c. Market price per share should be assigned to the dividend shares.

    d. A small stock dividend ordinarily will have an effect on par value per share of stock.

11. (LO 3) Orlando Company has a beginning balance in retained earnings of $100,000. During the year, it had a net loss of $20,000, declared cash dividends of $3,000, and declared a small stock dividend that had a market value of $7,000 and a par value of $1,000. The ending balance in retained earnings is:

    a. $120,000.   **c.** $79,000.

    b. $80,000.   **d.** $70,000.

12. (LO 4) In the stockholders' equity section of the balance sheet, common stock is:

    a. listed before preferred stock.

    b. added to total capital stock.

    c. part of paid-in capital.

    d. part of additional paid-in capital.

13. (LO 4) Which of the following is **not** reported under additional paid-in capital?

    a. Paid-in capital in excess of par.

    b. Common stock.

    c. Paid-in capital in excess of stated value.

    d. Paid-in capital from treasury stock.

14. (LO 4) Jackson Inc. reported net income of $186,000 during 2022 and paid dividends of $26,000 on common stock. It also has 10,000 shares of 6%, $100 par value, noncumulative preferred stock outstanding and paid dividends of $60,000 on preferred stock. Common stockholders' equity was $1,200,000 on January 1, 2022, and $1,600,000 on December 31, 2022. The company's return on common stockholders' equity for 2022 is:

    a. 10.0%.   **c.** 7.1%.

    b. 9.0%.   **d.** 13.3%.

*15. **(LO 5)** When a stockholders' equity statement is presented, it is not necessary to prepare a (an):

    a. retained earnings statement.

    b. balance sheet.

    c. income statement.

    d. None of the answer choices is correct.

*16. **(LO 6)** The ledger of JFK, Inc. shows common stock, common treasury stock, and no preferred stock. For this company, the formula for computing book value per share is:

    a. total paid-in capital and retained earnings divided by the number of shares of common stock issued.

    b. common stock divided by the number of shares of common stock issued.

    c. total stockholders' equity divided by the number of shares of common stock outstanding.

    d. total stockholders' equity divided by the number of shares of common stock issued.

Solutions

1. c. Government regulations are a disadvantage of a corporation. The other choices are advantages of a corporation.

2. b. Additional taxes are a disadvantage of a corporation. The other choices are advantages of a corporation.

3. d. Par value has no relationship with market price, and many states today do not require a par value. The other choices are true statements.

4. c. Common Stock should be credited for $10,000 and Paid-in Capital in Excess of Par should be credited for $2,000. The stock is par value stock, not stated value stock, and this excess is contributed, not earned, capital. The other choices are therefore incorrect.

5. d. Preferred stock usually does not have voting rights and therefore does not have priority over common stock on this issue. The other choices are true statements.

6. a. Treasury Stock should be credited for $1,000 (100 shares × $10, the acquisition cost). Paid-in Capital from Treasury Stock should be credited for the difference between the $1,000 and the cash received of $1,300 (100 shares × $13), or $300. The other choices are therefore incorrect.

7. a. The cost of treasury stock is deducted from total paid-in capital and retained earnings. The other choices are therefore incorrect.

8. d. The preferred stockholders will receive a total of $240,000 of dividends [dividends in arrears ($80,000 × 2 years) + current-year dividends ($80,000)]. If U-Bet wants to pay a total of $375,000 in 2022, then common stockholders will receive $135,000 ($375,000 − $240,000), not (a) $0, (b) $295,000, or (c) $215,000.

9. a. Entries are required for dividends on the declaration date and the payment date, but not the record date. The other choices are therefore incorrect.

10. c. Because the stock dividend is considered small, the fair value (market price), not the par value, is assigned to the shares. The other choices are incorrect because (a) a debit to Retained Earnings for the fair value of the shares issued should be made; (b) a small stock dividend changes the composition of total stockholders' equity, but does not change the total; and (d) a small stock dividend will have no effect on par value per share.

11. d. The ending balance in retained earnings is $70,000. It is computed by subtracting from the beginning balance of $100,000 the following items: net loss of $20,000, cash dividends of $3,000, and stock dividends of $7,000. Note that market value of the cash dividend should be used instead of its par value. The other choices are therefore incorrect.

12. c. Common stock is part of paid-in capital. The other choices are incorrect because common stock (a) is listed after preferred stock, (b) is not added to total capital stock but is part of capital stock, and (d) is part of capital stock, not additional paid-in capital.

13. b. Common stock is reported in the capital stock section of paid-in capital, not in the additional paid-in capital section. The other choices are true statements.

14. b. Return on common stockholders' equity = Net income available to common stockholders ÷ Average common stockholders' equity. Net income available to common stockholders = Net income − Preferred dividends = $126,000 [$186,000 − (10,000 × .06 × $100)]. The company's return on common stockholders' equity for the year is therefore 9.0% [$126,000 ÷ ($1,200,000 + $1,600,000) ÷ 2)], not (a) 10.0%, (c) 7.1%, or (d) 13.3%.

*15. **a.** When a stockholders' equity statement is presented, a retained earnings statement is unnecessary as the information would be redundant. Choices (b) balance sheet and (c) income statement are required statements. Choice (d) is wrong because there is a correct answer given.

*16. **c.** When a company has only one class of stock outstanding, Book value per share = Total stockholders' equity ÷ Number of shares of common stock outstanding. The other choices are therefore incorrect.

Practice Brief Exercises

1. (LO 2) On April 10, Leury Corporation issues 3,000 shares of $5 par value common stock for cash at $14 per share. Journalize the issuance of the stock.

Prepare entries for issuance of par value common stock.

Solution

1. April 10	Cash (3,000 × $14)	42,000	
	Common Stock (3,000 × $5)		15,000
	Paid-in Capital in Excess of Par—		
	Common Stock (3,000 × $9)		27,000

Prepare entries for treasury stock transactions.

2. (LO 2) On June 1, Omar Corporation purchases 600 shares of its $5 par value common stock for the treasury at a cash price of $10 per share. Journalize the treasury stock transaction.

Solution

2. June 1	Treasury Stock (600 × $10)	6,000	
	Cash		6,000

Prepare entries for a cash dividend.

3. (LO 3) Giovanni Corporation has 70,000 shares of common stock outstanding. It declares a $2 per share cash dividend on November 15 to stockholders of record on December 15. The dividend is paid on December 31. Prepare the entries on the appropriate dates to record the declaration and payment of the cash dividend.

Solution

3. Nov. 15	Cash Dividends (70,000 × $2)	140,000	
	Dividends Payable		140,000
Dec. 31	Dividends Payable	140,000	
	Cash		140,000

Show before-and-after effects of a stock dividend.

4. (LO 3) The stockholders' equity section of Ynoa Corporation consists of common stock ($5 par) $3,000,000 and retained earnings $1,000,000. A 15% stock dividend (90,000 shares) is declared when the market price per share is $11. Show the before-and-after effects of the dividend on (a) the components of stockholders' equity, (b) shares outstanding, and (c) par value per share.

Solution

	Before Dividend	After Dividend
4. a. Stockholders' equity		
Paid-in capital		
Common stock, $5 par	$3,000,000	$3,450,000
In excess of par	—	540,000
Total paid-in capital	3,000,000	3,990,000
Retained earnings	1,000,000	10,000
Total stockholders' equity	$4,000,000	$4,000,000
b. Outstanding shares	600,000	690,000
c. Par value per share	$5.00	$5.00

Prepare stockholders' equity section.

5. (LO 4) Navarez Corporation has the following accounts at December 31: Common Stock, $2 par, 50,000 shares issued, $100,000; Paid-in Capital in Excess of Par—Common Stock $40,000; Retained Earnings $65,000; and Treasury Stock, 2,000 shares, $17,000. Prepare the stockholders' equity section of the balance sheet.

Solution

5. Stockholders' equity	
Paid-in capital	
Common stock, $2 par value, 50,000 shares issued, and 48,000 shares outstanding	$100,000
In excess of par—common stock	40,000
Total paid-in capital	140,000
Retained earnings	65,000
Total paid-in capital and retained earnings	205,000
Less: Treasury stock (2,000 common shares)	17,000
Total stockholders' equity	$188,000

Practice Exercises

1. **(LO 2)** Maci Co. had the following transactions during the current period.

Journalize issuance of common and preferred stock and purchase of treasury stock.

Mar. 2   Issued 5,000 shares of $5 par value common stock to attorneys in payment of a bill for $35,000 for services performed in helping the company to incorporate.

June 12   Issued 60,000 shares of $5 par value common stock for cash of $370,000.

July 11   Issued 1,000 shares of $100 par value preferred stock for cash at $112 per share.

Nov. 28   Purchased 2,000 shares of treasury stock for $70,000.

Instructions

Journalize the transactions.

Solution

1.

Mar. 2	Organization Expense	35,000	
	Common Stock (5,000 × $5)		25,000
	Paid-in Capital in Excess of Par—		
	Common Stock		10,000
June 12	Cash	370,000	
	Common Stock (60,000 × $5)		300,000
	Paid-in Capital in Excess of Par—		
	Common Stock		70,000
July 11	Cash (1,000 × $112)	112,000	
	Preferred Stock (1,000 × $100)		100,000
	Paid-in Capital in Excess of Par—		
	Preferred Stock (1,000 × $12)		12,000
Nov. 28	Treasury Stock	70,000	
	Cash		70,000

2. **(LO 3, 4)** On January 1, Chong Corporation had 95,000 shares of no-par common stock issued and outstanding. The stock has a stated value of $5 per share. During the year, the following occurred.

Journalize cash dividends; indicate statement presentation.

Apr. 1   Issued 25,000 additional shares of common stock for $17 per share.

June 15   Declared a cash dividend of $1 per share to stockholders of record on June 30.

July 10   Paid the $1 cash dividend.

Dec. 1   Issued 2,000 additional shares of common stock for $19 per share.

     15   Declared a cash dividend on outstanding shares of $1.20 per share to stockholders of record on December 31.

Instructions

a. Prepare the entries, if any, on each of the three dividend dates.

b. How are dividends and dividends payable reported in the financial statements prepared at December 31?

Solution

2. a. June 15	Cash Dividends [(95,000 + 25,000) × $1]	120,000	
	Dividends Payable		120,000
July 10	Dividends Payable	120,000	
	Cash		120,000
Dec. 15	Cash Dividends [(120,000 + 2,000) × $1.20]	146,400	
	Dividends Payable		146,400

b. In the retained earnings statement, dividends of $266,400 ($120,000 + $146,400) will be deducted. In the balance sheet, Dividends Payable of $146,400 will be reported as a current liability.

Practice Problem

Journalize transactions and prepare stockholders' equity section.

(LO 2, 4) Rolman Corporation is authorized to issue 1,000,000 shares of $5 par value common stock. In its first year, the company has the following stock transactions.

Jan. 10	Issued 400,000 shares of stock at $8 per share.
July 1	Issued 100,000 shares of stock for land. The land had an asking price of $900,000. The stock is currently selling on a national exchange at $8.25 per share.
Sept. 1	Purchased 10,000 shares of common stock for the treasury at $9 per share.
Dec. 1	Sold 4,000 shares of the treasury stock at $10 per share.

Instructions

a. Journalize the transactions.

b. Prepare the stockholders' equity section, assuming the company had ending retained earnings of $200,000 at December 31.

Solution

a.

Date	Account	Debit	Credit
Jan. 10	Cash	3,200,000	
	Common Stock		2,000,000
	Paid-in Capital in Excess of		
	Par—Common Stock		1,200,000
	(To record issuance of 400,000		
	shares of $5 par value stock)		
July 1	Land	825,000	
	Common Stock		500,000
	Paid-in Capital in Excess of		
	Par—Common Stock		325,000
	(To record issuance of 100,000		
	shares of $5 par value stock for land)		
Sept. 1	Treasury Stock	90,000	
	Cash		90,000
	(To record purchase of 10,000		
	shares of treasury stock at cost)		
Dec. 1	Cash	40,000	
	Treasury Stock		36,000
	Paid-in Capital from Treasury Stock		4,000
	(To record sale of 4,000 shares of treasury		
	stock above cost)		

b.

Rolman Corporation
Balance Sheet (partial)

Stockholders' equity		
Paid-in capital		
Capital stock		
Common stock, $5 par value, 1,000,000 shares		
authorized, 500,000 shares issued, 494,000		
shares outstanding		$2,500,000
Additional paid-in capital		
In excess of par—common stock	$1,525,000	
From treasury stock	4,000	
Total additional paid-in capital		1,529,000
Total paid-in capital		4,029,000
Retained earnings		200,000
Total paid-in capital and retained earnings		4,229,000
Less: Treasury stock (6,000 shares)		54,000
Total stockholders' equity		$4,175,000

WileyPLUS

Brief Exercises, DO IT! Exercises, Exercises, Problems, and many additional resources are available for practice in WileyPLUS.

Note: All asterisked Questions, Exercises, and Problems relate to material in the appendices to the chapter.

Questions

1. Joe, a student, asks your help in understanding the following characteristics of a corporation: (a) separate legal existence, (b) limited liability of stockholders, and (c) transferable ownership rights. Explain these characteristics to Joe.

2. **a.** Your friend G. C. Jones cannot understand how the characteristic of corporation management is both an advantage and a disadvantage. Clarify this problem for G. C.

   b. Identify and explain two other disadvantages of a corporation.

3. **a.** The following terms pertain to the forming of a corporation: (1) charter, (2) by-laws, and (3) organization costs. Explain the terms.

   b. Nona James believes a corporation must be incorporated in the state in which its headquarters' office is located. Is Nona correct? Explain.

4. What are the basic ownership rights of common stockholders in the absence of restrictive provisions?

5. **a.** What are the two principal components of stockholders' equity?

   b. What is paid-in capital? Give three examples.

6. How does the balance sheet for a corporation differ from the balance sheet for a proprietorship?

7. The corporate charter of Gage Corporation allows the issuance of a maximum of 100,000 shares of common stock. During its first two years of operations, Gage sold 70,000 shares to shareholders and reacquired 4,000 of these shares. After these transactions, how many shares are authorized, issued, and outstanding?

8. Which is the better investment—common stock with a par value of $5 per share, or common stock with a par value of $20 per share? Why?

9. What factors help determine the market price of stock?

10. Why is common stock usually not issued at a price that is less than par value?

11. Land appraised at $80,000 is purchased by issuing 1,000 shares of $20 par value common stock. The market price of the shares at the time of the exchange, based on active trading in the securities market, is $95 per share. Should the land be recorded at $20,000, $80,000, or $95,000? Explain.

12. For what reasons might a company like **IBM** repurchase some of its stock (treasury stock)?

13. Monet, Inc. purchases 1,000 shares of its own previously issued $5 par common stock for $11,000. Assuming the shares are held in the treasury, what effect does this transaction have on (a) net income, (b) total assets, (c) total paid-in capital, and (d) total stockholders' equity?

14. Monet, Inc. purchases 1,000 shares of its own previously issued $5 par common stock for $11,000. Monet then resells this treasury stock for $16,000. What effect does this resale transaction have on (a) net income, (b) total assets, (c) total paid-in capital, and (d) total stockholders' equity?

15. **a.** What are the principal differences between common stock and preferred stock?

   b. Preferred stock may be cumulative. Discuss this feature.

   c. How are dividends in arrears presented in the financial statements?

16. Identify the events that result in credits and debits to retained earnings.

17. Indicate how each of the following accounts should be classified in the stockholders' equity section.

   a. Common stock.

   b. Paid-in capital in excess of par—common stock.

   c. Retained earnings.

   d. Treasury stock.

   e. Paid-in capital from treasury stock.

   f. Paid-in capital in excess of stated value—common stock.

   g. Preferred stock.

18. Jan Kimler maintains that adequate cash is the only requirement for the declaration of a cash dividend. Is Jan correct? Explain.

19. **a.** Three dates are important in connection with cash dividends. Identify these dates, and explain their significance to the corporation and its stockholders.

   b. Identify the accounting entries that are made for a cash dividend and the date of each entry.

20. Contrast the effects of a cash dividend and a stock dividend on a corporation's balance sheet.

21. Doris Angel asks, "Since stock dividends don't change anything, why declare them?" What is your answer to Doris?

22. Jayne Corporation has 170,000 shares of $15 par value common stock outstanding when it announces a 3-for-1 stock split. Before the split, the stock had a market price of $120 per share. After the split, how many shares of stock will be outstanding? What will be the approximate market price per share?

23. The board of directors is considering either a stock split or a stock dividend. They understand that total stockholders' equity will remain the same under either action. However, they are not sure of the different effects of the two types of actions on other aspects of stockholders' equity. Explain the differences to the board of directors.

24. What is the purpose of a retained earnings restriction? Identify the possible causes of retained earnings restrictions.

25. What is the formula for the payout ratio? What does it indicate?

*26. What is the formula for computing book value per share when a corporation has only common stock?

*27. Emko Inc.'s common stock has a par value of $1, a book value of $24, and a current market price of $18. Explain why these amounts are all different.

Brief Exercises

List the advantages and disadvantages of a corporation.

BE11.1 (LO 1), K Angie Baden is studying for her accounting midterm examination. Identify for Angie the advantages and disadvantages of the corporate form of business organization.

Journalize issuance of par value common stock.

BE11.2 (LO 2), AP On May 10, Pilar Corporation issues 2,500 shares of $5 par value common stock for cash at $13 per share. Journalize the issuance of the stock.

Prepare entries for issuance of no-par value common stock.

BE11.3 (LO 2), AP On June 1, Noonan Inc. issues 4,000 shares of no-par common stock at a cash price of $6 per share. Journalize the issuance of the shares assuming the stock has a stated value of $1 per share.

Prepare entries for issuance of stock in a noncash transaction.

BE11.4 (LO 2), AP Lei Inc.'s $10 par value common stock is actively traded at a market price of $15 per share. Lei issues 5,000 shares to purchase land advertised for sale at $85,000. Journalize the issuance of the stock in acquiring the land.

Journalize issuance of preferred stock.

BE11.5 (LO 2), AP Layes Inc. issues 8,000 shares of $100 par value preferred stock for cash at $106 per share. Journalize the issuance of the preferred stock.

Prepare entries for treasury stock transactions.

BE11.6 (LO 2), AP On July 1, Raney Corporation purchases 500 shares of its $5 par value common stock for the treasury at a cash price of $9 per share. On September 1, it sells 300 shares of the treasury stock for cash at $11 per share. Journalize the two treasury stock transactions.

Prepare entries for a cash dividend.

BE11.7 (LO 3), AP Basse Corporation has 7,000 shares of common stock outstanding. It declares a $1 per share cash dividend on November 1 to stockholders of record on December 1. The dividend is paid on December 31. Prepare the entries on the appropriate dates to record the declaration and payment of the cash dividend.

Prepare entries for a stock dividend.

BE11.8 (LO 3), AP Langley Corporation has 50,000 shares of $10 par value common stock outstanding. It declares a 15% stock dividend on December 1 when the market price per share is $16. The dividend shares are issued on December 31. Prepare the entries for the declaration and issuance of the stock dividend.

Show before-and-after effects of a stock dividend.

BE11.9 (LO 3), AP The stockholders' equity section of Mabry Corporation's balance sheet consists of common stock ($8 par) $1,000,000 and retained earnings $300,000. A 10% stock dividend (12,500 shares) is declared when the market price per share is $19. Show the before-and-after effects of the dividend on (a) the components of stockholders' equity and (b) the shares outstanding.

Determine retained earnings balance.

BE11.10 (LO 4), AP For the year ending December 31, 2022, Soto Inc. reports net income $170,000 and cash dividends $85,000. Determine the balance in retained earnings at December 31 assuming the balance in retained earnings on January 1, 2022, was $220,000.

Prepare a stockholders' equity section.

BE11.11 (LO 4), AP Sudz Corporation has these accounts at December 31: Common Stock, $10 par, 5,000 shares issued, $50,000; Paid-in Capital in Excess of Par Value $22,000; Retained Earnings $42,000; and Treasury Stock, 500 shares, $11,000. Prepare the stockholders' equity section of the balance sheet.

Compute book value per share.

*** BE11.12 (LO 6), AP** The balance sheet for Lauren Inc. shows the following: total paid-in capital and retained earnings $877,000, total stockholders' equity $817,000, common stock issued 44,000 shares, and common stock outstanding 38,000 shares. Compute the book value per share. (No preferred stock is outstanding.)

DO IT! Exercises

DO IT! 11.1a (LO 1), C Indicate whether each of the following statements is true or false. If false, indicate how to correct the statement.

_____ **1.** The corporation is an entity separate and distinct from its owners.

_____ **2.** The liability of stockholders is normally limited to their investment in the corporation.

_____ **3.** The relative lack of government regulation is an advantage of the corporate form of business.

_____ **4.** There is no journal entry to record the authorization of capital stock.

_____ **5.** No-par value stock is quite rare today.

Analyze statements about corporate organization.

DO IT! 11.1b (LO 1), AP At the end of its first year of operation, Goss Corporation has $1,000,000 of common stock and net income of $236,000. Prepare (a) the closing entry for net income and (b) the stockholders' equity section at year-end.

Close net income and prepare stockholders' equity section.

DO IT! 11.2a (LO 2), AP Beauty Island Corporation began operations on April 1 by issuing 60,000 shares of $5 par value common stock for cash at $13 per share. On April 19, it issued 2,000 shares of common stock to attorneys in settlement of their bill of $27,500 for organization costs. In addition, Beauty Island issued 1,000 shares of $1 par value preferred stock for $6 cash per share. Journalize the issuance of the common and preferred shares, assuming the shares are not publicly traded.

Journalize issuance of stock.

DO IT! 11.2b (LO 2), AP Fouts Corporation purchased 2,000 shares of its $10 par value common stock for $130,000 on August 1. It will hold these shares in the treasury until resold. On December 1, the corporation sold 1,200 shares of treasury stock for cash at $72 per share. Journalize the treasury stock transactions.

Journalize treasury stock transactions.

DO IT! 11.3a (LO 3), AP Herr Corporation has 3,000 shares of 8%, $100 par value preferred stock outstanding at December 31, 2022. At December 31, 2022, the company declared a $105,000 cash dividend. Determine the dividend paid to preferred stockholders and common stockholders under each of the following scenarios.

Determine dividends paid to preferred and common stockholders.

1. The preferred stock is noncumulative, and the company has not missed any dividends in previous years.

2. The preferred stock is noncumulative, and the company did not pay a dividend in each of the two previous years.

3. The preferred stock is cumulative, and the company did not pay a dividend in each of the two previous years.

DO IT! 11.3b (LO 3), AP Spears Company has had 4 years of record earnings. Due to this success, the market price of its 400,000 outstanding shares of $2 par value common stock has increased from $6 per share to $50. During this period, paid-in capital remained the same at $2,400,000. Retained earnings increased from $1,800,000 to $12,000,000. CEO Don Ames is considering either (1) a 15% stock dividend or (2) a 2-for-1 stock split. He asks you to show the before-and-after effects of each option on (a) retained earnings, (b) total stockholders' equity, and (c) par value per share.

Determine effects of stock dividend and stock split.

DO IT! 11.4a (LO 4), AP Hoyle Corporation has issued 100,000 shares of $5 par value common stock. It was authorized to sell 500,000 shares. The paid-in capital in excess of par on common stock is $263,000. The corporation has reacquired 7,000 common shares at a cost of $46,000 and is currently holding those shares.

The corporation also has 2,000 shares issued and outstanding of 9%, $100 par value preferred stock. It was authorized 10,000 shares. The paid-in capital in excess of par value on the preferred stock is $23,000. Retained earnings is $372,000. Prepare the stockholders' equity section of the balance sheet.

Prepare stockholders' equity section.

DO IT! 11.4b (LO 4), AP On January 1, 2022, Vahsholtz Corporation purchased 5,000 shares of treasury stock. Other information regarding Vahsholtz Corporation is provided as follows.

Compute return on stockholders' equity and discuss changes.

	2022	2021
Net income	$110,000	$100,000
Dividends on preferred stock	$ 30,000	$ 30,000
Dividends on common stock	$ 25,000	$ 20,000
Weighted-average number of common shares outstanding	45,000	50,000
Common stockholders' equity beginning of year	$750,000	$600,000
Common stockholders' equity end of year	$830,000	$750,000

(a) Compute return on common stockholders' equity for each year, and (b) discuss the changes from 2021 to 2022.

Exercises

Identify characteristics of a corporation.

E11.1 (LO 1), C Andrea has prepared the following list of statements about corporations.

1. A corporation is an entity separate and distinct from its owners.

2. As a legal entity, a corporation has most of the rights and privileges of a person.

3. Most of the largest U.S. corporations are privately held corporations.

4. Corporations may buy, own, and sell property; borrow money; enter into legally binding contracts; and sue and be sued.

5. The net income of a corporation is not taxed as a separate entity.

6. Creditors have a legal claim on the personal assets of the owners of a corporation if the corporation does not pay its debts.

7. The transfer of stock from one owner to another requires the approval of either the corporation or other stockholders.

8. The board of directors of a corporation legally owns the corporation.

9. The chief accounting officer of a corporation is the controller.

10. Corporations are subject to fewer state and federal regulations than partnerships or proprietorships.

Instructions

Identify each statement as true or false. If false, indicate how to correct the statement.

Identify characteristics of a corporation.

E11.2 (LO 1), C Khalid has come to you with statements about corporations.

1. Corporation management is both an advantage and a disadvantage of a corporation compared to a proprietorship or a partnership.

2. Limited liability of stockholders, government regulations, and additional taxes are the major disadvantages of a corporation.

3. When a corporation is formed, organization costs are recorded as an asset.

4. Each share of common stock gives the stockholder the ownership rights to vote at stockholder meetings, share in corporate earnings, keep the same percentage ownership when new shares of stock are issued, and share in assets upon liquidation.

5. The number of issued shares is always greater than or equal to the number of authorized shares.

6. A journal entry is required for the authorization of capital stock.

7. Publicly held corporations usually issue stock directly to investors.

8. The trading of capital stock on a securities exchange involves the transfer of already issued shares from an existing stockholder to another investor.

9. The market price of common stock is usually the same as its par value.

10. Retained earnings is the total amount of cash and other assets paid in to the corporation by stockholders in exchange for capital stock.

Instructions

Identify each statement as true or false. If false, indicate how to correct the statement.

Journalize issuance of common stock.

E11.3 (LO 2), AP During its first year of operations, Mona Corporation had these transactions pertaining to its common stock.

| Jan. 10 | Issued 30,000 shares for cash at $5 per share. |
| July 1 | Issued 60,000 shares for cash at $7 per share. |

Instructions

a. Journalize the transactions, assuming that the common stock has a par value of $5 per share.

b. Journalize the transactions, assuming that the common stock is no-par with a stated value of $1 per share.

Journalize issuance of common stock.

E11.4 (LO 2), AP Osage Corporation issued 2,000 shares of stock.

Instructions

Prepare the entry for the issuance under the following independent assumptions.

a. The stock had a par value of $5 per share and was issued for a total of $52,000.

b. The stock had a stated value of $5 per share and was issued for a total of $52,000.

c. The stock had no par or stated value and was issued for a total of $52,000.

d. The stock had a par value of $5 per share and was issued to attorneys for services provided during incorporation valued at $52,000.

e. The stock had a par value of $5 per share and was issued for land worth $52,000.

E11.5 (LO 2, 3), AP Hodge Corporation issued 100,000 shares of $20 par value, cumulative, 6% preferred stock on January 1, 2021, for $2,300,000. In December 2023, Hodge declared its first dividend of $500,000.

Differentiate between preferred and common stock dividends.

Instructions

a. Prepare Hodge's journal entry to record the issuance of the preferred stock.

b. If the preferred stock is **not** cumulative, how much of the $500,000 would be paid to **common** stockholders?

c. If the preferred stock is cumulative, how much of the $500,000 would be paid to **common** stockholders?

E11.6 (LO 2), AP As an auditor for the CPA firm of Hinkson and Calvert, you encounter the following situations in auditing different clients.

Journalize noncash common stock transactions.

1. LR Corporation is a closely held corporation whose stock is not publicly traded. On December 5, the corporation acquired land by issuing 5,000 shares of its $20 par value common stock. The owners' asking price for the land was $120,000, and the fair value of the land was $110,000.

2. Vera Corporation is a publicly held corporation whose common stock is traded on the securities markets. On June 1, it acquired land by issuing 20,000 shares of its $10 par value stock. At the time of the exchange, the land was advertised for sale at $250,000. The stock was selling at $11 per share.

Instructions

Prepare the journal entries for each of the situations above.

E11.7 (LO 2), AP Rinehart Corporation purchased from its stockholders 5,000 shares of its own previously issued stock for $255,000. It later resold 2,000 shares for $54 per share, then 2,000 more shares for $49 per share, and finally 1,000 shares for $43 per share.

Journalize treasury stock transactions.

Instructions

Prepare journal entries for the purchase of the treasury stock and the three sales of treasury stock.

E11.8 (LO 2), AP Quay Co. had the following transactions during the current period.

Journalize issuance of common and preferred stock and purchase of treasury stock.

Mar.	2	Issued 5,000 shares of $5 par value common stock to attorneys in payment of a bill for $30,000 for services performed in helping the company to incorporate.
June	12	Issued 60,000 shares of $5 par value common stock for cash of $375,000.
July	11	Issued 1,000 shares of $100 par value preferred stock for cash at $110 per share.
Nov.	28	Purchased 2,000 shares of treasury stock for $80,000.

Instructions

Journalize the transactions.

E11.9 (LO 2), AP On January 1, 2022, the stockholders' equity section of Newlin Corporation shows common stock ($5 par value) $1,500,000; paid-in capital in excess of par $1,000,000; and retained earnings $1,200,000. During the year, the following treasury stock transactions occurred.

Journalize treasury stock transactions.

Mar.	1	Purchased 50,000 shares for cash at $15 per share.
July	1	Sold 10,000 treasury shares for cash at $17 per share.
Sept.	1	Sold 8,000 treasury shares for cash at $14 per share.

Instructions

a. Journalize the treasury stock transactions.

b. Restate the entry for September 1, assuming the treasury shares were sold at $12 per share.

E11.10 (LO 2, 4), AP Penland Corporation is authorized to issue both preferred and common stock. The par value of the preferred stock is $50. During the first year of operations, the company had the following events and transactions pertaining to its preferred stock.

Journalize preferred stock transactions and indicate statement presentation.

Feb.	1	Issued 40,000 shares for cash at $51 per share.
July	1	Issued 60,000 shares for cash at $56 per share.

Instructions

a. Journalize the transactions.

b. Post to the stockholders' equity accounts. (Use T-accounts.)

c. Discuss the statement presentation of the accounts.

Answer questions about stockholders' equity section.

E11.11 (LO 2, 4), C The stockholders' equity section of Lachlin Corporation's balance sheet at December 31 is presented here.

Lachlin Corporation
Balance Sheet (partial)

Stockholders' equity	
Paid-in capital	
Preferred stock, cumulative, 10,000 shares authorized,	
6,000 shares issued and outstanding	$ 600,000
Common stock, no par, 750,000 shares authorized,	
580,000 shares issued	2,900,000
Total paid-in capital	3,500,000
Retained earnings	1,158,000
Total paid-in capital and retained earnings	4,658,000
Less: Treasury stock (6,000 common shares)	32,000
Total stockholders' equity	$4,626,000

Instructions

From a review of the stockholders' equity section, answer the following questions.

a. How many shares of common stock are outstanding?

b. Assuming there is a stated value, what is the stated value of the common stock?

c. What is the par value of the preferred stock?

d. If the annual dividend on preferred stock is $36,000, what is the dividend rate on preferred stock?

e. If dividends of $72,000 were in arrears on preferred stock, what would be the balance reported for retained earnings?

Prepare correct entries for capital stock transactions.

E11.12 (LO 2), AP Gilliam Corporation recently hired a new accountant with extensive experience in accounting for partnerships. Because of the pressure of the new job, the accountant was unable to review his understanding of corporation accounting. During the first month, the accountant made the following entries for the corporation's capital stock.

May 2	Cash		130,000	
		Capital Stock		130,000
		(Issued 10,000 shares of $10 par value		
		common stock at $13 per share)		
	10	Cash	600,000	
		Capital Stock		600,000
		(Issued 10,000 shares of $50 par value		
		preferred stock at $60 per share)		
	15	Capital Stock	15,000	
		Cash		15,000
		(Purchased 1,000 shares of common		
		stock for the treasury at $15 per share)		
	31	Cash	8,000	
		Capital Stock		5,000
		Gain on Sale of Stock		3,000
		(Sold 500 shares of treasury stock at $16		
		per share)		

Instructions

On the basis of the explanation for each entry, prepare the entry that should have been made for the capital stock transactions.

E11.13 (LO 3), AP On January 1, Graves Corporation had 60,000 shares of no-par common stock issued and outstanding. The stock has a stated value of $4 per share. During the year, the following transactions occurred.

Journalize cash dividends; indicate statement presentation.

Apr.	1	Issued 9,000 additional shares of common stock for $11 per share.
June	15	Declared a cash dividend of $1.50 per share to stockholders of record on June 30.
July	10	Paid the $1.50 cash dividend.
Dec.	1	Issued 4,000 additional shares of common stock for $12 per share.
	15	Declared a cash dividend on outstanding shares of $1.60 per share to stockholders of record on December 31.

Instructions

a. Prepare the entries, if any, on each of the three dates that involved dividends.

b. How are dividends and dividends payable reported in the financial statements prepared at December 31?

E11.14 (LO 3), AP On January 1, 2022, Lenne Corporation had $1,200,000 of common stock outstanding that was issued at par and retained earnings of $750,000. The company issued 30,000 shares of common stock at par on July 1 and earned net income of $400,000 for the year.

Journalize stock dividends.

Instructions

Journalize the declaration of a 15% stock dividend on December 10, 2022, for the following two independent assumptions.

a. Par value is $10 and market price is $15.

b. Par value is $5 and market price is $8.

E11.15 (LO 3), AP On October 31, the stockholders' equity section of Manolo Company's balance sheet consists of common stock $648,000 and retained earnings $400,000. Manolo is considering the following two courses of action: (1) declaring a 5% stock dividend on the 81,000 $8 par value shares outstanding or (2) effecting a 2-for-1 stock split that will reduce par value to $4 per share. The current market price is $17 per share.

Compare effects of a stock dividend and a stock split.

Instructions

Prepare a tabular summary of the effects of the alternative actions on the company's stockholders' equity and outstanding shares. Use these column headings: **Before Action, After Stock Dividend,** and **After Stock Split.**

E11.16 (LO 3), AP Before preparing financial statements for the current year, the chief accountant for Toso Company discovered the following errors in the accounts.

Prepare correcting entries for dividends and a stock split.

1. The declaration and payment of a $50,000 cash dividend was recorded as a debit to Interest Expense $50,000 and a credit to Cash $50,000.

2. A 10% stock dividend (1,000 shares) was declared on the $10 par value stock when the market price per share was $18. The only entry made was Stock Dividends (Dr.) $10,000 and Dividend Payable (Cr.) $10,000. The shares have not been issued.

3. A 4-for-1 stock split involving the issue of 400,000 shares of $5 par value common stock for 100,000 shares of $20 par value common stock was recorded as a debit to Retained Earnings $2,000,000 and a credit to Common Stock $2,000,000.

Instructions

Prepare the correcting entries at December 31.

E11.17 (LO 4), AP On January 1, 2022, Eddy Corporation had retained earnings of $610,000. During the year, Eddy had the following selected events.

Determine retained earnings balance.

1. Declared cash dividends $120,000.

2. Earned net income $350,000.

3. Declared stock dividends $90,000.

Instructions

Determine the retained earnings balance at the end of the year.

Determine retained earnings balance.

E11.18 (LO 4), AP Newland Company reported retained earnings at December 31, 2021, of $330,000. Newland had 200,000 shares of common stock outstanding at the beginning of 2022.

The following transactions occurred during 2022.

1. A cash dividend of $0.50 per share was declared and paid.

2. A 5% stock dividend was declared and distributed when the market price per share was $15 per share.

3. Net income was $285,000.

Instructions

Compute the ending balance in retained earnings at the end of 2022.

Classify stockholders' equity accounts.

E11.19 (LO 4), AP The ledger of Rolling Hills Corporation contains the following accounts: Common Stock, Preferred Stock, Treasury Stock, Paid-in Capital in Excess of Par—Preferred Stock, Paid-in Capital in Excess of Stated Value—Common Stock, Paid-in Capital from Treasury Stock, and Retained Earnings.

Instructions

Classify each account using the following table headings.

| | Paid-in Capital | | | |
| | Capital | Additional | Retained | |
Account	Stock		Earnings	Other

Prepare a stockholders' equity section.

E11.20 (LO 4), AP The following accounts appear in the ledger of Horner Inc. after the books are closed at December 31, 2022.

Common Stock, no par, $1 stated value, 400,000 shares authorized; 300,000 shares issued	$ 300,000
Common Stock Dividends Distributable	30,000
Paid-in Capital in Excess of Stated Value—Common Stock	1,200,000
Preferred Stock, $5 par value, 8%, 40,000 shares authorized; 30,000 shares issued	150,000
Retained Earnings	800,000
Treasury Stock (10,000 common shares)	74,000
Paid-in Capital in Excess of Par—Preferred Stock	344,000

Instructions

Prepare the stockholders' equity section at December 31, 2022, assuming retained earnings is restricted for plant expansion in the amount of $100,000 (use Note R).

Prepare a stockholders' equity section.

E11.21 (LO 4), AP Dirk Company reported the following balances at December 31, 2021: common stock $500,000, paid-in capital in excess of par—common stock $100,000, and retained earnings $250,000. During 2022, the following transactions affected stockholders' equity.

1. Issued preferred stock with a par value of $125,000 for $200,000.

2. Purchased treasury stock (common) for $40,000.

3. Earned net income of $180,000.

4. Declared and paid cash dividends of $56,000.

Instructions

Prepare the stockholders' equity section of Dirk Company's December 31, 2022, balance sheet.

Prepare an income statement and compute return on equity.

E11.22 (LO 4), AP In 2022, Pennington Corporation had net sales of $600,000 and cost of goods sold of $360,000. Operating expenses were $153,000, and interest expense was $7,500. The corporation's tax rate is 30%. The corporation declared preferred dividends of $15,000 in 2022, and its average common stockholders' equity during the year was $200,000.

Instructions

a. Prepare a multiple-step income statement for Pennington Corporation.

b. Compute Pennington Corporation's return on common stockholders' equity for 2022.

E11.23 (LO 4), AN The following financial information is available for Flintlock Corporation.

Calculate ratios to evaluate dividend and earnings performance.

(in millions)	2022	2021
Average common stockholders' equity	$2,532	$2,591
Dividends declared for common stockholders	298	611
Dividends declared for preferred stockholders	40	40
Net income	504	555

Instructions

Calculate the payout ratio and return on common stockholders' equity for 2022 and 2021. Comment on your findings.

E11.24 (LO 4), AN Suppose the following financial information is available for **Walgreens**.

Calculate ratios to evaluate dividend and earnings performance.

(in millions)	2022	2021
Average common stockholders' equity	$13,622.5	$11,986.5
Dividends declared for common stockholders	471	394
Dividends declared for preferred stockholders	0	0
Net income	2,006	2,157

Instructions

Calculate the payout ratio and return on common stockholders' equity for 2022 and 2021. Comment on your findings.

*****E11.25 (LO 4, 6), AP** A recent stockholders' equity section of **Aluminum Company of America (Alcoa)** showed the following (in alphabetical order): additional paid-in capital $6,101, common stock $925, preferred stock $56, retained earnings $7,428, and treasury stock $2,828. (All dollar data are in millions.)

Prepare a stockholders' equity section.

The preferred stock has 557,740 shares authorized, with a par value of $100 and an annual $3.75 per share cumulative dividend preference. At December 31 of the current year, 557,649 shares of preferred are issued and 546,024 shares are outstanding. There are 1.8 billion shares of $1 par value common stock authorized, of which 924.6 million are issued and 844.8 million are outstanding at December 31.

Instructions

a. Prepare the stockholders' equity section of the current year, including disclosure of all relevant data.

b. Compute the book value per share of common stock, assuming there are no preferred dividends in arrears. (Round to two decimals.)

*****E11.26 (LO 6), AP** At December 31, Gorden Corporation has total stockholders' equity of $3,200,000. Included in this total are preferred stock $500,000 and paid-in capital in excess of par—preferred stock $50,000. There are 10,000 shares of $50 par value, 8% cumulative preferred stock outstanding. At year-end, 200,000 shares of common stock are outstanding.

Compute book value per share with preferred stock.

Instructions

Compute the book value per share of common stock under each of the following assumptions.

a. There are no preferred dividends in arrears, and the preferred stock does not have a call price.

b. Preferred dividends are one year in arrears, and the preferred stock has a call price of $60 per share.

Problems

P11.1A (LO 2, 4), AP DeLong Corporation was organized on January 1, 2022. It is authorized to issue 10,000 shares of 8%, $100 par value preferred stock, and 500,000 shares of no-par common stock with a stated value of $2 per share. The following stock transactions were completed during the first year.

Journalize stock transactions, post, and prepare paid-in capital section.

Jan. 10	Issued 80,000 shares of common stock for cash at $4 per share.
Mar. 1	Issued 5,000 shares of preferred stock for cash at $105 per share.
Apr. 1	Issued 24,000 shares of common stock for land. The asking price of the land was $90,000. The fair value of the land was $85,000.
May 1	Issued 80,000 shares of common stock for cash at $4.50 per share.
Aug. 1	Issued 10,000 shares of common stock to attorneys in payment of their bill of $30,000 for services performed in helping the company organize.
Sept. 1	Issued 10,000 shares of common stock for cash at $5 per share.
Nov. 1	Issued 1,000 shares of preferred stock for cash at $109 per share.

Instructions

a. Journalize the transactions.

c. Total paid-in capital $1,479,000

b. Post to the stockholders' equity accounts. (Use T-accounts.)

c. Prepare the paid-in capital section of stockholders' equity at December 31, 2022.

Journalize and post treasury stock transactions, and prepare stockholders' equity section.

P11.2A (LO 2, 4), AP Fechter Corporation had the following stockholders' equity accounts on January 1, 2022: Common Stock ($5 par) $500,000, Paid-in Capital in Excess of Par—Common Stock $200,000, and Retained Earnings $100,000. In 2022, the company had the following treasury stock transactions.

Mar. 1	Purchased 5,000 shares at $8 per share.
June 1	Sold 1,000 shares at $12 per share.
Sept. 1	Sold 2,000 shares at $10 per share.
Dec. 1	Sold 1,000 shares at $7 per share.

Fechter Corporation uses the cost method of accounting for treasury stock. In 2022, the company reported net income of $30,000.

Instructions

a. Journalize the treasury stock transactions, and prepare the closing entry at December 31, 2022, for net income.

b. Treasury Stock $8,000

c. Total stockholders' equity $829,000

b. Open accounts for (1) Paid-in Capital from Treasury Stock, (2) Treasury Stock, and (3) Retained Earnings. (Post to T-accounts.)

c. Prepare the stockholders' equity section of Fechter Corporation's balance sheet at December 31, 2022.

Journalize and post transactions, and prepare stockholders' equity section.

P11.3A (LO 2, 4), AP The stockholders' equity accounts of Castle Corporation on January 1, 2022, were as follows.

Preferred Stock (8%, $50 par, cumulative, 10,000 shares authorized)	$ 400,000
Common Stock ($1 stated value, 2,000,000 shares authorized)	1,000,000
Paid-in Capital in Excess of Par—Preferred Stock	100,000
Paid-in Capital in Excess of Stated Value—Common Stock	1,450,000
Retained Earnings	1,816,000
Treasury Stock (10,000 common shares)	50,000

During 2022, the corporation had the following transactions and events pertaining to its stockholders' equity.

Feb. 1	Issued 25,000 shares of common stock for $120,000.
Apr. 14	Sold 6,000 shares of treasury stock—common for $33,000.
Sept. 3	Issued 5,000 shares of common stock for a patent valued at $35,000.
Nov. 10	Purchased 1,000 shares of common stock for the treasury at a cost of $6,000.
Dec. 31	Determined that net income for the year was $452,000.

No dividends were declared during the year.

Instructions

a. Journalize the transactions and the closing entry for net income.

b. Enter the beginning balances in the accounts, and post the journal entries to the stockholders' equity accounts. (Use T-accounts.)

c. Total stockholders' equity $5,350,000

c. Prepare a stockholders' equity section at December 31, 2022, including the disclosure of the preferred dividends in arrears.

P11.4A (LO 3, 4), AP On January 1, 2022, Geffrey Corporation had the following stockholders' equity accounts.

Prepare dividend entries and stockholders' equity section.

Common Stock ($20 par value, 60,000 shares issued and outstanding)	$1,200,000
Paid-in Capital in Excess of Par—Common Stock	200,000
Retained Earnings	600,000

During the year, the following transactions occurred.

Feb.	1	Declared a $1 cash dividend per share to stockholders of record on February 15, payable March 1.
Mar.	1	Paid the dividend declared in February.
Apr.	1	Announced a 2-for-1 stock split. Prior to the split, the market price per share was $36.
July	1	Declared a 10% stock dividend to stockholders of record on July 15, distributable July 31. On July 1, the market price of the stock was $13 per share.
	31	Issued the shares for the stock dividend.
Dec.	1	Declared a $0.50 per share dividend to stockholders of record on December 15, payable January 5, 2023.
	31	Determined that net income for the year was $350,000.

Instructions

a. Journalize the transactions and the closing entries for net income and dividends.

b. Enter the beginning balances, and post the entries to the stockholders' equity accounts. (Use T-accounts.) (*Note:* Open additional stockholders' equity accounts as needed.)

c. Prepare the stockholders' equity section at December 31.

c. Total stockholders' equity $2,224,000

P11.5A (LO 2, 3, 4), AP The post-closing trial balance of Storey Corporation at December 31, 2022, contains the following stockholders' equity accounts.

Prepare stockholders' equity section and compute allocation of dividends.

Preferred Stock (15,000 shares issued)	$ 750,000
Common Stock (250,000 shares issued)	2,500,000
Paid-in Capital in Excess of Par—Preferred Stock	250,000
Paid-in Capital in Excess of Par—Common Stock	400,000
Common Stock Dividends Distributable	250,000
Retained Earnings	1,105,000

A review of the accounting records reveals the following.

1. No errors have been made in recording 2022 transactions or in preparing the closing entries.

2. Preferred stock is $50 par, 6%, and cumulative; 15,000 shares have been outstanding since January 1, 2021.

3. Authorized stock is 20,000 shares of preferred, 500,000 shares of common with a $10 par value.

4. The January 1 balance in Retained Earnings was $1,170,000.

5. On July 1, 20,000 shares of common stock were issued for cash at $16 per share.

6. A cash dividend of $250,000 was declared and properly allocated to preferred and common stock on October 1. No dividends were paid to preferred stockholders in 2021.

7. On December 31, a 10% common stock dividend was declared out of retained earnings on common stock when the market price per share was $16.

8. Net income for the year was $585,000.

9. On December 31, 2022, the directors authorized disclosure of a $200,000 restriction of retained earnings for plant expansion. (Use Note X.)

Instructions

a. Reproduce the Retained Earnings account (T-account) for 2022.

b. Prepare the stockholders' equity section at December 31, 2022.

c. Compute the allocation of the cash dividend to preferred and common stock.

b. Total stockholders' equity $5,255,000

Prepare entries for stock transactions and prepare stockholders' equity section.

P11.6A (LO 2, 3, 4), AP Irwin Corporation has been authorized to issue 20,000 shares of $100 par value, 10%, noncumulative preferred stock and 1,000,000 shares of no-par common stock. The corporation assigned a $2.50 stated value to the common stock. At December 31, 2022, the ledger contained the following post-closing balances pertaining to stockholders' equity.

Preferred Stock	$ 120,000
Paid-in Capital in Excess of Par—Preferred Stock	20,000
Common Stock	1,000,000
Paid-in Capital in Excess of Stated Value—Common Stock	1,800,000
Treasury Stock (1,000 common shares)	11,000
Paid-in Capital from Treasury Stock	1,500
Retained Earnings	82,000

All the preferred stock was issued for land having a fair value of $140,000. All common stock issued was for cash. In November, 1,500 shares of common stock were purchased for the treasury at a per share cost of $11. In December, 500 shares of treasury stock were sold for $14 per share. No dividends were declared in 2022.

Instructions

a. Prepare the journal entries for the:

1. Issuance of preferred stock for land.

2. Issuance of common stock for cash.

3. Purchase of common treasury stock for cash.

4. Sale of treasury stock for cash.

b. Total stockholders' equity
$3,012,500

b. Prepare the stockholders' equity section at December 31, 2022.

Prepare dividend entries and stockholders' equity section.

P11.7A (LO 2, 3, 4), AP On January 1, 2022, Primo Corporation had the following stockholders' equity accounts.

Common Stock ($10 par value, 75,000 shares issued and outstanding)	$750,000
Paid-in Capital in Excess of Par—Common Stock	200,000
Retained Earnings	540,000

During the year, the following transactions occurred.

Jan.	15	Declared a $1 cash dividend per share to stockholders of record on January 31, payable February 15.
Feb.	15	Paid the dividend declared in January.
Apr.	15	Declared a 10% stock dividend to stockholders of record on April 30, distributable May 15. On April 15, the market price of the stock was $14 per share.
May	15	Issued the shares for the stock dividend.
July	1	Announced a 2-for-1 stock split. The market price per share at the time of the announcement was $15. (The new par value is $5.)
Dec.	1	Declared a $0.60 per share cash dividend to stockholders of record on December 15, payable January 10, 2023.
	31	Determined that net income for the year was $250,000.

Instructions

a. Journalize the transactions and the closing entries for net income and dividends.

b. Enter the beginning balances, and post the entries to the stockholders' equity accounts. (*Note:* Open additional stockholders' equity accounts as needed.)

c. Total stockholders' equity
$1,566,000

c. Prepare a stockholders' equity section at December 31, 2022.

Prepare stockholders' equity statement.

* **P11.8A (LO 5), AP** On January 1, 2022, Goodhue Inc. had the following stockholders' equity balances.

Common Stock (400,000 shares issued)	$800,000
Paid-in Capital in Excess of Par—Common Stock	500,000
Common Stock Dividends Distributable	120,000
Retained Earnings	600,000

During 2022, the following transactions and events occurred.

1. Issued 60,000 shares of $2 par value common stock as a result of 15% stock dividend declared on December 15, 2021.

2. Issued 30,000 shares of common stock for cash at $4 per share.

3. Purchased 25,000 shares of common stock for the treasury at $5 per share.

4. Declared and paid a cash dividend of $111,000.

5. Sold 8,000 shares of treasury stock for cash at $5 per share.

6. Earned net income of $360,000.

Instructions

Prepare a stockholders' equity statement for the year.

Total stockholders' equity
$2,304,000

*P11.9A (LO 5, 6), AP The following stockholders' equity accounts (post-closing) arranged alphabetically are in the ledger of Westin Corporation at December 31, 2022.

Prepare stockholders' equity section; compute book value per share.

Common Stock ($10 stated value)	$1,500,000
Paid-in Capital from Treasury Stock	6,000
Paid-in Capital in Excess of Par—Preferred Stock	42,400
Paid-in Capital in Excess of Stated Value—Common Stock	690,000
Preferred Stock (8%, $100 par, noncumulative)	360,000
Retained Earnings	776,000
Treasury Stock—Common (7,000 shares)	92,000

Instructions

a. Prepare the stockholders' equity section of the balance sheet at December 31, 2022.

b. Compute the book value per share of the common stock, assuming the preferred stock has a call price of $110 per share.

a. Total stockholders' equity
$3,282,400

Continuing Case

Cookie Creations

(*Note:* This is a continuation of the Cookie Creations case from Chapters 1 through 10.)

CC11 After establishing their company's fiscal year-end to be October 31, Natalie and Curtis began operating Cookie & Coffee Creations Inc. on November 1, 2020. On that date, they issued both preferred and common stock. After the first year of operations, Natalie and Curtis want to prepare financial information for the year.

Go to **WileyPLUS** *for complete case details and instructions*

leungchopan/
Shutterstock.com

Comprehensive Accounting Cycle Review

ACR11.1 Hawkeye Corporation's balance sheet at December 31, 2021, is presented as follows.

Journalize transactions and prepare financial statements.

Hawkeye Corporation
Balance Sheet
December 31, 2021

Cash	$ 24,600		Accounts payable	$ 25,600
Accounts receivable	45,500		Common stock ($10 par)	80,000
Allowance for doubtful			Retained earnings	127,400
accounts	(1,500)			$233,000
Supplies	4,400			
Land	40,000			
Buildings	142,000			
Accumulated depreciation—				
buildings	(22,000)			
	$233,000			

During 2022, the following transactions occurred.

1. On January 1, 2022, Hawkeye issued 1,200 shares of $40 par, 7% preferred stock for $49,200.

2. On January 1, 2022, Hawkeye also issued 900 shares of the $10 par value common stock for $21,000.

3. Hawkeye performed services for $320,000 on account.

4. On April 1, 2022, Hawkeye collected cash of $36,000 in advance for services to be performed evenly from April 1, 2022, to March 31, 2023.

5. Hawkeye collected $276,000 from customers on account.

6. Hawkeye bought $35,100 of supplies on account.

7. Hawkeye paid $32,200 on accounts payable.

8. Hawkeye reacquired 400 shares of its common stock on June 1, 2022, for $28 per share.

9. Paid other operating expenses of $188,200.

10. On December 31, 2022, Hawkeye declared the annual preferred stock dividend and a $1.20 per share dividend on the outstanding common stock, all payable on January 15, 2023.

11. An account receivable of $1,700 which originated in 2021 is written off as uncollectible.

Adjustment data:

1. A count of supplies indicates that $5,900 of supplies remain unused at year-end.

2. Recorded revenue from item 4 above.

3. The allowance for doubtful accounts should have a balance of $3,500 at year end.

4. Depreciation is recorded on the building on a straight-line basis based on a 30-year life and a salvage value of $10,000.

5. The income tax rate is 30%, and the taxes remain unpaid at year-end. (*Hint:* Prepare the income statement up to income before income taxes and multiply by 30% to compute the amount.)

Instructions

(You may want to set up T-accounts to determine ending balances.)

a. Prepare journal entries for the transactions listed above and adjusting entries.

b. Totals $740,690

c. Net income $81,970
Tot. assets $421,000

b. Prepare an adjusted trial balance at December 31, 2022.

c. Prepare an income statement and a retained earnings statement for the year ending December 31, 2022, and a classified balance sheet as of December 31, 2022.

Journalize transactions and prepare financial statements.

ACR11.2 Karen Noonan opened Clean Sweep Inc. on February 1, 2022. During February, the following transactions and events occurred.

Feb.	1	Issued 5,000 shares of Clean Sweep common stock for $13,000. Each share has a $1.50 par.
	1	Borrowed $8,000 on a 2-year, 6% note payable.
	1	Paid $9,020 to purchase used floor and window cleaning equipment from a company going out of business ($4,820 was for the floor equipment and $4,200 was for the window equipment).
	1	Paid $220 for February Internet and phone services.
	3	Purchased cleaning supplies for $980 on account.
	4	Hired 4 employees. Each will be paid $480 per 5-day work week (Monday–Friday). Employees will begin working Monday, February 9.
	5	Obtained insurance coverage for $9,840 per year. Coverage runs from February 1, 2022, through January 31, 2023. Karen paid $2,460 cash for the first quarter of coverage.
	5	Discussions with the insurance agent indicated that providing outside window cleaning services would cost too much to insure. Karen sold the window cleaning equipment for $3,950 cash.
	16	Billed customers $3,900 for cleaning services performed through February 13, 2022.
	17	Received $540 from a customer for 4 weeks of cleaning services to begin February 21, 2022. (By paying in advance, this customer received 10% off the normal weekly fee of $150.)
	18	Paid $300 on amount owed on cleaning supplies.
	20	Paid $3 per share to buy 300 shares of Clean Sweep common stock from a shareholder who disagreed with management goals. The shares will be held as treasury shares.
	23	Billed customers $4,300 for cleaning services performed through February 20.
	24	Paid cash for employees' wages for 2 weeks (February 9–13 and 16–20).
	25	Collected $2,500 cash from customers billed on February 16.
	27	Paid $220 for Internet and phone services for March. (*Hint:* Use Prepaid Expenses.)
	28	Declared and paid a cash dividend of $0.20 per share.

Instructions

a. Journalize the February transactions. (You do not need to include an explanation for each journal entry.)

b. Post to the ledger accounts. (Use T-accounts.)

c. Prepare a trial balance at February 28, 2022.

c. Totals $30,420

d. Journalize the following adjustments. (Round all amounts to whole dollars.)

1. Services performed for customers through February 28, 2022, but unbilled and uncollected were $3,800.

2. Received notice that a customer who was billed $200 for services performed February 10 has filed for bankruptcy. Clean Sweep does not expect to collect any portion of this outstanding receivable.

3. Clean Sweep uses the allowance method to estimate bad debts. Clean Sweep estimates that 3% of its month-end receivables will not be collected.

4. Record 1 month of depreciation for the floor equipment. Use the straight-line method, an estimated life of 4 years, and $500 salvage value.

5. Record 1 month of insurance expense.

6. An inventory count shows $400 of supplies on hand at February 28.

7. One week of services were performed for the customer who paid in advance on February 17.

8. Accrue for wages owed through February 28, 2022.

9. Accrue for interest expense for 1 month.

10. Karen estimates a 20% income tax rate. (*Hint:* Prepare an income statement up to income before income taxes to help with the income tax calculation.)

e. Post adjusting entries to the T-accounts.

f. Prepare an adjusted trial balance.

g. Prepare a **multiple-step income statement, a retained earnings statement,** and a **properly classified balance sheet** as of February 28, 2022.

g. Net income $3,117
Tot. assets $26,101

h. Journalize closing entries.

Expand Your Critical Thinking

Financial Reporting Problem: Apple Inc.

CT11.1 The stockholders' equity section of **Apple Inc.**'s balance sheet is shown in the Consolidated Statement of Financial Position in Appendix A. The complete annual report, including the notes to its financial statements, is available at the company's website.

Instructions

Answer the following questions.

a. What is the par or stated value per share of Apple's common stock?

b. What percentage of Apple's authorized common stock was issued at September 29, 2018? (Round to the nearest full percent.)

c. How many shares of common stock were outstanding at September 30, 2017, and at September 29, 2018?

d. Calculate the payout ratio, earnings per share, and return on common stockholders' equity for 2018.

Comparative Analysis Problem: PepsiCo, Inc. vs. The Coca-Cola Company

CT11.2 **PepsiCo, Inc.**'s financial statements are presented in Appendix B. Financial statements of **The Coca-Cola Company** are presented in Appendix C. The complete annual reports of PepsiCo and Coca-Cola, including the notes to the financial statements, are available at each company's respective website.

Instructions

a. What percentage of authorized shares was issued by Coca-Cola at December 31, 2018, and by PepsiCo at December 29, 2018?

b. How many shares are held as treasury stock by Coca-Cola at December 31, 2018, and by PepsiCo at December 29, 2018?

c. How many Coca-Cola common shares are outstanding at December 31, 2018? How many PepsiCo shares of common stock are outstanding at December 29, 2018?

d. Compute earnings per share and return on common stockholders' equity for both companies for 2018. Assume PepsiCo's weighted-average shares were 1,415 million and Coca-Cola's weighted-average shares were 4,259 million. Can these measures be used to compare the profitability of the two companies? Why or why not?

e. What was the total amount of dividends paid by each company in 2018? (*Hint:* Use the statement of cash flows.)

Comparative Analysis Problem: Amazon.com, Inc. vs. Walmart Inc.

CT11.3 Amazon.com, Inc.'s financial statements are presented in Appendix D. Financial statements of **Walmart Inc.** are presented in Appendix E. The complete annual reports of Amazon and Walmart, including the notes to the financial statements, are available at each company's respective website. Assume that Walmart has 11,000 million shares authorized and has 2,878 million shares issued and outstanding.

Instructions

a. What percentage of authorized shares was issued by Amazon at December 31, 2018, and by Walmart at January 31, 2019?

b. How many shares are held as treasury stock by Amazon at December 31, 2018, and by Walmart at January 31, 2019?

c. How many Amazon common shares are outstanding at December 31, 2018? How many Walmart shares of common stock are outstanding at January 31, 2019?

d. What are the basic earnings per share for both Amazon and Walmart as of December 31, 2018, and January 31, 2019, respectively?

e. What was the total amount of dividends, if any, paid by Amazon for the year ending December 31, 2018? What was the total dividends paid by Walmart for the year ending January 31, 2019? (*Hint:* Use the statement of cash flows.)

Real-World Focus

CT11.4 Use the stockholders' equity section of an annual report and identify the major components.

Instructions

Select a well-known company, search the Internet for its most recent annual report, and then answer the following questions.

a. What is the company's name?

b. What classes of capital stock has the company issued?

c. For each class of stock:

    1. How many shares are authorized, issued, and/or outstanding?

    2. What is the par value?

d. What are the company's retained earnings?

e. Has the company acquired treasury stock? How many shares?

Decision-Making Across the Organization

CT11.5 The stockholders' meeting for Percival Corporation has been in progress for some time. The chief financial officer for Percival is presently reviewing the company's financial statements and is explaining the items that comprise the stockholders' equity section of the balance sheet for the current year. The stockholders' equity section of Percival Corporation at December 31, 2022, is as follows.

Percival Corporation
Balance Sheet (partial)
December 31, 2022

Paid-in capital		
Capital stock		
Preferred stock, authorized 1,000,000 shares		
cumulative, $100 par value, $8 per share, 6,000		
shares issued and outstanding		$ 600,000
Common stock, authorized 5,000,000 shares, $1 par		
value, 3,000,000 shares issued, and 2,700,000 outstanding		3,000,000
Total capital stock		3,600,000
Additional paid-in capital		
In excess of par—preferred stock	$ 50,000	
In excess of par—common stock	25,000,000	
Total additional paid-in capital		25,050,000
Total paid-in capital		28,650,000
Retained earnings		900,000
Total paid-in capital and retained earnings		29,550,000
Less: Treasury stock (300,000 common shares)		9,300,000
Total stockholders' equity		$20,250,000

At the meeting, stockholders have raised a number of questions regarding the stockholders' equity section.

Instructions

With the class divided into groups, answer the following questions as if you were the chief financial officer for Percival Corporation.

a. "What does the cumulative provision related to the preferred stock mean?"

b. "I thought the common stock was presently selling at $29.75, but the company has the stock stated at $1 per share. How can that be?"

c. "Why is the company buying back its common stock? Furthermore, the treasury stock has a debit balance because it is subtracted from stockholders' equity. Why is treasury stock not reported as an asset if it has a debit balance?"

Communication Activity

CT11.6 Earl Kent, your uncle, is an inventor who has decided to incorporate. Uncle Earl knows that you are an accounting major at U.N.O. In a recent letter to you, he ends with the question, "I'm filling out a state incorporation application. Can you tell me the difference in the following terms: (1) authorized stock, (2) issued stock, (3) outstanding stock, and (4) preferred stock?"

Instructions

In a brief note, differentiate for Uncle Earl among the four different stock terms. Write the letter to be friendly, yet professional.

Ethics Case

CT11.7 The R&D division of Pele Corp. has just developed a chemical for sterilizing the vicious Brazilian "killer bees" which are invading Mexico and the southern United States. The president of the company is anxious to get the chemical on the market to boost the company's profits. He believes his job is in jeopardy because of decreasing sales and profits. The company has an opportunity to sell this chemical in Central American countries, where the laws are much more relaxed than in the United States.

The director of Pele's R&D division strongly recommends further testing in the laboratory for side-effects of this chemical on other insects, birds, animals, plants, and even humans. He cautions the president, "We could be sued from all sides if the chemical has tragic side-effects that we didn't even test for in the labs." The president answers, "We can't wait an additional year for your lab tests. We can avoid losses from such lawsuits by establishing a separate wholly owned corporation to shield Pele from such lawsuits. We can't lose any more than our investment in the new corporation, and we'll invest in just the patent covering this chemical. We'll reap the benefits if the chemical works and is safe, and avoid the losses from lawsuits if it's a disaster." The following week, Pele creates a new wholly owned corporation called Cabo Inc., sells the chemical patent to it for $10, and watches the spraying begin.

Instructions

a. Who are the stakeholders in this situation?

b. Are the president's motives and actions ethical?

c. Can Pele shield itself against losses of Cabo Inc.?

All About You

CT11.8 A high percentage of Americans own stock in corporations. As a shareholder in a corporation, you will receive an annual report. One of the goals of this course is for you to learn how to navigate your way around an annual report.

Instructions

Use **Apple**'s 2018 annual report (see Appendix A) to answer the following questions.

a. What CPA firm performed the audit of Apple's financial statements?

b. What was the amount of Apple's earnings per share in 2018?

c. What were net sales in 2018?

d. How much cash did Apple spend on capital expenditures in 2018?

e. Over what life does the company depreciate its buildings?

f. What were the proceeds from issuance of common stock in 2018?

FASB Codification Activity

CT11.9 If your school has a subscription to the FASB Codification, log in and prepare responses to the following.

a. What is the stock dividend?

b. What is a stock split?

c. At what percentage point does the issuance of additional shares qualify as a stock dividend, as opposed to a stock split?

A Look at IFRS

LEARNING OBJECTIVE 7

Compare the accounting for stockholders' equity under GAAP and IFRS.

The accounting for transactions related to stockholders' equity, such as issuance of shares and purchase of treasury stock, is similar under both IFRS and GAAP. Major differences relate to terminology used, introduction of items such as revaluation surplus, and presentation of stockholders' equity information.

Key Points

Following are the key similarities and differences between GAAP and IFRS as related to stockholders' equity, dividends, retained earnings, and income reporting.

Similarities

- Aside from the terminology used, the accounting for the issuance of shares, the purchase of treasury stock, and dividends is similar.

- Like GAAP, IFRS does not allow a company to record gains or losses on purchases of its own shares.

- The computations related to earnings per share are essentially the same under IFRS and GAAP.

Differences

- Under IFRS, the term **reserves** is used to describe all equity accounts other than those arising from contributed (paid-in) capital. This would include, for example, reserves related to retained earnings, asset revaluations, and fair value differences.

- Many countries have a different mix of investor groups than in the United States. For example, in Germany, financial institutions like banks are not only major creditors of corporations but often are the largest corporate stockholders as well. In the United States, Asia, and the United Kingdom, many companies rely on substantial investment from private investors.

- There are often terminology differences for equity accounts. The following summarizes some of the common differences in terminology.

GAAP	IFRS
Common stock	Share capital—ordinary
Stockholders	Shareholders
Par value	Nominal or face value
Authorized stock	Authorized share capital
Preferred stock	Share capital—preference
Paid-in capital	Issued/allocated share capital
Paid-in capital in excess of par—common stock	Share premium—ordinary
Paid-in capital in excess of par—preferred stock	Share premium—preference
Retained earnings	Retained earnings or Retained profits
Retained earnings deficit	Accumulated losses

As an example of how similar transactions use different terminology under IFRS, consider the accounting for the issuance of 1,000 shares of $1 par value common stock for $5 per share. Under IFRS, the entry is as follows.

Cash	5,000	
Share Capital—Ordinary		1,000
Share Premium—Ordinary		4,000

- A major difference between IFRS and GAAP relates to the account Revaluation Surplus. Revaluation surplus arises under IFRS because companies are permitted to revalue their property, plant, and equipment to fair value under certain circumstances. This account is part of general reserves under IFRS and is not considered contributed capital.

- IFRS often uses terms such as **retained profits** or **accumulated profit or loss** to describe retained earnings. The term retained earnings is also often used.

- Equity is given various descriptions under IFRS, such as shareholders' equity, owners' equity, capital and reserves, and shareholders' funds.

IFRS Practice

IFRS Self-Test Questions

1. Which of the following is **true**?

   a. In the United States, the primary corporate stockholders are financial institutions.

   b. Share capital means total assets under IFRS.

   c. Share Capital—Ordinary is an account used under IFRS.

   d. The accounting for treasury stock differs extensively between GAAP and IFRS.

2. Under IFRS, the amount of capital received in excess of par value would be credited to:

   a. Retained Earnings.

   b. Contributed Capital—Ordinary.

   c. Share Premium—Ordinary.

   d. Retained Profits.

3. Which of the following is **false**?

   a. Under GAAP, companies cannot record gains on transactions involving their own shares.

   b. Under IFRS, companies cannot record gains on transactions involving their own shares.

   c. Under IFRS, the statement of stockholders' equity is a required statement.

   d. Under IFRS, treasury shares are not permitted.

4. Which of the following does **not** represent a pair of GAAP/IFRS-comparable terms?

   a. Additional paid-in capital/Share premium.

   b. Treasury stock/Repurchase reserve.

   c. Common stock/Share capital.

   d. Preferred stock/Preference shares.

5. The basic accounting for cash dividends and stock dividends:

   a. is different under IFRS versus GAAP.

   b. is the same under IFRS and GAAP.

   c. differs only for the accounting for cash dividends between GAAP and IFRS.

   d. differs only for the accounting for stock dividends between GAAP and IFRS.

6. Which item is **not** considered part of reserves?

   a. Unrealized loss on available-for-sale investments

   b. Revaluation surplus.

   c. Retained earnings.

   d. Issued shares.

7. Which set of terms can be used to describe total stockholders' equity under IFRS?

   a. Shareholders' equity, capital and reserves, other comprehensive income.

   b. Capital and reserves, shareholders' equity, shareholders' funds.

   c. Capital and reserves, retained earnings, shareholders' equity.

   d. All of the answer choices are correct.

8. Earnings per share computations related to IFRS and GAAP:

   a. are essentially similar.

   b. result in an amount referred to as earnings per share.

   c. must deduct preferred (preference) dividends when computing earnings per share.

   d. All of the answer choices are correct.

IFRS Exercises

IFRS11.1 On May 10, Jaurez Corporation issues 1,000 shares of $10 par value ordinary shares for cash at $18 per share. Journalize the issuance of the shares.

IFRS11.2 Meenen Corporation has the following accounts at December 31, 2022 (in euros): Share Capital—Ordinary, €10 par, 5,000 shares issued, €50,000; Share Premium—Ordinary €10,000; Retained Earnings €45,000; and Treasury Shares—Ordinary, 500 shares, €11,000. Prepare the equity section of the statement of financial position (balance sheet).

IFRS11.3 Overton Co. had the following transactions during the current period.

Mar.	2	Issued 5,000 shares of $1 par value ordinary shares to attorneys in payment of a bill for $30,000 for services performed in helping the company to incorporate.
June	12	Issued 60,000 shares of $1 par value ordinary shares for cash of $375,000.
July	11	Issued 1,000 shares of $100 par value preference shares for cash at $110 per share.
Nov.	28	Purchased 2,000 treasury shares (ordinary) for $80,000.

Instructions

Journalize the above transactions.

International Financial Reporting Problem: **Louis Vuitton**

IFRS11.4 The financial statements of **Louis Vuitton** are presented in Appendix F. The complete consolidated financial statements, including the notes to its financial statements, are available at the company's website.

Instructions

Use the company's 2018 consolidated financial statements to answer the following questions.

   a. Determine the following amounts at December 31, 2018: (1) total equity, (2) total revaluation reserve, and (3) number of treasury shares.

   b. Examine the equity section of the company's balance sheet. For each of the following, provide the comparable label that would be used under GAAP: (1) share capital and (2) share premium.

   c. Did the company declare and pay any dividends for the year ended December 31, 2018?

   d. Compute the company's return on ordinary shareholders' equity for the year ended December 31, 2018.

   e. What was Louis Vuitton's earnings per share for the year ended December 31, 2018?

Answers to IFRS Self-Test Questions

1. c 2. c 3. d 4. b 5. b 6. d 7. b 8. d

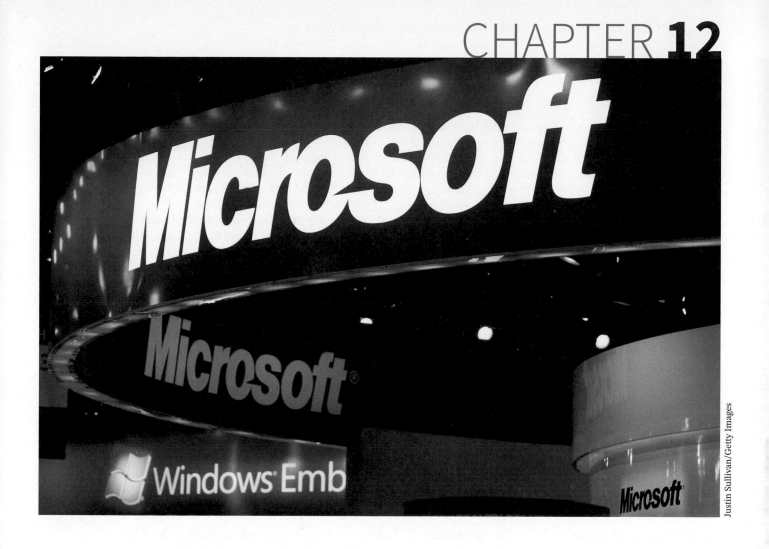

CHAPTER 12

Justin Sullivan/Getty Images

Statement of Cash Flows

Chapter Preview

The balance sheet, income statement, and retained earnings statement do not always show the whole picture of the financial condition of a company or institution. In fact, looking at the financial statements of some well-known companies, a thoughtful investor might ask questions like these: How did **Eastman Kodak** finance cash dividends of $649 million in a year in which it earned only $17 million? How could **United Air Lines** purchase new planes that cost $1.9 billion in a year in which it reported a net loss of over $2 billion? How did the companies that spent a combined fantastic $3.4 trillion on mergers and acquisitions in a recent year finance those deals? Answers to these and similar questions can be found in this chapter, which presents the statement of cash flows.

Feature Story

Got Cash?

Companies must be ready to respond to changes quickly in order to survive and thrive. This requires careful management of cash. One company that managed cash successfully in its early years was **Microsoft**. During those years, the company paid much of its payroll with stock options (rights to purchase company stock in the future at a given price) instead of cash. This conserved cash and turned more than a thousand of its employees into millionaires.

In recent years, Microsoft has had a different kind of cash problem. Now that it has reached a more "mature" stage in life, it generates so much cash—roughly $1 billion per month—that it cannot always figure out what to do with it. At one time, Microsoft had accumulated $60 billion.

The company said it was accumulating cash to invest in new opportunities, buy other companies, and pay off pending lawsuits. Microsoft's stockholders complained that holding all this cash was putting a drag on the company's profitability. Why? Because Microsoft had the cash invested in very low-yielding government securities. Stockholders felt that the company either should find new investment projects that would bring higher returns, or return some of the cash to stockholders.

Finally, Microsoft announced a plan to return cash to stockholders by paying a special one-time $32 billion dividend. This special dividend was so large that, according to the U.S. Commerce Department, it caused total personal income in the United States to rise by 3.7% in one month—the largest increase ever recorded by the agency. (It also made the holiday season brighter, especially for retailers in the Seattle area.) Microsoft also doubled its regular annual dividend to $3.50 per share. Further, it announced that it would spend another $30 billion buying treasury stock.

Apple also has encountered this cash "problem." Recently, Apple had nearly $100 billion in liquid assets (cash, cash equivalents, and investment securities). The company was generating $37 billion of cash per year from its operating activities but spending only about $7 billion on plant assets and purchases of patents. In response to shareholder pressure, Apple announced that it would begin to pay a quarterly dividend of $2.65 per share and buy back up to $10 billion of its stock. Analysts noted that the dividend consumes only $10 billion of cash per year. This leaves Apple wallowing in cash. The rest of us should have such problems.

Source: "Business: An End to Growth? Microsoft's Cash Bonanza," *The Economist* (July 23, 2005), p. 61.

Chapter Outline

LEARNING OBJECTIVES	REVIEW	PRACTICE
LO 1 Discuss the usefulness and format of the statement of cash flows.	• Usefulness of the statement of cash flows • Classification of cash flows • Significant noncash activities • Format of the statement of cash flows	**DO IT! 1** Classification of Cash Flows
LO 2 Prepare a statement of cash flows using the indirect method.	• Indirect and direct methods • Indirect method—Computer Services Company • Step 1: Operating activities • Summary of conversion to net cash provided by operating activities • Step 2: Investing and financing activities • Step 3: Net change in cash	**DO IT! 2a** Cash Flows from Operating Activities **DO IT! 2b** Indirect Method
LO 3 Analyze the statement of cash flows.	• Free cash flow	**DO IT! 3** Free Cash Flow

Go to the Review and Practice section at the end of the chapter for a review of key concepts and practice applications with solutions.

Visit WileyPLUS for additional tutorials and practice opportunities.

Usefulness and Format of the Statement of Cash Flows

LEARNING OBJECTIVE 1

Discuss the usefulness and format of the statement of cash flows.

The balance sheet, income statement, and retained earnings statement provide only limited information about a company's cash flows (cash receipts and cash payments). For example, comparative balance sheets show the net increase in property, plant, and equipment during the year. But, they do not show how the additions were financed or paid for. The income statement shows net income based on the accrual basis of accounting. But, it does not indicate the amount of cash generated by operating activities. The retained earnings statement shows cash dividends declared but not the cash dividends paid during the year. None of these statements presents a detailed summary of where cash came from and how it was used.

Usefulness of the Statement of Cash Flows

The **statement of cash flows** reports the cash receipts, cash payments, and net change in cash resulting from operating, investing, and financing activities during a period. The information in a statement of cash flows helps investors, creditors, and others assess the following.

1. **The entity's ability to generate future cash flows.** By examining relationships between items in the statement of cash flows, investors can better predict the amounts, timing, and uncertainty of future cash flows than they can from accrual-basis data.

2. **The entity's ability to pay dividends and meet obligations.** If a company does not have adequate cash, it cannot pay employees, settle debts, or pay dividends. Employees, creditors, and stockholders should be particularly interested in this statement because it alone shows the flows of cash in a business.

3. **The reasons for the difference between net income and net cash provided (used) by operating activities.** Net income provides information on the success or failure of a business. However, some financial statement users are critical of accrual-basis net income because it requires many estimates (see **Ethics Note**). As a result, users often challenge the reliability of the number. Such is not the case with cash. Many readers of the statement of cash flows want to know the reasons for the difference between net income and net cash provided by operating activities. Then, they can assess for themselves the reliability of the net income number.

4. **The cash investing and financing transactions during the period.** By examining a company's investing and financing transactions, a financial statement reader can better understand why assets and liabilities changed during the period.

ETHICS NOTE

Though we discourage reliance on cash flows to the exclusion of accrual accounting, comparing net cash provided by operating activities to net income can reveal important information about the "quality" of reported net income. Such a comparison can reveal the extent to which net income provides a good measure of actual performance.

Classification of Cash Flows

The statement of cash flows classifies cash receipts and cash payments as operating, investing, and financing activities. Transactions and other events characteristic of each kind of activity are as follows.

1. **Operating activities** include the cash effects of transactions that generate revenues and expenses. They thus enter into the determination of net income.

2. **Investing activities** include (a) acquiring and disposing of investments and property, plant, and equipment, and (b) lending money and collecting the loans.

3. **Financing activities** include (a) obtaining cash from issuing debt and repaying the amounts borrowed, and (b) obtaining cash from stockholders, repurchasing shares, and paying dividends.

The operating activities category is the most important. It shows the cash provided by company operations. This source of cash is generally considered to be the best measure of a company's ability to generate sufficient cash to continue as a going concern.

Illustration 12.1 lists typical cash receipts and cash payments within each of the three classifications. *Study the list carefully; it will prove very useful in solving homework exercises and problems.*

Typical receipt and payment classifications

Operating activities

Investing activities

Financing activities

Types of Cash Inflows and Outflows

Operating activities—Income statement items
  Cash inflows:
    From sale of goods or services.
    From interest received and dividends received.
  Cash outflows:
    To suppliers for inventory.
    To employees for wages.
    To government for taxes.
    To lenders for interest.
    To others for expenses.

Investing activities—Changes in investments and long-term assets
  Cash inflows:
    From sale of property, plant, and equipment.
    From sale of investments in debt or equity securities of other entities.
    From collection of principal on loans to other entities.
  Cash outflows:
    To purchase property, plant, and equipment.
    To purchase investments in debt or equity securities of other entities.
    To make loans to other entities.

Financing activities—Changes in long-term liabilities and stockholders' equity
  Cash inflows:
    From sale of common and preferred stock.
    From issuance of debt (bonds and notes).
  Cash outflows:
    To stockholders as dividends.
    To redeem long-term debt or reacquire capital stock (treasury stock).

Note the following general guidelines:

1. Operating activities involve income statement items.

2. Investing activities involve cash flows resulting from changes in investments and long-term asset items.

3. Financing activities involve cash flows resulting from changes in long-term liability and stockholders' equity items.

Companies classify as operating activities some cash flows related to investing or financing activities. For example, receipts of investment revenue (interest and dividends) are classified as operating activities. So are payments of interest to lenders. Why are these considered operating activities? **Because companies report these items in the income statement, where results of operations are shown**.

Significant Noncash Activities

Not all of a company's significant activities involve cash. Examples of significant noncash activities are as follows.

1. Direct issuance of common stock to purchase assets.

2. Conversion of bonds into common stock.

3. Direct issuance of debt to purchase assets.

4. Exchanges of plant assets.

Companies do not report in the body of the statement of cash flows significant financing and investing activities that do not affect cash. Instead, they report these activities in either a **separate schedule** at the bottom of the statement of cash flows or in a **separate note or supplementary schedule** to the financial statements (see **Helpful Hint**). The reporting of these noncash activities in a separate schedule satisfies the **full disclosure principle**.

In solving homework assignments, you should present significant noncash investing and financing activities in a separate schedule at the bottom of the statement of cash flows (see the last item in Illustration 12.2 below).

HELPFUL HINT

Do not include noncash investing and financing activities in the body of the statement of cash flows. Report this information in a separate schedule.

Accounting Across the Organization   Target Corporation

Darren McCollester/
Getty Images

Net *What*?

Net income is not the same as net cash provided by operating activities. The table shows some results from recent annual reports (dollars in millions), including **Target Corporation**. Note how the numbers differ greatly across the list even though all these companies engage in retail merchandising.

Company	Net Income	Net Cash Provided by Operating Activities
Kohl's Corporation	$ 889	$ 1,884
Walmart Inc.	16,669	25,591
J. C. Penney Company, Inc.	(1,388)	(1,814)
Costco Wholesale Corp.	20,391	3,437
Target Corporation	1,971	6,520

In general, why do differences exist between net income and net cash provided by operating activities? (Go to WileyPLUS for this answer and additional questions.)

Format of the Statement of Cash Flows

The general format of the statement of cash flows presents the results of the three activities discussed previously—operating, investing, and financing—plus the significant noncash investing and financing activities. **Illustration 12.2** shows a widely used form of the statement of cash flows.

ILLUSTRATION 12.2

Format of statement of cash flows

Company Name Statement of Cash Flows For the Period Covered		
Cash flows from operating activities		
(List of individual items)	XX	
Net cash provided (used) by operating activities		XXX
Cash flows from investing activities		
(List of individual inflows and outflows)	XX	
Net cash provided (used) by investing activities		XXX
Cash flows from financing activities		
(List of individual inflows and outflows)	XX	
Net cash provided (used) by financing activities		XXX
Net increase (decrease) in cash		XXX
Cash at beginning of period		XXX
Cash at end of period		XXX
Noncash investing and financing activities		
(List of individual noncash transactions)		XXX

The cash flows from operating activities section always appears first, followed by the investing activities section and then the financing activities section. The sum of the operating, investing, and financing sections equals the net increase or decrease in cash for the period.

This amount is added to the beginning cash balance to arrive at the ending cash balance—the same amount reported on the balance sheet. The FASB now requires that restricted cash be included with cash and cash equivalents when reconciling the beginning and ending amounts on the statement of cash flows.

ACTION PLAN

- Identify the three types of activities used to report all cash inflows and outflows.
- Report as operating activities the cash effects of transactions that generate revenues and expenses and enter into the determination of net income.
- Report as investing activities transactions that (a) acquire and dispose of investments and long-term assets and (b) lend money and collect loans.
- Report as financing activities transactions that (a) obtain cash from issuing debt and repay the amounts borrowed and (b) obtain cash from stockholders and pay them dividends.

DO IT! 1 | Classification of Cash Flows

During its first week, Duffy & Stevenson Company had these transactions.

1. Issued 100,000 shares of common stock at par for $800,000 cash.
2. Borrowed $200,000 from Castle Bank, signing a 5-year note bearing 8% interest.
3. Purchased two semi-trailer trucks for $170,000 cash.
4. Paid employees $12,000 for salaries and wages.
5. Collected $20,000 cash for services performed.

Classify each of these transactions by type of cash flow activity. (*Hint:* Refer to Illustration 12.1.)

Solution

1. Financing activity.
2. Financing activity.
3. Investing activity.
4. Operating activity.
5. Operating activity.

Related exercise material: **BE12.1, BE12.2, BE12.3, DO IT! 12.1, E12.1, E12.2, and E12.3.**

Preparing the Statement of Cash Flows—Indirect Method

LEARNING OBJECTIVE 2

Prepare a statement of cash flows using the indirect method.

Companies prepare the statement of cash flows differently from the three other basic financial statements. First, it is not prepared from an adjusted trial balance. It requires detailed information concerning the changes in account balances that occurred between two points in time. An adjusted trial balance will not provide the necessary data. Second, the statement of cash flows deals with cash receipts and payments. As a result, the company **adjusts** the effects of the use of accrual accounting **to determine cash flows**.

The information to prepare this statement usually comes from three sources:

- **Comparative balance sheets.** Information in the comparative balance sheets indicates the amount of the changes in assets, liabilities, and stockholders' equity from the beginning to the end of the period.

- **Current income statement.** Information in this statement helps determine the amount of net cash provided or used by operating activities during the period.
- **Additional information.** Such information includes transaction data that are needed to determine how cash was provided or used during the period.

Preparing the statement of cash flows from these data sources involves three major steps, explained in **Illustration 12.3**.

ILLUSTRATION 12.3

Three major steps in preparing the statement of cash flows

Step 1: Determine net cash provided/used by operating activities by converting net income from an accrual basis to a cash basis.

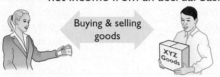

Buying & selling goods

This step involves analyzing not only the current year's income statement but also comparative balance sheets and selected additional data.

Step 2: Analyze changes in noncurrent asset and liability accounts and stockholders' equity accounts and report as investing and financing activities, or disclose as noncash transactions.

Investing   Financing

This step involves analyzing comparative balance sheet data and selected additional information for their effects on cash.

Step 3: Compare the net change in cash on the statement of cash flows with the change in the Cash account reported on the balance sheet to make sure the amounts agree.

Year 1   Year 2   Difference

The difference between the beginning and ending cash balances can be easily computed from comparative balance sheets.

Indirect and Direct Methods

In order to perform Step 1, a company **must convert net income from an accrual basis to a cash basis**. This conversion may be done by either of two methods: (1) the indirect method or (2) the direct method. **Both methods arrive at the same amount** for "Net cash provided by operating activities." They differ in **how** they arrive at the amount.

The **indirect method** adjusts net income for items that do not affect cash. A great majority of companies (98%) use this method. Companies favor the indirect method for two reasons: (1) it is easier and less costly to prepare, and (2) it focuses on the differences between net income and net cash flow from operating activities.

The **direct method** shows operating cash receipts and payments. It is prepared by adjusting each item in the income statement from the accrual basis to the cash basis. The FASB has expressed a preference for the direct method but allows the use of either method.

The next section illustrates the more popular indirect method. Appendix 12A illustrates the direct method.

Indirect Method—Computer Services Company

To explain how to prepare a statement of cash flows using the indirect method, we use financial information from Computer Services Company. **Illustration 12.4** presents Computer Services' current- and previous-year balance sheets, its current-year income statement, and related financial information for the current year.

ILLUSTRATION 12.4

Comparative balance sheets, income statement, and additional information for Computer Services Company

Computer Services Company
Comparative Balance Sheets
December 31

	2022	2021	Change in Account Balance Increase/Decrease
Assets			
Current assets			
Cash	$ 55,000	$ 33,000	$ 22,000 Increase
Accounts receivable	20,000	30,000	10,000 Decrease
Inventory	15,000	10,000	5,000 Increase
Prepaid expenses	5,000	1,000	4,000 Increase
Property, plant, and equipment			
Land	130,000	20,000	110,000 Increase
Buildings	160,000	40,000	120,000 Increase
Accumulated depreciation—buildings	(11,000)	(5,000)	6,000 Increase
Equipment	27,000	10,000	17,000 Increase
Accumulated depreciation—equipment	(3,000)	(1,000)	2,000 Increase
Total assets	$398,000	$138,000	
Liabilities and Stockholders' Equity			
Current liabilities			
Accounts payable	$ 28,000	$ 12,000	$ 16,000 Increase
Income taxes payable	6,000	8,000	2,000 Decrease
Long-term liabilities			
Bonds payable	130,000	20,000	110,000 Increase
Stockholders' equity			
Common stock	70,000	50,000	20,000 Increase
Retained earnings	164,000	48,000	116,000 Increase
Total liabilities and stockholders' equity	$398,000	$138,000	

Computer Services Company
Income Statement
For the Year Ended December 31, 2022

Sales revenue		$507,000
Cost of goods sold	$150,000	
Operating expenses (excluding depreciation)	111,000	
Depreciation expense	9,000	
Loss on disposal of plant assets	3,000	
Interest expense	42,000	315,000
Income before income tax		192,000
Income tax expense		47,000
Net income		$145,000

Additional information for 2022:

1. Depreciation expense was comprised of $6,000 for building and $3,000 for equipment.

2. The company sold equipment with a book value of $7,000 (cost $8,000, less accumulated depreciation $1,000) for $4,000 cash.

3. Issued $110,000 of long-term bonds in direct exchange for land.

4. A building costing $120,000 was purchased for cash. Equipment costing $25,000 was also purchased for cash.

5. Issued common stock at par for $20,000 cash.

6. The company declared and paid a $29,000 cash dividend.

We now apply the three steps for preparing a statement of cash flows to the information provided for Computer Services Company.

Step 1: Operating Activities

Determine Net Cash Provided/Used by Operating Activities by Converting Net Income from an Accrual Basis to a Cash Basis

To determine net cash provided by operating activities under the indirect method, companies **adjust net income in numerous ways**. A useful starting point is to understand **why** net income must be converted to net cash provided by operating activities.

Under generally accepted accounting principles (GAAP), most companies use the accrual basis of accounting. This basis requires that companies record revenue when a performance obligation is satisfied and record expenses when incurred. Revenues include credit sales for which the company has not yet collected cash. Expenses incurred include some items that have not yet been paid in cash. Thus, under the accrual basis, net income is not the same as net cash provided by operating activities.

Therefore, under the **indirect method**, companies must adjust net income to convert certain items to the cash basis. The indirect method (or reconciliation method) starts with net income and converts it to net cash provided by operating activities. **Illustration 12.5** lists the three types of adjustments.

Net Income	+/−	Adjustments	=	Net Cash Provided/ Used by Operating Activities
		• **Add back noncash expenses**, such as depreciation expense and amortization expense.		
		• **Deduct gains and add losses** that resulted from investing and financing activities.		
		• **Analyze changes** to noncash current asset and current liability accounts.		

ILLUSTRATION 12.5

Three types of adjustments to convert net income to net cash provided by operating activities

We explain the three types of adjustments in the next three sections.

Depreciation Expense

Computer Services' income statement reports depreciation expense of $9,000. Although depreciation expense reduces net income, it does not reduce cash. In other words, depreciation expense is a noncash charge. The company must add it back to net income to negate the effect of the expense to arrive at net cash provided by operating activities (see **Helpful Hint**). Computer Services reports depreciation expense in the statement of cash flows as in **Illustration 12.6**.

HELPFUL HINT

Depreciation is similar to any other expense in that it reduces net income. It differs in that it does not involve a current cash outflow. That is why it must be *added back* to net income to arrive at net cash provided by operating activities.

Cash flows from operating activities	
Net income	$145,000
Adjustments to reconcile net income to net cash provided by operating activities:	
Depreciation expense	**9,000**
Net cash provided by operating activities	$154,000

ILLUSTRATION 12.6

Adjustment for depreciation

As the first adjustment to net income in the statement of cash flows, companies frequently list depreciation and similar noncash charges such as amortization of intangible assets and bad debt expense.

Loss on Disposal of Plant Assets

Illustration 12.1 states that cash received from the sale (disposal) of plant assets is reported in the investing activities section. Because of this, **companies eliminate from net income all gains and losses related to the disposal of plant assets, to arrive at net cash provided by operating activities.**

In our example, Computer Services' income statement reports a $3,000 loss on the disposal of plant assets (book value $7,000, less $4,000 cash received from disposal of plant assets). The journal entry to record this transaction would have been as follows.

Cash	4,000	
Accumulated Depreciation—Equipment	1,000	
Loss on Disposal of Plant Assets	3,000	
Equipment		8,000

The company's loss of $3,000 should be added to net income in order to determine net cash provided by operating activities. The loss reduced net income but did not reduce cash. **Illustration 12.7** shows that the $3,000 loss is eliminated by adding $3,000 back to net income to arrive at net cash provided by operating activities. (The cash received of $4,000 will be reported in the investing activities section, as discussed later.)

ILLUSTRATION 12.7

Adjustment for loss on disposal of plant assets

Cash flows from operating activities		
Net income		$145,000
Adjustments to reconcile net income to net cash		
provided by operating activities:		
Depreciation expense	$9,000	
Loss on disposal of plant assets	**3,000**	12,000
Net cash provided by operating activities		$157,000

If a gain on disposal occurs, the company deducts the gain from net income in order to determine net cash provided by operating activities. **In the case of either a gain or a loss, companies report the actual amount of cash received from the sale in the investing activities section of the statement of cash flows.**

Changes to Noncash Current Asset and Current Liability Accounts

A final adjustment in reconciling net income to net cash provided by operating activities involves examining all changes in current asset and current liability accounts. The accrual-accounting process records revenues in the period in which the performance obligation is satisfied and expenses as incurred. For example, Accounts Receivable reflects amounts owed to the company for sales that have been made but for which cash collections have not yet been received. Prepaid Insurance reflects insurance that has been paid for but has not yet expired (therefore has not been expensed). Similarly, Salaries and Wages Payable reflects salaries and wages expense that has been incurred but has not been paid.

As a result, companies need to adjust net income for these accruals and prepayments to determine net cash provided by operating activities. Thus, they must analyze the change in each current asset and current liability account to determine its impact on net income and cash.

Changes in Noncash Current Assets The adjustments required for changes in non-cash current asset accounts are as follows. **Deduct from net income increases in current asset accounts, and add to net income decreases in current asset accounts, to arrive at net cash provided by operating activities.** We observe these relationships by analyzing the accounts of Computer Services.

Decrease in Accounts Receivable Computer Services' accounts receivable decreased by $10,000 (from $30,000 to $20,000) during the period. For Computer Services, this means that cash receipts were $10,000 higher than sales revenue. The Accounts Receivable account in **Illustration 12.8** shows that Computer Services had $507,000 in sales revenue (as reported on the income statement), but it collected $517,000 in cash.

ILLUSTRATION 12.8

Analysis of accounts receivable

		Accounts Receivable			
1/1/22	Balance	30,000	**Receipts from customers**	517,000
	Sales revenue	**507,000**		
12/31/22	Balance	20,000		

As shown in Illustration 12.9, to adjust net income to net cash provided by operating activities, the company **adds** to net income the decrease of $10,000 in accounts receivable. When the Accounts Receivable balance increases, cash receipts are lower than sales revenue earned under the accrual basis. Therefore, the company **deducts** from net income the amount of the increase in accounts receivable, to arrive at net cash provided by operating activities.

Increase in Inventory Computer Services' inventory increased $5,000 (from $10,000 to $15,000) during the period. The change in the Inventory account reflects the difference between the amount of inventory purchased and the cost of inventory sold. For Computer Services, this means that the cost of merchandise purchased exceeded the cost of goods sold by $5,000. As a result, cost of goods sold does not reflect $5,000 of cash payments made for merchandise. The company **deducts** from net income this inventory increase of $5,000 during the period, to arrive at net cash provided by operating activities (see Illustration 12.9). If inventory decreases, the company **adds** to net income the amount of the change, to arrive at net cash provided by operating activities.

Increase in Prepaid Expenses Computer Services' prepaid expenses increased during the period by $4,000. This means that cash paid for prepaid expenses is greater than the actual expenses reported on an accrual basis. In other words, the company has made cash payments in the current period that will not be charged to expenses until future periods. To adjust net income to net cash provided by operating activities, the company **deducts** from net income the $4,000 increase in prepaid expenses (see **Illustration 12.9**).

Cash flows from operating activities		
Net income		$145,000
Adjustments to reconcile net income to net cash provided by operating activities:		
Depreciation expense	$ 9,000	
Loss on disposal of plant assets	3,000	
Decrease in accounts receivable	**10,000**	
Increase in inventory	**(5,000)**	
Increase in prepaid expenses	**(4,000)**	13,000
Net cash provided by operating activities		$158,000

If prepaid expenses decrease, reported expenses are greater than the expenses paid. Therefore, the company **adds** to net income the decrease in prepaid expenses, to arrive at net cash provided by operating activities.

Changes in Current Liabilities The adjustments required for changes in current liability accounts are as follows. **Add to net income increases in current liability accounts and deduct from net income decreases in current liability accounts, to arrive at net cash provided by operating activities.**

Increase in Accounts Payable For Computer Services, Accounts Payable increased by $16,000 (from $12,000 to $28,000) during the period. That means the company received $16,000 more in goods than it actually paid for. As shown in **Illustration 12.10**, to adjust net income to determine net cash provided by operating activities, the company adds to net income the $16,000 increase in Accounts Payable.

Decrease in Income Taxes Payable When a company incurs income tax expense but has not yet paid its taxes, it records income taxes payable. A change in the Income Taxes Payable account reflects the difference between income tax expense incurred and income tax actually paid. Computer Services' Income Taxes Payable account decreased by $2,000. That means the $47,000 of income tax expense reported on the income statement was $2,000 less than the amount of taxes paid during the period of $49,000. As shown in Illustration 12.10, to adjust net income to a cash basis, the company must reduce net income by $2,000.

Illustration 12.10 shows that after starting with net income of $145,000, the sum of all of the adjustments to net income was $27,000. This resulted in net cash provided by operating activities of $172,000.

Cash flows from operating activities

Net income		$145,000
Adjustments to reconcile net income to net cash		
provided by operating activities:		
Depreciation expense	$ 9,000	
Loss on disposal of plant assets	3,000	
Decrease in accounts receivable	10,000	
Increase in inventory	(5,000)	
Increase in prepaid expenses	(4,000)	
Increase in accounts payable	**16,000**	
Decrease in income taxes payable	**(2,000)**	27,000
Net cash provided by operating activities		$172,000

Summary of Conversion to Net Cash Provided by Operating Activities—Indirect Method

As shown in the previous illustrations, the statement of cash flows prepared by the indirect method starts with net income. It then adds or deducts items to arrive at net cash provided by operating activities. The required adjustments are of three types:

1. Noncash charges such as depreciation and amortization.
2. Gains and losses on the disposal of plant assets.
3. Changes in noncash current asset and current liability accounts.

Illustration 12.11 provides a summary of these changes and required adjustments.

		Adjustments Required to Convert Net Income to Net Cash Provided by Operating Activities
Noncash Charges	Depreciation expense	Add
	Amortization expense	Add
Gains and Losses	Loss on disposal of plant assets	Add
	Gain on disposal of plant assets	Deduct
Changes in Current Assets and Current Liabilities	Increase in current asset account	Deduct
	Decrease in current asset account	Add
	Increase in current liability account	Add
	Decrease in current liability account	Deduct

Anatomy of a Fraud

For more than a decade, the top executives at the Italian dairy products company **Parmalat** engaged in multiple frauds that overstated cash and other assets by more than $1 billion while understating liabilities by between $8 and $12 billion. Much of the fraud involved creating fictitious sources and uses of cash. Some of these activities incorporated sophisticated financial transactions with subsidiaries created with the help of large international financial institutions. However, much of the fraud employed very basic, even sloppy, forgery of documents. For example, when outside auditors requested confirmation of bank accounts (such as a fake $4.8 billion account in the Cayman Islands), documents were created on scanners, with signatures that were cut and pasted from other documents. These were then passed through a fax machine numerous times to make them look real (if difficult to read). Similarly, fictitious bills were created in order to divert funds to other businesses owned by the Tanzi family (who controlled Parmalat).

Total take: Billions of dollars

The Missing Control

Independent internal verification. Internal auditors at the company should have independently verified bank accounts and major transfers of cash to outside companies that were controlled by the Tanzi family.

DO IT! 2a | Cash Flows from Operating Activities

Josh's PhotoPlus reported net income of $73,000 for 2022. Included in the income statement were depreciation expense of $7,000 and a gain on disposal of plant assets of $2,500. Josh's comparative balance sheets show the following balances.

	12/31/21	12/31/22
Accounts receivable	$17,000	$21,000
Accounts payable	6,000	2,200

Calculate net cash provided by operating activities for Josh's PhotoPlus.

Solution

Cash flows from operating activities		
Net income		$73,000
Adjustments to reconcile net income to net cash		
provided by operating activities:		
Depreciation expense	$ 7,000	
Gain on disposal of plant assets	(2,500)	
Increase in accounts receivable	(4,000)	
Decrease in accounts payable	(3,800)	(3,300)
Net cash provided by operating activities		$69,700

Related exercise material: **BE12.4, BE12.5, BE12.6, DO IT! 12.2a, E12.4, E12.5, E12.6, and E12.7.**

ACTION PLAN

- **Add noncash charges such as depreciation back to net income to compute net cash provided by operating activities.**
- **Deduct from net income gains on the disposal of plant assets, or add losses back to net income, to compute net cash provided by operating activities.**
- **Use changes in noncash current asset and current liability accounts to compute net cash provided by operating activities.**

Step 2: Investing and Financing Activities

Analyze Changes in Noncurrent Asset and Liability Accounts and Stockholders' Equity Accounts and Report as Investing and Financing Activities, or as Noncash Investing and Financing Activities

Increase in Land   As indicated from the change in the Land account and the additional information, Computer Services purchased land for $110,000. This activity is generally classified as an investing activity. However, by directly exchanging bonds for land, the issuance of bonds payable for land has no effect on cash. But, it is a significant noncash investing and financing activity that merits disclosure in a separate schedule (see Illustration 12.14).

Increase in Buildings   As the additional data indicate, Computer Services acquired an office building for $120,000 cash. This is a cash outflow reported in the investing activities section (see Illustration 12.14).

Increase in Equipment   The Equipment account increased $17,000. The additional information explains that this net increase resulted from two transactions: (1) a purchase of equipment for $25,000, and (2) the sale for $4,000 of equipment costing $8,000. These transactions are investing activities (see **Helpful Hint**). The company should report each transaction separately. Thus, it reports the purchase of equipment as an outflow of cash for $25,000. It reports the sale as an inflow of cash for $4,000. The T-account in **Illustration 12.12** shows the reasons for the change in this account during the year.

HELPFUL HINT

The investing and financing activities are measured and reported the same way under both the direct and indirect methods.

ILLUSTRATION 12.12

Analysis of equipment

Equipment

1/1/22	Balance	10,000	Cost of equipment sold	8,000
	Purchase of equipment	**25,000**		
12/31/22	Balance	27,000		

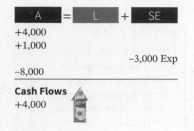

A	=	L	+	SE
+4,000				
+1,000				
				−3,000 Exp
−8,000				

Cash Flows
+4,000

ILLUSTRATION 12.13

Analysis of retained earnings

The following entry shows the details of the equipment sale transaction.

Cash	4,000	
Accumulated Depreciation—Equipment	1,000	
Loss on Disposal of Plant Assets	3,000	
Equipment		8,000

Increase in Bonds Payable The Bonds Payable account increased $110,000. As indicated in the additional information, the company acquired land from the issuance of these bonds. It reports this noncash transaction in a separate schedule at the bottom of the statement.

Increase in Common Stock The balance sheet reports an increase in Common Stock of $20,000. The additional information section notes that this increase resulted from the issuance of new shares of stock for cash at par. This is a cash inflow reported in the financing activities section (see **Helpful Hint**).

Increase in Retained Earnings Retained earnings increased $116,000 during the year. This increase can be explained by two factors: (1) net income of $145,000 increased retained earnings, and (2) dividends declared of $29,000 decreased retained earnings. The company adjusts net income to net cash provided by operating activities in the operating activities section. The T-account shown in **Illustration 12.13** shows the reasons for the change in this account during the year.

Retained Earnings

Dividends declared	29,000	1/1/22	Balance		48,000
			Net income		145,000
		12/31/22	Balance		164,000

Payment of the dividends (not the declaration) is a **cash outflow that the company reports as a financing activity**. Since the balance sheet does not report a Cash Dividends Payable account, the declared cash dividends of $29,000 must have been paid.

Statement of Cash Flows—2022

Using the previous information, we can now prepare a statement of cash flows for 2022 for Computer Services Company as shown in **Illustration 12.14** (see **Helpful Hint**).

ILLUSTRATION 12.14

Statement of cash flows, 2022—indirect method

Computer Services Company
Statement of Cash Flows—Indirect Method
For the Year Ended December 31, 2022

Cash flows from operating activities		
Net income		$145,000
Adjustments to reconcile net income to net cash		
provided by operating activities:		
Depreciation expense	$ 9,000	
Loss on disposal of plant assets	3,000	
Decrease in accounts receivable	10,000	
Increase in inventory	(5,000)	
Increase in prepaid expenses	(4,000)	
Increase in accounts payable	16,000	
Decrease in income taxes payable	(2,000)	27,000
Net cash provided by operating activities		172,000
Cash flows from investing activities		
Purchase of building	(120,000)	
Purchase of equipment	(25,000)	
Sale of equipment	4,000	
Net cash used by investing activities		(141,000)
Cash flows from financing activities		
Issuance of common stock	20,000	
Payment of cash dividends	(29,000)	
Net cash used by financing activities		(9,000)
Net increase in cash		22,000
Cash at beginning of period		33,000
Cash at end of period		$ 55,000
Noncash investing and financing activities		
Issuance of bonds payable to purchase land		$110,000

Step 3: Net Change in Cash

Compare the Net Change in Cash on the Statement of Cash Flows with the Change in the Cash Account Reported on the Balance Sheet to Make Sure the Amounts Agree

Illustration 12.14 indicates that the net change in cash during the period was an increase of $22,000. This agrees with the change in Cash account reported on the comparative balance sheets in Illustration 12.4.

Accounting Across the Organization

iStock.com/Soubrette

Burning Through Our Cash

Box (cloud storage), **Cyan** (game creator), **FireEye** (cyber security), and **MobileIron** (mobile security of data) are a few of the tech companies that recently have issued or are about to issue stock to the public. Investors now have to determine whether these tech companies have viable products and high chances for success.

An important consideration in evaluating a tech company is determining its financial flexibility—its ability to withstand adversity if an economic setback occurs. One way to measure financial flexibility is to assess a company's cash burn rate, which determines how long its cash will hold out if the company is expending more cash than it is receiving.

FireEye, for example, used cash in excess of $50 million in 2013. But the company also had over $150 million as a cash cushion, so it would have taken over 30 months for it to run out of cash. And even though Box has a much lower cash burn rate than FireEye, it still has over a year's cushion. Compare that to the tech companies in 2000, when over one-quarter of them were on track to run out of cash within a year. And many did. Fortunately, the tech companies of today seem to be better equipped to withstand an economic setback.

Source: Shira Ovide, "Tech Firms' Cash Hoards Cool Fears of a Meltdown," *Wall Street Journal* (May 14, 2014).

What implications does a company's cash burn rate have for its survival? (See WileyPLUS for this answer and additional questions.)

DO IT! 2b | Indirect Method

Use the following information to prepare a statement of cash flows using the indirect method.

Reynolds Company
Comparative Balance Sheets
December 31

	2022	2021	Change Increase/Decrease
Assets			
Cash	$ 54,000	$ 37,000	$ 17,000 Increase
Accounts receivable	68,000	26,000	42,000 Increase
Inventory	54,000	–0–	54,000 Increase
Prepaid expenses	4,000	6,000	2,000 Decrease
Land	45,000	70,000	25,000 Decrease
Buildings	200,000	200,000	–0–
Accumulated depreciation—buildings	(21,000)	(11,000)	10,000 Increase
Equipment	193,000	68,000	125,000 Increase
Accumulated depreciation—equipment	(28,000)	(10,000)	18,000 Increase
Totals	$569,000	$386,000	

ACTION PLAN
- Determine net cash provided/used by operating activities by adjusting net income for items that did not affect cash.
- Determine net cash provided/used by investing activities and financing activities.
- Determine the net increase/decrease in cash.

	2022	2021	Change Increase/ Decrease
Liabilities and Stockholders' Equity			
Accounts payable	$ 23,000	$ 40,000	$ 17,000 Decrease
Accrued expenses payable	10,000	–0–	10,000 Increase
Bonds payable	110,000	150,000	40,000 Decrease
Common stock ($1 par)	220,000	60,000	160,000 Increase
Retained earnings	206,000	136,000	70,000 Increase
Totals	$569,000	$386,000	

Reynolds Company
Income Statement
For the Year Ended December 31, 2022

Sales revenue		$890,000
Cost of goods sold	$465,000	
Operating expenses	221,000	
Interest expense	12,000	
Loss on disposal of plant assets	2,000	700,000
Income before income taxes		190,000
Income tax expense		65,000
Net income		$125,000

Additional information:

1. Operating expenses include depreciation expense of $33,000, $10,000 for the building and $23,000 for the equipment.

2. Land was sold at its book value for cash.

3. Cash dividends of $55,000 were declared and paid in 2022.

4. Equipment with a cost of $166,000 was purchased for cash. Equipment with a cost of $41,000 and a book value of $36,000 was sold for $34,000 cash.

5. Bonds of $40,000 were redeemed at their face value for cash.

6. Common stock ($1 par) was issued at par for $160,000 cash.

Solution

Reynolds Company
Statement of Cash Flows—Indirect Method
For the Year Ended December 31, 2022

Cash flows from operating activities		
Net income		$ 125,000
Adjustments to reconcile net income to net cash provided by operating activities:		
Depreciation expense	$ 33,000	
Loss on disposal of plant assets	2,000	
Increase in accounts receivable	(42,000)	
Increase in inventory	(54,000)	
Decrease in prepaid expenses	2,000	
Decrease in accounts payable	(17,000)	
Increase in accrued expenses payable	10,000	(66,000)
Net cash provided by operating activities		59,000
Cash flows from investing activities		
Sale of land	25,000	
Sale of equipment	34,000	
Purchase of equipment	(166,000)	
Net cash used by investing activities		(107,000)

Cash flows from financing activities		
Redemption of bonds	(40,000)	
Issuance of common stock	160,000	
Payment of cash dividends	(55,000)	
Net cash provided by financing activities		65,000
Net increase in cash		17,000
Cash at beginning of period		37,000
Cash at end of period		$ 54,000

Related exercise material: **BE12.4, BE12.5, BE12.6, BE12.7, DO IT! 12.2b, E12.4, E12.5, E12.6, E12.7, E12.8, and E12.9.**

Analyzing the Statement of Cash Flows

LEARNING OBJECTIVE 3
Analyze the statement of cash flows.

Traditionally, investors and creditors used ratios based on accrual accounting. These days, cash-based ratios are gaining increased acceptance among analysts.

Free Cash Flow

In the statement of cash flows, net cash provided by operating activities is intended to indicate the cash-generating capability of a company. Analysts have noted, however, that **net cash provided by operating activities fails to take into account that a company must invest in new fixed assets** just to maintain its current level of operations. Companies also must at least **maintain dividends at current levels** to satisfy investors. The measurement of free cash flow provides additional insight regarding a company's cash-generating ability. **Free cash flow** describes the net cash provided by operating activities after adjustment for capital expenditures and dividends.

Consider the following example. Suppose that MPC produced and sold 10,000 personal computers this year. It reported $100,000 net cash provided by operating activities. In order to maintain production at 10,000 computers, MPC invested $15,000 in equipment. It chose to pay $5,000 in dividends. Its free cash flow was $80,000 ($100,000 – $15,000 – $5,000). The company could use this $80,000 either to purchase new assets to expand the business or to pay an $80,000 dividend and continue to produce 10,000 computers. In practice, free cash flow is often calculated with the formula in **Illustration 12.15**. (Alternative definitions also exist.)

Free Cash Flow	=	Net Cash Provided by Operating Activities	–	Capital Expenditures	–	Cash Dividends

ILLUSTRATION 12.15
Free cash flow

Illustration 12.16 provides basic information excerpted from the 2018 statement of cash flows of **Tootsie Roll Industries**.

Tootsie Roll's cash flow
information
($ in thousands)

Real World

Tootsie Roll Industries
Statement of Cash Flows (partial)
December 31, 2018

Net cash provided by operating activities		$100,929
Cash flows from investing activities		
Capital expenditures	$(27,612)	
Purchases of trading securities	(4,378)	
Sale of trading securities	1,255	
Sale and maturity of available for sale securities	64,602	
Net cash used in investing activities		$ 44,510
Dividends paid in cash		$ 22,978

Tootsie Roll's free cash flow is computed as shown in **Illustration 12.17**. Tootsie Roll generated approximately $50.3 million of free cash flow. This is a significant amount of cash generated in a single year. It is available for the acquisition of new assets, the buyback and retirement of stock or debt, or the payment of dividends.

Calculation of Tootsie Roll's
free cash flow
($ in thousands)

Net cash provided by operating activities	$100,929
Less: Capital expenditures	27,612
Dividends paid	22,978
Free cash flow	$ 50,339

Tootsie Roll's cash from operations of $100,929,000 exceeds its 2018 net income of $56,805,000 by $44,124,000. This lends credibility to Tootsie Rolls' income number as an indicator of potential future performance.

ACTION PLAN

- Compute free cash flow as Net cash provided by operating activities – Capital expenditures – Cash dividends.

DO IT! 3 | Free Cash Flow

Chicago Corporation issued the following statement of cash flows for 2022.

Chicago Corporation
Statement of Cash Flows—Indirect Method
For the Year Ended December 31, 2022

Cash flows from operating activities		
Net income		$ 19,000
Adjustments to reconcile net income to net cash		
provided by operating activities:		
Depreciation expense	$ 8,100	
Loss on disposal of plant assets	1,300	
Decrease in accounts receivable	6,900	
Increase in inventory	(4,000)	
Decrease in accounts payable	(2,000)	10,300
Net cash provided by operating activities		29,300
Cash flows from investing activities		
Sale of investments	1,100	
Purchase of equipment	(19,000)	
Net cash used by investing activities		(17,900)

Cash flows from financing activities		
Issuance of common stock	10,000	
Payment on long-term note payable	(5,000)	
Payment of cash dividends	(9,000)	
Net cash used by financing activities		(4,000)
Net increase in cash		7,400
Cash at beginning of year		10,000
Cash at end of year		$ 17,400

(a) Compute free cash flow for Chicago Corporation. (b) Explain why free cash flow often provides better information than "Net cash provided by operating activities."

Solution

a. Free cash flow = $29,300 – $19,000 – $9,000 = $1,300

b. Net cash provided by operating activities fails to take into account that a company must invest in new plant assets just to maintain the current level of operations. Companies must also maintain dividends at current levels to satisfy investors. The measurement of free cash flow provides additional insight regarding a company's cash-generating ability.

Related exercise material: **BE12.8, BE12.9, BE12.10, BE12.11, DO IT! 12.3, E12.8, and E12.10.**

Appendix 12A	# Statement of Cash Flows—Direct Method

LEARNING OBJECTIVE *4

Prepare a statement of cash flows using the direct method.

To explain and illustrate the direct method for preparing a statement of cash flows, we use the transactions of Computer Services Company for 2022. **Illustration 12A.1** presents information related to 2022 for the company.

To prepare a statement of cash flows under the direct method, we apply the three steps outlined in Illustration 12.3 for the indirect method.

Step 1: Operating Activities

Determine Net Cash Provided/Used by Operating Activities by Converting Net Income Components from an Accrual Basis to a Cash Basis

Under the **direct method**, companies compute net cash provided by operating activities by **adjusting each item in the income statement** from the accrual basis to the cash basis. To simplify and condense the operating activities section, companies **report only major classes of operating cash receipts and cash payments**. For these major classes, the difference between cash receipts and cash payments is the net cash provided by operating activities. These relationships are as shown in **Illustration 12A.2**.

An efficient way to apply the direct method is to analyze the items reported in the income statement in the order in which they are listed. We then determine cash

Computer Services Company
Comparative Balance Sheets
December 31

	2022	2021	Change in Account Balance Increase/Decrease
Assets			
Current assets			
Cash	$ 55,000	$ 33,000	$ 22,000 Increase
Accounts receivable	20,000	30,000	10,000 Decrease
Inventory	15,000	10,000	5,000 Increase
Prepaid expenses	5,000	1,000	4,000 Increase
Property, plant, and equipment			
Land	130,000	20,000	110,000 Increase
Buildings	160,000	40,000	120,000 Increase
Accumulated depreciation—buildings	(11,000)	(5,000)	6,000 Increase
Equipment	27,000	10,000	17,000 Increase
Accumulated depreciation—equipment	(3,000)	(1,000)	2,000 Increase
Total assets	$398,000	$138,000	
Liabilities and Stockholders' Equity			
Current liabilities			
Accounts payable	$ 28,000	$ 12,000	$ 16,000 Increase
Income taxes payable	6,000	8,000	2,000 Decrease
Long-term liabilities			
Bonds payable	130,000	20,000	110,000 Increase
Stockholders' equity			
Common stock	70,000	50,000	20,000 Increase
Retained earnings	164,000	48,000	116,000 Increase
Total liabilities and stockholders' equity	$398,000	$138,000	

Computer Services Company
Income Statement
For the Year Ended December 31, 2022

Sales revenue		$507,000
Cost of goods sold	$150,000	
Operating expenses (excluding depreciation)	111,000	
Depreciation expense	9,000	
Loss on disposal of plant assets	3,000	
Interest expense	42,000	315,000
Income before income tax		192,000
Income tax expense		47,000
Net income		$145,000

Additional information for 2022:

1. Depreciation expense was comprised of $6,000 for building and $3,000 for equipment.

2. The company sold equipment with a book value of $7,000 (cost $8,000, less accumulated depreciation $1,000) for $4,000 cash.

3. Issued $110,000 of long-term bonds in direct exchange for land.

4. A building costing $120,000 was purchased for cash. Equipment costing $25,000 was also purchased for cash.

5. Issued common stock at par for $20,000 cash.

6. The company declared and paid a $29,000 cash dividend.

ILLUSTRATION 12A.2 **Major classes of cash receipts and payments**

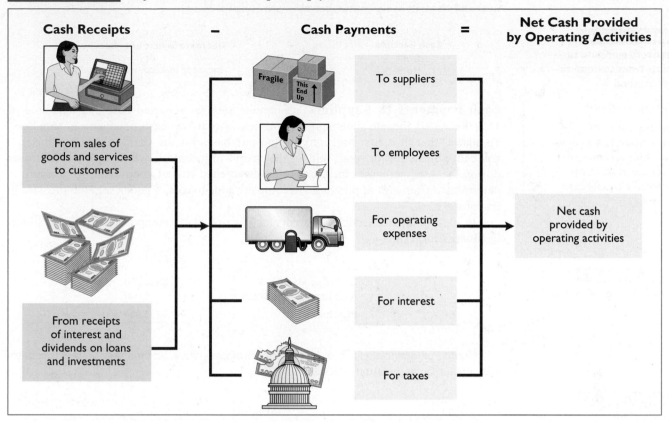

receipts and cash payments related to these revenues and expenses. The following presents the adjustments required to prepare a statement of cash flows for Computer Services Company using the direct method.

Cash Receipts from Customers The income statement for Computer Services reported sales revenue from customers of $507,000. How much of that was cash receipts? To answer that, a company considers the change in accounts receivable during the year. When accounts receivable increase during the year, revenues on an accrual basis are higher than cash receipts from customers. Operations led to revenues, but not all of those revenues resulted in cash receipts.

To determine the amount of cash receipts, a company deducts from sales revenue the increase in accounts receivable. On the other hand, there may be a decrease in accounts receivable. That would occur if cash receipts from customers exceeded sales revenue. In that case, a company adds to sales revenue the decrease in accounts receivable. For Computer Services, accounts receivable decreased $10,000. Thus, cash receipts from customers were $517,000, computed as shown in **Illustration 12A.3**.

Sales revenue	$507,000
Add: Decrease in accounts receivable	10,000
Cash receipts from customers	**$517,000**

ILLUSTRATION 12A.3

Computation of cash receipts from customers

Computer Services can also determine cash receipts from customers from an analysis of the Accounts Receivable account, as shown in **Illustration 12A.4**.

Accounts Receivable

1/1/22	Balance	30,000	**Receipts from customers**	**517,000**
	Sales revenue	507,000		
12/31/22	Balance	20,000		

ILLUSTRATION 12A.4

Analysis of accounts receivable

Illustration 12A.5 shows the relationships among cash receipts from customers, sales revenue, and changes in accounts receivable (see **Helpful Hint**).

Cash Receipts from Customers	=	Sales Revenue	+ Decrease in Accounts Receivable or − Increase in Accounts Receivable

HELPFUL HINT

The T-account in Illustration 12A.4 shows that sales revenue plus decrease in accounts receivable equals cash receipts.

Cash Payments to Suppliers Computer Services reported cost of goods sold of $150,000 on its income statement. How much of that was cash payments to suppliers? To answer that, it is first necessary to find purchases for the year. To find purchases, a company adjusts cost of goods sold for the change in inventory. When inventory increases during the year, purchases for the year have exceeded cost of goods sold. As a result, to determine the amount of purchases, a company adds to cost of goods sold the increase in inventory.

In 2022, Computer Services' inventory increased $5,000. It computes purchases as shown in **Illustration 12A.6**.

ILLUSTRATION 12A.6

Computation of purchases

Cost of goods sold	$150,000
Add: Increase in inventory	5,000
Purchases	**$155,000**

Computer Services can also determine purchases from an analysis of the Inventory account, as shown in **Illustration 12A.7**.

ILLUSTRATION 12A.7

Analysis of inventory

	Inventory			
1/1/22	Balance	10,000	Cost of goods sold	150,000
	Purchases	**155,000**		
12/31/22	Balance	15,000		

After computing purchases, a company can determine cash payments to suppliers. This is done by adjusting purchases for the change in accounts payable. When accounts payable increase during the year, purchases on an accrual basis are higher than they are on a cash basis. As a result, to determine cash payments to suppliers, a company deducts from purchases the increase in accounts payable. On the other hand, if cash payments to suppliers exceed purchases, there will be a decrease in accounts payable. In that case, a company adds to purchases the decrease in accounts payable. For Computer Services, cash payments to suppliers were $139,000, computed as shown in **Illustration 12A.8**.

ILLUSTRATION 12A.8

Computation of cash payments to suppliers

Purchases	$155,000
Deduct: Increase in accounts payable	16,000
Cash payments to suppliers	**$139,000**

Computer Services also can determine cash payments to suppliers from an analysis of the Accounts Payable account, as shown in **Illustration 12A.9**.

ILLUSTRATION 12A.9

Analysis of accounts payable

	Accounts Payable			
Payments to suppliers	**139,000**	1/1/22	Balance	12,000
			Purchases	155,000
		12/31/22	Balance	28,000

HELPFUL HINT

The T-account shows that purchases less increase in accounts payable equals payments to suppliers.

Illustration 12A.10 shows the relationships among cash payments to suppliers, cost of goods sold, changes in inventory, and changes in accounts payable (see **Helpful Hint**).

Cash Payments to Suppliers	=	Cost of Goods Sold		+ Increase in Inventory or − Decrease in Inventory		+ Decrease in Accounts Payable or − Increase in Accounts Payable

ILLUSTRATION 12A.10

Formula to compute cash payments to suppliers—direct method

Cash Payments for Operating Expenses   Computer Services reported on its income statement operating expenses of $111,000. How much of that amount was cash paid for operating expenses? To answer that, we need to adjust this amount for any changes in prepaid expenses and accrued expenses payable. For example, if prepaid expenses increased during the year, cash paid for operating expenses is higher than operating expenses reported on the income statement. To convert operating expenses to cash payments for operating expenses, a company adds the increase in prepaid expenses to operating expenses. On the other hand, if prepaid expenses decrease during the year, it deducts the decrease from operating expenses.

Companies must also adjust operating expenses for changes in accrued expenses payable. When accrued expenses payable increase during the year, operating expenses on an accrual basis are higher than they are in a cash basis. As a result, to determine cash payments for operating expenses, a company deducts from operating expenses an increase in accrued expenses payable. On the other hand, a company adds to operating expenses a decrease in accrued expenses payable because cash payments exceed operating expenses.

Computer Services' cash payments for operating expenses were $115,000, computed as shown in **Illustration 12A.11**.

Operating expenses	$111,000
Add: Increase in prepaid expenses	4,000
Cash payments for operating expenses	**$115,000**

ILLUSTRATION 12A.11

Computation of cash payments for operating expenses

Illustration 12A.12 shows the relationships among cash payments for operating expenses, changes in prepaid expenses, and changes in accrued expenses payable.

Cash Payments for Operating Expenses	=	Operating Expenses		+ Increase in Prepaid Expenses or − Decrease in Prepaid Expenses		+ Decrease in Accrued Expenses Payable or − Increase in Accrued Expenses Payable

ILLUSTRATION 12A.12

Formula to compute cash payments for operating expenses—direct method

Depreciation Expense and Loss on Disposal of Plant Assets   Computer Services' depreciation expense in 2022 was $9,000. Depreciation expense is not shown on a statement of cash flows under the direct method because it is a noncash charge. If the amount for operating expenses includes depreciation expense, operating expenses must be reduced by the amount of depreciation to determine cash payments for operating expenses.

The loss on disposal of plant assets of $3,000 is also a noncash charge. The loss on disposal of plant assets reduces net income, but it does not reduce cash. Thus, the loss on disposal of plant assets is not shown on the statement of cash flows under the direct method.

Other charges to expense that do not require the use of cash, such as the amortization of intangible assets and bad debt expense, are treated in the same manner as depreciation.

Cash Payments for Interest   Computer Services reported on the income statement interest expense of $42,000. Since the balance sheet did not report interest payable for 2021 or 2022, the amount reported as interest expense is the same as the amount of interest paid.

Cash Payments for Income Taxes   Computer Services reported income tax expense of $47,000 on the income statement. Income taxes payable, however, decreased $2,000. This decrease means that income taxes paid were more than income tax expense reported in the income statement. Cash payments for income taxes were therefore $49,000 as shown in **Illustration 12A.13**.

ILLUSTRATION 12A.13
Computation of cash payments for income taxes

Income tax expense	$47,000
Add: Decrease in income taxes payable	2,000
Cash payments for income taxes	**$49,000**

Computer Services can also determine cash payments for income taxes from an analysis of the Income Taxes Payable account, as shown in **Illustration 12A.14**.

ILLUSTRATION 12A.14
Analysis of income taxes payable

Income Taxes Payable				
Cash payments for income taxes	49,000	1/1/22	Balance	8,000
			Income tax expense	47,000
		12/31/22	Balance	6,000

Illustration 12A.15 shows the relationships among cash payments for income taxes, income tax expense, and changes in income taxes payable.

ILLUSTRATION 12A.15
Formula to compute cash payments for income taxes—direct method

$$\text{Cash Payments for Income Taxes} = \text{Income Tax Expense} \begin{cases} + & \text{Decrease in Income Taxes Payable} \\ & \text{or} \\ - & \text{Increase in Income Taxes Payable} \end{cases}$$

The operating activities section of the statement of cash flows of Computer Services is shown in **Illustration 12A.16**.

ILLUSTRATION 12A.16
Operating activities section of the statement of cash flows

Cash flows from operating activities		
Cash receipts from customers		$517,000
Less: Cash payments:		
To suppliers	$139,000	
For operating expenses	115,000	
For interest expense	42,000	
For income taxes	49,000	345,000
Net cash provided by operating activities		$172,000

When a company uses the direct method, it must also provide in a **separate schedule** (not shown here) the net cash flows from operating activities as computed under the indirect method. Note that whether a company uses the indirect or direct method, the net cash provided by operating activities is the same for both methods.

Step 2: Investing and Financing Activities

Analyze Changes in Noncurrent Asset and Liability Accounts and Stockholders' Equity Accounts and Record as Investing and Financing Activities, or Disclose as Noncash Transactions

Increase in Land   As indicated from the change in the Land account and the additional information, Computer Services purchased land of $110,000 by directly exchanging bonds for land. The exchange of bonds payable for land has no effect on cash. But, it is a significant noncash investing and financing activity that merits disclosure in a separate schedule (see Illustration 12A.18).

Increase in Buildings As the additional data indicate, Computer Services acquired an office building for $120,000 cash. This is a cash outflow reported in the investing activities section (see Illustration 12A.18).

Increase in Equipment The Equipment account increased $17,000. The additional information explains that this was a net increase that resulted from two transactions: (1) a purchase of equipment of $25,000, and (2) the sale for $4,000 of equipment costing $8,000. These transactions are investing activities (see **Helpful Hint**). The company should report each transaction separately. The statement in Illustration 12A.18 reports the purchase of equipment as an outflow of cash for $25,000. It reports the sale as an inflow of cash for $4,000. The T-account in **Illustration 12A.17** shows the reasons for the change in this account during the year.

> **HELPFUL HINT**
>
> The investing and financing activities are measured and reported the same under both the direct and indirect methods.

> **ILLUSTRATION 12A.17**
>
> Analysis of equipment

	Equipment			
1/1/22	Balance	10,000	Cost of equipment sold	8,000
	Purchase of equipment	**25,000**		
12/31/22	Balance	27,000		

The following entry shows the details of the equipment sale transaction.

Cash	4,000	
Accumulated Depreciation—Equipment	1,000	
Loss on Disposal of Plant Assets	3,000	
Equipment		8,000

A = L + SE
+4,000
+1,000
−3,000 Exp
−8,000

Cash Flows
+4,000

Increase in Bonds Payable The Bonds Payable account increased $110,000. As indicated in the additional information, the company acquired land by directly exchanging bonds for land. Illustration 12A.18 reports this noncash transaction in a separate schedule at the bottom of the statement.

Increase in Common Stock The balance sheet reports an increase in Common Stock of $20,000. The additional information section notes that this increase resulted from the issuance of new shares of stock. This is a cash inflow reported in the financing activities section in Illustration 12A.18 (see **Helpful Hint**).

Increase in Retained Earnings Retained earnings increased $116,000 during the year. This increase can be explained by two factors: (1) net income of $145,000 increased retained earnings, and (2) dividends of $29,000 decreased retained earnings. **Payment** of the dividends (not the declaration) is a **cash outflow that the company reports as a financing activity in Illustration 12A.18**.

> **HELPFUL HINT**
>
> When companies issue stocks or bonds for cash, the actual proceeds will appear in the statement of cash flows as a financing inflow (rather than the par value of the stocks or face value of bonds).

Statement of Cash Flows—2022

Illustration 12A.18 shows the statement of cash flows for Computer Services Company.

ILLUSTRATION 12A.18
Statement of cash flows, 2022—direct method

Computer Services Company
Statement of Cash Flows—Direct Method
For the Year Ended December 31, 2022

Cash flows from operating activities		
Cash receipts from customers		$ 517,000
Less: Cash payments:		
To suppliers	$ 139,000	
For operating expenses	115,000	
For income taxes	49,000	
For interest expense	42,000	345,000
Net cash provided by operating activities		172,000
Cash flows from investing activities		
Sale of equipment	4,000	
Purchase of building	(120,000)	
Purchase of equipment	(25,000)	
Net cash used by investing activities		(141,000)
Cash flows from financing activities		
Issuance of common stock	20,000	
Payment of cash dividends	(29,000)	
Net cash used by financing activities		(9,000)
Net increase in cash		22,000
Cash at beginning of period		33,000
Cash at end of period		$ 55,000
Noncash investing and financing activities		
Issuance of bonds payable to purchase land		$ 110,000

Step 3: Net Change in Cash

Compare the Net Change in Cash on the Statement of Cash Flows with the Change in the Cash Account Reported on the Balance Sheet to Make Sure the Amounts Agree

Illustration 12A.18 indicates that the net change in cash during the period was an increase of $22,000. This agrees with the change in balances in the Cash account reported on the balance sheets in Illustration 12A.1.

Appendix 12B

Worksheet for the Indirect Method

LEARNING OBJECTIVE *5
Use a worksheet to prepare the statement of cash flows using the indirect method.

When preparing a statement of cash flows, companies may need to make numerous adjustments to net income. In such cases, they often use **a worksheet to assemble and classify the data that will appear on the statement**. The worksheet is merely an aid in preparing the statement. Its use is optional. **Illustration 12B.1** shows the skeleton format of the worksheet for preparation of the statement of cash flows.

The following guidelines are important in preparing a worksheet.

1. In the balance sheet accounts section, **list accounts with debit balances separately from those with credit balances**. This means, for example, that Accumulated Depreciation appears under credit balances and not as a contra account under debit

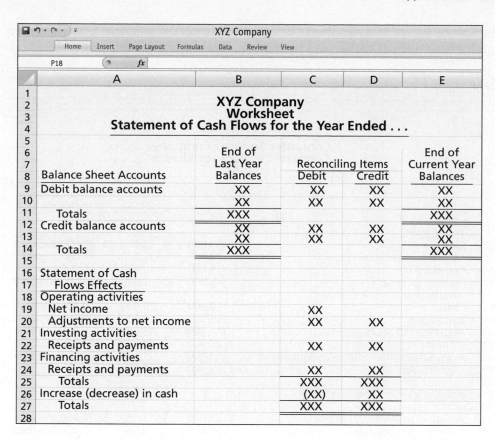

ILLUSTRATION 12B.1

Format of worksheet

balances. Enter the beginning and ending balances of each account in the appropriate columns. Enter as reconciling items in the two middle columns the transactions that caused the change in the account balance during the year.

   After all reconciling items have been entered, each line pertaining to a balance sheet account should "foot across." That is, the beginning balance plus or minus the reconciling item(s) must equal the ending balance. When this agreement exists for all balance sheet accounts, all changes in account balances have been reconciled.

2. The bottom portion of the worksheet consists of the operating, investing, and financing activities sections. It provides the information necessary to prepare the formal statement of cash flows. **Enter inflows of cash as debits in the reconciling columns. Enter outflows of cash as credits in the reconciling columns.** Thus, in this section, the sale of equipment for cash at book value appears as a debit under investing activities. Similarly, the purchase of land for cash appears as a credit under investing activities.

3. **The reconciling items shown in the worksheet are not entered in any journal or posted to any account.** They do not represent either adjustments or corrections of the balance sheet accounts. They are used only to facilitate the preparation of the statement of cash flows.

Preparing the Worksheet

Preparing a worksheet involves a series of prescribed steps. The steps in this case are:

1. Enter in the balance sheet accounts section the balance sheet accounts and their beginning and ending balances.

2. Enter in the reconciling columns of the worksheet the data that explain the changes in the balance sheet accounts other than cash and their effects on the statement of cash flows.

3. Enter on the cash line and at the bottom of the worksheet the increase or decrease in cash. This entry should enable the totals of the reconciling columns to be in agreement.

   To illustrate the preparation of a worksheet, we will use the 2022 data for Computer Services Company. Your familiarity with these data (from the chapter) should help you understand the use of a worksheet. For ease of reference, the comparative balance sheets, income statement, and selected data for 2022 are presented in **Illustration 12B.2**.

ILLUSTRATION 12B.2

Comparative balance sheets, income statement, and additional information for Computer Services Company

Computer Services Company

	A	B	C	D
		Computer Services Company		
		Comparative Balance Sheets		
		December 31		
				Change in Account Balance
		2022	**2021**	Increase/Decrease
7	Assets			
8	Current assets			
9	Cash	$ 55,000	$ 33,000	$ 22,000 Increase
10	Accounts receivable	20,000	30,000	10,000 Decrease
11	Inventory	15,000	10,000	5,000 Increase
12	Prepaid expenses	5,000	1,000	4,000 Increase
13	Property, plant, and equipment			
14	Land	130,000	20,000	110,000 Increase
15	Buildings	160,000	40,000	120,000 Increase
16	Accumulated depreciation—buildings	(11,000)	(5,000)	6,000 Increase
17	Equipment	27,000	10,000	17,000 Increase
18	Accumulated depreciation—equipment	(3,000)	(1,000)	2,000 Increase
19	Total assets	$398,000	$138,000	
20				
21	Liabilities and Stockholders' Equity			
22	Current liabilities			
23	Accounts payable	$ 28,000	$ 12,000	$ 16,000 Increase
24	Income taxes payable	6,000	8,000	2,000 Decrease
25	Long-term liabilities			
26	Bonds payable	130,000	20,000	110,000 Increase
27	Stockholders' equity			
28	Common stock	70,000	50,000	20,000 Increase
29	Retained earnings	164,000	48,000	116,000 Increase
	Total liabilities and stockholders' equity	$398,000	$138,000	

Computer Services Company

	A	B	C	D
1		**Computer Services Company**		
2		**Income Statement**		
3		**For the Year Ended December 31, 2022**		
4				
5	Sales revenue			$507,000
6	Cost of goods sold		$150,000	
7	Operating expenses (excluding depreciation)		111,000	
8	Depreciation expense		9,000	
9	Loss on disposal of plant assets		3,000	
10	Interest expense		42,000	315,000
11	Income before income taxes			192,000
12	Income tax expense			47,000
13	Net income			$145,000
14				

Additional information for 2022:

1. Depreciation expense was comprised of $6,000 for building and $3,000 for equipment.

2. The company sold equipment with a book value of $7,000 (cost $8,000, less accumulated depreciation $1,000) for $4,000 cash.

3. Issued $110,000 of long-term bonds in direct exchange for land.

4. A building costing $120,000 was purchased for cash. Equipment costing $25,000 was also purchased for cash.

5. Issued common stock at par for $20,000 cash.

6. The company declared and paid a $29,000 cash dividend.

Determining the Reconciling Items

Companies can use one of several approaches to determine the reconciling items. For example, they can first complete the changes affecting net cash provided by operating activities, and then can determine the effects of financing and investing transactions. Or, they can analyze the balance sheet accounts in the order in which they are listed on the worksheet. We will follow this latter approach for Computer Services, except for cash. As indicated in Step 3, **cash is handled last**.

Accounts Receivable   The decrease of $10,000 in accounts receivable means that cash collections from sales revenue are higher than the sales revenue reported in the income statement. To convert net income to net cash provided by operating activities, we add the decrease of $10,000 to net income. The entry in the reconciling columns of the worksheet is:

a.	Operating—Decrease in Accounts Receivable	10,000	
	Accounts Receivable		10,000

Inventory   Computer Services' inventory balance increases $5,000 during the period. The Inventory account reflects the difference between the amount of inventory that the company purchased and the amount that it sold. For Computer Services, this means that the cost of merchandise purchased exceeds the cost of goods sold by $5,000. As a result, cost of goods sold does not reflect $5,000 of cash payments made for merchandise. We deduct this inventory increase of $5,000 during the period from net income to arrive at net cash provided by operating activities. The worksheet entry is:

b.	Inventory	5,000	
	Operating—Increase in Inventory		5,000

Prepaid Expenses   An increase of $4,000 in prepaid expenses means that expenses deducted in determining net income are less than expenses that were paid in cash. We deduct the increase of $4,000 from net income in determining net cash provided by operating activities. The worksheet entry is:

c.	Prepaid Expenses	4,000	
	Operating—Increase in Prepaid Expenses		4,000

Land   The increase in land of $110,000 resulted from a purchase through the issuance of long-term bonds. The company should report this transaction as a significant noncash investing and financing activity (see **Helpful Hint**). The worksheet entry is:

d.	Land	110,000	
	Bonds Payable		110,000

HELPFUL HINT
These amounts are asterisked in the worksheet to indicate that they result from a significant noncash transaction.

Buildings   The cash purchase of a building for $120,000 is an investing activity cash outflow. The entry in the reconciling columns of the worksheet is:

e.	Buildings	120,000	
	Investing—Purchase of Building		120,000

Equipment   The increase in equipment of $17,000 resulted from a cash purchase of $25,000 and the disposal of plant assets (equipment) costing $8,000. The book value of the equipment was $7,000, the cash proceeds were $4,000, and a loss of $3,000 was recorded. The worksheet entries are:

f.	Equipment	25,000	
	Investing—Purchase of Equipment		25,000
g.	Investing—Sale of Equipment	4,000	
	Operating—Loss on Disposal of Plant Assets	3,000	
	Accumulated Depreciation—Equipment	1,000	
	Equipment		8,000

Accounts Payable We must add the increase of $16,000 in accounts payable to net income to determine net cash provided by operating activities. The worksheet entry is:

h. Operating—Increase in Accounts Payable	16,000	
Accounts Payable		16,000

Income Taxes Payable When a company incurs income tax expense but has not yet paid its taxes, it records income taxes payable. A change in the Income Taxes Payable account reflects the difference between income tax expense incurred and income taxes actually paid. Computer Services' Income Taxes Payable account decreases by $2,000. That means the $47,000 of income tax expense reported on the income statement was $2,000 less than the amount of taxes paid during the period of $49,000. To adjust net income to a cash basis, we must reduce net income by $2,000. The worksheet entry is:

i. Income Taxes Payable	2,000	
Operating—Decrease in Income Taxes Payable		2,000

Bonds Payable The increase of $110,000 in this account resulted from the issuance of bonds for land. This is a significant noncash investing and financing activity. Worksheet entry (d) above is the only entry necessary.

Common Stock The balance sheet reports an increase in Common Stock of $20,000. The additional information section notes that this increase resulted from the issuance of new shares of common stock at par for cash. This is a cash inflow reported in the financing section. The worksheet entry is:

j. Financing—Issuance of Common Stock	20,000	
Common Stock		20,000

Accumulated Depreciation—Buildings, and Accumulated Depreciation—Equipment Increases in these accounts of $6,000 and $3,000, respectively, resulted from depreciation expense. Depreciation expense is a **noncash charge that we must add to net income** to determine net cash provided by operating activities. The worksheet entries are:

k. Operating—Depreciation Expense	6,000	
Accumulated Depreciation—Buildings		6,000
l. Operating—Depreciation Expense	3,000	
Accumulated Depreciation—Equipment		3,000

Retained Earnings The $116,000 increase in retained earnings resulted from net income of $145,000 and the declaration and payment of a $29,000 cash dividend. Net income is included in net cash provided by operating activities, and the dividends are a financing activity cash outflow. The entries in the reconciling columns of the worksheet are:

m. Operating—Net Income	145,000	
Retained Earnings		145,000
n. Retained Earnings	29,000	
Financing—Payment of Dividends		29,000

Disposition of Change in Cash The firm's cash increased $22,000 in 2022. The final entry on the worksheet, therefore, is:

o. Cash	22,000	
Increase in Cash		22,000

As shown in the worksheet, we enter the increase in cash in the reconciling credit column as a **balancing** amount. This entry should complete the reconciliation of the changes in the balance sheet accounts. Also, it should permit the totals of the reconciling columns to be in agreement. When all changes have been explained and the reconciling columns are in agreement, the reconciling columns are ruled to complete the worksheet. The completed worksheet for Computer Services Company is shown in **Illustration 12B.3**.

Computer Services Company

| Home | Insert | Page Layout | Formulas | Data | Review | View |

P18   fx

	A	B	C	D	E
1	**Computer Services Company**				
2	**Worksheet**				
3	**Statement of Cash Flows for the Year Ended December 31, 2022**				
4					
5		Balance	Reconciling Items		Balance
6	Balance Sheet Accounts	12/31/21	Debit	Credit	12/31/22
7	Debits				
8	Cash	33,000	(o) 22,000		55,000
9	Accounts Receivable	30,000		(a) 10,000	20,000
10	Inventory	10,000	(b) 5,000		15,000
11	Prepaid Expenses	1,000	(c) 4,000		5,000
12	Land	20,000	(d)110,000*		130,000
13	Buildings	40,000	(e)120,000		160,000
14	Equipment	10,000	(f) 25,000	(g) 8,000	27,000
15	Total	144,000			412,000
16	Credits				
17	Accounts Payable	12,000		(h) 16,000	28,000
18	Income Taxes Payable	8,000	(i) 2,000		6,000
19	Bonds Payable	20,000		(d)110,000*	130,000
20	Accumulated Depreciation—Buildings	5,000		(k) 6,000	11,000
21	Accumulated Depreciation—Equipment	1,000	(g) 1,000	(l) 3,000	3,000
22	Common Stock	50,000		(j) 20,000	70,000
23	Retained Earnings	48,000	(n) 29,000	(m)145,000	164,000
24	Total	144,000			412,000
25					
26	Statement of Cash Flows Effects				
27	Operating activities				
28	Net income		(m)145,000		
29	Decrease in accounts receivable		(a) 10,000		
30	Increase in inventory			(b) 5,000	
31	Increase in prepaid expenses			(c) 4,000	
32	Increase in accounts payable		(h) 16,000		
33	Decrease in income taxes payable			(i) 2,000	
34	Depreciation expense		{(k) 6,000		
35			{(l) 3,000		
36	Loss on disposal of plant assets		(g) 3,000		
37	Investing activities				
38	Purchase of building			(e)120,000	
39	Purchase of equipment			(f) 25,000	
40	Sale of equipment		(g) 4,000		
41	Financing activities				
42	Issuance of common stock		(j) 20,000		
43	Payment of dividends			(n) 29,000	
44	Totals		525,000	503,000	
45	Increase in cash			(o) 22,000	
46	Totals		525,000	525,000	
47					

* Significant noncash investing and financing activity.

Appendix 12C | # Statement of Cash Flows—T-Account Approach

LEARNING OBJECTIVE *6

Use the T-account approach to prepare a statement of cash flows.

Many people like to use T-accounts to provide structure to the preparation of a statement of cash flows. The use of T-accounts is based on the accounting equation:

Assets = Liabilities + Stockholders' Equity

Now, let's rewrite the left-hand side as:

Cash + Noncash Assets = Liabilities + Stockholders' Equity

Next, rewrite the equation by subtracting Noncash Assets from each side to isolate Cash on the left-hand side:

Cash = Liabilities + Stockholders' Equity − Noncash Assets

Finally, if we insert the Δ symbol (which means "change in"), we have:

Δ Cash = Δ Liabilities + Δ Stockholders' Equity − Δ Noncash Assets

What this means is that the change in cash is equal to the change in all of the other balance sheet accounts. Another way to think about this is that if we analyze the changes in all of the noncash balance sheet accounts, we will explain the change in the Cash account. This, of course, is exactly what we are trying to do with the statement of cash flows.

To implement this approach, first prepare a large Cash T-account with sections for operating, investing, and financing activities. Then, prepare smaller T-accounts for all of the other noncash balance sheet accounts. Insert the beginning and ending balances for each of these accounts. Once you have done this, then walk through the steps outlined in Illustration 12.3. As you walk through the steps, enter debit and credit amounts into the affected accounts. When all of the changes in the T-accounts have been explained, you are done. To demonstrate, we apply this approach to the example of Computer Services Company that is presented in the chapter. Each of the adjustments in **Illustration 12C.1** is numbered so you can follow them through the T-accounts.

1. Post net income as a debit to the operating section of the Cash T-account and a credit to Retained Earnings. Make sure to label all adjustments to the Cash T-account. It also helps to number each adjustment so you can trace all of them if you make an error.

2. Post depreciation expense as a debit to the operating section of Cash and a credit to each of the appropriate accumulated depreciation accounts.

3. Post any gains or losses on the sale of property, plant, and equipment. To do this, it is best to first prepare the journal entry that was recorded at the time of the sale and then post each element of the journal entry. For example, for Computer Services the entry was as follows.

Cash	4,000	
Accumulated Depreciation—Equipment	1,000	
Loss on Disposal of Plant Assets	3,000	
Equipment		8,000

The $4,000 cash entry is a source of cash in the investing section of the Cash account. Accumulated Depreciation—Equipment is debited for $1,000. The Loss on Disposal of Plant Assets (equipment) is a debit to the operating section of the Cash T-account. Finally, Equipment is credited for $8,000.

4–8. Next, post each of the changes to the noncash current asset and current liability accounts. For example, to explain the $10,000 decline in Computer Services' accounts receivable, credit Accounts Receivable for $10,000 and debit the operating section of the Cash T-account for $10,000.

ILLUSTRATION 12C.1 **T-account approach**

Cash

Operating				
(1) Net income	145,000	5,000	Inventory (5)	
(2) Depreciation expense	9,000	4,000	Prepaid expenses (6)	
(3) Loss on equipment	3,000	2,000	Income taxes payable (8)	
(4) Accounts receivable	10,000			
(7) Accounts payable	16,000			
Net cash provided by operating activities	172,000			
Investing				
(3) Sold equipment	4,000	120,000	Purchased building (10)	
		25,000	Purchased equipment (11)	
		141,000	Net cash used by investing activities	
Financing				
(12) Issued common stock	20,000	29,000	Dividend paid (13)	
		9,000	Net cash used by financing activities	
Net increase in cash	22,000			

Accounts Receivable		Inventory		Prepaid Expenses		Land	
30,000		10,000		1,000		20,000	
	10,000 (4)	(5) 5,000		(6) 4,000		(9) 110,000	
20,000		15,000		5,000		130,000	

Buildings		Accumulated Depreciation—Buildings		Equipment		Accumulated Depreciation—Equipment	
40,000			5,000	10,000			1,000
(10) 120,000			6,000 (2)	(11) 25,000	8,000 (3)	(3) 1,000	3,000 (2)
160,000			11,000	27,000			3,000

Accounts Payable		Income Taxes Payable		Bonds Payable		Common Stock		Retained Earnings	
	12,000		8,000		20,000		50,000		48,000
	16,000 (7)	(8) 2,000			110,000 (9)		20,000 (12)		145,000 (1)
	28,000		6,000		130,000		70,000	(13) 29,000	
									164,000

9. Analyze the changes in the noncurrent accounts. Land was purchased by issuing bonds payable. This requires a debit to Land for $110,000 and a credit to Bonds Payable for $110,000. Note that this is a significant noncash event that requires disclosure at the bottom of the statement of cash flows.

10. Buildings is debited for $120,000, and the investing section of the Cash T-account is credited for $120,000 as a use of cash from investing.

11. Equipment is debited for $25,000 and the investing section of the Cash T-account is credited for $25,000 as a use of cash from investing.

12. Common Stock is credited for $20,000 for the issuance of shares of stock, and the financing section of the Cash T-account is debited for $20,000.

13. Retained Earnings is debited to reflect the payment of the $29,000 dividend, and the financing section of the Cash T-account is credited to reflect the use of Cash.

At this point, all of the changes in the noncash accounts have been explained. All that remains is to subtotal each section of the Cash T-account and compare the total change in cash with the change shown on the balance sheet. Once this is done, the information in the Cash T-account can be used to prepare a statement of cash flows.

Review and Practice

Learning Objectives Review

1 Discuss the usefulness and format of the statement of cash flows.

The statement of cash flows provides information about the cash receipts, cash payments, and net change in cash resulting from the operating, investing, and financing activities of a company during the period. Operating activities include the cash effects of transactions that enter into the determination of net income. Investing activities involve cash flows resulting from changes in investments and long-term asset items. Financing activities involve cash flows resulting from changes in long-term liability and stockholders' equity items.

2 Prepare a statement of cash flows using the indirect method.

The preparation of a statement of cash flows involves three major steps. (1) Determine net cash provided/used by operating activities by converting net income from an accrual basis to a cash basis. (2) Analyze changes in noncurrent asset and liability accounts and stockholders' equity accounts and report as investing and financing activities, or disclose as noncash transactions. (3) Compare the net change in cash on the statement of cash flows with the change in the Cash account reported on the balance sheet to make sure the amounts agree.

3 Analyze the statement of cash flows.

Free cash flow indicates the amount of cash a company generated during the current year that is available for the payment of additional dividends or for expansion.

*4 Prepare a statement of cash flows using the direct method.

The preparation of the statement of cash flows involves three major steps. (1) Determine net cash provided/used by adjusting each item in the income statement from the accrual basis to the cash basis. (2) Analyze changes in noncurrent asset and liability accounts and stockholders' equity accounts and record as investing and financing activities, or disclose as noncash transactions. (3) Compare the net change in cash on the statement of cash flows with the change in the Cash account reported on the balance sheet to make sure the amounts agree. The direct method reports cash receipts less cash payments to arrive at net cash provided by operating activities.

*5 Use a worksheet to prepare the statement of cash flows using the indirect method.

When there are numerous adjustments, a worksheet can be a helpful tool in preparing the statement of cash flows. Key guidelines for using a worksheet are as follows. (1) List accounts with debit balances separately from those with credit balances. (2) In the reconciling columns in the bottom portion of the worksheet, show cash inflows as debits and cash outflows as credits. (3) Do not enter reconciling items in any journal or account, but use them only to help prepare the statement of cash flows.

The steps in preparing the worksheet are as follows. (1) Enter beginning and ending balances of balance sheet accounts. (2) Enter debits and credits in reconciling columns. (3) Enter the increase or decrease in cash in two places as a balancing amount.

*6 Use the T-account approach to prepare a statement of cash flows.

To use T-accounts to prepare the statement of cash flows: (1) prepare a large Cash T-account with sections for operating, investing, and financing activities; (2) prepare smaller T-accounts for all other noncash accounts; (3) insert beginning and ending balances for all balance sheet accounts; and (4) follows the steps in Illustration 12C.1, entering debit and credit amounts as needed.

Glossary Review

*Direct method A method of preparing a statement of cash flows that shows operating cash receipts and payments. It is prepared by adjusting each item in the income statement from the accrual basis to the cash basis. (pp. 12-7, 12-19).

Financing activities Cash flow activities that include (a) obtaining cash from issuing debt and repaying the amounts borrowed and (b) obtaining cash from stockholders, repurchasing shares, and paying dividends. (p. 12-3).

Free cash flow   Net cash provided by operating activities adjusted for capital expenditures and cash dividends paid. (p. 12-17).

Indirect method   A method of preparing a statement of cash flows in which net income is adjusted for items that do not affect cash, to determine net cash provided by operating activities. (pp. 12-7, 12-9).

Investing activities   Cash flow activities that include (a) purchasing and disposing of investments and property, plant, and equipment using cash and (b) lending money and collecting the loans. (p. 12-3).

Operating activities   Cash flow activities that include the cash effects of transactions that generate revenues and expenses and thus enter into the determination of net income. (p. 12-3).

Statement of cash flows   A basic financial statement that provides information about the cash receipts, cash payments, and net change in cash during a period, resulting from operating, investing, and financing activities. (p. 12-3).

Practice Multiple-Choice Questions

1. (LO 1) Which of the following is **incorrect** about the statement of cash flows?

   a. It is a fourth basic financial statement.

   b. It provides information about cash receipts and cash payments of an entity during a period.

   c. It reconciles the ending Cash account balance to the balance per the bank statement.

   d. It provides information about the operating, investing, and financing activities of the business.

2. (LO 1) Which of the following is **not** reported in the statement of cash flows?

   a. The net change in stockholders' equity during the year.

   b. Cash payments for plant assets during the year.

   c. Cash receipts from sales of plant assets during the year.

   d. How acquisitions of plant assets during the year were financed.

3. (LO 1) The statement of cash flows classifies cash receipts and cash payments into these activities:

   a. operating and nonoperating.

   b. investing, financing, and operating.

   c. financing, operating, and nonoperating.

   d. investing, financing, and nonoperating.

4. (LO 1) Which is an example of a cash flow from an operating activity?

   a. Payment of cash to lenders for interest.

   b. Receipt of cash from the sale of common stock.

   c. Payment of cash dividends to the company's stockholders.

   d. None of the answer choices is correct.

5. (LO 1) Which is an example of a cash flow from an investing activity?

   a. Receipt of cash from the issuance of bonds payable.

   b. Payment of cash to repurchase outstanding common stock.

   c. Receipt of cash from the sale of equipment.

   d. Payment of cash to suppliers for inventory.

6. (LO 1) Cash dividends paid to stockholders are classified on the statement of cash flows as:

   a. an operating activity.

   b. an investing activity.

   c. a combination of an operating activity and an investing activity.

   d. a financing activity.

7. (LO 1) Which is an example of a cash flow from a financing activity?

   a. Receipt of cash from sale of land.

   b. Issuance of debt for cash.

   c. Purchase of equipment for cash.

   d. None of the answer choices is correct.

8. (LO 1) Which of the following is **incorrect** about the statement of cash flows?

   a. The direct method may be used to report net cash provided by operating activities.

   b. The statement shows the net cash provided (used) for three categories of activity.

   c. The operating section is the last section of the statement.

   d. The indirect method may be used to report net cash provided by operating activities.

Use the indirect method to solve Questions 9 through 11.

9. (LO 2) Net income is $132,000, accounts payable increased $10,000 during the year, inventory decreased $6,000 during the year, and accounts receivable increased $12,000 during the year. Under the indirect method, what is net cash provided by operating activities?

   a. $102,000.   **c.** $124,000.

   b. $112,000.   **d.** $136,000.

10. (LO 2) Items that are added back to net income in determining net cash provided by operating activities under the indirect method do **not** include:

   a. depreciation expense.

   b. an increase in inventory.

   c. amortization expense.

   d. loss on disposal of plant assets.

11. (LO 2) The following data are available for Bill Mack Corporation.

Net income	$200,000
Depreciation expense	40,000
Dividends paid	60,000
Gain on sale of land	10,000
Decrease in accounts receivable	20,000
Decrease in accounts payable	30,000

Net cash provided by operating activities is:

   a. $160,000.   **c.** $240,000.

   b. $220,000.   **d.** $280,000.

12. (LO 2) The following data are available for Orange Peels Corporation.

Proceeds from sale of land	$100,000
Proceeds from sale of equipment	50,000
Issuance of common stock	70,000
Purchase of equipment	30,000
Payment of cash dividends	60,000

Net cash provided by investing activities is:

a. $120,000.   **c.** $150,000.

b. $130,000.   **d.** $190,000.

13. (LO 2) The following data are available for Retique!

Increase in accounts payable	$ 40,000
Increase in bonds payable	100,000
Sale of investment	50,000
Issuance of common stock	60,000
Payment of cash dividends	30,000

Net cash provided by financing activities is:

a. $90,000.   **c.** $160,000.

b. $130,000.   **d.** $170,000.

14. (LO 3) The statement of cash flows should **not** be used to evaluate an entity's ability to:

a. generate net income.   **c.** pay dividends.

b. generate future cash flows.   **d.** meet obligations.

15. (LO 3) Free cash flow provides an indication of a company's ability to:

a. manage inventory.

b. generate cash to pay additional dividends.

c. generate cash to invest in new capital expenditures.

d. both generate cash to pay additional dividends and invest in new capital expenditures.

Use the direct method to solve Questions 16 and 17.

*16. **(LO 4)** The beginning balance in accounts receivable is $44,000, the ending balance is $42,000, and sales during the period are $129,000. What are cash receipts from customers?

a. $127,000.

b. $129,000.

c. $131,000.

d. $141,000.

*17. **(LO 4)** Which of the following items is reported on a statement of cash flows prepared by the direct method?

a. Loss on sale of building.

b. Increase in accounts receivable.

c. Depreciation expense.

d. Cash payments to suppliers.

*18. **(LO 5)** In a worksheet for the statement of cash flows, a decrease in accounts receivable is entered in the reconciling columns as a credit to Accounts Receivable and a debit in the:

a. investing activities section.

b. operating activities section.

c. financing activities section.

d. None of the answer choices is correct.

*19. **(LO 5)** In a worksheet for the statement of cash flows, a worksheet entry that includes a credit to accumulated depreciation will also include a:

a. credit in the operating activities section and a debit in another section.

b. debit in the operating activities section.

c. debit in the investing activities section.

d. debit in the financing activities section.

Solutions

1. c. The statement of cash flows does not reconcile the ending cash balance to the balance per the bank statement. The other choices are true statements.

2. a. The net change in stockholders' equity during the year is not reported in the statement of cash flows. The other choices are true statements.

3. b. Operating, investing, and financing activities are the three classifications of cash receipts and cash payments used in the statement of cash flows. The other choices are therefore incorrect.

4. a. Payment of cash to lenders for interest is an operating activity. The other choices are incorrect because (b) receipt of cash from the sale of common stock is a financing activity, (c) payment of cash dividends to the company's stockholders is a financing activity, and (d) there is a correct answer.

5. c. Receipt of cash from the sale of equipment is an investing activity. The other choices are incorrect because (a) the receipt of cash from the issuance of bonds payable is a financing activity, (b) payment of cash to repurchase outstanding common stock is a financing activity, and (d) payment of cash to suppliers for inventory is an operating activity.

6. d. Cash dividends paid to stockholders are classified as a financing activity, not (a) an operating activity, (b) an investing activity, or (c) a combination of an operating and an investing activity.

7. b. Issuance of debt for cash is a financing activity. The other choices are incorrect because (a) the receipt of cash from the sale of land is an investing activity, (c) the purchase of equipment for cash is an investing activity, and (d) there is a correct answer.

8. c. The operating section of the statement of cash flows is the first, not the last, section of the statement. The other choices are true statements.

9. d. Net cash provided by operating activities is computed by adjusting net income for the changes in the three current asset/current liability accounts listed. An increase in accounts payable ($10,000) and a decrease in inventory ($6,000) are added to net income ($132,000), while an increase in accounts receivable ($12,000) is subtracted from net income, or $132,000 + $10,000 + $6,000 − $12,000 = $136,000, not (a) $102,000, (b) $112,000, or (c) $124,000.

10. b. An increase in inventory is subtracted, not added, to net income in determining net cash provided by operating activities. The other choices are incorrect because (a) depreciation expense,

(c) amortization expense, and (d) loss on disposal of plant assets are all added back to net income in determining net cash provided by operating activities.

11. b. Net cash provided by operating activities is $220,000 (Net income $200,000 + Depreciation expense $40,000 – Gain on sale of land $10,000 + Decrease in accounts receivable $20,000 – Decrease in accounts payable $30,000), not (a) $160,000, (c) $240,000, or (d) $280,000.

12. a. Net cash provided by investing activities is $120,000 (Sale of land $100,000 + Sale of equipment $50,000 – Purchase of equipment $30,000), not (b) $130,000, (c) $150,000, or (d) $190,000. Issuance of common stock and payment of cash dividends are financing activities.

13. b. Net cash provided by financing activities is $130,000 (Increase in bonds payable $100,000 + Issuance of common stock $60,000 – Payment of cash dividends $30,000), not (a) $90,000, (c) $160,000, or (d) $170,000. Increase in accounts payable is an operating activity and sale of investment is an investing activity.

14. a. The statement of cash flows is not used to evaluate an entity's ability to generate net income. The other choices are true statements.

15. d. Free cash flow provides an indication of a company's ability to generate cash to pay additional dividends and invest in new capital

expenditures. Choice (a) is incorrect because other measures besides free cash flow provide the best measure of a company's ability to manage inventory. Choices (b) and (c) are true statements, but (d) is the better answer.

*16. c. Cash from customers amount to $131,000 ($129,000 + a decrease in accounts receivable of $2,000). The other choices are therefore incorrect.

*17. d. Cash payments to suppliers are reported on a statement of cash flows prepared by the direct method. The other choices are incorrect because (a) loss on sale of building, (b) increase in accounts receivable, and (c) depreciation expense are reported in the operating activities section of the statement of cash flows when the indirect, not direct, method is used.

*18. b. Because accounts receivable is a current asset, the debit belongs in the operating activities section of the worksheet, not in the (a) investing activities or (c) financing activities section. Choice (d) is incorrect as there is a right answer.

*19. b. A worksheet entry that includes a credit to accumulated depreciation will also include a debit to depreciation expense. This debit in the operating activities section of the statement of cash flows will be added to the net income to determine net cash provided by operating activities. The other choices are therefore incorrect.

Practice Brief Exercises

1. (LO 1) The following is a summary of the Cash account of Covey Company:

Identify investing activity transactions.

Cash (Summary Form)

Balance, Jan. 1	8,000		
Receipts from customers	364,000	Payments for goods	200,000
Dividends on stock investments	6,000	Payments for operating expenses	140,000
Proceeds from sale of land	96,000	Purchase of equipment	70,000
Proceeds from issuance of bonds		Taxes paid	8,000
payable	300,000	Dividends paid	50,000
Balance, Dec. 31	306,000		

What amount of net cash provided (used) by investing activities should be reported in the statement of cash flows?

Solution

1. Cash flows from investing activities

Proceeds from sale of land	$96,000
Purchase of equipment	(70,000)
Net cash provided by investing activities	$26,000

Note the dividends on stock investments is classified as an operating cash flow.

2. (LO 2) Engel, Inc. reported net income of $1.6 million in 2022. Depreciation for the year was $140,000, accounts receivable increased $250,000, and accounts payable increased $210,000. The company also had a gain on disposal of plant assets of $19,000. Compute net cash provided by operating activities using the indirect method.

Compute net cash provided by operating activities—indirect method.

Solution

2. Net income $1,600,000
  Adjustments to reconcile net income to net cash
    provided by operating activities
    Depreciation expense $ 140,000
    Gain on disposal of plant assets   (19,000)
    Accounts receivable increase   (250,000)
    Accounts payable increase   210,000   81,000
      Net cash provided by operating activities $1,681,000

Calculate free cash flow.

3. **(LO 3)** Goldberg Corporation reported net cash provided by operating activities of $410,000, net cash used by investing activities of $200,000 (including cash spent for equipment of $160,000), and net cash provided by financing activities of $60,000. Dividends of $110,000 were paid. Calculate free cash flow.

Solution

3. Free cash flow = $410,000 − $160,000 − $110,000 = $140,000

Practice Exercises

Prepare journal entries to determine effect on statement of cash flows.

1. **(LO 2)** Furst Corporation had the following transactions.

   1. Paid salaries of $14,000.
   2. Issued 1,000 shares of $1 par value common stock for equipment worth $16,000.
   3. Sold equipment (cost $10,000, accumulated depreciation $6,000) for $3,000.
   4. Sold land (cost $12,000) for $16,000.
   5. Issued another 1,000 shares of $1 par value common stock for $18,000.
   6. Recorded depreciation of $20,000.

Instructions

For each transaction above, **(a)** prepare the journal entry, and **(b)** indicate how it would affect the statement of cash flows. Assume the indirect method.

Solution

1. 1. **a.** Salaries and Wages Expense   14,000
        Cash   14,000

   b. Salaries and wages expense is not reported separately on the statement of cash flows. It is part of the computation of net income in the income statement and is included in the net income amount on the statement of cash flows.

   2. **a.** Equipment   16,000
        Common Stock   1,000
        Paid-in Capital in Excess of Par—Common Stock   15,000

   b. The issuance of common stock for equipment ($16,000) is reported as a noncash financing and investing activity at the bottom of the statement of cash flows.

3. a. Cash | | 3,000 |
 Loss on Disposal of Plant Assets | | 1,000 |
 Accumulated Depreciation—Equipment | | 6,000 |
 Equipment | | | 10,000

   b. The cash receipt ($3,000) is reported in the investing section. The loss ($1,000) is added to net income in the operating section.

4. a. Cash | | 16,000 |
 Land | | | 12,000
 Gain on Disposal of Plant Assets | | | 4,000

   b. The cash receipt ($16,000) is reported in the investing section. The gain ($4,000) is deducted from net income in the operating section.

5. a. Cash | | 18,000 |
 Common Stock | | | 1,000
 Paid-in Capital in Excess of Par—Common Stock | | | 17,000

   b. The cash receipt ($18,000) is reported in the financing section.

6. a. Depreciation Expense | | 20,000 |
 Accumulated Depreciation—Equipment | | | 20,000

   b. Depreciation expense ($20,000) is added to net income in the operating section.

2. **(LO 2, 3)** Strong Corporation's comparative balance sheets are as follows.

Prepare statement of cash flows and compute free cash flow.

Strong Corporation
Comparative Balance Sheets
December 31

	2022	2021
Cash	$ 28,200	$ 17,700
Accounts receivable	24,200	22,300
Investments	23,000	16,000
Equipment	60,000	70,000
Accumulated depreciation—equipment	(14,000)	(10,000)
Total	$121,400	$116,000
Accounts payable	$ 19,600	$ 11,100
Bonds payable	10,000	30,000
Common stock	60,000	45,000
Retained earnings	31,800	29,900
Total	$121,400	$116,000

Additional information:

1. Net income was $28,300. Dividends declared and paid were $26,400. Depreciation expense was $5,200.

2. Equipment which cost $10,000 and had accumulated depreciation of $1,200 was sold for $4,300.

3. All other changes in noncurrent accounts had a direct effect on cash flows, except the change in accumulated depreciation.

Instructions

   a. Prepare a statement of cash flows for 2022 using the indirect method.

   b. Compute free cash flow.

Solution

2. a.

Strong Corporation
Statement of Cash Flows
For the Year Ended December 31, 2022

Cash flows from operating activities		
Net income		$ 28,300
Adjustments to reconcile net income		
to net cash provided by operating activities:		
Depreciation expense	$ 5,200	
Loss on disposal of plant assets	4,500*	
Increase in accounts payable	8,500	
Increase in accounts receivable	(1,900)	16,300
Net cash provided by operating activities		44,600
Cash flows from investing activities		
Sale of equipment	4,300	
Purchase of investments	(7,000)	
Net cash used by investing activities		(2,700)
Cash flows from financing activities		
Issuance of common stock	15,000	
Retirement of bonds	(20,000)	
Payment of dividends	(26,400)	
Net cash used by financing activities		(31,400)
Net increase in cash		10,500
Cash at beginning of period		17,700
Cash at end of period		$ 28,200

*[$4,300 − ($10,000 − $1,200)]

b. Free cash flow = $44,600 − $0 − $26,400 = $18,200

Practice Problem

Prepare statement of cash flows using indirect and direct methods.

(LO 2, 4) The income statement for the year ended December 31, 2022, for Kosinski Manufacturing Company contains the following condensed information.

Kosinski Manufacturing Company
Income Statement
For the Year Ended December 31, 2022

Sales revenue		$6,583,000
Cost of goods sold	$2,810,000	
Operating expenses (excluding depreciation)	2,086,000	
Depreciation expense	880,000	
Loss on disposal of plant assets	24,000	5,800,000
Income before income taxes		783,000
Income tax expense		353,000
Net income		$ 430,000

The $24,000 loss resulted from selling equipment for $270,000 cash. New equipment was purchased for $750,000 cash.

The following balances are reported on Kosinski's comparative balance sheets at December 31.

Kosinski Manufacturing Company
Comparative Balance Sheets (partial)

	2022	2021
Cash	$672,000	$130,000
Accounts receivable	775,000	610,000
Inventory	834,000	867,000
Accounts payable	521,000	501,000

Income tax expense of $353,000 represents the amount paid in 2022. Dividends declared and paid in 2022 totaled $200,000.

Instructions

a. Prepare the statement of cash flows using the indirect method.

*b. Prepare the statement of cash flows using the direct method.

Solution

a.

Kosinski Manufacturing Company
Statement of Cash Flows—Indirect Method
For the Year Ended December 31, 2022

Cash flows from operating activities		
Net income		$ 430,000
Adjustments to reconcile net income to net cash		
provided by operating activities:		
Depreciation expense	$ 880,000	
Loss on disposal of plant assets	24,000	
Increase in accounts receivable	(165,000)	
Decrease in inventory	33,000	
Increase in accounts payable	20,000	792,000
Net cash provided by operating activities		1,222,000
Cash flows from investing activities		
Sale of equipment	270,000	
Purchase of equipment	(750,000)	
Net cash used by investing activities		(480,000)
Cash flows from financing activities		
Payment of cash dividends	(200,000)	
Net cash used by financing activities		(200,000)
Net increase in cash		542,000
Cash at beginning of period		130,000
Cash at end of period		$ 672,000

*b.

Kosinski Manufacturing Company
Statement of Cash Flows—Direct Method
For the Year Ended December 31, 2022

Cash flows from operating activities		
Cash collections from customers		$6,418,000*
Less: Cash payments:		
To suppliers	$2,757,000**	
For operating expenses	2,086,000	
For income taxes	353,000	5,196,000
Net cash provided by operating activities		1,222,000

Cash flows from investing activities		
Sale of equipment	270,000	
Purchase of equipment	(750,000)	
Net cash used by investing activities		(480,000)
Cash flows from financing activities		
Payment of cash dividends	(200,000)	
Net cash used by financing activities		(200,000)
Net increase in cash		542,000
Cash at beginning of period		130,000
Cash at end of period		$ 672,000

Direct-Method Computations:

*Computation of cash collections from customers:

Sales revenue	$6,583,000
Deduct: Increase in accounts receivable	(165,000)
Cash collections from customers	$6,418,000

**Computation of cash payments to suppliers

Cost of goods sold per income statement	$2,810,000
Deduct: Decrease in inventories	(33,000)
Deduct: Increase in accounts payable	(20,000)
Cash payments to suppliers	$2,757,000

WileyPLUS

Brief Exercises, DO IT! Exercises, Exercises, Problems, and many additional resources are available for practice in WileyPLUS.

Note: All asterisked Questions, Exercises, and Problems relate to material in the appendices to the chapter.

Questions

1. a. What is a statement of cash flows?

   b. Pat Marx maintains that the statement of cash flows is an optional financial statement. Do you agree? Explain.

2. What questions about cash are answered by the statement of cash flows?

3. Distinguish among the three types of activities reported in the statement of cash flows.

4. a. What are the major sources (inflows) of cash?

   b. What are the major uses (outflows) of cash?

5. Why is it important to disclose certain noncash transactions? How should they be disclosed?

6. Helen Powell and Paul Tang were discussing the format of the statement of cash flows of Baumgarten Co. At the bottom of Baumgarten's statement of cash flows was a separate section entitled "Noncash investing and financing activities." Give three examples of significant noncash transactions that would be reported in this section.

7. Why is it necessary to use comparative balance sheets, a current income statement, and certain transaction data in preparing a statement of cash flows?

8. Contrast the advantages and disadvantages of the direct and indirect methods of preparing the statement of cash flows. Are both methods acceptable? Which method is preferred by the FASB? Which method is more popular?

9. When the total cash inflows exceed the total cash outflows in the statement of cash flows, how and where is this excess identified?

10. Describe the indirect method for determining net cash provided (used) by operating activities.

11. Why is it necessary to convert accrual-basis net income to cash-basis income when preparing a statement of cash flows?

12. The president of Murquery Company is puzzled. During the last year, the company experienced a net loss of $800,000, yet its cash increased $300,000 during the same period of time. Explain to the president how this could occur.

13. Identify five items that are adjustments to convert net income to net cash provided by operating activities under the indirect method.

14. Why and how is depreciation expense reported in a statement of cash flows prepared using the indirect method?

15. Why is the statement of cash flows useful?

16. During 2022, Slivowitz Doubleday Company converted $1,700,000 of its total $2,000,000 of bonds payable into common stock. Indicate how the transaction would be reported on a statement of cash flows, if at all.

17. In its 2018 statement of cash flows, what amount did **Apple** report for net cash (a) provided by operating activities, (b) used for investing activities, and (c) used for financing activities?

*18. Describe the direct method for determining net cash provided by operating activities.

*19. Give the formulas under the direct method for computing (a) cash receipts from customers and (b) cash payments to suppliers.

*20. Harbinger Inc. reported sales of $2 million for 2022. Accounts receivable decreased $150,000 and accounts payable increased $300,000. Compute cash receipts from customers, assuming that the receivable and payable transactions are related to operations.

*21. In the direct method, why is depreciation expense not reported in the cash flows from operating activities section?

*22. Why is it advantageous to use a worksheet when preparing a statement of cash flows? Is a worksheet required to prepare a statement of cash flows?

Brief Exercises

BE12.1 (LO 1), C Each of these items must be considered in preparing a statement of cash flows for Irvin Co. for the year ended December 31, 2022. For each item, state how it should be shown in the statement of cash flows for 2022.

Indicate statement presentation of selected transactions.

   a. Issued bonds for $200,000 cash.

   b. Purchased equipment for $180,000 cash.

   c. Sold land costing $20,000 for $20,000 cash.

   d. Declared and paid a $50,000 cash dividend.

BE12.2 (LO 1), C Classify each item as an operating, investing, or financing activity. Assume all items involve cash unless there is information to the contrary.

Classify items by activities.

   a. Purchase of equipment.   **d.** Cash received from sale of goods.

   b. Proceeds from sale of building.   **e.** Payment of dividends.

   c. Redemption of bonds payable.   **f.** Issuance of common stock.

BE12.3 (LO 1), AP The following T-account is a summary of the Cash account of Alixon Company.

Identify financing activity transactions.

Cash (Summary Form)

Balance, Jan. 1	8,000		
Receipts from customers	364,000	Payments for goods	200,000
Dividends on stock investments	6,000	Payments for operating expenses	140,000
Proceeds from sale of equipment	36,000	Interest paid	10,000
Proceeds from issuance of		Taxes paid	8,000
bonds payable	300,000	Dividends paid	40,000
Balance, Dec. 31	316,000		

What amount of net cash provided (used) by financing activities should be reported in the statement of cash flows?

BE12.4 (LO 2), AP Miguel, Inc. reported net income of $2.5 million in 2022. Depreciation for the year was $160,000, accounts receivable decreased $350,000, and accounts payable decreased $280,000. Compute net cash provided by operating activities using the indirect method.

Compute net cash provided by operating activities—indirect method.

BE12.5 (LO 2), AP The net income for Mongan Co. for 2022 was $280,000. For 2022, depreciation on plant assets was $70,000, and the company incurred a loss on disposal of plant assets of $28,000. Compute net cash provided by operating activities under the indirect method, assuming there were no other changes in the company's accounts.

Compute net cash provided by operating activities—indirect method.

BE12.6 (LO 2), AP The comparative balance sheets for Gale Company show these changes in noncash current asset accounts: accounts receivable decreased $80,000, prepaid expenses increased $28,000, and inventories increased $40,000. Compute net cash provided by operating activities using the indirect method, assuming that net income is $186,000.

Compute net cash provided by operating activities—indirect method.

Determine cash received from sale of equipment.

BE12.7 (LO 2), AN The T-accounts for Equipment and the related Accumulated Depreciation—Equipment for Goldstone Company at the end of 2022 are shown here.

Equipment					Accum. Depr.—Equipment			
Beg. bal.	80,000	Disposals	22,000		Disposals	5,100	Beg. bal.	44,500
Acquisitions	41,600						Depr. exp.	12,000
End. bal.	99,600						End. bal.	51,400

In addition, Goldstone's income statement reported a loss on the disposal of plant assets of $3,500. What amount was reported on the statement of cash flows as "cash flow from sale of equipment"?

Calculate free cash flow.

BE12.8 (LO 3), AP Suppose that during 2022 **Cypress Semiconductor Corporation** reported net cash provided by operating activities of $89,303,000, cash used in investing of $43,126,000, and cash used in financing of $7,368,000. In addition, cash spent for fixed assets during the period was $25,823,000. No dividends were paid. Calculate free cash flow.

Calculate free cash flow.

BE12.9 (LO 3), AP Sprouts Corporation reported net cash provided by operating activities of $412,000, net cash used by investing activities of $250,000, and net cash provided by financing activities of $70,000. In addition, cash spent for capital assets during the period was $200,000. No dividends were paid. Calculate free cash flow.

Calculate free cash flow.

BE12.10 (LO 3), AP Suppose **Shaw Communications** reported net cash used by operating activities of $104,539,000 and sales revenue of $2,867,459,000 during 2022. Cash spent on plant asset additions during the year was $79,330,000. Calculate free cash flow.

Calculate and analyze free cash flow.

BE12.11 (LO 3), AN The management of Uhuru Inc. is trying to decide whether it can increase its dividend. During the current year, it reported net income of $875,000. It had net cash provided by operating activities of $734,000, paid cash dividends of $92,000, and had capital expenditures of $310,000. Compute the company's free cash flow, and discuss whether an increase in the dividend appears warranted. What other factors should be considered?

Compute receipts from customers—direct method.

* **BE12.12 (LO 4), AP** Suppose **Columbia Sportswear Company** had accounts receivable of $299,585,000 at January 1, 2022, and $226,548,000 at December 31, 2022. Assume sales revenue was $1,244,023,000 for the year 2022. What is the amount of cash receipts from customers in 2022?

Compute cash payments for income taxes—direct method.

* **BE12.13 (LO 4), AP** Hoffman Corporation reported income taxes of $370,000,000 on its 2022 income statement and income taxes payable of $277,000,000 at December 31, 2021, and $528,000,000 at December 31, 2022. What amount of cash payments were made for income taxes during 2022?

Compute cash payments for operating expenses—direct method.

* **BE12.14 (LO 4), AP** Pietr Corporation reports operating expenses of $90,000, excluding depreciation expense of $15,000, for 2022. During the year, prepaid expenses decreased $7,200 and accrued expenses payable increased $4,400. Compute the cash payments for operating expenses in 2022.

DO IT! Exercises

Classify transactions by type of cash flow activity.

DO IT! 12.1 (LO 1), C Moss Corporation had the following transactions.

1. Issued $160,000 of bonds payable.
2. Paid utilities expense.
3. Issued 500 shares of preferred stock for $45,000.
4. Sold land and a building for $250,000.
5. Loaned $30,000 to Dead End Corporation, receiving Dead End's 1-year, 12% note.

Classify each of these transactions by type of cash flow activity (operating, investing, or financing). (*Hint:* Refer to Illustration 12.1.)

Calculate net cash from operating activities.

DO IT! 12.2a (LO 2), AP PK Photography reported net income of $100,000 for 2022. Included in the income statement were depreciation expense of $6,300, patent amortization expense of $4,000, and a gain on disposal of plant assets of $3,600. PK's comparative balance sheets show the following balances.

	12/31/22	12/31/21
Accounts receivable	$21,000	$27,000
Accounts payable	9,200	6,000

Calculate net cash provided by operating activities for PK Photography.

DO IT! 12.2b (LO 2), AN Alex Company reported the following information for 2022.

Prepare statement of cash flows—indirect method.

Alex Company
Comparative Balance Sheets
December 31

Assets	2022	2021	Change Increase/Decrease	
Cash	$ 59,000	$ 36,000	$ 23,000	Increase
Accounts receivable	62,000	22,000	40,000	Increase
Inventory	44,000	–0–	44,000	Increase
Prepaid expenses	6,000	4,000	2,000	Increase
Land	55,000	70,000	15,000	Decrease
Buildings	200,000	200,000	–0–	No change
Accumulated depreciation—buildings	(21,000)	(14,000)	7,000	Increase
Equipment	183,000	68,000	115,000	Increase
Accumulated depreciation—equipment	(28,000)	(10,000)	18,000	Increase
Totals	$560,000	$376,000		

Liabilities and Stockholders' Equity	2022	2021	Change Increase/Decrease	
Accounts payable	$ 43,000	$ 40,000	$ 3,000	Increase
Accrued expenses payable	–0–	10,000	10,000	Decrease
Bonds payable	100,000	150,000	50,000	Decrease
Common stock ($1 par)	230,000	60,000	170,000	Increase
Retained earnings	187,000	116,000	71,000	Increase
Totals	$560,000	$376,000		

Alex Company
Income Statement
For the Year Ended December 31, 2022

Sales revenue		$941,000
Cost of goods sold	$475,000	
Operating expenses	231,000	
Interest expense	12,000	
Loss on disposal of plant assets	2,000	720,000
Income before income taxes		221,000
Income tax expense		65,000
Net income		$156,000

Additional information:

1. Operating expenses include depreciation expense of $40,000.
2. Land was sold at its book value for cash.
3. Cash dividends of $85,000 were declared and paid in 2022.
4. Equipment with a cost of $166,000 was purchased for cash. Equipment with a cost of $51,000 and a book value of $36,000 was sold for $34,000 cash.
5. Bonds of $50,000 were redeemed at their face value for cash.
6. Common stock ($1 par) was issued at par for $170,000 cash.

Use this information to prepare a statement of cash flows using the indirect method.

Compute and discuss free cash flow.

DO IT! 12.3 (LO 3), AP Moskow Corporation issued the following statement of cash flows for 2022.

Moskow Corporation Statement of Cash Flows—Indirect Method For the Year Ended December 31, 2022		
Cash flows from operating activities		
Net income		$ 59,000
Adjustments to reconcile net income to net cash provided by operating activities:		
Depreciation expense	$ 9,100	
Decrease in accounts receivable	9,500	
Increase in inventory	(5,000)	
Decrease in accounts payable	(2,200)	
Loss on disposal of plant assets	3,300	14,700
Net cash provided by operating activities		73,700
Cash flows from investing activities		
Sale of investments	3,100	
Purchase of equipment	(24,200)	
Net cash used by investing activities		(21,100)
Cash flows from financing activities		
Issuance of common stock	20,000	
Payment on long-term note payable	(10,000)	
Payment of cash dividends	(13,000)	
Net cash used by financing activities		(3,000)
Net increase in cash		49,600
Cash at beginning of year		13,000
Cash at end of year		$ 62,600

a. Compute free cash flow for Moskow Corporation.

b. Explain why free cash flow often provides better information than "Net cash provided by operating activities."

Exercises

Classify transactions by type of activity.

E12.1 (LO 1), C Kiley Corporation had these transactions during 2022.

a. Purchased a machine for $30,000, giving a long-term note in exchange.

b. Issued $50,000 par value common stock for cash.

c. Issued $200,000 par value common stock upon conversion of bonds having a face value of $200,000.

d. Declared and paid a cash dividend of $13,000.

e. Sold a long-term investment with a cost of $15,000 for $15,000 cash.

f. Collected $16,000 from sale of goods.

g. Paid $18,000 to suppliers.

Instructions

Analyze the transactions and indicate whether each transaction is an operating activity, investing activity, financing activity, or noncash investing and financing activity.

Classify transactions by type of activity.

E12.2 (LO 1), C An analysis of comparative balance sheets, the current year's income statement, and the general ledger accounts of Hailey Corp. uncovered the following items. Assume all items involve cash unless there is information to the contrary.

a. Exchange of land for patent.

b. Sale of building at book value.

c. Payment of dividends.

d. Depreciation of plant assets.

e. Conversion of bonds into common stock.

f. Issuance of capital stock.

g. Amortization of patent.

h. Issuance of bonds for land.

i. Purchase of land.

j. Loss on disposal of plant assets.

k. Retirement of bonds.

Instructions

Indicate where each item should be presented in the statement of cash flows (indirect method) using these four major classifications: operating activity (that is, the item would be listed among the adjustments to net income to determine net cash provided by operating activities under the indirect method), investing activity, financing activity, or significant noncash investing and financing activity.

E12.3 (LO 1), AP Cushenberry Corporation had the following transactions.

    1. Sold land (cost $12,000) for $15,000.

    2. Issued common stock at par for $20,000.

    3. Recorded depreciation on buildings for $17,000.

    4. Paid salaries of $9,000.

    5. Issued 1,000 shares of $1 par value common stock for equipment worth $8,000.

    6. Sold equipment (cost $10,000, accumulated depreciation $7,000) for $1,200.

Prepare journal entry and determine effect on cash flows.

Instructions

For each transaction above, (a) prepare the journal entry, and (b) indicate how it would affect the statement of cash flows using the indirect method.

E12.4 (LO 2), AP Sosa Company reported net income of $190,000 for 2022. Sosa also reported depreciation expense of $35,000 and a loss of $5,000 on the disposal of plant assets. The comparative balance sheets show an increase in accounts receivable of $15,000 for the year, a $17,000 increase in accounts payable, and a $4,000 increase in prepaid expenses.

Prepare the operating activities section—indirect method.

Instructions

Prepare the operating activities section of the statement of cash flows for 2022. Use the indirect method.

E12.5 (LO 2), AP The current sections of Sunn Inc.'s balance sheets at December 31, 2021 and 2022, are presented here. Sunn's net income for 2022 was $153,000. Depreciation expense was $27,000.

Prepare the operating activities section—indirect method.

	2022	2021
Current assets		
Cash	$105,000	$ 99,000
Accounts receivable	80,000	89,000
Inventory	168,000	172,000
Prepaid expenses	27,000	22,000
Total current assets	$380,000	$382,000
Current liabilities		
Accrued expenses payable	$ 15,000	$ 5,000
Accounts payable	85,000	92,000
Total current liabilities	$100,000	$ 97,000

Instructions

Prepare the operating activities section of the company's statement of cash flows for the year ended December 31, 2022, using the indirect method.

E12.6 (LO 2), AP The following information is available for Stamos Corporation for the year ended December 31, 2022.

Prepare statement of cash flows—indirect method.

Beginning cash balance	$ 45,000
Accounts payable decrease	3,700
Depreciation expense	162,000
Accounts receivable increase	8,200
Inventory increase	11,000
Net income	284,100
Cash received for sale of land at book value	35,000
Cash dividends paid	12,000
Income taxes payable increase	4,700
Cash used to purchase building	289,000
Cash used to purchase treasury stock	26,000
Cash received from issuing bonds	200,000

Instructions

Prepare a statement of cash flows using the indirect method.

Prepare partial statement of cash flows—indirect method.

E12.7 (LO 2), AN The following three accounts appear in the general ledger of Beiber Corp. during 2022.

Equipment

Date		Debit	Credit	Balance
Jan. 1	Balance			160,000
July 31	Purchase of equipment	70,000		230,000
Sept. 2	Purchase of equipment	53,000		283,000
Nov. 10	Cost of equipment sold		49,000	234,000

Accumulated Depreciation—Equipment

Date		Debit	Credit	Balance
Jan. 1	Balance			71,000
Nov. 10	Accumulated depreciation on equipment sold	16,000		55,000
Dec. 31	Depreciation for year		28,000	83,000

Retained Earnings

Date		Debit	Credit	Balance
Jan. 1	Balance			105,000
Aug. 23	Dividends (cash)	14,000		91,000
Dec. 31	Net income		72,000	163,000

Instructions

From the postings in the accounts, indicate how the information is reported on a statement of cash flows using the indirect method. The loss on disposal of plant assets was $8,000.

Prepare statement of cash flows and compute free cash flow.

E12.8 (LO 2, 3), AP Rojas Corporation's comparative balance sheets are presented below.

Rojas Corporation
Comparative Balance Sheets
December 31

	2022	2021
Cash	$ 14,300	$ 10,700
Accounts receivable	21,200	23,400
Land	20,000	26,000
Buildings	70,000	70,000
Accumulated depreciation—buildings	(15,000)	(10,000)
Total	$110,500	$120,100
Accounts payable	$ 12,370	$ 31,100
Common stock	75,000	69,000
Retained earnings	23,130	20,000
Total	$110,500	$120,100

Additional information:

1. Net income was $22,630. Dividends declared and paid were $19,500.

2. No noncash investing and financing activities occurred during 2022.

3. The land was sold for cash of $4,900.

Instructions

a. Prepare a statement of cash flows for 2022 using the indirect method.

b. Compute free cash flow.

E12.9 (LO 2), AP The following are comparative balance sheets for Mitch Company.

Prepare statement of cash flows—indirect method.

Mitch Company
Comparative Balance Sheets
December 31

	2022	2021
Assets		
Cash	$ 68,000	$ 22,000
Accounts receivable	88,000	76,000
Inventory	167,000	189,000
Land	80,000	100,000
Equipment	260,000	200,000
Accumulated depreciation—equipment	(66,000)	(32,000)
Total	$597,000	$555,000
Liabilities and Stockholders' Equity		
Accounts payable	$ 39,000	$ 43,000
Bonds payable	150,000	200,000
Common stock ($1 par)	216,000	174,000
Retained earnings	192,000	138,000
Total	$597,000	$555,000

Additional information:

1. Net income for 2022 was $93,000.

2. Depreciation expense was $34,000.

3. Cash dividends of $39,000 were declared and paid.

4. Bonds payable with a carrying value of $50,000 were redeemed for $50,000 cash.

5. Common stock was issued at par for $42,000 cash.

6. No equipment was sold during 2022.

7. Land was sold for its book value.

Instructions

Prepare a statement of cash flows for 2022 using the indirect method.

E12.10 (LO 2, 3), AP Rodriquez Corporation's comparative balance sheets are as follows.

Prepare statement of cash flows—indirect method and compute free cash flow.

Rodriquez Corporation
Comparative Balance Sheets
December 31

	2022	2021
Cash	$ 15,200	$ 17,700
Accounts receivable	25,200	22,300
Investments	20,000	16,000
Equipment	60,000	70,000
Accumulated depreciation—equipment	(14,000)	(10,000)
Total	$106,400	$116,000
Accounts payable	$ 14,600	$ 11,100
Bonds payable	10,000	30,000
Common stock	50,000	45,000
Retained earnings	31,800	29,900
Total	$106,400	$116,000

Additional information:

1. Net income was $18,300. Dividends declared and paid were $16,400.

2. Equipment which cost $10,000 and had accumulated depreciation of $1,200 was sold for $3,300.

3. No noncash investing and financing activities occurred during 2022.

4. Bonds were retired at their carrying value.

Instructions

a. Prepare a statement of cash flows for 2022 using the indirect method.

b. Compute free cash flow.

Compute net cash provided by operating activities—direct method.

*E12.11 (LO 4), AP Zimmer Company completed its first year of operations on December 31, 2022. Its initial income statement showed that Zimmer had sales revenue of $198,000 and operating expenses of $83,000. Accounts receivable and accounts payable at year-end were $60,000 and $23,000, respectively. Assume that accounts payable related to operating expenses. Ignore income taxes.

Instructions

Compute net cash provided by operating activity using the direct method.

Compute cash payments—direct method.

*E12.12 (LO 4), AP Suppose the 2022 income statement for **McDonald's Corporation** shows cost of goods sold $5,178.0 million and operating expenses (including depreciation expense of $1,216.2 million) $10,725.7 million. The comparative balance sheets for the year show that inventory decreased $5.3 million, prepaid expenses increased $42.2 million, accounts payable (inventory suppliers) increased $15.6 million, and accrued expenses payable increased $199.8 million.

Instructions

Using the direct method, compute (a) cash payments to suppliers and (b) cash payments for operating expenses.

Compute cash flow from operating activities—direct method.

*E12.13 (LO 4), AP The 2022 accounting records of Megan Transport provide the following information.

Payment of interest	$ 10,000	Payment of salaries and wages	$ 53,000
Cash sales	48,000	Depreciation expense	16,000
Receipt of dividend revenue	18,000	Proceeds from sale of vehicles	812,000
Payment of income taxes	12,000	Purchase of equipment for cash	22,000
Net income	38,000	Loss on sale of vehicles	3,000
Payment for merchandise	97,000	Payment of dividends	14,000
Payment for land	74,000	Payment of operating expenses	28,000
Collection of accounts receivable	195,000		

Instructions

Prepare the cash flows from operating activities section using the direct method.

Calculate cash flows—direct method.

*E12.14 (LO 4), AN The following information is taken from the 2022 general ledger of Preminger Company.

Rent	Rent expense	$ 30,000
	Prepaid rent, January 1	5,900
	Prepaid rent, December 31	7,400
Salaries	Salaries and wages expense	$ 54,000
	Salaries and wages payable, January 1	2,000
	Salaries and wages payable, December 31	8,000
Sales	Sales revenue	$160,000
	Accounts receivable, January 1	16,000
	Accounts receivable, December 31	7,000

Instructions

In each case, compute the amount that should be reported in the operating activities section of the statement of cash flows under the direct method.

Prepare a worksheet.

*E12.15 (LO 5), AP Comparative balance sheets for International Company are as follows.

International Company
Comparative Balance Sheets
December 31

	2022	2021
Assets		
Cash	$ 73,000	$ 22,000
Accounts receivable	85,000	76,000
Inventory	180,000	189,000
Land	75,000	100,000
Equipment	250,000	200,000
Accumulated depreciation—equipment	(66,000)	(42,000)
Total	$597,000	$545,000

	2022	2021
Liabilities and Stockholders' Equity		
Accounts payable	$ 34,000	$ 47,000
Bonds payable	150,000	200,000
Common stock ($1 par)	214,000	164,000
Retained earnings	199,000	134,000
Total	$597,000	$545,000

Additional information:

1. Net income for 2022 was $135,000.

2. Cash dividends of $70,000 were declared and paid.

3. Bonds payable with a carrying value of $50,000 were redeemed for $50,000 cash.

4. Common stock was issued at par for $50,000 cash.

5. Depreciation expense was $24,000.

6. Sales revenue for the year was $978,000.

7. Land was sold at cost, and equipment was purchased for cash.

Instructions

Prepare a worksheet for a statement of cash flows for 2022 using the indirect method. Enter the reconciling items directly on the worksheet, using letters to cross-reference each entry.

Problems

P12.1A (LO 1, 2), C You are provided with the following information regarding events that occurred at Moore Corporation during 2022 or changes in account balances as of December 31, 2022.

Distinguish among operating, investing, and financing activities.

	(1) Statement of Cash Flow Section Affected	(2) If Operating, Did It Increase or Decrease Reported Cash from Operating Activities?
a. Depreciation expense was $80,000.		
b. Interest Payable account increased $5,000.		
c. Received $26,000 from sale of plant assets.		
d. Acquired land by issuing common stock to seller.		
e. Paid $17,000 cash dividend to preferred stockholders.		
f. Paid $4,000 cash dividend to common stockholders.		
g. Accounts Receivable account decreased $10,000.		
h. Inventory increased $2,000.		
i. Received $100,000 from issuing bonds payable.		
j. Acquired equipment for $16,000 cash.		

Instructions

Moore prepares its statement of cash flows using the indirect method. Complete the first column of the table, indicating whether each item affects the operating activities section (O) (that is, the item would be listed among the adjustments to net income to determine net cash provided by operating activities under the indirect method), investing activities section (I), financing activities section (F), or is a noncash (NC) transaction reported in a separate schedule. For those items classified as operating activities (O), indicate whether the item is added (A) or subtracted (S) from net income to determine net cash provided by operating activities.

P12.2A (LO 2), AN The following account balances relate to the stockholders' equity accounts of Molder Corp. at year-end.

Determine cash flow effects of changes in equity accounts.

	2022	2021
Common stock, 10,500 and 10,000 shares, issued and outstanding, respectively, for 2022 and 2021	$160,800	$140,000
Preferred stock, 5,000 shares, issued and outstanding	125,000	125,000
Retained earnings	300,000	270,000

A small stock dividend was declared and issued in 2022. The market price of the shares was $8,800. Cash dividends of $20,000 were declared and paid in both 2022 and 2021. The common stock and preferred stock have no par or stated value.

Instructions

a. Net income $58,800

a. What was the amount of net income reported by Molder Corp. in 2022?

b. Determine the amounts of any cash inflows or outflows related to the common stock and dividend accounts in 2022.

c. Indicate where each of the cash inflows or outflows identified in (b) would be classified on the statement of cash flows.

Prepare the operating activities section—indirect method.

P12.3A (LO 2), AP The income statement of Munsun Company is presented here.

Munsun Company
Income Statement
For the Year Ended November 30, 2022

Sales revenue		$7,600,000
Cost of goods sold		
Beginning inventory	$1,900,000	
Purchases	4,400,000	
Goods available for sale	6,300,000	
Ending inventory	1,600,000	
Total cost of goods sold		4,700,000
Gross profit		2,900,000
Operating expenses		
Selling expenses	450,000	
Administrative expenses	700,000	1,150,000
Net income		$1,750,000

Additional information:

1. Accounts receivable decreased $380,000 during the year, and inventory decreased $300,000.
2. Prepaid expenses increased $150,000 during the year.
3. Accounts payable to suppliers of inventory decreased $350,000 during the year.
4. Accrued expenses payable decreased $100,000 during the year.
5. Administrative expenses include depreciation expense of $110,000.

Instructions

Net cash provided $1,940,000

Prepare the operating activities section of the statement of cash flows for the year ended November 30, 2022, for Munsun Company, using the indirect method.

Prepare the operating activities section—direct method.

Net cash provided—
oper. act. $1,940,000

*P12.4A (LO 4), AP Data for Munsun Company are presented in P12.3A.

Instructions

Prepare the operating activities section of the statement of cash flows using the direct method.

Prepare the operating activities section—indirect method.

P12.5A (LO 2), AP Rewe Company's income statement contained the following condensed information.

Rewe Company
Income Statement
For the Year Ended December 31, 2022

Service revenue		$970,000
Operating expenses, excluding depreciation	$614,000	
Depreciation expense	55,000	
Loss on disposal of plant assets	16,000	685,000
Income before income taxes		285,000
Income tax expense		56,000
Net income		$229,000

Rewe's balance sheets contained the following comparative data at December 31.

	2022	2021
Accounts receivable	$70,000	$60,000
Accounts payable	41,000	32,000
Income taxes payable	13,000	7,000

Accounts payable pertain to operating expenses.

Instructions

Prepare the operating activities section of the statement of cash flows using the indirect method.

*P12.6A **(LO 4), AP** Data for Rewe Company are presented in P12.5A.

Instructions

Prepare the operating activities section of the statement of cash flows using the direct method.

P12.7A **(LO 2, 3), AP** Presented here are the financial statements of Warner Company.

Net cash provided $305,000

Prepare the operating activities section—direct method.

Net cash provided $305,000

Prepare a statement of cash flows—indirect method, and compute free cash flow.

Warner Company
Comparative Balance Sheets
December 31

	2022	2021
Assets		
Cash	$ 35,000	$ 20,000
Accounts receivable	20,000	14,000
Inventory	28,000	20,000
Property, plant, and equipment	60,000	78,000
Accumulated depreciation	(32,000)	(24,000)
Total	$111,000	$108,000
Liabilities and Stockholders' Equity		
Accounts payable	$ 19,000	$ 15,000
Income taxes payable	7,000	8,000
Bonds payable	17,000	33,000
Common stock	18,000	14,000
Retained earnings	50,000	38,000
Total	$111,000	$108,000

Warner Company
Income Statement
For the Year Ended December 31, 2022

Sales revenue		$242,000
Cost of goods sold		175,000
Gross profit		67,000
Selling expenses	$18,000	
Administrative expenses	6,000	24,000
Income from operations		43,000
Interest expense		3,000
Income before income taxes		40,000
Income tax expense		8,000
Net income		$ 32,000

Additional data:

1. Depreciation expense was $17,500.

2. Dividends declared and paid were $20,000.

3. During the year equipment was sold for $8,500 cash. This equipment cost $18,000 originally and had accumulated depreciation of $9,500 at the time of sale.

4. Bonds were redeemed at their carrying value.

5. Common stock was issued at par for cash.

Instructions

a. Prepare a statement of cash flows using the indirect method.

b. Compute free cash flow.

a. Net cash provided—
   oper. act. $38,500

Prepare a statement of cash flows—direct method, and compute free cash flow.

*P12.8A (LO 3, 4), AP Data for Warner Company are presented in P12.7A. Further analysis reveals the following.

1. Accounts payable pertain to merchandise suppliers.
2. All operating expenses except for depreciation were paid in cash.
3. All depreciation expense is in the selling expense category.
4. All sales and inventory purchases are on account.

Instructions

a. Net cash provided—
  oper. act. $38,500

a. Prepare a statement of cash flows for Warner Company using the direct method.
b. Compute free cash flow.

Prepare a statement of cash flows—indirect method.

P12.9A (LO 2), AP Condensed financial data of Granger Inc. follow.

Granger Inc.
Comparative Balance Sheets
December 31

	2022	2021
Assets		
Cash	$ 80,800	$ 48,400
Accounts receivable	87,800	38,000
Inventory	112,500	102,850
Prepaid expenses	28,400	26,000
Long-term investments	138,000	109,000
Plant assets	285,000	242,500
Accumulated depreciation	(50,000)	(52,000)
Total	$682,500	$514,750
Liabilities and Stockholders' Equity		
Accounts payable	$102,000	$ 67,300
Accrued expenses payable	16,500	21,000
Bonds payable	110,000	146,000
Common stock	220,000	175,000
Retained earnings	234,000	105,450
Total	$682,500	$514,750

Granger Inc.
Income Statement Data
For the Year Ended December 31, 2022

Sales revenue		$388,460
Less:		
Cost of goods sold	$135,460	
Operating expenses, excluding depreciation	12,410	
Depreciation expense	46,500	
Income tax expense	27,280	
Interest expense	4,730	
Loss on disposal of plant assets	7,500	233,880
Net income		$154,580

Additional information:

1. New plant assets costing $100,000 were purchased for cash during the year.
2. Old plant assets having an original cost of $57,500 and accumulated depreciation of $48,500 were sold for $1,500 cash.
3. Bonds payable matured and were paid off at face value for cash.
4. A cash dividend of $26,030 was declared and paid during the year.
5. Common stock was issued at par for cash.
6. There were no significant noncash transactions.

Instructions

Net cash provided—
  oper. act. $176,930

Prepare a statement of cash flows using the indirect method.

Prepare a statement of cash flows—direct method.

*P12.10A (LO 4), AP Data for Granger Inc. are presented in P12.9A. Further analysis reveals that accounts payable pertain to merchandise creditors.

Instructions

Prepare a statement of cash flows for Granger Inc. using the direct method.

Net cash provided—
  oper. act. $176,930

P12.11A (LO 2), AP The comparative balance sheets for Spicer Company as of December 31 are as follows.

Prepare a statement of cash flows—indirect method.

Spicer Company
Comparative Balance Sheets
December 31

	2022	2021
Assets		
Cash	$ 68,000	$ 45,000
Accounts receivable	50,000	58,000
Inventory	151,450	142,000
Prepaid expenses	15,280	21,000
Land	145,000	130,000
Buildings	200,000	200,000
Accumulated depreciation—buildings	(60,000)	(40,000)
Equipment	225,000	155,000
Accumulated depreciation—equipment	(45,000)	(35,000)
Total	$749,730	$676,000
Liabilities and Stockholders' Equity		
Accounts payable	$ 44,730	$ 36,000
Bonds payable	300,000	300,000
Common stock, $1 par	200,000	160,000
Retained earnings	205,000	180,000
Total	$749,730	$676,000

Additional information:

1. Operating expenses include depreciation expense of $42,000 ($20,000 of depreciation expense for buildings and $22,000 for equipment).
2. Land was sold for cash at book value.
3. Cash dividends of $12,000 were declared and paid.
4. Net income for 2022 was $37,000.
5. Equipment was purchased for $92,000 cash. In addition, equipment costing $22,000 with a book value of $10,000 was sold for $8,000 cash.
6. 40,000 shares of $1 par value common stock were issued in exchange for land with a fair value of $40,000.

Instructions

Prepare a statement of cash flows for the year ended December 31, 2022, using the indirect method.

Net cash provided—
  oper. act. $94,000

*P12.12A (LO 5), AP Condensed financial data of Oakley Company are as follows.

Prepare a worksheet—indirect method.

 Excel

Oakley Company
Comparative Balance Sheets
December 31

	2022	2021
Assets		
Cash	$ 82,700	$ 47,250
Accounts receivable	90,800	57,000
Inventory	126,900	102,650
Investments	84,500	87,000
Equipment	255,000	205,000
Accumulated depreciation—equipment	(49,500)	(40,000)
	$590,400	$458,900
Liabilities and Stockholders' Equity		
Accounts payable	$ 57,700	$ 48,280
Accrued expenses payable	12,100	18,830
Bonds payable	100,000	70,000
Common stock	250,000	200,000
Retained earnings	170,600	121,790
	$590,400	$458,900

Oakley Company
Income Statement
For the Year Ended December 31, 2022

Sales revenue		$297,500
Gain on disposal of plant assets		8,750
		306,250
Less:		
Cost of goods sold	$99,460	
Operating expenses (excluding depreciation expense)	14,670	
Depreciation expense	49,700	
Income tax expense	7,270	
Interest expense	2,940	174,040
Net income		$132,210

Additional information:

1. Equipment costing $97,000 was purchased for cash during the year.

2. Investments were sold at their carrying value.

3. Equipment costing $47,000 was sold for $15,550, resulting in gain of $8,750.

4. A cash dividend of $83,400 was declared and paid during the year.

Reconciling items total
$610,210

Instructions

Prepare a worksheet for the statement of cash flows using the indirect method. Enter the reconciling items directly in the worksheet columns, using letters to cross-reference each entry.

Continuing Case

Cookie Creations

(*Note:* This is a continuation of the Cookie Creations case from Chapters 1 through 11.)

CC12 Natalie has prepared the balance sheet and income statement of Cookie & Coffee Creations Inc. and would like you to prepare the statement of cash flows.

Go to **WileyPLUS** *for complete case details and instructions.*

leungchopan/
Shutterstock.com

Expand Your Critical Thinking

Financial Reporting Problem: Apple Inc.

CT12.1 The financial statements of **Apple Inc.** are presented in Appendix A.

Instructions

Answer the following questions.

a. What was the amount of net cash provided by operating activities for the year ended September 29, 2018? For the year ended September 30, 2017?

b. What was the amount of increase or decrease in cash and cash equivalents for the year ended September 29, 2018?

c. Which method of computing net cash provided by operating activities does Apple use?

d. From your analysis of the September 29, 2018, statement of cash flows, was the change in accounts receivable a decrease or an increase? Was the change in inventories a decrease or an increase? Was the change in accounts payable a decrease or an increase?

e. What was the net cash provided (generated) by investing activities for the year ended September 29, 2018?

f. What was the amount of interest paid in the year ended September 29, 2018? What was the amount of income taxes paid for the same period?

Comparative Analysis Problem: PepsiCo, Inc. vs. The Coca-Cola Company

CT12.2 **PepsiCo**'s financial statements are presented in Appendix B. Financial statements of **The Coca-Cola Company** are presented in Appendix C. The complete annual reports of PepsiCo and Coca-Cola, including the notes to the financial statements, are available at each company's respective website.

Instructions

a. Based on the information contained in these financial statements, compute the 2018 fiscal year free cash flow for each company.

b. What conclusions concerning the management of cash can be drawn from these data?

Comparative Analysis Problem: Amazon.com, Inc. vs. Walmart Inc.

CT12.3 **Amazon.com, Inc.**'s financial statements are presented in Appendix D. Financial statements of **Walmart Inc.** are presented in Appendix E. The complete annual reports of Amazon and Walmart, including the notes to the financial statements, are available at each company's respective website.

Instructions

a. Based on the information contained in these financial statements, compute the 2018 fiscal year free cash flow for each company.

b. What conclusions concerning the management of cash can be drawn from these data?

Decision-Making Across the Organization

CT12.4 Pete Kent and Maria Robles are examining the following statement of cash flows for Sullivan Company for the year ended January 31, 2022.

Sullivan Company Statement of Cash Flows For the Year Ended January 31, 2022	
Sources of cash	
From sales of merchandise	$385,000
From sale of capital stock	405,000
From sale of investment (purchased below)	80,000
From depreciation	55,000
From issuance of note for truck	20,000
From interest on investments	6,000
Total sources of cash	951,000
Uses of cash	
For purchase of fixtures and equipment	$320,000
For merchandise purchased for resale	258,000
For operating expenses (including depreciation)	170,000
For purchase of investment	75,000
For purchase of truck by issuance of note	20,000
For purchase of treasury stock	10,000
For interest on note payable	3,000
Total uses of cash	856,000
Net increase in cash	$ 95,000

Pete claims that Sullivan's statement of cash flows is an excellent portrayal of a superb first year, with cash increasing $95,000. Maria replies that it was not a superb first year. Rather, she says, the year was an operating failure, that the statement is presented incorrectly, and that $95,000 is not the actual increase in cash. The cash balance at the beginning of the year was $140,000.

Instructions

With the class divided into groups, answer the following.

a. Using the data provided, prepare a statement of cash flows in proper form using the indirect method. The only noncash items in the income statement are depreciation and the gain from the sale of the investment.

b. With whom do you agree, Pete or Maria? Explain your position.

Real-World Focus

CT12.5 Purpose: Learn about the **Securities and Exchange Commission (SEC)**.

Instructions

Go to the SEC website, choose **About**, and then answer the following questions.

  a. How many enforcement actions does the SEC take each year against securities law violators? What are typical infractions?

  b. After the Depression, Congress passed the Securities Acts of 1933 and 1934 to improve investor confidence in the markets. What two "common sense" notions are these laws based on?

  c. Who was the president of the United States at the time of the creation of the SEC? Who was the first SEC chairperson?

CT12.6 You can use the Internet to view **SEC** filings.

Instructions

Choose a company, go to the **Yahoo! Finance** website, and then answer the following questions.

  a. What company did you select?

  b. What is its stock symbol? What is its selling price?

  c. What recent SEC filings are available for your viewing? (*Hint:* Use the Profile link.)

  d. Which filing is the most recent? What is the date?

Communication Activity

CT12.7 Walt Jax, the owner-president of Computer Services Company, is unfamiliar with the statement of cash flows that you, as his accountant, prepared. He asks for further explanation.

Instructions

Write him a brief memo explaining the form and content of the statement of cash flows as shown in Illustration 12.14.

Ethics Case

CT12.8 Pendleton Automotive Corp. is a medium-sized wholesaler of automotive parts. It has 10 stockholders who have been paid a total of $1 million in cash dividends for 8 consecutive years. The board's policy requires that, for this dividend to be declared, net cash provided by operating activities as reported in Pendleton Automotive's current year's statement of cash flows must exceed $1 million. President and CEO Hans Pfizer's job is secure so long as he produces annual operating cash flows to support the usual dividend.

At the end of the current year, controller Kurt Nolte presents president Hans Pfizer with some disappointing news: The net cash provided by operating activities is calculated by the indirect method to be only $970,000. The president says to Kurt, "We must get that amount above $1 million. Isn't there some way to increase operating cash flow by another $30,000?" Kurt answers, "These figures were prepared by my assistant. I'll go back to my office and see what I can do." The president replies, "I know you won't let me down, Kurt."

Upon close scrutiny of the statement of cash flows, Kurt concludes that he can get the operating cash flows above $1 million by reclassifying the proceeds from the $60,000, 2-year note payable listed in the financing activities section as "Proceeds from bank loan—$60,000." He will report the note instead as "Increase in payables—$60,000" and treat it as an adjustment to net income in the operating activities section. He returns to the president, saying, "You can tell the board to declare their usual dividend. Our net cash flow provided by operating activities is $1,030,000." "Good man, Kurt! I knew I could count on you," exults the president.

Instructions

  a. Who are the stakeholders in this situation?

  b. Was there anything unethical about the president's actions? Was there anything unethical about the controller's actions?

  c. Are the board members or anyone else likely to discover the misclassification?

All About You

CT12.9 In this chapter, you learned that companies prepare a statement of cash flows in order to keep track of their sources and uses of cash and to help them plan for their future cash needs. Planning for short- and long-term cash needs is every bit as important for you as it is for a company.

Instructions

Read the online article ("Financial Uh-Oh? No Problem") and answer the following questions. To access this article, it may be necessary to register at no cost.

a. Describe the three factors that determine how much money you should set aside for short-term needs.

b. How many months of living expenses does the article suggest to set aside?

c. Estimate how much you should set aside based upon your current situation. Are you closer to Cliff's scenario or to Prudence's?

FASB Codification Activity

CT12.10 If your school has a subscription to the FASB Codification, log in and prepare responses to the following. Use the Master Glossary to determine the proper definitions.

a. What are cash equivalents?

b. What are financing activities?

c. What are investing activities?

d. What are operating activities?

e. What is the primary objective for the statement of cash flow? Is working capital the basis for meeting this objective?

f. Do companies need to disclose information about investing and financing activities that do not affect cash receipts or cash payments? If so, how should such information be disclosed?

A Look at IFRS

LEARNING OBJECTIVE 7

Compare the procedures for the statement of cash flows under GAAP and IFRS.

As in GAAP, the statement of cash flows is a required statement for IFRS. In addition, the content and presentation of an IFRS statement of cash flows is similar to the one used for GAAP. However, the disclosure requirements related to the statement of cash flows are more extensive under GAAP. *IAS 7* ("Cash Flow Statements") provides the overall IFRS requirements for cash flow information.

Key Points

Following are the key similarities and differences between GAAP and IFRS as related to the statement of cash flows.

Similarities

- Companies preparing financial statements under IFRS must also prepare a statement of cash flows as an integral part of the financial statements.

- Both IFRS and GAAP require that the statement of cash flows have three major sections—operating, investing, and financing activities—along with changes in cash and cash equivalents.

- Similar to GAAP, the statement of cash flows can be prepared using either the indirect or direct method under IFRS. In both U.S. and international settings, companies choose for the most part to use the indirect method for reporting net cash flows from operating activities.

- The definition of cash equivalents used in IFRS is similar to that used in GAAP. A major difference is that in certain situations, bank overdrafts are considered part of cash and cash equivalents under IFRS (which is not the case in GAAP). Under GAAP, bank overdrafts are classified as financing activities in the statement of cash flows and are reported as liabilities on the balance sheet.

Differences

- IFRS requires that noncash investing and financing activities be excluded from the statement of cash flows. Instead, these noncash activities should be reported elsewhere. This requirement is interpreted to mean that noncash investing and financing activities should be disclosed in the notes to the financial statements instead of in the financial statements. Under GAAP, companies may present this information on the face of the statement of cash flows.

- One area where there can be substantial differences between IFRS and GAAP relates to the classification of interest, dividends, and taxes. The following table indicates the differences between the two approaches.

Item	IFRS	GAAP
Interest paid	Operating or financing	Operating
Interest received	Operating or investing	Operating
Dividends paid	Operating or financing	Financing
Dividends received	Operating or investing	Operating
Taxes paid	Operating—unless specific identification with financing or investing activity	Operating

- Under IFRS, some companies present the operating section in a single line item, with a full reconciliation provided in the notes to the financial statements. This presentation is not seen under GAAP.

IFRS Practice

IFRS Self-Test Questions

1. Under IFRS, interest paid can be reported as:
   a. only a financing activity.
   b. a financing activity or an investing activity.
   c. a financing activity or an operating activity.
   d. only an operating activity.

2. IFRS requires that noncash items:
   a. be reported in the section to which they relate, that is, a noncash investing activity would be reported in the investing section.
   b. be disclosed in the notes to the financial statements.
   c. do not need to be reported.
   d. be treated in a fashion similar to cash equivalents.

3. Under IFRS:
   a. taxes are always treated as an operating activity.
   b. the income statement uses the headings operating, investing, and financing.
   c. dividends received can be either an operating or investing activity.
   d. dividends paid can be either an operating or investing activity.

4. Which of the following is **correct?**
   a. Under IFRS, the statement of cash flows is optional.
   b. IFRS requires use of the direct method in preparing the statement of cash flows.
   c. The majority of companies following GAAP and the majority following IFRS employ the indirect method to the statement of cash flows.
   d. Under IFRS, companies offset financing activities against investing activities.

IFRS Exercises

IFRS12.1 Discuss the differences that exist in the treatment of bank overdrafts under GAAP and IFRS.

IFRS12.2 Describe the treatment of each of the following items under IFRS versus GAAP.
   a. Interest paid
   b. Interest received
   c. Dividends paid.
   d. Dividends received.

International Financial Reporting Problem: Louis Vuitton

IFRS12.3 The financial statements of **Louis Vuitton** are presented in Appendix F. The complete consolidated financial statements, including the notes to its financial statements, are available at the company's website.

Instructions

Use the company's 2018 consolidated cash flow statement to answer the following questions.
   a. In which section (operating, investing, or financing) does Louis Vuitton report interest paid (finance costs)?
   b. In which section (operating, investing, or financing) does Louis Vuitton report dividends received?
   c. If Louis Vuitton reported under GAAP rather than IFRS, how would its treatment of bank overdrafts differ?

Answers to IFRS Self-Test Questions

1. c 2. b 3. c 4. c

CHAPTER 13

Daniel Acker/Bloomberg/Getty Images

Financial Analysis: The Big Picture

Chapter Preview

We can all learn an important lesson from Warren Buffett: Study companies carefully if you wish to invest. Do not get caught up in fads but instead find companies that are financially healthy. Using some of the basic decision tools presented in this text, you can perform a rudimentary analysis on any company and draw basic conclusions about its financial health. Although it would not be wise for you to bet your life savings on a company's stock relying solely on your current level of knowledge, we strongly encourage you to practice your new skills wherever possible. Only with practice will you improve your ability to interpret financial numbers.

Before we unleash you on the world of high finance, we present a few more important concepts and techniques as well as one more comprehensive review of corporate financial statements. We use all of the decision tools presented in this text to analyze a single company, with comparisons to a competitor and industry averages.

13-1

Feature Story

It Pays to Be Patient

A recent issue of *Forbes* magazine listed Warren Buffett as the second richest person in the world. His estimated wealth was $69 billion, give or take a few million. How much is $69 billion? If you invested $69 billion in an investment earning just 4%, you could spend $7.6 million per day—every day—forever.

So, how does Buffett spend his money? Basically, he doesn't! He still lives in the same house that he purchased in Omaha, Nebraska, in 1958 for $31,500. He still drives his own car (a Cadillac DTS). And, in case you were thinking that his kids are riding the road to Easy Street, think again. Buffett has committed to donate virtually all of his money to charity before he dies.

How did Buffett amass this wealth? Through careful investing. Buffett epitomizes a "value investor." He applies the basic techniques he learned in the 1950s from the great value investor Benjamin Graham. He looks for companies that have good long-term potential but are currently underpriced. He invests in companies that have low exposure to debt and that reinvest their earnings for future growth. He does not get caught up in fads or the latest trends.

For example, Buffett sat out on the dot-com mania in the 1990s. When other investors put lots of money into fledgling high-tech firms, Buffett didn't bite because he did not find dot-com companies that met his criteria. He didn't get to enjoy the stock price boom on the way up, but on the other hand, he didn't have to ride the price back down to Earth. When the dot-com bubble burst, everyone else was suffering from investment shock. Buffett swooped in and scooped up deals on companies that he had been following for years.

In 2012, the stock market had again reached near record highs. Buffett's returns had been significantly lagging the market. Only 26% of his investments at that time were in stock, and he was sitting on $38 billion in cash. One commentator noted that "if the past is any guide, just when Buffett seems to look most like a loser, the party is about to end."

If you think you want to follow Buffett's example and transform your humble nest egg into a mountain of cash, be warned. His techniques have been widely circulated and emulated, but never practiced with the same degree of success. You should probably start by honing your financial analysis skills. A good way for you to begin your career as a successful investor is to master the fundamentals of financial analysis discussed in this chapter.

Source: Jason Zweig, "Buffett Is Out of Step," *Wall Street Journal* (May 7, 2012).

Chapter Outline

LEARNING OBJECTIVES	REVIEW	PRACTICE
LO 1 Apply the concepts of sustainable income and quality of earnings.	• Sustainable income • Quality of earnings	**DO IT! 1** Unusual Items
LO 2 Apply horizontal analysis and vertical analysis.	• Horizontal analysis • Vertical analysis	**DO IT! 2** Horizontal Analysis
LO 3 Analyze a company's performance using ratio analysis.	• Liquidity ratios • Solvency ratios • Profitability ratios • Financial analysis and data analytics • Comprehensive example	**DO IT! 3** Ratio Analysis

Go to the Review and Practice section at the end of the chapter for a targeted summary and practice applications with solutions.

Visit WileyPLUS for additional tutorials and practice opportunities.

Sustainable Income and Quality of Earnings

> **LEARNING OBJECTIVE 1**
> Apply the concepts of sustainable income and quality of earnings.

Sustainable Income

The value of a company like **Google** is a function of the amount, timing, and uncertainty of its future cash flows. Google's current and past income statements are particularly useful in helping analysts predict these future cash flows. In using this approach, analysts must make sure that Google's past income numbers reflect its **sustainable income**, that is, they do not include unusual (out-of-the-ordinary) revenues, expenses, gains, and losses.

Sustainable income is, therefore, the most likely level of income to be obtained by a company in the future. Sustainable income differs from actual net income by the amount of unusual revenues, expenses, gains, and losses included in the current year's income. Determining sustainable income requires an understanding of discontinued operations, comprehensive income, and changes in accounting principle. Analysts are interested in sustainable income because it helps them derive an estimate of future earnings without the "noise" of unusual items.

Discontinued Operations

Discontinued operations refers to the disposal of a **significant component** of a business, such as the elimination of a major class of customers or an entire activity. For example, to downsize its operations, **General Dynamics Corp.** sold its missile business to **Hughes Aircraft Co.** for $450 million. In its income statement, General Dynamics reported the sale in a separate section entitled "Discontinued operations."

When a company has discontinued operations, the company should report on its income statement both income from continuing operations and income (or loss) from discontinued operations. **The income (loss) from discontinued operations consists of two parts: the income (loss) from operations of the component and the gain (loss) on disposal of the component.** The income from continuing operations as well as the discontinued component are reported net of tax.

To illustrate, assume that during 2022 Acro Energy Inc. has income before income taxes of $800,000. During 2022, Acro discontinued and sold its unprofitable chemical division. The loss in 2022 from the chemical division's operations (net of $60,000 taxes) was $140,000. The loss on disposal of the chemical division (net of $30,000 taxes) was $70,000. Assuming a 30% tax rate on income, **Illustration 13.1** shows Acro's income statement (see **Helpful Hint**).

Note that the statement uses the caption "Income from continuing operations" and adds a new section "Discontinued operations." **The new section reports both the operating loss and the loss on disposal net of applicable income taxes.** This presentation clearly indicates the separate effects of continuing operations and discontinued operations on net income.

Income statement

HELPFUL HINT

Observe the dual disclosures: (1) the results of operation of the discontinued division must be separated from the results of continuing operations, and (2) the company must also report the gain or loss on disposal of the division.

Acro Energy Inc.		
Income Statement (partial)		
For the Year Ended December 31, 2022		
Income before income taxes		$800,000
Income tax expense		240,000
Income from continuing operations		560,000
Discontinued operations		
Loss from operation of chemical division, net of $60,000 income tax savings	$140,000	
Loss from disposal of chemical division, net of $30,000 income tax savings	70,000	210,000
Net income		$350,000

Investor Insight

iStock.com/Andrey Armiagov

What Does "Non-Recurring" Really Mean?

Many companies incur restructuring charges as they attempt to reduce costs. They often label these items in the income statement as "non-recurring" charges, to suggest that they are isolated events, unlikely to occur in future periods. The question for analysts is, are these costs really one-time, "non-recurring events" or do they reflect problems that the company will be facing for many periods in the future? If they are one-time events, then they can be largely ignored when trying to predict future earnings.

But, some companies report "one-time" restructuring charges over and over again. For example, **Procter & Gamble** reported a restructuring charge in 12 consecutive quarters, and **Motorola** had "special" charges in 14 consecutive quarters. On the other hand, other companies have a restructuring charge only once in a 5- or 10-year period. There appears to be no substitute for careful analysis of the numbers that comprise net income.

If a company takes a large restructuring charge, what is the effect on the company's current income statement versus future ones? (Go to WileyPLUS for this answer and additional questions.)

Comprehensive Income

Most revenues, expenses, gains, and losses are included in net income. However, as discussed in earlier chapters, certain gains and losses that bypass net income are reported as part of a more inclusive earnings measure called comprehensive income. **Comprehensive income** is the sum of net income and other comprehensive income items.[1]

Illustration of Comprehensive Income Accounting standards require that companies adjust most investments in stocks and bonds up or down to their market price at the end of each accounting period. For example, assume that during 2022, its first year of operations, Stassi Corporation purchased **IBM** bonds for $10,500 as an investment, which it intends to sell sometime in the future. At the end of 2022, Stassi was still holding the investment, but the bonds' market price was now $8,000. In this case, Stassi is required to reduce the recorded value of its IBM investment by $2,500. The $2,500 difference is an "unrealized" loss. A gain or loss is referred to as unrealized when an asset has experienced a change in value but the owner has not sold the asset. The sale of the asset results in "realization" of the gain or loss.

---

[1]The FASB's Conceptual Framework describes comprehensive income as including all changes in stockholders' equity during a period except those changes resulting from investments by stockholders and distributions to stockholders.

Should Stassi include this $2,500 unrealized loss in net income? It depends on whether Stassi classifies the IBM bonds as a trading security or an available-for-sale security. A **trading security** is bought and held primarily for sale in the near term to generate income on short-term price differences. Companies report unrealized losses on trading securities in the "Other expenses and losses" section of the income statement. The rationale: It is likely that the company will realize the unrealized loss (or an unrealized gain), so the company should report the loss (gain) as part of net income.

If Stassi did not purchase the investment for trading purposes, it is classified as available-for-sale. **Available-for-sale securities** are held with the intent of selling them sometime in the future. Companies do not include unrealized gains or losses on available-for-sale securities in net income. Instead, they report them as part of "Other comprehensive income," which is not included in net income.

Format   Companies report other comprehensive income in a separate statement of comprehensive income. For example, assuming that Stassi Corporation has a net income of $300,000 and a 20% tax rate, the unrealized loss would be reported below net income, net of tax, as shown in **Illustration 13.2**.

ILLUSTRATION 13.2
Statement of comprehensive income

Stassi Corporation	
Statement of Comprehensive Income	
For the Year Ended December 31, 2022	
Net income	$300,000
Other comprehensive income	
Unrealized loss on available-for-sale securities,	
net of $500 income tax savings	2,000
Comprehensive income	$298,000

Companies report the cumulative amount of other comprehensive income from all years as a separate component of stockholders' equity. To illustrate, assume Stassi has common stock of $3,000,000, retained earnings of $300,000, and accumulated other comprehensive loss of $2,000. (To simplify, we are assuming that this is Stassi's first year of operations. Since it has only operated for one year, the cumulative amount of other comprehensive income is this year's loss of $2,000.) **Illustration 13.3** shows the balance sheet presentation of the accumulated other comprehensive loss.

ILLUSTRATION 13.3
Accumulated other comprehensive loss in stockholders' equity section

Stassi Corporation	
Balance Sheet (partial)	
Stockholders' equity	
Common stock	$3,000,000
Retained earnings	300,000
Total paid-in capital and retained earnings	3,300,000
Accumulated other comprehensive loss	**2,000**
Total stockholders' equity	$3,298,000

Note that the presentation of the accumulated other comprehensive loss is similar to the presentation of the cost of treasury stock in the stockholders' equity section. (An unrealized gain would be added in this section of the balance sheet.)

Income Statement and Statement of Comprehensive Income As discussed, many companies report net income and other comprehensive income in separate statements, such as those shown for Pace Corporation in **Illustration 13.4**.

ILLUSTRATION 13.4

Income statement and statement of comprehensive income

Pace Corporation
Income Statement
For the Year Ended December 31, 2022

Net sales		$440,000
Cost of goods sold		260,000
Gross profit		180,000
Operating expenses		110,000
Income from operations		70,000
Other revenues and gains		5,600
Other expenses and losses		9,600
Income before income taxes		66,000
Income tax expense ($66,000 × 30%)		19,800
Income from continuing operations		46,200
Discontinued operations		
Loss from operation of plastics division, net of		
income tax savings $18,000 ($60,000 × 30%)	**$42,000**	
Gain on disposal of plastics division, net of		
$15,000 income taxes ($50,000 × 30%)	35,000	7,000
Net income		$39,200

Pace Corporation
Statement of Comprehensive Income
For the Year Ended December 31, 2022

Net income	$39,200
Other comprehensive income	
Unrealized gain on available-for-sale securities,	
net of income taxes ($15,000 × 30%)	10,500
Comprehensive income	**$49,700**

Note how the income statement shown in Illustration 13.4 presents the types of items usually found on this statement, such as net sales, cost of goods sold, operating expenses, and income taxes. Together, the income statement and statement of comprehensive income show how companies report discontinued operations and other comprehensive income (high-lighted in red).

Changes in Accounting Principle

For ease of comparison, users of financial statements expect companies to prepare their statements on a basis **consistent** with the preceding period. A **change in accounting principle** occurs when the principle used in the current year is different from the one used in the preceding year. An example is a change in inventory costing methods (such as FIFO to average-cost). Accounting rules permit a change when management can show that the new principle is preferable to the old principle.

Companies report most changes in accounting principle retroactively.[2] That is, they report both the current period and previous periods using the new principle. As a result, the same principle applies in all periods. This treatment improves the ability to compare results across years.

Investor Insight   United Parcel Service (UPS)

Larry MacDougal/
Canadian Press Images

More Frequent Ups and Downs

In the past, U.S. companies used a method to account for their pension plans that smoothed out the gains and losses on their pension portfolios by spreading gains and losses over multiple years. Many felt that this approach was beneficial because it reduced the volatility of reported net income. However, recently some companies have opted to adopt a method that comes closer to recognizing gains and losses in the period in which they occur. Some of the companies that have adopted this approach are **United Parcel Service (UPS)**, **Honeywell International**, **IBM**, **AT&T**, and **Verizon Communications**. The CFO at UPS said he favored the new approach because "events that occurred in prior years will no longer distort current-year results. It will result in better transparency by eliminating the noise of past plan performance." When UPS switched, it resulted in a charge of $827 million from the change in accounting principle.

Source: Bob Sechler and Doug Cameron, "UPS Alters Pension-Plan Accounting," *Wall Street Journal* (January 30, 2012).

When predicting future earnings, how should analysts treat the one-time charge that results from a switch to the different approach for accounting for pension plans? (Go to WileyPLUS for this answer and additional questions.)

Quality of Earnings

The quality of a company's earnings is of extreme importance to analysts. A company that has a high **quality of earnings** provides full and transparent information that will not confuse or mislead users of the financial statements.

Recent accounting scandals suggest that some companies are spending too much time managing their income and not enough time managing their business. Here are some of the factors affecting quality of earnings.

Alternative Accounting Methods

Variations among companies in the application of generally accepted accounting principles (GAAP) may hamper comparability and reduce quality of earnings. For example, suppose one company uses the FIFO method of inventory costing, while another company in the same industry uses LIFO. If inventory is a significant asset to both companies, it is unlikely that their current ratios are comparable. For example, if **General Motors Corporation** used FIFO instead of LIFO for inventory valuation, its inventories in a recent year would have been 26% higher, which significantly affects the current ratio (and other ratios as well).

In addition to differences in inventory costing methods, differences also exist in reporting such items as depreciation and amortization. Although these differences in accounting methods might be detectable from reading the notes to the financial statements, adjusting the financial data to compensate for the different methods is often difficult, if not impossible.

Pro Forma Income

Companies whose stock is publicly traded are required to present their income statement following GAAP. In recent years, many companies have been also reporting a second measure of

---

[2]An exception to the general rule is a change in depreciation methods. The effects of this change are reported prospectively in current and future periods. Discussion of this approach is left for more advanced courses.

income, called pro forma income. **Pro forma income** usually excludes items that the company thinks are unusual or non-recurring.

For example, in a recent year, **Cisco Systems** (a high-tech company) reported a quarterly net loss under GAAP of $2.7 billion. Cisco reported pro forma income for the same quarter as a profit of $230 million. This large difference in profits between GAAP income numbers and pro forma income is not unusual. For example, during one nine-month period, the 100 largest companies on the Nasdaq stock exchange reported a total pro forma income of $19.1 billion but a total loss as measured by GAAP of $82.3 billion—a difference of about $100 billion!

To compute pro forma income, companies generally exclude any items they deem inappropriate for measuring their performance. Many analysts and investors are critical of the practice of using pro forma income because these numbers often make companies look better than they really are. As the financial press noted, pro forma numbers might be called "earnings before bad stuff." Companies, on the other hand, argue that pro forma numbers more clearly indicate sustainable income because they exclude unusual and non-recurring expenses. "Cisco's technique gives readers of financial statements a clear picture of Cisco's normal business activities," the company said in a statement issued in response to questions about its pro forma income accounting.

Recently, the SEC provided some guidance on how companies should present pro forma information. Stay tuned: Everyone seems to agree that pro forma numbers can be useful if they provide insights into determining a company's sustainable income. However, many companies have abused the flexibility that pro forma numbers allow and have used the measure as a way to put their companies in a more favorable light.

Improper Recognition

Because some managers feel pressure from Wall Street to continually increase earnings, they manipulate earnings numbers to meet these expectations. The most common abuse is the improper recognition of revenue. One practice that some companies use is called **channel stuffing**. Offering deep discounts, companies encourage customers to buy early (stuff the channel) rather than later. This boosts the seller's earnings in the current period, but it often leads to a disaster in subsequent periods because customers have no need for additional goods. To illustrate, **Bristol-Myers Squibb** at one time indicated that it used sales incentives to encourage wholesalers to buy more drugs than they needed. As a result, the company had to issue revised financial statements showing corrected revenues and income.

Another practice is the improper capitalization of operating expenses as assets. **WorldCom** capitalized over $7 billion of operating expenses in order to report positive net income. In other situations, companies fail to report all their liabilities. **Enron** promised to make payments on certain contracts if financial difficulty developed, but these guarantees were not reported as liabilities. In addition, disclosure was so lacking in transparency that it was impossible to understand what was happening at the company.

ACTION PLAN

• Show discontinued operations and other comprehensive income net of tax.

DO IT! 1 | Unusual Items

In its proposed 2022 income statement, AIR Corporation reports income before income taxes $400,000, unrealized gain on available-for-sale securities $100,000, income taxes $120,000 (not including unusual items), loss from operation of discontinued flower division $50,000, and loss on disposal of discontinued flower division $90,000. The income tax rate is 30%. Prepare a correct partial income statement, beginning with "Income before income taxes," and a statement of comprehensive income.

Solution

AIR Corporation		
Income Statement (partial)		
For the Year Ended December 31, 2022		
Income before income taxes		$400,000
Income tax expense		120,000
Income from continuing operations		280,000
Discontinued operations		
Loss from operation of flower division,		
net of $15,000 income tax savings	$35,000	
Loss on disposal of flower division,		
net of $27,000 income tax savings	63,000	98,000
Net income		$182,000

AIR Corporation	
Statement of Comprehensive Income	
For the Year Ended December 31, 2022	
Net income	$182,000
Other comprehensive income	
Unrealized gain on available-for-sale	
securities, net of $30,000 income taxes	70,000
Comprehensive income	$252,000

Related exercise material: **BE13.1, BE13.2, DO IT! 13.1, E13.1,** and **E13.2.**

Horizontal Analysis and Vertical Analysis

LEARNING OBJECTIVE 2

Apply horizontal analysis and vertical analysis.

In assessing the financial performance of a company, investors are interested in the core or sustainable earnings of a company. In addition, investors are interested in making comparisons from period to period. Throughout this text, we have relied on three types of comparisons to improve the decision-usefulness of financial information:

1. **Intracompany basis.** Comparisons within a company are often useful to detect changes in financial relationships and significant trends. For example, a comparison of **Kellogg**'s current year's cash amount with the prior year's cash amount shows either an increase or a decrease. Likewise, a comparison of Kellogg's year-end cash amount with the amount of its total assets at year-end shows the proportion of total assets in the form of cash.

2. **Intercompany basis.** Comparisons with other companies provide insight into a company's competitive position. For example, investors can compare Kellogg's total sales for the year with the total sales of its competitors in the breakfast cereal area, such as **General Mills**.

3. **Industry averages.** Comparisons with industry averages provide information about a company's relative position within the industry. For example, financial statement readers can compare Kellogg's financial data with the averages for its industry compiled by financial rating organizations such as **Dun & Bradstreet**, **Moody's**, and **Standard & Poor's**, or with information provided on the Internet by organizations such as **Yahoo!** on its financial site.

We use three basic tools in financial statement analysis to highlight the significance of financial statement data:

1. Horizontal analysis.
2. Vertical analysis.
3. Ratio analysis.

In previous chapters, we relied primarily on ratio analysis, supplemented with some basic horizontal and vertical analysis. In the remainder of this section, we introduce more formal forms of horizontal and vertical analysis. In the next section, we review ratio analysis in some detail.

Horizontal Analysis

Horizontal analysis, also known as trend analysis, is a technique for evaluating a series of financial statement data over a period of time. Its purpose is to determine the increase or decrease that has taken place, expressed as either an amount or a percentage. For example, here are recent net sales figures (in thousands) of Chicago Cereal Company:

2022	2021	2020	2019	2018
$11,776	$10,907	$10,177	$9,614	$8,812

If we assume that 2018 is the base year, we can measure all percentage increases or decreases relative to this base-period amount with the formula shown in **Illustration 13.5**.

ILLUSTRATION 13.5

Horizontal analysis—computation of changes since base period

$$\text{Change Since Base Period} = \frac{\text{Current-Year Amount} - \text{Base-Year Amount}}{\text{Base-Year Amount}}$$

Using horizontal analysis, we can determine that net sales for Chicago Cereal increased approximately 9.1% [($9,614 − $8,812) ÷ $8,812] from 2018 to 2019. Similarly, we can also determine that net sales increased by 33.6% [($11,776 − $8,812) ÷ $8,812] from 2018 to 2022.

Alternatively, we can express current-year net sales as a percentage of the base period. To do so, we divide the current-year amount by the base-year amount, as shown in **Illustration 13.6**.

ILLUSTRATION 13.6

Horizontal analysis—computation of current year in relation to base year

$$\text{Current Results in Relation to Base Period} = \frac{\text{Current-Year Amount}}{\text{Base-Year Amount}}$$

Current-period net sales expressed as a percentage of the base period for each of the five years, using 2018 as the base period, are shown in **Illustration 13.7**.

Chicago Cereal Company				
Net Sales (in thousands)				
Base Period 2018				
2022	**2021**	**2020**	**2019**	**2018**
$11,776	$10,907	$10,177	$9,614	$8,812
133.6%	123.8%	115.5%	109.1%	100%

ILLUSTRATION 13.7

Horizontal analysis of net sales

The large increase in net sales during 2019 would raise questions regarding possible reasons for such a significant change. Chicago Cereal's 2019 notes to the financial statements explain that the company completed an acquisition of Elf Foods Company during 2019. This major acquisition would help explain the increase in net sales highlighted by horizontal analysis.

To further illustrate horizontal analysis, we use the financial statements of Chicago Cereal Company. Its two-year condensed balance sheets for 2022 and 2021, showing dollar and percentage changes, are presented in **Illustration 13.8** (see **Helpful Hint**).

ILLUSTRATION 13.8

Horizontal analysis of balance sheets

HELPFUL HINT

When using horizontal analysis, be sure to examine both dollar amount changes and percentage changes.

Chicago Cereal Company				
Condensed Balance Sheets				
December 31 (in thousands)				
			Increase (Decrease) during 2022	
	2022	**2021**	**Amount**	**Percent**
Assets				
Current assets	$ 2,717	$ 2,427	$290	**11.9**
Property, plant, and equipment (net)	2,990	2,816	174	**6.2**
Other assets	5,690	5,471	219	**4.0**
Total assets	$11,397	$10,714	$683	**6.4**
Liabilities and Stockholders' Equity				
Current liabilities	$ 4,044	$ 4,020	$ 24	**0.6**
Long-term liabilities	4,827	4,625	202	**4.4**
Total liabilities	8,871	8,645	226	**2.6**
Stockholders' equity				
Common stock	493	397	96	**24.2**
Retained earnings	3,390	2,584	806	**31.2**
Treasury stock (cost)	(1,357)	(912)	445	**48.8**
Total stockholders' equity	2,526	2,069	457	**22.1**
Total liabilities and stockholders' equity	$11,397	$10,714	$683	**6.4**

The comparative balance sheets show that a number of changes occurred in Chicago Cereal's financial position from 2021 to 2022. In the assets section, current assets increased $290,000, or 11.9% ($290 ÷ $2,427), and property, plant, and equipment (net) increased $174,000, or 6.2%. Other assets increased $219,000, or 4.0%. In the liabilities section, current liabilities increased $24,000, or 0.6%, while long-term liabilities increased $202,000, or 4.4%. In the stockholders' equity section, we find that retained earnings increased $806,000, or 31.2%.

Illustration 13.9 presents two-year comparative income statements of Chicago Cereal Company for 2022 and 2021, showing dollar and percentage changes (see **Helpful Hint**).

ILLUSTRATION 13.9

Horizontal analysis of income statements

HELPFUL HINT

The increase in the Amount column of $99 results from adding and subtracting the amounts shown. In the Percent column, the 9.9% cannot be determined by adding and subtracting the percentages shown.

Chicago Cereal Company
Condensed Income Statements
For the Years Ended December 31 (in thousands)

	2022	2021	Increase (Decrease) during 2022 Amount	Percent
Net sales	$11,776	$10,907	$869	**8.0**
Cost of goods sold	6,597	6,082	515	**8.5**
Gross profit	5,179	4,825	354	**7.3**
Selling and administrative expenses	3,311	3,059	252	**8.2**
Income from operations	1,868	1,766	102	**5.8**
Interest expense	321	294	27	**9.2**
Income before income taxes	1,547	1,472	75	**5.1**
Income tax expense	444	468	(24)	**(5.1)**
Net income	$ 1,103	$ 1,004	$ 99	**9.9**

Horizontal analysis of the income statements shows the following changes. Net sales increased $869,000, or 8.0% ($869 ÷ $10,907). Cost of goods sold increased $515,000, or 8.5% ($515 ÷ $6,082). Selling and administrative expenses increased $252,000, or 8.2% ($252 ÷ $3,059). Overall, gross profit increased 7.3% and net income increased 9.9%. The increase in net income can be attributed to the increase in net sales and a decrease in income tax expense.

The measurement of changes from period to period in percentages is relatively straightforward and quite useful. However, complications can result in making the computations. If an item has no value in a base year or preceding year and a value in the next year, no percentage change can be computed.

Vertical Analysis

Vertical analysis, also called common-size analysis, is a technique for evaluating financial statement data that expresses each item in a financial statement as a **percentage of a base amount**. For example, on a balance sheet we might express current assets as 22% of total assets (total assets being the base amount). Or, on an income statement we might express selling expenses as 16% of net sales (net sales being the base amount).

Presented in **Illustration 13.10** are the comparative balance sheets of Chicago Cereal for 2022 and 2021, analyzed vertically. The base for the asset items is **total assets**, and the base for the liability and stockholders' equity items is **total liabilities and stockholders' equity**.

ILLUSTRATION 13.10

Vertical analysis of balance sheets

Chicago Cereal Company
Condensed Balance Sheets
December 31 (in thousands)

	2022 Amount	Percent*	2021 Amount	Percent*
Assets				
Current assets	$ 2,717	**23.8**	$ 2,427	**22.6**
Property, plant, and equipment (net)	2,990	**26.2**	2,816	**26.3**
Other assets	5,690	**50.0**	5,471	**51.1**
Total assets	$11,397	**100.0**	$10,714	**100.0**

	2022		2021	
	Amount	Percent*	Amount	Percent*
Liabilities and Stockholders' Equity				
Current liabilities	$ 4,044	35.5	$ 4,020	37.5
Long-term liabilities	4,827	42.4	4,625	43.2
Total liabilities	8,871	77.9	8,645	80.7
Stockholders' equity				
Common stock	493	4.3	397	3.7
Retained earnings	3,390	29.7	2,584	24.1
Treasury stock (cost)	(1,357)	(11.9)	(912)	(8.5)
Total stockholders' equity	2,526	22.1	2,069	19.3
Total liabilities and stockholders' equity	$11,397	100.0	$10,714	100.0

*Numbers have been rounded to total 100%.

ILLUSTRATION 13.10
(continued)

In addition to showing the relative size of each item on the balance sheets, vertical analysis can show the percentage change in the individual asset, liability, and stockholders' equity items. Current assets increased $290,000 from 2021 to 2022, and they increased from 22.6% to 23.8% of total assets. Property, plant, and equipment (net) decreased from 26.3% to 26.2% of total assets. Other assets decreased from 51.1% to 50.0% of total assets. Retained earnings increased by $806,000 from 2021 to 2022, and total stockholders' equity increased from 19.3% to 22.1% of total liabilities and stockholders' equity.

This switch to a higher percentage of equity financing has two causes.

1. While total liabilities increased by $226,000, the percentage of liabilities declined from 80.7% to 77.9% of total liabilities and stockholders' equity.

2. Retained earnings increased by $806,000, from 24.1% to 29.7% of total liabilities and stockholders' equity.

Thus, the company shifted toward equity financing by relying less on debt and by increasing the amount of retained earnings.

Vertical analysis of the comparative income statements of Chicago Cereal, shown in **Illustration 13.11**, reveals that cost of goods sold **as a percentage of net sales** increased

ILLUSTRATION 13.11
Vertical analysis of income statements

Chicago Cereal Company
Condensed Income Statements
For the Years Ended December 31 (in thousands)

	2022		2021	
	Amount	Percent*	Amount	Percent*
Net sales	$11,776	100.0	$10,907	100.0
Cost of goods sold	6,597	56.0	6,082	55.8
Gross profit	5,179	44.0	4,825	44.2
Selling and administrative expenses	3,311	28.1	3,059	28.0
Income from operations	1,868	15.9	1,766	16.2
Interest expense	321	2.7	294	2.7
Income before income taxes	1,547	13.2	1,472	13.5
Income tax expense	444	3.8	468	4.3
Net income	$ 1,103	9.4	$ 1,004	9.2

*Numbers have been rounded to total 100%.

from 55.8% to 56.0%, and selling and administrative expenses increased from 28.0% to 28.1%. Net income as a percentage of net sales increased from 9.2% to 9.4%. Chicago Cereal's increase in net income as a percentage of sales is due primarily to the decrease in income tax expense as a percentage of sales.

Vertical analysis also enables you to compare companies of different sizes. For example, one of Chicago Cereal's competitors is Giant Mills. Giant Mills' sales are 1,000 times larger than those of Chicago Cereal. Vertical analysis enables us to meaningfully compare the condensed income statements of Chicago Cereal and Giant Mills, as shown in **Illustration 13.12**.

ILLUSTRATION 13.12

Intercompany comparison by vertical analysis

Condensed Income Statements				
For the Year Ended December 31, 2022				
	Chicago Cereal (in thousands)		Giant Mills, Inc. (in millions)	
	Amount	Percent*	Amount	Percent*
Net sales	$11,776	100.0	$17,910	100.0
Cost of goods sold	6,597	56.0	11,540	64.4
Gross profit	5,179	44.0	6,370	35.6
Selling and administrative expenses	3,311	28.1	3,474	19.4
Income from operations	1,868	15.9	2,896	16.2
Interest expense	321	2.7	196	1.1
Income before income taxes	1,547	13.2	2,700	15.1
Income tax expense	144	3.8	876	4.9
Net income	$ 1,103	9.4	$ 1,824	10.2

*Numbers have been rounded to total 100%.

Although Chicago Cereal's net sales are much less than those of Giant Mills, vertical analysis eliminates the impact of this size difference for our analysis. Chicago Cereal has a higher gross profit percentage of 44.0%, compared to 35.6% for Giant Mills. But, Chicago Cereal's selling and administrative expenses are 28.1% of net sales, while those of Giant Mills are 19.4% of net sales. Looking at net income, we see that Chicago Cereal's net income as a percentage of net sales is 9.4%, compared to 10.2% for Giant Mills.

Anatomy of a Fraud

Sometimes relationships between numbers can be used to detect fraud. Financial ratios that appear abnormal or statistical abnormalities in the numbers themselves can reveal fraud. For example, the fact that **WorldCom**'s line costs, as a percentage of either total expenses or revenues, differed significantly from those of its competitors should have alerted people to the possibility of fraud. Or, consider the case of a bank manager, who cooperated with a group of his friends to defraud the bank's credit card department. The manager's friends would apply for credit cards and then run up balances of slightly less than $5,000. The bank had a policy of allowing bank personnel to write off balances of less than $5,000 without seeking supervisor approval.

The fraud was detected by applying statistical analysis based on Benford's Law. Benford's Law states that in a random collection of numbers, the frequency of lower digits (e.g., 1, 2, or 3) should be much higher than that of higher digits (e.g., 7, 8, or 9). In this case, bank auditors analyzed the first two digits of amounts written off. There was a spike at 48 and 49, which was not consistent with what would be expected if the numbers were random.

Total take: Thousands of dollars

The Missing Control

Independent internal verification. While it might be efficient to allow employees to write off accounts below a certain level, it is important that these write-offs be reviewed and verified periodi-cally. Such a review would likely call attention to an employee with large amounts of write-offs, or in this case, write-offs that were frequently very close to the approval threshold.

Source: Mark J. Nigrini, "I've Got Your Number," *Journal of Accoun-tancy Online* (May 1999).

DO IT! 2 | Horizontal Analysis

Summary financial information for Rosepatch Company is as follows.

	December 31, 2022	December 31, 2021
Current assets	$234,000	$180,000
Plant assets (net)	756,000	420,000
Total assets	$990,000	$600,000

Compute the amount and percentage changes in 2022 using horizontal analysis, assuming 2021 is the base year.

ACTION PLAN

- Find the percentage change by dividing the amount of the increase by the 2021 amount (base year).

Solution

	Increase in 2022	
	Amount	**Percent**
Current assets	$ 54,000	30% [($234,000 − $180,000) ÷ $180,000]
Plant assets (net)	336,000	80% [($756,000 − $420,000) ÷ $420,000]
Total assets	$390,000	65% [($990,000 − $600,000) ÷ $600,000]

Related exercise material: **BE13.4, BE13.6, BE13.7, BE13.9, DO IT! 13.2, E13.3, E13.5, and E13.6.**

Ratio Analysis

LEARNING OBJECTIVE 3

Analyze a company's performance using ratio analysis.

Ratio analysis expresses the relationship among selected items of financial statement data. A **ratio** expresses the mathematical relationship between one quantity and another. The rela-tionship is expressed in terms of either a percentage, a rate, or a simple proportion.

To illustrate, in a recent year, **Nike, Inc.** had current assets of $13,626 million and cur-rent liabilities of $3,926 million. We can find the relationship between these two measures by dividing current assets by current liabilities. The alternative means of expression are as follows.

Percentage: Current assets are 347% of current liabilities.
Rate: Current assets are 3.47 times current liabilities.
Proportion: The relationship of current assets to liabilities is 3.47:1.

To analyze the primary financial statements, we can use ratios to evaluate liquidity, solvency, and profitability. **Illustration 13.13** describes these classifications.

ILLUSTRATION 13.13
Financial ratio classifications

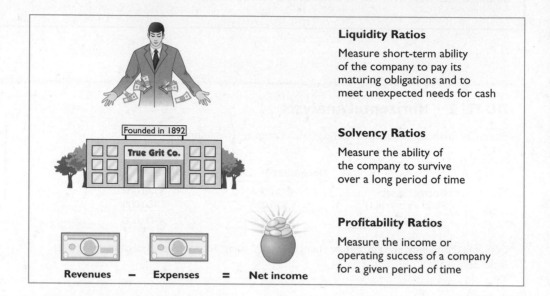

Liquidity Ratios

Measure short-term ability of the company to pay its maturing obligations and to meet unexpected needs for cash

Solvency Ratios

Measure the ability of the company to survive over a long period of time

Profitability Ratios

Measure the income or operating success of a company for a given period of time

Ratios can provide clues to underlying conditions that may not be apparent from individual financial statement components. However, a single ratio by itself is not very meaningful. Thus, in the discussion of ratios we will use the following types of comparisons.

1. **Intracompany comparisons** for two years for Chicago Cereal.
2. **Industry average comparisons** based on median ratios for the industry.
3. **Intercompany comparisons** based on Giant Mills as Chicago Cereal's principal competitor.

Liquidity Ratios

Liquidity ratios (Illustration 13.14) measure the short-term ability of the company to pay its maturing obligations and to meet unexpected needs for cash. Short-term creditors such as bankers and suppliers are particularly interested in assessing liquidity.

ILLUSTRATION 13.14
Summary of liquidity ratios

Liquidity Ratios

1. Current ratio	$\dfrac{\text{Current assets}}{\text{Current liabilities}}$
2. Inventory turnover	$\dfrac{\text{Cost of goods sold}}{\text{Average inventory}}$
3. Days in inventory	$\dfrac{365 \text{ days}}{\text{Inventory turnover}}$
4. Accounts receivable turnover	$\dfrac{\text{Net credit sales}}{\text{Average net accounts receivable}}$
5. Average collection period	$\dfrac{365 \text{ days}}{\text{Accounts receivable turnover}}$

Investor Insight

Nova Stock/SuperStock

How to Manage the Current Ratio

The apparent simplicity of the current ratio can have real-world limitations because adding equal amounts to both the numerator and the denominator causes the ratio to decrease.

Assume, for example, that a company has $2,000,000 of current assets and $1,000,000 of current liabilities. Its current ratio is 2:1. If it purchases $1,000,000 of inventory on account, it will have $3,000,000 of current assets and $2,000,000 of current liabilities. Its current ratio decreases to 1.5:1. If, instead, the company pays off $500,000 of its current liabilities, it will have $1,500,000 of current assets and $500,000 of current liabilities. Its current ratio increases to 3:1. Thus, any trend analysis should be done with care because the ratio is susceptible to quick changes and is easily influenced by management.

How might management influence a company's current ratio? (Go to WileyPLUS for this answer and additional questions.)

Solvency Ratios

Solvency ratios (Illustration 13.15) measure the ability of the company to survive over a long period of time. Long-term creditors and stockholders are interested in a company's long-run solvency, particularly its ability to pay interest as it comes due and to repay the balance of debt at its maturity.

Solvency Ratios

6. Debt to assets ratio

$$\frac{\text{Total liabilities}}{\text{Total assets}}$$

7. Times interest earned

$$\frac{\text{Net income} + \text{Interest expense} + \text{Income tax expense}}{\text{Interest expense}}$$

8. Free cash flow

$$\frac{\text{Net cash provided}}{\text{by operating activities}} - \frac{\text{Capital}}{\text{expenditures}} - \frac{\text{Cash}}{\text{dividends}}$$

ILLUSTRATION 13.15
Summary of solvency ratios

Profitability Ratios

Profitability ratios (Illustration 13.16) measure the income or operating success of a company for a given period of time. A company's income, or lack of it, affects its ability to obtain debt and equity financing, its liquidity position, and its ability to grow. As a consequence, creditors and investors alike are interested in evaluating profitability. Profitability is frequently used as the ultimate test of management's operating effectiveness.

Profitability Ratios

9. Return on common stockholders' equity

$$\frac{\text{Net income} - \text{Preferred dividends}}{\text{Average common stockholders' equity}}$$

10. Return on assets

$$\frac{\text{Net income}}{\text{Average total assets}}$$

11. Profit margin

$$\frac{\text{Net income}}{\text{Net sales}}$$

12. Asset turnover

$$\frac{\text{Net sales}}{\text{Average total assets}}$$

13. Gross profit rate

$$\frac{\text{Gross profit}}{\text{Net sales}}$$

14. Earnings per share

$$\frac{\text{Net income} - \text{Preferred dividends}}{\text{Weighted-average common shares outstanding}}$$

15. Price-earnings ratio

$$\frac{\text{Market price per share}}{\text{Earnings per share}}$$

16. Payout ratio

$$\frac{\text{Cash dividends paid on common stock}}{\text{Net income}}$$

ILLUSTRATION 13.16
Summary of profitability ratios

Financial Analysis and Data Analytics

In the age of "Big Data," opportunities for investors to apply data analytics to financial data are boundless. Immense quantities and types of data are available to investors. Free financial data about corporations, for example, can be obtained from the SEC's Edgar database and other sources. Alternatively, database services such as Compustat and WorldScope sell financial and other information regarding a wide range of company and industry characteristics. In addition, each day massive amounts of trading data are collected from financial exchanges.

Professional analysts employ sophisticated computerized valuation models that use financial, nonfinancial, and trading data to identify investment opportunities. Since these valuation models frequently rely heavily on accounting data, it is important to have a sound understanding of the financial accounting standards on which the numbers used in the models are based. If you desire to someday use data analytics to evaluate companies, the accounting skills and financial analysis tools acquired in this course are a good start.

Comprehensive Example of Ratio Analysis

In this section, we provide a comprehensive review of ratios used for evaluating the financial health and performance of a company. We use the financial information in **Illustrations 13.17** through **13.20** to calculate Chicago Cereal Company's 2022 ratios. You can use these data to review the computations.

ILLUSTRATION 13.17

Chicago Cereal Company's balance sheets

Chicago Cereal Company
Balance Sheets
December 31 (in thousands)

	2022	2021
Assets		
Current assets		
Cash	$ 524	$ 411
Accounts receivable (net)	1,026	945
Inventory	924	824
Prepaid expenses and other current assets	243	247
Total current assets	2,717	2,427
Property, plant, and equipment (net)	2,990	2,816
Other assets	5,690	5,471
Total assets	$11,397	$10,714

ILLUSTRATION 13.17

(continued)

	2022	2021
Liabilities and Stockholders' Equity		
Current liabilities	$ 4,044	$ 4,020
Long-term liabilities	4,827	4,625
Stockholders' equity—common	2,526	2,069
Total liabilities and stockholders' equity	$11,397	$10,714

ILLUSTRATION 13.18

Chicago Cereal Company's income statements

Chicago Cereal Company
Condensed Income Statements
For the Years Ended December 31 (in thousands)

	2022	2021
Net sales	$11,776	$10,907
Cost of goods sold	6,597	6,082
Gross profit	5,179	4,825
Selling and administrative expenses	3,311	3,059
Income from operations	1,868	1,766
Interest expense	321	294
Income before income taxes	1,547	1,472
Income tax expense	444	468
Net income	$ 1,103	$ 1,004

ILLUSTRATION 13.19

Chicago Cereal Company's statements of cash flows

Chicago Cereal Company
Condensed Statements of Cash Flows
For the Years Ended December 31 (in thousands)

	2022	2021
Cash flows from operating activities		
Cash receipts from operating activities	$11,695	$10,841
Cash payments for operating activities	(10,192)	(9,431)
Net cash provided by operating activities	1,503	1,410
Cash flows from investing activities		
Purchases of property, plant, and equipment	(472)	(453)
Other investing activities	(129)	8
Net cash used in investing activities	(601)	(445)
Cash flows from financing activities		
Issuance of common stock	163	218
Issuance of debt	2,179	721
Reductions of debt	(2,011)	(650)
Payment of cash dividends	(475)	(450)
Repurchase of common stock and other items	(645)	(612)
Net cash provided (used) by financing activities	(789)	(773)
Increase (decrease) in cash and cash equivalents	113	192
Cash and cash equivalents at beginning of year	411	219
Cash and cash equivalents at end of year	$ 524	$ 411

ILLUSTRATION 13.20

Additional information for Chicago Cereal Company

Additional information:

	2022	2021
Weighted-average common shares outstanding (thousands)	418.7	418.5
Stock price at year-end	$52.92	$50.06

As indicated in the chapter, we can classify ratios into three types for analysis of the primary financial statements:

1. **Liquidity ratios.** Measures of the short-term ability of the company to pay its maturing obligations and to meet unexpected needs for cash.

2. **Solvency ratios.** Measures of the ability of the company to survive over a long period of time.

3. **Profitability ratios.** Measures of the income or operating success of a company for a given period of time.

As a tool of analysis, ratios can provide clues to underlying conditions that may not be apparent from an inspection of the individual components of a particular ratio. But, a single ratio by itself is not very meaningful. Accordingly, in this discussion we use the following three comparisons.

1. **Intracompany comparisons** covering two years for Chicago Cereal (using comparative financial information from Illustrations 13.17 through 13.20). The ratios for 2021 are given and not calculated because the beginning balances are not provided for this year.

2. **Intercompany comparisons** using Giant Mills as one of Chicago Cereal's competitors.

3. **Industry average comparisons** based on **MSN.com** median ratios for manufacturers of flour and other grain mill products and comparisons with other sources. For some of the ratios that we use, industry comparisons are not available (denoted "na").

Liquidity Ratios

Liquidity ratios measure the short-term ability of the company to pay its maturing obligations and to meet unexpected needs for cash.

- Short-term creditors such as bankers and suppliers are particularly interested in assessing liquidity.

- The measures used to determine the company's short-term debt-paying ability are the current ratio, the accounts receivable turnover, the average collection period, the inventory turnover, and days in inventory. In addition, another measure used to assess liquidity is working capital. Working capital is current assets less current liabilities.

1. **Current ratio.** The **current ratio** expresses the relationship of current assets to current liabilities, computed by dividing current assets by current liabilities. It is widely used for evaluating a company's liquidity and short-term debt-paying ability. The 2022 and 2021 current ratios for Chicago Cereal and comparative data are shown in **Illustration 13.21.**

ILLUSTRATION 13.21 Current ratio

Ratio	Formula	Chicago Cereal		Giant Mills	Industry Average
		2022	2021	2022	
Current ratio	$\dfrac{\text{Current assets}}{\text{Current liabilities}}$	$\dfrac{\$2,717}{\$4,044} = .67$	.60	.67	1.06

What do the measures tell us?

- Chicago Cereal's 2022 current ratio of .67 means that for every dollar of current liabilities, it has $0.67 of current assets. (We sometimes state such ratios as .67:1 to reinforce this interpretation.)

- Its current ratio—and therefore its liquidity—increased significantly in 2022.

- Its ratio is well below the industry average but the same as that of Giant Mills.

2. **Accounts receivable turnover.** Analysts can measure liquidity by how quickly a company converts certain assets to cash. A low value for the current ratio can sometimes be compensated for if some of the company's current assets are highly liquid.

How liquid, for example, are the receivables? The ratio used to assess the liquidity of the receivables is the **accounts receivable turnover**, which measures the number of times, on average, a company collects receivables during the period. The accounts receivable turnover is computed by dividing net credit sales (net sales less cash sales) by average net accounts receivable during the year. The accounts receivable turnover for Chicago Cereal is shown in **Illustration 13.22**.

ILLUSTRATION 13.22 Accounts receivable turnover

Ratio	Formula	Chicago Cereal 2022	Chicago Cereal 2021	Giant Mills 2022	Industry Average
Accounts receivable turnover	$\dfrac{\text{Net credit sales}}{\text{Average net accounts receivable}}$	$\dfrac{\$11{,}776}{(\$1{,}026 + \$945) \div 2} = 11.9$	12.0	12.2	11.2

In computing the rate, we assumed that all Chicago Cereal's sales are credit sales.

- Its accounts receivable turnover declined slightly in 2022.
- The turnover of 11.9 times is higher than the industry average of 11.2 times, and slightly lower than Giant Mills' turnover of 12.2 times.
- A higher value suggests better liquidity because the receivables are being collected more quickly.

3. **Average collection period.** A popular variant of the accounts receivable turnover converts it into an **average collection period** in days. This is done by dividing the accounts receivable turnover into 365 days. The average collection period for Chicago Cereal is shown in **Illustration 13.23**.

ILLUSTRATION 13.23 Average collection period

Ratio	Formula	Chicago Cereal 2022	Chicago Cereal 2021	Giant Mills 2022	Industry Average
Average collection period	$\dfrac{\text{365 days}}{\text{Accounts receivable turnover}}$	$\dfrac{365}{11.9} = 30.7$	30.4	29.9	32.6

Chicago Cereal's 2022 accounts receivable turnover of 11.9 times is divided into 365 days to obtain approximately 31 days.

- This means that the average collection period for receivables is about 31 days.
- Its average collection period is slightly longer than that of Giant Mills and shorter than that of the industry.
- A shorter collection period means receivables are being collected more quickly and thus are more liquid.

Analysts frequently use the average collection period to assess the effectiveness of a company's credit and collection policies. The general rule is that the collection period should not greatly exceed the credit term period (i.e., the time allowed for payment, which is 30 days for many companies).

4. **Inventory turnover.** The **inventory turnover** measures the number of times average inventory was sold during the period. Its purpose is to measure the liquidity of the inventory. A high measure indicates that inventory is being sold and replenished frequently. The inventory turnover is computed by dividing the cost of goods sold by the average inventory during the period. Unless seasonal factors are significant, average inventory can be computed using the beginning and ending inventory balances. Chicago Cereal's inventory turnover is shown in **Illustration 13.24**.

ILLUSTRATION 13.24 Inventory turnover

Ratio	Formula	Chicago Cereal 2022	Chicago Cereal 2021	Giant Mills 2022	Industry Average
Inventory turnover	$\dfrac{\text{Cost of goods sold}}{\text{Average inventory}}$	$\dfrac{\$6{,}597}{(\$924 + \$824) \div 2} = 7.5$	7.9	7.4	6.7

Chicago Cereal's inventory turnover decreased slightly in 2022.

- The turnover of 7.5 times is higher than the industry average of 6.7 times and similar to that of Giant Mills.
- Generally, the faster the inventory turnover, the less cash is tied up in inventory and the less the chance of inventory becoming obsolete.
- A downside of high inventory turnover is that it sometimes results in lost sales because if a company keeps less inventory on hand, it is more likely to run out of inventory when it is needed.

5. **Days in inventory.** A variant of the inventory turnover is the **days in inventory**, which measures the average number of days inventory is held. The days in inventory for Chicago Cereal is shown in **Illustration 13.25**.

ILLUSTRATION 13.25 Days in inventory

Ratio	Formula	Chicago Cereal 2022	Chicago Cereal 2021	Giant Mills 2022	Industry Average
Days in inventory	$\dfrac{365 \text{ days}}{\text{Inventory turnover}}$	$\dfrac{365}{7.5} = 48.7$	46.2	49.3	54.5

Chicago Cereal's 2022 inventory turnover of 7.5 divided into 365 is approximately 49 days.

- An average selling time of 49 days is faster than the industry average and similar to that of Giant Mills.
- However, inventory turnovers vary considerably among industries. For example, grocery store chains have a turnover of 10 times and an average selling period of 37 days. In contrast, jewelry stores have an average turnover of 1.3 times and an average selling period of 281 days.
- Within a company, there may even be significant differences in inventory turnover among different types of products. Thus, in a grocery store the turnover of perishable items such as produce, meats, and dairy products is faster than the turnover of soaps and detergents.

To conclude, nearly all of these liquidity measures suggest that Chicago Cereal's liquidity changed little during 2022. Its liquidity appears acceptable when compared to the industry as a whole and when compared to Giant Mills.

Solvency Ratios

Solvency ratios measure the ability of the company to survive over a long period of time.

- Long-term creditors and stockholders are interested in a company's long-run solvency, particularly its ability to pay interest as it comes due and to repay the face value of debt at maturity.
- The debt to assets ratio and times interest earned provide information about debt-paying ability.
- In addition, free cash flow provides information about the company's solvency and its ability to pay additional dividends or invest in new projects.

6. **Debt to assets ratio.**   The **debt to assets ratio** measures the percentage of total financing provided by creditors. It is computed by dividing total liabilities (both current and long-term debt) by total assets. This ratio indicates the degree of financial leveraging. It also provides some indication of the company's ability to withstand losses without impairing the interests of its creditors. The higher the percentage of debt to assets, the greater the risk that the company may be unable to meet its maturing obligations. Thus, from the creditors' point of view, a low ratio of debt to assets is desirable. Chicago Cereal's debt to assets ratio is shown in **Illustration 13.26**.

ILLUSTRATION 13.26 Debt to assets ratio

Ratio	Formula	Chicago Cereal		Giant Mills	Industry Average
		2022	2021	2022	
Debt to assets ratio	$\dfrac{\text{Total liabilities}}{\text{Total assets}}$	$\dfrac{\$8,871}{\$11,397} = 78\%$	81%	55%	55%

Chicago Cereal's 2022 ratio means that creditors have provided financing sufficient for 78% of the company's total assets.

- Alternatively, the ratio indicates that the company would have to liquidate 78% of its assets at their book value in order to pay off all of its debts.
- Chicago Cereal's ratio is above the industry average of 55%, as well as that of Giant Mills.
- This suggests that it is less solvent than the industry average and Giant Mills. Chicago Cereal's solvency improved slightly from that in 2021.

The adequacy of this ratio is often judged in light of the company's earnings. Generally, companies with relatively stable earnings, such as public utilities, have higher debt to assets ratios than cyclical companies with widely fluctuating earnings, such as many high-tech companies.

Another ratio with a similar meaning is the **debt to equity ratio**.

- It shows the relative use of borrowed funds (total liabilities) compared with resources invested by the owners.
- If debt and assets are defined as above (all liabilities and all assets), then when the debt to assets ratio equals 50%, the debt to equity ratio is 1:1.

7. **Times interest earned.**   The **times interest earned** (also called interest coverage) indicates the company's ability to meet interest payments as they come due. It is computed by dividing the sum of net income, interest expense, and income tax expense by interest expense. Note that this ratio uses income before interest expense and income taxes because this amount represents what is available to cover interest. Chicago Cereal's times interest earned is shown in **Illustration 13.27**.

ILLUSTRATION 13.27 Times interest earned

Ratio	Formula	Chicago Cereal		Giant Mills	Industry Average
		2022	2021	2022	
Times interest earned	$\dfrac{\text{Net Income} + \text{Interest expense} + \text{Income tax expense}}{\text{Interest expense}}$	$\dfrac{\$1,103 + \$321 + \$444}{\$321} = 5.8$	6.0	9.9	5.5

For Chicago Cereal, the 2022 interest coverage was 5.8 times, which indicates that income before interest and taxes was 5.8 times the amount needed for interest expense.

- This is less than the rate for Giant Mills, but it slightly exceeds the rate for the industry.
- The debt to assets ratio decreased for Chicago Cereal during 2022, and its times interest earned held relatively constant.
- A low debt to assets ratio and high times interest earned suggest better solvency.

8. **Free cash flow.**   One indication of a company's solvency, as well as of its ability to pay dividends or expand operations, is the amount of excess cash it generated after investing in capital expenditures and paying dividends. This amount is referred to as **free cash flow**. For example, if you generate $100,000 of net cash provided by operating activities but you spend $30,000 on capital expenditures and pay $10,000 in dividends, you have $60,000 ($100,000 − $30,000 − $10,000) to use either to expand operations, pay additional dividends, or pay down debt. Chicago Cereal's free cash flow is shown in **Illustration 13.28.**

ILLUSTRATION 13.28 Free cash flow

Ratio	Formula			Chicago Cereal		Giant Mills	Industry Average
				2021	2022	2022	
Free cash flow	Net cash provided by operating activities	− Capital expenditures	− Cash dividends	$1,503 − $472 − $475 = $556 (in thousands)	$507	$895 (in millions)	na

Chicago Cereal's free cash flow increased slightly from 2021 to 2022.

- During both years, the net cash provided by operating activities was more than enough to allow it to acquire additional productive assets and maintain dividend payments.
- It could have used the remaining cash to reduce debt if necessary.
- Given that Chicago Cereal is much smaller than Giant Mills, we would expect Chicago Cereal's free cash flow to be substantially smaller, which it is.

Profitability Ratios

Profitability ratios measure the income or operating success of a company for a given period of time.

- A company's income, or the lack of it, affects its ability to obtain debt and equity financing, its liquidity position, and its ability to grow.
- As a consequence, creditors and investors alike are interested in evaluating profitability.
- Analysts frequently use profitability as the ultimate test of management's operating effectiveness.

The relationships among measures of profitability are very important. Understanding them can help management determine where to focus its efforts to improve profitability. **Illustration 13.29** diagrams these relationships. Our discussion of Chicago Cereal's profitability is structured around this diagram.

9. **Return on common stockholders' equity (ROE).**   A widely used measure of profitability from the common stockholders' viewpoint is the **return on common stockholders' equity (ROE)**. This ratio shows how many dollars of net income the company earned for each dollar invested by the owners. It is computed by dividing net income minus any

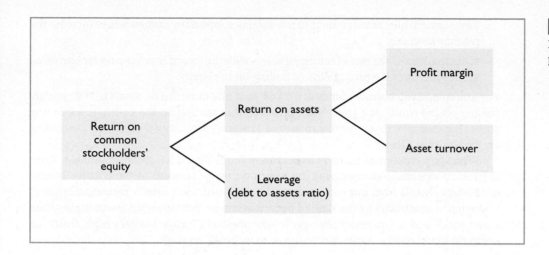

ILLUSTRATION 13.29
Relationships among profitability measures

preferred dividends—that is, income available to common stockholders—by average common stockholders' equity. The return on common stockholders' equity for Chicago Cereal is shown in **Illustration 13.30**.

ILLUSTRATION 13.30   **Return on common stockholders' equity**

Ratio	Formula	Chicago Cereal 2022	Chicago Cereal 2021	Giant Mills 2022	Industry Average
Return on common stockholders' equity	$\dfrac{\text{Net Income} - \text{Preferred dividends}}{\text{Average common stockholders' equity}}$	$\dfrac{\$1{,}103 - \$0}{(\$2{,}526 + \$2{,}069) \div 2} = 48\%$	46%	25%	19%

Chicago Cereal's 2022 return on common stockholders' equity is unusually high at 48%. The industry average is 19% and Giant Mills' return is 25%. In the subsequent sections, we investigate the causes of this high return.

10. **Return on assets.**   The return on common stockholders' equity is affected by two factors: the **return on assets** and the degree of leverage. The return on assets measures the overall profitability of assets in terms of the income earned on each dollar invested in assets. It is computed by dividing net income by average total assets. Chicago Cereal's return on assets is shown in **Illustration 13.31**.

ILLUSTRATION 13.31   **Return on assets**

Ratio	Formula	Chicago Cereal 2022	Chicago Cereal 2021	Giant Mills 2022	Industry Average
Return on assets	$\dfrac{\text{Net income}}{\text{Average total assets}}$	$\dfrac{\$1{,}103}{(\$11{,}397 + \$10{,}714) \div 2} = 10.0\%$	9.4%	6.2%	5.3%

Chicago Cereal had a 10.0% return on assets in 2022. This rate is significantly higher than that of Giant Mills and the industry average.

Note that its rate of return on common stockholders' equity (48%) is substantially higher than its rate of return on assets (10%). The reason is that it has made effective use of **leverage**.

- **Leveraging** or **trading on the equity** at a gain means that the company has borrowed money at a lower rate of interest than the rate of return it earns on the assets it purchased with the borrowed funds.

- Leverage enables management to use money supplied by nonowners to increase the return to owners.
- A comparison of the rate of return on assets with the rate of interest paid for borrowed money indicates the profitability of trading on the equity.

For example, if you borrow money at 8% and your rate of return on assets is 11%, you are trading on the equity at a gain. Note, however, that trading on the equity is a two-way street. For example, if you borrow money at 11% and earn only 8% on it, you are trading on the equity at a loss.

Chicago Cereal earns more on its borrowed funds than it has to pay in interest. Thus, the return to stockholders exceeds the return on assets because of the positive benefit of leverage. Recall from our earlier discussion that Chicago Cereal's percentage of debt financing, as measured by the ratio of debt to assets (or debt to equity), was higher than Giant Mills' and the industry average. It appears that Chicago Cereal's high return on common stockholders' equity is due in part to its use of leverage.

11. **Profit margin.**   The return on assets is affected by two factors, the first of which is the profit margin. The **profit margin**, or rate of return on sales, is a measure of the percentage of each dollar of sales that results in net income. It is computed by dividing net income by net sales for the period. Chicago Cereal's profit margin is shown in **Illustration 13.32**.

ILLUSTRATION 13.32

Profit margin

| Ratio | Formula | Chicago Cereal | | Giant Mills | Industry |
		2022	2021	2022	Average
Profit margin	$\dfrac{\text{Net income}}{\text{Net sales}}$	$\dfrac{\$1,103}{\$11,776} = 9.4\%$	9.2%	8.2%	6.1%

Chicago Cereal experienced a slight increase in its profit margin from 2021 to 2022 of 9.2% to 9.4%.

- Its profit margin was higher, indicating the company earned more profit out of each dollar of net sales, than the industry average and that of Giant Mills.
- High-volume (high inventory turnover) businesses such as grocery stores and pharmacy chains generally have low profit margins.
- Low-volume businesses such as jewelry stores and airplane manufacturers typically have high profit margins.

12. **Asset turnover.**   The other factor that affects the return on assets is the asset turnover. The **asset turnover** measures how efficiently a company uses its assets to generate sales. It is determined by dividing net sales by average total assets for the period. The resulting number shows the dollars of net sales produced by each dollar invested in assets. **Illustration 13.33** shows the asset turnover for Chicago Cereal.

ILLUSTRATION 13.33

Asset turnover

| Ratio | Formula | Chicago Cereal | | Giant Mills | Industry |
		2022	2021	2022	Average
Asset turnover	$\dfrac{\text{Net sales}}{\text{Average total assets}}$	$\dfrac{\$11,776}{(\$11,397 + \$10,714) \div 2} = 1.07$	1.02	.76	.87

The asset turnover shows that in 2022, Chicago Cereal generated sales of $1.07 for each dollar it had invested in assets.

- The ratio rose from 2021 to 2022.
- Its asset turnover is above the industry average and that of Giant Mills.
- Asset turnovers vary considerably among industries. The average asset turnover for utility companies is .45, for example, while the grocery store industry has an average asset turnover of 3.49.

In summary, Chicago Cereal's return on assets increased from 9.4% in 2021 to 10.0% in 2022. Underlying this increase was an increased profitability on each dollar of net sales (as measured by the profit margin) and a rise in the sales-generating efficiency of its assets (as measured by the asset turnover). The combined effect of the profit margin and asset turnover yields the return on assets for Chicago Cereal shown in **Illustration 13.34**.

ILLUSTRATION 13.34 **Composition of return on assets**

Ratios:	Profit Margin	×	Asset Turnover	=	Return on Assets
	$\dfrac{\text{Net Income}}{\text{Net Sales}}$	×	$\dfrac{\text{Net Sales}}{\text{Average Total Assets}}$	=	$\dfrac{\text{Net Income}}{\text{Average Total Assets}}$
Chicago Cereal					
2022	9.4%	×	1.07 times	=	10.1%*
2021	9.2%	×	1.02 times	=	9.4%

*Difference from value in Illustration 13.31 due to rounding.

13. **Gross profit rate.**   One factor that strongly influences the profit margin is the gross profit rate. The **gross profit rate** is determined by dividing gross profit (net sales less cost of goods sold) by net sales. This rate indicates a company's ability to maintain an adequate unit selling price above its unit cost of goods sold.

  As an industry becomes more competitive, this ratio typically declines.

- For example, in the early years of the personal computer industry, gross profit rates were quite high.
- Today, because of increased competition and a belief that most brands of personal computers are similar in quality, gross profit rates have become thin.
- Analysts should closely monitor gross profit rates over time.

Illustration 13.35 shows Chicago Cereal's gross profit rate.

ILLUSTRATION 13.35

Gross profit rate

Ratio	Formula	Chicago Cereal 2022	Chicago Cereal 2021	Giant Mills 2022	Industry Average
Gross profit rate	$\dfrac{\text{Gross profit}}{\text{Net sales}}$	$\dfrac{\$5,179}{\$11,776} = 44\%$	44%	34%	30%

Chicago Cereal's gross profit rate remained constant from 2021 to 2022, and exceeded that of Giant Mills and of the industry average.

14. **Earnings per share (EPS).**   Stockholders usually think in terms of the number of shares they own or plan to buy or sell. Expressing net income earned on a per share basis provides a useful perspective for evaluating profitability. **Earnings per share** is a measure of the net income earned on each share of common stock. It is computed by dividing net income by the average number of common shares outstanding during the year.

  The terms "net income per share" and "earnings per share" refer to the amount of net income applicable to each share of **common stock**. Therefore, when we compute earnings per share, if there are preferred dividends declared for the period, we must deduct them from net income to arrive at income available to the common stockholders. Chicago Cereal's earnings per share is shown in **Illustration 13.36**. There were no shares of preferred stock outstanding and no preferred stock dividends.

ILLUSTRATION 13.36
Earnings per share

Ratio	Formula	Chicago Cereal 2022	2021	Giant Mills 2022	Industry Average
Earnings per share (EPS)	$\dfrac{\text{Net income} - \text{Preferred dividends}}{\text{Weighted-average common shares outstanding}}$	$\dfrac{\$1{,}103 - \$0}{418.7} = \$2.63$	$2.40	$2.90	na

Note that no industry average is presented in Illustration 13.36.

- Industry data for earnings per share are not reported, and in fact the Chicago Cereal and Giant Mills ratios should not be compared.
- Such comparisons are not meaningful because of the wide variations in the number of shares of outstanding stock among companies.
- Chicago Cereal's earnings per share increased 23 cents per share in 2022. This represents a 9.6% increase from the 2021 EPS of $2.40.

15. **Price-earnings ratio.** The **price-earnings (P-E) ratio** is an oft-quoted statistic that measures the ratio of the market price of each share of common stock to the earnings per share of common stock. The price-earnings ratio reflects investors' assessments of a company's future earnings. It is computed by dividing the market price per share by earnings per share. Chicago Cereal's price-earnings ratio is shown in **Illustration 13.37**.

ILLUSTRATION 13.37
Price-earnings ratio

Ratio	Formula	Chicago Cereal 2022	2021	Giant Mills 2022	Industry Average
Price-earnings ratio	$\dfrac{\text{Market price per share}}{\text{Earnings per share}}$	$\dfrac{\$52.92}{\$2.63} = 20.1$	20.9	24.3	35.8

At the end of 2022 and 2021, the market price of Chicago Cereal's stock was $52.92 and $50.06, respectively.

- In 2022, each share of Chicago Cereal's stock sold for 20.1 times the amount that was earned on each share.
- Chicago Cereal's price-earnings ratio is lower than Giant Mills' ratio of 24.3 and lower than the industry average of 35.8 times.
- Its lower P-E ratio suggests that the market is less optimistic about Chicago Cereal than about Giant Mills, but it might also signal that Chicago Cereal's stock is underpriced.

16. **Payout ratio.** The **payout ratio** measures the percentage of earnings distributed in the form of cash dividends. It is computed by dividing cash dividends paid on common stock by net income. Companies that have high growth rates are characterized by low payout ratios because they reinvest most of their net income in the business. The payout ratio for Chicago Cereal is shown in **Illustration 13.38**.

ILLUSTRATION 13.38
Payout ratio

Ratio	Formula	Chicago Cereal 2022	2021	Giant Mills 2022	Industry Average
Payout ratio	$\dfrac{\text{Cash dividends paid on common stock}}{\text{Net income}}$	$\dfrac{\$475}{\$1{,}103} = 43\%$	45%	54%	37%

The 2022 and 2021 payout ratios for Chicago Cereal are lower than that of Giant Mills (54%) but higher than the industry average (37%).

- A lower payout ratio means a company has chosen to pay out a lower percentage of its net income as dividends.
- Management has some control over the amount of dividends paid each year, and companies are generally reluctant to reduce a dividend below the amount paid in a previous year.
- The payout ratio will actually increase if a company's net income declines but the company keeps its total dividend payment the same. (Of course, unless the company returns to its previous level of profitability, maintaining this higher dividend payout ratio is probably not possible over the long run.)

Before drawing any conclusions regarding Chicago Cereal's dividend payout ratio, we should calculate this ratio over a longer period of time to evaluate any trends and also try to find out whether management's philosophy regarding dividends has changed recently. The "Selected Financial Data" section of Chicago Cereal's Management Discussion and Analysis shows that over a 5-year period, earnings per share rose 45%, while dividends per share grew only 19%.

In terms of the types of financial information available and the ratios used by various industries, what can be practically covered in this text gives you the "Titanic approach." That is, you are only seeing the tip of the iceberg compared to the vast databases and types of ratio analysis that are available electronically. The availability of information is not a problem. The real trick is to be discriminating enough to perform relevant analysis and select pertinent comparative data.

DO IT! 3 | Ratio Analysis

The condensed financial statements of John Cully Company, for the years ended June 30, 2022 and 2021, are presented as follows.

John Cully Company
Balance Sheets
June 30

	(in thousands)	
	2022	**2021**
Assets		
Current assets		
Cash and cash equivalents	$ 553.3	$ 611.6
Accounts receivable (net)	776.6	664.9
Inventory	768.3	653.5
Prepaid expenses and other current assets	204.4	269.2
Total current assets	2,302.6	2,199.2
Investments	12.3	12.6
Property, plant, and equipment (net)	694.2	647.0
Other assets	876.7	849.3
Total assets	$3,885.8	$3,708.1
Liabilities and Stockholders' Equity		
Current liabilities	$1,497.7	$1,322.0
Long-term liabilities	679.5	637.1
Stockholders' equity—common	1,708.6	1,749.0
Total liabilities and stockholders' equity	$3,885.8	$3,708.1

ACTION PLAN

- **Remember that the current ratio includes all current assets.**
- **Use average balances for turnover ratios like inventory, accounts receivable, and return on assets.**

John Cully Company
Income Statements
For the Years Ended June 30

	(in thousands)	
	2022	**2021**
Net sales	$6,336.3	$5,790.4
Expenses		
Cost of goods sold	1,617.4	1,476.3
Selling and administrative expenses	4,007.6	3,679.0
Interest expense	13.9	27.1
Total expenses	5,638.9	5,182.4
Income before income taxes	697.4	608.0
Income tax expense	291.3	232.6
Net income	$ 406.1	$ 375.4

Compute the following ratios for 2022 and 2021.

   a. Current ratio.

   b. Inventory turnover. (Inventory on 6/30/20 was $599.0.)

   c. Profit margin.

   d. Return on assets. (Assets on 6/30/20 were $3,349.9.)

   e. Return on common stockholders' equity. (Stockholders' equity on 6/30/20 was $1,795.9.)

   f. Debt to assets ratio.

   g. Times interest earned.

Solution

	2022	**2021**
a. Current ratio:		
$2,302.6 ÷ $1,497.7 =	1.5:1	
$2,199.2 ÷ $1,322.0 =		1.7:1
b. Inventory turnover:		
$1,617.4 ÷ [($768.3 + $653.5) ÷ 2] =	2.3 times	
$1,476.3 ÷ [($653.5 + $599.0) ÷ 2] =		2.4 times
c. Profit margin:		
$406.1 ÷ $6,336.3 =	6.4%	
$375.4 ÷ $5,790.4 =		6.5%
d. Return on assets:		
$406.1 ÷ [($3,885.8 + $3,708.1) ÷ 2] =	10.7%	
$375.4 ÷ [($3,708.1 + $3,349.9) ÷ 2] =		10.6%
e. Return on common stockholders' equity:		
($406.1 − $0) ÷ [($1,708.6 + $1,749.0) ÷ 2] =	23.5%	
($375.4 − $0) ÷ [($1,749.0 + $1,795.9) ÷ 2] =		21.2%
f. Debt to assets ratio:		
($1,497.7 + $679.5) ÷ $3,885.8 =	56.0%	
($1,322.0 + $637.1) ÷ $3,708.1 =		52.8%
g. Times interest earned:		
($406.1 + $13.9 + $291.3) ÷ $13.9 =	51.2 times	
($375.4 + $27.1 + $232.6) ÷ $27.1 =		23.4 times

Related exercise material: **BE13.10, BE13.11, BE13.12, BE13.13, BE13.14, BE13.15, DO IT! 13.3, E13.7, E13.8, E13.9, E13.10, E13.11, E13.12, and E13.13.**

Review and Practice

Learning Objectives Review

1 Apply the concepts of sustainable income and quality of earnings.

Sustainable income analysis is useful in evaluating a company's performance. Sustainable income is the most likely level of income to be obtained by the company in the future and omits unusual items. Discontinued operations and other comprehensive income items are presented separately to highlight their unusual nature. Items below income from continuing operations must be presented net of tax.

A high quality of earnings provides full and transparent information that will not confuse or mislead users of the financial statements. Issues related to quality of earnings are (1) alternative accounting methods, (2) pro forma income, and (3) improper recognition.

2 Apply horizontal analysis and vertical analysis.

Horizontal analysis is a technique for evaluating a series of data over a period of time to determine the increase or decrease that has taken place, expressed as either a dollar amount or a percentage.

Vertical analysis is a technique that expresses each item in a financial statement as a percentage of a relevant total or a base amount.

3 Analyze a company's performance using ratio analysis.

Financial ratios are provided in Illustration 13.14 (liquidity), Illustration 13.15 (solvency), and Illustration 13.16 (profitability). Analysis is enhanced by intracompany, intercompany, and industry comparisons of these three classes of ratios.

Glossary Review

Accounts receivable turnover   A measure of the liquidity of receivables; computed as net credit sales divided by average net accounts receivable. (p. 13-21).

Asset turnover   A measure of how efficiently a company uses its assets to generate net sales; computed as net sales divided by average total assets. (p. 13-26).

Available-for-sale securities   Securities that are held with the intent of selling them sometime in the future. (p. 13-5).

Average collection period   The average number of days that receivables are outstanding; calculated as accounts receivable turnover divided into 365 days. (p. 13-21).

Change in accounting principle   Use of an accounting principle in the current year different from the one used in the preceding year. (p. 13-6).

Comprehensive income   The sum of net income and other comprehensive income items. (p. 13-4).

Current ratio   A measure used to evaluate a company's liquidity and short-term debt-paying ability; calculated as current assets divided by current liabilities. (p. 13-20).

Days in inventory   A measure of the average number of days that inventory is held; computed as inventory turnover divided into 365 days. (p. 13-22).

Debt to assets ratio   A measure of the percentage of total financing provided by creditors; computed as total liabilities divided by total assets. (p. 13-23).

Discontinued operations   The disposal of a significant component of a business. (p. 13-3).

Earnings per share   The net income earned by each share of outstanding common stock; computed as net income less preferred dividends divided by the weighted-average common shares outstanding. (p. 13-27).

Free cash flow   A measure of solvency. Cash remaining from operating activities after adjusting for capital expenditures and dividends paid. (p. 13-24).

Gross profit rate   Gross profit expressed as a percentage of net sales; computed as gross profit divided by net sales. (p. 13-27).

Horizontal analysis   A technique for evaluating a series of financial statement data over a period of time to determine the increase (decrease) that has taken place, expressed as either a dollar amount or a percentage. (p. 13-10).

Inventory turnover   A measure of the liquidity of inventory. Measures the number of times average inventory was sold during the period; computed as cost of goods sold divided by average inventory. (p. 13-21).

Leveraging   Borrowing money at a lower rate of interest than can be earned by using the borrowed money; also referred to as *trading on the equity*. (p. 13-25).

Liquidity ratios   Measures of the short-term ability of the company to pay its maturing current obligations and to meet unexpected needs for cash. (p. 13-16).

Payout ratio   A measure of the percentage of earnings distributed in the form of cash dividends; calculated as cash dividends paid on common stock divided by net income. (p. 13-28).

Price-earnings (P-E) ratio   A comparison of the market price of each share of common stock to the earnings per share; computed as the market price of the stock divided by earnings per share. (p. 13-28).

Profitability ratios   Measures of the income or operating success of a company for a given period of time. (p. 13-17).

Profit margin   A measure of the net income generated by each dollar of net sales; computed as net income divided by net sales. (p. 13-26).

Pro forma income   A measure of income that usually excludes items that a company thinks are unusual or non-recurring. (p. 13-8).

Quality of earnings   Indicates the level of full and transparent information that is provided to users of the financial statements. (p. 13-7).

Ratio   The mathematical relationship between one quantity and another. The relationship may be expressed either as a percentage, a rate, or a simple proportion. (p. 13-15).

Ratio analysis   A technique for evaluating financial statements that expresses the relationship between selected financial statement data. (p. 13-15).

Return on assets A profitability measure that indicates the amount of net income generated by each dollar of assets; calculated as net income divided by average total assets. (p. 13-25).

Return on common stockholders' equity (ROE) A measure of the dollars of net income earned for each dollar invested by the owners; computed as income available to common stockholders divided by average common stockholders' equity. (p. 13-24).

Solvency ratios Measures of the ability of a company to survive over a long period of time, particularly to pay interest as it comes due and to repay the balance of debt at its maturity. (p. 13-17).

Sustainable income The most likely level of income to be obtained by a company in the future. (p. 13-3).

Times interest earned A measure of a company's solvency and ability to meet interest payments as they come due; calculated as the sum of net income, interest expense, and income tax expense divided by interest expense. (p. 13-23).

Trading on the equity *See leveraging.* (p. 13-25).

Trading securities Securities bought and held primarily for sale in the near term to generate income on short-term price differences. (p. 13-5).

Vertical analysis A technique for evaluating financial statement data that expresses each item in a financial statement as a percentage of a base amount. (p. 13-12).

Practice Multiple-Choice Questions

1. (LO 1) In reporting discontinued operations, the income statement should show in a special section:

  a. gains on the disposal of the discontinued component.

  b. losses on the disposal of the discontinued component.

  c. neither gains nor losses on the disposal of the discontinued component.

  d. both gains and losses on the disposal of the discontinued component.

2. (LO 1) Cool Stools Corporation has income before taxes of $400,000 and a loss on discontinued operations of $100,000. If the income tax rate is 25% on all items, the income statement should report income from continuing operations and discontinued operations, respectively, of

  a. $325,000 and $100,000.

  b. $325,000 and $75,000.

  c. $300,000 and $100,000.

  d. $300,000 and $75,000.

3. (LO 1) Which of the following would be considered an "Other comprehensive income" item?

  a. Gain on disposal of discontinued operations.

  b. Unrealized loss on available-for-sale securities.

  c. Loss related to flood.

  d. Net income.

4. (LO 1) Which situation below might indicate a company has a low quality of earnings?

  a. The same accounting principles are used each year.

  b. Revenue is recognized when the performance obligation is satisfied.

  c. Maintenance costs are capitalized and then depreciated.

  d. The company's P-E ratio is high relative to competitors.

5. (LO 2) In horizontal analysis, each item is expressed as a percentage of the:

  a. net income amount.

  b. stockholders' equity amount.

  c. total assets amount.

  d. base-year amount.

6. (LO 2) Adams Corporation reported net sales of $300,000, $330,000, and $360,000 in the years 2020, 2021, and 2022, respectively.

If 2020 is the base year, what percentage do 2022 net sales represent of the base?

  a. 77%.   **c.** 120%.

  b. 108%.   **d.** 130%.

7. (LO 2) The following schedule is a display of what type of analysis?

	Amount	Percent
Current assets	$200,000	25%
Property, plant, and equipment	600,000	75%
Total assets	$800,000	

  a. Horizontal analysis.   **c.** Vertical analysis.

  b. Differential analysis.   **d.** Ratio analysis.

8. (LO 2) In vertical analysis, the base amount for depreciation expense is generally:

  a. net sales.

  b. depreciation expense in a previous year.

  c. gross profit.

  d. fixed assets.

9. (LO 3) Which measure is an evaluation of a company's ability to pay current liabilities?

  a. Accounts receivable turnover.

  b. Current ratio.

  c. Both accounts receivable turnover and current ratio.

  d. None of the answer choices is correct.

10. (LO 3) Which measure is useful in evaluating the efficiency in managing inventories?

  a. Inventory turnover.

  b. Days in inventory.

  c. Both inventory turnover and days in inventory.

  d. None of the answer choices is correct.

11. (LO 3) Which of these is **not** a liquidity ratio?

  a. Current ratio.

  b. Asset turnover.

  c. Inventory turnover.

  d. Accounts receivable turnover.

12. (LO 3) Plano Corporation reported net income $24,000, net sales $400,000, and average assets $600,000 for 2022. What is the 2022 profit margin?

  a. 6%.   **c.** 40%.

  b. 12%.   **d.** 200%.

Use the following financial statement information as of the end of each year to answer Questions 13–17.

	2022	2021
Inventory	$ 54,000	$ 48,000
Current assets	81,000	106,000
Total assets	382,000	326,000
Current liabilities	27,000	36,000
Total liabilities	102,000	88,000
Common stockholders' equity	240,000	198,000
Net sales	784,000	697,000
Cost of goods sold	306,000	277,000
Net income	134,000	90,000
Income tax expense	22,000	18,000
Interest expense	12,000	12,000
Dividends paid to preferred stockholders	4,000	4,000
Dividends paid to common stockholders	15,000	10,000

13. (LO 3) Compute the days in inventory for 2022.

  a. 64.4 days.   **c.** 6 days.

  b. 60.8 days.   **d.** 24 days.

14. (LO 3) Compute the current ratio for 2022.

  a. 1.26:1.   **c.** 0.80:1.

  b. 3.0:1.   **d.** 3.75:1.

15. (LO 3) Compute the profit margin for 2022.

  a. 17.1%.   **c.** 37.9%.

  b. 18.1%.   **d.** 5.9%.

16. (LO 3) Compute the return on common stockholders' equity for 2022.

  a. 54.2%.   **c.** 61.2%.

  b. 52.5%.   **d.** 59.4%.

17. (LO 3) Compute the times interest earned for 2022.

  a. 11.2 times.   **c.** 14.0 times.

  b. 65.3 times.   **d.** 13.0 times.

Solutions

1. d. Gains and losses from the operations of a discontinued component and gains and losses on the disposal of the discontinued component are shown in a separate section immediately after continuing operations in the income statement. Choices (a) and (b) are correct, but (d) is the better answer. Choice (c) is wrong as there is a correct answer.

2. d. Income tax expense = 25% × $400,000 = $100,000; therefore, income from continuing operations = $400,000 − $100,000 = $300,000. The loss on discontinued operations is reported net of tax, $100,000 × 75% = $75,000. The other choices are therefore incorrect.

3. b. Unrealized gains and losses on available-for-sale securities are part of other comprehensive income. The other choices are incorrect because they are reported on the income statement as follows: (a) a gain on the disposal of discontinued operations is reported as an unusual item, (c) loss related to a flood is reported among other expenses and losses, and (d) net income is a separate line item.

4. c. Capitalizing and then depreciating maintenance costs suggests that a company is trying to avoid expensing certain costs by deferring them to future accounting periods to increase current-period income. The other choices are incorrect because (a) using the same accounting principles each year and (b) recognizing revenue when the performance obligation is satisfied is in accordance with GAAP. Choice (d) is incorrect because a high P-E ratio does not suggest that a firm has low quality of earnings.

5. d. Horizontal analysis converts each succeeding year's balance to a percentage of the base year amount, not (a) net income amount, (b) stockholders' equity amount, or (c) total assets amount.

6. c. The trend percentage for 2022 is 120% ($360,000 ÷ $300,000), not (a) 77%, (b) 108%, or (d) 130%.

7. c. The data in the schedule are a display of vertical analysis because the individual asset items are expressed as a percentage of total assets. The other choices are therefore incorrect. Horizontal analysis is a technique for evaluating a series of data over a period of time.

8. a. In vertical analysis, net sales is used as the base amount for income statement items, not (b) depreciation expense in a previous year, (c) gross profit, or (d) fixed assets.

9. c. Both the accounts receivable turnover and the current ratio measure a firm's ability to pay current liabilities. Choices (a) and (b) are correct but (c) is the better answer. Choice (d) is incorrect because there is a correct answer.

10. c. Both inventory turnover and days in inventory measure a firm's efficiency in managing inventories. Choices (a) and (b) are correct but (c) is the better answer. Choice (d) is incorrect because there is a correct answer.

11. b. Asset turnover is a measure of profitability. The other choices are incorrect because the (a) current ratio, (c) inventory turnover, and (d) accounts receivable turnover are all measures of a firm's liquidity.

12. a. Profit margin = Net income ($24,000) ÷ Net sales ($400,000) = 6%, not (b) 12%, (c) 40%, or (d) 200%.

13. b. Inventory turnover = Cost of goods sold ÷ Average inventory {$306,000 ÷ [($54,000 + $48,000) ÷ 2]} = 6 times. Thus, days in inventory = 60.8 (365 ÷ 6), not (a) 64.4, (c) 6, or (d) 24 days.

14. b. Current ratio = Current assets ÷ Current liabilities ($81,000 ÷ $27,000) = 3.0:1, not (a) 1.26:1, (c) 0.80:1, or (d) 3.75:1.

15. a. Profit margin = Net income ÷ Net sales ($134,000 ÷ $784,000) = 17.1%, not (b) 18.1%, (c) 37.9%, or (d) 5.9%.

16. d. Return on common stockholders' equity = Net income ($134,000) − Dividends to preferred stockholders ($4,000) ÷ Average common stockholders' equity [($240,000 + $198,000) ÷ 2] = 59.4%, not (a) 54.2%, (b) 52.5%, or (c) 61.2%.

17. c. Times interest earned = (Net income + Interest expense + Income tax expense) ÷ Interest expense [($134,000 + $12,000 + $22,000) ÷ $12,000] = 14.0 times, not (a) 11.2, (b) 65.3, or (d) 13.0 times.

Practice Brief Exercises

Prepare a discontinued operations section.

1. (LO 1) On September 30, Reynaldo Corporation discontinued its operations in Africa. During the year, the operating income was $100,000 before taxes. On September 1, Reynaldo disposed of its African facilities at a pretax loss of $350,000. The applicable tax rate is 30%. Show the discontinued operations section of the income statement.

Solution

1.

Reynaldo Corporation
Income Statement (partial)

Income from operations of discontinued division, net of $30,000 income taxes ($100,000 × 30%)	$ 70,000	
Loss from disposal of discontinued division, net of $105,000 income tax savings ($350,000 × 30%)	245,000	$175,000

Prepare horizontal analysis.

2. (LO 2) Using the following data from the comparative balance sheet of Alfredo Company, perform horizontal analysis.

	December 31, 2022	December 31, 2021
Accounts payable	$ 300,000	$ 200,000
Common stock	700,000	600,000
Total liabilities and equity	2,000,000	1,800,000

Solution

2.

	December 31, 2022	December 31, 2021	Increase or (Decrease) Amount	Percent*
Accounts payable	$ 300,000	$ 200,000	$100,000	50%
Common stock	700,000	600,000	100,000	17
Total liabilities and stockholders' equity	2,000,000	1,800,000	200,000	11

*100 ÷ 200 = 50%; 100 ÷ 600 = 16.7%; 200 ÷ 1,800 = 11.1%

Calculate ratios.

3. (LO 3) Gonzalez Company has beginning inventory of $400,000, cost of goods sold of $2,200,000, and days in inventory of 73. What is Gonzalez' inventory turnover and ending inventory?

Solution

3. Days in inventory = 365 ÷ Inventory turnover
         73 = 365 ÷ Inventory turnover.
   Inventory turnover = 5 (365 ÷ 73)

   Inventory turnover = Cost of goods sold ÷ Average inventory
         5 = $2,200,000 ÷ Average inventory
   Average inventory = $2,200,000 ÷ 5 = $440,000.

   Since beginning inventory is $400,000, ending inventory must be $480,000:
   ($400,000 + $480,000) ÷ 2 = $440,000.

Practice Exercises

1. **(LO 2)** The comparative condensed balance sheets of Roadway Corporation are as follows.

Prepare horizontal and vertical analyses.

Roadway Corporation
Condensed Balance Sheets
December 31

	2022	2021
Assets		
Current assets	$ 76,000	$ 80,000
Property, plant, and equipment (net)	99,000	90,000
Intangible assets	25,000	40,000
Total assets	$200,000	$210,000
Liabilities and Stockholders' Equity		
Current liabilities	$ 40,800	$ 48,000
Long-term liabilities	143,000	150,000
Stockholders' equity	16,200	12,000
Total liabilities and stockholders' equity	$200,000	$210,000

Instructions

a. Prepare a horizontal analysis of the balance sheet data for Roadway Corporation using 2021 as a base.

b. Prepare a vertical analysis of the balance sheet data for Roadway Corporation in columnar form for 2022.

Solution

1. **a.**

Roadway Corporation
Condensed Balance Sheets
December 31

	2022	2021	Increase (Decrease)	Percent Change from 2021
Assets				
Current assets	$ 76,000	$ 80,000	$ (4,000)	(5.0%)
Property, plant, and equipment (net)	99,000	90,000	9,000	10.0%
Intangible assets	25,000	40,000	(15,000)	(37.5%)
Total assets	$200,000	$210,000	$(10,000)	(4.8%)
Liabilities and Stockholders' Equity				
Current liabilities	$ 40,800	$ 48,000	$ (7,200)	(15.0%)
Long-term liabilities	143,000	150,000	(7,000)	(4.7%)
Stockholders' equity	16,200	12,000	4,200	35.0%
Total liabilities and stockholders' equity	$200,000	$210,000	$(10,000)	(4.8%)

b.

Roadway Corporation		
Condensed Balance Sheet		
December 31, 2022		
	Amount	**Percent**
Assets		
Current assets	$ 76,000	38.0%
Property, plant, and equipment (net)	99,000	49.5%
Intangibles	25,000	12.5%
Total assets	$200,000	100.0%
Liabilities and Stockholders' Equity		
Current liabilities	$ 40,800	20.4%
Long-term liabilities	143,000	71.5%
Stockholders' equity	16,200	8.1%
Total liabilities and stockholders' equity	$200,000	100.0%

Compute ratios.

2. (LO 3) Rondo Corporation's comparative balance sheets are presented here.

Rondo Corporation		
Balance Sheets		
December 31		
	2022	**2021**
Cash	$ 5,300	$ 3,700
Accounts receivable (net)	21,200	23,400
Inventory	9,000	7,000
Land	20,000	26,000
Buildings	70,000	70,000
Accumulated depreciation—buildings	(15,000)	(10,000)
Total	$110,500	$120,100
Accounts payable	$ 10,370	$ 31,100
Common stock	75,000	69,000
Retained earnings	25,130	20,000
Total	$110,500	$120,100

Rondo's 2022 income statement included net sales of $120,000, cost of goods sold of $70,000, and net income of $14,000.

Instructions

Compute the following ratios for 2022.

a. Current ratio.

b. Accounts receivable turnover.

c. Inventory turnover.

d. Profit margin.

e. Asset turnover.

f. Return on assets.

g. Return on common stockholders' equity.

h. Debt to assets ratio.

Solution

2. a. ($5,300 + $21,200 + $9,000) ÷ $10,370 = 3.42:1

b. $120,000 ÷ [($21,200 + $23,400) ÷ 2] = 5.38 times

c. $70,000 ÷ [($9,000 + $7,000) ÷ 2] = 8.8 times

d. $14,000 ÷ $120,000 = 11.7%

e. $120,000 ÷ [($110,500 + $120,100) ÷ 2] = 1.04 times

f. $14,000 ÷ [($110,500 + $120,100) ÷ 2] = 12.1%

g. $14,000 ÷ [($100,130 + $89,000) ÷ 2] = 14.8%

h. $10,370 ÷ $110,500 = 9.4%

Practice Problem

(LO 1) The events and transactions of Dever Corporation for the year ended December 31, 2022, resulted in the following data.

Prepare an income statement and a statement of comprehensive income.

Cost of goods sold	$2,600,000
Net sales	4,400,000
Other expenses and losses	9,600
Other revenues and gains	5,600
Selling and administrative expenses	1,100,000
Income from operations of plastics division	70,000
Gain from disposal of plastics division	500,000
Unrealized loss on available-for-sale securities	60,000

Analysis reveals the following:

1. All items are recorded before the applicable income tax rate of 30%.
2. The plastics division was sold on July 1.
3. All operating data for the plastics division have been segregated.

Instructions

Prepare an income statement and a statement of comprehensive income for the year.

Solution

Dever Corporation		
Income Statement		
For the Year Ended December 31, 2022		
Net sales		$4,400,000
Cost of goods sold		2,600,000
Gross profit		1,800,000
Selling and administrative expenses		1,100,000
Income from operations		700,000
Other revenues and gains		5,600
Other expenses and losses		9,600
Income before income taxes		696,000
Income tax expense ($696,000 × 30%)		208,800
Income from continuing operations		487,200
Discontinued operations		
Income from operation of plastics division, net of $21,000 income taxes ($70,000 × 30%)	$ 49,000	
Gain from disposal of plastics division, net of $150,000 income taxes ($500,000 × 30%)	350,000	399,000
Net income		$886,200

Dever Corporation	
Statement of Comprehensive Income	
For the Year Ended December 31, 2022	
Net income	$886,200
Unrealized loss on available-for-sale securities, net of $18,000 income tax savings ($60,000 × 30%)	42,000
Comprehensive income	$844,200

WileyPLUS

Brief Exercises, DO IT! Exercises, Exercises, Problems, and many additional resources are available for practice in WileyPLUS.

Questions

1. Explain sustainable income. What relationship does this concept have to the treatment of discontinued operations on the income statement?

2. Hogan Inc. reported 2021 earnings per share of $3.26 and had no discontinued operations. In 2022, earnings per share on income from continuing operations was $2.99, and earnings per share on net income was $3.49. Do you consider this trend to be favorable? Why or why not?

3. Moosier Inc. has been in operation for 3 years and uses the FIFO method of inventory costing. During the fourth year, Moosier changes to the average-cost method for all its inventory. How will Moosier report this change?

4. What amount did **Apple** report as "Other comprehensive earnings" in its consolidated statement of comprehensive income ending September 29, 2018? By what percentage did Apple's "Comprehensive income" differ from its "Net income"?

5. Identify and explain factors that affect quality of earnings.

6. Explain how the choice of one of the following accounting methods over the other raises or lowers a company's net income during a period of continuing inflation.

   a. Use of FIFO instead of LIFO for inventory costing.

   b. Use of a 6-year life for machinery instead of a 9-year life.

   c. Use of straight-line depreciation instead of declining-balance depreciation.

7. Two popular methods of financial statement analysis are horizontal analysis and vertical analysis. Explain the difference between these two methods.

8. **a.** If Erin Company had net income of $300,000 in 2021 and it experienced a 24.5% increase in net income for 2022, what is its net income for 2022?

   b. If 6 cents of every dollar of Erin's revenue results in net income in 2021, what is the dollar amount of 2021 revenue?

9. **a.** Gina Jaimes believes that the analysis of financial statements is directed at two characteristics of a company: liquidity and profitability. Is Gina correct? Explain.

   b. Are short-term creditors, long-term creditors, and stockholders interested in primarily the same characteristics of a company? Explain.

10. **a.** Distinguish among the following bases of comparison: intracompany, intercompany, and industry averages.

    b. Give the principal value of using each of the three bases of comparison.

11. Name the major ratios useful in assessing (a) liquidity and (b) solvency.

12. Vern Thoms is puzzled. His company had a profit margin of 10% in 2022. He feels that this is an indication that the company is doing well. Tina Amos, his accountant, says that more information is needed to determine the company's financial well-being. Who is correct? Why?

13. What does each type of ratio measure?

    a. Liquidity ratios.

    b. Solvency ratios.

    c. Profitability ratios.

14. What is the difference between the current ratio and working capital?

15. Handi Mart, a retail store, has an accounts receivable turnover of 4.5 times. The industry average is 12.5 times. Does Handi Mart have a collection problem with its receivables?

16. Which ratios should be used to help answer each of these questions?

    a. How efficient is a company in using its assets to produce net sales?

    b. How near to sale is the inventory on hand?

    c. How many dollars of net income were earned for each dollar invested by the owners?

    d. How able is a company to meet interest charges as they become due?

17. At year-end, the price-earnings ratio of **General Motors** was 11.3, and the price-earnings ratio of **Microsoft** was 28.14. Which company did the stock market favor? Explain.

18. What is the formula for computing the payout ratio? Do you expect this ratio to be high or low for a growth company?

19. Holding all other factors constant, indicate whether each of the following changes generally signals good or bad news about a company.

    a. Increase in profit margin.

    b. Decrease in inventory turnover.

    c. Increase in current ratio.

    d. Decrease in earnings per share.

    e. Increase in price-earnings ratio.

    f. Increase in debt to assets ratio.

    g. Decrease in times interest earned.

20. The return on assets for Ayala Corporation is 7.6%. During the same year, Ayala's return on common stockholders' equity is 12.8%. What is the explanation for the difference in the two rates?

21. Which two ratios do you think should be of greatest interest in each of the following cases?

    a. A pension fund considering the purchase of 20-year bonds.

    b. A bank contemplating a short-term loan.

    c. A common stockholder.

22. Keanu Inc. has net income of $200,000, average shares of common stock outstanding of 40,000, and preferred dividends of $20,000 that were declared and paid during the period. What is Keanu's earnings per share of common stock? Fred Tyme, the president of Keanu, believes that the computed EPS of the company is high. Comment.

Brief Exercises

BE13.1 (LO 1), AP On June 30, Flores Corporation discontinued its operations in Mexico. During the year, the operating income was $200,000 before taxes. On September 1, Flores disposed of the Mexico facility at a pretax loss of $640,000. The applicable tax rate is 25%. Show the discontinued operations section of Flores's income statement.

Prepare a discontinued operations section of an income statement.

BE13.2 (LO 1), AP An inexperienced accountant for Silva Corporation showed the following in the income statement: net income $337,500 and unrealized gain on available-for-sale securities (before taxes) $70,000. The unrealized gain on available-for-sale securities is subject to a 25% tax rate. Prepare a correct statement of comprehensive income.

Prepare a statement of comprehensive income including unusual items.

BE13.3 (LO 1), C On January 1, 2022, Bryce Inc. changed from the LIFO method of inventory costing to the FIFO method. Explain how this change in accounting principle should be treated in the company's financial statements.

Indicate how a change in accounting principle is reported.

BE13.4 (LO 2), AP Using these data from the comparative balance sheets of Rollaird Company, perform horizontal analysis.

Prepare horizontal analysis.

	December 31, 2022	December 31, 2021
Accounts receivable (net)	$ 460,000	$ 400,000
Inventory	780,000	650,000
Total assets	3,164,000	2,800,000

BE13.5 (LO 2), AP Using these data from the comparative balance sheets of Rollaird Company, perform vertical analysis.

Prepare vertical analysis.

	December 31, 2022	December 31, 2021
Accounts receivable (net)	$ 460,000	$ 400,000
Inventory	780,000	650,000
Total assets	3,164,000	2,800,000

BE13.6 (LO 2), AP Net income was $500,000 in 2020, $485,000 in 2021, and $518,400 in 2022. What is the percentage of change (a) from 2020 to 2021, and (b) from 2021 to 2022? Is the change an increase or a decrease?

Calculate percentage of change.

BE13.7 (LO 2), AP If Coho Company had net income of $382,800 in 2022 and it experienced a 16% increase in net income over 2021, what was its 2021 net income?

Calculate net income.

BE13.8 (LO 2), AP Vertical analysis (common-size) percentages for Palau Company's net sales, cost of goods sold, and expenses are listed here.

Analyze change in net income.

Vertical Analysis	2022	2021	2020
Net sales	100.0%	100.0%	100.0%
Cost of goods sold	60.5	62.9	64.8
Expenses	26.0	26.6	27.5

Did Palau's net income as a percent of net sales increase, decrease, or remain unchanged over the 3-year period? Provide numerical support for your answer.

BE13.9 (LO 2), AP Writing Horizontal analysis (trend analysis) percentages for Phoenix Company's net sales, cost of goods sold, and expenses are listed here.

Analyze change in net income.

Horizontal Analysis	2022	2021	2020
Net sales	96.2%	104.8%	100.0%
Cost of goods sold	101.0	98.0	100.0
Expenses	105.6	95.4	100.0

Explain whether Phoenix's net income increased, decreased, or remained unchanged over the 3-year period.

BE13.10 (LO 3), AP Suppose these selected condensed data are taken from recent balance sheets of **Bob Evans Farms** (in thousands).

Calculate current ratio.

	2022	2021
Cash	$ 13,606	$ 7,669
Accounts receivable (net)	23,045	19,951
Inventory	31,087	31,345
Other current assets	12,522	11,909
Total current assets	$ 80,260	$ 70,874
Total current liabilities	$245,805	$326,203

Compute the current ratio for each year and comment on your results.

Evaluate collection of accounts receivable.

BE13.11 (LO 3), AN Writing The following data are taken from the financial statements of Colby Company.

	2022	**2021**
Accounts receivable (net), end of year	$ 550,000	$ 540,000
Net sales on account	4,300,000	4,000,000
Terms for all sales are 1/10, n/45		

Compute for each year (a) the accounts receivable turnover and (b) the average collection period. What conclusions about the management of accounts receivable can be drawn from these data? At the end of 2020, accounts receivable (net) was $520,000.

Evaluate management of inventory.

BE13.12 (LO 3), AN Writing The following data were taken from the financial records of Mydorf Company.

	2022	**2021**
Net sales	$6,420,000	$6,240,000
Beginning inventory	960,000	840,000
Purchases	4,840,000	4,661,000
Ending inventory	1,020,000	960,000

Compute for each year (a) the inventory turnover and (b) days in inventory. What conclusions concerning the management of the inventory can be drawn from these data?

Calculate profitability ratios.

BE13.13 (LO 3), AN Staples, Inc. is one of the largest suppliers of office products in the United States. Suppose it had net income of $738.7 million and net sales of $24,275.5 million in 2022. Its total assets were $13,073.1 million at the beginning of the year and $13,717.3 million at the end of the year. What is Staples, Inc.'s (a) asset turnover and (b) profit margin? (Round to two decimals.) Provide a brief interpretation of your results.

Calculate profitability ratios.

BE13.14 (LO 3), AN Hollie Company has stockholders' equity of $400,000 and net income of $72,000. It has a payout ratio of 18% and a return on assets of 20%. How much did Hollie pay in cash dividends, and what were its average total assets?

Calculate and analyze free cash flow.

BE13.15 (LO 3), AN Selected data taken from a recent year's financial statements of trading card company **Topps Company, Inc.** are as follows (in millions).

Net sales	$326.7
Current liabilities, beginning of year	41.1
Current liabilities, end of year	62.4
Net cash provided by operating activities	10.4
Total liabilities, beginning of year	65.2
Total liabilities, end of year	73.2
Capital expenditures	3.7
Cash dividends	6.2

Compute the free cash flow. Provide a brief interpretation of your results.

DO IT! Exercises

Prepare a partial income statement and a statement of comprehensive income.

DO IT! 13.1 (LO 1), AP In its proposed 2022 income statement, Hrabik Corporation reports income before income taxes $500,000, income taxes $100,000 (not including unusual items), loss on operation of discontinued music division $60,000, gain on disposal of discontinued music division $40,000, and unrealized loss on available-for-sale securities $150,000. The income tax rate is 20%. Prepare a correct partial income statement, beginning with income before income taxes, and a statement of comprehensive income for the year ended December 31, 2022.

Prepare horizontal analysis.

DO IT! 13.2 (LO 2), AP Summary financial information for Gandaulf Company is as follows.

	Dec. 31, 2022	**Dec. 31, 2021**
Current assets	$ 200,000	$ 220,000
Plant assets	1,040,000	780,000
Total assets	$1,240,000	$1,000,000

Compute the amount and percentage changes in 2022 using horizontal analysis, assuming 2021 is the base year.

DO IT! 13.3 (LO 3), AP The condensed financial statements of Murawski Company for the years 2021 and 2022 are presented as follows. (Amounts in thousands.)   *Compute ratios.*

Murawski Company
Balance Sheets
December 31

	2022	2021
Current assets		
Cash and cash equivalents	$ 330	$ 360
Accounts receivable (net)	470	400
Inventory	460	390
Prepaid expenses	120	160
Total current assets	1,380	1,310
Investments	10	10
Property, plant, and equipment (net)	420	380
Intangibles and other assets	530	510
Total assets	$2,340	$2,210
Current liabilities	$ 900	$ 790
Long-term liabilities	410	380
Stockholders' equity—common	1,030	1,040
Total liabilities and stockholders' equity	$2,340	$2,210

Murawski Company
Income Statements
For the Years Ended December 31

	2022	2021
Net sales	$3,800	$3,460
Expenses		
Cost of goods sold	955	890
Selling & administrative expenses	2,400	2,330
Interest expense	25	20
Total expenses	3,380	3,240
Income before income taxes	420	220
Income tax expense	126	66
Net income	$ 294	$ 154

Compute the following ratios for 2022 and 2021.

a. Current ratio.

b. Inventory turnover. (Inventory on 12/31/20 was $340.)

c. Profit margin.

d. Return on assets. (Assets on 12/31/20 were $1,900.)

e. Return on common stockholders' equity. (Stockholders' equity—common on 12/31/20 was $900.)

f. Debt to assets ratio.

g. Times interest earned.

Exercises

Prepare a correct partial income statement.

E13.1 (LO 1), AN Writing For its fiscal year ending October 31, 2022, Haas Corporation reports the following partial data.

Income before income taxes	$540,000
Income tax expense (20% × $420,000)	84,000
Income from continuing operations	456,000
Loss on discontinued operations	120,000
Net income	$336,000

The loss on discontinued operations was comprised of a $50,000 loss from operations and a $70,000 loss from disposal. The income tax rate is 20% on all items.

Instructions

a. Prepare a correct partial income statement, beginning with income before income taxes.

b. Explain in memo form why the original income statement data are misleading.

Prepare a partial income statement and a statement of comprehensive income.

E13.2 (LO 1), AP Trayer Corporation has income from continuing operations of $290,000 for the year ended December 31, 2022. It also has the following items (before considering income taxes).

1. An unrealized loss of $80,000 on available-for-sale securities.

2. A gain of $30,000 on the discontinuance of a division (comprised of a $10,000 loss from operations and a $40,000 gain on disposal).

Assume all items are subject to income taxes at a 20% tax rate.

Instructions

Prepare a partial income statement, beginning with income from continuing operations, and a statement of comprehensive income.

Prepare horizontal analysis.

E13.3 (LO 2), AP Here is financial information for Glitter Inc.

	December 31, 2022	December 31, 2021
Current assets	$106,000	$ 90,000
Plant assets (net)	400,000	350,000
Current liabilities	99,000	65,000
Long-term liabilities	122,000	90,000
Common stock, $1 par	130,000	115,000
Retained earnings	155,000	170,000

Instructions

Prepare a schedule showing a horizontal analysis for 2022, using 2021 as the base year.

Prepare vertical analysis.

E13.4 (LO 2), AP Operating data for Joshua Corporation are presented as follows.

	2022	2021
Net sales	$800,000	$600,000
Cost of goods sold	520,000	408,000
Selling expenses	120,000	72,000
Administrative expenses	60,000	48,000
Income tax expense	30,000	24,000
Net income	70,000	48,000

Instructions

Prepare a schedule showing a vertical analysis for 2022 and 2021.

E13.5 (LO 2), AP Hypothetical comparative condensed balance sheets of **Nike, Inc.** are presented here.

Prepare horizontal and vertical analyses.

Nike, Inc.
Condensed Balance Sheets
May 31
($ in millions)

	2022	2021
Assets		
Current assets	$ 9,734	$ 8,839
Property, plant, and equipment (net)	1,958	1,891
Other assets	1,558	1,713
Total assets	$13,250	$12,443
Liabilities and Stockholders' Equity		
Current liabilities	$ 3,277	$ 3,322
Long-term liabilities	1,280	1,296
Stockholders' equity	8,693	7,825
Total liabilities and stockholders' equity	$13,250	$12,443

Instructions

a. Prepare a horizontal analysis of the balance sheet data for Nike, using 2021 as a base. (Show the amount of increase or decrease as well.)

b. Prepare a vertical analysis of the balance sheet data for Nike for 2022.

E13.6 (LO 2), AP Here are the comparative condensed income statements of Delaney Corporation.

Prepare horizontal and vertical analyses.

Delaney Corporation
Condensed Income Statements
For the Years Ended December 31

	2022	2021
Net sales	$598,000	$500,000
Cost of goods sold	477,000	420,000
Gross profit	121,000	80,000
Operating expenses	80,000	44,000
Net income	$ 41,000	$ 36,000

Instructions

a. Prepare a horizontal analysis of the income statement data for Delaney Corporation, using 2021 as a base. (Show the amounts of increase or decrease.)

b. Prepare a vertical analysis of the income statement data for Delaney Corporation for both years.

E13.7 (LO 3), AP **Nordstrom, Inc.** operates department stores in numerous states. Selected hypothetical financial statement data (in millions) for 2022 are presented below.

Compute liquidity ratios.

	End of Year	Beginning of Year
Cash and cash equivalents	$ 795	$ 72
Accounts receivable (net)	2,035	1,942
Inventory	898	900
Other current assets	326	303
Total current assets	$4,054	$3,217
Total current liabilities	$2,014	$1,601

For the year, net credit sales were $8,258 million, cost of goods sold was $5,328 million, and net cash provided by operating activities was $1,251 million.

Instructions

Compute the current ratio, accounts receivable turnover, average collection period, inventory turnover, and days in inventory for the current year.

Perform current ratio analysis.

E13.8 (LO 3), AP Gwynn Incorporated had the following transactions involving current assets and current liabilities during February 2022.

Feb. 3 Collected accounts receivable of $15,000.
    7 Purchased equipment for $23,000 cash.
    11 Paid $3,000 for a 1-year insurance policy.
    14 Paid accounts payable of $12,000.
    18 Declared cash dividends, $4,000.

Additional information:
As of February 1, 2022, current assets were $120,000 and current liabilities were $40,000.

Instructions

Compute the current ratio as of the beginning of the month and after each transaction.

Compute selected ratios.

E13.9 (LO 3), AP Lendell Company has these comparative balance sheet data:

Lendell Company
Balance Sheets
December 31

	2022	2021
Cash	$ 15,000	$ 30,000
Accounts receivable (net)	70,000	60,000
Inventory	60,000	50,000
Plant assets (net)	200,000	180,000
	$345,000	$320,000
Accounts payable	$ 50,000	$ 60,000
Bonds payable (15%)	100,000	100,000
Common stock, $10 par	140,000	120,000
Retained earnings	55,000	40,000
	$345,000	$320,000

Additional information for 2022:

1. Net income was $25,000.

2. Sales on account were $375,000. Sales returns and allowances amounted to $25,000.

3. Cost of goods sold was $198,000.

4. Net cash provided by operating activities was $48,000.

5. Capital expenditures were $25,000, and cash dividends paid were $10,000.

6. The bonds payable are due in 2035.

Instructions

Compute the following ratios at December 31, 2022.

a. Current ratio.   d. Inventory turnover.

b. Accounts receivable turnover.   e. Days in inventory.

c. Average collection period.   f. Free cash flow.

Compute selected ratios.

E13.10 (LO 3), AP Selected hypothetical comparative statement data for the giant bookseller **Barnes & Noble** are presented here. All balance sheet data are as of the end of the fiscal year (in millions).

	2022	2021
Net sales	$5,121.8	$5,286.7
Cost of goods sold	3,540.6	3,679.8
Net income	75.9	135.8
Accounts receivable (net)	81.0	107.1
Inventory	1,203.5	1,358.2
Total assets	2,993.9	3,249.8
Total common stockholders' equity	921.6	1,074.7

Instructions

Compute the following ratios for 2022.

a. Profit margin.

b. Asset turnover.

c. Return on assets.

d. Return on common stockholders' equity.

e. Gross profit rate.

E13.11 (LO 3), AP Here is the income statement for Myers, Inc.

Compute selected ratios.

Myers, Inc.
Income Statement
For the Year Ended December 31, 2022

Net sales	$400,000
Cost of goods sold	230,000
Gross profit	170,000
Expenses (including $16,000 interest and $24,000 income taxes)	98,000
Net income	$ 72,000

Additional information:

1. Common stock outstanding January 1, 2022, was 32,000 shares, and 40,000 shares were outstanding at December 31, 2022. (Use a simple average for weighted-average.)

2. The market price of Myers stock was $14 on December 31, 2022.

3. Cash dividends of $21,000 were declared and paid.

Instructions

Compute the following measures for 2022.

a. Earnings per share.

b. Price-earnings ratio.

c. Payout ratio.

d. Times interest earned.

E13.12 (LO 3), AP Panza Corporation experienced a fire on December 31, 2022, in which its financial records were partially destroyed. It has been able to salvage some of the records and has ascertained the following balances.

Compute amounts from ratios.

	December 31, 2022	December 31, 2021
Cash	$ 30,000	$ 10,000
Accounts receivable (net)	72,500	126,000
Inventory	200,000	180,000
Accounts payable	50,000	90,000
Notes payable	30,000	60,000
Common stock, $100 par	400,000	400,000
Retained earnings	113,500	101,000

Additional information:

1. The inventory turnover is 3.8 times.

2. The return on common stockholders' equity is 22%. The company had no additional capital accounts.

3. The accounts receivable turnover is 11.2 times.

4. The return on assets is 18%.

5. Total assets at December 31, 2021, were $605,000.

Instructions

Compute the following for Panza Corporation.

a. Cost of goods sold for 2022.

b. Net credit sales for 2022.

c. Net income for 2022.

d. Total assets at December 31, 2022.

Compute ratios.

E13.13 (LO 3), AP The condensed financial statements of Ness Company for the years 2021 and 2022 are as follows.

Ness Company
Balance Sheets
December 31 (in thousands)

	2022	2021
Current assets		
Cash and cash equivalents	$ 330	$ 360
Accounts receivable (net)	470	400
Inventory	460	390
Prepaid expenses	130	160
Total current assets	1,390	1,310
Investments	10	10
Property, plant, and equipment (net)	410	380
Other assets	530	510
Total assets	$2,340	$2,210
Current liabilities	$ 820	$ 790
Long-term liabilities	480	380
Stockholders' equity—common	1,040	1,040
Total liabilities and stockholders' equity	$2,340	$2,210

Ness Company
Income Statements
For the Year Ended December 31 (in thousands)

	2022	2021
Net sales	$3,800	$3,460
Expenses		
Cost of goods sold	970	890
Selling and administrative expenses	2,400	2,330
Interest expense	10	20
Total expenses	3,380	3,240
Income before income taxes	420	220
Income tax expense	168	88
Net income	$ 252	$ 132

Compute the following ratios for 2022 and 2021.

a. Current ratio.

b. Inventory turnover. (Inventory on December 31, 2020, was $340.)

c. Profit margin.

d. Return on assets. (Assets on December 31, 2020, were $1,900.)

e. Return on common stockholders' equity. (Stockholders' equity—common on December 31, 2020, was $900.)

f. Debt to assets ratio.

g. Times interest earned.

Problems

P13.1A (LO 2, 3), AN Writing Here are comparative financial statement data for Duke Company and Lord Company, two competitors. All data are as of December 31, 2022, and December 31, 2021.

Prepare vertical analysis and comment on profitability.

	Duke Company		Lord Company	
	2022	**2021**	**2022**	**2021**
Net sales	$1,849,000		$546,000	
Cost of goods sold	1,063,200		289,000	
Operating expenses	240,000		82,000	
Interest expense	6,800		3,600	
Income tax expense	62,000		28,000	
Current assets	325,975	$312,410	83,336	$ 79,467
Plant assets (net)	526,800	500,000	139,728	125,812
Current liabilities	66,325	75,815	35,348	30,281
Long-term liabilities	113,990	90,000	29,620	25,000
Common stock, $10 par	500,000	500,000	120,000	120,000
Retained earnings	172,460	146,595	38,096	29,998

Instructions

a. Prepare a vertical analysis of the 2022 income statement data for Duke Company and Lord Company.

b. Comment on the relative profitability of the companies by computing the 2022 return on assets and the return on common stockholders' equity for both companies.

P13.2A (LO 3), AP The comparative statements of Wahlberg Company are presented here.

Compute ratios from balance sheets and income statements.

Wahlberg Company
Income Statements
For the Years Ended December 31

	2022	**2021**
Net sales	$1,890,540	$1,750,500
Cost of goods sold	1,058,540	1,006,000
Gross profit	832,000	744,500
Selling and administrative expenses	500,000	479,000
Income from operations	332,000	265,500
Other expenses and losses		
Interest expense	22,000	20,000
Income before income taxes	310,000	245,500
Income tax expense	92,000	73,000
Net income	$ 218,000	$ 172,500

Wahlberg Company
Balance Sheets
December 31

	2022	**2021**
Assets		
Current assets		
Cash	$ 60,100	$ 64,200
Debt investments (short-term)	74,000	50,000
Accounts receivable (net)	117,800	102,800
Inventory	126,000	115,500
Total current assets	377,900	332,500
Plant assets (net)	649,000	520,300
Total assets	$1,026,900	$852,800

	2022	2021
Liabilities and Stockholders' Equity		
Current liabilities		
Accounts payable	$ 160,000	$145,400
Income taxes payable	43,500	42,000
Total current liabilities	203,500	187,400
Bonds payable	220,000	200,000
Total liabilities	423,500	387,400
Stockholders' equity		
Common stock ($5 par)	290,000	300,000
Retained earnings	313,400	165,400
Total stockholders' equity	603,400	465,400
Total liabilities and stockholders' equity	$1,026,900	$852,800

All sales were on credit. Net cash provided by operating activities for 2022 was $220,000. Capital expenditures were $136,000, and cash dividends paid were $70,000.

Instructions

Compute the following ratios for 2022.

a. Earnings per share.
b. Return on common stockholders' equity.
c. Return on assets.
d. Current ratio.
e. Accounts receivable turnover.
f. Average collection period.

g. Inventory turnover.
h. Days in inventory.
i. Times interest earned.
j. Asset turnover.
k. Debt to assets ratio.
l. Free cash flow.

Perform ratio analysis, and discuss changes in financial position and operating results.

⮕ Excel

P13.3A (LO 3), AN Writing Condensed balance sheet and income statement data for Jergan Corporation are presented here.

Jergan Corporation
Balance Sheets
December 31

	2022	2021	2020
Cash	$ 30,000	$ 20,000	$ 18,000
Accounts receivable (net)	50,000	45,000	48,000
Other current assets	90,000	95,000	64,000
Investments	55,000	70,000	45,000
Property, plant, and equipment (net)	500,000	370,000	358,000
	$725,000	$600,000	$533,000
Current liabilities	$ 85,000	$ 80,000	$ 70,000
Long-term debt	145,000	85,000	50,000
Common stock, $10 par	320,000	310,000	300,000
Retained earnings	175,000	125,000	113,000
	$725,000	$600,000	$533,000

Jergan Corporation
Income Statements
For the Years Ended December 31

	2022	2021
Sales	$740,000	$600,000
Less: Sales returns and allowances	40,000	30,000
Net sales	700,000	570,000
Cost of goods sold	425,000	350,000
Gross profit	275,000	220,000
Operating expenses (including income taxes)	180,000	150,000
Net income	$ 95,000	$ 70,000

Additional information:

1. The market price of Jergan's common stock was $7.00, $7.50, and $8.50 for 2020, 2021, and 2022, respectively.

2. You must compute dividends declared. All declared dividends were paid in cash in the year of declaration.

Instructions

a. Compute the following ratios for 2021 and 2022.

  1. Profit margin.

  2. Gross profit rate.

  3. Asset turnover.

  4. Earnings per share.

  5. Price-earnings ratio.

  6. Payout ratio.

  7. Debt to assets ratio.

b. Based on the ratios calculated, discuss briefly the improvement or lack thereof in the financial position and operating results from 2021 to 2022 of Jergan Corporation.

P13.4A (LO 3), AN The following financial information is for Priscoll Company.

Compute ratios; comment on overall liquidity and profitability.

Priscoll Company
Balance Sheets
December 31

	2022	2021
Assets		
Cash	$ 70,000	$ 65,000
Debt investments (short-term)	55,000	40,000
Accounts receivable (net)	104,000	90,000
Inventory	230,000	165,000
Prepaid expenses	25,000	23,000
Land	130,000	130,000
Building and equipment (net)	260,000	185,000
Total assets	$874,000	$698,000
Liabilities and Stockholders' Equity		
Notes payable (current)	$170,000	$120,000
Accounts payable	65,000	52,000
Accrued liabilities	40,000	40,000
Bonds payable, due 2025	250,000	170,000
Common stock, $10 par	200,000	200,000
Retained earnings	149,000	116,000
Total liabilities and stockholders' equity	$874,000	$698,000

Priscoll Company
Income Statements
For the Years Ended December 31

	2022	2021
Net sales	$882,000	$790,000
Cost of goods sold	640,000	575,000
Gross profit	242,000	215,000
Operating expenses	190,000	167,000
Net income	$ 52,000	$ 48,000

Additional information:

1. Inventory at the beginning of 2021 was $115,000.

2. Accounts receivable (net) at the beginning of 2021 were $86,000.

3. Total assets at the beginning of 2021 were $660,000.

4. No common stock transactions occurred during 2021 or 2022.

5. All sales were on credit.

Instructions

a. Indicate, by using ratios, the change in liquidity and profitability of Priscoll Company from 2021 to 2022. (*Note:* Not all profitability ratios can be computed, nor can cash-basis ratios be computed.)

b. The following are three **independent** situations and a ratio that may be affected. For each situation, compute the affected ratio (1) as of December 31, 2022, and (2) as of December 31, 2023, after giving effect to the situation.

Situation	Ratio
1. 18,000 shares of common stock were sold at par on July 1, 2023. Net income for 2023 was $54,000, and there were no dividends.	Return on common stockholders' equity
2. All of the notes payable were paid in 2023. All other liabilities remained at their December 31, 2022, levels. Total assets on December 31, 2023, were $900,000.	Debt to assets ratio
3. The market price of common stock was $9 and $12 on December 31, 2022 and 2023, respectively. Net income for 2023 was $54,000. (Use a simple average calculation for EPS).	Price-earnings ratio

Compute selected ratios, and compare liquidity, profitability, and solvency for two companies.

P13.5A (LO 3), AN Selected hypothetical financial data of **Target** and **Walmart** for 2022 are presented here (in millions).

	Target Corporation	Walmart Inc.
Income Statement Data for Year		
Net sales	$65,357	$408,214
Cost of goods sold	45,583	304,657
Selling and administrative expenses	15,101	79,607
Interest expense	707	2,065
Other income (expense)	(94)	(411)
Income tax expense	1,384	7,139
Net income	$ 2,488	$ 14,335
Balance Sheet Data (End of Year)		
Current assets	$18,424	$ 48,331
Noncurrent assets	26,109	122,375
Total assets	$44,533	$170,706
Current liabilities	$11,327	$ 55,561
Long-term debt	17,859	44,089
Total stockholders' equity	15,347	71,056
Total liabilities and stockholders' equity	$44,533	$170,706
Beginning-of-Year Balances		
Total assets	$44,106	$163,429
Total stockholders' equity	13,712	65,682
Current liabilities	10,512	55,390
Total liabilities	30,394	97,747
Other Data		
Average net accounts receivable	$ 7,525	$ 4,025
Average inventory	6,942	33,836
Net cash provided by operating activities	5,881	26,249
Capital expenditures	1,729	12,184
Cash dividends paid	496	4,217

Instructions

a. For each company, compute the following ratios. Assume all sales were on credit.

1. Current ratio.
2. Accounts receivable turnover.
3. Average collection period.
4. Inventory turnover.
5. Days in inventory.
6. Profit margin.
7. Asset turnover.
8. Return on assets.
9. Return on common stockholders' equity.
10. Debt to assets ratio.
11. Times interest earned.
12. Free cash flow.

b. Compare the liquidity, solvency, and profitability of the two companies.

Continuing Case

Cookie Creations

(*Note:* This is a continuation of the Cookie Creations case from Chapters 1 through 12.)

CC13 Natalie and Curtis have comparative balance sheets and income statements for Cookie & Coffee Creations Inc. They have been told that they can use these financial statements to prepare horizontal and vertical analyses, to calculate financial ratios, to analyze how their business is doing, and to make some decisions they have been considering.

Go to **WileyPLUS** *for complete case details and instructions.*

leungchopan/
Shutterstock.com

Expand Your Critical Thinking

Financial Reporting Problem: Apple Inc.

CT13.1 Your parents are considering investing in **Apple Inc.** common stock. They ask you, as an accounting expert, to make an analysis of the company for them. Financial statements of Apple are presented in Appendix A. The complete annual report, including the notes to its financial statements, is available at the company's website.

Instructions

a. Make a 5-year trend analysis, using 2014 as the base year, of (1) net sales and (2) net income. Comment on the significance of the trend results.

b. Compute for 2018 and 2017 the (1) debt to assets ratio and (2) times interest earned. (See Note 3 for interest expense.) How would you evaluate Apple's long-term solvency?

c. Compute for 2018 and 2017 the (1) profit margin, (2) asset turnover, (3) return on assets, and (4) return on common stockholders' equity. How would you evaluate Apple's profitability? Total assets at September 24, 2016, were $321,686 million and total stockholders' equity at September 24, 2016, was $128,249 million.

d. What information outside the annual report may also be useful to your parents in making a decision about Apple?

Comparative Analysis Problem: PepsiCo, Inc. vs. The Coca-Cola Company

CT13.2 **PepsiCo**'s financial statements are presented in Appendix B. Financial statements of **The Coca-Cola Company** are presented in Appendix C. The complete annual reports of PepsiCo and Coca-Cola, including the notes to the financial statements, are available at each company's respective website.

Instructions

a. Based on the information contained in these financial statements, determine each of the following for each company.

1. The percentage increase (decrease) in (i) net sales and (ii) net income from 2017 to 2018.

2. The percentage increase in (i) total assets and (ii) total common stockholders' (shareholders') equity from 2017 to 2018.

3. The basic earnings per share and price-earnings ratio for 2018. (For both PepsiCo and Coca-Cola, use the basic earnings per share.) Coca-Cola's common stock had a market price of $47.35 at the end of fiscal-year 2018, and PepsiCo's common stock had a market price of $110.48.

b. What conclusions concerning the two companies can be drawn from these data?

Comparative Analysis Problem: Amazon.com, Inc. vs. Walmart Inc.

CT13.3 The financial statements of **Amazon.com, Inc.** are presented in Appendix D. Financial statements of **Walmart Inc.** are presented in Appendix E.

Instructions

a. Based on the information in the financial statements, determine each of the following for each company:

1. The percentage increase (i) in total net sales for Amazon and net sales for Walmart, and (ii) in net income between the two most recent years provided.

2. The percentage increase (i) in total assets and (ii) in total stockholders' equity between the two most recent years provided.

3. The basic earnings per share for the most recent year provided.

b. What conclusions concerning the two companies can be drawn from these data?

Decision-Making Across the Organization

CT13.4 You are a loan officer for White Sands Bank of Taos. Paul Jason, president of P. Jason Corporation, has just left your office. He is interested in an 8-year loan to expand the company's operations. The borrowed funds would be used to purchase new equipment. As evidence of the company's debt-worthiness, Jason provided you with the following facts.

	2022	2021
Current ratio	3.1	2.1
Asset turnover	2.8	2.2
Net income	Up 32%	Down 8%
Earnings per share	$3.30	$2.50

Jason is a very insistent (some would say pushy) man. When you told him that you would need additional information before making your decision, he acted offended and said, "What more could you possibly want to know?" You responded that, at a minimum, you would need complete, audited financial statements.

Instructions

With the class divided into groups, answer the following.

a. Explain why you would want the financial statements to be audited.

b. Discuss the implications of the ratios provided for the lending decision you are to make. That is, does the information paint a favorable picture? Are these ratios relevant to the decision?

c. List three other ratios that you would want to calculate for this company, and explain why you would use each.

Real-World Focus

CT13.5 You can use the Internet to employ comparative data and industry data to evaluate a company's performance and financial position.

Instructions

Identify two competing companies and then go to the **MarketWatch** website. Type one of the company names in the search box (e.g., **Best Buy**) and then use the information from the Profile tab to answer the following questions.

a. Evaluate the company's liquidity relative to the industry averages and to the competitor that you chose.

b. Evaluate the company's solvency relative to the industry averages and to the competitor that you chose.

c. Evaluate the company's profitability relative to the industry averages and to the competitor that you chose.

CT13.6 The April 25, 2012, edition of the *Wall Street Journal* contains an article by Spencer Jakab entitled "Amazon's Valuation Is Hard to Justify."

Instructions

Read the article and answer the following questions.

a. Explain what is meant by the statement that "On a split-adjusted basis, today's share price is the equivalent of $1,166."

b. The article says that **Amazon.com** nearly doubled its capital spending on items such as fulfillment centers (sophisticated warehouses where it finds, packages, and ships goods to customers). Discuss the implications that this spending would have on the company's return on assets in the short-term and in the long-term.

c. How does Amazon's P-E ratio compare to that of **Apple**, **Netflix**, and **Walmart**? What does this suggest about investors' expectations about Amazon's future earnings?

d. What factor does the article cite as a possible hurdle that might reduce Amazon's ability to raise its operating margin back to previous levels?

Communication Activity

CT13.7 Larry Dundee is the chief executive officer of Palmer Electronics. Dundee is an expert engineer but a novice in accounting. Dundee asks you, as an accounting student, to explain (a) the bases for comparison in analyzing Palmer's financial statements and (b) the factors affecting quality of earnings.

Instructions

Write a memo to Larry Dundee that explains the basis for comparison and the factors affecting quality of earnings.

Ethics Case

CT13.8 René Kelly, president of RL Industries, wishes to issue a press release to bolster her company's image and maybe even its stock price, which has been gradually falling. As controller, you have been asked to provide a list of 20 financial ratios and other operating statistics for RL Industries' first-quarter financials and operations.

Two days after you provide the data requested, Erin Lourdes, the public relations director of RL, asks you to prove the accuracy of the financial and operating data contained in the press release written by the president and edited by Erin. In the news release, the president highlights the sales increase of 25% over last year's first quarter and the positive change in the current ratio from 1.5:1 last year to 3:1 this year. She also emphasizes that production was up 50% over the prior year's first quarter.

You note that the release contains only positive or improved ratios and none of the negative or deteriorated ratios. For instance, no mention is made that the debt to assets ratio has increased from 35% to 55%, that inventories are up 89%, and that although the current ratio improved, the accounts receivable turnover fell from 12 to 9. Nor is there any mention that the reported profit for the quarter would have been a loss had not the estimated lives of RL plant and machinery been increased by 30%. Erin emphasized, "The Pres wants this release by early this afternoon."

Instructions

a. Who are the stakeholders in this situation?

b. Is there anything unethical in the president's actions?

c. Should you as controller remain silent? Does Erin have any responsibility?

All About You

CT13.9 In this chapter, you learned how to use many tools for performing a financial analysis of a company. When making personal investments, however, it is most likely that you won't be buying stocks and bonds in individual companies. Instead, when most people want to invest in stock, they buy mutual funds. By investing in a mutual fund, you reduce your risk because the fund diversifies by buying the stock of a variety of different companies, bonds, and other investments, depending on the stated goals of the fund.

Before you invest in a fund, you will need to decide what type of fund you want. For example, do you want a fund that has the potential of high growth (but also high risk), or are you looking for lower risk and a steady stream of income? Do you want a fund that invests only in U.S. companies, or do you want one that invests globally? Many resources are available to help you with these types of decisions.

Instructions

Do an Internet search on "Motley Fool Here's How to Determine Your Ideal Asset Allocation Strategy" and then complete the investment allocation questionnaire. Add up your total points to determine the type of investment fund that would be appropriate for you.

FASB Codification Activity

CT13.10 If your school has a subscription to the FASB Codification, log in and prepare responses to the following. Use the Master Glossary for determining the proper definitions.

  a. Discontinued operations.

  b. Comprehensive income.

A Look at IFRS

LEARNING OBJECTIVE 4

Compare financial statement analysis and income statement presentation under GAAP and IFRS.

The tools of financial statement analysis are the same throughout the world. Techniques such as vertical and horizontal analysis, for example, are tools used by analysts regardless of whether GAAP- or IFRS-related financial statements are being evaluated. In addition, the ratios provided in the text are the same ones that are used internationally.

As in GAAP, the income statement is a required statement under IFRS. In addition, the content and presentation of an IFRS income statement is similar to the one used for GAAP. *IAS 1* (revised), "Presentation of Financial Statements," provides general guidelines for the reporting of income statement information. In general, the differences in the presentation of financial statement information are relatively minor.

Key Points

Following are the key similarities between GAAP and IFRS as related to financial statement analysis and income statement presentation. There are no significant differences between the two standards.

- The tools of financial statement analysis covered in this chapter are universal and therefore no significant differences exist in the analysis methods used.

- The basic objectives of the income statement are the same under both GAAP and IFRS. As indicated in the text, a very important objective is to ensure that users of the income statement can evaluate the sustainable income of the company. Thus, both the IASB and the FASB are interested in distinguishing normal levels of income from unusual items in order to better predict a company's future profitability.

- The basic accounting for discontinued operations is the same under IFRS and GAAP.

- The accounting for changes in accounting principles and changes in accounting estimates are the same for both GAAP and IFRS.

- Both GAAP and IFRS follow the same approach in reporting comprehensive income.

IFRS Practice

IFRS Self-Test Questions

1. The basic tools of financial analysis are the same under both GAAP and IFRS **except** that:
   a. horizontal analysis cannot be done because the format of the statements is sometimes different.
   b. vertical analysis cannot be done under IFRS.
   c. the current ratio cannot be computed because current liabilities are often reported before current assets in IFRS statements of position.
   d. None of the answer choices is correct.

2. Presentation of comprehensive income must be reported under IFRS in:
   a. the statement of stockholders' equity.
   b. the income statement ending with net income.
   c. the notes to the financial statements.
   d. a statement of comprehensive income.

3. In preparing its income statement for 2022, Parmalane assembles the following information.

Net sales	$500,000
Cost of goods sold	300,000
Operating expenses	40,000
Loss on discontinued operations	20,000

   Ignoring income taxes, what is Parmalane's income from continuing operations for 2022 under IFRS?
   a. $260,000.
   b. $250,000.
   c. $240,000.
   d. $160,000.

International Financial Reporting Problem: **Louis Vuitton**

IFRS13.1 The financial statements of **Louis Vuitton** are presented in Appendix F. The complete consolidated financial statements, including the notes to its financial statements, are available at the company's website.

Instructions

Use the company's 2018 consolidated financial statements to answer the following questions.
   a. What was the company's profit margin for 2018? Has it increased or decreased from 2017?
   b. What was the company's operating profit for 2018?
   c. The company reported comprehensive income of €6,337 million in 2018. What are the other comprehensive gains and losses reported in 2018?

Answers to IFRS Self-Test Questions

1. d   2. d   3. d

Specimen Financial Statements:
Apple Inc.

Once each year, a corporation communicates to its stockholders and other interested parties by issuing a complete set of audited financial statements. The **annual report**, as this communication is called, summarizes the financial results of the company's operations for the year and its plans for the future. Many annual reports are attractive, multicolored, glossy public relations pieces, containing pictures of corporate officers and directors as well as photos and descriptions of new products and new buildings. Yet the basic function of every annual report is to report financial information, almost all of which is a product of the corporation's accounting system.

The content and organization of corporate annual reports have become fairly standardized. Excluding the public relations part of the report (pictures, products, etc.), the following are the traditional financial portions of the annual report:

- Financial Highlights
- Letter to the Stockholders
- Management's Discussion and Analysis
- Financial Statements
- Notes to the Financial Statements

- Management's Responsibility for Financial Reporting
- Management's Report on Internal Control over Financial Reporting
- Report of Independent Registered Public Accounting Firm
- Selected Financial Data

The official SEC filing of the annual report is called a **Form 10-K**, which often omits the public relations pieces found in most standard annual reports. On the following pages, we present **Apple Inc.**'s financial statements taken from the company's 2018 Form 10-K. The complete Form 10-K, including notes to the financial statements, is available at the company's website.

Apple Inc.
Consolidated Statements of Operations
(in millions, except number of shares which are reflected in thousands and per share amounts)

	Years ended		
	September 29, 2018	September 30, 2017	September 24, 2016
Net sales	$ 265,595	$ 229,234	$ 215,639
Cost of sales	163,756	141,048	131,376
Gross margin	101,839	88,186	84,263
Operating expenses:			
Research and development	14,236	11,581	10,045
Selling, general and administrative	16,705	15,261	14,194
Total operating expenses	30,941	26,842	24,239
Operating income	70,898	61,344	60,024
Other income/(expense), net	2,005	2,745	1,348
Income before provision for income taxes	72,903	64,089	61,372
Provision for income taxes	13,372	15,738	15,685
Net income	$ 59,531	$ 48,351	$ 45,687
Earnings per share:			
Basic	$ 12.01	$ 9.27	$ 8.35
Diluted	$ 11.91	$ 9.21	$ 8.31
Shares used in computing earnings per share:			
Basic	4,955,377	5,217,242	5,470,820
Diluted	5,000,109	5,251,692	5,500,281

See accompanying Notes to Consolidated Financial Statements.

Apple Inc.
Consolidated Statements of Comprehensive Income
(in millions)

	Years ended		
	September 29, 2018	**September 30, 2017**	**September 24, 2016**
Net income	$59,531	$48,351	$45,687
Other comprehensive income/(loss):			
Change in foreign currency translation, net of tax effects of $(1), $(77) and $8, respectively	(525)	224	75
Change in unrealized gains/losses on derivative instruments:			
Change in fair value of derivatives, net of tax benefit/(expense) of $(149), $(478) and $(7), respectively	523	1,315	7
Adjustment for net (gains)/losses realized and included in net income, net of tax expense/(benefit) of $(104), $475 and $131, respectively	382	(1,477)	(741)
Total change in unrealized gains/losses on derivative instruments, net of tax	905	(162)	(734)
Change in unrealized gains/losses on marketable securities:			
Change in fair value of marketable securities, net of tax benefit/(expense) of $1,156, $425 and $(863), respectively	(3,407)	(782)	1,582
Adjustment for net (gains)/losses realized and included in net income, net of tax expense/(benefit) of $21, $35 and $(31), respectively	1	(64)	56
Total change in unrealized gains/losses on marketable securities, net of tax	(3,406)	(846)	1,638
Total other comprehensive income/(loss)	(3,026)	(784)	979
Total comprehensive income	$56,505	$47,567	$46,666

See accompanying Notes to Consolidated Financial Statements.

Apple Inc.
Consolidated Balance Sheets
(in millions, except number of shares which are reflected in thousands and par value)

	September 29, 2018	September 30, 2017
ASSETS:		
Current assets:		
Cash and cash equivalents	$ 25,913	$ 20,289
Marketable securities	40,388	53,892
Accounts receivable, net	23,186	17,874
Inventories	3,956	4,855
Vendor non-trade receivables	25,809	17,799
Other current assets	12,087	13,936
Total current assets	131,339	128,645
Non-current assets:		
Marketable securities	170,799	194,714
Property, plant and equipment, net	41,304	33,783
Other non-current assets	22,283	18,177
Total non-current assets	234,386	246,674
Total assets	$365,725	$375,319
LIABILITIES AND SHAREHOLDERS' EQUITY:		
Current liabilities:		
Accounts payable	$ 55,888	$ 44,242
Other current liabilities	32,687	30,551
Deferred revenue	7,543	7,548
Commercial paper	11,964	11,977
Term debt	8,784	6,496
Total current liabilities	116,866	100,814
Non-current liabilities:		
Deferred revenue	2,797	2,836
Term debt	93,735	97,207
Other non-current liabilities	45,180	40,415
Total non-current liabilities	141,712	140,458
Total liabilities	258,578	241,272
Commitments and contingencies		
Shareholders' equity:		
Common stock and additional paid-in capital, $0.00001 par value: 12,600,000 shares authorized; 4,754,986 and 5,126,201 shares issued and outstanding, respectively	40,201	35,867
Retained earnings	70,400	98,330
Accumulated other comprehensive income/(loss)	(3,454)	(150)
Total shareholders' equity	107,147	134,047
Total liabilities and shareholders' equity	$365,725	$375,319

See accompanying Notes to Consolidated Financial Statements.

Apple Inc.
Consolidated Statements of Shareholders' Equity
(in millions, except number of shares which are reflected in thousands and per share amounts)

	Common Stock and Additional Paid-In Capital		Retained Earnings	Accumulated Other Comprehensive Income/(Loss)	Total Shareholders' Equity
	Shares	**Amount**			
Balances as of September 26, 2015	5,578,753	$27,416	$92,284	$ (345)	$119,355
Net income	—	—	45,687	—	45,687
Other comprehensive income/(loss)	—	—	—	979	979
Dividends and dividend equivalents declared at $2.18 per share or RSU	—	—	(12,188)	—	(12,188)
Repurchase of common stock	(279,609)	—	(29,000)	—	(29,000)
Share-based compensation	—	4,262	—	—	4,262
Common stock issued, net of shares withheld for employee taxes	37,022	(806)	(419)	—	(1,225)
Tax benefit from equity awards, including transfer pricing adjustments	—	379	—	—	379
Balances as of September 24, 2016	5,336,166	31,251	96,364	634	128,249
Net income	—	—	48,351	—	48,351
Other comprehensive income/(loss)	—	—	—	(784)	(784)
Dividends and dividend equivalents declared at $2.40 per share or RSU	—	—	(12,803)	—	(12,803)
Repurchase of common stock	(246,496)	—	(33,001)	—	(33,001)
Share-based compensation	—	4,909	—	—	4,909
Common stock issued, net of shares withheld for employee taxes	36,531	(913)	(581)	—	(1,494)
Tax benefit from equity awards, including transfer pricing adjustments	—	620	—	—	620
Balances as of September 30, 2017	5,126,201	35,867	98,330	(150)	134,047
Cumulative effect of change in accounting principle	—	—	278	(278)	—
Net income	—	—	59,531	—	59,531
Other comprehensive income/(loss)	—	—	—	(3,026)	(3,026)
Dividends and dividend equivalents declared at $2.72 per share or RSU	—	—	(13,735)	—	(13,735)
Repurchase of common stock	(405,549)	—	(73,056)	—	(73,056)
Share-based compensation	—	5,443	—	—	5,443
Common stock issued, net of shares withheld for employee taxes	34,334	(1,109)	(948)	—	(2,057)
Balances as of September 29, 2018	4,754,986	$40,201	$70,400	$(3,454)	$107,147

See accompanying Notes to Consolidated Financial Statements.

Apple Inc.
Consolidated Statements of Cash Flows
(in millions)

	Years ended		
	September 29, 2018	September 30, 2017	September 24, 2016
Cash and cash equivalents, beginning of the year	$20,289	$20,484	$21,120
Operating activities:			
Net income	59,531	48,351	45,687
Adjustments to reconcile net income to cash generated by operating activities:			
Depreciation and amortization	10,903	10,157	10,505
Share-based compensation expense	5,340	4,840	4,210
Deferred income tax expense/(benefit)	(32,590)	5,966	4,938
Other	(444)	(166)	486
Changes in operating assets and liabilities:			
Accounts receivable, net	(5,322)	(2,093)	527
Inventories	828	(2,723)	217
Vendor non-trade receivables	(8,010)	(4,254)	(51)
Other current and non-current assets	(423)	(5,318)	1,055
Accounts payable	9,175	8,966	2,117
Deferred revenue	(44)	(626)	(1,554)
Other current and non-current liabilities	38,490	1,125	(1,906)
Cash generated by operating activities	77,434	64,225	66,231
Investing activities:			
Purchases of marketable securities	(71,356)	(159,486)	(142,428)
Proceeds from maturities of marketable securities	55,881	31,775	21,258
Proceeds from sales of marketable securities	47,838	94,564	90,536
Payments for acquisition of property, plant and equipment	(13,313)	(12,451)	(12,734)
Payments made in connection with business acquisitions, net	(721)	(329)	(297)
Purchases of non-marketable securities	(1,871)	(521)	(1,388)
Proceeds from non-marketable securities	353	126	—
Other	(745)	(124)	(924)
Cash generated by/(used in) investing activities	16,066	(46,446)	(45,977)
Financing activities:			
Proceeds from issuance of common stock	669	555	495
Payments for taxes related to net share settlement of equity awards	(2,527)	(1,874)	(1,570)
Payments for dividends and dividend equivalents	(13,712)	(12,769)	(12,150)
Repurchases of common stock	(72,738)	(32,900)	(29,722)
Proceeds from issuance of term debt, net	6,969	28,662	24,954
Repayments of term debt	(6,500)	(3,500)	(2,500)
Change in commercial paper, net	(37)	3,852	(397)
Cash used in financing activities	(87,876)	(17,974)	(20,890)
Increase/(Decrease) in cash and cash equivalents	5,624	(195)	(636)
Cash and cash equivalents, end of the year	$25,913	$20,289	$20,484
Supplemental cash flow disclosure:			
Cash paid for income taxes, net	$10,417	$11,591	$10,444
Cash paid for interest	$ 3,022	$ 2,092	$ 1,316

See accompanying Notes to Consolidated Financial Statements.

Specimen Financial Statements: PepsiCo, Inc.

PepsiCo, Inc. is a world leader in convenient snacks, foods, and beverages. The following are PepsiCo's financial statements as presented in its 2018 annual report. The complete annual report, including notes to the financial statements, is available at the company's website.

Consolidated Statement of Income
PepsiCo, Inc. and Subsidiaries
Fiscal years ended December 29, 2018, December 30, 2017 and December 31, 2016
(in millions except per share amounts)

	2018	2017	2016
Net Revenue	$64,661	$63,525	$62,799
Cost of sales	29,381	28,796	28,222
Gross profit	35,280	34,729	34,577
Selling, general and administrative expenses	25,170	24,453	24,773
Operating Profit	10,110	10,276	9,804
Other pension and retiree medical benefits income/(expense)	298	233	(19)
Interest expense	(1,525)	(1,151)	(1,342)
Interest income and other	306	244	110
Income before income taxes	9,189	9,602	8,553
(Benefit from)/provision for income taxes (See Note 5)	(3,370)	4,694	2,174
Net income	12,559	4,908	6,379
Less: Net income attributable to noncontrolling interests	44	51	50
Net Income Attributable to PepsiCo	$12,515	$ 4,857	$ 6,329
Net Income Attributable to PepsiCo per Common Share			
Basic	$ 8.84	$ 3.40	$ 4.39
Diluted	$ 8.78	$ 3.38	$ 4.36
Weighted-average common shares outstanding			
Basic	1,415	1,425	1,439
Diluted	1,425	1,438	1,452

See accompanying notes to the consolidated financial statements.

Consolidated Statement of Comprehensive Income
PepsiCo, Inc. and Subsidiaries
Fiscal years ended December 29, 2018, December 30, 2017 and December 31, 2016
(in millions)

	2018	2017	2016
Net income	$12,559	$4,908	$6,379
Other comprehensive income/(loss), net of taxes:			
Net currency translation adjustment	(1,641)	1,109	(302)
Net change on cash flow hedges	40	(36)	46
Net pension and retiree medical adjustments	(467)	(159)	(316)
Net change on available-for-sale securities	6	(68)	(24)
Other	—	16	—
	(2,062)	862	(596)
Comprehensive income	10,497	5,770	5,783
Comprehensive income attributable to noncontrolling interests	(44)	(51)	(54)
Comprehensive Income Attributable to PepsiCo	$10,453	$5,719	$5,729

See accompanying notes to the consolidated financial statements.

Consolidated Statement of Cash Flows
PepsiCo, Inc. and Subsidiaries
Fiscal years ended December 29, 2018, December 30, 2017 and December 31, 2016
(in millions)

	2018	2017	2016
Operating Activities			
Net income	$12,559	$ 4,908	$ 6,379
Depreciation and amortization	2,399	2,369	2,368
Share-based compensation expense	256	292	284
Restructuring and impairment charges	308	295	160
Cash payments for restructuring charges	(255)	(113)	(125)
Charge related to the transaction with Tingyi	—	—	373
Pension and retiree medical plan expenses	221	221	501
Pension and retiree medical plan contributions	(1,708)	(220)	(695)
Deferred income taxes and other tax charges and credits	(531)	619	452
Other net tax benefits related to international reorganizations	(4,347)	—	—
Net tax (benefit)/expense related to the TCJ Act	(28)	2,451	—
Change in assets and liabilities:			
Accounts and notes receivable	(253)	(202)	(349)
Inventories	(174)	(168)	(75)
Prepaid expenses and other current assets	9	20	10
Accounts payable and other current liabilities	882	201	981
Income taxes payable	333	(338)	329
Other, net	(256)	(305)	70
Net Cash Provided by Operating Activities	9,415	10,030	10,663

(continues)

	2018	2017	2016
Investing Activities			
Capital spending	$ (3,282)	$(2,969)	$(3,040)
Sales of property, plant and equipment	134	180	99
Acquisition of SodaStream, net of cash and cash equivalents acquired	(1,197)	—	—
Other acquisitions and investments in noncontrolled affiliates	(299)	(61)	(212)
Divestitures	505	267	85
Short-term investments, by original maturity:			
More than three months - purchases	(5,637)	(18,385)	(12,504)
More than three months - maturities	12,824	15,744	8,399
More than three months - sales	1,498	790	—
Three months or less, net	16	2	16
Other investing, net	2	29	7
Net Cash Provided by/(Used for) Investing Activities	4,564	(4,403)	(7,150)
Financing Activities			
Proceeds from issuances of long-term debt	—	7,509	7,818
Payments of long-term debt	(4,007)	(4,406)	(3,105)
Cash tender and exchange offers/debt redemptions	(1,589)	—	(2,504)
Short-term borrowings, by original maturity:			
More than three months - proceeds	3	91	59
More than three months - payments	(17)	(128)	(27)
Three months or less, net	(1,352)	(1,016)	1,505
Cash dividends paid	(4,930)	(4,472)	(4,227)
Share repurchases - common	(2,000)	(2,000)	(3,000)
Share repurchases - preferred	(2)	(5)	(7)
Proceeds from exercises of stock options	281	462	465
Withholding tax payments on RSUs, PSUs and PEPunits converted	(103)	(145)	(130)
Other financing	(53)	(76)	(58)
Net Cash Used for Financing Activities	(13,769)	(4,186)	(3,211)
Effect of exchange rate changes on cash and cash equivalents and restricted cash	(98)	47	(252)
Net Increase in Cash and Cash Equivalents and Restricted Cash	112	1,488	50
Cash and Cash Equivalents and Restricted Cash, Beginning of Year	10,657	9,169	9,119
Cash and Cash Equivalents and Restricted Cash, End of Year	$10,769	$10,657	$ 9,169

See accompanying notes to the consolidated financial statements.

Consolidated Balance Sheet
PepsiCo, Inc. and Subsidiaries
December 29, 2018 and December 30, 2017
(in millions except per share amounts)

	2018	2017
ASSETS		
Current Assets		
Cash and cash equivalents	$ 8,721	$10,610
Short-term investments	272	8,900
Restricted cash	1,997	—
Accounts and notes receivable, net	7,142	7,024
Inventories	3,128	2,947
Prepaid expenses and other current assets	633	1,546
Total Current Assets	21,893	31,027
Property, Plant and Equipment, net	17,589	17,240
Amortizable Intangible Assets, net	1,644	1,268
Goodwill	14,808	14,744
Other indefinite-lived intangible assets	14,181	12,570
Indefinite-Lived Intangible Assets	28,989	27,314
Investments in Noncontrolled Affiliates	2,409	2,042
Deferred Income Taxes	4,364	—
Other Assets	760	913
Total Assets	$77,648	$79,804
LIABILITIES AND EQUITY		
Current Liabilities		
Short-term debt obligations	$ 4,026	$ 5,485
Accounts payable and other current liabilities	18,112	15,017
Total Current Liabilities	22,138	20,502
Long-Term Debt Obligations	28,295	33,796
Deferred Income Taxes	3,499	3,242
Other Liabilities	9,114	11,283
Total Liabilities	63,046	68,823
Commitments and contingencies		
Preferred Stock, no par value	—	41
Repurchased Preferred Stock	—	(197)
PepsiCo Common Shareholders' Equity		
Common stock, par value 1⅔¢ per share (authorized 3,600 shares; issued, net of repurchased common stock at par value: 1,409 and 1,420 shares, respectively)	23	24
Capital in excess of par value	3,953	3,996
Retained earnings	59,947	52,839
Accumulated other comprehensive loss	(15,119)	(13,057)
Repurchased common stock, in excess of par value (458 and 446 shares, respectively)	(34,286)	(32,757)
Total PepsiCo Common Shareholders' Equity	14,518	11,045
Noncontrolling interests	84	92
Total Equity	14,602	10,981
Total Liabilities and Equity	$77,648	$79,804

See accompanying notes to the consolidated financial statements.

Consolidated Statement of Equity
PepsiCo, Inc. and Subsidiaries
Fiscal years ended December 29, 2018, December 30, 2017 and December 31, 2016
(in millions)

	2018		2017		2016	
	Shares	**Amount**	Shares	Amount	Shares	Amount
Preferred Stock						
Balance, beginning of year	0.8	$ 41	0.8	$ 41	0.8	$ 41
Conversion to common stock	(0.1)	(6)	—	—	—	—
Retirement of preferred stock	(0.7)	(35)	—	—	—	—
Balance, end of year	—	—	0.8	41	0.8	41
Repurchased Preferred Stock						
Balance, beginning of year	(0.7)	(197)	(0.7)	(192)	(0.7)	(186)
Redemptions	—	(2)	—	(5)	—	(6)
Retirement of preferred stock	0.7	199	—	—	—	—
Balance, end of year	—	—	(0.7)	(197)	(0.7)	(192)
Common Stock						
Balance, beginning of year	1,420	24	1,428	24	1,448	24
Share issued in connection with preferred stock conversion to common stock	1	—	—	—	—	—
Change in repurchased common stock	(12)	(1)	(8)	—	(20)	—
Balance, end of year	1,409	23	1,420	24	1,428	24
Capital in Excess of Par Value						
Balance, beginning of year		3,996		4,091		4,076
Share-based compensation expense		250		290		289
Equity issued in connection with preferred stock conversion to common stock		6		—		—
Stock option exercises, RSUs, PSUs and PEPunits converted[a]		(193)		(236)		(138)
Withholding tax on RSUs, PSUs and PEPunits converted		(103)		(145)		(130)
Other		(3)		(4)		(6)
Balance, end of year		3,953		3,996		4,091
Retained Earnings						
Balance, beginning of year		52,839		52,518		50,472
Cumulative effect of accounting changes		(145)		—		—
Net income attributable to PepsiCo		12,515		4,857		6,329
Cash dividends declared - common[b]		(5,098)		(4,536)		(4,282)
Cash dividends declared - preferred		—		—		(1)
Retirement of preferred stock		(164)		—		—
Balance, end of year		59,947		52,839		52,518
Accumulated Other Comprehensive Loss						
Balance, beginning of year		(13,057)		(13,919)		(13,319)
Other comprehensive (loss)/income attributable to PepsiCo		(2,062)		862		(600)
Balance, end of year		(15,119)		(13,057)		(13,919)

(*continues*)

	2018		2017		2016	
	Shares	**Amount**	Shares	Amount	Shares	Amount
Repurchased Common Stock						
Balance, beginning of year	**(446)**	**$(32,757)**	(438)	$(31,468)	(418)	$(29,185)
Share repurchases	**(18)**	**(2,000)**	(18)	(2,000)	(29)	(3,000)
Stock option exercises, RSUs, PSUs and PEPunits converted	**6**	**469**	10	708	9	712
Other	**—**	**2**	—	3	—	5
Balance, end of year	**(458)**	**(34,286)**	(446)	(32,757)	(438)	(31,468)
Total PepsiCo Common Shareholders' Equity		**14,518**		11,045		11,246
Noncontrolling Interests						
Balance, beginning of year		**92**		104		107
Net income attributable to noncontrolling interests		**44**		51		50
Distributions to noncontrolling interests		**(49)**		(62)		(55)
Currency translation adjustment:		**—**		—		4
Other, net		**(3)**		(1)		(2)
Balance, end of year		**84**		92		104
Total Equity		**$ 14,602**		$ 10,981		$ 11,199

(a) Includes total tax benefits of $110 million in 2016.
(b) Cash dividends declared per common share were $3.5875, $3.1675 and $2.96 for 2018, 2017 and 2016, respectively.

See accompanying notes to the consolidated financial statements.

Specimen Financial Statements:
The Coca-Cola Company

The Coca-Cola Company is a global leader in the beverage industry. It offers hundreds of brands, including soft drinks, fruit juices, sports drinks, and other beverages, in more than 200 countries. The following are Coca-Cola's financial statements as presented in its 2018 annual report. The complete annual report, including notes to the financial statements, is available at the company's website.

The Coca-Cola Company and Subsidiaries
Consolidated Statements of Income

Year Ended December 31,	2018	2017	2016
(in millions except per share data)			
NET OPERATING REVENUES	**$31,856**	$35,410	$41,863
Cost of goods sold	**11,770**	13,255	16,465
GROSS PROFIT	**20,086**	22,155	25,398
Selling, general and administrative expenses	**10,307**	12,654	15,370
Other operating charges	**1,079**	1,902	1,371
OPERATING INCOME	**8,700**	7,599	8,657
Interest income	**682**	677	642
Interest expense	**919**	841	733
Equity income (loss)—net	**1,008**	1,071	835
Other income (loss)—net	**(1,121)**	(1,764)	(1,265)
INCOME FROM CONTINUING OPERATIONS BEFORE INCOME TAXES	**8,350**	6,742	8,136
Income taxes from continuing operations	**1,623**	5,560	1,586
NET INCOME FROM CONTINUING OPERATIONS	**6,727**	1,182	6,550
Income (loss) from discontinued operations (net of income taxes of $126, $47 and $0, respectively)	**(251)**	101	—
CONSOLIDATED NET INCOME	**6,476**	1,283	6,550
Less: Net income attributable to noncontrolling interests	**42**	35	23
NET INCOME ATTRIBUTABLE TO SHAREOWNERS OF THE COCA-COLA COMPANY	**$ 6,434**	$ 1,248	$ 6,527
Basic net income per share from continuing operations[1]	**$ 1.58**	$ 0.28	$ 1.51
Basic net income (loss) per share from discontinued operations[2]	**(0.07)**	0.02	—
BASIC NET INCOME PER SHARE	**$ 1.51**	$ 0.29[3]	$ 1.51
Diluted net income per share from continuing operations[1]	**$ 1.57**	$ 0.27	$ 1.49
Diluted net income (loss) per share from discontinued operations[2]	**(0.07)**	0.02	—
DILUTED NET INCOME PER SHARE	**$ 1.50**	$ 0.29	$ 1.49
AVERAGE SHARES OUTSTANDING—BASIC	**4,259**	4,272	4,317
Effect of dilutive securities	**40**	52	50
AVERAGE SHARES OUTSTANDING—DILUTED	**4,299**	4,324	4,367

[1]Calculated based on net income from continuing operations less net income from continuing operations attributable to noncontrolling interests.

[2]Calculated based on net income (loss) from discontinued operations less net income from discontinued operations attributable to noncontrolling interests.

[3]Per share amounts do not add due to rounding.

Refer to Notes to Consolidated Financial Statements.

The Coca-Cola Company and Subsidiaries
Consolidated Statements of Comprehensive Income

Year Ended December 31,	2018	2017	2016
(in millions)			
CONSOLIDATED NET INCOME	**$6,476**	$1,283	$6,550
Other comprehensive income:			
Net foreign currency translation adjustments	**(2,035)**	861	(626)
Net gains (losses) on derivatives	**(7)**	(433)	(382)
Net unrealized gains (losses) on available-for-sale securities	**(34)**	188	17
Net change in pension and other benefit liabilities	**29**	322	(53)
TOTAL COMPREHENSIVE INCOME	**4,429**	2,221	5,506
Less: Comprehensive income attributable to noncontrolling interests	**95**	73	10
TOTAL COMPREHENSIVE INCOME ATTRIBUTABLE TO SHAREOWNERS OF THE COCA-COLA COMPANY	**$4,334**	$2,148	$5,496

Refer to Notes to Consolidated Financial Statements.

The Coca-Cola Company and Subsidiaries
Consolidated Balance Sheets

December 31,	**2018**	2017
(in millions except par value)		
ASSETS		
CURRENT ASSETS		
Cash and cash equivalents	**$ 8,926**	$ 6,006
Short-term investments	**2,025**	9,352
TOTAL CASH, CASH EQUIVALENTS AND SHORT-TERM INVESTMENTS	**10,951**	15,358
Marketable securities	**5,013**	5,317
Trade accounts receivable, less allowances of $489 and $477, respectively	**3,396**	3,667
Inventories	**2,766**	2,655
Prepaid expenses and other assets	**1,962**	2,000
Assets held for sale	**—**	219
Assets held for sale—discontinued operations	**6,546**	7,329
TOTAL CURRENT ASSETS	**30,634**	36,545
EQUITY METHOD INVESTMENTS	**19,407**	20,856
OTHER INVESTMENTS	**867**	1,096
OTHER ASSETS	**4,139**	4,230
DEFERRED INCOME TAX ASSETS	**2,667**	330
PROPERTY, PLANT AND EQUIPMENT—net	**8,232**	8,203
TRADEMARKS WITH INDEFINITE LIVES	**6,682**	6,729
BOTTLERS' FRANCHISE RIGHTS WITH INDEFINITE LIVES	**51**	138
GOODWILL	**10,263**	9,401
OTHER INTANGIBLE ASSETS	**274**	368
TOTAL ASSETS	**$83,216**	$87,896
LIABILITIES AND EQUITY		
CURRENT LIABILITIES		
Accounts payable and accrued expenses	**$ 8,932**	$ 8,748
Loans and notes payable	**13,194**	13,205
Current maturities of long-term debt	**4,997**	3,298
Accrued income taxes	**378**	410
Liabilities held for sale	**—**	37
Liabilities held for sale—discontinued operations	**1,722**	1,496
TOTAL CURRENT LIABILITIES	**29,223**	27,194
LONG-TERM DEBT	**25,364**	31,182
OTHER LIABILITIES	**7,638**	8,021
DEFERRED INCOME TAX LIABILITIES	**1,933**	2,522
THE COCA-COLA COMPANY SHAREOWNERS' EQUITY		
Common stock, $0.25 par value; Authorized—11,200 shares; Issued—7,040 and 7,040 shares, respectively	**1,760**	1,760
Capital surplus	**16,520**	15,864
Reinvested earnings	**63,234**	60,430
Accumulated other comprehensive income (loss)	**(12,814)**	(10,305)
Treasury stock, at cost—2,772 and 2,781 shares, respectively	**(51,719)**	(50,677)
EQUITY ATTRIBUTABLE TO SHAREOWNERS OF THE COCA-COLA COMPANY	**16,981**	17,072
EQUITY ATTRIBUTABLE TO NONCONTROLLING INTERESTS	**2,077**	1,905
TOTAL EQUITY	**19,058**	18,977
TOTAL LIABILITIES AND EQUITY	**$83,216**	$87,896

Refer to Notes to Consolidated Financial Statements.

The Coca-Cola Company and Subsidiaries
Consolidated Statements of Cash Flows

Year Ended December 31,	2018	2017	2016
(In millions)			
OPERATING ACTIVITIES			
Consolidated net income	$ 6,476	$ 1,283	$ 6,550
(Income) loss from discontinued operations	251	(101)	—
Net income from continuing operations	6,727	1,182	6,550
Depreciation and amortization	1,086	1,260	1,787
Stock-based compensation expense	225	219	258
Deferred income taxes	(450)	(1,256)	(856)
Equity (income) loss—net of dividends	(457)	(628)	(449)
Foreign currency adjustments	(38)	281	158
Significant (gains) losses on sales of assets—net	189	1,459	1,146
Other operating charges	558	1,218	647
Other items	682	(269)	(224)
Net change in operating assets and liabilities	(1,202)	3,464	(225)
Net cash provided by operating activities	7,320	6,930	8,792
INVESTING ACTIVITIES			
Purchases of investments	(7,789)	(17,296)	(16,626)
Proceeds from disposals of investments	14,977	16,694	17,842
Acquisitions of businesses, equity method investments and nonmarketable securities	(1,040)	(3,809)	(838)
Proceeds from disposals of businesses, equity method investments and nonmarketable securities	1,362	3,821	1,035
Purchases of property, plant and equipment	(1,347)	(1,675)	(2,262)
Proceeds from disposals of property, plant and equipment	245	104	150
Other investing activities	(60)	(93)	(305)
Net cash provided by (used in) investing activities	6,348	(2,254)	(1,004)
FINANCING ACTIVITIES			
Issuances of debt	27,339	29,857	27,281
Payments of debt	(30,568)	(28,768)	(25,615)
Issuances of stock	1,476	1,595	1,434
Purchases of stock for treasury	(1,912)	(3,682)	(3,681)
Dividends	(6,644)	(6,320)	(6,043)
Other financing activities	(243)	(91)	79
Net cash provided by (used in) financing activities	(10,552)	(7,409)	(6,545)
CASH FLOWS FROM DISCONTINUED OPERATIONS			
Net cash provided by (used in) operating activities from discontinued operations	307	111	—
Net cash provided by (used in) investing activities from discontinued operations	(421)	(58)	—
Net cash provided by (used in) financing activities from discontinued operations	205	(38)	—
Net cash provided by (used in) discontinued operations	91	15	—
EFFECT OF EXCHANGE RATE CHANGES ON CASH, CASH EQUIVALENTS, RESTRICTED CASH AND RESTRICTED CASH EQUIVALENTS	(262)	241	(5)
CASH, CASH EQUIVALENTS, RESTRICTED CASH AND RESTRICTED CASH EQUIVALENTS			
Net increase (decrease) in cash, cash equivalents, restricted cash and restricted cash equivalents during the year	2,945	(2,477)	1,238
Cash, cash equivalents, restricted cash and restricted cash equivalents at beginning of year	6,373	8,850	7,612
Cash, cash equivalents, restricted cash and restricted cash equivalents at end of year	9,318	6,373	8,850
Less: Restricted cash and restricted cash equivalents at end of year	392	367	295
Cash and cash equivalents at end of year	$ 8,926	$ 6,006	$ 8,555

Refer to Notes to Consolidated Financial Statements.

The Coca-Cola Company and Subsidiaries
Consolidated Statements of Shareowners' Equity

Year Ended December 31,	2018	2017	2016
(in millions except per share data)			
EQUITY ATTRIBUTABLE TO SHAREOWNERS OF THE COCA-COLA COMPANY			
NUMBER OF COMMON SHARES OUTSTANDING			
Balance at beginning of year	4,259	4,288	4,324
Treasury stock issued to employees related to stock compensation plans	48	53	50
Purchases of stock for treasury	(39)	(82)	(86)
Balance at end of year	4,268	4,259	4,288
COMMON STOCK	$ 1,760	$ 1,760	$ 1,760
CAPITAL SURPLUS			
Balance at beginning of year	15,864	14,993	14,016
Stock issued to employees related to stock compensation plans	467	655	589
Tax benefit (charge) from stock compensation plans	—	—	130
Stock-based compensation expense	225	219	258
Other activities	(36)	(3)	—
Balance at end of year	16,520	15,864	14,993
REINVESTED EARNINGS			
Balance at beginning of year	60,430	65,502	65,018
Adoption of accounting standards[1]	3,014	—	—
Net income attributable to shareowners of The Coca-Cola Company	6,434	1,248	6,527
Dividends (per share—$1.56, $1.48 and $1.40 in 2018, 2017 and 2016, respectively)	(6,644)	(6,320)	(6,043)
Balance at end of year	63,234	60,430	65,502
ACCUMULATED OTHER COMPREHENSIVE INCOME (LOSS)			
Balance at beginning of year	(10,305)	(11,205)	(10,174)
Adoption of accounting standards[1]	(409)	—	—
Net other comprehensive income (loss)	(2,100)	900	(1,031)
Balance at end of year	(12,814)	(10,305)	(11,205)
TREASURY STOCK			
Balance at beginning of year	(50,677)	(47,988)	(45,066)
Treasury stock issued to employees related to stock compensation plans	704	909	811
Purchases of stock for treasury	(1,746)	(3,598)	(3,733)
Balance at end of year	(51,719)	(50,677)	(47,988)
TOTAL EQUITY ATTRIBUTABLE TO SHAREOWNERS OF THE COCA-COLA COMPANY	$16,981	$17,072	$23,062
EQUITY ATTRIBUTABLE TO NONCONTROLLING INTERESTS			
Balance at beginning of year	$ 1,905	$ 158	$ 210
Net income attributable to noncontrolling interests	42	35	23
Net foreign currency translation adjustments	53	38	(13)
Dividends paid to noncontrolling interests	(31)	(15)	(25)
Contributions by noncontrolling interests	—	—	1
Business combinations	101	1,805	—
Deconsolidation of certain entities	—	(157)	(34)
Other activities	7	41	(4)
TOTAL EQUITY ATTRIBUTABLE TO NONCONTROLLING INTERESTS	$ 2,077	$ 1,905	$ 158

[1]Refer to Note 1, Note 3, Note 4 and Note 15.

Refer to Notes to Consolidated Financial Statements.

Specimen Financial Statements:
Amazon.com, Inc.

Amazon.com, Inc. is the world's largest online retailer. It also produces consumer electronics —notably the Kindle e-book reader and the Kindle Fire Tablet computer—and is a major provider of cloud computing services. The following are Amazon's financial statements as presented in the company's 2018 annual report. The complete annual report, including notes to the financial statements, is available at the company's website.

Amazon.com, Inc.
Consolidated Statements of Cash Flows
(in millions)

	Year Ended December 31,		
	2016	2017	2018
CASH, CASH EQUIVALENTS, AND RESTRICTED CASH, BEGINNING OF PERIOD	$16,175	$19,934	$21,856
OPERATING ACTIVITIES:			
Net income	2,371	3,033	10,073
Adjustments to reconcile net income to net cash from operating activities:			
Depreciation of property and equipment and other amortization, including capitalized content costs	8,116	11,478	15,341
Stock-based compensation	2,975	4,215	5,418
Other operating expense, net	160	202	274
Other expense (income), net	(20)	(292)	219
Deferred income taxes	(246)	(29)	441
Changes in operating assets and liabilities:			
Inventories	(1,426)	(3,583)	(1,314)
Accounts receivable, net and other	(3,436)	(4,780)	(4,615)
Accounts payable	5,030	7,100	3,263
Accrued expenses and other	1,724	283	472
Unearned revenue	1,955	738	1,151
Net cash provided by (used in) operating activities	17,203	18,365	30,723
INVESTING ACTIVITIES:			
Purchases of property and equipment	(7,804)	(11,955)	(13,427)
Proceeds from property and equipment incentives	1,067	1,897	2,104
Acquisitions, net of cash acquired, and other	(116)	(13,972)	(2,186)
Sales and maturities of marketable securities	4,577	9,677	8,240
Purchases of marketable securities	(7,240)	(12,731)	(7,100)
Net cash provided by (used in) investing activities	(9,516)	(27,084)	(12,369)
FINANCING ACTIVITIES:			
Proceeds from long-term debt and other	618	16,228	768
Repayments of long-term debt and other	(327)	(1,301)	(668)
Principal repayments of capital lease obligations	(3,860)	(4,799)	(7,449)
Principal repayments of finance lease obligations	(147)	(200)	(337)
Net cash provided by (used in) financing activities	(3,716)	9,928	(7,686)
Foreign currency effect on cash, cash equivalents, and restricted cash	(212)	713	(351)
Net increase (decrease) in cash, cash equivalents, and restricted cash	3,759	1,922	10,317
CASH, CASH EQUIVALENTS, AND RESTRICTED CASH, END OF PERIOD	$19,934	$21,856	$32,173
SUPPLEMENTAL CASH FLOW INFORMATION:			
Cash paid for interest on long-term debt	$ 290	$ 328	$ 854
Cash paid for interest on capital and finance lease obligations	206	319	575
Cash paid for income taxes, net of refunds	412	957	1,184
Property and equipment acquired under capital leases	5,704	9,637	10,615
Property and equipment acquired under build-to-suit leases	1,209	3,541	3,641

See accompanying notes to consolidated financial statements.

Amazon.com, Inc.
Consolidated Statements of Operations
(in millions, except per share data)

	Year Ended December 31,		
	2016	**2017**	**2018**
Net product sales	$94,665	$118,573	$141,915
Net service sales	41,322	59,293	90,972
Total net sales	135,987	177,866	232,887
Operating expenses:			
Cost of sales	88,265	111,934	139,156
Fulfillment	17,619	25,249	34,027
Marketing	7,233	10,069	13,814
Technology and content	16,085	22,620	28,837
General and administrative	2,432	3,674	4,336
Other operating expense, net	167	214	296
Total operating expenses	131,801	173,760	220,466
Operating income	4,186	4,106	12,421
Interest income	100	202	440
Interest expense	(484)	(848)	(1,417)
Other income (expense), net	90	346	(183)
Total non-operating income (expense)	(294)	(300)	(1,160)
Income before income taxes	3,892	3,806	11,261
Provision for income taxes	(1,425)	(769)	(1,197)
Equity-method investment activity, net of tax	(96)	(4)	9
Net income	$ 2,371	$ 3,033	$ 10,073
Basic earnings per share	$ 5.01	$ 6.32	$ 20.68
Diluted earnings per share	$ 4.90	$ 6.15	$ 20.14
Weighted-average shares used in computation of earnings per share:			
Basic	474	480	487
Diluted	484	493	500

See accompanying notes to consolidated financial statements.

Amazon.com, Inc.
Consolidated Statements of Comprehensive Income
(in millions)

	Year Ended December 31,		
	2016	**2017**	**2018**
Net income	$2,371	$3,033	$10,073
Other comprehensive income (loss):			
Foreign currency translation adjustments, net of tax of $(49), $5, and $6	(279)	533	(538)
Net change in unrealized gains (losses) on available-for-sale debt securities:			
Unrealized gains (losses), net of tax of $(12), $5, and $0	9	(39)	(17)
Reclassification adjustment for losses (gains) included in "Other income (expense), net," net of tax of $0, $0, and $0	8	7	8
Net unrealized gains (losses) on available-for-sale debt securities	17	(32)	(9)
Total other comprehensive income (loss)	(262)	501	(547)
Comprehensive income	$2,109	$3,534	$ 9,526

See accompanying notes to consolidated financial statements.

Amazon.com, Inc.
Consolidated Balance Sheets
(in millions, except per share data)

	December 31,	
	2017	**2018**
ASSETS		
Current assets:		
Cash and cash equivalents	$ 20,522	$ 31,750
Marketable securities	10,464	9,500
Inventories	16,047	17,174
Accounts receivable, net and other	13,164	16,677
Total current assets	60,197	75,101
Property and equipment, net	48,866	61,797
Goodwill	13,350	14,548
Other assets	8,897	11,202
Total assets	$131,310	$162,648
LIABILITIES AND STOCKHOLDERS' EQUITY		
Current liabilities:		
Accounts payable	$ 34,616	$ 38,192
Accrued expenses and other	18,170	23,663
Unearned revenue	5,097	6,536
Total current liabilities	57,883	68,391
Long-term debt	24,743	23,495
Other long-term liabilities	20,975	27,213
Commitments and contingencies (Note 7)		
Stockholders' equity:		
Preferred stock, $0.01 par value:		
Authorized shares—500		
Issued and outstanding shares—none	—	—
Common stock, $0.01 par value:		
Authorized shares—5,000		
Issued shares—507 and 514		
Outstanding shares—484 and 491	5	5
Treasury stock, at cost	(1,837)	(1,837)
Additional paid-in capital	21,389	26,791
Accumulated other comprehensive loss	(484)	(1,035)
Retained earnings	8,636	19,625
Total stockholders' equity	27,709	43,549
Total liabilities and stockholders' equity	$131,310	$162,648

See accompanying notes to consolidated financial statements.

Amazon.com, Inc.
Consolidated Statements of Stockholders' Equity
(in millions)

	Common Stock			Additional Paid-In Capital	Accumulated Other Comprehensive Income (Loss)	Retained Earnings	Total Stockholders' Equity
	Shares	Amount	Treasury Stock				
Balance as of January 1, 2016	471	$5	$(1,837)	$13,394	$ (723)	$ 2,545	$13,384
Net income	—	—	—	—	—	2,371	2,371
Other comprehensive income (loss)	—	—	—	—	(262)	—	(262)
Exercise of common stock options	6	—	—	1	—	—	1
Excess tax benefits from stock-based compensation	—	—	—	829	—	—	829
Stock-based compensation and issuance of employee benefit plan stock	—	—	—	2,962	—	—	2,962
Balance as of December 31, 2016	477	5	(1,837)	17,186	(985)	4,916	19,285
Cumulative effect of a change in accounting principle related to stock-based compensation	—	—	—	—	—	687	687
Net income	—	—	—	—	—	3,033	3,033
Other comprehensive income (loss)	—	—	—	—	501	—	501
Exercise of common stock options	7	—	—	1	—	—	1
Stock-based compensation and issuance of employee benefit plan stock	—	—	—	4,202	—	—	4,202
Balance as of December 31, 2017	484	5	(1,837)	21,389	(484)	8,636	27,709
Cumulative effect of changes in accounting principles related to revenue recognition, income taxes, and financial instruments	—	—	—	—	(4)	916	912
Net income	—	—	—	—	—	10,073	10,073
Other comprehensive income (loss)	—	—	—	—	(547)	—	(547)
Exercise of common stock options	7	—	—	—	—	—	—
Stock-based compensation and issuance of employee benefit plan stock	—	—	—	5,402	—	—	5,402
Balance as of December 31, 2018	491	$5	$(1,837)	$26,791	$(1,035)	$19,625	$43,549

See accompanying notes to consolidated financial statements.

Specimen Financial Statements:
Walmart Inc.

The following are **Walmart Inc.**'s financial statements as presented in the company's 2019 annual report. The complete annual report, including notes to the financial statements, is available at the company's website.

Walmart Inc.
Consolidated Statements of Income

	Fiscal Years Ended January 31,		
(Amounts in millions, except per share data)	**2019**	**2018**	**2017**
Revenues:			
Net sales	$510,329	$495,761	$481,317
Membership and other income	4,076	4,582	4,556
Total revenues	514,405	500,343	485,873
Costs and expenses:			
Cost of sales	385,301	373,396	361,256
Operating, selling, general and administrative expenses	107,147	106,510	101,853
Operating income	21,957	20,437	22,764
Interest:			
Debt	1,975	1,978	2,044
Capital lease and financing obligations	371	352	323
Interest income	(217)	(152)	(100)
Interest, net	2,129	2,178	2,267
Loss on extinguishment of debt	—	3,136	—
Other (gains) and losses	8,368	—	—
Income before income taxes	11,460	15,123	20,497
Provision for income taxes	4,281	4,600	6,204
Consolidated net income	7,179	10,523	14,293
Consolidated net income attributable to noncontrolling interest	(509)	(661)	(650)
Consolidated net income attributable to Walmart	$ 6,670	$ 9,862	$ 13,643
Net income per common share:			
Basic net income per common share attributable to Walmart	$ 2.28	$ 3.29	$ 4.40
Diluted net income per common share attributable to Walmart	2.26	3.28	4.38
Weighted-average common shares outstanding:			
Basic	2,929	2,995	3,101
Diluted	2,945	3,010	3,112
Dividends declared per common share	$ 2.08	$ 2.04	$ 2.00

See accompanying notes.

Walmart Inc.
Consolidated Statements of Comprehensive Income

	Fiscal Years Ended January 31,		
(Amounts in millions)	2019	2018	2017
Consolidated net income	$7,179	$10,523	$14,293
Consolidated net income attributable to noncontrolling interest	(509)	(661)	(650)
Consolidated net income attributable to Walmart	6,670	9,862	13,643
Other comprehensive income (loss), net of income taxes			
Currency translation and other	(226)	2,540	(3,027)
Net investment hedges	272	(405)	413
Cash flow hedges	(290)	437	21
Minimum pension liability	131	147	(397)
Unrealized gain on available-for-sale securities	—	1,501	145
Other comprehensive income (loss), net of income taxes	(113)	4,220	(2,845)
Other comprehensive (income) loss attributable to noncontrolling interest	188	(169)	210
Other comprehensive income (loss) attributable to Walmart	75	4,051	(2,635)
Comprehensive income, net of income taxes	7,066	14,743	11,448
Comprehensive (income) loss attributable to noncontrolling interest	(321)	(830)	(440)
Comprehensive income attributable to Walmart	$6,745	$13,913	$11,008

See accompanying notes.

Walmart Inc.
Consolidated Balance Sheets

	As of January 31,	
(Amounts in millions)	2019	2018
ASSETS		
Current assets:		
Cash and cash equivalents	$ 7,722	$ 6,756
Receivables, net	6,283	5,614
Inventories	44,269	43,783
Prepaid expenses and other	3,623	3,511
Total current assets	61,897	59,664
Property and equipment:		
Property and equipment	185,810	185,154
Less accumulated depreciation	(81,493)	(77,479)
Property and equipment, net	104,317	107,675
Property under capital lease and financing obligations:		
Property under capital lease and financing obligations	12,760	12,703
Less accumulated amortization	(5,682)	(5,560)
Property under capital lease and financing obligations, net	7,078	7,143
Goodwill	31,181	18,242
Other long-term assets	14,822	11,798
Total assets	$219,295	$204,522

(continues)

(Amounts in millions)	As of January 31,	
	2019	**2018**
LIABILITIES AND EQUITY		
Current liabilities:		
Short-term borrowings	$ 5,225	$ 5,257
Accounts payable	47,060	46,092
Accrued liabilities	22,159	22,122
Accrued income taxes	428	645
Long-term debt due within one year	1,876	3,738
Capital lease and financing obligations due within one year	729	667
Total current liabilities	77,477	78,521
Long-term debt	43,520	30,045
Long-term capital lease and financing obligations	6,683	6,780
Deferred income taxes and other	11,981	8,354
Commitments and contingencies		
Equity:		
Common stock	288	295
Capital in excess of par value	2,965	2,648
Retained earnings	80,785	85,107
Accumulated other comprehensive loss	(11,542)	(10,181)
Total Walmart shareholders' equity	72,496	77,869
Noncontrolling interest	7,138	2,953
Total equity	79,634	80,822
Total liabilities and equity	$219,295	$204,522

See accompanying notes.

Walmart Inc.
Consolidated Statements of Shareholders' Equity

(Amounts in millions)	Common Stock Shares	Common Stock Amount	Capital in Excess of Par Value	Retained Earnings	Accumulated Other Comprehensive Income (Loss)	Total Walmart Shareholders' Equity	Noncontrolling Interest	Total Equity
Balances as of February 1, 2016	3,162	$317	$1,805	$90,021	$(11,597)	$80,546	$3,065	$83,611
Consolidated net income	—	—	—	13,643	—	13,643	650	14,293
Other comprehensive income (loss), net of income taxes	—	—	—	—	(2,635)	(2,635)	(210)	(2,845)
Cash dividends declared ($2.00 per share)	—	—	—	(6,216)	—	(6,216)	—	(6,216)
Purchase of Company stock	(120)	(12)	(174)	(8,090)	—	(8.276)	—	(8,276)
Cash dividend declared to noncontrolling interest	—	—	—	—	—	—	(519)	(519)
Other	6	—	740	(4)	—	736	(249)	487
Balances as of January 31, 2017	3,048	305	2,371	89,354	(14,232)	77,798	2,737	80,535
Consolidated net income	—	—	—	9,862	—	9,862	661	10,523
Other comprehensive income (loss), net of income taxes	—	—	—	—	4,051	4,051	169	4,220
Cash dividends declared ($2.04 per share)	—	—	—	(6,124)	—	(6,124)	—	(6,124)
Purchase of Company stock	(103)	(10)	(219)	(7,975)	—	(8,204)	—	(8,204)
Cash dividend declared to noncontrolling interest	—	—	—	—	—	—	(687)	(687)
Other	7	—	496	(10)	—	486	73	559

(*continues*)

(Amounts in millions)	Common Stock		Capital in Excess of Par Value	Retained Earnings	Accumulated Other Comprehensive Income (Loss)	Total Walmart Shareholders' Equity	Noncontrolling Interest	Total Equity
	Shares	Amount						
Balances as of January 31, 2018	2,952	$295	$2,648	$85,107	$(10,181)	$77,869	$2,953	$80,822
Adoption of new accounting standards on February 1, 2018, net of income taxes		—	—	2,361	(1,436)	925	(1)	924
Consolidated net income	—	—	—	6,670	—	6,670	509	7,179
Other comprehensive income (loss), net of income taxes	—	—	—	—	75	75	(188)	(113)
Cash dividends declared ($2.08 per share)	—	—	—	(6,102)	—	(6,102)	—	(6,102)
Purchase of Company stock	(80)	(8)	(245)	(7,234)	—	(7,487)	—	(7,487)
Cash dividend declared to noncontrolling interest	—	—	—	—	—	—	(488)	(488)
Noncontrolling interest of acquired entity	—	—	—	—	—	—	4,345	4,345
Other	6	1	562	(17)	—	546	8	554
Balances as of January 31, 2019	2,878	$288	$2,965	$80,785	$(11,542)	$72,496	$7,138	$79,634

See accompanying notes.

Walmart Inc.
Consolidated Statements of Cash Flows

(Amounts in millions)	Fiscal Years Ended January 31,		
	2019	2018	2017
Cash flows from operating activities:			
Consolidated net income	$ 7,179	$10,523	$14,293
Adjustments to reconcile consolidated net income to net cash provided by operating activities:			
Depreciation and amortization	10,678	10,529	10,080
Unrealized (gains) and losses	3,516	—	—
(Gains) and losses for disposal of business operations	4,850	—	—
Deferred income taxes	(499)	(304)	761
Loss on extinguishment of debt	—	3,136	—
Other operating activities	1,734	1,210	206
Changes in certain assets and liabilities, net of effects of acquisitions:			
Receivables, net	(368)	(1,074)	(402)
Inventories	(1,311)	(140)	1,021
Accounts payable	1,831	4,086	3,942
Accrued liabilities	183	928	1,280
Accrued income taxes	(40)	(557)	492
Net cash provided by operating activities	27,753	28,337	31,673
Cash flows from investing activities:			
Payments for property and equipment	(10,344)	(10,051)	(10,619)
Proceeds from the disposal of property and equipment	519	378	456
Proceeds from the disposal of certain operations	876	1,046	662
Purchase of available for sale securities	—	—	(1,901)
Payments for business acquisitions, net of cash acquired	(14,656)	(375)	(2,463)
Other investing activities	(431)	(77)	(31)
Net cash used in investing activities	(24,036)	(9,079)	(13,896)
Cash flows from financing activities:			
Net change in short-term borrowings	(53)	4,148	(1,673)
Proceeds from issuance of long-term debt	15,872	7,476	137
Repayments of long-term debt	(3,784)	(13,061)	(2,055)
Premiums paid to extinguish debt	—	(3,059)	—
Dividends paid	(6,102)	(6,124)	(6,216)
Purchase of Company stock	(7,410)	(8,296)	(8,298)
Dividends paid to noncontrolling interest	(431)	(690)	(479)
Purchase of noncontrolling interest	—	(8)	(90)
Other financing activities	(629)	(261)	(398)
Net cash used in financing activities	(2,537)	(19,875)	(19,072)
Effect of exchange rates on cash, cash equivalents and restricted cash	(438)	487	(452)
Net increase (decrease) in cash, cash equivalents and restricted cash	742	(130)	(1,747)
Cash, cash equivalents and restricted cash at beginning of year	7,014	7,144	8,891
Cash, cash equivalents and restricted cash at end of period	$ 7,756	$ 7,104	$ 7,144
Supplemental disclosure of cash flow information:			
Income taxes paid	3,982	6,179	4,507
Interest paid	2,348	2,450	2,351

See accompanying notes.

Specimen Financial Statements:
Louis Vuitton

Louis Vuitton is a French company and is one of the leading fashion houses in the world. Louis Vuitton has been named the world's most valuable luxury brand. Note that its financial statements are IFRS-based and are presented in euros (€). The complete consolidated financial statements, including notes to the financial statement, are available at the company's website.

Consolidated Income Statement				
(EUR millions, except for earnings per share)	Notes	**2018**	**2017**[1][2]	**2016**[1]
Revenue	23	**46,826**	42,636	37,600
Cost of sales		(15,625)	(14,783)	(13,039)
Gross margin		**31,201**	27,853	24,561
Marketing and selling expenses		(17,755)	(16,395)	(14,607)
General and administrative expenses		(3,466)	(3,162)	(2,931)
Income/(loss) from joint ventures and associates	7	23	(3)	3
Profit from recurring operations	23–24	**10,003**	8,293	7,026
Other operating income and expenses	25	(126)	(180)	(122)
Operating profit		**9,877**	8,113	6,904
Cost of net financial debt		(117)	(137)	(133)
Other financial income and expenses		(271)	78	(185)
Net financial income/(expense)	26	**(388)**	(59)	(318)
Income taxes	27	(2,499)	(2,214)	(2,133)
Net profit before minority interests		**6,990**	5,840	4,453
Minority interests	17	(636)	(475)	(387)
Net profit, Group share		**6,354**	5,365	4,066
Basic Group share of net earnings per share *(EUR)*	28	**12.64**	10.68	8.08
Number of shares on which the calculation is based		502,825,461	502,412,694	502,911,125
Diluted Group share of net earnings per share *(EUR)*	28	**12.61**	10.64	8.06
Number of shares on which the calculation is based		503,918,140	504,010,291	504,640,459

(1) The financial statements as of December 31, 2017 and December 31, 2016 have been restated to reflect the retrospective application with effect from January 1, 2016 of IFRS 9 Financial Instruments. See Note 1.2.

(2) The financial statements as of December 31, 2017 have been restated to reflect the definitive allocation of the purchase price of Christian Dior Couture. See Note 2.

Consolidated Statement of Comprehensive Gains and Losses

(EUR millions)	Notes	2018	2017[1][2]	2016[1]
Net profit before minority interests		**6,990**	**5,840**	**4,453**
Translation adjustments		274	(958)	78
Amounts transferred to income statement		(1)	18	-
Tax impact		15	(49)	(9)
	15,4,17	**288**	**(989)**	**69**
Change in value of hedges of future foreign currency cash flows		3	372	47
Amounts transferred to income statement		(279)	(104)	(26)
Tax impact		79	(77)	(1)
		(197)	**191**	**20**
Change in value of the cost of hedging instruments		(271)	(91)	(273)
Amounts transferred to income statement		148	210	180
Tax impact		31	(35)	24
		(92)	**84**	**(69)**
Gains and losses recognized in equity, transferable to income statement		**(1)**	**(714)**	**20**
Change in value of vineyard land	6	8	(35)	30
Amounts transferred to consolidated reserves		-	-	-
Tax impact		(2)	82	108
		6	**47**	**138**
Employee benefit commitments: change in value resulting from actuarial gains and losses		28	57	(88)
Tax impact		(5)	(24)	17
		23	**33**	**(71)**
Gains and losses recognized in equity, not transferable to income statement		**29**	**80**	**67**
Comprehensive income		**7,018**	**5,206**	**4,540**
Minority interests		(681)	(341)	(433)
Comprehensive income, Group share		**6,337**	**4,865**	**4,107**

(1) The financial statements as of December 31, 2017 and December 31, 2016 have been restated to reflect the retrospective application with effect from January 1, 2016 of IFRS 9 Financial Instruments. See Note 1.2.

(2) The financial statements as of December 31, 2017 have been restated to reflect the definitive allocation of the purchase price of Christian Dior Couture. See Note 2.

Consolidated Balance Sheet

ASSETS (EUR millions)	Notes	2018	2017[1][2]	2016[1]
Brands and other intangible assets	3	17,254	16,957	13,335
Goodwill	4	13,727	13,837	10,401
Property, plant and equipment	6	15,112	13,862	12,139
Investments in joint ventures and associates	7	638	639	770
Non-current available for sale financial assets	8	1,100	789	744
Other non-current assets	9	986	869	777
Deferred tax		1,932	1,741	2,053
Non-current assets		**50,749**	**48,694**	**40,219**
Inventories and work in progress	10	12,485	10,888	10,546
Trade accounts receivable	11	3,222	2,736	2,685
Income taxes		366	780	280
Other current assets	12	2,868	2,919	2,342
Cash and cash equivalents	14	4,610	3,738	3,544
Current assets		**23,551**	**21,061**	**19,397**
Total assets		**74,300**	**69,755**	**59,616**

LIABILITIES AND EQUITY (EUR millions)	Notes	2018	2017[1][2]	2016[1]
Share capital	15.1	152	152	152
Share premium account	15.1	2,298	2,614	2,601
Treasury shares and LVMH share-settled derivatives	15.2	(421)	(530)	(520)
Cumulative translation adjustment	15.4	573	354	1,165
Revaluation reserves		875	1,111	799
Other reserves		22,462	19,903	18,125
Net profit, Group share		6,354	5,365	4,066
Equity, Group share		32,293	28,969	26,388
Minority interests	17	1,664	1,408	1,510
Equity		**33,957**	**30,377**	**27,898**
Long-term borrowings	18	6,005	7,046	3,932
Non-current provisions	19	2,430	2,484	2,342
Deferred tax		5,036	4,989	4,137
Other non-current liabilities	20	10,039	9,870	8,497
Non-current liabilities		**23,510**	**24,389**	**18,908**
Short-term borrowings	18	5,027	4,530	3,447
Trade accounts payable	21.1	5,314	4,539	4,184
Income taxes		538	763	428
Current provisions	19	369	404	352
Other current liabilities	21.2	5,585	4,753	4,399
Current liabilities		**16,833**	**14,989**	**12,810**
Total liabilities and equity		**74,300**	**69,755**	**59,616**

(1) The financial statements as of December 31, 2017 and December 31, 2016 have been restated to reflect the retrospective application with effect from January 1, 2016 of IFRS 9 Financial Instruments. See Note 1.2.

(2) The financial statements as of December 31, 2017 have been restated to reflect the definitive allocation of the purchase price of Christian Dior Couture. See Note 2.

Consolidated Statement of Changes in Equity

(EUR millions)	Number of shares	Share capital	Share premium account	Treasury shares and LVMH-share settled derivatives	Cumulative translation adjustment	Available for sale financial assets	Hedges of future foreign currency cash flows and cost of hedging instruments	Vineyard land	Employee benefit commitments	Net profit and other reserves	Group share	Minority interests	Total
Notes		15.1		15.2	15.4							17	
As of December 31, 2015	507,139,110	152	2,579	(241)	1,137	103	(10)	965	(107)	19,762	24,340	1,460	25,800
Impact of changes in accounting standards[1]	-	-	-	-	-	(103)	(61)	-	-	160	(4)	-	(4)
As of January 1, 2016, after restatement	507,139,110	152	2,579	(241)	1,137	-	(71)	965	(107)	19,922	24,336	1,460	25,796
Gains and losses recognized in equity					28		(44)	113	(56)	-	41	46	87
Net profit										4,066	4,066	387	4,453
Comprehensive income		-	-	-	28	-	(44)	113	(56)	4,066	4,107	433	4,540
Stock option plan and similar expenses										39	39	2	41
(Acquisition)/disposal of treasury shares and LVMH share-settled derivatives				(321)						(21)	(342)	-	(342)
Exercise of LVMH share subscription options	907,929		64								64	-	64
Retirement of LVMH shares	(920,951)		(42)	42							-	-	-
Capital increase in subsidiaries											-	41	41
Interim and final dividends paid										(1,811)	(1,811)	(272)	(2,083)
Changes in control of consolidated entities										(5)	(5)	22	17
Acquisition and disposal of minority interests' shares										(58)	(58)	(34)	(92)
Purchase commitments for minority interests' shares										58	58	(142)	(84)
As of December 31, 2016	507,126,088	152	2,601	(520)	1,165	-	(115)	1,078	(163)	22,190	26,388	1,510	27,898
Gains and losses recognized in equity					(811)		245	36	30	-	(500)	(134)	(634)
Net profit										5,365	5,365	475	5,840
Comprehensive income		-	-	-	(811)	-	245	36	30	5,365	4,865	341	5,206
Stock option plan and similar expenses										55	55	7	62
(Acquisition)/disposal of treasury shares and LVMH share-settled derivatives				(50)						(11)	(61)	-	(61)
Exercise of LVMH share subscription options	708,485		53								53	-	53
Retirement of LVMH shares	(791,977)		(40)	40							-	-	-
Capital increase in subsidiaries											-	44	44
Interim and final dividends paid										(2,110)	(2,110)	(261)	(2,371)
Changes in control of consolidated entities										(6)	(6)	114	108
Acquisition and disposal of minority interests shares										(86)	(86)	(56)	(142)
Purchase commitments for minority interests' shares										(129)	(129)	(291)	(420)
As of December 31, 2017	507,042,596	152	2,614	(530)	354	-	130	1,114	(133)	25,268	28,969	1,408	30,377
Gains and losses recognized in equity					219	-	(259)	3	20	-	(17)	45	28
Net profit										6,354	6,354	636	6,990
Comprehensive income		-	-	-	219	-	(259)	3	20	6,354	6,337	681	7,018
Stock option plan and similar expenses										78	78	4	82
(Acquisition)/disposal of treasury shares and LVMH share-settled derivatives				(256)						(26)	(282)	-	(282)
Exercise of LVMH share subscription options	762,851		49							-	49	-	49
Retirement of LVMH shares	(2,775,952)		(365)	365						-	-	-	-
Capital increase in subsidiaries										-	-	50	50
Interim and final dividends paid										(2,715)	(2,715)	(345)	(3,060)
Changes in control of consolidated entities										(9)	(9)	41	32
Acquisition and disposal of minority interests shares										(22)	(22)	(19)	(41)
Purchase commitments for minority interests' shares										(112)	(112)	(156)	(268)
As of December 31, 2018	505,029,495	152	2,298	(421)	573	-	(129)	1,117	(113)	28,816	32,293	1,664	33,957

(1) The financial statements as of December 31, 2017 and December 31, 2016 have been restated to reflect the retrospective application with effect from January 1, 2016 of IFRS 9 Financial Instruments. See Note 1.2.

Consolidated Cash Flow Statement

(EUR millions)	Notes	2018	2017[1][2]	2016[1]
I. OPERATING ACTIVITIES AND OPERATING INVESTMENTS				
Operating profit		9,877	8,113	6,904
Income/(loss) and dividends from joint ventures and associates	7	5	25	18
Net increase in depreciation, amortization and provisions		2,302	2,376	2,143
Other computed expenses		(141)	(43)	(177)
Other adjustments		(78)	(66)	(155)
Cash from operations before changes in working capital		**11,965**	**10,405**	**8,733**
Cost of net financial debt: interest paid		(113)	(129)	(122)
Tax paid		(2,275)	(2,790)	(1,923)
Net cash from operating activities before changes in working capital		**9,577**	**7,486**	**6,688**
Change in working capital	14.2	(1,087)	(514)	(512)
Net cash from operating activities		**8,490**	**6,972**	**6,176**
Operating investments	14.3	(3,038)	(2,276)	(2,265)
Net cash from operating activities and operating investments (free cash flow)		**5,452**	**4,696**	**3,911**
II. FINANCIAL INVESTMENTS				
Purchase of non-current available for sale financial assets[a]	8	(445)	(125)	(28)
Proceeds from sale of non-current available for sale financial assets	8	45	87	91
Dividends received		18	13	55
Tax paid related to non-current available for sale financial assets and consolidated investments		(2)	-	(461)
Impact of purchase and sale of consolidated investments	2	(17)	(6,306)	310
Net cash from (used in) financial investments		**(401)**	**(6,331)**	**(33)**
III. TRANSACTIONS RELATING TO EQUITY				
Capital increases of LVMH SE	15.1	49	53	64
Capital increases of subsidiaries subscribed by minority interests	17	41	44	41
Acquisition and disposals of treasury shares and LVMH share-settled derivatives	15.2	(295)	(67)	(352)
Interim and final dividends paid by LVMH SE	15.3	(2,715)	(2,110)	(1,859)
Tax paid related to interim and final dividends paid		(36)	388	(145)
Interim and final dividends paid to minority interests in consolidated subsidiaries	17	(339)	(260)	(267)
Purchase and proceeds from sale of minority interests	2	(236)	(153)	(95)
Net cash from (used in) transactions relating to equity		**(3,531)**	**(2,105)**	**(2,613)**
Change in cash before financing activities		**1,520**	**(3,740)**	**1,265**
IV. FINANCING ACTIVITIES				
Proceeds from borrowings	18.1	1,529	5,931	913
Repayment of borrowings	18.1	(2,174)	(1,760)	(2,181)
Purchase and proceeds from sale of current available for sale financial assets[a]	13	(147)	92	(104)
Net cash from (used in) financing activities	14.2	**(792)**	**4,263**	**(1,372)**
V. EFFECT OF EXCHANGE RATE CHANGES		**67**	**(242)**	**54**
NET INCREASE (DECREASE) IN CASH AND CASH EQUIVALENTS (I+II+III+IV+V)		**795**	**281**	**(53)**
CASH AND CASH EQUIVALENTS AT BEGINNING OF PERIOD	14.1	**3,618**	**3,337**	**3,390**
CASH AND CASH EQUIVALENTS AT END OF PERIOD	14.1	**4,413**	**3,618**	**3,337**
TOTAL TAX PAID		**(2,314)**	**(2,402)**	**(2,529)**

(a) The cash impact of non-current available for sale financial assets used to hedge net financial debt (see Note 18) is presented under "IV Financing activities" as "Purchase and proceeds from sale of current available for sale financial assets".

(1) The financial statements as of December 31, 2017 and December 31, 2016 have been restated to reflect the retrospective application with effect from January 1, 2016 of IFRS 9 Financial Instruments. See Note 1.2.

(2) The financial statements as of December 31, 2017 have been restated to reflect the definitive allocation of the purchase price of Christian Dior Couture. See Note 2.1.

Time Value of Money

Appendix Preview

Would you rather receive $1,000 today or a year from now? You should prefer to receive the $1,000 today because you can invest the $1,000 and then earn interest on it. As a result, you will have more than $1,000 a year from now. What this example illustrates is the concept of the **time value of money**. Everyone prefers to receive money today rather than in the future because of the interest factor.

Appendix Outline

LEARNING OBJECTIVES

1. Compute interest and future values.	• Nature of interest • Future value of a single amount • Future value of an annuity
2. Compute present values.	• Present value variables • Present value of a single amount • Present value of an annuity • Time periods and discounting • Present value of a long-term note or bond
3. Compute the present value in capital budgeting situations.	• Using alternative discount rates
4. Use a financial calculator to solve time value of money problems.	• Present value of a single sum • Present value of an annuity • Future value of a single sum • Future value of an annuity • Internal rate of return • Useful financial calculator applications

Interest and Future Values

> **LEARNING OBJECTIVE 1**
>
> Compute interest and future values.

Nature of Interest

Interest is payment for the use of another person's money. It is the difference between the amount borrowed or invested (called the **principal**) and the amount repaid or collected. The amount of interest to be paid or collected is usually stated as a rate over a specific period of time. The rate of interest is generally stated as an annual rate.

The amount of interest involved in any financing transaction is based on three elements:

1. **Principal (*p*):** The original amount borrowed or invested.
2. **Interest Rate (*i*):** An annual percentage of the principal.
3. **Time (*n*):** The number of periods over which the principal is borrowed or invested.

Simple Interest

Simple interest is computed on the principal amount only. It is the return on the principal for one period (we use an annual interest rate unless stated otherwise). Simple interest is usually expressed as shown in **Illustration G.1**.

ILLUSTRATION G.1

Interest computation

Interest	=	Principal p	×	Rate i	×	Time n

For example, if you borrowed $5,000 for 2 years at a simple interest rate of 12% annually, you would pay $1,200 in total interest, computed as follows.

$$\text{Interest} = p \times i \times n$$
$$= \$5,000 \times .12 \times 2$$
$$= \$1,200$$

Compound Interest

Compound interest is computed on principal **and** on any interest earned that has not been paid or withdrawn. It is the return on (or growth of) the principal for two or more time periods. Compounding computes interest not only on the principal but also on the interest earned to date on that principal, assuming the interest is left on deposit.

To illustrate the difference between simple and compound interest, assume that you deposit $1,000 in Bank Two, where it will earn simple interest of 9% per year, and you deposit another $1,000 in Citizens Bank, where it will earn compound interest of 9% per year compounded annually. Also assume that in both cases you will not withdraw any cash until three years from the date of deposit. **Illustration G.2** shows the computation of interest to be received and the accumulated year-end balances.

ILLUSTRATION G.2   **Simple versus compound interest**

	Bank Two				Citizens Bank		
	Simple Interest Calculation	Simple Interest	Accumulated Year-End Balance		Compound Interest Calculation	Compound Interest	Accumulated Year-End Balance
Year 1	$1,000.00 × 9%	$ 90.00	$1,090.00		Year 1	$1,000.00 × 9%	$ 90.00	$1,090.00
Year 2	$1,000.00 × 9%	90.00	$1,180.00		Year 2	$1,090.00 × 9%	98.10	$1,188.10
Year 3	$1,000.00 × 9%	90.00	$1,270.00		Year 3	$1,188.10 × 9%	106.93	$1,295.03
		$ 270.00		$25.03 Difference		$ 295.03	

Note in Illustration G.2 that simple interest uses the initial principal of $1,000 to compute the interest in all three years. Compound interest uses the accumulated balance (principal plus interest to date) at each year-end to compute interest in the succeeding year—which explains why your compound interest account is larger.

Obviously, if you had a choice between investing your money at simple interest or at compound interest, you would choose compound interest, all other things—especially risk—being equal. In the example, compounding provides $25.03 of additional interest income. For practical purposes, compounding assumes that unpaid interest earned becomes a part of the principal, and the accumulated balance at the end of each year becomes the new principal on which interest is earned during the next year.

Most business situations use compound interest. Simple interest is generally applicable only to short-term situations of one year or less.

Future Value of a Single Amount

The **future value of a single amount** is the value at a future date of a given amount invested, assuming compound interest. For example, in Illustration G.2, $1,295.03 is the future value of the $1,000 investment earning 9% for three years. The $1,295.03 is determined more easily by using the formula shown in **Illustration G.3**.

$$FV = p \times (1 + i)^n$$

ILLUSTRATION G.3

Formula for future value

where:

FV = future value of a single amount
p = principal (or present value; the value today)
i = interest rate for one period
n = number of periods

The $1,295.03 is computed as follows.

$$
\begin{aligned}
FV &= p \times (1 + i)^n \\
&= \$1,000 \times (1 + .09)^3 \\
&= \$1,000 \times 1.29503 \\
&= \$1,295.03
\end{aligned}
$$

The 1.29503 is computed by multiplying (1.09 × 1.09 × 1.09). The amounts in this example can be depicted in the time diagram shown in **Illustration G.4**.

ILLUSTRATION G.4 Time diagram

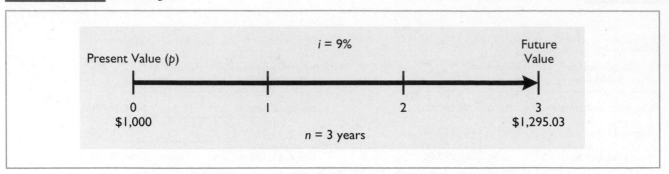

Another method used to compute the future value of a single amount involves a compound interest table. This table shows the future value of 1 for *n* periods. **Table 1** is such a table.

TABLE 1 Future Value of 1

(n) Periods	4%	5%	6%	7%	8%	9%	10%	11%	12%	15%
0	1.00000	1.00000	1.00000	1.00000	1.00000	1.00000	1.00000	1.00000	1.00000	1.00000
1	1.04000	1.05000	1.06000	1.07000	1.08000	1.09000	1.10000	1.11000	1.12000	1.15000
2	1.08160	1.10250	1.12360	1.14490	1.16640	1.18810	1.21000	1.23210	1.25440	1.32250
3	1.12486	1.15763	1.19102	1.22504	1.25971	1.29503	1.33100	1.36763	1.40493	1.52088
4	1.16986	1.21551	1.26248	1.31080	1.36049	1.41158	1.46410	1.51807	1.57352	1.74901
5	1.21665	1.27628	1.33823	1.40255	1.46933	1.53862	1.61051	1.68506	1.76234	2.01136
6	1.26532	1.34010	1.41852	1.50073	1.58687	1.67710	1.77156	1.87041	1.97382	2.31306
7	1.31593	1.40710	1.50363	1.60578	1.71382	1.82804	1.94872	2.07616	2.21068	2.66002
8	1.36857	1.47746	1.59385	1.71819	1.85093	1.99256	2.14359	2.30454	2.47596	3.05902
9	1.42331	1.55133	1.68948	1.83846	1.99900	2.17189	2.35795	2.55803	2.77308	3.51788
10	1.48024	1.62889	1.79085	1.96715	2.15892	2.36736	2.59374	2.83942	3.10585	4.04556
11	1.53945	1.71034	1.89830	2.10485	2.33164	2.58043	2.85312	3.15176	3.47855	4.65239
12	1.60103	1.79586	2.01220	2.25219	2.51817	2.81267	3.13843	3.49845	3.89598	5.35025
13	1.66507	1.88565	2.13293	2.40985	2.71962	3.06581	3.45227	3.88328	4.36349	6.15279
14	1.73168	1.97993	2.26090	2.57853	2.93719	3.34173	3.79750	4.31044	4.88711	7.07571
15	1.80094	2.07893	2.39656	2.75903	3.17217	3.64248	4.17725	4.78459	5.47357	8.13706
16	1.87298	2.18287	2.54035	2.95216	3.42594	3.97031	4.59497	5.31089	6.13039	9.35762
17	1.94790	2.29202	2.69277	3.15882	3.70002	4.32763	5.05447	5.89509	6.86604	10.76126
18	2.02582	2.40662	2.85434	3.37993	3.99602	4.71712	5.55992	6.54355	7.68997	12.37545
19	2.10685	2.52695	3.02560	3.61653	4.31570	5.14166	6.11591	7.26334	8.61276	14.23177
20	2.19112	2.65330	3.20714	3.86968	4.66096	5.60441	6.72750	8.06231	9.64629	16.36654

In Table 1, *n* is the number of compounding periods, the percentages are the periodic interest rates, and the 5-digit decimal numbers in the respective columns are the future value of 1 factors. To use Table 1, you multiply the principal amount by the future value factor for the specified number of periods and interest rate. For example, the future value factor for two periods at 9% is 1.18810. Multiplying this factor by $1,000 equals $1,188.10—which is the accumulated balance at the end of year 2 in the Citizens Bank example in Illustration G.2. The $1,295.03 accumulated balance at the end of the third year is calculated from Table 1 by multiplying the future value factor for three periods (1.29503) by the $1,000.

The demonstration problem in **Illustration G.5** shows how to use Table 1.

ILLUSTRATION G.5 Demonstration problem—Using Table 1 for *FV* of 1

John and Mary Rich invested $20,000 in a savings account paying 6% interest at the time their son, Mike, was born. The money is to be used by Mike for his college education. On his 18th birthday, Mike withdraws the money from his savings account. How much did Mike withdraw from his account?

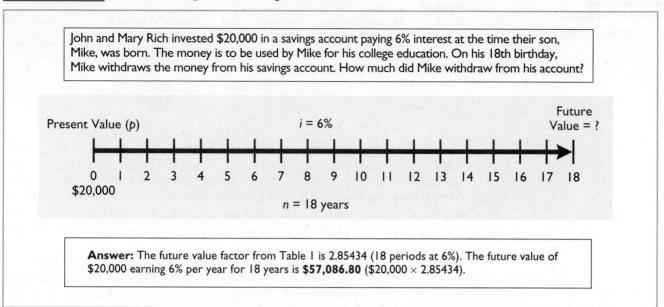

Answer: The future value factor from Table 1 is 2.85434 (18 periods at 6%). The future value of $20,000 earning 6% per year for 18 years is **$57,086.80** ($20,000 × 2.85434).

Future Value of an Annuity

The preceding discussion involved the accumulation of only a single principal sum. Individuals and businesses frequently encounter situations in which a **series** of equal dollar amounts are to be paid or received at evenly spaced time intervals (periodically), such as loans or lease (rental) contracts. A series of payments or receipts of equal dollar amounts is referred to as an **annuity**.

The **future value of an annuity** is the sum of all the payments (receipts) plus the accumulated compound interest on them. In computing the future value of an annuity, it is necessary to know (1) the interest rate, (2) the number of payments (receipts), and (3) the amount of the periodic payments (receipts).

To illustrate the computation of the future value of an annuity, assume that you invest $2,000 at the end of each year for three years at 5% interest compounded annually. This situation is depicted in the time diagram in **Illustration G.6**.

ILLUSTRATION G.6 Time diagram for a three-year annuity

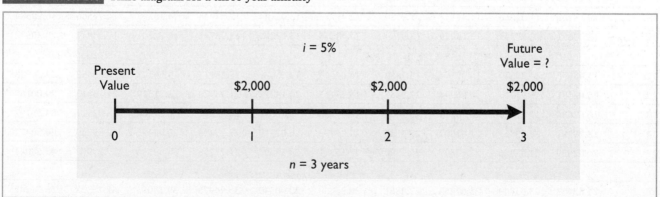

The $2,000 invested at the end of year 1 will earn interest for two years (years 2 and 3), and the $2,000 invested at the end of year 2 will earn interest for one year (year 3). However, the last $2,000 investment (made at the end of year 3) will not earn any interest. Using the future value factors from Table 1, the future value of these periodic payments is computed as shown in **Illustration G.7**.

ILLUSTRATION G.7
Future value of periodic payment computation

Invested at End of Year	Number of Compounding Periods	Amount Invested	×	Future Value of 1 Factor at 5%	=	Future Value
1	2	$2,000		1.10250		$2,205
2	1	2,000		1.05000		2,100
3	0	2,000		1.00000		2,000
				3.15250		**$6,305**

The first $2,000 investment is multiplied by the future value factor for two periods (1.1025) because two years' interest will accumulate on it (in years 2 and 3). The second $2,000 investment will earn only one year's interest (in year 3) and therefore is multiplied by the future value factor for one year (1.0500). The final $2,000 investment is made at the end of the third year and will not earn any interest. Thus, $n = 0$ and the future value factor is 1.00000. Consequently, the future value of the last $2,000 invested is only $2,000 since it does not accumulate any interest.

Calculating the future value of each individual cash flow is required when the periodic payments or receipts are not equal in each period. However, when the periodic payments (receipts) are **the same in each period**, the future value can be computed by using a future value of an annuity of 1 table. **Table 2** is such a table.

TABLE 2   Future Value of an Annuity of 1

(n) Payments	4%	5%	6%	7%	8%	9%	10%	11%	12%	15%
1	1.00000	1.00000	1.00000	1.0000	1.00000	1.00000	1.00000	1.00000	1.00000	1.00000
2	2.04000	2.05000	2.06000	2.0700	2.08000	2.09000	2.10000	2.11000	2.12000	2.15000
3	3.12160	3.15250	3.18360	3.2149	3.24640	3.27810	3.31000	3.34210	3.37440	3.47250
4	4.24646	4.31013	4.37462	4.4399	4.50611	4.57313	4.64100	4.70973	4.77933	4.99338
5	5.41632	5.52563	5.63709	5.7507	5.86660	5.98471	6.10510	6.22780	6.35285	6.74238
6	6.63298	6.80191	6.97532	7.1533	7.33592	7.52334	7.71561	7.91286	8.11519	8.75374
7	7.89829	8.14201	8.39384	8.6540	8.92280	9.20044	9.48717	9.78327	10.08901	11.06680
8	9.21423	9.54911	9.89747	10.2598	10.63663	11.02847	11.43589	11.85943	12.29969	13.72682
9	10.58280	11.02656	11.49132	11.9780	12.48756	13.02104	13.57948	14.16397	14.77566	16.78584
10	12.00611	12.57789	13.18079	13.8164	14.48656	15.19293	15.93743	16.72201	17.54874	20.30372
11	13.48635	14.20679	14.97164	15.7836	16.64549	17.56029	18.53117	19.56143	20.65458	24.34928
12	15.02581	15.91713	16.86994	17.8885	18.97713	20.14072	21.38428	22.71319	24.13313	29.00167
13	16.62684	17.71298	18.88214	20.1406	21.49530	22.95339	24.52271	26.21164	28.02911	34.35192
14	18.29191	19.59863	21.01507	22.5505	24.21492	26.01919	27.97498	30.09492	32.39260	40.50471
15	20.02359	21.57856	23.27597	25.1290	27.15211	29.36092	31.77248	34.40536	37.27972	47.58041
16	21.82453	23.65749	25.67253	27.8881	30.32428	33.00340	35.94973	39.18995	42.75328	55.71747
17	23.69751	25.84037	28.21288	30.8402	33.75023	36.97351	40.54470	44.50084	48.88367	65.07509
18	25.64541	28.13238	30.90565	33.9990	37.45024	41.30134	45.59917	50.39593	55.74972	75.83636
19	27.67123	30.53900	33.75999	37.3790	41.44626	46.01846	51.15909	56.93949	63.43968	88.21181
20	29.77808	33.06595	36.78559	40.9955	45.76196	51.16012	57.27500	64.20283	72.05244	102.44358

Table 2 shows the future value of 1 to be received periodically for a given number of payments. It assumes that each payment is made at the **end** of each period. We can see from Table 2 that the future value of an annuity of 1 factor for three payments at 5% is 3.15250. The future value factor is the total of the three individual future value factors shown in Illustration G.7. Multiplying this amount by the annual investment of $2,000 produces a future value of $6,305.

The demonstration problem in **Illustration G.8** shows how to use Table 2.

ILLUSTRATION G.8   Demonstration problem—Using Table 2 for *FV* of an annuity of 1

John and Char Lewis's daughter, Debra, has just started high school. They decide to start a college fund for her and will invest $2,500 in a savings account at the end of each year she is in high school (4 payments total). The account will earn 6% interest compounded annually. How much will be in the college fund at the time Debra graduates from high school?

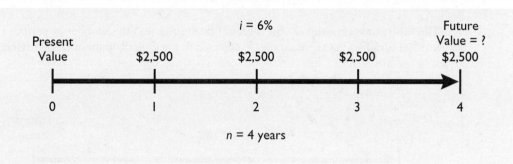

Answer: The future value factor from Table 2 is 4.37462 (4 payments at 6%). The future value of $2,500 invested each year for 4 years at 6% interest is **$10,936.55** ($2,500 × 4.37462).

Present Values

LEARNING OBJECTIVE 2
Compute present values.

Present Value Variables

The **present value** is the value now of a given amount to be paid or received in the future, assuming compound interest. The present value, like the future value, is based on three variables: (1) the dollar amount to be received (future amount), (2) the length of time until the amount is received (number of periods), and (3) the interest rate (the discount rate). The process of determining the present value is referred to as **discounting the future amount**.

Present value computations are used in measuring many items. For example, the present value of principal and interest payments is used to determine the market price of a bond. Determining the amount to be reported for notes payable and lease liabilities also involves present value computations. In addition, capital budgeting and other investment proposals are evaluated using present value computations. Finally, all rate of return and internal rate of return computations involve present value techniques.

Present Value of a Single Amount

To illustrate present value, assume that you want to invest a sum of money today that will provide $1,000 at the end of one year. What amount would you need to invest today to have $1,000 one year from now? If you want a 10% rate of return, the investment or present value is $909.09 ($1,000 ÷ 1.10). The formula for calculating present value is shown in **Illustration G.9**.

ILLUSTRATION G.9

Formula for present value

$$\text{Present Value } (PV) = \text{Future Value } (FV) \div (1 + i)^n$$

The computation of $1,000 discounted at 10% for one year is as follows.

$$
\begin{aligned}
PV &= FV \div (1 + i)^n \\
&= \$1{,}000 \div (1 + .10)^1 \\
&= \$1{,}000 \div 1.10 \\
&= \$909.09
\end{aligned}
$$

The future amount ($1,000), the discount rate (10%), and the number of periods (1) are known. The variables in this situation are depicted in the time diagram in **Illustration G.10**.

ILLUSTRATION G.10

Finding present value if discounted for one period

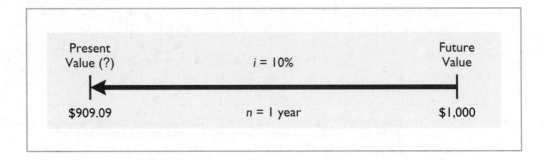

If the single amount of $1,000 is to be received **in two years** and discounted at 10%, the formula $PV = \$1{,}000 \div (1 + .10)^2$ is used, where $(1 + .10)^2$ is equal to 1.21 (1.10 × 1.10). Its present value is $826.45 ($1,000 ÷ 1.21), depicted in **Illustration G.11**.

ILLUSTRATION G.11

Finding present value if discounted for two periods

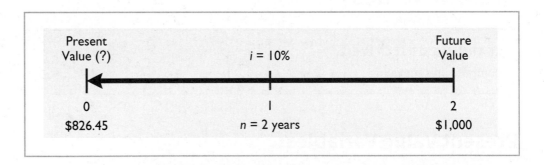

The present value of 1 may also be determined through tables that show the present value of 1 for n periods. In **Table 3**, n is the number of discounting periods involved. The percentages are the periodic interest rates or discount rates, and the 5-digit decimal numbers in the respective columns are the present value of 1 factors.

TABLE 3 Present Value of 1

(n) Periods	4%	5%	6%	7%	8%	9%	10%	11%	12%	15%
1	.96154	.95238	.94340	.93458	.92593	.91743	.90909	.90090	.89286	.86957
2	.92456	.90703	.89000	.87344	.85734	.84168	.82645	.81162	.79719	.75614
3	.88900	.86384	.83962	.81630	.79383	.77218	.75132	.73119	.71178	.65752
4	.85480	.82270	.79209	.76290	.73503	.70843	.68301	.65873	.63552	.57175
5	.82193	.78353	.74726	.71299	.68058	.64993	.62092	.59345	.56743	.49718
6	.79031	.74622	.70496	.66634	.63017	.59627	.56447	.53464	.50663	.43233
7	.75992	.71068	.66506	.62275	.58349	.54703	.51316	.48166	.45235	.37594
8	.73069	.67684	.62741	.58201	.54027	.50187	.46651	.43393	.40388	.32690
9	.70259	.64461	.59190	.54393	.50025	.46043	.42410	.39092	.36061	.28426
10	.67556	.61391	.55839	.50835	.46319	.42241	.38554	.35218	.32197	.24719
11	.64958	.58468	.52679	.47509	.42888	.38753	.35049	.31728	.28748	.21494
12	.62460	.55684	.49697	.44401	.39711	.35554	.31863	.28584	.25668	.18691
13	.60057	.53032	.46884	.41496	.36770	.32618	.28966	.25751	.22917	.16253
14	.57748	.50507	.44230	.38782	.34046	.29925	.26333	.23199	.20462	.14133
15	.55526	.48102	.41727	.36245	.31524	.27454	.23939	.20900	.18270	.12289
16	.53391	.45811	.39365	.33873	.29189	.25187	.21763	.18829	.16312	.10687
17	.51337	.43630	.37136	.31657	.27027	.23107	.19785	.16963	.14564	.09293
18	.49363	.41552	.35034	.29586	.25025	.21199	.17986	.15282	.13004	.08081
19	.47464	.39573	.33051	.27615	.23171	.19449	.16351	.13768	.11611	.07027
20	.45639	.37689	.31180	.25842	.21455	.17843	.14864	.12403	.10367	.06110

When using Table 3, the future value is multiplied by the present value factor specified at the intersection of the number of periods and the discount rate.

For example, the present value factor for one period at a discount rate of 10% is .90909, which is the value used to compute $909.09 ($1,000 × .90909) in Illustration G.10. For two periods at a discount rate of 10%, the present value factor is .82645, which is the value used to compute $826.45 ($1,000 × .82645) in Illustration G.11.

Note that a higher discount rate produces a smaller present value. For example, using a 15% discount rate, the present value of $1,000 due one year from now is $869.57 ($1,000 × .86957), versus $909.09 at 10%. Also note that the farther in the future that the future value is, the smaller the present value. For example, using the same discount rate of 10%, the present value of $1,000 due in **five years** at 10% is $620.92 ($1,000 × .62092). The present value of $1,000 due in **one year** is $909.09, a difference of $288.17.

The following two demonstration problems (**Illustrations G.12 and G.13**) illustrate how to use Table 3.

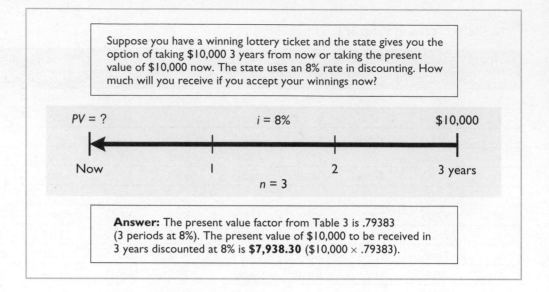

Suppose you have a winning lottery ticket and the state gives you the option of taking $10,000 3 years from now or taking the present value of $10,000 now. The state uses an 8% rate in discounting. How much will you receive if you accept your winnings now?

PV = ?   i = 8% $10,000

Now   1   2   3 years

n = 3

Answer: The present value factor from Table 3 is .79383 (3 periods at 8%). The present value of $10,000 to be received in 3 years discounted at 8% is **$7,938.30** ($10,000 × .79383).

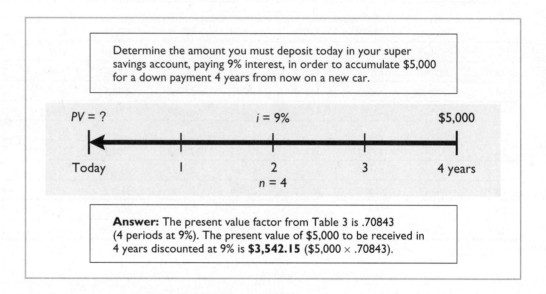

Determine the amount you must deposit today in your super savings account, paying 9% interest, in order to accumulate $5,000 for a down payment 4 years from now on a new car.

PV = ?   i = 9% $5,000

Today   1   2   3   4 years

n = 4

Answer: The present value factor from Table 3 is .70843 (4 periods at 9%). The present value of $5,000 to be received in 4 years discounted at 9% is **$3,542.15** ($5,000 × .70843).

Present Value of an Annuity

The preceding discussion involved the discounting of only a single future amount. Businesses and individuals frequently engage in transactions in which a series of equal dollar amounts are to be received or paid at evenly spaced time intervals (periodically). Examples of a series of periodic receipts or payments are loan agreements, installment sales, mortgage notes, lease (rental) contracts, and pension obligations. As discussed earlier, these periodic receipts or payments are **annuities**.

The **present value of an annuity** is the value now of a series of future receipts or payments, discounted assuming compound interest. In computing the present value of an annuity, it is necessary to know (1) the discount rate, (2) the number of payments (receipts), and (3) the amount of the periodic receipts or payments. To illustrate the computation of the present value of an annuity, assume that you will receive $1,000 cash annually for three years at a time when the discount rate is 10%. This situation is depicted in the time diagram in **Illustration G.14**. **Illustration G.15** shows the computation of its present value in this situation.

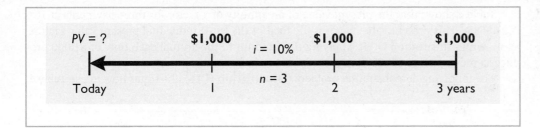

Time diagram for a three-year annuity

Future Amount	×	Present Value of 1 Factor at 10%	=	Present Value
$1,000 (1 year away)		.90909		$ 909.09
1,000 (2 years away)		.82645		826.45
1,000 (3 years away)		.75132		751.32
		2.48686		$2,486.86

Present value of a series of future amounts computation

This method of calculation is required when the periodic cash flows are not uniform in each period. However, when the future receipts are the same in each period, an annuity table can be used. As illustrated in **Table 4**, an annuity table shows the present value of 1 to be received periodically for a given number of payments. It assumes that each payment is made at the end of each period.

TABLE 4   **Present Value of an Annuity of 1**

(n) Payments	4%	5%	6%	7%	8%	9%	10%	11%	12%	15%
1	.96154	.95238	.94340	.93458	.92593	.91743	.90909	.90090	.89286	.86957
2	1.88609	1.85941	1.83339	1.80802	1.78326	1.75911	1.73554	1.71252	1.69005	1.62571
3	2.77509	2.72325	2.67301	2.62432	2.57710	2.53130	2.48685	2.44371	2.40183	2.28323
4	3.62990	3.54595	3.46511	3.38721	3.31213	3.23972	3.16986	3.10245	3.03735	2.85498
5	4.45182	4.32948	4.21236	4.10020	3.99271	3.88965	3.79079	3.69590	3.60478	3.35216
6	5.24214	5.07569	4.91732	4.76654	4.62288	4.48592	4.35526	4.23054	4.11141	3.78448
7	6.00205	5.78637	5.58238	5.38929	5.20637	5.03295	4.86842	4.71220	4.56376	4.16042
8	6.73274	6.46321	6.20979	5.97130	5.74664	5.53482	5.33493	5.14612	4.96764	4.48732
9	7.43533	7.10782	6.80169	6.51523	6.24689	5.99525	5.75902	5.53705	5.32825	4.77158
10	8.11090	7.72173	7.36009	7.02358	6.71008	6.41766	6.14457	5.88923	5.65022	5.01877
11	8.76048	8.30641	7.88687	7.49867	7.13896	6.80519	6.49506	6.20652	5.93770	5.23371
12	9.38507	8.86325	8.38384	7.94269	7.53608	7.16073	6.81369	6.49236	6.19437	5.42062
13	9.98565	9.39357	8.85268	8.35765	7.90378	7.48690	7.10336	6.74987	6.42355	5.58315
14	10.56312	9.89864	9.29498	8.74547	8.24424	7.78615	7.36669	6.98187	6.62817	5.72448
15	11.11839	10.37966	9.71225	9.10791	8.55948	8.06069	7.60608	7.19087	6.81086	5.84737
16	11.65230	10.83777	10.10590	9.44665	8.85137	8.31256	7.82371	7.37916	6.97399	5.95424
17	12.16567	11.27407	10.47726	9.76322	9.12164	8.54363	8.02155	7.54879	7.11963	6.04716
18	12.65930	11.68959	10.82760	10.05909	9.37189	8.75563	8.20141	7.70162	7.24967	6.12797
19	13.13394	12.08532	11.15812	10.33560	9.60360	8.95012	8.36492	7.83929	7.36578	6.19823
20	13.59033	12.46221	11.46992	10.59401	9.81815	9.12855	8.51356	7.96333	7.46944	6.25933

Table 4 shows that the present value of an annuity of 1 factor for three payments at 10% is 2.48685.[1] This present value factor is the total of the three individual present value factors, as shown in Illustration G.15. Applying this amount to the annual cash flow of $1,000 produces a present value of $2,486.85.

The following demonstration problem (**Illustration G.16**) illustrates how to use Table 4.

ILLUSTRATION G.16

Demonstration problem—
Using Table 4 for *PV* of an
annuity of 1

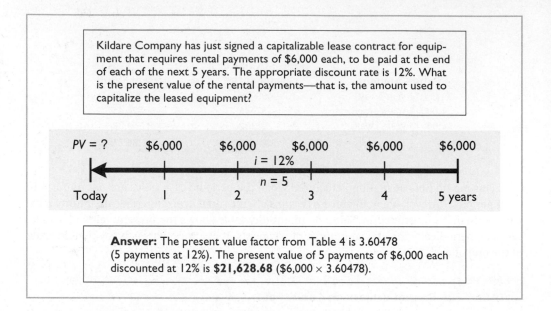

> Kildare Company has just signed a capitalizable lease contract for equipment that requires rental payments of $6,000 each, to be paid at the end of each of the next 5 years. The appropriate discount rate is 12%. What is the present value of the rental payments—that is, the amount used to capitalize the leased equipment?

Answer: The present value factor from Table 4 is 3.60478 (5 payments at 12%). The present value of 5 payments of $6,000 each discounted at 12% is **$21,628.68** ($6,000 × 3.60478).

Time Periods and Discounting

In the preceding calculations, the discounting was done on an annual basis using an annual interest rate. Discounting may also be done over shorter periods of time such as monthly, quarterly, or semiannually.

When the time frame is less than one year, it is necessary to convert the annual interest rate to the applicable time frame. Assume, for example, that the investor in Illustration G.14 received $500 **semiannually** for three years instead of $1,000 annually. In this case, the number of periods becomes six (3 × 2), the discount rate is 5% (10% ÷ 2), the present value factor from Table 4 is 5.07569 (6 periods at 5%), and the present value of the future cash flows is $2,537.85 (5.07569 × $500). This amount is slightly higher than the $2,486.86 computed in Illustration G.15 because interest is computed twice during the same year. That is, during the second half of the year, interest is earned on the first half-year's interest.

Present Value of a Long-Term Note or Bond

The present value (or market price) of a long-term note or bond is a function of three variables: (1) the payment amounts, (2) the length of time until the amounts are paid, and (3) the discount rate. Our example uses a five-year bond issue.

The first variable (dollars to be paid) is made up of two elements: (1) a series of interest payments (an annuity) and (2) the principal amount (a single sum). To compute the present value of the bond, both the interest payments and the principal amount must be discounted—two different computations. The time diagrams for a bond due in five years are shown in **Illustration G.17**.

---

[1]The difference of .00001 between 2.48686 and 2.48685 is due to rounding.

ILLUSTRATION G.17   **Time diagrams for the present value of a bond**

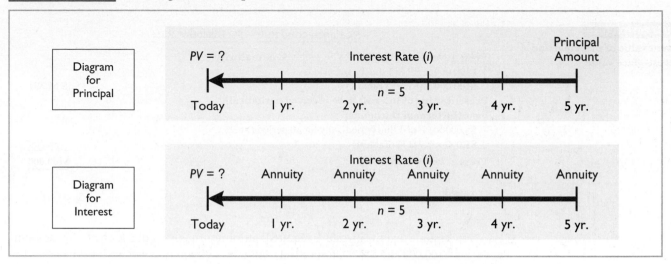

When the investor's market interest rate is equal to the bond's contractual interest rate, the present value of the bonds will equal the face value of the bonds. To illustrate, assume a bond issue of 5%, 10-year bonds with a face value of $100,000 with interest payable **annually** on January 1. If the discount rate is the same as the contractual rate, the bonds will sell at face value. In this case, the investor will receive (1) $100,000 at maturity and (2) a series of ten $5,000 interest payments ($100,000 × 5%) over the term of the bonds. The length of time is expressed in terms of interest periods—in this case, 10—and the discount rate per interest period, 5%. The time diagram in **Illustration G.18** depicts the variables involved in this discounting situation.

ILLUSTRATION G.18   **Time diagram for present value of a 5%, 10-year bond paying interest annually**

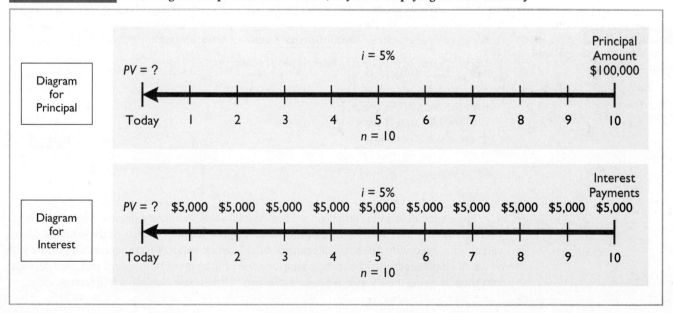

Illustration G.19 shows the computation of the present value of these bonds.

ILLUSTRATION G.19

Present value of principal and interest—face value

<table>
<tr><td colspan="2" align="center">**5% Contractual Rate—5% Discount Rate**</td></tr>
<tr><td>**Present value of principal to be received at maturity**</td><td></td></tr>
<tr><td>$100,000 × PV of 1 due in 10 periods at 5%</td><td></td></tr>
<tr><td>$100,000 × .61391 (Table 3)</td><td>$ 61,391</td></tr>
<tr><td>**Present value of interest to be received periodically**</td><td></td></tr>
<tr><td>**over the term of the bonds**</td><td></td></tr>
<tr><td>$5,000 × PV of 1 due periodically for 10 periods at 5%</td><td></td></tr>
<tr><td>$5,000 × 7.72173 (Table 4)</td><td>38,609*</td></tr>
<tr><td>**Present value of bonds**</td><td>**$100,000**</td></tr>
</table>

*Rounded

Now assume that the investor's required rate of return is 6%, not 5%. The future amounts are again $100,000 and $5,000, respectively, but now a discount rate of 6% must be used. The present value of the bonds is $92,639, as computed in **Illustration G.20**.

ILLUSTRATION G.20

Present value of principal and interest—discount

<table>
<tr><td colspan="2" align="center">**5% Contractual Rate—6% Discount Rate**</td></tr>
<tr><td>**Present value of principal to be received at maturity**</td><td></td></tr>
<tr><td>$100,000 × .55839 (Table 3)</td><td>$55,839</td></tr>
<tr><td>**Present value of interest to be received periodically**</td><td></td></tr>
<tr><td>**over the term of the bonds**</td><td></td></tr>
<tr><td>$5,000 × 7.36009 (Table 4)</td><td>36,800</td></tr>
<tr><td>**Present value of bonds**</td><td>**$92,639**</td></tr>
</table>

Conversely, if the discount rate is 4% and the contractual rate is 5%, the present value of the bonds is $108,111, computed as shown in **Illustration G.21**.

ILLUSTRATION G.21

Present value of principal and interest—premium

<table>
<tr><td colspan="2" align="center">**5% Contractual Rate—4% Discount Rate**</td></tr>
<tr><td>**Present value of principal to be received at maturity**</td><td></td></tr>
<tr><td>$100,000 × .67556 (Table 3)</td><td>$ 67,556</td></tr>
<tr><td>**Present value of interest to be received periodically**</td><td></td></tr>
<tr><td>**over the term of the bonds**</td><td></td></tr>
<tr><td>$5,000 × 8.11090 (Table 4)</td><td>40,555*</td></tr>
<tr><td>**Present value of bonds**</td><td>**$108,111**</td></tr>
</table>

*Rounded

The above discussion relied on present value tables in solving present value problems. Calculators may also be used to compute present values without the use of these tables. Many calculators, especially financial calculators, have present value (PV) functions that allow you to calculate present values by merely inputting the proper amount, discount rate, and periods, and then pressing the PV key. We discuss the use of financial calculators in a later section.

Capital Budgeting Situations

LEARNING OBJECTIVE 3

Compute the present value in capital budgeting situations.

The decision to make long-term capital investments is best evaluated using discounting techniques that recognize the time value of money. To do this, many companies calculate the present value of the cash flows involved in a capital investment.

To illustrate, Nagel-Siebert Trucking Company, a cross-country freight carrier in Montgomery, Illinois, is considering adding another truck to its fleet because of a purchasing opportunity. **Navistar Inc.**, Nagel-Siebert's primary supplier of overland rigs, is overstocked and offers to sell its biggest rig for $154,000 cash payable upon delivery. Nagel-Siebert knows that the rig will produce a net cash flow per year of $40,000 for five years (received at the end of each year), at which time it will be sold for an estimated salvage value of $35,000. Nagel-Siebert's discount rate in evaluating capital expenditures is 10%. Should Nagel-Siebert commit to the purchase of this rig?

The cash flows that must be discounted to present value by Nagel-Siebert are as follows.

Cash payable on delivery (today): $154,000.

Net cash flow from operating the rig: $40,000 for five years (at the end of each year).

Cash received from sale of rig at the end of five years: $35,000.

The time diagrams for the latter two cash flows are shown in **Illustration G.22**.

ILLUSTRATION G.22   **Time diagrams for Nagel-Siebert Trucking Company**

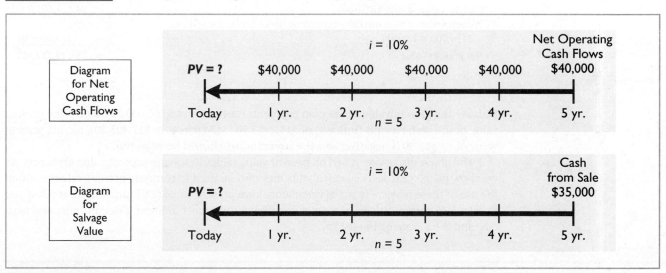

Notice from the diagrams that computing the present value of the net operating cash flows ($40,000 at the end of each year) is **discounting an annuity** (Table 4), while computing the present value of the $35,000 salvage value is **discounting a single sum** (Table 3). The computation of these present values is shown in **Illustration G.23**.

ILLUSTRATION G.23
Present value computations at 10%

Present Values Using a 10% Discount Rate

Present value of net operating cash flows received annually over 5 years	
$40,000 × PV of 1 received annually for 5 years at 10%	
$40,000 × 3.79079	$ 151,631.60
Present value of salvage value (cash) to be received in 5 years	
$35,000 × PV of 1 received in 5 years at 10%	
$35,000 × .62092	21,732.20
Present value of cash **inflows**	173,363.80
Present value of cash **outflows** (purchase price due today at 10%)	
$154,000 × PV of 1 due today	
$154,000 × 1.00000	(154,000.00)
Net present value	**$ 19,363.80**

Because the present value of the cash receipts (inflows) of $173,363.80 ($151,631.60 + $21,732.20) exceeds the present value of the cash payments (outflows) of $154,000.00, the net present value of $19,363.80 is positive, and **the decision to invest should be accepted**.

Now assume that Nagel-Siebert uses a discount rate of 15%, not 10%, because it wants a greater return on its investments in capital assets. The cash receipts and cash payments by Nagel-Siebert are the same. The present values of these receipts and cash payments discounted at 15% are shown in **Illustration G.24**.

ILLUSTRATION G.24
Present value computations at 15%

Present Values Using a 15% Discount Rate

Present value of net operating cash flows received annually over 5 years at 15%	
$40,000 × 3.35216	$ 134,086.40
Present value of salvage value (cash) to be received in 5 years at 15%	
$35,000 × .49718	17,401.30
Present value of cash **inflows**	$ 151,487.70
Present value of cash **outflows** (purchase price due today at 15%)	
$154,000 × 1.00000	(154,000.00)
Net present value	**$ (2,512.30)**

Because the present value of the cash payments (outflows) of $154,000.00 exceeds the present value of the cash receipts (inflows) of $151,487.70 ($134,086.40 + $17,401.30), the net present value of $2,512.30 is negative, and **the investment should be rejected**.

The above discussion relied on present value tables in solving present value problems. As we show in the next section, calculators may also be used to compute present values without the use of these tables. Financial calculators have present value (PV) functions that allow you to calculate present values by merely identifying the proper amount, discount rate, and periods, and then pressing the PV key.

Using Financial Calculators

LEARNING OBJECTIVE 4
Use a financial calculator to solve time value of money problems.

Business professionals, once they have mastered the underlying time value of money concepts, often use a financial calculator to solve these types of problems. To use financial calculators, you enter the time value of money variables into the calculator. **Illustration G.25** shows the five most common keys used to solve time value of money problems.[2]

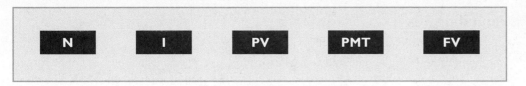

ILLUSTRATION G.25

Financial calculator keys

where:

N	=	number of periods
I	=	interest rate per period (some calculators use I/YR or i)
PV	=	present value (occurs at the beginning of the first period)
PMT	=	payment (all payments are equal, and none are skipped)
FV	=	future value (occurs at the end of the last period)

In solving time value of money problems in this appendix, you will generally be given three of four variables and will have to solve for the remaining variable. The fifth key (the key not used) is given a value of zero to ensure that this variable is not used in the computation.

Present Value of a Single Sum

To illustrate how to solve a present value problem using a financial calculator, assume that you want to know the present value of $84,253 to be received in five years, discounted at 11% compounded annually. **Illustration G.26** depicts this problem.

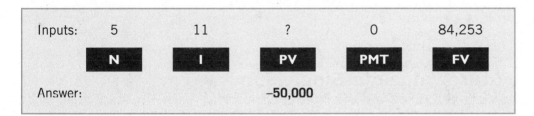

ILLUSTRATION G.26

Calculator solution for present value of a single sum

Illustration G.26 shows you the information (inputs) to enter into the calculator: N = 5, I = 11, PMT = 0, and FV = 84,253. You then press PV for the answer: −$50,000. As indicated, the PMT key was given a value of zero because a series of payments did not occur in this problem.

Plus and Minus

The use of plus and minus signs in time value of money problems with a financial calculator can be confusing. Most financial calculators are programmed so that the positive and negative cash flows in any problem offset each other. In the present value problem above, we identified the $84,253 future value initial investment as a positive (inflow); the answer −$50,000 was shown as a negative amount, reflecting a cash outflow. If the 84,253 were entered as a negative, then the final answer would have been reported as a positive 50,000.

Hopefully, the sign convention will not cause confusion. If you understand what is required in a problem, you should be able to interpret a positive or negative amount in determining the solution to a problem.

Compounding Periods

In the problem above, we assumed that compounding occurs once a year. Some financial calculators have a default setting, which assumes that compounding occurs 12 times a year. You

---

[2]On many calculators, these keys are actual buttons on the face of the calculator; on others, they appear on the display after the user accesses a present value menu.

must determine what default period has been programmed into your calculator and change it as necessary to arrive at the proper compounding period.

Rounding

Most financial calculators store and calculate using 12 decimal places. As a result, because compound interest tables generally have factors only up to five decimal places, a slight difference in the final answer can result. In most time value of money problems, the final answer will not include more than two decimal places.

Present Value of an Annuity

To illustrate how to solve a present value of an annuity problem using a financial calculator, assume that you are asked to determine the present value of rental receipts of $6,000 each to be received at the end of each of the next five years, when discounted at 12%, as pictured in **Illustration G.27**.

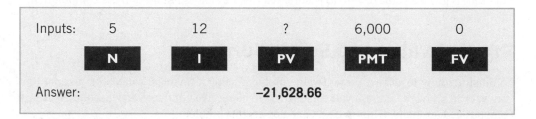

In this case, you enter N = 5, I = 12, PMT = 6,000, and FV = 0, and then press PV to arrive at the answer of −$21,628.66.

Future Value of a Single Sum

Now let us look at an investment to illustrate how to solve a future value problem using a financial calculator. Assume that you will invest $20,000 today in a fund and you intend to leave it there for 15 years. The fund earns 7% interest. **Illustration G.28** shows how to compute the future value of the fund at the end of year 15.

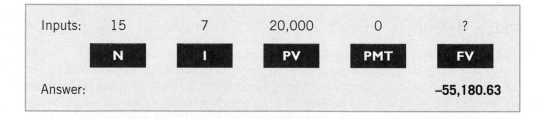

In this case, you enter N = 15, I = 7, PV = 20,000, and PMT = 0, and then press FV to calculate the future value of −$55,180.63.

Future Value of an Annuity

You can use a financial calculator to solve a future value of an annuity problem for an annuity investment. Assume that you will invest $8,000 in a fund at the end of each of the next eight years. The fund earns 9% interest. **Illustration G.29** shows how to compute the future value of the fund at the end of the eighth year.

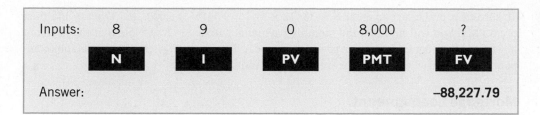

In this case, you enter N = 8, I = 9, PV = 0, and PMT = 8,000, and then press FV to determine the future value of −$88,227.79.

Internal Rate of Return

You can also use these same calculator keys to compute the internal rate of return of an investment that has equal cash flows. Suppose that a purchase of a piece of equipment with a seven-year life requires an initial investment of $54,000, has positive cash flows of $7,800 per year, and has an estimated salvage value of $11,000. The computation is shown in **Illustration G.30**.

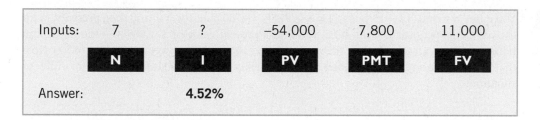

In this case, you enter N = 7, PV = −54,000 (we entered as a negative, since it is an outflow), PMT = 7,800, and FV = 11,000, and then press FV to determine the answer of 4.52%. Notice that the advantage to this approach is that you arrive at a much more precise result, rather than the rough approximation provided by the present value tables. To determine the internal rate of return using your calculator for an investment with unequal cash flows, you need to employ the cash flow key (CF) and the internal rate of return key (IRR). The use of these function keys varies across calculators, so you should consult the user manual for your calculator or the manufacturer's website for specific information.

Useful Applications of the Financial Calculator

With a financial calculator, you can solve for any interest rate or for any number of periods in a time value of money problem. Here are some examples of these applications.

Auto Loan

Assume you are financing the purchase of a used car with a three-year loan. The loan has a 9.5% stated annual interest rate, compounded monthly. The price of the car is $6,000, and you want to determine the monthly payments, assuming that the payments start one month after the purchase. This problem is pictured in **Illustration G.31**.

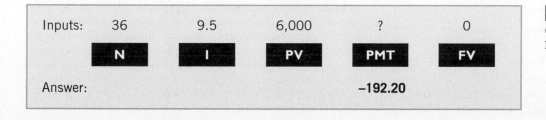

To solve this problem, you enter N = 36 (12 × 3), I = 9.5, PV = 6,000, and FV = 0, and then press PMT. You will find that the monthly payments will be $192.20. Note that the payment key is usually programmed for 12 payments per year. Thus, you must change the default (compounding period) if the payments are other than monthly.

Mortgage Loan Amount

Say you are evaluating financing options for a loan on a house (a mortgage). You decide that the maximum mortgage payment you can afford is $700 per month. The annual interest rate is 8.4%. If you get a mortgage that requires you to make monthly payments over a 15-year period, what is the maximum home loan you can afford? **Illustration G.32** depicts this problem.

ILLUSTRATION G.32

Calculator solution for mortgage amount

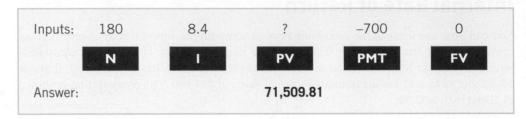

Inputs:	180	8.4	?	−700	0
	N	I	PV	PMT	FV
Answer:			71,509.81		

You enter N = 180 (12 × 15 years), I = 8.4, PMT = −700, and FV = 0, and then press PV. With the payments-per-year key set at 12, you find a present value of $71,509.81—the maximum home loan you can afford, given that you want to keep your mortgage payments at $700. Note that by changing any of the variables, you can quickly conduct "what-if" analyses for different situations.

Review

Learning Objectives Review

1 Compute interest and future values.

Simple interest is computed on the principal only, while compound interest is computed on the principal and any interest earned that has not been withdrawn.

To solve for future value of a single amount, prepare a time diagram of the problem. Identify the principal amount, the number of compounding periods, and the interest rate. Using the future value of 1 table, multiply the principal amount by the future value factor specified at the intersection of the number of periods and the interest rate.

To solve for future value of an annuity, prepare a time diagram of the problem. Identify the amount of the periodic payments (receipts), the number of payments (receipts), and the interest rate. Using the future value of an annuity of 1 table, multiply the amount of the payments by the future value factor specified at the intersection of the number of periods and the interest rate.

2 Compute present values.

The following three variables are fundamental to solving present value problems: (1) the future amount, (2) the number of periods, and (3) the interest rate (the discount rate).

To solve for present value of a single amount, prepare a time diagram of the problem. Identify the future amount, the number of discounting periods, and the discount (interest) rate. Using the present value of a single amount table, multiply the future amount by the present value factor specified at the intersection of the number of periods and the discount rate.

To solve for present value of an annuity, prepare a time diagram of the problem. Identify the amount of future periodic receipts or payments (annuities), the number of payments (receipts), and the discount (interest) rate. Using the present value of an annuity of 1 table, multiply the amount of the annuity by the present value factor specified at the intersection of the number of payments and the interest rate.

To compute the present value of notes and bonds, determine the present value of the principal amount and the present value of the interest payments. Multiply the principal amount (a single future amount) by the present value factor (from the present value of 1 table) intersecting at the number of periods (number of interest payments) and the discount rate. To determine the present value of the series of interest payments, multiply the amount of the interest payment by the present value factor (from the present value of an annuity of 1 table) intersecting at the number of periods (number of interest payments) and the discount rate. Add the present value of the principal amount to the present value of the interest payments to arrive at the present value of the note or bond.

3 Compute the present value in capital budgeting situations.

Compute the present values of all cash inflows and all cash outflows related to the capital budgeting proposal (an investment-type decision). If the **net** present value is positive, accept the proposal (make the investment). If the **net** present value is negative, reject the proposal (do not make the investment).

4 Use a financial calculator to solve time value of money problems.

Financial calculators can be used to solve the same (and additional) problems as those solved with time value of money tables. Enter into the financial calculator the amounts for all of the known elements of a time value of money problem (periods, interest rate, payments, future or present value), and it solves for the unknown element. Particularly useful situations involve interest rates and compounding periods not presented in the tables.

Glossary Review

Annuity A series of equal dollar amounts to be paid or received at evenly spaced time intervals (periodically). (p. G-5).

Compound interest The interest computed on the principal and any interest earned that has not been paid or withdrawn. (p. G-2).

Discounting the future amount(s) The process of determining present value. (p. G-7).

Future value of an annuity The sum of all the payments (receipts) plus the accumulated compound interest on them. (p. G-5).

Future value of a single amount The value at a future date of a given amount invested, assuming compound interest. (p. G-3).

Interest Payment for the use of another person's money. (p. G-2).

Present value The value now of a given amount to be paid or received in the future, assuming compound interest. (p. G-7).

Present value of an annuity The value now of a series of future receipts or payments, discounted assuming compound interest. (p. G-10).

Principal The amount borrowed or invested. (p. G-2).

Simple interest The interest computed on the principal only. (p. G-2).

WileyPLUS

Many additional resources are available for practice in WileyPLUS.

Brief Exercises

(Use tables to solve exercises BEG.1 to BEG.23.)

BEG.1 (LO 1), AP Jozy Altidore invested $6,000 at 5% annual interest, and left the money invested without withdrawing any of the interest for 12 years. At the end of the 12 years, Jozy withdrew the accumulated amount of money. (a) What amount did Jozy withdraw, assuming the investment earns simple interest? (b) What amount did Jozy withdraw, assuming the investment earns interest compounded annually?

Compute the future value of a single amount.

BEG.2 (LO 1), C For each of the following cases, indicate (a) what interest rate columns and (b) what number of periods you would refer to in looking up the future value factor.

Use future value tables.

1. In Table 1 (future value of 1):

	Annual Rate	Number of Years Invested	Compounded
Case A	5%	3	Annually
Case B	12%	4	Semiannually

2. In Table 2 (future value of an annuity of 1):

	Annual Rate	Number of Years Invested	Compounded
Case A	3%	8	Annually
Case B	8%	6	Semiannually

Compute the future value of a single amount.

BEG.3 (LO 1), AP Liam Company signed a lease for an office building for a period of 12 years. Under the lease agreement, a security deposit of $9,600 is made. The deposit will be returned at the expiration of the lease with interest compounded at 4% per year. What amount will Liam receive at the time the lease expires?

Compute the future value of an annuity.

BEG.4 (LO 1), AP Bates Company issued $1,000,000, 10-year bonds. It agreed to make annual deposits of $78,000 to a fund (called a sinking fund), which will be used to pay off the principal amount of the bond at the end of 10 years. The deposits are made at the end of each year into an account paying 6% annual interest. What amount will be in the sinking fund at the end of 10 years?

Compute the future value of a single amount and of an annuity.

BEG.5 (LO 1), AP Andrew and Emma Garfield invested $8,000 in a savings account paying 5% annual interest when their daughter, Angela, was born. They also deposited $1,000 on each of her birthdays until she was 18 (including her 18th birthday). How much was in the savings account on her 18th birthday (after the last deposit)?

Compute the future value of a single amount.

BEG.6 (LO 1), AP Hugh Curtin borrowed $35,000 on July 1, 2022. This amount plus accrued interest at 8% compounded annually is to be repaid on July 1, 2027. How much will Hugh have to repay on July 1, 2027?

Use present value tables.

BEG.7 (LO 2), C For each of the following cases, indicate (a) what interest rate columns and (b) what number of periods you would refer to in looking up the discount rate.

1. In Table 3 (present value of 1):

	Annual Rate	Number of Years Involved	Discounts per Year
Case A	12%	7	Annually
Case B	8%	11	Annually
Case C	10%	8	Semiannually

2. In Table 4 (present value of an annuity of 1):

	Annual Rate	Number of Years Involved	Number of Payments Involved	Frequency of Payments
Case A	10%	20	20	Annually
Case B	10%	7	7	Annually
Case C	6%	5	10	Semiannually

Determine present values.

BEG.8 (LO 2), AP **a.** What is the present value of $25,000 due 9 periods from now, discounted at 10%?

b. What is the present value of $25,000 to be received at the end of each of 6 periods, discounted at 9%?

Compute the present value of a single amount investment.

BEG.9 (LO 2), AP Messi Company is considering an investment that will return a lump sum of $900,000 6 years from now. What amount should Messi Company pay for this investment to earn an 8% return?

Compute the present value of a single amount investment.

BEG.10 (LO 2), AP Lloyd Company earns 6% on an investment that will return $450,000 8 years from now. What is the amount Lloyd should invest now to earn this rate of return?

Compute the present value of an annuity investment.

BEG.11 (LO 2), AP Robben Company is considering investing in an annuity contract that will return $40,000 annually at the end of each year for 15 years. What amount should Robben Company pay for this investment if it earns an 8% return?

Compute the present value of an annual investment.

BEG.12 (LO 2), AP Kaehler Enterprises earns 5% on an investment that pays back $80,000 at the end of each of the next 6 years. What is the amount Kaehler Enterprises invested to earn the 5% rate of return?

Compute the present value of bonds.

BEG.13 (LO 2), AP Dempsey Railroad Co. is about to issue $400,000 of 10-year bonds paying an 11% interest rate, with interest payable annually. The discount rate for such securities is 10%. How much can Dempsey expect to receive for the sale of these bonds?

Compute the present value of bonds.

BEG.14 (LO 2), AP Dempsey Railroad Co. is about to issue $400,000 of 10-year bonds paying an 11% interest rate, with interest payable annually. The discount rate for such securities is 12%. How much can Dempsey expect to receive from the sale of these bonds?

Compute the present value of a note.

BEG.15 (LO 2), AP Neymar Taco Company receives a $75,000, 6-year note bearing interest of 4% (paid annually) from a customer at a time when the discount rate is 6%. What is the present value of the note received by Neymar?

BEG.16 (LO 2), AP Gleason Enterprises issued 6%, 8-year, $2,500,000 par value bonds that pay interest annually on April 1. The bonds are dated April 1, 2022, and are issued on that date. The discount rate of interest for such bonds on April 1, 2022, is 8%. What cash proceeds did Gleason receive from issuance of the bonds?

Compute the present value of bonds.

BEG.17 (LO 2), AP Frazier Company issues a 10%, 5-year mortgage note on January 1, 2022, to obtain financing for new equipment. Land is used as collateral for the note. The terms provide for semiannual installment payments of $48,850. What are the cash proceeds received from the issuance of the note?

Compute the present value of a note.

BEG.18 (LO 2), AP If Colleen Mooney invests $4,765.50 now and she will receive $12,000 at the end of 12 years, what annual rate of interest will Colleen earn on her investment? (*Hint:* Use Table 3.)

Compute the interest rate on a single amount.

BEG.19 (LO 2), AP Tim Howard has been offered the opportunity of investing $36,125 now. The investment will earn 11% per year and at the end of that time will return Tim $75,000. How many years must Tim wait to receive $75,000? (*Hint:* Use Table 3.)

Compute the number of periods of a single amount.

BEG.20 (LO 2), AP Joanne Quick made an investment of $10,271.38. From this investment, she will receive $1,200 annually for the next 15 years starting one year from now. What rate of interest will Joanne's investment be earning for her? (*Hint:* Use Table 4.)

Compute the interest rate on an annuity.

BEG.21 (LO 2), AP Kevin Morales invests $7,793.83 now for a series of $1,300 annual returns beginning one year from now. Kevin will earn a return of 9% on the initial investment. How many annual payments of $1,300 will Kevin receive? (*Hint:* Use Table 4.)

Compute the number of periods of an annuity.

BEG.22 (LO 3), AP Barney Googal owns a garage and is contemplating purchasing a tire retreading machine for $12,820. After estimating costs and revenues, Barney projects a net cash inflow from the retreading machine of $2,700 annually for 7 years. Barney hopes to earn a return of 9% on such investments. What is the present value of the retreading operation? Should Barney Googal purchase the retreading machine?

Compute the present value of a machine for purposes of making a purchase decision.

BEG.23 (LO 3), AP Snyder Company is considering purchasing equipment. The equipment will produce the following cash inflows: Year 1, $25,000; Year 2, $30,000; and Year 3, $40,000. Snyder requires a minimum rate of return of 11%. What is the maximum price Snyder should pay for this equipment?

Compute the maximum price to pay for a machine.

BEG.24 (LO 4), AP Carly Simon wishes to invest $18,000 on July 1, 2022, and have it accumulate to $50,000 by July 1, 2032. Use a financial calculator to determine at what exact annual rate of interest Carly must invest the $18,000.

Determine interest rate.

BEG.25 (LO 4), AP On July 17, 2021, Keith Urban borrowed $42,000 from his grandfather to open a clothing store. Starting July 17, 2022, Keith has to make 10 equal annual payments of $6,500 each to repay the loan. Use a financial calculator to determine what interest rate Keith is paying.

Determine interest rate.

BEG.26 (LO 4), AP As the purchaser of a new house, Carrie Underwood has signed a mortgage note to pay the Nashville National Bank and Trust Co. $8,400 every 6 months for 20 years, at the end of which time she will own the house. At the date the mortgage is signed, the purchase price was $198,000 and Underwood made a down payment of $20,000. The first payment will be made 6 months after the date the mortgage is signed. Using a financial calculator, compute the exact rate of interest earned on the mortgage by the bank.

Determine interest rate.

BEG.27 (LO 4), AP Using a financial calculator, solve for the unknowns in each of the following situations.

Various time value of money situations.

a. On June 1, 2021, Jennifer Lawrence purchases lakefront property from her neighbor, Josh Hutcherson, and agrees to pay the purchase price in seven payments of $16,000 each, the first payment to be payable June 1, 2022. (Assume that interest compounded at an annual rate of 7.35% is implicit in the payments.) What is the purchase price of the property?

b. On January 1, 2021, Gerrard Corporation purchased 200 of the $1,000 face value, 8% coupon, 10-year bonds of Sterling Inc. The bonds mature on January 1, 2031, and pay interest annually beginning January 1, 2022. Gerrard purchased the bonds to yield 10.65%. How much did Gerrard pay for the bonds?

BEG.28 (LO 4), AP Using a financial calculator, provide a solution to each of the following situations.

Various time value of money situations.

a. Lynn Anglin owes a debt of $42,000 from the purchase of her new sport utility vehicle. The debt bears annual interest of 7.8% compounded monthly. Lynn wishes to pay the debt and interest in equal monthly payments over 8 years, beginning one month hence. What equal monthly payments will pay off the debt and interest?

b. On January 1, 2022, Roger Molony offers to buy Dave Feeney's used snowmobile for $8,000, payable in five equal annual installments, which are to include 7.25% interest on the unpaid balance and a portion of the principal. If the first payment is to be made on December 31, 2022, how much will each payment be?

Determine internal rate of return.

BEG.29 (LO 4), AP Renolds Corporation is considering two alternative investments in excavating equipment. Investment A requires an initial investment of $184,000, has positive cash flows of $27,500 per year, and has an estimated salvage value of $21,000. Investment B requires an initial investment of $234,000, has positive cash flows of $32,800 per year, and has an estimated salvage value of $19,000. Each piece of equipment is expected to have a 12-year useful life. Use a financial calculator to determine the internal rate of return of each project to decide which is more desirable. (Round to two decimal places, e.g., 9.74%.)

Reporting and Analyzing Investments

Appendix Preview

Some companies believe in aggressive growth through investing in the stock of existing companies. Besides purchasing stock, companies also purchase other securities, such as bonds issued by corporations or by governments. Companies can make investments for a short or long period of time, as a passive investment, or with the intent to control another company. As you will see in this appendix, the way in which a company accounts for its investments is determined by a number of factors.

Appendix Outline

LEARNING OBJECTIVES	REVIEW	PRACTICE
1. Explain how to account for debt investments.	• Why corporations invest • Accounting for debt investments	**DO IT! 1** Debt Investments
2. Explain how to account for stock investments.	• Holdings of less than 20% • Holdings between 20% and 50% • Holdings of more than 50%	**DO IT! 2** Stock Investments
3. Discuss how debt and stock investments are reported in the financial statements.	• Debt securities • Equity securities • Balance sheet presentation • Presentation of realized and unrealized gain or loss	**DO IT! 3a** Trading and Available-for-Sale Debt Securities **DO IT! 3b** Financial Statement Presentation of Investments

Go to the Review and Practice Section at the end of the appendix for a review of key concepts and practice applications with solutions.

Accounting for Debt Investments

LEARNING OBJECTIVE 1
Explain how to account for debt investments.

Why Corporations Invest

Corporations purchase investments in debt or equity securities generally for one of three reasons. First, a corporation may **have excess cash** that it does not need for the immediate purchase of operating assets. For example, many companies experience seasonal fluctuations in sales. A Cape Cod marina has more sales in the spring and summer than in the fall and winter. The reverse is true for an Aspen ski shop. Thus, at the end of an operating cycle, many companies may have cash on hand that is temporarily idle until the start of another operating cycle. These companies may invest the excess funds to earn—through interest and dividends—a greater return than they would get by just holding the funds in the bank. **Illustration H.1** shows the role that such temporary investments play in the operating cycle.

ILLUSTRATION H.1

Temporary investments and
the operating cycle

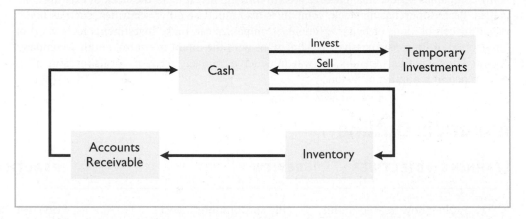

A second reason some companies such as banks purchase investments is to generate **earnings from investment income**. Although banks make most of their earnings by lending money, they also generate earnings by investing in primarily debt securities. Banks purchase investment securities because loan demand varies both seasonally and with changes in the economic climate. Thus, when loan demand is low, a bank must find other uses for its cash.

Some companies attempt to generate investment income through speculative investments. That is, they are speculating that the investment will increase in value and thus result in positive returns. Therefore, they invest mostly in the common stock of other corporations.

Third, companies also invest for **strategic reasons**. A company may purchase a non-controlling interest in another company in a related industry in which it wishes to establish a presence. Or, a company can exercise some influence over one of its customers or suppliers by purchasing a significant, but not controlling, interest in that company. Another option is for a corporation to purchase a controlling interest in another company in order to enter a new industry without incurring the costs and risks associated with starting from scratch.

In summary, businesses invest in other companies for the reasons shown in **Illustration H.2**.

ILLUSTRATION H.2

Why corporations invest

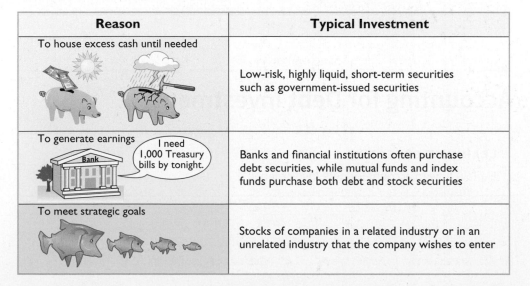

Reason	Typical Investment
To house excess cash until needed	Low-risk, highly liquid, short-term securities such as government-issued securities
To generate earnings *I need 1,000 Treasury bills by tonight.*	Banks and financial institutions often purchase debt securities, while mutual funds and index funds purchase both debt and stock securities
To meet strategic goals	Stocks of companies in a related industry or in an unrelated industry that the company wishes to enter

Accounting for Debt Investments

Debt investments are investments in government and corporation bonds. In accounting for debt investments, companies must make entries to record (1) the acquisition, (2) the interest revenue, and (3) the sale.

Recording Acquisition of Bonds

At acquisition, debt investments are recorded at cost. Cost includes all expenditures necessary to acquire these investments, such as the price paid plus brokerage fees (commissions), if any.

For example, assume that Kuhl Corporation acquires 50 Doan Inc. 8%, 10-year, $1,000 bonds on January 1, 2022, at a cost of $50,000. Kuhl records the investment as:

Jan. 1	Debt Investments	50,000	
	Cash		50,000
	(To record purchase of 50 Doan Inc. bonds)		

A = L + SE
+50,000
−50,000

Cash Flows
−50,000

Recording Bond Interest

The Doan Inc. bonds pay interest of $4,000 annually on January 1 ($50,000 × 8%). If Kuhl Corporation's fiscal year ends on December 31, it accrues the interest of $4,000 earned since January 1. The adjusting entry is:

Dec. 31	Interest Receivable	4,000	
	Interest Revenue		4,000
	(To accrue interest on Doan Inc. bonds)		

A = L + SE
+4,000
+4,000 Rev

Cash Flows
no effect

Kuhl reports Interest Receivable as a current asset in the balance sheet. It reports Interest Revenue under "Other revenues and gains" in the income statement.

Kuhl records receipt of the interest on January 1 as follows.

Jan. 1	Cash	4,000	
	Interest Receivable		4,000
	(To record receipt of accrued interest)		

A = L + SE
+4,000
−4,000

Cash Flows
+4,000

A credit to Interest Revenue at this time would be incorrect. Why? Because the company earned and accrued the interest revenue in the preceding accounting period.

Recording Sale of Bonds

When Kuhl Corporation sells the bond investments, it credits the investment account for the cost of the bonds. The company records as a gain or loss any difference between the net proceeds from the sale (sales price less brokerage fees) and the cost of the bonds (see **Helpful Hint**).

Assume, for example, that Kuhl receives net proceeds of $53,000 on the sale of the Doan Inc. bonds on January 1, 2023, after receiving the interest due. Since the securities cost $50,000, Kuhl has realized a gain of $3,000. It records the sale as follows.

> **HELPFUL HINT**
>
> The accounting for short-term debt investments and long-term debt investments is similar. Any exceptions are discussed in more advanced courses.

Jan. 1	Cash	53,000	
	Debt Investments		50,000
	Gain on Sale of Debt Investments		3,000
	(To record sale of Doan Inc. bonds)		

A = L + SE
+53,000
−50,000
+3,000 Rev

Cash Flows
+53,000

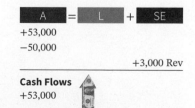

Kuhl reports the gain on the sale of debt investments under "Other revenues and gains" in the income statement and reports losses under "Other expenses and losses."

ACTION PLAN

- Record bond investments at cost.
- Record interest when accrued.
- When bonds are sold, credit the investment account for the cost of the bonds.
- Record any difference between the cost and the net proceeds as a gain or loss.

DO IT! 1 | Debt Investments

Waldo Corporation had the following transactions pertaining to debt investments.

Jan. 1, 2022 Purchased 30 $1,000 Hillary Co. 10% bonds for $30,000. Interest is payable annually on January 1.
Dec. 31, 2022 Accrued interest on Hillary Co. bonds in 2022.
Jan. 1, 2023 Received interest on Hillary Co. bonds.
Jan. 1, 2023 Sold 15 Hillary Co. bonds for $14,600.
Dec. 31, 2023 Accrued interest on Hillary Co. bonds in 2023.

Journalize the above transactions, including the accrual of interest on December 31, 2022.

Solution

Jan. 1 (2022)	Debt Investments	30,000	
	Cash		30,000
	(To record purchase of 30 Hillary Co. bonds)		
Dec. 31 (2022)	Interest Receivable	3,000	
	Interest Revenue ($30,000 × 10%)		3,000
	(To accrue interest on Hillary Co. bonds)		
Jan. 1 (2023)	Cash	3,000	
	Interest Receivable		3,000
	(To record receipt of interest on Hillary Co. bonds)		
Jan. 1 (2023)	Cash	14,600	
	Loss on Sale of Debt Investments	400	
	Debt Investments [$30,000 × (15 ÷ 30)]		15,000
	(To record sale of 15 Hillary Co. bonds)		
Dec. 31 (2023)	Interest Receivable	1,500	
	Interest Revenue ($15,000 × 10%)		1,500
	(To accrue interest on Hillary Co. bonds)		

Accounting for Stock Investments

LEARNING OBJECTIVE 2

Explain how to account for stock investments.

Stock investments are investments in the capital stock of corporations. When a company holds stock (and/or debt) of several different corporations, the group of securities is an **investment portfolio**.

The accounting for investments in common stock depends on the extent of the investor's influence over the operating and financial affairs of the issuing corporation (the **investee**). **Illustration H.3** shows the general guidelines.

Companies are required to use judgment instead of blindly following the guidelines.[1] We explain and illustrate the application of each guideline next.

---

[1]Among the factors that companies should consider in determining an investor's influence are whether (1) the investor has representation on the investee's board of directors, (2) the investor participates in the investee's policy-making process, (3) there are material transactions between the investor and the investee, and (4) the common stock held by other stockholders is concentrated or dispersed.

Investor's Ownership Interest in Investee's Common Stock	Presumed Influence on Investee	Accounting Guidelines
Less than 20%	Insignificant	Cost method
Between 20% and 50%	Significant	Equity method
More than 50%	Controlling	Consolidated financial statements

ILLUSTRATION H.3

Accounting guidelines for stock investments

Holdings of Less Than 20%

In the accounting for stock investments of less than 20%, companies use the cost method. Under the **cost method**, companies record the investment at cost and recognize revenue only when cash dividends are received.

Recording Acquisition of Stock

At acquisition, stock investments are recorded at cost. Cost includes all expenditures necessary to acquire these investments, such as the price paid plus brokerage fees (commissions), if any.

Assume, for example, that on July 1, 2022, Sanchez Corporation acquires 1,000 shares (10% ownership) of Beal Corporation common stock at $40 per share. The entry for the purchase is:

July 1	Stock Investments	40,000	
	Cash		40,000
	(To record purchase of 1,000 shares of Beal common stock)		

A = L + SE
+40,000
−40,000

Cash Flows
−40,000

Recording Dividends

During the time the company holds the stock, it makes entries for any cash dividends received. Thus, if Sanchez Corporation receives a $2 per share dividend on December 31, the entry is:

Dec. 31	Cash (1,000 × $2)	2,000	
	Dividend Revenue		2,000
	(To record receipt of a cash dividend)		

A = L + SE
+2,000
          +2,000 Rev

Cash Flows
+2,000

Sanchez reports Dividend Revenue under "Other revenues and gains" in the income statement.

Recording Sale of Stock

When a company sells a stock investment, it recognizes the difference between the net proceeds from the sale (sales price less brokerage fees) and the cost of the stock as a gain or a loss.

Assume, for instance, that Sanchez Corporation receives net proceeds of $39,500 on the sale of its Beal Corporation stock on February 10, 2023. Because the stock cost $40,000, Sanchez has incurred a loss of $500. It records the sale as:

Feb. 10	Cash	39,500	
	Loss on Sale of Stock Investments	500	
	Stock Investments		40,000
	(To record sale of Beal common stock)		

A = L + SE
+39,000
          −500 Exp
−40,000

Cash Flows
+39,500

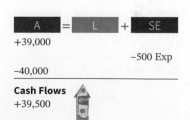

Sanchez reports the loss account under "Other expenses and losses" in the income statement and shows a gain on sale under "Other revenues and gains."

Holdings Between 20% and 50%

When an investor company owns only a small portion of the shares of stock of another company, the investor cannot exercise control over the investee. But when an investor owns between 20% and 50% of the common stock of a corporation, it is presumed that the investor has significant influence over the financial and operating activities of the investee. The investor probably has a representative on the investee's board of directors. Through that representative, the investor begins to exercise some control over the investee—and the investee company in some sense becomes part of the investor company.

For example, even prior to purchasing all of **Turner Broadcasting**, **Time Warner** owned 20% of Turner. Because it exercised significant control over major decisions made by Turner, Time Warner used an approach called the equity method. Under the **equity method, the investor records its share of the net income of the investee in the year when it is earned**. An alternative might be to delay recognizing the investor's share of net income until a cash dividend is declared. But that approach would ignore the fact that the investor and investee are, in some sense, one company, making the investor better off by the investee's net income.

Under the **equity method**, the company initially records the investment in common stock at cost. After that, it adjusts the investment account **annually** to show the investor's equity in the investee. Each year, the investor does the following. (1) It increases (debits) the investment account and increases (credits) revenue for its share of the investee's net income.[2] (2) The investor also decreases (credits) the investment account for the amount of dividends received. The investment account is reduced for dividends received because payment of a dividend decreases the net assets of the investee.

Recording Acquisition of Stock

Assume that Milar Corporation acquires 30% of the common stock of Beck Company for $120,000 on January 1, 2022. The entry to record this transaction is:

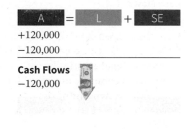

+120,000
−120,000

Cash Flows
−120,000

Jan. 1	Stock Investments		120,000	
	Cash			120,000
	(To record purchase of Beck common stock)			

Recording Revenue and Dividends

For 2022, Beck reports net income of $100,000. It declares and pays a $40,000 cash dividend. Milar must record (1) its share of Beck's income, $30,000 (30% × $100,000), and (2) the reduction in the investment account for the dividends received, $12,000 (30% × $40,000). The entries are:

(1)

+30,000
+30,000 Rev

Cash Flows
no effect

Dec. 31	Stock Investments		30,000	
	Revenue from Stock Investments			30,000
	(To record 30% equity in Beck's 2022 net income)			

(2)

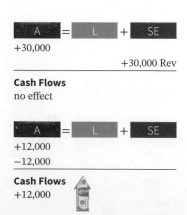

+12,000
−12,000

Cash Flows
+12,000

Dec. 31	Cash		12,000	
	Stock Investments			12,000
	(To record dividends received)			

[2]Conversely, the investor increases (debits) a loss account and decreases (credits) the investment account for its share of the investee's net loss.

After Milar posts the transactions for the year, the investment and revenue accounts are as shown in **Illustration H.4**.

Stock Investments				Revenue from Stock Investments	
Jan. 1	120,000	Dec. 31	**12,000**	Dec. 31	**30,000**
Dec. 31	**30,000**				
Dec. 31	Bal. 138,000				

During the year, the investment account increased by $18,000. This $18,000 is explained as follows: (1) Milar records a $30,000 increase in revenue from its stock investment in Beck, and (2) Milar records a $12,000 decrease due to dividends received from its stock investment in Beck.

Note that the difference between reported revenue under the cost method and reported revenue under the equity method can be significant. For example, Milar would report only $12,000 of dividend revenue (30% × $40,000) if it used the cost method.

Holdings of More Than 50%

A company that owns more than 50% of the common stock of another entity is known as the **parent company**. The entity whose stock is owned by the parent company is called the **subsidiary (affiliated) company**. Because of its stock ownership, the parent company has a **controlling interest** in the subsidiary company.

When a company owns more than 50% of the common stock of another company, it usually prepares **consolidated financial statements**. Consolidated financial statements present the assets and liabilities of the parent and subsidiary companies. They also present the total revenues and expenses of the parent and subsidiary companies. Companies prepare consolidated statements **in addition to** the financial statements for the individual parent and subsidiary companies.

As noted earlier, prior to acquiring all of **Turner Broadcasting**, **Time Warner** accounted for its investment in Turner using the equity method. Time Warner's net investment in Turner was reported in a single line item—Other investments. After the merger, Time Warner instead consolidated Turner's results with its own. Under this approach, Time Warner included the individual assets and liabilities of Turner with its own assets. That is, Turner's plant and equipment were added to Time Warner's plant and equipment, its receivables were added to Time Warner's receivables, and so on. A similar sort of consolidation went on when **AOL** merged with Time Warner (see **Helpful Hint**).

Consolidated statements are useful to the stockholders, board of directors, and management of the parent company. Consolidated statements indicate to creditors, prospective investors, and regulatory agencies the magnitude and scope of operations of the companies under common control. For example, regulators and the courts undoubtedly used the consolidated statements of **AT&T** to determine whether a breakup of the company was in the public interest. **Illustration H.5** lists three companies that prepare consolidated statements and some of the companies they have owned.

HELPFUL HINT

If the parent (A) has three wholly owned subsidiaries (B, C, and D), there are four separate legal entities but only one economic entity from the viewpoint of the shareholders of the parent company.

PepsiCo	Avis Budget Group	The Walt Disney Company
Frito-Lay	Avis Car Rental	Capital Cities/ABC, Inc.
Tropicana	Budget Car Rental	Disneyland, Disney World
Quaker Oats	Payless Car Rental	Anaheim Ducks
Pepsi-Cola	Apex Car Rentals	Anaheim Angels
Gatorade	Zipcar	ESPN

DO IT! 2 | Stock Investments

The following are two independent situations.

1. Rho Jean Inc. acquired 5% of the 400,000 shares of common stock of Stillwater Corp. at a total cost of $6 per share on May 18, 2022. On August 30, Stillwater declared and paid a $75,000 dividend. On December 31, Stillwater reported net income of $244,000 for the year.

2. Debbie, Inc. obtained significant influence over North Sails by buying 40% of North Sails' 60,000 outstanding shares of common stock at a cost of $12 per share on January 1, 2022. On April 15, North Sails declared and paid a cash dividend of $45,000. On December 31, North Sails reported net income of $120,000 for the year.

Prepare all necessary journal entries for 2022 for (1) Rho Jean Inc. and (2) Debbie, Inc.

Solution

1. May 18	Stock Investments (400,000 × 5% × $6)	120,000	
	Cash		120,000
	(To record purchase of 20,000 shares		
	of Stillwater Co. stock)		
Aug. 30	Cash	3,750	
	Dividend Revenue ($75,000 × 5%)		3,750
	(To record receipt of cash dividend)		
2. Jan. 1	Stock Investments (60,000 × 40% × $12)	288,000	
	Cash		288,000
	(To record purchase of 24,000 shares		
	of North Sails' stock)		
Apr. 15	Cash	18,000	
	Stock Investments ($45,000 × 40%)		18,000
	(To record receipt of cash dividend)		
Dec. 31	Stock Investments ($120,000 × 40%)	48,000	
	Revenue from Stock Investments		48,000
	(To record 40% equity in North Sails' net income)		

Reporting Investments in Financial Statements

LEARNING OBJECTIVE 3

Discuss how debt and stock investments are reported in the financial statements.

The value of debt and stock investments may fluctuate greatly during the time they are held. For example, in a 12-month period, the stock of **Time Warner** hit a high of $58\frac{1}{2}$ and a low of 9. In light of such price fluctuations, how should companies value investments at the balance sheet date? Valuation could be at cost, at fair value, or at the lower-of-cost-or-market value.

Many people argue that fair value offers the best approach because it represents the expected cash realizable value of securities. **Fair value** is the amount for which a security could be sold in a normal market. Others counter that unless a security is going to be sold soon, the fair value is not relevant because the price of the security will likely change again.

Debt Securities

For purposes of valuation and reporting at a financial statement date, debt investments are classified into three categories:

1. **Trading securities** are bought and held primarily for sale in the near term to generate income on short-term price differences.
2. **Available-for-sale securities** are held with the intent of selling them sometime in the future.
3. **Held-to-maturity securities** are debt securities that the investor has the intent and ability to hold to maturity.[3]

Illustration H.6 shows the valuation guidelines for these debt securities.

ILLUSTRATION H.6 Valuation guidelines for debt securities

Trading Securities

Trading securities are held with the intention of selling them in a short period of time (generally less than three months and sometimes less than a full day). **Trading** means frequent buying and selling. As indicated in Illustration H.6, companies adjust trading securities to fair value at the end of each period (an approach referred to as **mark-to-market** accounting). They report changes from cost **as part of net income**. The changes are reported as **unrealized gains or losses** because the securities have not been sold. The unrealized gain or loss is the difference between the **total cost** of trading securities and their **total fair value**. Companies classify trading securities as a current asset.

As an example, **Illustration H.7** shows the costs and fair values for investments classified as trading securities for Pace Corporation on December 31, 2022. Pace has an unrealized gain of $7,000 because total fair value ($147,000) is $7,000 greater than total cost ($140,000).

Trading Securities, December 31, 2022

Investments	Cost	Fair Value	Unrealized Gain (Loss)
Yorkville Company bonds	$ 50,000	$ 48,000	$(2,000)
Kodak Company bonds	90,000	99,000	9,000
Total	$140,000	$147,000	**$ 7,000**

ILLUSTRATION H.7
Valuation of trading securities

HELPFUL HINT
Companies report an unrealized gain or loss in the income statement because of the likelihood that the securities will be sold at fair value since they are a short-term investment.

The fact that trading securities are a short-term investment increases the likelihood that Pace will sell them at fair value for a gain. Pace records fair value and the unrealized gain through an adjusting entry at the time it prepares financial statements (see **Helpful Hint**).

[3]This category is provided for completeness. The accounting and valuation issues related to held-to-maturity securities are discussed in more advanced accounting courses.

In this entry, the company uses a valuation allowance account, Fair Value Adjustment—Trading, to record the difference between the total cost and the total fair value of the securities. The adjusting entry for Pace is:

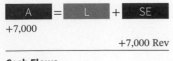

+7,000

+7,000 Rev

Cash Flows
no effect

Dec. 31	Fair Value Adjustment—Trading	7,000	
	Unrealized Gain or Loss—Income		7,000
	(To record unrealized gain on trading securities)		

The use of the Fair Value Adjustment—Trading account enables the company to maintain a record of the investment cost. Actual cost is needed to determine the gain or loss realized when the securities are sold. The company adds the debit balance (or subtracts a credit balance) of the Fair Value Adjustment—Trading account to the cost of the investments to arrive at a fair value for the trading securities.

The fair value of the securities is the amount companies report on the balance sheet. They report the unrealized gain on the income statement under "Other revenues and gains." The term **income** in the account title indicates that the gain affects net income.

If the total cost of the trading securities is greater than total fair value, an unrealized loss has occurred. In such a case, the adjusting entry is a debit to Unrealized Gain or Loss—Income and a credit to Fair Value Adjustment—Trading. Companies report the unrealized loss under "Other expenses and losses" in the income statement.

The Fair Value Adjustment—Trading account is carried forward into future accounting periods. No entries are made to this account during the period. At the end of each reporting period, a company adjusts the balance in the account to the difference between cost and fair value at that time. It closes the Unrealized Gain or Loss—Income account at the end of the reporting period.

Available-for-Sale Securities

As indicated earlier, available-for-sale securities are held with the intent of selling them sometime in the future. If the intent is to sell the securities within the next year or operating cycle, a company classifies the securities as current assets in the balance sheet. Otherwise, it classifies them as long-term assets in the investments section of the balance sheet.

Companies also report available-for-sale securities at fair value. The procedure for determining fair value and unrealized gain or loss for these securities is the same as that for trading securities. To illustrate, assume that Shelton Corporation has two securities that are classified as available-for-sale. **Illustration H.8** provides information on the cost, fair value, and amount of the unrealized gain or loss on December 31, 2022. There is an unrealized loss of $9,537 because total cost ($293,537) is $9,537 more than total fair value ($284,000).

ILLUSTRATION H.8

Valuation of available-for-sale securities

Available-for-Sale Securities, December 31, 2022

Investments	Cost	Fair Value	Unrealized Gain (Loss)
Campbell Soup Co. bonds	$ 93,537	$103,600	$10,063
Hershey Foods bonds	200,000	180,400	(19,600)
Total	$293,537	$284,000	$(9,537)

Both the adjusting entry and the reporting of the unrealized loss from Shelton's available-for-sale securities differ from those illustrated for trading securities. The differences result because these securities are not going to be sold in the near term. Thus, prior to actual sale it is much more likely that changes in fair value may reverse the unrealized loss. Therefore, Shelton does not report an unrealized loss in the income statement. Instead, the company reports it as an item of other comprehensive income in the statement of comprehensive income. In the adjusting entry, Shelton identifies the fair value adjustment account with available-for-sale securities, and identifies the unrealized gain or loss account with stockholders' equity (see **Helpful Hint**). The adjusting entry for Shelton to record the unrealized loss of $9,537 is as follows.

HELPFUL HINT

The entry is the same regardless of whether the securities are considered short-term or long-term.

Dec. 31	Unrealized Gain or Loss—Equity	9,537	
	Fair Value Adjustment—Available-for-Sale		9,537
	(To record unrealized loss on available-for-sale securities)		

| A | = | L | + | SE |

−9,537 Eq

−9,537

Cash Flows
no effect

If total fair value exceeds total cost, Shelton would record the adjusting entry as an increase (debit) to Fair Value Adjustment—Available-for-Sale and a credit to Unrealized Gain or Loss—Equity.

Shelton's unrealized loss of $9,537 would appear in the statement of comprehensive income as shown in **Illustration H.9**.

Shelton Corporation
Statement of Comprehensive Income
For the Year Ended December 31, 2022

Net income	$118,000
Other comprehensive income	
Unrealized loss on available-for-sale securities	(9,537)
Comprehensive income	$108,463

ILLUSTRATION H.9

Statement of comprehensive income

ETHICS NOTE

Recently, the SEC accused investment bank **Morgan Stanley** of overstating the value of certain bond investments by $75 million. The SEC stated that, in applying fair value accounting, Morgan Stanley used its own more optimistic assumptions rather than relying on external pricing sources.

For available-for-sale securities, the company carries forward the Unrealized Gain or Loss—Equity account to future periods. At each future balance sheet date, the account is adjusted with the Fair Value Adjustment—Available-for-Sale account to show the difference between cost and fair value at that time (see **Ethics Note**).

DO IT! 3a │ Trading and Available-for-Sale Debt Securities

Some of Powderhorn Corporation's investment debt securities are classified as trading securities and some are classified as available-for-sale. The cost and fair value of each category at December 31, 2022, are as follows.

	Cost	Fair Value	Unrealized Gain (Loss)
Trading securities	$93,600	$94,900	$1,300
Available-for-sale securities	$48,800	$51,400	$2,600

At December 31, 2021, the Fair Value Adjustment—Trading account had a debit balance of $9,200, and the Fair Value Adjustment—Available-for-Sale account had a credit balance of $5,750. Prepare the required journal entries for each group of securities for December 31, 2022.

ACTION PLAN
- Mark trading securities to fair value and report the adjustment in current-period income.
- Mark available-for-sale securities to fair value and report the adjustment as a separate component of stockholders' equity.

Solution

Trading securities:

Unrealized Gain or Loss—Income	7,900*	
Fair Value Adjustment—Trading		7,900
(To record unrealized loss on trading securities)		

*$9,200 − $1,300

Available-for-sale securities:

Fair Value Adjustment—Available-for-Sale	8,350**	
Unrealized Gain or Loss—Equity		8,350
(To record unrealized gain on available-for-sale securities)		

**$5,750 + $2,600

Equity Securities

The valuation and reporting of equity securities at a financial statement date depends on the levels of influence involved, as shown in **Illustration H.10**.

ILLUSTRATION H.10

Accounting and reporting for equity securities by category

Category	Valuation	Unrealized Gains or Losses	Other Income Effects
Holdings less than 20%	Fair value	Recognized in net income	Dividends declared; gains and losses from sale
Holdings between 20% and 50%	Equity	Not recognized	Proportionate share of investee's net income
Holdings more than 50%	Consolidation	Not recognized	Not applicable

When an investor has an interest of less than 20%, it is presumed that the investor has little or no influence over the investee. In such cases, if market prices are available subsequent to acquisition, the company values and reports the stock investment using the fair value method.

Illustration of Stock Holdings Less Than 20%

At December 31, 2022, Shelton Corporation has two equity securities in which it has less than a 20% ownership interest and therefore has little or no influence over these companies. Shelton has the following cost and fair value for these two companies, as shown in **Illustration H.11**.

ILLUSTRATION H.11

Computation of fair value adjustment—equity security portfolio (2022)

Investments	Cost	Fair Value	Unrealized Gain (Loss)
Twitter Co.	$259,700	$275,000	$15,300
Campbell Soup Co.	317,500	304,000	(13,500)
Totals	$577,200	$579,000	$ 1,800

For Shelton's equity securities portfolio, the gross unrealized gain is $15,300 and the gross unrealized loss is $13,500, resulting in a net unrealized gain of $1,800. That is, the fair value of the equity securities portfolio is above cost by $1,800.

Shelton records the net unrealized gains and losses related to changes in the fair value equity securities in an Unrealized Gain or Loss—Income account. In this case, Shelton prepares an adjusting entry debiting the Fair Value Adjustment—Stock account and crediting the Unrealized Gain or Loss—Income account to record the increase in fair value and to record the gain as follows.

December 31, 2022		
Fair Value Adjustment—Stock	1,800	
Unrealized Gain or Loss—Income		1,800
(To record unrealized gain on equity securities)		

Similar to trading securities, Shelton adjusts the balance in the Fair Value Adjustment—Stock account for the difference between cost and fair value. In addition, the unrealized gain related to Shelton's equity securities is reported in the "Other revenues and gains" section of the income statement.

Balance Sheet Presentation

In the balance sheet presentation, companies must classify investments as either short-term or long-term.

Short-Term Investments

Short-term investments (also called **marketable securities**) are securities held by a company that are (1) **readily marketable** and (2) **intended to be converted into cash** within the next year or operating cycle, whichever is longer (see **Helpful Hint**). Investments that do not meet **both criteria** are classified as **long-term investments**.

Readily Marketable **An investment is readily marketable when it can be sold easily whenever the need for cash arises.** Short-term paper[4] meets this criterion because a company can readily sell it to other investors. Stocks and bonds traded on organized securities markets, such as the New York Stock Exchange, are readily marketable because they can be bought and sold daily. In contrast, there may be only a limited market for the securities issued by small corporations and no market for the securities of a privately held company.

Intent to Convert **Intent to convert means that management intends to sell the investment within the next year or operating cycle, whichever is longer.** Generally, this criterion is satisfied when the investment is considered a resource that the company will use whenever the need for cash arises. For example, a ski resort may invest idle cash during the summer months with the intent to sell the securities to buy supplies and equipment shortly before the next winter season. This investment is considered short-term even if lack of snow cancels the next ski season and eliminates the need to convert the securities into cash as intended.

Because of their high liquidity, companies list short-term investments immediately below Cash in the current assets section of the balance sheet. Short-term investments are reported at fair value. For example, Weber Corporation would report its trading securities as shown in **Illustration H.12**.

HELPFUL HINT

Trading securities are always classified as short-term. Available-for-sale securities can be either short-term or long-term.

Weber Corporation	
Balance Sheet (partial)	
Current assets	
Cash	$21,000
Debt investments (at fair value)	**60,000**

ILLUSTRATION H.12

Balance sheet presentation of short-term investments

Long-Term Investments

Companies generally report long-term investments in a separate section of the balance sheet immediately below "Current assets," as shown in **Illustration H.13**. Long-term investments in available-for-sale securities are reported at fair value. Investments in common stock accounted for under the equity method are reported at equity.

Weber Corporation		
Balance Sheet (partial)		
Investments		
Debt investment (at fair value)	$100,000	
Stock investments (at fair value)	**50,000**	
Stock investments (at equity)	**150,000**	
Total investments		$300,000

ILLUSTRATION H.13

Balance sheet presentation of long-term investments

---

[4]Short-term paper includes (1) certificates of deposits (CDs) issued by banks, (2) money market certificates issued by banks and savings and loan associations, (3) Treasury bills issued by the U.S. government, and (4) commercial paper issued by corporations with good credit ratings.

Presentation of Realized and Unrealized Gain or Loss

Companies must present in the financial statements gains and losses on investments, whether realized or unrealized. In the income statement, companies report gains and losses, as well as interest and dividend revenue, in the nonoperating activities section under the categories listed in **Illustration H.14**.

ILLUSTRATION H.14

Nonoperating items related to investments

Other Revenues and Gains	Other Expenses and Losses
Interest Revenue	Loss on Sale of Investments
Dividend Revenue	Unrealized Loss
Gain on Sale of Investments	
Unrealized Gain	

Companies report the cumulative amount of other comprehensive income items from the current and previous years as a separate component of stockholders' equity. To illustrate, assume that Muzzillo Inc. has common stock of $3,000,000, retained earnings of $1,500,000, and an accumulated other comprehensive loss of $100,000. **Illustration H.15** shows the financial statement presentation of the accumulated other comprehensive loss.

ILLUSTRATION H.15

Unrealized loss in stockholders' equity section

Muzzillo Inc.
Balance Sheet (partial)

Stockholders' equity	
Common stock	$3,000,000
Retained earnings	1,500,000
Total paid-in capital and retained earnings	4,500,000
Accumulated other comprehensive loss	**(100,000)**
Total stockholders' equity	$4,400,000

A classified balance sheet is shown in **Illustration H.16**. This balance sheet includes the following items (highlighted in red): short-term and long-term debt investments, stock investments, and accumulated other comprehensive income.

ILLUSTRATION H.16

Classified balance sheet

Pace Corporation
Balance Sheet
December 31, 2022

Assets

Current assets		
Cash		$ 21,000
Debt investments (at fair value)		**147,000**
Accounts receivable	$ 84,000	
Less: Allowance for doubtful accounts	4,000	80,000
Inventory, at FIFO cost		43,000
Prepaid insurance		23,000
Total current assets		314,000
Investments		
Debt investments (at fair value)	**20,000**	
Stock investments (at fair value)	**30,000**	
Stock investments (at equity)	**150,000**	
Total investments		200,000

Property, plant, and equipment

Land		200,000
Buildings	$800,000	
Less: Accumulated depreciation—buildings	200,000	600,000
Equipment	180,000	
Less: Accumulated depreciation—equipment	54,000	126,000
Total property, plant, and equipment		926,000

Intangible assets

Goodwill		270,000
Total assets		$1,710,000

Liabilities and Stockholders' Equity

Current liabilities

Accounts payable		$ 185,000
Federal income taxes payable		60,000
Interest payable		10,000
Total current liabilities		255,000

Long-term liabilities

Bonds payable, 10%, due 2027	$ 300,000	
Less: Discount on bonds	10,000	
Total long-term liabilities		290,000
Total liabilities		545,000

Stockholders' equity

Paid-in capital

Common stock, $10 par value, 200,000 shares authorized, 80,000 shares issued and outstanding	800,000	
In excess of par—common stock	100,000	
Total paid-in capital	900,000	
Retained earnings (Note 1)	255,000	
Total paid-in capital and retained earnings	1,155,000	
Add: Accumulated other comprehensive income	**10,000**	
Total stockholders' equity		1,165,000
Total liabilities and stockholders' equity		$1,710,000

Note 1. Retained earnings of $100,000 is restricted for plant expansion.

DO IT! 3b | Financial Statement Presentation of Investments

Identify where each of the following items would be reported in the financial statements.

1. Interest earned on investments in bonds.
2. Fair value adjustment—stock.
3. Unrealized gain or loss—equity.
4. Gain on sale of investments in stock.
5. Unrealized gain—income.

Use the following possible categories:

Balance sheet:

Current assets	Current liabilities
Investments	Long-term liabilities
Property, plant, and equipment	Stockholders' equity
Intangible assets	

Income statement:

Other revenues and gains	Other expenses and losses

ACTION PLAN

- **Classify investments as current assets if they will be held for less than one year.**
- **Report unrealized gains or losses on trading securities in income.**
- **Report unrealized gains or losses on available-for-sale securities in equity.**
- **Report realized gains and losses on investments in the income statement as "Other revenues and gains" or as "Other expenses and losses."**

Solution

Item	Financial Statement	Category
1. Interest earned on investments in bonds.	Income statement	Other revenues and gains
2. Fair value adjustment—stock	Balance sheet	Investments
3. Unrealized gain or loss—equity.	Balance sheet	Stockholders' equity
4. Gain on sale of investments in stock.	Income statement	Other revenues and gains
5. Unrealized gain—income.	Income statement	Other revenues and gains

Review and Practice

Learning Objectives Review

1 Explain how to account for debt investments.

Corporations invest for three common reasons: (a) they have excess cash, (b) they view investment income as a significant revenue source, and (c) they have strategic goals such as gaining control of a competitor or supplier or moving into a new line of business.

Entries for investments in debt securities are required when companies purchase bonds, receive or accrue interest, and sell bonds.

2 Explain how to account for stock investments.

Entries for investments in common stock are required when companies purchase stock, receive dividends, and sell stock. When ownership is less than 20%, the cost method is used—the investment is recorded at cost. When ownership is between 20% and 50%, the equity method should be used—the investor records its share of the net income of the investee in the year it is earned.

When a company owns more than 50% of the common stock of another company, consolidated financial statements are usually prepared. These statements are especially useful to the stockholders, board of directors, and management of the parent company.

3 Discuss how debt and stock investments are reported in the financial statements.

Investments in debt securities are classified as trading, available-for-sale, or held-to-maturity for valuation and reporting purposes. Trading securities are reported as current assets at fair value, with changes from cost reported in net income. Available-for-sale securities are also reported at fair value, with the changes from cost reported as items of other comprehensive income. Available-for-sale securities are classified as short-term or long-term depending on their expected realization.

Investments in stock when ownership is less than 20% are reported at fair values, with changes from cost reported in net income.

Short-term investments are securities held by a company that are readily marketable and intended to be converted to cash within the next year or operating cycle, whichever is longer. Investments that do not meet both criteria are classified as long-term investments.

Glossary Review

Available-for-sale securities   Securities that are held with the intent of selling them sometime in the future. (p. H-9).

Consolidated financial statements   Financial statements that present the assets and liabilities controlled by the parent company and the total revenues and expenses of the subsidiary companies. (p. H-7).

Controlling interest   Ownership of more than 50% of the common stock of another entity. (p. H-7).

Cost method   An accounting method in which the investment in common stock is recorded at cost and revenue is recognized only when cash dividends are received. (p. H-5).

Debt investments   Investments in government and corporation bonds. (p. H-3).

Equity method   An accounting method in which the investment in common stock is initially recorded at cost, and the investment account is then adjusted annually to show the investor's equity in the investee. (p. H-6).

Fair value   Amount for which a security could be sold in a normal market. (p. H-8).

Held-to-maturity securities   Debt securities that the investor has the intent and ability to hold to maturity. (p. H-9).

Long-term investments   Investments that are not readily marketable or that management does not intend to convert into cash within the next year or operating cycle, whichever is longer. (p. H-13).

Mark-to-market   A method of accounting for certain investments that requires that they be adjusted to their fair value at the end of each period. (p. H-9).

Parent company   A company that owns more than 50% of the common stock of another entity. (p. H-7).

Short-term investments (marketable securities)   Investments that are readily marketable and intended to be converted into cash within the next year or operating cycle, whichever is longer. (p. H-13).

Stock investments Investments in the capital stock of corporations. (p. H-4).

Subsidiary (affiliated) company A company in which more than 50% of its stock is owned by another company. (p. H-7).

Trading securities Securities bought and held primarily for sale in the near term to generate income on short-term price differences. (p. H-9).

Practice Multiple-Choice Questions

1. **(LO 1)** Which of the following is **not** a primary reason why corporations invest in debt and equity securities?

   a. They wish to gain control of a competitor.

   b. They have excess cash.

   c. They wish to move into a new line of business.

   d. They are required to by law.

2. **(LO 1)** Debt investments are initially recorded at:

   a. cost.

   b. cost plus accrued interest.

   c. fair value.

   d. face value.

3. **(LO 1)** Hanes Company sells debt investments costing $26,000 for $28,000. In journalizing the sale, credits are to:

   a. Debt Investments and Loss on Sale of Debt Investments.

   b. Debt Investments and Gain on Sale of Debt Investments.

   c. Stock Investments and Gain on Sale of Stock Investments.

   d. None of the answer choices is correct.

4. **(LO 2)** Pryor Company receives net proceeds of $42,000 on the sale of stock investments that cost $39,500. This transaction will result in reporting in the income statement a:

   a. loss of $2,500 under "Other expenses and losses."

   b. loss of $2,500 under "Operating expenses."

   c. gain of $2,500 under "Other revenues and gains."

   d. gain of $2,500 under "Operating revenues."

5. **(LO 2)** The equity method of accounting for long-term investments in stock should be used when the investor has significant influence over an investee and owns:

   a. between 20% and 50% of the investee's common stock.

   b. 20% or more of the investee's common stock.

   c. more than 50% of the investee's common stock.

   d. less than 20% of the investee's common stock.

6. **(LO 2)** Assume that Horicon Corp. acquired 25% of the common stock of Sheboygan Corp. on January 1, 2022, for $300,000. During 2022, Sheboygan Corp. reported net income of $160,000 and paid total dividends of $60,000. If Horicon uses the equity method to account for its investment, the balance in the investment account on December 31, 2022, will be:

   a. $300,000.

   b. $325,000.

   c. $400,000.

   d. $340,000.

7. **(LO 2)** Assume that Horicon Corp. acquired 25% of the common stock of Sheboygan Corp. on January 1, 2022, for $300,000. During 2022, Sheboygan Corp. reported net income of $160,000 and paid total dividends of $60,000. If Horicon uses the equity method to account for its investment, what entry would Horicon make to record the receipt of the dividend from Sheboygan?

   a. Debit Cash and credit Revenue from Stock Investments.

   b. Debit Cash Dividends and credit Revenue from Stock Investments.

   c. Debit Cash and credit Stock Investments.

   d. Debit Cash and credit Dividend Revenue.

8. **(LO 2)** You have a controlling interest if:

   a. you own more than 20% of a company's stock.

   b. you are the president of the company.

   c. you use the equity method.

   d. you own more than 50% of a company's stock.

9. **(LO 2)** Which of the following statements is **false**? Consolidated financial statements are useful to determine:

   a. the profitability of specific subsidiaries.

   b. the total profitability of companies under common control.

   c. the breadth of a parent company's operations.

   d. the full extent of total obligations of companies under common control.

10. **(LO 3)** At the end of the first year of operations, the total cost of the trading securities portfolio is $120,000. Total fair value is $115,000. The financial statements should show:

    a. a reduction of an asset of $5,000 and a realized loss of $5,000.

    b. a reduction of an asset of $5,000 and an unrealized loss of $5,000 in the stockholders' equity section.

    c. a reduction of an asset of $5,000 in the current assets section and an unrealized loss of $5,000 in "Other expenses and losses."

    d. a reduction of an asset of $5,000 in the current assets section and a realized loss of $5,000 in "Other expenses and losses."

11. **(LO 3)** At December 31, 2022, the fair value of available-for-sale debt securities is $41,300 and the cost is $39,800. At January 1, 2022, there was a credit balance of $900 in the Fair Value Adjustment— Available-for-Sale account. The required adjusting entry would be:

    a. Debit Fair Value Adjustment—Available-for-Sale for $1,500 and credit Unrealized Gain or Loss—Equity for $1,500.

    b. Debit Fair Value Adjustment—Available-for-Sale for $600 and credit Unrealized Gain or Loss—Equity for $600.

    c. Debit Fair Value Adjustment—Available-for-Sale for $2,400 and credit Unrealized Gain or Loss—Equity for $2,400.

    d. Debit Unrealized Gain or Loss—Equity for $2,400 and credit Fair Value Adjustment—Available-for-Sale for $2,400.

12. **(LO 3)** If a company wants to increase its reported income by manipulating its investment accounts, which should it do?

    a. Sell its "winner" trading securities and hold its "loser" trading securities.

    b. Hold its "winner" trading securities and sell its "loser" trading securities.

c. Sell its "winner" available-for-sale securities and hold its "loser" available-for-sale securities.

d. Hold its "winner" available-for-sale securities and sell its "loser" available-for-sale securities.

13. (LO 3) In the balance sheet, a debit balance in Unrealized Gain or Loss—Equity is reported as a(n):

a. increase to stockholders' equity.

b. decrease to stockholders' equity.

c. loss in the income statement.

d. loss in the retained earnings statement.

14. (LO 3) Short-term debt investments must be readily marketable and expected to be sold within:

a. 3 months from the date of purchase.

b. the next year or operating cycle, whichever is shorter.

c. the next year or operating cycle, whichever is longer.

d. the operating cycle.

Solutions

1. d. Corporations are not required to by law to invest in debt and equity securities. The other choices are reasons why corporations invest in debt and equity securities.

2. a. When debt investments are purchased, they are recorded at cost, not (b) cost plus accrued interest, (c) fair value, or (d) face value.

3. b. Credits are made to Debt Investments $26,000 and Gain on Sale of Debt Investments $2,000 ($28,000 − $26,000). The other choices are therefore incorrect.

4. c. Because the cash received ($42,000) is greater than the cost ($39,500), this sale results in a gain, not a loss, which will be reported under "Other revenues and gains" in the income statement. The other choices are therefore incorrect.

5. a. The equity method is used when the investor can exercise significant influence and owns between 20% and 50% of the investee's common stock. The other choices are therefore incorrect.

6. b. Horicon records the acquisition of the stock investment by debiting Stock Investments $300,000 and crediting Cash $300,000. Then, Horicon records (1) its share in Sheboygan Corp.'s net income ($160,000 × .25) by debiting Stock Investments $40,000 and crediting Revenue from Stock Investments $40,000 and (2) the reduction in the investment account for the dividends received ($60,000 × .25) by debiting Cash $15,000 and crediting Stock Investments $15,000. Thus, the balance in the investment account on December 31 will be $325,000 ($300,000 + $40,000 − $15,000), not (a) $300,000, (c) $400,000, or (d) $340,000.

7. c. Horicon records the receipt of the dividend from Sheboygan by debiting Cash and crediting Stock Investments. The other choices are therefore incorrect.

8. d. You have a controlling interest if you own more than 50% of a company's stock, not (a) 20% of a company's stock, (b) are president of the company, or (c) use the equity method.

9. a. Consolidated financial statements are not useful in determining the profitability of specific subsidiaries (legal entities) because consolidated financial statements represent the results of the single economic entity. The other choices are true statements.

10. c. The difference between the fair value ($115,000) and total cost ($120,000) of trading securities at the end of the first year would result in a reduction of an asset of $5,000 through the valuation allowance account in the current assets section and an unrealized loss of $5,000 in "Other expenses and losses." The other choices are therefore incorrect.

11. c. In this case, there is an unrealized gain of $1,500 because total fair value of $41,300 is $1,500 greater than the total cost of $39,800. The desired balance in the market adjustment account is $1,500 debit. The required adjusting entry considers the existing credit balance of $900 and is a debit to Fair Value Adjustment—Available-for-Sale for $2,400 ($1,500 + $900) and a credit to Unrealized Gain or Loss—Equity for $2,400 ($1,500 + $900). The other choices are therefore incorrect.

12. c. When a company sells its winners as related to available-for-sale securities, it has a realized gain that increases net income. Selling the winners will affect the balance in Unrealized Holding Gain or Loss—Equity, but any change in this balance does not affect net income. Choices (a) and (b) are incorrect because trading securities' gains and losses related to changes in valuation are reported in net income. Thus, when a company sells a trading security, it should have no effect on net income because the value change was recognized in net income previously. Choice (d) is incorrect because selling the losing available-for-sale securities will decrease net income.

13. b. A debit balance in Unrealized Gain or Loss—Equity is reported on the balance sheet as a separate component of stockholders' equity, decreasing stockholders' equity. The other choices are therefore incorrect.

14. c. Short-term investments are current assets that are expected to be consumed, sold, or converted to cash within one year or the operating cycle, whichever is longer. The other choices are therefore incorrect.

Practice Brief Exercises

Journalize entries for debt investments.

1. (LO 1) Liriano Corporation purchased debt investments for 85,000 on January 1, 2022. On July 1, 2022, Liriano received cash interest of $6,800. Journalize the purchase and the receipt of interest. Assume that no interest has been accrued.

Solution

1.	Jan. 1	Debt Investments	85,000	
		Cash		85,000
	July 1	Cash	6,800	
		Interest Revenue		6,800

2. (LO 2) On June 1, Willyjuan Company buys 2,000 shares of Minaya common stock for $57,000 cash. On October 15, Willyjuan sells the stock investments for $54,000 in cash. Journalize the purchase and sale of the common

Journalize entries for stock investments.

Solution

2.	June 1	Stock Investments	57,000	
		Cash		57,000
	Oct. 15	Cash	54,000	
		Loss on Sale of Stock Investments	3,000	
		Stock Investments		57,000

3. (LO 3) The cost of the trading securities of Dylan Company at December 31, 2022, is $46,000. At December 31, 2022, the fair value of the securities is $50,000. (a) Prepare the adjusting entry to record the securities at fair value. (b) Show the financial statement presentation at December 31, 2022.

Prepare adjusting entry and indicate statement presentation using fair value.

Solution

3. a.	Dec. 31	Fair Value Adjustment—Trading	4,000	
		Unrealized Gain or Loss—Income		4,000
		($50,000 – $46,000)		

b.   **Balance Sheet**

Current assets

   Short-term investments, at fair value $50,000

Income Statement

Other revenues and gains

   Unrealized gain—income $4,000

Practice Exercises

1. (LO 1) Potter Company purchased 50 Quinn Company 6%, 10-year, $1,000 bonds on January 1, 2022, for $50,000. The bonds pay interest annually. On January 1, 2023, after receipt of interest, Potter Company sold 30 of the bonds for $28,100.

Journalize debt investment transactions, accrue interest, and record sale.

Instructions

Prepare the journal entries to record the transactions described above.

Solution

1.

2022				
Jan. 1	Debt Investments		50,000	
	Cash			50,000
Dec. 31	Interest Receivable		3,000	
	Interest Revenue ($50,000 × 6%)			3,000
2023				
Jan. 1	Cash		3,000	
	Interest Receivable			3,000
Jan. 1	Cash		28,100	
	Loss on Sale of Debt Investments		1,900	
	Debt Investments [(30 ÷ 50) × $50,000]			30,000

Journalize transactions for investments in stocks.

2. (LO 2) Lucy Inc. had the following transactions in 2022 pertaining to investments in common stock.

Jan. 1 Purchased 4,000 shares of Morgan Corporation common stock (5% interest) for $180,000 cash.
July 1 Received a cash dividend of $3 per share.
Dec. 1 Sold 600 shares of Morgan Corporation common stock for $32,000 cash.
Dec. 31 Received a cash dividend of $3 per share.

Instructions

Journalize the transactions.

Solution

2.

Jan. 1	Stock Investments		180,000	
	Cash			180,000
July 1	Cash (4,000 × $3)		12,000	
	Dividend Revenue			12,000
Dec. 1	Cash		32,000	
	Stock Investments [$180,000 × (600 ÷ 4,000)]			27,000
	Gain on Sale of Stock Investments			5,000
Dec. 31	Cash [(4,000 − 600) × $3]		10,200	
	Dividend Revenue			10,200

Prepare adjusting entries for fair value, and indicate statement presentation for two classes of securities.

3. (LO 3) Remy Company started business on January 1, 2022, and has the following data at December 31, 2022.

Debt Securities	**Cost**	**Fair Value**
Trading	$120,000	$132,000
Available-for-sale	100,000	86,000

The available-for-sale securities are held as a long-term investment.

Instructions

a. Prepare the adjusting entries to report each class of securities at fair value.

b. Indicate the statement presentation of each class of securities and the related unrealized gain (loss) accounts.

Solution

3.

a. Dec.	31	Fair Value Adjustment—Trading		
		($132,000 – $120,000)	12,000	
		Unrealized Gain or Loss—Income		12,000
Dec.	31	Unrealized Gain or Loss—Equity		
		($100,000 – $86,000)	14,000	
		Fair Value Adjustment—Available-for-Sale		14,000

b.

Balance Sheet

Current assets	
Short-term investments, at fair value	$132,000
Investments	
Debt investment, at fair value	86,000
Stockholders' equity	
Less: Accumulated other comprehensive income	$14,000

Income Statement

Other revenues and gains	
Unrealized gain—income	$12,000

Practice Problem

(LO 2, 3) In its first year of operations, DeMarco Company had the following selected transactions in stock investments (holdings less than 20%).

Journalize transactions and prepare adjusting entry to record fair value.

June 1	Purchased for cash 600 shares of Sanburg common stock at $24 per share.
July 1	Purchased for cash 800 shares of Cey Corporation common stock at $33 per share.
Sept. 1	Received a $1 per share cash dividend from Cey Corporation.
Nov. 1	Sold 200 shares of Sanburg common stock for cash at $27 per share.
Dec. 15	Received a $0.50 per share cash dividend on Sanburg common stock.

At December 31, the fair values per share were Sanburg $25 and Cey $30.

Instructions

a. Journalize the transactions.

b. Prepare the adjusting entry at December 31 to report the securities at fair value.

Solution

a. June 1	Stock Investments	14,400	
	Cash (600 × $24)		14,400
	(To record purchase of 600 shares of		
	Sanburg common stock)		
July 1	Stock Investments	26,400	
	Cash (800 × $33)		26,400
	(To record purchase of 800 shares of Cey		
	common stock)		
Sept. 1	Cash (800 × $1.00)	800	
	Dividend Revenue		800
	(To record receipt of $1 per share cash		
	dividend from Cey Corporation)		

Nov. 1	Cash (200 × $27)		5,400	
	Stock Investments (200 × $24)			4,800
	Gain on Sale of Stock Investments			600
	(To record sale of 200 shares of Sanburg common stock)			
Dec. 15	Cash [(600 − 200) × $0.50]		200	
	Dividend Revenue			200
	(To record receipt of $0.50 per share dividend from Sanburg)			
b. Dec. 31	Unrealized Gain or Loss—Income		2,000	
	Fair Value Adjustment—Stock			2,000
	(To record unrealized loss on trading securities)			

Investment	Cost	Fair Value	Unrealized Gain (Loss)
Sanburg common stock	$ 9,600ᵃ	$10,000ᵇ	$ 400
Cey common stock	26,400ᶜ	24,000ᵈ	(2,400)
Totals	$36,000	$34,000	$(2,000)

ᵃ400 × $24; ᵇ400 × $25; ᶜ800 × $33; ᵈ800 × $30

WileyPLUS

Many additional resources are available for practice in WileyPLUS.

Questions

1. What are the reasons that companies invest in securities?

2. **a.** What is the cost of an investment in bonds?

   b. When is interest on bonds recorded?

3. Geena Jaymes is confused about losses and gains on the sale of debt investments. Explain these issues to Geena:

   a. How the gain or loss is computed.

   b. The statement presentation of gains and losses.

4. Heliy Company sells bonds that cost $40,000 for $45,000, including $1,000 of accrued interest. In recording the sale, Heliy books a $5,000 gain. Is this correct? Explain.

5. What is the cost of an investment in stock?

6. To acquire Gaines Corporation stock, Palmer Co. pays $61,500 in cash. What entry should be made for this investment, assuming the stock is readily marketable?

7. **a.** When should a long-term investment in common stock be accounted for by the equity method?

   b. When is revenue recognized under the equity method?

8. Stetson Corporation uses the equity method to account for its ownership of 30% of the common stock of Pike Packing. During 2022, Pike reported a net income of $80,000 and declares and pays cash dividends of $10,000. What recognition should Stetson Corporation give to these events?

9. What constitutes "significant influence" when an investor's financial interest is less than 50%?

10. Distinguish between the cost and equity methods of accounting for investments in stocks.

11. What are consolidated financial statements?

12. What are the valuation guidelines for trading and available-for-sale debt investments at a balance sheet date?

13. Pat Ernst is the controller of J-Products, Inc. At December 31, the end of its first year of operations, the company's investments in trading debt securities cost $74,000 and have a fair value of $70,000. Indicate how Pat would report these data in the financial statements prepared on December 31.

14. Pat Ernst is the controller of J-Products, Inc. At December 31, the end of its first year of operations, the company's investments in trading debt securities cost $74,000 and have a fair value of $70,000. How would Pat report the data if the investments were long-term and the debt securities were classified as available-for-sale?

15. Boise Company's investments in equity securities at December 31 show total cost of $202,000 and total fair value of $210,000. Boise has less than a 20% ownership interest in the equity securities. Prepare the adjusting entry.

16. Where is Accumulated Other Comprehensive Loss reported on the balance sheet?

17. Bargain Wholesale Supply owns stock in Cyrus Corporation, which it intends to hold indefinitely because of some negative tax consequences if sold. Should the investment in Cyrus be classified as a short-term investment? Why?

Brief Exercises

BEH.1 (LO 1), AP Craig Corporation purchased debt investments for $40,800 on January 1, 2022. On July 1, 2022, Craig received cash interest of $1,660. Journalize the purchase and the receipt of interest. Assume no interest has been accrued.

Journalize entries for debt investments.

BEH.2 (LO 2), AP On August 1, Snow Company buys 1,000 shares of BCN common stock for $35,600 cash. On December 1, the stock investments are sold for $38,000 in cash. Journalize the purchase and sale of the common stock.

Journalize entries for stock investments.

BEH.3 (LO 2), AP Tote Company owns 25% of Toppe Company. For the current year, Toppe reports net income of $150,000 and declares and pays a $60,000 cash dividend. Record Tote's equity in Toppe's net income and the receipt of dividends from Toppe.

Journalize transactions under the equity method.

BEH.4 (LO 3), AP Cost and fair value data for the trading debt securities of Lecler Company at December 31, 2022, are $62,000 and $59,600, respectively. Prepare the adjusting entry to record the securities at fair value.

Prepare adjusting entry using fair value.

BEH.5 (LO 3), AP Cost and fair value data for the trading debt securities of Lecler Company at December 31, 2022, are $62,000 and $59,600, respectively. Show the financial statement presentation of the trading securities and related accounts.

Indicate statement presentation using fair value.

BEH.6 (LO 3), AP In its first year of operations, Machin Corporation purchased available-for-sale debt securities costing $72,000 as a long-term investment. At December 31, 2022, the fair value of the securities is $69,000. Prepare the adjusting entry to record the securities at fair value.

Prepare adjusting entry using fair value.

BEH.7 (LO 3), AP In its first year of operations, Machin Corporation purchased available-for-sale debt securities costing $72,000 as a long-term investment. At December 31, 2022, the fair value of the securities is $69,000. Show the financial statement presentation of the securities and related accounts. Assume the securities are noncurrent.

Indicate statement presentation using fair value.

BEH.8 (LO 3), AP Perth Corporation has these long-term investments: common stock of Vejas Co. (10% ownership), cost $108,000, fair value $112,000; common stock of Penn Inc. (30% ownership), cost $210,000, equity $230,000; and debt investment, cost $90,000, fair value, $150,000. Prepare the investments section of the balance sheet.

Prepare investments section of balance sheet.

DO IT! Exercises

DO IT! H.1 (LO 1), AP Kurtyka Corporation had the following transactions relating to debt investments:

Make entries for bond investment.

Jan. 1, 2022   Purchased 50, $1,000, 10% Spiller Company bonds for $50,000. Interest is payable annually on January 1.
Dec. 31, 2022   Accrued interest on Spiller Company bonds.
Jan. 1, 2023   Received interest from Spiller Company bonds.
Jan. 1, 2023   Sold 30 Spiller Company bonds for $29,000.

Journalize the above transactions, including the adjusting entry for the accrual of interest on December 31, 2022.

DO IT! H.2 (LO 2), AP The following are two independent situations:

Make journal entries for stock investments.

1. Edelman Inc. acquired 10% of the 500,000 shares of common stock of Schuberger Corporation at a total cost of $11 per share on June 17, 2022. On September 3, Schuberger declared and paid a $160,000 dividend. On December 31, Schuberger reported net income of $550,000 for the year.

2. Wen Corporation obtained significant influence over Hunsaker Company by buying 30% of Hunsaker's 100,000 outstanding shares of common stock at a cost of $18 per share on January 1, 2022. On May 15, Hunsaker declared and paid a cash dividend of $150,000. On December 31, Hunsaker reported net income of $270,000 for the year.

Prepare all necessary journal entries for 2022 for (a) Edelman and (b) Wen.

Make journal entries for trading and available-for-sale securities.

DO IT! H.3a (LO 3), AP Some of Tollakson Corporation's investments in debt securities are classified as trading securities and some are classified as available-for-sale. The cost and fair value of each category at December 31, 2022, are as follows.

	Cost	Fair Value	Unrealized Gain (Loss)
Trading securities	$96,300	$84,900	$(11,400)
Available-for-sale securities	$59,000	$63,200	$ 4,200

At December 31, 2021, the Fair Value Adjustment—Trading account had a debit balance of $3,200, and the Fair Value Adjustment—Available-for-Sale account had a credit balance of $5,750. Prepare the required journal entries for each group of securities for December 31, 2022.

Indicate financial statement presentation of investments.

DO IT! H.3b (LO 3), K Identify where each of the following items would be reported in the financial statements.

1. Loss on sale of investments in stock.

2. Unrealized gain or loss—equity.

3. Fair value adjustment—trading.

4. Interest earned on investments in bonds.

5. Unrealized loss on trading securities.

Use the following possible categories:

Balance sheet:

Current assets	Current liabilities
Investments	Long-term liabilities
Property, plant, and equipment	Stockholders' equity
Intangible assets	

Income statement:

Other revenues and gains	Other expenses and losses

Exercises

Journalize debt investment transactions, and accrue interest.

EH.1 (LO 1), AP Chopin Corporation had these transactions pertaining to debt investments:

Jan. 1 Purchased 90 Martine Co. 10% bonds (each with a face value of $1,000) for $90,000 cash. Interest is payable annually on December 31.

Dec. 31 Received annual interest on Martine Co. bonds.

31 Sold 30 Martine Co. bonds for $32,000.

Instructions

Journalize the transactions.

Journalize stock investment transactions, and explain income statement presentation.

EH.2 (LO 2, 3), AP Soylent Company had these transactions pertaining to stock investments:

Feb. 1 Purchased 1,200 shares of BJ common stock (2% of outstanding shares) for $8,400.

July 1 Received cash dividends of $2 per share on BJ common stock.

Sept. 1 Sold 500 shares of BJ common stock for $5,400.

Dec. 1 Received cash dividends of $1 per share on BJ common stock.

Instructions

a. Journalize the transactions.

b. Explain how dividend revenue and the gain (loss) on sale should be reported in the income statement.

EH.3 (LO 2), AP Cooper Inc. had these transactions pertaining to investments in common stock:

Jan.	1	Purchased 1,200 shares of Gate Corporation common stock (5% of outstanding shares) for $59,200 cash.
July	1	Received a cash dividend of $7 per share.
Dec.	1	Sold 900 shares of Gate Corporation common stock for $47,200 cash.
	31	Received a cash dividend of $7 per share.

Instructions

Journalize the transactions.

EH.4 (LO 2), AP On January 1, Lyon Corporation purchased a 25% equity investment in Shane Corporation for $150,000. At December 31, Shane declared and paid a $80,000 cash dividend and reported net income of $380,000.

Instructions

a. Journalize the transactions.

b. Determine the amount to be reported as an investment in Shane stock at December 31.

EH.5 (LO 2), AP These are two independent situations:

1. Sosey Cosmetics acquired 12% of the 300,000 shares of common stock of Elite Fashion at a total cost of $14 per share on March 18, 2022. On June 30, Elite declared and paid a $75,000 dividend. On December 31, Elite reported net income of $244,000 for the year. At December 31, the market price of Elite Fashion was $16 per share.

2. Williams Inc. obtained significant influence over Kasey Corporation by buying 25% of Kasey's 30,000 outstanding shares of common stock at a total cost of $11 per share on January 1, 2022. On June 15, Kasey declared and paid a cash dividend of $35,000. On December 31, Kasey reported a net income of $120,000 for the year.

Instructions

Prepare all the necessary journal entries for 2022 for (a) Sosey Cosmetics and (b) Williams Inc.

EH.6 (LO 3), AP At December 31, 2022, the trading debt securities for Gwynn, Inc. are as follows.

Security	Cost	Fair Value
A	$18,100	$16,000
B	12,500	14,800
C	23,000	18,000
Total	$53,600	$48,800

Instructions

a. Prepare the adjusting entry at December 31, 2022, to report the securities at fair value.

b. Show the balance sheet and income statement presentation at December 31, 2022, after adjustment to fair value.

EH.7 (LO 3), AP Writing At December 31, 2022, available-for-sale debt securities for Gwynn, Inc. are as follows. The securities are considered to be a long-term investment.

Security	Cost	Fair Value
A	$18,100	$16,000
B	12,500	14,800
C	23,000	18,000
Total	$53,600	$48,800

Instructions

a. Prepare the adjusting entry at December 31, 2022, to report the securities at fair value.

b. Show the statement presentation at December 31, 2022, after adjustment to fair value.

c. Pam Jenks, a member of the board of directors, does not understand the reporting of the unrealized gains or losses on trading debt securities and available-for-sale debt securities. Write a letter to Ms. Jenks explaining the reporting and the purposes it serves.

Prepare adjusting entries for fair value, and indicate statement presentation for two classes of securities.

EH.8 (LO 3), AP Weston Company has these data at December 31, 2022, the end of its first year of operations.

Debt Securities	Cost	Fair Value
Trading	$110,000	$122,000
Available-for-sale	100,000	96,000

The available-for-sale securities are held as a long-term investment.

Instructions

a. Prepare the adjusting entries to report each class of securities at fair value.

b. Indicate the statement presentation of each class of securities and the related unrealized gain (loss) accounts.

Problems

Journalize debt investment transactions.

PH.1 (LO 1), AP Penn Farms is a grower of hybrid seed corn for Bend Genetics Corporation. It has had two exceptionally good years and has elected to invest its excess funds in bonds. The following selected transactions relate to bonds acquired as an investment by Penn Farms, whose fiscal year ends on December 31.

2022

Jan. 1   Purchased at par $600,000 of Dover Corporation 10-year, 7% bonds dated January 1, 2022, directly from the issuing corporation. The bonds pay interest annually on January 1.

Dec. 31   Accrual of interest at year-end on the Dover bonds.

Assume that all intervening transactions and adjustments have been properly recorded and the number of bonds owned has not changed from December 31, 2022, to December 31, 2024.

2025

Jan. 1   Received the annual interest on the Dover bonds.

1   Sold $300,000 of Dover bonds at 110.

Dec. 31   Accrual of interest at year-end on the Dover bonds.

Instructions

Journalize the listed transactions for the years 2022 and 2025.

Journalize investment transactions, prepare adjusting entry, and show financial statement presentation.

PH.2 (LO 1, 2, 3), AP In January 2022, the management of Northern Company concludes that it has sufficient cash to purchase some short-term investments in debt and stock securities. During the year, the following transactions occurred.

Jan. 1   Purchased 70 $1,000, 8% TRC bonds for $70,000. Interest is payable annually on December 31.

Feb. 1   Purchased 1,200 shares of LAF common stock for $51,600.

Mar. 1   Purchased 500 shares of NCL common stock for $18,500.

July 1   Received a cash dividend of $0.80 per share on the LAF common stock.

Aug. 1   Sold 200 shares of LAF common stock at $42 per share.

Sept. 1   Received $2 per share cash dividend on the NCL common stock.

Dec. 31   Received the annual interest on the TRC bonds.

31   Sold the TRC bonds for $75,700.

At December 31, the fair values of the LAF and NCL common stocks were $39 and $30 per share, respectively. These stock investments by Northern Company provide less than a 20% ownership interest.

Instructions

a. Journalize the transactions and post to the accounts Debt Investments and Stock Investments. (Use the T-account form.)

b. Prepare the adjusting entry at December 31, 2022, to report the investments at fair value.

c. Show the balance sheet presentation of investment securities at December 31, 2022.

d. Identify the income statement accounts and give the statement classification of each account.

PH.3 (LO 2, 3), AP On December 31, 2021, the end of its first year of operations, Botani Associates owned the following securities that are held as long-term investments.

Journalize transactions, prepare adjusting entry for stock investments, and show balance sheet presentation.

Common Stock	Shares	Cost
C Co.	1,000	$48,000
D Co.	5,000	36,000
E Co.	1,200	24,000

On this date, the total fair value of the securities was equal to its cost. The securities are not held for influence or control over the investees. In 2022, the following transactions occurred.

July	1	Received $2.00 per share semiannual cash dividend on D Co. common stock.
Aug.	1	Received $0.50 per share cash dividend on C Co. common stock.
Sept.	1	Sold 1,000 shares of D Co. common stock for cash at $9 per share.
Oct.	1	Sold 300 shares of C Co. common stock for cash at $53 per share.
Nov.	1	Received $1 per share cash dividend on E Co. common stock.
Dec.	15	Received $0.50 per share cash dividend on C Co. common stock.
	31	Received $2.20 per share semiannual cash dividend on D Co. common stock.

At December 31, the fair values per share of the common stocks were C Co. $47, D Co. $7, and E Co. $24. These investments should be classified as long-term.

Instructions

a. Journalize the 2022 transactions and post to the account Stock Investments. (Use the T-account form.)

b. Prepare the adjusting entry at December 31, 2022, to show the securities at fair value. Botani has less than a 20% ownership interest in all these common stocks (C Co., D Co., and E Co.).

c. Show the balance sheet presentation of the investments at 2022. These investments should be classified as long-term.

PH.4 (LO 2), AP **Writing** Wellman Company acquired 30% of the outstanding common stock of Grinwold Inc. on January 1, 2022, by paying $1,800,000 for 60,000 shares. Grinwold declared and paid a $0.50 per share cash dividend on June 30 and again on December 31, 2022. Grinwold reported net income of $800,000 for the year.

Prepare entries under cost and equity methods, and prepare memorandum.

Instructions

a. Prepare the journal entries for Wellman Company for 2022, assuming Wellman cannot exercise significant influence over Grinwold. (Use the cost method.)

b. Prepare the journal entries for Wellman Company for 2022, assuming Wellman can exercise significant influence over Grinwold. (Use the equity method.)

c. The board of directors of Wellman Company is confused about the differences between the cost and equity methods. Prepare a memorandum for the board that explains each method and shows in tabular form the account balances under each method at December 31, 2022.

PH.5 (LO 2, 3), AP Here is Kalvin Company's portfolio of long-term stock investments at December 31, 2021, the end of its first year of operations.

Journalize stock transactions, and show balance sheet presentation.

	Cost
1,400 shares of Batone Inc. common stock	$73,500
1,200 shares of Mendez Corporation common stock	84,000
800 shares of P. Tillman Corporation preferred stock	33,600

On December 31, the total cost of the portfolio equaled the total fair value. Kalvin had the following transactions related to the securities during 2022.

Jan. 20   Sold 1,400 shares of Batone Inc. common stock at $55 per share.

    28   Purchased 400 shares of $10 par value common stock of P. Wahl Corporation at $78 per share.

    30   Received a cash dividend of $1.25 per share on Mendez Corporation common stock.

Feb. 8   Received cash dividends of $0.40 per share on P. Tillman Corporation preferred stock.

    18   Sold all 800 shares of P. Tillman preferred stock at $35 per share.

July 30   Received a cash dividend of $1.10 per share on Mendez Corporation common stock.

Sept. 6   Purchased an additional 600 shares of the $10 par value common stock of P. Wahl Corporation at $82 per share.

Dec. 1   Received a cash dividend of $1.50 per share on P. Wahl Corporation common stock.

At December 31, 2022, the fair values of the securities were:

Mendez Corporation common stock	$65 per share
P. Wahl Corporation common stock	$77 per share

Kalvin uses separate account titles for each investment, such as Investment in Mendez Corporation Common Stock.

Instructions

a. Prepare journal entries to record the transactions.

b. Prepare the adjusting entry at December 31, 2022, to report the portfolio at fair value.

c. Show the balance sheet presentation at December 31, 2022.

Prepare a balance sheet.

PH.6 (LO 3), AP The following data, presented in alphabetical order, are taken from the records of Manfreid Corporation.

Accounts payable	$ 150,000
Accounts receivable	90,000
Accumulated depreciation—buildings	180,000
Accumulated depreciation—equipment	52,000
Allowance for doubtful accounts	6,000
Bonds payable (10%, due 2033)	350,000
Buildings	900,000
Cash	63,000
Common stock ($5 par value; 500,000 shares authorized, 240,000 shares issued)	1,200,000
Debt investments (at fair value)	400,000
Discount on bonds payable	20,000
Dividends payable	50,000
Equipment	275,000
Goodwill	190,000
Income taxes payable	70,000
Inventory	170,000
Land	410,000
Notes payable (due 2023)	70,000
Paid-in capital in excess of par value	464,000
Prepaid insurance	16,000
Retained earnings	310,000
Stock investments (Horton Inc. stock, 30% ownership, at equity)	240,000
Stock investments (short-term, at fair value)	128,000

Instructions

Prepare a balance sheet at December 31, 2022.

Company Index

Subject Index

BASIC ACCOUNTING EQUATION (Chapter 2)

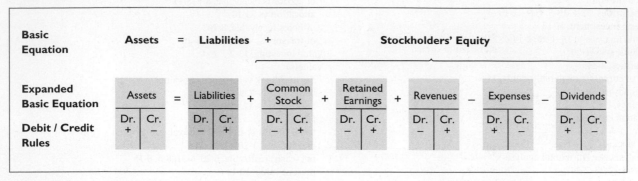

ADJUSTING ENTRIES (Chapter 3)

	Type	Adjusting Entry	
Deferrals	1. Prepaid expenses	Dr. Expenses	Cr. Assets
	2. Unearned revenues	Dr. Liabilities	Cr. Revenues
Accruals	1. Accrued revenues	Dr. Assets	Cr. Revenues
	2. Accrued expenses	Dr. Expenses	Cr. Liabilities

Note: Each adjusting entry will affect one or more income statement accounts and one or more balance sheet accounts.

INTEREST (Chapter 3)

Interest Computation

Interest = Face value of note × Annual interest rate × Time in terms of one year

ACCOUNTING CONCEPTS (Appendix 3B)

Fundamental Qualities	Enhancing Qualities	Assumptions	Principles	Constraint
Relevance	Comparability	Monetary unit	Historical cost	Cost
Faithful representation	Verifiability	Economic entity	Fair value	
	Timeliness	Periodicity	Revenue recognition	
	Understandability	Going concern	Expense recognition	
			Full disclosure	

Two other important accounting concepts are materiality and consistency.

CLOSING ENTRIES (Chapter 4)

Purpose

1. Update the Retained Earnings account in the ledger by transferring net income (loss) and dividends to retained earnings.
2. Prepare the temporary accounts (revenue, expense, dividends) for the next period's postings by reducing their balances to zero.

ACCOUNTING CYCLE (Chapter 4)

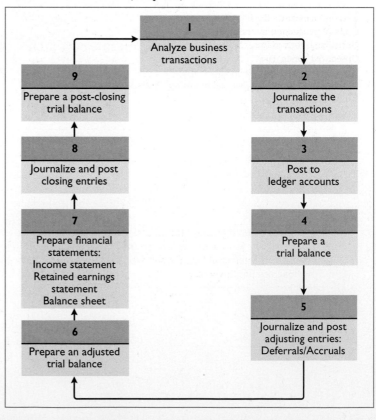

Chapter Content

INVENTORY (Chapters 5 and 6)

Ownership

Freight Terms	Ownership of goods on public carrier resides with:
FOB shipping point	Buyer
FOB destination	Seller

Perpetual vs. Periodic Journal Entries

Event	Perpetual	Periodic
Purchase of goods	Inventory 　Cash (A/P)	Purchases 　Cash (A/P)
Freight (shipping point)	Inventory 　Cash	Freight-In 　Cash
Return of purchased goods	Cash (or A/P) 　Inventory	Cash (or A/P) 　Purchase Returns and 　　Allowances
Sale of goods	Cash (or A/R) 　Sales Revenue Cost of Goods Sold 　Inventory	Cash (or A/R) 　Sales Revenue No entry
Return of sold goods	Sales Returns and Allowances 　Accounts Receivable Inventory 　Cost of Goods Sold	Sales Returns and Allowances 　Accounts Receivable No entry
End of period	No entry	Closing or adjusting entry required

FRAUD, INTERNAL CONTROL, AND CASH (Chapter 7)

Principles of Internal Control

Establishment of responsibility
Segregation of duties
Documentation procedures
Physical controls
Independent internal verification
Human resource controls

The Fraud Triangle

Opportunity

Financial
pressure

Rational-
ization

Bank Reconciliation

Per Bank Statement	Per Books
Adjustments to the bank balance 　Deposits in transit (+) 　Outstanding checks (−)	Adjustments to the book balance 　EFT collections and other deposits (+) 　NSF (bounced) checks (−) 　Service charges and other payments (−)

Note: 1. Errors should be offset (added or deducted) on the side that made the error.
2. Adjusting journal entries should only be made for items affecting books.
3. The adjusted cash balance per the bank should equal the adjusted cash balance per the books.

RAPID REVIEW
Chapter Content

RECEIVABLES (Chapter 8)

Two Methods to Account for Uncollectible Accounts

Direct write-off method	Record bad debt expense when the company determines a particular account to be uncollectible.
Allowance method	At the end of each period, estimate the amount of uncollectible receivables. Debit Bad Debt Expense and credit Allowance for Doubtful Accounts in an amount that results in a balance in the allowance account equal to the estimate of uncollectibles. As specific accounts become uncollectible, debit Allowance for Doubtful Accounts and credit Accounts Receivable.

PLANT ASSETS (Chapter 9)

Computation of Annual Depreciation Expense

Straight-line	$\dfrac{\text{Cost} - \text{Salvage value}}{\text{Useful life (in years)}}$
Declining-balance	Book value at beginning of year × Declining balance rate* *Declining-balance rate $= 1 \div$ Useful life (in years)
Units-of-activity	$\dfrac{\text{Cost} - \text{Salvage value}}{\text{Useful life (in units)}} \times$ Units of activity during year

Note: If depreciation is calculated for partial periods, the straight-line and declining-balance methods must be adjusted for the relevant proportion of the year. Multiply the annual depreciation expense by the number of months expired in the year divided by 12 months.

ISSUANCE OF BONDS (Chapter 10)

Premium	Market interest rate < Contractual interest rate
Face Value	Market interest rate = Contractual interest rate
Discount	Market interest rate > Contractual interest rate

Computation of Annual Bond Interest Expense

Interest expense = Interest paid (payable) + Amortization of discount
(OR − Amortization of premium)

Bond Amortization (Appendices 10A and 10B)

Straight-line amortization	$\dfrac{\text{Bond discount (premium)}}{\text{Number of interest periods}}$	
Effective-interest amortization (preferred method)	Bond interest expense	Bond interest paid
	Carrying value of bonds at beginning of period × Effective-interest rate	Face amount of bonds × Contractual interest rate

STOCKHOLDERS' EQUITY (Chapter 11)

No-Par Value vs. Par Value Stock Journal Entries

No-Par Value	**Par Value**

Cash
    Common Stock
	Cash
	    Common Stock (par value)
	    Paid-in Capital in Excess of Par

Comparison of Dividend Effects

	Cash	**Common Stock**	**Retained Earnings**
Cash dividend	↓	No effect	↓
Stock dividend	No effect	↑	↓
Stock split	No effect	No effect	No effect

STATEMENT OF CASH FLOWS (Chapter 12)

Cash flows from operating activities (**indirect method**)

Net income

Add:	Amortization and depreciation	$ X
	Losses on disposals of assets	X
	Decreases in noncash current assets	X
	Increases in current liabilities	X
Deduct:	Increases in noncash current assets	(X)
	Decreases in current liabilities	(X)
	Gains on disposals of assets	(X)
	Net cash provided (used) by operating activities	$ X

Cash flows from operating activities (**direct method**)

Cash receipts

(Examples: from sales of goods and services to customers, from receipts of interest and dividends) $ X

Cash payments

(Examples: to suppliers, for operating expenses, for interest, for taxes)   (X)

Net cash provided (used) by operating activities $ X

FINANCIAL STATEMENT ANALYSIS (Chapter 13)

Discontinued operations	Income statement (presented separately after Income from continuing operations)
Changes in accounting principle	In most instances, use the new method in current period and restate previous years' results using new method. For changes in depreciation and amortization methods, use the new method in the current period, but do not restate previous periods.

INVESTMENTS (Appendix H)

Comparison of Long-Term Bond Investment and Liability Journal Entries

Event	Investor	Investee

Purchase/issue of bonds	Debt Investments
	  Cash
		Cash
		  Bonds Payable

Interest receipt/payment	Cash
	  Interest Revenue
		Interest Expense
		  Cash

Comparison of Cost and Equity Methods of Accounting for Long-Term Stock Investments

Event	Cost	Equity

Acquisition	Stock Investments
	  Cash
		Stock Investments
		  Cash

Investee reports earnings	No entry	Stock Investments Investment Revenue

Investee pays dividends	Cash
	  Dividend Revenue
		Cash
		  Stock Investments

Debt Investments

Trading	Report at fair value with changes reported in net income.
Available-for-sale	Report at fair value with changes reported in other comprehensive income.

Stock Investments

Category	Valuation	Unrealized Gains or Losses	Other Income Effects
Holdings less than 20%	Fair value	Recognized in net income	Dividends declared; gains and losses from sale.
Holdings between 20% and 50%	Equity	Not recognized	Proportionate share of investee's net income.
Holdings more than 50%	Consolidation	Not recognized	Not applicable.

RAPID REVIEW
Financial Statements

Order of Preparation	Date
1. Income statement	For the period ended
2. Retained earnings statement	For the period ended
3. Balance sheet	As of the end of the period
4. Statement of cash flows	For the period ended

Income Statement (perpetual inventory system)

Name of Company **Income Statement** **For the Period Ended**		
Sales		
Sales revenue	$ X	
Less: Sales returns and allowances	X	
Sales discounts	X	
Net sales		$ X
Cost of goods sold		X
Gross profit		X
Operating expenses		
(Examples: store salaries, advertising, delivery, rent, depreciation, utilities, insurance)		X
Income from operations		X
Other revenues and gains		
(Examples: interest, gains)	X	
Other expenses and losses		
(Examples: interest, losses)	X	X
Income before income taxes		X
Income tax expense		X
Net income		$ X

Name of Company **Statement of Comprehensive Income** **For the Period Ended**	
Net income	$XX
Other comprehensive income	XX
Comprehensive income	$XX

Retained Earnings Statement

Name of Company **Retained Earnings Statement** **For the Period Ended**	
Retained earnings, beginning of period	$ X
Add: Net income (or deduct net loss)	X
	X
Deduct: Dividends	X
Retained earnings, end of period	$ X

Income Statement (periodic inventory system)

Name of Company **Income Statement** **For the Period Ended**			
Sales			
Sales revenue		$ X	
Less: Sales returns and allowances		X	
Sales discounts		X	
Net sales			$ X
Cost of goods sold			
Beginning inventory		X	
Purchases	$ X		
Less: Purchase returns and allowances	X		
Net purchases	X		
Add: Freight-in	X		
Cost of goods purchased		X	
Cost of goods available for sale		X	
Less: Ending inventory		X	
Cost of goods sold			X
Gross profit			X
Operating expenses			
(Examples: store salaries, advertising, delivery, rent, depreciation, utilities, insurance)			X
Income from operations			X
Other revenues and gains			
(Examples: interest, gains)		X	
Other expenses and losses			
(Examples: interest, losses)		X	X
Income before income taxes			X
Income tax expense			X
Net income			$ X

Note: Net income (loss) presented on the retained earnings statement must equal the net income (loss) presented on the income statement.

RAPID REVIEW
Financial Statements

Balance Sheet

Name of Company Balance Sheet As of the End of the Period			
Assets			
Current assets			
(Examples: cash, short-term investments,			
accounts receivable, inventory, prepaids)			$ X
Long-term investments			
(Examples: investments in bonds,			
investments in stocks)			X
Property, plant, and equipment			
Land		$ X	
Buildings and equipment	$ X		
Less: Accumulated depreciation	X	X	X
Intangible Assets			X
Total assets			$ X
Liabilities and Stockholders' Equity			
Liabilities			
Current liabilities			
(Examples: notes payable, accounts			
payable, accruals, unearned revenues,			
current portion of notes payable)			$ X
Long-term liabilities			
(Examples: notes payable, bonds			
payable)			X
Total liabilities			X
Stockholders' equity			
Common stock			X
Retained earnings			X
Total liabilities and stockholders'			
equity			$ X

Note: Total assets on the balance sheet must equal total liabilities plus stockholders' equity; and, ending retained earnings on the balance sheet must equal ending retained earnings on the retained earnings statement.

Statement of Cash Flows

Name of Company Statement of Cash Flows For the Period Ended	
Cash flows from operating activities	
Note: May be prepared using the direct	
or indirect method	
Net cash provided (used) by operating	
activities	$ X
Cash flows from investing activities	
(Examples: purchase/sale of long-term assets)	
Net cash provided (used) by investing activities	X
Cash flows from financing activities	
(Examples: issue/repayment of long-term	
liabilities, issue of stock, payment of dividends)	
Net cash provided (used) by financing activities	X
Net increase (decrease) in cash	X
Cash, beginning of the period	X
Cash, end of the period	$ X

Note: Cash, end of the period, on the statement of cash flows must equal cash presented on the balance sheet.

RAPID REVIEW
Using the Information in the Financial Statements

Ratio	Formula	Purpose or Use
Liquidity Ratios		
1. Current ratio	$\dfrac{\text{Current assets}}{\text{Current liabilities}}$	Measures short-term debt-paying ability.
2. Acid-test (quick) ratio	$\dfrac{\text{Cash + Short-term investments + Accounts receivable (net)}}{\text{Current liabilities}}$	Measures immediate short-term liquidity.
3. Accounts receivable turnover	$\dfrac{\text{Net credit sales}}{\text{Average net accounts receivable}}$	Measures liquidity of receivables.
4. Inventory turnover	$\dfrac{\text{Cost of goods sold}}{\text{Average inventory}}$	Measures liquidity of inventory.
Profitability Ratios		
5. Profit margin	$\dfrac{\text{Net income}}{\text{Net sales}}$	Measures net income generated by each dollar of sales.
6. Asset turnover	$\dfrac{\text{Net sales}}{\text{Average total assets}}$	Measures how efficiently assets are used to generate sales.
7. Return on assets	$\dfrac{\text{Net income}}{\text{Average total assets}}$	Measures overall profitability of assets.
8. Return on common stockholders' equity	$\dfrac{\text{Net income − Preferred dividends}}{\text{Average common stockholders' equity}}$	Measures profitability of stockholders' investment.
9. Earnings per share (EPS)	$\dfrac{\text{Net income − Preferred dividends}}{\text{Weighted-average common shares outstanding}}$	Measures net income earned on each share of common stock.
10. Price-earnings (P-E) ratio	$\dfrac{\text{Market price per share of stock}}{\text{Earnings per share}}$	Measures the ratio of the market price per share to earnings per share.
11. Payout ratio	$\dfrac{\text{Cash dividends paid on common stock}}{\text{Net income}}$	Measures percentage of earnings distributed in the form of cash dividends.
Solvency Ratios		
12. Debt to assets ratio	$\dfrac{\text{Total liabilities}}{\text{Total assets}}$	Measures percentage of total assets provided by creditors.
13. Times interest earned	$\dfrac{\text{Net income + Interest expense + Income tax expense}}{\text{Interest expense}}$	Measures ability to meet interest payments as they come due.
14. Free cash flow	Net cash provided by operating activities − Capital expenditures − Cash dividends	Measures the amount of cash generated during the current year that is available for the payment of additional dividends or for expansion.